PATERNOSTER DIGITAL LIBRARY

New Horizons in Hermeneutics
The Theory and Practice of Transforming Biblical Reading

A full listing of all titles in this series will be found at the close of this book.

PATERNOSTER DIGITAL LIBRARY

The resources of modern printing technology now enable us to respond to the on-going demand for classical biblical and theological studies which would otherwise have been too expensive to keep in stock. All titles in the series are important scholarly works in their own right and fresh titles will continue to be added at regular intervals. Readers who missed these books when they originally appeared now have the opportunity to enhance their collections, and new theological libraries in developing countries will welcome this opportunity to update their holdings with essential textbooks.

PATERNOSTER DIGITAL LIBRARY

New Horizons in Hermeneutics

The Theory and Practice of Transforming Biblical Reading

Anthony C. Thiselton

Copyright © 1992 Anthony C. Thiselton

First published in 1992 by Marshall Pickering

This digital edition 2006

Paternoster is an imprint of Authentic Media,
PO Box 6 326, Bletchley, Milton Keynes,
MK1 9GG

The right of Anthony C. Thiselton to be identified
as the Author of this Work has been asserted in accordance
with the Copyright, Designs and Patents Act 1988.

*All rights reserved. No part of the publication may be reproduced, stored in a retrieval system,
or transmitted in any form or by any means, electric, mechanical, photocopying, recording or otherwise,
without the prior permission of the publisher or the license permitting restricted copying. In the U.K. such
licenses are issued by the Copyright Licensing Agency, Hay's Galleria, Shackleton House, 4 Battle Bridge
Ln, London SE1 2HX*

British Library Cataloguing in Publication Data
a Catalogue record for this book is
available from the British Library

ISBN-13: 978-1-84227-455-2

CONTENTS

Preface and Acknowledgements   xi

INTRODUCTION: NEW HORIZONS

1 Aims and Concerns   1
2 Hermeneutics in the University, and the Bible and the Church   4
3 New Horizons for Readers: Reading with Transforming Effects   8
4 New Horizons in the Development of Hermeneutics   10
5 The New Horizons of Fresh Argument and Transforming the Reading-Paradigm   16
Notes to Introduction [n. 1-31]   25

I TRANSFORMING TEXTS: PRELIMINARY OBSERVATIONS

1 The Capacity of Texts to Transform Readers   31
2 The Capacity of Readers and Texts to Transform Texts: Different Notions of Intertextuality   35
3 Situational and Horizonal Factors in Transforming Texts   42
4 Factors Arising from Semiotics, Theories of Hermeneutics, and Theories of Textuality   47
Notes to Chapter I   52

II WHAT IS A TEXT? SHIFTING PARADIGMS OF TEXTUALITY

1 Are Authors Part of Texts? Introductory Issues   55
2 Are Situations or Readers Part of Texts?   58
3 Theological Claims about the Givenness and Actualization of Biblical Texts   63
4 Further Theological Issues: Disembodied Texts or Communicative Address?   68
Notes to Chapter II   75

III FROM SEMIOTICS TO DECONSTRUCTION AND POST-MODERNIST THEORIES OF TEXTUALITY

1 Code in Semiotic Theory: The Nature of Semiotic Theory   80
2 Need Semiotics Lead to Deconstructionism? Different Understandings of the Implications of Semiotic Theory   84

Contents

3 Roland Barthes: From Hermeneutics through Semiotics to Intralinguistic World, and to Text as Play ... 92
4 Difficulties and Questions: the Inter-Mixture of Semiotics and World-View ... 94
5 Jacques Derrida: an Endless Series of Signs under Erasure ... 103
6 Postmodernist and Deconstructionist Approaches in Biblical Interpretation ... 114
7 Further Philosophical Evaluations and Critiques of Deconstructionism, Some in Dialogue with Wittgenstein ... 125
Notes to Chapter III ... 132

IV PRE-MODERN BIBLICAL INTERPRETATION: THE HERMENEUTICS OF TRADITION

1 Relations between Pre-Modern, Modern and Post-Modern Perspectives: some Parallels and Contrasts ... 142
2 Tradition as Context of Understanding: the Two Testaments, Gnosticism and the Relevance of Irenaeus ... 148
3 Varied Issues in Allegorical Interpretation: its Demythologizing Function in Pre-Christian and Philonic Interpretation ... 157
4 The Beginnings of Christian Allegorical Interpretation ... 163
5 Allegory or Application? The Development of Pastoral Hermeneutical Consciousness in Origen and a Contrast with Chrysostom ... 167
Notes to Chapter IV ... 173

V THE HERMENEUTICS OF ENQUIRY: FROM THE REFORMATION TO MODERN THEORY

1 The Three Polemical Contexts which Give 'Claritas Scripturae' its Currency: Epistemology, 'Higher' Meanings, and Efficacy ... 179
2 Questioning in the Service of Faith: Christ and Reflective Criteria in Luther ... 186
3 Further Reflection on Interpretation in Calvin and in English Reformers ... 190
4 The Rise and Development of Modern Hermeneutical Theory ... 194
Notes to Chapter V ... 198

VI SCHLEIERMACHER'S HERMENEUTICS OF UNDERSTANDING

1 Schleiermacher's Most Distinctive Contribution to the Subject ... 204
2 The Broader Context: Romanticism, Pietism, Culture, and Hermeneutics ... 209

Contents

3 Schleiermacher's System of Hermeneutics: 'Grammatical' (Shared Language) and 'Psychological' (Language-Use) Axes	216
4 Schleiermacher's System of Hermeneutics: the Hermeneutical Circle and a 'Better' Understanding than the Author	221
5 Theological Ambiguities and Hermeneutical Achievements	228
Notes to Chapter VI	233

VII PAULINE AND OTHER TEXTS IN THE LIGHT OF A HERMENEUTICS OF UNDERSTANDING

1 Paul, Pauline Texts, and Schleiermacher's Hermeneutical Circle	237
2 The Hermeneutical Circle and the Quest for a 'Centre' of Pauline Thought	242
3 A Hermeneutics of 'Life-World' Reconstruction in Dilthey and Betti: 'Re-living' and 'Openness'	247
4 Pauline Texts and Reconstruction: A 'Better' Understanding than the Author?	253
5 Understanding the Author of an Anonymous Text: the Epistle to the Hebrews	261
Notes to Chapter VII	267

VIII THE HERMENEUTICS OF SELF-INVOLVEMENT: FROM EXISTENTIALIST MODELS TO SPEECH-ACT THEORY

1 Reader-Involvement, Address, and States of Affairs: The Contrasting Assumptions of Existentialist Hermeneutics and 'the Logic of Self-Involvement' in Austin and Evans	272
2 The Hermeneutics of the Earlier Heidegger and Bultmann's Approach to Paul	279
3 Christological Texts in Paul and in the Synoptic Gospels in the Light of Speech-Act Theory in Austin, Evans, Searle, and du Plessis	283
4 Illocutionary Acts in J.R. Searle and F. Recanati: Directions of Fit between Words and the World	291
5 The 'World-to-Word Fit' of a Hermeneutic of Promise: Types of Illocutions; the Work of Christ in Paul; Promise in the Old Testament	298
Notes to Chapter VIII	307

IX THE HERMENEUTICS OF METACRITICISM AND THE FOUNDATIONS OF KNOWLEDGE

1 The Context of the Paradigm-shift to Radical Metacritical Hermeneutics and the Nature of Gadamer's Hermeneutics	313

2 Gadamer's Claim for 'the Universality of the Hermeneutical
  Problem' and the Development of Critiques of
  Language and of Knowledge   322
3 Pannenberg's Metacritical Unifying of a Hermeneutics
  of Universal History with the Scientific Status of Theology   331
  Notes to Chapter IX   338

X THE HERMENEUTICS OF SUSPICION AND RETRIEVAL:
PAUL RICOEUR'S HERMENEUTICAL THEORY

1 Human Fallibility, Hermeneutical Suspicion, and Freudian
  Psychoanalysis: Idols, Dreams, and Symbols   344
2 Paul Ricoeur on Metaphor and Narrative: Possibility, Time,
  and Transformation   351
3 Metacriticism, Fiction, History, and Truth: Some Assessments
  Largely in the Light of Speech-Act Theory   358
4 Some Consequences for Ricoeur's Approach to Biblical
  Hermeneutics   368
  Notes to Chapter X   373

XI THE HERMENEUTICS OF SOCIO-CRITICAL THEORY: ITS RELATION TO
SOCIO-PRAGMATIC HERMENEUTICS AND TO LIBERATION THEOLOGIES

1 The Nature of Socio-Critical Hermeneutics:
  Habermas on Hermeneutics, Knowledge, Interest,
  and an Emancipatory Critique   379
2 Habermas's Theory of Communicative Action in the
  Double Context of Social Theory in Marx, Weber
  and Parsons, and Speech-Act Theory: Habermas and
  Biblical Interpretation   385
3 Richard Rorty's Socio-Pragmatic Contextualism *vs.* Karl-Otto
  Apel's Cognitive Anthropology as Transcendental Metacritique   393
  Notes to Chapter XI   405

XII THE HERMENEUTICS OF LIBERATION THEOLOGIES AND
FEMINIST THEOLOGIES: SOCIO-CRITICAL AND
SOCIO-PRAGMATIC STRANDS

1 The Major Concerns, Development, and Dual Character
  of Latin American Liberation Hermeneutics   411
2 Parallels and Contrasts with Black Hermeneutics: the Varied
  Approaches of Cone, Boesak, Goba, Mosala, and other Writers   419
3 Further Examples of Marxist or 'Materialist' Readings:
  Belo and Clévenot   427
4 The Nature and Development of Feminist Biblical Hermeneutics 430

5 The Use of Socio-Critical and Socio-Pragmatic Methods and
 Epistemologies in Feminist Hermeneutics: Ruether, Fiorenza,
 Tolbert, and other Writers   439
6 Further Complexities in Feminist Hermeneutics:
 Parallels between Demythologizing and Depatriarchalizing   452
 Notes to Chapter XII   463

XIII THE HERMENEUTICS OF READING IN THE CONTEXT
OF LITERARY THEORY

1 Problematic and Productive Aspects of the Literary Approach
 and the Legacy of the New Criticism   471
2 A Closer Examination of Narrative Theory   479
3 Formalist and Structuralist Approaches to Biblical
 Narrative Texts   486
4 From Post-Structuralism to Semiotic Theories of Reading:
 Intertextuality and the Paradigm-Shift to 'Reading'   495
5 The Paradigm of 'Reading' in Biblical Studies and
 Intertextuality in Biblical Interpretation   499
 Notes to Chapter XIII   508

XIV THE HERMENEUTICS OF READING IN READER-RESPONSE
THEORIES OF LITERARY MEANING

1 Wolfgang Iser's Theory of Reader-Interaction and its
 Utilization in Biblical Studies   516
2 Umberto Eco's Semiotic and Text-Related Reader-Response
 Theories and their Implications for Biblical Texts   524
3 Differences among More Radical Reader-Response Theories:
 The Psychoanalytical Approach of Holland and the
 Socio-Political Approach of Bleich   529
4 Further Observations on the Reader-Orientated Semiotics of
 Culler and on the Social Pragmatism of Fish   534
5 What Fish's Counterarguments Overlook about Language:
 Fish and Wittgenstein   540
6 The Major Difficulties and Limited Value of Fish's Later
 Theory for Biblical Studies and for Theology   546
 Notes to Chapter XIV   550

XV THE HERMENEUTICS OF PASTORAL THEOLOGY:
(I) TEN WAYS OF READING TEXTS IN RELATION TO
VARIED READING-SITUATIONS

1 Life-Worlds, Intentional Directedness, and Enquiring Reading
 in Reconstructionist Models   558

x   *Contents*

2 Disruptions of Passive Reading in Existentialist Models   563
3 Drawing Readers into Biblical Narrative-Worlds:
   Four Theories of Narrative in Relation
   to Reading-Situations   566
4 Biblical Symbols: Productive and Spiritual Reading,
   with Questions partly from Freud and Jung
   for Pastoral Theology   575
5 Models Five through to Eight on Variable Reader-Effects:
   Semiotic Productivity, Reader-Response,
   Socio-Pragmatic Contextualization, and Deconstruction   582
   Notes to Chapter XV   592

XVI THE HERMENEUTICS OF PASTORAL THEOLOGY:
     (2) FURTHER READING-SITUATIONS, PLURALISM, AND
     'BELIEVING' READING

1 Some Implications of Speech-Act Models for Enquiring and
   Believing Reading (Ninth Model); and the
   Socio-Critical Quest to Transcend Instrumental
   Uses of Texts (Tenth Model)   597
2 'The Present Situation' in Hermeneutical Approaches to
   Pastoral Theology and to Social Science:
   Criteria of Relevance in Alfred Schutz and the
   Critique of the Cross   604
3 The Transformation of Criteria of Relevance and Power
   in the New Horizons of the Cross and Resurrection:
   Towards a New Understanding of Hermeneutical
   Pluralism   611
   Notes to Chapter XVI   619

   Bibliography   621
   Index of authors   662
   Index of subjects (including index to definition of terms)   673
   Index of biblical references   695
   Index of ancient extra-biblical sources   702

PREFACE AND ACKNOWLEDGEMENTS

I have described the aims, scope, and main arguments of this volume in the Introduction. There I have also suggested the range of readerships to which these are primarily directed. Nevertheless particular readers may be drawn more readily (at least initially) to certain specific chapters.

The Introduction may well invite attention from the viewpoint of all interests. Those with more immediately practical interests, however, may perhaps find hopes most readily fulfilled in chapters, I, II, VII, VIII, and XII, and most especially in XV and XVI. These last two chapters explicitly summarize the value of particular models in relation to specific biblical texts and specific reader-related situations and goals.

Chapter XVI constitutes the climax of a sustained argument. Foundational issues are explored in chapters II through to XIV. Gadamer (chapter IX) and Ricoeur (chapter X) represent key figures and turning-points for contemporary theory. Post-Gadamerian hermeneutics diverge sharply in the contrast between socio-critical hermeneutics in Habermas and Apel (chapter XI) and socio-contextual pragmatism in Rorty and Fish (chapters XI and XIV). This has profound implications for practical issues about biblical reading. Issues in black hermeneutics and feminist hermeneutics (chapter XII) illustrate this. Chapters XIII-XIV (in addition to III) seek to take account of the enormous impact of contemporary literary theory on biblical studies.

Chapter III explores semiotics, deconstruction and postmodernism with particular reference to Barthes and to Derrida. With hindsight, I may have been too easily seduced by Jeanrond's arguments that the nature of texts and textuality need logically to be explored before hermeneutics. As I explain more fully in the Introduction, in the end each set of issues mutually depends on the other. Chapter III is placed early in the argument to carry forward the fundamental questions about textuality which have been raised more broadly in chapter II. But this has an unintended side-effect. It places a complex, heavily technical, chapter at a point before the argument has gained momentum, where it may constitute a disincentive for all but the most robust to persevere. Some may wish therefore to postpone this chapter until they have reached XIV, where the arguments and conclusions of these two chapters clearly interact with those of III in practical ways.

The debts of gratitude which I wish to acknowledge remain great and numerous. Mrs Doreen Ayling, my Personal Assistant until June 1990, showed a great kindness which was invaluable as an impetus to put pen to paper. At the beginning of my four months of study-leave, she tactfully 'expected' regular batches of manuscript for her desk, and took infinite pains with this work, often after office hours. When she moved to London, she continued to work on the indices of authors and references.

Mrs Aileen Jones succeeded Mrs Ayling as my Personal Assistant in June 1990. She gave meticulous and unstinted care to this work alongside almost impossible pressures in my office. Without her administrative initiatives and her willingness, like Mrs Ayling, to take on a massive work-load, the task of finishing this manuscript alongside other heavy administrative, pastoral, and teaching commitments, would simply have been too much.

Mrs Jones and Mrs Ayling were ably assisted in this work throughout by the considerable talents, accurate eye, and ever-ready help of Mr Eugene Ginty. Mr wife, Rosemary gave much practical help with checking work and arranging bibliographical material. She also suffered a severely unsocial home-life for eighteen months. Dr and Mrs Ward offered invaluable help at a particular stage, and I am grateful to Dr N. T. Wright for identifying the need for a number of corrections shortly after the book had left my desk for the publishers.

Ms Christine Whitell of HarperCollins has been a ready source of help, constant encouragement, and good advice. I have valued her help, together with that of Dr Stan Gundry, who has been a personal contact with the American publishers over some years. Debts to academic colleagues remain too numerous to specify. I have always valued my very close links with the Departments of Philosophy and of Linguistics over sixteen years in the University of Sheffield. Likewise I appreciated my year in an interdisciplinary research team as a Fellow of Calvin College, Grand Rapids. My American colleagues have always been warmly supportive of this kind of work, and I have always returned from visits across the Atlantic with renewed vision.

ANTHONY C. THISELTON
St John's College
University of Durham
June 1991

INTRODUCTION

New Horizons

1. Aims and Concerns

This book originated in a promise to provide an advanced textbook on hermeneutics. It includes a description and critical evaluation of all the major theoretical models and approaches which characterize current hermeneutical theory, or which have contributed to its present shape. Equally, it suggests how these theoretical models may be exemplified in concrete approaches to specific biblical texts or to issues in biblical interpretation.

I also seek to offer more than a tool for teaching, study and research. A number of arguments put forward in these chapters remain distinctive to this volume, and attempt to carry the subject forward in creative and constructive ways. The title and the sub-title reflect a three-fold word-play. First, texts may enlarge the horizons of readers. When this occurs, horizons move and become new horizons. Reading may also produce transforming effects. In this sense, reading biblical texts can become eventful as transforming biblical reading.

New horizons, in a second sense, have been opened in the development of hermeneutics as an interdisciplinary area over the last twenty years. Advances in the subject have re-shaped its agenda and re-defined its growing edges. Among many more recent developments, the nature and goals of readers' interactions and engagements with texts form part of this revised agenda. Recent hermeneutical theory may invite us to re-consider our assumptions about what it is to read, to interpret, or to understand texts. Hermeneutics may transform our notion of reading; transforming biblical reading may be one effect of hermeneutical enquiry.

These chapters also try to open new horizons which, in a third sense, move beyond those already established within the discipline. Some distinctive arguments advanced in this volume go beyond previous work, but also reflect some continuity with my earlier approach in *The Two Horizons* (1980). We review the nature of these arguments in the final section of this introduction. One concerns the diversity of directions for which Gadamer's work has been taken as a point of departure, and their theoretical significance for different types of liberation hermeneutics. For example, Latin American, black, or feminist hermeneutics which operate within the frame of socio-critical theory adopted by Habermas function very differently from those which derive their theoretical validity from the contextual pragmatism of Rorty and of others.

A second distinctive area explores speech-act theory. I remain unconvinced by those who try to restrict speech-act theory to oral discourse. Legal texts, for example, clearly embody commitments and set up transactions which potentially function as acts: acts of transferring property, acts of authorization, and so forth. Some types of biblical texts also potentially function as acts of promise, acts of pardon, acts of commission, or acts of judgment or love. The claims of Searle and Recanati about "directions of fit" or "directions of correspondence" between language and extra-linguistic states of affairs provides a theoretical starting-point for a detailed exploration of these issues in chapter VIII. I argue that this approach sheds light on Christological texts, as well as texts which embody potential promise, potential blessing, or other kinds of acts.

A third sense of "transforming reading" emerges in the context of some distinctive arguments about the impact of theories of sign-systems, or semiotics, on biblical interpretation and on hermeneutics. Some writers replace traditional terminology about biblical "interpretation" by the term "reading" simply for cosmetic purposes. But other writers use "reading" to signal a paradigm-shift in which a new agenda focusses on semiotic and literary issues. I argue that this brings significant gains but also possible losses. Each of the terms "understanding", "interpretation", and "reading" needs to be broadened to include hermeneutical issues about understanding, knowledge, communication, and truth, as well as questions about the competency of the reader at the semiotic level.

I hope to reach two distinct reading audiences. One includes all who undertake teaching, study, or research in the multidisciplinary area of hermeneutics. The other extends to Christians who are concerned about how the Bible is read and used. The very questions in multidisciplinary hermeneutical theory about the nature of enquiry, language, and understanding which address the whole academic community also address the Christian community with parallel urgency to ask how the language of the biblical writings may speak creatively, and may be read and understood with transforming effects. How we read, understand, interpret, and use biblical texts relates to the very identity of Christian faith and stands at the heart of Christian theology.

In particular, *what effects biblical texts produce* on thought and on life, and especially *on what basis these effects come about* not only challenges our theological integrity but also constitutes a burning concern for all who have some interest in the nurture of faith and its communication in the modern world. These chapters address those who undertake teaching, study, or research in the university, but also all who long for a more authentic, effective, and productive engagement between readers and biblical texts.

In 1970 I introduced into the Department of Biblical Studies in the University of Sheffield a course in hermeneutics which, to my knowledge, was the first of its kind to be offered in a British university. It was designed for advanced students who specialized in biblical studies for over one half of their degree, but who also studied philosophy, linguistics or literature for the other half of their work. I enjoyed the opportunity at Sheffield, while I taught this course, to work closely with colleagues in philosophy and in linguistics, with whom I also shared some teaching and some doctoral supervision of research.

Twenty years of teaching hermeneutics has convinced me that no adequate textbook on the subject yet exists, at least at an advanced level. I recommend to students the two anthologies of extracts from primary sources in hermeneutical theory, edited respectively by Kurt Mueller-Vollmer (1985-86) and by David Klemm (1986).[1] But these inevitably leave little room for detailed critical evaluation of the extracts, and fail to exemplify how the general theories might apply to the interpretation of biblical texts. The dilemma about books may be summarized as follows: some major on theory, but offer little on practices of biblical interpretation; others offer critical surveys of how biblical scholars have approached texts, but remain seriously short on theory; a third category allows some interaction to occur between theory and practice, but tends to concentrate on particular models, approaches, or theories of language, rather than seeking to provide a comprehensive discussion of the wide range of hermeneutical issues and resources of which students need to be aware.

Two recent examples of the British antipathy towards theory in biblical interpretation appeared in 1990. One occurs in *Liberating Exegesis*, a book on liberation hermeneutics written co-jointly by Christopher Rowland and Mark Corner. They argue explicitly and rightly that we cannot expect to reach an adequate understanding of the biblical hermeneutics of liberation theologies unless we examine the work of Ricoeur and of Habermas. But throughout their otherwise helpful two hundred pages I can find no further reference, beyond this comment itself, to Ricoeur; and only one paragraph and one sentence on Habermas.[2] Similarly in her book *The Art of Performance* Frances Young explores the analogy (which I also used and discussed in 1980) between the actualization of textual meaning and the performance of music and art. But apart from two short footnotes and a quotation from Gadamer about Aristotle, Frances Young does not seek to engage with Gadamer's theory of the actualization of art, festivals, or games in her otherwise constructive study, even though she acknowledges that in theology his theory has been "the catalyst of the discussion".[3]

I have attempted, therefore, to provide a tool which is as comprehensive as possible, and which interweaves hermeneutical theory with specific practical questions about biblical interpretation and particular biblical texts. Thus, for example, the theory of understanding found in Schleiermacher, Dilthey, and Betti, first receives assessment on its own terms as a general theory (chapter VI and parts of VII), and is then exemplified in relation to specific biblical texts and to problems of Pauline interpretation (chapter VII). I have documented primary sources in considerable detail, as well as major secondary critical literature. Each theory is approached both sympathetically and critically. This attempt to integrate theory and practice becomes most evident in the final chapter. Chapters XV and XVI explore ten theological models, each with examples of biblical texts, and evaluate their operative value in relation to a variety of reading-situations. Here, as in parts of chapter II, explicitly theological concerns also emerge. The relation between different hermeneutical models and the variables of reader-situations raises issues for pastoral theology, as well as for a theology of biblical interpretation.

2. Hermeneutics in the University, and the Bible and the Church

A major aim in this book is that of seeking to reach two sets of readers, namely those who teach, study, or pursue research in the university, and those who address practical questions about the use of the biblical writings with firm Christian concern. This point invites further amplification. I wish to argue that *within a multidisciplinary frame these two sets of concerns become one single set of concerns in hermeneutics*. Four brief introductory examples will illustrate the issue.

One major hermeneutical tradition begins with Schleiermacher, develops through Dilthey, and finds recent expression in Betti. I discuss and evaluate this tradition in chapters VI and VII with reference both to general theory and to the interpretation of specific biblical texts. Part of Dilthey's general theory of understanding turns on what it is to try to stand in the shoes of someone else. This raises *both* philosophical issues about whether such an exercize is possible *and* pastoral issues about how we reach an understanding of persons and of texts.

Emilio Betti develops this hermeneutical approach further by underlining the part played by *openness* towards others and towards texts. He argues that hermeneutical awareness is fundamental for the humanities and for the sciences in universities and also in social and political life, for hermeneutics encourages reciprocal listening, tolerance, and mutual respect. Betti's work does call attention to the role of openness and listening; but he also expresses concern that listening alone could run the risk of surrendering critical evaluation for credulity. Schleiermacher's question of how we hold together what he termed the "feminine" quality of creative, intuitive, immediacy, with what he regarded as the "masculine" quality of comparison and critical distance, remains equally central to multidisciplinary hermeneutics (including especially literature and sociology) and to issues of Christian faith.

A second major type of example arises from the work of Paul Ricoeur, whose hermeneutical theory is explicitly multidisciplinary. I discuss his hermeneutics in detail in chapter X. Ricoeur examines the contribution of Freudian categories as methodological tools of suspicion and criticism. But he also seeks to retrieve the creative power of symbols, metaphors, and narratives in texts and especially in religious discourse. He calls attention, among other things, to the creativity of language: the symbol gives rise to thought. Among the biblical texts he has particular interests in the wisdom literature of the Old Testament and in the Book of Job. In general hermeneutical terms he aims to shift the focus of attention from whatever lies "behind" the text to what occurs "in front of" the text. Traditional biblical studies, he argues, concentrates too narrowly on reconstructing the history out of which the text arose. What is important for hermeneutics is how texts impinge on readers: *what processes they set in motion, and whether these processes are valid.*

This approach carries considerable import for theological and pastoral questions in the Christian community. In Ricoeur's words, adequate use of suspicion and self-criticism in hermeneutics is essential if we are not to worship idols, by projecting our own wishes and images onto revelation. Freud's account of the capacity of the self to deceive itself stands not far distant from theological assertions about the deceitfulness of the human heart. No less relevant to Christian concerns, the shift of emphasis to what *effects* a text *produces creatively* provides a welcome corrective to more antiquarian and purely informational approaches. Common to Ricoeur and to some important strands in recent literary theory is the question: what does this text *do?*

The very formulation of this question, however, raises a multitude of critical questions in philosophy, theories of language, and socio-critical theory. Can we, or should we, seek to find criteria which determine the validity of what a text *does* within this or that community or for this or that occasion? Can we welcome a pluralism that might be satisfied as long as texts *do something?* A key issue which hermeneutics faces in the wake of Gadamer and Ricoeur concerns the possibility and role of metacriticism:

can we critically rank the different criteria by which we judge what counts as *meaningful* or *productive effects of texts within this or that context in life?*

Precisely the same issue confronts multidisciplinary hermeneutics in the university as that which confronts the Christian community in everyday life. At one end of a spectrum stands contextual-relative socio-*pragmatic* hermeneutics: "This is the effect of the text on me and my community". It runs through pietism, radical reader-response theory, pragmatic forms of narrative theology, and post-modern elements of literary theory. At the other end of the spectrum stands *metacritical* and *socio-critical* hermeneutics. Here the search for some metacritical ranking is not given up: some trans-contextual basis is sought for the comparative evaluation of contextual criteria of interpretation and indeed for the purposes in relation to which each set of criteria gains its currency.

A third example of the commonality of interest shared by multidisciplinary hermeneutics and the Christian community arises from the hermeneutical models used by Gadamer. Gadamer's main concern comes from his philosophical conviction that post-Enlightenment rationalism has set us on the wrong track by its pre-occupation with "method" as the means of grasping truth. "Method" presupposes an abstract generality. Like the later Wittgenstein, Gadamer urges the importance of the particular case within human life. We approach questions of knowledge, or we seek to understand, from within horizons already bounded by our finite situatedness within the flow of history. But it is possible for these finite and historically conditioned horizons to be enlarged, and to expand. In actualizations of understanding or encounter between readers and texts, the boundaries of horizons may be extended and moved, and thus come to constitute *new* horizons.

This model, or cognitive metaphor, has immediate relevance for theology and for the church. In theological terms, horizons which initially are centred on the individual or corporate self *may expand in such a way as to de-centre the self*. But is this not, in the Christian tradition, the heart of the message of the cross and the resurrection, and one of the most fundamental functions which biblical texts can perform?

The convergence between theology, Christian action, and multidisciplinary hermeneutics becomes still clearer in the light of post-Gadamerian developments. A fourth example can be found in the development of socio-critical hermeneutics. Socio-critical hermeneutics seeks to unmask uses of texts which serve self-interests or the interests of dominating power-structures. Texts can be used for social manipulation or control, or to authorize, or to appear to authorize, values which serve the interests of some individual or corporate entity. Here the socio-critical theory of Habermas and others offers a *critical* frame which can provide theoretical tools for approaches under the heading of liberation theologies. The notion of freedom from bondage to the interests of self in Christian pietism has parallels with the goal of liberation from oppressive structures in the liberation hermeneutics of Latin American, black, and feminist theologies.

The radical consequences of apparently relatively small shifts in hermeneutical theory can have massive consequences for theology in the area under consideration. Habermas, Apel, and others aim to develop an *emancipatory critique* in hermeneutics which reaches beyond the horizons of particular persons or communities. The historically and socially finite, contingent, or particular, finds expression in Habermas' use of Dilthey's concept of *life-world*. But a trans-contextual critique also operates at the level of *system*. This provides a foundation for a *socio-critical* hermeneutic. But some other writers, by contrast, most notably Rorty and the later Fish, insist that a trans-contextual critique, almost by definition, cannot be formulated because all criteria remain relative to what is perceived to *count* as criteria within a given social community. Hermeneutics is not capable of producing critical theory; it can only give a *pragmatic* account of what reader-effects become operative in given contexts.

The key consequence of this is that *socio-pragmatic hermeneutics turns on its head, and reverses, the emancipatory critiques, or liberation hermeneutics, which socio-critical hermeneutics sets in motion*. For if there can be no critique *from outside* of a community, hermeneutics *serves only to affirm its corporate self, its structures, and its corporate values. It can use texts only by the same ploy as that which oppressors and oppressive power-structures use, namely in the service of its own interests*. Therefore it can leave no room for a theology of the cross. The cross is controlled, domesticated, and transposed into a construct of the linguistic world of some given community. The cross performs no trans-contextual function.

The early Church Fathers glimpsed something of this issue when they rejected gnostic attempts to turn the cross into a docetic idea, no longer firmly anchored in the extra-linguistic world of temporal events. In the theology of the Fathers, as in that of Paul, the message of the cross challenged the corporate constructs, expectations, and wish-fulfilments of communities or of individuals as a scandalous reversal of human expectations and values. Far from reflecting pre-existing social horizons, the cross and the resurrection gave birth to new horizons, which in turn effected a trans-contextual liberating critique and individual and social transformation. This is a far cry from the notion that communities can only project their own image onto texts, thereby to construct their meanings. It questions the notion that, in Fish's words, they are so "embedded in a context of practice" that socio-contextual conditioning restricts their models of reading solely to "doing what comes naturally".[4] In transposing theology into questions about the community (i.e. into ecclesiology), or knowledge into contextual practice (i.e. into social history) socio-pragmatic hermeneutics leaves no room for the new creation as the work of grace in

Christian theology, and no room for new horizons in hermeneutics. Once again, certain fundamental issues in hermeneutical theory go hand in hand with some central issues in Christian theology.

3. New Horizons for Readers: Reading with Transforming Effects

We noted earlier that "New Horizons" and "Transforming Biblical Reading" both signified a triple word-play. We may now explore each aspect further. Texts, first, we argue, open new horizons for readers. Because of their capacity to bring about change, texts and especially biblical texts engage with readers in ways which can productively transform horizons, attitudes, criteria of relevance, or even communities and inter-personal situations. *In this sense we may speak of transforming biblical reading.* The very process of reading may lead to a re-ranking of expectations, assumptions, and goals which readers initially bring to texts.

Gadamer points out, however, that such a process does not occur inevitably or automatically. *Only if we respect the distinctiveness of the horizons of the text* as against the distinctiveness of our own reader-horizon can a creative and productive interaction of horizons occur. The distance between the reader and the text performs a positive hermeneutical function. *Premature assimilation* into the perspectives projected by the horizons of readers leaves the reader trapped within his or her own prior horizons. Worse, in such a case the reader may stand under the illusion that the texts have fully addressed him or her. Still more significantly, interaction between the two horizons of texts and readers will, if premature assimilation has taken place, appear *uneventful, bland, routine, and entirely unremarkable.*

Within the Christian community the reading of biblical texts often takes this uneventful and bland form. For the nature of the reading-process is governed by horizons of expectation already pre-formed by the community of readers or by the individual. Preachers often draw from texts what they had already decided to say; congregations sometimes look to biblical readings only to affirm the community-identity and life-style which they already enjoy. The biblical writings, in such a situation become assimilated into the function of creeds: they become primarily institutional mechanisms to ensure continuity of corporate belief and identity.

This is not to deny that prior understanding of biblical texts can become corporately embodied in the tradition which shapes our horizons. The concern that biblical reading should be eventful, creative, and transforming, should not be interpreted as the kind of iconoclasm which simply sees all

Christian tradition as negative. Reading does not constantly destroy and break up traditions. That which is authentically creative, rather than merely novel or eccentric, springs from productive events which occur within the broader context of a stable tradition of continuity. Postmodernist and deconstructionist approaches in hermeneutical theory stress the iconoclastic role of texts in repeatedly de-stabilizing any resting point which might become transposed into an incipient tradition. But tradition itself moves under the pressures of creative questioning and new contexts. It yields, in Wittgenstein's language, sufficient regularities of beliefs and practices to offer an identifiable continuity within the public world, but sufficient development, change, and particularity to allow for the growth of new socio-linguistic horizons as new socio-historical contexts emerge. The drive towards constant iconoclasm can itself become an artificial idol. Nevertheless interpretations of texts and of earlier traditions can also become institutionalized and fossilized into forms which defeat the original vision which they emerged to serve. Traditions can absorb error, and be overtaken by new understandings and contexts.

It is equally misleading, therefore, to see all biblical texts either as predictable, bland, affirmations of traditions, or as destructive iconoclastic critiques. Credal mechanisms occur in the biblical writings, of which the *Shema*, "Hear, O Lord, the Lord our God is one Lord" (Deut. 6:4) provides a classic example. Creeds also occur in the New Testament, as in the quotation of I Cor. 8:4 "there is no God but one". These have an affirming function in relation to prior tradition. But iconoclasm also occurs in the speeches of Job, the explorations of Ecclesiastes, and Jesus's parables of reversal. These constitute critiques which de-centre prior systems. In the Book of Job, as my former colleague David Clines maintains, "the deconstructive strategy eliminates dogma as dogma."[5]

Luther and Calvin argued that the word of God encounters readers most sharply when it addresses us as adversary, to correct and to change our prior wishes and expectations. This corresponds at a formal level to the correction of a tradition. Grace and judgment, holiness and love, may recall us to new and better paths.

The creativity of texts also varies in its nature in the case of different kinds of texts. Ricoeur stresses the creative effect of symbols, metaphors, and narratives, on imagination and on thought. These project new possibilities which can reach beyond prior boundaries of thought-systems. Umberto Eco draws a constructive distinction between types of texts that transmit a given content, and types which operate as semiotic networks or matrices to generate further meaning. Eco and Iser explore the active roles of readers in contributing to creative textual meaning. More radical reader-response theories, however, can become over-extended into radically pragmatic accounts of meaning. In this case contextual meanings are seen as meaning-*effects* wholly determined by community-horizons. The creative dimension of the texts themselves then becomes inhibited. Some of these theoretical approaches can be applied to biblical texts; others, not. Some apply to certain categories of biblical texts, but not to all types of texts among the biblical writings.

The exploration of such a variety of theoretical models remains essential to the hermeneutical task of evaluating ways in which texts function eventfully and creatively. If processes of routinization threaten to reduce encounters with familiar texts to processes and experiences which are bland, since reader-horizons are always shifting this represents an inadequate paradigm of readers' engagements with biblical texts. Biblical reading, when horizons engage and interact, has the capacity to be transforming reading.

4. New Horizons in the Development of Hermeneutics

When I first taught hermeneutics at an advanced level in 1970, the shape of the course looked very different from the more complex issues which face students of the subject today. A good half of the course focussed on comparisons between, and evaluations of, three major theoretical models: first, that of Schleiermacher, Dilthey, and Betti and the Romanticist tradition; second, the so-called existential interpretation of Bultmann, and its philosophical background in the earlier Heidegger and in related thinkers; and third, the hermeneutical system of Gadamer, in which understanding and conscious judgments are founded on broader realities accessible through language as, in principle, a universal phenomenon. In this sense, Gadamer sees his hermeneutics as taking an *ontological* turn towards language (like the late Heidegger). But the *actualizations* of this broad linguistic tradition occur only in *changing, historically-finite, events*. A game, or a work of art, projects a "world" which shapes the judgments of the player or the interpreter who enters it. The reality of a game clearly transcends the content of the consciousness of a player; its structure, its goals, and its variable shape as a series of particular temporal events, determine what counts as appropriate knowledge and action for the player. No one game is simply a replica of another. Similarly interpretation or understanding is not static. As a paradigm of hermeneutics, Gadamer's work offers a distinctive third approach, in contrast to the so-called Romanticist models of Schleiermacher and Dilthey, and to the existentialist models of Bultmann and others.

These three basic models provided a core for a course on hermeneutics in the early 1970s. But such a course needed also to include further issues, some more traditional, and others more recent. The history of biblical interpretation demanded exploration of the relation between the Two Testaments, allegorical interpretation, mediaeval understandings of the four senses of scripture, and Reformation issues. More recent developments up to around 1970 invited examination of the new hermeneutic of Fuchs and Ebeling, the emergence of structuralism, issues in semantics, the early beginnings of Latin American liberation hermeneutics, and the earlier work of Paul Ricoeur.

Ten years later by the beginning of the 1980s, however, the horizons of the growing edges of the subject assumed a new shape. Post-Gadamerian hermeneutics represents and embodies three or four different directions of response to Gadamer's work. If Gadamer's work is perceived as a crossroads or as an intersection, some theorists move forward with a firmer emphasis on *metacritical evaluations* of theoretical criteria and pragmatic operations. Others move in the direction of exploring the socio-ethical aspects of historical tradition and language, and expound a hermeneutics which embodies a *socially relevant critical theory*. A third direction leads towards the very opposite conclusion. The finite, context-relative actualizations of an otherwise inaccessible reality and truth are perceived to inhibit any metacritical exploration, and hermeneutics comes to represent a descriptive account, even a narrative account, of *the pragmatic effects of texts within given social communities*. Finally, some attempt to turn back from Gadamer's position, and offer defences of more *traditional* approaches in hermeneutics.

Gadamer's emphasis on practical wisdom, in contrast to theoretical reason, provides a starting-point for *metacritical* developments of his work. The historical flow of tradition transmits practical judgments of communities as a continuous process in which established patterns and practices become embedded in language. This gives contingent, historically finite, conscious, acts of judgment their currency. Enlightenment rationalism is perceived to rest on the error of elevating the status of instrumental theoretical reason to something more. "Method" reflects theory abstracted from the contextual contingencies and broader life-flow of history. It represents only a derivative and over-generalized tool. Rationality rests on a broader base. Pannenberg, Habermas, Apel, and arguably Ricoeur, all take up, and then modify, some kind of metacritical approach which embodies these insights.

Other theorists, however, interpret Gadamer's work in a second, quite different direction. Since each "actualization" of texts or of historical language differs from previous or subsequent actualizations, it is possible to argue that all particularizations of truth remain radically context-relative. On this view, knowledge or truth can be actualized only fleetingly, in fluid moments in the flow of history. In history each given historically finite horizon moves on to merge with the next. No two "performances" of the play, the score, or the game are replicas of the other, or they would not *count as* plays, concerts, or games. We cannot predict, through some overview or metacritical formula, how one performance will differ from another in a new context.

Richard Rorty remains probably the best known exponent of this context-relative socio-pragmatic aspect of hermeneutics. Indeed in these chapters Rorty and Fish represent paradigms or models of *socio-pragmatic hermeneutics* in contrast to the socio-critical hermeneutics of Habermas and Apel. We shall note the argument in due course, put forward by Robert Corrington, that *pragmatic* approaches to hermeneutics, with their emphasis on reading-*effects*, have taken root most distinctively on American soil, where C.S. Peirce and Josiah Royce initiated a pragmatic tradition as a context for questions about meaning and interpretation. Both stressed the role of community and *community-conventions and values* in this area, paving the way for socio-pragmatic hermeneutics.

Gadamer's hermeneutics also provides a starting-point for a third possible direction of development. Habermas and Apel criticize Gadamer for insufficient sensitivity towards the socio-ethical implications of hermeneutics. They argue that *given social interests* and not merely bare, finite contextual contingencies, lie behind different actualizations of texts or of truth. The task of *socio-critical* hermeneutics is to unmask these social interests through an emancipatory critique, which serves freedom, justice, and truth. In his earlier work Habermas examines the relation between knowledge and human "interests". In his later work, he argues convincingly that the questions raised by hermeneutics at a metacritical and social level necessitate exploration of *both* the historically finite contingencies of the hermeneutical *life-world and* a broader trans-contextual critique involving, in some sense, *system*.[6] Pannenberg's volume *Theology and the Philosophy of Science* reflects a similar dual concern, but with perhaps a more controlling interest in system.

Karl-Otto Apel also attempts to move beyond the given of social and linguistic practices in particular contexts to some kind of provisional or anticipatory notion of the universal as a basis for metacriticism. But like Gadamer, he appreciates the contextual boundaries of historical finitude. Following Wittgenstein, he accepts the particularity of given language-games in the public world. But unlike Rorty and Fish, Apel does not believe that this locks the interpreter or the philosopher into some localized ethnocentric world. Apel also seeks a broader understanding of human rationality, and refuses to restrict enquiry to the socio-pragmatic level. Human inter-subjectivity, he argues, reaches beyond particular communities.

We have identified three distinct directions which begin with Gadamer: the metacritical, the socio-pragmatic, and the socio-critical. A fourth direction from an intersection or cross-roads is the option of turning back. A return to more traditional hermeneutical models is still advocated by many. In the American discussion, the model of meaning and intention outlined by E.D. Hirsch remains influential in some quarters, and most recently has been defended as the major theoretical model for biblical interpretation by Elliott E. Johnson (1990).[7] On the other hand, others endorse Frank Lentricchia's verdict that Hirsch's approach represents "a hermeneutics of innocence" which cannot be sustained in a post-Gadamerian era.[8]

The warnings offered by Hirsch about the radical consequences of too readily surrendering humanist paradigms without remainder in exchange for post-modernist assumptions deserve to be noted. In the case of certain *kinds* of texts many but not all of his arguments can be sustained. Nevertheless his largely pre-Wittgensteinian conceptual and methodological tools do not match the complexity of the issues formulated in post-Gadamerian theory. First, Hirsch's language about the importance of author's intention needs to be transposed into the kind of post-Wittgensteinian theoretical terms adopted by Searle and others in claims about the "directedness" of texts.[9] (This is distinct from Hirsch's use of Wittgenstein's "language game" for genre). Some of the issues raised by philosophers about human agency and linguistic communicative interaction need to be introduced at this point also. Second, it only postpones rather than solves the problem if we follow Hirsch in restricting "meaning" to a largely *semantic* notion of meaning or only to more straightforward models of inter-personal communication. It does not help to use the term "significance" as a catch-all for more complex and more context-relative examples as if these functioned only as subjective connotations, all of the same kind. What meaning *is*, as Wittgenstein observes, depends on the language-game from within which meaning-currency is drawn.

This is *not*, however, to reduce all kinds of textual meaning to socio-pragmatic meaning-*effects*. For, as Wittgenstein urges, we presuppose some kind of criteria which will allow us to determine when some "mistake" or misunderstanding has occurred. If meaning were only meaning-effects, texts could never be misunderstood. Intersubjective regularities in the public world prevent the collapse of communicative meaning into what Wittgenstein termed, in his own technical sense, "private" language, i.e. that for which no criteria of *what might count as a mistake* could be sustained. This provides a more constructive ground on which to examine the various claims of post-Gadamerian hermeneutics than to turn back to Hirsch's own over-simplified arguments. For this reason I do not devote much further discussion to Hirsch in this present study, even though I sympathize with his concerns.

A further distinctive feature of post-Gadamerian hermeneutics emerges from the increasing attention which has been given to psycho-analytic models in formulating what Ricoeur and others term "a hermeneutic of suspicion". Neither language nor the human mind is transparent or straightforward. In terms of their world-view, it may be tempting for Christian thinkers to dismiss the work of the three so-called masters of suspicion, Freud, Marx, and Nietzsche, as incompatible with the claims of Christian theology. But their insistence that the human mind can deceive itself in varieties of ways, often in the interests of individual or of social power, resonates with biblical and theological assertions about the deceitfulness, opaqueness, and duplicity of the human heart.

On this basis Ricoeur presses into the service of hermeneutics the critical tools of Freudian theory. Freud's interpretation of dreams, and his notions of dream-text and dream work, offer parallels for Ricoeur with interpretations of myths, symbols, metaphors, and other multi-layered or double-layered texts. Freud's concept of overdetermination underlines the complexity of interpreting complex processes for which different levels of explanation can be suggested, or in which different levels of understanding may operate.

Side by side with a critical use of tools of suspicion, Ricoeur also aims to recover the power of symbols, metaphor, and narrative. Critical tools serve to destroy the idols which we project into the sacred Word; a hermeneutic of retrieval aims at restoring the power of language for creative and productive purposes. This also, for Ricoeur, hinges on the multiform character of language. A relevant crux in the interpretation of biblical texts is cited in the work of my colleague, Robert Fyall, on imagery in Job.[10] Is Leviathan in Job 41: 1–34 a referential allusion to a particular water-creature, perhaps a hippopotamus, or a multi-layered image which also points to some larger reality? To suggest that Job can only leave in God's hands the threat of the untamable chaos-monster, the Kraken, the primaeval force which threatens to dissolve the order of the cosmos into confusion and meaninglessness, is to say more than that Job cannot create a hippopotamus.

Two other major features characterize new horizons in hermeneutics over the last ten years. Liberation hermeneutics has moved to a second phase in Latin America, and black and feminist hermeneutics have entered the scene in force. Black South African hermeneutics include theoretical models drawn from materialist and Marxist approaches to texts; but black hermeneutics assume a different form in North American and in black African states. The most striking feature in feminist hermeneutics from the point of view of hermeneutical theory is the different, even opposing, theoretical models which different strands within feminist theologies represent. Some seek a universal critique in the name of freedom and justice, appealing to trans-contextual criteria which identify them as *socio-critical* approaches. Others seek from hermeneutics the affirmation of particular community-relative social norms, and presuppose a *socio-pragmatic* rejection of the possibility of any such trans-contextual critique. In effect, if not causally, the figures of Habermas and Rorty stand respectively behind each set of opposing theoretical assumptions.

The impact of literary theory on hermeneutics also raises a multitude of distinct and separable issues. These include for example, the development of narrative theory; the transposition of post-structuralist accounts of sign-systems into theories of reader-competency; and the general shift in focus from texts to readers. In narrative theory earlier developments in narrative grammar on the part of Greimas and others lead on to the work of Genette, Seymour Chatman, and others. Jonathan Culler has explored the transposition of structuralist and post-structuralist theories into a reader-orientated "framing" of texts.[11] Reader-response theories emerge in more careful and philosophically-based forms in Iser, in more balanced and comprehensive semiotic forms in Eco, and in less restrained and more far-reaching pragmatic forms in Bleich, Holland, and Fish. All these issues and areas are explored below, mainly in chapters XIII and XIV.

Finally, controversies have arisen about the very nature of texts. Such questions are implied by reader-response theories, which see readers as co-authors of texts. Texts are neither complete nor fully "given" until the community of readers creates for them a particular working currency. In post-modernism and in theories of deconstructionism texts assume the form of shifting textures. Their shape and function undergo constant transposition as new intertextual contexts and reading-contexts re-define their meaning-matrices and their effects. Again, the American tradition of hermeneutical pragmatism, with its tendency to equate meaning with meaning-effect, provides fruitful soil for this movement which originated partly in France. But this intermixture of literary theory and philosophical world-view encounters higher resistance in Britain. In Britain, the empirical tradition, with its emphasis on the status of particular cases, encourages the identification of stubborn counterexamples which, like jagged rocks, may puncture the pretensions of such sweeping theories. It is perhaps more constructive to focus first, as Umberto Eco does, on what *kinds* of texts might be thought to operate in relatively stable or unstable ways. The genuinely creative emerges from within a stable framework; otherwise no criterion distinguishes the creatively novel from the eccentric and idiosyncratic.

At the same time genuine concerns about the nature of texts lie behind these issues. These place in sharp focus the central issue of what it is to *read* texts. Our second sense of "new horizons" is matched by a second sense of *transforming biblical reading*. The kind of reflection invited by contemporary hermeneutical theory may invite *transformation of the ways in which we read biblical texts*. We can no longer take for granted traditional assumptions about the nature of reading processes. Where the major emphasis from Schleiermacher to Gadamer lay on theories of understanding, on intersubjective traditions, and on human judgments, with the impact of literary and semiotic theory the focus shifts to the processes that operate in the interaction and encounters between texts and readers. From the point of view of more traditional theorists, this may be *transforming biblical reading into something else*. From the viewpoint of post-modernism this movement may be seen as *transforming biblical reading from routine and predictable processes to more creative and productive ones*.

5. The New Horizons of Fresh Argument and Transforming the Reading-Paradigm

With the possible exception of the first chapter and one or two other sections, I have attempted to include in each main chapter arguments which have not been put forward in other studies. The consequent degree of novelty or creativity, however, if such there is, varies from chapter to chapter.

The first chapter, which otherwise represents only a low-key introduction to the subject, anticipates certain claims about speech-acts which are later elaborated more fully in chapter VIII. It may therefore be appropriate to offer here a word of comment about how I came to place particular value on this theoretical model in my own teaching and research. By 1964 I was strongly attracted to the work of J.L. Austin, as well as to that of the later Wittgenstein. In a series of oral conversations between 1965 and 1969 I became increasingly impressed by George Caird's oral comments concerning the potential importance for New Testament studies of D.D. Evans's use of Austin's work in his book *The Logic of Self-Involvement* (1963). Caird urged the essential importance of interdisciplinary work (his comments are discussed further in chapter VIII). As a result, in 1970 I published a study on the hermeneutics of the parables of Jesus which compared the new hermeneutic of Ernst Fuchs with speech-act theory in Austin, also against the further background of Wittgenstein.[12] Both Fuchs and Austin, I argued, rightly focussed on the capacity of language *to perform acts*: in the case of some parables, to *make pledges or offers*, to *effect acts of forgiveness*, to *subvert* institutional assumptions, and so forth.

All this harmonized with Wittgenstein's insistence that uses of language constituted "part of an activity" anchored in the public world of interactive human life. Fuchs's philosophical tradition differed from that of Austin and Wittgenstein, in that the language-effects which generated the parable-world remained for Fuchs primarily linguistic or intra-linguistic. For Fuchs, even the resurrection of Jesus remains essentially a "linguistic" event. But for Austin the effectiveness of illocutionary speech-acts depended on whether certain states of affairs were the case in the public world, including institutional authorizations and states of affairs in inter-personal relationships.

These considerations suggested two sets of related concerns about hermeneutics. One arose from Wittgenstein's notion of the language-game, his work on context, training, pattern, "following a rule", and his distinction between public and (in a special, technical, sense) "private" language. In *The Two Horizons* (1980) I argued at length that Wittgenstein's approach offered a theoretical apparatus for hermeneutical reflection.[13] I compared with his work in particular the hermeneutics of Heidegger, Bultmann, and Gadamer, and exemplified the consequences of using this theoretical model for interpreting "truth", "faith" and justification by grace through faith, as these appeared in biblical texts.

The other direction remained to be explored: what role is played in hermeneutical theory by the notion of language-uses as *acts* which have *effects*? Can we suggest criteria for the validity of effects which language produces, or can we only describe what effects occur? In Wittgenstein's language, is it possible to conceive of any kind of textual-effect as a "mistake"? Even more fundamentally, why in hermeneutical theory up to 1970 had so little attention been given to the capacity of biblical texts *to produce certain transforming effects*, rather than only to transmit certain disclosures?

This was my question long before I read Ricoeur, and before the emergence of reader-response theory. When reader-response theory did finally make an entrance into hermeneutics and biblical studies, it became clear that the angle of approach was quite different from that of Austin and Searle. For Austin and Searle extra-linguistic factors influence the operative currency of language-effects. For reader-response theories, effects may depend on little more than reader-perceptions and reader-expectations against a background of linguistic conventions within given communities or traditions. In my publication of 1970 I followed the path of Austin's concerns. I am most appreciative of J.G. du Plessis's generous comment that this study "introduced speech-act theory (which was developed by Austin, 1962) into parable research", and that his own work "is conceived as an extension of the line of research initiated by Thiselton (1970), Aurelio (1977) and Arens (1982)".[14]

Can speech-act theory, however, be applied to written texts? The parables of Jesus originated as oral discourse. Inter-personal situations of oral speech offer the clearest examples of speech which effects acts: "I forgive you . . .", "I hereby authorize you . . .", "Take it, it is yours . . .", all constitute *acts* of extra-linguistic transaction. But, as I argue in chapter I, legal wills, love letters, and written promises can also function as effective *acts* which change situations in the public domain. The biblical writings, it may be argued, embody an institutional framework of covenant in which commitments and effects become operative in acts of promise, acts of blessing, acts of forgiveness, acts of pronouncing judgment, acts of repentance, acts of worship, acts of authorization, acts of communion, and acts of love. Because these particular features of biblical language have always seemed to me to lie near the heart of what the Bible is all about, I have always retained a section on speech-act theory and performative language in my courses on hermeneutics.

In 1974 I developed this approach in a publication which examined the "power of words" in the biblical writings.[15] I argued that an adequate examination of the wider implications of Austin's theory saves us from having to accept the bizarre explanations about blessings, cursings, and other "powerful" words which a number of Old Testament specialists had proposed. These implied that the Hebrews, or the so-called "Hebraic mind", held a very primitive and simplistic view of language akin to that of word-magic. Appeal was made to the work of Malinowski and others, and much was made of similes of military weaponry. The alleged reason why Isaac could not recall the blessing which he had, through Jacob's deceit, given to Jacob, or why Balaam could not call back his blessing at the command of Balak, was because their words were like missiles armed with a time-fuse, or like delayed explosives, the effects of which were causally inevitable.

Nevertheless it is not necessary, I argued, to suggest that Hebrews held this primitive view of language. It is implausible to claim that they could not distinguish between words and things, on the ground that *dabhar* could mean "word" or "thing". In Austin's terms, some speech-acts carry no institutional procedure for withdrawal, even if others do. In some churches and societies (but not in all) the speech-act "I do" in a marriage-service can be effectively undone in an act of divorce. But there is no procedure for saying (as far as I know) "I unbaptize this infant . . .", or "I uncommit his or her ashes to the ground . . .". Isaac could not unbless Jacob because no *procedure* existed which could *authorize* such an unblessing.

I shall argue in Chapter VIII that some of the speech-acts enacted by Jesus in the gospels rest equally on assumptions about authorization which, in turn, carry implications for Christology. Similarly promissory speech-acts raise issues about commitments, on one side, and conditions, expectations, and changes, on the other. Much of the religious currency of biblical texts depends on whether readers have *sufficient cause to act* on the basis of what these promise, proclaim, or direct, as Luther insisted in his debate about *claritas scripturae* with Erasmus. Of all the issues discussed in this volume, however, the ground-breaking argument which has given me most satisfaction to formulate arises from noting the consequences of speech-act theory in Searle and in Recanati for a re-appraisal of the arguments of E.P. Sanders concerning Pauline language about the work of Christ in Paul.

In Chapter VIII I argue that atonement language in Paul belongs to the category of language in which, to use the terminology of Searle and Recanati, the "direction of fit" or "direction of correspondence" is that in which words express states of affairs. On the other hand, "participatory" language in Paul, which speaks of sharing in the having-died and being-been-raised of Christ, belongs to the category of promissory or eschatological language, in which, in the terms used by Searle and Recanati, the world is changed in accordance with the word: there is a "world-to-word" direction of fit. Sanders may well be correct to see the "participatory" language as forward-looking, and atonement language as relating to the past. But it is misleading when he suggests that the atonement language on this basis becomes less central or less important than participatory language. For in terms of speech-act theory, this language *describes* the contextual and institutional presuppositions without which the *promissory* language of participation in the resurrection would be null and void. Without the presupposition of atonement, the promise of participation in the resurrection *would not constitute an effective act*, carrying far-reaching consequences.

One minor point which also arises from the theory of Searle and Recanati deserves brief introductory mention. Biblical specialists often fail to distinguish between changes of linguistic content and changes of linguistic force when a passage or sentence is re-contextualized within the biblical writings. In chapter I an example is cited from the work of Michael Fishbane; and in chapter XII, from Phyllis Trible. Fishbane implies that Ex. 34: 6,7, receives a different meaning in Nahum 1: 2,3. But Searle and Recanati, following the tradition of Wittgenstein, distinguish between the picture, image, or propositional content (p) and its functions, application, or *force* (F). Indeed Recanati explicitly entitles his book *Meaning and Force*.[16] A change of *force*, however, cannot be described as a "contradiction" without de-historicizing and de-contextualizing each text as if it were a context-free statement. In everyday parlance, I may declare "God is great", in one situation as an assurance; in another, as a warning; in a third, as an act of praise. To speak of "contradictions" in such contexts suggests an inaccurate and indeed misleading use of terminology.

I have ventured into one area where I am not as confident as in most of the rest of the book. The argument is finely balanced for initiating a discussion of textuality as soon as in chapters II and III. Werner Jeanrond (1988) has urged that theorists should not discuss the interpretation and reading of texts *before* they have established what they mean by "texts".[17] But a dilemma arises because the problem can *also* be formulated the other way round: what theorists count as reading or as interpretation serves to condition their view about the nature of texts. Does Fish's socio-pragmatic theory of human perception and interpretation, for example, determine his view of the nature of texts, or does his theory of texts lead to his socio-contextual pragmatism? Like the hermeneutical circle, the understanding of the one conditions the evaluation of the other. Hence, we must emphasize, *the arguments of chapters II and III remain provisional on conclusions reached later in the book*, including not least chapters VI, VII, VIII, X, XIII and XIV.

In chapter II I introduce broad issues about the nature of texts. Again, for the sake of readers who may be relatively new to the subject, the discussion at this stage remains undemanding, and is qualified with more rigour in chapters III, XIII, and XIV. But textuality cannot remain for ever in the abstract and at a merely general level. Just as Wittgenstein and Austin conclusively demonstrated that the question "What is meaning?", and even the question "What is the meaning of a word?", produces only confusion in abstraction from some context and purpose, so the question "What is a text?" invites parallel observations. In chapter XIII I note Umberto Eco's helpful comments on different categories and species of texts. Specific biblical texts may be primarily transmissive (perhaps Philemon) or productive (perhaps Revelation); author-orientated (perhaps I Corinthians) or relatively context-free (perhaps Jonah), and even these provisional evaluations depend on given traditions of interpretative judgments, within given frameworks.

Inevitably, therefore, some of the arguments of chapters II and III are negative. I attack sweeping, wholesale attempts to strip *all* written texts and certainly all biblical texts, from authors and from situations in life. Questions about the nature of texts also arise from within given contexts and address certain purposes. Where these contexts and purposes are provided by the Christian community, certain theological constraints condition answers about textuality in relation to biblical material. If in theological terms the central paradigm-case of the word of God made accessible and intelligible is that of the enfleshed word, in which word and deed are interwoven, it would not remain consonant with the nature of the gospel to disembody *all* biblical texts as literary effects disengaged from the public world which gave them operative currency.

To put forward such arguments, however, is by no means to depend on a representational or narrowly referential theory of language. The issues about *how* language and meaning engage with historical life-worlds, or with what Wittgenstein terms "the stream of life" are far more complex and subtle. We are not obliged to choose between *either* a representational and wholly transparent view of language *or* a postmodernist notion of language as a multi-layered matrix of effects generated by shifting community-attitudes and social conventions. The gospels may embody productive texts; but they also witness to events initiated by divine grace. Even if we were to grant Michael Wadsworth's questionable claim that "saving event and community response become one", they are more than matrices of meaning out of which communities of readers are invited to create their own gospels.[18]

Nevertheless it remains true that the capacity of texts to shape and to transform readers become actualized within the temporal horizons of readers. The latter section of chapter II and the initial sections of chapter III introduce these issues. The setting of worship acquires special significance here, as an instanciation of hermeneutical openness and listening in corporate expectancy of an eventful communicative or productive act. I note the emphasis of Eastern Orthodox hermeneutics, in which the liturgy of the word provides a classic setting for this creative moment.

Chapter III includes some difficult and demanding reading, which some may prefer to postpone until near the end of the book. The aim of the chapter is to try to disentangle semiotic theory from a particular world-view associated with the work of Barthes, Derrida, and others. I suggest an analogy with A.J. Ayer's exposition of logical positivism in the 1930s. Ayer's work became influential and fashionable because he presented it to the reading public as a *theory of language*. Whatever could not be verified in principle, he argued, could not convey cognitive *meaning*. But Ayer's system was eventually unmasked as *positivism in linguistic dress*, and its spell was broken. By analogy, Barthes, Derrida, and other post-modernist and deconstructionist writers often seem plausible as exponents of *literary and semiotic* theory. If the sign-system matrix (cf. Saussure's *langue*) becomes subject to successive transpositions on the ground that it is arbitrary how can linguistic anchorage in the public world remain sufficiently stable to communicate assertions about states of affairs or extra-linguistic reality? Everything becomes fluid.

I argue, however, that Barthes and Derrida, among others, carry semiotic theory beyond the limits which semiotics itself strictly reaches. In practice, they press for *a post-modernist world-view in semiotic dress*. As we have noted and shall expound in fuller detail, such an approach would invalidate Wittgenstein's careful distinction between public-domain language which reflected testable regularities (albeit developing ones) and uncheckable "private language" (in his own sense of the term) which lacked observable engagements with the extra-linguistic public world of behaviour. All languages would effectively become "private" language, because there could be no criteria for what might count as a *mistake* in its use. It is true that some texts serve to de-stabilize traditions for iconoclastic purposes; but these de-stabilizing functions are parasitic on more regular and stable traditions. In Wittgenstein's terminology, doubt comes only after belief; lying is a language-game that is dependent on practices of truthful communication.

It would be a mistake to put forward arguments about contemporary hermeneutical theory as if this had no pre-history which has contributed to its present shape. I have chosen *not* to try to offer a detailed history of hermeneutics or of biblical interpretation. Books on the latter are numerous. But I have given attention to those perennial issues which re-appear in modern debates, and those which assume a new form in the light of the current discussion.

The discussion of Patristic and mediaeval allegorical interpretation, together with its origins and pre-history in Philo and in the Stoics, takes on new dimensions in the light of contemporary issues in hermeneutics. In his *Symbolism and Interpretation* (Eng. 1982) Tzvetan Todorov distinguishes two major interpretative strategies in the history of interpretation. He traces an "operational" or "philological" strategy through Spinoza, Wolf, Ast, and Boeckh, and a "finalist" strategy of interpretation through the Patristic writers, and then in Marxist and Freudian criticism. Each strategy operates with two or more "texts". In operational hermeneutics the "input text" is that of the author, and the "output text" that of the interpreter. Todorov writes: "The two types of interpretation that abound in the history of hermeneutics... correspond to two... possibilities: imposing constraints on the *operations* that correct the input text with the output text, or else on the output text itself."[19] Patristic interpretation, he argues, does not utilize the constraint of the input text, but undergoes "ceaseless confrontation with another text (that of Christian doctrine)".[20]

A number of post-modernist theorists argue that the Patristic and mediaeval eras of interpretation reflect the role of communities in ways which stand in contrast to the individualism of post-Reformation and Enlightenment rationalism and modernism. In terms of social history, the Fathers, they argue, operated a pragmatic hermeneutic which affirmed this community.

In chapter IV I argue that any claim about parallels between the pre-Reformation Church and post-modernism should be viewed with caution. Two factors invite special attention. First, in contrast to post-modernist readings, the *lectio divina* or "spiritual reading" of the Patristic and mediaeval church took place within the theological boundaries of a stable tradition. I have called this general perspective a *hermeneutics of tradition*. It is not enough for biblical texts to operate productively; what counts as productive reading is partly determined, as Todorov notes, by the "text" of Christian doctrine. In *The Two Horizons* I discussed in some detail the relation between biblical exegesis and systematic theology, especially in the light of Gadamer's hermeneutics.[21]

Claims about community-relative criteria in the interpretation of the Fathers also invite careful evaluation. I discuss Irenaeus's concept of tradition in chapter IV, but I find unconvincing the arguments of Elaine Pagels and others that gnostic exegesis is no less rational, responsible, or justifiable within its socio-contextual frame than Patristic exegesis is within its own tradition. Wittgenstein's injunction that we should "look and see" before accepting theories too readily reveals a striking variety among Patristic and gnostic sources which relativizes these claims about contextual frames. Even within gnostic contextual frames, transpositions of biblical texts into instrumental devices often transparently entail what Laeuchli identifies as semantic disintegration and breakdown. On the other hand Origen makes a decisive hermeneutical advance. Even if he often uses allegorical interpretation, some of the examples often cited in this category represent careful and considered pastoral applications of texts. Karen Torjesen's work on Origen's hermeneutics (1986) not only confirms this point, but also demonstrates that Origen also develops a hermeneutic of reader-effects as a *pastoral* resource.

I am aware that I could have addressed in more detail issues raised by mediaeval interpretation. In this area, however, Gillian R. Evans has already produced accurate, detailed and constructive work, and I refer to her writings in the chapters concerned. Her books include careful accounts of theories of language and logic which belong to this period.[22]

A major issue for Protestant readers of the bible emerges from Luther's notion of *claritas scripturae*, and from Calvin's emphasis on scripture's perspicuity. I have argued in chapter V that Luther develops this category as a polemic against Erasmus in the context of theories of knowledge. Erasmus argued that the biblical texts offer insufficient coherence and clarity to offer a firm *basis for action*. Luther insisted that such a suspension of judgment constituted a self-defeating paralysis. He urged that the way ahead was always clear enough to indicate the next practical step. Moreover, the interpreter of scripture, in Luther's judgment, had no need to resort to finding "higher" meanings in the text in order to justify action. The biblical texts function with operative effectiveness in "promoting Christ".

All the same, Luther and Calvin, followed by the English Reformers, saw the need for questioning and enquiry in the interpretation of biblical texts. *Theirs was a hermeneutic of enquiry*. The nature of these questions and their development towards modern hermeneutics receives further exploration in these chapters.

Schleiermacher's hermeneutics is the subject of detailed and sympathetic treatment in chapter VI. He offers *a hermeneutics of understanding*. His theory is complex, and has generally been oversimplified and undervalued. I argue that his contrasts between the grammatical and psychological axes of hermeneutics anticipate Saussure's distinction between shared language as an intersubjective system (*langue*), and language-uses in particular acts of communication (*parole*). The dual role which Schleiermacher establishes between creative, intuitive, *immediacy* of inter-personal *understanding*, and comparative, objective, *distanced*, *criticism* still remains fundamental in hermeneutics. Habermas as we have noted, develops this kind of contrast in terms of *life-world* and *system*.

The hermeneutics of understanding expounded by Schleiermacher, Dilthey, and Betti, receives concrete and specific application to biblical interpretation and to biblical texts in chapter VII. I do not know of other attempts to test their theoretical models in this detailed way. In particular I apply their theory to Pauline texts, drawing on a variety of work in Pauline studies. From among these studies the work of J. Christiaan Beker on contingency and coherence in Paul represents the most immediately relevant and suggestive approach. One additional by-product is to note the awareness of Schleiermacher and Betti that understandings of texts remain provisional and corrigible in relation to the systems within which they operate. But unlike some more recent relativistic and pluralistic theories, they do not surrender, on this ground, their quest for advances in corrigible knowledge, or claims for its working status as provisional but testable knowledge. It is precisely because for him understanding can be trans-contextual that Betti makes so much of the need for listening, openness, tolerance, and mutual respect.

I have already outlined the distinctive contribution of chapter VIII, in which the work of Searle and Recanati on speech-act theory serves as a resource and model for the exploration of a hermeneutic of self-involvement. I have tried to demonstrate briefly that speech-act theory offers a more balanced and less one-sided model of self-involvement than existential interpretation. I have not enlarged on Heidegger and Bultmann, since I did so in *The Two Horizons*. The ultimate test of this approach, however, is whether speech-act theory sheds light on the issues in biblical texts which I seek to illuminate. These include most especially texts concerning Paul's theology of the work of Christ against the interpretative background of questions raised by Schweitzer, Sanders, and others, as we have noted.

Gadamer's approach to hermeneutics has also already been outlined in this introduction. In *The Two Horizons* I offered a critical exposition of Gadamer's hermeneutics, and attempted to suggest how his theory might shed light on retrospective contextualization in the Fourth Gospel. I have not covered the same ground here. My major concern in chapter IX has been to trace the contours of the philosophical background, including work on the critique of language, which necessitated the rejection of rationalism and the turn towards metacritical theory. In any case Gadamer's rejection of any notion of "method" as a determinate procedure which is not wholly context-dependent, together with his change of focus from the critical to the metacritical, places a question mark against attempts to find any "model" for interpretation in Gadamer's philosophical hermeneutics. He is more concerned with broader fundamental questions about the relation between the two major hermeneutical axes: the contingent, particular, historical axis of variable finite actualizations and textual performances, and the general linguistic axis of the universal ontological ground which these finite acts presuppose.

My critique of Gadamer stands close to those of Richard Bernstein and especially Georgia Warnke. A deep ambiguity in Gadamer allows the interpreter of his system to stress either of two aspects. He or she may stress, on one side, the universality of language and of effective-histories which transmit community-judgments of practical wisdom as tradition. Alternatively the emphasis may be seen to lie on the variable and unpredictable nature of the historically finite actualizations of texts and traditions in context-relative events. If interpreters emphasize only variable finite *effects*, this suggests some support for a *socio-pragmatic* hermeneutic. If, however, they emphasize that these effects *presuppose* universals of language and continuities of tradition, this suggests that Gadamer is laying the foundations for a *metacritical* hermeneutic. I criticize those pragmatists who attend to only one side of Gadamer's system, but I recognize the difficulty of reconciling the two sides, and acknowledge the ambiguity of Gadamer's own work.

Pannenberg acknowledges the problem of historical finitude which Gadamer addresses. But his notion of Christian eschatology as providing horizons of ultimacy and of universality allows him to give substance to the otherwise unduly empty concept of the universal in Gadamer. The God of Christian theology stands as the source, creator, and goal, of all; theology therefore has a universal character and claim. This transcends the hermeneutical life-world of any one ghetto-like "religious" tradition. Indeed in his later work partly anticipating parallels in Habermas, Pannenberg argues that the *hermeneutical lifeworld*, which represents the axis of historical finitude and contingent event, cannot be isolated from a relation of dialogue with *critical system* which provides a metacritical and coherent frame, and becomes more decisive for the nature of theology.

Provided that we recognize that anticipations of "system" remain in principle corrigible, incomplete, and open-ended, I argue that Pannenberg's approach is constructive. Increasingly in the social sciences and to a more limited extent, even in some of the physical sciences, the task of bringing the hermeneutical life-world of the community of interpreters into engagement with critical, expanding open systems, is seen as an important one for a variety of disciplines. Pannenberg's appeal to the principles implied by a Christian eschatology also carry the discussion forward constructively. Only in the context of the whole, he argues, can that which is partial in principle achieve genuine meaning. A work of art, for example, cannot be judged prior to its completion. For Christian theology, the eschatological horizon of divine promise sheds light on the meaning of the present. The event of Jesus Christ and his resurrection offers provisional anticipation of this eschatological goal of promise. This projects meaning within a frame which transcends the unfinished history of any particular community. James McHann (1987) argues that I should have paid more attention to Pannenberg's eschatological horizon in my work *The Two Horizons*. I did not dissent from this when I examined his doctoral dissertation, which he presented under the title *The Three Horizons*.[23]

I have already indicated the nature of my approach to the hermeneutics of Paul Ricoeur. The heart of hermeneutical theory finds clearest expression in Ricoeur's axiom: "Hermeneutics seems to me to be animated by this double motivation: willingness to suspect, willingness to listen, vow of rigour, vow of obedience."[24] The first addresses the task of "doing away with idols", namely becoming critically aware of when we project our own wishes and constructs into texts, so that they no longer address us from beyond ourselves as "other". The second concerns the need to listen in openness to symbol and to narrative and thereby to allow creative events to occur "in front of" the text, and to have their effect on us.

Nevertheless I also pursue one major line of argument which expresses a hesitation about the comprehensiveness of Ricoeur's hermeneutical model. Searle and Recanati, among others, go further than Ricoeur in elaborating the differences of logical and presuppositional mechanisms on the basis of which fictional and non-fictional texts achieve their respective effects. Recanati, in a suggestive image, distinguishes between linguistic acts performed "on stage" and those which operate "behind the scenes", or after the curtain falls.[25] Many biblical texts undeniably function as fiction. Many (probably not all) of the parables of Jesus fall into this category. Some texts may embody mixed modes. Some including perhaps the narrative of Jonah, presuppose operational conditions in which in Hans Frei's terminology the distinction between "realistic history-like narrative" and referential historical narrative fades and cannot be sharply sustained.[26] But this operational merging of boundaries does not apply to every category of biblical narrative texts.

This need not imply a crude series of ostensive references for each component of the text. It may rest on a broader extra-linguistic anchorage in the public world through less transparent and more complex networks of multiple interweavings with human life, behaviour, and situation. But within a particular sub-category of examples, historical narrative is more than "history-like". It does not miss the point in these instances to ask what occurred or what the author thought occurred, as if this were only a "modern" question.

Evidence for this claim arises from placing together two sets of considerations. First Searle argues convincingly that while "roughly speaking, whether or not a work is literature is for the readers to decide, whether or not it is fiction is for the author to decide."[27] The latter has to do with the particular set of commitments, responsibilities, and purposes which the author chooses either to adopt or to suspend. But the theory of texts adopted by Ricoeur accords a minimal role to what authors may have decided about their responsibilities and commitments. These drop from view as soon as oral speech takes the form of written texts, when we read texts as literature.

Second, the response of the early Church Fathers to second- and third-century gnostic sources suggests that conscious distinctions between history and history-like narrative were made long before formulations of theories took place in eighteenth-century hermeneutics about ostensive reference. Samuel Laeuchli demonstrates in convincing detail that the interpretation of biblical narrative texts as only "history-like" in such sources as *The Gospel of Truth* transposed many biblical texts into a different key, of which both the gnostics and the Fathers were fully aware. In post-modernist language, *The Gospel of Truth* may well embody linguistic creativity in which multi-layered textual matrices produce fresh meanings on the basis of intertextuality. But the cost of this, as Laeuchli argues, is "semantic breakdown". because "the frame within which exegesis operates has no history", and "interpretation has long ceased to be historical".[28] This does *not* call into question the constructive value of Ricoeur's important work on the creative power of symbols, metaphors, and narratives. It invites caution in evaluating how comprehensively his hermeneutical models apply to different sub-categories of biblical texts.

The distinctive arguments of chapters XI and XII have already been broadly outlined. If Latin American hermeneutics, black hermeneutics, and feminist hermeneutics seek to evolve a genuinely liberating critique of injustice and oppression, in which uses of biblical texts in the interests of oppressors are unmasked, it becomes essential to disentangle those strands within them which utilize socio-critical theoretical models from others which crumble and collapse into socio-pragmatic systems of hermeneutics. Socio-contextual pragmatism can achieve nothing beyond the attempt to fight oppressors with the oppressors' own oppressive weapons. Whoever is the most militant, the most articulate, the most manipulative, the most self-confident (sometimes even the most supposedly pious) appears to win this rhetorical power struggle. If his metaphor is barbed, Jonathan Culler nevertheless offers an unforgettable image when he identifies the power-rhetoric of contextual "success" on which Rorty and others rely as a "pragmatism whose complacency seems altogether appropriate to the Age of Reagan".[29]

Socio-pragmatic hermeneutics remain explicitly ethnocentric. The community cannot be corrected and reformed as Fish concedes, from outside itself. Its only hope of change is to imperialize other communities by extending its own boundaries until it disintegrates under its own weight and internal pluralism. But this is to exchange hermeneutical understanding for the random contingencies of social history. It is daring to call this "hermeneutics" when the hermeneutical tradition began by asking what it is to stand in the shoes of the other and to listen in openness. By contrast, Habermas and Apel seek to unmask the social interests of particular communities and groups on some broader basis. In theological terms socio-pragmatism would immunize the church against a theology of the cross which de-centres individual and corporate self-interest as a critique extended to the church itself.

The issues which arose from the impact of literary and semiotic theory on biblical interpretation receive evaluation in chapters XIII and XIV. New tools are added to the hermeneutical repertoire, but more fundamental questions emerge than the evaluation of particular procedures and devices. Numerous semiotic cross-currents flow in the wake of the transposition of structuralism into post-structuralist and post-modernist approaches. Traditional notions of what kind of processes are involved in the reading of texts become subverted. Whereas the hermeneutical tradition tended to focus on processes of *human understanding* within *life-worlds grounded in historical inter-subjectivity*, semiotic approaches tend to focus on processes in which *sign-systems* become operative as *sub-systems grounded in contextualizing frames of intertextuality*. Networks of signs become matrices which generate meanings in relation to other texts.

While this brings certain advances in identifying semiotic dimensions in reading-processes and in questions concerning reader-competency, the price of the advance may be in many cases to neglect the cognitive dimension of human understanding and to substitute a concern for literary *productiveness* in place of concerns for *communication*. In this respect the sub-title "transforming biblical readings" now takes on a third sense. Where the change from "interpretation" to "reading" is more than cosmetic and indicates a conscious paradigm-shift, writers tend to focus on encounters with texts as semiotic processes of literary production, rather than as acts of communication which transmit some cognitive context. One advantage of the otherwise cumbersome term "hermeneutics" is that its all-embracing and neutral character avoids restricting discussion to any single sub-category otherwise suggested by theories of "interpretation", "understanding", or "reading". The present study concerns *both* communication *and* productiveness; *both* the transforming effects of texts upon readers, *and* the truth-conditions which render those effects operative or valid in the extra-linguistic world of human life.

The dimension of textual effect remains fundamental for hermeneutics. But meanings of texts cannot be equated entirely with their pragmatic effects, not least because the traditional question of what counts as a deception or mistake in processes of interpretation also retains a central place in this subject. In Christian theology the critique of the cross stands in judgment on any use of biblical texts that serves self-affirmation or self-legitimation if this rests on illusion, deceit, or self-interest. Authorization on the basis of truth is a different matter. Transforming biblical reading de-centres individual or corporate self-interests, and allows readers to share the new horizons projected by what "addresses" them from beyond them as "other".[30] In the words of David Kelsey, recently endorsed by Frances Young, part of what it means to call a text "Christian scripture" is that "it functions to shape persons' identities so decisively as to transform them".[31] The practical implications of this last point are explored in detail in our final chapter.

NOTES TO INTRODUCTION

1. Kurt Mueller-Volmer (ed.) *The Hermeneutics Reader: Texts of the German Tradition from the Enlightenment to the Present*, Oxford: Blackwell, 1986 and Continuum Publishing 1985; and David E. Klemm (ed.) *Hermeneutical Inquiry: I, The Interpretation of Texts*, and *II, The Interpretation of Existence* (2 vols.) Atlanta: Scholars Press (A.A.R. Studies in Religion, 43) 1986.
2. Christopher Rowland and Mark Corner, *Liberating Exegesis: The Challenge of Liberation Theology to Biblical Studies*, London: S.P.C.K., 1990, 76 and 78–9.
3. Frances Young, *The Art of Performance. Towards a Theology of Holy Scripture*, London: Darton, Longman, and Todd, 1990, 32n; cf. 64n. and 185. My first reference to the "performance" model occurred in my discussion of Gadamer in Anthony C. Thiselton, *The Two Horizons: New Testament Hermeneutics and Philosophical Description with Special Reference to Heidegger, Bultmann, Gadamer, and Wittgenstein*, Grand Rapids: Eerdmans, and Exeter: Paternoster, 1980, 298.
4. Stanley Fish, *Doing What Comes Naturally. Change, Rhetoric, and the Practice of Theory in Literary and Legal Studies*, Oxford: Clarendon Press, 1989, ix.
5. David J.A. Clines "Deconstructing the Book of Job" in Martin Warner (ed.) *The Bible as Rhetoric. Studies in Biblical Persuasion and Credibility*, London and New York: Routledge, 1990, 79; cf. 65–80.
6. J. Habermas, *The Theory of Communicative Action: The Critique of Functionalist Reason*, 2 vols., Eng. Cambridge: Polity Press, 1984 and 1987. Cf. also *Knowledge and Human Interests*, Eng., London: Heinemann, 2nd edn. 1978.
7. Elliott E. Johnson, *Expository Hermeneutics: An Introduction* Grand Rapids: Academie, 1990, 54–69 *et passim*; cf. E.D.. Hirsch, *Validity in Interpretation*, New Haven: Yale University Press, 1967; and *The Aims of Interpretation*, Chicago: University of Chicago Press, 1976, especially 1–13 and 17–49.
8. Frank Lentriccia, *After the New Criticism*, Chicago: University of Chicago Press, 1980, 256–87.
9. John R. Searle, *Intentionality. An Essay on the Philosophy of Mind*, Cambridge: Cambridge University Press, 1983, 141–232 *et passim*.
10. Robert Fyall, "How God Treats His Friends: God, Job, and Satan", Unpublished Seminar Paper, Durham, November 1990; cf. further his doctoral thesis *Imagery in the Book of Job*, University of Edinburgh, 1991.

11. Jonathan Culler, *Framing the Sign. Criticism and its Institutions*, Oxford: Blackwell, 1988, especially ix.
12. Anthony C. Thiselton, "The Parables as Language-Event: Some Comments on Fuchs's Hermeneutics in the Light of Linguistic Philosophy", *Scottish Journal of Theology* 23, 1970, 437–68.
13. Anthony C. Thiselton, *The Two Horizons: New Testament Hermeneutics and Philosophical Description with Special Reference to Heidegger, Bultmann, Gadamer, and Wittgenstein*, Grand Rapids: Eerdmans, and Exeter: Paternoster, 1980, especially 357–427.
14. J.G. du Plessis, *Clarity and Obscurity. A Study in Textual Communication of the Relation between Sender Parable and Receiver in the Synoptic Gospels*, Stellenbosch: University of Stellenbosch D. Theol. Dissertation, 1985, 2; cf. 3 and 62.
15. Anthony C. Thiselton, "The Supposed Power of Words in the Biblical Writings", *Journal of Theological Studies* n.s. 25, 1974, 282–99.
16. François Recanati, *Meaning and Force. The Pragmatics of Peformative Utterances*, Eng. Cambridge: Cambridge University Press, 1987.
17. Werner Jeanrond, *Text and Interpretation as Categories of Theological Thinking*, Dublin: Gill and MacMillan, 1988, 73–103.
18. Michael Wadsworth, "Making and Interpreting Scripture" in M. Wadsworth (ed.) *Ways of Reading the Bible*, Sussex: Harvester Press and New Jersey: Barnes and Noble, 1981, 20; cf. 7–22.
19. Tzvetan Todorov, *Symbolism and Interpretation*, Eng. Ithaca: Cornell University Press, 1982, 167.
20. *Ibid* 98.
21. Anthony C. Thiselton, *The Two Horizons*, 314–26.
22. Gillian R. Evans, *The Language and Logic of the Bible: the Earlier Middle Ages*, Cambridge: Cambridge University Press, 1984; and *The Language and Logic of the Bible: the Road to the Reformation*, Cambridge: Cambridge University Press, 1985.
23. James C. McHann Jr., *The Three Horizons: A Study in Biblical Hermeneutics with Special Reference to Wolfhart Pannenberg*, Aberdeen: University of Aberdeen Ph.D. Dissertation, 1987.
24. Paul Ricoeur, *Freud and Philosophy: An Essay on Interpretation*, Eng. New Haven and London: Yale University Press, 1970, 27.
25. F. Recanati, *op. cit.* 266.
26. Hans W. Frei, *The Eclipse of Biblical Narrative. A Study in Eighteenth and Nineteenth Century Hermeneutics*, New Haven and London: Yale University Press, 1974, 10–16, 51–104, *et passim*.
27. John R. Searle, "The Logical Status of Fictional Discourse" in *Expression and Meaning. Studies in the Theory of Speech Acts*, Cambridge: Cambridge University Press, 1979, 59; cf. 58–75.
28. Samuel Laeuchli, *The Language of Faith: An Introduction to the Semantic Dilemma of the Early Church*, London: Epworth Press, 1965, 89, 69 and 72.
29. Jonathan Culler, *op. cit.* 55.
30. On the notion of texts as "address", cf. Dick Leith and George Myerson, *The Power of Address. Exploration in Rhetoric*, London and New York: Routledge, 1989, xii *et passim*.
31. Frances Young, *op. cit.* 173; cf. David Kelsey, *The Uses of Scripture in Recent Theology*, London: S.C.M., 1975, 90.

CHAPTER I

Transforming Texts: Preliminary Observations

The phrase "transforming texts" can be interpreted in two ways. Texts can actively shape and transform the perceptions, understanding, and actions of readers and of reading communities. Legal texts, medical texts, and biblical texts provide examples. But texts can also suffer transformation at the hands of readers and reading communities. Readers may misunderstand and thereby misuse them; they may blunt their edge and domesticate them; or they may consciously or unconsciously transform them into devices for maintaining and confirming prejudices or beliefs which are imposed on others in the name of the text. Readers and interpreters may also endow texts with new life in the context of new situations.

1. The capacity of texts to transform readers

Hermeneutics entails a study of the processes and operative conditions of transforming texts, in both senses of the phrase. It also raises a large network of related questions about goals and models of interpretation, and what each may be thought to presuppose and to effect. The transforming effects of a text remain no more than *potential* ones all the while its writing, printing, or electronic display (or more debatably, sound) constitute nothing more than physical-spatial objects of visual (or tactile or aural) perception. Their potential begins to become *actualized* when a reader or reading community perceives that the signs constitute an intelligible sub-system of some larger linguistic or semiotic code, and processes of interpretation begin. When the necessary conditions for interpretation become operational, an event of communication takes place *within the temporal flow of the reader's life and experience*. The example of musical texts illustrate the relevance of this temporal axis well. The potential of the physical-spatial shapes of crotchets and quavers in a musical score become actualized only in the temporal flow of the performance, or when a skilled musician "reads" the score in his or her head.

In what way this temporal actualization of the text will be creative or transforming depends partly on the nature of the text in question. Hermeneutics has suffered grievously from the attempts of theorists to use one particular hermeneutical paradigm as an explanatory model for a large variety of texts. Briefly in *The Two Horizons* (1980) and in *The Responsibility of Hermeneutics* (1985) I tried to argue that the notion of speech-acts, alongside that of projected narrative-worlds, offered at least two explanatory models of how texts make a creative impact on readers.[1] Speech act theory, as we noted in the Introduction, is associated especially with the work of J.L. Austin and J.R. Searle, although its pre-history began with the later Wittgenstein. It has been further developed and modified by F. Recanati (French, 1981, Eng. 1987), by Geoffrey Leech (1983) and by others.[2] Recently a number of biblical specialists have re-opened questions about the relevance of speech-act theory for biblical interpretation in a volume of *Semeia* (41) edited by Hugh C. White under the title, *Speech Act Theory and Biblical Criticism* (1988).

Some legal texts of a certain kind offer an excellent example of the operational significance of texts which constitute speech acts. Parallels with biblical texts will soon become clear. A text which constitutes a valid will, duly signed and witnessed, bequeaths an estate or a legacy to a named beneficiary. Even if a will lies forgotten, unnoticed, or misplaced for a period, it becomes operative as soon as it has been proven, and the text becomes an effective *act* of transferring property. An operational text thereby changes the life of a beneficiary, perhaps giving rise to new hopes, new attitudes, and new actions. In the case of the biblical writings, the persistence of the terms Old and New "Testament" serve to remind us of a covenantal context in which pledge and promise feature prominently. The biblical writings abound in promises, invitations, verdicts, confessions, pronouncements of blessing, commands, namings, and declarations of love. In his book *Conversation with the Bible* Markus Barth writes: "The unique power of the Bible flows from the fact that the biblical words are words of love. . . . between God and man. The reading of the Bible therefore should be compared to reading love-letters rather than the study and use of a law book".[3] The recipient of a love letter does not normally respond by acknowledging receipt of information. Reading here often (but not always) becomes *transactional*. It entails acts of acceptance, sometimes commitment, and probably deeper bonding.

Nevertheless speech-act theory does not offer a comprehensive paradigm for all biblical texts, let alone all non-biblical texts. Texts shape and transform readers in many different ways. For example, a narrative may draw the hearer into a projected narrative-world in which a flow of events and feelings are imaginatively experienced at a pre-reflective level. In this case, the "transaction" lies in the reader's willingness to step into this world, and to let his or her feelings and imagination be directed by the world of the text. The Book of Jonah, for example, invites us to travel in imagination with this self-important prophet. We hear him give his orthodox testimony to the sailors; we witness his prayers for death and his formalized thanksgiving for deliverance from death, carefully modelled like one of the psalms. We eventually follow him to Nineveh, and finally, to our horror, experience the shock of observing and feeling Jonah's intense concern about the welfare of a castor-oil plant which forms part of his immediate "world" against the background of his persistent unconcern about the welfare of Nineveh which never seriously becomes part of his own world of concerns (Jonah 1: 2,9; 2: 2–9; 4: 1–11)[4]. Spending time with Jonah in the narrative-world projected by the text transforms feelings and attitudes about the wider world at a level which might not be reached by a theological sermon or treatise on mission or evangelism as a principle of life.

A quite different approach to the transforming potential of texts is suggested by the tradition of hermeneutical theory from Dilthey to Betti. The goal of interpretation according to Dilthey and Betti is to come to understand the mind, life-processes, and life-world of a text's author. The reader must learn what it is to stand in the shoes of the author. This produces what Emilio Betti views as a cast of mind essential for the modern world, with its trends towards political confrontations and polarizations. He writes: "For humankind, nothing lies so close to the heart as understanding one's fellow human beings"[5]. The process entails a recognition of the limits of my own understanding, and learning to listen, with patience and respect, not only to what the other person says, but also to why the other person says it.

In Christian spirituality or in pastoral theology we should probably describe this orientation initially as one of openness. To be open is to let oneself be sufficiently vulnerable to be influenced by the other towards self-change. According to Dilthey and Betti it would be false to set up a contrast between "pastoral skills of listening" and reading ancient or modern texts with hermeneutical training and awareness. An openness to be willing to listen, to see the other person's point of view, and to be changed, characterizes any hermeneutically sensitive reading of texts, no less than in encounters between persons in everyday life.

These three models of textual activity, that of the speech-act, that of the narrative-world, and that of inter-personal understanding, do not exhaust the variety of ways in which texts, and especially biblical texts, can have transforming effects. As a fourth example in this chapter, we consider a model which is suggested by a hermeneutical category used by Hans Robert Jauss. Jauss was a former pupil of Gadamer, and is regarded as a leading exponent of Reception Theory. He follows Husserl, Heidegger, Gadamer, and others in using the notion of "horizon", and in particular regards the central category of "horizon of expectation" as his "methodological centrepiece"[6]. Every reader brings a horizon of expectation to the text. This is a mind-set, or system of references, which characterizes the reader's finite viewpoint amidst his or her situatedness in time and history. Patterns of habituation in the reader's attitudes, experiences, reading-practices, and life, define and strengthen his or her horizon of expectation.

A text, however, can surprise, contradict, or even reverse such a horizon of expectation. In earlier literary theory, the Russian formalist writer Viktor Shklovski had already explored this kind of phenomenon. He argued that the effective actualization of a work of creative literary art lay in its power to "de-habitualize" the perceptions of readers.

In the case of the material of New Testament texts, Jesus, Paul and the apostolic community regarded the message of the cross as bringing to sharpest possible focus a clash with, and potential reversal of, very widespread horizons of expectation. Paul writes: "For the word of the cross is folly to those who are perishing, but to us who are being saved it is the power of God...We preach a Christ crucified, a stumbling block to Jews and folly to Gentiles, but to those who are called, both Jews and Gentiles, Christ the power of God and the wisdom of God" (1 Cor. 1: 18,,23,24). The message of the cross brings about a reversal of evaluations, and a change in the mind-set and system of references which had previously constituted a horizon of expectation.

The hermeneutical operation of this principle in some of the parables of Jesus had been explored, as is now well known, by Ernst Fuchs and other exponents of the so-called new hermeneutic. For example, in the parable of the labourers in the vineyard (Matt. 20: 1–15), the labourers and the readers share a horizon of expectation which is shaped and determined by the demands of justice. But this horizon is shattered, eclipsed, and transformed by a verdict which communicates the generosity of grace. I have considered other examples elsewhere (e.g. Luke 18: 9–14; Luke 10: 29–37)[7] The teaching of Jesus constantly clashes with horizons of expectation: "Many that are first will be last, and the last shall be first". (Mark 10:31). "Whoever would be great among you must be your servant". (10:44). Even more sharply: "Whoever would save his life will lose it; and whoever loses his life for my sake and the gospel's will save it" (Mark 8:35: *par.* Matt. 10:39; Luke 17:33; John 12:25).

As Dietrich Bonhoeffer and others point out, such a reversal of expectations finds expression in the beatitudes: "Blessed are the *poor* . . . Blessed are those who *mourn*...Blessed are those who *hunger*..." (Matt. 5: 3–6, and especially Luke 6: 20–22). Bonhoeffer comments on the principle that is involved, not as part of a hermeneutical theory at such, but as a comment on the signifance of the biblical texts from the viewpoint of Christian theology, and in particular, a theology of the cross. In his book *Meditating on the Word* he writes: "Either I determine the place in which I will find God, or I allow God to determine the place where he will be found. If it is I who say where God will be, I will always find there a God who in some way corresponds to me, is agreeable to me, fits in with my nature. But if it is God who says where He will be, then that will truly be a place which at first is not agreeable to me at all, which does not fit so well with me. That place is the cross of Christ. And whoever will find God there must draw near to the cross in the manner which the sermon on the Mount requires. This does not correspond to our nature at all".[8] In hermeneutical terms, our horizons of expectation need to be open to change and to transformation.

The history of the effects of texts bears witness to many experiences of this principle of transformation and reversal in the lives of a variety of people and communities. Perhaps the most widely celebrated example in Protestant Christendom is that of Martin Luther, who recounted the impact made on him by Paul's words: "He who by faith is righteous shall live" (Rom. 1:17). Luther recalls the sense of anger and fear with which he had hitherto reflected on biblical texts and on the gospels. But, he continues, when I came "to understand" both the text of Rom. 1:17 and its larger context, I felt that I was altogether "born again" and "entered paradise". A totally other face of the entire Scripture showed itself to me. In place of anger and fear, there came a love "as great as the hatred with which I had hated the word 'righteousness of God'"[9].

2. The capacity of readers and texts to transform texts: different notions of intertextuality

All the same, if texts can transform readers, readers can and do transform texts. Hermeneutics traces paths by which this process occurs. Sometimes readers transform texts through ignorance, blindness, or misunderstanding. Sometimes readers either consciously or through processes of self-deception find ways of rendering harmless texts which would otherwise prove to be disturbing and call for change. It is customarily acknowledged that understanding may be difficult in cases where the subject-matter of a text or its genre or code may be distant from the reader's assumptions and expectations and entirely unfamiliar. But texts may be transformed, no less, by habituated patterns of individual or corporate familiarity which rob the text of its power to speak to the reader as "*other*". If, for example, biblical and other religious texts are to deliver us from self-centredness and to convey messages of judgment or of love, encounters with texts involve, as David Klemm insists, encounters with "otherness".[10]

In Paul Ricoeur's view, an authentic encounter with texts occurs when the reader both "conquer(s) a remoteness" and meets with the other: "It is thus the growth of his own understanding of himself that he pursues through his understanding of the other. Every hermeneutics is thus, explicitly or implicitly, self-understanding by means of understanding others".[11] This represents, in the judgment of Ricoeur and others, an entirely different starting-point from that of the isolated individualism of Descartes' *Cogito*. If the reader's expectations and assumptions, especially those which have been ingrained by individual or corporate habit, transform the text into a reflection of the reader's own local and domestic concerns, the text's capacity to speak from within a horizon of otherness has evaporated.

What are we to say, however, about the kind of transformation which occurs when texts are placed in new contexts, or re-contextualized in new situations or in developing traditions? Again, hermeneutics has suffered because many theorists seek to formulate general answers to this question independently of the kind of text, or theory of texts, which is in view, and without specifying what theory of meaning each answer implies. It is well known that Gadamer insists that the development of traditions, and contexts within traditions, lead to changes of meaning, while Hirsch insists that what changes is not meaning but significance.[12]

In an essay entitled "Meaning in the Bible" Richard Swinburne argues that developments in the meanings of biblical texts occur, as small units are placed first within a context perhaps in pre-literary tradition, then in the editorial construction of a biblical book, then in the context of the biblical canon as scripture, and finally in the context of ecclesial creeds.[13] This principle, he argues, is not confined to biblical texts. He suggests the example of a speech or document which is quoted verbatim, and then is later placed in between a preface and an appendix in which the author explains that he or she no longer holds some of the views expressed in the document, or that the document is to be understood in some unusual or unexpected sense.[14]

Are these changes of "meaning", or transformations of function, role, or significance? The work of Brevard Childs on the canonical context of the Old Testament (1979) and the canonical context of the New (1984) seems to suggest that more than significance may be involved.[15] The work of J.A. Sanders (1972 and 1984) on canonical contexts stresses, rather, the processes by which later biblical writers use earlier biblical traditions, but both Childs and Sanders trace the re-contextualizations of meaning which occur when successive communities apply inherited texts to new situations, or place them in the context of some larger body of writing.[16] While Sanders' work relates primarily to the Old Testament, James Dunn makes some parallel points about the processes which lead towards a canonical text of the New Testament. Dunn comments concerning the stages or levels through which these processes advance: "At each of these levels the tradition in question functioned as constitutive and normative for the self-understanding of the communities who used them".[17] He continues: "All this involves the recognition that God was heard to speak differently at different periods".[18] He argues that the final composition level gives greatest promise of providing a normative control, although the message of any document may be qualified by its being included in a larger canon.[19]

In what sense does this distinction between levels and successive contexts determine changes of meaning rather than changes of significance? One writer, commenting on the work of B.S. Childs, speaks of the phenomenon of "re-signification". For example, he compares an earlier meaning of "Zion" in Isa. 31: 4,5, where the term refers to Zion as a political entity with a later use in Isa. 61: 2,3, where Zion becomes the place to which all come.[20] In Psalm 8: 4–6 "Son of Man" seems to mean humankind in general, whereas in the context of Hebrews 2: 7,8 the quotation of the Psalm seems as Hagner and others agree, to refer to Jesus Christ.[21] However, we should not make judgments too hastily about these passages. At least one writer, Walter C. Kaiser insists at the end of a study on the subject, that such passages "yield the same basic meaning in both Testaments."[22]

A fascinating question concerning the meaning of a text arises from Wittgenstein's *Tractatus*. During the years 1919 and 1920 Wittgenstein discussed the meaning of his work with Russell both by correspondence and in face-to-face conversation. Russell undertook to write an introduction for its publication. But in May, 1920, Wittgenstein wrote to Russell that the introduction contained much misunderstanding. Meanwhile, the publisher with whom Wittgenstein had been negotiating decided to reject the manuscript. In July, 1920 Wittgenstein wrote to Russell that he no longer wished to be bothered by whether the work was published, and that Russell could do what he liked with it. In due course, the *Tractatus* appeared with an introduction by Russell which could not but influence how many readers understood the book. Only with the publication many years later, after the death of both men, of *Letters from Ludwig Wittgenstein* and other work did the full extent of Wittgenstein's radical dissociation from Russell's positivism become clear.[23] In the concluding propositions of the Tractatus Wittgenstein spoke of the "mystical" and ended: "What we cannot speak about we must pass over in silence".[24] For Russell these were the needless confusions of metaphysics and religion; the "non-sense" of Ayer and the Vienna Circle. But for Wittgenstein they were the most important things of all; too profound to be caught in the net of purely descriptive language.

Is this an example of change in meaning which depends on change of a document's context, or is it, as Hirsch might claim, simply an example of the restoration of a valid interpretation in the light of the author's own intention?

This question is complex and cannot be answered in the present chapter. But we may indicate the kind of issues which arise if the question is ever to receive a satisfactory answer. On one side, the very idea of "the author's intention" has suffered a series of heavy attacks, first from the so-called New Criticism and then from theories of texts associated with reader-response theory and from post-structuralism or deconstructionism. The case for the traditional view has not been helped by the insistence of Gadamer and Ricoeur that once a text has been committed to writing, it no longer "belongs" to the horizon of the author.

On the other side, Hirsch insists that meaning is to be understood primarily in terms of the author's will or intention. He sees a sinister and destructive philosophical trend in the movement which seeks to locate meaning purely in the texts themselves. The trend begins with the New Criticism and ends in the post-modern deconstructionist dissolution of the consciousness of the subject, in which the production of meaning is seen wholly in terms of an interplay of signs within intralinguistic sign systems.[25] By contrast, the principle of intentionality in language has been defended by H.P. Grice, P.D. Juhl, and, more strictly within the context of speech-act theory, by John R. Searle and François Recanati.[26]

There are at least six distinct levels at which readers may consciously or unconsciously bring about a transformation of texts and their meaning, for good or ill. We might provisionally categorize the six as: (i) inter-textual; (ii) situational or temporally contingent; (iii) horizonal; (iv) semiotic; (v) hermeneutical; and (vi) relating to theories of texts. We shall introduce the first and the fourth only provisionally, since they become subjects of major discussion later. Others may be treated more briefly, since I have discussed them elsewhere.[27]

Intertextual factors. The term "intertextuality", probably first coined as a technical term by Julia Kristeva, has been used in two or three distinct ways. Jonathan Culler uses it to denote any "prior body of discourse" in terms of which a given text becomes intelligible: that which the text "implicitly or explicitly takes up, prolongs, cites, refutes, transposes..." For Culler it is almost equivalent to "presuppositions" or to the technical term "pre-understanding". Some other writers, including M. Riffaterre, use the term more specifically to indicate self-referring or intralinguistic relations between texts, and a survey of current theories and approaches concerning the nature of intertextuality is available in the introductory essay of the volume entitled *Intertextuality: Theories and Practices*, edited by Michael Worton and Judith Still (1990)[28].

As Michael Worton and Judith Still indicate, the notion of intertextuality has become a complex and technical one in literary theory and in post-structuralist theories of signs. It entails more than allusions suggested by one text to another. We discuss these technical dimensions in detail in chapter XIII (especially in XIII. 4), and note there the emergence of recent work on intertextuality in biblical studies. Texts function in this approach as generative matrices of further meaning projected by other texts through a textual network or textual grid. The layered textuality of parts of the Book of Revelation provides the clearest examples among the biblical texts. But it is also possible to work with simpler models of intertextuality as a starting-point. In this preliminary discussion we note simply examples of texts which become framed or re-contextualized in different ways within different biblical texts.

The intertextual framework of smaller units of biblical material has been examined in detail within the framework of Old Testament studies by Michael Fishbane, among others, in his book *Biblical Interpretation in Ancient Israel*. Fishbane offers numerous detailed examples of what he calls "inner-biblical" exegesis. These are instances in which, to use Fishbane's own terminology, a later biblical (Old Testament) writer takes up an earlier biblical text in order to "re-use", "re-contextualize", "extend", "reformulate", "re-interpret" or "*transform*" it.[29] Thus the pre-existing text as "deposit of tradition" (*traditium*) is pressed into the service of the actively ongoing tradition (*traditio*).

The Chronicler, for example, extends or makes more specific, a number of judgments conveyed in the texts of the Books of Kings. Thus whereas in 1 Kings 15: 11–15 Asa receives commendation in more *general* terms for "doing what was right in the eyes of the Lord", including especially the removal of most (not all) of the cultic abominations, in 2 Chron. 14: 1–4 the outline of 1 Kings 15 is repeated, but with the *additional specification* that "doing right" also included "commanding Judah...to keep the law and the commandment."[30] Fishbane offers a broader example in the re-contextualization of imagery from Genesis 1 in Isaiah 45:18 and some other related passages. Here the image of "chaos and darkness" (Gen. 1:2) is explicated in a way which guards against the possibility of a dualistic or anthropomorphic understanding of Gen. 1:2. Chaos is not a pre-existent or quasi-existent reality "out of which" God created the world. He alone pre-exists all that is part of his creatures.

A more complex and significant example is offered in the *multiple* "re-uses" for which Fishbane argues in the case of Jer. 25: 9–12.[31] In 25: 11,12 Jeremiah prophesies that "This whole land shall become a ruin and a waste, and these nations shall serve the king of Babylon seventy years. Then after seventy years are completed, I will punish the king of Babylon and that nation. . ." As is often pointed out, an explicit allusion to this passage in Jeremiah occurs in Dan. 9:2: "I, Daniel, perceived in the books the number of years which, according to the word of the Lord to Jeremiah the prophet, must pass before the end of the desolations of Jerusalem, namely seventy years." But in Dan. 9:24 this becomes "seventy weeks of years." Fishbane, however, argues further that a more complex intertextual network is involved.[32]

In 2 Chron. 36: 18–21 two different allusions to texts seem to play a part. Fishbane suggests that the Chronicler brings together Jeremiah's seventy years and material in Lev. 26: 34–35 which tells how "the land shall make up for its sabbaths; for all this time that it lies desolate shall the land rest" The land thus lies fallow to recover from its pollution, and Jer. 25 is now re-interpreted in terms of sabbatical cycles. But a full understanding of the implications seems to rest also on Lev. 25: 1–55, where a jubilee cycle of forty-nine years represents both the maximal period for indentured servitude and the maximal length of time when the land was alienated from inherited ownership. Daniel's interpretation of Jeremiah 25 in terms of "seventy sabbatical cycles, or ten jubilees", Fishbane concludes, "was presumably stimulated by 2 Chron. 36:21, which, owing to its re-use of Lev. 26: 34–5, seems to have understood the seventy years of Jeremiah's oracle as ten sabbatical cycles."[33] If Fishbane's suggestion is more than a hypothesis, this represents a complex example of inter-textual determinants of meaning.

Fishbane's work includes examples of more radical "transformations" of textual meaning. Fishbane finds one such example in Nahum 1:2,3: Nahum, he writes, considers the fate of the Assyrian army, and "envisages the imminence of divine vengeance portrayed through a series of vengefully re-applied references and allusions to Exod. 34: 6–7. The older *traditium* is thus *transformed* by a *traditio* which preaches wrath and doom, with no trace of mitigating divine mercy".[34] Exodus 34: 6,7 portrays the character of God both as "gracious and compassionate, long forbearing, and abundant in faithful love", and yet also as the God who "will not acquit guilt, but will requite the iniquity of fathers on their children..." (34: 6,7).

The subject of inter-textual relations within the Old Testament, however, remains a delicate, complex and specialized one. David Clines, for example, has examined Neh. 10:31–40 and argued that Nehemiah offers supplementary interpretation of the intention of Pentateuchal law (Lev. 6: 5,6); while H.G.M. Williamson concludes that there are grounds for differing from Fishbane on questions of detail, although not on the general principle which has been "observed piecemeal by previous commentators."[35] From the point of view of the present study, four brief observations may be added.

First, it is notoriously difficult to distinguish between resonances and shared uses of familiar imagery or language and conscious quotation. Here is one instance in which, if literary theory discourages questions about conscious intentions on the part of a writer, resultant enquiries about "meaning" become more difficult, and the notion of "transforming" an earlier text more problematic. Second, it may sometimes be worth while to observe a distinction between image, picture, or representational or propositional content and function or illocutionary force. For example, the proposition "the Lord is of great might" (Nahum 1:3) could be *used* in various ways or operate with different *force* in different speech-acts: the words could be spoken as a *warning*, as an act of *comfort*, or to lend support to a *promise*. When we speak of "re-using" or "re-applying" textual meaning are we speaking of transforming a propositional content, of re-directing an illocutionary force, or some change of meaning such as an innovative extension of metaphor? The basic distinction between propositional content and illocutionary force is central to the speech-act theory of John Searle and F. Recanati, and to the Pragmatics of Geoffrey Leech. We take up the distinction as it features in Searle in chapter VIII, below, where we apply it to a variety of biblical texts and to some current issues in biblical interpretation.

Third, the extent to which we shall regard inter-textual factors as "transforming" texts will depend partly on whether we regard the texts in question as providing a new frame of reference for interpretation and understanding. Does it constitute what in semiotic theory would be called a new signifying system? One positive example of the capacity of inter-textuality to offer a frame which brings about re-signification concerns what Brevard Childs has called "broken myth". The images of Rahab, Leviathan, and the Dragon (Psalm 74: 13,14; 104:26; Job 41:1; Isa. 51:9; Rev. 12: 3–17; 16:13), I have argued elsewhere, no longer operate in the biblical writings with the dream-like and unselfconscious or uncritical signification of myth, but as myth-consciously-used-as-symbol, or, to use the term favoured by Childs and Caird, "broken" myth.[36]

Fourth, while the importance of *intertextuality* at this modest or obvious level cannot be doubted, the debate takes a very different turn when the term is used as an implicit polemic in literary theory as that which stands in some writers in implied opposition to *intersubjectivity*, as if texts were merely semiotic systems which could operate without reference to *persons* or to *situations*. It is to this technical and specialist sense that Raymond Tallis alludes in his recent volume *Not Saussure* when he speaks of "the contemporary obsession with 'intertextuality'".[37] We introduce these issues in the next chapter, wrestle with them more deeply in chapter III when we examine questions about semiotics and deconstructionism, and include a formal discussion in chapter XIII, section 4, and chapter XIV, sections 1 and 3. Here it is worth noting that in principle, some theorists regard intertextuality as an all-encompassing and infinitely expanding system or systems of signification. These provide the matrices of meaning which generate what Umberto Eco, following Lotman, calls "productive" in contrast to "transmissive" texts. We discuss Eco's theory in chapter XIV.

Thus Julia Kristeva (to whose work we shall later refer) writes: "The term *inter-textuality* denotes this transposition of one (or several) sign-system(s) into another; but since the term has often been unhistorical in the broad sense of 'study of sources' we prefer the term *transposition*".38 A new frame of reference, in other words, can transpose the original meaning-unit into a new key. Jonathan Culler, in the work to which we have referred, defines intertextuality broadly, so that it becomes virtually equivalent to "presupposition", while, as we have noted, in Riffaterre it suggests the self-referential nature of texts or literary works.

The insertion of one text into the frame of another text cannot be judged either to "enrich" the text or to do "violence" to the text without prior reference to other questions about the choice of hermeneutical goals and the nature of what we regard as "meaning" in this or that context. In the biblical traditions inter-textuality in its broad sense is simply a fact of life. Janet Martin Soskice, one of my former research students, writes: "In ways similar to the allusive techniques of any literary tradition, certain metaphors and models of God's presence and gracious acts, models which often stand as significant in their own right without historical glosses, have been used and re-used in the central texts of Christianity and in subsequent expositions of texts. So, to explain what it means to Christians to say that God is a fountain of living water, or a vine-keeper, or a rock or fortress or king requires an account not merely of fountains, rocks, vines, and kings, but of a whole tradition of experiences and of their literary tradition which records and interprets them."39

3. Situational and Horizonal Factors in Transforming Texts

Situational or temporally-contingent factors. Some biblical texts are not specific to certain situations. They are not temporally contingent. The principle that "the fear of the Lord is the beginning of knowledge; fools despise wisdom" (Prov. 1:7) is universal in meaning and application, and almost has the status of a logically analytical statement, from the viewpoint of the biblical traditions. Into the same category we could place "the earth is the Lord's and the fulness thereof" (Ps.24:1), or a verse which I have on my desk as I write: "His steadfast love endures for ever" (Ps. 136:26). But very many biblical texts are specific to certain states of affairs or situations. Some of the regulations in Leviticus or Deuteronomy, for example, presuppose life in a pre-industrial, pre-modern agrarian society. Richard Rohrbaugh argues that we cannot fully understand the meaning of the narrative of Ahab's seizure of Naboth's vineyard (1 Kings 21: 1–29) unless we presuppose socio-historical conditions quite different from those of a modern industrial society in which land constituted, among other things, a sign of the covenant. Rohrbaugh writes: "Elijah is not rebuking Ahab for some private sin; for having fallen prey to the temptation of greed, but he is calling Ahab and indeed all Israel to recognize and return to the Sinai covenant."[40] Ken Bailey also discusses the importance of the pre-industrial agrarian background in relation of the gospels.[41]

Paul's discussion of the issues raised by "food offered to idols" at Corinth similarly presupposes a given socio-cultural situation from which we are separated in time (1 Cor. 8: 1–13; 10: 19–11:1). Even within this one social context, two different social situations are distinguished: sharing in cultic meals held on ceremonial occasions, and eating in the house of a host who serves meat which had been associated with pagan rites. Indeed Gerd Theissen argues that we cannot fully grasp the meanings of Paul's references to "the strong" and "the weak" in conscience (1 Cor. 8:7) and the issues in 1 Cor. 8:1–11:1 unless we take account of a combination of historical factors from which we are temporally and culturally distant: that wealthy people at Corinth could afford to eat meat more often than others, while most people subsisted on a diet of flour-based cerials; that the enjoyment of meat depended for this poorer majority on public distributions organized around quasi-sacred ceremonial occasions; and that the claim to possess "knowledge" (*gnosis*, 1. Cor. 8:1) was formulated from "the standpoint of the strong" who claimed to represent the whole Christian community,but may well have represented a class-specific orientation.[42]

Theissen convincingly concludes that in this grey area Paul feels that he has to urge a compromise: "The wishes (or prejudices) of the weak are upheld just as is the knowledge (and social privilege) of the strong...It is realistic and practicable."[43] Needless to say, the modern interpreter can "extend" the ethical criteria which Paul formulates (especially in terms of love and concern for the "weaker" brother or sister) to a different temporally-contingent or socio-cultural situation. But language about "idol-food" cannot be transplanted *directly* without first respecting the temporal and situational particularity of the text.

The illocutionary force, or more generally the language-*functions*, of particular biblical texts even more clearly presuppose given temporal and situational factors. Promises and warnings may sometimes be general or universal, but sometimes they relate to particular personal or institutional sets of conditions, such as the presence or absence of humble trust or self-confident pride. We shall argue in the next chapter and in chapter VIII that such speech-acts as promises are actualized with the time-horizon of the reader in inter-personal communication, but there is a presupposition of some kind of "match" or truth-condition relating to a situation if the speech-act is to be effective. Could someone who is planning unjust military oppression or murder credibly appropriate as an encouragement and authority for action: "The Lord is on my side to help me" (Ps. 118:7)?

In his incisive article "Unmeant Meanings of Scripture" Abraham Cronbach rightly points out that the words "the Lord watch between you and me when we are absent one from the other" (Gen. 31:49) is frequently misconstrued in popular piety because a difference of situation between two kinds of "partings" is overlooked.44 In religious folk-lore the text is often invoked as an assurance and a *benediction*. But the illocutionary force in the biblical text is different. In the context of heated exchanges and recriminatory charges of cheating and deceit, Jacob and Laban invoke the presence of God as a *virtual threat* to provide protection from being defrauded further by the other when absence prevents their protecting their own interests.

We need not explore this issue further at this point. In *The Two Horizons* I have discussed the bearing of this temporal and situational differentiation on questions concerning cultural relativism, as well as issues about the logic of so-called "timeless" propositions.45 The questions about cultural relativism remain important ones, but they arise equally from the factors which we have provisionally described as horizonal, semiotic, and hermeneutical.

Horizonal factors. Comments about the horizons of the reader and the horizons of texts remain preliminary until our later discussion of the issues. Those who stand in the hermeneutical tradition of Schleiermacher, of Heidegger, or of Bultmann usually speak at this point of "pre-understanding." But there are difficulties about varied uses of this term, and there is a tendency to jump to conclusions too hastily about what "pre-understanding" entails. We shall try to guard against this by avoiding the term except in certain necessary contexts. In some ways it might be preferable to speak of a *horizon of expectation*, provided that several qualifications are made. First, this includes a network of provisional working *assumptions* which are open to revision and change; second, the reader or interpreter may not be *conscious* of all that the horizon of expectation sets in motion, makes possible, or excludes. The expectations and assumptions concern the kind of questions and issues which we anticipate the text will address, and even the types of genre or mode of communication which it might use. For once, the over-worked phrase about the need "to ask the right questions" genuinely comes into its own and has its place.

The fact that a horizon is by definition both a limitation and yet also capable of movement and expansion as the subject of perception moves focusses the dual element of the strange and the familiar in processes of seeking to understand texts. To understand a musical score or an algebraic formula presupposes that I know what kind of thing music or algebra is; but I may never have seen *this* particular melody or equation before. My horizons must contain a space within which the text can be intelligibly "slotted" in terms of provisional linkages with the familiar that allow patterns of recognition. On the other hand the realization that what seems familiar is not quite what I had expected or assumed it to be, necessitates an expansion of my horizons to make room for what is new.

In this respect the term "horizon" offers an important advantage over the term "presupposition" which has unfortunately become familiar to English-speaking readers as a technical term in the English translation of Rudolf Bultmann's very well-known essay "Is Exegesis without Presuppositions Possible?"[46] Bultmann actually uses Schleiermacher's term, or here especially *Dilthey's* term "pre-understanding" (*Vorverständnis*). For Dilthey himself, whose work Bultmann is discussing, this preliminary to understanding is a relation to *life*, as it was also to be for the later Wittgenstein. My pre-conceptual relation in life to music, to mathematics, to law, or to love, would both influence, and provide operative conditions for, how I came to understand texts of music, mathematics, law, poems, or letters or declarations of love. But the term "presuppositions" seems to suggest a different flavour. It conveys the impression of rooted beliefs and doctrines which are not only cognitive and conceptual, but which also can only be changed and revised with pain, or at least with difficulty. Neither element is *necessarily* involved in "horizon".

The practical, behavioural, and pre-conceptual nature of horizon is also well captured by a term which probably represents its nearest equivalent in the broader climate of Anglo-American philosophy of language. John Searle expounds what he calls "the hypothesis of the background", or "*pre-intentional background*".[48] This rids us of the phenomenological, almost quasi-mentalist, overtones of "horizon" in Heidegger. Meaning is communicated and perceived, Searle argues, not only in the context of a "directedness" on the part of the author or speaker, but also "against a Background of capacities and social practices."[49] We understand what it is "to open a door", or "to open a meeting", or "to open fire"; but do not understand what it would be, Searle urges, "to open a mountain" or "to open the grass", because up to the present we have no common Background of common practices which could constitute a frame of reference for understanding the meaning of such language.

I explored this kind of argument in *The Two Horizons* with reference to Wittgenstein's understanding of patterns and traditions of public behaviour.[50] We understand what it is for God to pledge himself in addressing to us *acts of love*, because we can perceive patterns of God's loving action in the public traditions of Israel and of his deeds in Christ. But in turn, this understanding is inevitably coloured by experiences of people's love to us, and by our own capacity to love others. This approach shows *both* the positive role of background or horizons in making understanding possible *and* the negative possibility of transforming meaning unwittingly by failing to note the *differences and distinctiveness* which characterize the horizons of the biblical text, in contrast to our own. Analogies with experiences provide no more than starting-points.

The horizon or pre-intentional background is thus a network of revisable expectations and assumptions which a reader brings to the text, *together with* the shared patterns of behaviour and belief with reference to which processes of interpretation and understanding become operative. The term "horizon" calls attention to the fact that our finite situatedness in time, history, and culture defines the present (though always expanding) limits of our "world", or more strictly the limits of *what we can "see"*. The term "background" calls attention to the fact that these boundaries embrace not only what we can draw on in conscious reflection, but also the pre-cognitive dispositions or competences which are made possible by our participation in the shared practices of a social and historical world. The meaning of biblical texts, however, can be transformed when a serious mis-match of horizons occurs. For example, how we understand "hearing God's voice" (Ps.95:7; Hebs. 3:7,15; 4:7) may depend partly on the nature of the shared practices of "listening to God" which take place in our local church community, our ecclesial tradition, or our wider cultural situation. We may also explore questions about biblical history, biblical language, and genre, but it is likely that horizonal factors will play some part in interpretation.

A different kind of example concerns biblical texts which use literal or metaphorical language about fatherhood. Paul writes, "although you have countless guides, you do not have many fathers. For I became your father in Christ Jesus" (1 Cor. 4:15). Whether such an image enters the horizons of a reader negatively as "patriarchal" or positively as "intimate, loving, and inviting trust" will have something to do with parental attitudes and practices in the family in which the reader reached adulthood, as well as with a network of assumptions and beliefs about Paul, the Bible, and the world. These two examples, however, call attention to the value of the term "horizon" over both "pre-understanding", "presupposition", and "pre-intentional background". For although we are using metaphor, what is implied by the metaphor is true. Hans-Georg Gadamer reminds us that there are *two* component elements to the notion of "horizon": First, "it represents a standpoint that limits the possibility of vision . . . The horizon is the range of vision that includes everything that may be seen from a particular vantage-point."[51] But, second, we speak of "the *possible expansion* of horizon, the *opening up of new horizons . . . Horizons change for a person who is moving*".[52] This is part of the process in which texts transform readers.

4. Factors arising from Semiotics, Theories of Hermeneutics, and Theories of Textuality

Semiotic factors. Factors which arise from semiotics, or theories of signs are considered in detail in chapter III, and more generally in chapters XIII and XIV. There we consider the particular role played by semiotic "code", as the term has been used by Roman Jakobson, Roland Barthes, and others. A number of consequences follow from the notion both that a text can constitute a signifying system or sub-system, and also that a text can be inserted into the frame of some new or different signifying system. In the first case, it may be suggested on the basis of semiotic theory that texts constitute systems of meaning which are *quasi-independent of the human subject* who produced the text. In the second case, it may be suggested that the new or different signifying system into which the text is placed *radically* transforms its possible range of meaning and function. The entry of semiotic theory into hermeneutics marks the point of departure for a post-modern understanding of texts and hermeneutics. Here the focus of attention moves from the human subject as author or producer of meaning to the semiotic interplay of forces of meaning within the text.

The starting-point of semiotic theory lies in two parallel but independent contributions to thought on the part of Ferdinand de Saussure and Charles S. Peirce. Saussure argued that the operational nature of signs or speech (*parole*) depended on inter-relationships of similarity and difference within a language-*system* (*langue*) or sign-system. Peirce argued that the capacity of signs to signify depended partly on habit, and that signs, in effect, point to other signs. In chapter three we examine the roots of semiotic theory and trace its development up to Roland Barthes, Jacques Derrida, and its marriage with a post-Nietzschean and post-Freudian world-view which transforms semiotics into deconstructionism. Part of our argument is summed up in the question: need semiotic theory lead to deconstructionism? In chapter XIV we discuss whether semiotics leads, as it does for Umberto Eco to reader-response theory, or, as it does for Culler, to reader-orientated interpretation.

For biblical interpretation two developments which emerge from all this acquire decisive importance. One concerns theories of textuality, which we shall consider shortly. The other concerns the "encoding" and "decoding" of biblical texts in terms of different semiotic systems or layers of meta-language, which, it is claimed, unmask what may otherwise seem natural or "right" in the light of a text as a coded device for establishing or subverting some structure of power. This approach lies at the heart of socio-critical hermeneutics, and depends on "a hermeneutic of suspicion". The figures of Nietzsche, Marx, and Freud stand prominently in the immediate background. The hermeneutics of some liberation theologies, black theologies, and feminist theologies also draw on this general perspective of a hermeneutic of suspicion. In chapter X, section 1 we note Ricoeur's use of Freudian categories in the service of a hermeneutic of suspicion; and in chapter XII we examine how far socio-critical theory features in liberation, black, and feminist hermeneutics.

Several writers argue, for example, that what is "really going on" in the Gospel of Mark in its finished form is the manipulation of readers in the interets of a particular ecclesial power-system. Graham Shaw argues that Mark's is no innocent portrayal of Jesus, but one which seeks to manipulate the reader.[53] Fernando Belo makes explicit use of Roland Barthes's work on semiotic theory, drawing both on his earlier or more structuralist period and on his later emphasis on texts as processes of production of meaning in which many voices speak.[54] Like Barthes, Fernando Belo's agenda is heavily political. The upshot is his highly complex and difficult work entitled *A Materialist Reading of the Gospel of Mark*. Mark's text has been transformed, but the methodological basis of the "re-reading" lies in a theory and application of semiotics along the lines of a Barthesian model. In our third chapter, therefore, we examine the foundations of Barthes's theory of semiotics, as well as the theory of textuality with which it is interwoven. Then in chapter XII we return to examine Belo's work in more detail, together with other materialist readings of biblical texts, including that of I. Mosala in the black hermeneutics of South Africa.

Hermeneutical factors. If the effect of semiotic factors seems to be more radical in effect than the application of different models in hermeneutical theory, should we not move from hermeneutics to semiotics, rather than from semiotics to hermeneutics? It is true that hermeneutics is most frequently defined as the theory of interpretation. But two factors, among others, make hermeneutics a genuinely radical discipline. First, hermeneutics embodies reflection on the very *conditions which make any understanding of texts possible*. Second, hermeneutics entails an *evaluation of the range of possible hermeneutical models* which may become operative, and entails an *assessment of their respective value or validity in relation to particular kinds of texts*. In this sense, hermeneutics stands in relation to interpretation as a meta-discipline. It employs meta-criticism, in the sense that it embodies reflection about the validity or operational conditions of the interpretative activity which is under examination. We examine the metacritical nature of hermeneutical theory in chapter IX, and the contrast between meta-critique in Ricoeur, Habermas and Apel and contextual pragmatism in Rorty in chapters X and XI.

Radical disagreements about the message and meaning of given texts sometimes spring not from differences between two or more sets of exegetical conclusions, but from prior disagreements about the *goals* of interpretation. An argument for the importance of this conclusion has been put forward recently by Robert Morgan, who writes: "Some disagreements about what the Bible means stem not from obscurities in the texts, but from the conflicting aims of the interpreters."[55] For example, if a parable of Jesus which functions to draw the reader into its narrative-world is merely "used" as a text for the purpose of historical re-construction of situations, or for its didactic content alone, it is arguable that interpreters have transformed not only its function but its meaning. Conversely, if a text which genuinely portrays historical processes and events is judged only to project a "history-like" (intralinguistic) narrative-world, we have again transformed the meaning of a text, this time in a reverse direction to that of the previous example. The use of semiotic or deconstructionist models of reading also represents decisions to adopt given hermeneutical methods and goals. Hence the evaluation of such decisions remains part of the hermeneutical task.

Factors arising from theories of textuality. The most radical question of all in hermeneutics concerns the nature of texts, because the decision to adopt given interpretative goals depends not simply on the needs of the modern reading community but also, more fundamentally, on the nature of the particular text which is to be understood. This is the case if such a decision is to be theologically, rationally, and ethically responsible. But the nature of texts can no longer be regarded as self-evident. Is a text, as it is regarded in modern hermeneutics from Schleiermacher to Betti, primarily the expression of the experience and thought of an author, with the implication that the goal of interpretation is to understand the author's experience and mind? Or does a text, as the New Criticism of the 1940s and 1950s imply, stand as an autonomous world of meaning, to which its author and situation relate only in the most minimal way? Or are texts to be viewed primarily as invitations to readers to contribute to or "complete" textual meaning, as reader-response theory in some of its versions suggests? What are we to make of the post-modernist view that texts are primarily open-ended processes, which set going an infinite chain of significations rather than conveying some specific "content" which is bounded by closure?

It is not difficult to appreciate how radical such paradigms of textuality may be in relation to the traditional approaches of biblical studies. In the 1980s there has been increasing interest in "literary" rather than "historical" paradigms, but often this entailed only catching up on some of the literary devices and techniques which emerged in the context of formalism or the New Criticism. Whereas, for example, patterns of repetition, tension, contradiction or omission were seen within the historical paradigm as evidence of "sources" and perhaps clumsy or unfinished editing, within the literary paradigm these very same features acquired an entirely positive significance. They were effective literary devices, designed to make an impact on the reader. Thus Robert Alter urges that Old Testament narrative "insists on parallels of situation and reiterations of motif that provide... commentary on each other." The use of recurrent motifs is "ubiquitous in narrative literature."[56] The literary critic looks for such features in Ruth and in Esther as "dialectical tension between antitheses", and changes of narrative tempo, or in the Davidic succession narratives for "paradoxical foci", ambiguities, and multiple meaning.[57] Constructive studies of narrative techniques emerged in David Gunn's work on Saul and Adele Berlin's study of David.[58]

In literary theory, however, the paradigm of the New Criticism's autonomous text was disappearing even before it began to be taken seriously in biblical studies. Formalism became unsatisfactory for a variety of reasons. In chapter XIII section 4 we see in detail how structures which were once perceived as *formal*, logical or "natural" systems are later perceived to be products of social history and *convention*. In particular formalism was unsatisfactory to philosophical realists, who in the search for some anchorage of the text in the real world, found this anchor in the reader and the reader's response rather than in the author, the subject-matter, or context-of-situation of the text. More significantly and in greater numbers, post-Kantian philosophical Idealists could no longer remain convinced by the pseudo-objectivity of an autonomous text. Everything was seen to depend on the perceptions of the reader and reading communities. For some literary theorists, like Stanley Fish, the interpretative perceptions, pre-understandings, grid of expectations and active responses of communities of readers came to constitute, if not the text, at least its effective meaning. Aphoristically Fish writes: "Interpretation is the source of texts, facts, authors, and intentions."[59]

The positive gain in the shift of focus to the reader is potentially significant for biblical interpretation. The reader is no longer seen merely as a passive recipient of a message, but as actively engaged in a process of reading-transactions and responses. However, the losses remain serious ones. Without the constraints imposed on meaning by the text's context or situation and the directedness of the author's utterance, meaning becomes almost infinitely variable and polyvalent. Even if this constitutes a model of textuality for certain biblical parables, it cannot stand as a model for most biblical texts. In chapters XIII and XIV we also note the difficulties of this model for a Christian theology of revelation if it were to be viewed as a comprehensive model of textuality. We also note its weakness as a philosophical theory of language.

The most radical and far-reaching shift in paradigms of textuality, however, is reached in postmodernism in the shape of deconstructionism. The role of the conscious judgments of the human subject becomes swallowed up in an endless sea of signifying systems. Texts become processes which move us on, but never end, because any "final" meaning is called into question by the never-ending network of intertextuality which surrounds all texts and places them within new signifying systems. This theory of texts reaches its philosophical climax in Jacques Derrida, who supports it with a world-view shaped by Nietzsche and Freud, and with philosophical devices drawn from the later Heidegger. The consequences of such a theory of texts for biblical interpretation can be seen partly in Fernando Belo's use of Barthes in his work on Mark, but more especially in a series of studies offered by John Dominic Crossan. Biblical texts become primarily iconoclastic in function, and constitute, for Crossan, parables of parables, and metaphors of metaphors.

Clearly these last three paradigms of textuality have profoundly transforming effects on more traditional understandings of biblical material. A genuinely *radical* hermeneutic, in the sense of a meta-critical theory of interpretation which seeks to go to the root of things, must begin with an assessment of theories of textuality. This must include a theological evaluation of what kind of theory of texts might be appropriate for Christian scriptures, and philosphical and literary-theoretical critique of the grounds on which various paradigms of textuality are put forward. In the next chapter, therefore, we consider shifting paradigms of textuality, and ask what kind of theory might be consonant with Christian theology in the case of biblical texts. In chapter three we embark on what is probably the most difficult and complex part of the book. There we question whether semiotic theory as such can support the weight of deconstructionism, and examine both the validity of the approach and its consequences for biblical interpretation. Nevertheless, as we have noted, these arguments remain provisional until we have completed the further discussions of texts and reading in chapters XIII and XIV.

Some readers may wish to postpone the section on Derrida because of its unavoidable difficulty. But we cannot ignore the subject. David Couzens Hoy reminds us that Derrida represents "a thoroughgoing challenge" to all traditions of hermeneutical thought. His notion of "undecidable meaning" becomes "both the bane of hermeneutical philosophy and the hallmark of grammatological philosophy".[60] By contrast, John Caputo urges that Derrida represents the climax of post-modern hermeneutics. He declares, "Derrida does not overthrow hermeneutics but makes it radical."[61] Either way, therefore, we are obliged to include an assessment of Derrida's thought.

NOTES TO CHAPTER I

1. Anthony C. Thiselton: *The Two Horizons*, 335–51 (on narrative-world) and 133, 374–77, 384–85, and 436–37 (on speech-acts); with Clare Walhout and Roger Lundin, *The Responsibility of Hermeneutics*, Grand Rapids: Eerdmans, and Exeter: Paternoster 1985, especially 107–113; cf. also 42–57.
2. F. Recanati, *op. cit.*; cf. Geoffrey Leech, *Principles of Pragmatics*, London and New York: Longman, 1983. The two most relevant works by J.R Searle are his *Speech Acts: An Essay in the Philosophy of Language*, Cambridge: Cambridge University Press, 1969; and *Expression and Meaning: Studies in the Theory of Speech Acts*, Cambridge: Cambridge University Press, 1979. But cf. also J.R. Searle, F. Kiefer, and M. Bierwisch (eds.) *Speech Act Theory and Pragmatics*, Dordrecht: Reidel, 1980; and Stephen C. Levinson, *Pragmatics*, Cambridge: Cambridge University Press, 1983. On speech-act theory in biblical studies, see Hugh C. White (ed.) *Speech Act Theory and Biblical Criticism*, Semeia 41, (1988).
3. Markus Barth, *Conversation with the Bible*, New York: Holt, Rinehart and Winston, 1964, 9.
4. Cf. Edwin M. Good, *Irony in the Old Testament*: London: S.P.C.K. 1965, 39–55; and Kornelis H. Miskotte, *When the Gods are Silent*, Eng., London: Collins, 1967, 422–38.
5. Emilio Betti, *Die Hermeneutik als allgemeine Methodik des Geisteswissenschaften*, 2nd edn. Tübingen: Mohr, 1972,7.
6. Hans Robert Jauss, *Towards an Aesthetic of Reception*, Eng. Minneapolis, University of Minnesota Press, 1982, especially "Literary History as a Challenge to Literary Theory", 3–45; and *Aesthetic Experience and Literary Hermeneutics* Eng. Minneapolis: University of Minnesota Press, 1982. On Reception Theory in general cf. Robert C. Holub, *Reception Theory. A Critical Introduction*, London: Methuen, 1984; and D.W. Fokkema and Elrud Kunne-Ibsch, *Theories of Literature in the Twentieth Century*, London: Hurst & Co., 1978, 136–64.
7. Anthony C. Thiselton "The New Hermeneutic" in I.H. Marshall (ed.) *New Testament Interpretation*, Grand Rapids, Eerdmans and Exeter: Paternoster, 1977, 308–33; and *The Two Horizons* 12–17 (Luke 18: 9–14) and 344–52 (Luke 15:11–32, Luke 10:29–37.
8. Dietrich Bonhoeffer, *Meditating on the Word*, Cambridge, Mass.: Cowley Publications 1986, 44–45.
9. *Luther's Works* (ed. J.J. Pelikan and H.T. Lehmann) St. Louis, Philadelphia: Concordia Publishing House. 1955– , 336–37 .
10. David E. Klemm, *Hermeneutical Inquiry: I, The Interpretation of Texts*, Atlanta: Scholars Press, 1986, 3. .
11. Paul Ricoeur, *The Conflict of Interpretations: Essays in Hermeneutics*, Evanston: Northwestern University Press, 1974, 17. .
12. Hans-Georg Gadamer, *Truth and Method*, Eng. London: Sheed & Ward, 1975, especially 267–78 and 295–341, and E.D. Hirsch, *Validity in Interpretation*, New Haven: Yale University Press, 1967, 62–64, 140–41, and 212–24 and 247–51.
13. Richard Swinburne, "Meaning in the Bible" in S.R. Sutherland and T.A. Roberts (ed.) *Religion, Reason, and the Self. Essays in Honour of H.D. Lewis* Cardiff: University of Wales Press,1989. 1–33. .
14. *Ibid* 14. .

15. Brevard S. Childs, *Introduction to the Old Testament as Scripture*, London: S.C.M., 1979; and *The New Testament as Canon: An Introduction*, London: S.C.M., 1979.
16. J.A. Sanders, *Torah and Canon*, Philadelphia: Fortress, 1972, and *Canon and Community*, Philadephia: Fortress, 1984.
17. James D.G. Dunn, "Levels of Canonical Authority", *New Horizons in Biblical Theology* 4 (1982) 13–60; and *The Living Word*, London: S.C.M., 1987.
18. *Ibid* 30.
19. *Ibid* 40–41.
20. Terence Keegan, *Interpreting the Bible. A Popular Introduction to Biblical Hermeneutics*. New York: Paulist Press, 1985, 142–44.
21. Donald A. Hagner, "The Old Testament in the New", in Samuel J. Schultz and Morris A. Inch, (ed.) *Interpreting the Word of God. Festschrift in Honor of Steven Barabas*, Chicago: Moody Press, 1976, 78–104 esp. 102.
22. Walter C. Kaiser, *The Uses of the Old Testament in the New*, Chicago: Moody Press, 1985, 226.
23. Paul Engelmann, *Letters from Ludwig Wittgenstein* Oxford: Blackwell, 1967; and Allen Janik and Stephen Toulmin, *Wittgenstein's Vienna*, London: Wiedenfeld and Nicolson, 1973.
24. Ludwig Wittgenstein, *Tractatus Logico-Philosophicus*, London: Routledge and Kegan Paul, 1961, 7 (p.151) cf. Anthony C. Thiselton, *The Two Horizons* 359–70.
25. E.D. Hirsch Jr., *The Aims of Interpretation*, Chicago: University of Chicago Press, 1978 (1976) 146–58.
26. H.P. Grice: "Meaning" in P.F. Strawson (ed.) *Philosophical Logic*, Oxford: Oxford University Press, 1967, 47; cf. 39–48. Cf. P.D. Juhl, *Interpretation. An Essay in the Philosophy of Literary Criticism*, Princeton: Princeton University Press, 1980; John R. Searle, *Intentionality. An Essay in the Philosophy of Mind*, Cambridge: Cambridge University Press, 1983; and François Recanati, *Meaning and Force: The Pragmatics of Performative Utterances*, Cambridge: Cambridge University Press, 1987.
27. Anthony C. Thiselton, *The Two Horizons*, 3–23, 103–14, 154–61 (on horizon); 51–103, (on temporal contingency).
28. Jonathan Culler, *The Pursuit of Signs: Semiotics, Literature, Deconstruction*, London: Routledge & Kegan Paul, 1981, 101; cf. 100–18. See further Michael Worton and Judith Still (eds.) *Intertextuality: Theories and Practices*, Manchester: Manchester University Press, 1990, esp. the introductory essay by Worton and Still.
29. Michael Fishbane, *Biblical Interpretation in Ancient Israel*, Oxford: Clarendon Press, 1985, 1, 140, 410, 414, 440, 473 *et passim*.
30. *Ibid* 385–86.
31. *Ibid* 324–26.
32. *Ibid* 479–84.
33. *Ibid* 482.
34. *Ibid* 347.
35. David J.A. Clines, "Nehemiah 10 as an Example of Early Jewish Biblical Exegesis" in *Journal for the Study of the Old Testament* 21, 1981, 111–17; and H.G.M. Williamson "History" in Don A. Carson and H.G.M. Williamson (eds.) *It is Written: Scripture Citing Scripture: Essays in Honour of Barnabas Lindars*, Cambridge: Cambridge University Press, 1988, 25–38.
36. Brevard S. Childs, *Myth and Reality in the Old Testament*, London: S C M, 1962, 42; Anthony C. Thiselton, "Myth, Mythology" *Zondervan Pictorial Encyclopedia of*

the Bible, Grand Rapids: Zondervan, 1975, vol.4, 333–43; and George B. Caird, *The Language and Imagery of the Bible*, London: Duckworth, 1980, 219–42.
37. Raymond Tallis, *Not Saussure. A Critique of Post-Saussurean Literary Theory*, London: MacMillan, 1988, 31.
38. Julia Kristeva, *Revolution in Poetic Language*, Eng. New York: Columbia University Press, 1984, 59–60.
39. Janet Martin Soskice, *Metaphor and Religious Language*, Oxford: Clarendon Press, 1985, 158.
40. Richard L. Rohrbaugh, *The Biblical Interpreter. An Agrarian Bible in an Industrial Age*, Philadelphia: Fortress 1978, 61; cf. 55–68.
41. Ken E. Bailey, *Poet and Peasant*, Grand Rapids: Eerdmans, 1976.
42. Gerd Theissen, *The Social Setting of Pauline Christianity. Essays on Corinth.*, Eng. Philadelphia: Fortress, 1982, 121–43.
43. *Ibid* 139.
44. Abraham Cronbach, "Unmeant Meanings of Scripture", *Hebrew Union College Annual* 36, 1965, 99–122.
45. Anthony C. Thiselton, *The Two Horizons* 51–84, 92–103.
46. Rudolf Bultmann, *Existence and Faith. Shorter Writings of Rudolf Bultmann*, Eng. London: Fontana edn. 1964, 342–51.
47. Rudolf Bultmann, *Glauben und Verstehen. Gesammelte Aufsätze* (4 vols.) Tübingen: Mohr, 1964–5, III 142–50.
48. John Searle, *Intentionality. An Essay in the Philosophy of Mind*, Cambridge: Cambridge University Press, 1983, 19–20 and 144–59.
49. *Ibid* 147.
50. Anthony C. Thiselton, *The Two Horizons*, 357–427 esp. 379–85.
51. Hans-Georg Gadamer, *Truth and Method*, 269.
52. *Ibid* 269 and 271.
53. Graham Shaw, *The Cost of Authority. Manipulation and Freedom in the New Testament*, London: S.C.M., 1983, 190–268.
54. Fernando Belo, *A Materialist Reading of the Gospel of Mark*, Eng. New York: Orbis Books, 1981.
55. Robert Morgan (with John Barton) *Biblical Interpretation*, Oxford: Oxford University Press, 1988, 8.
56. Robert Alter, *The Art of Biblical Narrative*, New York: Basic Books, 1981, 91.
57. *Ibid* 34, 63, 92 and 123.
58. David M. Gunn, *The Fate of King Saul. An Interpretation of a Biblical Story*, Sheffield: J.S.O.T. Press, Suppl. 14, 1980; and Adele Berlin, *Poetics and Interpretation of Biblical Narrative*, Sheffield: Almond, 1983.
59. Stanley Fish, *Is There a Text in This Class? The Authority of Interpretive Communities*, Cambridge: Harvard University Press, 1980, 16.
60. David Couzens Hoy, "Must We Say What We Mean? The Grammatological Critique of Hermeneutics" in Bruce R. Wachterhauser (ed.) *Hermeneutics and Modern Philosophy*, New York: Albany State University of New York Press, 1986, 397–98; cf. 397–415.
61. John D. Caputo, *Radical Hermeneutics: Repetition, Deconstruction, and the Hermeneutical Project*, Bloomington: Indiana University Press, 1987, 4.

CHAPTER II

What is a Text?
Shifting Paradigms of Textuality

1. Are Authors Part of Texts? Introductory Issues

Why should it be necessary to spend time on a discussion of the nature of texts? Is not the meaning of the word "text" self-evident, at least from the vantage-point of common sense? If we are reading literature, a text, we might assume, represents a more or less unified stretch of written language which has a beginning and a closure. If we are interpreting extra-linguistic or quasi-linguistic signs, the notion of "text" may be extended metaphorically to include messages generated by such sign-systems as traffic signals, religious or civic rituals, styles of dress, non-verbal body-language, or electronically coded indicators. In the case of the biblical writings, certainly the whole Bible, or whole books of the Bible, constitute texts. But what is the smallest working unit that can be called a text? In the context of language in general, John Lyons speaks of "utterance-units", to which such terms as "statement", "question", and "command" are applicable, but which are also "heavily context-dependent".[1] We may not be able to decide between certain possibilities of meaning "without drawing upon the information that is given in the co-text or context of situation."[2] These utterance-units may be seen as "basic units of language-behaviour".[3]

All this remains valid up to a point, but it takes us into highly controversial territory. What is controversial is not simply a matter of definition: differences between theories of the nature of texts and textuality carry with them fundamentally different conceptions of what it is for a text to convey meaning. In particular, different theories of textuality either link the text's author and context of situation inseparably with its meaning, or view meaning as a more pluralistic range of possibilities generated either by the sign-system of the text itself and its relation to other texts, or by the relation between a text and successive readers or reading communities, or by both.

Until recently the classical-humanist paradigm of textuality has dominated the history of biblical interpretation. In this tradition, texts are stretches of language which serve to express the thoughts and ideas of their authors, and to refer to states of affairs in the extra-linguistic world. Even with the rise of Romanticist hermeneutics in the nineteenth century, a relatively minor change of emphasis shifted from the "thought" of authors to the shared "life" of authors, although some account was also taken of the "life-worlds" of readers. Texts were still seen as linguistically mediating inter-personal communication. In the case of biblical texts, there was room for the idea that God, Jesus or one of the prophets or apostles could "speak" directly through texts. In effect, it was as if the author and the situation out of which the author spoke formed part of the "text" itself. Theologically this approach fits very comfortably with the view that revelation is "given" through biblical texts; that the revealed word is enfleshed primarily in Jesus Christ as *the* Word of God; and that this word is also embodied in the lives and deeds of the apostolic community and in the history of Israel as the people of God. Revelation through texts is given, not made; it is interpersonal address; and it is enfleshed and embodied, rather than functioning purely as a language abstracted from life.

None of these traditional assumptions, however, can escape question if some of the competing claims about texts and textuality which have entered recent theory are deemed to be convincing or true. The collapse of many traditional assumptions and the need at very least to re-assess and to re-formulate them arises from the invasion of hermeneutics by three sets of forces: movements in literary theory; the development of certain strands in semiotics and deconstructionism; and the development of a tradition of sociology that owes much to the sociology of knowledge. A further significant factor arises from the important work of Walter Ong, Werner Kelber, and others, on the difference between textuality and orality. A print-orientated hermeneutic, Kelber maintains, especially in our study of the Bible, invites different hermeneutical dynamics from those of an oral hermeneutic.

In common with a number of other biblical specialists, Kelber appeals at a key point in his argument to the hermeneutical theory of Paul Ricoeur.[4] Ricoeur asserts: "Writing renders the text autonomous with respect to the intention of the author. What the text signifies no longer coincides with what the author meant."[5] The text is a work, or a structured totality, which cannot be reduced to the sentences out of which it is composed. It does indeed remain a "production" on the part of an author. But, in his essay entitled "What is a Text?", Ricoeur insists: "The reader is absent from the act of writing; the writer is absent from the act of reading. The text thus produces a double eclipse of the reader and the writer. It thereby replaces the relation of dialogue, which directly connects the voice of one to the hearing of the other".[6] The text becomes "emancipated" from the oral situation, and from "the situation, the surroundings, and the circumstantial milieu of discourse".[7] This principle forms part of what

Ricoeur calls the phenomenon of "distanciation", which leads to an eclipse of "the circumstantial world" in the "quasi-world" of texts.[8]

Jacques Derrida and Roland Barthes develop this principle much further, and radicalize the whole notion of textuality. In his essay "Living On"/"Border Lines" Derrida writes: "The question of the text . . . has been transformed in the last dozen or so years".[9] A text is "no longer a finished corpus of writing, some content enclosed in a book or its margins, but a differential network, a fabric of traces, referring endlessly to something other than itself, to other differential traces".[10] Barthes agrees in seeing the text as a "metaphor" of "network", which no longer bears its author's signature.[11] "The text is plural: it achieves plurality of meaning, an *irreducible* plurality."[12] A text, for Barthes, is not so much a "given" as an invitation to activity. On biblical interpretation he comments: "Some of the 'texts' of the Scriptures that have traditionally been recuperated by theological (historial or anagogical) monism may perhaps lend themselves to diffraction of meaning."[13]

If we leave aside, for the moment, the effects of the invasion of hermeneutics by semiotic theory, it is not difficult to see why many biblical interpreters find the paradigms of textuality which are offered by literary theory and the sociology of knowledge to be attractive and constructive. Ricoeur draws a contrast between the text-world "in front of" the text and the text-world behind it.[14] If we stand in front of the text, we experience its operative effects. The text projects forward a "world" which we may enter, and which may renew and transform us. In his work on Philemon and other Pauline epistles, for example, Norman Petersen argues that the Pauline texts project forward a "world" which is both a literary narrative-world of temporal sequence and also a sociological "world" of meanings, generated by perceptions of social relationships and social systems.[15] These social and epistemological constructs reflect ways in which members of a society categorize their experience, so that they may give it order and form.

In contrast to this, what occured "behind" the text may appear to reflect a more remote and antiquarian set of concerns. Traditionally biblical studies have presupposed a notion of textuality which leans heavily on a historical paradigm. We look behind the text at the situation which provided its raison d'etre. But should we start here? Recently Robert Morgan has criticized what he regards as an over-preoccupation with this historical paradigm in biblical interpretation.[16] In an attempt "to make explicit a model for bridging the gulf between critical scholarship and religious faith" Morgan argues that problems and tensions can be "eased by the switch to a literary paradigm for biblical interpretation".[17] In particular he attacks an approach in which biblical texts are used not with a view to asking what they project or set in motion, but as instruments for the different task of re-constructing a history. All too easily, he points out, a necessary use of historical *methods* slides into a use of texts with solely historical *aims*.[18] Morgan observes: "Historical reconstruction of biblical persons, events, and traditions is an entirely legitimate activity, but possibly less fruitful for theology than the newly emerging literary approaches."[19] What he terms a "breakthrough" which amounts to a paradigm-shift consists in the movement away from persons and events behind the text "to the now available texts and their impact upon present-day hearers and readers".[20] In my judgment, this paradigm-shift brings both gains and potential losses, and the hermeneutical consequences of such a shift need to be examined in greater detail. I have discussed Morgan's specific arguments in another volume.[21]

Meanwhile Norman Petersen, in the book to which we have referred, rightly argues that what is at issue is the relation between text and context within the framework of questions about textuality. The key issue, he asserts, is "which should dominate in textual interpretation, the information internal (intrinsic) to the text, or contextual information that is external (extrinsic) to the text, like the author's intent, his biography, or the historical and cultural climate of his times."[22] He alludes to the New Criticism in mid-century theories of literature, with its emphasis on the intrinsic autonomy of the text, and to the later course of the debate in literary theory among such writers as Wolfgang Iser and Jacques Derrida. We cannot undertake even a brief study of textuality without reference to these writers, and so we need to examine the issues which they raise. Derrida's work is examined in the next chapter; the hermeneutics of Paul Ricoeur in chapter X, and reader-response theory more fully in chapter XIV. Meanwhile a wider and more fundamental account and evaluation of the impact of literary theory on biblical hermeneutics is offered in chapter XIII.

2. Are Situations or Readers Part of Texts?

The so-called New Criticism arose in reaction against perspectives of the nineteenth and early twentieth centuries which had concerned themselves with material extrinsic to the text as an aid to understanding and interpreting it. By the mid 1950s it represented an established orthodoxy in the literary theory of the Anglo-American world, and its influence is currently still felt in biblical interpretation especially in terms of those discussions which focuss on such literary devices as ambiguity, metaphor, irony, tension, and paradox. Probably the most influential text-book which reflected the movement was René Wellek's and Austin Warren's *Theory of Literature* (1949). Wellek and Warren argued that the paradigm of textuality and interpretation which had been inherited by previous generations too narrowly fitted the particular needs of classical studies and philology. This classical-humanist paradigm could be seen for example in the hermeneutical and critical theory of Philip August Boeckh, whose *Encyclopedia and Methodology of the Philological Sciences* was revised and published by one of his students in 1877, and then in 1886. Significantly Boeckh had been a pupil of Schleiermacher, and like his teacher he argued that the interpreter must look behind the text to the situations, experiences, and intentions which gave rise to the text, some of which may not even have entered the author's awareness. Boeckh had produced a serious work of hermeneutics and criticism, but from the standpoint of a historical philologist of the time. We briefly examine Boeckh's contribution to hermeneutical theory in section 4 of chapter V.

Against such a background, Wellek and Warren urged that the whole idea of the author's intention, at least as a criterion of meaning in literature "seems quite mistaken". "The total meaning of a work of art cannot be defined merely in terms of its meaning for the author and his contemporaries."[23] The text is autonomous: it speaks on its own terms.

This approach received further support in the same era with the publication of Wimsatt's and Beardsley's essay entitled "The Intentional Fallacy".[24] To use the intention of an author as a criterion for judging the "success" of a work of literary art, they claimed, rested on a fallacy. For the author's intention represented a private state of mind, which was virtually inaccessible except through the text itself. If, on the one hand, the author had not wholly succeeded in his or her intention, it was useless to appeal to the text as evidence of it. If, on the other hand, the intention was fully successful, this intention was identical with the text, and there was no need to go "behind" the text. In this essay and in a later revised version of the argument, the possible relevance of biographical information was not entirely excluded, and it was allowed that intention may have some role in "practical" utterances. But the notion of going behind the text to ascertain criteria of success or meaning was said to embody not only an intentional, but also a "genetic", fallacy, derived largely from romanticism. Wimsatt and Beardsley stress the inadequacy of intention not only as a criterion of "success", but also as a criterion of meaning.

Wimsatt and Beardsley were addressing a pre-Wittgensteinian notion of intention as inner mental processes. H.P. Grice, John Searle and others have since argued firmly that what an utterance means is explicable in terms of what a *person* means by his or her utterance.[25] There are ways of expressing intention which identify the directedness of a speech-act without presupposing some pychological notion of "inner mental states". I attempt this in chapter XV, section 1. But the New Criticism faced more serious philosophical difficulties. It rested on the model of an autonomous self-contained text which addressed a reader who, in misplaced hermeneutical innocence, presupposed that with uncommitted neutrality, he or she could understand the text purely on its own terms. Wellek and Warren believed that "we can experience quite directly how things are" with literary texts. Such an innocent objectivism could not be sustained as the second half of this century advanced. It attempted to replace classical humanism by modern mid-century liberal humanism. But in literary and semiotic theory this kind of perspective was radically questioned by such thinkers as Roland Barthes, and in hermeneutical theory, almost by definition, it could not survive the work of major twentieth-century theorists.

In his book *After the New Criticism* Frank Lentricchia identifies the publication of Northrop Frye's *The Anatomy of Criticism* (1957) as marking a point of transition which both looks back to the New Criticism and looks forward to post-modernism. He comments: "The great hope for literary critics in 1957, when the hegemony of the New Criticism was breaking, was that the muse would be demystified ... and that younger critics would somehow link up poetry with the world again", that they would bring art "to the place in which the forbidden subjects of history, intention, and cultural dynamics could be taken up once again."[26] But this "great hope" was not to be fulfilled by a return to the text's relation to the *author* or to the world of *reality to which it referred*. If the text related to anything beyond itself, this would prove to be the *reader*, or simply *other texts*. In her introduction to a volume of essays on audience and interpretation, Susan Suleiman speaks of the movement away from the New Critical emphasis on "the text itself" towards "a recognition (or a re-recognition) of the relevance of context".[27] But here this is not the context of the author and the author's situation; it is the context of the reader or the audience.

A further paradigm-shift in the notion of texts and textuality can be seen, therefore, in the Reception theory of Hans Robert Jauss and Wolfgang Iser in Germany and in the related movement of Reader-response theory in America with the work of Stanley Fish, David Bleich, Wayne Booth, and others. Wolfgang Iser writes: "The text only takes on life when it is realized. . . . The convergence of text and reader *brings the literary work into existence*".[28] Susan Suleiman and Inge Crosman entitle their work on reader-response theory *The Reader in the Text* to underline "the notion of the reader 'in' the text".[29] In an essay in this volume Robert Crosman argues that readers "make" meaning: "We arrive at the 'author's meaning' precisely when we decide we have arrived there: we *make* the author's meaning".[30] Stanley Fish questions the "givenness" of texts in any purely objective or objectivist sense. He writes: "I 'saw' what my interpretive principles permitted or directed me to see, and then I turned around and attributed what I had 'seen' to a text and an intention. What my principles direct me to 'see' are readers performing acts. The points at which I find (or to be more precise, declare) these acts to have been performed become (by sleight of hand) demarcations *in* the text."[31] But these "do not lie innocently in the world; rather they are themselves constituted by an interpretive act."[32] Jauss is more concerned, like Gadamer, with the relation between hermeneutics and tradition. However, his central category is that of the reader's "horizon of expectation". We examine the views of Fish, Bleich, and Iser in detail in chapter XIV.

All this may be thrown into relief by noting how far the conception of texts and textuality which these approaches imply has moved from that of the classical world, Renaissance humanism, and the Reformers. From Aristotle until the end of the eighteenth century texts were seen as vehicles which conveyed the thoughts and ideas of their authors, and by this means also referred to the external world. Interpretation or intelligent reading entailed searching out leading concepts. The process, as it was borrowed by Cicero from Aristotle, was known as *inventio*. Aristotle called these leading concepts *topoi*; Cicero called them *loci*. Melanchthon and Erasmus wrote *loci* on biblical texts at the time of the Reformation. Calvin and Chladenius came to see that the selection and identification of *topoi* by the interpreter might arbitrarily disrupt the contextual flow of the text, and Calvin therefore used the method of running commentary. Calvin's work effectively represented the beginnings of the modern commentary. In his work on the epistles he saw it as his task to come to understand and to expound "the mind of Paul".[33] We discuss these points in chapter V.

Can such a view of textuality still be held with integrity today? We began this chapter by noting that John Lyons, a current exponent of linguistics and author of a standard work on semantics, views texts and text-sentences in a fairly traditional way, as sub-sets of utterance-units which constitute particular instances of language-behaviour, and to which such terms as 'statement', 'question', and 'command' are applicable.[34] Lyons also views with some favour the earlier work of J.R. Firth on the importance of context-of-situation for meaning.[35] Firth, who held the first Chair of Linguistics in the University of London, understands all utterances as instances of linguistic behaviour, the meaning of which consists in "a serial contextualization of our facts, context within context, each one being a function, an organ of a bigger context, and all contexts finding a place in what might be called the context of culture".[36] Lyons acknowledges that Firth's approach has limitations and invites criticisms, but concludes that we cannot afford to dismiss his insights.

In recent hermeneutical theory Werner G. Jeanrond expresses most clearly a view of textuality which explicitly regards the situation of communication as part of the "text". Internal organization and the "external relatedness" of linguistic acts *together constitute* the text. Textuality, Jeanrond writes, represents "more than a stringing together of single assertions".[37] The meanings of utterances, he continues, are "not determined solely by the choice of words or the manner in which the sentence is structured but also by the context in which an expression is embedded. This embedding comes about through the linguistic context on the one hand and, on the other, through the situation of communication which is also constitutive of meaning." Jeanrond concludes: "This external relatedness of linguistic acts and its internal organization compel us to treat as foundational for linguistic studies that unit which can best do justice to those two relational characteristics of linguistic expression: the text".38

Such comments serve to underline that questions about the nature of texts not only remain entirely open and in need of further debate, but also interact closely with issues about the nature of meaning and also the hermeneutical goals of the interpreter. In his article "What is the Meaning of a Text?" Jeffrey Stout argues that there is a circularity in the relationship between interpreters' own formulation of questions about "the meaning of a text" and their respective emphases on the author's intention, contextual significance, or the present reader's orientation. He comments: "The controversial notion that interpreters *create* meaning in the texts they interpret can be explicated as the true but innocuous idea that different interests quite naturally issue in different readings of texts. Only when we think of the task of interpretation as discovering *the meaning* of a text does such a doctrine seem paradoxical."39 As we shall note in chapter XIV, Stout's approach is compatible with a reader-orientated contextual pragmatism. In his recent book on biblical interpretation Robert Morgan makes a similarly pluralistic observation about biblical texts: "Texts, like dead men and women, have no rights, no aims, no interests. They can be used in whatever way readers or interpreters choose. If interpreters choose to respect an author's intentions, that is because it is in their interest to do so".40

Just how far, if at all, interpreters remain free to "choose" what goals effectively define textuality for them in the case of biblical texts raises such a number of complex issues that we cannot attempt to provide a full answer until we have considered at very least the following questions: (1) do considerations which emerge from Christian theology contribute any fresh factors concerning the nature of textuality in the case of biblical texts? (2) do issues which emerge from semiotic theory offer new constraints or new freedoms to the choices of interpreters, or new factors in determining the nature of textuality? (3) What light is shed on these issues by acts and processes of interpretation? (4) Does hermeneutical theory offer any criteria for the assessment and ranking of particular hermeneutical goals in relation to these issues? We shall consider these questions in the context of current theory, beginning with some distinctively theological issues which are raised by the present discussion of textuality. The remainder of the present chapter therefore focusses primarily but not exclusively on theological issues which bear on questions about textuality. Then in chapter III we consider issues raised by semiotics, and the basis of deconstructionist claims about the nature of texts. After we have examined pre-modern and modern theories of hermeneutics, we return in chapter IX to metacritical questions of hermeneutics, and in chapters X through to XIV to the bearing on these issues of further literary and socio-critical approaches.

3. Theological Claims about the Givenness and Actualization of Biblical Texts

It is often argued that hermeneutics begins, in François Bovon's words, with "a reflection on our status as readers". This exposes the problem that "a text does not have a single door nor a single key".[41] Since the work of Schleiermacher, many writers have defined hermeneutics in terms of the problem of human understanding, and have begun their study of the discipline by an examination of the interpretative processes of the human subject. Some critics of modern hermeneutics see this as opening the door to an inevitable relativism in biblical interpretation. They blame a starting-point which begins with interpretative processes and human subjectivity for introducing into theology a subjectivism and a relativism which is, in the view of these critics, at variance with the stable objectivity and givenness of Christian revelation.

For this reason, the present study, which reflects a positive, even passionate, conviction that hermeneutics represents a fundamental, unavoidable, and fruitful discipline, begins consciously and deliberately with a consideration of texts, rather than with the human subject. Only when we have completed our enquiry about textuality shall we feel free to proceed with questions about interpretation, understanding, and hermeneutical theories. Traditional Christian theology finds a "given" not primarily in human processes of interpretation, but in biblical texts and in the messages which they convey, even if the role of interpretation in shaping what we *count as* a given is *also* duly recognized.

At first sight, any re-definition of textuality which loosens it from its anchorage in the flow of the historical processes of which it is part may seem to compromise the status of a text and its message as "given". Still more clearly, a reader-orientated or audience-orientated definition of texts which locates the reader "in" the text itself as part of the text will seem to relativize and to project into a more subjective (or at least inter-subjective) realm the whole notion of what "the message of the text" might seem to be. But here judgments should be made with care. The logic of "gift" and "givenness" in the biblical traditions themselves invites deeper reflection. When God "gave" the promised land to Joshua and to Israel, what this giving consisted in, or amounted to, became visible and evidential in the people's capacity to enter it and to appropriate it (Joshua 1: 2–5, 13–14; 6:2; 8:1; 10:12; 11:23). "Gifts" of the Holy Spirit, including the capacity to teach, to heal, or to have special faith (1 Cor. 12: 4–11) become operative only in the activities of teaching, healing, or exercizing special faith. The "gifts" given by the risen and ascended Christ in Ephesians (Eph. 4: 7–13) likewise become actualized in processes of evangelism, pastoral care, teaching, and the building up of God's people. The heavier the emphasis which is placed upon gifts and grace in the biblical writings, the greater the correlative emphasis on the possibility and necessity of actualizing the gift in question through appropriate human response. It is the response which makes the grace "cashable" and evidential, as the Epistle of James so forcefully reminds us (Jas.2:14–26).

These considerations may influence some of our assessments about the relation between our discussions of shifting paradigms in textuality and the notion of a givenness as a quality of biblical texts, or of revelation through these texts, in Christian theology. First of all, we suggest that an appropriate emphasis on givenness *in no way conflicts with the basic distinction in virtually all theories of textuality between: (a) the capacity of the text, as a sub-system of signs operative within a life-world to communicate a message; and (b) the actualization of the text as a particular act of communication within the time-horizon of a reader or a reading community.*

For Christian theology it is not even enough to say that this view of texts remains congruent or consonant with Christian theological doctrine and Christian experience. More than this, such a view of texts calls attention to the living *eventfulness* of the text in the context of the work of the Holy Spirit in the worshipping community. In most Christian traditions, a self-consistency is noted between the Holy Spirit's inspiration of the biblical texts in their origin and transmission, and the Spirit's actualization of the message of these texts in the lives of successive generations of readers. Distinctions between different *time-horizons* should be kept logically distinct, at the least in the present discussion, from different questions about where the *interpretative constraints* of a text might lie. When biblical texts are actualized within the time-horizon of the present community, for example, these texts characteristically "speak" in the setting of liturgy and worship: at the Lord's Supper, in corporate prayer, in preaching and teaching, in corporate waiting on God in silence and expectancy.

In his book *The Power of the Word in the Worshipping Church* John Breck discusses this eventfulness of the word in liturgy. Like Georges Florovsky, who also writes on hermeneutics from an Eastern Orthodox angle, Breck sets the active, eventful, word in the context of the church's tradition and worship, and he concludes that in relation to so-called Protestant individualism and Roman Catholic sacramentalism, this emphasis remains a distinctive feature of Eastern Orthodox hermeneutics.[42] But virtually all Christian traditions which have a serious theology of the Holy Spirit and an adequate ecclesiology see the eventfulness of the actualized word in these terms.

The model in which the reader confronts the text purely as an isolated individual, cut off from the activities of the community, arises only because the time-horizon of the act of reading is something artificially abstracted from the processes which lead up to it and follow it. In practice, a reader reads in the privacy of his or her own room only in the light of horizons of expectation which have been derived from, and shaped by, the communities to which the individual reader belongs: indeed a community of communities, ranging from the local church and church traditions to learning-processes and assumptions inherited through the family, school, and mass media, contributes decisively to this horizon of expectation. While a reader's *transactional* relation with the text may operate at the level of individual response, the processes of *reading and interpretation* which make any such transaction possible, owe more to community-factors than to those which are peculiar to the individual. We may note in passing that whereas the New Criticism in literary theory tended to operate with the model of the isolated lone reader, semiotic and reader-response approaches stress the role of the reading-community in reading texts.

We now move to a second consideration. It may readily be granted, without any difficulty, that *some* (or even in principle many) biblical texts do function in ways which invite a reader-orientated hermeneutic. Undeniably some or many parables of Jesus operate in this way. In the 1930s C.H. Dodd made the uncontroversial comment that some parables leave the mind in sufficient doubt about their precise application "to tease it into active thought".[43] As recent interpreters including Funk and Crossan have argued, Jülicher was mistaken in viewing many, all, or most parables as vehicles for general truths. It is arguable that Job and Ecclesiastes also function not to supply some packaged piece of information, but to place the reader in a position where he or she can work their way towards certain perspectives or even conclusions at first-hand. In neither case could a digest of contents or a bare description of "the message of the book" be the same thing as actually reading it. Behind both books lies the recognition that if some packaged "answer" were to be offered independently of the reader's struggle, the reader would perhaps cease prematurely to worry away at the problem.

Even Eccles. 12:13 and Job 42: 10–17, do not really constitute "answers" to the questions which their writers have raised, whatever their time of composition in relation to that of the main body of these books.[44] Such texts as Job, Ecclesiastes, and the parables do not function *primarily* as raw-material for Christian doctrine. If they are used in this way, a responsible hermeneutic would demand that they are read in interaction and conjunction with other texts whose meaning is less dependent on where the reader stands. Their primary function is to invite or to provoke the reader to wrestle actively with the issues, in ways that may involve adopting a series of comparative angles of vision. Kierkegaard recognized the unique importance of *this* kind of "indirect communication" in certain situations. In reader-reponse theory of a more moderate kind Iser works with this principle, and Umberto Eco recognizes that the applicability of different reader-response models *depends on the nature of the text in question*.

Nevertheless, our third point qualifies all this. In the case of different categories of biblical texts, there remain *some* texts which cannot be up-anchored from the contextual setting in life and history, which decisively shapes their meaning. In such passages this setting imposes constraints on the range of interpretative options which remain open to the responsible reader. The argument put forward by Stout and by Morgan that the reader or interpreter has liberty to *choose* whether what he or she regards as "the meaning of the text" is true only, up to a point, in a secondary or derivative sense. It is true in the sense that the interpreter's hermeneutical goals inevitably determine what *counts* as "the meaning of the text", at least within a given framework. But not all choices can be defended with the same level of rational or ethical justification. Some texts, by their very nature, draw part of their meaning from the actions, history, and life with which they are inextricably interwoven.

To select a key example from the point of view of the earliest Christian communities, the statement "and they crucified Him" (Mark 15:24; *par* Matt. 27:35; Luke 23:33; John 19:18) draws the referential dimension of meaning from the historical state of affairs which it depicts, as well as from its broader theological and narrative context. Theoretically a modern reader might choose to read it only as a narrative-event within the projected narrative-worlds of the evangelists and no more, but this would consciously transform the function of the texts from that which they clearly performed in the theological thought, life, and purposes of the communities in which they were written and transmitted. Two millennia of interpretative tradition cohere with this purpose. A particular justification for such an innovative interpretative choice would therefore need to be offered if it were to be taken seriously on rational and ethical grounds. This does not indeed imply that no interpretative judgment is required of the reader; or that we can take it for granted, without careful reflection, that history-likeness in this example is history.[45] On the contrary, as David Tracy reminds us, every time we deliberate or make a judgment, we interpret.[46] We return to these questions in chapters VIII, IX, X, XI, XIII and XIV–XVI.

A more extended example may be suggested in Jesus' language about the Kingdom of God. In his book *Jesus and the Language of the Kingdom*

Norman Perrin puts forward the case that "Kingdom of God is a *symbol* rather than a *conception* in the message of Jesus".[47] Using Philip Wheelwright's terminology, he argues that it is a "tensive" symbol rather than a steno-symbol.[48] Part of the process of the proclamation of the Kingdom, therefore, is to use parable, metaphor, paradox, image; indeed the kind of language and hermeneutic to which we alluded in earlier paragraphs. Nevertheless, partly perhaps because he chooses to place too much weight on the term "myth", Perrin's arguments seem to run out just when they have bcome most interesting. Even granted that the hearer or reader needs to make his or her own judgments about the meaning of "Kingdom of God", nevertheless another principle operates: the frame of reference presented by Jesus himself is that of *his own life and deeds* as well as that of the larger developing verbal context of his teaching with which his deeds were interwoven.

The double function of these texts about the Kingdom of God is explored constructively by Lategan and Vorster in their book *Text and Reality: Aspects of Reference in Biblical Texts* (1985).[49] Jesus used language, Lategan argues, which is unusal and foreign enough to be inviting, but familiar enough to recognize.[50] It is not simply flat description. But, Vorster insists, Jesus used language *about* the Kingdom.[51] Jesus referred to a reality which could not be reduced entirely to language. In particular this language must be understood against the extra-linguistic background and context of Jesus' own *deeds*. These are "seminal events in the ongoing stream of life and history."[52] The Kingdom of God is present, in a sense, in the deeds of Jesus (Luke 11:20; *par* Matt. 12:28). These, at very least, "relativize the autonomy of the text", by constituting a context of situation which remains *part of the text*. It does not undermine this referential or extra-linguistic dimension if we regard "Kingdom", with Perrin, as a metaphor. Paul Ricoeur and others have argued that metaphor is not imprisoned within a merely intra-linguistic world, and a careful argument for the capacity of metaphor to *refer*, even if within the framework of developing traditions of language and life, has been put forward in detail by Janet Martin Soskice.[53] In chapter VIII we take these issues further by examining Christological texts in the light of speech-act theory. Some Christological utterances, we shall argue, would be empty and inoperative if they did not presuppose situations in the extra-linguistic world.

A third and admittedly more controversial example might be suggested in the triple dating with which Luke introduces the ministry of John the Baptist (Luke 3:1,2). The material is peculiar to Luke, and dates the ministry of John first with reference to Tiberius Caesar and Pontius Pilate; then with reference to Herod, Philip and Lysanias; and finally with reference to the high-priesthood of Annas and Caiaphas. The style reflects that of classical historians especially Thucydides, as well as Polybius and Josephus. But is this, as Norman Petersen and others would maintain, part of the stage-setting of a Lucan narrative-world? [54] Or does it represent Luke's genuine concern to anchor the history of salvation in the broader context of world-history itself, in which Luke-Acts seems to reflect a special redactional interest? Luke's concern expressed in his prologue (Luke 1:1–4) concerning sources, and eyewitnesses, and traditions might also arguably bear on the issues. What he has received from earlier witnesses has a quality of givenness about it, which he is eager for "Theophilus", his actual or implied reader, to note. The broader issues which this example raises in relation to literary criticism are examined more fully in chapters III, X, XIII and XIV.

The theological understanding of biblical texts as given, then, does not short-circuit questions about the reader and the reader's response. It does not foreclose questions which we have yet to examine about processes of interpretation and understanding. No less important, it does not call into doubt the basic contrast in theories of textuality between the text as a sub-set of signs or signals transmitted through some code and medium and the text's actualization in an act or event of communication within the time-horizons of the reader or readers. This issue will be clarified further in the light of the necessary process of semiotic encoding and de-coding which we describe at the beginning of the next chapter. Nevertheless, these considerations place serious question marks against theories which attempt to dispense altogether with authors or with extra-linguistic contexts of situation, regardless of the nature of the particular texts under examination. In many cases (although not in every case) these place constraints on the range of options which are available to the responsible reader. How serious these constraints might be, and whether they are weak or strong, awaits further discussion when we consider the nature of interpretation, and of the part played by the choice and ranking of different hermeneutical goals.

4. Further Theological Issues: Disembodied Texts or Communicative Address?

At the centre of all theological considerations about revelation and its relation to biblical texts stands the Christological affirmation that Christ himself is *the* Word made flesh. Supremely and paradigmatically the truth of God is revealed and focussed in the *person* of Jesus of Nazareth. In Christ the truth of God is *spoken, embodied, and lived*. The language of Jesus is addressed to those who will hear, as *inter-personal* communication. It is of course possible to distinguish between strong and weaker senses of "address". Dick Leith and George Myerson write: "Language is always addressed to someone else, even if that someone is not immediately present, or is actually unknown or imagined. The term is preferable to *communication* since this word is often linked in people's minds with an unproblematic "transfer" of "information" from one person to another".[55] In this chapter it is used in a generally stronger sense but does not entail less than that which Leith and Myerson indicate.

The Christian church has always been suspicious of doceticism: the tendency to spiritualize away the bodily enfleshment of Christ. But is the Word made flesh to become purely and exclusively "word" again, when the oral message of Jesus, *embodied* in his life and deeds, takes the form of *a written text which can be transmitted independently of the life-context which it presupposes*? In the Fourth Gospel word and deed are presented as interwoven in a flow of acted "signs". These sustain the principle that Jesus speaks through an enfleshed and acted-out word. (John 2:11, 20:30). His claim to be the Bread of Life has a frame of reference in the feeding of the five thousand (John 6:35; cf. 6:1–14); his description of himself as the light of the world operates against the background of his giving sight to the blind (John 8:12; cf. 9:1–11); his self-designation as the resurrection and the life comes in the context of the "raising" of Lazarus (John 11:25; cf.11:38–44). His language about service is framed by the episode of his washing the feet of his disciples (John 13: 5–11; cf. 12–17). The Johannine commission does not seem to suggest that this pattern of relationship between word and deed should discontinue after the resurrection. "As the Father has sent me, even so I send you". (John 20:21). The disciples of Jesus are to function as apostolic witnesses to the word. The question which we shall raise in chapters VIII and XIII, however, especially in the light of work by Searle and by Recanati, is whether this "action" dimension is simply part of Johannine stage scenery. Is deed or act, after all, *only* deed or act *on stage* (i.e. within the text which disappears when the lights go up)?

In Paul this pattern is heavily pronounced. Paul can appeal to a consistency of conduct on his part that matched the words of the gospel (1 Thess. 2:7; 1 Cor. 9: 12–23; 2 Cor. 1:9,12,24; 4:2–12; 6:3–10; 12:9,15; 13:4). Often when he speaks of "power" in contrast to "word" Paul means that which is effectively operative in life, as against mere speech (1 Thess. 1:5; 1 Cor.4: 19,20). Yet Paul uses writing and written texts. Does this therefore imply, as Ricoeur and others might seem to suggest in their theories of textuality, that the written text becomes a disembodied voice, detached from the author and the author's situation, and no longer constituting an act of inter-personal communication?

Theologically this contrast between oral speech and written language would become increasingly problematic if it involved not only a disembodiment of the language of the gospel, but also a reduction of its capacity to function as inter-personal address. In traditional Christian theology, the biblical writings are perceived to function not only as words *about* God, but also as words *from* God. If we recall Markus Barth's analogy between biblical texts and love letters, only in the living situation shared by two lovers in which the letter is read as address, can the letter itself constitute an *act* of love. Outside this situation, for lawyers, detectives, or biographers it is only a record from which inferences may be drawn. To compare a more mundane example suggested by the philosopher John L. Austin, when an angry parent responds to a neighbour's complaint with the words: "He promises, don't you Willie?" the logic of the utterance is different from that of first-person commitment and address. Does Jesus, or God in Christ, say "I forgive you" or "I love you" only *on stage*?

Language concerning divine promise and address raises complex issues, and we discuss this language in detail in chapter VIII. We may begin to address the problem at a more modest level by returning, in the first place, to our observations about the language of Jesus and Paul. Does the transformation of their speech into written texts mean the kind of "hermeneutical distanciation" which removes the author and the author's life from the field of the text? Is this what the work of Ricoeur and others implies, when Ricoeur states that in writing as opposed to speech, the writer is "absent" from the reading?[56]

Werner Kelber has carried out some pioneering research on texts of the New Testament in relation to this contrast between oral speech and writing. His work has also been discussed by Lou Silberman, Walter Ong, and others in a recent number of *Semeia* (1987). Kelber argues that our study of the Bible is dominated by "a disproportionately print-orientated hermeneutic".[57] The thrust of his work is to draw a carefully-argued distinction between an oral model of textuality which is appropriate to Paul, to Q, and to the pre-literary Synoptic tradition, and a written model of textuality which is applicable above all to Mark.

On the Pauline writings, Kelber convincingly takes account of the work of Robert Funk and others, to confirm that the Pauline travelogue, as a minimal starting-point is "harbinger of oral words and personal presence". He declares: "Oral analogies are the key to the Pauline gospel".[58] In Pauline language "the ear triumphs over the eye."[59] Kelber rightly sees that for Paul words must always be matched by deeds. To borrow a simile from Wittgenstein, words from Paul are like paper money which is always backed by the gold of action.[60] This "equivalence of word and deed" in Paul (to use Kelber's phrase) can be seen from such passages as 1 Cor.4:11,12; 9: 1–19; 2 Cor. 4:7–14; 6:3–13; 10:11; 11:7–15; 12:13–16; 1 Thess.2: 8,9; and 2 Thess.3:8,9. Kelber notes: "The teacher lives a life that is paradigmatic in terms of his message. Because in oral hermeneutics words have no existence apart from persons, participation in the message is inseparable from imitation of the speaker: 'We decided to share with you not only the Gospel of God but also ourselves' (1 Thess.2:8,9)"[61]

In the pre-Synoptic traditions, Kelber finds "a speaking of living words in social contexts . . . Voiced words well up in a person . . . Spoken language consists in speech acts".[62] He also attributes this kind of orality to the sayings-source Q. But Mark, he argues, is a very different matter. Mark disrupted the oral life-world. Mark has brought about "a freezing of oral life into textual still- life". Kelber quotes Ricoeur: "The reader is absent from the writing of the book; the writer is absent from its reading".[63] There is a "decontextualization of words from their oral matrix"; a "de-activation" of the dynamistic component".[64] By placing himself outside the life-flow, Mark can now manipulate the text. He can construct his own coherent narrative. But the price is distanciation. Mark is donor of the text, who also hides behind it.[65] He loses control over the process of interpretation.

In a critical discussion in *Semeia* one writer views Kelber's work on Mark as a "breakthrough". But Silberman and Ong emphasize the still greater significance of orality as a hermeneutical model for texts which nevertheless took written form. Silberman alludes with more than a hint of scepticism to the deconstructionist assumption that a written text belongs "absolutely" to the reader; and he asks: "What if the text is vocally constructed? Can the author's voice be silenced?"[66] Walter Ong endorses the basic writing-orality distinction as a matter of hermeneutical principle. However, he points out that a written text in an oral culture does not yet possess the dynamics of a hermeneutic of written texts as such. Attention should be given to a "persistently oral milieu" which may "envelop even a highly developed textuality", and "deeply effect both the composition of texts and their interpretation".[67] Rather than viewing Mark as representing an "explosive" discontinuity with the pre-Marcan oral tradition, Ong prefers to speak of Mark as an *interpreter* of the tradition which he received.[68]

Such a view of Mark does not seem to conflict with the emphasis found in a number of recent studies on Mark which portray the evangelist as an interpreter of tradition who creatively combines elements of tradition into a unified and holistic narrative or story. Ernest Best's study *Mark: the Gospel as Story* provides a good example, although others could also be mentioned.[69] Mark's particular achievement was to provide a continuous narrative structure, in which the structuring of the material conveyed the message: this is how the pieces make sense. For example, Mark's use of *euthus* (immediately) some thirty-one times, leads the reader on at a rapid pace, but the pace begins to slow down in Mark 9 and 10 when the Passion sayings are introduced. The cross is the goal to which all the narrative movement is leading. In so ordering his material, Mark interprets it in terms of the centrality of the cross. There is no contradiction between an apparently causal chain of events in the life of Jesus and the fulfilment of the divine purpose. In the absence of infancy narratives, the only introductory framework is that of the Old Testament and John the Baptist. Sometimes one episode is fitted inside the frame of another. There are also omissions and silences, loose ends and rough edges, which invite the reader to ask questions and to engage actively with the text.

In response to the claim that Mark is primarily "interpreting" rather than disrupting the pre-Marcan tradition, Kelber re-asserts some of the discontinuities with tradition which he finds in Mark, especially the "role-reversal" of the disciples in Mark: "the insiders are turned into outsiders", and the narrator's viewpoint is distanced from that of the disciples within the Marcan narrative.[70] But this kind of discontinuity, if this is what it is, does not represent decisive evidence for a clear-cut contrast between the dynamics of oral speech as inter-personal communication and a hermeneutic of written texts. What may readily be granted is that Mark does choose to step back out of the scene as anonymous narrator who knows the end from the beginning. With Patrick Grant and other literary theorists whom we discuss in chapter XIII, we may admit that Mark's "voice" functions in a different way from Paul's. Secrecy, overview, and narrative distance, play an important part, and the text is at times, to use Eco's contrast, creative and generative, and not simply a vehicle of transmission. Nevertheless, while Kelber is no doubt right to claim that Mark has stepped back from his text in a way that differentiates his literary role from that of Paul, it remains doubtful whether this difference has become one of *kind*, rather than of *degree*. It still makes sense to speak of *Mark's* theology, and of *Mark's* theological purpose. Mark is a purposive agent; not a semiotic construct. His object is not simply to let readers "make what they like" of his work. Our view of Kelber's work will depend ultimately on whether we are willing to follow Paul Ricoeur and others in drawing such a very sharp contrast between speech and writing. In the case of biblical texts, there are both theological and hermeneutical reasons for firm caution about accepting such a clear-cut distinction, and these will emerge in the subsequent pages of the present work. The issue forms part of a wider discussion about inter-personal communication, speech-acts, and the relation between intertextuality and intersubjectivity. Moreover, as we shall now see, Ricoeur's claims about revelation as declaration and address do not seem to fit entirely comfortably this aspect of his theory of textuality.

Can revelation through biblical texts include the notion of inter-personal address from God? We have already argued that such an address, if we can conceive of it in these terms, would occur not simply through a disembodied text, but through a text interwoven at certain key points with life and history. It may be helpful to try to view part of this problem in dialogue with the work of Paul Ricoeur, since Ricoeur has attempted simultaneously to affirm the absence of the author from processes of reading written texts (notably in his books *Interpretation Theory* and *Hermeneutics and the Human Sciences*) and also to acknowledge that biblical revelation embodies *irreducibly first-person and second-person address* (mainly in his *Essays on Biblical Interpretation*).71 The direction of a path towards the reconciliation of these two standpoints can be found especially in his essays "Towards a Hermeneutic of the Idea of Revelation" and "Biblical Hermeneutics".72 This initial discussion of Ricoeur's hermeneutics will be developed more fully in chapter X.

Ricoeur distinguishes between five primary modes of discourse in the biblical texts, which are not exhaustive: prophetic, narrative, hymnic, prescriptive, and wisdom modes. The prophetic mode represents an address not simply from the prophet, but also from God. Nevertheless this *model* of revelation is *qualified* by the other four modes, and in particular by the wisdom mode. He alludes here to Ian Ramsey's work on models and qualifiers.73 For Ricoeur, even the notion of inter-personal communication between God and man remains a *personal model* that needs to be *qualified by divine transcendence and hiddenness*. Hence he dissociates himself from the "personalism" of Martin Buber and Gabriel Marcel.74

In the prophetic mode of discourse, Ricoeur fully allows that "the prophet presents himself as not speaking in his own name, but in the name of another, in the name of Yahweh".75 There is a *"double author* of speech and writing" (Jer.2:1,2; 3:12; 4:27). Likewise in hymnic modes of discourse, such as in the Psalms, hymns of praise, thanksgiving, and supplication are addressed *to* God. Celebration transforms story into invocation.76 In narrative, typically in the Pentateuch, the Synoptic Gospels, and Acts, the author often disappears, as if events recounted themselves; but the essential ingredient is the emphasis on founding events "as the imprint, mark, or trace of God's act".77 Prescriptive discourse expresses the will of God. It represents a relationship of commanding and obeying within the framework which the term 'covenant' broadly conveys: "The idea of covenant designates a whole complex of relations", running from meticulous obedience to the Law to loving Yahweh your God with all your heart, with all your soul, with all your strength" (Deut. 6:5,6) and a new heart and spirit (Ezk.11:19).78 Jesus sums up this mode in the Golden Rule (Matt.7:12). But there remains the revelatory mode of wisdom. Wisdom speaks to every person through limit-situations, Ricoeur argues: through experiences of solitude, anguish, suffering, and death. Hebraic wisdom interprets these as signifying "the incomprehensibility of God – as the silence and absence of God".79

Over the years Ricoeur has developed a special interest in the Book of Job. He regards it as the outstanding example of wisdom in the Old Testament, and it is not surprising, in the light of his sustained reflection on Job, that he refuses to subordinate the wisdom model of revelation to that of the prophetic mode. For our present discussion what is most significant is the simultaneous presence of dialogue, of silence, of indirect communication, and of what is perceived as the absence of God, or at very least his hiddenness. In his earlier work *The Symbolism of Evil* Ricoeur comments on Job 23:8, 30:20; "Faced with the torturing absence of God, the man (Job) dreams of his own absence".[80] While, in his later essay "Religion, Atheism, and Faith" he declares that Job receives no "answer" to his questions. Ricoeur also asserts: "The fact that the Lord *speaks* is what is essential. He does not speak *about* Job; he speaks *to* Job".[81] Ricoeur therefore tries to hold together the notion of divine *address* with a qualifying attention to divine transcendence which in Job 42: 1–6 "cannot be transcribed by speech or *logos*".[82] Wisdom reveals "a hidden God" who takes as his mask "the anonymous and non-human course of events".[83] Job is brought to the point where he is no longer pre-occupied by the need for self-protection. Alluding to Bonhoeffer, Ricoeur sees Job as encountering the God of the Crucified One, where "dialogue is in itself a mode of consolation".[84]

Does God reveal Himself through inter-personal address in biblical texts? Ricoeur can offer an affirmative answer only with strict qualifications. God remains hidden, "infinitely above human thought and speech".[85] Hence every model of communication, including that of inter-personal address, is decisively "modified" so that it speaks of or from the "Wholly Other" analogically or in symbol.[86] The first-person prophetic model and the second-person hymnic model also remain valid to a degree, provided that we understand these inter-personal models *analogically*. In chapter X we explore these issues in much fuller detail, noting both the philosophical and theological contexts which serve to shape Ricoeur's approach. Among the evaluations of Ricoeur's approach, we note the theological assessments offered by Kevin J. Vanhoozer among others.[87]

Although defences of analogy have rested partly on a theology of the image of God in humankind, the case becomes more decisive when emphasis is placed on the belief that the fullest and uniquely definitive revelation of God has occurred in the person of Jesus Christ (Hebrews 1:2,3; Col. 1:15,19; John 14:6–9). But while it remains entirely clear that analogy enters into our understanding of *descriptions* about God it is less self-evident in what sense the category of address is analogical. In an obvious but philosophically unremarkable sense, analogy comes into play in the sense that if someone cannot "hear" God, we do not advise him or her to purchase a deaf-aid. Yet when we have allowed for analogy in *this* sense, *address remains an integral aspect of the logical grammar of what it is for God to "speak" at all*. Wittgenstein makes the *conceptual* observation: "'You can't hear God speak to someone else; you can hear him only if you are being addressed.' This is a grammatical remark."[88]

What is a Text?

There remains therefore some internal tension between the claim that, even if analogically, God may *address* his people through modes of language embodied in a text, while the text is also said to have become detached or "*distanciated*" from a speaker and the speaker's context of utterance. The importance of the role of context of situation and of the relation between the text and its author becomes important, as Vern Poythress argues in some detail, when we are considering the notion of what Poythress calls "the Divine meaning of scripture".[89] The work of the Spirit of God, he concludes, concerns not simply the texts, but also the lives and actions with which the text is interwoven.[90]

A hermeneutic which is orientated towards a view of textuality dependent on the role of intra-linguistic worlds and intertextuality, then, may stand in contrast to a hermeneutic which is orientated towards a theory of texts in which texts are embedded in inter-subjective situations of interpersonal communication. This contrast will emerge regularly as we proceed. Theologically a hermeneutic of an *embodied* text reflects an incarnational Christology, in which revelation operates through the interwovenness of word and deed. It also coheres with a theological account of the role of the community in which their actions and witness give credibility to, and facilitate understanding of, the word which is spoken and read. *The text is more than a "docetic" or disembodied system of signifiers.*

At the same time we cannot attempt to formulate any theory of textuality simply on the basis of what may cohere with our theology. We must also evaluate theories of texts on their own terms. The most powerful arguments about disembodied systems of signifiers arise not only from literary formalism (to which we return in chapter XIII) but also from particular applications of semiotic theory. We therefore turn in the next chapter to the work of Saussure, Peirce, and other more recent writers in semiotics, and we ask in particular whether semiotic theory as such necessarily leads to purely intralinguistic theories of texts, or even to deconstructionism. The theories of texts associated with Barthes and with Derrida which we discuss in the next chapter also raise questions about truth and truth-claims, and to these truth issues we shall return again in chapters VIII through to XIV.

NOTES TO CHAPTER II

1. John Lyons, *Semantics* (2 vols) Cambridge: Cambridge University Press, 1977, 2, 633.
2. *Ibid* 634.
3. *Ibid* 633.

4. Werner H. Kelber, *The Oral and the Written Gospel, The Hermeneutics of Speaking and Writing in the Synoptic Tradition, Mark, Paul and Q*, Philadelphia: Fortress Press, 1983.
5. Paul Ricoeur, *Hermeneutics and the Human Sciences*, Cambridge and New York: Cambridge University Press, 1981, 139.
6. *Ibid* 147.
7. *Ibid* 148.
8. *Ibid* 149; cf. 131–44, on distanciation, and 145–64 on textuality. See further, Paul Ricoeur, *Interpretation Theory. Discourse and the Surplus of Meaning*, Fort Worth: Texas Christian University Press, 1976, 25–44.
9. Jacques Derrida "Living On"/"Border Lines", in Harold Bloom, Paul de Man, Jacques Derrida et al., *Deconstruction and Criticism*, London: Routledge and Kegan Paul, 1979, 83, cf. 75–176. .
10. *Ibid* 84 .
11. Roland Barthes, "From Work to Text" in Josué V. Harari (ed), *Textual Strategies. Perspectives in Post-Structuralist Criticism*, Ithaca: Cornell University Press, 1979, 78; cf. 73–81.
12. *Ibid* 76.
13. *Ibid* 77–8 .
14. Paul Ricoeur, *Hermeneutics and the Human Sciences* 142–44.
15. Norman R. Petersen, *Rediscovering Paul. Philemon and the Sociology of Paul's Narrative World*, Philadelphia: Fortress Press, 1985, 17–32 *et passim*.
16. Robert Morgan (with John Barton) *Biblical Interpretation*, 10, 196–200, 287 *et passim*.
17. *Ibid* 25 and 198.
18. *Ibid* 287.
19. *Ibid* 203.
20. *Ibid* 221.
21. Anthony C. Thiselton, "On Models and Methods: A Conversation with Robert Morgan" in David J.A. Clines, Stephen E Fowl, and Stanley E Porter (eds.) *The Bible in Three Dimensions: Essays in Celebration of Forty Years of Biblical Studies in the University of Sheffield*, Sheffield: Sheffield Academic Press (J.S.O.T. Suppl. Ser. 87) 1990, 337–56.
22. Norman Petersen, *op. cit.* 6.
23. Rene Wellek and Austin Warren, *Theory of Literature*, London: Penguin Books, 1973 (1949), 42.
24. William K. Wimsatt and Monroe Beardsley, "The Intentional Fallacy" in W.K. Wimsatt, *The Verbal Icon: Studies in the Meaning of Poetry*, New York: Noonday Press, 1966 (1954); cf. "Genesis: A Fallacy Re-visited" in Peter Demetz *et al*, *The Disciplines of Criticism: Essays in Literary Theory, Interpretation and History*, New Haven: Yale University Press, 1968, 193–225; and "The Intentional Fallacy" in David De-Newton Molina (ed.) *On Literary Intention*, Edinburgh: Edinburgh University Press, 1976, 1–13. See further, John Barton, *Reading the Old Testament: Method in Biblical Study*, London: Darton, Longman & Todd, 1984, 147–53; and David Couzens Hoy, *The Critical Circle: Literature, History and Philosophical Hermeneutics*, Berkeley: University of California Press, 1982, 25–29.
25. H.P. Grice, "Meaning" in P.F. Strawson (ed.) *Philosophical Logic*, Oxford: Oxford University Press, 1971, 39–48; and "Utterance-Meaning, Sentence-Meaning,

and Word-Meaning" in J.R. Searle (ed.), *The Philosophy of Language*, London: Oxford University Press, 1971, 54–70; John R Searle, *Intentionality. An Essay in the Philosophy of Mind*, Cambridge: Cambridge University Press, 1983, 160–79 *et passim*; and F. Recanati, *op. cit.*

26. Frank Lentricchia, *After the New Criticism*, Chicago: University of Chicago Press, 1980, 7; cf. 3–26.
27. Susan R. Suleiman and Inge Crosman (eds.) *The Reader in the Text: Essays on Audience and Interpretation*, Princeton: Princeton University Press, 1980, 5.
28. Wolgang Iser, *The Implied Reader: Patterns of Communication in Prose Fiction from Bunyan to Beckett*, Baltimore: Johns Hopkins University Press, 1974, 274–75, (my italics).
29. S.R. Suleiman and I. Crosman (eds.) *op. cit* ; vii. .
30. Robert Crosman, "Do Readers Make Meaning?" *op cit* 161; cf. 149–64. .
31. Stanley Fish, *Is There a Text in This Class? The Authority of Interpretive Communities*, Cambridge, Mass.: Harvard University Press, 1980, 12–13.
32. *Ibid* 13.
33. See Calvin on 1 Cor. 16:19, and 2 Cor. 11:3. Cf. further T.H.L. Parker, *Calvin's New Testament Commentaries*, London: S.C.M. Press, 1971, 26–68. .
34. John Lyons, *op. cit.* vol. 2, 622–35.
35. *Ibid* 607–13.
36. J.R. Firth, *Papers in Linguistics*, 1934–51, London: Oxford University Press, 1957, 32–3.
37. Werner G. Jeanrond, *Text and Interpretation as Categories of Theological Thinking*, Eng, Dublin: Gill and MacMillan, 1988, 7.
38. *Ibid* 76.
39. Jeffrey Stout, "What is the Meaning of a Text?" *New Literary History*, 14, 1982, 7, cf. 1–12 (Stout's italics).
40. Robert Morgan (with John Barton) *Biblical Interpretation*, 7.
41. François Bovon, *Exegesis. Problems of Method and Exercizes in Reading* Eng. Pittsburgh: Pickwick Press, 1978, 1.
42. John Breck, *The Power of the Word in the Worshipping Church*, New York: St. Vladamir's Seminary Press, 1986, 93–139. Cf. Georges Florovsky, *Bible, Church, Tradition: An Eastern Orthodox View*, Belmont: Nordland Publishing Co., 1972, 37–72.
43. C.H. Dodd, *The Parables of the Kingdom*, London: Nisbet, 1935, 16. .
44. In addition to the standard commentaries cf. John Dominic Crossan (ed.)"The Book of Job and Ricoeur's Hermeneutics" *Semeia* 19, 1981, 41–46 *et passim*.
45. Cf. Hans Frei, *The Eclipse of Biblical Narrative. A Study in Eighteenth and Nineteenth Century Hermeneutics*, New Haven: Yale University Press, 1974.
46. David Tracy, *Plurality and Ambiguity: Hermeneutic, Religion, Hope*, San Francisco: Harper and Row, 1987, 9.
47. Norman Perrin, *Jesus and the Language of the Kingdom. Symbol and Metaphor in New Testament Interpretation*, London: S C M. 1976, 197 (Perrin's italics).
48. *Ibid* 29–30.
49. Bernard Lategan and Willem Vorster, *Text and Reality: Aspects of Reference in Biblical Texts*, Atlanta: Scholars Press, 1985.
50. *Ibid* 67–93.
51. Willem Vorster, *loc. cit.* 64.

52. Bernard Lategan *Ibid* 67–93.
53. Janet Martin Soskice, *Metaphor and Religious Language*, 148–61 *et passim*. Cf. Paul Ricoeur, *The Rule of Metaphor* Eng. London: Routledge and Kegan Paul, 1978.
54. Norman R. Petersen, *Literary Criticism for New Testament Critics*, Philadelphia: Fortress Press, 1978, 81–92.
55. Dick Leith and George Myerson, *The Power of Address: Explorations in Rhetoric*, London & New York: Routledge, 1989, xii.
56. Paul Ricoeur, *Interpretation Theory*, 25–44; *Hermeneutics and the Human Sciences*, 131–44.
57. Werner H. Kelber, *The Oral and the Written Gospel: The Hermentutics of Speaking and Writing in the Synoptic Tradition, Mark, Paul and Q*, Philadelphia: Fortress Press 1983, xv.
58. *Ibid* 141.
59. *Ibid* 143.
60. Ludwig Wittgenstein, *The Blue and Brown Books* 2nd edn. Oxford: Blackwell, 1969, 48.
61. Werner H. Kelber, *op. cit.* 151.
62. *Ibid* 33.
63. *Ibid* 92; cf. Paul Ricoeur, *Interpretation Theory* 25–44.
64. Werner H. Kelber *op. cit.* 94.
65. *Ibid* 115.
66. Lou H. Silberman "Reflections on Orality, Aurality, and Perhaps More", *Semeia* 39 (1987) 4; cf. 1–6.
67. Walter Ong, "Text as Interpretation: Mark and After" *Ibid* 19 and 21.
68. *Ibid* 7–26.
69. Ernest Best, *Mark: The Gospel as Story*, Edinburgh: Clark, 1983, esp. 93–147; cf. David Rhoads and Donald Michie, *Mark as Story*, Philadephia: Fortress Press, 1982.
70. Werner Kelber, "Biblical Hermeneutics and the Ancient Art of Communication" *Semeia* 39, 1987, 102; cf. 97–105.
71. Paul Ricoeur, *Interpretation Theory* 25–44; *Hermeneutics and the Human Sciences* 131–64; *Essays on Biblical Interpretation* (ed. L.S. Mudge) London: S.P.C.K., 1981.
72. Paul Ricoeur, "Biblical Hermeneutics" *Semeia* 4, 1975, 29–148; and *Essays on Biblical Interpretation* 73–118.
73. Paul Ricoeur, *Essays on Biblical Interpretation* 75–95, and *Semeia* 4, 1975, 107–22.
74. Paul Ricoeur, *Essays on Biblical Interpretation* 89.
75. *Ibid* 75.
76. *Ibid* 88–9.
77. *Ibid* 79.
78. *Ibid* 83–4.
79. *Ibid* 86.
80. Paul Ricoeur, *The Symbolism of Evil*, Eng. Boston: Beacon Press, 1969 (1967) 319.
81. Paul Ricoeur, *The Conflict of Interpretations. Essays in Hermeneutics* (ed. Don Ihde), Evanston: Northwestern University Press, 1974, 461 (my italics).
82. Paul Ricoeur, *Essays in Biblical Interpretation* 87.
83. *Ibid* 89.

84. Paul Ricoeur, *The Conflict of Interpretation*, 460–61.
85. Paul Ricoeur, *Essays in Biblical Interpretation*, 93.
86. Paul Ricoeur, *Semeia* 4, 1975, 107–9.
87. Kevin J Vanhoozer, *Biblical Narrative in the Philosophy of Paul Ricoeur*, Cambridge: Cambridge University Press, 1990.
88. Ludwig Wittgenstein, *Zettel*, Oxford: Blackwell, 1967, sect. 717.
89. Vern Sheridan Poythress, "Divine Meaning of Scripture", *Westminster Theological Journal* 48, 1986, 241–79.
90. *Ibid* 258–62.

CHAPTER III

From Semiotics to Deconstruction and Post-Modernist Theories of Textuality

1. Code in Semiotic Theory: the Nature of Semiotic Theory

In general terms semiotics is the theory of signs. But in practice semiotic theory achieves its most distinctive importance in two particular areas, both of which we have yet to consider more adequately with reference to our discussion of textuality. The first area concerns the nature and status of the *codes* through which texts communicate meanings. The second concerns those forms of *non-verbal social behaviour* which, through the presupposition of a code, become signifying messages. All texts presuppose code. The text of a medical prescription, for example, has been encoded by a medical practitioner in accordance with the conventions of the profession, and invites a pharmacist to de-code it for action in the light of these shared conventions. A music score has been encoded by a composer, and waits to be de-coded by an orchestra or singers in a musical event.

In these examples, however, the *code* is not the items of information which constitute the "message". The code is the sign-*system, lattice, or network, in terms of which* the linguistic choices which convey the message are expressed. The musical code which enables the composer to specify the production of a particular note for a particular length of time is not the note itself (which would be the message); but the stave or staff of five parallel horizontal lines (together with the clef and the specified areas where possible choices about key signature and time would be supplied) which constitute the *structure in terms of which* given notes can be chosen and their properties specified.

Complex texts may presuppose several different layers of code. For example, the Apocalypse of John at one level presupposes the range of possible lexical and grammatical choices available in hellenistic Greek (albeit the Apocalyptist's Greek presses the code at times to its limits!) But it also operates on the basis of a system of conventions used by earlier apocalyptic.[1] Some allusions to earlier texts such as Ezekiel, Zechariah, and Daniel are not merely reminders about earlier traditions. Sometimes they perform not a stylistic but a *semiotic* function, providing yet another level of encoding in terms of which a message is to be read. In these cases we have examples of what Julia Kristeva in her work on semiotics has called *intertextuality*. She writes "The term intertextuality denotes this transposition of one (or several) sign system(s) into another; but since this term has often been understood in the broad sense of 'study of sources' we prefer the term *transposition* because it specifies that the passage from one signifying system to another demands a new articulation. . . ."[2]

To make a mistake about the semiotic code, therefore, violates the text and distorts its meaning. Language in the Apocalypse of John about "one hundred and forty-four thousand" (Rev.7:4) presupposes a code which is different from that which generates meaning in the case of mathematical propositions. In the code of mathematics, the network of choices operates in terms of a contrast which opposes or excludes "one hundred and forty-four thousand and one" or "one hundred and forty-three thousand and ninety nine." But the text of Revelation presupposes contrastive networks which signal differences between completeness and incompleteness with reference to a history of traditions about "twelve" which have become familiar enough to represent a convention among certain communities. Where horses' heads seem to become merged with heads of lions (Rev. 9:10) the code which is presupposed is not that of empirical visual observation and description. The "measuring" of the temple (Rev.11:1,2) may perhaps involve several layers of signifying systems of intertextuality, as John Court's exegesis may imply.[3]

The culture-specific nature of codes is underlined when we examine the second feature to which we referred in semiotics, namely the role of non-verbal behaviour. The conventions of apocalyptic can be no more strange to the modern western world than the code which forms the basis for the operation of traffic lights might seem to the ancient world. The existence of such a code (based on arbitrary colour-contrasts) gives rise to extended and metaphorical applications. A modern pietist might say: "I prayed, and God gave me a green light". Flowers in their natural habitat do not usually convey a message. But if they are woven into a wreath, and sent to a funeral, they become a *sign* of sympathy and respect, on the basis of a shared social code. To mistake the code, and to send a funeral-wreath to a wedding would be to commit a social gaffe, comparable to interpreting the Apocalypse as empirical description. Clothes can become signs which convey given signals on particular occasions. Negative signals can be generated by a given choice of clothes either because someone makes a mistake, or because they consciously revolt against the shared conventions of the social group which holds them.

Roland Barthes has explored, with interesting effects, a wide range of non-verbal social behaviour which has the capacity to generate signs on the basis of code: film, furniture, cooking, sport, the use of political slogans, dress-fashions, beards, perfumes, advertising, striptease, cars, and photography.[4] In these examples the *code* is not the particular choice of a particular car or item of clothing, but the network of possible options in relation to which a particular car or choice of clothing becomes "significant". Umberto Eco makes a parallel point. He asserts: "To communicate is to use the entire world as a semiotic apparatus. I believe that *culture* is that, and nothing else". For example: "I am speaking through my clothes. If I were wearing a Mao suit, if I were without a tie, the ideological connotations of my speech would be changed."[5]

It might seem that we have already exposed the "radical" character of code for meaning and for the interpretation of meaning. But we have barely begun. The very serious philosophical issue which all this raises for Roland Barthes and others is the relation between language and the world, or more especially, the relation between language and social culture. In the thought of Barthes and of Julia Kristeva semiotic theory constitutes a meta-language or second-order critique of language and signs.[6] In Julia Kristeva's words, "No form of semiotics can exist other than as a critique of semiotics."[7] What such meta-reflection suggests for Barthes is that the effect of semiotic theory is radically to unmask the status of codes which are often assumed to mirror the world as no more than particular *habits of mind* or *cultural constructs*.

If, however, language-operations depend on linguistic codes, Barthes argues, this principle applies to all language as such. People assume that language mirrors the external world. They trust language to allow the possibility of objectivity. But its relation to the world is culture-bound and arbitrary. At this point Barthes borrows the terminology and some of the ideology of Marxism. Bourgeois cultures utilize this confused "mystification" whereby they and the masses remain subject to the illusion that we encounter "nature" or "objectivity" in the systems of the culture. The task of the semioticist is to unmask this pseudo-objectivity; to "decipher" a meaning-network which "conceals" or "naturalizes" what amount to no more than conventions. Mystification is a tool whereby bourgeois cultures transmit their own values under the guise of objective truth. The consequences which follow from all this are radical: the subject-matter of language and texts remains intra-linguistic; they do not describe states of affairs about the external world; texts and meanings are endlessly fluid and plural.[8]

We must ask, however: are the implications of modern semiotic theory as radical as Barthes and others maintain? The pre-history of semiotics can be traced back into classical antiquity. Hippocrates stressed the role of signs in medical diagnosis and prognosis. Aristotle distinguished between necessary signs (for example, fever as a sign of illness) and those which depended only on probability (whether fast breathing constituted a sign of fever). Augustine noted the capacity of signs to point beyond themselves, and like Locke, viewed linguistic signs as identifying markers of thoughts or ideas. Hobbes and Locke held theories about the nature of signs in language. Nevertheless the pre-history of the subject throws up none of the most sensitive issues.

The two major innovative thinkers who founded semiotics as a modern discipline were Charles S. Peirce (1839–1914) and Ferdinand de Saussure (1857–1913). The Swiss linguistician Saussure never envisaged that his work would lead to the kind of conclusions advocated by Barthes, Derrida, and the post-structuralist deconstructionists, even if Derrida insists that Saussure's work logically implies the outcome when it is "radicalized". Indeed the immediate impact of Saussure's work lay in the founding of modern general linguistics as a sober scientific discipline of linguistic description. John Lyons expresses the mainstream view in that discipline that Saussure is effectively the founder of the subject.[9]

Nevertheless, Saussure did insist on three fundamental principles, which we shall shortly explore. First, he insisted on what he called "the *arbitrary nature of the sign*" as a key principle.[10] Second, he argued that language functions as "a system of interdependent terms".[11] Meaning is generated by relations of *difference* within this system. For example, in a sub-system of colour-words, "orange" derives its meaning from its difference from its next-door neighbours in the continuum, "red" and "yellow", rather than from pointing to oranges on trees. Third, Saussure distinguished between concrete acts of speech (*parole*) and the language-system *(langue)* which represents a purely *formal or abstract* structure; a network of possibilities out of which concrete utterances could be generated. *Langue* does not "exist" in the external world.

More than fifty years after Saussure's death, Jacques Derrida was to radicalize his principles of *arbitrariness* and *difference* into an anti-metaphysical view of language, thought, and the world. "Difference" becomes a key anti-ontological category. What Barthes describes as the process of "mystification" whereby the merely cultural is endowed with pseudo-objectivity is an illusion easier to maintain, Derrida suggests, in oral speech than in writing or written texts. Only vocal or oral utterance can appear to support the illusion of "a metaphysics of presence", centred on the word, as if the word itself mirrored the world and reality. But writing calls attention to the absence of the writer, and invites a greater plurality of interpretations of possible meanings. If language is a differential network, and if differences generate meanings, we should focus not on linguistic "entities" ("Logocentrism") but on the differences between signs. It then becomes an operative principle of interpretation for Derrida that *differentiation* (Fr. *différence*) leads to and invites *defer-ment* (Fr. *différance*).[12] We can never reach any "final" point in the interpretation of meaning. One semiotic process leads on to another, and none is grounded in "reality" or in the external world.

These claims will bring us back to Saussure, when we attempt to revaluate the implications of the three principles which he expounds. But a preliminary comment is also invited on the influence of Charles S. Peirce. Peirce is often associated with the philosophy of pragmatism, although in Peirce this principle related primarily to his work on meaning, and less explicitly to theories of truth, as was the case in William James. Nevertheless, several principles formulated by Peirce were to have very broadly parallel effects to those of the "radicalization" of Saussure. First, Peirce stressed the fallible character of all human knowledge, beliefs and statements. Beliefs amount largely to "habits of behaviour". Second, thinking or thought has to do with the use of signs. Yet signs point beyond themselves to other signs and sign-relations. Finally, meaning is to be seen primarily in terms of meaning-*effect*. It is here that Peirce's pragmatism has its most far-reaching effects. What is important and "cashable" about meaning is its bearing on the conduct of life.

Recently Robert S. Corrington has put forward a detailed case for the view that Peirce laid the foundations for American hermeneutics, or for a hermeneutical tradition which is distinctive of modern American philosophical thought.[13] He traces a tradition in America which, it might be argued, is comparable to the radicalization of Saussure in Europe. Corrington stresses that for Peirce there is "no 'pure' given". He adds (with an additional allusion to Josiah Royce): "Reality consists of signs and sign relations". This emphasis must be coupled with Peirce's pragmatic interest in meaning-*effects*. Against such a background, audience-criticism and reader-related theories of textuality, hermeneutics, and literary theory find ready hospitality. The fundamental question which these two parallel trends in Europe and in America raise, therefore, is: are these "radical" implications the genuine and inescapable implications of mainstream semiotic theory? To begin to answer this question we must look more closely at the work of Saussure, and at its effects in semiotics, linguistics, and biblical interpretation.

2. Need Semiotics Lead to Deconstructionism? Different Understandings of the Implications of Semiotic Theory

Saussure insists that, as a first principle, "the arbitrary nature of the sign" constitutes an axiom which "dominates all the linguistics of language; its consequences are numberless".[15] It is arbitrary, for example, that French speakers use two words, *bon marché*, where English speakers use one, *cheap*.

It is also arbitrary that English splits up the colour-spectrum semiotically in such a way that this language has one word for "blue", while Russians have to decide whether to use *goluboj*, "light blue", or *sinij*, "dark blue". French speakers have to choose between *brun* and *marron* for a segment of the spectrum which in English is merely "brown". It is arbitrary that Latin and Greek use the one-word forms *amo* and *philo* or *ero*, where English and German use two-word forms: *I love* and *ich liebe*. Such grammatical categories as substantive verbs, or adjectives, Saussure comments, represent abstract distinctions of habit, convention and convenience. They are not imposed by the nature of the world: "they are not linguistic realities".[16]

In the second place, every linguistic sign that carries meaning does so by virtue of its being part of a *system or structure* which generates the value, force, or meaning of its component elements through the interplay of similarities and differences within the system. Saussure writes: "Language is a system of interdependent terms in which the value (*la valeur*) of each term results solely from the simultaneous presence of the others."[17] He illustrates the principle from the "value" of a given piece in chess. This depends on the state of the whole board, and draws its operational significance from its relation to other pieces in the structure of the game. Meaning is generated and assessed not by how a sign-unit mirrors or fails to mirror some entity in the external world, but by how it relates to other sign-units within the system.

The lattice of the system has a vertical and a horizontal axis. Meanings are generated by relations and differences along each axis. Fundamental differences are generated vertically by the possibility of *alternative choices* of words where the use of one excludes the use of the other. They may have the same syntactic function, but different meanings. Such words stand in *paradigmatic* relations to each other. For example in the context of speech about traffic signals, "red" and "green" stand in paradigmatic relation to each other as alternative linguistic choices which could be slotted into the same space in an appropriate sentence. Each draws part of its meaning from its contrast to the other. But there is also a horizontal axis of difference. Both "red" and "green" are colour-words, but they are different from the verbal forms "see", "notice", "signal". These other terms provide the horizontal context, or *syntagmatic* relationship into which the colour-words can be slotted as adjacent terms in a sentence. Part of the meaning of "red" is that in syntagmatic terms, it is the kind of word which can be the object of the verb "I see", and an adjective applicable to "signal". It makes sense in the chain of language: "I see a red signal". Part of its meaning in paradigmatic terms, is drawn from its difference from "green". Both axes entail *differences*.

This brings us to the third main principle from Saussure which concerns us. The speaker does not verbally or orally explore the entire repertoire of alternative possibilities from which he or she may choose, each time an utterance occurs. The lattice or structure of differing but inter-related terms, represents not a concrete actuality but an *abstract potentiality* until a speaker actualizes a particular choice in a concrete use of a specific piece of language. Saussure drew attention to this distinction by consistently using the term *langue* for what he called "the storehouse" of language; *langue* consists in the abstract of "a collection of necessary conventions". On the other hand, he uses the word *parole* to denote a *concrete act* of speech; one which is made possible on the basis of *langue*. *Langue* represents the formal, abstract, structure; *parole* represents the specific, concrete, utterance.

I have discussed the work of Saussure and its implications for biblical studies in greater detail elsewhere.[18] Saussure's distinction between *langue* and *parole* remains fundamental both in linguistics and in semiotics. In semiotics it marks the difference between a sign, or more strictly the use of a given sign on a given occasion, and the differential network of relations between signs on the basis of which the given sign itself bears meaning. The distinction between *langue* and *parole* in Saussure's "semiology" corresponds to Roman Jakobson's later formulation of the contrast between *code* and *message*, and is parallel to Charles Peirce's distinction between *type* and *token*. *Tokens*, in Peirce's semiotic theory, are particular, even unique, physical objects or events located at a given place in space or time. *Types* are patterns or abstract classes of which *tokens* constitute actual instanciations.

What is the relation between signs, signification, and the external world in C.S. Peirce's semiotic theory? His semiotics are complex, but they entail the following principles. Peirce distinguished three possible modes of relation between a sign and what it signifies. If a sign functions purely as an *index*, the relationship may be primarily of a physical or quasi-physical cause-effect kind. For example, a weather vane carries a message about wind direction. An index "is a sign which refers to the Object that it denotes by virtue of its being really affected by that Object".[19] Signs which function as *icons* are related to their objects by similarity of structure. For example, a map, diagram, or representational picture corresponds either isomorphically or at least by "fitness", to the elements of what it portrays and their relation to each other. Signs which function as *symbols* Peirce stresses, have no such causal, quasi-physical or "fitness" characteristics: in this respect their use as signs is arbitrary, or at least due to regularly *habituated patterns* of association. Here a process of pattern-recognition involving *type* allows the interpreter to perceive a relation of meaning: "A symbol is a sign which refers to the Object that it denotes by virtue of a law, usually an association of general ideas, which operates to cause the symbol to be interpreted as referring to that Object. It is thus itself a general type or law, that is, a *Legisign*".[20]

Peirce viewed semiotics as a branch of logic and philosophy. But are *types* and *legisigns* products of logical necessity, or generalizations based only on regularities and associations of habit observed as contingent data of experience? Here Peirce's thought becomes more complex, and is capable of more than one possible interpretation. The complexity is partly due to Peirce's insistence that indices, icons, and symbols are not three distinct *kinds* of sign, but three distinct *modes* by which signs operate which may be simultaneously present, or present in varying degrees. But the most crucial difference among implications drawn from Peirce reflect a contrast between a fundamentally pragmatic, behavioural and functional semiotics, and one which takes more seriously his concerns about logic and the place which he accords to the inter-subjective judgments of the community. In due course we shall note, in this connection, Karl-Otto Apel's understanding of his semiotics.

Charles W. Morris is generally regarded as Peirce's successor in American semiotic theory. Morris developed a theory of signs in terms of what he called goal-seeking sign-behaviour. Some of his models are drawn from stimulus-response situations in behavioural psychology. His central formulation of a theory of meaning turns on a "disposition to respond". He developed from Peirce a more clear-cut distinction between areas within semiotics: *syntactics* concerns internal relations between signs; *semantics* concerns the relations between signs and that to which they point; while *pragmatics* concerns the relations between signs and human sign-*users*. But whereas in 1938 Morris understood pragmatics to involve "the relations between signs and *interpreters*" (my italics), in 1946 he was concerned to re-define this in more behaviourist terms as "the origins, uses, and effects of signs within the behaviour in which they occur".[21] This behaviourist emphasis signals a great gulf between Morris and Peirce, as Sándor Hervey rightly argues.[22] Peirce saw semiotics as a branch of logic which raised questions about types, patterns, constraints, and principles. Morris's primary interest lay in empirically observable semiotic acts, processes, speech-tokens, and meaning-effects, and the responses which they produced. Philosophically his sympathies lay with the anti-metaphysical logical positivism of Rudolf Carnap.

This functional emphasis on meaning-*effect* finds expression in the American tradition in a wide variety of forms. It underlies approaches to meaning in linguistics (Leonard Bloomfield, 1933); behavioural psychology (B.F. Skinner, 1957); philosophy of language (partly, W.V.O. Quine, 1960; fully, Richard Rorty, 1979); and audience-orientated literary theory (Norman Holland, 1975; Stanley Fish, 1980).[23] It underlines the claims put forward by Robert Corrington about the foundation of a distinctively American philosophical hermeneutic in Peirce and Royce. Ideas are fallible; there are no "pure" givens; knowledge depends on signs which point to other signs; "laws" appear at first sight to be derived from logic, but turn out to be only habituated patterns of behaviour which generate associations of ideas. The only ontology of which Corrington can speak is "the ontology of the community".[24]

Later in this chapter we shall note how the radical interpretation of Saussure carried out in the French philosophical and literary tradition of Barthes and Derrida is developed in American literary theory by Paul de Man, Harold Bloom and Geoffrey Hartman and in American theology by J.D. Crossan, Mark Taylor, and Carl Raschke. Crossan speaks of "the necessity of a break-out from ontotheology".[25] Carl Raschke sees texts as "neither message nor medium".[26] Textual meanings are "liberated" into infinite fluidity to point beyond themselves in the "melting" of the "lattice of 'signs' which has been fixed . . . by habits".[27] Mark C. Taylor draws on Saussurean difference, Derrida's *différance*, and Hegel's "negativity" to formulate a postmodern theological perception in which "'biblical' revelation" can find no place.[28] In an excellent study of postmodernism David Harvey observes: "Fragmentation, indeterminacy and intense distrust of all universal or 'totalizing' discourses . . . are the hallmark of postmodernist thought."[29]

All the same, there are other ways of responding to Peirce's semiotics. In Europe the most important thinkers for semiotics and hermeneutics who have drawn partly on Peirce include Karl-Otto Apel and Julia Kristeva. If Christopher Norris is right in comparing "the same giddy limit" of scepticism in Jacques Derrida and David Hume, then it is all the more notable that for Karl-Otto Apel, Charles Peirce is "the Kant of American philosophy".[30] In 1952 Jürgen von Kempski had examined parallels between Peirce's work on the relation between logical form and categories of habituated experience with Kant's work on the relation between categories and judgments. Apel examines Peirce's work not only in the context of Kant, but in relation to theories of language in the later thought of Wittgenstein and of Gadamer. In all three writers, he concludes, especially when taken together, there is a convincing case that "the achievement of inter-subjective agreement" constitutes the pre-condition for effective sign-operations and communication.[31] Gadamer's emphasis on the trans-cultural horizons of tradition and community and Wittgenstein's work on public criteria of meaning combine to harmonize with a conception which, Apel believes, is centrally implied by Peirce and Royce. This "regulative principle", Apel writes, is *"that unlimited community of interpretation which is presupposed by everyone who takes part in critical discussion* (that is, by everyone who thinks!) *as an ideal controlling instance"*.[32]

Apel's inter-subjective community is not an empirical culture-bound community which has simply generated a cultured code of its own by habit and convention. This "ideal" community embodies "various nations, classes, language-games and life-forms".[33] The "habits" to which Peirce refers cannot be reduced simply to " an object of the empirical social sciences".[34] To speak disparagingly of merely "conventional" elements of cognition betrays an individualistic rather than inter-subjective standpoint. In speaking of "everyone who thinks" Apel has in his view not "consensus" but broad criteria of rationality. Wittgenstein imagines a critic confusing the two issues in this way. He writes: "'So you are saying that human agreement decides what is true and what is false?' – It is what human beings *say* that is true and false; and they agree in the *language* they use. That is not agreement in opinions but in form of life. If language is to be a means of communication there must be agreement not only in definitions but also (queer as this may sound) in judgments. This seems to abolish logic, but does not do so."35 Apel does not claim that Peirce produced an adequate hermeneutic. But he offers what he calls "the transcendental hermeneutic interpretation of Peirce's semiotics" in which the focus is on "the interpreting community as an interacting community."36

Several writers have commented on the subtlety of Peirce's thought, and its consequent capacity to be interpreted in various ways, with various indirect effects.37 The "semiology" of Saussure has, to no less an extent, been applied and interpreted in different directions. His most immediate impact was to set the agenda for modern linguistics which he provided with a programmatic foundation. In spite of Derrida's accusation of Saussure's "blindness" about "writing", Saussure bequeathed to linguisticians the traditionally-agreed principle that spoken language is primary. Phonological description represents a recognized area of the subject. Saussure's working distinction between diachronic and synchronic description also constitutes a principle of linguistics. But most important of all, the three key principles which we outlined above remain operative in the discipline, although without the philosophical implications drawn by Derrida. First, because linguistic signs are arbitrary or conventional, linguistics remains a *descriptive*, not prescriptive, discipline. Second, the distinction between *langue* and *parole* remains fundamental, and is sometimes expounded (in Chomsky's terminology) in terms of a contrast between linguistic competence and linguistic performance. Third, and most important, because language (*langue*) is a system of relations, or a set of inter-related systems, all linguistics is in principle *structural* linguistics, although this term is sometimes reserved for more formalist approaches in linguistics.

This emphasis on structure began to acquire the status of a doctrine (structuralism) as well as a tool of method around 1929, when the Prague Linguistic Circle formulated the principle on the basis of Saussure that linguisticians should begin not with individual "facts" of language, but from the system which gave them their significance. The linguistics model was no longer item-centred, but relation-centred. Less explicitly, trends which were later to culminate in a structuralist approach could be detected in Eduard Sapir's book *Language* (1921) published in America, and in the Russian formalism of Viktor Shklovsky and others. In 1931 J. Trier formulated the axiom of field semantics that "only within a field" and "only as part of a whole" does a word carry meaning.[38] In the year that L. Bloomfield published his book *Language* (1933) N. Trubetzkoy from the Prague Circle argued that structuralism in linguistics could provide a model for other academic disciplines.

These rapid theoretical developments which emerged from 1929 to 1933 were taken further in the 1950s by Roman Jakobson and by Claude Lévi-Strauss. In 1956 Roman Jakobson diagnosed problems of speech aphasia in terms of Saussure's two structural axes of syntagmatic (horizontal) and paradigmatic (vertical) relations. Patients found difficulty *either* over the selective (paradigmatic, metaphoric) axis, *or* over the combinatory (syntagmatic, metonymic) axis, but seldom if ever over both. In Jakobson's terminology, a "message" is a *combination* of elements, *selected* from the possibilities offered by *"code"*.

Structuralism was finally applied to other disciplines and brought to the centre of the stage in Claude Lévi-Strauss's book *Structural Anthropology* (1958). He asked "whether the different aspects of social life ... cannot be studied with the help of concepts similar to those employed in linguistics."[39] Linguistics and social phenomena are "the same" in the sense of being a language which structures or codes. In his doctoral dissertation he had examined kinship terms. Rules of kinship and rules of language, he concludes, "are caused by identical unconscious structures".[40] His work, Julia Kristeva comments, "reconfirms the equivalence between the symbolic and the social."[41] The structure is a relation of relations: brother-sister, husband-wife, father-son, uncle-nephew. Controversially, Lévi-Strauss sees the network as a marriage-system, which generates a kind of "logic" about the availability or "value" of women for marriage, or what he calls their "circulation".[42] Lévi-Strauss finds examples of code and signification in marriage laws, ceremonies, rituals, and even methods of cooking. Many binary oppositions (cf. Saussure's associative or paradigmatic relations) are culturally significant: left hand *vs.* right hand; raw *vs.* cooked; examples of spatial opposition such as earth *vs.* sky, land *vs.* sea, dry *vs.* wet, city *vs.* desert.

Lévi-Strauss's widest interest, however, was in the structure and significance of myth. Here the fundamental oppositions include life *vs.* death; man *vs.* God; good *vs.* bad. Whether or not we know the codes of a given culture "a myth is still felt as a myth by any reader anywhere in the world."[43] Myth is deep structure, a universal narrative model freed from temporal and cultural conditioning. Myth itself is anonymous. Yet particular mythological stories and folk-tale texts, including the "mythemes" or constituent-units of which myths are composed, depend on structures that are culture-relative. There is an element of ambivalence in Lévi-Strauss about whether all codes or systems are culture-relative, or whether trans-cultural universal features dictate the code that is presupposed at least by myth as such. Despite Lévi-Strauss's appeal to the difference between the scientific objectifying perceptions of the "engineer" and the more meta-critical perspectives of the *bricoleur*, this ambivalence is noted by Derrida and by such commentators as Leach, Lentricchia, and Scholes.[44] Leach ascribes it partly to Lévi-Strauss's desire to effect a synthesis in social anthropology between the approaches of Malinowski and of Radcliffe-Brown.

This earlier phase of structuralism, however, which traced formal or quasi-universal structural categories in texts and in other phenomena soon gave way to a recognition of the implications of community-relativity and convention. In chapter XIII, section 3, I discuss the formalist notion of narrative-grammar developed by A.J. Greimas and applied repeatedly in biblical studies of the 1970s, especially in earlier volumes of *Semeia*. In section 4 of chapter XIII I trace the transposition of structuralism into semiotic accounts of reading-competencies and of reading-processes, based on the social conventions of matrices of meaning-systems inherited by given communities.

Two approaches to biblical texts may be mentioned here, as representing perspectives which are distinctive, but not unrelated to these issues. Northrop Frye's book *The Great Code: The Bible and Literature* (1982) is "structural" rather than "structuralist". The Bible, he argues, reflects traces of "a total structure", with a beginning and an end, in which a structure of recurring patterns becomes evident.[45] Images such as the city, the mountain, bread, wine, garden, tree, oil and fountain recur so often as to indicate "some kind of unifying principle". The biblical texts reflect a unified structure of narrative and imagery.

Erhardt Güttgemanns, by contrast, offers a fully structuralist approach, which appeals repeatedly to Saussure and to Saussure's contrast between *langue* and *parole*.[46] Terminologically, the designation "generative poetics" sounds like a post-structuralist and literary theory of the productivity of intertextual play. But Güttgemanns looks to the *formal* model of Noam Chomsky's generative transformational grammar, and this, in turn, looks to the *logical-universals* of Descartes and of mathematical method; not to the contingent particularities of social history and art. Güttgemanns describes his approach as "a new method of linguistic textual analysis that is applicable to all human texts".[47] "*Langue* is ontologically pre-given to speaking *parole*."[48]

None of the varied semiotic or structural approaches which we have reviewed, however, demands the kind of transposition of more traditional approaches to textuality which Barthes, Derrida, and other deconstructionists believe is necessitated by the work of Saussure and his successors in semiotics. Even allowing for the *critical* turn, in which Roland Barthes and Julia Kristeva see *semiotics as a critique of semiotics*, the conclusions which deconstructionists draw *rest not simply on semiotic theory alone, but on an intermixture of semiotics and post-modernist, often neo-Nietzschean, world-view.*

Here an illuminating parallel suggests itself. In 1936 A.J. Ayer published his book *Language, Truth, and Logic*, which became very influential in Britain in the 1930s and 1940s. One component in its widespread appeal was its common-sense empirical approach, which British readerships have always found congenial. But its influence was due to a more profound reason. Ayer *seemed* to argue for logical positivism on the basis of an account of language and meaning, put forward as the result of description and observation. In practice, however, his book served to promote the *philosophical doctrine* of positivism by *clothing it in linguistic dress*. Only by the early 1950s, nearly twenty years later, had this issue become sufficiently clear to the popular mind for its spell to be broken. This possible parallel suggests that we ask again: what elements of deconstructionist theories of texts and language genuinely rest on principles of *semiotics* rather than on a doctrine or world-view which is *clothed in semiotic dress?*

3. Roland Barthes: From Hermeneutics through Semiotics to Intralinguistic World, and to Text as Play

At least four factors play a part in shaping the theories of textuality which we find in Roland Barthes (1915–1980). First, the earlier Barthes is strongly motivated by socio-political concerns of a radically "left" or broadly neo-Marxist sympathy. Second, the influence of Marx, Freud, and Nietzsche, as the three great "masters of suspicion", inspire a range of models of socio-critical hermeneutics in the context of a general war against hermeneutical "innocence", and Barthes's work constitutes an example of those who draw on Freudian and Marxist traditions or terminology. Third, his view of the relation between perception and language and the notion of intra-linguistic world should be seen against the background of the philosophy of Maurice Merleau-Ponty. Fokkema and Kunne-Ibsch (1978) make this point, and Dwyer's study of Merleau-Ponty and Wittgenstein (1990) adds plausibility to it.[49] Barthes notes that Merleau-Ponty was the first to introduce Saussure into French philosophy; but Merleau-Ponty's interpretation of Saussure is acknowledged by many to be idiosyncratic and uneven. This may have influenced Barthes's use of Saussure and the nature of appeals to Saussure in deconstructionism. Fourthly, Barthes presses semiotic theory into the service of his political and literary concerns, entering into explicit dialogue with Saussure and extending the notion of "code" along similar lines to Lévi-Strauss.

From the publication of his first book, *Writing Degree Zero* (Fr.1953) Barthes combines a standpoint in literary theory with what we shall describe later in this study as a *socio-critical model of hermeneutical theory*. In this model texts which may appear to have a relatively neutral objective, or innocent status are unmasked in a process of interpretation as supporting *interests* in maintaining given power-structures and power-relations within a society, culture, or religion. *Writing Degree Zero* examines the literature of French classicism from the seventeenth to the nineteenth century, offering the *hermeneutical* diagnosis that what seemed at the time to give it a quality of inherent "rightness" was not some natural or objective feature but its status as an expression of the bourgeois life and values of the time. With the break-up of the classical style, Barthes traces subsequent developments, arguing that even attempts at a "style-less" (zero degree) writing cannot but become yet another "style". Neutral writing is impossible. Even the goal of "lucidity" or "clarity" in seventeenth-century France is not a natural virtue but "a class idiom", reflecting the élitism of privilege. Barthes confirms this diagnosis in his later book *Criticism and Truth* (1966).[50]

All this raises fundamental *hermeneutical* questions, although it is a socio-critical hermeneutic of a particular kind. In accordance with hermeneutical principles, Barthes unmasks what he regards as the naïve innocence of French literary theorists who detach questions of this kind from what, in hermeneutical theory, we should call the historicity of language: the capacity of language to be conditioned by the historical horizon of the writer and by the historical horizon of the reader or interpreter. As we have suggested, a Marxist background shapes Barthes's concerns about ideologies and bourgeois culture; while the legacy of Nietzsche encourages questions about power and iconoclasm. Barthes endorses whole-heartedly the Freudian exposure of the "innocence" of any academic activity which fails to take account of psychoanalysis and the unconscious. Freud's work would play a major part in the deconstructionism of Jacques Lacan and in Julia Kristeva's semiotics.

Barthes took this hermeneutical iconoclasm further, at a more popular level, in his next-but-one book *Mythologies* (Fr.1957). Here he unmasks as illusory the supposed descriptive objectivity of a variety of phenomena. He examines photography, in which both the clothing and posture of the subject and the conventions and methods of the photographer convey messages over and above bare description.[51] He considers the cover of a magazine, where the picture of a black soldier saluting the French flag attempts to re-inforce imperialist assumptions in the Algerian situation.[52] He discusses the spectacle of wrestling, where the action serves more as a ritual than as a genuine contest.[53] This book has been written, Barthes tells us frankly, out of "a feeling of impatience at the sight of the 'naturalness' with which newspapers, art, and common sense constantly dress up reality ... I resented seeing Nature and History confused at every turn."[54]

The last section of the book, sub-titled "Myth Today" serves to make two broad and basic points. First, Barthes argues that "myth", in the sense in which he has used the term, is a semiological system. Here he introduces Saussure to his readers. The face-value of the myths depend on one level of signification; but if they are placed within "a greater semiological system", we perceive a second-order meaning which unmasks them.[55] There is a parallel here, Barthes suggests, with Freud's interpretation principle of a second-order of meaning which lies below the surface. In both cases we can "decipher" what is signified.[56] Second, myths themselves appear to be neutral or non-political. But the "deciphering" of myth, virtually by definition of the role of myth as a tool of the Establishment or the bougeoisie, will be undertaken by members of the political Left.

Semiotics, or "semiology" (to use Saussure's term) offers, or seems to offer, an explanatory model for de-coding, de-mystifying, or de-ideologizing, not only language but cultural phenomena. Lévi-Strauss, in this very year, was preparing his *Structural Anthropology* for the press. At the risk of beginning to over-stretch what Roman Jakobson meant by "code", Barthes sees semiotics as performing a task at two levels: the descriptive and the meta-linguistic. First the traditional codes which generated *prima facie* messages embodied bourgeois values. A description of the semiotic process could unmask the illusion of objective innocence as such that it was. Second, semiotics seemed to offer a meta-language: a system of language-description which somehow stood outside the language which it was describing. At both levels semiotics seemed to offer a tool for Barthes's literary and political concerns.

The text in which Barthes follows Saussure most closely is his *Elements of Semiology* (Fr. 1964) He follows and expounds Saussure's arguments about system, about syntagmatic and associative or paradigmatic relations, about oppositions and differences within the system, and enters into dialogue with linguisticians who have sought to refine Saussure's work, especially Jakobson, Hjelmslev and Martinet. Barthes is careful about how he substitutes such systems as the garment-system, food-system, furniture-system, and architecture-system for systems that were otherwise purely linguistic.[57] For example juxtapositions in clothing or in items of furniture represent the syntagma, and allow for associative or paradigmatic choices. But Barthes carefully allows for the possibility that choices sometimes depend in life on other factors. Thus someone's choice between a long skirt and a short skirt may either have semiological significance, or be due to considerations about protection from the weather.[58]

Oppositions in a paradigmatic field may be simple binary patterns, like the talking drum of the Congo tribes, which has two notes; or like dots and dashes of the morse code, or digital systems of computers. Or we can have multilateral proportional oppositions, like the combinations of colour-variations and oppositions of circle and triangle in the Highway Code.[59] Marked and unmarked terms in a privative opposition can be explained in more than one possible way (e.g. in the examples dog/bitch, man/wife, nurse/male nurse, the first term is the unmarked or "neutral" term in the opposition). For Barthes, this is the "zero degree" of the opposition which is "a significant absence" in "a pure differential state".[60] Binary oppositions are not the only ones. Barthes points out that Saussure did not conceive of the associative or paradigmatic field as only binary, and approves of Martinet's conclusion that "binarism" is neither universal nor dictated by nature rather than culture.[61] In such cultural systems as clothing fashions Barthes argues that the network of contrasts is polysemic. Barthes points out that the applications of these linguistic and semiotic models to social life is something which Saussure envisaged, and of which he therefore would have approved.[62]

All this remains compatible with traditional semiotic theory. Semiotics still serves a *hermeneutical* theory in which language-uses are still grounded in the historicity of language-using communities. The emphasis in the later writings, from 1966 onwards, on meaning and interpretation as an endless succession of semiotically-generated variants has not yet become explicit. But Barthes begins to foresee the logical problem entailed in the idea of ascribing to semiotic theory the status of a meta-language which deciphers and de-codes everyday language and literature. He is not satisfied, as the Marxist literary theorist Fredric Jameson is, to view Marxism as the final great "interpretive master code" which forms the "untranscendable horizon" of all textual interpretation. For Barthes foresees the possibility of the criticism of his work which is in fact put forward, in spite of Barthes's later shift in emphasis, by Sándor Hervey. Commenting on "the paradox of 'semioclasm'" Hervey declares, "In a nutshell the irony is that Barthesianism has been overtaken by the necessary fate of successful ideologies; it has become a dogma."[64] A meta-language can in theory become a vehicle for new mythologies and new traditions. Hence Barthes argues that there is no reason in principle why one meta-language should not be scrutinized and "deciphered" by another. In principle there can be an infinite series of semiotic layers, in which no "final" reading or semiotic system can be reached. Meanings must therefore be infinitely plural.

Some identify the moment of a shift in thought in Barthes with the publication of *Criticism and Truth* in 1966.[65] This work constitutes a counter-reply to Raymond Picard's criticisms of his earlier book *On Racine* which had appeared in 1963. Picard had argued that the "new"

"new criticism" turned language into a game of chance by imposing the primary meanings of Racine's words as they would have been understood in the seventeenth century, and substituting such "readings" as might be suggested by the subjectivities of psychoanalytical or other extrinsic frames of reference. In the first part of his reply, Barthes argues on hermeneutical grounds. What appears to be "evident truth" depends on hermeneutical frames of reference, and depends on interpretative "choices".[66] But in the second part he goes further. He declares, "Each age can indeed believe that it holds the canonical meaning of the work, but it suffices to have a slightly broader historical perspective in order for this circular meaning to be transformed into a plural meaning, and the closed work to be transformed into an open work. The very definition of the work is changing: it is no longer a historical fact . . . *The work is not surrounded, designated, protected, or directed by any situation, no practical life is there to tell us the meaning which should be given to it.*"[67] If we ask about the reader's situation, rather than the author's, "this situation, as it changes, *composes* the work and does not rediscover it."[68]

Barthes has now shifted his ground away from the hermeneutical suspicion which is grounded in historicality. He appeals to *generative* models in linguistics and in semiotics as models to be applied to texts and literature. In these disciplines, we may note, these generative models concern possibilities of *production* and *composition* at the level of the *langue*; not the understanding or interpretation of *parole*, or "message". Barthes is aware that he is moving between different semiotic levels. The theoretical justification for such movement, if it exists, can be found in the five pages in *Elements of Semiology* which discussed staggered systems, connotative semiotics and meta-language. Barthes's hypothetical and theoretical claims about an infinite series of connotative and meta-linguistic language-layers show that this shift from history to formal language-system had been envisaged in principle two years earlier in 1964. If we begin with a language-system of denotation, this gives rise to a system "above" it of secondary connotation. But the language-system which we use to undertake a description and critique of the denotation language-system constitutes a meta-language "below" it. Theoretically, it would be possible to account for the meta-language in terms of a meta-metalinguistic system at a still lower level. Like mirror-images in a mirror, the layers could be repeated endlessly in either direction, except that the layers do not constitute representational images, but sign-systems based on arbitrary sign-relations.

Barthes explains this in the following terms. He writes: "In connotative semiotics the signifiers of the second system are constituted by the signs of the first;[69] this is reversed in meta-language: there the signifiers of the second system "takes over" a first language. But "nothing in principle prevents a meta-language from becoming in its turn the language-object of a new meta-language".⁷⁰ As history advances, there could be "a diachrony of meta-languages, and each science, including of course semiology, would contain the seeds of its own death, in the shape of the language destined to speak it."⁷¹ Hence the objective function of the "decipherer" has only a relative and provisional objectivity, because it is subject to the history which renews languages.

This may partly answer the difficulty outlined by Sándor Hervey as the "paradox of semioclasm", except that semantic pluralism is now the new dogma. But the application of the linguistic and semiotic model in this way no longer involves matters of linguistic science; it has brought us into the domain of philosophy. For when *linguisticians* speak of "connotation" as *secondary implication*, the assumption is retained that the denotative system remains the primary one. Likewise, metalinguistic systems *serve* the primary language-system under consideration in terms of the inter-subjective judgments of the language-using community or linguistic observers. But a constant flow of movement in which each meta-language is perceived to change its level to that of primary language banishes the realities of the inter-subjective world, and places language, rather than the inter-subjective world, at the centre of the system. Linguistic *method* has now become a linguistic *world-view*. Whether or not this happens to be right or wrong, it is no more a semiotic *method* than it is a scientific *method* when positivists turn scientific method into a scientific *world-view*. *To replace inter-subjectivity by intertextuality is a philosophical, not a semiotic or linguistic move.*

Fokkema and Kunne-Ibsch are probably correct when they suggest that, as we have noted, Barthes is to some extent indebted to a view of perception and its relation to language which has been inspired by Maurice Merleau-Ponty.⁷² Even though he puts it forward "at the risk of some misunderstanding" Robert Detweiler's rule-of-thumb contrast between phenomenology and radical structuralism is helpful: the effect is "not to discover how consciousness forms a system of being and meaning, but how system forms the being and meaning of consciousness."⁷³

Barthes has now gone further than his intention in *On Racine* "to amputate literature from the individual".⁷⁴ In his book *S/Z* (1970) he compares unfavourably those types of literature which project "a view", or some standpoint located in history, which "writerly" (*scriptible*) texts in which signifiers have free play, and readers are thereby invited to participate in the *production* of the text. In such texts *language itself* has become the object of study, rather than what is said, or even what is heard through language. Barthes begins *S/Z* with a repudiation of those versions of structuralism which see universals in narrative grammar. This signals a move from his references to "the typology of actants proposed by A.J. Greimas" and to T. Todorov and to V. Propp in 1966.⁷⁵ In contrast to this approach Barthes now declares that "all the stories in the world" do not add up to one universal narrative grammar; to pursue the notion of single narrative model is "exhausting" and "undesirable". In *S/Z* Barthes examines a short story by Balzac called "Sarrasine" with a view to achieving two aims. First he wants to show that Balzac's view of life or "reality" was already encoded and produced by his own linguistic and semiotic world. Second, he wants to de-code or to trans-code the story at various levels in a way which will release it to become a "writerly" text; one which is capable of generating a plurality of meanings in the production of which readers can share.

The contrast between "readerly" and "writerly" texts reflects Barthes's earlier distinction (1960) between the kind of writer who uses language for extra-linguistic purposes (the *écrivant*) and the kind of writer who writes language "intransitively" as a purely linguistic activity (the *écrivain*). In the writing of the *écrivain* meaning is plural, and therefore "postponed". John Sturrock comments that in Barthes's view the *écrivain* will "cede initiative to words". He continues: "the text is a sort of verbal carnival . . . a linguistic spectacle, and the reader is required to enjoy that spectacle for its own sake rather than to look through language to the world."[76] James Joyce's *Finnegan's Wake* represents an example of the *écrivain's* activity. In this sense, it is *text* rather than a *work*.

In *S/Z* Barthes deconstructs the apparently content-orientated nature of Balzac's "Sarrasine" by two methodological devices. First, he does away with Balzac's own divisions of his story in terms of paragraphs or episodes. The story is read in a single linear continuum, broken up into a succession of 561 "lexemes" or reading-units.[77] Second, he introduces not one "code" but five: a hermeneutic code, a cultural code, a symbolic code, a semic code, and an actional code.[78] The symbolic code is probably closest to anything implied by Saussure's *langue*, Jakobson's *code*, or the use of code in Lévi-Strauss. It constitutes a system of contrasts and categorizations presupposed by the temporal progress of the story. The semic code represents a particular and variant example of the symbolic code. The hermeneutic code is a network of questions which are resolved as the momentum of the narrative approaches its closure. The actional code relates to successive stages of the action. Finally, the cultural code is virtually an epistemological category. It represents a system of knowledge and values which are "accepted", stereotyped, or perceived in the story as "common knowledge".

These devices transform "Sarrasine" from the work of an author, Balzac, into a *process* of the *production* of meaning in which many voices, including successive readers, are involved. It matches exactly Barthes's definition of textuality in his 1971 essay "From Work to Text". He writes: "The Text must not be thought of as a defined object . . . The Text is a methodological field".[79] He continues: "The Text is experienced only as an activity, a production. It follows that the Text cannot stop."[80] In harmony with Derrida, Barthes asserts, "The Text, on the contrary, practises the infinite deferral of the signified".[81] This infinity of deferral is *not* to be identified, Barthes insists, with the mere corrigibility of a "hermeneutic process of deepening, but rather with a serial movement of dislocations ... variations ... an *irreducible* plurality.[82] As Barthes repeats in his book *The Pleasure of the Text* (Fr. 1973), the "I" or the "subject" who was the author has become a "paper" entity only, who has "come undone", as if a spider were to become dissolved into its web.[83] The Text itself now "plays", in all its pluralities of possible meanings, and the reader "plays twice over: playing the text as one plays a game", namely to "re-produce" the Text; and "playing the Text as one would play music".[84] Barthes compares the notion in post-serial music of the hearer's becoming "co-author" of the score.

4. Difficulties and Questions: the Inter-Mixture of Semiotics and World-View

All this is part of a heavily political agenda. In traditional Protestant bourgeois capitalism a privileged élite, namely authors, expressed ideas which presupposed traditional codes of values and patterns. These ideas were gathered to form a privileged "canon", and regarded as "classics" of literature or religion. The bourgeoisie delegated to professional "interpreters", who formed another élite, the task of safeguarding "the" meanings of the texts in question. But post-modern theories of literature and semiotics allow us to dispense with these models, according to Barthes. The author, as human subject "comes undone"; texts do not convey messages; they are simply processes which cannot stop; in which *anyone* is invited to participate. They are cut off from authors, from situations, and from the extralinguistic world, to constitute an infinite open system of endless signification. Barthes concludes, "As an institution the author is dead: his civil status, his biographical person have disappeared".[85]

We have already put forward the argument that Barthes's work after 1966 goes well beyond the principles suggested, let alone demanded, by the semiotic theory of Saussure and his successors in linguistics. This later emphasis in *S/Z* and in *The Pleasure of the Text* however, turns Saussure's distinction between *langue* and *parole* on its head. For it is *langue* as an *abstract* and theoretical construct which generates *possibilities*; *parole*, which *presupposes a speaking subject* constitutes the actuality in language *using* situations. It is not the case, in Saussure, that *parole* can be generated by a subjectless system, in isolation from the *constraints* on possibility imposed by the purposive *choices of the speaking subject*.

If we have succeeded in demonstrating some distance between Barthes and Saussure, however, would it be legitimate to go further, and to claim that Barthes's pluralistic theory of texts is not dictated primarily by semiotic considerations? In the very broad and philosophically unimportant sense that everything *can* become a sign of something else, Barthesian thought is semiotic. But in this very broad sense, the same could be said of a traditional "sacramental" view of the world in Christian theology: water can point to inner cleansing; Spring can point to resurrection; wind can point to the invigorating and refreshing power of the Holy Spirit. In the more technical sense of the term, however, the answer depends on what aspect of Barthes's literary theory is in view. Two questions remain central if an answer is to be defended.

(1) First, are *possibilities* of meaning merely *linguistic or hermeneutical* possibilities which remain subject to the constraints of interpretative choices, and choices about the selection, use and application of what the system generates; or are these possibilities to be seen as *conditions of possibility, in the philosophical sense*, inherited from Hegel and Marx? Semiotics as such cannot carry responsibility for a philosophical doctrine about conditions of possibility independent of the human subject.

(2) Second, are we examining the *presuppositions* of communication (intertextuality or inter-subjective community and tradition) or *acts* of communication (texts which are written and read) and their relationship to operative conditions of meaning (codes, patterns, or practices in relation to which choices of language or speech-behaviour are made)? It is arguable that intertextuality remains a semiotic concept, but the relation between intertextuality and inter-subjectivity becomes a philosophical issue. Similarly, it is arguable that the view that texts *can* be pluralistic in meaning rests on hermeneutical decisions about interpretative goals and strategy. But the doctrine that all texts *are* pluralistic in meaning, and that this plurality is irreducible and infinite, is at best a very particular version of semiotics, and at worst a particular philosophy of language which masquerades as semiotics.

(3) A confusing misunderstanding about the nature of "possibility" in Saussure's theory of language and signs entered French intellectual life in the late 1940s when Maurice Merleau-Ponty first introduced Saussure into French philosophy.[86] James Schmidt accurately documents a devastating critique of Merleau-Ponty's attempt to interpret the relation between "existence" and "possibility" in Saussure as categories which could address the deeper philosophical issues about possibility identified by Hegel and Marx.[87] Schmidt shows that Merleau-Ponty misunderstood Saussure at two levels. First, there are particular mistakes of detail. For example, Merleau-Ponty seemed to think that Saussure correlated isomorphically *langue* with diachronic perspective and *parole* with synchronic perspectives.[88]

He applied Saussure's "difference" not to Saussure's "sound-images" or "concepts", but to his own notion of a perceptual chain. Differentiation is also applied to *parole*. But the most fundamental confusion was at a second level. The key move was to translate Saussure's semiotic terminology into philosophical categories, so that Saussure's work was interpreted as providing a philosophical foundation for questions about *conditions of possibility*. Schmidt documents statements from Saussure and from Merleau-Ponty which expose the inappropriateness of such an interpretation, which Schmidt describes as "loose" and "idiosyncratic".[89]

It is easy to see how such an interpretation might encourage the theory that metalinguistic description would entail not, as in Saussure, drawing on the *langue* which was also presupposed by the language to be described, but by a series of *different* systems operating *at different levels*. But for Saussure *langue* is not primarily a diachronic category, although Saussure does also consider it diachronically. Barthes speaks, as we have seen, of "a diachrony of metalanguages" which are so radically discontinuous as to cause the "death" of a previous language-system.[90] But Saussure saw the diachronic dimensions of *langue* in terms of a gradually evolving system which could in principle be transformed on the basis of *parole*; of specific choices of language drawn from the system as it existed synchronically at the time of the *parole*. T.K. Seung observes: "Roland Barthes has given his semiology the appearance of being a universal science . . . by overextending the linguistic categories".[91] I had already completed this chapter when I discovered the incisive, if at times uneven, critique of Barthes and Derrida offered by Raymond Tallis under the brilliant title *Not Saussure* (1988). Tallis rightly accuses Barthes and Derrida of being unfaithful to Saussure in several fundamental respects, including their lack of reference to the extra-linguistic world and their confusions between sign-systems (*langue*) and *uses* of signs (*parole*).[92]

(4) Some penetrating observations by Jonathan Culler show the bearing of this difficulty on the second issue, namely the relation between Barthes's theory of texts and intertextuality. Culler notes the presence of a paradox in Saussure: "Everything in *la langue*, as Saussure says, must have first been in *parole*. But *parole* is made possible by *la langue*, and if one attempts to identify any utterance or text as a moment of origin one finds that they depend upon prior codes. A codification, one might say, can only originate or be originated if it is already encoded in a prior code; more simply, it is in the nature of codes to be always already in existence, to have lost origins. 'Intertextuality' thus has a double focus. On the one hand, it calls our attention to the importance of prior texts, insisting that the autonomy of texts is a misleading notion . . . Yet in so far as it focusses on intelligibility, on meaning, 'intertextuality' leads us to consider prior texts as contributions to a code which makes possible the various effects of signification".[93]

These two aspects of intertextuality find a firm semiotic base, provided that they are not defined so narrowly as to isolate them from broader questions about inter-subjective judgments, traditions and practices, and situated acts of human choice, purpose, and judgment within given horizons. The two aspects are closely parallel to the later Wittgenstein's understanding of training, tradition, and patterns of practice on the one hand (cf. "the importance of prior texts") and to public criteria of meaning on the other (cf. contributions to a code which makes possible the various effects of signification). The notion of a code's "lost origin" is parallel to Wittgenstein's observation that "'obeying a rule' is a practice. . . . It is not possible to obey a rule 'privately'".[94] But in conjunction with his recognition of the inextricably close inter-wovenness of thought and language and of the trans-personal or trans-individual basis of communication, Wittgenstein, like Saussure, refused to equate language-*use* with a linguistic network of possibility. Thus he remarks, "Naming is so far not a move in the language-game – any more than putting a piece in its place on the board is a move in chess."[95]

To extend the metaphor, the state of the board, or the code, may determine what kind of moves, and what range of moves, are open to me; but a *move* will be the outcome of a human judgment at a particular time and place. Wittgenstein agreed that "A *picture* held us captive. And we could not get outside it, for it lay in our language and language seemed to repeat it to us inexorably."[96] But this is why struggle and judgment includes "a battle against bewitchment of our intelligence by means of language".[97] For a picture, which as a semiotic sub-system has various possibilities of meaning, can be *applied* in some particular way. For Wittgenstein the spell of the picture arises when a language-system is amputated from life; application arises from situatedness in life coupled with human judgment.[98] Confusions arise when language is "free"; or in Wittgenstein's words, "like an engine idling, not when it is doing work".[99] To recognize, then, that with certain qualifications intertextuality represents a constructive category in semiotics is one thing. It is quite another to regard Barthes's particular theory of texts as having semiotic validity as a theory for all texts.

(5) As a more speculative footnote, we may also observe the kinds of criticisms which have been made by philosophers and linguisticians against the theory of language and its relation to thought put forward by B.L. Whorf fashionable in the late 1950s and early 1960s. The so-called Whorfian hypothesis tried to revive, on the basis of socio-anthropological observations, the linguistic relativity approach associated with Wilhelm von Hamboldt, and associated with E. Sapir. The linguistic system, he wrote, "is not merely a reproducing instrument", but is "itself the shapes of ideas . . . We dissect nature along lines laid down by our native language . . . We cut nature up, organize it into

concepts . . . because we are party to an agreement to organize it in this way."[100]

Whorf's formulation of his theory received hostile criticism from such writers as Nida and Max Black, mainly, but not exclusively, because he saw the influence of language on thought more in the simplistic terms of vocabulary-stock and grammar than in terms of conceptual patterns reflected in language uses.[101] But for the purposes of our discussion of texts, two features of the critical response invite interest. First, in the examination of concrete examples, most notably the system of colour-words, some argued that considerations about semantic or semiotic habit remained incomplete without due regard for extra-linguistic factors such as bio-physical or neuro-physical elements in genetic coding which *also* shaped the structures of perception. The work of B. Berlin and P. Kay on colour-terms and colour-perception provides an example of this research.[102] Second, the availability of circumlocution and a basic level of inter-translatability in languages suggests that while language-habits *condition* the possibilities of thought and language, they do not *determine* their limits. Habituated patterns make new or different language-uses harder or easier; they demand greater or lesser critical struggle and imaginative innovation; but they do not wholly determine angles of vision or possibilities of communication. I have discussed Whorf's work briefly in *The Two Horizons*, and at greater length elsewhere.[103]

These five sets of considerations serve to warn us against the validity of suggestions that deconstructionist theories of textuality deliver literary theorists or biblical interpreters from any obligation to probe the substantial philosophical doctrines that are built into them. As a theory of texts, they are not "demanded" by semiotic considerations as such. Even an appeal to post-modernist perspectives need not become an all-or-nothing affair. As Andreas Huyssen has argued in his book *After the Great Divide* (1986) rather than constituting a new self-contained movement, post-modernism may serve to identify contradictions and tensions within modernism which impede or limit its further forward development.[104] We note, in due course, the opposing evaluations of modernism represented by J. Habermas and by J.F. Lyotard.

5. Jacques Derrida: an Endless Series of Signs under Erasure

Deconstructionism in literary theory is often perceived as the strongest philosophical context of post-modernism, and Derrida as one of its most forceful exponents in this dual area. The present discussion might have been extended to the Yale school of Paul de Man, Harold Bloom, Geoffrey Hartman, and others. But in biblical interpretation and in theology most attention has been focussed in the later Barthes and on the earlier Derrida as primary representatives of deconstructionism, and this chapter therefore is largely restricted to their approach.

Although differences, especially in philosophy, exist between them, Jacques Derrida's view of textuality comes close in its net effect to that of Barthes. In his discussion of Saussure he remarks that writing entails "the absence of signatory" and "the absence of the referent. Writing is the name of these two absences".[105] A text does not have a signature and a referential realm outside its frame: "it is no longer a finished corpus of writing, some context enclosed in a book or its margins, but a differential network, a fabric of traces referring endlessly to something other than itself, to other differential traces".[106] But the path by which Derrida reaches this view of textuality is an explicitly philosophical one.

Born in 1930, he read philosophy as a student in Paris, where he officially teaches philosophy. As his close collaborator and translator Gayatri Spivak points out, "his acknowledged 'precursors'" are Nietzsche, Freud, Husserl, and Heidegger. She writes in the preface to Derrida's *Grammatology* concerning Nietzsche, Freud, and Heidegger: "All three protogrammatologues: Nietzsche a philosopher who cut away the grounds of knowing; Freud a psychologist who put the psyche in question; Heidegger an ontologist who put Being under erasure. It was for Derrida to 'produce' their power and 'discover' grammatology".[107] Husserl's philosophy was the subject of Derrida's first book. Here he examined relations between subjective and objective structures with reference to Husserl's thought on the origins and logical status of geometry.

Probably Derrida's best-known work is his *Grammatology* (1967). The pre-condition of grammatology, he writes, "is certainly the undoing (*sollicitation*) of logocentrism".[108] Grammatology is "the theory of writing" or "the science of writing".[109] Derrida argues for the priority of writing over oral speech. At first sight this claim may seem absurd when one recalls that both in the development of children and in the history of societies writing follows oral speech. But he uses the term "writing" to convey all communicative systems which are other than vocal: "We say 'writing' for all that gives rise to inscription ... cinematography, choreography ... pictorial, musical, sculptural 'writing'."[110] In particular Derrida attacks Saussure's claim that in the two systems of spoken language and writing "the second exists for the sole purpose of representing the first".[111]

Derrida acknowledges that this Saussurean view of writing has a long tradition which reaches back to Plato and to Aristotle. Writing has been seen as mere "clothing" for prior utterance.[112] But the assumption which lies behind this arises from the place given to psychologizing processes which link together sound and sense, and which relate them to the presence of the signified. By contrast we may compare the *"empty"* symbolism of a written mathematical formula.[113] Logical and mathematical notation demands neither the presence of an author nor any reference to the extra-linguistic world. What Saussure "saw without seeing" is that every sign refers to a sign. But the "'sign of a sign' signifies writing".[114] Derrida challenges "in the very name of the arbitrariness of the sign the Saussurean definition of writing as 'image' – hence as natural symbol – of language".[115]

Derrida believes that Saussure was unable to see clearly enough the implications of his own work because he was heir to the insufficiently critical metaphysical tradition which extends from Plato to modern times, and includes even Marxism and structuralism. Apart from the advances towards an end of metaphysics anticipated partially in Nietzsche, in Freud, and in later Heidegger, one of the few semiotic theorists to have an inkling of the issues was Charles Peirce. Derrida comments, "Logic, according to Peirce, is only a semiotic . . . Peirce goes very far in the direction that I have called the de-construction of the transcendental signified."[116] Peirce recognizes that "the thing itself is a sign. . . . The self-identity of the signified conceals itself unceasingly and is always on the move".[117] We think only in signs. In this respect Peirce is more radical, and indeed more genuinely phenomenological, than Husserl.

The development of Saussure's key category of "difference" into Derrida's notion of defer-ment (*différance*) has already been noted in the first section of this chapter. Probably the clearest account of this development is offered by Derrida in his collection of essays entitled *Speech and Phenomena and Other Essays on Husserl's Theory of Signs*.[118] *Différance* provisionally refers "to differing, both as spacing/temporalizing and as the movement that structures every dissociation".[119] Derrida cannot help noting that the letter *a* in *différance*, in contrast to the *e* of *différence* is written or read, but cannot be heard as a phonological entity. The temporal and spatial differentiations, however, are themselves products of prior differentiations, and in turn give rise to others. Hence *différence* gives rise to the *différance* entailed in an endless series, in which writing constitutes *"traces"* in the double sense of the term: "marks" and "tracks" which proceed forward to allow movement.[120]

Granted that Derrida engages in dialogue with Peirce and Saussure, and that his conclusions are intimately bound up with a given theory of signs, how much of Derrida's argument depends on philosophical issues which may be distinguished from the demands of semiotic theory? In his essay in *Speech and Phenomena* which Derrida begins in dialogue with Saussure, he soon moves on to extend the dialogue to include Hegel, Nietzsche, Freud, and Heidegger. But is this because he wants to work out the implications of semiotic theory for philosophy, or because his fundamental concerns reside in the larger philosophical issues in which his semiotic theory is grounded? In one sense, the two aspects are inseparable, since all philosophy *can* be seen as a critique of language. Fritz Mauthner (1849–1923), a slightly earlier contemporary of Husserl, had argued for this view, which we discuss in chapter IX.

Derrida's starting-point as a thinker lay initially with issues in Husserl, and in Husserl a theory of signification was intertwined with broader philosophical issues about the nature of subjectivity and intentionality, time-consciousness and temporality, and structures, logic, and essence. However, this gives added point to our question, rather than disposing of it. Can we separate Derrida's semiotic theory and his theory of texts from the philosophical themes and perspectives that surround it? When Derrida criticized Husserl, and moved far beyond him, it was in dialogue not only with Husserl's notion of temporal structure, but also with concepts and categories of thinking which were distinctive to the late Heidegger, including Heidegger's "reading" of Nietzsche. It was primarily within this framework that the work of Saussure and his successors in linguistic theory took on a new status and a particular meaning. Within this framework, too, Freudian beliefs and categories made their own particular contribution.

Derrida has pointed out that there have been misunderstandings of his relation of thought to the later Heidegger.[121] But for the most part such misunderstandings arose not from overestimating Heidegger's thought as a point of departure for Derrida, but from underestimating their radical differences. Derrida dissents radically from Heidegger's view of language as *logos* and from his assertion that "thinking cuts furrows into the soil of Being".[122] But Derrida shares the later Heidegger's deep misgivings about the Western tradition of philosophy since Plato, and presses many of Heidegger's conceptual-methodological devices into the service of his own thought. Commentators have spoken of Derrida as "Heidegger's pupil" and have assessed Heidegger's influence in various ways.[123]

Nearly a hundred pages of my book *The Two Horizons* concern the development of Heidegger's earlier and later thought with particular reference to his views on interpretation and language.[124] I do not propose to cover the same ground again here. However, two or three very major points about his later thought may be underlined with reference to this new context of discussion, and some additional points also be noted. The major difference from Derrida lies in Heidegger's continuing concern to address the question of Being. In 1954 on a visit to Japan he underlined this ontological concern as belonging to both periods. His oral comment was published in his book on language in 1959: "What mattered to me then and still does is to bring out the Being of beings – though no longer in the manner of metaphysics."[125] Heidegger shares with Derrida the belief that metaphysics has reached the end of the road. Both have a negative view of the Western tradition of philosophy since Plato, which Heidegger expresses as the tragedy of having "fallen out of Being".[126] Quoting Nietzsche's *The Twilight of Idols*, Heidegger sees this tradition as pursuing "the last cloudy streak of evaporating reality".[127] He himself had to abandon the quest for Being which was begun in *Being and Time*, even though he had begun from within existential and phenomenological horizons. The projected second volume never appeared, because the task was *in principle* impossible. In his *Introduction to Metaphysics* he agrees that the word 'Being' "no longer applies to anything".[128]

How, then, can it make any sense for Heidegger to speak of continuing the quest? The answer hinges on a contrast between two radically different kinds of *language*. This difference is the key to his later thought. In harmony with Derrida, Heidegger believes that the language which serves to articulate human concepts merely reflects prior language and concepts from which it is derived. Language that is conceptual, or which has been used in the service of life, simply throws humankind "onto paths which he himself has laid out". We are "mired" in our own paths, because language takes us only where we have been many times before. It leads humankind "round and round in our own circle".[129] But Heidegger sees the possibility of a glimmer of hope in something beyond human "concepts" and their functional or descriptive language. Poetic vision may be caught. If we "know how to wait, even a whole life-time", we may come to see an "Opening".[130] We must "step back out of metaphysics" because here we try to make Being the object of *thought*. In his seminar on "Time and Being" Heidegger explains: "In the step back, openness as such *appears* as what is to be *thought*. But, in what direction does it *shine*? . . . The 'whither' cannot be determined."[131] He adds: "Their indeterminacy exists only for knowledge, but is rather an indeterminacy of the *manner of being of the whither itself*."[132] Yet even such forms of expression are "inadequate" or subject to erasure, because all we can know is "the 'that' of the *place* of the 'whither'"; *not* "how this place is".[133] Heidegger quotes a line of the poet Stefan George: "Where word breaks off, no thing may be".[134]

Here is the philosophical soil in which a deconstructionist theory of textuality can grow and flourish. Texts provide a space for an indeterminate "whither", and seem to hold a promise to take us forward, where conceptual or content-related language would merely throw us back onto paths already laid out. Moreover in the later Heidegger humankind as intersubjectivity or as the speaking subject has abdicated its role to language itself: "*language speaks* (Heidegger's italics) . . . language speaks by saying, that is, by showing". Heidegger asks: "On what does the being of language rest?", and reflects: "Perhaps we are missing the very nature of language when we ask for grounds?"[135] But can we even "think" or "see" language itself? Reflection "has come only within sight of *the way of language* it is seeking

(Heidegger's italics); it is barely *on its traces*" (my italics).¹³⁶ For Derrida, as we have noted, texts are an endless series of "traces" or "tracks"; they are traces in the sense of being products of previous traces, and tracks in the sense of moving "on the way to" other traces. But language has no external ground that is not illusory. Here, as we shall see, Friedrich Nietzsche (and Heidegger's "reading" of Nietzsche) also enters the picture. If language is like a chess-board, as both Saussure and Wittgenstein had suggested, Derrida uses the metaphor of the "bottomless chessboard": there is no underlying ground to support it, and play has no meaning beyond itself.¹³⁷ Even for the later Heidegger, in language "the farewell of all 'it is' comes to pass".¹³⁸

At the same time there is an ambivalence in the later Heidegger which Derrida wishes to eliminate. Heidegger can still suggest that because the being of beings resides in the word "therefore . . . Language is the house of Being".¹³⁹ The contexts in which he uses this phrase imply that it is a metaphor, or at least an extension of language rather than an ontological statement. He admits that this phrase is "clumsy", and insists that it "does not provide a concept of the nature of language".¹⁴⁰ He writes "The notion proves invalid as soon as we think of the ambiguity of 'Being' . . . I do not mean the Being of beings represented metaphysically."¹⁴¹ What Heidegger is doing is letting the word play a fleeting role in his text before withdrawing it, and moving on. In Derrida's terminology, it is "given" only to be placed immediately "under erasure". It is difficult at this point to know which thinker adopts a perspective more true to the spirit of deconstruction. Derrida's exclusion of Being might be said to betray more "metaphysical confidence", even in the service of an anti-metaphysical philosophy. Heidegger's hesitant and oscillating ambiguity represents a drawn-out *process* of hint, suggestion, and erasure.

The methodological device of *erasure* suggests a still closer link between Derrida and the later Heidegger. Derrida himself readily acknowledges that Heidegger is the originator and "authority" for this methodological device which is central to his own thought. Derrida writes: "The order of the signified is never contemporary, is at best the subtly discrepant inverse or parallel – discrepant by the time of a breath – from the order of the signifier."¹⁴² Because the sign is a *trace* or a *mark*, it needs to be left intact. But because the sign is a *trace* in the sense of a *track* that encourages onward movement, the mark *also* needs to be erased. It stands both as a fleeting presence, and as that which must be "under erasure" (*sous rature*). Thus Derrida will write a word, cross it out because it is not accurate, and print both the word and its deletion because, in his judgment, both are necessary. Derrida acknowledges that Heidegger invented this procedure in his book *On the Question of Being* (Germ. 1956). We have already discussed Heidegger's dilemma about the word *Being*. He knows that he wants to talk about Being, but that such talk cannot strictly take place. Hence he writes: "A thoughtful glance ahead into this realm of 'Being' can only write it as B̶e̶i̶n̶g̶"(sic).[143] The drawing of these crossed lines "wards off" certain linguistic habits of interpretation. But the erasure is not simply a negative sign which totally withdraws the word; it simultaneously puts it forward and draws it back as part of a *process*.

Derrida does not follow Heidegger, however, in reserving this notion of standing "under erasure" only for those signs which, from Heidegger's viewpoint, hover near the edge of metaphysics. Gayatri Spivak comments, "Derrida's notion of '*sous rature*' differs from that of Heidegger. Heidegger's Being (*sic*) might point to an articulable presence. Derrida's t̶r̶a̶c̶e̶ is the mark of the absence of a presence, an always already absent present."[144] *Absence* becomes a key theme in Derrida. In *The Post Card* (1980) he reflects on Heidegger's notion of "there is" (*es gibt*) as he also does in *Writing and Difference* and elsewhere. Heidegger had described this (lit.) "it gives" as a "giving" which also "holds itself back and withdraws."[145] Derrida comments, "the gift itself is given *on the basis of* 'something', which is nothing, which is not something."[146] In his volume *Signéponge* Derrida plays the game of "sign-punning" (as Heidegger was notoriously wont to do) especially between the name of the major French poet for whose Colloquium Derrida spoke, namely Francis *Ponge*, and the use of the *sponge (l'éponge)*. "The sponge expunges the proper name . . . effaces it and loses it . . . But simultaneously the sponge can also retain the name, absorb it, shelter it . . . It holds clean and proper water as well as dirty water."[147] The sponge becomes a metaphor for simultaneous erasure and preservation based on absence between the sponge and what is sponged. Indeed, where the author of a text offers his or her signature, a further metaphor is also used: the heraldic concept of *mise en abyme*, where word-play brings together the notions of placement in decay (*abîme*), "self-representation" in heraldry (*abyme*) and placement in abyss (*abîme*).[148] The metaphor of "abyss" features regularly in Derrida's book *The Truth in Painting*.[149]

Two or three final comments on Derrida's use of devices and categories borrowed from the later Heidegger need still to be mentioned. The first concerns the word "deconstruction". This is not Derrida's favourite term which he would most readily use to describe his own theory of texts, but he uses it and does not disown it. The actual *Destruktion* comes from Heidegger. In his seminars later published under the title *The Ear of the Other* Derrida notes: "When I made use of this word, I had the sense of translating two words from Heidegger at a point where I needed them in the context. These two words are *Destruktion*, which Heidegger uses, explaining the *Destruktion* is not a destruction but precisely a destructuring that dismantles structural layers in the system, and so on. The other word is *Abbau*, which has a similar meaning." What this deconstruction was applied to was "the whole history of Western philosophy."[151]

Second, Heidegger's deliberate attempt to "re-read" rather than to expound the classic writings of Western philosophy from Plato to Nietzsche does two things. First, it initiates a model for the kind of "reading of classic texts which occurs in deconstructionist circles. Second, it allows Derrida to draw extensively on Nietzsche without *appearing* to treat Nietzsche as a source of metaphysical dogma. Heidegger's "reading" of Nietzsche therefore comes close in its influence on Derrida to that of the later Heidegger's own thought. Nietzsche's direct influence is also powerful, but, as G.V. Spivak observes, "Heidegger stands between Derrida and Nietzsche. Almost on every occasion that Derrida writes of Nietzsche, Heidegger's reading is invoked."[142] The reason for this is the very opposite of any notion that Heidegger interprets Nietzsche "correctly". In one sense Heidegger falsifies Nietzsche, Derrida claims, by making him a figure "within the history of metaphysics". But the "text" of Nietzsche cannot end with Nietzsche; otherwise it constitutes a "given" or a dogma, and Nietzsche proclaimed the illusion of all givens and dogmata.[153] Being "caught in the circle", as both Heidegger and Derrida put it, means that, in Derrida's words in *Writing and Difference* "This is what allows these destroyers to destroy each other reciprocally – for example, Heidegger regarding Nietzsche – with as much lucidity and rigor as bad faith and misconstruction, as the last metaphysician, the last 'Platonist'. One could do the same for Heidegger himself, for Freud, or for a number of others".[154]

Derrida's affinities with Nietzsche, as he himself acknowledges, lie in this shared distrust of metaphysics, their shared suspicions concerning the illusory nature of "truth", and especially their shared belief that doctrines, fixed contents, or fixed meanings are really generated by a "mobile army of metaphors" whose metaphorical and mobile status has been repressed, forgotten, or unnoticed. Derrida observes, "Nietzsche stretches the limits of the metaphorical to such a point that he attributes metaphorical power to every use of sound in speaking."[155] Truths, for Nietzsche, are illusory "metaphors, metonymies and anthropomorphisms" which have been rhetorically sublimated and transposed, with the result that after long and habitual use they now appear "solid, canonical, unavoidable."[156] Their metaphorical and illusory nature has been forgotten, and they become like coins thinned down by over-use into mere pieces of metal. The Nietzschean critique of metaphysics, Derrida comments, substitutes "the concepts of play, interpretation, and sign (sign without present truth) for the illusory categories of Being and truth."[157]

As Derrida points out in this same essay, "Structure, Sign and Play" the Nietzschean perspective, "de-centres" any notion of structure, meaning, or system, and substitutes what Lentricchia calls "a new hedonism" of "play", "joy", "activity" and their variants.158 This becomes the theme, as Lentricchia argues, in the work of Derrida's Yale colleagues in literary theory Paul de Man, Geoffrey Hartman, and J. Hillis Miller. Derrida writes: "The centre . . . closes off the play which it opens up."159 The history of thought has produced a succession of "centres", or metaphors around which system, doctrine, and meaning have been organized. By contrast, "the Nietzschean affirmation . . . is the joyous affirmation of the play of the world; and the innocence of becoming; the affirmation of a world of signs without fault, without truth."160

This process of affirmation and act of human will, Nietzsche argues, leads humankind to impose notions of fixity and logic onto the world; but this is only to make our own existence possible. We simply give the name "truth" to a process. In his book *Spurs: Nietzsche's Styles* and in his *Otobiographies* Derrida urges that we read Nietzsche not as a promulgator of relativist "doctrine", but as one who starts us along a road which we, the readers, must complete.161 Derrida therefore comments that we should be "immeasurably wary whenever we think we are reading Nietzsche's signature or 'autograph' . . . The effects or structure of a text are not reducible to its 'truth', to the intended meaning of its presumed author."162 Derrida quotes Nietzsche: "I *want* no 'believers'". He is "no man", but "a collision *against* everything that had been believed."163 Nietzsche does not expect "ears" for what he says in his own time.164 We are reminded of Kierkegaard's device of attacking what he himself had written under pseudonyms, in order that the truth could not be packaged, but had to be subject to struggle, engagement, and decision on the part of readers.

To complete our account of Derrida's theory of textuality and language, one more contributory factor needs to be noted. This is his use of Freud. Nietzsche and Freud both challenge the priority of consciousness over the unconscious "often in a very similar way."165 Christopher Norris and Gayatri Spivak identify further parallels between Nietzsche and Freud which are important for Derrida.166 At the most general level, both exercize hermeneutical suspicion of all conscious articulation, on the ground that this may reflect disguises thrown up by unconscious forces. The Psyche is "protected" from certain stimuli of perception. In his essay "Freud and the Sense of Writing" Derrida shows the extent to which Freud has recourse to metaphorical models, most of which are drawn not from oral speech but from writing (in the broad sense in which this term is used by Derrida).167 The conscious mind experiences a series of momentary perceptions; but these leave "traces" in the unconscious long after the event. To decipher traces which lie deep in the unconscious requires something more than the traditional language of statement. Here Freud's psychoanalytic method takes on key importance. In his book *The Interpretation of Dreams* and in other works Freud discussed the interplay of disclosure and concealment.

This notion, Gayatri Spivak comments, "that the concealment is itself a revelation and vice versa, brings Nietzsche and Freud together."[168] Derrida is conscious here of the agenda of Paul Ricoeur, but answers the questions addressed by Ricoeur in a radically different, non-theistic, way.

Other post-modernist writers, most notably Jacques Lacan and Julia Kristeva regard Freud's work as being foundational for their theories of the relationship between language, texts, and human persons. But in Derrida a very radical implication is drawn from Freud: *the priority of written texts over the human psyche itself.* This is more fundamental in terms of theory and method than the growing practice in Derrida's later writings of using psychoanalysis and an increasingly sexual vocabulary as categories of "interpretation". In general terms, like Lacan, Ricoeur, and Julia Kristeva, Derrida uses the Freudian categories of "condensation" and "displacement" along lines which in the semiotic systems of Saussure and Jakobson would respectively stand for metaphor, paradigmatic relations, or gaps, and metonymy, syntagma, or movement from a focal point.[169] The multiplication of these processes in polyvalent meaning was called "overdetermination" in Freudian thought. But one metaphor remains no less suggestive for Derrida than these "fundamental concepts", as Lacan calls them. This is Freud's notion of the unconscious as a "mystic writing pad".[170]

Freud expounded the metaphor in detail. A sheet of transparent celluloid is placed over a thin sheet of translucent waxed paper, which rests, in turn, on a slab of resin or wax. Perceptions of events or objects are like the scratching of a stilus on the surface of the celluloid. The celluloid "protects" the thin paper and vulnerable paper which represents the conscious self. But this wax slab, below the level of immediate consciousness, exhibits the traces made by the stilus. "The layer which received the stimuli forms no permanent traces ... The 'perceived' may be read only in the past, beneath perceptions and after it."[171] For Derrida this not only inverts the traditional priority of conscious over unconscious, and of speech over writing; it also leads to a radical inversion of the relation between writing and the psyche. We do not simply have a good set of questions about the psyche; rather Freud's metaphor prompts the question: *What is a text, and what must the psyche be if it can be represented by a text?"* Derrida concludes: "The trace is the erasure of selfhood, of one's own presence."[173]

We have now moved far beyond the demands of semiotic theory into a philosophical world-view which puts forward huge claims not simply about how language, texts, or signs operate, but about the nature of thought and language itself, and about their relation to human consciousness and to the intersubjective world. We cannot simply detach those aspects of Derrida's thought which concern texts and literature from the philosophical framework to which they belong. Yet there are a number of writers who see value for Christian theology and for biblical interpretation in an approach which regards texts as "a fabric to traces referring endlessly ... to other differential traces."[174] They see such a model of textuality as delivering us from bondage to fixed entities and to false securities, and as allowing language to point *towards* the transcendent by polyvalent parable, rather than by having to articulate the transcendent in or through conceptual language. Some also see this approach as, in Harari's words, "a definition of a post-modern critical attitude", or welcome it as heralding the necessary "post-modern crisis."[175] Do not believe, Hilary Lawson exhorts us, "that the world of the true and false, the world of status and idols – the fixed and immobile – can survive for long".[176]

The post-modernist attack on the fixed and immobile accords with hermeneutical insights after Hegel and after Dilthey into the historical, contextual, and finite nature of human understanding and of language. But this insight is to be distinguished from post-modernist suggestions that all truth and falsehood and all critiques of idolatry remain so contextually conditioned as to become *unstable* and radically pluralistic. This distinction emerges in our discussions of radically socio-contextual interpretations of Gadamer (chapter IX), of the respective claims of Apel, Habermas, Rorty, and Lyotard (chapters XI–XII), of certain kinds of socio-literary and reader-response theory (chapters XIII–XIV), and of issues raised by hermeneutical pluralism (chapters XV–XVI). It is worth recalling again that A.J. Ayer's logical positivism attempted to sell a given world-view dressed up as a theory of language. But in spite of the problematic nature of this world-view, and of the seriously over-simplified view of language which it implied, the legacy of the falsification principle which formed part of it offered some limited value for questions about meaning in certain contexts. For certain specific purposes of enquiry (not for all) we may allow the limited value of the falsification principle in the context of theological truth-claims.

We shall therefore need to consider exploring two distinct but related questions. First, can the kind of approach to texts associated with Derrida and with Barthes offer anything positive for biblical interpretation? What gains or losses, if any, have emerged when this kind of perspective has been adopted in the interpretation of biblical texts? Second, if a post-modernist or deconstructionist theory of texts has any validity, one of two possible propositions must be true: *either* (a) it must stand on its own feet as a theory of texts or as a descriptive theory of semiotics, independently of some philosophical frame or world-view in which it is embedded; *or* (b) we must be convinced of the validity *both* of the philosophical frame and world-view *and* the theory of textuality which belongs to it. But do either of these two propositions invite or compel assent?

6. Postmodernist and Deconstructionist Approaches in Biblical Interpretation

Before describing post-modernist or deconstructionist approaches to biblical texts, and before assessing the validity of the theory of language which they imply, it may be helpful at this point to remind ourselves of the degree of incompatibility which has now emerged between deconstructionist theories of texts and the theological considerations about the nature of biblical texts which we outlined in the second half of our second chapter. There are deep difficulties, in particular, about the status of biblical texts as vehicles, or even potential vehicles, for inter-personal communication, for the language of personal address, and for the incarnational principle of an embodied text which has as its system of reference the enfleshed life of Jesus of Nazareth and the apostolic witness of a living community. For Derrida and for Barthes the inter-subjective world has been replaced by intertextuality; the self stands under erasure; presence is governed by absence.

This is not to claim, however, that deconstructionism is irrelevant *to certain specific examples of texts* within the biblical writings. I have already alluded in the introduction to David Clines's "deconstruction" of dialogues in Job, where the function of the Book of Job is clearly not to expose the inadequacies of one doctrine by replacing it with some new substitute doctrine in equally packaged form. As we shall see, J.D. Crossan offers operational examples of certain parables which subvert worlds, and traces the iconoclastic effects of Ecclesiastes. But careful distinctions must be drawn. Prophetic discourse becomes problematic, especially if the prophet is divorced from the text. Hymnic modes and prescriptive discourse are difficult. Within Ricoeur's categories discussed in chapter II, the wisdom mode probably remains the closest or best model, in which all language is indirect, and God remains either absent or hidden. Certainly God is beyond human thought, and texts function as subversive explorations, moving the reader on from false securities. Derrida is at home with the "Apocalyptic tone", as long as the promised future of apocalyptic never materializes, but is always *on the way*.[177] Derrida views "Living On" as *différance* "between archaeology and eschatology, as *différance in* apocalypse"; but adds: "That will be a while in coming."[178]

It may be suggested that the priority of writing over human consciousness suggests something about the primacy of the word, as this is conceived of in the Johannine writings: "In the beginning was the word" (John 1:1). But nothing could be further from the Johannine theology of the incarnation. We argued in our second chapter that in the biblical traditions there was an interweaving of language and practice, of word, witness, and life, which achieves its culmination in the embodiment of the word, in the Word made flesh. (John 1:14) In his Preface to his collection *Deconstruction and Criticism* (which includes essays by Derrida, Harold Bloom, and Paul de Man) Geoffrey Hartman declares: "Deconstruction, as it has come to be called, refuses to identify the force of literature with any concept of embodied meaning, and shows how deeply such logocentric or incarnationist perspectives have influenced the way we think about art . . . But the opposite can also be urged . . . Everything remains within an 'intertextual' sphere."[179] The word, if it ever could have been made flesh, has now become only word again.

Our aim here is not to try to "answer" deconstructionist problems on the basis of Christian theology, but first to point out what theological considerations are compatible, or incompatible, with this kind of approach to textuality. We shall address, in due course, on the grounds of a philosophy of language, the misplaced assumption that language or semiotic systems can be divorced from life. But this will be on the basis of the kind of considerations put forward by Wittgenstein, and developed by Searle. Wittgenstein was keenly aware of the impossibility of standing "outside" language. When, surprisingly, in his book entitled *Wittgenstein and Derrida*, Henry Staten attempts to argue that Wittgenstein's approach to language is deconstructionist, certain "parallels" between these "allies" are legitimate to the extent that Wittgenstein's *diagnosis* of the problems anticipate Derrida's in some respects.[180] But Wittgenstein's *cure* is very different. For Wittgenstein, patterns of *life* and *action* which embody *particular cases and judgments* are like the gold which gives currency to the paper-money of the sign-system.

In the area of biblical interpretation there is inevitably an element of arbitrariness in the selection of particular examples for consideration. However, some writers are more explicit than others about their interest in *irreducible* textual polyvalency, and one writer who has moved consistently towards the kind of approach that we have in view is John Dominic Crossan. In his first book entitled *In Parables: the Challenge of the Historical Jesus* (1973), he already views history in intra-linguistic terms, and views the texts of the parables as setting in motion operative processes rather than as media through which a content or message is conveyed.[181] Parables reverse reader-expectations. Metaphor founds and establishes a language-world, and conceptual description cannot articulate the Wholly Other.[182] The emphasis falls on reader-effects on the part of the text.

In a helpful critical assessment of Crossan's approach, Lynn M. Poland identifies the main literary influence at this stage of his writing as the so-called New Criticism.[183] Crossan cites such writers as Cleanth Brooks, Ezra Pound, and T.S. Eliot. In *The Two Horizons* I had indicated that his work owed something to the influence of the later Heidegger and Ernst Fuchs, not only because of Crossan's explicit interest in Heidegger and the so-called New Quest of the Historical Jesus, but also because of very close affinities with the work of Robert Funk on metaphor in the parables of Jesus in which Funk acknowledges his debt to Heidegger, Fuchs, and Merleau-Ponty.[184] No doubt both sets of influences play their part. At all events, Lynn Poland draws attention to two methodological features in Crossan's work: first, he subsumes history within language; second, he emphasizes form and function at the expense of cognitive content. Crossan writes: "The term 'historical' Jesus really means the language of Jesus and most especially the parables themselves."[185] Lynn Poland comments: "Like the New Critics, Crossan focusses on the structure and function at the expense of the content of the meanings and beliefs embodied in the story ... He does not seem to see that the content, as well as the function, of metaphor is also dependent on the concrete situation that the narrative depicts and the auditors recognize."[186] Lynn Poland rightly sees metaphor here as an extension of ordinary meanings "in a given cultural situation."[187] While metaphor may shock or surprise, he concludes, the revealing of truth involves more than this.

Crossan's progress towards a more radical theory of language advances further in his next book, *The Dark Interval* (1975).[188] Parables are iconoclastic. While myths serve to re-assure us, parables subvert. What they do is to move us on. But this is all we can expect of language, at least when really important things are at stake. Crossan appeals here to the *early* Wittgenstein: we must be silent about that of which we cannot speak.[189] This applies firmly to what masquerade as metaphysical propositions. The best that can be done is to tell a variety of stories which function as parable. Otherwise we shall end in illusion and idolatry.

This is applied to all language about God, with the result that language itself seems to impose an inescapable dilemma. We cannot ask "what is 'out there' apart from the story in which 'it' is envisioned". But "if there is only one story", then God is either "*inside*" my story and, in that case ... an idol I have created; or God is *outside* my story, and ... completely unknowable."[190] As Lynn Poland comments, "All language now seems to be not only 'indirect' but also non-referential ... All attempts to speak of God are idolatrous ... The parables are not disclosive but subversive".[191] Moreover, we may add, parables are the only effective linguistic resource that we have. The nub of the matter is that the best thing we can hope for in biblical texts is that "parables give God room."[192] Inevitably this is achieved by telling us that we have built our home "above an earthquake fault"; and parable destroys our security by preparing us for the experience of transcendence in "the dark night of story."[193]

Crossan's next book *Raid on the Articulate: Comic Eschatology in Jesus and Borges* (1976) picks up Eliot's phrase "raid on the inarticulate." In his Preface Crossan expresses his fascination for structuralist *philosophy* rather than structuralist methodology.[194] When he appeals to Roland Barthes, Crossan's major concern is with iconoclasm. We know reality "only in language", but this is an "unreal reality" or perhaps even "a real unreality."[195] We are trapped in our linguistic world, except that there may be "cracks" or "fissures" through which we catch a hint of transcendence through "comedy too deep for laughter."[196] Crossan takes up the notion of language and textuality as play. Like Derrida and Barthes, however, the play takes us through both apparent affirmation and withdrawal. "We are children preparing with infinite seriousness an eternal game of hide-and-seek."[197] Following J. Ehrmann, Crossan agrees: "Play is not played against a background of a fixed, stable, reality."[198] Following Derrida, Crossan leads us into a field of textual "freeplay, that is to say, a field of infinite substitutions."[199]

What, then, is the purpose and nature of biblical interpretation? Jesus stands, like Moses, as a destroyer of idols. Crossan looks for the "comic" (i.e. iconoclastic) dimension in irony, parody, parable, and paradox within the biblical texts. A first example is the "comic questioning" with which the Book of Ruth takes up the question of mixed marriages. The Ezra-Nehemiah tradition prohibits marriage to foreign women, but we are not allowed to forget that Ruth is a foreigner (Ruth 1:16; 4: 17–22). A more convincing example is perhaps that of Ecclesiastes as parody of the inherited Wisdom tradition. The writer dons the mask of Solomon to declare: "The wise man dies like the fool" (Eccles.2:16). "The race is not to the swift, nor the battle to the strong, nor bread to the wise" (9:11). Crossan concludes: "God cannot be caught in the nets of Wisdom any more than in the nets of the Law."[200]

In most of these instances, including the language of Jesus, the literary device identified by V. Shklovsky as "defamiliarization" is used. The poetic, aphoristic, or parabolic image makes strange what was otherwise habitual (in these cases, established biblical traditions) by presenting it in a novel light or in some unexpected context. For example, in the language of Jesus it appears at first sight that we are offered a development of the familiar tradition of case-law in Matt. 5: 39–41 (*par* Luke 6:29). If anyone strikes you on the right cheek, turn to him the other also; and if anyone would sue you and take your coat, let him have your cloak as well; and if anyone forces you to go one mile, go with him two miles" (*par* Luke 6:29). In Crossan's view this represents "case parody, a deliberate subversion of the wise and prudent necessity of case law."[201] It uses the familiar forms of case-law, but ends with the strange injunction "to join in our own despoiling". Jesus is challenging the legal tradition.

Crossan returns to his own home ground when he expounds the paradoxical character of Jesus's parables of reversal. He identifies three metonymic parables of paradox: the Good Samaritan (Luke 10: 30–37);

the Pharisee and the Tax Collector (Luke 18: 9–14); and the Rich Man and Lazarus (Luke 16: 19–31). The Samaritan, the pharisee, and Lazarus are metonyms in the sense that they stand for a wider religious and social world. The metaphoric parables of paradox include the Prodigal Son (Luke 15: 11–32) and the Great Supper (Luke 14: 16–24). They open up worlds of metaphorical meaning which are then called into question. Crossan allows that other parables may function in other ways. But all, on the basis of his theory of language, reflect the notion of text-as-process-of-play and language as iconoclastic "destruction". The parable of the sower, for example (Mark 4: 3–20; *par* Matt. 13: 1–9, 18–23) becomes an allegorical parable. But "an allegorical parable will generate interpretations that are both *multiple* and *paradoxical*".[202]

With the parables of Jesus Crossan compares the parables of Jorge Luis Borges. For Borges, there is no "system" of belief, but paradoxes in which any assertion implies its own denial, and the clash of opposites. Their function therefore is not to describe or to assert, but to change, or to move on, a reader's viewpoint. This equally well reflects Crossan's philosophy of language as well as his theology. We experience transcendence not as the revelation of some truth, but as "glad acceptance of our finitude."[203] "Jesus has taught us to the limits of word and the form in the name of Israel's aniconic God ... Borges has taught us the limits of book ... in the name of ... playful laughter."[204]

Crossan's allusion to the parable of the Hidden Treasure (Matt.13:44; cf. Thom. 76 and 109) which he briefly discusses in *Raid on the Articulate* becomes associated with a radically post-modern theory of textuality in his next book *Finding is the First Act: Trove Folktales and Jesus' Treasure Parable* (1979).[205] In rabbinic parables the two acts of selling/buying and finding follow the sequence: (i) transference of ownership, (ii) finding treasure. But Jesus transposes the sequence, making the series of actions dubious from a moral viewpoint. The Jewish parable has a didactic content about value of work-ethics which leads to discovery. According to Crossan, the point of Jesus's utterance is that it simply points to a present opportunity which remains unspecified. Obtaining the field procures the space for discovery; but the content remains hidden. The parable therefore shows us how language fails to refer beyond itself: "I will tell you, it says, what the Kingdom of God is like. Watch carefully how, and as I *fail* to do so and learn that *it cannot be done* ... the more magnificent my failure, the greater my success."[206]

Finally, Crossan's book *Cliffs of Fall: Paradox and Polyvalence in the Parables of Jesus* (1980) radicalizes to the limits the notion of polyvalent meaning, and develops themes explored in "Waking the Bible" and in his paper "A Metamodel for Polyvalent Narration".[207] In *Cliffs of Fall* the notion of texts and language as play is brought into conjunction with the category which must sharply distinguish post-modern from modern thought: reflection is replaced by *reflexivity*,. Now we have not so much parables as such, but rather "parables of parables" in an infinite series of self-referring signs. Lynn Poland offers a critical assessment: "As Crossan extends the dominion of language he shifts, or at least clarifies, his theological intention. The parables do not, even enigmatically, reveal something of the character of the transcendent, because it is a wholly unknowable divine. God's action is not "hiddenly present" . . . but present only as void, as the absence of meaning and order".[208] She concludes: "Jesus is now less a prophetic figure, shocking us into an awareness of the falsity and complacency of our stories, than he is an 'ancient Palestinian mystic' whose "serene and iconoclastic spirit places him in the company of the Zen masters, Dionysius the Areopagite, and the anonymous author of the Cloud of Unknowing . . . Why Derrida is attractive to Crossan is understandable, for he is, in Meyer Abram's apt characterization, the Zen master of Western philosophy."[209]

I had noted in an article on the parables as language-event in 1970 that the later Heidegger's influence on Fuchs and the new hermeneutic led in a direction where parable became like the Zen Buddhist *koan*. I noted the later Heidegger's comment on Zen Buddhist writing of Suzuki: "this is what I have been trying to say in all my writings."[210] Joseph Prabhu, as a *critic* of theological deconstructionism, and Thomas Altizer and Mark Taylor as enthusiastic *exponents* of theological deconstructionism agree that there is a close resemblance between "a deconstructed Christianity" and Buddhism. Taylor adds: "More specifically, certain aspects of Derridean deconstruction bear a significant similarity to the form of Madhyamaka Buddhism, or 'the *Middle* Way', developed by Nagarjuna."[211]

In this light, it is scarcely surprising that Crossan takes up and develops Derrida's understanding of metaphor as "a metaphor of metaphor" for his model of polyvalent narration in the parables of Jesus.[212] Crossan distinguishes between two different philosophies which enter the labyrinth of language. In the labyrinth the existentialist experiences nausea and "ontological disappointment" because there is no centre to the labyrinth. But in "structuralist" or post-modern thought we know that "we create the labyrinth ourselves, that it has no centre, that it is infinitely expansible, that we create it as play and for play."[213] For the background to this notion of text as play Crossan goes back to semiotic theory, referring his readers briefly to Charles Morris and to Saussure before he turns to Barthes and Derrida. Texts can be played continuously. The paradox of parable "precludes canonical interpretation."[214] In *Cliffs of Fall* parables are "metaparables": parables about parabling.[215] A parable is a "perfect mirror", not of the world or the kingdom but "of itself."

Some of Crossan's work of biblical interpretation is more orientated towards a "content", but his interest remains focussed on the "play of (often opposing) forces" within a text which "moves on". For example, in his "Structural Analysis of John 6" (1980) he identifies different and opposing sets of textual processes depending on whether the meanings of the metaphors used by Jesus about bread and "eating" and about his flesh and blood (John 6: 35, 41, 52–66) are "completed" by the disciples or "completed" by the Jews. "Although addressed to 'the Jews', this final reaction is not recorded yet."[216]

Consistent with his approach in *Cliffs of Fall* Crossan seems more ready to ask questions concerning Derrida than to make assertions about his thought in the volume of *Semeia* entitled *Derrida and Bible Studies* (1982). In particular he raises questions about the relation between *différance* (which invites endless textual play) and a theology of *via negativa*. Derrida, on the one hand, maintains that God cannot be recognized, in the language of negation, as "a superior, inconceivable, ineffable mode of being", because *différance* involves no category of being, present or absent "not even in the most negative order of negative theology."[217] Crossan appreciates the dilemma: which is the less "metaphysical" position? Should one *assert* the impossibility of negative theology (a metaphysical assertion?) Or would it be less metaphysical to allow the *possibility* of *via negativa*? He finds it attractive that negative theology "has been suspected of unorthodoxy at best and of atheism at worst."[218] This may indicate something "profound". But on the horns of such a dilemma, Crossan must defer any answer: "Certain questions beget not so much answers as different ways of phrasing themselves."[219] The conclusion is true to the spirit of Derrida.

Crossan's two books *In Parables* and *Raid on the Articulate* offer a contribution to biblical interpretation. They clarify the semiotic and functional dynamics of *some* (not all) parables, and they call attention to those uncomfortable elements within the biblical traditions which serve to question and to undermine complacently "static" interpretations of earlier biblical traditions. The relation between Ruth and Ezra, or between Ecclesiastes and Proverbs, delivers us from the supposition that any single element of the biblical canon can be made a "centre" or controlling model at the expense of others. In positive terms "God is given a little room in which to be God".[220] In more recent work Crossan seeks to offer a "generative model" for Jesus's aphorisms, which allow "free-play" within the "aphoristic core".[221] It might be argued that such language begins to move away, to a small extent, from deconstructionist "de-centering". In the event, any theory of texts which *mainly* concerns iconoclasm, and suspicion, and "play" becomes self-defeating, or at least parasitic on what it seeks to undermine. Kierkegaard was fully aware of this. This is why he insisted that a prophet of subversion can never be more than "a little piece of cinnamon".

David Clines's essay "Deconstructing the Book of Job" (1990) is written in the light of many years of research on the Hebrew text of Job. My former Sheffield colleague takes up that aspect of deconstruction in which a discourse is perceived to "undermine the philosophy it asserts, or the hierarchical oppositions on which it relies."[222] This does not mean, for Clines, simply showing some incoherence in the text. The key point is that the undermining processes remain latent, less explicit than the surface-argument.

Clines sees two explicit philosophies in confrontation in Job. The traditional dogma that the righteous person is rewarded, and that only the wicked suffer is not uniformly denied. In Job 1: 1–3, 1: 9 and elsewhere the framework seems to be affirmed. But a second and stronger principle confronts it, namely the righteous also suffer, and that piety does not necessarily lead to prosperity. Neither, however, "undermines" the other latently; at this level the conflict is entirely above board. The deconstruction process appears in the epilogue in Job 42: 7–17. It brings discomfort to the assertion of the second philosophy, which in practice represents the dominant theme of the whole book. It does not contradict it but it undermines it, and pulls the rug from beneath it.

Other deconstructive processes are also at work. Job appears to provide a model counter-example against the traditional doctrine for all who bear human suffering disproportionate to their deeds. Yet, Clines observes, Job is both explicitly a model and yet one which we can embrace or apply only with discomfort. The narrative asserts that Job has a right to protest, but is the Book, he asks, "also an indirect warning that no good will come of behaving like Job unless one is in Job's moral position to begin with? If that is so, we no longer know whether the book offers an encouragement or a warning. Is it saying Behave like Job, or Don't behave like Job? What we are told about Job deconstructs the example he affords."[223]

Clines's treatment undoubtedly asks pertinent questions about the text of Job, and is probably the best example of a use of deconstructionist approaches to biblical texts that can be found. He concludes that the purpose here of the deconstructionist strategy is to eliminate dogma as dogma. But this thrust coheres with the strategies of such texts as Job and perhaps Ecclesiastes, and with specific selected parables of Jesus, in ways which many other biblical texts would support less readily. Clines's approach in this respect belongs to a different order from the work of Mark C. Taylor, whose earlier work, at least, seeks to apply Derridean deconstructionism not to selected texts but to Christian theology as such. Mark Taylor explicitly calls Derrida "the most important philosopher now writing", and traces his own intellectual foundations from Hegel's work on identity and difference through Kierkegaard, Nietzsche, and Heidegger, to Derrida.

The decisive advance of post-modernism, Taylor urges, is to move from the necessity of interpretation to that of "interpreting interpretation".[224] This is the move from "reflection" to "reflexion". But this meta-critical move supposedly "unmasks" the fictional status of all that we believe in, including the unity of the self: "One of the characteristics of post-modernism is the death of selfhood."[225] Taylor endorses Barthes's assertions about the "death of the author", and Derrida's "critique of present." Textuality now becomes a "ceaseless flux" in which any boundary can be crossed. Taylor theologizes Derrida's critique of presence as a kind of incarnational "*Kenosis* of all absolute self-presence."[226] The biblical texts exhibit an endless play of a "cruciform word" in which the activity of deferment, deconstruction, or erasure has metaphorical extension in the experience of the cross and ethical "selflessness". Like Crossan, Taylor tells us that he is engaged in "the iconoclasm of *radical* criticism."[227] The "domino effect" of Kierkegaard, Hegel, Nietzsche, and Derrida together have made "post-modernism" inevitable. Here "the world becomes an undecidable and irresolvable play of masks"; textual play takes place where "revelation is reveilation"; and all this "makes erring endless."[228]

It is tempting for someone writing in Britain, where so-called common sense philosophies have often prevailed, to raise the standard question about what would or could count as counter-examples or as falsifications in the face of such a theory. Once again, when deconstructionist and postmodernist insights of iconoclastic method become inflated into some world-view which is allegedly anti-metaphysical but in practice comes to function as a metaphysic, the whole system becomes self-defeating, a mere negative against someone else's positive. To set this up as a model of *textuality as such* is to imperialize all texts within a single system, while superficially rejecting any notion of system. Philosophers and theologians have been aware of the possibility of a polarized opposition between theories of reality as metaphysical Being and as ever-changing flux since the speculations of Parmenides and of Heraclitus of Ephesus in the fifth and sixth centuries B.C. Heraclitus compared the nature of reality and a drink of *kykeōn* (a mixture of wine, barley-meal and grated cheese, Homer, *Iliad* 11 624, 641) which "falls apart if it is not being stirred" (Heraclitus, *Fragments* 125). He saw reality as that which is constituted by strife, conflict, movement, and variable tensions between opposites. The logical status and implications of such a philosophy have always been disputed. Aristotle accused Heraclitus of violating the logic of contradiction. Even Taylor readily concedes that the model of deconstruction is equally hospitable to "Christian selflessness" or to "Jewish exile" or to "Buddhist emptiness".[229]

P.J. Hartin applies deconstruction in two recent studies (1988 and 1991) to New Testament parable texts along lines invited by Roland Barthes's view of texts as no longer "defined objects". Hartin insists that deconstruction is not a single "method"; but it frees texts from the "hegemony" of their author, or, in Barthes's language, detaches them from "the father's signature". In his essay of 1991 Hartin argues that the parable of the sower (Mark 4:1–9) is capable of endless readings as it is re-contextualized among various "intertexts". He endorses Taylor's conclusion that texts are "ever unfinished", transforming readers into authors.[230] Such a view of meaning, he freely allows, differs radically from that of traditional historical criticism.

Some theological writers sympathize with certain aspects of Derridean or deconstructionist thought, but are unwilling to go the whole way with it. Carl A. Raschke, for example, accepts Derrida only as a point of departure. He accepts Derrida's philosophy of signs, and draws on his notion of *différance* to establish the relativity and self-referring nature of signs: "The sign abolishes its own intent of signification."[231] But rather than moving from Heidegger to Derrida, Raschke moves from Derrida back to Heidegger: "The deconstruction of language is the liberation of language for its power to *mean*".[232] "Radical hermeneutics", as Raschke names the process, aims to liberate "semantic potentials" from the written text.[233] The upshot is to reach a conclusion at variance with that of Derrida, and which reflects aspects of Ricoeur, Gadamer, and Heidegger. "Theology becomes dialogy."[234] Language is to be rescued from the "I-It" relationship of sign-systems ... All signs are idols ... The Word of God must be released from its tutelage to the written letter. Dialogue does not take place between words, but between living persons. Such is the eschatological significance of the theology of the *logos* become flesh."[235] By contrast, in Derrida "the primal voice is mute. One can only write and re-write. Although he does not seem explicitly to allude to Derrida's Jewish roots, Raschke concludes: "Derrida's method, therefore, is pre-eminently Talmudic."[236]

As a final example we may briefly note that Derrida himself expresses a special interest in apocalyptic and in the Johannine Apocalypse. The emphasis here, he urges, is on process and promise: "Be awake ... I shall come to you" (Rev. 3:1–3). What appeals to Derrida is that "Nothing is less conservative than the apocalyptic genre: apocryptic, apocryphal, masked, coded ... " It flows on subversively "by its very tone, the mixing of voices, genres, codes ... "[237] It thereby misleads the vigilance of the Roman establishment, to establish a different vigilance. Its complex language, embodying allusions to allusions and interpretations of interpretations constitutes, like music, a "tonality", a "tonal network". In parallel with his own "Living On"/"Border Lines", Derrida claims, the repetitive invitation "Come" (Rev. 6: 3,5,7; 17: 1; 21:9; 22:17) launches repercussions, echoes, resonances, and movements. This is "apocalyptic tone". We need not be surprised at Derrida's interest in the Johannine Apocalypse. He writes: "A text is a text only if it conceals, from the first glance, from the first comer, the law of its composition and the rule of its game."[238]

7. Further Philosophical Evaluations and Critiques of Deconstructionism, Some in Dialogue with Wittgenstein

We offer four general conclusions to add to the observations which we have already made in this chapter. The first is a brief acknowledgement that the value of post-modern theories of textuality is not entirely negative for biblical interpretation. The remaining three concluding observations constitute serious criticism of deconstructionism. Part of the discussion is in conversation with the later Wittgenstein. But in this section I am not concerned with expository details of Wittgensteinian interpretation, which I consider elsewhere. The points are put forward in this section not as an exposition of Wittgenstein, but as a way of formulating some of the difficulties involved in deconstructionist philosophy.

(1) The journey undertaken in this chapter has not been entirely negative. The philosophical problems left by Peirce about the relation between social habit and logic still need further clarification, and the conceptual tools given to us by Saussure and developed in more recent semiotic theory remain indispensable for questions concerning meaning, code, and text. Roland Barthes's suspicious questions about the codes embodied in cultural traditions remain an important component in the basic model of a hermeneutic of suspicion, and this remains closely relevant to a variety of approaches in socio-critical hermeneutics, including those of Marxist, feminist, and black theologies.

Crossan's work on the parables of Jesus and on the relations between different biblical traditions is primarily but not exclusively iconoclastic. He questions the complacent assumption that we can somehow "finish" reading a biblical text. His work on parable, on aphorism, and on inter-textual relations between different biblical traditions all have a positive place in biblical interpretation. Clines's deconstructionist approach to Job reveals otherwise unnoticed features in the text. Mere *interpretations* of texts can themselves take on the status of controlling paradigms in our lives, which, when they become both all-powerfully directive and unchallengeably "for-ever fixed" begin to assume a quasi-idolatrous role, as securities in which we place *absolute* trust. Illusions need to be dispelled, and where a doctrine or an interpretation rests entirely on a metaphor, the metaphorical basis of thought and action needs to be explored. Wittgenstein speaks of: "a whole cloud of philosophy condensed into a drop of grammar."[240] The metaphor of the text as movement or as growing texture, rather than a fixed and static entity, calls attention to the capacity of biblical texts to lead us ever further on; not to let us rest in the illusion that by once reading them we have completed a finished journey, as if we had "mastered" them. Wittgenstein's comment about language-utterances in his *Culture and Value* apply to some biblical texts: "There are remarks that sow, and remarks that reap."[241]

This model has firmly to be qualified, however, and cannot be a comprehensive paradigm of textuality, especially in the case of the biblical texts. Even if we grant the role played by what Michael Fishbane calls "inner-biblical" relations and dynamics, or the play of forces which arise from intertextuality, this is not the whole story. What are the implications of the claim of the earliest Christian communities that in Jesus Christ, words spoken to earlier generations in "partial and piecemeal ways" had now achieved a definitive, final, or eschatological status? Jacob Neusner expresses a preference for the post-modern metaphor of "texture" or "web of a loom" for Talmudic texts, where Shamma Friedman had spoken of their "stratification".[242] In his collection *Ways of Reading the Bible* (1981) Michael Wadsworth makes some parallel points. But can the message of the New Testament be said to be in any sense eschatological, or to embody a Christological truth-criterion, if textuality, rather than the ongoing interpretation of texts, is governed by the metaphor of process and flux? In our sections on socio-pragmatic hermeneutics and on Fish's reader-response theory, we resist the conclusion that disclosure and critique cannot come from *outside* given communities as they wrestle with texts, as if interpretation were *only* a product of their social history.

(2) We must distinguish here between world-view and *method*. If we grant that meaning does not reside in simple referential relations between language-components and the extra-linguistic world, and if we grant that hermeneutics entails interpretations of interpretations of texts, why should this give rise either to the notion of an infinite chain of signs, or to an infinity of layers of metalanguage or code? Even if we were to accept the view of language formulated by Heidegger, we might still in theory select the philosophical option of following Hubert Dreyfus, for example, within this framework and ground the signs in a pre-linguistic realm of *shared practices*. Dreyfus's "holism" substitutes shared practices for an inter-linguistic "play of differences".[243] The "post-modern turn", as Richard Palmer comments seeks to move beyond human subjectivity and consciousness, and the theory that a semiotic system can generate meaning without references to the judgment of a human subject seems at first sight to allow just such a move.[244] But there is a fatal flaw: the system, *langue* remains potential and abstract until it is activated in *parole* which presupposes *human choice and judgment*.

We have argued that Saussure's notion, and that of his successors, of the "arbitrariness of the sign", his distinction between *langue* and *parole*, and his category of "difference", do no more than open up the *possibility* of post-modern theory and only when it is *combined with a world view based on Freudian and Nietzschean suspicion, and the "re-reading" of Western philosophy* undertaken by the later Heidegger. However, the *use of a hermeneutic of suspicion as a method* is an entirely different matter from the *transformation of the principle of suspicion into a world-view*. In chapter X we see this principle recognized in Paul Ricoeur's use of Freudian methods, while he rejects a Freudian *world-view*. The parallel would be for a specialist in the physical sciences to transform the legitimate and necessary *use* of positivist or *scientific method* into a positivist or *scientific world-view*. But this is the transformation which deconstructionists have imposed on semiotic theory. A linguistic model which genuinely applies as a *method* to language has become the model for a *world-view* which *equates* language and reality.

It does not escape the difficulty when deconstructionists make two standard counter-moves. The first is to claim that since all our *perceptions are linguistic* we cannot step outside language; therefore language *constitutes* our reality. But this is like the argument on which the philosophy of solipsism is based: all I can know are my own states of mind; therefore I have no grounds for believing in anything except my own states of mind. If epistemological solipsism is turned into ontological solipsism, i.e. a *world-view*, the conclusion is offered that my own states of mind *constitute* all there is of reality. The critic cannot logically *prove to me* that he or she is not a projection of my mind, although he or she knows that this is not the case. When Crossan says, "we swim in language like fish in the sea", at one level this is no more philosophically informative than affirming that "we swim in the sea of our own states of mind". To *both* kinds of statements Wittgenstein responds that what the solipsist or the philosopher of language *means* here is correct, but the affirmation neither really *helps* or makes a *constructive* point, because it is difficult to see how either proposition influences the realities of life in the inter-subjective world of human conduct and practices. As this book goes to press, it is announced that Don Cupitt is publishing a work on theology which draws on arguments concerning the linguistic nature of our perceptions, and our place within intra-linguistic textuality, arguing for a reduction of the sense of theology to such a realm. We shall explicate the difficulties of such a view in chapters XIV – XVI.

Wittgenstein's "answer" (though he would not have called it that) to *both* philosophical dilemmas which are of the same kind lay in his exposition of the necessity for *public criteria of meaning*. Once we see how language actually *engages* with the intersubjective world, we have found a way of cashing our linguistic paper money into something more solid. The problem about debates between Realists and Solipsists (or, in the present instance with those who equate reality-as-we-have-access-to-it with the strictly intra-linguistic world) is that "one party attack the normal form of expression as if they were attacking a statement; the others defend it, as if they were stating facts recognized by every reasonable human being."[245]

But, as Wittgenstein declares in *Zettel*, "How words are understood is not told by words alone."[246]

The second counter-move by Derrideans is to deny that a Nietzschean scepticism provides a *world-view* as such since Nietzsche is no more than a channel for a flow of perspectives and questions which are radically "re-read" first by the later Heidegger and then by other readers. But is this theory of texts-as-processes the cause or the effect of deconstructionism? Does this theory stand on its own feet, or is it a semiotically-disguised version of the standard philosophical move which addresses the so-called "paradox of scepticism": how do I know that I do not know? As we saw clearly in our discussion of Mark Taylor's work, the Derridean move is *not* the traditional one, in the sense that, rather than operate within the inherited frame of assertion or denial, the post-modern perspective rests on distinctions between layers of meta-languages (systems below or within systems; texts dependent on other texts; interpretations of interpretations of interpretations) which dissolve this frame. This allows ground-rules to be changed so that normal assertions and denials no longer have the character of assertions or denials.

(3) A further key difficulty is the loss of the role of the "speaking subject" in Derrida and Barthes. As we have noted, this represents a key characteristic of the "post-modern turn", to use Palmer's term. Once again, it does not do justice to Saussure's original model to conceive of language as network of systems (*langue* or even idiolects) the possibilities of which do fail to become concretely actualized in events of *parole* which result from *conscious judgments* on the part of speakers. On this particular point E.D. Hirsch's interpretation of Saussure together with the incisive argument of Tallis, is entirely correct.[247] Even the theoretical construct of some new emerging system which is generated as a *meta*-system cannot but grow out of specific uses and habits of *parole* which represents earlier choices of human judgment. Admittedly the network provides the basis for the *possibility* of the judgment and conditions it; but, Wittgenstein observes: "Every sign by itself seems dead. *What* gives it life? In use it is *alive*."[248] It is tempting, Wittgenstein notes, to think that in understanding an order, for example, there is "nothing but sounds, ink-marks. . . . As if the signs were precariously trying to produce understanding in us. . . . Here it is easy to get into that dead-end in philosophy . . . having to describe phenomena that are hard to get hold of, the present experience that slips quickly by."[249] How, for example, does an arrow "point"? "'No, not the dead line on paper'; . . . The arrow points only in *the application that a living being makes of it.*" "*Only in the stream of thought and life* do words have meaning."[250]

In Wittgenstein's later philosophy this is no merely simplistic return to a notion of meanings as "entities", nor are they "mental events", nor processes of reference within a world in which "thought" and "world" are other than linguistic, in the sense that we cannot "step outside" what is shaped by language. But language abstracted from the speaking subject and from *inter-subjective judgments and practices* has neither stability nor purchase-power. Without public criteria of meaning, I can only evaluate meanings in terms of my own meaning-assumptions, which is the same "as if someone were to buy several copies of the morning paper to assure himself that what it said was true."[251] Language abstracted from patterns of life and judgment in the inter-subjective world is like "a wheel that can be turned though nothing else moves with it is not part of the mechanism."[252]

Language does indeed presuppose patterns, regularities, or "rules" of a system; but unless a human being makes a judgment about their *application* (Wittgenstein's *Anwendung*; cf. Saussure's *parole*) within a context of inter-subjective life, then: "here the rules would really hang in the air; for the institution of their use (*Anwendung*) is lacking."[253] Rules about the interpretation of rules do not entail, as they do for Roland Barthes, an infinite series of meta-languages, but, as they do for Wittgenstein and Gadamer a pattern of linguistic experience and critical judgment which can be called "training" (*Abrichtung*).[254] To inherit a language-system is like having the chess pieces set out on the chess-board. But the speech-act or *parole* results from a judgment, like moving a piece on the board. We have noted Wittgenstein's comment: "Naming is so far not a move in the language-game - any more than putting a piece in its place on the board is a move in chess."[255]

Karl-Otto Apel is profoundly aware of the genuine relationship between semiotic theory and the elements in post-modern thought which must be taken seriously. As "a self-reflexive medium" and as "a meta-institution", he concedes, language "represents the instance of criticism for all unreflected social norms and, at the same time, as the meta-*institution* of all institutions" it carries the individual beyond "their merely subjective reasoning."[256] This is the kind of point which Barthes and most post-modernists would wish to make. But, Apel continues, this "compels them to participate in intersubjective communication or social norms." This socio-critical hermeneutic presupposes community and that linguistic signs are related "to possible praxis and possible experience." Pragmatic semiotics entails both interactive judgments related to social life and "the undeniable reference of interpretation to a human subject who is himself historical."[257]

A significant participant is this particular debate about human agents or subjects, largely because she is in other respects relatively close to Derrida, is Julia Kristeva (b. 1941). She left her native Bulgaria to study linguistics and semiotics in Paris, and was taught by Roland Barthes. Following Jacques Lacan, she combined a post-structuralist, post-modernist approach to semiotics with psychoanalytical Freudian methods and models. Her re-instatement of "the speaking subject" into semiotics, in contrast to

Derrida's approach, reflects her concerns about relations between language and the human body, and leads to what amounts to foundations for sociology of literature.[258]

Julia Kristeva does not return in any way to traditional notions of the author behind a text. Texts have not "authors", but a "writing subject". We have already noted that intertextuality becomes a key concept for her. The "writing subject" brings to the text unconscious modes of being as well as conscious production or response. Julia Kristeva shares with Barthes the view that semiotics can unmask cultural, literary, and political ideologies hidden in language. She observes "No form of semiotics can exist other than as a critique of semiotics".[259] But in her book *Revolution in Poetic Language* she distinguishes between the semiotic and the symbolic as, in effect, bio-physical and sociological preconditions of language. Bio-socio-physical drives "displace and condense both energies and their inscription."[260] "Drives" cause "energies" to flow through the body, and leave "marks" which are bio-socially conditioned by primitive relationships, especially that between mother and infant. The symbolic is a *social* effect.[261]

Julia Kristeva follows Barthes and Derrida in viewing texts as expanding, unfinished, textures. But the system *also* entails the "speaking *subject*".[262] It would not be legitimate to claim that her work questions deconstructionism in post-modernism. But what it achieves, for critical evaluation, is to show that in the end some kind of operational purchase is needed between language and bio-socio-physical embodiment. From this it is a shorter distance to travel to Wittgenstein's public world of behaviour, or to Habermas and Apel on communicative interaction.

(4) We turn, finally, to the notion of "textual play". Music can be endlessly played and enjoyed, without our necessarily asking about the conscious horizons and situation of the composer. No doubt some examples of fictional literature, especially poetic literature, fall into this category. But it becomes an entirely different matter if we place biblical texts (or at least the overwhelming majority of biblical texts) within the boundaries of this model. The same difficulty applies to most philosophical texts, theological texts and biographical, legal and historical texts. Yet many deconstructionist writers seem to extend this model as if it constituted a *general* theory of texts as such.

On the question of the status of biblical texts, it is worth noting the strength of conviction with which the well-known biblical scholar Amos N. Wilder expresses reservations about recent literary and semiotic theory. This is all the more striking because Wilder's comments appeared in 1982, one year after J.D. Crossan, whose enthusiasm for deconstructionism we have noted, published the volume *A Fragile Craft: the Work of Amos Wilder* in which he congratulated Wilder on his venturesome hospitality to literary theory in biblical interpretation. Wilder's work, Crossan claims, is "structural and relational rather than substantial and objectional."[263] In this light, Wilder's comments must have had the quality of a bombshell. Wilder warns: "By a kind of irony, some have been 'overconverted' to a literary approach . . . The point is that 'what is written' in this case of texts like these (i.e. the Gospels including the parables) is profoundly *referential* and does not belong only to some detached 'story world'".[264]

Wilder continues to make this point with reference to the use of both formalist and deconstructionist models in biblical interpretation. He writes: "I urge that the biblical rhetorics, even the most figurative, have a certain robust quality because like the prophetic oracles . . . or the parables of Jesus they are rooted in dense empirical actuality . . . Here one tendency, encouraged by 'deconstruction' theory and its open view of signs and signifiers, and stressing the aspect of plurivalence, is to extract the parables from this historical context . . . to relate them . . . to modern literary or oriental paradoxes and riddles. Thus their import may be identified with some supposed iconoclastic wisdom."[265] What we miss here, Wilder asserts, is the historical and cosmic transformation evoked by Jesus, and the rootedness of his words and work in time and place. He concludes: "a recurrent error in literary criticism is that which would assimilate the literary arts to the non-referential art of music . . . The authorised urgency and realism are lost sight of when the 'fictional world' is thus assigned autonomy". Where there is biblical language, even symbols, "all are anchored in and controlled by this personal and historical realism . . . Above all, there can be no question – with our deconstructionists – of 'decentering' the discourse." The biblical witness was "not by word alone . . . the witness in word was inseparable from the witness in action and behaviour."[266]

On the broader question of textuality as such a number of standard criticisms have been expressed. Frank Lentricchia, for example, points out that a theoretical rejection of criteria in practice seems to bring back a criterion of pleasure, or ethical hedonism.[267] It may be granted that Derrida does not view deconstructionism as "a method".[268] But if *some* texts are read for the joy of reading, or *some* biblical texts inspire celebration, there is no ground for elevating this principal to a *universal*, least of all on the basis of a philosophy that allows for no universal. In his "Structure, Sign and Play", Derrida writes that while one interpretation of interpretation "concerns truth", the other reflects Nietzsche's "joyous affirmation of the play of the world . . . without truth."[268] One cannot "choose", he urges, between these; fate, in effect, imposes the criticism of pleasure.[270]

In his influential book *Contest of Faculties: Philosophy and Theory after Deconstruction* Christopher Norris makes two complementary points about this emphasis. There is an "unsettling co-existence", he argues, especially in Paul de Man, between "a rhetoric of textual *undecidability* and a constant demand for *logical* precision". He adds: "What complicates matters in de Man's case is the insistence that each reading must 'undo' the other."[271] This sheds light, in his view, on one of the problems raised by the acceptance of Derrida's *philosophical* beliefs in American *literary* circles. Norris rightly comments: "Clearly there are pressing institutional motives for this readiness among literary critics to accept the broader drift of Derrida's arguments. It is agreeable to be told, after all, – and on good 'philosophical' authority – that criticism is not just a poor relation of philosophy but possesses the rhetorical means to dismantle philosophy's claims to truth. But there remains a great difference between Derrida's scrupulous thinking of these issues and the way that his *conclusions* are taken as read by many of his American admirers." [272] Norris argues that Derrida's notion of textual play is more complex than mere "interpretative licence".[273]

Leith and Myerson use "play" to mean only that an utterance will always go beyond the conscious control of the speaker or writer, and there will thus be 'looseness' or play of meaning, in the sense of a mechanical "play" between loose parts.[274] On the other hand in Julia Kristeva's play (*jouissance*) becomes an umbrella term for liberated spiritual and sexual ecstasy, derived as a model from Jacques Lacan's psychological analytical approach. But, as Wittgenstein observes, *some* language-uses operate with blurred edges; others, not. In Umberto Eco's terms, some texts are transmissive and communicative; others, productive and polyvalent. If *all* texts are subsumed under the model of play, texts no longer function as a basis for rational action. The very egalitarianism which, in some socio-literary circles, withdrew "privilege" from authors and from "trained" interpreters, threatens to dissolve into the anarchy and instability in which texts might equally well give rise to quite different courses of action, or equally again suggest inaction. From their own particular political perceptive, Louis Althusser and Terry Eagleton press this kind of point.

David Tracy rightly complains that in such a context it is difficult even to engage in fruitful conversation: "The conversation stops."[275] Roger Lundin, with whom I worked very closely for a year at Calvin College, Grand Rapids, charts what he calls "the retreat from action to pleasure" in literary and aesthetic theory.[276] He traces the role of philosophical, theological, and political factors which have led to the isolation of the criterion of "pleasure", and to the setting up of artificial and unnecessary alternatives between the didactic, the aesthetic, and the pragmatic. To isolate one single goal is a symptom of being trapped within one particular philosophical and aesthetic tradition. By contrast, the biblical texts transcend any single goal: they teach, but they also invite us to celebrate with joy the deeds and reign of God. They make truth-claims about the world and reality; but they also make us uncomfortable recipients of judgment and comfortable recipients of grace. They subvert our idols, but they also address us, heal us, build us, and transform us. Any theory of textuality which cannot make room for these textual functions cannot be given a paradigmatic place in biblical interpretation.

NOTES TO CHAPTER III

1. Cf. John M. Court, *Myth and History in the Book of Revelation*, London: S.P.C.K., 1979, especially 45–59, 82–7, 91–105 and 164–69; George B. Caird, *The Language and Imagery of the Bible*, London: Duckworth, 1980, 250–71; G.R. Beasley-Murray, *The Book of Revelation*, London: Oliphants 1974, 16–17.
2. Julia Kristeva, *Revolution in Poetic Language*, Eng, New York: Columbia University Press, 1984, 59–60 (her italics).
3. John M. Court, *op. cit.*; 85–7. Cf. G.R. Beasley-Murray *op. cit.*, 181–82, and John Sweet, *Revelation*, London: S C M 1979, 183.
4. Roland Barthes, *Elements of Semiology*, Eng. London: Jonathan Cape, 1967, 13–28; Cf. *Mythologies*, Eng. London: Jonathan Cape, 1972 *passim*. .
5. Umberto Eco, "Social Life as a Sign System" in David Robey (ed) *Structuralism. An Introduction*, Oxford: Clarendon Press, 1973, 57, 59; Cf. 57–72.
6. Roland Barthes, *Elements of Semiology* 92.
7. Julia Kristeva, "From Symbol to Sign" rp. in Toril Moi (ed.) *The Kristeva Reader*, New York: Columbia University Press, 1986, 79.
8. In addition to *Elements of Semiology* and *Mythologies* cf. Roland Barthes, *S/Z* Eng. London: Jonathan Cape, 1975, and *The Pleasure of the Text* Eng. London: Jonathan Cape, 1976.
9. John Lyons, *Introduction to Theoretical Linguistics*, Cambridge: Cambridge University Press 1968, 38.
10. Ferdinand de Saussure, *Course in General Linguistics*, Eng. London: Owen, 1960, 68; *Cours de linguistique générale* (*édition critique* by R. Engler, Wiesbaden: Harasowitz 1967, 152–53.
11. *Ibid* 114 (*édition critique*) Fasc, 2, 259.
12. Jacques Derrida, *Speech and Pheonomena, and Other Essays on Husserl's Theory of Signs*. Eng. Evanston: North Western University Press, 1973, 129–60.
13. Robert S. Corrington, *The Community of Interpreters: On the Hermeneutics of Nature and the Bible in the American Philosophical Tradition*, Macon Ga: Mercer University Press, 1987, 1–29.
14. *Ibid* 2, 16.
15. Ferdinand de Saussure, *op. cit.* 68 (*édition critique*, 152–3) .
16. *Ibid* 110.
17. *Ibid* 114.
18. Anthony C. Thiselton, "Semantics and New Testament Interpretation" in I.H Marshall (ed.) *New Testament Interpretation*, Grand Rapids: Eerdmans, and Exeter: Paternoster Press, 1977, 75–104, especially 79–89.
19. Charles S. Peirce, *The Collected Papers of Charles Sanders Peirce*, (eds. Charles Hartshorne and Paul Weiss) Cambridge, Mass.: Harvard University Press, 1934–36, vol.2, 248; cf. especially 227–92.

20. *Ibid* vol. 2, 249.
21. Charles W. Morris, *Writings on the General Theory of Signs*, The Hague: Mouton, 1971 (includes *Foundations of the Theory of Signs* (1938) and *Signs, Language, and Behaviour*, 1946), 6 and 219.
22. Cf. Sándor Hervey, *Semiotic Perspectives*, London: Allen and Unwin 1982, 38–58.
23. Leonard Bloomfield, *Language*, London, Allen & Unwin 1935 (1933); B.F. Skinner, *Verbal Behaviour*, New York: Appleton Crofts, 1957; W.V.O. Quine, *Word and Object*, Cambridge, Mass.: M.I.T. Press, 1960; Richard Rorty, *Philosophy and the Mirror of Nature*, Princeton: Princeton University Press, 1980 (1979); Norman N. Holland, *Five Readers Reading*, New Haven: Yale University Press, 1975; *Poems in Persons: An Introduction to the Psychoanalysis of Literature*, New York: Norton, 1973; and "Transactive Criticism: Re-Creation through Identity", *Criticism* 18, 1976, 334–52; and Stanley Fish *op. cit.*.
24. Robert S. Corrington, *op. cit.* 15.
25. John Dominic Crossan, "Difference and Divinity" in Robert Detweiler (ed.) *Derrida and Biblical Studies, Semeia* 23, 1982, 38; cf. 29–40 .
26. Carl A. Raschke, *The Alchemy of the Word: Language and the End of Theology*, Missoula: Scholars Press, 1979 (A.A.R. Studies in Religion 20) 67.
27. *Ibid* 17.
28. Mark C. Taylor, *Deconstructing Theology*, New York: Crossroad, and Chico: Scholars Press, 1982 (A.A.R. Studies in Religion 28) xiv and 99.
29. David Harvey, *The Condition of Postmodernity*, Oxford: Blackwell, 1989, 9.
30. Karl-Otto Apel, *Towards a Transformation of Philosophy*, Eng, London: Routledge & Kegan Paul, 1980, 80; Christopher Norris, *Deconstruction. Theory and Practice*, London: Methuen, 1982, xii. .
31. Karl-Otto Apel, *op. cit.*, 111 .
32. *Ibid* 123 .
33. *Ibid* .
34. *Ibid* 110 .
35. Ludwig Wittgenstein, *Philosophical Invertigations* sect. 241 and 242 .
36. Karl-Otto Apel, *op. cit.*, 110 .
37. Sándor Hervey, *Semiotic Perspectives*, London: Allen and Unwin, 1982, 37 (cf.17–37); John Lyons, *Semantics* vol.1, 99; Terence Hawkes, *Structuralism and Semiotics* London: Methuen 1977, 130.
38. J. Trier, *Der Deutsche Wortschatz im Sinnbezirk des Verstandes*, Heidelberg: Winter, 1931, 6.
39. Claude Lévi-Strauss, *Structural Anthropology*, Eng. London and New York: Basic Books 1963, 62.
40. *Ibid*.
41. Julia Kristeva, *Revolution in Poetic Language*, 72.
42. Cf. the criticism of Dan Sperber in John Sturrock (ed.) *Structuralism and Since: From Lévi Strauss to Derrida*, Oxford: Oxford University Press, 1979, 23–25. .
43. Claude Lévi-Strauss, *op. cit.* 210.
44. Edmund Leach, "Structuralism in Social Anthropology" in David Robey (ed.) *Structuralism. An Introduction*, Oxford: Clarendon Press, 1973, 38–39; cf. 37–56; Robert Scholes, *Structuralism in Literature*, New Haven: Yale University Press, 1974, 71–72; Frank Lentricchia, *After the New Criticism*, Chicago: Chicago University Press, 1980, 128–29.

45. Northrop Frye, *The Great Code. The Bible and Literature*, New York and London: Harcourt Brace Jovanovich, 1982, xiii.
46. Erhardt Güttgemanns, *Candid Questions Concerning Gospel From Criticism*, Eng. Pittsburgh: Pickwick Press, 1979, 59–63; "Generative Poetics" in *Semeia* 6, 1976, 3–8, 197–201; and "'Text' und 'Geschichte' als Grundkategorien der Generativen Poetik", *Linguistica Biblica* 11–12, 1972, 2–12.
47. E. Güttgemanns, *Semeia* 6, 1976, 2.
48. E. Güttgemanns, *Candid Questions*, 60.
49. D.W. Fokkema and Elrud Kunne-Ibsch, *Theories of Literature in the Twentieth Century*, London: Hurst, 1978, 56; and Philip Dwyer, *Sense and Subjectivity. A Study of Wittgenstein and Merleau-Ponty*, Leiden: Brill, 1990, 1–47.
50. Roland Barthes, *Criticism and Truth*, Eng. Minneapolis: University of Minnesota Press, 1987, 46–49; cf. *Writing Degree Zero*, Eng. London: Jonathan Cape, 1967.
51. Roland Barthes, *Mythologies*, Eng. London: Jonathan Cape, 1972, 91–93.
52. *Ibid* 116.
53. *Ibid* 15–25.
54. *Ibid* 11.
55. *Ibid* 116.
56. *Ibid* 120.
57. Roland Barthes, *Elements of Semiology*, Eng. London: Jonathan Cape 1967, 25–30, 58–88.
58. *Ibid* 68.
59. *Ibid* 79, 81.
60. *Ibid* 77.
61. *Ibid* 81, 82.
62. Ferdinand de Saussure, *op. cit.* 15, 16.
63. Fredric Jameson, *The Political Unconscious. Narrative as a Socially Symbolic Act*, Ithaca: Cornell University Press, 1981, 10.
64. Sándor Hervey, *op. cit.* 152.
65. Frank Lentricchia, *op. cit.* 130.
66. Roland Barthes, *Criticism and Truth*, 39.
67. *Ibid* 67, 71.
68. *Ibid* 72.
69. Roland Barthes, *Elements of Semiology*, 92.
70. *Ibid* 93.
71. *Ibid*.
72. D. W. Fokkema and Elrud Kunne-Ibsch, *Theories of Literature in the Twentieth Century. Structuralism, Marxism, Aesthetics of Reception, Semiotics*, 56.
73. Robert Detweiler, *Story, Sign and Self. Phenomenology and Structuralism as Literary-Critical Methods*, Philadelphia: Fortress, and Missoula: Scholars Press, 1978, 17.
74. Roland Barthes, *On Racine*, Eng. New York: Hill and Wang, 1964, 162.
75. Roland Barthes, *Introduction to the Structural Analysis of Narrative,*. Communications 8, 1966, 3; cf. 1–27.
76. John Sturrock, *Structuralism and Since: From Levi-Strauss to Derrida*, Oxford: Oxford University Press, 1979, 67, 69.
77. Roland Barthes, *S/Z*, Eng. London: Jonathan Cape, 1975, 13.
78. *Ibid* 14–21.

79. Roland Barthes, "From Work to Text" in Josué V. Harari (ed.) *op. cit.* 74.
80. *Ibid* 75.
81. *Ibid* 76.
82. *Ibid*.
83. *Ibid* 78; and Roland Barthes, *The Pleasure of the Text*, London: Jonathan Cape, 1975.
84. Roland Barthes, "From Work to Text", 80.
85. Roland Barthes, *The Pleasure of the Text*, 27.
86. Roland Barthes, *Elements of Semiology* 24.
87. James Schmidt, *Maurice Merleau-Ponty. Between Phenomenology and Structuralism*, London: MacMillan, 1985, 105–111.
88. *Ibid* 106.
89. *Ibid* 105, 107, and 108.
90. Roland Barthes, *Elements of Semiology* 93.
91. T.K. Seung, *Structuralism and Hermeneutics*, New York: Columbia University Press, 1982, 125.
92. Raymond Tallis, *Not Saussure. A Critique of Post-Saussurean Literary Theory*, London: MacMillan, 1988, 83–96, 211–13 *et passim*.
93. Jonathan Culler, *The Pursuit of Signs. Semiotics, Literature, Deconstruction*, London: Routledge and Kegan Paul, 1981,103.
94. Ludwig Wittgenstein, *Philosophical Investigations* sect.202 .
95. *Ibid* sect. 49.
96. *Ibid* sect. 115.
97. *Ibid* sect. 109.
98. *Ibid* sects. 140, 146, 374, 422–26, and p.11.
99. *Ibid* sect. 132.
100. Benjamin L. Whorf, *Language, Thought and Reality: Selected Writings of Benjamin Lee Whorf*, ed. J.B. Carroll, Cambridge, Mass.: M.I.T. Press, 1956, 212–14.
101. Eugene A. Nida, "The Implications of Contemporary Linguistics for Biblical Scholarship" *J.B.L.* 91, 1972, 73–89; Max Black, "Linguistic Relativity: The Views of Benjamin Lee Whorf", *Philosophical Review* 68, 1959, 228–38; David Crystal, *Linguistics, Language and Religion*, London: Burns and Oates 1965,John Lyons, *Semantics* vol.1, 245–50, and *Structural Semantics: An Analysis of Part of the Vocabulary of Plato*, Oxford: Blackwell, 1969, 39–44.
102. B. Berlin and P. Kay, *Basic Color Terms*, Berkley: University of California Press, 1969.
103. Anthony C. Thiselton, *The Two Horizons*, 136–39, and "Semantics and New Testament Interpretation" in I.H. Marshall (ed) *op. cit.* 75–104.
104. Andreas Huyssen, *After the Great Divide. Modernism, Mass Culture, Post-Modernism*, Bloomington: Indiana University Press, 1986, 217.
105. Jacques Derrida, *Of Grammatology* Eng. Baltimore London: Johns Hopkins University Press, 1976, 40 and 41.
106. Jacques Derrida "Living On/Border Lines" in *Deconstruction and Criticism* 84.
107. Guyatri C. Spivak, "Translator's Preface" to *Of Grammatology*, xxi.
108. Jacques Derrida, *Of Grammatology* 74.
109. *Ibid* 27 and 74–5.
110. *Ibid* 9.
111. *Ibid* 30 (cf. Ferdinand de Saussure, *op. cit.* 45).

112. *Ibid* 35.
113. *Ibid* 40 (Derrida's italics).
114. *Ibid* 43.
115. *Ibid* 45.
116. *Ibid* 48.
117. *Ibid* 49.
118. Jacques Derrida, *Speech and Phenomena and Other Essays on Husserl's Theory of Signs*, 129–60.
119. *Ibid* 130.
120. *Ibid* 135–41.
121. Jacques Derrida, "Positions", *Diacritics* 3, 1973, 39–40; cf. 33–46.
122. Martin Heidegger, *On the Way to Language*, Eng. New York: Harper and Row, 1971, 70; cf. *An Introduction to Metaphysics* Eng. New Haven: Yale University Press, 1959.
123. Mark C. Taylor, *op. cit.* 95; Guyatri Spivak, *loc cit.* xxxii-liv; Christopher Norris, *Deconstruction: Theory and Practice*, London: Methuen 1982, 68–70; John Sallis (ed.) *Deconstruction and Philosophy. The Texts of Jacques Derrida*, Chicago: University of Chicago Press, 1987, xii-xv, 34–5; 161–96 Richard Rand, in Jacques Derrida, *Signéponge*, New York: Columbia University Press, 1984, x, David Couzens Hoy, *The Critical Circle. Literature, History, and Philosophical Hermeneutics*, Berkeley: University of California Press, 1982, 78–81.
124. Anthony C. Thiselton, *The Two Horizons*, 143–204 and 327–55.
125. Martin Heidegger, *On the Way to Language*, 30.
126. Martin Heidegger, *An Introduction to Metaphysics*, 36 & 37.
127. *Ibid*.
128. *Ibid* 40.
129. *Ibid* 158.
130. *Ibid* 206 .
131. Martin Heidegger, *On Time and Being*, Eng. New York: Harper and Row, 1972, 30 (my italics).
132. *Ibid* (my italics).
133. *Ibid* (my italics).
134. Martin Heidegger, *On the Way to Language*, 64 .
135. *Ibid* 124.
136. *Ibid* 125.
137. Jacques Derrida, *Speech and Phenomena*, 154.
138. Martin Heidegger, *On the Way to Language* 54.
139. *Ibid* 163.
140. *Ibid* 5, 21.
141. *Ibid* 26.
142. Jacques Derrida, *Of Grammatology* 18.
143. Martin Heidegger, *The Question of Being*, Eng. New York: Vision, 1958, 80; cf. Jacques Derrida, *Of Grammatology* xiv-xvii.
144. G.C. Spivak, *loc. cit.* xvii.
145. Martin Heidegger, *On Time and Being* 8.
146. Jacques Derrida, *The Post Card. From Socrates to Freud and Beyond* Eng. Chicago: University of Chicago Press, 1987, 63; cf. *Writing and Difference* Eng. London: Routledge and Kegan Paul, 1978, 90–92.

147. Jacques Derrida, *Signéponge*, New York: Columbia University Press, 1984, 64–5.
148. *Ibid* 28–9; cf. ix and 157.
149. Jacques Derrida, *The Truth in Painting* Eng. Chicago, University of Chicago Press, 1987, 16, 291–2.
150. Jacques Derrida et al. *The Ear of the Other. Otobiography, Transference, Translation* (ed. C V McDonald) Eng. New York: Schocken Books, 1985, 86.
151. *Ibid* 87.
152. G.V. Spivak, *loc. cit* xxxiii.
153. Jacques Derrida, *Of Grammatology* 19.
154. Jacques Derrida, *Writing and Difference* 281–82.
155. Jacques Derrida, "White Metaphor: Metaphor in the Text of Philosophy", *New Literary History* 6, 1971, 26; cf. 5–74.
156. Friedrich Nietzsche, *Werke* vol.3, Munich: Hanser, 1956, 311.
157. Jacques Derrida, *Writing and Difference* 280.
158. *Ibid* 278–93; cf. Frank Lentricchia, *op. cit.* 169.
159. Jacques Derrida, *Writing and Difference* 279.
160. *Ibid* 292.
161. Jacques Derrida, *Spurs: Nietzsche's Styles*, Eng. Chicago: Chicago University Press, 1972; and "Otobiographies" in *The Ear of the Other* 3–38.
162. Jacques Derrida, "Otobiographies" *loc. cit.* 9 and 29.
163. *Ibid* 31–32.
164. *Ibid* 20.
165. Jacques Derrida, *Speech and Phenomena* 148.
166. Christopher Norris, *Derrida*, London: Fontana 1987, 203–13; G.V. Spivak, *loc. cit.* xxi–xlix.
167. Jacques Derrida, *Writing and Difference*, 199; cf. 196–231 .
168. G.V. Spivak, *loc. cit.* xlvi.
169. Jacques Lacan, *The Four Fundamental Concepts of Psychoanalysis* Eng. London: Penguin edn. 1979; Paul Ricoeur, *Freud and Philosophy: An Essay on Interpretation* Eng. New Haven: Yale University Press, 1970, 93; cf. Julia Kristeva, *Revolution in Poetic Language* Eng. New York: Columbia University Press 1984, 28. and *The Kristeva Reader* 109–111.
170. Jacques Derrida, *Writing and Difference* 199, 221–31.
171. *Ibid* 224.
172. *Ibid* 199 (my italics).
173. *Ibid* 230.
174. Jacques Derrida, "Living On/Border Lines" *loc. cit.* 84.
175. Hilary Lawson, *Reflexivity. The Post-Modern Predicament*, London; Hutchinson 1985, 7; Josué V. Harari (ed.) *Textual Strategies*, 69.
176. Hilary Lawson *op. cit.* 129.
177. Jacques Derrida, "Of an Apocalyptical Tone Recently Adopted in Philosophy" in *Semeia* 23, 1982: *Derrida and Biblical Studies* 63–97.
178. Jacques Derrida, "Living On/Border Lines" *loc. cit.* 94; cf. Jacques Derrida, *De l'esprit: Heidegger et la question*, Paris: Galilée, 1987, 126–29.
179. Geoffrey Hartman, *ibid* vii–viii.
180. Henry Staten, *Wittgenstein and Derrida*, Lincoln and London: University of Nebraska Press 1984, xiv *et passim*.
181. John Dominic Crossan, *In Parables. The Challenge of the Historical Jesus*, New

York: Harper and Row, 1973, 64.
182. *Ibid* 13, 16.
183. Lynn M. Poland, *Literary Criticism and Biblical Hermeneutics: A Critique of Formalist Approaches*, Chicago: Scholars Press, 1985 (A.A.R. Academy Series 48) 108–14.
184. Robert W. Funk, *Language, Hermeneutic and Word of God*, New York: Harper and Row, 1966, xiv; cf. 133–222.
185. J.D. Crossan, *op. cit* xiii.
186. Lynn M. Poland *op. cit.* lll.
187. *Ibid.*
188. John Dominic Crossan, *The Dark Interval. Towards a Theology of Story*, Niles: Argus Communications 1975.
189. *Ibid* 22.
190. *Ibid* 40–41.
191. Lynn Poland, *op. cit.* 116.
192. J.D. Crossan, *The Dark Interval* 121.
193. *Ibid* 57 and 60.
194. John Dominic Crossan, *Raid on the Articulate. Comic Eschatology in Jesus and Borges*, New York: Harper and Row, 1976, xiv.
195. *Ibid* 39–40.
196. *Ibid* 9.
197. *Ibid* 23.
198. *Ibid* 27.
199. *Ibid* 34.
200. *Ibid* 60.
201. *Ibid* 67.
202. *Ibid* 129.
203. *Ibid* 148.
204. *Ibid* 92.
205. John Dominic Crossan, *Finding is the First Act: Trove Folktales and Jesus' Treasure Parable*, Missoula: Scholars Press and Philadelphia: Fortress Press, 1979 (*Semeia Supplements* 9) esp. 104–06.
206. *Ibid* 120 (my italics).
207. John Dominic Crossan, *Cliffs of Fall: Paradox and Polyvalence in the Parables of Jesus*, New York: Seabury Press, 1980; "Waking the Bible", *Interpretation* 32, 1978, 269–85; "A Metamodel for Polyvalent Narration" *Semeia* 9, 1977, 105–47.
208. Lynn M. Poland, *op. cit.* 118–9.
209. *Ibid* 119.
210. Anthony C. Thiselton, "The Parables as Language-Event: Some Comments on Fuchs's Hermeneutics in the Light of Linguistic Philosophy", *Scottish Journal of Theology* 23, 1970, 437–68; cf. and "The New Hermeneutic" in I. H. Marshall (ed.) *New Testament Interpretation*, 323.
211. Mark C. Taylor, "Masking: Domino Effect" in "On Deconstructing Theology: A Symposium on *Erring: a Postmodern A/Theology*", *Journal of the American Academy of Religion* 54, 1986, 553; cf. 547–57; Thomas J.J. Altizer *Ibid* 525–29; T.J.J. Altizer *et al.*, *Deconstruction and Theology*, New York: Crossroad, 1982; and Joseph Prabhu, "The Blessing of the Bathwater", J.A.A.R. *loc. cit.* 534–43,

cf. also Mark C. Taylor, *Erring: A Postmodern A/Theology* Chicago: University of Chicago Press, 1984.
212. J.D. Crossan, "A Metamodel for Polyvalent Narration" *loc. cit.* 108–9.
213. *Ibid* 112.
214. *Ibid* 140.
215. John Dominic Crossan, *Cliffs of Fall* 94.
216. John Dominic Crossan, "A Structuralist Analysis of John 6" in Richard A. Spencer (ed.) *Orientation by Disorientation. Studies in Literary Criticism and Biblical Literary Criticism in Honor of W.A. Bearsdlee* Pittsburgh, Pickwick Press, 1980, 248; cf. 235–49.
217. J.D. Crossan, "Difference and Divinity" *Semeia* 23 1982, 38; cf. 29–40, and J. Derrida, *Speech and Phenomena* 134–35.
218. *Ibid* 38–9.
219. *Ibid.*
220. J.D. Crossan, *Dark Interval* 176.
221. J.D. Crossan "Kingdom and Children: A Study in the Aphoristic Tradition", *Semeia* 29, 1983, 95; cf. 75–95, and *In Fragments. The Aphorisms of Jesus* New York: Harper, 1983.
222. David J.A. Clines, "Deconstructing the Book of Job" in Martin Warner (ed.) *The Bible as Rhetoric. Studies in Biblical Persuasion and Credibility*, London & New York: Routledge, 1990, 65; cf. 65–80.
223. *Ibid* 77.
224. Mark C. Taylor, *Deconstructing Theology*, New York: Crossroad and Chicago: Scholars Press, 1982, 81.
225. *Ibid* 89.
226. Mark C. Taylor, *Erring. A Postmodern A/Theology*, Chicago: University of Chicago Press, 1984, 120.
227. Mark C. Taylor "Masking: Domino Effect" *Journal of the Academy of Religion* 54, 1986, 554. (Taylor's italics).
228. *Ibid.*
229. *Ibid.*
230. P.J. Hartin, "Disseminating the Word: A Deconstructive Reading of Mark 4:1–9 and Mark 4:13–20" in P.J. Hartin and J.H. Petzer (eds.) Text and Interpretation. *New Approaches in the Criticism of the New Testament*, Leiden: Brill, 1991, 195; cf. 187–200; see also P.J. Hartin, "Angst in the Household: A Deconstructive Reading of the Parable of the Supervising Servant (Luke 12: 41–48) "in *Neotestamentica* 22, 1988, 373–90.
231. Carl A. Raschke, *The Alchemy of the Word: Language and the End of Theology*, Missoula: Scholars Press, 1979, 24–29.
232. *Ibid* 43.
233. *Ibid* 66 .
234. *Ibid* 85.
235. *Ibid* 91.
236. *Ibid* 86.
237. Jacques Derrida "Of An Apocalyptic Tone Recently Adopted in Philosophy" *Semeia* 23, 1982, 89–91; cf. 63–97.
238. Jacques Derrida *La Dissemination*, Paris: Seuil, 1972, 71.
239. Anthony C. Thiselton, *The Two Horizons* 357–432, and also below.
240. L. Wittgenstein, *Philosophical Investigations* II xi, 222.

241. Ludwig Wittgenstein, *Culture and Value* Eng. & Germ. 2nd edn. Oxford: Blackwell, 1980, 78e.
242. Jacob Neusner, "Introduction: Metaphor and Exegesis" in *Semeia* 27, 1983, 41 in "Contemporary Exegesis of Talmudic Literature" 37–116.
243. Hubert L. Dreyfus, "Holism and Hermeneutics", *Review of Metaphysics* 34, 1980, 3–55.
244. Richard E. Palmer, "Toward a Postmodern Interpretive Self Awareness", *Journal of Religion* 55, 1975, 313–26, esp. 322. See also Richard E. Palmer, "What are We *Doing* When We Interpret a Text? – Variations on the Theme of Hermeneutic Handeln", *Eros* 7, 1980, 1–45.
245. Ludwig Wittgenstein, *The Blue and Brown Books: Preliminary Studies for the "Philosophical Investigations"* Oxford: Blackwell 1969, 48–49, 57–59, 64, 71; *Philosophical Investigations* sects. 206, 257–309, 402–03, *Zettel*, Germ. and Eng., Oxford: Blackwell 1967, sects. 142–44, 173; *Culture and Value*, 78–79.
246. Ludwig Wittgenstein, *Zettel* sect. 144.
247. E.D. Hirsch, *Validity in Interpretation*, 231–33, cf. Raymond Tallis, *Not Saussure* 65–99 and 205–34.
248. L. Wittgenstein, *Philosophical Investigations* sect. 432. .
249. *Ibid* sect. 436.
250. *Ibid* sect. 454 (my italics) and *Zettel* sect. 173. (my italics).
251. L. Wittgenstein, *Philosophical Investigations* sect. 265. .
252. *Ibid* sect. 271.
253. *Ibid* sect. 380.
254. *Ibid* sect. 86; cf. sects. 5,6,9,143; *Zettel* sects. 186 and 318; Hans-Georg Gadamer, *Truth and Method*, 238–45, cf. 247–78.
255. L. Wittgenstein, *Philosophical Investigations* sect. 49.
256. Karl-Otto Apel, *op. cit.* 119.
257. *Ibid* 124.
258. Julia Kristeva, "The System and the Speaking Subject", *Times Literary Supplement*, 12 Oct, 1973, 1249–52; rp. in *The Kristeva Reader*, 27, cf. 25–32.
259. Julia Kristeva, "From Symbol to Sign" *loc.cit.* 79; cf. 78–80.
260. Julia Kristeva, *Revolution in Poetic Language*, Eng. New York: Columbia University Press, 1984, 25.
261. *Ibid* 29.
262. Julia Kristeva, "The System and the Speaking Subject", *loc. cit.*.
263. John Dominic Crossan, *A Fragile Craft: The Work of Amos Niven Wilder* (S.B. L. Centennial 1980) Chicago: Scholars Press, 1981, 69 & 71.
264. Amos N. Wilder, *Jesus' Parables and the War of Myths. Essays on Imagination in the Scriptures*, Philadelphia: Fortress, 1982, 29.
265. *Ibid* 31.
266. *Ibid* 36 & 37.
267. Frank Lentricchia, *op. cit.* 169.
268. Christopher Norris, *Derrida*, London: Fontana, 1987, 18–19; cf. Robert Detweiler, "Introduction" *Semeia* 23 (*Derrida and Biblical Studies*) 1982, 2.
269. Jacques *Derrida, Writing and Difference* 292.
270. *Ibid* 293.
271. Christopher Norris, *Contest of Faculties: Philosophy and Theory after Deconstruction*, London & New York: Methuen 1985, 75.

272. *Ibid* 73.
273. *Ibid* 220.
274. Dick Leith and George Myerson, *The Power of Address: Explorations in Rhetoric*, London and New York: Routledge, 1989, xii.
275. David Tracy, *Plurality and Ambiguity: Hermeneutics, Religion, Hope*, San Francisco: Harper and Row, 1987, 59.
276. Roger Lundin, Clarence Walhout and Anthony C. Thiselton, *The Responsibility of Hermeneutics*, Grand Rapids: Eerdmans and Exeter: Paternoster, 1985, 14.

CHAPTER IV

Pre-Modern Biblical Interpretation: The Hermeneutics of Tradition

1. Relations between Pre-Modern, Modern, and Post-Modern Perspectives: Some Parallels and Contrasts

It would be a mistake to generalize too readily about the pre-modern era of biblical interpretation. For the Church Fathers and the mediaeval church, not to mention the New Testament itself, embrace a wide variety of approaches to interpretation. The most widely-known point of contrast arises from the very different attitudes towards allegorical intepretation represented on the one hand by Origen (c.186–254) and on the other by Theodore of Mopsuestia (c.350–428) and by John Chrysostom (c.347–407). But there are numerous other points of contrast. The stress on ongoing tradition or the rule of faith (*paradosis, traditio*) as a necessary framework for biblical interpretation is central for Irenaeus (d.202) in his struggle against gnosticism; whereas for Cyprian (d.258) the notion of doctrinal tradition more readily belongs to the Bible itself.

Even more strikingly symptomatic of pre-modern differences is the role of *lectio divina*, or of holy or spiritual reading, especially in mediaeval monastic life. Rupert of Deutz (1070–c.1129) allows gentle contemplation to move amidst a kaleidoscope of ever-changing biblical imagery in a way which almost anticipates the post-modernist notion of textual play. His near-contemporary Anselm of Canterbury (1033–1109) reads the Bible rigorously for exegetical and doctrinal purposes. Some of these differences of approach are due to wider differences of theology and philosophical perspective. Thus Origen, who was perhaps the first to formulate something approaching a theory of biblical interpretation, explains the principles which underlie his use of allegorical interpretation.[1] The reservations of the Antiochene Fathers concerning this method of interpretation may well be due, as Richard Longenecker recently argues, to their "livelier sense of historical development."[2]

In full awareness of these important caveats, however, it is also possible to identify a number of broad characteristics which mark most pre-modern examples of biblical interpretation, and which also offer some instructive points of similarity and difference in relation to modern and post-modern interpretation. Surprisingly the major contrast does not simply lie between pre-modern or "pre-critical" interpretation on the one hand, and modern and post-modern interpretation on the other. In certain respects pre-modern perspectives represent a reversed mirror-image of some post-modernist concerns, where there are both parallels and radical inversions. By way of introduction we suggest three examples.

(1) Modernism, in contrast to both pre-modernism and post-modernism is profoundly individualistic. The rationalism of Descartes typically signals the transition into the modern era. He evolves a system of rationalism by placing the individual thinking self at the centre of thought, and submitting everything else to methodological doubt. This has coloured two centuries of method in biblical interpretation. By contrast, in pre-modern and in post-modern thought the individual belongs to a community in which shared beliefs, practices, conventions, and traditions, decisively shape the individual's understanding. The individual is not a rationally self-sufficient entity.

At this point, however, the paths of pre-modernism and post-modernism radically and sharply diverge. For the pre-modern ecumenical Christian world sees these corporately shared beliefs and practices as testimonies to be respected, as creeds to be revered, and as traditions of faith and conduct to be guarded. In the post-modern world, after Freud, Nietzsche, and Marx, they become merely conventions to be suspected, interests to be unmasked, and myths to be explained and exploded. A hermeneutic of radical suspicion replaces a hermeneutic of potential or initial trust. This does not imply that pre-modern thinkers did not raise critical questions; but that the basic frame of reference within which doubt or questions were expressed remained a fundamentally theological one which, informed by Christology and the creeds, was perceived to deserve at least provisional trust. On the basis of belief in God, *trust* assumes the kind of methodological role which *doubt* assumes for modernism as exemplified in Cartesian rationalism, and which *suspicion* assumes for post-modernism in socio-critical hermeneutics and in deconstructionism.

(2) Pre-modernism and post-modernism both allow more room for the notion of texts as processes and variables than either the concern about didactic ideas in modern rationalism or the expressions of human experience in modern Romanticism. This tentative suggestion must quickly be qualified, however, for much, if not most, biblical interpretation in the Patristic and mediaeval era was undertaken for the purpose of instruction, doctrine, or the evaluation of ideas. Nevertheless, allegorical interpretation allowed texts to generate other levels of meaning. Northrop Frye argues that one of the commonest experiences in reading is "the sense of further

discoveries to be made within the same structure of words."[3] The key to generating new meaning is "a new context in our experience;" but it remains "a single process growing in subtlety and comprehensiveness, not different senses, but different intensities or wider contexts."[4]

Frye alludes to Dante's exemplification of the four "levels" of context and meaning familiar in mediaeval biblical interpretation. He takes as a textual example Ps. 114: 2: "When Israel went forth from Egypt, the house of Jacob from a people of strange language, Judah became his sanctuary, Israel his dominion." The *historical* level of meaning is the immediate extra-linguistic referent: the historical exodus in the time of Moses. Sense-experience is the foundation of knowledge. But the context of Christian experience and doctrine allows a contemplative dimension, which sees an *allegorical* level of meaning in terms of Christ's redemption of the world. There is a pattern or type which transforms the particular or token historical event into something which resonates more broadly. Contemplation, however, gives way to practical application. The *moral* level of meaning is that of a summons to enter into the new inheritance. Finally, we lift our eyes to the ultimate horizon of eternity and future destiny. The *anagogic* level sees the passage as a pointer to the beatific vision, when everything is under God's dominion.

In response to Milton's later "modern" criticism that "no passage of Scripture is to be interpreted in more than one sense", Frye maintains that this fourfold schema is not one of polyvalent meaning in any arbitrary sense, but that which is brought about by a series of widening contexts or horizons, until a final context of ultimacy is achieved. This well illustrates how the pre-modern perspective is both more closely parallel with the post-modern and yet also constitutes a radical inversion of it. On the one hand, Christian theology and tradition provides what amounts to a series of semiotic systems which allow meanings to be generated outside the primary (historical) semiotic system. On the other hand, the series of systems does not stretch to infinity without closure. When Origen criticized the allegorical interpretation of the gnostics, his target was not the use of allegorical interpretation as such, but the borrowing of artificial and arbitrary systems by which to generate meaning.

A still more striking example of parallels and differences between pre-modernism and post-modernism might be suggested by the practice of contemplative *lectio divina* in the monastic life. Gillian Evans offers a comparison between the very different approaches of Rupert of Deutz and Anselm of Canterbury. What most engaged Rupert about the biblical texts was their "myriad pictures counterchanging and reflecting one another in its pages . . . the figurative meanings of Scripture where he found an infinity of subtleties. . . . Everywhere Rupert finds aesthetic satisfaction in Scripture which is inseparable from spiritual understanding . . . a joy in the pleasures of the senses heightened and made spiritual."[6]

This seems at first sight to have a close parallel with the Barthesian and Derridean notions of textuality as joyous play, which we examined in the previous chapter. But if there are parallels, there is also a radical inversion. For we could find no criterion of effectiveness, validity, productiveness, or appropriateness in Barthes and Derrida other than the hedonism of pleasure. But Rupert's contemplation *presupposes a tradition and context in which the goal of "spiritual" reading is well understood.* His "reading community" includes his near-contemporary Anselm who approaches the biblical texts differently from Rupert. Anselm is not attracted to allegorical interpretation, but uses biblical texts sparingly and rigorously in the service of his theological work on the nature of truth and on the incarnation.[7] *Anselm is one of those who helps to shape the framework of tradition within the boundaries of which Rupert can engage in contemplation.* The images and figurative meanings of the biblical writings are thus placed in contexts which constitute, for him, trustworthy frameworks which have both a centre and an ultimacy.

(3) There is one sense of the word "hermeneutics" which applies to reflection on interpretation since the time of the Stoics, Plato, Aristotle, and the rabbis Hillel and Ishmael, and Eliezer. Here hermeneutics entails reflection on the methods of interpretation which will reach a given goal. Thus Plato discussed the Stoics' allegorical interpretation of Homer and Hesiod; and Hillel formulated seven "rules" of interpretation, or devices which allowed extensions and re-applications of the text. In another later sense of the term, however, hermeneutics represents a fully meta-critical evaluation of the foundations, goals, and conditions of possibility for understanding. In this sense the discipline cannot strictly arise until after the emergence of transcendental questions in Kant and his successors. If critical thinking is said to take its rise from Descartes' replacing of trust by doubt in any methodological approach to tradition, hermeneutical thinking follows Kant's work on the limits of thought, and in most traditions also Dilthey's explorations of the role of the social flow of life as a condition for understanding. It also presupposes, as we argue in chapter IX, the critique of language undertaken by such thinkers as Mauthner, Wittgenstein, Gadamer and others. John Caputo distinguishes a further metacritical development in which "radical" hermeneutics stems from Kierkegaard and moves to Derrida. This is what he calls "the great project of hermeneutical trouble-making" which is "only for the hardy."[8]

By contrast with this meta-critical approach, pre-modern theories of interpretation might seem to represent a hermeneutic of innocence. But this is because, in contrast to Cartesian modernism, pre-modernist Christian thinkers realized how much depended on the contextual framework of tradition. The crucial difference is that, whereas in post-modernism the recurring patterns of tradition are viewed as objects of intense suspicion, as devices of power to sanction monarchical, feudal, or bourgeois socio-political values, in the pre-modern ecumenical Christian world the framework remains an object of trust, because it embodies the testimony of the community to the historic apostolic faith as definitively revealed in Christ. Irenaeus, Tertullian, Origen and Augustine did not doubt that a wilful departure from the boundaries of that tradition projected the individual into a sea of uncharted relativism. Both a hermeneutic of trust and a hermeneutic of suspicion equally recognize, as modernist individualism does not, the importance of the trans-individual frame within which understanding and interpretation operate.

At this point, however, care must be taken over what is meant by "tradition". With the exception of Clement of Alexandria, who falls into the gnostic trap of appealing to "secret traditions of true knowledge", the Fathers in general appeal to an ongoing community-testimony to apostolic faith and practice which is both public and testable in the light of truth-criteria of coherence, continuity, and performative endorsement of the common faith.[9] It became an operative frame of reference for biblical interpretation, but it had not yet become the pre-Reformation ecclesial *magisterium*. Virtually all the Fathers, R.P.C. Hanson writes, "regarded the rule as open to being proved from the Bible, but . . . none of them regarded the Bible as open to being supported in its authority by the rule . . . The case for the rule of faith as original, authentic tradition independent of the Bible breaks down."[10] Only with Cyril of Alexandria in the fifth century did the practice fully emerge of placing "proofs from the Fathers" systematically alongside "proofs from Scripture", and this emerged as a polemic in the context of his controversy with Nestorius.[11]

The epistemological status of tradition as a framework which invites trust, but which is also open to revision and question, is most clearly seen in the light of two kinds of comment. The first concerns the origins of tradition in the Old Testament writings, with its re-interpretation within the framework of a tradition in the New. The second arises from Gadamer's comments about the peculiarly negative understanding of tradition in the Enlightenment beginnings of modernism. On the first aspect, C.H. Dodd admirably captures the point at issue when he writes that the biblical traditions are mediated "by a whole community, whose experience through many generations tests, confirms, and revises them . . . We may well turn away from the *narrow scene of individual experience at the moment* to the spacious prospect we command in the Bible . . . Here we trace the long history of a *community which through good fortune and ill tested* their belief in God and experimented too in varieties of belief."[12] Dodd concludes that this pattern of corporate experience and memory helps us "to a true objectivity of judgment... When once the corporate factor in Christian experience is admitted, the factor of historical tradition cannot be excluded." [13]

This introduces the second observation which needs to be made. Hans-Georg Gadamer, perhaps more than any other, has attacked what he calls "the abstract antithesis between tradition and historical research."[14] "Understanding" Gadamer continues, is not so much "an action of one's own subjectivity", but "the placing of oneself within a process of tradition, in which past and present are constantly fused."[15] This tradition or context of understanding colours our "expectation of meaning". The notion of viewing any tradition, context, or community as "authority", which is rejected in modernism, and anathematized in post-modernism, rests, Gadamer urges, on an utterly *rational* principle that some given community, tradition, or persons may actually know more about what we seek to understand than we do. It rests, Gadamer explains, on "an act of reason itself which, aware of its own limitations, accepts that others have better understanding."[16] Authority, in this sense, "has nothing to do with blind obedience."[17]

As Georgia Warnke rightly points out, we may distinguish between two or three issues in Gadamer's argument here.[18] First, interpreting and understanding is related to the principle in Husserl and Heidegger that to interpret something is to see it *as* something. But what we see it *as* often depends on a component which is not "given" in the perception of that object, but rooted in what Searle calls "Background" experience, and Husserl and Heidegger call "horizon" of interpretation. For example, we interpret objects which we may perhaps see from the window of the house as three-dimensional, even though we may be able to see them only in two dimensions. We project anticipated or expected meanings onto these objects. In *theory*, if we were to live by Cartesian criticism or by a hermeneutic of suspicion, we should never give these perceptions the benefit of the doubt, without first checking them, or assuming that some institutional or political authority is trying to deceive us about the view from the window. In *practice* we have no choice but to approach what has to be understood from a given perspective (cf. Heidegger's notions of "pre-viewing" or "conceiving in advance"). Against Descartes, Gadamer believes that all understanding involves projections which arise out of one's situation within ongoing patterns of belief and practice.

This is not to suggest that we should read a post-Gadamerian or post-modern account of tradition into the ideas of tradition held within the Patristic church or the pre-modern period. But it alerts us to the perennial nature of the dilemma in which Irenaeus and other Fathers found themselves when they wanted to assert *both* the importance of a given tradition of faith and practice as a context of understanding for biblical interpretation *and* the arbitrary or irrational nature of the interpretations of their opponents. We shall examine these issues in the modern and post-modern context in chapter IX. Meanwhile we may note that the work of Thomas Kuhn, Paul Feyerabend, and Mary Hesse in the philosophy of science, of Peter Winch, Jürgen Habermas and Karl-Otto Apel in the area of philosophy and the social sciences, have raised radical questions about whether what may be seen to *count* as rational or coherent can be asked in isolation from given "open-systems" of ongoing intersubjective belief and practice.[19]

For many Protestant Christians today the status of "ongoing tradition" poses a genuine and very practical dilemma about the Bible. Confronted with biblical interpretations put forward by minor sects or by major cults, it is tempting to use arguments about "how the mainstream churches understand the Bible". On the other hand, as heirs to the Reformation Protestant Christians also know that if the Bible has no capacity to question the presupposed framework of tradition, we cannot speak of a sharply-focussed "biblical" faith in contrast to what folk-religion makes of the Bible.

2. Tradition as Context of Understanding: the Two Testaments, Gnosticism, and the Relevance of Irenaeus

According to the earliest pre-Pauline formulae or creeds within the New Testament, the Jewish scriptures constitute a definite context of understanding within which the events of the death and resurrection of Jesus Christ are to be interpreted. Thus Paul receives, and in turn transmits, an already-formulated tradition (*paradosis*), which is itself situated within a tradition, "that Christ died for our sins in accordance with the scriptures, that he was buried, that he was raised on the third day in accordance with the Scriptures, and that he appeared to Cephas, then to the twelve" (1 Cor. 15: 3–5). The phrase "in accordance with the scriptures" is not used to isolate and identify some specific predictive passage, but to provide the pattern of divine action and promise which makes the cross and resurrection intelligible as an act of God "for our sins". The Old Testament offers a selected or privileged frame of reference; by implication it excludes such potentially competing frames as that of political martyrdom or tragic miscalculation. Jesus died and was raised not primarily as a martyr or primarily as a political victim, but as the fulfilment of God's purposes already partly disclosed in a pattern of redemptive suffering and vindication which constitutes a theme in the Jewish scriptures.

The earliest event in the life of the post-resurrection Christian church is likewise placed in the context of an interpretative tradition to provide or to facilitate understanding. The phenomena of Pentecost (Acts 2:1–14) receive an interpretation in Peter's speech (Acts 2: 15–21) which utilizes Joel 2: 28–36 as a frame of reference. Similarly on the Emmaus road the risen Christ opens the understanding of the two disciples with whom He is speaking by using as a frame of reference, or context of interpretation, "the law of Moses and all the prophets" (Luke 24:27).

In the case of Paul himself, Ulrich Luz comments: "For Paul, the Old Testament is not in the first place something to understand; but *it itself creates understanding.*"[20] Luz, A.T. Hanson, Richard Longenecker, and most recently J.W. Aageson and D. Moody Smith stress that the hundred or so quotations of the Old Testament which Paul cites mainly in Romans, 1 and 2 Corinthians and Galatians, not only constitute a vital ingredient in his own theology but also do more.[21] The temporal and historical horizon of the Jewish Scriptures unfolds a tradition which is the basis for understanding what God has now done in Christ "when the time had fully come" (Gal. 4:4). The dimensions of understanding set up by the Old Testament traditions are both temporal-historical and corporate. D. Moody Smith convincingly declares: "The integrity of Paul's theology cannot, on these terms, be established against the horizon of the *individual's* existence only".[22] In this sense "one must take seriously Paul's appropriation of the Old Testament and his understanding of it as providing the *framework*, if not the root, of his theology." Paul's "horizon of meaning", Smith concludes, "is a scripturally conceived framework of history over which God rules, and within which his revelation of his purpose may be perceived."[23] Such a framework prohibits a merely individualistic or existential understanding of Paul's message, and embodies a judgment that his use of the Old Testament is much more than an *ad hominem* polemical device for debate with Jewish Christians.

A.T. Hanson stresses some parallel points about the understanding of God and of history; and he also underlines the Christological significance of the use of the Old Testament by Paul and other New Testament writers. He comments: "Paul in fact claimed the Jewish scriptures for Christ and in this respect set a model for the early church ... Without Paul's strong conviction that the scriptures are full of references to Christ, the Christian church might have set off on its career in history without a bible."[24] Of the many instances of the use of frames of reference or contexts of understanding which Hanson suggests, one striking example concerns an understanding of the unexpectedness of God's mode of salvation in Christ, even though the work of Christ represented the climax or centre of God's purposes for Israel and the world. The New Testament writers find the context for understanding the "folly" of the cross (1.Cor. 1:18) in such passages as: "The very stone which the builders rejected has become the head of the corner" (Ps. 118: 22; cf. Luke 20: 17; 1 Pet. 2:7); or: "I will destroy the wisdom of the wise . . ." (Isa. 29: 14; cf. 1 Cor. 1:19); or: "I do a deed in your days, a deed you never will believe . . ." (Hab. 1:5; cf. Acts. 13: 41).[25]

Although the primary emphasis concerns the use of the Old Testament as a context of understanding, it is also the case that the New Testament writers see Christ as an interpretative key for the interpretation and understanding of the Old Testament. Luke 24: 27 and 45 uses the Old Testament as a frame of reference for understanding Christ, and Christ as an interpretative key for understanding the Old Testament. In Goppelt's words, each facilitates understanding by pointing to the other.[26] Beale and Carson affirm both principles in terms of the Apocalypse, Gospel, and Epistles of John. In Revelation "the Christ-event is *the* key to understanding the Old Testament, and yet reflection back on the Old Testament leads the way to further comprehension of this event."[27] The earliest Christians, Carson writes, "needed *biblical* categories to make sense of the shattering event of the cross."[28] *The key point is that the Old Testament was not simply invoked, as a "support" or as a "proof" in the context of polemical debate for a message which had been understood independently of it.*

Graham Stanton thus observes concerning Matthew's use of the Old Testament, "The Old Testament is woven into the warp and woof of this gospel." With regard to Matthew's ten formula-quotations in particular, "all comment on the story of Jesus and draw out its deeper significance by stressing that all its main features are in fulfilment of Scripture."[29] Sometimes the New Testament writers may become aware of potential sources of tension with the Old Testament. Morna Hooker comments on some Markan examples, including that of Jesus's healing on the sabbath day (Mark 3: 1–6). She concludes, however, that, rather than substituting some different context of understanding for Mark, the issue becomes "the way in which the law is interpreted."[30] This principle applies to the well-known examples in Matthew of Jesus's re-interpretation of the law (Matt. 5: 21–26) and especially to the notorious exegetical crux which introduces them: "Think not that I have come to abolish (*katalusai*) the law and the prophets; I have not come to abolish them but to fulfil (*plerosai*) them. For truly I say to you, till heaven and earth pass away, not an iota, not a dot, will pass from the law until all is accomplished (*panta genetai*)" (Matt. 5: 17,18). As David Hill rightly argues, the general principle is likely to represent, for Matthew, a safeguard against the possible misunderstanding of the sequence of re-interpretations which follow: "You have heard it said to the men of old . . . , but I say to you . . ." (5: 21–26). This wider context, and its relation to questions about the rôle of the law in Matthew's community, contribute decisively to the meaning of *plērōsai* (validate? set forth in its true meaning? bring into being that to which it points?) in 5:17. In accordance with a regular Jewish use, "the law and the prophets" may denote the whole Old Testament. Hence, the thrust of the passage is that the whole of the Old Testament points forward to Christ; but within this framework Jesus's own interpretation takes place as a dialectic embodying both continuity and novelty, because Christ himself represents the definitive revelation of the will of God.

To interpret the present in the light of a biblical context of understanding is not peculiar to the New Testament and the early Church. Peter's phrase as it is recounted on the day of Pentecost "This was that which was spoken by the prophet . . ." (Act. 2:16) may reflect a formulaic introduction to a scriptural citation which is also used by the community of Qumran in connection with what is often called *pesher* interpretation. The term *pesher* is used some thirty times in Daniel for the "interpretation" of dreams (Dan. 2:4,7,16,28, cf. 5:7–16) and was later employed by the Qumran community of the "unriddling" of passages which were perceived to offer contexts of understanding for the last generation. For example, in 1 *Qp Hab.* 1:1–2, Hab. 1:1–2a is cited with the comment: "The *pesher* of the passage concerns everything Habakkuk prophesied regarding the beginning of the generation of the visitation in the latter days." The significance of *pesher* interpretation is discussed further by M.P. Horgan, Bruce Chilton, A.T. Hanson, D. Patte and R. Longenecker, among others.[31]

Patte, Hanson and Chilton also examine interpretation in different Targumic traditions. Chilton argues that Jesus himself referred to the tradition of the Isaiah Targum in the preaching of his message.[32] Patte concludes that in non-sectarian Judaism scripture performed two main functions: it gave the Jewish community its identity as a people with a particular vocation; and it provided criteria for working out how to fulfill this vocation in new situations. Thus the interpretative role of the Mishnah and Talmud extends and elaborates the original horizons of the scriptural text. One of the best-known examples from the Mishnah concerns the application to more specific situations of the general prohibition against work on the sabbath (Ex. 20: 8–11). What mitigating circumstances might allow certain re-definitions of work? (being at the top of a tree?). Another example concerns the "official" rabbinic Targum tradition on diet. What gives rise to the well-known Jewish dietary prohibition against eating meat products and milk products at the same meal is not a scriptural passage in isolation from a context of understanding, but the Targum Onqelos *interpretation* of Ex. 23: 19 (cf. Ex. 24:26): "You shall not boil a kid in its mother's milk."

In the Christian church questions about the relation between interpretation and tradition as a context of understanding became especially critical in the second century, when a crisis involving biblical interpretation developed on two fronts. On one side Marcion questioned the status of the Old Testament as a "Christian" text at all; let alone as a definitive source of understanding and a norm of truth for the church. On the other side gnostic teachers and writers employed the vocabulary and imagery of the New Testament itself to expound and to support gnostic systems of thought, giving thereby new meanings to familiar phrases and concepts in the New Testament. In the face of these two types of challenge, Irenaeus stressed the unity and wholeness of the biblical writings, in contrast to a more atomistic use of this language, and re-affirmed the role of apostolic testimony and the development of a public apostolic tradition as a context of understanding. It is difficult to judge how much his emphasis on tradition as a context of understanding owes to these two polemical concerns. If we compare the earlier writings of Justin Martyr, Justin seems to imply, as Willis Shotwell's specialist study confirms, that understanding operates primarily on the level of individual human rationality: "The person of intelligence can understand "(*ho nouneches katalabein dunēsetai*).[33] But for Irenaeus understanding is achieved within the *community* of faith.[34] He is acutely conscious, and makes explicit complaint, that other competing systems of thought are being put forward in the name of being faithful to the biblical writings themselves, but place scripture in a foreign context.[35]

In order to appreciate the nature of the difficulty which Irenaeus faced, it is helpful to consider examples of gnostic uses of biblical texts. Some comparisons are offered by Samuel Laeuchli and by the two books of Elaine Pagels entitled *The Gnostic Paul* and *The Johannine Gospel in Gnostic Exegesis*.[36] Paul's language in 1 Corinthians is either free of gnostic implications, or, some have argued, consciously anti-gnostic, in the sense of attacking an undeveloped "proto-gnosticism". At all events the statement that "all of us possess knowledge (*gnōsis*)" (1 Cor. 8:1) not only almost certainly represents a quotation from the Corinthians' own letter to Paul, but is in any case firmly qualified by the principle "knowledge puffs up; but love builds up" (8:1 b). The same principle applies to language in Corinthians about "the spiritual person" (1 Cor. 2:15; cf. 1 Cor. 12:1). Paul responds to his readers' claim to be a "spiritual" kind of person: "But I, brethren, could not address you as 'spiritual' men . . ." (3:1). I have discussed elsewhere the Corinthians' use of "persuasive definition" over the term "spiritual".[37] Paul's language about imparting "a wisdom among the mature . . . a secret and hidden wisdom of God" (1 Cor. 2: 6,7) provides a third example. In *the Gospel of Truth*, Sophia is "revealed" to gnostic people "for the aeons" (*Ev. Ver.* 23: 16–21); but the connection of thought is far from Pauline.

Elaine Pagels is sympathetic with the suggestion that gnostic exegesis seems no more "arbitrary" than that of Irenaeus and Tertullian, once each is seen as system-relative to a given context of understanding. It is true that, as she writes, "Irenaeus, Hippolytus, Clement and Origen clearly have little interest in examining gnostic exegesis on its own terms."[38] But Laeuchli seems to be on firmer ground when he argues that while the meanings of biblical words and phrases depend to a considerable extent on the frame or context of thought within which they are used, gnostic systems lend themselves to "semantic breakdown" and frequent idiosyncrasy of a kind which less readily characterizes the Fathers. A reading of *The Gospel of Truth*, in the light of Grobel's brief commentary seems to confirm this. For example, the writer accounts for the "ninety-nine sheep" which the good shepherd leaves behind (Matt. 18: 12–14) in terms of the folk-custom of counting on the fingers of the hand, whereby the "hundred" switches the focus of attention from the left to the right hand (*Ev. Ver* 32: 4,5). The eschatological goal involves "that which is perfect" (1 Cor. 13:10), eclipsing the fragmentary and the partial. But whereas the decisive factor for Paul is the eschatological character of love, in *Ev. Ver* 25: 2,3 it is knowledge. "Members" (*melos*, 1 Cor. 12:12) remains a social or ecclesiological term in Paul; but it becomes cosmological in *Ev. Ver.* 18:40.

Examples are not confined, however, to *The Gospel of Truth*. The *Apocryphon of John* radically re-casts the Genesis narratives to accommodate a speculative metaphysic in which wisdom and thought beget a quasi-divine being Ialdabaoth. It is Ialdabaoth who speaks as a "jealous" God in Ex. 20: 5, and the heavenly powers who "make men in our image" (Gen. 1:26). Examples of a wide range of gnostic uses of the biblical writings can be found in Werner Foerster's two-volume collection of gnostic texts.[39]

Laeuchli argues that although, for example, John uses concepts which occur frequently in Gnostic literature, in the *Gospel of Truth* "Christ as a man of flesh and blood cannot be meaningful because Gnostic language cannot grasp man as a creature of flesh and spirit in unity".[40] He comments further: "Though Gnostic texts still use the Old Testament vocabulary, this vocabulary is no longer understood. . . . A comparison between 1 Cor. and the *Gospel of Truth* shows two conflicting concepts of the body of the faithful".[41] Laeuchli concludes that how ever self-consistent gnostic interpretation may be claimed to be "underneath lies a failure to think *in the biblical frame*".[42] The problem becomes one of "semantic breakdown" because "peripheral speech . . . becomes the centre."[43] What constitutes "canonical" language is not the use of a biblical vocabulary, but the inter-relations between biblical concepts and the use of these concepts for given purposes within'a given frame. "The familiar biblical concepts" in some, though not all, gnostic writings "hold the key to the reversal of meaning of seemingly biblical terms."[44]

A re-play of the same kind of debate as that into which Laeuchli and Pagels enter over Irenaeus and the gnostic writings occurs in partly parallel claims made by R.C. Gregg and D.E. Groh about the respective interpretations of scripture offered by Athanasius and by the Arians.45 The Arians could plausibly appeal, Gregg and Groh argue, to such passages as Hebrews 1–4. God appoints Christ for service (Heb 1:2; 1:9; 3:2); and so Christ has been exalted with glory and honour (1:4; 2:9; 5:6). The Son "learns obedience" (Heb. 5:8). He who sanctifies and those who are sanctified are "all out of one" (2:11), and he is like a brother (2: 14,16). On his side, Athanasius claims that an Arian interpretation of Hebrews fails to keep in view the broad sweep or "scope" (*skopos*) of Hebrews.46 Gregg and Groh argue: "The Arian fires could be fueled by the same texts read according to the Arian insistence that Christ was essentially different from God".47 Surprisingly, they admit, "ready-made Arian texts like Hebs. 2: 11,14 and 5: 1–10 are absent from our sources", but use is made of this Epistle.

Against this kind of background we can more readily appreciate why Irenaeus responded to Marcion and the gnostics by making two related but parallel moves. First, he appealed to the continuity of a rule of faith based on apostolic testimony as the only appropriate or adequate context of understanding for biblical interpretation. The scriptures are like a field which contains the hidden treasure of Christ Himself. (cf. Matt. 13:46). When they are read outside a Christian context of understanding they become merely "like a fable." But when they are read "by the Christians, it is a treasure, hid indeed in a field, but brought to light by the cross of Christ."48 Irenaeus's allusion to the problems facing Jewish readers in this context reflects Paul's retrospective analysis of his pre-conversion Jewish reading of a text which seemed, by comparison with Christian experience, to be covered by a veil (2.Cor.3:14). In the context of his own time Irenaeus underlines the corporate character of this Christian context of understanding, and today it stands in contrast with the more individualistic "reading" of our print-orientated culture. Perhaps with a reference not only to ecclesiological continuity but also, as Joseph P. Smith suggests, to the role of elders as a historical link with the apostolate, Irenaeus defines this context as "diligently reading the scripture in company with the presbyters of the church."49

The second move made by Irenaeus lay in his appeal to an understanding of the wholeness of scripture. This emerges partly in his polemics against Marcion, who not only divorced the Old Testament from the New, but also recognized only a smaller number of New Testament books as functionally definitive or authoritative, in contrast to wider Christian practice. It would be partly anachronistic to say that Marcion worked with a smaller canon, but this reflects the reality of a situation which later became formalized. Marcion's dualistic system, with its radical opposition between Pauline gospel and Jewish law, shaped not only Marcionite biblical interpretation, but also the Marcionite canon. This contained ten edited epistles of Paul and a severely edited version of Luke.

Adolf Harnack places on record Franz Overbeck's comment that "in the second century nobody understood Paul except Marcion, who misunderstood him."[50] But Marcion's readiness to resort to the knife (to use Tertullian's phrase) confirms that it is *not* the case that any or every system could be supported on the basis of biblical interpretation, provided that what is kept in view is the *wholeness* of the biblical writings. Admittedly, unlike Marcion, a number of the Fathers as well as the gnostics made interpretation less stable by using allegorical interpretation; but they nevertheless had confidence in the conjunction and combination of three constraining principles: (i) the rule of apostolic faith as a context of understanding; (ii) the wholeness of scripture as a comprehensive theological horizon; and (iii) the biblical and ecclesial witness to Christ as the "centre" of the biblical texts and their subsequent interpretation.

One weakness in Irenaeus's interpretative practice was his willingness to resort to allegorical interpretation, although often this is either more strictly typology (a correspondence between patterns of events, not simply ideas) and often it reflects allegorical imagery which had already become common coinage in the church. The practice had begun in pre-Christian interpretation, and was found in the sub-apostolic writings. We shall discuss the origins and purposes of allegorical interpretation in the next section. Allegorical interpretation also arises because Irenaeus believes that every part of scripture carries significance and points ultimately to Christ, or serves the gospel. Andrew Louth, as we point out elsewhere, makes much of this theological role of allegory in the Fathers.[51] Thus in his attempt to use Old Testament material otherwise viewed as "unedifying" Irenaeus is carried along into questionable and artificial allegorizations of such episodes as the incest of Lot's daughters (Gen. 19: 30–38), and offers a Trinitarian interpretation of the visit of Joshua's spies to Jericho (Jos. 2:1). Irenaeus follows the Epistle of Barnabas and Justin in seeing allegorical meaning in Moses' stretching out of his arms to ensure victory over the Amalekites (Ex. 17: 11,12). Moses represents "Jesus . . . stretching forth his hands" on the cross to bring us into the kingdom.[52] There is word-play, rather than strictly allegory, in his reference to the tree of Eden (Gen. 3:1–6). Irenaeus writes, "the sin that was wrought through the tree was undone by the obedience of the tree, whereby the Son of Man was nailed to the tree, destroying the knowledge of evil".[53] This is more like reflection on an *Urzeit-Endzeit* motif than an allegory. Irenaeus interprets Jacob's words about a future ruler from Judah who washes his garment in the blood of the grape (Gen. 49:11) as that which is fulfilled in Christ's "cleansing and redeeming us with his blood."[54] Again, however, there is a parallel with the language of Justin, and this may be nearer to typology than to allegory. [55]

Deviations in details of practice do not invalidate the basic principles, especially when a number reflect precedents which may have already become almost standard imagery. In principle Irenaeus rejects atomistic exegesis of isolated texts.[56] In spite of F.W. Farrar's dismissive comments a century ago, and Elaine Pagels' arguments that differences in relation to gnostic interpretation are effectively entirely system-relative, R.P.C. Hanson correctly asserts: "There is no allegorization into general moral sentiments nor into philosophical speculation of a Philonic sort."[57] Irenaeus's complaint that his gnostic opponents "garble" biblical passages in fanciful ways is only partly, not wholly, system-relative. Above all he complains about the esoteric and semantically innovative nature of interpretation which rests on idiosyncratic individualism. This is like prescribing medicines "in accordance with the patient's whims."[58] The wholeness of the biblical text entails a hermeneutical "seeing . . . as . . ." Thus gnostic interpretation is "as if one, when a beautiful image of king has been constructed by some skilful artist out of precious jewels, should take this . . . to pieces, should re-arrange the gems, and so fit them together as to make them into the form of a dog or of a fox . . . and declare that *this* was the beautiful image of the king".[59] Gnostic interpreters cite biblical phrases and expressions, but taking advantage of the words and terminology "they have transferred them to their own system".[60]

Irenaeus's thought brings together a number of issues which remain matters of recurring concern. As Kelly and Louth point out, his understanding of the actual content of the *regula fidei* comes extemely close in verbal form to the wording of the Apostles' Creed.[61] His appeal to the centrality of Christ as a hermeneutical principle or key, together with his concern about the wholeness of scripture, anticipate two of the fundamental concerns of Luther and the Reformers. His work, Skevington Wood concludes, leads on to the Reformation principle of scripture's being allowed to be "its own interpreter."[62] Superficially it might appear to suggest precisely the opposite. But if "tradition", in the sense of the rule of faith, is seen as a context of understanding which has continuity with the earliest context of understandings, which in turn were focussed on Christ, the principle not only becomes more intelligible but also more credible. Continuity operates with a frame of regular and repeated patterns of belief and practice. It entails inter-subjective judgments. The context of understanding is corporate rather than individual, and given rather than made. On this basis it is no merely circular argument when Irenaeus pleads that more obscure passages be interpreted in the light of clearer ones. On the other hand Irenaeus maintains that the extreme subjectivism of individualism can give rise to a circular process, because thereby the individual has rejected "the very method of discovery" and remains on a continuous journey of unanswered enquiry.[63]

3. Varied Issues in Allegorical Interpretation: its De-mythologizing Function in Pre-Christian and Philonic Interpretation

The value of allegorical interpretation depends on a number of factors, including the purpose of interpretation, the nature of the text to be interpreted, and how broadly or narrowly the term "allegorical" is defined. Clearly, for example, if a text presents a series of allegories, as is the case with John Bunyan's *Pilgrim's Progress*, the only appropriate method of interpretation is the allegorical one. When Christian is imprisoned in Doubting Castle by Giant Despair, we know that this should not be read as a spatio-temporal event enacted by an agent of large physical proportions. The scope of the term "allegory" also raises questions. In the first century Heraclitus Stoicus defined it as "saying one thing and meaning something other than what it says. (*ho gar alla men agoreuōn tropos, hetera de ōn legei sēmainōn epōnymōs allēgoria kateitai*).64 But does this mean, as Leslie Barnard claims on the basis of usage in Greek rhetoric, that allegory is "a series of metaphors"?65 John Bunyan wished to convey a determinate and didactic content by his use of allegory. But Umberto Eco finds examples in Patristic and mediaeval allegorical interpretation a "beautiful case of unlimited semiosis".66 This, however, brings us back to the world of postmodern theory and deconstructionism in which Crossan sees biblical language as metaphors of metaphors.67

The purpose for which allegorical interpretation is undertaken also constitutes a major factor in assessing its validity as an interpretative tool. Biblical specialists would perhaps still have been more ready to dismiss allegorical interpretation out of hand (except specifically in the case of interpreting biblical allegories) when, to use Morgan's phrase, the historical paradigm reigned supreme and unchallenged. But in recent years allegorical interpretation of the biblical texts has had some defenders. Andrew Louth argues, for example, that hostility towards this approach rests on a mistaken assumption that it is somehow a *dishonest* procedure, smuggling in the interpreter's own ideas which are then "read" from the authoritative texts.68 But allegorical interpretation, Louth argues, allows for an advancing corporate horizon of interpretation on the part of the interpreting community. For example, it allows them to read texts in the light of the development of Christian doctrine. Allegory presents not just the author's historical meaning, but, in Origen's metaphor, the polyphonic harmony of "God's symphony". We thus plumb "the depth of its signification."69 Allegory, in Louth's view, brings us face to face with "the ultimate 'difficulty' of the Scriptures, a difficulty, a mystery, which challenges us to revise our understanding of what might be meant by meaning."70

Such an approach simply underlines, in the first place, how closely bound up together are theories of meaning which interpreters and reading communities consciously or unconsciously adopt with questions about the purposes which are those of the author or those of the reader. As we have already seen from the example of Rupert of Deutz, *lectio divina*, or contemplative reading, can draw on layers of meaning for the stimulation and refreshment of meditation within a pre-existing framework of belief and understanding which enjoys trust. But if the purpose of interpretation has to do with an investigation of the thought of a biblical author, or with the content of biblical theology or ethics, allegorical transposition gives rise to Luther's trenchant tongue-in-cheek rejoinder: "I can easily prove from the scriptures that beer is better than wine."[71] It is for this reason that many have viewed the standard methods of historical reconstruction, form criticism, redaction criticism, and related approaches, as a legitimate legacy of the classical Reformers.

In assessing the purposes for which allegorical interpretation functioned in the history of the subject, we may compare the *"demythologizing"*, *de-objectifying*, or *de-particularizing* purpose which marks most pre-Christian Greek and Jewish allegorical interpretation with the Christian, Patristic, and mediaeval purpose of *"spiritualizing"*, or providing *Christological or moral particularization and application*. Umberto Eco describes the contrast only slightly differently: in the pre-Christian era allegorical interpretation generated *secular* meanings from religious texts; in the Patristic and mediaeval church it generated more intensely *religious* meanings from texts which seemed otherwise to offer only history-like narrative or statements about the world.[72]

It is probable that the origins of allegorical interpretation go back to the sixth century BC with Theagenes of Rhegium, although his writings are no longer extant. According to Stoic tradition, Theagenes interpreted parts of Homer allegorically, expounding Homer's anthropomorphic stories about the doings of gods and godesses as symbolic language about natural forces, or as moral tales told to impart ethical values. In the fifth century Metrodorus of Lampsacus allegorized the Homeric pantheon as parts of the human body: Apollo signified bile; Demeter signified the liver; and so on. This procedure probably implies three assumptions. First, it implies a content-criticism or *Sachkritik* which signals an unease with what the text says as it stands; second, it presupposes a wish to "use" a respected text in supposedly more "contemporary" ways; third, it may also reflect a belief that the author was inspired to say more than he knew. In his earliest work Plato subscribes to the belief that the god speaks through Homer.[73]

In the Stoics the Homeric deities become allegories of forces of nature, and Zeno also interpreted Hesiod allegorically. Heraclitus Stoicus admits that a literal interpretation of Homer would result in absurdly anthoropomorphic notions of divinity. He offers a good parallel in pre-historical terms to Bultmann's programme of demythologizing: what appears in the *Illiad* to be an *objective* description of Athene's restraining Achilles by pulling his hair must be *de-objectified* in interpretation as portraying only Achilles' subjective sense of restraint. Stories about Ares, Poseidon and Hephaestus refer to changes in the property of iron when it is placed in water. The story of Odysseus stopping his ears against the seductive songs of the Sirens represented, for some of the Stoics, an allegory of the defence of the righteous against the seductions of evil. Nevertheless among the Greeks themselves, there was also some deep suspicion of the method of allegorical interpretation. Up to the first century the word *hyponoia*, "under-meaning", was used rather than *allegoria*. In the *Republic* Plato expressed reservations about allegorical interpretations of anthropomorphic deities. Plutarch was prepared to accept the "de-objectifying" interpretation, but not the metaphorical extension of supposed deities to signify forces of nature.

For Jewish writers many of the anthropomorphisms of the Old Testament posed parallel questions about meaning. Some describe the interpretative work of the Jewish writer Aristobulus of Alexandria, at the end of the second century BC, as an example of allegorical interpretation. Here, however, we have an awareness of the metaphorical dimensions of language which lies only at the very edge of allegory. Aristobulus let theology engage with biblical interpretation. Thus theology, shaped by the wholeness of the biblical texts, asserted that God is omnipresent. But the biblical texts spoke of God's "descending" onto Mount Sinai (Ex. 19:18) and of Moses's "going up to God" on Sinai (Ex. 19:3). They signify some extension of what the verb would convey in normal contexts. Similarly, God's "resting" on the seventh day of creation (Gen. 2:2) refers not to any supposed cessation from activity, but to the completion of the particular work of creation which has just been described.

Aristobulus stands in contrast to the so-called *Letter of Aristeas* (c.100BC), a pseudonymous Jewish writing also from Alexandria. Here allegorical interpretation is used more radically to cover over what are perceived as potential embarrassments about the Levitical law in the eyes of educated Greeks. Thus the verse "whatever parts of the hoof end is cloven-footed and chews the cud, among the animals, you may eat" (Lev. 11:3) is interpreted as an allegorical injection to wise discernment.

Philo of Alexandria (c.20BC–c.AD50) stands as the most important example of Jewish allegorical interpretation of the scriptures. Philo specialists differ about whether, following E.R. Goodenough, we should regard him as genuinely representative of a hellenized Judaism in the diaspora; or whether following H. Wolfson, we see him as related more closely to a broader version of pharisaic Judaism; or whether, with Samuel Sandmel, we regard him as in many ways unique in the context of a broadly hellenistic Judaism.74 But on one major point all are agreed. Philo was primarily an apologist who is firm in his Jewish faith, but is "poised . . . between the Greek and Jewish thought-worlds."75 In particular, he chooses the role of a philosophical and theological exegete of scripture, but works on the basis of a Greek text with Greek conceptual tools.76 Klaus Otte argues that Philo's theory of language is also bound up with this amalgam of Jewish and Greek ideas, including the Therapeutae, the Essenes, and the translators of the Septuagint.77

Philo went as far as he could towards adopting the ideas and thought-forms of the educated Greek intellectual, while remaining in principle loyal to the teaching of the Jewish Scriptures. These two poles, the Greek and the Jewish, provide the frame of reference which determines all his thinking, and not least his use of allegorical interpretation. On the one hand, Scripture is "the holy word", "the divine word", and "the sacred oracles".78 It is the inspired word of God. On the other hand, Philo frequently quotes Homer, Pindar, Euripides, or Sophocles, and is saturated in the thought of Zeno, Cleanthes, and the Pythagoreans, and quotes and speaks of "the great Plato". Philo's criteria for the use of allegorical interpretation arise not from the style or genre of biblical texts, but from questions about their theological implications especially for a doctrine of God; from apparent logical contradictions; and from passages which would seem to be entirely culture-relative to Judaism from a wider hellenistic perspective. As Umberto Eco observed, Philo uses allegorical interpretation *to broaden meaning* in accordance with a less narrowly religious frame whereas the Fathers use allegorical interpretation *to focus meaning more narrowly* on Christological doctrine. Thus Philo comments on the reference to Adam's hiding himself from God (Gen. 3:8) that since God is all-seeing, "some other meaning" than the *prima facie* one must be sought. There is a logical difficulty about how Cain could build "a city" or find a wife (Gen. 4:17) when there is an implication from the narrative that the population numbers four; so the literal meaning of the verse cannot be the right one.79 Of the two creation accounts, Gen. 2:7 describes the creation of humankind, while Gen. 1:27 concerns the creation of the "ideal" (in Plato's sense), or "spiritual", man.80 Paul may perhaps indirectly allude to such an interpretation in his reversal of the sequence in 1 Cor. 15: 46.

Philo also uses allegorical interpretation to broaden what would otherwise be *time-specific* or *spatial-specific* references. The scriptures do not simply concern the "petty state" of the land of Israel, but "a greater country, namely this whole world."81 Thus the journey of Abraham represents not a temporal event in which Abraham moves from one specific place to another, but the human journey from sensual understanding to contemplation of higher realities. (Gen. 12: 1–8). When Jacob crosses the river Jordan with his staff, the staff signifies the discipline with which baseness (the

Jordan) is overcome. There is some justification for the verdict that, in his eagerness to convey "timeless" truth, Philo shows a measure of contempt for narrative as temporal narrative. Philo becomes particularly anxious about narrative acts ascribed to God which are embarrassingly anthropomorphic. To suggest that God "planted a garden in Eden" (Gen. 2:8) is "fabulous nonsense"; the verse signifies that God "plants" virtue in the human race.[82] The river that flows out of Eden is "goodness" and its four heads are not geographical entitites but Plato's four cardinal virtues. Pheison (Gen. 2:11) may be derived from *pheidomai*, meaning I spare; hence it supposedly designates "prudence". Gihon (Gen. 2:13) becomes "courage" by a more complicated linguistic route. Cain and Abel represent character-types which can be found in every age and place: Cain stands for the person who is fluent in speech but deficient in character; Abel is a solid person whose speech is halting. In the Patriarchal age, figures often represent virtues: Jacob designates virtue acquired after struggle; Lot signifies sensuality; and Rachel represents innocence.[83]

Clearly there are parallels between Philo's allegorical interpretation and that of the Stoics. That the relation is a conscious one has been argued by Sandmel, on the basis of a comparison between a Stoic allegorical interpretation of Odysseus, Penelope, Penelope's maidens and the suitors, and Philo's allegorizations of Abraham, Sarah, and Hagar. In each case there can be no co-union with "wisdom" (Penelope, Sarah) until "the encyclical studies" (the maidens, Hagar) have first become known. The key to Philo's purpose in the use of allegorical interpretation is his awareness of, and often embarrassment by, what Alan Richardson and others have called "the scandal of particularity" in the Hebrew-Christian tradition. Sandmel rightly observes, "The grand Allegory enables Philo to transform Scripture into the nature and experience of every man."[84] Thus biblical narrative becomes allegorically the journey which each person can make towards spiritual perfection.

It is not unduly anachoronistic to see pre-Christian allegorical interpretation as a partial anticipation of what Bultmann would later call "demythologizing". Bultmann writes: "The real purpose of myth is not to present an objective picture of the world . . . , but to express man's understanding of himself in the world in which he lives. Myth should be interpreted not cosmologically but anthropologically, or better existentially."[85] Bultmann's three criteria for changing the *prima facie* meaning of a "mythological" text are: (i) a need to "de-objectify" what look like descriptions of particularized states of affairs into more widely cashable self-involving language; (ii) a need to respond to symptoms of *prima facie* contradiction or absurdity in the text; and (iii) a need to re-interpret what might suggest an outdated anthropomorphic understanding of divine transcendence or of cosmology. I have discussed these three criteria in considerable detail elsewhere.[86] There are two crucial *differences*, however, between Philo and Bultmann. First, Bultmann firmly rejects what he sees as a "liberal" notion of timeless truth, especially when it is imparted in the form of didactic *ideas*. In continuity with his work on form criticism Bultmann urges that the gospel is proclaimed as a temporal *event*: it is not a timeless idea, but *kerygma*. Bultmann writes: "The charge against liberal theology is that it has sought to remove this stumbling-block or to minimize it.[87] Second, Bultmann also rejects any idealist contrast between the "natural" and the "inner". He is not concerned about "inner" psychological processes, but about practical orientations of human will.

In other respects, however, parallels between Bultmann's programme and pre-Christian allegorical interpretation are unmistakeable, and are recognized by Bultmann himself. He writes: "Earlier attempts at demythologizing (include) . . . allegorical interpretation (which) . . . spiritualizes the mythical events so that they become symbols of processes going on in the soul."[88] Hence Philo identifies as one clear example of a "myth" which cries out to be transposed the "speaking" of the serpent in Gen. 3:1. This text Philo writes, seems to portray "prodigies and wonders . . . But by deploying explanations derived from the deeper sense, the mythical vanishes from sight, and the truth becomes manifest."[89] At the same time, Philo does not dismiss the spatio-temporal or "outward" meaning of all texts as altogether valueless. Anticipating Origen, he observes: "We ought to look on the outward . . . as resembling the body, and the inner meaning as resembling the soul. Just as we then provide for the body, in as much as it is the cloak of the soul, so we must attend to the letter of the laws. If we keep these, we shall obtain an understanding of those things of which these are the symbols."[90]

Much of Philo's concern is therefore theological. But we should not underestimate the part played by Platonic idealism in his thought. As Klaus Otte argues, for Philo language is like a door to "Being", but in accordance with Platonic thought reality lies *above the sensory realm*. Hence, as Goppelt declares: "for Philo, allegorizing is the same as advancing from the visible world to the higher world of ideas."[91] The parallel between the body and the soul makes the point well: "we provide for the body", but only because it is "the abode of the soul". Spatio-temporal signification does not, Goppelt argues concerning Philo's view, speak of "God's dealings" with his people or with the world in public events in history, but of human qualities, practical attitudes, values, or states of soul. It is not strictly the case that, as Eco claims, pre-Christian allegory is "secularizing" language; Philo seeks to eliminate the historical particularity which is at odds with a Platonic understanding of ultimacy or spirituality. It is possible to express this judgment in a positive or in a negative way, depending on the extent of one's sympathies with a Platonic world-view. In a plea for a more serious and positive approach to allegory, Gerald Bostock writes that "allegory in this period is the literary mode of a Platonism which interprets the world as the ambivalent image of a higher reality. It is the means whereby the hidden connection between two levels of reality is indicated and expounded."[92] By contrast, Frederic Farrar dismisses Philo's method as a device for finding in the Bible "the common places of philosophy."[93]

4. The Beginnings of Christian Allegorical Interpretation

In Gal. 4:24–26 Paul comments on Gen. 16:15 and 21:2 concerning the births of Ishmael as son of the bond-woman Hagar and of Isaac as son of the free woman Sarah. He observes, "Now this is an allegory ("is stated allegorically", *allegoroumena*, v.24): these women are two covenants. One is from Mount Sinai, bearing children for slavery; she is Hagar. Now Hagar is Mount Sinai in Arabia; she corresponds to the present Jerusalem, for she is in slavery with her children. But the Jerusalem above is free, and she is our mother." Paul concludes "we, like Isaac, are children of the promise. . . . children of the free woman" (28,31). Origen appealed to the precedent of this passage for his own widespread use of allegorical interpretation. But is this a genuine example of what is usually thought of as allegorizing?

The vast majority of Pauline specialists, including F.F. Bruce and C.K. Barrett, answer broadly in the affirmative at least until or unless finer distinctions are drawn between narrower sub-categories, although Otto Michel prefers to see this as an example of *typology*.[94] We have already suggested that typology represents a parallel, analogy, or correspondence between two or more *historical events*; whereas allegory represents an extension of meaning in terms of parallels, analogies or correspondences between two or more *ideas*. Lampe and Woollcombe define typology as "the establishment of historical connections between certain events, persons, or things in the Old Testament and similar events, persons or things in the New Testament."[95] Earle Ellis also stresses this historical dimension in typology, and places it in opposition to allegorical interpretation which sees the Old Testament "as a book of metaphors hiding a deeper meaning." Typology, Ellis argues, entails "two principles, historical correspondence and escalation."[96] The New Testament anti-type complements and transcends the Old Testament type. More recently J.W. Aageson has taken up Ellis's discussion, together with Gerhard von Rad's notion of "correspondences", and concludes that with the possible exception of Rom. 5: 12–21 and 1 Cor. 10: 1–13, where Paul explicitly uses the word "type" "the term *correspondence* is more appropriate than typology for describing this linkage in Paul's application of scripture."[97]

Whether we use the word allegory, typology, or correspondence, it is clear that Paul has in view God's deeds in history, and the situational character of the analogy which he wishes to draw. His approach is different from that which we have considered in Philo. Although he has reservations about the application of the word "typology" here, R.P.C. Hanson writes, "Paul is not trying to emancipate the meaning of the passage from its historical context and transmute it into a moral sentiment or a philosophical truth, which is the almost invariable faction of Alexandrian allegory ... He is envisaging a critical situation which took place under the Old Covenant ... as forecasting and repeated by a situation under the New Covenant".[98] In any case, if we do choose to describe these verses as allegorical interpretation, this passage remains entirely uncharacteristic of Paul's approach to the Old Testament. Thus Longenecker, who uses the term "allegory" here, argues that this image or analogy "may very well represent an extreme form of Palestinian allegorical interpretation that was triggered by polemic debate and is strongly circumstantial and *ad hominem*".[99] We may note in passing that the Reformers were divided about Gal. 4: 24–26. Luther acknowledges that allegory is being used, which he thinks is "seemly ... when the foundation is well laid"; but Calvin dismisses Origen's appeal to the passage as "an occasion of twisting Scripture this way and that, away from the genuine sense" (*a genuino sensu*).[100]

It is clear that the number of examples of "allegorical interpretation" which we find in the New Testament depends partly on how broadly or how technically we define allegory. Thus in 1 Cor. 9: 9,10 Paul certainly places in broader frame the principle articulated in Deut. 25:4 "You shall not muzzle an ox that treads out the grain." His theological context of understanding suggests to him that this principle is formulated primarily "for our sake". In 1 Cor. 10: 1–4 the supply of water from the rock in the wilderness is attributed to Christ with the words "the rock was Christ." Mark 12: 1–9 extends an already familiar analogy, correspondence, or allegory, in which Israel is compared to God's vineyard (Isa. 5: 1,2). Although R.M. Grant and E.C. Blackman find parallels between the use of the Old Testament in the Epistle to the Hebrews and Philo's methods of interpretation (e.g. Heb. 4: 8,9; 7: 1–3), Ronald Williamson underlines important differences, especially in terms of the historical and eschatological emphasis in Hebrews, together with a temporal horizon which is virtually absent from Philo.[101] In general, whereas allegorical interpretation over-rides the immediate semantic frame by transposing it in terms of some larger extrinsic system, the New Testament writers for the most part take up Old Testament passages "as *wholes* ... as pointers to the whole context ..."[102] We need not revise C.H. Dodd's earlier conclusion that "It is the *total context* that is in view", and that this context was in general respected "upon the basis of a certain understanding of history."[103] Dodd urges: "In general (they) remain true to the main intention of their writers".[104] Where exceptions occur, this is more likely to be due to some particular factor in the situation in view, rather than because allegorical interpretation features as a regular interpretative device among the New Testament writers.

As we noted in Irenaeus, it is not always easy to draw a clear line between allegorical interpretation and uses of Old Testament material as images which have acquired a particular theological resonance in the life of a community. Thus in the sub-apostolic literature, 1 Clement (c.AD 95) suggests that the scarlet thread placed in the window of Rahab's house (Jos. 2:18,21) "makes evident beforehand" (*prodēlon poiountes*) that those who trust in God shall find deliverance "through the blood of the Lord" (1 Clem. 13:7). But the possibility that this simply represents an image that may already have become more widely symbolic is strengthened by the fact that allegorical interpretation is not characteristic of Clement. In the *Didache* (c.100–110) and in the genuine *Epistles of Ignatius* (c.110–120) there is likewise little or no allegory. On the other hand, *The Epistle of Barnabas* contains allegorical interpretations of Old Testament Levitical laws as timeless moral principles (*Barnabas* 10: 1–12), and an allegory on the three-hundred-and-eighteen trained men of Abraham (Gen. 14:14) which depends on theories of numerology (*Barnabas* 9:8).

Systematic allegorization, however, emerges in gnosticism and in Clement of Alexandria, and in a particular sense yet to be discussed, also in Origen. In the Valentinian tradition allegory does not represent only some "added" or optional extra to the situational or narrative meaning of biblical text. As Elaine Pagels asserts, in Heracleon and in other Valentinian writings hermeneutics is governed by "the metaphysical principle of the *three ontological levels* of exegesis."[105] These correspond to the *respective frames of reference*, or *contexts of understanding*, brought to the texts by the "hylic" (materially minded) person, the "psychic", (broadly religious) person, and the "pneumatic" (spiritual or gnostic) person. A secret revelation of *gnosis* provides the pre-condition for a necessary level of meaning which lies above and beyond *"open", public, or rational enquiry*. For Heracleon, therefore, the spatio-temporal or situational meaning cannot, by virtue of his hermeneutical principle, constitute the primary meaning. His method is that of "systematically translating *somatic* (material) 'images' into spiritual truth."[106] Hence the woman of Samaria (John 4: 7–26) is not primarily a female person who lived in Samaria; but the spiritual elect whose "true husband" is the gnostic *pleroma*. Mount Gerizim is the sense-experience of ordinary "hylic" (materially-minded) people; Jerusalem is the "religious" experience of the "psychical"; but the "spiritual" worship in Spirit and in truth (John 4:23).

Clement of Alexandria (c.200) comes nearer than any other church Father to sharing a gnostic hermeneutic. Clement's "tradition", or context of understanding, is not the *publicly accessible pattern of belief and practice* that it was for Irenaeus. The revelation of "knowledge" takes a different form for the gnostic or the "spiritual" believer than that which the ordinary "simple" believer can appreciate. The tradition and the revelation *cannot* be plain and open, because truth about God can by very definition be conveyed only "in enigmas and symbols, in allegories and metaphors, and in similar figures."[107] Veiled teaching stimulates enquiry. If biblical language were clear, it could not communicate its message, and revelatory "knowledge" would be unnecessary. Thus the Psalms (Ps.78: 2) say of Christ: "He will open his mouth in parables."[108] The style of the scriptures is parabolic.[109] But parables remain veiled: "seeing, they do not see" (Matt. 13:13).

According to Gunneweg, Clement of Alexandria is the first explicitly to use the word "Testament" (*diatheke*, also covenant) for the *two* parts of the biblical writings which effectively constitute the Old and New Testaments, although Paul had spoken of the Jews "reading the old covenant (*diatheke*)" (II Cor. 3:14).[110] But Clement is also the first to achieve the more questionable and dubious goal of using allegorical interpretation systematically, as "grand allegory" on the basis of a theology of *gnosis*, at least among the Fathers. Richard Hanson aptly observes: Clement "has reached the stage where he can see the text of scripture as containing a hidden meaning everywhere. He is the first Christian scholar to formulate this doctrine, and he has borrowed it from Philo."[111] Eco's claim that allegory allows "unlimited semiosis . . . a puzzling web" now becomes applicable to Christian interpretation for the first time. Thus, to take virtually random examples, in the parable of the pearl of great price (Matt. 13: 45,46), Clement transposes the signification by extending the pearl into a set of originating conditions concerning the oyster and oyster-shell which, in turn, signify truths about the incarnation.[112] In the parable of the Prodigal Son (Luke 15: 11–32), the best robe (15:22) signifies immortality; the ring, the mystery of the Trinity; and the feast, the eucharist.

Wider questions about the relationship between Christian spirituality and individualism are raised by Louth's defence of Clement's notion of the *gnostic* as representing "the spiritual director as the organ of tradition" in a context which witnesses to "the notion of tradition as silence." Louth relates this to the Eastern tradition in which Christians would visit a Desert Father "to ask for a word." By comparison, the public and corporate emphasis of Irenaeus not only embodies a more stable frame of meaning and of continuity, but also stands closer to the concerns of the Reformers about a publicly accessible and testable tradition which can be questioned about its authenticity as a witness to Christ.

5. Allegory or Application? The Development of Pastoral Hermeneutical Consciousness in Origen and a Contrast with Chrysostom

Clement's successor at Alexandria was Origen, whose writings span much of the first half of the third century (d.254) In Book IV of his *De Principiis* he explicitly discusses his view of scriptural inspiration (IV.1) and of the "spiritual" interpretation and understanding of the biblical writings (IV. 2,3). Origen's theory of biblical interpretation has been the subject of a number of specialist studies, including recently Karen Jo Torjesen's impressive study of Origen's hermeneutical procedure, which calls attention to his pastoral concern about *reader-effect*, as well as Gerald Bostock's brief defence of Origen's use of allegory.[114] It is tempting at first sight simply to categorize Origen along with Clement, as if he allegorized the Two Testaments simply in a Philonic or infinitely polyvalent sense. R.B. Tollinton, for example, observes that Origen's "whole exegesis rests upon the principle that Scripture says one thing and means another; that every narrative, every injunction, is really a mystery, shrouding a secret sense which alone is of real value ... He found in scripture what he wished to find".[115] But Origen's approach is more deeply rooted in a *theology of the incarnation* and a "sacramental" view of the world, and Tollinton paints only part of a wider picture.

Karen Torjesen and Hans Urs Von Balthasar both stress, apparently independently, the centrality of the Logos principle for Origen's interpretation of the Bible. Christ the Logos communicates to us in three "incarnational" modes: in his historical and risen body; in his body, the church; and in his "body" of the scriptures whose letters are brought to life by the Holy Spirit.[116] The Johannine Logos occupies a central place in Origen's thinking. Hence Origen *does not despise the particular or the spatio-temporal*; these are necessary vehicles through which the glory and truth of Christ is made manifest in signs. He *begins* with the "literal". If the linguistic and semantic constraints of the biblical text had been unimportant to him, it would be hard to imagine why he had laboured to create the *Hexapla*; a compendium of versions of the Old Testament designed to allow comparisons between variant manuscript readings. Contrary to the custom of many teachers of the time, Origen studied Hebrew and the Hebrew text as well as the Greek versions. In his many commentaries, especially on Romans, he discusses grammar, vocabulary, and differences between semantic meanings in different contexts. Indeed it has been seen as a weakness of Origen that he reads too much into linguistic and semantic differences.

Nevertheless if he begins with the literal sense, Origen cannot end there. In his commentary on John, the "spiritual gospel" he writes: "What we have now to do is to transform the sensible gospel (*aistheton euaggelion*) into a spiritual one (*euaggelion noetou kai pneumatikou*). For what would the narrative of the sensible gospel amount to if it were not developed into a spiritual one? . . . Any one can read it and assure himself of the facts it tells – no more. But our whole energy is now to be directed to penetrate to the deep things of the meaning of the gospel, and to search out the truth that is in it when divested of types."[117] In an incisive, sustained and compelling argument, Karen Torjesen interprets Origen's concern not as a philosophical or quasi-gnostic one but as a *pastoral* concern about the *reader-effects* of the biblical texts. When Origen insists that we must go beyond "the letter", the first point which he wishes to make is that no-one will be moved, persuaded, or transformed, by "the rude vessel of words" alone, in contrast not to allegory but to the *flow of argument* and teaching which the words *signify*. The words must be brought to *life*.[118] This is achieved "in demonstration of the (Holy) spirit and power" (*en apodeixei pneumatos kai dynameos* 1 Cor. 2:4). Origen's doctrine of the inspiration of scripture in Book IV chapter 1 of *De Principiis* concerns not simply the origin of the biblical writings but their *capacity to become effective within the time-horizon of the present*. If a person reads the text diligently and reverently "in that very act he . . . will recognize that the books he reads have not been produced in a human way, but are words of God".[119] Without the Holy Spirit, the words remain only "earthen vessels".

Origen formulates his well-known image of three "levels" of meaning of the text in the context of a theory of interpretation which is *pastorally* orientated. In the context of interpreting the text for the community, he writes: "As man is said to consist of body, soul, and spirit, so also does sacred Scripture which has been granted by the divine bounty for the salvation of man."[120] This idea is suggested partly by the allusion to "things threefold in counsel and knowledge so that words of truth may be separated and distinguished". (Origen's reading of Prov. 22:20). It partly reflects Paul's warning and promise that "the letter (R.S.V. written code; Greek, *to gramma*) kills, but the Spirit gives life" (2. Cor. 3:6). But K.J. Torjesen, in contrast to most other writers on this subject, argues that "we do not as yet have a principle which says that each verse must be interpreted on these three different levels, a principle which would be parallel to the mediaeval four-fold sense of scripture."[121] The congregation to whom the scriptures are expounded contains at least three groups with what Origen pastorally perceives to be "differing spiritual capabilities". The body of scripture is the text itself as it is read in the context of worship; the soul of scripture belongs to the category of what edifies or benefits; the third level "means understanding the text as a shadow of the coming blessings."[122] These are progessive steps in spiritual growth.

All this might remain unsubstantiated theory about Origen's hermeneutical goals, were it not for the fact that it is possible to show how this understanding of Origen is exemplified in his handling of a variety of concrete passages. One example arises from Origen's exposition of Psalm 38. The first level of meaning emerges when Origen invites us to reflect on the Psalmist's *situation*: "Thy arrows have sunk into me, and thy hand has come down on me" (Ps. 38:2). Origen expounds the arrows as the piercing of conscience, and God's hand as one of discipline. The next level of meaning concerns *spiritual attitude*: the psalmist is praying, and addressing God as "Thou". The final step is what today is often called "application": "Origen addresses *his hearers* . . . the words of the Psalm are now spoken as if by his hearers . . . tying this confession back into the words of the Psalmist as the hearer's own."[123] More strictly there are four elements here: (i) What are the words of the Psalmist? (ii) What attitude do they express? (iii) What attitude should the present hearer have in order to say these words? (iv) What should the hearer pray?

On the other hand, Origen allows that a different hermeneutic operates in the case of the Gospels. Especially in the case of John, as we have noted, the "sensible gospel" must become the "spiritual gospel." Here the hearer stands directly before the Logos, and the wholeness of the Logos includes both the historical body and the divine fulness. The inspiration of scripture achieves its goal when "the doctrines presented in historical and material form have reached, and taken form in, the hearer . . . Scripture understood as an activity of the Logos requires a hearing and receiving subject who is acted upon."[124]

The standard examples which are usually cited of Origen's "allegorical" interpretation must be understood within this broader hermeneutical and pastoral frame. Some examples come within the broad category of "extensions" of language, rather than allegory. Like Philo, Origen is aware that the notion of God's "planting trees in the garden of Eden" (Gen. 2:8), or of there being a first "day" before the creation of sun and moon (Gen. 1:5,16) cannot be taken at face value as spatio-physical events.[125] Origen, like Philo, collects a batch of what have sometimes been called "modern" difficulties ranging from Adam's "hiding" from God (Gen. 3:8) and the dimensions of Noah's ark (Gen. 6:15) to Jesus' surveying the kingdoms of the world from "a very high mountain" (Matt. 4:8), and invites his readers to use their intelligence about what this language is meant to convey.[126]

Other examples are more genuinely allegorical. Following what he takes to be Pauline precedent in Gal. 4: 21–24, Origen allegorizes Sarah and

Hagar in terms of the blindness that has befallen Israel. Parts of the Mosaic law are interpreted ethically and spiritually, and de-historicized. Even the prayer "Give us this day our daily bread" (Matt. 6:11) points beyond a request for food to a request for Christ, the true manna. Origen insists that this follows the example of Paul in such passages as 1 Cor. 10: 1–4: "You observe how greatly the sense Paul gives us differs from the narrative of the texts."[127] The most striking examples of Origen's allegorization occur in his treatment of the parables of the Labourers in the Vineyard and the Good Samaritan. Of those who are called to work in the vineyard (Matt. 20: 1–16) the ones who toil all day represent humankind from Adam to Noah; those who are called at the third hour are the generations from Noah to Abraham; those who begin at the sixth hour belong to the period from Abraham to Moses; the last represent generations from Joshua to Christ. In the Parable of the Good Samaritan (Luke 10: 30–37) the man who journeys to Jericho and is left half dead is humanity in its sin and corruption; the priest represents the law, and the Levite, the prophets; the oil used by the Samaritan, who is Christ, is mercy; the inn signifies the church, and the innkeeper, the apostles. The two denarii signify various possibilities, including the two Testaments.[128]

On the basis of this extreme example of radical allegory it is understandable why in the context of modern historical models of interpretation Adolf von Harnack should have described this approach as "biblical alchemy." But it is not entirely characteristic of Origen, and it is not, in the end, an infinitely "unending" semiosis, because while historical and semantic constraints on meaning have here disappeared, Origen will not move, at least in theory, outside the frame of biblical tradition. He wishes to interpret scripture in the light of scripture. Where Origen has most radically transformed the text, however, in its change of *function*. Parable and allegory *perform different functions* and *address different audiences*.

The narrative-world of a parable draws the hearer in, so that within this "world" values and attitudes may be challenged and changed at a pre-cognitive level. Parables are used to address *critics*, *enquirers* or *observers*. But an allegory presupposes the possession of an interpretative key which can be used by *insiders* to unlock the code by a series of transpositional exercizes on the individual components of the narrative. Thus a parable speaks as a whole which operates at a pre-cognitive level; allegory is didactic and cerebral, and treats the narrative as a series of separate translatable units. Eta Linnemann observes: "Anyone who does not have this key can read the words, but the deeper meaning is hidden from him. Allegories therefore may serve to transmit encoded information, which is only intelligible to the initiated . . . The parable speaks (for preference) to opponents; the allegory, to the initiated. The parable is used to reconcile opposition, the allegory presupposes an understanding."[129] Even Bunyan's

Pilgrim's Progress, as an allegory, presupposes a certain level of biblical understanding on the part of the reader.

If the earlier comments about Origen's pastoral concern are valid, the transformation of a parable into an allegory may rest partly on the change of audience which Origen is addressing. This does *not* imply that his is the "correct" way of re-interpreting these two parables; only that Origen is probably aware of the hermeneutical problem which a change of audience entails. If his wish was to convey the particular theological message which his allegory suggests he could have communicated it more responsibly on the basis of some other biblical text or set of passages.

We may conclude, then, that Origen's "allegorical" interpretation takes a variety of forms, and operates with varying degrees of hermeneutical success and failure, depending largely on his aim in particular cases. At times "allegorical interpretation" comes closer to representing what we should nowadays call pastoral application, and here Origen is at his best. At times it represents a common-sense insistence that much biblical language is metaphorical or at least extended beyond a *prima facie* spatio-temporal application. As R.P.C. Hanson reminds us, Origen faced not only Marcionite traditions of thought which devalued the Old Testament by drawing attention to its anthropomorphic language about God and its *prima facie* contradictions, but also criticism of the Bible as a whole by those outside the church who pressed their criticisms by means of literalist interpretations of the text.[130] They drew attention to such "modern secular" difficulties as Zechariah's language about God's "seven eyes" (Zech. 4:10), or the Psalmist's allusion to God's "wings" (Ps.91:4) At other times Origen's methods can result in the banal and bizarre. In his eagerness to accommodate "secular" and other criticism, Origen went too far, as Kugel and Greer argue, in emptying certain biblical texts effectively of their narrative meaning.[131] Nevertheless he does not look for a polyvalent meaning which is totally arbitrary. His is not the "grand allegory" of Philo and Clement, even if selected examples of arbitrary interpretation can be found.

Raymond Williams contributes a suggestive article in which he makes certain comparisons between semiotic transposition in Origen's biblical interpretation and Levi-Strauss's view of transpositions in myth. Origen, he argues, follows "a careful logic which he believed to be the logic of the Word".[132] Texts open doors to other texts, and we find something like a notion of *intertextuality* in which scripture is interpreted always by scripture. "Origen was more concerned with the letter than most, because only through the letter could he reach the heights of spiritual interpretation."[133] But in the end, as Duncan Ferguson also concludes, the Antiochene Fathers were right in their claim that Origen and the other Alexandrians failed to achieve an adequately *historical* understanding of the broad temporal unfolding of the divine purposes in word and deed in scripture.[134] Williams sees here a parallel with the structuralist pre-occupation with transpositions in a-historical systems.

In his recent article on allegory in Origen Gerald Bostock endorses the principle that Origen places limits and constraints, or what he calls "safeguards", against the undue proliferation of polyvalent meaning. These include the unity of scripture, the interpretation of scripture in the light of scripture, and the church's rule of faith.[135] But he is more generous in his assessment of Origen's attitude towards history, because he believes that for Origen the contingent events of biblical history and the recurring events of existential human experience represent a "both . . .and . . .", not an either/or. He compares C.S. Lewis's comment: "When you accepted the exodus of Israel from Egypt as a type of the soul's escape from sin, you did not on that account abolish the exodus as a historical event." The events of the incarnation and of the crucifixion are concrete historical events which *also* "look forward to an existential reality".[136] Thus Origen writes: "In this way his crucifixion contains the truth indicated by the words '*I have been crucified with Christ* (Gal. 2:20) . . . So also his burial extends to those who are conformed to his death . . . , as Paul says: 'By baptism we were buried with him' (Rom. 6:4), and we have risen together with him."[137]

While these caveats and qualifications may be accepted, there remains a greater emphasis on history and a related suspicion of polyvalent meaning among the Antiochene Fathers. This may suggest another point of contrast. Origen, as we earlier noted, drew a distinction between "mere words" and the frame within which a text was understood. But the orientation remains largely *inter-textual*, or at least concerns the relation between intertextual transposition and *the reader*. John Chryostom (c.347–407), by contrast, explicates the following primary hermeneutical dictum: "We must not examine the words as bare words . . . nor examine the language by itself, but we must mark *the mind of the writer*".[138] Chryostom expounds this principle in terms of life-understanding: understanding our neighbour, and the patterns of action around us.[139] In today's vocabulary we should say that where the Alexandrians stressed *reader-related intertextuality*, the Antiochenes stressed *author-related intersubjectivity*. This led them to more effective and realistic constraints on polyvalency of meaning.

Just as the conclusions of this chapter suggest that we should be cautious even in generalizing about Alexandrian interpretation, even so varied purposes and practices occur within the Antiochene school. John Chrysostom does sometimes use allegorical interpretation. In Proverbs, for example, there is a passage in which he seems to echo Origen: the "corner of the roof" (Prov. 21:9) seems to signify a good action, brought to light by the "sun" of righteousness. But in principle and mostly in practice Chrysostom's criteria of meaning remain historical and contextual. The contention, for example, that Paul's language about marriage (2 Cor. 7:1ff) applies to priests, is excluded in Chrysostom's view by "judging from what follows". "Paul himself interprets his meaning in the words which follow."[140] It is fundamental to reflect on "the aim of the speaker". This includes the context of situation. Thus in 1 Cor. 8:4, where Paul discussed the status of belief in idols, Chrysostom asserts that we must carefully observe whether the Apostle states something absolutely (*apolelumenos*, effectively context-free) or from a circumstantial position towards certain persons. This contributes in an important way, he stresses, to how we apprehend his words. The interpreter is to seek the "literal" meaning in this contextual and purposive sense. The "literal" may include the use of metaphor or other figures of speech, if this is the meaning which the purpose of the author and the linguistic context suggest. The role, then, which is performed by inter-relations between texts for Origen seems to be parallelled, with different effects, by the relation between a text and the life-situation of its author for Chrysostom. This contrast between signifying systems and persons, or between intertextuality and intersubjectivity will be taken up and directly addressed in our examination of Schleiermacher's hermeneutics, and in subsequent chapters.

NOTES TO CHAPTER IV

1. Origen, *De Principiis* IV. 1:7–20.
2. Richard N. Longenecker "Three Ways of Understanding Relations between the Testaments" in Gerald F. Hawthorne and Otto Betz (eds.) *Tradition and Interpretation in the New Testament: Essays in Honor of E Earle Ellis*, Grand Rapids: Eerdmans and Tubingen: Mohr, 1987, 28; cf. 22–29.
3. Northrop Frye, *The Great Code* 220.
4. *Ibid* 221.
5. *Ibid* 222–23.
6. G.R. Evans, *The Language and Logic of the Bible: the Earlier Middle Ages*, Cambridge: Cambridge University Press, 1984,14, 15.
7. *Ibid* 24, 25.
8. John D. Caputo, *Radical Hermeneutics*, 2.
9. Clement of Alexandria, *Stromata* I:12.56.2.
10. Richard P.C. Hanson, *Tradition in the Early Church*, London: S.C.M. , 1962, 125 and 127; cf. 75–129.
11. Cyril of Alexandria, *Epistles* 1 and 4; cf. Johannes Quasten, *Patrology* Eng. Westminster: Christian Classics, 1984 (1950) vol. 3, 135–36.
12. C.H. Dodd, *The Authority of the Bible*, London: Nisbet, 1938, 289 and 298 (my italics).
13. *Ibid* 299.
14. H.G. Gadamer, *Truth and Method* 251; cf. 245–58.
15. *Ibid* 258.
16. *Ibid* 248.

17. *Ibid.*
18. Georgia Warnke, *Gadamer: Hermeneutics, Tradition, and Reason*, Cambridge: Polity Press, 1987, 75–82.
19. Thomas S. Kuhn, *The Essential Tension: Selected Studies in a Scientific Tradition and Change* Chicago: University of Chicago Press, 1977; Jürgen Habermas, *Knowledge and Human Interests*, Eng. London: Heinemann, 2nd edn. 1978; Richard J. Bernstein, *Beyond Objectivism and Relativism: Science, Hermeneutics, and Praxis*, Oxford: Blackwell, 1983; Peter Winch, *The Idea of a Social Science and its Relation to Philosophy*, London: Routledge & Kegan Paul, 1958.
20. Ulrich Luz, *Das Geschichtsverständnis des Paulus*, Munich: Kaiser, 1968, 134 (my italics).
21. Anthony T. Hanson, *The Living Utterances of God: The New Testament Exegesis of the Old*, London: Darton, Longman & Todd, 1983, 44–62, and *The New Testament Interpretation of Scripture*, London: S.P.C.K., 1980; Richard N Longenecker, *Biblical Exegesis in the Apostolic Period*, Grand Rapids: Eerdmans, 1975; J.W. Aageson, "Scripture and Structure in the Development of the Argument in Romans 9–11" *Catholic Biblical Quarterly* 48, 1986, 268–89, and "Typology, Correspondence, and the Application of Scripture in Romans 9–11" *Journal for the Study of the New Testament* 31, 1987, 51–72; D. Moody Smith, "The Pauline Literature" in D.A. Carson and H.G.M. Williamson (eds.) *It is Written: Scripture Citing Scripture. Essays in Honour of Barnabas Lindars*, Cambridge: Cambridge University Press, 1988, 265–91.
22. D. Moody Smith, *loc. cit.* 287 (my italics).
23. *Ibid* 288 (my italics).
24. A.T. Hanson, *The Living Utterances of God*, 62.
25. *Ibid* 233–34.
26. Leonhard Goppelt, *Typos: The Typological Interpretation of the Old Testament in the New*, Eng., Grand Rapids: Eerdmans, 1982, 237.
27. G.K. Beale, "Revelation" in Don A. Carson and H.G.M. Williamson (eds.) *op. cit.* 333 (Beale's italics).
28. D.A. Carson, "John and the Johannine Epistles" *Ibid* 259. .
29. Graham Stanton, "Matthew", *Ibid* 205 and 217.
30. Morna Hooker, *Ibid* 228, cf. Klaus Berger, *Die Gesetzesauslegung Jesu. Ihr historischer Hintergrund im Judentum und im Alten Testament*, Neukirchen-Vluyn: Neukirchener, 1972.
31. Bruce D. Chilton, "Commentary in the Old Testament" in D.A. Carson and H.G.M. Williamson (eds.) *op. cit.* 122–40; M.P. Horgan, *Pesharim: Qumran Interpretations of Biblical Books*, Washington: Catholic Biblical Quarterly Monograph, 1979; Daniel Patte, *Early Jewish Hermeneutic in Palestine*, Missoula: Scholars Press, 1975, 301–08, cf. 211–31; A.T. Hanson, *The Living Utterances of God* 14–43; Richard Longenecker, *op. cit.* 38–45.
32. Bruce D. Chilton, *A Galilean Rabbi and his Bible: Jesus' own Interpretation of Isaiah*, London: S.P.C.K., 1984.
33. Justin, *Apologia* I, 46. Cf. Willis A. Shotwell, *The Biblical Exegesis of Justin Martyr*, London: S.P.C.K. 1965, 2–8.
34. Irenaeus, *Adversus Haereses* IV. 26:2 and IV. 21:3.
35. Irenaeus, IV. 27:1.
36. Elaine H. Pagels, *The Johannine Gospel in Gnostic Exegesis: Heracleon's Commentary*

Pre-Modern Biblical Interpretation 175

on *John*, Nashville & New York: Abingdon Press, 1973; and *The Gnostic Paul: Gnostic Exegesis of the Pauline Letters*, Philadelphia: Fortress, 1975; Samuel Laeuchli, *The Language of Faith: An Introduction to the Semantic Dilemma of the Early Church*, London: Epworth Press, 1965.

37. Anthony C. Thiselton, "Realized Eschatology at Corinth", *New Testament Studies* 24, 1978, 510–26.
38. E.H. Pagels, *The Johannine Gospel in Gnostic Exegesis*, 35.
39. Werner Foerster (ed.), *Gnosis: A Selection of Gnostic Texts* (2 vols.) Eng. Oxford: Clarendon Press, 1972 and 1974; cf. Kendrick Grobel, *The Gospel of Truth*, London: Black, 1960.
40. Samuel Laeuchli, *op. cit.* 77.
41. *Ibid* 84 and 86.
42. *Ibid* 88.
43. *Ibid* 89.
44. *Ibid* 43.
45. Robert C. Gregg and Dennis E. Groh, *Early Arianism. A View of Salvation*, London: S.C.M., 1981.
46. Athanasius, *Orationes contra Arianos* III. 29.
47. R.C. Gregg and D.E. Groh, *op. cit.* 166–67.
48. Irenaeus IV. 26:1.
49. Irenaeus IV. 33:6; cf. *Proof of the Apostolic Preaching*, (ed. Joseph P Smith) New York: Newman, 1952, 36.
50. Adolf Harnack, *History of Dogma* Eng. London: Williams & Norgate, vol. 1, 3rd edn., 1895, 89.
51. Irenaeus, IV. 28:1, cf. Andrew Louth, *Discerning the Mystery. An Essay on the Nature of Theology*, Oxford: Clarendon Press, 1983.
52. Irenaeus, *Proof of the Apostolic Preaching*, 46; cf. *Epistle of Barnabas* 12:2; and Justin, *Dialogue* 91; 112; 131.
53. Irenaeus, *Proof*, 34.
54. Irenaeus, *Proof*, 57.
55. Justin, *Apologia* 1:32 and *Dialogue* 54.
56. Irenaeus, *Adversus Haereses* II. 28:3 and I. 8:1.
57. Richard P.C. Hanson, *Allegory and Event. A Study of the Sources and Significance of Origen's Interpretation of Scripture*, London: S.C.M. 1959, 111.
58. Irenaeus, *Adversus Haereses* I. 11:1 and II. 5:2.
59. Irenaeus I. 8:1.
60. Irenaeus I. 9:2.
61. Andrew Louth, *Discerning the Mystery. An Essay on the Nature of Theology*, 84.
62. A. Skevington Wood, *The Principles of Biblical Interpretation as Enunciated by Irenaeus, Origen, Augustine, Luther and Calvin*, Grand Rapids: Zondervan, 1967, 31.
63. Irenaeus, *Adversus Haereses* II:27. On Irenaeus, see further, Frances Young, *op. cit.* 45–65.
64. Heraclitus Stoicus, *Quaestiones Homerieae*, 22.
65. Leslie W. Barnard, "To Allegorize or Not to Allegorize?" *Studia Theologica* 36, 1982, 1; cf. 1–10.
66. Umberto Eco, *Semiotics and the Philosophy of Language*, London: MacMillan, 1984, 148.

67. Above, chapter III, section 5.
68. Andrew Louth, *op. cit.*, 97; cf 96–131.
69. *Ibid* 112 and 113; Origen, Philokalia VI.2.
70. *Ibid* 111.
71. Luther, *Works*, Weimar edn. VI.301.
72. Umberto Eco, *Semiotics and the Philosophy of Language* 147 .
73. Plato, *Ion* 534d.
74. Erwin R. Goodenough, *An Introduction to Philo Judaeus*, 2nd edn. Oxford: Blackwell, 1962; Harry A. Wolfson, *Philo* (2 vols.) Cambridge: Harvard University Press, 1947; Samuel Sandmel, *Philo of Alexandria. An Introduction*, Oxford: Oxford University Press, 1979; and *Philo's Place in Judaism* 2nd edn. New York: Ktav, 1971.
75. David Winston, *Philo of Alexandria: The Contemplative Life, the Giants, and Selections*, London: S.P.C.K., 1981, xi (comment from John Dillon's Preface).
76. V. Nikiprowetzky, *Le commentaire de l'écriture chez Philon d'Alexandrie*, Leiden: Brill, 1977, 50 ff.
77. Klaus Otte, *Das Sprachverständnis bei Philo von Alexandrien: Sprache als Mittel der Hermeneutik*, Tübingen: Mohr, 1968, pp. 1–44; cf 105–118.
78. Philo, *De mutatione nominum* 8; *Quis rerum divinarum heres sit* 53; *De vita Mosis* III.23.
79. Philo, *De Posteritate Caini* 11 and 14.
80. Philo, *Legum Allegoriae* III. 12 and 16.
81. Philo, *De ebrietate* 36.
82. Philo, *De plantatione* 8.
83. Philo, *De congressu quaerendae eruditionis gratia* 1–6. .
84. S. Sandmel, *Philo of Alexandria* 24.
85. Rudolf Bultmann, "New Testament and Mythology" in Hans Werner Bartsch *Kerygma and Myth* (2 vols.), Eng. 2nd edn. London: S.P.C.K. 1964, & 1962, vol. I, 10.
86. Anthony C. Thiselton, *The Two Horizons* 252–92.
87. Rudolf Bultmann, *Faith and Understanding I*, Eng. London: S.C.M. 1969, 29; cf *The Two Horizons* 218–26.
88. Rudolf Bultmann, "New Testament and Mythology" *loc. cit.* 13.
89. Philo, De Agricultura, 96, 97.
90. Philo, *De migratione Abrahami*, 93.
91. Leonhard Goppelt, *Typos: The Typological Interpretation of the Old Testament in the New*, Eng. Grand Rapids: Eerdmans, 1982, 52.
92. Gerald Bostock, "Allegory and the Interpretation of the Bible in Origen", *Journal of Literature and Theology* I, 1987, 39; cf 39–53.
93. Frederic W Farrar, *History of Interpretation*, Grand Rapids: Baker, rp. 1961, 140.
94. J. Bonsirven, *Exégèse rabbinique et exégèse paulinienne*, Paris: Beauchesne, 1939, 309–10; C. K. Barrett, in *The Cambridge History of the Bible* I (ed. Peter R. Ackroyd and C.F. Evans), Cambridge: Cambridge University Press, 1970, 391–92; F.F. Bruce, *This is That: The New Testament Development of Old Testament Themes*, Exeter: Paternoster, 1968, 54, and *The Epistle of Paul to the Galatians. A Commentary on the Greek Text*, Grand Rapids: Eerdmans, 1982, 217 ff.; R.N. Longenecker, *op. cit.* 127–29; and Otto Michel, *Paulus und seine Bibel*, Gutersloh: Bertelsmann, 1929, 110.

95. Geoffrey W.H. Lampe and K.J. Woollcombe, *Essays on Typology*, London: S.C.M. 1957, 39.
96. E. Earl Ellis, "Foreword" in L. Goppelt, *op. cit.* x.
97. J.W. Aageson, "Typology, Correspondence, and the Application of Scripture in Romans 9–11" *Journal for the Study of the N.T* 31, 1987, 66; cf 51–72.
98. R.P.C. Hanson, *Allegory and Event* 82.
99. R.N. Longenecker, *op. cit.* 129.
100. Martin Luther, *A Commentary on St. Paul's Epistle to the Galatians* Eng. London: Clarke, 1953, 417; John Calvin, *The Epistles of Paul the Apostle to the Galatians, Ephesians, Philippians and Colossians* Eng. Edinburgh: Oliver & Boyd 1965, 85.
101. Ronald Williamson, *Philo and the Epsitle to the Hebrews*, Leiden: Brill, 1970; cf also R.P.C. Hanson, *op. cit.* 83; E.C. Blackman, *Biblical Interpretation* London: Independent Press, 1957, 88–9.
102. C.H. Dodd, *According to the Scriptures*, London: Fontana edn. 1963, 109 (his italics).
103. *Ibid* 126 and 128 (Dodd's italics).
104. *Ibid* 130.
105. Elaine Pagels, *The Johannine Gospel in Gnostic Exegesis*, 52.
106. *Ibid* 66–67.
107. Clement, *Stromata* V 21:4.
108. Clement, *Stromata* V 12.
109. Clement, *Stromata* VI 15.
110. A.H.J. Gunneweg, *Understanding the Old Testament* Eng. London: S.C.M. 1978, 36.
111. R.P.C. Hanson, *Allegory and Event*, 117.
112. Clement, *Fragments from the Hypotyposes* V.
113. Andrew Louth, *op. cit.* 94.
114. Karen Jo Torjesen, *Hermeneutical Procedure and Theological Method in Origen's Exegesis*, Berlin: Walter de Gruyter, 1986, especially 36 ff; Gerald Bostock "Allegory and the Interpretation of the Bible in Origen" *loc. cit.*; B. de Margerie, *Introduction a l'histoire de l'exégese* (3 vols.), Paris: Les Editions du Cerf, 1980–83); R.B. Tollinton, *Selections from the Commentaries and Homilies of Origen*, London: S.P.C.K. 1929; R.P.C. Hanson, *Allegory and Event*; Joseph W. Trigg, Origen: *The Bible and Philosophy in the Third-century Church*, London: S.C.M. 1983.
115. R.B. Tollinton, *op. cit.* xxvi and xxxiii.
116. Hans Urs Von Balthasar, "Preface" to Rowan A. Greer (ed.) *Origen: An Exhortation to Martyrdom, Prayer, and Selected Works*, London: S.P.C.K. 1979, xii; Karen Torjesen, *op. cit.* 43–9.
117. Origen, *Commentary on John* I.10.
118. Origen, *De Principiis* IV 1:7; cf Karen Torjesen, *op. cit.* 38.
119. Origen, *De Principiis* IV 1:6.
120. Origen, *De Principiis* IV 1:11.
121. Karen Torjesen *op. cit.* 40.
122. *Ibid.*
123. *Ibid* 27–28; cf 26–29.
124. *Ibid* 146.
125. Origen, *De Principiis* IV 3:1.
126. Origen, *Contra Celsum* 4:41; *De Principiis* IV 3:1,2.

127. Origen, *Homilies in Exodus* 5:1.
128. Origen, *Homilies in Luke*, 34.
129. Eta Linnemann, *Parables of Jesus. Introduction and Exposition* Eng. London: S.P.C.K. 1966, 7.
130. R.P.C. Hanson, *op. cit.* 133–61.
131. James L. Kugel and Rowan A. Greer, *Early Biblical Interpretation*, Philadelphia: Westminster, 1986, 179.
132. Raymond B. Williams, "Origen's Interpretation of the Old Testament and Lévi-Strauss' Interpretation of Myth" in A.L. Merrill and T.W. Overholt (eds.) *Scripture in History and Theology: Essays in Honour of J.C. Rylaarsdam*, Pittsburgh: Pickwick Press, 1977, 297; cf 279–99.
133. *Ibid* 289–90.
134. Duncan S. Ferguson, *Biblical Hermeneutics. An Introduction*, London: S.C.M. 1986, 148.
135. Gerald Bostock, *loc. cit.* 51–2.
136. *Ibid* 42.
137. Origen, *Contra Celsum* II.69; Gerald Bostock, *loc. cit.* 51.
138. John Chrysostom X 675A (my italics).
139. Frederic H. Chase, *Chrysostom, A Study in the History of Biblical Interpretation* Cambridge: Deighton, Bell & Co., 1887, 157.
140. John Chrysostom IX. 531 D.

CHAPTER V

The Hermeneutics of Enquiry: From the Reformation to Modern Theory

1. Three Polemical Contexts which Give "Claritas Scripturae" its Currency: Epistemology, "Higher" Meanings, and Efficacy

The doctrine of the perspicuity (*claritas*) of scripture, which is associated so closely with the Reformers and with classical Protestantism, might superficially seem to point in either of two directions as far as theories of interpretation are concerned. On the one hand, it has been interpreted in certain strands of Christian pietism as a signal that hermeneutical theory and endeavour is scarcely necessary, since all believers, irrespective of particular competence or training, find scripture clear in its meaning and application. On the other hand, it has been taken, in the other direction, to signify a coming of age from dependency on tradition or on the magisterium of the church, and thereby to constitute an invitation to purely rational reflection, on the ground that the meaning of scripture is open to straightforward enquiry, provided that this is conducted on the right basis.

Neither of these two interpretations can be fully convincing in the light of the Reformers' own practices. With regard to the first, Calvin in particular, but also Luther and other Reformers, wrote numerous exegetical and expository commentaries on the text, and discussed issues concerning the problem of biblical interpretation. They could have spared themselves immense labours if the first interpretation were to be taken at its face value. But there are also difficulties about the second. Although the Reformers believed that the scriptures stood, as it were, on their own feet rather than being dependent for their use and understanding on the *magisterium* of the church of the day, Luther and Calvin deeply respected the early patristic traditions. It is true that, as the Wittenberg University Luther Symposuim *Luther and Learning* has amply demonstrated, Luther's early scholastic training, his intense concern about university education, and his intimate knowledge of humanistic scholarship, all underline his stature as a thinker for whom learning and scholarship were indispensable tools.[1] Nevertheless

Luther and Calvin also stressed the limitations of rational enquiry outside a firm framework of Christian faith and understanding.

To appreciate what is genuinely at issue in the emphasis of Luther and Calvin on *claritas scripturae* we need to examine with care how it emerged in various polemical contexts, and also its formulation in the context of questions about the status of human knowledge. In relation to the claim that we noted, for example, in Clement of Alexandria and others that the meaning of scripture is *in principle* puzzling and polyvalent, the perspicuity of scripture emerges as a *hermeneutical* principle. In relation to the claim that scripture can be interpreted only in the light of the received *magisterium* of the church, it becomes a *Christological, ecclesiological and critical* principle. In relation to the claim that no *knowledge* can be sufficiently certain to allow theological judgments to result in radical action, the perspicuity of scripture becomes an *epistemological* principle.

If we are to judge from the respective degrees of intensity with which Luther asserts the perspicuity of scripture in different writings, it is most appropriate to begin with his controversy with Erasmus about the status of knowledge in the form which this issue takes in Luther's work *On the Bondage of the Will* (1525). James Atkinson admirably identifies what was at issue.[2] Up until about 1524 Erasmus forwarded the Reformation both positively, by reviving classical, biblical, and patristic studies; and also negatively by exposing the inadequacies, excesses, and distortions of assumptions and practices within the church of the day. Erasmus sought to restore the church to greater simplicity and purity. But he had two reservations in relation to Luther. First, he did not share Luther's confidence that the foundations of knowledge were clear enough to allow the radical action which Luther urged; second, he did not fully share Luther's doctrines of sin, grace, and human nature.

The watershed came somewhere between 1520 and 1524. James Atkinson writes: "As long as reformation was being *discussed*, Erasmus went along with the idea. As soon as Luther burned the papal bull and the decretals in 1520, and had taken his stand at Worms in 1521, Erasmus began to withdraw."[3] Atkinson points out that Erasmus's very decency and goodness paradoxically constituted an obstacle to his fully appreciating the radical nature of grace and sin which Luther emphasized. The same might be said of his theory of knowledge, where his generosity of judgment could give the opponent sufficient benefit of the doubt to question a theological decision that could result in firm action, at least in supposedly "inessential" matters. Richard H. Popkin sums up the epistemological point: "Erasmus's . . . dislike of rational theological discussions led him to suggest a kind of *sceptical basis* for remaining within the Catholic Church . . . Human affairs are so obscure and various that nothing can be clearly known."[4] Popkin's philosophical discussion provides a most helpful contextual interpretation.

The Hermeneutics of Enquiry

This is the primary context in which Luther formulates his theme of the "clarity" of scripture, especially in his work *On the Bondage of the Will*. Luther rejects Erasmus's claim that it is impossible to reach genuinely firm conclusions which will provide a basis for innovative action because the teaching of the scriptures is in no way equivocal or uncertain. Luther is not speaking initially of certainty or clarity about the exegesis of particular passages, but of the capacity of scripture as a whole to provide criteria of knowledge. He writes, "If the laws were equivocal and uncertain, not only would no issues be settled, but no sure standards of conduct would exist."[5] That which is to be a measure and yardstick must be clear and determinate in meaning. Otherwise, how could the Psalmist experience and describe God's word as a lamp and a light? (Psalm 119: 105). Scripture is called a path by reason of its "entire certainty". In the New Testament, Luther urges, Christ is a light (John 8:12) and Christians have "a sure word of prophecy" (II Pet. 1:19). How can scripture be obscure if God has given it? It is "a shameless blasphemy that the scriptures are obscure . . . Those who deny the perfect clarity and plainness of the scriptures leave us nothing but darkness . . . I would say in the whole of Scripture that I do not allow any part of it to be called obscure".[6] Luther writes: "You see, then that the entire content of the scriptures has now been brought to light, even though some passages which contain unknown words remain obscure."[7] "Nothing whatsoever is left obscure or ambiguous."[8]

This contextual understanding of Luther, however, should also be extended to Erasmus. Reventlow shows that Erasmus advocated toleration and caution only on matters which he regarded as "inessential". Reventlow claims that Erasmus is the first to put forward "the need to distinguish between essential and inessential principles of faith . . . Erasmus also coined the description of doctrines 'by which the church stands and falls'."[9] Nevertheless, Erasmus also makes less carefully qualified statements. In his book *The Praise of Folly* he asserts: "Human affairs are so obscure and various that nothing can be *clearly* known."[10] In his *The Freedom of the Will* (1524) he argues that this lack of clarity characterizes even scripture, at least in contrast to the confidence with which Luther uses it. His debt to Neoplatonism reduces the significance of the literal, contextual, or historical meaning of the text, as against the spiritual or allegorical. He appeals to scriptural language about "hidden" wisdom.

In reply, Luther asserts: "You would readily take up the sceptics' position whenever the inviolate authority of Holy Scripture or the Church's decisions permit."[11] But: "what Christian can endure the idea that we should deprecate *assertions*?"[12] Luther accepts Erasmus' citation of Rom. 11:33 to the effect that God's will is inscrutable, in that we cannot plumb the depths or the limit of God's being and will. But this is not a basis for scepticism, because who could direct himself according to a will that is wholly inscrutable and incapable of expression? Erasmus has "cherished a Lucian, or some other hog of Epicurus' herd. . . . (But) the Holy Spirit is no sceptic, and the things he has written in our hearts are not doubts or opinion, but assertions – surer and more certain than sense and life itself."[13]

None of this offers any ground for suggesting that questions of interpretation and hermeneutics need not be taken seriously. In the first context of epistemology, what Luther attacks is the denial of the possibility of making *truth-claiming assertions* on the basis of the biblical writings. Whereas for Erasmus, the inconclusive nature of biblical interpretation re-enforces a gentle working scepticism, for Luther the belief that scripture as a whole carries a contextual meaning which *in principle* can be understood re-enforces a firm programme of faith and action.

The work of Heinrich Bornkamm, among others, reminds us of the many points on which Luther had to fight during the period 1521–30, to which *On the Bondage of the Will* belongs.[14] If the primary context of thought for Luther's *claritas scripturae* was epistemological, other contexts, no less polemical, also played their part. These related to hermeneutics, to Christian faith, and to the church. All three aspects are discussed in a specialist treatment of this subject by Friedrich Beisser.[15] Luther did not question that the interpretation of specific biblical texts might invite enquiry and controversy, and require strenuous effort to resolve. But he rejected the notion that ecclesiastical *magisterium* could settle such questions by *fiat*. This would be like "adding to the word of God or taking away from it (Deut. 4:2)"[16] Luther was concerned not only about the self-preserving interpretations of those in ecclesiastical office, but also about claims to possess secret esoteric keys to meaning made on the basis of supposed revelations by the Spirit to selected individuals.

Luther's position here, however, is sometimes misunderstood. He attacked an authoritarian and self-serving appeal to tradition as a means of forcing scripture to speak with a certain voice. But he did not seek to substitute individual opinion for tradition in a way akin to the mood of post-Enlightenment rationalism. It was important to Luther, for example, to consult the writings of the Fathers of the Church, provided that undue weight was not given to them. Commenting on Luther's work as expositor Jaroslav Pelikan concludes "in opposing traditionalism, therefore, Luther claimed to be opposing not the tradition itself, or even the proper use of the tradition in theology, but the abuse of the tradition. He took the position of defending the tradition against its abusers."[17] The Fathers themselves, he urged, had not wished to elevate their interpretations into articles of faith.

If scripture is to serve, however, not as a mere reflection of existing tradition, but, rather, as a *critical test and corrective* of it, Luther saw that this called into question the *multiplex intelligentia* of scripture which characterized many mediaeval and scholastic writers. In the previous chapter we noted the contrast between the *lectio divina* of Rupert of Deutz (c.1070–c.1129) and the more historical and contextual interpretation of Anselm of Canterbury. Both traditions, although predominately the former, characterized Christian biblical interpretation from the time of Gregory the Great (c. 540–604) until the time of Luther. Origen's "three senses" and Alexandrian interpretation influenced Augustine through Ambrose, and the approach of Augustine and Gregory dominated much of the mediaeval tradition.

Although the notion of the four-fold sense probably originated in the first half of the fifth century, and is used by Augustine, Gregory formulates it explicitly: (i) the literal meaning, which may include figurative language or metaphor, arises from the historical situation and context of the text; (ii) the allegorical interpretation, as we have noted, may be a theological, Christological, or devotional extension or transposition of the historical meaning; (iii) the moral meaning embodies a practical application for present conduct; (iv) the anagogical meaning embraces the horizon of the future consummation. Gregory himself does not apply this four-fold scheme uniformly or consistently.[18] In the mediaeval tradition there are those who, like Anselm, placed primary emphasis on the historical sense. These included, for example, Hugh of St. Victor (c.1096–1141) and Thomas Aquinas (c.1225–1274).[19] But for the most part Bede (672–735) and others follow the pattern suggested by Gregory, and many of the Franciscan preachers, it is claimed, considered all four senses to be of equal importance.[20]

Luther acknowledges that in his earlier years as a monk, he, too "allegorized everything".[21] In his younger years, he recalls, he dealt in allegories and analogies, but now "I know they are nothing but rubbish."[22] It is important to bear in mind this chronological development when Luther is accused of gross inconsistency in his view of allegorical interpretation. The earlier Luther used the fourfold scheme of mediaeval interpretation. The later Luther could also use it in instances where he believed that a point which was being made had been, or would be, established on other independent grounds. But if scripture is to consitutute not only a word from God but also a *criterion* and potential *corrective* for current tradition, how can the ordinary believer appeal to the open meaning of the biblical text if a dignitary of the church, or a person of esoteric learning, can reply that the historical and contextual meaning of a text is nothing more than a door to some supposedly "higher" meaning?

Luther's appeal to a "plain" or "natural" meaning, therefore, is not the fruit of naïve objectivism, as if to imply that nothing depended on some existing context of understanding. Beisser, and others, discuss this issue, to which we shall return shortly. The point of the semantic contrast turns primarily on the difference between "natural" meaning and "multiple" or allegorical meaning. Even if the latter stimulates imaginative meditation, it cannot serve for the formulation of true assertions about God and the gospel, at least in its own right, rather than as an illustration of what can be proved from scripture elsewhere. Gerhard Ebeling rightly underlines the point to which we alluded: if the mature Luther uses allegory, this is usually only for homiletical or illustrative purposes, relating to what has been proved on other grounds.[23]

Luther therefore declares: "The Christian reader should make it his first task to seek out the literal sense, as they call it. For it alone is the whole substance of faith and Christian theology; it alone holds its ground in trouble and trial".[24] Elsewhere he comments: "it is the historical sense alone which supplies the true and sound doctrine".[25] Although he respects Origen as a teacher, Luther considers his allegorization to have been disastrous. It is on this basis that Karlstadt transposes the meaning of scripture by pure juggling. Although he prefers to speak of the "plain" or the "natural" meaning, Luther accepts the use of the term "literal". In contrast to allegory, he roundly declares, "The literal sense does it – in it there is life, comfort, power, instruction and skill. The other is tomfoolery."[26]

If we place together the three polemical contexts in which Luther insists on the perspicuity of scripture, one further point emerges. *Claritas scripturae* is a relational, contextual, or functional concept. As G.C. Berkouwer, following H. Bavinck, asserts: "Clarity does not mean that scientific exegesis would be unnecessary."[27] Friedrich Beisser carefully examines the distinction in Luther's thought between "internal" and "external" perspicuity. Luther writes, "If you speak of *internal* perspicuity the truth is that nobody who has not the Spirit of God sees a jot of what is in the Scriptures. All men have their hearts darkened, so that even when they can discuss and quote all that is in Scripture they do not understand or really know any of it."[28] But even external clarity remains a clarity which is relative to a given goal, and to certain needs and purposes. As Beisser notes, Luther understands external clarity as that which is seen "where the word of God is preached."[29] Luther, Beisser argues, is not speaking of scriptures in the abstract, but in their capacity to mediate the presence of Christ: "Take Christ from the scriptures, and what more will you find in them?"[30] *Claritas scripturae*, then, does not denote the idea of a context-free "obviousness" of meaning in the biblical texts. It is more closely related, as Berkouwer, Bavinck and Bernard Ramm note, to the functional concepts of "efficacy" or "sufficiency", concerning which it is appropriate to ask: efficacious for what? Or, sufficient for what?[31] The answer in the context of epistemology would be: scripture provides a ground on which we may confidently *proceed*. The context in the context of theology would be: scripture provides a witness to Christ to which we may confidently *respond*. The notion of the perspicuity of scripture, as Luther uses it, in no way offers any short-cut through the problems of interpretation and hermeneutics.

In his Microfiche concordance to Calvin's *Institutes* of 1559, F.L. Battles' work reveals that there are few uses of the actual term *claritas* in the *Institutes*, and that for the most part neither the noun *claritas* nor the adjective *clarus* bears on this discussion.[32] *Perspicuitas* is for Calvin a rhetorical concept. T.F. Torrance and T.H.L. Parker point out that Calvin is influenced here by Cicero's notion that the *interpreter* allows a text to become *perspicuous*, in the sense that the intentions of the author are allowed to flow from the text like living speech.[33] Calvin does speak, however, of the need for the interpreter to arrive at the "natural" meaning of the text, in contrast to polyvalent layers of meaning. The goal is to apprehend *verum sensum scripturae, qui germanus est et simplex*.[34] Calvin also speaks of "clarity" in the *Institutes* of scripture's power to transform human vision. Just as those who have poor sight, Calvin writes, "are scarcely to make out two consecutive words (in a book), but when aided by glasses, begin to read distinctly, so Scripture, gathering together the impressions of Deity . . . dissipates the darkness and shows us the true God clearly."[35]

Calvin is even less tolerant of allegorical interpretation than Luther. A broadly parallel function in Calvin's thought to that which Luther's notion of perspicuity performs in a different set of contexts is focused by Calvin's varied language about the powerful *effectiveness* of scripture. The meaning of the biblical text itself is like an arrow heading for its mark. Demosthenes or Cicero may move or enchant, but scripture, Calvin urges, "will so affect you, so pierce your heart, so work its way into your very marrow, that in comparison of the impression so produced, that of orator and philosopher will almost disappear, making it manifest that there is a truth divine".[36] Its authority is seen in action, not at the level of theoretical arguments about its internal properties.

In some strands of post-Reformation Protestant thought the concept of the perspicuity of scripture did undergo some change into a more isolated and less context-related idea.[37] In the century following Luther and Calvin it became more capable of being invoked by pietists as a defensive slogan against the need for strenuous thought concerning biblical interpretation. But this departs from Luther's usage. In the three polemical contexts in which Luther formulates the principle, it has the opposite effective of making biblical interpretation and enquiry about its nature more urgent. In this respect Luther leads away from the mediaeval world and points to questions of the modern era, and paves the way for fundamental questions about interpretation.

2. Questioning in the Service of Faith: Christ and Reflective Criteria in Luther

There is a technical sense in which "critical" theories of knowledge could not arise until after Kant, because Kant was the first thinker to formulate explicitly a genuinely critical philosophy which examined the limits of knowledge, and the pre-conditions under which knowledge and judgment were possible. Similarly, in the technical sense of the term, "critical" biblical interpretation is often said to begin either with the emergence of the methodological principle of doubt employed in the rationalist philosophy of Descartes, or in the isolation of historical enquiry from theology, as this emerges partially in Spinoza and Reimarus, and more fully in J.S. Semler. Thus Henning Graf Reventlow sees English Deism as "the climax of biblical criticism";[38] and Krentz and others single out Descartes and Reimarus as decisive transitional points.[39]

If we define "critical reflection" more broadly, however, as a questioning which can take place within the framework of faith and theology in order to examine the foundations of belief, should we remain fully justified in drawing an imaginary line, for example, between on one side John Collet, Laurentius Valla, Erasmus, Descartes and Hobbes, whose attitude is more "critical"; and on the other side, Luther, Tyndale, Calvin, and Hooker, who would be seen as supposedly less "critical" in terms of the seriousness with which they engaged in open enquiry? Does this not presuppose an Enlightenment definition and understanding of what may be said to constitute critical reflection, which is the very point at issue?

Luther, Tyndale, and Calvin sought public interpretative *criteria* within a framework of faith. Is "critical awareness", therefore, to be defined in terms of the extent to which the enquirer is detached from, or independent of, theology; or in terms of a willingness and capacity to *test truth*? We have already traced in Gadamer his persistent argument that critical *rationality* should not necessarily be defined in the Enlightenment way, in terms of the enthronement of individual subjective judgment as over against the witness of communities against a background of regularities of inter-subjective judgment in developing traditions. Yet critical judgment cannot be defined, either, as the freedom of the individual to reach certain judgments within some firmly bounded intellectual limits, as if tradition always had the last word, and exploration were merely a pretence or an exercise confined to a regional area. T.F. Torrance defines the intellectual freedom of the Reformers as "a repentant readiness to re-think all preconceptions and presuppositions, to put all traditional ideas to the test."[40]

The example of Descartes may be instructive. Krentz argues that he used three methodological principles which became decisive for biblical criticism. First, human individual subjective consciousness is placed at the centre of enquiry as its focus and starting-point. Second, everything is to be doubted except what is self-evident, or what may be inferred from the self-evident. Third, reason constitutes and provides the sole criterion of firm knowledge. This is an accurate account of the Cartesian *method*; but Descartes formulated it within a context of understanding in which belief in God was fundamental both as a foundation and as a frame. Within this context, Decartes explored the value of mathematical models of knowledge in philosophy, as a way of overcoming the challenges and difficulties of scepticism. Descartes' "rationalist criticism" operated as a model for critical testing, for him, only within the framework of a personal theistic faith.

With these questions in mind, we may return to Luther and the other Reformers. Does their insistence on the limitations of human reason apart from faith disqualify the seriousness with which they also stress the need to test truth and truth-claims, and to establish criteria? Luther firmly insists on the limitation and fallibility of human reason alone. In his *Prefaces to the Old Testament* he writes, "These are the scriptures which make fools of all the wise and understanding, and are open only to the small and simple, as Christ says in Matthew 11:25. Therefore dismiss your own opinions and feelings, and think of the scriptures as the loftiest and noblest of holy things, as the richest of mines which can never be sufficiently explored, in order that you may find that divine wisdom which God here lays before you in such simple guise as to quench all pride. Here you will find the swaddling clothes and the manger in which Christ lies."[41] "The saints could err ... the scriptures cannot err".[42] "The Holy Scriptures require a humble reader who shows reverence and fear towards the Word of God, and constantly says, 'Teach me, teach me, teach me'" "The Spirit resists the proud".[43] Luther continues: "Prior to faith reason is darkness ... Reason is subject to vanity, as all of God's creatures are subject to vanity, that is, to folly".[44]

Nevertheless Luther, like Paul, sees reason also as a tool which can be used well or badly, and for good or for ill. He cites an analogy: "David used a bow, a sword, and weapons, and he said, 'Not in my bow do I trust' (Psalm 44:6); but he did not spurn the resource."[45] Without the use of assessment or critical evaluation, there would be no discernment in the handling and hearing of scripture. Luther writes, for example, "One must deal cleanly with the scriptures. From the very beginning the word has come to us in various ways. It is not enough simply to look and see whether this is God's word, whether God has sent it; rather we must look and see *to whom it has been spoken, whether it fits us*. That makes all the difference between night and day. God said to David, 'Out of you shall come the king' (2 Sam. 7:13). But this does not pertain to me ... Upon that word which does pertain to me I can boldly trust and rely, as upon a strong rock. But if it does not pertain to me, then I should stand still. The false prophets pitch in and say, 'Dear people, this is the word of God'. That is true . . . But we are not the people. God has not given *us* the directive."[46]

The historical context of Luther's statements helps our understanding of their significance. Luther faced at least two sets of opponents, at this particular point. In his struggle against the "Babylonian captivity" of the church to Rome, he sought to free human judgment to examine whether the Christ of the Church was indeed the Christ of the scriptures. But he also faced opponents who had once been his followers. The quotations which we have just cited come in his treatise *How Christians Should Regard Moses*, where the particular issue at this point is not primarily the difference between law and gospel, but the attempts of Thomas Münzer and others to use the biblical writings as a blue-print for government in sixteenth-century Europe in the context of the Peasants' Revolt in 1525.[47] Luther did not support the anti-establishment stance of the radical enthusiasts who took Reformation principles too far. Rational reflection and critical discernment were called for, not merely a mindless appeal to scripture, to see that passages which *historically* related to the Jewish theocracy in the Old Testament could not simply be transferred to non-Jewish governments in the sixteenth century.

Luther's attitude to biblical interpretation also emerges more fully in his controversy with other "enthusiasts" or "fanatics" (*Schwärmer*). Andreas Karlstadt, in Luther's judgment, mishandles biblical passages, but not because he lacks any firmness of belief or subjective certainty. He and his followers "boast of possessing the Spirit, more than the apostles."[48] Luther observes, "A Christian never holds so standfastly to his Christ or . . . a fanatic holds to his teaching, for although a Christian also continues to believe until he dies, yet he often stumbles and begins to doubt. This is not so in the case of fanatics, who stand firm".[49] Nevertheless, according to Luther, biblical passages are "forced out of context" at their hands and special meanings are "added and patched on", like fastening a sea-shell to a cape.[50] The result is that Karlstadt "*constructs his own Christ*".[51]

This brings us to the heart of the issue. *Any* understanding of the Bible's witness to *Christ* needs to be tested, and where necessary corrected. Critical reflection within the framework of a Christological interpretation of scripture arises from belief in the *fallibility of the church*, including the fallibility of the church's *current understanding and interpretation* of the biblical writings. For "Christ", as Luther saw, can be only the Christ of the scriptures. *Without the Bible*, as James Smart expresses it, "*the remembered Christ becomes the imagined Christ*"; a Christ constructed and shaped "by the religiosity and unconscious desires of his worshippers".[52] If faith is to be anchored in Christ, rather than in human subjectivity, experience, and imagination, it is fundamental, Luther urged, that scripture should not be turned into a "wax nose", to be pushed into any kind of shape. Luther's Christological focus does not by-pass the need for critical reflection and evaluation; it makes it all the more urgent. When he declares: "Here, (in the Bible) you will find the swaddling clothes and manger in which Christ lies. Luther adds "Simple and lovely are these swaddling clothes, but dear is the treasure, Christ, who lies in them.".[53] He asserts, "This much is beyond question, that all the scriptures point to Christ alone".[54]

All this gives added urgency to the need for rigorous reflection about criteria of truth and levels of meaning. As Hummel remarks, Luther's emphasis "*was Christum treibt*" does not lead to a "subjective" stress on faith, gospel, and Christ *as against* exegetical struggle and hermeneutical reflection; this is "what must always be *central* in exegesis, not something which could be pitted against it."[55] The relationship in Luther between scripture, tradition, spiritual experience, and reason, is complex and carefully balanced to avoid simplistic antitheses. John Goldingay observes: "the aim of his polemic is to put an end to what are relatively novel practices . . . He opposes the overthrowing of tradition when it is not inconsistent with scripture. Though concerned for the priority of text over tradition, he also asserts the priority of tradition over rationalism and over enthusiasm."[56]

All of this necessitates *assessments*: about what others claim about Christ; about traditions; about claims for "spiritual" experience, and about interpretations of scripture. Assessments, in turn, are made by using *criticism*. Luther's concern in this direction is reflected in his selective use of humanist learning and studies; and second in his burning concern for public university education and its reform. In his essay "Luther and Humanism" Lewis Spitz examines the intellectual and conceptual tools which Luther used in his work as a professor of biblical studies for thirty-three years.[57] James Kittelson points out that Luther rapidly acquired skills in the humanistic disciplines "that would lead by and thereafter to a thorough reform of the curriculum of his own university and thence to many others . . . The Reformation itself may be rightly understood as a massive educational undertaking that in time affected entire populaces."[58] In the treatise *To the Christian Nobility* of 1520 he clearly endorsed the humanist educational programme.[59] Luther was particularly concerned that pastors should receive a high level of education.

Kittelson provides statistics for various areas which show that the ratio of university-educated clergy rose dramatically from the middle to the end of the sixteenth century.[60]

Kittelson concludes: "It was the Enlightenment and . . . John Locke who divided the heart from the head . . . But it was Luther, above all, who brought education to the public."[61] The education and equipment of clergy and also laypeople remained a central and major concern both for Luther and for Calvin. It was not enough simply to repeat inherited words and liturgical actions without the involvement of the whole person, including the mind. In particular the mind of the reader or hearer should be able to engage with the mind expressed in the biblical text.

We need not enter here into the wide-ranging discussions of Lutheran hermeneutics which debate whether Luther should be seen as, on the one side, a forerunner of biblical criticism, or, on the other side, committed to a view of scripture which would preclude methods associated with modern historical criticism. In a volume entitled *Studies in Lutheran Hermeneutics* John Reumann surveys the discussion.[62] Kurt Marquart champions the second view.[63] M. Reu warns us not to jump to hasty conclusions by invoking, outside their historical and theological contexts, Luther's well-known comments about the epistle of James as "a letter of straw".[64] Luther was able simultaneously, as Bornkamm points out, to discern both the "Jewishness" of the Old Testament and yet also its witness to Christ and to divine grace.[65] Luther used questioning in the service of faith, and his insistence that even the scriptures would be nothing without Christ made reflection about criteria in biblical interpretation not something to be avoided but a theological and intellectual necessity. In this respect, the mature Luther should not be interpreted in the light of the younger Luther.[66] The progress of his thought needs to be traced through his successive conflicts, and the stages of theological, intellectual, and pastoral reflection to which these give rise.

3. Further Reflection on Interpretation in Calvin and in English Reformers

In his introduction to his 1965 edition of Tyndale's works, Gervase Duffield describes William Tyndale as one of the first in England to reflect on and to set out principles of biblical interpretation.[67] In *The Obedience of a Christian Man* (1528) Tyndale discusses and explicitly rejects the mediaeval doctrine of the four senses of scripture. Scripture has "one simple, literal, sense, whose light the owls cannot abide ... the root and ground of all."[68] This literal sense, which may include proverb, riddle or allegory *where scripture itself uses such figures*, becomes a critical *criterion* for what others derive from supposedly higher levels of meaning. For "of what text thou provest hell, will another prove purgatory; another *limbo patrum* ... and another shall prove of the same text that an ape hath a tail."[69]

Tyndale's understanding of the Old Testament is as near to what today we should call a *historical* understanding as the times could allow. Old Testament laws and ceremonies belonged to a particular era in the unfolding of the divine purpose for the world. Such ceremonies may be compared with the ABC which a child begins in the process of learning to read, as with milk by which a nurse feeds an infant. It is "after their own capacity."[70] Gillian Evans comments, "The precepts of the Old Testament could, then, be taken literally, but as applying literally *in their time and place*; as not unworthy, but, on the contrary, a merciful dispensation of the divine lawgiver."[71] Tyndale's warnings against the dangers of "private interpretation" (2 Peter 1: 20–21) invite the participation of *corporate testing* by the community. He writes: "When I allege any Scripture, *look thou on the text whether I interpret it right* . . ."[72] This testing involves both examining the circumstances and processes, and a faith response to Christ. Dean Freiday speaks of "Tyndale's repeated warning against 'private interpretation'."[73] Tyndale's deeply pastoral concern also led him to relate questions of judgment not only primarily to reason in the abstract, but to *human life.*

Tyndale's emphasis on public, historical, corporate, and practical criteria of meaning and truth, set in contrast to some private or esoteric tradition, places him among those who use critical reflection in the service of faith, and in the course of biblical interpretation. Melanchthon's evaluation and use of rational enquiry is even more explicit. Partly in order to serve Luther's vision about the need for rapid and radical education of pastors, Melanchthon used the Ciceronian method, expounding the content of scripture in terms of themes or *loci*. The general conception of academic method which he followed is set out in his *De Methodo*. It is "the art or way of teaching correctly, by defining, dividing, and connecting true lines of argument, and by unravelling and refuting arguments that are false and do not hang together."[74] T.H.L. Parker comments: "The programme is quite clear: the critic's (*sic*) way is one of search and discovery, his purpose to find and co-ordinate the major concepts, his office to reduce confusion to order. He is an explorer . . . His journey is *inventio*, his specimens *loci*."[75]

Contrary to popular myth, John Calvin was deeply concerned not to impose theological doctrine *onto* the biblical texts. Hence, in contrast to Melanchthon he takes two particular steps to ensure that the biblical writings will speak for themselves. First, he rejects the classical method of *loci* used by Melanchthon, and prefers the method of running commentary. Second, in the second edition of the *Institutes* (1539) he declares in his "Epistle to the Reader" that in his exegetical writings he need not and will not digress into doctrinal discussions, not least because it has been his strategy to deal with these separately in the *Institutes*. In the same year Calvin completed his commentary on Romans, and by 1551 had completed commentaries on all of the epistles. Between 1553 and 1557 he produced commentaries on the gospels, and then devoted his attention to commentaries on the Old Testament. Like Chrysostom, Calvin was concerned to understand and to expound "the mind of the biblical author" (*mens auctoris*).77 Access to the mind of the writer is gained through the text, its context, and through the author's language, but the context of situation in history also demands attention.78

As we have already noted Calvin rejected Origen's appeal both to Gal. 4: 22–24 and to 2 Cor. 3:6 as a precedent for allegory. Paul's contrast between the "letter" and the "Spirit" has nothing to do with any alleged distinctions between a literal and spiritual meaning of scripture. To isolate the Spirit from the word as it is spoken in its historical context is the error of the "enthusiasts".79 Calvin's contention that "Letter . . . means . . . dead and ineffective preaching . . . Spirit . . . means spiritual teaching" comes close to Westerholm's fairly recent conclusion in *New Testament Studies* that "'letter' and 'spirit' express not two ways of reading scripture, but the essence of service under the two covenants."80 Origen's interpretation, Calvin's comments, "became the source of much evil. It not only gave license for corrupting the true meaning of scripture, but also led to the notion that the more unprincipled the allegorizer, the more expert he was as an interpreter of Scripture."81

In his recent work on the hermeneutics of Calvin T.F. Torrance elucidates further a claim that he has consistently made in earlier writings that Calvin is concerned with both linguistic interpretation and epistemological clarification. Because, as Calvin asserts at the beginning of the *Institutes*, knowledge of God and knowledge of ourselves are closely bound together, language about God has *both* an objective *and* self-involving quality or logic. "Without knowledge of ourselves knowledge of God does not take place; but without knowledge of God there is no clear knowledge of ourselves. In ourselves we are nothing, for we live and move and have our subsistence only in God."82 Torrance continues: "The full place given here to the human person as a self-possessed subject in the knowledge of God is very significant, for it is part of the transition which Calvin effected, not without help from Franciscan teaching, from the mediaeval to the modern mode of theological thinking."83 Here the "personal" and the "objective" come together, although it is not an epistemological relationship in which the subject and object are fully separated and split apart.

G.R. Evans has shown in her book on mediaeval biblical interpretation how closely underlying theories of meaning and language influenced perspectives, assumptions, and possibilities in textual interpretation.84 In the mediaeval period, she argues, most theories of signification were derived ultimately from one of two traditions. One went back to Augustine of Hippo (354–430); and the other looked back to Boethius (c.480–524) including the latter's commentaries on Aristotle's *De Interpretatione*.85 Augustine focussed on the word as the unit of meaning, and in effect expounded a theory of meaning as reference. He recalls that in his infancy, by frequently hearing words, "I gradually identified the objects which the words stood for . . . I exchanged with those about me the verbal signs by which we express our wishes . . ."[86] Boethius saw languages as *systems* which split up a conceptual continuum or perceptual chain in different ways. The divisions of each language served practical convenience rather than "nature" or logic. In allegorical interpretation, G.R. Evans argues, there is a point-by-point correspondence between analogy and analogue which extends a given distance. But, within the framework of the four senses of the Gregorian system, the anagogical comparison is not so direct, and involves "several stages of removal from the original sign."[87] Finally the tropological sense entails "a deliberate 'bending' to make it instructive about human behaviour."[88] These "senses" owe more to "*contemplatio*" than to inferential logic. There is no effective check on the relations between the different semiotic systems.

This principle, however, in Calvinist theology, is perceived to shift the initiative and givenness of judgment from the givenness of the public meaning of the word and text to the creative imagination of the hearer or reader. Torrance draws attention to Calvin's work *De Scandalis*, which, he allows, owes much to Luther. He comments, "It could be argued that the whole of this work of Calvin is an elaboration of Luther's contention that the point *where we feel ourselves under attack from the Scripture*, where our natural reason is offended by it, and where we are flung into tumults, is *the very point where genuine interpretation can take place and profound understanding be reached*. It is then . . . that we can let ourselves be told something which we cannot tell ourselves, and really learn something new which we cannot think up for ourselves."[89]

Such an attitude is radically different from the individualist strands within pietism which emerged in the post-Reformation period. In later reactions against theological controversy, Stuart Allen writes, there emerged "a type of believer whose only interest in the Bible is what he gets out of it for himself and his own comfort . . . His aim is self and his own particular experience . . . In a subtle way it keeps this sort of person pre-occupied with himself, instead of being occupied with Christ and God's great and glorious redemptive plan."[90] By contrast, Calvin's concerns were broader, more objective, and related to the wider dimensions of human life, including *human society*. Torrance sees it as highly significant that Calvin not only received a thorough grounding in humanistic learning, but that especially through his training in law, he related logic and language to *action in the public world*.[91] The 1970 Report of the Calvin College Curriculum Study Committee makes the point in a parallel way, focussing on Calvin's concern about education. The Report states: "Calvin himself put a great deal of effort into the founding of the Genevan Academy; he campaigned for funds . . . and was one of the lecturers. Under Calvinist auspices the University of Heidelberg was reformed . . . The Christian gospel demanded the reformation of society in general, as well as of the individual and the church."92

Among other sixteenth-century Reformers, most Anglican Reformers followed the general principles which we have observed in Luther, Tyndale, and Calvin, but with an explicit emphasis on the value of Patristic and Reformation tradition, as well as rational reflection, but under scripture.93 Thomas Cranmer (1489–1556) felt himself to be on most solid ground where there was a consensus between scripture, the Fathers, and the theologians of the Reformation.94 Richard Hooker (c.1554–1600) argued, as against some of the Puritans, that tradition, reason, and common sense are required in conjunction with scripture, not only because some biblical texts apply only to particular times and persons, but also because scripture is *silent on many practical issues of the time*. The Puritans look to the Bible for guidance on "taking up of a rush or straw", but "scripture in many things doth neither command nor forbid, but use silence."95 This does not mean that for Hooker the Bible is other than supreme in authority. Indeed he compares the Continental practice of placing a greater emphasis on longer sermons with the Anglican discipline of the extensive use of the lectionary with the words: "When we reade or recite the scripture, we then deliver to the people *properlie* the word of God. As for our sermons, be they never so sound and perfect, his worde they are not, as the sermons of the prophets were; no, they are but ambiguoustic, termed his worde."96 It is not difficult to see why the label "the judicious Hooker" has survived. Commitment first to the Bible and then to the church is no enemy of reason and common sense.

4. The Rise and Development of Modern Hermeneutical Theory

Apart from its rather different meaning in Aristotle, it is generally agreed that the first explicit use of the term "hermeneutics" as the title of a study emerged in J.C. Dannhauer's *Hermeneutica Sacra* of 1654. In his brief historical survey of hermeneutics, Ebeling, however, mentions also two predecessors to Dannhauer: Heinrich Bullinger, whose work on the authority of the Bible appeared in 1538, and Matthias Flacius Illyricus, who published his *Clavis scripturae sacrae* in 1567.97 Bullinger argued that the interpreter should take account of such contingent factors as peculiarities of the author and differences in historical periods, but also especially of the thrust of the whole passage under consideration. The circumstances, including the time and occasion of a text are important: *causa, locus, occasio, tempus, instrumentum, modus* and other conditions under which the passage was written.[98] Bullinger seems to have anticipated something roughly akin to the later notion of the hermeneutical circle, in that he grasped and expounded the principle that an understanding of the situational and linguistic components of a text and its content depend on some awareness of where the argument as a whole leads. On the other hand, to grasp the nature of the author's argument, on which everything hinges, the interpreter must examine situational and linguistic details.

Bullinger's near-contemporary Flacius also reflected these two emphases. On the one hand, the wholeness of scripture is the key to its interpretation. On the other hand, detailed lexicographical and grammatical enquiry remains essential. Flacius stressed the wholeness of scripture, however, not primarily, like Irenaeus, in continuity with early tradition, but as a polemic which stood in contrast to the traditions of the church of the day.

Towards the end of the seventeenth century, hermeneutics became a broader discipline. In 1689 the jurist Johannes von Felde sought to establish principles of interpretation which would be valid for all kinds of texts. Similarly in 1713 Christian Wolff published work on interpretation, which attempted to distinguish between approaches to historical and dogmatic texts. The latter, he urged, invite judgments about the strength of the arguments employed; the former depend also on author-related and situational factors. Wolff uses the notion of "author's intention", although one writer warns us that this is not employed with quite the same meaning as the term is usually understood to convey today.[99] In the eighteenth century a considerable number of works on hermeneutics appeared. In 1728 Jean Alphonse Turretinus of Geneva argued that the goal of interpretation was to place oneself with the surroundings and times of the biblical authors, and enquire what concepts could arise for those who lived at the time.

Probably the three most significant theorists of this century, however, are Johann Martin Chladinius (1710–1759) Johann August Ernesti (1707–1781) and Johann Salomo Semler of Halle (1725–1791). Hans Frei in his study of eighteenth and nineteenth-century hermeneutics describes Ernesti and Semler as the two usually "regarded as fathers to 'general' biblical hermeneutics".[100] Ernesti drew a sharp distinction between the task of understanding the *language* of a text, which is the task of general hermeneutics and understanding its *content* which is the task of theology. Hermeneutics is concerned with meaning; theology, with truth. The author's use of the language of the time, the author's intention, and the historical situation of the text, represent the three major concerns of hermeneutical enquiry. By contrast, Semler insisted that hermeneutics not only embraced both tasks, namely of apprehending both the meaning and the truth of biblical texts, but also that interpretation should proceed independently of all theological or dogmatic considerations.

Semler had moved away from the pietism in which he was brought up, and came under the influence of English Deism. He was also influenced, as John Rogerson reminds us, by the earlier biblical criticism of Richard Simon (1678) and Spinoza (1670).[101] Semler's hermeneutics focussed also on three tasks. First, the interpreter must examine the language of the texts appropriately and precisely. Second, all particularities, or peculiarities, marking its historical cirucmstances should be taken into account. Third, the interpreter should re-articulate the subject-matter of the text in such a way as to take full account of changes in times or situation.

A few years earlier Chladenius had published his *Introduction to the Correct Interpretation of Reasonable Discourses and Books* (1742). He defined hermeneutics as the art of reaching a full understanding of utterances, whether these be oral speech or written texts. In contrast to the later Romanticist emphasis on "life" and "experience" as major hermeneutical categories, Chladenius retained the Enlightenment emphasis on reason. However, he also stressed that to understand and to interpret entails seeing something *from a particular perspective* (*Sehe-Punkt*). Chladenius writes: "Hermeneutics teaches us to discover and to avoid misunderstanding and misrepresentations; for these have caused much evil in the world."[102] But how do misunderstandings so easily arise? For the most part, he answers, they arise because "different people perceive that which happens in the world differently, so that if many people describe an event, each would attend to something in particular."[103] For example, three spectators at a battle which is under way will probably see different aspects of the single event, and their viewpoint will depend on such factors as their physical location and the focus of their attention and concern. Thus a rebellion in political life will be perceived in one way by a loyal subject; in another way by a rebel who perceives himself to have been oppressed. "This is the nature of all histories ... This is especially true when human actions are related to us from a viewpoint which differs from the one we have previously held."[104]

We have not yet reached the stage in Chladenius of moving from reason to "life", which becomes a key hermeneutical principle in the so-called Romanticist hermeneutical tradition of Schleiermacher, Dilthey, and Betti. Neither have we yet reached the critical moment of the publication of Kant's *Critique of Pure Reason* (1781), which would, through its implications, transform the course of hermeneutical theory. However, the notion of "viewpoint" begins to move towards what will later be elaborated by Husserl and Heidegger into the concept of "horizon". To understand a writing, we must understand the writer's point of view, as well as the language and situation from which the text emerges. It is a relatively short logical step to raise questions about the point of view of the interpreter, which Schleiermacher and Dilthey would in due course duplicate, partly against the background of Kant. What remains fully consonant with Reformation and Protestant theology, as a recent essay of Vern Poythress reminds us, is the emphasis on inter-personal communication between author and reader.[105] We noted in chapters two and three that this is a different emphasis from that which is involved in recently-shifting paradigms of textuality and in post-modernism.

With Friedrich Schleiermacher (1768–1834) we reach a decisive turning-point in hermeneutics. We move from a hermeneutics of enquiry to a hermeneutics of understanding. Hermeneutics becomes not a matter of formulating criteria in relation to a context of understanding which is already presupposed (whether Christian, as in Luther and Calvin, or anti-supernaturalist as in Semler) but a matter of examining the pre-conditions for understanding in itself. Because Schleiermacher's system of hermeneutics is complex and of critical importance, and because it is often expounded one-sidedly and even unfairly, we shall devote the next chapter entirely to this subject.

Before we reach the more familiar ground of the twentieth century, however, two more thinkers must be mentioned. Wilhelm von Humboldt (1767–1835) was an almost exact contemporary of Schleiermacher. Like Schleiermacher he saw that the basis of understanding was both linguistic and inter-personal. Like Schleiermacher he grounds hermeneutics in the nature of thinking and speaking. But perhaps more clearly than Scheiermacher, Humboldt anticipates the late twentieth-century emphasis that, as Mueller-Vollmer acutely summarizes Humboldt's more lengthy language: "Meaning must be seen . . . as the co-production of speaker and listener, where both share in the same active power of linguistic competence."[106]

A trio of hermeneutical theorists who belong together are Friedrich Ast, F.A. Wolf, and Philip August Boeckh of Berlin (1785–1867). We discuss Ast and Wolf in our chapter on Schleiermacher. Boeckh's major contributions were made as a classicist and philologist; not as a biblical scholar or philosopher. Much of his work simply underlined in greater detail methods of enquiry about historical, linguistic, and literary factors. The point of greatest interest lies in the claim, found already in Schleiermacher, that the task of hermeneutics is to understand an author *"better"* than the author understands his or her own writings, or the author's self-knowledge.[107] This is because by historical enquiry and reconstruction of causal chains of events, the interpreter can come to perceive elements and factors within the author's horizon of which the author may have been unaware. This principle would in the late twentieth century become fundamental in post-Freudian and Neo-Marxist hermeneutics of suspicion.

Meanwhile, in biblical criticism in the nineteenth century some rough kind of parallel can be observed in the work of Ferdinand Christian Baur in his study of Paul and the "parties" at Corinth according to 1 Cor. 1:12

(1831); his *Paulus* (1845); and his broader accounts of development in the New Testament period (1853, 1864). Paul was governed, according to Baur, by *constraints of circumstances* of which he could scarcely be fully aware.[108] Historical criticism in the service of a suspicious hermeneutic is not simply a matter of evaluating whether certain events took place; it assigns causes and processes which may be extrinsic to the text and its author, as a methodological device for understanding "better" than the author. Since Freud did not publish his *Studies in Hysteria* and *The Interpretation of Dreams* until 1895 and 1899, it is noteworthy that before, at the very latest, 1867, Boeckh could write: "the interpreter must bring to clear awareness what the author has *unconsciously* created, and in so doing many things will be opened to him, many windows will be unlocked which may have been closed to the author himself."[109]

Clearly we have now entered the atmosphere of the twentieth century. It is no longer necessary to chart theories of interpretation in terms of chronological development. It is more constructive to distinguish between different major models of approach in hermeneutical theory. The so-called "Romanticist" model of Schleiermacher, which we are about to consider in detail, underwent further development by Wilhelm Dilthey (1833–1911). Dilthey's work towards a "critique of historical reason", which he saw as a parallel achievement for hermeneutics to that of Kant's *Critique of Pure Reason* for philosophy, was produced towards the end of his life. It was published for the first time in 1926.[110] This work looked back behind Schleiermacher to Herder and Ast, but by making *life* (*Leben*) a key hermeneutical category in place of reason or in place of "spirit", Dilthey also laid a foundation, as Bauman maintains, for a twentieth-century hermeneutics of the social sciences.[111] *Leben* is a shared activity, in which understanding is conditioned by the interpreter's own place in history and society.

NOTES TO CHAPTER V

1. Marilyn J. Harran (ed.) *Luther and Learning, The Wittenberg University Luther Symposium*, Selinsgrove: Susquehanna University Press and London: Associated University Press, 1985, 69–94 *et passim*.
2. James Atkinson, *The Great Light. Luther and the Reformation*, Grand Rapids: Eerdmans, and Exeter: Paternoster, 1968, 78–81.
3. *Ibid* 80 (Atkinson's italics).
4. Richard H. Popkin, *The History of Scepticism from Erasmus to Spinoza*, Berkeley: University of California Press, 1979, 5; cf. 1–17, cf. J.B.Payne, in B. Fatio and P. Fraenkel (eds.) *Histoire de l'exégèse au XVIe siècle*, Geneva: Droz, 1978, 312–30 and Richard Popkin, *Introduction to the Philosophy of the Sixteenth and Seventeenth centuries*. New York: Freeborn, 1966.

5. Martin Luther, *On the Bondage of the Will*, Eng. Edinburgh: Clarke, 1957, 125.
6. *Ibid* 128 and 129.
7. *Ibid* 71.
8. *Ibid* 74.
9. Henning Graf Reventlow, *The Authority of the Bible and the Rise of the Modern World*, Eng. London: S.C.M. 1984, 48; cf. 39–47.
10. Desiderius Erasmus, *The Praise of Folly*, Eng. Chicago: Packard, 1946, 84 (my italics).
11. Martin Luther, *On the Bondage of the Will* 66.
12. *Ibid* 67 (my italics).
13. *Ibid* 67 (my italics).
14. Heinrich Bornkamm, *Luther in Mid-Career 1521–30*, London: Darton, Longman, & Todd, 1983.
15. Friedrich Beisser, *Claritas Scripturae bei Martin Luther*, Göttingen: Vandenhoeck & Ruprecht, 1966.
16. Martin Luther, *Luther's Works: vol.* 35: Word and Sacrament I, Philadephia: Muhlinberg Press, 1960, 132.
17. Jaroslav Pelikan, *Luther's Works: Companion Volume, Luther the Expositor*, St. Louis: Concordia, 1959, 81.
18. Cf. Dietram Hofmann, *Die geistige Auslegung der Schrift bei Gregor dem Grossen*, Munsterschwarzach: Vier-Türme Verlag, 1968.
19. On Hugh of St. Victor, see Beryl Smalley, *The Study of the Bible in the Middle Ages*, 3rd edn. Oxford: Blackwell, 1983; and G.R. Evans, *The Language and Logic of the Bible*, 67–71.
20. Robert M. Grant and David Tracy, *A Short History of the Interpretation of the Bible*, 2nd edn. Philadephia: Fortress 1984, 86.
21. Martin Luther, *Luther's Works* vol. 54, (Philadephia edn.) 47.
22. *Ibid* 406.
23. Gerhard Ebeling, *Luther. An Introduction to his Thought*, Eng. London: Collins, Fontana edn. 1972, 107–9; cf G.S. Robbert, *Luther as Interpreter of Scripture*, St. Louis: Concordia, 1982, and Duncan Ferguson, *op.cit.* 159–60.
24. Martin Luther *Luther's Works* vol. 9, 24.
25. *Luther's Works* vol. 1, 283.
26. Luther's Works vol. 54, 406.
27. G.C. Berkouwer, *Studies in Dogmatics: Holy Scripture*, Eng. Grand Rapids: Eerdmans 1975, 271; cf. 267–98.
28. Martin Luther, *On the Bondage of the Will*, 73; cf. 172.
29. Friedrich Beisser, *op. cit.* 82.
30. Martin Luther, *On the Bondage to the Will*, 71; F. Beisser, *op.cit.* 81.
31. G.C. Berkouwer, *op cit.* 272; Bernard Ramm *Protestant Biblical Interpretation* 3rd edn. Grand Rapids: Baker, 1970.
32. Ford L. Battles and Richard Wevers, *A Concordance to Calvin's Instituatio* 1559, Grand Rapids: Calvin College and Eerdmans (n.d. continuing) cf. *Institutes* III: 8:7; III: 11: 6,23; III: 19:3; III: 22:7; III: 25:8 (*claritas*); cf. II. 11:10; III:24:4; II: 10:23 (on 2 Cor. 3).
33. Thomas F. Torrance, *The Hermeneutics of John Calvin*, Edinburgh: Scottish Academic Press, 1988, 111, and T.H.C. Parker, *op.cit.* 51.
34. John Calvin, *The Epistles of Paul to the Galatians, Ephesians, Philippians and Colossians*,

Edinburgh; Oliver & Boyd, 1965, 85, on Gal. 5:22. (on Gal. 5:22).
35. John Calvin, *Institutes of the Christian Religion*, Eng. Edinburgh: Clarke 1957, vol. I, I.vi.1 (64).
36. *Ibid* vol. I, I.viii.1 (75).
37. G.C. Berkouwer, *op. cit.* 275, stresses this point. There is a shift, he argues, to questions about the *words* of scripture, and questions are isolated from more functional contexts.
38. See the magisterial survey in Hemming Graf Reventlow, *op.cit.* esp 289–410.
39. Cf. Edgar Krentz, *The Historical-Critical Method*, Philadelphia: Fortress Press, 1975, 10–14 (on Descartes) and Netherlands Reformed Church *The Bible Speaks Again*, Eng. London: S.C.M. 1969, 42 (on Reimarus).
40. Thomas F. Torrance *Theological Science*, Oxford: Oxford University Press, 1969, 75.
41. Martin Luther, *Luther's Works vol.* 35: Prefaces to the Old Testament, 236.
42. *Luther's Works vol.* 36: The Misuse of the Mass, 137.
43. *Luther's Works vol.* 54, 379; *Table Talk*, 5017.
44. *Ibid.* 183 *Table Talk* 2938b.
45. *Ibid.*
46. *Luther's Works vol.* 35: How Christians Should Regard Moses, 170.
47. Cf. James Atkinson, *op.cit.* 81–87; Heinrich Bornkamm, *op.cit.*; and A. Skevington Wood, *Captive to the Word: Martin Luther: Doctor of Sacred Scripture*, Exeter: Paternoster 1969, 105–115.
48. *Luther's Works vol.* 40: Against the Heavenly Prophets, 222.
49. *Luther's Works* vol. 54, 435; *Table Talk*, 5568.
50. *Luther's Works vol.* 40: Against the Heavenly Prophets, 156–7 (my italics) cf. vol. 37, 40–45.
51. *Ibid* (my italics).
52. James Smart, *The Strange Silence of the Bible in the Church: A study in Hermeneutics*, London: S.C.M. 1970, 25 (my italics).
53. *Martin Luther's Works*, vol. 35: Prefaces to the Old Testament, 236.
54. *Ibid: Avoiding the Doctrines of Men* 132.
55. Horace D. Hummel, "The Outside Limits of Lutheran Confessionalism in Contemporary Biblical Interpretation." *The Springfielder* 35, 1971, 265; (his italics); cf. 103–25, 264–73, and 1972, 37–53, and 212–22.
56. John Goldingay, "Luther and the Bible" *Scottish Journal of Theology* 35, 1982, 41; cf. 33–58.
57. Lewis W. Spitz, "Luther and the Humanism" in Marilyn J. Harran (ed.)*Luther and Learning. The Wittenberg University Luther Symposium*, Ithaca: Cornell University Press, 1979, 69–94.
58. J. Kittelson, in M.J. Harran (ed.) *op. cit.* 95; cf. 96–114.
59. *Ibid* 99.
60. *Ibid* 105.
61. *Ibid* 111.
62. John Reumann (ed.) *Studies in Lutheran Hermeneutics*, Philadephia: Fortress 1979, esp. 1–76.
63. *Ibid* 313–34; cf. 44 and 59.
64. M. Reu, *Luther and the Scriptures*, Columbus, Ohio: Wartburg Press, 1944 esp. 38–48; cf. also Horace Hummel, *loc.cit.*

65. Heinrich Bornkamm, *Luther and the Old Testament*, Eng. Philadelphia; Fortress, 1969, esp. sect. IIIA; A.H.J. Gunneweg, *op.cit.* 45–55 and 116–18.
66. J.S. Preus, *From Shadow to Promise: Old Testament Interpretation from Augustine to the Young Luther*, Cambridge: Harvard University Press, 1969.
67. Gervase E. Duffield (ed.) *The Work of William Tyndale*, Appleford: Sutton Courtenay Press and Philadelphia: Fortress, 1965, xxxiv On Tyndale, see further Henning Graf Reventlow, *op.cit.* 105–12.
68. William Tyndale, *ibid* 31–32 and 339.
69. *Ibid* 330.
70. *Ibid* 59–60.
71. G.R. Evans, *The Language and Logic of the Bible: The Road to The Reformation*, Cambridge: Cambridge University Press, 1985, 43 (my italics).
72. William Tyndale, *op.cit.*; 337 (my italics).
73. Dean Freiday, *The Bible: Its Criticism, Interpretation, and Use in Sixteenth and Seventeenth Century England*, Pittsburgh: Catholic and Quaker Studies no. 4, 1979, 34. For a different approach to "private interpretation" cf. Peter Toon, *The Right of Private Judgment. The Study and Interpretation of Scripture in Today's Church*, Portland: Western Conservative Baptist Seminary 1975.
74. Methanchthon, *Corpus Reformatorum*, cited in T.H.L. Parker, *Calvin's New Testament Commentaries*, London: S.C.M. 1971, 32–3.
75. T.H.L. Parker, *op.cit.* 33.
76. *Ibid* 51–54.
77. John Calvin, "Epistle to Simon Gryneaus on the Commentary on Romans" in *Calvin: Commentaries*, (Library of Christian Classics 23) London: S.C.M., 1958, 73, Cf. also B. Fatio and P. Fraenkel (ed.) *Histoire de l'exégèse au XVIe Siècle*, Geneva: Droz, 1978, 312–30.
78. John Calvin, *Institutes* III. 17: 14 and IV. 16:13.
79. T.H.L. Parker, *op.cit.* 67.
80. John Calvin, *Commentary on the Epistles of Paul the Apostle to the Corinthians* rp. in *Calvin: Commentaries* 107.
81. John Calvin, *ibid* 108; cf. S. Westerholm "'Letter' and 'Spirit'; the Foundation of Pauline Ethics" *New Testament Studies* 30, 1984, 240; cf. 229–48, and R.M. Grant, *The Letter and the Spirit* London: S.P.C.K., 1957, esp. 34,37,48 and 54–5.
82. Thomas F. Torrance, *The Hermeneutics of John Calvin*, 162.
83. Cf. Thomas F. Torrance, *Theology in Reconstruction*, London: S.C.M., 1965, 76–98 (on speech about God in Calvin) and *Theological Science* Oxford: Oxford University Press, 1969.
84. Gillian R. Evans, *The Language and Logic of the Bible. The Earlier Middle Ages* 51–124.
85. *Ibid* 72–76.
86. Augustine, *Confessions* I.8.13 in *Confessions and Enchiridion*, London: S.C.M., 1955, 38.
87. G.R. Evans, *loc. cit.* 117.
88. *Ibid* 119.
89. T.F. Torrance *The Hermeneutics of John Calvin*, 158 (my italics).
90. Stuart Allen, *The Interpretation of Scripture*, London: Berean Publishing Trust, 1967, 18.
91. T.F. Torrance, *loc cit* 100–101.

92. Calvin College Curriculum Study Committee, *Christian Liberal Arts Education* Grand Rapids: Calvin College and Eerdmans, 1970, 14–15.
93. Cf. Frederick H. Borsch (ed.) *Anglicanism and the Bible,* Wilton: Morehouse Barlow 1984, 11–80. The dependence of Anglicans on the Fathers is somewhat overrated, however, in Andrew Louth, "The Hermeneutical Question Approached through the Fathers" *Sobornost* 7, 1978, 541–549.
94. J.I.Packer "Introduction" to G.E. Duffield (ed.) *The Work of Thomas Cranmer,* Appleford: Sutton Courtenay and Philadephia: Fortress, 1965, xii-xvii.
95. Richard Hooker, *Works,* Oxford: Oxford University Press, 1886, II; 1:2, and II. 5,7; cf Dean Freiday, *op.cit.* 46.
96. Richard Hooker, *Of the Lawes of Ecclesiasticall Politic* v.22: 10, cited in F.H. Borsch (ed.) *op.cit.* 73. On Hooker, see further Henning Graf Reventlow, *op.cit* 116–19 and Richard H. Wilmer, "Hooker on Authority" *Anglican Theological Review* 32 1951. 102–8.
97. Gerhard Ebeling, "Hermeneutik", in *Die Religion in Geschichte und Gegenwart* 3rd edn. Tübingen: Mohr vol. III, 1959, cols. 242–62; col. 259.
98. Cf. T.H.L. Parker, *op.cit.* 38–40.
99. Kurt Mueller-Vollmer (ed.) *The Hermeneutics Reader,* Oxford: Blackwell, 1986, 4.
100. Hans W. Frei, *The Eclipse of Biblical Narrative. A Study in Eighteenth and Nineteenth Century Hermeneutics,* New Haven: Yale University Press, 1974, 246–47.
101. John W. Rogerson, *Old Testament Criticism in the Nineteenth Century: England and Germany,* London: S.P.C.K., 1984, 16.
102. Johann Martin Chladenius, *Einleitung zur richtigen Auslegung vernunftiger Reden and Schriften* (1742), rp. Düsseldorf: Stern, 1969, sect. 194; translated in Kurt Mueller-Vollmer, *op.cit* 64.
103. *Ibid* sect. 308; Eng. *loc cit* 65.
104. *Ibid* sect. 308 and 312; Eng. *loc cit* 66 and 67.
105. Vern S. Poythress, "What Does God Say Through Human Authors?" in Harvey M. Conn (ed.) *Inerrancy and Hermeneutic. A Tradition, A Challenge, A Debate,* Grand Rapids: Baker 1988, 81–99.
106. Kurt Mueller-Vollmer, *op.cit.* 14.
107. Philip August Boeckh, *On Interpretation and Criticism,* Eng. Norman, Oklahoma: University of Oklahoma Press, 1968. The longer German text was edited after Boeckh's death: *Enzyklopädie und Methodologie der philologischen Wissenschaften,* 2nd edn. Leipzig: Teubner, 1886.
108. An excellent essay on this aspect of F.C. Baur's thought is offered by Christophe Senft, "Ferdinand Christian Baur: Methodological Approach and Interpretation of Luke 15: 11–32" in François Bovon and Grégoire Rouiller (eds.) *Exegesis: Problems of Method and Exercises in Reading,* Eng. Pittsburgh: Pickwick, 1978, 77–96. Cf. also Werner G. Kummel, *The New Testament: History of the Investigation of its Problems,* Eng. London: S.C.M. and Nashville, 1972, 126–42.
109. P.A. Boeckh, *op.cit;* r.p. in K. Mueller-Vollmer (ed.) *op.cit.* 139.
110. Wilhelm Dilthey, *Gesammelte Schriften,* vol. 7, Göttingen: Vandenhoeck & Ruprecht, 1926; partly translated in "The Development of Hermeneutics" in H.P. Rickman (ed.) *Selected Writings,* Cambridge: Cambridge University Press, 1976, with part selections in K. Mueller-Vollmer, *op cit* 149–64, and in David E. Klemm, *Hermeneutical Inquiry* (2 vols.) Atlanta: Scholars Press, I, 93–106 and

also "Types of World-View and Their Development in the Metaphysical Systems" (1911) *ibid* II, 33–34.
111. Zygmunt Bauman, *Hermeneutics and Social Science. Approaches to Understanding*, London: Hutchinson, 1978, 18–19, 49, 69–71.

CHAPTER VI

Schleiermacher's Hermeneutics of Understanding

1. Schleiermacher's Most Distinctive Contributions to the Subject

The contribution of Friedrich Schleiermacher (1768–1834) to hermeneutical theory is more subtle and more far reaching than is often supposed. He is often credited with being the first to formulate as a clear hermeneutical goal the aim of re-living and re-thinking the thoughts and feelings of an author. This way of construing the goals of hermeneutics is central to the romanticist model to which Schleiermacher was a contributor. But Schleiermacher's own formulation of this principle is carefully qualified and occurs in a particular context of thought. On the other hand we may question the assumption that is sometimes popularly made that Schleiermacher was the first major thinker to formulate the principle of the hermeneutical circle. Other writers before him had noted that in order to understand the individual components of a stretch of writing some grasp of the whole message of the text needed to be presupposed. Schleiermacher was probably the first to address seriously the theoretical and practical implications of the problem for hermeneutics.

Schleiermacher's more distinctive contribution to hermeneutics lies in a combination of several closely related elements. At first sight none seems of itself to constitute a major turning point in the discipline, but on closer examination each has profound implications which significantly change the direction and content of its agenda. They raise fresh questions about method. We may identify the following areas by way of introduction.

(i) Schleiermacher departed from his predecessors in no longer conceiving of hermeneutics as serving some particular areas of studies. Other thinkers before him had conceived of hermeneutics as serving such areas as our understanding of the classical texts of the Graeco-Roman world or of the biblical writings. By contrast Schleiermacher saw hermeneutics as the *problem of human understanding as such*. The far reaching consequences of the contrast may perhaps best be explained by the use of an analogy. We may draw a parallel contrast between the study of language and the study of specific languages. To study Greek, Hebrew, or French is to study some particular area of language, in which the agenda for study will focus largely on the grammar, vocabulary and literature of a given language. But this is a different agenda from that which arises when we study language as such. In general in linguistics or in philosophy of language we do not primarily study specific grammar, vocabularies, or bodies of literature; we are concerned with the wider principles on the basis of which language functions as language.

In broadening therefore the scope of hermeneutics as a discipline, Schleiermacher thereby transformed its working agenda. Different kinds of questions arise when we deregionalise the subject. In Schleiermacher's case the most radical effect is to place hermeneutics in the context of theories of knowledge. Central to hermeneutics is the question: how do we understand something as the thing which it is? Schleiermacher's distinctive questions about language and about our understanding of human persons emerge from within this context.

(ii) A second distinctive development emerges from the first. Prior to the work of Schleiermacher, the formulation of hermeneutical principles had been undertaken on the assumption that on the basis of a retrospective knowledge, a given route to successful interpretation could be mapped out and explained to others. Hermeneutics was in effect a pedagogic discipline which allowed other interpreters to reach the position advocated, at least in the broadest terms, by the theorist. The guidelines or rules which were formulated served to test possible areas of *mis*understanding within a broader horizon of already *assumed* understanding. By contrast, Schleiermacher asked not how an assumed understanding had been arrived at, but what were the conditions under which human understanding could take place at all. *In this sense it raised transcendental questions: it enquired into the basis and possibility of human understanding.* This aspect is parallel to Kant's approach to the theory of knowledge. Kant had enquired into the conditions under which human knowledge was possible at all. This marks a second point of departure for modern hermeneutics.

(iii) Since hermeneutics is now no longer simply to be regarded as some kind of checking procedure which follows a prior process of assumed understanding, Schleiermacher now stresses a role of creative processes within the human mind within the process of understanding. Logical deduction and rational reflection alone may test, but cannot create, understanding, at least understanding of human persons and human life. A checking procedure may be merely mechanical; *but human understanding is more akin, in Schleiermacher's judgment, to what is involved in seeking to understand a friend.* This is the aspect of Schleiermacher's thought which Dilthey most heavily emphasized and developed. However, for Schleiermacher himself it remains one of two essential axes of the same hermeneutical problem.

Understanding a text involves both a concern about the individuality of the author who produced it, and a study of the language-sitatuion and language-world out of which the text arose.

(iv) The work of Heinz Kimmerle has drawn attention to Schleiermacher's concern about language, or "grammatical" interpretation, alongside his parallel emphasis on the author, or "psychological" (or "technical") interpretation. Prior to the critical edition of Schleiermacher's *Hermeneutics: The Handwritten Manuscripts* (1959) prepared by Kimmerle, his work in this area was known partly through the edition of his writings entitled *Hermeneutics and Criticism* (1838) edited shortly after Schleiermacher's death by his former pupil F.Lucke, and through the interpretation, writings, and *Life of Schleiermacher* which came from Dilthey. Kimmerle insisted that the emphasis on language or grammatical interpretation was never eclipsed by the increasing emphasis on psychological or technical interpretation which is reflected especially in Schleiermacher's later work.[1]

Kimmerle's claims have received some criticism. Martin Redeker, among others, believes that Dilthey's *Life of Schleiermacher* remains a definitive account of his thought, in which it appears that Schleiermacher moved away from his earlier concerns. But the *Handwritten Manuscripts* offer undeniable evidence that the emphasis on tracing what gives rise to the thought of the author, which is the central feature of Romanticist hermeneutics, is never Schleiermacher's sole concern. In his *Compendium* of 1819, confirmed by his marginal notes of 1828, Schleiermacher writes: "Understanding always involves two moments: to understand what is said in the context of the *language* with its possibilities and to understand it as a fact in the thinking of the *speaker* . . . these two hermeneutical tasks are completely equal, and it would be incorrect to label grammatical interpretation the 'lower' and psychological interpretation as the 'higher' task."[2]

Schleiermacher therefore explicity raised for the first time a question which remains of permanent importance for hermeneutics: can we interpret the meaning of texts purely with reference to their language, or purely with reference to their authors' intention, *or does textual meaning reside somehow in the inter-relation or inter-action between both?* As he wrestles with this question, Schleiermacher sees that it also reveals another: is rational reflection or logical deduction the only hermeneutical tool which is needed? To grasp the content of a text as a flow of thought emerging from a given situation, he believes, both critical reflection or comparison is needed, and the capacity to "divine", or proleptically to perceive in a way which is more than merely logical or rational. In a way which points to the later work of Wittgenstein, he notes in one of his early sentence-jottings: "Every child comes to understand the meaning of words only through hermeneutics."[3]

(v) Does this concern about "divining" or perceiving narrow hermeneutics to a concern only about the personal perceptions or capacities of the addressee or of the interpreter? Some critics of Schleiermacher regard his hermeneutics as reductionist in this sense. Gordon E. Michalson insists "With Schleiermacher we commit the fatal error of permitting the cultural despisers [the addressees of his *On Religion: Speeches to its Cultural Despisers* (1799)] to define the theological agenda".4 Partly because of his influence "theology gradually becomes hermeneutical . . . made theologically respectable by rendering apparently historical claims into propositions of a self-referential sort".5 There is no doubt that Schleiermacher's thought *can* give rise to this kind of development. "Religious consciousness" comes to occupy a more central place than a theology of the acts of God. Nevertheless, Schleiermacher is not concerned with the subjectivity of the isolated individual. Interpretation involves "listening", and *stepping "out of one's own frame of mind".*6 Part of the very possibility of interpretation lies in an already pre-given, shared language, an established linguistic system which opens the possibility of communication.

Schleiermacher explicity addresses the problem of the relationship between individual consciousness and an individual's potential capacity for *inter-personal communication on the basis of shared language.* In hermeneutical terms, the problem turns on the relationship between thinking, speaking, understanding, and the nature of language. He writes "Hermeneutics is part of the art of thinking".7 But by this he means more than some mental process within individual consciousness, even though it may include this. He asserts, "The art of speaking and the art of understanding stand in relation to each other, speaking being only the outer side of thinking . . . Speaking is the medium for the communality of thought . . . Every act of speaking is related to both the totality of the language and the totality of the speaker's thoughts."8 This is true both of the socio-linguistic context presupposed in inter-personal communication and in the context of theological claims about knowledge or understanding of God. Schleiermacher would have endorsed Calvin's dictum that "Knowledge of God and knowledge of ourselves are bound together by a mutual tie."9 Indeed Calvin earlier observes "As these are connected together by many ties, it is not easy to determine which of the two precedes, and gives birth to the other."10 Schleiermacher's attention to individual consciousness did not make his hermeneutics merely subjectivist or individualist; for he also presupposed a linguistic and inter-personal interaction in which the individuality of the self was not only enhanced but also transcended and perhaps transformed.

(vi) To Schleiermacher must also go the credit for being one of the first to formulate the *comprehensive* significance of several different factors in consideration of a text and the text's author. He insists, "The idea of the work . . . can be understood only by the joint consideration of two factors: the *content* of the text and the *range of effects*".11 In turn these effects depend on the character and situation of the addressee. The interpreter should take into account "who these people were, and what effect their passages were to have on them . . . since these factors determine the composition of the work."[12] To evolve what amounts to the beginnings of a theory of *reader-effects* in nineteenth-century hermeneutics constitutes a major advance, which is usually ignored or forgotten when Schleiermacher's theory is described as merely "genetic" or reconstructionist.

Schleiermacher's conception of the goals of interpretation, then, is far broader than is often allowed, especially when he is described as formulating a "genetic" model about the origins of texts, or accused of focussing exclusively on the author "behind" the text. Indeed, although more than a century would elapse before explicit reader-response models in hermeneutics were to emerge, it can be said that Schleiermacher took some account of both the original audience, the later reader, and effects of the text upon each. Inter-action with the text through the shared world of language provides one condition for the development of self-awareness, even perhaps self-identity, on the part of the individual reader. As we noted in the previous point, the individuality of the reader is both enhanced and transcended in this inter-subjective process.

James Duke argues this point at some length, noting that for Schleiermacher "Language overcomes solipsism and opens up a social world which is sharable by all, *through* each individual perceiver and relates to that world from his own particular point of vantage".[13] This emerges especially from Schleiermacher's comments about "divining" and from his emphasis on language which Duke and Kimmerle underline. Divining the author's purpose, Schleiermacher writes, leads "the interpreter to transform himself, so to speak, into the author".[14] Schleiermacher's conception of the hermeneutical task, therefore, is very broad. It involves the author's thought, experience, and situation; the content, context, language, and effects of the text; the first readers of the text, including their linguistic and other capacities and competences; and the consciousness and experience of later interpretation.

(vii) Schleiermacher is ready to bring all these factors to bear on the hermeneutics of the biblical writings. He urged, for example, that the whole point of the subject known as "Introduction to the New Testament", with its concerns about the authorship, date, language, and settings of various New Testament writings was precisely that of "placing us (by gathering historical knowledge) in the position of the original readers for whom the New Testament authors wrote."[15] The question which Schleiermacher raises for biblical studies is that of how far the biblical writings themselves may be said to exemplify the issues which are raised in general hermeneutical theory. He does not believe that any particular theory of inspiration by the Holy Spirit exempts the biblical material from the relevance of these broader questions, because the Bible, whatever else it may be, remains a text written in language addressed to human situations and human persons. This is not to suggest any conclusion about the adequacy or otherwise of Schleiermacher's theological evaluation of the Bible or scripture. The point is a more simple and modest one: Schleiermacher led the way in addressing a new range of hermeneutical questions to the language of the biblical writings. These were not addressed only to the language of the classical world, or to the language of literature, and law.

2. The Broader Context: Romanticism, Pietism, Culture, and Hermeneutics

Schleiermacher has been described as both "the founder of modern hermeneutics" and as "the founder of modern Protestant theology".[16] Karl Barth applies to Schleiermacher the words which Schleiermacher himself used of Frederick the Great in his Academy address entitled "What goes to make a great man?": He declares, "He did not found a school, but an era".[17] Barth adds, "He will in fact live for every age".[18] Of some thirty volumes of writings, roughly a third concern theology; a third, philosophy; and a third are sermons. In 1805 Schleiermacher committed to writing some notes on hermeneutics in the form of maxims, or preliminary observations of a sentence or two in length. He wrote a first draft of a manuscript on hermeneutics in 1809–10 and produced a developed study in 1819, known as the *Compendium*, which formed the basis of his lecture-course on hermeneutics in the University of Berlin, where he taught from its foundation in 1810 to his death in 1834. In 1828 he added some further marginal notes. His two Academy Addresses of 1829 directly identify areas of similarity to, and difference from, the hermeneutics of Wolf and Ast. His work on hermeneutics, therefore, developed in the context of a wider range of theological and philosophical concerns and interests. The works for which Schleiermacher is most widely known are his books *On Religion: Speeches to its Cultural Despisers* (1799) and *The Christian Faith* (1821). Hermeneutical concerns, however, often remain in the background. On the title page of *The Christian Faith* he cites a motto from Anselm: "He who has not experienced will not understand". It is difficult to appreciate the subtlety and force of Schleiermacher's contribution to hermeneutics without noting the complexity of concerns which he drew from his own intellectual, religious, and cultural worlds.

(i) A first major consideration concerns Schleiermacher's relation to *Romanticism*. In this connexion his friendship with Friedrich Schlegel, with whom he shared rooms in Berlin for a time (from 1797) played a significant part. Martin Redeker warns us not to overestimate his indebtedness to Romanticism, but in the years immediately before the publication of his speeches *On Religion*, Schleiermacher met regularly with a small circle of Romantic poets, and it was Schlegel who was urging him to write.[19] Rudolf Otto, in his preface to a later edition of the speeches, describes this work as a "veritable manifesto of the Romantics", in its view of nature and history.[20]

Schleiermacher did not share all of the attitudes and values of Schlegel or the Romantic poets. But in common with them he believed in the creative power of human feeling and in the importance of lived experience, in contrast to the more cerebral rationalism of the Enlightenment. These comments can be illustrated with reference to Schleiermacher's short writing *The Celebration of Christmas: A Conversation* (1805) as B.A. Gerrish observes.[21] The life and joy of Christmas, it is suggested in this fictional narrative, comes to expression better in music than in theological discourse.[22] It is also expressed in the simplicity of childhood. Such understanding is intuitive, and therefore, Schleiermacher believes, more firmly rooted in the feminine than in the masculine.[23] The women express the spirit of Christmas in their warm reminiscences of human life, and in their persons. By contrast, the men introduce an alien spirit by engaging in theological argument about the incarnation. On the last page of the *Christmas Dialogue*, the spirit of Christmas is expressed as "a long caressing kiss which I gave to the world... Let us be cheerful and sing something devout and glad."[24]

Schleiermacher shares with the spirit of Romanticism a distrust of how much can be achieved by rational argument and reflection alone. Jack Forstman examines the relationships of the "Romantic triangle" of Schleiermacher, Novalis, and Schlegel.[25] As we shall see, Schleiermacher's romanticism was tempered and modified by other important elements in his thinking. In his hermeneutics there is always interaction between what he saw as a "feminine" intuitive perception of meaning and the supposedly "masculine" work of comparison and deduction. Nevertheless he shares with Herder and others the urge to reach "behind" formulations, arguments, states of affairs, or institutions to the creative moments in human life of which they are merely the products. Perhaps the most important hermeneutical model of all for Schleiermacher is that of the intuitive understanding between two friends.

J. Arundel Chapman has offered a suggestive comparison between Schleiermacher's romanticism and Wordsworth's poetry, which sprang from the same period.[26] We may indeed note the same themes in Wordsworth as we have observed in Schleiermacher's *The Celebration of Christmas*. In 1798, seven years earlier and only a year before the *Speeches on Religion*, Wordsworth expresses his view of the comparison between reason and creative feeling in the poem which begins "Up, up, my friend, and quit your books". He writes:

> Sweet is the lore which Nature brings;
> Our meddling intellect
> Mis-shapes the beauteous forms of things:-
> We murder to dissect.

Where Schleiermacher looks for the powerful vision of the child's simplicity, Wordsworth writes:

> Heaven lies about us in our infancy.
> Shades of the prison house begin to close
> Upon the growing boy.

Neither Schleiermacher nor Wordsworth reflects the raw Romanticism of Rousseau or Schlegel, but they share the same emphasis on feeling, on life, on creative imagination, on the sense of the infinite and the unity of the whole. "Analytic industry", says Wordsworth, sees only difference; vision of the whole comes from "creative agency."[27] If, for Wordsworth, poetry is born out of "emotion recollected in tranquillity", for Schleiermacher interpretation reaches back behind the poetic form, to the emotion that produced it.

(ii) Before we mention some of the more philosophical influences associated with Romanticism, we must explore further Schleiermacher's early roots in Christian pietism. He grew up in a home where his father was a chaplain of the Reformed Church, and his early piety was that of the Moravians. At the age of sixteen he writes of Christ as the one who "washed me there in his blood from each and every sin".[28] Later he rejected a substitutionary and expiatory theology of the work of Christ, but he never lost the conviction characteristic of pietism that Christian faith lies neither in the acceptance of certain doctrinal ideas, nor in adopting some pattern of moral conduct, but in a trustful and experiential relationship with God. Thus in *The Christian Faith* Schleiermacher identifies as the heart of all true piety "the consciousness of being absolutely dependent" or "being in a relationship with God."[29] The combination of this emphasis on pious feeling together with a deep concern for intellectual integrity and a desire to gain a hearing by faith's "cultural despisers" has led G.P. Fisher and B.A. Gerrish to label Schleiermacher "a liberal evangelical".[30]

We may doubt whether Schleiermacher's theology takes sufficient account of the effects of human sin on the human situation to be called "evangelical" in the fullest sense of the word; but the feeling of which he speaks is not simply that which is generated by human persons. Redeker observes "It is an activity of grace which Schleiermacher described in nearly the same manner as that the pietists used to describe their conversion experience. Men can contribute nothing to it. Intuition and feeling are not activities of the human spirit by means of which reality is brought under control; rather they represent that primal act of the spirit in which reality is not yet divided into subject and object. Intuition does not mean sense perception . . . ; rather it means allowing the activity of the infinite present in the finite to work upon it."[31]

In spite of his intellectual commitment to wrestle with the philosophical issues of the day, or perhaps (as one would like to think) because of it, Schleiermacher remained fully committed to his vocation as a preacher. In 1805 he wrote of preaching as his "proper office", and preached regularly in Berlin while he held his university Chair. Karl Barth, who speaks also as a keen critic of his theology, writes warmly of his commitment to preaching, and in his critical study chooses first to view Schleiermacher as a preacher. Barth writes: "The tenor of his later utterances shows that it is here that we must seek, on his own view, the centre of his work . . . Preaching to the congregation to awaken faith was by far the sweetest desire of his life".[32] But in preaching, as in hermeneutics, communication which entails understanding is not a matter of "forcing our way of thinking either upon this or a future generation": it involves "striking up the music" to "move" the hearers; awaking "the slumbering spark" so that they will catch the vision.[33]

(iii) The picture which has so far emerged, however, needs to be qualified partly by Schleiermacher's commitment to some aspects (although by no means all) of the intellectual mood of the Enlightenment, and partly by his serious engagement with some of the philosophical issues of his day. Early in his life his pietist faith nurtured in the Moravian community seemed to come into conflict with broader intellectual challenges. In 1785 he had entered a seminary at Barby to prepare for ordination. The seminary policy was to seek to shelter ordinands from the philosophical thinking and secular literature of the time. But the young Schleiermacher became disenchanted with a ghetto-like approach. In 1787 he entered the neighbouring University of Halle, where he was introduced fully into the Enlightenment climate of the day in theology and in philosophy. Here he became familiar with the biblical criticism of the Halle scholar J.S.Semler, whose aim was to interpet the Bible as historical writings, free from any dogmatic considerations about the special status of the biblical writings as scripture. Kant's *Critique of Pure Reason* had appeared only six years earlier in 1781, and the philosopher J.A. Eberhard gave Schleiermacher a thorough grounding in Kant's philosophy.

Schleiermacher became increasingly absorbed in fundamental philosophical and ethical questions. In 1794 he was appointed assistant pastor in Landsberg, but the development of his thought in these years also reflects his discovery of Spinoza. In this period he began work on the *Soliloquies* in which he wrestles with how the infinite is revealed in the finite. It can hardly be doubted that in the background he is conscious of Spinoza's pantheistic monism, in which "Whatever is, is God", and "Without God nothing can be, or be conceived". In the same year, 1794, J.G.Fichte (1762–1814) published his *Theory of Knowledge*. Fichte might be said to provide a bridge from Kant to a philosopophy of Romanticism. He developes Kant's transcendental questions about the conditions for the possibility of knowledge, but he identified "God" with Being, with all that is. Later in 1810 Fichte would serve as the first Rector of the University of Berlin, where Schleiermacher held his Chair; but earlier affinities and influences, as well as differences, may be discovered. Richard Brandt offers a critical evaluation of the philosophical influence on Schleiermacher of both Fichte and Schelling, and H.Suskind earlier provided a special study of Schelling's influence.[34] With the philosophy of Schelling we have moved firmly into the thought of the Romanticist movement, especially in his philosophy of nature, his view of art, and his work on individuality, identity, and unity. Creativity, for Schelling, springs from something deeper than rational consciousness.

Schleiermacher does not take over the system of any one philosopher, but he wrestles seriously with the issues which they have formulated. This has an effect in two different directions. First, as T. Foreman has forcefully argued, Schleiermacher developes an understanding of the religious consciousness as that which alone can fulfill the human desire for the highest personal culture (*Bildung*).[35] His *Speeches* are addressed to the *cultured* despisers (*an die Gebildeten unter ihren Verachtern*). "Culture" consituites a quest for high personal values, and he seeks to address his contemporaries on this basis. Second, Schleiermacher's work on hermeneutics reflects an awareness of these issues. In the spirit of Kant's critical philospy, he does not begin with some prior "given", as if the interpreter already understood the nature, content, and meaning independently of the very processes of understanding which are under examination. He therefore enquires into the conditions which first make understanding possible. But unlike Kant, he does not postulate the notion of an absolute or universal which can be known only through the moral imperative. The infinite is revealed neither as an idea nor as an imperative but in the finite particularities of individual or corporate human life.

Knowledge, in the sense of logical deduction or rational reflection, depends on abstracting or universalising concepts in terms of general classes. But human life consists of individual particularities. Hence hermeneutical understanding is concerned not with logical deduction alone, but with the *inter-relation between the general and the particular*. This principle provided the starting-point for Dilthey's development of Schleiermacher's hermeneutics. But Schleiermacher has formulated the issues against the background of the philosophy of the time. The axis of generality would find expression primarily though not exclusively in

Schleiermacher's "grammatical" hermeneutics of language; the axis of particularity would find expression (thought not exclusively) in his "psychological" or "technical" hermeneutics. But neither could be abstracted from the other: language exhibits particularities as well as general features; and "divining" meaning and purpose presupposes an intuitive perception of the whole.

(iv) Schleiermacher also inherited the *hermeneutical* endeavours of his predecessors. Some principles of interpretation could be taken for granted; others provided points of departure for new developments. Work on biblical, classical, and legal texts provided an important background to Schleiermacher's hermeneutics. As we noted in the previous chapter, this went back initially to the Renaissance and the Reformers, and included such writers as Dannhauer, Johannes von Felde, Ernesti and Chladenius. Schleiermacher explicitly interacts with the work of Ernesti, and more especially with his contemporaries Friedrich Wolf and Friedrich Ast. Schleiermacher's "Academy Address" of 1829 bore the title: "On the Concept of Hermeneutics, with Reference to F.A. Wolf's Instructions and Ast's Textbook".[36]

Friedrich Wolf (1759–1824) taught classical language and literature in the University of Halle when Schleiermacher was a student there. Schleiermacher's major criticism of Wolf's work is that "it did not amount even to a sketch of a general hermeneutical theory". It was "directed" specifically to the literature of classical antiquity."[37] Wolf sees hermeneutics and criticism as preparatory to philology, but in Schleiermacher's judgment his work remains primarily a collection of philological observations. He complains that he views interpretation mainly as the use of tools for the understanding of particular written texts. But Wolf goes beyond merely philosophical concerns. He believes that the author's aims and subtleties of purpose must be grasped by interpretation, and he draws explicit distinctions between three levels of understanding. He first operates on the level of linguistic knowledge and clarification. This is distinguished from the level of reconstructive understanding, which draws on historical knowledge of the situation of the author and the text. Third, there is a reflective or philosophical level at which critical evaluation is undertaken to assess these interpretative understandings. Even if Schleiermacher criticizes Wolf for not adequately following through the implications of these distinctions in a more developed way, points of affinity and common concern are clear.

Friedrich Ast (1778–1841) addresses issues which are even closer to those of Schleiermacher. He was ten years junior to Schleiermacher, and published his *Hermeneutics and Criticism* in 1808. But Joachim Wach confirms what Schleiermacher also acknowledges, namely that Ast anticipated him in formulating the principle of the hermeneutical circle.[38] Ast's major concern was the role and function of the classical literature and culture of Greece and Rome in the European world of the nineteenth century. From the Renaissance to the Enlightenment the classics were admired, but treated on the whole as a remote, timeless, "object of study" within the framework of a kind of static scholasticism. But Ast shared with the Romantic thinkers a vision of the classical world as more than a merely passive "object" of cerebral thought, but as the legacy of creative forces, whose significance might once again become a living reality for later generations. These creative forces could speak out of their own context of life to the lived experience and history of the modern world. The study of documents, laws, institutions, and historical events, was not merely to satisfy antiquarian curiosity about "what was the case" in the past. Like J.G.Herder, Ast believed that the culture of a people is the product of its creative spirit. If the culture is to "speak", the modern world must look *behind* the documents, institutions, laws, and events, seeking to understand the spirit which gave them birth. The goal of understanding then for Ast is "the capture of the Spirit" which expresses itself through these now objectified legacies of creative life.

Here in the form of a hermeneutical theory is the Romanticist conviction that life itself, or the human spirit, is always fuller than any of its verbal, artistic, or institutional expressions. Hence, alongside philological study of languages, the interpreter must seek to divine what lies *behind* the language. Like Wolf, Ast postulates three distinct levels of the hermeneutical task: a historical understanding of the situation and content of a work; a linguistic or "grammatical" study; and a "spiritual", intuitive, vision of the whole creation of the author in the context of his or her own values and individuality and the spirit of the age. Ast recognizes the inter-dependence of the various aspects of this process. Thus Schleiermacher acknowledges his formulation of the hermeneutical circle, and writes: "The hermeneutical principle which Ast has proposed and in several respects developed quite extensively is that just as the whole is understood from the parts, so the parts can be understood only from the whole. This principle is . . . so incontestable that one cannot even begin to interpret without using it."[39]

Ast and Schleiermacher, then, share common concerns, and many common perspectives. What they have in common is further developed by their younger contemporary Philip August Boeckh (1785–1867) whom Schleiermacher also taught. Boeckh took up in particular the notion that on the basis of looking both at and behind the language of texts, the interpreter should aim in principle at understanding a linguistic text or artifact "better", or more fully, than its author. But Schleiermacher operates within a broader frame than Ast, and has a more comprehensive grasp of the varied dimensions involved in the hermeneutical task. He insists that Ast's "formula" cannot operate successfully for any and every kind of text.[40] Schleiermacher would probably have claimed that his account of the relation between the general and the particular was more subtle, and the interaction between "grammatical" and "psychological" interpretation more complex and closely intertwined than Ast allows. The four sets of major contexts, influences, and concerns which we have identified invited Schleiermacher to work on a larger canvas than Ast, and the seven distinctive contributions which we outlined at the beginning of this chapter remain essentially Schleiermacher's achievement.

3. Schleiermacher's System of Hermeneutics: "Grammatical" (Shared Language) and "Psychological" (Language-Use) Axes

Various studies of Schleiermacher's hermeneutics are available which rightly identify some major themes: (a) understanding consists in re-experiencing the mental processes of the author of a text; (b) it is grasping the meaning of the parts through divining the whole, and understanding the whole through grasping the parts; (c) it involves perceiving the individuality of the author as a human user of shared language; (d) it seeks to understand more than a text may have explicitly expressed, and hence to achieve a fuller grasp of the author's thoughts or purpose than the author articulated or perhaps understood. We can speak of the "infinite significance of the Holy Scriptures", but "only historical interpretation can do justice to the rootedness of the New Testament authors in this time and place".[41] "Each text was addressed to specific people, and their writings could not be properly understood in the future unless these first readers could understand them".[42] All these represent themes in Schleiermacher's thought. But their particular force and deepest significance for hermeneutical theory cannot be fully appreciated without seeing how they cohere together as a single system of thought. It is the tightly-woven texture of Schleiermacher's hermeneutical thought which gives most impressive force to his observations. This coherence also serves to explain why he is so dissatisfied with his predecessors' "collection of observations". We may trace the following steps in his ordered argument.

(i) Schleiermacher begins with the belief that "Hermeneutics is a part of the art of thinking, and is therefore philosophical."[43] But "thinking" is not merely a solipsistic self-interrogation, in the sense that it *presupposes* percepts, concepts, or habits of linguistic articulation, which could not have arisen apart from the givenness of shared experience and language. To construe "thinking" in merely individual terms is to miss Schleiermacher's point. (It could also be said to miss the point of more recent debates about the so-called Private Language argument. I have argued elsewhere that the points made by Wittgenstein on this issue remain convincing, and that Ayer's defence of the *concept* of "private" language does not genuinely address Wittgenstein's arguments.44 Schleiermacher presupposes a position which would accord more closely with Wittgenstein than with Ayer). Speaking, for Schleiermacher, is the "outer side" of thinking. (More recent debates might prefer the term "public"). It is "the medium for the communality of thought".45 This issue remains all the more relevant in the context of current debates about *intertextuality, intersubjectivity*, and the respective roles played by *linguistic*, by *philosophical* and by *literary* theories, in contemporary hermeneutics.

(ii) Simply to observe what occurs in inter-personal communication is to discern that thinking, or understanding, always entails *two inseparable but distinct axes: that of generality and particularity*. Because we use language, inherited concepts, and shared conventions of speech, there is an axis of *generality* (some modern writers might speak of rule-governed, or at least recognisably common, patterns). This generality emerges, for example, when we look at language as a system which generates certain possibilities of choice. In linguistics after Ferdinand de Saussure, this angle of perspective identifies shared language-possibilities as *la langue*.46 The second axis is that of the individual or particular. We are concerned here with the specific content of a particular utterance in the flow of human life, together with the particular character which it derives from the distinctive individuality of the author. This approaches the idea of Saussure's term *la parole*. This individuality is grasped by comparison and contrast. J. Duke and J. Forstman correctly observe: "Does not Schleiermacher force interpreters once again to consider how the relationship between *la langue* and *la parole* affects hermeneutics?"47

(iii) The third step in Schleiermacher's hermeneutics is to develop a further contrast between *grammatical* hermeneutics, which concerns language, and *psychological* (or technical) hermeneutics which concerns human persons and their expressions of thought. But this causes a complication: how does this contrast relate to the previous one? It is tempting to assume that grammatical hermeneutics concerns the general structures of shared language, and that psychological interpretation concerns the particularities of human personhood and historical events and agencies. But Schleiermacher sees particularities as well as generalities in language; and he sees the need to "divine" intuitively how to understand the person, as well as making general and comparative observations about the thought expressed by the individual person.

Is a given language-*use* to be understood, then, as a particular example of *language* (grammatical hermeneutics), or as the expression of a particular *speaker* (psychological hermeneutics)? Schleiermacher makes it clear that the psychological has no absolute privilege as over against the grammatical –

nor the grammatical, as over against the psychological. Neither does the particular have privilege or priority, in any final or absolute sense, against the general, nor the general, as against the particular. If it seems that priority is accorded this arises only from *decisions of strategy* determined by the interpreter in accordance with chosen tasks and goals. We can now see in what way the two sets of contrasts (grammatical and psychological hermeneutics; general language-systems and particular utterance-acts) are inter-related. *Each provides a conceptual frame in which the significance of the other contrast becomes clear.* Thus Schleiermacher declares, "An act of speaking cannot even be understood *as* [my italics] a moment in a person's development unless it is also understood in relation to language." "Every act of speaking is related both to the totality of the language and the totality of the speaker's thoughts . . . Understanding . . . always involves two moments: to understand what is said in the language with its possibilities [cf. Saussure's *la langue*] and to understand it in the thinking of the speaker [cf. *la parole*]."[48]

This principle now illuminates in what sense the two hermeneutical tasks of psychological and grammatical interpretation are said to be interdependent and "completely equal". Schleiermacher writes: "Psychological interpretation is higher when one regards the language exclusively as a means by which a *person communicates his thoughts* . . . Grammatical interpretation and language . . . are higher only when one regards the person and his speaking as *occasions for the language to reveal itself.*"[49] We cannot ask which should be the prior hermeneutical goal: where to start, or where to place the emphasis, is open to *decision* in the light of pressing questions; but the interpreter will not progress far, if anywhere at all, without the mutual inter-action of both operations.

We cannot refrain from noting Schleiermacher's closeness to the late Wittgenstein at these two or three points. First, language is not only a system of signs. Wittgenstein observes: "The speaking of language is part of an activity, or of a form of life".[50] It is "a totality consisting of the language and the actions into which it is woven".[51] "Only in the stream of thought and life do words have meaning".[52] Second, as against any urge towards abstract generality, we are warned against "the contemptuous attitude towards the particular case."[53] Yet language is shared and embodies "regular use of signposts, a custom . . . It is not possible that there should have been only one occasion on which someone obeyed a rule."[54] Third, many of the contrasts and hierarchies presupposed in given philosophies and theories of meaning are no more than functional ones which are relative to the purposes of the enquirer. They collapse into meaninglessness outside the context of given questions, agenda, or life-situations. The question "Does meaning reside in the author or in the text?" turns on just such a contrast, as Schleiermacher rightly saw.

The relative importance of the grammatical and psychological sides, Schleiermacher acknowledges, may be due partly to the nature of the text as well as to the concerns of the interpreter. In classical texts, for example, it may be appropriate to focus especially on their language, particularly if they exhibit unusual features of linguistic form or development. "A statement is maximally significant for the psychological side when it is highly individualized", as for example, "in dealing with letters, especially personal letters".[55] When we move from historical to didactic material, and then from didactic material to letters, there is a steady continuum which moves in this direction. We shall take up this point, in due course, with reference to the interpretation of the Pauline epistles.

(iv) The next stage in the argument is explicitly to draw out the implication, which emerges from the above, that *neither grammatical nor psychological interpretation can achieve a "final" or complete result.* There is a provisionality or corrigibility about the ongoing process, which, to borrow Wittgenstein's phrase again, means that "understanding" does not have a sharp boundary. The interpreter certainly cannot reach "complete" understanding by following mechanical rules or scientific deduction. Schleiermacher writes: "In order to complete the grammatical side of the interpretation it would be necessary to have a complete knowledge of the language. In order to complete the psychological side it would be necessary to have a complete knowledge of the person. Since in both cases such complete knowledge is impossible, it is necessary to move back and forth between the grammatical and psychological sides, and no rules can stipulate exactly how to do this."[56]

These observations about the provisional nature of understanding relate directly to Schleiermacher's conception of hermeneutics as a universal or "de-regionalized" area which does not presuppose some already-achieved understanding. He draws a working contrast between three levels of communication. At the routine level of everyday conversation in the street or marketplace, understanding may indeed be merely "mechanical". But there is a second level of communication and thinking which presupposes some particular experience or observation. Here we move from the merely mechanical to the level of shared experience. But where the creative expression of an individual's distinctive thought becomes the issue, we move to the level at which understanding has become an "art". The possibility of misunderstanding, and the plurality of competing attempts at understanding, gives rise to hermeneutics, in Schleiermacher's sense of the term. In his early "aphorisms" or notes Schleiermacher compares what he calls "two divergent maxims for understanding: (1) I am understanding everything until I encounter a contradiction or nonsense. (2) I do not understand anything that I cannot perceive and comprehend as necessary."[57] But I cannot understand "everything" without a complete understanding of both the author and the language out of which the text has been born; and no understanding is "necessary" all the while plausible competing choices about thought and meaning cannot finally be excluded.

Paul Ricoeur rightly observes that this position is to be seen against the background of both critical and Romanticist philosophy. He writes: "The proposal to struggle against misunderstanding in the name of the human adage 'there is hermeneutic where there is misunderstanding' is critical; the proposal 'to understand an author as well as, and even better than, he understands himself' is Romantic."[58] Karl Barth also summarizes the position clearly. He explains, "Where understanding is not an art [cf. the distinctions above] it proceeds on the assumption that understanding is natural, and our only job is to avoid misunderstanding. Where it is an art, however, it proceeds on the assumption that mis-understanding is natural, and the first concern is to seek understanding at every point. Is there some *necessary* and *compelling* insight into the expressed thoughts of someone else? 'No', replies Schleiermacher . . . in view of the multiplicity of historical and linguistic factors that have to be taken into account, and especially in view of the individuality of the author, where is there not the possibility of a *different* understanding from that which is *most* likely? The art of hermeneutics, then, is an art of relative *approximation* to the goal of an absolutely certain understanding." [59]

Schleiermacher draws out some implications for biblical hermeneutics. First, the biblical writings offer an example of the level at which understanding does indeed become an "art" rather than a mechanical operation. For the biblical writers offer an outstanding example of individuality and creativity. Indeed the dogmatic principle that we are to regard the Holy Spirit as the author of scripture is, at first, one-sided in its account of the biblical writings, for either it softens and reduces the individuality of the human writers, or "it must attribute the undeniable changes of mood and modification of view to the Holy Spirit".[60] Paul and John, especially, stand among "the more individualistic writers."[61] Indeed their very individuality witnesses to the flesh-and-blood reality of their relationship to Christ. This calls, therefore, for something more than merely mechanical interpretation on the part of human interpreters. "Each text has been addressed to specific people, and their writings could not be properly understood in the future unless these first readers could understand them . . . Their first readers would have looked for what was specifically related to their own situations . . . Even if the authors had been merely passive tools of the Holy Spirit, the Holy Spirit could have spoken through them only as they themselves would have spoken".[62]

Second, it is hazardous to restrict biblical hermeneutics only to "difficult" passages, as if "easier" ones could first be interpreted wholly through mechanical or philosophical means. This is because not only "quantitative" misunderstanding can arise about the degree of importance, emphasis, or effect, of a passage; but also "qualitative" misunderstanding about what it all adds up to together as a message, or about what we might call the "point". Schleiermacher insists "Quantitative and qualitative understanding deserve equal attention. Consequently, the interpreter should not begin solely with the difficult passages, but should also deal with the easy ones, and with both the formal and material elements of the language".[63]

4. Schleiermacher's System of Hermeneutics: the Hermeneutical Circle and a "Better" Understanding than the Author

It has now become clear that Schleiermacher's own formulation of the hermeneutical circle is more subtle and far-reaching than that of Ast. It concerns not only the mutual dependence of an understanding of the parts and of the whole of a message, or text, but also the interaction between grammatical and psychological hermeneutics and between different levels of understanding. The context of his description of the hermeneutical circle is that of a double principle: (a) "To understand the text . . . as well as and then even better than its author"; and (b) "the interpreter must put himself both objectively and subjectively in the position of the author."[64] This includes a grasp of "the vocabulary and history of an author's age" as well as the distinctive thought and experience of the author.

(v) Within this framework Schleiermacher formulates his version of the hermeneutical circle. He asserts: "Complete knowledge always involves an apparent circle, that each part can be understood only out of the whole to which it belongs, and vice-versa . . . To put oneself in the position of an author means to follow through with this relationship between the whole and the parts . . . The more we learn about an author, the better equipped we are for interpretation. A text can never be understood right away. On the contrary, every reading puts us in a better position to understand . . . Only in the case of insignificant texts (i.e. those of the market place) are we satisfied with what we understand on first reading."[65] This amplifies and develops his earlier maxim that "to complete the grammatical side of interpretation it would be necessary to have a complete knowledge of the person."[66]

Although the two axes or dimensions of parts and whole, remain inter-dependent, Schleiermacher commits himself to the observation that in practice the process must begin with a preliminary attempt to grasp the whole; to perceive what the text or the author's thought is about; to see its point. He writes "The process is as follows: The unity of the whole is grasped and then seen in its relation to the various sections within the whole . . . Once an overall aim of the work has been gained, this view is applied to the details . . . First task: Finding the inner unity of the theme of the work."67 But clearly such a preliminary assessment of the whole remains provisional upon confirmation, disconfirmation, or modifications by subsequent examination of the details. "The provisional grasp of the whole . . . will necessarily be incomplete . . . Our initial grasp of the whole is only provisional and imperfect."68 But the process of revision continues: "Even after we have revised our initial concept of a work, our understanding is still only provisional".69

We are now well on the way towards a conception of the hermeneutical circle in which the emphasis lies not only on the inter-action between the parts and the whole, but on a process of revision which modifies the interpreter's exploratory understanding in the light of the text. This mature understanding of the hermeneutical circle, sometimes re-defined as a hermeneutical spiral, finds fullest expression in Hans-George Gadamer.70 The logical extension of Schleiermacher's perspective would be to offer an explanatory account of the reason for trends, fashions, movements, and developments in the history of biblical interpretation. We shall attempt to offer a comment on this issue in due course.

(vi) This circular or spiral process, however, moves not only between grammatical and psychological hermeneutics, and between the general and the particular, but also between the divinatory and the comparative. As Barth observes, there is a broad but by no means constant correlation between the psychological and the divinatory poles.71 Schleiermacher writes: "Psychological interpretation seeks to understand the creative ideas, including those fundamental thoughts which give rise to the entire train of thought."72 "In the psychological task we cannot avoid giving greater emphasis to divination . . . But we cannot be too careful in examining from every angle a picture that has been sketched in such hypothetical fashion".73 Conversely, in the examination of language and textual form "the other method is by the very nature predominantly comparative . . . But even so there is originally a measure of divination in the way one poses the question about a work".74 To "divine" without comparative philological or critical study is to become a hermeneutical "nebulist"; to engage in comparative philological questions without a living, intuitive, perception of the spirit of the subject-matter and its author is to remain a hermeneutical *"pedant"*.75

Schleiermacher's particular understanding of "divining" plays an influential part in his hermeneutics and indeed in his whole thought. We noted earlier in our comments on his *Christmas Dialogue* of 1805 that he associated this creative, intuitive, capacity especially with the feminine. He reiterates this view for hermeneutics in his *Compendium* of 1819. He writes:

"Divinatory knowledge is *the feminine strength in knowing people*: comparative knowledge, the masculine . . . the divinatory is based on the assumption that each person is not only a unique individual in his own right, but that he has a receptivity to the uniqueness of every other person".[76] The interpreter must "transform himself, so to speak, into the author".[77] As we have noted, the fundamental model used by Schleiermacher is that of the *intuitive rapport which can exist between friends*. He declares, "The divinatory (*divinatorische*) method seeks to gain an immediate comprehension of the author as an individual".[78]

Customary textbook expositions of Schleiermacher speak of his appeal to the use of sympathetic imagination. This is part of his concern, but it is more especially a matter of "getting inside" the author's thoughts and feelings. There is a standard rejoinder by existentialist psychoanalytical and post-modern theorists to the effect that no-one can identify that closely with any other human individual, since "I" am not "him" or "her". But two rejoinders must be borne in mind. First, Schleiermacher appeals to the experience of intuitive perceptiveness which can sometimes (not necessarily often) be found in close human relationships. Rightly or wrongly, we do tend to think of a few particular individuals as having outstanding pastoral or personal gifts of potential *rapport* with other human persons. They are the kind of counsellors, friends, or spouses who can genuinely say "I understand . . . there is no need to explain". Second, as we note in chapter XV, Schleiermacher's emphasis on "sharing the form of *life*" *prohibits a merely psychologistic interpretation of this principle*. "Life" reflects something akin to Searle's "Background" (discussed in chapters VIII, X, and XV).

Schleiermacher is at pains, also, not to isolate the role of feeling or intuition from comparative or critical reflection. Psychological or technical interpretation "involves two methods: a divinatory and a comparative. Since each method refers back to the other, the two should never be separated."[79] The comparative method allows us to see the individual who has produced the text as a type within a given category, who writes out of a context of shared concerns and through the use of a common style, vocabulary, and linguistic code. Thus, if we were to apply these two methods to an understanding of the Pauline epistles, we should need to live with Paul until we establish some sense of *rapport* with his concerns, his passions, and his purposes, but we should also need to understand him as an example of a Christian missionary-pastor, itinerant in the Graeco-Roman world of the first century, who used the letter-forms and conventions of his day, and belonged to a worshipping Christian community. Comparative study would note relative similarities and differences in relation to other hellenistic language-users, other religious thinkers of the period, other itinerant missionaries or preachers and other representatives of the apostolic community. Intuitive insight would seek to perceive what made Paul the unique person that he was. Both dimensions, which cannot be separated, belong to the task of New Testament interpretation.

Yet Schleiermacher attributes both methods not only to the work of "psychological" interpretation, but also to the "grammatical" or linguistic area. It is easy to see why the comparative method is fundamental. Under the heading "grammatical interpretation" Schleiermacher asserts: "First canon: a more precise determination of any point in a given text must be decided on the basis of the use of *language common to the author and his original public.*"[80] Indeed we noted at the beginning of this discussion that for Schleiermacher speaking is the medium for the communality of thought, and is therefore "related to both the totality of the language and the totality of the speaker's thoughts."[81] He then stipulates that the "second canon" in grammatical interpretation is to determine "the meaning of each word in a passage . . . *by the context in which it occurs*".[82]

Schleiermacher offers a dozen or so pages of comment on the application of this principle to New Testament interpretation. He argues, for example, that we cannot determine the meaning of New Testament language without careful reference to similarities with, and differences from, Greek language-uses in the Septuagint; Semitic colouring in the New Testament itself; special considerations about Greek particles and narrative connections; and the interactions between choices of language and the didactic or historical purposes of an author. All this, it is stressed, entails two tasks: "to regard the text as unity, that is, as a general view, (and) to regard it in its particularity, that is, as personally delimited."[83] But the *second* task transcends merely comparative method. Schleiermacher writes, "In grammatical interpretation individuality cannot be grasped by a concept. Individuality must be intuited".[84] Linguistic interpretation must grasp *both* how a work is related "to similar works of the same type" *and* the creative moments where distinctive experience or insights operate.[85] In his early notes Schleiermacher draws attention to the importance of studying synonymy and multiple meanings.[86] Similarly in the "loose" page from 1810–11 he observes, "One must know all the possibilities that were at the author's disposal – tools for grasping this are analogy, writers of a similar sort, antithesis."[87]

We return, then, finally to what is probably the most widely-known formulation of Schleiermacher's hermeneutical goal. In his Academy Address of 1829 he repeats: "The task of hermeneutics is to reproduce the whole internal process of an author's way of combining thoughts . . . Explanations of words and contents are not themselves interpretation but only elements of it."[88] Richard Palmer aptly comments: "It is the reverse of composition, for it starts with the fixed and finished expression and goes back to the mental life from which it arose."[89] But when Schleiermacher's complex system is summarised under some short slogan as merely "genetic" or "reconstructionist" its subtlety and multiformity is lost from view. The various polarities in Schleiermacher's system of hermeneutics overlap and criss-cross or as Karl Barth has observed "cross wires". [90] It would be difficult, if not impossible, to summarize the process in one single schematic form. If we were compelled to attempt it, the following dual scheme is perhaps a partial representation of certain aspects of the process:

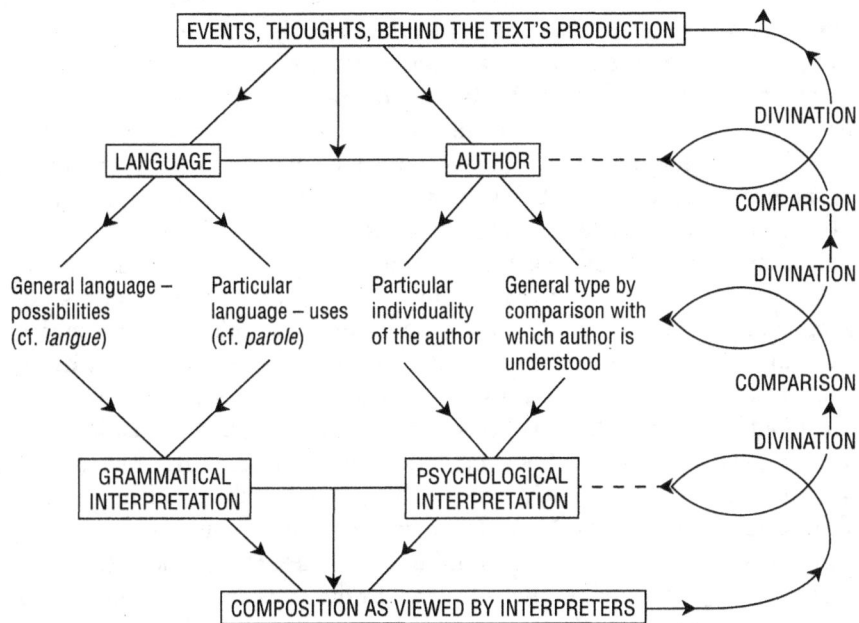

(vii) All of the six elements within Schleiermacher's system of hermeneutics which we have outlined turn on polarities or contrasts; between thinking and speaking, between generality and particularity, between language-possibilities and language-uses, between grammatical interpretation and psychological interpretation, between parts and whole, between divination and comparison. This list must now be extended to include one more polarity. On the one hand Schleiermacher insists that the meaning of a text is rooted in its original situation, which is determined with reference to its historical and linguistic context. On the other hand he believes that the interpreter can grasp the meaning of the text better, or more fully, even than its author. He declares, "The task is to be formulated as follows: 'To understand the text at first as well as, and then even better than, its author' ... The task is infinite."[91]

Both sides of this polarity deserve emphasis and clarification for different reasons. The first has sometimes received insufficient emphasis, and Schleiermacher's concern for historical interpretation, been underestimated. The second arises from the influence of Romanticism. Duke and Forstman follow Patsch's research in tracing it initially to the particular influence of Schlegel, although Schleiermacher himself developed it into a central point in his hermeneutics. Schlegel and Schleiermacher shared J. G. Herder's assumption that what was important in the understanding of a literary text or a work of art was the spirit that "underlay" the text or work itself. Hence meaning is always "more" than has been objectively embodied in the work which remains as a monument to the creative moment of human subjectivity and agency.

The first of the two principles begins to emerge in Schleiermacher's work on language. Today we should call it the semantic aspect. He writes, "The meaning of each word in a passage must be determined by the context in which it occurs."[92] But this specificity is not only linguistic; it is also historical. This is seen most clearly in Schleiermacher's comments about the interpretation of the New Testament. These writings, he insists, were not addressed "to all of Christendom", but "each text was addressed to a specific people".[93] The starting-point for determining their meaning was how the "first readers" understood them. This entailed "what was specifically related to their own situations."[94] Hence "the interpreter must put himself both objectively and subjectively in the position of the author", which includes knowing "the vocabulary and the history of an author's age".[95] In his early notes Schleiermacher distinguished between various levels of context. Every level from the most immediate to the most general remains relevant to determining the message of the utterance. In biblical interpretation, he later observes in the *Compendium*, "*only historical interpretation* can do justice to the rootedness of the New Testament authors in their time and place".[96] His only qualification of this principle is the timely warning that historical explanation must not be reductionist. It must not seek to account for the new and creative merely in terms of pre-existing concepts and categories. This kind of historical interpretation, he acknowledges, can be one-sided; but it is improper to reject historical interpretation altogether, simply because it is capable of being misused.

This approach to meaning is confirmed and underlined in Schleiermacher's discussion of allegorical interpretations of New Testament material. Once again, his remarks are sophisticated and modern. We cannot dismiss *all* allegorical interpretation, he points out, in the name of some abstract or dogmatic principle that texts can have only *one* meaning, for where parable or allegory are actually used by a biblical writer, such a principle is patently false. Whenever biblical language is even *allusive*, allusions always involve a second meaning. Nevertheless, where the author does not expect readers to pick up allusion or allegorical meanings, to look for them is simply "an error".[97] Once again, the historical research embodied in what are known as "New Testament introductions" are indispensable, Schleiermacher believes, for placing us where the author stood in the matter of language-uses, historical situation, and what should nowadays be called linguistic code.

In view of this emphasis on the original language-situation and the author, how does the second side of this last polarity emerge, that the interpreter must seek a "better" understanding than the author? We have noted that with Herder, Schlegel, and other Romantics, Schleiermacher held the view that a written text or a work of art could never fully and exhaustively embody the creative spirit which produced it. At first sight the logical inference might seem to be that if an interpreter has access only to the text, the interpretation can only be *less* than what the author wished to express. From where could this "more" be derived? The answer lies in what is entailed in going "behind" the text. Schleiermacher proposes that the interpreter examine *every* feature which might contribute to the author's competence, performance, and will to express what lies in the text. But even the author would not have been aware of *all* these contributory factors. The interpreter can gather together data and critical evaluations of which the author may have been, at most, only dimly conscious.

The relationship of this line of reasoning to the philosophical background of Schelling cannot be accidental. We have already noted Schelling's influence on Schleiermacher's thought and the evaluations of this influence offered by Suskind and Brandt. Schelling's philosophy of nature took its point of departure from Fichte. How did the reflective or self-limiting activities of the mind, as Fichte expounded them, relate to the infinite? Schelling views nature as a system of developing stages which culminated in self-consciousness. Nature, in effect, is a product of mind, but not of conscious mind. It is an unconscious dialectic, moving towards conscious expression when the individual ego reproduces in thought what has been unconscious in nature. Consciousness and nature are therefore one, and infinite, although conscious thought in its actual expression takes finite and delimited form. Schelling formulated these ideas initially in his *Ideas for Philosophy of Nature* (1797), and then in his *First Sketch of a System of Nature Philosophy* (1799). In his *System of Transcendental Idealism* (1800) he developed these approaches into a philosophy of knowledge. As consciousness emerges in the transition from sensation to perception, perception then moves to reflection, and finally reflection to will.

Apart from Plato's notion of knowledge as recollection, this is perhaps the first formulation in the history of ideas of what might be termed a philosophical doctrine of the unconscious, and certainly the first formulation of a philosophy of artistic creativity in these terms. As Brandt observes, Schlegel insisted that in spite of their differences in character or personality, the philosophies of Schelling and Schleiermacher were very close during this period which was formative for both of them.[98] If the interpreter of a work of art, or of a written text, could reach behind the conscious product to the conscious and unconscious forces which drove the thoughts to expression, then the will or purpose of the author in writing or producing could be perceived, in principle even with better insight than the author. Schleiermacher writes: "We must try to become aware of many things of which he himself [the author] may have been unconscious, except insofar as he reflects in his own work and became his own reader ... So formulated, the task is infinite."[99]

It would be roughly a century before Freud laid out more detailed notions of the unconscious in his *The Interpretation of Dreams* (1899) and subsequent works on the basis of which other writers, including most notably Ricoeur, have developed a "hermeneutic of suspicion". *Yet Schleiermacher hints at anticipations of this self-deception:* "Active misunderstanding . . . occurs when one reads something into a text because of one's own bias. In such a case the author's meaning cannot possibly emerge."[100] Hence we must undertake a succession of readings, each of which may put us in a better position to understand, because it increases our knowledge of the material. The interpreter must even guard against illusion and deception here, however, when independent research should not be sacrificed for linguistic and historical research which is questionable or is itself the product of questionable interpretation. He observes, "In New Testament studies especially it can be said that the questionableness and arbitrariness of interpretation is due in large measure to this failure".[101] Needless to say, the need for a divinatory leap into "an overview of the whole" is fraught with the possibility of misunderstanding; but it remains the inevitable starting-point. It constitutes, however, no more than the beginning of a long process in which compassion and critical reflection have their parts to play. Whatever role he assigns to feeling and intuition, how ever great his affinity with the Romantic spirit, there is shrewdness and sophistication in Schleiermacher's system of hermeneutics, as well as a recognition of the limitation of rational reflection alone.

5. Theological Ambiguities and Hermeneutical Achievements

Assessments of Schleiermacher have often been quicker to note his theological ambiguities or shortcomings than the brilliance, in the context of the time, of his hermeneutical achievements. He was the first thinker to balance a focus on the author with a focus on the text, and see that which was emphasized more was bound up with decisions concerning hermeneutical goals and interpretative strategies. He was the first thinker to complement what is often dismissively and simplistically called his "re-constructionist" or "genetic" hermeneutic with questions about reader-effects at different levels. But is his hermeneutical system any the less constructive as a hermeneutic of understanding because of the acknowledged theological ambiguities and weaknesses which also form part of Schleiermacher's thought?

We may acknowledge, as we have already noted, that there are serious inadequacies in Schleiermacher's theology. Critic after critic has repeated H.R.Mackintosh's damning verdict that "for him theology is less concerned with God than with man's consciousness of God."[102] Would Schleiermacher himself admit the claim, Mackintosh asks, that his theology is no more than "a systematic exploitation of the contents of the Christian soul"? He would probably reject it on the ground that for him "feeling" is much more than a psychological state of mind. A feeling of the infinite signifies not simply a purely human mode of apprehension, perception, or emotion, but God's presence as immediately known. Nevertheless Mackintosh rightly concludes that, at best, Schleiermacher's language is "equivocal".[103] The same kind of ambivalence, we might argue, characterizes the role of "faith" in semi-Pelagian strands of pietism, where it is argued that grace depends for its effectiveness on human appropriation, and most notably of all in Paul Tillich's use of the term "ultimate concern" which he explicitly describes both as a human mode of understanding or appropriation and also as the reality which is appropriated and lies beyond conceptual understanding. In the case of Tillich and Schleiermacher the philosophical background of Fichte and Schelling has some significance.

Three theological areas in particular give cause for concern. First, while Schleiermacher endeavours to do justice to the particularity of Christology, it is too easy to come away with the impression that for him the distinctive issue lies in Christ's experience of a universal God-consciousness which simply attains a unique degree. The account of Christ and Christianity in the *Speeches* certainly convey this impression.[104] Second, his immanentism and Romanticism scarcely leave room for an adequately serious view of the consequences of human sin. It is not clear how this affects the human situation and human orientation, rather than simply the content of human consciousness. It is by no means an accident, as Karl Barth acutely observed, that Schleiermacher found the Old Testament an uncongenial text for preaching, and that he felt little rapport with Old Testament literature and theology.

Schleiermacher also gives cause for a third area of concern, which is both predictable and yet also surprising. His approach to questions about the uniqueness and inspiration of the biblical writings is, from one point of view, predictable, because he does not wish to accommodate a supernaturalist interventionist view of inspiration. But from another viewpoint, as Barth points out, he leaves behind the subtlety and concern for balance which he so often shows in other areas, in insisting on a choice between two extreme alternatives in his theology of the status of the Bible. Because of the individuality and creativity of the biblical writers, Schleiermacher excludes, understandably, any mechanistic or "dictation" view of biblical inspiration. But on this basis he wishes to treat the Bible like any other book, except for its distinctive features of language and human creativity.

If, then, we acknowledge that these difficulties exist, are they fatal to any search for value in Schleiermacher's system of hermeneutics? Helmut Thielicke and Barth suggest that this might be so. The concern, it is argued, has moved from God to the 'I'. Thielicke brands this approach as a "Cartesian" theology.[105] He writes, "Certainty about God cannot be based, then, on a 'God says'. Before the word 'God' can mean anything it must be shown to be prepared for in my subjectivity, and to have a place in its structure. This is why Schleiermacher opens the *Christian Faith*, not with the doctrine of God, but with an analysis of subjectivity."[106]

The strands of criticism within this argument have to be unravelled. First, it is inappropriate to describe Schleiermacher as "Cartesian" in an individualistic ego-centred sense, from the viewpoint of his philosophy of language and especially *his hermeneutics*. Schleiermacher makes a deliberate point of expounding the relationship between thought as a supposedly individual activity and the *inter-subjective reality of language*. Descartes isolates the individual consciousness from everything except the activity of logical reasoning. Schleiermacher knows that the individual cannot even begin to acquire self-knowledge without inter-action with other persons through a given framework of shared language. We have discussed these issues in detail above, noting that interpretation entails stepping "out of one's own frame of mind."[107] For this reason we questioned Michaelson's verdict that Schleiermacher's hermeneutical perspective turned theology into a system of self-referring prepositions. In Schleiermacher's words, "Speaking is the medium for the communality of thought."[108]

This criticism takes a more plausible form when it relates not to Descartes' individualistic self, but rather to his beginning with doubt as the starting-point for knowledge. This is the deeper ground of Barth's unease, which Thielicke and Michaelson also share. Can Schleiermacher found a hermeneutical system on the belief that all prior interpretations (either of the biblical writings or of other literature) must be open to doubt or to alternative understanding? Can interpretation genuinely *begin* with the divinatory leap by the interpreter into the subject-matter and language of the text? Barth opposes this starting-point with a theological question: "Why should not God have spoken to man in a way that is necessarily and compellingly understandable?" Might it not be "without any qualitative or quantitative possibilities of misunderstanding the truth or Word of God?"[109]

Such a question places us in a logical dilemma. For if we could be sure that no qualitative or quantitative misunderstanding ever could or ever would arise, on Schleiermacher's own frank admission, there would be no need for hermeneutics. The dilemma for Protestant theology arises from a desire to assert and affirm both the givenness of the word of God and the fallibility of human interpretation, including even the church's current corporate perceptions of that word. Hermeneutics presupposes the *possibility* of misunderstanding, and the *possibility* of the need for correction and for fresh perception. What Schleiermacher wishes to emphasize is the *provisionality* of interpretation pending confirmation or disconfirmation as reading and understanding proceed. He himself does not in practice begin from a blank sheet. As Richard Niebuhr points out, in spite of its weaknesses his Christology begins with the givenness of a historical particularity.[110] But in the context of *hermeneutics*, rather than theology, the fallibility of human understanding, even fallible Christian understanding, is the reason for the whole enterprise.

We may tentatively suggest an analogy. In the philosophy of religion it is valuable to expose the strengths, weaknesses and logical status of arguments for the existence of God. It would seem odd to question the logical and philosophical value of the exercise on the ground that even to consider the question implies doubt about God, or an agnostic or atheistic "presupposition". Similarly the consideration of *psychological factors* in religious experience or *sociological factors* in the development of Christian churches does not imply a psychological or sociological *"explanation"* of this reality. In the same way, Schleiermacher's hermeneutics contain often subtle and sometimes brilliant insights into the processes of interpretation and understanding which stand on their own feet as contributions within this specific area. We select five of the more important achievements by way of summary.

(i) Schleiermacher set hermeneutics in the context of theories of knowledge. This stands in contrast to both the pre-modern and post-modern models. In the former, it is perhaps too readily assumed that the interpreter, or community of interpretation, already in principle "knows" what the text is all about; hermeneutics tends in practice to furnish explanations for the different routes whereby other interpreters or communities have reached different conclusions. In the ancient world and in Patristic thought hermeneutics encouraged reflection on interpretation within a framework of trust which might include innocence and obedience, but also, on occasion, credulity and self-deception. The Reformation marked a transition towards a hermeneutic of enquiry, which increasingly raised questions about the nature of knowledge and understanding itself. Schleiermacher's hermeneutics become, after Kant, transcendental: he enquires into the linguistic and inter-subjective conditions which make understanding possible. Although, as Gadamer notes, Schleiermacher did not fully face the issues raised by the historical-conditionedness of tradition and inter-subjectivity, this does not imply that he has nothing to say.[111] His work remains an ingredient, although not more than an ingredient, in any serious contemporary hermeneutical theory, provided that its complexity and subtlety is properly understood.

(ii) Popular interpretations of Schleiermacher often expound too superficially his contrast between "grammatical" and "psychological" hermeneutics. We have noted that various categories in his hermeneutics criss-cross and overlap. His attention to language as both a shared, corporate, social phenomenon (cf. *la langue*) and as particularities which take the form of language-uses (cf. *la parole*) facilitates a formulation of the hermeneutical task which is neither merely individualistic nor merely psychological. Most important of all, he avoids giving absolute privilege either to focus on the *text at the expense of forgetting the author, or on the author at the expense of the text. Meaning arises from the single unity of author-and-text.* To use a later terminology, language includes the actions or life with which it is interwoven. But Schleiermacher, anticipating twentieth-century linguistic perspectives, recognizes that the emphasis may fall on occasion more on one aspect than the other, depending on the *chosen* purposes of the interpreter.

(iii) There are both gains and losses in Schleiermacher's pre-occupation with processes "behind" the text. The Romanticist devaluing of thought and language as a mere residue or deposit of creative experience lurks in the background. But it is not as decisive for Schleiermacher as for other Romantics. Moreover it opens the interpreter's appreciation of the necessity of historical reconstruction as something far more profound and important than a pedant's concern for antiquarian worlds, or a merely genetic approach to truth-questions. In any case Schleiermacher's genius is such that his concern for what lies behind the text does not blind him to the importance of questions about its *effects. Content, context, situation, author, effect, first readers, and subsequent readers, all stand within the area of his active concern.*

(iv) Schleiermacher's formulation of the hermeneutical circle is not the simplified model which popular interpretations often make of it. It is more than a straightforward relation between the parts and the whole of texts. These processes of understanding involve distinctions between a divinatory intuitive perception of wholeness and comparative judgement and critical assessments about linguistic elements, categories, and genre; distinctions between language-possibilities and language-uses; distinctions between human individuality and patterns of structure or generality. In biblical interpretation this principle focuses the relationship between painstaking exegesis and broader theological and historical judgements about the "point" of a biblical book, or the "mind" of a biblical author. It may also perhaps suggest a reason for trends and fashions in biblical scholarship which sometimes have the appearance of moving merely in cycles, but actually serve to *advance corporate understanding,* as different sets of questions are addressed to the text in a sequence which may repeat earlier questions, but now in the light of other enquiries.

(v) Schleiermacher still speaks to the contemporary debate about whether meaning goes "beyond" the horizon or consciousness of a text's author, or whether it is rooted in the historical situation out of which it was born. It is typical of Schleiermacher as a "mediation" thinker that he wants to hold together both poles of the debate. Because of the importance of context, situation, and the language on which the author draws, the historical rootedness of the text remains decisive for the meaning. Nevertheless, the interpreter may become aware of factors which evade the author's consciousness, even though they play a part in the formulation of the text and its message. The implications of this for biblical interpretation of the New Testament are discussed further below. They range from questions of the kind raised by F.C. Baur, and noted in the previous chapter, about historical constraint and necessity, to questions raised by orthodox Christians about whether the New Testament writings can be said to imply a theology of the Holy Trinity.

NOTES TO CHAPTER VI

1. F.D.E. Schleiermacher, *Hermeneutics: The Handwritten Manuscripts* edited by H. Kimmerle, Eng.Missoula: Scholars Press 1977 (A.A.R. Text and Translation series 1, Tr. by J. Duke and J. Forstman) 21–40 and 229–34 [German edition: *Hermeneutik: Abhandlung der Heidelberger Akademie der Wissenschaften* (Heidelberg: Carl Winter, 1959), 9–24]. Cf. also Manfred Frank (ed.) *Hermeneutik und Kritik. Mit einem Anhang sprachphilosophischer Texte Schleiermachers* Frankfurt a/M: Suhrkamp 1977. See also Heinz Kimmerle, "Hermeneutical Theory or Ontological Hermeneutics" in *Journal for Theology and the Church,* 4: *History and Hermeneutic,* Tübingen: Mohr and New York: Harper & Row, 1967 107–121.
2. F.D.E. Schleiermacher, *Hermeneutics: The Handwritten Manuscripts,* 98, 99.
3. F.D.E. Schleiermacher, *Hermeneutics,* 52 (German edn 40).
4. Gordon E. Michalson Jr., *Lessing's 'Ugly Ditch': A Study of Theology and History,* Pennsylvania State University Press 1985, ix.
5. *Ibid,* 18.
6. F.D.E. Schleiermacher, *Hermeneutics,* 42 and 109.
7. *Ibid* 97.
8. *Ibid* 97–8.
9. John Calvin, *Institutes of the Christian Religion* (Eng. Edinburgh: Clarke, 1957) I.1.3, (Eng. edn 39).
10. *Ibid* I.1.1 (Eng. edn 37).

11. F.D.E. Schleiermacher, *Hermeneutics* 151 (my italics).
12. *Ibid.*
13. James O. Duke, *The Prospects for Theological Hemeneutics: Hegel versus Schleiermacher?* (Dissertation for Vanderbilt Ph.D. Ann Arbor: University Microfilms 1979) 76; cf 61–97, and Duke's introduction to his English translation of *Hermeneutics* 11–15. On the contrast betweeen Schleiermacher and Hegel see further H.-G. Gadamer, *Truth and Method* 147–50.
14. F.D.E. Schleiermacher, *Hermeneutics* 150; cf 100, 101, and 113.
15. *Ibid* 38, cf 107,113.
16. David E. Klemm, *Hermeneutical Inquiry: I The Interpretation of Texts*, 55; Kurt Mueller-Vollmer (ed) *The Hermeneutics Reader*, 72. Cf. Robert W. Funk, (ed.) *Schleiermacher as Contemporary: Journal for Theology and Church*, 7, New York: Herder, 1970.
17. Karl Barth, *Protestant Theology in the Nineteenth Century*, Eng. London: SCM 1972, 425, cf 425–73.
18. *Ibid* 428.
19. Martin Redeker, *Schleiermacher's Life and Thought* Eng. Philadelphia: Fortress Press, 1973, 61.
20. F.D.E. Schleiermacher, *On Religion, Speeches to its Cultural Despisers*, Eng. New York, Harper edn, 1958, xi (from Otto's introduction).
21. F.D.E. Schleiermacher, "Die Weihnachtsfeier. Ein Gespräch", (rp.in Schleiermacher *Werke* IV, Aalen: Scientia Verlag, 1967 (from the 2nd Leipzig edn. of 1928) 475–532; cf B.A. Gerrish, *A Prince of the Church. Schleiermacher and the Beginning of Modern Theology*, London: SCM, 1984, 13–18.
22. Schleiermacher *Werke* IV 479, 495–6.
23. *Werke IV*, 477–83; cf *Hermeneutics* 150.
24. *Werke IV*, 532.
25. Jack Forstman, *A Romantic Triangle: Schleiermacher and Early German Romanticism*, Missoula: Scholars Press (A.A.R. Studies in Religion 13) 1977, esp 95–113.
26. J. Arundel Chapman, *An Introduction to Schleiermacher*, London: Epworth Press, 1932, 100–125.
27. William Wordsworth, *The Prelude* 2, 379–82. There is only a two year difference between Wordsworth's date of birth (1770–1850) and Schleiermacher's.
28. M. Redeker, *op.cit.* 11.
29. F.D.E. Schleiermacher, *The Christian Faith*. Eng.Edinburgh: Clarke, 1948, 12.
30. B.A. Gerrish, *op. cit.*. 18–20.
31. M. Redeker, *op. cit.*. 39.
32. Karl Barth, *The Theology of Schleiermacher. Lectures at Göttingen* 1923–24. Eng. Grand Rapids: Eerdmans 1982, xviii.
33. F.D.E. Schleiermacher, *On Religion* 119–20.
34. Richard Brandt, *The Philosophy of Schleiermacher*, New York: Greenwood Press 1968 (1941) 42–70; Hermann Suskind, *Der Einfluss Schellings auf die Entwicklung von Schleiermachers System*, Tübingen: Mohr, 1909.
35. Terry H. Foreman, *Religion as the Heart of Humanistic Culture. Schleiermacher as Exponent of Bildung in the Speeches on Religion of 1799* (Dissertation for Yale Ph.D) Ann Arbor: University Microfilms 1977.
36. F.D.E. Schleiermacher *Hermeneutics* 175–214.
37. *Ibid* 116.

38. *Ibid* 195–6.
39. *Ibid.*
40. *Ibid* 208–9.
41. *Ibid* 55 and 104. Cf. H.-G. Gadamer, *Truth and Method* 148–49.
42. F.D.E. Schleiermacher, *Hermeneutics*, 107.
43. *Ibid* 97. Cf. Georgia Warnke, *Gadamer. Hermeneutics, Tradition, and Reason*, Cambridge: Polity Press 1988, 12–15.
44. Anthony C. Thiselton, *The Two Horizons*, 379–85. Cf. O.R. Jones (ed.) *The Private Language Argument*, London: Macmillan, 1971; R. Rhees, *Discussions of Wittgenstein*, London: Routledge & Kegan Paul, 1970; L. Wittgenstein, *Philosophical Investigations*, esp. sections 198–9, 202, 257 and 265, 275, 293, and "Notes for Lectures on Private Experience and 'Sense Data'" in *Philosophical Review* 77 (1968) 271–320.
45. F.D.E. Schleiermacher, *Hermeneutics*, 97.
46. F. de Saussure, *Cours de linguistique générale* 181–2; cf. *Course in General Linguistics*, (Eng. London: Owen, 1960) 81.
47. Translators' Introduction to Schleiermacher: *Hermeneutics*, 12.
48. *Ibid* 97–8 and 99.
49. *Ibid* 97–98.
50. L. Wittgenstein, *Philosophical Investigations*, Sect.23.
51. *Ibid* Sect.7.
52. L. Wittgenstein, *Zettel*, Germ. & Eng. Oxford, Blackwell, 1967 sect 173.
53. L. Wittgenstein, *The Blue and Brown Books*, Oxford, Blackwell 1958 18.
54. L. Wittgenstein, *Philosophical Investigations* sects. 198–9.
55. F.D.E. Schleiermacher, *Hermeneutics*, 102, 103.
56. *Ibid* 100.
57. *Ibid* 41.
58. Paul Ricoeur, *Hermeneutics and the Human Sciences*, Eng. Cambridge: Cambridge University Press 1981, 46.
59. Karl Barth, *The Theology of Schleiermacher* 179.
60. F.D.E. Schleiermacher, *Hermeneutics*, 139.
61. *Ibid.*
62. *Ibid* 107.
63. *Ibid* 142.
64. *Ibid* 112–13.
65. *Ibid* 113.
66. *Ibid* 100.
67. *Ibid* 168.
68. *Ibid* 200.
69. *Ibid* 203.
70. H.-G. Gadamer, *Truth and Method* 235–45, 258–74, 325–41.
71. K. Barth, *The Theology of Schleiermacher* 182.
72. F.D.E. Schleiermacher, *Hermeneutics* 223.
73. *Ibid* 207.
74. *Ibid* 208.
75. *Ibid* 205.
76. *Ibid* 150.
77. *Ibid.*

78. *Ibid* (German, Lücke edn. *Werke IV* 153).
79. *Ibid.*
80. *Ibid* 177 (my italics).
81. *Ibid* 97–8.
82. *Ibid* 127 (my italics).
83. *Ibid* 162.
84. *Ibid* 64.
85. *Ibid* 205.
86. *Ibid* 51.
87. *Ibid* 91.
88. *Ibid* 188 and 211.
89. Richard E. Palmer, *op. cit.*, 86.
90. Karl Barth, *The Theology of Schleiermacher* 182.
91. F.D.E. Schleiermacher, *Hermeneutics*, 246 n.12.
92. *Ibid* 127.
93. *Ibid* 107.
94. *Ibid.*
95. *Ibid* 113.
96. *Ibid* 104 (my italics).
97. *Ibid* 105.
98. Richard B. Brandt *op. cit.*. 161.
99. F.D.E. Schleiermacher, *Hermeneutics* 112.
100. *Ibid* 111.
101. *Ibid* 114.
102. H. R. Mackintosh, *Types of Modern Theology: Schleiermacher to Barth*, London: Nisbet, 1937, 94. For more recent discussions of Schleiermacher's theology, however, cf. Robert Williams, *Schleiermacher the Theologian. The Construction of the Doctrine of God*, Philadelphia: Fortress, 1978; Richard R. Niebuhr, *Schleiermacher on Christ and Religion: A New Introduction*, New York: Scribner 1964; and John E. Thiel, *God and World in Schleiermacher's 'Dialektik und Glaubenslehre'*, Bern, Frankfurt a.M.: Lang, 1981.
103. H.R. Mackintosh *op. cit.*.
104. Cf. F.D.E. Schleiermacher, *On Religion*, esp.246–9.
105. Helmut Thielicke, *The Evangelical Faith I*, Eng, Grand Rapids: Eerdmans, 1974 38–40; 43–49.
106. *Ibid* 303.
107. F.D.E. Schleiermacher, *Hermeneutics*, 42 and 109. See above, section 1.
108. *Ibid* 97.
109. K. Barth, *The Theology of Schleiermacher*, 183.
110. Richard R. Niebuhr, *Schleiermacher on Christ and Religion*, New York: Scribner 1964.
111. Hans-Georg Gadamer, *Truth and Method*, 162–73; cf. *Kleine Schriften* (4 vols) Tübingen: Mohr 1967–72, and 1977, III, 133–34.

CHAPTER VII

Pauline and other Texts in the Light of a Hermeneutics of Understanding

1. Paul, Pauline Texts, and Schleiermacher's Hermeneutical Circle

Schleiermacher's careful and detailed formulation of the principle of the hermeneutical circle, which we have closely examined in the previous chapter, can readily be applied and illustrated with reference to Pauline texts. On the one hand, there is no substitute for painstaking exegesis of the flow of the texts, detail by detail. If, for example, we wish to understand Paul's view of the law, part of the process entailed will be to examine the Greek text with the aid of standard commentaries such as those by Cranfield, Barrett, or Dunn.[1] This, in Schleiermacher's view, entails comparative assessment of an analytical or supposedly "masculine" nature. On the other hand, the exegetical conclusions at which the interpreter arrives cannot be isolated from his or her provisional understanding of the mind of Paul, or of Pauline thought as a whole.

This does not presuppose that Paul writes as a systematic theologian who seeks to expound a tightly organized system of theology. *It does imply, however, that we interpret this or that utterance against the background of a broader understanding of the speaker;* and that in this respect a quality of perception above and beyond that of detailed rational analysis is involved. Schleiermacher chose to describe this as a more intuitive or supposedly "feminine" quality of perception. *This creative and wholistic aspect goes beyond purely rational or mechanical scientific method.* It also entails more than "psychological" imagination and rapport. As we have stressed, and as we urge again in chapter XV, *it implies entering a life-world, or sharing a form of life which we contextualize within our own horizons of understanding.*

This emphasis may still broadly be termed "Romanticist" in as much as to perceive Paul as a living *person* who wrote his epistles amidst the flow and pressures of life suggests that interpretation, as a process of understanding, cannot be reduced to the level of purely rational analysis alone. The Romanticist reaction against rationalism found later a parallel in a cycle of emphasis in Pauline interpretation. At the end of the nineteenth century it was fashionable, as Munck expressed it, to have a "one-sided view" of Paul as a theologian: "People make him a Christian thinker who goes out from his study into the rough-and-tumble of the day's controversy as the keen logical representative of his own ideas (Paulinism)".[2] This was followed by what Munck calls "the liberal period, with its emphasis on the deep emotions of the apostle's religious life . . . Paul's place is not in theology, but in religion".[3] Thus Adolf Deissmann could write in his book *Paul* (1912) that if Paul's sermons had really taken the form of treatises on "Paulinism", then "the people of Iconium, Thessalonica, and Corinth would all have been overtaken by the fate of Eutychus of Troas."[4]

Munck, however, rejects Deissmann's undervaluation of Paul's status as a thinker. Pannenberg likewise observes, "In trusting the Spirit, Paul in no way spared himself thinking and arguing."[5] Munck therefore urges that it is primarily as a missionary-pastor who thinks theologically that Paul is best understood. His thinking serves his apostolic, pastoral, and missionary vocation and vision. Munck declares: "His theology arises from his work as apostle and directly serves that work."[6] To return to Schleiermacher's hermeneutics, we are not simply concerned to understand a set of concepts, but the relationship between Pauline utterances and the man who made them in given life-situations.

If this is the case, however, this principle confirms Schleiermacher's emphasis on the fallibility and corrigibility of individual interpretation. Exegetical conclusions remain provisional, in the sense that they await a complete understanding of Paul both as human person and as a commissioned apostle. Yet the interpreter's picture of the "whole" Paul depends theoretically on a definitive exegesis of the extant Pauline texts, and also on an understanding of the effects generated by other processes in the socio-historical and pastoral situations which the New Testament texts take for granted or imply. Our *corporate* understanding of Paul remains therefore in principle a historically-expanding process, even if particular interpretative developments may sometimes entail backward-steps and reversals, which may lose, for a period, the gains of earlier corporate advances.

The moral which we drew in *The Two Horizons* is that mistakes can be made in either of two directions.[7] On one side, it would be a mistake to allow systematic theology to swallow up patient historical exegesis, in the interests of a premature desire to formulate an understanding of the mind of Paul as a whole. On the other side, however, endlessly to postpone the formulation of a Pauline theology in the supposed interests of respect for situational and historical particularity, actually has the effect of undermining and betraying the exegetical process itself. For understanding the particularities depends on and presupposes a provisional grasp of the broader whole. The formulation of this wider understanding simply makes explicit, and therefore *publicly open to criticism and assessment*, what would otherwise remain a set of hidden working assumptions; or, alternatively, we should engage in a suspension of judgment which inhibits exploratory exegesis. The overriding qualification to all this, remains the provisionality and corrigibility of "Pauline theology", which must, in turn, be re-submitted to exegetical testing and enquiry of a contingent-historical nature.

The dual necessity for, and provisionality of, so-called "keys" to the theological mind of Paul has been heavily underlined by J. Christiaan Beker in his book *Paul the Apostle*. Beker reviews what he terms "the search for a doctrinal centre."[8] The Reformers focussed this centre in Paul's anti-Judaistic debate, and formulated it in terms of a theology of justification by grace through faith. At the end of the nineteenth and beginning of the twentieth centuries, the history-of-religions school produced first Wilhelm Bousset's "cultic Paul"; then Deissmann's "mystic Paul"; and finally Albert Schweitzer's notion of Pauline mysticism within a decisive framework of Jewish-Christian eschatology.[9] Up to the middle of the twentieth century, debate turned on differences between evaluations of the heart of Pauline thinking as perceived from a hellenistic framework (represented for example by W.L Knox) and evaluations as perceived from within a rabbinic framework (represented especially by W.D. Davies).[10] During these middle decades Rudolf Bultmann found the Pauline "centre" in Paul's view of human nature and human existence. Thus Bultmann asserts: "Paul's theology can best be treated as his doctrine of man."[11] From the 1950s to the 1970s Munck and Stendahl stressed the central role of salvation-history for Paul; while Käsemann stressed the centrality of divine grace and the righteousness of God, as this was to be understood particularly within the framework of apocalyptic.[12]

That the "centre" of Pauline thought emerges in the context of historical situations and pastoral dialogue has been emphasized by many, including Georg Eichholz and by George Howard.[13] But Beker rightly insists that Pauline thought can best be understood by allowing it to come into focus in a way which reveals not only its heart but also its *coherence*. Beker comments: "Our habit of systematic denotative thinking in terms of *finished* structures of thought and restrictive conceptual units has too often suggested false alternatives, as when scholars oppose 'doctrine' and propose 'mysticism' because of their abhorrence of a 'rationalistic' Paul. Paul's centre is not a *theoretical* proposition that is subsequently applied to sociological contingencies."[14] Nevertheless, he argues, Paul's call to proclaim Christ within a framework that leads to the apocalyptic consummation of history does provide a source of coherence.

Thus, Beker declares, Paul's "hermeneutic consists in the constant interaction between the coherent center of the gospel and its contingent interpretation."[15] On the one hand, he observes, "Paul locates the coherent center of the gospel in the apocalyptic interpretation of the Christ-event."[16]

On the other hand, as we argued in relation to incarnation and embodiment in chapter two, Paul "enfleshes" the gospel "into human particularity . . . The one gospel . . . achieves incarnational depth and relevance in every particularity and variety of the human situation."[17]

Beker might almost be quoting Schleiermacher directly when he asserts that "The intent and thrust of Paul's thought is inseparable from the specific situation that evokes it." We cannot understand Paul, he continues, if we abstract him "from the historical nexus of his thinking that addresses the partner(s) in the dialogue."[18] When, for example, in Gal. 3:6 Paul uses the words of Gen. 15:6, it is essential to relate them contextually to the central role played by the figure of Abraham in the theology of Paul's opponents.[19]

When we move on to Romans, the interpreter will be keenly aware of the arguments for and against the contextual character of this epistle. Some of the issues in this discussion are summarized in the collection of essays edited by Karl Donfried under the title *The Romans Debate*.[20] Beker represents what seems to be a convincing and perhaps majority view when he interprets the epistle contextually against the background of relations between Gentile-Christian and Jewish-Christian groups within the church at Rome. Arguing that the pastoral problem at Rome concerned misplaced feelings of superiority on the part of the Gentile Christians as over against the Jewish Christian group (cf. Rom. 14:15; 15:1), Beker asserts: "The hermeneutical key to Romans is primarily situational."[21] On this basis it embodies a consideration of the question about Israel's role in salvation-history. Robert Jewett similarly argues that the key issue in Romans is formulated in Rom. 15:7. Gentile and Jewish Christians are to "welcome one another"; for all have come to faith on the same basis, namely the *grace* of God.[22] The epistle is "to assist the Gentile Christian majority, who are the primary addressees of the letter, to live together with the Jewish Christians in one congregation."[23]

Jewett's historical reconstruction and exegesis also remains inseparable from the fresh picture of Paul as a pastor, and theologian and human person which emerges from this study. Because he sees that the gospel is based on "radical grace", Paul, Jewett argues, comes to stand as the apostle of *tolerance* and even pluralism.[24] If the "strong" and the "weak" (Rom. 14:1) are respectively roughly equivalent to politically "liberal" and politically "conservative" believers, Paul's argument, Jewett urges, is that each must "accept" the other, even as Christ has accepted them.[25] Yet Jewett readily acknowledges that his picture of Paul does stand in tension with certain passages traditionally attributed to Paul. Not only do the Pastoral Epistles clearly suggest some qualification of this picture if they are regarded as Pauline; Jewett also has difficulty over several "interpolations in the main epistles including 1 Cor. 4:17; 7:17; and 11:16.[26]

The dialectical cross-checking between comparative judgments about the details of particular passages and "divinatory" or inter-personal perceptions about Paul himself therefore continues as the process which lies at the heart of Pauline interpretation. It may well be the case that Jewett rightly brings to our attention a neglected aspect of the wholeness of Paul; but this picture, in turn, is not a definitive or final one. It still needs to be qualified by further discussions about the limits of tolerance within the frame of apostolic truth. Schleiermacher's comments about the provisionality of the hermeneutical circle apply.

It is scarcely necessary to illustrate this principle further with reference to the Corinthian correspondence, where its relevance is even clearer. In our opening chapter we commented on the situational and socio-historical factors which facilitate our understanding of these texts, and we referred by way of constructive example to the work of Gerd Theissen, especially to his discussion of "food offered to idols" (1 Cor. 8:1 ff).[27] In 2 Corinthians, several approaches illustrate the interaction between exegesis and a wider understanding of Paul, but one of the most important is that of J.H. Schütz, (and to a lesser extent also Holmberg) on the nature of power and authority in Paul.[28] In 2 Corinthians, as Schütz argues, this relates closely and profoundly to the reality and experience of being conformed to the cross and to the dying of Jesus. (2. Cor. 4: 7–15; 5:14, 15; 6:3–10). It is not the "power" of self-assertion; but the power of the gospel of a crucified Christ in which self is renounced in identification with Christ on the cross. Here Schütz's work draws both on the sociological work of Weber and others, and also on the theological interpretation of Paul in Käsemann.

The hermeneutical principle under discussion also applies, no less, to more specific areas of Pauline thought. We select as an example Pauline texts about the Holy Spirit. The fundamental procedure here remains an exegetical one. But we cannot in practice wholly isolate this detailed exegetical work from provisional hypotheses about the function of passages within a broader frame. In his book *Baptism in the Holy Spirit* James Dunn warns us that it is all too easy to begin with some generalized assumption about Paul's view of the Spirit, and on this basis to construe which passages we regard as "clear" (i.e. those which fit in with the general assumption) and which texts about the Spirit seem "difficult" and "obscure" (i.e. they do not fit in with the expectation implied by the working assumption).[29] It is then tempting to regard the "clear" texts as controlling ones. Dunn distinguishes perspectives which he broadly characterizes as "Reformed" or "Protestant", "sacramentalist" and "Pentecostalist". Each tradition may be tempted to identify different passages as "clear". Thus the first group finds to be "clear" those which relate the Spirit to divine grace and human faith; the second, those texts which relate the Spirit to baptism; the third, those which relate the reception of the Spirit to "experience". Each may then interpret the obscure "problematic" passages from a pre-given angle.

The purpose of Dunn's warning is to underline the need for careful attention to the particularities of exegesis. But by implication it also reinforces the complementary point made earlier above. It facilitates our exegetical understanding if we make explicit whether or when such working assumptions have a part in the interpreter's processes of understanding. We are then in a better position to make comparative judgments about what exegetical options might become re-opened or modified if a different working re-construction of the broader area were also to be taken seriously as a possibility.

2. The Hermeneutical Circle and the Quest for a "Centre" of Pauline Thought

Beker and Dunn, we have noted, are keenly aware of the dialectical interaction which exercizes a two-way influence on exegesis and on wider perceptions of the mind of Paul. Beker points out that difficulties and one-sidedness too easily arise when interpreters become so pre-occupied with the search for a "centre" in Pauline thought that everything else becomes pushed to the side-lines. This, he notes, was the fallacy which led Marcion so firmly in one direction.[30] Wayne Meeks recalls Harnack's comment on the pathos of Marcion's position. Marcion was convinced that he, not mainstream Christianity, had genuinely understood Paul, and he perceived the mainstream church as surrendering Pauline freedom as it identified the Gods of Old and New Testament and became "thoroughly" 'Jewish'".[31]

One-sidedness, however, can result *either* from too hasty a desire to identify a Pauline centre and make every particularity revolve around it; *or* from so firm an insistence on a *contextual* attention to particularities that we become sceptical about whether we can genuinely speak of "Paul's theology". We shall look more closely at both sets of problems. A wide range of examples of interpretations pre-occupied with a supposed "centre" at the expense of exegetical and other detail appear in a collection of interpretations of Paul surveyed by Wayne Meeks.[32] He includes for example F.C. Baur's portrait of Paul created with heavily-painted strokes. Baur writes: "Who were the opponents to whom Paul and Barnabas had to offer so strenuous a resistance? Who else than the elder apostles themselves? . . . Thus there were now two Gospels . . . The two were to go on, side by side, separate and independent, without crossing each other's paths . . .

Up to the time when the apostle disappears from the scene of the history, we have before us nothing but differences and oppositions."33

Friedrich Nietzsche provides another example. He argues, "If we have read, *really read* the writings of St. Paul, not as the revelations of the 'Holy Ghost', but with honest and independent minds . . . it would have been all up with Christianity long ago . . . This man suffered from a fixed idea . . . What is the *meaning* of the Jewish law? . . . There never was more than one Christian, and he *died* on the Cross. The gospel *died* on the Cross. That which thenceforward was called 'gospel' was the reverse of that 'gospel' . . . 'evil tidings', a *dysangel*.34 This conception of Paul as a second founder of "pseudo-Christianity" is taken further by George Bernard Shaw. He declares, "No sooner had Jesus knocked over the dragon of superstition than Paul boldly set it on its legs again in the name of Jesus . . . There is not one word of Pauline Christianity in the characteristic utterances of Jesus."35

Wayne Meeks surveys these various portraits of Paul, including, among those of more recent times, that of Deissmann, Dibelius, Bultmann, Schoeps, and Stendahl. He concludes that "Paul is the Christian Proteus"; the *daimon* of the sea who could assume any form.36 This is because, Meeks explains, "We never see pure Pauline thought being developed at leisure by its own inner logic; rather we see Paul always thinking under pressure, usually in the heat of immediate controversy."37 But if Schleiermacher's hermeneutics have any validity, the apostolic testimony of Paul in word and deed is not to be reduced to the level of mere "thought being developed *at leisure*". If the incarnational principle of embodiment discussed in chaper two has any force, the witness and truth conveyed by biblical texts embraces precisely their *engagement with life as well as their truth-content as Christian theology*. Kierkegaard's criticisms of the unreality of "thought being developed at leisure" are well-known. Schleiermacher's point is that the ability to discern *what particularities of situations and experiences called forth the thought of an author* help us to understand this thought *better* than otherwise; they are not hindrances to understanding. This is because such an approach constitutes a more rounded understanding, which allows us to see persons as persons, and not simply as sources of ideas.

Nevertheless, there remains two key provisos or qualifications to all this. First, an interactive checking process must take place whereby wholistic judgments about the author are tested and modified in the light of detailed exegetical assessments. Even the consequent, modified, re-articulation of these assessments must be yet once again submitted to scrutiny, as part of an ongoing process of adjustment.

A fundamental epistemological and logical consideration constitutes the second proviso. To argue for a contextual understanding of Paul does *not* necessarily imply that Paul has no "theological system". The hermeneutical principle under discussion raises questions not about the *existence of* the theological content of Paul's thought as such, but about our way of *understanding and gaining access to* this thought. There is an analogy here with what has been called the dispositional account of belief, which I have discussed elsewhere with reference to Paul and James.38 Wittgenstein argues that it is perfectly possible in principle to think of "having beliefs" as a given state of mind. But this may cause confusions, he urges, when certain questions are asked. For example, does one stop "believing" when one falls asleep, or is occupied in other affairs? Does one believe "uninterruptedly"?39 The points at which belief *engages with reality* emerge in situations where it becomes *operatively effective* in terms of words, attitudes, orientation, and conduct. That is why Vernon Neufeld's conclusion about the nature of "confession" or "confessional belief" in the New Testament is not surprising: confession entails *both* a cognitive content *and* the dimension of nailing one's colours to the mast.40 Paul certainly formulated a "theology"; but we see different aspects of it in action as he engages with daily life as apostle, pastor, missionary, friend, adviser, listener (cf. 1 Cor. 7:1–11:1) and human person.

We offer two final examples of instances in Pauline interpretation which illustrate the interaction between exegetical detail and provisional attempts to perceive the wholeness of Pauline thought. The first concerns the eschatological approach to Paul. Three remarkable accounts of Paul have resulted from this approach. All are one-sided and require serious questioning in the light of painstaking exegesis; but all contain exceptionally perceptive observations about given texts and about Paul's place in the development of Christian thought. The three works which represent the eschatological approach are those of Albert Schweitzer; the Jewish scholar Hans Joachim Schoeps; and Martin Werner, who sees the development of doctrine as contingent on the delay of the parousia. For reasons of space we shall restrict our attention to Schweitzer.

I have discussed Schweitzer's interpretation of Paul in greater detail elsewhere.41 The key to Paul, Schweitzer believes, lies in the eschatological frame within which his thought operates. But this gives rise to a hermeneutical issue. Schweitzer writes: "The problem why Paul's teaching did not appear strange to the Christians of the first generation has its counterpart in the similarly puzzling fact that it did become strange to the immediately following generations."42 This gives a different significance to several aspects, if not all aspects, of Pauline thought, including his theology of the resurrection of Christ which Paul "cannot regard . . . as an isolated event."43 Jesus was raised as the "first-fruits" of the new community (1 Cor. 15:20). Christian believers become "capable of assuming the resurrection mode of existence before the general resurrection of the dead takes place."44

Paul's historical continuity with Jesus and the gospels can be seen in the fact that "everything depends upon the realization of fellowship with Jesus".[45] In Paul, however, this takes the form of sharing Jesus' having-died and being-raised: "I am crucified with Christ" (Gal. 2:20); "We have been buried with him by baptism" (Rom. 6:4); "if we have died with Christ, we believe that we shall also live with him (Rom. 6:8); "to know him, and the power of his resurrection and the fellowship (*koinonia*) of his sufferings, being conformed to his death, if by any means I might attain to the resurrection from the dead" (Phil. 3:10–11). This is what constitutes "belonging to Christ", or being-in-Christ. Within this framework, Schweitzer observes, "The concept being-in-Christ dominates Paul's thought." Believers carry about in their bodies the 'having died' of Jesus (2 Cor. 4:10–12). To bear "the marks of Jesus" (*stigmata*, Gal. 6:17) is to wear "the brandings by which a slave . . . was made recognizable as his master's property".[48] Thus fellowship with Christ entails suffering as well as resurrection. To receive the Holy Spirit is to receive "the life-principle of His Messianic personality."[49]

Schweitzer's account of Pauline thought contains brilliant insights, but because everything revolves around eschatology, it remains in the end seriously one-sided. Although he speaks of the believer's being under "the law of love", the basic thrust of Schweitzer's argument is that because law and eschatology are incompatible, the believer's relation to the law and to the natural world now becomes irrelevant. Not simply the former life, but also "the new being" is like a house sold for breaking up, repairs to which are irrational".[50] Righteousness by faith performs a minor role in Paul's thought, which, it is claimed, is unduly brought to prominence by controversy, and remains logically independent of being-in-Christ.[51] Nevertheless, Schweitzer shows, with convincing elements in his argument, how a different understanding, or even a lack of understanding, of Paul arose when the framework of interpretation was radically hellenized and removed from its eschatological setting.

The sharpest and most tellingly radical re-statement of this argument was later put forward by Martin Werner, although Werner drastically overstates the case.[52] This change of framework helps to account, probably, more than any other single factor, for the truth of Maurice Wiles's claim that although much is of value in Patristic interpretations of Paul, "nevertheless the total impression which [a less eschatological orientation] leaves upon the reader is that Paul has been *tamed*".[53]

Our final example arises from the work of E.P. Sanders. In Protestant theology it has become traditional to begin with Paul's account of the human plight and then to expound Paul's Christology and theology of salvation as the "answer" to the human situation. Stendahl questioned this approach in his essay "The Apostle Paul and the Introspective Conscience of the

West" (first published in 1963) in which he challenged the validity of the Augustinian and Lutheran paradigm as a way of understanding Paul.[54] In 1977 Sanders expanded and elaborated Stendahl's approach. The heart of the matter is indicated by his section-heading "The solution as preceding the problem."[55] In contrast to Bultmann, Conzelmann, and Bornkamm, Sanders argued that "Paul's thought did not run from plight to solution, but rather from solution to plight. The attempts to argue that Romans 7 shows the frustration which Paul felt during his life as a practising Jew have now mostly been given up . . . It may further be observed on the basis of Phil. 3 that Paul did not, while 'under the law', perceive himself to have a 'plight' from which he needed salvation."[56]

The *prior* conviction, Sanders urges, is that God has provided a saviour. His death was *necessary* for salvation. From this it *follows* that salvation cannot come in any other way, and *consequently* that all were, prior to the death and resurrection, in need of a saviour."[57] Sanders concludes: Paul "did not begin with the sin and transgression of man, but with the opportunity for salvation . . . Put another way, Paul did not preach about men, but about God."[58]

As we shall note further below, this has the effect of shifting the emphasis from the human "existential" situation to a proclamation of a cosmic and historical act of God. Nevertheless, it rests on interpretative judgments of the kind indicated by Schleiermacher's formulation of the hermeneutical circle. On one side stands a mass of detailed exegetical considerations in such passages as Rom. 7:7–25 and Phil. 3:4–7. On the other side these interact with perceptions of Paul as an apostle and as a human person. But the respective roles of what Schleiermacher called the comparative and the divinatory are no more clear-cut in Sanders than they were for Schleiermacher. Thus Sanders makes *comparative* judgments about "holistic patterns of religion", and what we might perceive as partially analytical and partially divinatory perceptions about the function of such passages as Rom. 7:7–25 within the flow of the epistle and within Paul's pastoral concern and theological thought.[59] Sanders's belief that "in Paul, or in Jewish literature, good deeds are the *condition* of remaining 'in', but they do not *earn* salvation" depends partly on his *particular* interpretations of such passages as Rom. 11:22 and 1 Cor. 6:9,10.[60] But it also depends on *general* judgments that "Paul was a coherent, but not systematic, thinker"; and that, as a *general* perception: "Paul's 'pattern of religion' cannot be described as 'covenantal nomism', and therefore Paul presents an essentially different type of religiousness from any found in Palestinian Jewish literature."[61]

Schleiermacher's formulation of the hermeneutical circle helps us not only to see more clearly how to approach the Pauline writings, but also to appreciate how it comes about that in modern interpretation of Paul appeals can often be made to the same groupings of texts for divergent understandings of Paul. It would be, on the one hand, too naïvely objectivistic to assume that an adequate holistic picture will necessarily emerge solely by adding together the results of mechanical attention to linguistic and exegetical detail. We are concerned with catching a creative vision, as well as with understanding nouns and verbs. On the other hand, it would be unduly cynical to give up the attempt at objective exegesis, on the ground that this is necessarily distorted, rather than at times facilitated, by a vision of the whole. We noted that from Irenaeus onwards the church has felt a need to appeal to this "wholeness" alongside investigation of detail. Both approaches are essential to understanding. Understanding falls apart when one comes to dominate the other. Before looking further at specific Pauline and other texts, we shall first trace the theoretical development of these principles up to modern times in the hermeneutics of Dilthey and Betti.

3. A Hermeneutics of "Life-World" Reconstruction in Dilthey and in Betti: "Re-living" and "Openness"

Wilhelm Dilthey (1831–1911) produced most of his work on hermeneutics between 1900 and 1910, although his earliest academic work entailed editing some of Schleiermacher's papers. He was heavily influenced by Schleiermacher's hermeneutics, which he sought to develop further. He formulated his theory of knowledge largely in dialogue with the work of Kant, but also drew from Hegel a concept of reality as a process of historical change. H.P. Rickman and others include him in a broadly Romanticist tradition because of his high evaluation of life and experience rather than thought alone.[62] Following Schleiermacher, he stressed the uniqueness and particularity of human individuals, as well as what they shared in common, and he also gave an important place to the creative power of human imagination. Hodges speaks of his "appreciative understanding of the meaning and value of the unique individual."[63]

The key category in Dilthey's hermeneutical theory remains that of "life" (*Leben*) or "lived experience" (*Erlebnis*). Looking back critically at the pre-Hegelian, "pre-historicist" theories of knowledge found in Locke, Hume, and even in Kant, he observes that "in the veins of the 'knowing subject' . . . *no real blood flows*".[64] "Life" represents the shared flow of human activities and experiences which together constitute human experience both in its social diversity and in its individual particularity. Dilthey writes: "What we grasp through experience and understanding is life as the interweaving of all mankind."[65] Thus: "understanding of other people and their expressions is developed on the basis of experience and self-understanding and the constant interaction between them."[66] These "expressions" (*Lebensäusserungen*) include signs, symbols, speech, writing, practices and actions. "Expressions can contain more of the psychological context than any introspection can discover. They lift it from depths which consciousness does not illuminate."[67] "Not through introspection but through history do we come to know ourselves."[68]

The task of the interpreter is to gain understanding of the other through "re-living" (*nacherleben*) the other's experience; by stepping into the other's shoes on the basis of "empathy" (*Hineinversetzen*) or "transposition" (*Transposition*).[69] Dilthey is only too keenly aware that the "I" differs from others. He would probably have been distressed by the claims of Manfred Mezger, Ernst Fuchs, and James Robinson that his notion of "re-living" someone else's experience, or of "putting myself in the skin of Moses or Paul" attempts a "short-cut" which ignores existential individuality.[70] Dilthey carefully explains that a number of specific factors are involved.

First, self-understanding actually depends not on introspection but on the revelation of similarities and differences, of variations and particularities, which emerge not simply in reflection but in social inter-action, and from which one learns sympathy and develops imagination. Second, "transposition" or "re-living" the other's experience depends on "transposing myself into the circumstances" which gave rise to the life-expression which invites my understanding.[71] Dilthey discusses the example of understanding Luther's writings. Here the interpreter needs not only to read through Luther's letters and writings, but also the records the councils and disputes, of dealings between Luther and officials of church and state, until one begins to enter into the "eruptive power and energy" in which life and death are at issue, but which is strictly "beyond the possibility of direct experience for a man of our time. But I can re-live it. I transpose myself into the circumstances."[72] Third, all this is to be understood within the framework of Dilthey's "Critique of Historical Reason." In a key sentence he observes: "Understanding (*Verstehen*) is a re-discovery of the I in the Thou: the mind rediscovers itself at ever higher levels of complex involvement . . . If in this way we know the mind-constructed world objectively, we may ask how much this contributes to solving the general problem of epistemology."[73]

This third point may need further clarification. It relates to Dilthey's central concern about the nature of historical understanding, and the problem of "objectification" in hermeneutics and in the social sciences (grouped together in German universities as the "human sciences" or *Geisteswissenschaften*). Kant's critique of pure reason had provided a turning-point for the history of ideas by establishing the boundaries and finitude of theoretical thought. Dilthey aimed to produce a critique of historical understanding which would apply not simply to Kant's abstract "subject of knowledge" or "knowing mind", but to a *flesh-and-blood historically-conditioned* subject who already stood within the flow of human life. At first sight, the contrast between the physical sciences on the one hand, and the humanities and social sciences on the other, appeared to present a contrast of order and chaos. Human life reflects diversities, particularities, and changing processes which seem to defy the application of "laws", norms, or criteria which appear to characterize science. But if this were genuinely the case, must we surrender the claim to objective understanding in the *Geisteswissenschaften*?

Kant had formulated the notion of "categories" as an ordering and organizing principle, but this was inapplicable, Dilthey believed, to the historical flow of human life. Dilthey now drew on all the conceptual devices formulated by Schleiermacher in his hermeneutics of understanding. Thus Dilthey declares, "The whole must be understood in terms of its individual parts; individual parts, in terms of the whole. To understand the whole of a work we must refer to its author and to related literature ... Understanding of the whole and of the individual parts are interdependent."[74] Every human expression must be understood in terms of the situations and experiences which led to its production. Understanding traces back in reverse the processes that led to composition: "Understanding as such moves in the reverse order to the sequence of events."[75]

Dilthey, however, develops these hermeneutical principles further in two specific directions. First, he takes a step in a direction associated with Husserl and later to be explored fully by Heidegger and existential hermeneutics. Whereas the data of the physical sciences remain, as it were "neutral" in relation to each other, as soon as we consider the historical subject of perception and understanding, it becomes clear that there is a *life-relation* between the self and the other. Dilthey writes: "In so far as things or people which make a demand on the self come to occupy a place in its existence, become sources of help or hindrance, objects of desire, striving or recoil . . . they acquire a meaning over and above our factual comprehension of them."[76] The individual person is thus characterized as a historical being, determined, at least in part, by a given place in space and time within given cultural systems and communities. Dilthey's second major development concerns "the connectedness" (*Zusammenhang*) of life and the principle of objectification.[77] Dilthey writes "Every word, every sentence . . . every political deed, is intelligible because the people who expressed themselves through them and those who understood them have something in common."[78] Howard Tuttle examines this aspect of Dilthey's thought. He writes "The 'inner' life of others – past or present – is of the same 'human stuff' as our own life, and therefore understandable."[79]

The heart of the hermeneutical approach, in contrast to the concern in the physical sciences about generality, is precisely *the relation between patterns of correspondence, analogy, or generality, and the particular, the unique, and the contingent.* For this reason, among others, Dilthey takes up and develops Schleiermacher's dual emphasis on comparative judgments which presuppose parallels and similarities, and divinatory or empathetic understandings of personal individuality in the flow of life. Also for this reason, made all the more urgent by Hegel's emphasis on historical processes, Dilthey sees hermeneutics as the foundation of knowledge in the "human" sciences. He writes: "The first, epistemological problem which confronts us in the human studies is the analysis of understanding. Hermeneutics, by starting from this problem and seeking its solution, becomes relevant to questions about the nature and foundation of the human studies which occupy present-day scholars." (i.e. in 1900).[80] The basis of hermeneutics is "not a logical abstraction", but the relation between the particular and the general in the context of an ongoing stream of life.

The "Romanticist" component which Dilthey inherits from Schleiermacher and others (perhaps ultimately from Herder) can be seen most clearly in his belief that "life-expressions" such as texts constitute in effect dead deposits left behind by "live" experience. They stand as "objectifications" of the living, creative, experience, for which they now serve as consequences and access-points. The interpreter must necessarily reach "behind" these objectified residues in order to understand what brought them to birth, and, hence, to understand the texts themselves. Dilthey's understanding of the interpreter as someone also conditioned by his or her place in history strengthens, rather than weakens, this perspective to which Schleiermacher also assented. It is this particular characteristic, rather than others, which allows us to retain the broad term "Romanticist" as well as Reconstructionist for this hermeneutic tradition.

From a theological viewpoint there are ambiguities about Dilthey's emphasis on the unity and correspondences which exist in human experiences alongside their particularities. On the one hand, the biblical texts themselves offer theologies of human nature which ascibe the same general capacities to humankind, self-interest, bondage, self-deception, and fallibility; but also the capacity for reflection, for self-knowledge, for repentance, for worship, and for fellowship with God. The corporate solidarity of humankind, whether in the old or the new Adam, stands as the framework within which more individualistic aspects of character-history, responsibility, decision and accountability are to be seen. On the other hand, as the horizon of understanding begins to expand indefinitely, this hermeneutical approach suggests, as Wolfhart Pannenberg notes, further questions about the ultimacy of the horizons of Christian eschatology.[81] Indeed, in a recent doctoral dissertation submitted to the University of

Aberdeen under the title *The Three Horizons*, James C. McHann Jr. argues for this point, allowing some of my claims in *The Two Horizons* to interact with Pannenberg's theology relating to a "third horizon" of eschatology.[82]

It is arguable that Dilthey's system as a whole fails in the attempt to offer a comprehensive critique of historical reason, and a foundation for interpersonal understanding in the humanities and social sciences. In sociology, in spite of affinities with Dilthey which we noted in the previous chapter, Weber opted for a view of "understanding" which entailed quasi-scientific "types" of a more general nature. At the other end of the hermeneutical spectrum Gadamer criticizes Dilthey for the very opposite trend, namely that of trying to seek any parallel to objective or scientific "method" at all. Gadamer declares: "He was always attempting to justify the knowledge of what was historically conditioned as the achievement of objective science, despite the fact of the knower's being conditioned himself".[83] But even if we remained unconvinced by his work as a comprehensive system of historical understanding, however, we may perhaps feel a greater sympathy for Dilthey than Gadamer does on two grounds. First, the relation between *general methods* and *individual particularities* of history and *theology* throw up similar questions to those with which Dilthey wrestled. We seek to ask how much in biblical studies belongs to "scientific" method, and how much to human judgment, vision, imagination and creative insight, not to mention receptive and enquiring faith. The second factor arises from changes in the notion of "object" and "objectivity" which have occurred in the philosophy of science, with re-appraisals of the status of the observer in several hard sciences. It is more than a generation ago that Michael Polanyi, successively Professor of Physical Chemistry and Professor of Social Studies in the University of Manchester, raised questions about the participatory nature of knowledge in all disciplines. I have discussed Dilthey's thought largely from a different angle in *The Two Horizons*, where I was concerned especially with Bultmann's use of his philosophy of life.[85] The grounds on which Gadamer dismisses the role of "method" in hermeneutics are examined and evaluated in chapter IX, below.

Our allusion to receptiveness, to openness, and to enquiry brings us to Emilio Betti, whose massive and detailed hermeneutical treatise appeared in Italian in 1955, and in German in 1967. He writes as a legal historian who is well versed in philosophy, especially that of Hegel and Hartmann. His two key concerns, with which he opens his book, relate to the nature of objectivity and the hermeneutics of understanding.[86] He follows Schleiermacher and Dilthey closely in their emphasis on reconstruction and on "life" and shares Dilthey's problem about the status of method in the human sciences.[87] But he parts company from Dilthey in separating meaning as it emerges in a given historical context-of-situation from what a person or text may be taken to mean by an interpreter in some new or broader context. Betti undertakes his discussion about objectivity in dialogue with Hegel's notion of process, and situatedness-within-history, and more especially with the neo-Kantian and neo-Hegelian philosopher Nicolai Hartmann. In the face of Kant's insistence that we ourselves shape our understandings of reality, and in the light of Hegel's diagnosis of the problems of historical-conditionedness, how can "understanding" operate with any chance of achieving objectivity? Betti finds a fruitful concept in the notion of openness or "open-mindedness" (*Aufgeschlossenheit*), and in "receptiveness" (*Empfänglichkeit*).[88] With Schleiermacher and with Dilthey, Betti sees understanding as a continuous, ongoing process, which is always open to correction and improvement, and which depends on this openness to continuous discovery.

This establishes hermeneutics, Betti believes, *as an intellectual discipline and educational training which is fundamental for life*. For what can be more important today than that humankind should recognize the need for patience and tolerance in understanding, and that they should *live in mutual understanding*? Whether we are interpreting a historical text, or listening to a conversation, we need to reach *behind* the words themselves to see what led to them, why they are being said, and what is the main train of thought which gives rise to them. Hence imaginative *reconstruction* (*Rekonstruktion*, or *nachvollziehen*), with the use of sympathy and insight, is required for understanding.[89] What has to be understood, however, transcends the semantic meaning of the text or utterance. The text is an "objectification" of the dynamic process in which one mind opens itself to another thinking person. As Gadamer observes, we have come very close to Schleiermacher here. Understanding is "a reversal or inversion of the creative process in which the interpreter has to make his hermeneutical way back along the creative path, carrying on the process of re-thinking".[90] Interpretation is the reverse process, in terms of direction, to that of composition.

This leads Betti to affirm Schleiermacher's dictum that there is a sense in which the interpeter can understand the author "better", or more fully, than the author could, because his or her historical, linguistic and psychological reconstruction might include factors of which the author was not fully aware. For example, a question for understanding may embody perceptions and evaluations based on "typifications", both in terms of language and social role. Betti writes: "In historical reconstruction the procedure of typification according to forms of speech is fully justified."[91] He includes a discussion of the notion of typification as this is employed in the sociological theory of Max Weber.[92] In the process of understanding, inter-subjective processes also assist the interpreter in seeking to arrive at, and to validate, interpretation. Like Dilthey, Betti sees self-understanding as the product not of introspection but of the flow of inter-subjective life and encounter. In this respect, once again, we are not far from the later

Wittgenstein and Apel. Indeed Betti, like Wittgenstein, can speak of "forms of life". Knowledge which is of a merely theoretical or introspective kind operates on a different level.

Finally, unlike Gadamer, who rejects the notion of hermeneutical "method", Betti suggests four "moments" in the hermeneutical process which together facilitate understanding. First, the interpreter investigates the linguistic phenomena of the speech or text. Second, in a critical "moment", the interpreter seeks to gain self-awareness of social interests, ideologies, commitments, or sources of intolerance that may hinder genuine openness to listen and to understand. Third, following Schleiermacher and especially Dilthey, Betti invites the interpreter to place himself or herself in the shoes of the person to be understood, using imagination and insight. Fourth, the reconstruction extends to the entire situation and set of conditions which work together to lead to the production of the utterance or the text.[93]

Betti argues that although much of this process is "retrospective" or "genetic" it also entails a "prospective" and "evolutionary" element. For what is to be understood is situated within a flow of historical life which both precedes and follows it in a process of development. As Schleiermacher saw, he urges, the historical-social reality as a whole invites both historical analysis and "divinatory" or "prophetic" insight.[94] The so-called "hermeneutical canons" which Betti then elaborates also remain, except in one respect, close to the outlook of Schleiermacher and Dilthey.[95] Betti affirms the value of Schleiermacher's hermeneutical circle both as a heuristic and as a checking principle. He argues that authors and texts must be understood in their historical particularity, both on their own terms and in accordance with the logic that they employ. Josef Bleicher notes the closeness of this position to Schleiermacher and to Dilthey.[96] In Pannenberg's view, however, Betti has taken a retrograde step. He has moved back "to a stage not only before Dilthey, who recognized values as products of the historical process itself, but also before Rickert, who did separate value and being, but still treated *all* historical knowledge as 'value-relative'".[97]

4. Pauline Texts and Reconstruction: "Better" Understanding than the Author?

It is arguable that the major Pauline epistles provide solid and helpful paradigmatic examples for the hermeneutical methods of Schleiermacher, Dilthey, and Betti. We have already discussed at length in the first two sections of this chapter how the exegesis of Pauline texts interacts with attempts to understand Paul and Pauline thought both exegetically and as a whole, especially in relation to Schleiermacher's particular formulation of the hermeneutical circle. We shall examine shortly the problem of applying this hermeneutical model to an anonymous text. But before we do this, we may first note how Pauline studies relate in at least three further ways to a hermeneutics of understanding and life-related reconstruction.

(i) First, Dilthey and Betti insist that the historical life-context in which a text is understood includes the realities of life and thought which surround the author and which give rise to his utterances. From among many biblical texts which might be chosen for discussion, one prime example is offered by Paul's Corinth. The first two questions for any interpreter of 1 Corinthians remain: (a) what was the shape of the Corinthians' own theology to which Paul responds? (b) what socio-historical factors shed light on the actual life of the church at Corinth which conditions both their theology and Paul's response? To answer these questions we have to hand numerous tools, including most notably J.C. Hurd's reconstruction of the Corinthian correspondence and the Corinthians' own theology; Gerd Theissen's work on socio-historical factors at Corinth; Peter Marshall's book *Enmity in Corinth*; and Jerome Murphy-O'Connor's study of relevant Greco-Roman texts, the edict of Claudius and pro-consulship of Gallio, and especially archaeological discoveries relating to house-churches, to temple banquets, and to Paul's probable work-conditions.[98]

We have already noted the far-reaching consequences which F.C. Baur drew for his theories about developments of historical necessity in the Pauline situation, largely on the basis of a starting-point in 1 Cor. 1:12: "Each one of you says, 'I belong to Paul' or 'I belong to Apollos', or 'I belong to Cephas', or 'I belong to Christ'". In his book *Paul* Baur interpreted this verse as reflecting, on the one hand, a Jewish-Christian faction (the so-called Peter-party and Christ-party) and a Gentile-orientated "party" (the so-called Paul faction and the Apollos faction). For many years it was generally assumed that the divisions implied in this verse were largely doctrinal. T.W. Manson, for example, while rejecting Baur's account of Paul's role in early Christianity, retained the notion of a Judaizing group at Corinth referred to here as the Peter party. Hence Gordon Fee observes in his recent commentary: "This verse is a crux in terms of how one is going to understand 1 Corinthians as a whole and especially the historical situation to which Paul is writing."[99]

In 1954, however, (English 1959) Munck put forward the argument that Corinth was a "church without factions". What was at issue concerned not *doctrinal* differences, but "disunity and bickerings", perhaps centred on leading Corinthian personalities.[100] Munck observes, "Paul is not arguing in chs. 1–4 against false doctrine."[101] The real problem is a theological and religious complacency which allows them to become triumphalistic about themselves and similarly to boast about the great names.[102] Gordon Fee rightly follows the broad direction of Munck's conclusion; but what is the specific evidence for it?[103]

Part of the argument turns on our reconstruction of theology at Corinth. What clinches the issue, however, is the archaeological reconstruction suggested by Jerome Murphy-O'Connor.[104] Private houses were the first centres of church life, and a villa from around A.D. 50 has been excavated at Corinth. Its fine mosaic suggests that it represented one of the larger residences for one of the wealthier citizens. Yet the *triclinium*, where the family and guests would dine, measures only around forty square meters, and the *atrium* or hallway, about thirty square meters. Space for couches and perhaps ornaments must be subtracted from the total, as well as (in the hall), the *impluvium* for the collection of water. Even if we average this with other larger second-century houses, the *atrium* would probably have held not more than between thirty and forty people. Murphy O'Connor concludes in the light of various additional considerations: "It seems likely that the various groups mentioned by Paul in 1 Cor. 1:12 would regularly have met separately. Such relative isolation would have meant that each group had a chance to develop its own theology, and virtually ensured that it took good root before being confronted by other opinions. The difficulty of getting the whole church together regularly in one place goes a long way towards explaining ... the divisions."[105]

This same archaeological reconstruction also sheds light on the meaning of Paul's words in 1 Cor. 11: 20–22 about the Lord's Supper: "It is not the Lord's Supper which you eat. For in eating each one goes ahead with his own meal, and one is hungry, and another drunk. What! Do you not have houses to eat and drink in? Or do you despise the church of God and humiliate those who have nothing?" Archaeological reconstruction invites us to imagine that, since not all could be accommodated in the *triclinium*, where perhaps nine or ten might recline on couches for the meal amidst decorous surroundings, late-comers would have to form an "overflow" meeting in the *atrium* outside the dining room. Thus "first-class believers were invited into the *triclinium* while the rest stayed outside."[106] One group reclined; the other group sat (cf. 1 Cor. 8:10; 14:30). Perhaps different food was served to each. At all events, the very function of the Lord's Supper in focussing on Christ's death and the equality and *oneness* of all believers in this light was not only undermined; as "the Lord's" Supper it entirely defeated its own ends in these circumstances. The *meaning* of Paul's texts is elucidated.

(ii) Schleiermacher, Dilthey, and Betti invite precisely this kind of reconstruction of socio-historical life-context which gives rise to the author's thought and writing. It reconstructs with insight the inter-subjective realities which Paul actually addresses, and therefore allows us to understand more fully what he writes. All the same, there is also a second level at which reconstructive interpretation is invited. Studies of Paul as a man, as a thinker, as a Christian believer and pastor and as an apostle, also facilitate understanding. In very general terms, in modern interpretation studies of Paul have offered hermeneutical assistance in two complementary ways. Many late nineteenth-century treatments, culminating perhaps in the work of Weiss and Schweitzer in the early years of this century, underline the distance between Paul and the thought-forms of the modern world, stressing his historical particularity, although perhaps with some over-readiness to 'modernize' Paul. Some contemporary treatments do the same, but others, more notably that of F.F. Bruce, bring Paul alive, on the other hand, as a man of deep faith and generous judgment to whom we can more readily relate.

Several late nineteenth-century and early twentieth-century studies underline what Gadamer calls "the tension between the text and the present", or in Dilthey's and Betti's terms his uniqueness and historical particularity.[107] Perhaps the most radical expression of tension or uniqueness can be found in Franz Overbeck's provocative aphorism: "Nowadays no one has understood Paul if he thinks he can agree with him." In his critical history of nineteenth-century Pauline interpretation Albert Schweitzer observes that such writers as Richard Lipsius (1863), Hermann Lüdemann (1872) and Otto Pfleiderer (1873) encounter blockages in understanding because they undertake merely conceptual examinations of Paul in abstraction from the life-situations and thought-contexts which give Pauline concepts their meaning and currency. They "fail to reckon with the possibility that the original significance of his utterances may rest on presuppositions which are not present to our apprehension."[108] Schweitzer finds this life-context in eschatology. Johnnes Weiss took account of Paul's indebtedness both to the Old Testament and to apocalyptic Judaism.[109] But he also paid special attention to the hermeneutical significance of Paul's conversion experience and call to mission. The "break in his life" took the form of an "immense 'cut' . . . everywhere in his thinking . . . There lies in this a real difficulty for men of later times . . . Most of us have not passed over from Judaism or heathenism to Christianity".[110] Apocalyptic, furthermore, provides the background against which we need to understand Paul's language about the new creation (2 Cor. 5:17).[111]

Up to the middle of this century the historical particularity of Paul was perhaps partially obscured, first by "hellenistic" interpretations of his thought and then by existential interpretation. But more recently Paul's uniqueness as a person has been considered in two quite different ways. On one side, Krister Stendahl has portrayed Paul as addressing problems which are not always ours. On the other side, F.F. Bruce has portrayed Paul as a Christian and pastor of deep compassion and humanity. Stendahl speaks repeatedly of "the uniqueness of Paul and his mission."[112] He is eager also to argue that "limitation is the turn of uniqueness".[113] He argues forcefully for the abandonment of a Lutheran or Augustinian approach to Paul which makes the human consciousness of sin a "common denominator" between Paul and humankind of all generations. He argues that at this point Paul adopts an unexpected and quite different stance, judging himself as concerning the righteousness required by the law to have been "flawless" (Phil. 3:6).[114] Stendahl stresses Paul's concern about more objective and circumstantial questions concerning the law and Judaism. He wishes to do for Paul what H.J. Cadbury hoped to achieve for gospel study in his book *The Peril of Modernizing Jesus*. But if this "estranges" aspects of Paul from our own world, we may recall T.F. Torrance's comment on the hermeneutics of Luther and Calvin, to the effect that a transforming understanding of the scriptures may be more likely to occur when we feel disturbed by the unexpected than when biblical texts have already been tamed of all that is strange or unfamiliar.

Nevertheless, any proposed portrait of Paul, as we noted in our discussion of the hermeneutical circle, must be cross-checked against exegetical detail. F.F. Bruce's study of Paul traces the development of his theological thought through a succession of detailed life-situations. The picture of Paul which finally emerges is one which facilitates sympathetic rapport. Paul, Bruce urges, was "sociable, gregarious. He delighted in the company of his fellows, both men and women."[115] Bruce argues that "the most incredible feature in the Paul of popular mythology is his alleged misogyny. He treated women as persons: we recall his commendation of Phoebe, the deacon of the church in Cenchreae . . . or his appreciation of Euodia and Syntyche of Philippi who worked side by side with him in the gospel" (Rom. 16: 1,2; Phil. 4: 2,3).[116] Paul's personality was of a kind which evoked devotion from friends: Aquila and Priscilla risked their lives for him (Rom. 16: 3,4); Epaphroditus exhausted his strength in order to be of help to Paul (Phil. 2: 25–30). When in Galatians Paul explodes, this is because he shares the sternness of Jesus about those who cause the weak or "the little" to stumble (Gal. 4:9; Luke 17: 2; cf. 2 Cor. 11:29). Paul protects the weak (1 Cor. 8:1–11); he is careless of his own comfort and safety in the service of the gospel (2 Cor. 11: 23–27; Phil. 2:17; Rom. 9:3); he is orientated to people, rather than to things or to abstract principles.[117]

In the 1980s several studies examine Paul in his social context with the added use of sociological or socio-historical categories. Ronald Hock, for example, attempts to challenge the prevailing consensus about the role of Paul's work as a tentmaker. We may doubt whether he fully establishes the case that Paul has in mind his work as one who made tents from leather when he speaks of boasting in his "weakness" (2 Cor. 11:30; 12: 9.10) or accepting "humiliation" (1 Cor. 4: 9–13). Nevertheless, Hock's approach draws attention to an important aspect of Paul's total life-context, as Betti would call it. This includes the world of the work-shop: "of artisan friends like Aquila, Barnabas, and perhaps Jason; of leather, knives, and awls; of wearying toil; of being bent over a workbench like a slave."[118]

Jerome Murphy-O'Connor's archaeological reconstruction adds further details to this picture: "The (workshop) doorway was the only source of light, and this would have created problems in the cold of winter. The heat of a brazier would have been counteracted by the wind ... Working conditions would have been decidedly uncomfortable. It is not at all improbable that Paul wrote with such big letters (Gal. 6:11) because he had to work barehanded in the cold."[119] On the other hand, "from a shop in a busy market Paul had access not only to co-workers and clients, but also the throng outside ... In times of stress ... believers could encounter him as clients ... In sum, therefore, the workshop was a very astute choice for a missionary center."[120]

Norman Petersen makes use of a sociological categorization of interpersonal and institutional roles in his study of the relation between Paul and the text of Philemon.[121] In one sense this admirably meets Betti's comments about the hermeneutical value of typification. On the other hand, the mixture of social theory and of a sociology-of-knowledge "construction" of reality *within* an *intra*-linguistic narrative-world adds complicating factors, which take us beyond the role of reconstruction and rapport in hermeneutics. The work of Peter Marshall, to which we have already alluded, explores social conventions in Paul's relations with the Corinthians, within a framework of less speculative linguistic assumptions, although questions about rhetorical function play a positive part in his argument.

(iii) Schleiermacher, Dilthey, and Betti insist that the kind of investigations which we have discussed will enable the intepreter to understand the author of a text *better, or more fully, than the author*. As we saw in the case of F.C. Baur's interpretation of New Testament history, *in principle* (whether or not Baur in actuality went beyond the evidence) there is always a possibility that the individual may be subject to historical forces of which he or she may not be fully aware. The fact that Baur's reconstruction drew to itself convincing criticism means only that this particular example remains hypothetical. The postulation of "historical constraints" must always remain a tentative matter subject to correction in the light of further argument or evidence. However, there are other kinds of factors of which the author may not be aware, not least those which involve later *conceptual developments which allow retrospective elucidation* of what has earlier been expressed in more general or in less developed terms. From among such examples two outstanding cases invite consideration. One concerns the subsequent development of psychological concepts; the other concerns the theological doctrine.

The psychological example which most strikingly claims attention emerges from Paul's language about the human heart (*kardia*). Paul inherits from the Old Testament the notion that the heart (Hebrew, *lebh*) embraces *hidden depths* of character which cannot necessarily be perceived in terms of superficial appearance. The semantic opposition which contributes decisively to the meaning of *lebh* in 1 Sam. 16:7 is that whereas human beings look "on the outward appearance; the Lord looks on the heart." Paul shares with the Old Testament a view of the heart as the seat of emotions, distress, or anxiety: "In my heart there is great grief and unceasing sorrow" (Rom. 9:2; cf. Psalm 22:14) The N.E.B. imaginatively and justifiably translates "my heart's desire" as "my deepest desire" (Rom. 10:1). If a decision is made which is a firm one, involving a deliberate and sustained attitude on the part of the whole person, this may be expressed as a "decision in his heart" (1 Cor. 7:37). A hardened heart signifies impenetrable obstinacy (Rom. 1:28; 2:5; 2 Cor. 3: 14,15). Talking to, or deliberating with, oneself, is "saying in (one's) heart" (Rom. 10: 6). The most characteristic use, however (which also reflects a theme of the Old Testament) is the notion that only God can "bring to light" the purposes of human hearts (1 Cor. 4:5; Rom. 8:27); and that God "searches", or brings to the surface, what otherwise *lies hidden* in the heart (1. Thess. 2:4).

Bultmann considers a number of these examples and concludes that in cases where will and intention are entailed, this "need not penetrate into *the field of consciousness at all*, but may designate the *hidden tendency* of the self."[122] Those who "want to make a good showing in the flesh" (Gal. 6:12) may well not understand their own *conscious* intentions, "but their secret motive (is) hidden even from themselves."[123] The "strivings" (*boulai*, 1 Cor. 4:5) of the heart may never reach the threshold of consciousness, and the heart can be "darkened" and be the victim of deception (Rom. 1:21; 16:18) as well as the agent of deception. It is clear that Bultmann comes very near to saying that if he had had access to post-Freudian concepts of the unconscious or the sub-conscious, Paul would have drawn on these conceptual tools and vocabulary. Similarly the modern and post-modern debate about hermeneutical "suspicion" cannot but come to mind when Robert Jewett writes concerning Paul's use of *kardia* in Romans: "It is from the darkened and senseless 'heart' (Rom. 1:21) that the thoughts which deliberately distort and suppress the truth about God and His creation flow."[124] We should also wish to argue, on this same ground, that this is the reason why salvation and sanctification entail the *pouring of the Holy Spirit* into the human *heart* (Rom. 5:5). Therapy is needed at the deepest level. It would be anachronistic and unhistorical to claim that *kardia* "means" the Freudian unconscious or sub-conscious in Paul. Yet it would be correct to use an adverbial phrase to say that when Paul speaks of the heart he means *what we are through and through*; and that post-Freudian clinical and conceptual tools enable *us* to understand *what this entails* even more clearly than Paul could have seen in the pre-modern world before this clinical experience had been evaluated. Further issues in this area are explored by Gerd Theissen in his *Psychological Aspects of Pauline Theology* (Eng. 1987).

The second example arises from the development of Christian theology, and may well appeal mainly to orthodox Christians. Most orthodox Christians claim to be "biblical" in doctrine yet also "Trinitarian". Many share the view expressed by Whiteley and by Kelly that the Pauline texts embody "traces of a Trinitarian ground-plan".[125] It is certainly the case that Paul unambiguously expresses the Christian belief in one God (1 Cor. 8:6), and that in many passages both associations and distinctions are drawn between God as Father, Christ as Lord, and the Holy Spirit (Rom. 1:4; Rom. 8: 11, 14–16; Col. 1:15). The relation between Christ and the Holy Spirit has been discussed in numerous studies, and it cannot be claimed that Paul's sentence "the Lord is the Spirit" (2 Cor. 3:17) contains an "is" of identity rather than meaning "is in the passage quoted . . . "[126] In two successive Reports of the Church of England Doctrine Commission, one published in 1987, the other in 1991, several of us urged that the origins of the doctrine of the Holy Trinity are to be found not in contingent factors arising from three centuries of historical and theological controversy, but in the Christian experience, shared by Paul and others, of being caught up "in a divine dialogue", in which prayer is articulated *by* the Holy Spirit *to* God as Father *through* Christ as Lord (Rom. 8: 14–17, 26,27).[127] It is impossible to describe fully and explicitly the actuality of the situation of the believer and of the believing community and their relation to God without drawing on Trinitarian language.

On the other hand, the earliest Christian creeds and confessions concerned not the Holy Trinity but confession of the Lordship of Christ (1 Cor. 12:3), and belief in his death and resurrection "for our sins" according to the scriptures (1 Cor. 15: 3–5; cf. 1 Cor. 11: 23–25; Rom. 4:25). At what stage, if at all, would Paul and the Pauline communities have expressed their creed in terms of a formal doctrine of the Holy Trinity? If 1 Cor. 8:6 represents the beginnings of such a creed, why does it stop abruptly at the second article? The orthodox answer is that the Christian doctrine of the Holy Trinity "explicates the logic" which is already implicit in the Pauline texts. But this would seem to suggest that *subsequent reflection* clarifies "where Pauline thought is leading" in a way that partially transcends Paul's own conscious horizons, and formulates a "better" or "fuller" understanding of these realities.

The difficulty here, however, concerns *criteria* for interpretative judgment. If we are concerned about what Paul *meant*, rather than with what we should like him to have meant, criteria must be employed to ascertain whether a speculative hypothesis about factors which escaped the author's awareness can be firmly established. Here the interpreter must balance hermeneutical faithfulness and responsibility with a measure of courage, if one is to interpret Pauline texts in new situations. For example, it is noteworthy that on the subject of Paul and the ministry of women one of the most cautious and conservative of British New Testament scholars makes a judgment about the "true" meaning of a range of Pauline texts in the following terms: Donald Guthrie asserts concerning the verse "there is neither male nor female . . . You are all one in Christ Jesus" (Gal. 3:28), "It must be regarded as the key for understanding his (Paul's) other statements."[128] Yet as Schleiermacher, Dilthey, and Betti urge, we could not begin to evolve any "fuller" understanding until we have *first* placed ourselves in the author's situation, and the historical context must remain the "control" for hypotheses about "fuller" meanings. The view of textuality discussed in chapter two which detaches the text from its life-world, and context of situation, is inconceivable in the case of the Pauline texts. The kind of data which emerges from Jerome Murphy-O'Connor and others establishes this beyond doubt. To borrow J.L. Austin's phrase, it may not be the last word, but it is certainly the first word.

5. Understanding the Author of an Anonymous Text: the Epistle to the Hebrews

The "hermeneutics of understanding" formulated by Schleiermacher, Dilthey and Betti operates on the basis not only of reconstruction but also of interpersonal understanding. Nevertheless we noted Schleiermacher's perceptive observation that the proportion or weight of attention that was paid respectively to the text or to its author depended in practice on issues of *interpretative strategy*. In the end what is important is not our knowledge of the *name and biography* of an author, but that the text which the author produces is understood not only with reference to its detailed parts, but also as a *wholeness which represents the vision of a human mind and which belongs to some larger context or life-world*.

In practice, the task of historical reconstruction in the case of an anonymous writing such as the Epistle to the Hebrews differs greatly in its degree of difficulty but not radically in kind, from reconstructing Paul's thought and situation from the Pauline texts. Paul's situations are easier to construct because, even if we were to be cautious about the use of material in Acts 9: 1–30 and 13:2–28: 31, Paul includes considerable autobiographical material in such passages as Gal. 1: 11 – 2:21; 2 Cor. 11: 21–33, and Phil.

3: 4–16 and we have a series of life-contexts in different epistles. His autobiographical reflections find no parallel in Hebrews, and here we have only a text. We can, however, re-construct the *kind* of thought and life-situation which characterizes the author and which finds expression in the text. At very least, we can arrive at what Betti and others refer to as typification, and we can attempt to gain insight into the wholeness of vision which directs the author's theological argument and pastoral concern. Indeed, in the case of the Epistle to the Hebrews we can go further, for the author expounds a theological vision which is unique within the New Testament and employs particular and distinctive conceptual schemes within a framework of eschatology and Christology which is uniquely his (or if the author could conceivably have been Priscilla, her) own. His practical paranetic material is not reserved, as it is often, but not always (cf. I Corinthians) in Paul, for the closing part of the argument, but is interdispersed repeatedly at various stages of the argument (Hebs. 2:1–4; 3:7–19; 4:14–16; 5:11 -6:12; 10:26–39; 12:1–17, 25–29). Thus it is easy to see the nature of his practical concerns about the readers, which call forth his arguments.

The Epistle to the Hebrews reflects a strongly eschatological vision. Robert Jewett entitles his study of Hebrews *Letter to Pilgrims* in which he sees Hebrews as "rejecting the illusions of lasting cities."[129] "Here we have no lasting city, but we seek the city which is to come" (Heb. 13:14). William Manson sees the congregation to whom the Epistle is directed as cautiously clinging to securities associated with the Jewish part of their former life, "living too much in the Jewish part of their Christianity, and so missing the true horizon of the eschatological calling".[130] Like the mobile imagery of the tabernacle rather than the institutional temple, they were to move on, and "go out". Abraham "went out, not knowing where he was to go" (Heb. 11:8; cf. Gen. 12: 1–8). Therefore "looking to Jesus the pioneer" (Hebs. 12:2) "let us go forth to him outside the camp" (Hebs. 13:13). Ernst Käsemann entitles his study of Hebrews *The Wandering People of God*, and takes as his starting point the paradigmatic model of Joshua as the pre-cursor of Jesus, leading his people in the wilderness. (The background to Käsemann's writing of the first draft arose from his challenge to the German church in 1937, when Hitler was Chancellor, to sit loose to earthly securities and to live as those whom Christ had set free. The first edition was written largely in prison, which was the response of National Socialism to his challenge.) Käsemann writes of "the existential necessity of wandering ... through the wilderness ... as antitype of Christianity ... Rest appears as promise only after the toil and restlessness of a sojourn".[131] "So then, there *remains* a sabbath rest for the people of God" (Hebs. 4:9). If the "rest" had simply been what Joshua (the name is the same in Greek as Jesus) had achieved for Israel, "God would not speak later of another 'day'" (Hebs. 4:8).

This eschatological pilgrim motif has more recently been expounded by Olfried Hofius, who entitles his entire study on Hebrews *Katapausis* (the word for "rest" in Hebs. 4:3 and 4:8). The image of the "eternal sabbath", Hofius argues, has nothing to do with alleged gnostic ideas in Hebrews, but is eschatological. It represents the future goal, to which eschatological pilgrimage finally leads.[132] Hebs. 4:3 ("entering into God's rest", *katapausis*). is "the day of final salvation."[133]

We can be certain on both internal and external grounds that Paul was not the author of this Epistle. Clement of Rome, writing as early as A.D. 95 usually mentions the name of an author whom he quotes; but he cites the text of Hebrews extensively without the use of a name. Clement of Alexandria, recognizing its un-Pauline Greek, postulated Pauline authorship on the ground that Luke was the translator, but his successor Origen admitted that no-one knew who wrote this Epistle. Tertullian and Hippolytus rejected the Pauline authorship. The tradition which associated the Epistle with Paul took firm hold only when Jerome and Augustine were involved in questions about the relation between apostolicity and canonicity. From the Reformation onwards its anonymity was recognized.

Internal evidence points conclusively in the same direction. The theology of the Epistle to the Hebrews reflects emphases that are not characteristic of Paul. First Paul focusses on the language of personal and social *relationship* to describe salvation. Reconciliation and justification become key terms.[134] But the author of the Epistle to the Hebrews focusses on the language of movement and *approach*. He uses the liturgical or worship imagery of "drawing near" (Hebs. 4:16; 7:25; 10:22): "Let us then with confidence *draw near* to the throne of grace" (4:16 though the distinctiveness of "drawing . . . . . .", Greek *proserchomai*, should not be exaggerated in the light of Paul's use of "access", Greek *prosagōgē*, in Rom. 5:2)." Second, Paul regularly speaks of Christ's exaltation as *resurrection*. Resurrection constitutes a centrally important category both for Christology, the work of Christ, and salvation in Paul. (Only Eph. 4:8–10 represents a possible exception in the Pauline corpus, although some would also include Phil. 2:5–11.) The Epistle to the Hebrews, by contrast, as Schrenk argues, has little reference to the resurrection (13:20) and speaks instead of Christ's *ascension*.[135] This coheres entirely with his other imagery of approach to God. As "pioneer" of faith, Christ leads the way for His people into the innermost "sanctuary" or heavenly presence of God. (Hebs. 10:12,13). Third, Paul discusses the role of the law in relation to grace, obedience, commandment, and achievement. The author of Hebrews, on the other hand, examines the role of the law as a system relating to priesthood, sacrifice, and *worship*. Fourth, Paul and the author of Hebrews use different techniques of *Old Testament quotation*. Graham Hughes shows how the forward-looking, "open", and dynamic-eschatological outlook which characterizes Hebrews influences the hermeneutic of Old Testament texts which is employed. Continuities and "connectedness" rest on convictions about the purposive action of God; but the Christian community addressed by the author of the Epistle "is forced to reckon with its own unfinality, as being still very much enmeshed in the processes of history."[136] The Old Testament texts point *beyond* merely past and present horizons.

The originality and uniqueness of the author as a creative thinker who puts a powerful theology to pastoral use, emerges in a variety of ways. First, the author uses conceptual tools which at first sight seem closely, if indirectly, related to Platonic thought, as mediated through Alexandrian culture, and possibly Philo. But the *conceptual tools are employed in a radically different and unexpected way by their incorporation into a firmly temporal eschatology*. Here Ronald Williamson's work assumes considerable importance. Williamson carefully and meticulously examines the conceptual relations between Hebrews and Philo, as current representative of Alexandrian Platonism, and identifies several major differences. He rightly observes, "The fundamental difference between the thought of Philo and that of the Epistle to the Hebrews is shown in their deeply differing attitudes to *time*."[137] Thus on the one side, the author invokes the broadly Platonic contrast between the imperfect, human, earthly, representation or "copy" (*hypodeigma*, Hebs. 8:5), and the perfect heavenly reality which constitutes the divine idea or purposive "pattern" (*kata ton typon*, Hebs. 8:5), of which the copy is an imperfect representation. The writer shares the general hellenistic-Jewish view, reflected also by the Stephen circle, that "the Most High does not dwell in houses made with hands" (Act 7: 48; Hebs. 9:24). Nevertheless, on the other side, the writer's eschatology transposes the Platonic *spatial* imagery into a *temporal* conceptual scheme: that which is *earthly and imperfect, including* the Jewish temple and its priests and sacrifices, *points forward to the heavenly realities of the eschaton*. Faith grasps what is "unseen" (Hebs. 11:1), not primarily in the sense of aspiring to the upper world, but in the sense of *reaching forward to that which God promises*, but which has not yet visibly taken place.

Second, the author now integrates this powerful eschatologizing of Alexandrian conceptual categories with a system of "fulfilment" and "waiting" which in turn entails a high and unique Christology. Some (but not all) "eschatological" or "perfect" realities have already entered history in a definitive and irreducible way. Thus, while prior to the coming of Christ divine revelation was "fragmentary" or partial, and piecemeal, "in these last days" God has spoken definitively in Christ (Hebs. 1:1).[138] Since Christ bears "the stamp of God's nature", the revelation of God in Christ does not, as Montefiore expresses it, merely "resemble certain aspects" of God, but "is the exact representation" of "what makes God be God."[139] Christ, however, is even more than a perfect revelation of God; his work of priestly offering and sacrifical atonement is perfect, entire, and complete. It is "finished" work: He "takes His seat" (1:3); his work is unrepeatable and once-for-all (*ephapax*, Hebs. 7:27; 9:12; 10:10; cf. 9: 26,28). This Christology and soteriology is now intergrated with the eschatological frame around an Alexandrian conceptual theme: "Christ entered, not into a sactuary made with hands, *copy* of a *true* one; but into *heaven itself*, now to appear in the presence of God on our behalf." (Hebs. 9:24).

The author now draws on yet one more conceptual model to clinch the point. As Buchanan and others argue, Psalm 110 has special importance in his thought.[140] Perhaps he had been reflecting on this Psalm before he formulated the argument of the epistle. At all events, he takes up the figure of Melchizedek, whose contemporary importance for Judaism is reflected in the Qumran texts, (cf. 11 Q. Melch; 4Q. Florilegium).[141] He applies Psalm 110:4 (cf. Gen. 14: 18–20) to Christ as a "complete" or "eternal" type of priesthood, in contrast to the ongoing and incomplete character of Aaronic priests who always left "unfinished" work for successors. Whereas the Jewish high-priests have continually to *repeat* their offerings because they are *incomplete* and *imperfect* (with an infinite regress of earthly successors), Jesus has *completed a perfect sacrifice and offering once-for-all* (*ephapax*).

All the same, a third feature now enters the picture. The readers themselves have *not yet achieved* eschatological finality and perfection. They still await the fulfilment of their final goal, when they will enter the "rest" (*katapausis*) which follows completed work. Like all God's pilgrim people of faith (Hebs. 11: 4–40) they must act now in the present boldly, and accept the hardship and endurance of pilgrim-travellers. They need a forward-looking faith which will appropriate, and act on, God's promises concerning the future purposes. Like Abraham, they must "venture forth" (Hebs. 11. 8,9). They need fresh vision, fresh courage, fresh perseverance, fresh heart, in the face of drifting, stultification, stagnation, and a desire to shelter within old securities. Hence, they are urged: "Let us run with patience the race that is set before us, looking to Jesus the *pioneer* and *perfecter* of our faith" (Hebs. 12:2). The "cloud of witnesses" (12:1) who have witnessed to this faith that God will bring them to future promised realities, (11: 4–40) encourages the community in this vision.

Our aim has been to reconstruct *the life-context which called forth* the thought of this unique and creative writer. He is one of the outstanding theologians of the New Testament, and his thought is breath-taking in its forceful originality. But have we achieved anything above and beyond examining the text, simply as a text? We readily allow that our evidence about the author comes from the text itself, and that our picture remains a construct, which has been largely established, unlike our understanding of Paul, in terms of what Betti refers to as typifications. But we have been trying to arrive at an understanding of how this pastor-theologian perceived the problems of the church which led him to write, and what conceptual resources he used to formulate the flow of argument in the text. We have consciously tried to pin-point those features which allow us to see a *unique* theological mind and pastoral heart addressing the readers. We have high-lighted those features which are distinctive, and which together represent a configuration which is unique. Qualities emerge in understanding a human person *as a person* which transcend explanations about a text *as a text*. A perception of his *vision, purpose,* and *pastoral concern*, take us, as Schleiermacher, Dilthey and Betti urge, beyond issues of "explanation" to a hermeneutics of "understanding".

We must conclude, however, with four important caveats or disclaimers. First, we doubt whether *every* biblical text needs to be treated in this particular way. We shall return to these issues in chapters X and XIII-XV. It is arguable that certain narrative-material (for example the Book of Jonah or Job) would convey their meaning as readily as self-contained textual "narrative-worlds" rather than as expressions or articulations of particular life-situations. Some historical situations simply cannot be recoverd with certainty, as is the case with the "floating" narrative-text which was eventually incorporated in John as John 7:53 – 8:11 (the woman caught in adultery). In some cases we have to make careful judgments. Some theories about the distinctive concerns of Matthew and Luke remain speculative and idiosyncratic. On the other hand, the established features of Matthew's sensitivity about Judaism and concern about the law, and Luke's deep concern for social and historical realities in wider society, have become solid working axioms. Once again, the notion of a hermeneutical circle, in which exegetical detail interacts and serves as a mutual cross-check with the larger picture, offers a tool for steady, though slow, corporate advance in interpretation.

Second, it would be a mistake to conclude that *no* understanding is possible without historical reconstruction. The point made carefully by Schleiermacher, Dilthey and Betti, and underlined by other writers including Heinrich Ott, is that *understanding is a process rather than a single event*.[142] We may sometimes experience "leaps" in understanding. But this does not necessarily imply that we have *no* understanding before such an experience; or, on the other hand, that subsequent understanding cannot improve still further. There are *degrees* of understanding. This is one reason why so often readers describe the Bible as "inexhaustible". The absence of historical construction may mean only that certain features of understanding may be missing, and that the constraints which prevent *mis*understanding are fewer and less effective than otherwise. In the Christian community, in practice, sometimes certain historical reconstructions are simply presupposed by some who do not consciously make them. They have been mediated, second-hand, from lecture-rooms or pulpits, and contribute unconsciously to what is perceived as the "natural" meaning. The inference of this is not that historical interpretation should be avoided, but that what is mediated needs to be based on responsible and careful judgments.

Third, we have urged, and shall underline again in our concluding chapter, that *Schleiermacher's emphasis on background and on linguistic system prohibits an unduly psychologistic interpretation of his hermeneutics.* We comment further on this issue in our observations on *intention* in chapter XV.

Fourth, while we have urged the importance of a hermeneutics of understanding as this is expounded by Schleiermacher, Dilthey, and Betti, we have not claimed, and do not claim, that this constitutes a *comprehensive theory* of hermeneutics. Our use of Pauline and other New Testament texts was designed to illustrate the value and application of the model. But, equally, it also *demonstrates what has been omitted.* Interpreting the biblical texts entails much more than understanding persons and texts as phenomena who speak in the past, or who help us to understand the language and events of the past. Other hermeneutical theories reflect concerns about relations between the text and reader, about textual effects, about the horizon of the present. To these other models and theories we now turn.

NOTES TO CHAPTER VII

1. Charles E.B. Cranfield, *A Critical and Exegetical Commentary on the Epistle to the Romans* (2 vols.) Edinburgh: Clark 1975 and 1979; C.K. Barrett, *A Commentary on the Epistle to the Romans*, 2nd edn. London, Black, 1962; James D.G. Dunn, *Romans* (Word Biblical Commentary 38, 2 vols.) Dallas: Word, 1988.
2. Johannes Munck, *Paul and the Salvation of Mankind*, Eng. London: S.C.M., 1959, 66.
3. *Ibid.*
4. Adolf Deissmann, *Paul. A Study in Social and Religious History*, Eng. 2nd edn. London: Hodder & Stoughton, 1926, 6.
5. Wolfhart Pannenberg *Basic Questions in Theology* (3 vols.) Eng. London: S.C.M. 1970, 1971 & 1973, II, 35.
6. J. Munck, *op. cit.* 67.
7. Anthony C. Thiselton, *The Two Horizons* 314–26.
8. J. Christiaan Beker, *Paul the Apostle. The Triumph of God in Life and Thought* Edinburgh: Clarke, Philadelphia: Fortress, 1980, 13.
9. Albert Schweitzer, *The Mysticism of Paul the Apostle*, Eng. London: Black, 1931.
10. W.D. Davies, *Paul and Rabbinic Judaism. Some Rabbinic Elements in Pauline Theology* (1948) 4th edn. Philadelphia: Fortress, 1980; London: S.P.C.K. 1981.
11. Rudolf Bultmann, *Theology of the New Testament* (2 vols.) Eng. London: S.C.M. 1952 and 1955, I, 191.
12. J. Munck, *op. cit.*, and *Christ and Israel. An Interpretation of Romans 9–11*, Eng. Philadelphia: Fortress, 1967; Krister Stendahl, *Paul Among Jews and Gentiles and Other Essays*, London: S.C.M. 1977 and Philadelphia: Fortress 1976; Ernst Käsemann, *New Testament Questions of Today*, Eng. London: S.C.M. and Philadelphia: Fortress, 1969, esp. 180–81; and *Perspectives on Paul*, London: S.C.M. and Philadelphia: Fortress, 1971.
13. Georg Eichholz, *Die Theologie des Paulus im Umriss*, Neukirchen-Vluyn: Neukirchener Verlag 2nd edn. 1977, 14–40; and George Howard, *Crisis in Galatia:*

A Study in Early Christian Theology, Cambridge: Cambridge University Press (S.N.T.S.M.S. 35) 1979.
14. J.C. Beker, *op. cit.* 15.
15. *Ibid* 11.
16. *Ibid* 18.
17. *Ibid* 35.
18. *Ibid* 38.
19. *Ibid* 47.
20. Karl P. Donfried (ed.) *The Romans Debate: Essays on the Origins and Purpose of the Epistle*, Minneapolis: Augsburg, 1977.
21. J.C. Beker, *op. cit.* 74.
22. Robert Jewett, *Christian Tolerance. Paul's Message to the Modern Church*, Philadelphia: Westminster, 1982, 29.
23. *Ibid.*
24. *Ibid* 21–22.
25. *Ibid* 23–42.
26. *Ibid* 17.
27. Gerd Theissen, *The Social Setting of Pauline Christianity*, esp. 121–44.
28. J.H. Schütz, *Paul and the Anatomy of Apostolic Authority*, Cambridge: Cambridge University Press, 1975 (S.N.T.S. Mon., 26); and Bengt Holmberg, *Paul and Power: The Structure of Authority in the Primitive Church as Reflected in the Pauline Epistles*, Coniectanea Biblica, Lund: Gleerup, 1978 and Philadelphia: Fortress, 1980, 198–99.
29. James D.G. Dunn, *Baptism in the Holy Spirit*, London: S.C.M., 1970, 103–05.
30. J.C. Beker, *op. cit.* 30.
31. Wayne A. Meeks (ed.) *The Writings of St Paul: Norton Critical Edition*, London & New York: Norton, 1972, 192.
32. *Ibid* esp. 176–364.
33. *Ibid* 281, 282 and 287, from *The Church History of the First Three Centuries* (1860).
34. *Ibid* 288, 289, from "The First Christians" in *The Dawn of Day* (1880); and 291, from "The Jewish Dysangelist" in *The Antichrist* (1888), sects. 39–43.
35. *Ibid* 299, from "Preface on the Prospects of Christianity" to *Androcles and the Lion* (1913).
36. *Ibid* 438.
37. *Ibid.*
38. Anthony C. Thiselton, *The Two Horizons*, 422–27.
39. Ludwig Wittgenstein, *Philosophical Investigations* II.x, 191–92; *Zettel*, sects. 75 and 85; cf. H.H. Price, *Belief*, London: Allen & Unwin, 1969, esp. 20–28, 290–314.
40. Vernon H. Neufeld, *The Earliest Christian Confessions*, Leiden: Brill, 1963.
41. Anthony C. Thiselton, "Schweitzer's Interpretation of Paul", *Expository Times* 90, 1979, 132–37.
42. Albert Schweitzer, *op. cit.* 38–39.
43. *Ibid* 98.
44. *Ibid* 101.
45. *Ibid* 107.
46. *Ibid* 121.
47. *Ibid* 124.
48. *Ibid* 143.

49. *Ibid* 165.
50. *Ibid* 194.
51. *Ibid* 223.
52. Martin Werner, *The Formation of Christian Dogma*, Eng. London: Black, 1957.
53. Maurice F. Wiles, *The Divine Apostle. The Intepretation of St Paul's Epistles in the Early Church*, Cambridge: Cambridge University Press, 1967, 139 (my italics).
54. Krister Stendahl, *Paul among Jews and Gentiles*, 78–96.
55. E.P. Sanders, *Paul and Palestinian Judaism. A Comparison of Patterns of Religion*, London: S.C.M. 1977, 442.
56. *Ibid* 443.
57. *Ibid* (my italics) 9.
58. *Ibid* 446.
59. *Ibid* 12–24.
60. *Ibid* 517.
61. *Ibid* 518 and 543.
62. Wilhelm Dilthey, *Selected Writings* (ed. H.P. Rickman) Cambridge: Cambridge University Press, 1976, 3–4.
63. H.A. Hodges, *The Philosophy of Wilhelm Dilthey*, London: Routledge & Kegan Paul, 1952, xiv.
64. Wilhelm Dilthey, *Gesammelte Schriften V: Die Geistige Welt. Einleitung in die Philosophie des Lebens*, Leipzig and Berlin: Teubner, 1927, 4. (my italics).
65. Wilhelm Dilthey, *Gesammelte Schriften VII: Der Aufbau der Geschichtlichen Welt in den Geisteswissenschaften*, Leipzig and Berlin: Teubner, 1927, 131; cf. *Selected Writings* 177–78.
66. W. Dilthey, *op. cit.* VII, 203; cf. *Selected Writings*, 218.
67. W. Dilthey, *op. cit.* VII, 206; *Selected Writings*, 219.
68. *Ibid* 279
69. W. Dilthey *op. cit.* VII, 213–14; *Selected Writings*, 226–27.
70. James M. Robinson and John B. Cobb Jr. (edn.) *New Frontiers in Theology: II, The New Hermeneutic*, New York: Harper and Row, 1964, 59.
71. W. Dilthey, *op. cit.* VII 215–16; *Selected Writings* 227.
72. *Ibid.*
73. W. Dilthey, *op. cit.* VII 191; *Selected Writings* 208.
74. W. Dilthey, *op. cit.* V 336; *Selected Writings* 262.
75. W. Dilthey, *op. cit.* VII, 214; *Selected Writings* 226.
76. W. Dilthey, *op. cit.* VII, 133–34; *Selected Writings* 180.
77. W. Dilthey, *op. cit.* VII 196–99 and 202–04; 146–57; cf. *Selected Writings* 191–207, 212–14.
78. W. Dilthey, *op. cit.* VII 146–47; *Selected Writings* 191.
79. Howard N. Tuttle, *Wilhelm Dilthey's Philosophy of Historical Understanding*, Leiden: Brill, 1969, 11.
80. W. Dilthey, "The Development of Hermeneutics", *Selected Writings* 262; cf. *op. cit.* V 336.
81. Wolfhart Pannenberg, *Theology and the Philosophy of Science*, Eng. Philadelphia: Westminster, 1976, 78–80, 130–131, in relation to W. Pannenberg, "Hermeneutics and Universal History" in Robert Funk (ed.) *Journal for Theology and the Church* 4, 1967, 122–52.
82. James C. McHann Jr., *The Three Horizons: A Study in Biblical Hermeneutics*

with Special Reference to Wolfhart Pannenberg, University of Aberdeen, Ph.D Dissertation, 1987.
83. H.-G. Gadamer, *Truth and Method* 204; cf. 460–62.
84. Michael Polanyi, *Personal Knowledge: Towards a Post-Critical Philosophy*, London: Routledge & Kegan Paul, (1958) 1962.
85. Anthony C. Thiselton, *The Two Horizons*, 234–40.
86. Emilio Betti, *Allgemeine Auslegungslehre als Methodik der Geisteswissenschaften*, Tübingen: Mohr, 1967, 1–61.
87. *Ibid* 169.
88. *Ibid* 21.
89. *Ibid* 158 and 211–16.
90. H.-G. Gadamer, *Truth and Method* 465; cf. E Betti, *op. cit.* 93–4.
91. Emilio Betti, *op. cit.* 98.
92. *Ibid* 472–77.
93. *Ibid* 204–16.
94. *Ibid* 211.
95. *Ibid* 216–40.
96. Josef Bleicher, *Contemporary Hermeneutics. Hermeneutics as Method, Philosophy, and Critique*, London: Routledge & Kegan Paul, 1980, 27–50; cf. 11–26.
97. W. Pannenberg, *Theology and the Philosophy of Science*, 166.
98. Jerome Murphy-O'Connor, *St Paul's Corinth: Texts and Archaeology*, Wilmington: Glazier, 1983; Gerd Theissen, *op. cit.*; John C. Hurd Jr. *The Origin of I Corinthians*, London: S.P.C.K., 1965; and Peter Marshall, *Enmity in Corinth: Social Conventions in Paul's Relations with the Corinthians*, Tübingen, Mohr, 1987.
99. Gordon D. Fee, *The First Epistle to the Corinthians*, Grand Rapids: Eerdmans, 1987 (N.I.C.N.T.) 55.
100. J. Munck, *Paul and the Salvation of Mankind* 135–67; 136.
101. *Ibid* 152.
102. *Ibid* 157–67.
103. Gordon D. Fee, *op. cit.* 59.
104. Jerome Murphy-O'Connor, *op. cit.* 153–61.
105. *Ibid* 158.
106. *Ibid* 159.
107. H.-G. Gadamer, *Truth and Method*, 273.
108. Albert Schweitzer, *Paul and his Interpreters. A Critical History*, London: Black, 1912, 37–8.
109. Johannes Weiss, "Earliest Christianity" vol.2, Eng. New York, Harper edn. 1959, 433–40.
110. *Ibid* 442.
111. *Ibid* 445–46.
112. Krister Stendahl, *Paul among Jews and Gentiles* 68, 70, 71, 75, *et. passim*.
113. *Ibid* 76.
114. *Ibid* 78–80.
115. F.F. Bruce, *Paul; Apostle of the Free Spirit*, Exeter: Paternoster, 1977, 457.
116. *Ibid*; cf. 456–63.
117. *Ibid* 463.
118. Ronald F. Hock, *The Social Context of Paul's Ministry: Tentmaking and Apostleship*, Philadelphia: Fortress, 1980, 67.

119. Jerome Murphy-O'Connor, *op. cit.* 169.
120. *Ibid* 170.
121. Norman R. Petersen, *Rediscovering Paul. Philemon and the Sociology of Paul's Narrative World*, Philadelphia: Fortress, 1985.
122. Rudolf Bultmann, *Theology of the New Testament* (2 vols.) Eng. London, S.C.M., 1952 and 1955, I, 223 (my italics); cf. 220–27.
123. *Ibid* 224 (my italics).
124. Robert Jewett, *Paul's Anthropological Terms. A Study of their Use in Conflict Settings*, Leiden: Brill, 1971, 332.
125. D.E.H. Whiteley, *The Theology of St Paul*, 2nd edn. Oxford: Blackwell, 1974, 128–29; cf. J.N.D. Kelly, *op. cit.* 21–22.
126. Cf. N.Q. Hamilton, *The Holy Spirit and Eschatology in St Paul*, Edinburgh: Oliver and Boyd, 1957, and arguments by Vincent Taylor, Hendry and others.
127. Church of England Doctrine Commission Report, *We believe in God*, London: Church House Publishing, 1987, 109 and 104–21; and *We Believe in the Holy Spirit*, London: Church House Publishing. 1991.
128. Donald Guthrie, *New Testament Theology*, London: Inter-Varsity Press, 1981, 775.
129. Robert Jewett, *Letter to Pilgrims. A Commentary on the Epistle to the Hebrews*, New York: Pilgrim Press, 1981, 16.
130. William Manson, *The Epistle to the Hebrews. An Historical and Theological Reconsideration*, London: Hodder & Stoughton, 1951, 24, 35, 36.
131. Ernst Käsemann, *The Wandering People of God. An Investigation of the Letter to the Hebrews*, Eng. Minneapolis: Augsburg, 1984, 19.
132. Olfried Hofius, *Katapausis. Die Vorstellung vom endzeitichen Ruheort im Hebraäerbrief*, Tübingen: Mohr, 1970, 17–21; 102; and 116–151.
133. *Ibid* 256.
134. Ralph P. Martin, *Reconciliation. A Study in Pauline Theology*, London: Marshall, Morgan & Scott, 1981.
135. G. Shrenk in G. Kittel and G. Friedrich (ed.), *Theological Dictionary of the New Testament*, Eng. Grand Rapids: Eerdmans, 1964, III, 274.
136. Graham Hughes, *Hebrews and Hermeneutics. The Epistle to the Hebrews as a New Testament Example of Biblical Interpretation*, Cambridge: Cambridge University Press, 1979, 108; cf. 104 *et passim*.
137. Ronald Williamson, *Philo and the Epistle to the Hebrews*, Leiden: Brill, 1970, 144–45.
138. Cf. F.F. Bruce, *The Epistle to the Hebrews*, London: Marshall, Morgan & Scott, 1964, 1–3.
139. Hugh W. Montefiore, *The Epistle to the Hebrews*, London: Black, 1964, 35.
140. George Wesley Buchanan, *To the Hebrews: A New Translation with Introduction and Commentary*, New York: Doubleday, 1972; cf. "The Present State of Scholarship on Hebrews" in J. Neusner (ed.) *Christianity, Judaism and other Greco-Roman Cults*, Leiden: Brill, 1975.
141. M. de Jonge and A.S. van der Woude, "11 Q Melchizedek and the New Testament", *New Testament Studies* 12, 1966, 301–26; and Joseph A. Fitzmyer, "Further Light on Melchizedek from Qumran Cave II" *Journal of Biblical Literature* 86, 1967, 25–41.
142. Heinrich Ott "What is Systematic Theology?" in James M. Robinson and J. Cobb Jr. (eds.) *New Frontiers in Theology: I The Later Heidegger and Theology*, New York: Harper & Row, 1963, 77–111, esp. 80–81.

CHAPTER VIII

The Hermeneutics of Self-Involvement: From Existentialist Models to Speech-Act Theory

1. Reader-Involvement, Address, and States of Affairs: The Contrasting Assumptions of Existentialist Hermeneutics and "the Logic of Self-Involvement" in Austin and Evans

In our second chapter we discussed the dimension of inter-personal address which we might expect from a theological point of view to characterize some biblical texts. We noted the inadequacy of a purely historical paradigm (to recall Robert Morgan's language) in which biblical texts are transformed simply into devices for the reconstruction of the ancient historical world. In the very early work of Karl Barth and in Rudolf Bultmann a hermeneutical shift occurs from purely historical enquiry into an attempt to let the New Testament texts speak as proclamation, as address, as promise or as warning, which involves the present reader. Behind both the dialectical theology of the early Barth and the hermeneutical theory of Bultmann stood the existentialist thought of Kierkegaard, although in the case of Bultmann a multiplicity of influences were at work ranging from Neo-Kantianism and the earlier Heidegger to Lutheran pietism and form criticism.

In the development of hermeneutical theory, however, the alliance of existentialist philosophy and dialectical theology constituted a false dawn for reader-related interpretation, at least as an attempt to offer a *comprehensive* model of hermeneutics. Existentialism is profoundly individualistic, and stands in tension with post-Gadamerian emphases on the positive role of traditions and reading-communities. Even more to the point, it sets up an unwarranted polarization between the two supposed *alternatives* of factual, descriptive functions of language, and value-laden, proclamatory, and transforming functions of language, as if the latter could or should operate independently of the former.

Nevertheless existentialist hermeneutics brought to biblical studies an emphasis on *reader-situations*, which remains entirely constructive and positive. Moreover, within a frame in which the role of the community in interpretation is otherwise acknowledged, a Kierkegaardian stress on the *disruption* of social and religious convention in transforming and creative understanding has a valuable place as a *supplementary* hermeneutical model. In chapter XV we explore both of these two aspects in greater detail, relating a variety of hermeneutical models to differing reading-situations, and also exploring Kierkegaard's own existential reading of the narrative of Abraham and the sacrifice of Isaac in Gen 22:1–19.

In the biblical texts themselves, biblical authors are concerned to address the hearer or the reader, and in particular both Jesus and Paul, as well as the author of Luke-Acts, allow their material, vocabulary, and mode of communication to take account of the nature of the audience whom they are addressing. The parables of Jesus provide classic examples of communication which is related to the capacity and stance of the hearers. As Ernst Fuchs rightly expresses the matter, Jesus does not simply throw down a message, but comes to *meet* the hearer in the parable-text. He writes: "Is not this the way of true love? Love does not just blurt out. Instead it provides in advance the sphere in which meeting takes place."[1] J. Arthur Baird traces the beginnings of audience criticism in studies of the language of Jesus back to T.W. Manson and to his comment: "As to matter and method, the teaching of Jesus is conditioned by the nature of the audience."[2]

Paul also provides a place of meeting by entering into the "world" of his readers. He applies in his own hermeneutic the principle which he enunciates in 1 Cor. 9: 20–23: "To the Jews I became a Jew . . . To those outside the law, I became as one outside the law . . . To the weak, I became weak . . . I have become all things to all men, that I might by all means save some. I do it all for the sake of the gospel". In different studies I have argued that Paul temporarily accepts and follows the logic of the Corinthians' definitions of "Spirit" and "spirituality", only to let them be transformed from within the shared "world" in the light of the reality of the cross.[3] It has often been argued that typical sermon-material in Luke-Acts is selected by the author to illustrate settings in relation to typified or distinctive audiences: Peter preaches to Jews in Jerusalem, alluding to scripture and the last days (Acts 2: 14–36); Paul and Barnabas preach to pagan villagers at Lystra, speaking not about "the last days" but about the need to turn from vain things to the living God (Acts 14: 15–18). To city-educated Greeks in Athens, the sermon embodies a more elaborate theology of creation (Acts 17: 22–31).

Existentialist models of hermeneutics have sought to capture the dimension of self-involvement and audience-related address which such texts presuppose. But the era of existentialism, associated especially with Heidegger and Bultmann, has largely passed, not least because of the two reasons already mentioned. But what are the losses, and what are the gains, in this shift of emphasis to other models of reading? Are there not insights in existentialist models of hermeneutics which should not be lost from view? If so, *are there better conceptual tools with which these insights might be preserved and expressed?* We shall argue in this chapter that self-involving hermeneutics remains fundamental to the larger hermeneutical enterprise, but that we should do better to draw here on the conceptual and logical work undertaken initially by J.L. Austin and in the use made of his work by Donald Evans, and then in the speech-act theory of John Searle, F. Recanati, and others.

Existentialist models of hermeneutics from Kierkegaard to Bultmann represent a narrower and more one-sided example of the hermeneutics of self-involvement than work which draws in other traditions in the philosophy of language, including the speech-act theory of J.L. Austin. Heidegger uses the word "involvement"; but it does not constitute one of his major terms. Donald Evans explored what he called "the logic of self-involvement" in a seminal and seriously undervalued book published in 1963.[4] Evans was heavily influenced by J.L. Austin's philosophy of language, and less directly by J.O. Urmson and by Ian Ramsey. He set himself the task of exploring the logical connections between utterances as texts and the "practical commitments, attitudes, and feelings" which are contextually related to them.[5] He applied this exploration in particular to biblical language relating to creation.

On the basis of a *purely descriptive* or *purely historical* hermeneutical model we might be tempted to interpret the creation accounts (Gen. 1:1–2:25) as doing little more than referring to past events through narrative and narrative-imagery, from which the reader was absent, and not involved at first hand. "By the word of the Lord were the heavens made . . . He spoke, and it came to be" (Psalm 33: 6,9). "The Lord God planted a garden in Eden, in the East; and there he put the man whom he had formed. And out of the ground the Lord God made to grow every tree that is pleasant to the sight and good for food" (Gen. 2: 8,9). But Evans, following implications from Austin, distinguishes between two different logical functions which characterize these creation texts. On the one hand, God, or the Word of God, acts as the agent of *causal power*. Here the emphasis falls on *events and states of affairs*. But on the other hand, the *fiats* of God *also* have "*exercitive force*". In these terms they take their place within Austin's category of performative language. If the words of creation have exercitive force, it is not simply the case that creation, including humankind, comes into *existence* (causal power); creation is also *appointed to a role* and *given a particular status*. In this case, language about creation *addresses the reader*: it addresses us about our own *creaturely status*, our *responsibilities as stewards* of the created order, and of the *divine evaluation* which is placed upon us as part of the good creation.

Evans devlops these points in detail against the background of speech-act theory. The self-involvement of the reader echoes Calvin's contention that knowledge of God and of ourselves remains inseparable; and it reflects Bultmann's claim that "Every assertion about God is simultaneously an assertion about man, and *vice versa*".[6] To call God Creator, Evans argues, is to use language which is self-involving in terms of human status, role, commitment, and orientation; it is not simply a flat statement about a process of cause and effect.

The relation between self-involving or existential functions of language and the language which asserts that certain states of affairs are or were the case brings us to the heart of the problem about existentialist hermeneutics. Austin, by contrast with Bultmann, declares that "for a certain performative utterance to be happy (i.e. effectively involve people and perform acts) certain *statements* have *to be true*".[7] Austin's theory of truth is more complex than at first it might seem, and Jon Wheatley and others provide an excellent critique of its status.[8] In this context, however, Austin is speaking of "correspondence to the facts". Evans takes up Austin's approach arguing that the *cause-effect* language of states of affairs provides a basis on which biblical language about creation is *also self-involving*. But existentialist models of hermeneutics reflect an utterly different approach. The more heavily they emphasize the language of self-involvement, human experience, and divine address, the further they move away from *description, narrative, report, and statement*.

Bultmann poses an either/or rather than a both . . . and . . . At the conclusion of his *Theology of the New Testament* he claims that the interpreter can *either* interrogate the New Testament as a "source" for the reconstruction of the history of primitive Christianity "*or* the reconstruction stands in the service of the interpretation of the New Testament writings under the presupposition that they have something to say to the present."[9] It *cannot* be both. Thus in *The History of the Synoptic Tradition* and in Bultmann's work on form criticism, the language of the Synoptic Gospels includes proclamation, address, polemic, challenge, pronouncement, preaching, apologetic, but only minimal report or description. Graham Stanton's book *Jesus of Nazareth in New Testament Preaching* provides a constructive corrective to the surprising allegation that the earliest Christians would not have been much interested in "reports" or "descriptions" concerning Jesus.[10]

Why does Bultmann polarize the either/or of history and faith, or description and address, with such uncompromising sharpness? It took me nearly a hundred pages to try to offer a detailed answer to this question in *The Two Horizons*.[11] Part of the issue turns on Bultmann's relation to neo-Kantian frameworks of thought mediated through his teacher Wilhelm Herrmann. One of my former doctoral students, Clive Garrett, has developed in detail the case for Herrmann's influence on Bultmann.[12] Herrmann stressed that faith was not a matter of "ideas", but of renewed practical response. Along with this, the philosophers of Neo-Kantianism, Cohen and Natorp, urged that we cannot speak of "objects" prior to conceptual thought-construction. In the physical sciences Heinrich Hertz and others were stressing the value of "models" or "constructs" which described objects in accordance with laws. Bultmann therefore associated description with human "construal" and construction, which in turn-of-the-century Lutheran pietism represented "works". The "grace" dimension, by contrast, sprang from address and call. The result was to encourage a dualism in which "works" of achievement were associated with "laws", "constructs", descriptions" and "objectification"; while "faith" was associated with "being addressed", "the present moment", and "decision". Thus to believe in the cross of Christ, Bultmann writes, "does not mean to concern ourselves ... with an objective event (*ein objectiv anschaubares Ereignis*) ... *but rather* (my italics) to make the cross of Christ our own, to undergo crucifixion with Him."[13]

More is at issue than what is popularly seen as the Neo-Kantian contrast between fact (the law polarity) and value (the faith polarity). Many other influences are at work: pietism; a network of assumptions about "myth" mediated through the history-of-religions school; the influence of dialectical theology; Dilthey's philosophy of "life" and life-world; Collingwood's view of history; and finally conceptual schemes and devices offered by the earlier philosophy of Heidegger. Behind all of these, however, stands the figure of Kierkegaard, who is usually regarded as the first major thinker to undertake an existentialist approach to questions of truth and of understanding. Kirkegaard influenced, in turn, not only the theology of the early Karl Barth and of Bultmann, but the philosophy of Jaspers and Heidegger.

Soren Kierkegaard (1813–1855) reacted vehemently against the philosophy of Hegel. The very notion of a universal "system" of truth, he urged, overlooked the concrete situatedness, orientation, and historical finitude of the individual. Truth exists only in as far as it engages with life, and the communication of truth must take full account of the orientation of the individual. Kierkegaard's theory of communication, if we may call it that, emerges most clearly in the small work published after his death under the title *The Point of View for My Work as an Author*. Kierkegaard had used pseudonyms for some of his writings, and had written from different points of view. The purpose behind this exercise was to try to prevent readers from responding prematurely merely in terms of *passive intellectual assent to or denial of ideas*.

This method of *indirect* communication necessitated a *reader-response that involved decision and commitment*. A reader could not passively accept a package; but must choose between the competing approaches offered. "Duplicity dates from the very start."[14] Kierkegaard cannot use "direct communication", because this presupposes "that the receiver's ability to receive is undisturbed. But here . . . an illusion stands in the way."[15] This illusion includes the false assumption that the reader has only to "assent to ideas", to understand and to appropriate what has been said. But such an assumption would be damaging and misleading. Kierkegaard writes: "Everyone who has a result merely as such does not possess it; for he has not *the way*."[16]

For Kierkegaard himself this principle rang true in at least three areas: the nature of Christianity, his own autobiographical experience, and the incarnation and paradox of the cross. The nature of Christianity, he argued, had been transposed into something different, namely the entity called "Christendom" in which everyone who could afford the fees of the Danish church for baptism and burial was automatically a "name-Christian". He blamed the "incalculable harm" done by Augustine in transposing biblical faith into the Platonic-Aristotelian notion of a belief situated in the intellect.[17] One has only to assent to the right formulae to "play the knavish trick" of "calling Christianity what is the exact opposite . . . and then thanking God . . . for the inestimable privilege of being a Christian."[18] As soon as we equate reader-response with bare assent to ideas, Christianity becomes "abolished by expansion." Kierkegaard explains: "Truth becomes untruth in this or that person's mouth."[19]

Second, Kierkegaard found this principle to be true in his own life. He was brought up "as a Christian", and even entered theological college at his father's bidding. But as life brought him through experiences of anguish, suffering, guilt, and despair, he came to believe that a merely theoretical and passive "hearing" of truth was worthless. Active first-hand engagement with truth was everything. If truth were genuinely truth, its effects would be transforming, and would reach through not simply to the mind, but to the sharpened awareness of one's whole personhood, which Kierkegaard called "subjectivity". Thus he writes: "*The objective account falls on WHAT is said; the subjective accent on how it is said* . . . Objectively the interest is focussed on the thought-content; subjectively, on the inwardness . . . This inward 'how' is the passion of the infinite (which) is precisely subjectivity, and thus subjectivity becomes the truth."[20]

Third, the concrete, the particular, and even the paradoxical is seen in the incarnation and the cross, which reveal truth in life and deeds, not primarily in ideas which transcend contradiction. Here above all to respond with "assent" rather than in personal commitment and re-orientation of life is simply to misunderstand the nature of the truth and to mis-hear the communication of the gospel. If the message is understood, it will be seen not as a "system" of general truth, but "a truth which is true *for me* . . . for which I can live and die."[21] The early Karl Barth recalls that what most attracted him to Kierkegaard in 1919 was the unrelenting incisiveness with which he pressed the absolute claims of the gospel for the individual and resisted attempts to make it "innocuous".[22]

At the beginning of this chapter we compared the way in which Austin and Evans interwove self-involvement with descriptive truth-claims as over against Bultmann's tendency to view the dimensions of objective description and existential address almost as mutually exclusive alternatives. Kierkegaard poses this problem even more acutely than Bultmann. Although he insists that interpretation and understanding entail participation and decision, the choices which have to be made cannot, for Kierkegaard, entail criteria which have any rational or logical basis, apart from sheer faith. His paradigm of faith-decision is that of Abraham's willingness to sacrifice the very son on whose survival the fulfilment of the divine promise depended. In his book *Fear and Trembling* Kierkegaard expounds the principle that Abraham's faith must involve self-contradiction and paradox, transcending ethical criteria (the prohibition of murder) and theological criteria (facilitating the fulfilment of the divine promise).[23] The concrete "existing" individual is too irremediably finite, too radically limited in his or her angle of viewpoint, to gain access to a point at which such a criterion could be found. We return to this example in greater detail in chapter XV.

This lack of criteria means that my subjectivity is fully and entirely engaged; for the decision is determined *wholly by the "I"*, and in *no* way imposed by the logic or strength of some given set of criteria. It would be difficult to conceive of any more radical emphasis on "self-involvement" than this; but it is achieved at the price of excluding any positive evaluation of the rational, corporate, or ultimately even the ethical. All are swallowed up in the subjectivity of the individual; although paradoxically, for Kierkegaard, this entailed the renunciation of the self.

Although he evolved contributions to questions about communication about truth, rather than explicitly about hermeneutics, Kierkegaard is generally regarded as contributing to the development of hermeneutical theory through his emphasis on life and self-involvement as that which both transcends and contextualizes bare reason. Thus in his book *Radical Reflection*, where he seeks to formulate "a hermeneutic of everyday life", Calvin Schrag observes that "the unique contribution of Nietzsche and particularly Kierkegaard was to register a mistrust of technical reason as the paradigm of rationality."[24] Kierkegaard begins the journey that culminates in post-Gadamerian hermeneutics in a contrast between "instrumental" reason and some broader, more historical, frame.

2. The Hermeneutics of the Earlier Heidegger and Bultmann's Approach to Paul

Kierkegaard's work on radical human finitude and the fragmentary or partial nature of understanding contributed to the thought of the two near-contemporaries Karl Jaspers (1883–1973) and Martin Heidegger (1884–1976). Heidegger was also heavily indebted to Husserl, from whom he derived the notion of a horizon which embodied a direction of concern. Both Jaspers and Heidegger stressed priority of "existence" as a "given" which preceded and conditioned the nature of knowledge or understanding.

In Heidegger "hermeneutics" denotes both a process of human interpretation or understanding from within a particular orientation, and also a transcendental or meta-critical discipline which seeks to explore the foundations on which the possibility of understanding is based. Thus Heidegger writes: "It designates this business of interpreting . . . This hermeneutic also becomes a 'hermeneutic' in the sense of working out the conditions on which the possibility of any ontological investigation depends."[25] Heidegger begins with three assumptions. First, the "horizon for the understanding of Being" is *time*.[26] We cannot escape questions of "historicality", or the way in which the interpreter is himself or herself historically conditioned. This is also the case with whatever the interpreter seeks to understand. Second, following Dilthey, Heidegger draws a sharp distinction between the "categorizations" of *science* and existential characterizations of *human life*. "*Objectification*" *amounts to* "*depersonalization*."[27] Hence we are not surprised to learn that bare "description" will not do justice to the particularities of life. We must move beyond the subject-object relationship. Third, the *givenness* of our "world" is seen as the "thrown-ness" or "facticity" of our "existence" and our being born into a situation which is not of our making or thinking. This constitutes the particularity of our being. For this reason Heidegger prefers to coin a new term, and to speak of our relation to "*being-there*" (*Dasein*) than to speak of our "being" in the abstract.

One more factor must be taken into account before we can achieve an initial grasp of the nature of Heidegger's hermeneutics. He argues that from the standpoint of our world, we "see" what lies around us in terms of its *relation to our practical concerns in life*. The "*objective*" may sometimes be merely the *artificial*. It would impose an artificial quasi-philosophizing projection onto our "world" to say, for example, that we see a hammer as a wooden handle joined to a piece of metal; or that we perceive a broken hammer as a piece of metal from which the wooden handle has become separated. We see a hammer as an *instrument for hammering* nails; we see a broken hammer as a temporarily *useless* implement. The first supposedly more "objective" view Heidegger terms "present-at-hand"; the second, more functional and "primordial" view he terms "readiness-to-hand".[28] In existentialist hermeneutics the relational, the directed, the projected, and the "possible", not the actual or objective, constitute the foundational.[29]

Understanding thus has the structure of seeing "something *as something*". But what we see it *as* depends on our horizons, our world, and the set of concerns which determine what is ready-to-hand. Heidegger writes: "In interpreting we do not, so to speak, throw a 'signification' over some naked thing which is present-at-hand; but when something within-the-world is encountered as such, the thing in question already has an involvement which is disclosed in our understanding of the world ... In every case this interpretation is grounded in something we have in advance ... An interpretation is never a presuppositionless apprehending of something presented to us."[30] We *"project" forward* certain anticipations which will make sense of the phenomenon to be understood. This involves, Heidegger allows, a hermeneutical circle. We can check-back, as it were, our preliminary understanding; this circle is not "a vicious one". Heidegger gives a name to the "as" in "interpreting as . . . " It is "the primordial 'as'" or "the existential-hermeneutical 'as'".[31]

In the second half of *Being and Time* Heidegger explores the question of "authentic" existence. In authentic existence the self discovers itself in "resoluteness" or decision. Heidegger writes: "'Resoluteness' signifies letting oneself be summoned out of one's lostness in the 'they'".[32] The "they" represent the anonymous crowd whose orientation is determined by convention which is dominated by "loud idle talk", rather than by resoluteness.[33] Authentic existence is "authentically futural".[34] In words very similar to those which Bultmann will use about human existence in Pauline theology, Heidegger concludes that when existence is inauthentic "it is loaded down with a legacy of a 'past'"; but when historicality is "authentic" it understands the present in terms of a "possibility" which becomes open "in a moment of vision."[35]

I have chosen to restrict and to summarize what would otherwise have been a much more extended exposition and assessment, because I have discussed elsewhere in much greater detail Heidegger's philosophy in *Being and Time* and the subsequent use which Rudolf Bultmann made of this work in his own theology.[36] Heidegger's existentialist approach to hermeneutics and to the question of "Being" provides Bultmann with *conceptual tools* for an existential interpretation of Pauline theology. Parallel with the contrast between inauthentic and authentic existence, Bultmann expounds Pauline thought under an organizing methodological contrast between "man prior to the revelation of faith" and "man under faith." Bultmann writes: "Paul's theology can best be treated as his doctrine of man."[37] Existence "according to the flesh" becomes, rightly reflecting

Pauline thought, "trust in one's self as being able to procure life by the use of the earthly and through one's own strength" (cf. Rom. 8:7).[38] The life orientated to "the flesh" is "the self-reliant of attitude of the man who puts his trust in his own strength and in that which is controllable by him" (cf. Phil. 3: 3–7,9).[39] One one side, sin and death signify bondage to the past, and the law represents a system whereby humankind is always trapped by criteria of achievements and failures based on a chain of cause-and-effect processes stemming from the past. On the other side justification constitutes God's "eschatological verdict"; a deed of grace which frees the believer from this orientation towards the past.[40] Faith is not primarily "belief" but a "decision-question".[41] Faith points towards the future" (Gal. 3:11).[42] "The decision of faith has done away with the past", although it must be constantly renewed.[43] The freedom of the Spirit is "nothing else than being open for the genuine future, letting oneself be determined by the future. So Spirit may be called the power of futurity."[44]

Here Bultmann's use of existentialist categories of interpretation serve certain aspects of Pauline thought very well. The existentialist interpretation of *sarx* (flesh) goes quickly to the centre of Paul's most characteristic and important theological use of the term. As John Macquarrie, Robert Jewett and others have argued, *sarx* is not a substantival term in the most characteristic Pauline texts, but signifies modes, aspects, or possibilities of human existence. The causal nexus related to the past which the law-principle entails stands in contrast to the creative opening to future possibilities by the freedom of the Holy Spirit. This conceptual contrast, expressed in temporal terms, captures, and gives existential resonance to, the Pauline antithesis between the old and the new creation. Nevertheless as a *comprehensive* exposition of Pauline theology it is irredeemably one-sided and selective. The *historical* questions about the Gentiles and Israel to which Stendahl and Sanders subsequently gave prominence scarcely feature at all, and the doctrine of the church is almost an incidental in an individualistic scheme of sin and salvation.

This one-sidedness becomes seriously damaging in Bultmann's attempt at a hermeneutical programme of demythologizing. Myth is not merely the use of imagery in order to describe the transcendent, although Bultmann includes this among his three definitions of myth. Neither does Bultmann's second definition of myth in terms of a belief in a "three-storey" universe in which supernatural forces intervene genuinely bring us to the heart of the matter.[45] The fundamental issue is the task of "*de-objectification*". Myth, according to Bultmann, *appears* to portray "objective" events, including the atonement and the resurrection; but in practice *the form disguises the function*. This language functions, according to Bultmann, only existentially or self-involvingly. It does not, in the intention of the writer, describe objective events. Language about the last judgment, Bultmann claims, does not describe or make statements about, a future judgment; it simply *invites an attitude of human responsibility*. Similarly, Bultmann declares, "To believe in the cross of Christ does not mean to concern ourselves with a mythical process wrought outside of us and our world, with an objective event . . . but rather to make the cross of Christ our own."[46]

Christology is perhaps the most serious casualty. In his lecture of 1951 relating to the Christological confession of the World Council of Churches Bultmann formulates as a key question: does Jesus help me because he is the Son of God, or is he the Son of God because he helps me? He agrees that a de-objectified and demythologized Christology may be cashed out in terms of soteriology. The New Testament offers a Christology *only* in terms of Christ's significance "for *me*".

The one-sidedness of existentialist interpretation would be disastrous for Christian theology and do violence to our understanding of the New Testament if it is regarded as a comprehensive hermeneutic. The corporate and public dimensions of the Christian faith receive less than adequate attention; large areas of concern disappear from sight; and the church's witness to the reality of God in Christ as an ultimate ground which transcends the boundaries of human experience is compromised. The church offers its praise to God "as it was in the beginning, is now, and shall be for ever." The wisdom of God stands "before the mountains had been shaped" (Prov. 8:25). Heavenly worship is offered to "the Lord God Almighty, who was, and is, and is to come" (Rev. 4:8).

The Psalmist articulates self-involving experience: "My hope is in thee . . . Hear my prayer, O Lord . . . He drew me up from the desolate pit . . . He put a new song in my mouth" (Psalm 39: 7,12; 40: 2,3). But these experiences are contextualized in a tradition of words and deeds which looks back to a past and forward to a promised future. Eventually as Wolfhart Pannenberg comments, "In those prophetic circles which were the starting-point of the apocalyptic movement, the whole history of Israel and of the world into the far future was understood for the first time as a continuing totality of divine activity, realizing a plan which had been decided at the beginning of creation."[47] Christians look forward to "the last eschatological event which binds history into a whole."[48]

The operative question for hermeneutical theory, then, is whether it is possible to draw on what is of value in the existentialist model, while avoiding its one-sidedness and reductionist view of history. In particular, Donald Evans draws on Austin to show that self-involving language *pre-supposes*, rather than offers an *alternative* to, the language which makes truth-claims about states of affairs or events. But Austin and Evans represent only the beginnings of what develops into a more complex and sophisticated speech-act theory. To explore this path further invites consideration of the work of John Searle, Recanati, Levinson, and other writers.

3. Christological Texts in Paul and in the Synoptic Gospels in the Light of Speech-Act Theory in Austin, Evans, Searle, and du Plessis

In the case of the Christological texts which we find in Paul, we may begin either with the aspect of self-involvement or with more objective and descriptive aspects of Paul's Christology. It may be helpful to follow Johannes Weiss in exploring first the practical, operative, or self-involving aspects of the earliest Christian pre-Pauline confession "Jesus is Lord" (1 Cor. 12:3). Weiss begins by observing "What it means in a practical, religious sense will best be made clear through the correlative concept of 'servant' or 'slave' of Christ" (Rom. 1:1; 1 Cor. 7: 22,23; Gal. 1:10; Phil. 1:1).[49]

A person who sees himself or herself as Christ's servant or slave is wholly at the disposal of his or her "Lord". But he or she can also look to this Lord, as the one to whom they are solely and wholly responsible, not only in obedience, but also in trust. For in the first-century world, the "Lord" provided what his slave needed; this was not the concern of the slave. As Bultmann rightly observes, spelling out the self-involving aspect: for Paul the believer "no longer bears the care for himself, for his own life, but lets this care go, yielding himself entirely ... 'If we live, we live to the Lord; and if we die, we die to the Lord; so whether we live or whether we die; we are the Lord's'" (Rom. 14: 7,8) ... He knows only one care: 'how he may please the Lord' (1 Cor. 7:32), and only one ambition: 'to please the Lord' (2 Cor. 5:9)".[50]

Werner Kramer retains this emphasis on self-involvement in this context, but he rightly expands the horizons of interpretation to include the community and also the future. He writes, "Because the Church (and the individual Christian, too) belongs wholly to the *Lord*, there is no place for fear, but only for confidence and for joy ... there is no limit, even in the future, to the power of the *Lord*, nor will the Church cease to belong to Him. What is true of the Lord now must continue to be true."[51]

All the same, this aspect of self-involvement logically depends on the truth of certain *assertions* about Christ. It is doubtful whether Bultmann is correct when he suggests that the Christological language of the gospels and of Paul tells us nothing "about the nature of Jesus."[52] J.L. Austin and D.D. Evans carefully examine the performative and illocutionary force of a number of verbs which we shall regard as characterizing the inter-personal involvement between *lord and servant* or slave.[53] Austin is concerned about the pre-conditions which must be operative when these verbs are effective as part of "the total speech-act". Austin and Evans expound the significance of the sub-category which they term "*exercitives*", as a way of describing the effectiveness of the words spoken by a person in authority.

It is not of great moment at *this* stage of the argument that where Austin and Evans used the term "Exercitive", John Searle, followed by François Recanati, Stephen Levinson, and Geoffrey Leech, prefer the near-equivalent term "Directive".[54] Thus, if "the word of the Lord" has power to *direct*, to *appoint*, to *authorize*, or to *order*, *directive authority is actually exercised in the exercitive or directive utterance*. Evans includes among his examples of exercitives: "I appoint . . . , I approve . . . , I authorize . . ., I give . . . , I order . . . "[55] Austin includes "the exercising of powers . . ., appointing . . . , urging, advising, warning, ordering, choosing, enacting, claiming, directing."[56] Clearly for these functions to be "performed" under *valid* and *effective* conditions, *more is at issue than the practical attitude of the servant or slave*. To ascribe "lordship" to someone who cannot rightfully exercise it, is from the linguistic viewpoint *empty* or logically arbitrary and from the theological viewpoint *idolatrous*. The words "Jesus is Lord" express *both* factual or institutional truth *and* self-involvement.

The Pauline texts confirm this supposition decisively. In Pauline language, *God* designated Christ "Lord" in the resurrection; Christ's exaltation, and his receiving the name "Lord", is effected by the ontological and institutional action of *God* (Rom. 1:4; 10:9; Phil. 2:11). In Rom. 10:9, Dunn comments: Paul brings together the two central emphases of the gospel: "God raised Him from the dead" and "Jesus is Lord."[57]

This aspect of the logic of self-involvement receives further clarification when we examine two further relevant sub-categories of performatives expounded by Austin and by Evans. The sub-category designated "verdictives" by Austin and Evans is classified as "declarative" by Searle and Recanati. This sub-category of *verdictives* includes "reckoning, requiting, ruling, assessing."[58] Thus Paul declares, "I am not aware of anything against myself, but I am not thereby acquitted; it is the *Lord* who *judges* me" (1 Cor. 4:4). In addition to this sub-category which relates to *verdicts* (Austin) or to *declarations* (Searle), Austin and Evans identify another, which relates to contexts of *behaviour*. Under Austin's "behabitives" (which are like Searle's "expressives") Austin and Evans include "commending, accusing, reprimanding, applauding."[59] Paul writes: "It is not the man who commends himself that is accepted, but the man whom the *Lord commends*" (2 Cor. 10.18).

Although there are other reasons for the choice of the word *kyrios* in the Pauline texts and in other parts of the New Testament (also in the LXX, of God), Whiteley and Cullmann are probably still correct in seeing some element of the notion of "rightful" lord in the use of the term of Jesus, as against the more "arbitrary" lordship or mastership implied more readily in *despotes*.[60] Cerfaux underlines the ontological or objective basis of the application of the term *kyrios* in its close association with the *parousia* of Christ. He argues on the basis of the analogy of the lord or ruler whose coming to his city occasions a festive reception: "we shall be caught up together in the clouds to meet the Lord" (1 Thess. 4:17).[61]

Even when he is examining the cultic or liturgical contexts of *kyrios* texts, Bultmann stresses the aspect of existential experience. Thus he sees a close parallel between early Christian experience of Christ's lordship and that of being at the disposal of the cult-deities from whom they were converted, in the terms described in W. Bousset's *Kyrios Christos* (1913 and 1921). But both aspects, the existential or self-involving, and the ontological or "institutional" belong to the logical function of *kyrios* texts. At the existential and self-involving level, they *invite trust, obedience, surrender and devotion*. They are not simply flat descriptions of abstract doctrinal truths or heavenly transactions. But at the level of their truth-claim about what is the case, the texts also speak of *God's instituting, appointing, or exalting Christ as Lord*. This aspect would remain *true* whether human consciousness wished to acknowledge it or not; but its operative *effects* and *hermeneutical currency* would be seen most clearly when such acknowledgement is made.

Questions about the *identity* of Jesus as Lord bring together not only these two distinct but related logical functions, but also provide a link between the Pauline texts and material in the Synoptic gospels. The basis on which Jesus invites trust and obedience arises *both* from God's exaltation and vindication of his work in the event of his resurrection *and* from his identity and character, disclosed in the words and deeds of his earthly ministry. James Dunn rightly sees this identity as a unifying focus within a variety of New Testament texts. Together they offer "the affirmation of the identity of the man Jesus with the risen Lord."[62]

In the Synoptic Gospels and especially in Mark there is a reticence, the reasons for which we shall shortly note, in stating truths explicitly about the Christological status of Jesus. Nevertheless, the self-involving aspects of Jesus' pronouncements imply Christological presuppositions. Bultmann observes that Jesus' call "is the *call to decision*: Something greater than Solomon . . . greater than Jonah, is here" (Luke 11:31,32) . . . "Follow me, and leave the dead to bury their own dead" (Matt. 8:22). Bultmann concedes that for the very earliest Christians "Jesus' call to decision implies a christology."[63] The words of Jesus perform a more-than-intralinguistic function: they call for, and effect, total renunciation and obedient discipleship (Luke 14:27); they re-interpret traditions of the Old Testament which shaped the pattern of first-century Jewish life (Matt. 5: 21–37); they proclaim the arrival of God's reign which characterizes and inaugurates the new age. Within the presuppositions of Jewish eschatology and apocalyptic, this arrival of the Kingdom in the coming of Jesus constitutes not simply a national but also a *cosmic* turning-point (Mark 1:15; cf. 2: 21,22).

In the triple tradition common to Mark, Matthew, and Luke, a sequence of utterances emerges especially in the early chapters, which, from the viewpoint of Austinian logical analysis may be viewed as *exercitive* language-functions within a broader category of *performative utterances*. Jesus says to the paralytic: "My son, your sins are [hereby] forgiven" (Mark 2:5; par. Matt. 9:2; Luke 5:20). Mark and Matthew use the present, which is typical of, though not decisive for, performative utterances (*aphientai*); Luke uses the perfect (*apheōntai*) which Marshall explains as expressing "the abiding *force*" (sic) of the forgiveness.[64] Jesus' effective words of exorcism (Mark 1:25, "be silent, come out of him") are interpreted in the triple tradition not primarily as miracle as such, but as Messianic verbal-deeds which *in the speaking constitute* the binding of the "strong man" and the *act of plundering* his goods (Mark 3: 23–27; par. Matt. 12: 22–30; Luke 11: 14,15, 17–23). They meet Austin's criterion for *illocutionary speech-acts*: "the performance of an act *in* saying something".[65] The sovereign, authoritative, *exercitive* utterance: "Peace! Be still", subjugates the winds and waves, similarly *in* the act of being uttered. (Mark 4:35–41; par. Matt. 8: 23–27; Luke 8:22–25). Matthew, Mark, and Luke, all make room for the reader to reflect on the presuppositions which allow the exercitive to function effectively: "Who, then, is this . . . (Matt. 8:27, what sort of person is this?) that even the wind and sea obey him?"

Interpreters and commentators, especially on the Matthean text, see at once existential parallels in the invitation to trust on the part of the storm-tossed church. Matthew's readers are invited to trust in their Lord. G. Bornkamm expounds this theme, in his essay on the Stilling of the Storm.[66] Matthew portrays Jesus, David Hill comments, as having "divine authority over creation, a man in whom absolute confidence may be placed because He is able to protect disciples in times of stress and danger".[67] The implications go even further. R.T. France adds: "In the Old Testament it was a mark of the sovereignty of God Himself that the sea obeyed His orders (Job. 38: 8–11, Psalm 65: 5–8; 89: 8,9); a passage like Psalm 107: 23–32 must have been in Matthew's mind as he narrated the story."[68]

If we move from the triple tradition to material which also reflects the theology of individual evangelists, we may identify a number of other examples of exercitive, verdictive, and behabitive categories (or in Searle's terminology, directive, declarative, and expressive speech-acts), each of which carries an existential resonance for the present reader which does not exhaust its further truth-claims. A number of writers, including Otto Michel, A. Vögtle, and B.J. Hubbard have examined the *act of authorization* in post-resurrection commissioning of the disciples (Matt. 28: 18–20). This, in Michel's view represents a key to Matthew's Christology: "All authority in heaven and on earth has been given me. Go, therefore, and make disciples of all nations . . . "⁶⁹ Here the logic on which the *exercitive speech-act of authorization depends* is made clear and fully explicit: "All authority in heaven and on earth has been given me." Graham Stanton approves of Bornkamm's comment that the text functions as an endorsement by the exalted Lord of the authority of the commands of the earthly Jesus for his church, and as a pledge of his presence.⁷⁰

Three sub-categories of performative or illocutionary force are used: "Go therefore and make disciples" (Matt. 28:19) constitutes an *exercitive* which appoints, commands and *assigns* an "institutional" *role*. "Teaching them to observe all that I have commanded you" (Matt. 28:20) combines the *exercitive* and *behabitive* dimensions of *authorization*. "Lo, I am with you always, to the close of the age." (Matt. 28:20) represents a classic example of the sub-category identified by Austin, Evans, Searle, and Recanati as *"commissives"*. Bornkamm observes that the words embody the self-commitment of a *pledge* or promise. If a present-day reader feels any sense of identification with the addressees, the effect of the language transcends information, or narrative report. A commission *assigns* a task and a role; an authorization *confers* a status; a pledge or a promise *invites* trust, and also action which takes the promise for its basis.

We have not yet answered the question, however, which arises about a relative reticence found in the words of Jesus, and often in the evangelists to make explicit statements about the basis on which his own illocutionary utterances and the disciples' existential commitments were valid. One part of the answer is that Christology remained incomplete before the resurrection awaiting divine corroboration. As James Dunn urges, Christology concerns not only the life and consciousness of the pre-resurrection Jesus, but "the whole Christ-event", including "reflection on, and elaboration of, Jesus' own sense of sonship and eschatological mission."⁷¹ But a further consideration also arises from Jesus' *uniqueness*. It was important that *an understanding of Jesus*, seen in his words and in his *completed work*, should *govern interpretations of conventional "messianic" language, rather than that ready-made assumptions about the meaning of such language should govern an understanding of Jesus.*

In this respect Perrin is right to note a certain open-ended quality, for example, in Jesus' language about the Kingdom of God.⁷² It cannot become wholly clear what is the nature of God's active reign until Jesus has demonstrated its context paradigmatically in his life and work, including the cross and resurrection. Similarly language about the Son of Man remains open to a variety of interpretations.⁷³ Whether we seek to use contemporary Aramaic, Dan. 7:13, 14, or Psalm 8:4 as a key to its interpretation, it allows no packaged pre-judgments about Jesus, but invites understanding of Jesus only on the grounds of an identity revealed in his authoritative and saving words and deeds. Language about the Kingdom of God, however, does include the dual dimensions of the ontological and the existential. The Kingdom of God in the apocalyptic tradition represents God's cosmic reign; "taking upon oneself the yoke of the Kingdom" in rabbinic traditions entails human obedience and response.

The evangelists themselves also include material which reflects a more explicit Christology. There is general agreement that Mark embodies a central concern about Christology, which he unfolds in a distinctively narrative form. Robert Fowler (1981) Rhoads and Michie (1982), Ernest Best (1983) and Eugene Boring (1985) all stress the Marcan use of narrative devices to involve the reader in reaching judgments about Christology, and we shall return to consider their arguments when we examine reader-response theory.[74] Graham Stanton distinguishes between Christological assumptions which operate *within* the narrative world of Mark, and what Mark addresses to the reader. Mark tells us in his opening line that Jesus is "Christ, the Son of God" (Mark 1:1): "As the story unfolds the true identity of Jesus is either kept secret from the participants in the story or misunderstood by them, but for the reader there is no secret."[75] In a recent number of *Semeia* on speech-act theory Hugh White and Michael Hancher relate speech-act theory to narrative hermeneutics.[76] But their main concern is the broader one of locating speech-act theory in relation to Ricoeur, Ebeling, Barthes, and Derrida rather than applying the theory more concretely to specific texts. Hancher rightly regards Derrida's interest in the theory as a paradoxical "betrayal" of it, since it is undermined if we eliminate the author. Form criticism itself embodies an emphasis on *kerygma* or "proclamation" (Kierkegaard), on functionalism (the early Heidegger), and on address (pietism), as against bare description and report.

Meanwhile Matthew's Christology demonstrates a relation to speech-act theory perhaps more clearly than Mark, not least because Matthew's interest lies in the authority of Jesus' *words and teaching*. Although he leaves his most explicit Christological declaration to the post-resurrection commissioning in Matt. 28: 18–20, throughout his gospel Matthew interweaves inextricably his account of Jesus's teaching and commands with an emphasis on the uniqueness of his person. John P. Meier admirably captures the Matthean perspective. Meier writes, "What Jesus teaches depends on his own person for its truth, validity, and permanence. Teacher and teaching become inextricably tied together. You do not fully understand what the teaching is unless you understand who the teacher is. You cannot accept the teaching as true unless you accept the teacher as your Lord . . . "[77] But why should this be the case, and why should the reader be involved? The answer concerns the Christological presuppositions on the basis of which the series of illocutionary acts depicted by Matthew operate: language which brings forgiveness; language which stills the storm; language which authorizes and assigns a role. If the implicit Christology is false, the entire performative and exercitive dimension collapses and falls to the ground as nothing more than a construct of pious human imagination.

Before we conclude this section, we should note the constructive and positive work undertaken by Johannes G. du Plessis in his Stellenbosch study *Clarity and Obscurity* (1985). Generously he comments about the origins of his research: "The present study is conceived as an extension of the line of research initiated by Thiselton (1970), Aurelio (1977) and Arens (1982). Thiselton introduced the speech-act theory (which was developed by Austin, 1962) into parable research . . . This was taken up by Aurelio . . . Arens distinguishes his study from Thiselton's and Aurelio's by pointing out that they attempted to analyse the parables as individual speech-acts.[78] Arens, on the other hand, turns his attention to a broader model of understanding within which the nature of the language of Jesus as communicative action becomes evident.

E. Arens rightly recognizes that if he wishes to construct a speech-act theory of parables which could become the basis for a broader theological theory of action, he must look "behind" the New Testament parable-texts to take account of the entire speech-acts which are performed. Johannes du Plessis accepts this, but also argues (with W.S. Vorster) that the context of speech-acts also embraces the wider textual embedding of the parables. The conclusion of du Plessis' detailed argument entirely coheres with the argument of the present chapter, with specific reference to the parables of Jesus. He writes: "The thesis of this study is that the primary function of the parables in the narrative world of the gospels is *to establish Jesus*, as the narrator of the parables, *in an authoritative position towards his addressees*. The clarity and/or obscurity of the parables are intrinsic aspects of the parables as symbolic discourse. Both these aspects are manipulated to support Jesus' authoritative position. The gospels report (*sic*) the relationship between Jesus and his addressees in order that the recipients of the gospels may enter into the same dependent *relationship with Jesus* . . . The obscurity and the perplexity are outshone by the focus on the power and authority of Jesus . . . The parables' main aim is to let the recipients *recognize Jesus' authority* as the sole source of a salvific relationship with God."[79]

J.G. du Plessis' arguments throughout his study, however, draw not on theology, but on a view of the parables as part of a process of communicative action, examined in the light of the work of Austin, Grice, Searle, T. Aurelio, E. Arens (1982) and Geoffrey N. Leech (1983). He discusses Grice's principle of co-operative goals in his maxims of conversational implicature, to which we allude in more detail later in this book in our discussion of Ricoeur's narrative theory. In the context of the parables du Plessis takes up Wolfgang Iser's work (1980) on the interaction between the explicit and the implicit, between revelation and concealment, in texts. He distinguishes between "fictionality", which is a possible attribute not of texts but of the process of communication between author and audience, and "fictiveness", which can characterize texts, textual content, or textual devices. "Fictive" denotes a product of the imagination; "fictional" denotes a certain mode or category of speech-act. Although he cautiously accepts the operational value of Ricoeur's notion of narrative as "redescription" (which we shall examine in chapter X), du Plessis calls attention to the referential and contextual frames which constrain its limits.

In chapters X and XV we develop these points further with reference to John Searle's essay on the logic of fiction and to the important work of Nicholas Wolterstorff in his valuable and closely-argued philosophical study *Works and Worlds of Art* (1980). With meticulous detail Wolterstorff demonstrates the role of human agency in performing actions which "*count as*" performances of other actions. His contrast between "cause-generation" and "count-generation" runs closely parallel to the contrast in Austin and Evans between causal and performative force, and he explicitly utilizes Searle's notion of "institutional facts" in which "X counts as Y in context C". On this basis we arrive at a philosophy of language in which the projection of "worlds" by human agents may include both a given propositional content *and a variety of possible illocutionary effects.*

It is important to note that Wolterstorff, Searle, and du Plessis all underline the fundamental *role of human agents within an extra-linguistic world for determining the operative nature and effect of certain speech-acts.* Differences between fiction, falsehood, historical report, or history-like narrative depends on what *status, stance, commitments and responsibilities* have been presupposed and accepted by authoral agents. They do not depend simply on judgments by communities of readers about systems of literary effects detached from the world of causal and count-generation. We elaborate these points in chapters X and XV, underlining the capacities of a single speech-act to perform a *variety* of illocutionary functions. In chapter XV we also relate these issues to the problem of "*author's intention*".

Du Plessis also notes, in common with Aurelio (and also my own earlier work) that parables may enact *various illocutionary acts at the same time.* Thus the Parable of the Lost Son (Luke 15: 11–32) *both directs and invites* a potentially hostile audience of critics to a relationship of unconditional sharing and receiving, on the basis of Jesus' own "commitment" to sinners. Du Plessis agrees with Robert Funk that the audience has freedom to opt either for grace or for justice. But he dissents from Funk that the message cannot be specified further. Its "implicatures" also reveal the estrangement of "elder sons" and the experience of "coming home" as the security of the father's creative and sharing love.

In contrast to the more open-ended and plurivalent interpretations of parables suggested by Funk, Crossan, Dan Otto Via, Susan Wittig, and Mary Ann Tolbert, J.G. du Plessis argues that their status and function as total speech-acts includes *both* their immediate conversational contexts in the gospel texts *and* their speech-relations to the speaker and to the audience. He insists that in many instances parables represent "gambits in a broader conversational pattern". They belong to a strategy of "*macro speech*", to which an *authoritative* dimension is integral. Du Plessis applies this approach to specific passages in a series of studies, in which he emphasizes extra-linguistic reality (1984), conversational implicature (1985, 1988, 1991) and the dimension of pragmatics (1987).[80] While he acknowledges the impetus of my work for his research (1970), he explores speech-act theory especially through Grice, Arens and Leech, whereas my own work enters into dialogue mainly with Searle and Recanati. By parallel routes we draw similar implications about the basis of operative currency for Christological texts, even if we do so in different ways. Christological truth constitutes the basis on which, to borrow Recanati's phrase, there is more than a merely textual or intralinguistic *claim* to perform acts in speech-utterances like those of actors on a stage; *the acts are effectively performed. They bring about a transformation in the extra-linguistic relationship between the speaker and the audience, and invite the reader to participate in that extra-linguistic transformation and relationship.*

4. Illocutionary Acts and Performatives in Searle and in Recanati: Directions of Fit between Words and the World

John R. Searle explicitly acknowledges an indebtedness to two of his former teachers, J.L. Austin and P.F. Strawson. Following Austin, and less directly the later Wittgenstein, Searle declares: "The unit of linguistic communication is not, as has generally been supposed, the symbol, word or sentence, or even the token of the word, symbol or sentence, but rather the production or issuance of the symbol or word or sentence in the performance of the speech-act".[81] Searle now elaborates a complex theoretical framework on the basis of which utterances perform a variety of specific acts, which in turn also entail a given propositional content. He draws attention to the nature of "speaking" as part of a rule-governed form of behaviour. But he also stresses that in Saussurian terms this does not imply that he is restricting his attention to Saussure's *parole*; Searle is also raising deeper questions about the presuppositions which constitute *langue*.[82]

This concern to construct a wider and deeper theoretical model represents a distinctive advance on Austin's work. For whereas Searle views his own work as a contributor to the philosophy of language, Austin had adopted the so-called "ordinary language" approach of Oxford linguistic philosophy. Although he raises philosophically serious questions about moral responsibility and truth in such essays as "A Plea for Excuses" and "Truth", and although the volume edited by K.T. Fann examines the philosophical issues which Austin raises, nevertheless his work on illocutionary acts and performative language tended to operate at the level of every-day examples.[83] Nevertheless it is worth pausing briefly to comment further on the background of speech-act theory in Austin's work, before introducing the specific methodological or theoretical devices with which we are most immediately concerned mainly from Searle but also from Recanati.

Austin does speak of the general contextual *presupposition* on the basis of which illocutionary acts operate, but he is more rigorous in his scrutiny of every-day examples than in a construction of a theoretical frame. His examples remain inimitable. He asks: how effective is the action of a team-captain in saying "I pick George", if George grunts "Not playing"?[84] If a conventional procedure has to be *accepted* for an utterance to constitute an act, what happens if someone concludes a quarrel with the words "My seconds will call on you", but we simply shrug it off?[85] How operative, if at all, are the words "I baptize thee", if the local minister is holding the wrong baby, or if he continues "I baptize thee infant no. 2704"?[86] What happens if the Vice Chancellor or the Archbishop says "I open this library", and the key snaps in the lock?[87]

Austin's examples serve to make clear the difference between *causal* power and *institutional* operativeness, which provided the basis for Evans' work on biblical texts. Thus a year after his work was published, Donald Evans's constructive book appeared. In 1974 I attempted to draw on Austin's work a second time (the first was the 1970 comparison between Austin and Fuchs in context of parable study) to challenge prevailing assumptions about the language of "power" and more specifically blessing and cursing, in the Old Testament.[88]

A very large number of Old Testament specialists had appealed to a supposedly "Hebraic" belief in the "innate power of words" to explain, for example, why Isaac, having been deceived into blessing the wrong son, could not revoke his words of blessing (Gen. 27: 33–37). The same explanation was offered to account for the fact that apparently Balaam could not revoke his blessing of Israel, in the face of pressure from Balak (Num. 23:20). Gerhard von Rad and many others claimed that Hebrews held a view of language akin to word-magic, which saw it as "an objective reality endowed with mysterious power."[89] Other scholars used colourful metaphors of military weaponry. Grether and Zimmerli ascribed to "Hebraic" thought a view of words as like "a missile with a time-fuse". Dürr described Hebrew words as "a power-laden" causal force. E. Jacob saw the Hebrew view of words as like "a projectile shot into the enemy camp whose explosion must sometimes be awaited but which is always inevitable."[90]

In Austin's terms, however, none of this line of reasoning was necessary. Isaac and Balaam were aware of operative conventional procedures for *blessings*. But *no procedure* existed or was *generally accepted* for *revoking* them. It would be like the bride or bridegroom saying solemnly "I do", and then expecting that the utterance, "Sorry, I have changed my mind", could function with equal *performative* force as part of a supplementary appendix to the marriage service. In Austinian terms, it would be like requesting a service of unbaptism. But "I unbaptize this infant . . . " would not be a *performative* utterance, because such a procedure neither exists nor is accepted. In the 1974 study I sought to apply this approach more broadly to other aspects of supposed "power of words". "Power", I concluded, does not function *causally* on the basis of a supposedly "Hebrew" view of language; but as operational force resting on procedures and presuppositions in a *context of promise* which related to the *covenantal* God. It related to *institutional* features in Israel's life which set the stage for *effective speech-acts*.

John Searle moved well beyond Austin in developing a wider, more rigorous, and more systematic framework of language-theory which addresses a broader range of issues. He published essays and collections in this area successively in 1969, 1979, 1980, 1983, and 1985 and at other intervals up to the present.[91] Austin had worked with the three-fold categories of locutionary, illocutionary, and perlocutionary acts. He defined these, respectively, as (i) a *locutionary* act *of* speaking which is "roughly equivalent to uttering a certain sentence with a certain sense and reference"; (ii) *illocutionary acts* such as informing, ordering, warning, undertaking, i.e. utterances which have a certain (conventional) force"; and (iii) *perlocutionary acts*: namely, "what we bring about or achieve *by* saying something, such as convincing, persuading, deterring."[92] The fundamental difference between the second and third categories is that the second involves broadly *institutional* procedures, whereas the third may involve only *causal* power.

Searle accepts, although with some reservation, Austin's term "illocutionary acts", which typically involve the use of such verbs as "warn", "order", "approve", "promise", and "request". But he supplements them with three additional cross-categories of language-function which partly overlap, but also draw attention to other aspects of wider issues: (i) *performing utterance acts*, in which words or sentences are uttered; (ii) *performing propositional acts*, in which referring and predicating take place; and (iii) *performing illocutionary acts*, in which statements, questions, promises, or commands become operative. Searle declares: "In performing an illocutionary act one characteristically performs propositional acts and utterance acts."[93]

This gives rise to a fundamental distinction which remains operative in Searle's entire body of writings, including his work on intentionality. He distinguishes between *"illocutionary force indicators"* (usually denoted by a variable F) and *"proposition indicators"* (denoted by p).94 The variable theoretical illocution "$F(p)$" may more specifically take the form of a warning "$W(p)$", or a promise "$Pr.(p)$". Thus for example, "I promise that I shall be there" may be represented as "F [I promise] (p) [I shall be there]" or as "$Pr(p)$". On the other hand, as Austin (followed by Recanati) acknowledges the F dimension may often be merely implicit rather than explicit: "I'll be there" may in some contexts be represented logically as ("$Pr(p)$", but not in all contexts. The negation of a propositional *content* can thus be kept distinct from the negation of illocutionary *force*. "I promise not to come" would be denoted by "$Pr.(-p)$"; whereas "I do not promise to come" would take the form "$-Pr(p)$".

This distinction is constructive for understanding the central issue discussed in the present chapter about hermeneutical theory and biblical texts. There are two separate points which need to be noted. First, Searle's distinction sheds light on the logical fallacy reflected in the overworn dualism of Kierkegaard, Heidegger, and Bultmann between on the one hand, description, objectification, report, and proposition, and on the other hand, address, promise, understanding and self-involvement. Biblical texts frequently *address the reader as warnings, commands, invitations, judgments, promises, or pledges of love.* But often these speech-acts also embody a propositional content. Thus, typically, the pattern of the earliest kerygma takes the form "$F(p)$", i.e. "We preach (F) a Christ crucified (p)" (1 Cor. 1:23). Sometimes the dual function, as Searle has pointed out, may simply be implied, each by the other in the same utterance. Thus in the previous section on Pauline Christology we argued that the confession "Jesus is Lord" (1 Cor. 12:3) is neither simply p nor simply F but $F(p)$, or more specifically a commissive which entails the assertion of a state of affairs: "$Com(p)$."

The second point is even more fundamental. In his book *Expression and Meaning*, Searle introduces an illuminating and *far-reaching difference between the logic of promise* (and related language-functions) and *the logic of assertion*. He described the difference as "*differences in the direction of fit between words and the world.*" Some illocutions have part of their purpose or "point", "*to get the words* (more strictly, their propositional content) *to match the world.*" This is the case with *assertions*. But others have the inverse function: "*to get the world to match the words*".95 This is the case with *promises* and *commands*.

By way of illustration from everyday life, Searle borrows an analogy from Elizabeth Anscombe's work on intention. We are asked to envisage a person who goes shopping, and is followed by a detective. The shopper has a list of words written on a slip of paper: "butter, eggs, bread, bacon . . ." His or her aim is so to transact the task as *to make the world of reality match the words* of the list. The transference of goods *changes the extra-linguistic world in accordance with the words* which embody *instructions, promises, or intentions.* The detective, on the other hand, does the converse. He carefully observes and notes down what takes place, i.e. describes the world as it is. The purpose of his list is to provide a *descriptive report in words which match the reality of the world.* The propositional *content* (p) of the two lists will be identical: butter, eggs, bread, bacon. Their *force* (F) will be quite different, and will reflect a *different direction of fit between language and the world.* A final point in this analogy brings home sharply the limitations and weakness of hermeneutics which concern only intra-linguistic worlds in handling biblical texts. If, on reaching home, the *detective* realizes that he or she has made a mistake in a word of his or her *report*, there is need only to erase "margarine" and substitute "butter". But if the *shopper* has made a parallel mistake in his or her *performing* of instructions, his or her spouse may well send the shopper back to the store to rectify the problem. It is not a merely "intra-linguistic" affair.

Recanati takes up the same analogy to illustrate differences in the "'direction of correspondence' between words and the world".[96] As we have seen, Searle, Austin, and Recanati diverge in their specific identifications of sub-categories of illocutionary acts, although Searle regards Austin's work as an "excellent basis" for development. More fundamentally, whereas Searle questions the sharpness of Austin's distinction between "meaning" and "force", Recanati defends it. Specifically, Recanati argues, "If in virtue of the meaning it expresses, an utterance presents itself as having a particular illocutionary force, there is no certainty that it really does have the force that it has . . . attributed to itself. Taken in Austin's sense, the force of an utterance must always go beyond its meaning; the latter includes a 'projection' of the utterance's illocutionary force, not *the force itself,* which must be inferred by the hearer on the basis of the supposed intentions of the speaker."[97] This entails a study of contextual inference.

For the purposes of this chapter, however, Austin, Searle, and Recanati offer very broadly similar sub-categories of illocutionary acts, and Searle and Recanati agree on the suggestive importance of the model of "direction of fit" or "direction of correspondence" between words and the world. These represent our two working sets of methodological tools for the remainder of this chapter. Searle revises Austin's sub-categories partly because he claims that Austin has confused illocutionary *acts* with illocutionary *verbs.* Searle proposes to substitute: *assertives, directives, commissives* (Austin's sub-category is accepted) *expressives* and *declarations.* These replace Austin's list of expositives, exercitives, behabitives, verdictives, and (commonly to Searle, Recanati, and Austin) commissives. To place "assertives" among sub-categories of force may seem surprising, but it brings some advantages.

It enables us to take account of different degrees of force with which an assertion states a propositional content: putting something forward as a tentative hypothesis stands at one end of the spectrum; insisting on the truth of something with total conviction stands at the other end. (This view has the further advantage of discouraging the disastrous Bultmannian antithesis between "faith", on the one hand, and positive response to the force of rational argument and evidence on the other. For affirmations of belief or faith combine *the two overlapping forces of assertions and commissives*).

It is not entirely clear, however, that Searle's scheme improves on Austin's at every point. Dieter Wunderlich argues, "There is no clear classification of speech acts. Neither Austin's nor Searle's nor anybody else's attempts are really convincing."[98] But the value of the categories is operational and pragmatic in relation to given arguments and purposes. Issues of interpretative strategy will determine which system better matches specific questions and purposes in view. The major advantage of Searle's system is the possibility of tracing his own clear correlation between this classification of illocutions and his *directional* analysis of a word-to-world or world-to-word fit. *Assertives* fit reality (as we have seen) in a *words-to-world* direction. *Directives* and *commissives* (which include commands and promises) fit reality in the opposite direction of *world-to-words*. *What is spoken shapes what will be. Expressives* may presuppose either direction of fit. *Declarations* in their very utterance *bring about* a particular direction of fit. Recanati's definition of declaratives is broader than Searle's. He argues that declarative sentences are "force-neutral", but also have illocutionary *potential*. All genuinely *performative* utterances "aim to *bring about*, not simply describe, the state of affairs they represent and that constitutes their propositional content."[99]

Care needs to be taken with the terminology adopted by Searle and by Recanati, which we shall consistently follow. In summary, linguistic *description* reflects or portrays prior states of affairs in word-*to-world* language; whereas world-*to*-word language in principle can bring about *change to the world to match the uttered word*, of which *promise* is the clearest paradigm. Searle retains these classifications and their corresponding directional relations in his subsequent book *Intentionality*.[100] From his work as a whole we may note two further points before we turn to the biblical texts. First, Searle underlines the importance of the institutional and extra-linguistic factors which were noted and expounded by Austin and Evans, but with special reference to *directives* (cf. Austin's *exercitives*). He declares, "It is *only given such institutions as the church, the law, private property, the state, and the special position of the speaker and hearer within these institutions* that we can excommunicate, appoint, give and bequeath . . ."[101]

Searle excepts from this principle only certain utterances of God "let there be light" (Gen. 1:3), and such intra-linguistic performances as "naming". But even here, many divine utterances perform actions because they operate commissively and directively as part of the covenant promise of God, and such intra-linguistic activities as "naming" often depend on institutional factors. For example, if Joe Bloggs, the ship's engineer, "names" the ship, this naming is of a different order from when the shipping magnate's wife names it *performatively* at the appropriate ceremony. The act of naming a child on the birth-certificate by parents is also *performative* in a way which is not the case if a "name" is suggested by a passing school enemy.

Second, Searle underlines the extra-linguistic factors involved in the logic of promise. Promise is typical of the force of many biblical texts. We cannot ignore the wishes and purposes of the speaker and the hearer in the promised commissive-transaction. In his book *Intentionality* this becomes part of Searle's wider and masterly discussion in which he insists, convincingly, that, provided that we do not view it primarily as a "mental act" the notion of the *purposive directedness of the author's intention against a background network of behavioural and contextual factors* is not only logically viable, but also logically *essential* for accounts of meaning that are balanced and comprehensive.[102] Whether we are speaking of intention or of promise, the logic of the concept and its practical operation in life presuppose some reference to the *wishes* of the speaker, and in the case of promise, both the speaker and the hearer.

If it were otherwise, we could not logically distinguish promise from threat. Searle observes, "A promise is a pledge to do something for you, not to you; but a threat is a pledge to do something to you, not for you. A promise is defective if the thing promised is something the promisee does *not want done*... Furthermore, a *promise*, unlike an *invitation*, normally requires some sort of *occasion or situation that calls for the promise*."[103] The essential feature of the logic of promising is the attitude of commitment on the part of the speaker: "It is the undertaking of an obligation to perform a certain act."[104]

Searle's work thus seems to embody several theoretical developments beyond Austin, which we shall now examine in relation to specific biblical texts. First, he has modified Austin's sub-categories of illocutionary acts. Second, he has classified and set in a broader theoretical frame the interpersonal and institutional backgrounds against which illocutions become operative. Third, he has defended the role of purpose, directedness, or intentionality on the part of the speaker. Fourth, he has paid special attention to the logic of promise and other commissives. Most important of all he has drawn a very important distinction between language which operates in the direction of word-to-world, and language which operates in the direction of world-to-word.

Recanati parts company from Searle at several major points, including the issue of whether utterance interpretation can be reduced to sentence interpretation. But from the point of view of the present argument, Recanati's emphasis on the role of speaker or writer and addressee in an extra-linguistic context strengthens the significance of his work. It is possible for an explicit performative to be self-referential, as Austin and Benveniste have urged. Sometimes this is marked by some such phrase as "hereby". But the intralinguistic markers of performative force are no guarantee of its effective extralinguistic operation. Hence, Recanati rightly concludes, if we want to assess performative force not, as it were, like the activities of actors on a stage but as real-life acts, we need to look "behind the scenes" at the extra-linguistic context.

5. The "World-to-Word Fit" of a Hermeneutic of Promise: Types of Illocutions; the Work of Christ in Paul; Promises in the Old Testament

We have spoken regularly of "transforming texts". When texts transform readers, situations, or reality, this force and function, as John Searle has pointed out, is characteristically that of *promise or pledge*, or sometimes that of *authorization or command.* The speaking of the words constitutes *an act which shapes a state of affairs, provided that* certain inter-personal or institutional states of affairs also hold. For example, as we saw in our discussion of Christological texts, whether the utterance "your sins are forgiven you" (Matt. 9:2) actually changes anything depends on the authority and institutional status of the speaker outside language, among other things. On the other hand, the declaration that a particular state of affairs is true ("Christ was buried, and was raised on the third day", 1 Cor. 15:4) has an *assertive* force, in which the *state of affairs* to be reported *determines the word* that is spoken. Characteristically *promise shapes world-to-word, assertion shapes word-to-world.*

Some biblical texts perform both functions simultaneously. Sometimes the two components remain distinct: "We preach a Christ crucified" $F(p)$, 1 Cor. 1:23. Sometimes the same form operates with dual force: "Jesus is Lord", $F(p)$, i.e. *commissive*, "We are Christ's bondslaves", (*world-to-word*); and *assertive* "God made Christ Lord" (*word-to-world*).

Although we note Searle's point that Austin sometimes confused illocutionary *acts* with a list of verbs in a given language which was used typically to perform such acts, the lists of such verbs drawn up under respective sub-headings by Austin, Evans, Recanati, and Searle himself help the interpreter to identify potential instances of illocutionary acts. A survey of a concordance to the biblical texts suggests that at least seventy verbs invite sub-classification as particular types of potential illocutionary acts. We may accept Dieter Wunderlich's assessment (noted above) that neither Austin's categories nor Searle's modifications of Austin, nor Recanati's modifications of Searle, may be regarded as definitive. The following verbs therefore are for the most part identified in terms of more than one system, and sometimes occur unavoidably in more than one sub-category. Wunderlich's call for a "workable" scheme is not invalidated by theoretical controversies between Searle, Recanati, and his own work.

Exercitives or *directives* include: appoint, adopt, bless, charge, choose, command, commission, confer, consecrate, convict, correct, curse, decree, direct, forbid, forgive, guarantee, hallow, invite, justify, name, ordain, pardon, preach, rebuke, send. *Commissives* include: acknowledge, adopt (also directive) bless (also directive), give, love (also expressive), magnify, obey, pledge, promise, repent (also expressive), swear, testify, trust, witness. *Declaratives* or *verdictives* include acquit, correct, declare, deny, excuse, judge, justify (also directive) love (also commissive and expressive), pardon, preach (also directive), proclaim, reckon, reproach (also expressive). *Expressives* or *behabitives* include: appeal, confess, cry, complain, comfort, encourage, entrust, exhort, intercede, love (also commissive), magnify, mourn, praise, rejoice, repent, salute, thank, urge, and worship. This list does not claim to be comprehensive.

The biblical texts abound in examples of occurrences of these verbs in institutional, situational, and inter-personal contexts which render them performative speech-acts. One such context is that of *liturgy or worship*, of which the Psalms contain many instances. Thus the utterance "*I give thanks* to Thee, O Lord, with my whole heart" (Psalm 138:1) does not function to inform God about a state of mind, but has the force of an *act* of thanksgiving. Similarly, "*We give thanks* to Thee, O God, *We give thanks* to Thee" (Psalm 75:1) is followed by an *act* of invocation and by an *act* of praise: "*We call on Thy name*, and recount Thy wondrous deeds." Liturgy typically involves what Searle terms expressive illocutions, and Austin, behabitive performatives.

Institutional roles also provide a setting for illocutions and performatives. As an *apostle*, Paul writes: "*I urge you*, then be imitators of me." (1 Cor. 4:18). In his role as *king* and *intercessor* for the nation, Hezekiah declares: "*the good Lord pardon* every one who sets his heart to seek God" (2 Chron. 30: 18,19). As bearer of the authority of God, Jesus declares "My son, your sins are *forgiven*" (Matt. 9:2; cf. John 20:23). The apostles combine exercitive authority and commissive promise in the utterance: "*Peace be to this house*" (Luke 10:5). Similarly, Jesus declares, "*Peace I leave with you*" (John 14:27), which constitutes the making of a promise and the giving of a gift, not simply a statement about a situation.

Some illocutions presuppose only a situation of inter-personal transaction, rather than more complex institutional factors. Thus the language of love can be spoken as an *act* of love: "*I love thee* O Lord, my strength ... my rock, my fortress, my deliverer" (Psalm 18: 1,2). The testimony of a witness may rest either on a formal or situational context: "*We testify* that the Father has sent the Son" (1 John 4:14) "*I affirm and testify* in the Lord ... " (Eph. 4:17). But other kinds of illocutions demand more formal relationships of status. In Zechariah an accusation is pre-empted by invoking the authority of God: "The Lord said, '*The Lord rebuke you* ... the Lord, who has chosen Jerusalem rebuke you'" (Zech. 3:2).

What is important about all these uses of language, however, is that they leave neither the speaker nor the hearer uninvolved and unchanged. In Evans's terminology they are self-involving; in Searle's terminology, all of the above examples operate in a *word-to-world* direction. Before we examine the effect of this principle for some major issues in biblical interpretation, we may note in passing that prior to Austin's work, the later Wittgenstein had noted this principle. He compares the respective logical force of "I am in pain" and "I love you." He comments, "One does not say: 'That was not true pain, or it would not have gone off so quickly'". But one *could* say this of *love*: "love is not a feeling."[105] Love, if it has operative meaning, has *commissive* consequences, so that the person who says "I love you" *behaves* in the way indicated by the words, or they become empty. One could not say "For a second I felt deep grief".[106] In contexts where we say "I believe", "I love", "I grieve", "I mourn", or "I give", Wittgenstein urges, "My own relation to my words is wholly different from other people."[107]

This constitutes, in effect, a further commentary on the logic and hermeneutic of promise. When God declares "I have loved you with an everlasting love" (Jer. 31:3) the utterance entails a *world-to-word fit* in which the word guarantees that compatible patterns of action and states of affairs will come about, and incompatible ones be excluded. We shall argue shortly that the "world-to-word fit" aspect of biblical texts arises from the prominence of the category of *promise* in the biblical writings. Divine promise bridges the gap between what "is" and what "ought to be", and is interwoven with the themes of covenant and of eschatology. Nevertheless the contextual and institutional frame within which promises become effective also concerns *states of affairs*. Side by side with *promissory word-to-world language*, therefore, we also find *world-to-word language of assertion*.

With this principle in mind, we turn to Pauline language about the power of the cross. We address in particular E.P. Sanders' claims about Paul. First, Sanders follows Stendahl in arguing against the traditional Lutheran interpretation that Paul first begins with the problem of human sin and then expounds the cross as its "solution". Second, Sanders draws a sharp distinction between "atonement" language and "participatory" language as ways of understanding Paul's theology of the cross. We shall argue that Sanders is wrong to give priority to the participatory model. Speech-act theory suggests that the *atonement language* constitutes *assertions about states of affairs* in which the *language reflects an accomplished reality*. But *participatory language* operates with the reverse direction of fit: it is *eschatological* and *promissory* language which *shapes actualities to the word*. It is part of the language of *transformation* but it depends for its operative effectiveness on the extra-linguistic state of affairs which the *atonement* language *asserts*.

In relation to current issues in Pauline interpretation, this seems partly to confirm (although also to modify) one recent emphasis and seriously to question another. First, it largely coheres with, but also sets in a new light, the emphasis since the 1970s (following initially some of Stendahl's questions in 1963) that Rom. 9:1–11:36 constitutes no mere appendix to Romans 1–8, but, rather, represents the theological crown, or at least continuation of the argument. Up until the 1970s, the common denominator between the reader and Paul was identified, as Stendahl expressed it, in the common human experience of bondage to sin which Paul articulates in Rom. 7:7–25. This approach matches both a Lutheran and an existential hermeneutic. But Stendahl, Sanders, and more recently others including Francis Watson and A.J.M. Wedderburn, have argued for a different emphasis.[108]

Sanders writes: "It seems likely ... that Paul's thought did not run from plight to solution, but rather from solution to plight. The attempts to argue that Romans 7 shows the frustration which Paul felt during his life as a practising Jew have now mostly been given up."[109] The "I" of these verses is not necessarily autobiographical. The major concern turns on how God determines to fulfil his covenant promises to his disobedient people.[110] What happens when God accepts the commissive force of a pledge, but his people effectively do not?

The key passages in Romans, including Romans 8, re-affirm the *world-to-word* effectiveness of the divine promise; but the realities of the human situation are also described in *word-to-world* assertions about the human plight. Nevertheless, this is not only a contextually-relevant state of affairs; it is also to be *asserted that God has acted decisively in Christ*. Two sets of assertions (word-to-world) provide the context for questions about the effective power of promise (world-to-word). Neither dimension is addressed without reference to the other. Stendahl is correct when he tartly observes that whether we try to interpret everything in existential terms depends on whether "we happen to be more interested in ourselves than in God or the fate of his creation."[111] In Markus Barth's judgment, the issue centres on the faithfulness of God and on the church's acknowledgement of her "sisterly co-existence with Israel".[112]

Here, however, a second and more complex issue arises. In what way is the believer's situation affected by the coming of Christ? Is the key concept, for Paul, the "participatory" one of being-in-Christ, or does the possibility of salvation depend on the work of Christ understood as atonement? Sanders argues that the former is more important and forward-looking to the future. Atonement language merely relates to the past. But how are these two "logics" in Paul related?

First, even the "participatory" logic of being-in-Christ is complex. Schweitzer was correct to argue that being-in-Christ is an *eschatological* concept. In our terms, it has a promissory dimension. Schweitzer argued that the term applied to the new creation who were "capable of assuming the resurrection mode of existence before the general resurrection of the dead takes place."[113] He rightly declares "Being-in-Christ is not a subjective experience."[114] It refers to the "one new entity" (Gal. 3:28) which shares in Christ's death and resurrection (Rom. 6:4,5,13). Sharing in the "mystical Body of Christ" stands in contrast to being "in Adam" (1 Cor. 15: 22–27, 45; Rom. 5: 12–21).[115] Deissmann's approach in terms of experience neglects eschatology.[116]

Alfred Wikenhauser developes Schweitzer's view further. He comments, "This union with Christ has an objective character."[117] It is "not merely a subjective feeling of Christ's nearness."[118] But it is *not* the language of *bare assertion*. For, first, Christ's resurrection constitutes a *pledge* (Rom. 6:8) of that of believers, who will be caught up in God's eschatological promise (1 Cor. 15: 20, Rom. 8:29). Second, it carries with it the self-involving dimension of Christ's "living in" believers (Gal. 2:20). Hence Wikenhauser concludes, rightly, that while the term "in Christ" is objective, the progressive dimension remains "incomplete". It is *"not something final"* but is *founded on promise*.

Robert Tannehill's interpretation of Paul's language about dying and rising with Christ, and A.T. Hanson's more recent work on the paradox of the cross, make a parallel point.[120] Some references to sharing the death and resurrection of Christ include the *word-to-world* force of *assertion*. They assert the uniqueness of God's saving deed in Christ. Other Pauline texts have *directive, promissory* or *commissive* force, and concern present transformation of *world-to-word*. (2 Cor. 4:10; Rom. 6:11). If we follow Recanati rather than Searle at this particular point, while all these references may be illocutionary, only some are performative *within* this category.

In this light we may now review E.P. Sanders's claims about the work of Christ in Paul. Sanders draws a sharp contrast between texts which stress the *participatory* significance of the cross and those which speak of its *atoning* significance. To the former category belongs the key verse: "One has died for all, therefore all have died ... that those who live might live no longer for themselves but for Him who for their sake died and was raised

(2 Cor. 5: 14,15). The thrust of Sanders's argument is that in Paul "the emphasis unquestionably falls . . . not *backwards* towards the expiation of past transgressions, but *forwards* towards the assurance of life with Christ . . . This, says Paul, is the *purpose* of Christ's death."[121]

Sanders is probably correct to trace two different kinds of "logic" to the "participation" texts and "atonement" texts respectively. N.T. Wright rightly resists the attempt to press too sharply any dual logic in Paul along the lines implied by Sanders; but a duality of operative principles was noted by J.K.S. Reid a number of years ago when he observed that the Pauline texts embody *both* "a principle of correspondence" ("because He lives, we shall live also"), *and* "a principle of contrariety": ("Christ wins these benefits for us, who Himself has no need of them").[122] But the ground on which Sanders singles out the participatory category as where Paul's "emphasis unquestionably falls" is very uncertain. For it is not merely a matter of *past versus future* orientation. In Searle's terminology, the language of *atonement* makes *assertions* about the finished work of Christ, in which the direction of fit is from *world-to-word*: the word of the cross, in this context, communicates and asserts the reality of what God *has done*. That it is *past* is part of the logic of its description as a *completed* work to which humankind can contribute nothing. But the language of *participation* is bound up with *promise, commitment, declaration, and directive*: it is *word-to-world* in that it *shapes the identity* of the Christian and *creates the reality of the new creation*.

This also helps us to see more clearly the issues discussed by Schweitzer and Wikenhauser about being in Christ. The phrase embodies a multi-layered logic. Its basis is objective, but in its eschatological frame it also operates with the logic of promise. Wikenhauser rightly stresses both its objectivity and its forward-looking self-involvement, inviting progressive transformation into the image of Christ. Robert Tannehill's work on death and resurrection with Christ and A.T. Hanson's book on the cross imply a similar conclusion. Some Pauline texts are *word-to-world directives*: "Reckon yourselves to be dead to sin" (Rom. 6:11). But other Pauline texts simultaneously assert a *world-to-word* deed of God in Christ and also create and shape reality, as promise, in a *word-to-world* direction. God's "eschatological deed" constitutes "an act by which the old world is invaded and a new life in a new world is created".[123]

The proclamation of this deed is the word of the cross, and its power lies in its *operative effectiveness to transform*. From the point of view of hermeneutical theory, the upshot of all this is that a hermeneutic of self-involvement rests, in turn, on a hermeneutic of understanding, in which historical reconstruction constitutes part of a more complex and more comprehensive process. Our account of assertions or of "propositional content" follows Searle more closely than Recanati. Recanati differs from Searle on several major points, including the nature and scope of the distinction between locutionary and illocutionary acts. He criticizes Searle for, in effect, equating locutions with the propositional contents of illocutionary acts. But both Searle and Recanati, together with Austin, Daniel Vanderveken and others, agree together that factors in the speaker's (and audience's) context of utterance contribute to the conditions which effect the *actual performance* (as opposed to mere *semantic indications* of performance) of the illocutionary act.[124] Although he finds border-line counterexamples which raise some difficulties, Levinson cautiously confirms this principle.[125]

The fundamental place of *promise* in the biblical texts is confirmed with reference to a substantial area of the Old Testament in the work of my former colleague David Clines on the theme of the Pentateuch. Clines convincingly expounds the argument that the Pentateuch as a whole "receives its impetus" from "the promise to the patriarchs, with its various elements and in the various formulations."[126] The patriarchal promise is declared in Gen. 12: 1–3: "Now the Lord said to Abram, 'Go from your country . . . to the land which I will show you, and I will make of you a great nation, and I will bless you, and make your name great, so that you will be a blessing. I will bless those who bless you . . . " Clines traces seven elements of the promise, which fall into three main groups: the promise of posterity, the promise of a relationship with God, and the promise of land. The Pentateuch sets forth a partial fulfilment and partial non-fulfilment of these promises. The posterity element is dominant in Gen. 12–50; the relationship element, in Exodus and Leviticus; and the land element, in Numbers and Deuteronomy.

Clines traces what amounts to a number of promissory-commissive illocutions in the text under each heading. The promise concerning posterity is "to your seed" (Gen. 12:7); "Count the stars . . . so shall your seed be" (Gen. 15: 4,5); "I will multiply your seed" (Gen. 16:10), "Sarah shall bear you a son . . . I will establish my covenant with him . . ." (Gen. 17: 19,20); "By myself have I sworn . . . that I will indeed bless you, and I will multiply your seed as the stars of heaven" (Gen. 22: 16–18). He includes some twenty examples under this heading. Under the promise of relationships, Clines includes several passages which allude to covenantal promises: "Behold, my covenant is with you" (Gen. 17: 1–11); "I will establish my covenant with him (Isaac) for an everlasting covenant" (Gen. 17: 17,18). The promise of relationship is formulated in different ways. Sometimes, for example, it takes the form of a pledge "to be with (you)" (Gen. 26: 3,24; 28:15). Clines comments, "The assurance that the God who speaks is the God who has pledged Himself to one's father and his descendants is a re-assurance of the hearer's own relationship to God".[127]

Clines compiles a list of nearly two hundred promises and allusions to the patriarchal promise in the Pentateuch.[128] Many constitute insistances of *world-to-word commissives*. Clearly spoken acts of commitment ("I will be your God"; Exod. 6:7; "This is my God", Exod. 15:2) bring about changes in situations or patterns of expectation and behaviour which would not otherwise take place. Associated with the promise, *directive* or *exercitive* world-to-word forces of utterance also operate. For example, Moses is addressed in language which begins as a *commissive* act of promise and becomes, in turn, an *exercitive* act of appointment or a *directive* act of commission: "I am the God of your father . . . I will send you . . ." (Exod. 3:6,10). The divine revelation constitutes an act of disclosure (Exod. 6:3,6). But some of these many instances have an assertive force. Exod. 6: 1–9 combines promise, commission, declaration and disclosure with propositional content. Thus "I will bring you to the land which I swore to give to Abraham, to Isaac, and to Jacob" (6:8) takes the form $F(p)$ or $Pr(p)$. These assertions operate in the direction of a *word-to-world* fit.

The language of divine promise belongs to the context of covenant (Exod. 34:10). The commissives "You shall be my own possession" and "All that Yahweh has spoken we will do" (Exod. 19: 5,8) frame the so-called covenant code. Similarly, the Book of Leviticus, Clines argues, presupposes that response to the divine promise will take the form of *acts* of worship, which are seen as institutional "statutes and ordinances" (Lev. 26: 46).[129] The sabbath (Lev. 26:43), the jubilee year (Lev. 27:23), confession of sin (Lev. 26:40) and tithes (Lev. 27:30) form part of an institutional context. On the other hand, the Book of Numbers gives the framework of promise a concrete form in terms of the physical *movement* towards the promised land. The "cloud" represents a *pledge* which moves with Israel towards entry into the land which God has promised (Num. 10: 11,12,29).

We need not depend on some particular interpretation or dating of the idea of covenant in the Old Testament texts in order to draw attention to the role of promise. A recent study of the covenant by Ernest Nicholson vindicates the view that the covenant in Israel did *not* represent a merely "word-to-world" legitimization of an existing social order.[130] Nicholson discusses and evaluates the influence of Weber's sociological theory on A. Alt, M. Noth, and others, and assesses the more recent work of L. Perlitt and of Kutsch. He concludes that the Hebrew prophets, especially Hosea (Hos. 6:7; 8:1) developed a theology of covenant precisely to *de*-legitimize existing social structures by stressing Israel's unique relationship to the sovereign God, who had initiated the relationship. Thus Nicholson's study of the covenant confirms the *world-to-word* dimension of covenantal promise which we have been examining. Provided that we place sufficient emphasis on divine initiative and transcendence, there is still force in W. Eichrodt's early comment on the commissive nature of the covenant, to the effect that on the basis of the covenant a relationship is established in which human persons know where they stand.[131] The world-to-word fit of promise (F) is a promise that can be defined also in terms of a content (p).

We add a brief postscript on the Johannine writings in order to make a parallel comment. The aim of the Fourth Gospel is explicit: "These things have been written that you may believe that Jesus is the Christ, the Son of God, and that believing, you might have life by His name." (John 20:31). It is a well-known issue of interpretation that this refers either to a deepening of Christian belief which is in view (present tense) or to an evangelistic purpose of bringing the reader to faith (aorist). Throughout the gospel a number of indicators of self-involving and commissive speech-acts occur. John stresses, for example, the commissive and declarative role of *witness* or *testimony*. John the Baptist performs the role of witness (Jn. 1:7,8,15,32,34; 3:26; 5:33). The woman of Samaria testifies to Jesus before her neighbours (Jn. 4:39); the disciples and the writer perform the role of witnesses (Jn. 15:27; 21:24); Jesus bears witness to the Father (Jn. 3:32,33), and the Father bears testimony to Jesus (Jn. 5:32,37; 8:18).

In the Johannine epistles "we testify" constitutes an illocution (1 Jn. 1:2; 4:14; cf. 5:6,9; 3 Jn.3). In the vast majority of cases, however, *that to which* witnesses testify can be expressed in terms of a given propositional content: "They believed because of the woman's testimony (F), 'He told me all that I ever did' (p)" (Jn. 4:39). The same principle applies to many instances of self-involving belief-utterances. The succession of Christological confessions, on the one hand, deeply affect and re-orientate the persons who utter or make them; on the other hand, they also embody a belief-content. The low-key beginnings in the earlier chapters: "He told me all that I ever did" (4:39) reach a grand climax in Thomas's Christological confession "My Lord and my God" (John 20:28).

The world-to-word direction of fit of belief-utterances in John is demonstrated by the connection between faith in Christ and *life*. It is no accident that the gift of life to Lazarus constitutes the climax of the section of the Gospel known as the Book of Signs (John 11: 1–44). In this context Jesus declares "He who believes in me, though he die, yet shall he live" (11:25). Once again, this has the force of a *promise* which has a *world-to-word* direction of fit. The transforming effects on the world of the words of Jesus are seen not only in the role of promise and self-involving confession, but also in the division, conflict, and verdictive force which they inevitably bring: "Many of the disciples drew back . . . Simon Peter said, 'Lord, to whom shall we go? You have the words of eternal life'" (John 6:66). "So there was a division among the people" (7:43). "Jesus said 'for judgment I came'" (9:39; cf. 16:8). But the call to faith, to decision, and to confession rests on the truth of certain states of affairs.

Raymond Brown argues that Bultmann's "existential interpretation" of the Fourth Gospel "has not done Johannine studies a disservice" because of John's emphasis on urgency and decision.[132] But Searle has reminded us that whenever promises, pledges, or other world-to-word utterances are effective and fully operative, a context and a background is presupposed concerning which word-to-world assertions can be made. In the enfleshment of the divine word of promise in the world in the incarnation of Jesus Christ (John 1:14) *these two "directions of fit" come together as one single transforming personal reality.* Jesus comes and addresses the reader in the Johannine writings as the word who, on the one hand, articulates a pre-existing ultimate reality (John 1: 1–18), but who, on the other hand, promises world-to-word transformation (John 20:31). In the post-resurrection era the word of Jesus, who is the truth (14:6), will be mediated through the Spirit of truth (16:13). The Paraclete will speak *truth* "in Christ's name" (14:26); but will speak on this basis in ways that will bring about *world-to-word transformation.*

NOTES TO CHAPTER VIII

1. Ernst Fuchs, *Studies of the Historical Jesus*, Eng. London: S.C.M. 1964, 129.
2. J. Arthur Baird, *Audience Criticism and the Historical Jesus*, Philadelphia: Westminster, 1969, 18.
3. Anthony C. Thiselton, "The Meaning of *Sarx* in I Cor 5:5: A Fresh Approach in the Light of Logical and Semantic Factors" *Scottish Journal of Theology* 26, 1973, 204–28, and "Realized Eschatology at Corinth," *New Testament Studies* 24, 1978, 510–26.
4. Donald D. Evans, *The Logic of Self-Involvement. A Philosophical Study of Everyday Language with Special Reference to the Christian Use of Language about God as Creator*, London: S.C.M. 1963; cf. Martin Heidegger, *Being and Time*, Eng. Oxford: Blackwell, 1962, 114–23.
5. D.D. Evans *op. cit.* 11.
6. Rudolf Bultmann, *Theology of the New Testament* vol.I, 190.
7. John L. Austin, *How to do Things with Words*, Oxford: Clarendon Press, 1962, 45. (Austin's italics.).
8. Jon Wheatley, "Austin on Truth" in K.T. Fann (ed.) *Symposium on J.L. Austin*, London: Routledge & Kegan Paul, 1969, 226–39.
9. Rudolf Bultmann, *Theology of the New Testament* II, 251.
10. Graham N. Stanton, *Jesus of Nazareth in New Testament Preaching*, Cambridge: Cambridge University Press, 1974 (S.N.T.S.M. 27).
11. Anthony C. Thiselton, *The Two Horizons*, 205–292.
12. Clive Garrett, *The Question of Development in Rudolf Bultmann's Theology*, University of Sheffield, Ph.D. Thesis 1981.
13. Rudolf Bultmann, "New Testament and Mythology" in H.-W. Bartsch (ed.) *Kerygma and Myth* (2 vols.) London: S.P.C.K. 1962 and 1964, I, 36, German H.-W. Bartsch (ed.) *Kerygma und Mythos. Ein theologisches Gespräch* (6 vols.), Hamburg: Reich & Heidrich, 1948 onwards, I, 46.

14. Søren Kierkegaard, *The Point of View for my Work as an Author*, Princeton, Princeton University Press, 1941 (rp. New York, 1962), 11.
15. *Ibid* 40.
16. Søren Kierkegaard, *The Concept of Irony*, Eng. London: Collins, 1966, 340.
17. Søren Kierkegaard, *The Last Years: Journals 1853–1855*, Eng. London: Collins, 1965, 99, and *The Attack upon "Christendom"* Eng. Princeton: Princeton University Press, 1944, 150.
18. *Ibid* 107; cf. 127.
19. Soren Kierkegaard, *Concluding Unscientific Postscript to the Philosophical Fragments*, Eng. Princeton: Princeton University Press, 1941, 181.
20. *Ibid* (Kierkegaard's italics).
21. Soren Kierkegaard, *The Journals of Soren Kierkegaard: A Selection* (ed. A. Dru) Eng. Oxford, 1938, under 1st August, 1835.
22. Cf. Anthony C. Thiselton, "Kierkegaard and the Nature of Truth", *Churchman* 89, 1975, 85–107.
23. Soren Kierkegaard, *Fear and Trembling* (with *The Sickness unto Death*) New York: Fontana edn. 1954, 27–64.
24. Calvin O. Schrag, *Radical Reflection and the Origins of the Human Sciences*, West Lafayette: Purdue University Press, 1980, 106.
25. M. Heidegger, *Being and Time* 62 and 39.
26. *Ibid* 73.
27. *Ibid* 95–107; cf. also 200–01.
28. *Ibid* 189.
29. *Ibid* 190–92.
30. *Ibid* 194.
31. *Ibid* 201.
32. *Ibid* 345.
33. *Ibid* 342.
34. *Ibid* 373.
35. *Ibid* 444.
36. Anthony C. Thiselton, *The Two Horizons*, 143–204 (on Heidegger's *Being and Time*) and 227–34 and 275–92 (on Bultmann's use of Heidegger).
37. Rudolf Bultmann, *Theology of the New Testament*, I, 191.
38. *Ibid* 239.
39. *Ibid* 240.
40. *Ibid* 276.
41. *Ibid* 300–01.
42. *Ibid* 319.
43. *Ibid* 322.
44. *Ibid* 335.
45. Rudolf Bultmann, "New Testament and Mythology" *loc. cit.*, Eng.I, Germ.11.
46. *Ibid* Eng.36; Germ. 46.
47. Wolfart Pannenberg, "The Revelation of God in Jesus" in James M. Robinson & John B. Cobb Jr. (eds.) *New Frontiers in Theology III, Theology as History*, New York: Harper & Row, 1967, 122.
48. *Ibid*.
49. J. Weiss, *op. cit.*, vol.2, 458.
50. R. Bultmann, *Theology of the New Testament* I 331 & 351.

51. Werner Kramer, *Christ, Lord, Son of God*, Eng. London: S.C.M. 1966, 181 & 182.
52. R. Bultmann, *Essays Philosophical and Theological*, London: S.C.M. 1955, 280, cf. 273–90; German *Glauben und Verstehen. Gesammelte Aufsätze* (4 vols.) Tübingen: Mohr, 1964–65, II, 252, cf. 246–61.
53. D.D. Evans, *op. cit.* 30–36, 46–78, 170–73; J.L. Austin, *op. cit.* 43–52, 78–90, 110–19, 150–61.
54. John R. Searle, *Expression and Meaning. Studies in the Theory of Speech Acts*, Cambridge: Cambridge University Press, 1979, 13–23; cf. 1–29; François Recanati, *Meaning and Force: The Pragmatics of Perfomative Utterances*, Eng. Cambridge: Cambridge University Press, 1987, 154–63; Stephen C. Levinson, *Pragmatics*, Cambridge: Cambridge University Press, 1983, 240–42; and Geoffrey Leech, *The Principles of Pragmatics*, London and New York: Longman, 1983, 205–12.
55. D.D. Evans, *op. cit.* 33.
56. J.L. Austin, *op. cit.* 150 & 154–55.
57. James D.G. Dunn, *Romans* 9–16, 616.
58. J.L. Austin *op. cit.* 152; J.R. Searle, *op. cit.* 16–20; and F. Recanati, *op. cit.* 138–54.
59. D.D. Evans, *op. cit.* 36; cf. J.L. Austin, *op. cit.* 159–60.
60. D.E.H. Whiteley, *op. cit.* 103; cf. Oscar Cullmann, *The Christology of the New Testament*, Eng. London: S.C.M. 1959, 200–13.
61. L. Cerfaux, *Christ in the Theology of St Paul*, Eng. Freiburg: Herder, 1959, 469.
62. James D.G. Dunn, *Unity and Diversity in the New Testament. An Inquiry into the Character of Earliest Christianity*, London: S.C.M. 1977, 227.
63. Rudolf Bultmann, *Theology of the New Testament* II, 9 & 43.
64. I. Howard Marshall, *The Gospel of Luke. A Commentary on the Greek Text*, Exeter: Paternoster, and Grand Rapids: Eerdmans, 1978, 213.
65. J.L. Austin, *op. cit.* 99; cf. 94–119.
66. G. Bornkamm, "The Stilling of the Storm" in G. Bornkamm, G. Barth, and H.J. Held, *Tradition and Interpretation in Matthew*, Eng. London: S.C.M. 1963, 52–57.
67. David Hill, *The Gospel of Matthew*, London: Oliphants & Marshall (New Century) 1972, 167.
68. R.T. France, *The Gospel according to Matthew. An Introduction and Commentary*, Leicester: I.V.P. and Grand Rapids: Eerdmans, 1985, 162.
69. Otto Michel, "The Conclusion of Matthew's Gospel. A Contribution to the History of the Easter Message", in Graham N. Stanton (ed.) *The Interpretation of Matthew*, Philadelphia: Fortress, and London: S.P.C.K., 1983, 30–41.
70. Graham N. Stanton, *ibid* 4; cf. G. Bornkamm, *loc. cit.* 228.
71. James D.G. Dunn, *Christology in the Making: A New Testament Inquiry into the Origins of the Doctrine of the Incarnation*, London: S.C.M., and Philadelphia: Westminster, 1980, 254.
72. Norman Perrin, *Jesus and the Language of the Kingdom*, London: S.C.M. 1976.
73. P. Maurice Casey, *Son of Man: The Interpretation and Influence of Daniel 7*, London: S.P.C.K. 1979; Morna D. Hooker, *The Son of Man in Mark*, London: S.P.C.K. 1967; and Barnabas Lindars, *Jesus Son of Man: A Fresh Examination of the Son of Man Sayings in the Gospels in the Light of Recent Research*, London: S.P.C.K., 1983.

74. Robert Fowler, *Loaves and Fishes. The Function of the Feeding Stories in the Gospel of Mark*, Chico: Scholars Press, 1981; Ernest Best, *op. cit.*; M. Eugene Boring, "The Christology of Mark: Hermeneutical Issues for Systematic Theology" in *Christology and Exegesis: New Approaches: Semeia* 30, 1985, 125–54; and David Rhoads and Donald Michie, *Mark as Story*, Philadelphia: Fortress Press, 1982
75. Graham N. Stanton, *The Gospels and Jesus*, Oxford: Oxford University Press, 1989, 28.
76. Hugh C. White (ed.) *Speech-Act Theory and Biblical Criticism: Semeia* 41, 1988; Michael Hancher, "Performative Utterances, the Word of God, and the Death of the Author", 27–40, and Hugh C. White, "The Value of Speech-Act Theory for Old Testament Hermeneutics", 41–63.(See especially 27).
77. John P. Meier, *The Vision of Matthew: Christ, Church, and Morality in the First Gospel*, New York: Paulist Press, 1979, 43; cf. 42–51.
78. Johannes G. du Plessis, *Clarity and Obscurity. A Study in Textual Communication of the Relation between Sender, Parable, and Receiver in the Synoptic Gospels*, Stellenbosch: University of Stellenbosch D.Theol. Dissertation, 1985, 2 and 3; cf. E. Arens, *Kommunikative Handlungen: die paradigmatische Bedeutung der Gleichnisse Jesu für eine Handlungstheorie*, Düsseldorf: Patmos, 1982, 355; T. Aurelio, *Disclosures in den Gleichnissen Jesu: Eine Anwendung der disclosure-Theorie von I.T. Ramsey*, Frankfurt a/M: Lang, 1977; and Anthony C. Thiselton, "The Parables as Language-Event: Some Comments on Fuchs' Hermeneutics in the Light of Linguistic Philosophy", *Scottish Journal of Theology* 23, 1970, 437–68.
79. Johannes G. du Plessis, *op. cit.* 5 and 269 (my italics).
80. J.G. du Plessis, "Speech Act Theory and New Testament Interpretation with Special Reference to G.N. Leech's Pragmatic Principles" in P.J. Hartin and J.H. Petzer (eds.) *Text and Interpretation. New Approaches in the Criticism of the New Testament*, Leiden: Brill, 1991, 129–42. Cf. also his "Pragmatic Meaning in Matthew 13: 1–23", *Neotestamentica* 21, 1987, 42–56; and "Did Peter Ask his Questions and How Did Jesus Answer Him? Or implicature in Luke 12: 35–48", *Neotestamentica* 22, 1988, 311–24. Cf. further Nicholas Wolterstorff, *Works and Worlds of Art*, Oxford: Clarendon Press. 1980; *loc. cit.* in chapters X, XV, and especially XVI below.
81. John R. Searle, *Speech Acts. An Essay in the Philosophy of Language*, Cambridge: Cambridge University Press, 1969, 16; cf. also vii.
82. *Ibid* 17.
83. John L. Austin, *Philosophical Papers*, Oxford: Clarendon Press, 1961, 85–101, and 123–154; and K.T. Fann (ed.) *Symposium on J.L. Austin*, London: Routledge & Kegan Paul, 1969.
84. John L. Austin, *How to Do Things with Words*, 28.
85. *Ibid* 27.
86. *Ibid* 35.
87. *Ibid* 37.
88. Anthony C. Thiselton, "The Supposed Power of Words in the Biblical Writings" *Journal of Theological Studies* 25, 1974, 283–99.
89. Gerhard von Rad, *Old Testament Theology*, vol.2, Eng. Edinburgh: Oliver & Boyd, 1965, 85.
90. W. Zimmerli, "Wort Gottes", *Religion in Geschichte und Gegenwart* vol.6 (Tübingen: 1962) col. 1810; O. Grether, *Name und Wort Gottes im Alten Testament*, Giessen:

1934, 103–7; Edmund Jacob, *Theology of the Old Testament* Eng. London: Hodder and Stoughton, 1958, 131; L. Dürr, *Der Wertung des göttlichen Wortes in Alten Testament und im antiken Orient*, Leipzig, 1938, 52, 61, and 71.

91. John R. Searle, *Speech Acts* (as cited) 1969; *Expression and Meaning. Studies in the Theory of Speech Acts*, Cambridge: Cambridge University Press, 1979; John R. Searle, Ferenc Kiefer and Manfred Bierwisch (eds.) *Speech-Act Theory and Pragmatics*, Dordrecht, London, and Boston: Reidel, 1980, esp. 221–32 (by Searle); John R. Searle, *Intentionality. An Essay in the Philosophy of Mind*, Cambridge: Cambridge University Press, 1983; and John R. Searle and Daniel Vanderveken, *Foundations of Illocutionary Logic*, Cambridge: Cambridge University Press, 1985.
92. J.L. Austin, *How to Do Things with Words*, 108.
93. J.R. Searle, *Speech-Acts* 24.
94. *Ibid* 31; cf. *Expression and Meaning*, 1; and *Intentionality* 5–7.
95. J.R. Searle, *Expression and Meaning*, 3 (Searle's italics).
96. F. Recanati, *op. cit.* 150; cf. 150–63.
97. *Ibid* 27.
98. Dieter Wunderlich, "Methodological Remarks on Speech-Act Theory" in J.R. Searle, F. Kiefer, and M. Bierwisch (eds.) *Speech-Act Theory and Pragmatics* 297; cf. 291–312.
99. F. Recanati, *op. cit.* 164 and 169 (his italics); and J.R. Searle, *Expression and Meaning* 18.
100. J.R. Searle, *Intentionality* 165–67.
101. J.R. Searle, *Expression and Meaning* 18.
102. J.R. Searle, *Intentionality* 1–36, 160–79 *et passim*.
103. J.R. Searle, *Speech-Acts*, 58 (my italics).
104. *Ibid* 60.
105. L. Wittgenstein, *Zettel* sect. 504.
106. L. Wittgenstein, *Philosophical Investigations* II i, 174.
107. *Ibid* II x, 192.
108. A.J.M. Wedderburn, *The Reasons for Romans*, Edinburgh: Clark, 1988; and Francis Watson, *Paul, Judaism and the Gentiles. A Sociological Approach*, Cambridge: Cambridge University Press (S.N.T.S. Mon. Ser. 56), 1986, 88–91 *et passim*.
109. E.P. Sanders, *Paul and Palestinian Judaism*, 443.
110. K. Stendahl, *Paul among Jews and Gentiles* 23–40; and 78–96.
111. *Ibid* 24.
112. Marcus Barth, *The People of God*, Sheffield: J.S.N.T.S. 5, 1983, 26.
113. A. Schweitzer, *The Mysticism of Paul the Apostle*, 101.
114. *Ibid* 117.
115. *Ibid* 123.
116. A. Deissmann, *Paul*, 161.
117. Alfred Wikenhauser, *Pauline Mysticism. Christ in the Mystical Teaching of St Paul*, Eng. Freiburg: Herder, and London: Nelson, 1960, 94.
118. *Ibid* 104.
119. *Ibid* 199; cf. 184 and 185.
120. Robert Tannehill, *Dying and Rising with Christ. A Study in Pauline Theology*, Berlin: Töpelmann, 1967, 1–47 and 75–129, and Anthony T. Hanson, *The Paradox of the Cross in the Thought of Paul*, Sheffield: J.S.N.T.S. 17, 1987, 24–78.
121. E.P. Sanders, *Paul and Palestinian Judaism*, 465 (first italics mine; second his).

122. J.K.S. Reid, *Our Life in Christ*, London: S.C.M. 1963, 91. cf. also N.T. Wright, "Jesus, Israel, and the Cross" in Kent H. Richards (ed.) *Society of Biblical Literature 1985 Seminar Papers*, Atlanta: Scholars Press, 1985, 75–95 (esp. 91–93); *The Messiah and the People of God*, D. Phil. Dissertation, University of Oxford, 1980; and especially *The Climax of the Covenant. Christ and the Law in Pauline Theology*, Edinburgh: Clark, 1991 4–9, 137–41, 258–67.
123. Robert Tannehill, *op. cit.* 70.
124. See also J.R. Searle and Daniel Vanderveken, *Foundations of Illocutionary Logic*, 74–86; Daniel Vanderveken, "Illocutionary Logic and Self-Defeating Speech Acts" in J.R. Searle, F. Kiefer, and M. Bierwisch (eds.), *Speech Act Theory and Pragmatics*, Dordrecht and Boston: Reidel 1980, 247–72; and F. Recanati, *op. cit.* 265–66.
125. Stephen C. Levinson, *Pragmatics*, 226–83, esp. 276–78.
126. David J.A. Clines, *The Theme of the Pentateuch*, Sheffield: J.S.O.T.S. Press, 11, 1978, 26 and 27.
127. *Ibid* 35.
128. *Ibid* 32–43.
129. *Ibid* 50–53.
130. Ernest W. Nicholson, *God and His People: Covenant and Theology in the Old Testament*, Oxford: Clarendon Press, 1986.
131. Walther Eichrodt, *Theology of the Old Testament* vol. 1, Engl London: S.C.M. 1961, 38.
132. Raymond E. Brown, *The Gospel according to John*, London: Chapman, 1971, lxxviii–lxxix.

CHAPTER IX

The Hermeneutics of Metacriticism and the Foundations of Knowledge

1. The Context of the Paradigm-Shift to Radical Metacritical Hermeneutics and the Nature of Gadamer's Hermeneutics

"Hans-Georg Gadamer, more than anyone else", Klemm rightly observes, "is responsible for intensifying and enlivening hermeneutical discussion since 1960."[1] Klemm refers to the year in which Gadamer (b. 1900) published the first edition of *Truth and Method*. David Tracy and many others underline the far-reaching importance of Gadamer's work not only for general hermeneutical theory, but also for the interpretation of biblical texts.[2] Yet Gadamer's work constitutes a full-scale attack on the role of *method* in hermeneutics. Whereas we have attempted to re-examine specific biblical texts in the light of models of interpretation suggested by the work of Schleiermacher, Dilthey, Betti, Bultmann, Austin, Searle, and even Heidegger, it is more difficult to cash out the immediate impact of Gadamer's hermeneutics for biblical interpretation. The reason for this, however, does not lie in some supposed defect in Gadamer's work. What has occurred is, rather, a paradigm-shift in the very nature of hermeneutics. Comparing Gadamer and Habermas, Paul Ricoeur rightly concludes that in both cases "hermeneutics ultimately claims to set itself up as a critique, or *meta-critique*."[3]

It is possible, however, to draw implications and analogues from Gadamer's work for biblical interpretation. This is not my present aim, which is, rather, to explore the deeper metacritical character of his work. But in my chapters on Gadamer in *The Two Horizons* I ventured to draw some practical inferences in three directions.[4] First, I drew on his notion of tradition and effective-history to discuss the nature of the relationship between biblical exegesis and systematic theology. Second, I explored his major category of the "world" of a work of art, and the "world" of the game, to shed light on the "worlds" projected by the parables of Jesus, especially in relation to the work of E. Fuchs and G. Ebeling and the so-called new hermeneutic. Third, I ventured some comments on the retrospective post-resurrection horizon of meaning which characterizes the Fourth Gospel.

One of my former doctoral research students, Stephen Fowl, has also explored parallels between Gadamer's hermeneutics and Brevard Childs's work on the biblical writings as canon.[5] But Fowl also identifies the problem to which we have alluded. He writes, "Gadamer talks about concepts such as 'judgment', 'tact', the *sensus communis, et al.* as guiding principles in determining what is, and what is not, justifiable in one's pre-understanding. On a theoretical level this sounds very helpful. When it comes to discussing how one might exercise these principles in certain situations, however, Gadamer is painfully silent. This reflects Gadamer's overall desire to avoid presenting a 'method' of understanding.[6]

Why, then, has Gadamer exercized such profound influence on contemporary hermeneutics? I shall not re-trace the same ground as that of my earlier study. Instead, I propose to draw attention primarily to Gadamer's role in focussing for hermeneutics, and addressing, a cluster of metacritical questions concerning the *basis* of understanding and of our possible relation to truth. Gadamer's distinctive way of addressing these questions not only constitutes a point of transition towards a new paradigm of hermeneutical theory; it also places him firmly on the boundary-line between modern and post-modern thought. Three outstanding critical discussions of Gadamer's hermeneutics have appeared since my work in 1980, and all three underline this distinctive, even ambiguous, boundary-crossing between modern and post-modern perspectives in Gadamer's work. In his excellent study Joel C Weinsheimer rightly observes: "Gadamer's triunion of art, play, and truth can be considered *either reactionary or post-modern.*"[7] In one sense, Gadamer's hermeneutics constitute "relativism with a vengeance . . . absolute relativism." This is because "the work exists nowhere but in its representations."[8] Hermeneutics is "ontological", precisely in the sense that *all reality is hermeneutical.* Works and thus "Truth" come to be only in their actualization as "performance". On the other hand, where there is no method or rule, there remains a part to be played by human judgment. In the unveiling of "truth" the interpreter may concede "yes, this is how it is."[9] The first aspect is post-modern; the second, almost literally, traditional. Qualities of "judgment" and common sense need to be employed precisely when the usual "rules" have run out and do not apply.

In her incisive and judicious study of 1987, Georgia Warnke also sets Gadamer in the context of the modern and post-modern debate.[10] From the angle of viewpoint of Habermas and Apel, she points out, Gadamer too readily substitutes acquiescence to the norms of tradition for more socially-orientated attempts to adjudicate the rationality of our beliefs and of our social practices. But this interpretation of Gadamer leaves some factors out of account. On the other side, however, Richard Rorty's attempt to appropriate Gadamer's work in the service of contextual pragmatism is even more one-sided.[11] Gadamer accepts the problems of historical pluralism; but "practical reason" may be advanced, Gadamer's work suggests, through dialogue, through judgment, and through a broadening inter-subjective "enculturalization" (*Bildung*) which takes effect in the context of history and tradition.

The third of the three most important studies is that of Richard Bernstein, who discusses Gadamer in a wider setting in relation to philosophies of the time, including those of Habermas, Rorty, and Hannah Arendt. Bernstein argues that "although the concept of truth is basic to Gadamer's entire project of philosophical hermeneutics, it turns out to be one of the most elusive concepts in his work . . . It is much easier to say what 'truth' does not mean than to give a positive account."[12] On the one hand, Gadamer makes much of developing a particular understanding of Aristotle's "practical wisdom" or *phronēsis*; but on the other hand he leaves us with the question: what is the basis for our critical judgments? Bernstein also expounds the relation between Gadamer's understanding of *phronēsis* and the problems of post-modern pluralism in another study.[13]

The paradigm-shift of hermeneutics to radical metacritical reflection raises complex issues about the post-Hegelian notion of historical finitude, about the critique of language and its relation to thought, and about the foundations of human enquiry. But before we move into this difficult and complex area of questions, we may perhaps pause briefly to offer a *simplified analogue* of what *metacritical* reflection in hermeneutics might be said to entail. We may step back, as it were, to note both the dilemmas posed by metacritical questions and also the opportunities which they afford for critical stock-taking of the foundations of the subject. But the following analogue is no more than a simplified model which for the moment side-steps round problems of post-modern thought, and the problem of historical finitude in post-Heideggerian philosophy.

At the *pre*-critical level, a reader finds himself or herself "reading texts" rather than consciously engaging in the task of "interpretation". Indeed it is sometimes argued that hermeneutical reflection can serve actually to *dis*-engage readers from being grasped by the text. In a short study of Jung, Frank Stach cites Jung's view that "the more we understand cognitively, the further we get away from what is really there. In Jung's words 'we get the feeling of having understood and explained something, but in so doing we are getting further away from the living mystery' . . . There is a sense in which interpretation does diminish the work of art."[14]

To illustrate the point, we might imagine that we have projected ourselves into the narrative world of a film. In this "world" of the film, we have been lowered into a lifeboat, and are battered by the roaring wind. Our stomachs turn as the boat rises high, then drops twenty feet into a trough between the waves. We hear the sound of the spray, and as lightning breaks across the sky we catch a last glimpse of the ship we have just left. Thunder rolls and reverberates. An awstruck voice whispers beside us "No one would ever think that the Director had used a two-foot model in a six-foot tank." The spell has been broken by the comment of a *critic*, who necessarily speaks on the basis of a *critical* approach.

In the film industry or in the publisher's office certain *critical* questions need to be asked: is this convincing? Is the narrative self-consistent? Do the period costumes accurately reflect the style of the day? What is the purpose of this particular segment of narrative in relation to the whole story? How well has it all been done? Robert Fowler discusses the difference of role imposed on the reader and on the critic.[15] As readers we allow ourselves to be mastered by the text. The text has its way with us. Our expectations are aroused and even at times manipulated. We feel what we are meant to feel; we live out the story. But the role of the critic reverses the relationship. The critic scrutinizes the text as his or her object of enquiry. The critic deliberately creates enough *distance* from the text, creates a high enough level of abstraction to ask: how does it work? What is going on here? The critic looks into the text from outside it; the reader accepts its invitation to enter in wherever it leads. Fowler rightly observes, however, that when readers are *solely* readers, and not critical readers, or when critics are *solely* critics and not reading, listening critics, the results are less than satisfactory. We need, he rightly urges, both "readerly passion" and "critical distance".[16]

Just as the first level of engaged reading can be submitted to *critical* evaluation by the critic, so too, in turn, the critic's own programme of criticism can be submitted to *meta-critical* evaluation. The critic's judgments relate directly to the film or book, even if they also operate at a higher level of abstraction. But where the critic may also speak of the success or failure of the film *as a film*, at a metacritical level discussion may turn on the *ranking of criteria* which the critic uses: is it more important for the film to be a success in bringing in funds through the box office, or to be a success in terms of providing a good acting-role for the director's wife; or to be a success in terms of conveying a socio-political message close to the heart of the author? What *counts* as "success", in terms of considerations more fundamental than conventional criteria agreed by the guild of professional critics? At this point a principle emerges which often seems to beset metacritical enquiry: *There seems to be no "objective" answer which is independent of the aims and interests of those involved.* To develop the analogy, the producer's commercial interests, the director's family interests, and the author's political interests may each seem more "fundamental" to the person concerned from their given point of view than the conventional criteria employed by the critic. But how could they agree among themselves *on the nature of the criterion used to formulate what would count as the most fundamental criteria* of success?

This provides some kind of parallel to the deepest problems of hermeneutics. At the *critical* level, the critic may employ criteria which are accepted *within given communities*, to ask and to answer given questions about texts: are they historically accurate? Do they project a coherent narrative world? Do they invite engagement and response from the reader? But at the *metacritical* level, is the criterion for hermeneutical "success" to be seen in terms of an interpreter's arriving at inter-personal understanding of the author, being nurtured in the faith, being mastered and transformed by the text (if so, into what?), or by seeing "how to go on" with what a text might seem to suggest, but not actually say? It is a major theme of Robert Morgan's book *Biblical Interpretation* that almost everything in interpretation rests on a *decision* made by the interpreter to opt for one or more such "interests". He writes: "Texts, like dead men and women have no rights, no aims, no interests. They can be used in whatever way readers or interpreters choose . . . .In all cases it is the interests or aims of the interpreter that are decisive, not the claims of the text as such. Any suggestion that the text has rights is a deception concealing someone else's interests."[17]

We should not, however, foreclose the enquiry as soon as this. Gadamer's contribution takes us forward, but not yet decisively forward, on this question. As we shall see, in one sense he acknowledges that what *counts* as a *rational* criterion depends on its context within a community and a tradition. In the view of some interpreters, this seems merely to relativize questions of truth into consensus or pragmatic questions about what is *accepted within the particular reading community* to which we belong. On the other hand, as Tracy argues, Gadamer makes much of the paradigm of "conversation" or "dialogue" as a vehicle out of which truth may "emerge".[18] Need we assume that in our analogue the director, producer, and author could not arrive at some mutually agreed ranking of criteria when every relevant factor had been placed honestly and openly on the table, and fresh perspectives had "emerged" from this to-and-fro of conversation? The discipline of hermeneutics may well have moved on, as Richard Rorty claims in his "Reply to Dreyfus and Taylor", from a study of *method* to the adopting of a fundamental *attitude*.[19] But it also constitutes a forum for continuing conversation between those who share the same family of concerns, or who wish rationally or ethically to defend certain models of interpretation as operative paradigms.

The metacritical level of the hermeneutical debate offers a positive contribution not least in relating the formulation of given models of interpretation to certain *interpretative purposes*. But we nevertheless resist the conclusion that the nature of texts themselves has no part in determining whether this or that given purpose remains appropriate from a rational, ethical, philosophical, literary, contextual, or theological point of view. A recognition of the role played by inter-subjectivity and communities of interpretation has led some writers to formulate only socio-pragmatic criteria about purposes of interpretation. But others draw different conclusions. This can be seen most sharply by comparing Habermas, Apel and probably Wittgenstein on the one hand, and Richard Rorty's attempt to appropriate the work of Wittgenstein and Gadamer on the other. To be sure, all this may call for what Calvin Schrag describes as "an expanded notion of reason". This "expanded" reason will include the "lived-through meanings" of practical life and community, and also "vision and insight", as against the "technical" reason of Enlightenment rationalism.[20] Given what Gadamer calls a "hermeneutically trained" judgment, or in Schrag's language an "expanded notion of reason", it does not seem a wholly impossible task to match the directedness of given biblical texts to the use of appropriate hermeneutical models. These do not necessarily function as competing models. The narrowest and least plausible option is for an interpreter to select any *one* given model of interpretation, and to use it as a comprehensive key for the interpretation of *every kind of text.*

We must return, however, to the philosophical context which provides the setting for Gadamer's metacritical philosophical hermeneutics. The cumulative problems which transform hermeneutics into radical metacriticism emerge from three directions. First, there is the problem of *radical historical finitude*, which gathers momentum as the issues move from Droysen and Dilthey, through Graf Yorck and Husserl, to Heidegger and Gadamer. Second, there is the problem of the *constitutive role of language* in inter-subjective and individual understanding. From tentative beginnings in Wilhelm von Humboldt, a variety of "critiques of language" emerge, from that of the little-known Fritz Mauthner to the well-known work of Wittgenstein. Third, Richard Bernstein identifies what he calls "the *unease*" that has beset numerous academic disciplines as they submit to re-appraisal what have been regarded as *"foundations" for their methods.*[21] Often, Bernstein argues, this unease takes the form of a quest to reach beyond the antitheses between objectivism and relativism. This struggle is apparent especially in the expansion of hermeneutics into the social sciences and in the conversation with deconstructionism in literary theory. A recent volume of essays edited by Bruce Wachterhauser charts this conversation between radical hermeneutics and post-modernism in this philosophical context, and includes an essay in which Gadamer addresses the orientation of Derrida.[22]

Schleiermacher had already *in principle* raised transcendental questions in a preliminary sense for hermeneutics. In principle, although not fully in practice, he had established the metacritical nature of the discipline.

But the problems which Schleiermacher addressed remained primarily within the frame of the a-historical difficulties formulated by Kant about the limits of pure reason. The problem of *historical* finitude and *historical*-conditionedness emerged fully only with Hegel and Kierkegaard. In Gadamer's view, it was Husserl who formulated most pointedly the implications of the "pre-givenness" of the "life-world" into which we are born, and which determines what we perceive *as* this or that. Gadamer writes: "The concept of 'life-world' is the antithesis of all objectivism. It is an essentially historical concept . . . Transcendental reflection, which is supposed to remove all the validity of the world and all the pre-givenness of anything else, must also regard itself as included in the life-world."[23]

Husserl himself had hoped to avoid the radical consequences of the historical situatedness which he had exposed by using the phenomenological method to "bracket out" the historical and social factors which surrounded human consciousness. He had, however, already taken the decisive step: things exist or are "given" only in the mode of "being known to consciouness" (*Bewusstsein*); they cannot be grasped as independent objects "out there". The radical consequences of human situatedness in history were carried through and developed, as we have seen, by his pupil, Heidegger. For Heidegger, what is "objective", including making assertions about "facts", is derivative from, and dependent on, hermeneutical understanding from within a given horizon. The fact-stating language of the sciences has its place, but only at a merely technical or instrumental level.

Heidegger's later thought provides a direct introduction to Gadamer. The later Heidegger's attack on "objectivism" takes the form of a consistent contrast between "calculative" (*method-based*) thinking and "meditative" thinking or "releasement" (*Gelassenheit*).[24] Although he allows that "each is justified and needed in its own way", Heidegger believes that "calculation" is merely technical or instrumental, and that our modern science-orientated culture is too "exclusively" pre-occupied with it.[25] *Gelassenheit* supposedly offers a new paradigm which "steps back" and reflects "the renunciation" of the poet.[26] Heidegger relates this view directly to the critique of language. For "what the poet learned to renounce is his formerly cherished view regarding the relation of the thing and the word."[27] Negatively, analysis, assertion, and subject-object thinking perform only technical tasks. Positively, Heidegger construes creative language and fundamental thinking as bringing together (*logos* signifies "collectedness") a "world" in which we experience "presence".[28]

Gadamer endorses not only Heidegger's radicalization of human historical finitude but also his exploration of art and "worlds" of art as new paradigms of operative communication and understanding. Gadamer's insistent rejection of *hermeneutics-as-method* stands in direct continuity with his former teacher's repudiation of "calculative" thinking as derivative and secondary. Human "situatedness" in the world cannot be overcome by scientific method. On the other hand, Gadamer develops Heidegger's model of "world" both in terms of the world projected by a work of art, and the *world presupposed and created in the playing of a game*. Gadamer writes: "Play fulfills its purpose only if the player loses himself in his play . . . . Only seriousness in playing makes the play wholly play . . . Play has its own essence, independently of the consciousness of those who play . . . The primacy of play over the consciousness of the player is fundamental . . . The structure of play absorbs the player."[29] Georgia Warnke paraphrases Gadamer's point: "In reading a book, viewing a painting, or playing a game, one is transported out of one's ordinary existence . . . Players enter a new and total environment . . . Players put aside their own concerns and desires, and submit to the purposes of the game itself."[30]

The weight which Gadamer places on this key metaphor and human experience as a paradigm for being open to truth situates him precisely on the borderline between modern and post-modern thought. In one direction he is "post-modern". Consciousness takes a secondary place, and reflection is replaced by reflexivity. Players simply *react* to tasks and rules which the *game* imposes. In Gadamer's words, "the game tends to master the players . . . The game is what holds the players in its spell."[31] Each game, Gadamer continues, has its own spirit and its own norms, often symbolized by the setting apart of some special space or area for the play. Its reality "surpasses" the individual players, and the player is an element of the whole which is presented to the spectators or audience.[32] It *exists* in the event of *interaction* with the audience: "What no longer exists is the players – with the poet or the composer being considered as one of the players."[33] Gadamer cites music as a paradigm case for what exists only in the performance.

At one level this may seem philosophically innocent. Gadamer plausibly declares: "A drama exists only when it is played . . . A festival exists only in being celebrated."[34] We argued in our second chapter that a biblical text *speaks* when it is actualized or "performed" in the present horizon and life-world of the hearer. But games, as part of this nature, vary in each performance; a game which rigidly *reproduces* each move of a previous game would not be a *game*. As Weinsheimer observes, then, in Gadamer's hermeneutics "there can be no determinate criterion for correct interpretation, nor any single, correct, canonical, interpretation."[35] This is the aspect which invites development into a radical philosophy of social contingency and pluralistic pragmatic contextualization.

On the other hand, as Weinsheimer and Georgia Warnke also point out, there is also a "conservative" aspect to Gadamer's thought. This aspect is incompatible with post-modernism. Gadamer does not accept the later Heidegger's negative evaluation of tradition since Plato. Rather, he traces a positive continuity of emphasis on "practical reason" from Socrates, Plato, and Aristotle, through Roman legal thought, to Vico, Shaftesbury, Thomas Reid, Hegel, and Bergson. English empiricism and Enlightenment rationalism represent *an artificial narrowing of this tradition in which positivistic, theoretical, and individual-centred reason becomes abstracted from tradition and community*. Thus Gadamer speaks approvingly and positively of the distinction which emerged in Socratic dialogue with the cynics between "the scholar and the wise man on whom the scholar depends."[36] Aristotle and late Roman legal science, he argues, rightly stressed the role of *phronēsis* as practical wisdom, rather than the more theoretical wisdom of *sophia*. Gadamer refers favourably to Plato's notion of "recognition", even in the context of the world of play.[37]

For Gadamer, Plato's most important contribution comes in his exposition of *dialogue* as a process in which truth "arises" in the to-and-fro of questions and of conversation.[38] A further event of importance occurs when Vico rightly takes up the notion of *sensus communis*, or common sense in his humanistic defence against Descartes and rationalist pre-occupations with the "methods of science".[39] One quality which characterizes the wise person in the context of *sensus communis* is that of judgment. But here "judgment" is not the intellectualizing kind of judgment that judges particulars under universal viewpoints, and can be reduced simply to deductive logic. It is, rather, a matter of knowing "what is important" within a practical and inter-subjective frame of reference. Similarly "taste" operates in community, and presupposes "culture" or *Bildung*.[40]

Entirely in harmony with his purpose of formulating a *metacritical* hermeneutics, Gadamer insists on the role of "pre-judgments" (translated "prejudices", in *Truth and Method*, German, *die Vorurteile*). Gadamer declares: "The prejudices (i.e. pre-judgments) of the individual, far more than his judgments, constitute the historical reality of his being."[41] But at this point Gadamer crosses over again to perspectives more akin to post-modernism. For he declares: "The self-awareness of the individual is only a flickering in the closed circuits of historical life."[42]

We have not yet seen *why* Gadamer seems to adopt a position which a number of recent critics, including his successor at Heidelberg, Reiner Wiehl, regard as ambiguous.[43] To understand more of Gadamer's concerns, we need to come to terms more closely with his metacritical re-appraisal of the inadequacy of the Enlightenment and rationalist notion of "reason", and to elucidate his understanding of what he calls "the universality of the hermeneutical problem".

2. Gadamer's Claim for "the Universality of the Hermeneutical Problem" and the Development of Critiques of Language and of Knowledge

Gadamer's essay under the title "The Universality of the Hermeneutical Problem" was written in 1966, and appears in the volume entitled *Philosophical Hermeneutics*.[44] Gadamer expresses here his dissatisfaction with any paradigm of hermeneutics which suggests that it might be "a technique" simply for avoiding misunderstanding. The opening part of his essay invites us to re-consider how much is *presupposed* in various branches of human enquiry. Schleiermacher and Dilthey were mistaken in restricting hermeneutics to the "human" sciences alone. The problem of hermeneutics "is really universal".[45] The physical sciences appear to operate on an empirical, rational, or observational basis, but in actuality there are pre-suppositions in "possibilities for knowing" which are left "half in the dark". For example, the science of statistics seems to be an exact observational and mathematical discipline based only on "the facts". But "which questions these facts answer, and which facts would begin to speak if other questions were asked, are *hermeneutical* questions."[46] Much depends in research in the sciences on "noticing the interesting fact", or the use of imagination, and on the posing of the right question. All this becomes more apparent when we examine "the linguistic constitution of the world" and note that "understanding is language-bound."[47] Hermeneutics concerns *all* human enquiry.

While we have noted and examined the problem of radical historical finitude which Gadamer addresses, we have not yet considered the background to his claims about language. Language, in Gadamer's view, constitutes a hermeneutical problem, because our understanding is restricted by the boundaries of our language; but more fundamentally it also provides positive hermeneutical conditions for understanding, because the linguistic world is the inter-subjective world which opens up the possibility of communication and has a "universal" dimension.

In the history of thought Gadamer perceives a significant advance in the work of Wilhelm von Humboldt (1767–1835). Humboldt argued that rather than mirroring the world, individual human languages function as "mirrors of the individual mentalities of the nations".[48] Without language, we should have no "world": "But this world is linguistic in nature."[49] On the other hand, Gadamer insists that Humboldt's critique of any conceptual independence of a linguistic world "is far from meaning that man's relationship to the world is imprisoned within a linguistically schematized habitat. On the contrary, . . . there is . . . freedom from the habitat . . . To rise above the habitat has from the outset a human, i.e. a linguistic significance . . . Matters of fact came into language."[50] Gadamer writes: "Whoever has language 'has' the world"; but language mediates this world intersubjectively rather than objectively.[51]

For Gadamer himself, the boundless intersubjectivity that characterizes all human language and communication constitutes the *"universal aspect of hermeneutics"*.[52] Language is "where 'I' and world meet", and gives hermeneutics "an ontological turn".[53] Gadamer is certainly not alone in suggesting that a critique of language has universal bearing on all disciplines and on all branches of knowledge or understanding. Some critiques of language, however, are more negative and even self-destructive. This is the case with the work of the relatively little-known Bohemian philosopher Fritz Mauthner (1849–1923) whose work not only anticipates certain features and devices used by Wittgenstein, but also, ahead of his time, postulates an almost Derridean type of approach. In his *Contributions to a Critique of Language* (1901–03) Mauthner coined the term *logocracy* to denote the illusion generated by the merely apparent truth-status of words. A critique carried out upon language (*Kritik an der Sprache*) was essential to bring about freedom from this illusion.[54] The deepest philosophical problems, Mauthner argued, could be "reduced to questions of linguistic usage" (*Sprachgebrauchs*).[55] He invited us to "see through" the conventionality and circularity of language, which holds us under its spell. Language is misleading, and there is a need rigorously to re-appraise its foundations both in universal terms and in particular cases. At the end of a full-length specialist study of Mauthner's *Critique* Gershon Weiler concludes: "The issue which is raised by Mauthner, namely the possibility for accounting for the *whole* of our language *and for whatever is expressed by means of language* in completely conventionalist terms, is still a living issue. His ultimate message, that analysis of language on a conventionalist assumption is self-destructive, may well be a lesson we have yet to learn."[56]

In his earlier work in the *Tractatus* Wittgenstein stated explicitly: "All philosophy is a 'critique of language'". [57] In this same sentence there occurs his only reference (to my knowledge) to Mauthner. The full proposition reads: "All philosophy is 'a critique of language' (though not in Mauthner's sense)." The similarities and differences between Wittgenstein and Mauthner are striking. In the *Tractatus* Wittgenstein asserts that "language disguises thought".[58] The aim in his earlier work was to determine *"the limits of my language"*, just as Kant had set himself to determine the limits of thought.[59] What language "disguised" was "the form of thought beneath it", or the nature of the proposition in terms of its formal logic. Logic itself, however, is foundational: "a proposition is a picture of reality."[60] "In a proposition there must be as many distinguishable parts as in the situation which it represents."[61]

The task of a critique of language for the earlier Wittgenstein consisted in a rigorous *logical* analysis which exposed the structure of *"simple objects"* (in the logical sense of the term), the analysis of combination *"elementary propositions"*, which depict simple states of affairs in the world, and their logical inter-relationship as *complex propositions* which could in principle depict everything "in" the world. Wittgenstein writes: "If all true elementary propositions are given, the result is a complete description of the world."[62] From this, however, Wittgenstein has to exclude the ethical and the mystical, which for him are real and important. But these can only be "shown"; they cannot be "said".[63] "The sense of the world must lie outside the world."[64]

Mauthner, on the other hand, entirely rejected such a distinction between language and thought. As Weiler argues, he would not have endorsed the statement that "a proposition is a picture of reality".[65] For Mauthner, *all* language universally falls under the category from which the early Wittgenstein exempts propositions about the natural world. Nevertheless both writers agree that the task of philosophy is to offer a critique of language, which will determine the *limits* of language. They also agree that, as Wittgenstein observed in his transitional or "middle" period: "I cannot get out of language by means of language."[66] In his later period Wittgenstein comes to share Mauthner's lack of faith in the power of logic alone, or the purely logical analysis of linguistic propositions to answer foundational human questions. Weiler argues the hypothesis that in his early period Wittgenstein read the first thirty pages of Mauthner's *Critique*, but then abandoned it because of the different nature of their projects at the time. But three themes from these pages appear in identical form in Wittgenstein's writings: the use of the ladder-image about the self-destructive nature of the critique of language; the comparison between the growth of a language and the growth of a city; and the notion of rules of a game as a central paradigm for the operation of language.[67] Weiler concludes that once he had abandoned his early view "Wittgenstein could now employ with profit the notion of *Spielregel*: perhaps remembering his early reading of Mauthner."[68]

For both Mauthner and Wittgenstein the critique of language assumed *universal* proportions. Both saw that this suggested the importance of *functional* and *practical* issues rather than merely theoretical questions about the foundations of intellectual enquiry. But whereas Mauthner spoke of illusion and "word-superstition", Wittgenstein remained aloof from sceptical and from radically pragmatic conclusions on the ground that what *counts as*, for example, "a mistake", depends on the interweaving of the thought and practices of humankind in networks of publicly recognizable operational intelligibility. Wittgenstein's philosophy comes very close to being a "universal hermeneutic". He observes, for example, that in some contexts the problem with the words "true" and "false" is that using them "is like saying 'it tallies with the facts or it doesn't'", when "the very thing that is in question is what 'tallying' is here." [69] Many of Wittgenstein's remarks invoke *practice* as a crucial element: "Giving grounds . . . justifying the evidence, comes to an end – but the end is not in certain propositions striking us immediately as true . . . It is our *acting* which lies at the bottom of the language-game."[70] Nevertheless *praxis* does not provide the whole story. Communication also presupposes "agreement not only in definitions but also . . . in judgments."[71] *Understanding* a formula, a practice, a pattern, or an activity is knowing "how to go on."[72] But this involves both cognitive, practical, and situational or hermeneutical factors, as well as "training".[73]

We have already noted how the later Heidegger combines an exposition of the problem of radical historical finitude and "calculative" thinking (cf. Gadamer's "method") with his own critique of language. Only the language of poetry, rather than the language of "analysis" which takes things apart can engage with anything foundational. (Heidegger calls this "Being" or "Being-as-Event".) Instrumental language merely reflects back the concepts which we already use, and which merely reflect "our" world.

Since we have already discussed the new hermeneutic in several other studies, we need not pursue further the issues raised here by Fuchs and Ebeling. But Ebeling's so-called "theological theory of language" is close to that of the later Heidegger. Ebeling speaks of "a profound crisis of language, and indeed a complete collapse of language."[74] "We threaten to die of language poisoning."[75] Theological hermeneutics must therefore seek "a theory of language with the widest possible horizon", and an account of "how breakdowns in language can be overcome."[76] Hermeneutics moves beyond "the mere sign-function of language (in which) words are reduced to ciphers . . . to a question of calculus."[77]

Gadamer claims that the problem of hermeneutics is universal to all disciplines not only because understanding is, in the sense discussed, linguistic, but also because *practical reason itself functions in the context of, and as part of, a tradition of effective history, not in opposition to it or in abstraction from it.* Although Gadamer does not develop the parallel, the principle is strikingly demonstrated in the part played by hermeneutics in the development of the social sciences. This area has been well charted in Zygmunt Bauman's study, *Hermeneutics and Social Science.*[78] We shall return to this work in chapter XV.

We shall undertake a more detailed discussion of this area in our examination of the hermeneutics of social and socio-political criticism in chapters XI and XII. Here we simply outline a broad development. Karl Marx, as Bauman observes, located the roots of miscomprehension not in the mind of the cognizing subject" (as would be the case in rationalism) "but in the structure . . . of domination which constitutes the object. That is to say: *Marx transforms epistemology into sociology*".[79]

But sociology, as Max Weber saw it, entails the attempt to understand "objectively" patterns of subjectively-orientated human behaviour. Weber believed that the possibility of achieving this depended on the emergence of the critical rationality that was distinctive to the modern era. But this evaluation of a critical rationality distinctive to a given historical era could be interpreted in a radically different way. Karl Mannheim (1893–1947) fastened on the corollary: *each historical era offers its own canons and criteria of rationality*. The search for truth thus remains relative to a given *Zeitgeist*, and can never strive for an "ultimate" truth which lies beyond history. Indeed, the relation to the spirit of the age *constitutes*, for Mannheim, the criterion of truth or rationality. For illusion and distortion spring either from *historically* lagging behind in applying anomalous ideology, or from *historically* leaping ahead in utopianism.[80] Thus Mannheim's introduction to the sociology of knowledge bears the title *Ideology and Utopia* (1936).[81]

We discuss Alfred Schutz's work later in fuller detail in chapter XV. Here, however, we may note the major role played by the notion of "life-world" which he draws from Dilthey, Husserl, and Heidgger and which he inter-relates with his other key concepts of *relevance* and *typification*.[82] In Schutz's view, *all* meaning arises from interpretation (i.e. is hermeneutical) in relation to given purposes and interests which emerge from within the life-world, but which also remain, in turn, open to constant revision as new patterns of relevance to new interests and developing purposes emerge. Perceptions and interpretations of social reality depend on relevances and typifications which shift in accordance with these patterns. Thomas Luckmann, Schutz's former pupil, colleague, and collaborator developed these perspectives further. The widely influential popular book *The Social Construction of Reality* (1966) comes from the pen of Peter Berger co-jointly with that of Thomas Luckmann. In their introduction Berger and Luckmann acknowledge the influence of the set of thinkers whom Bauman has identified as bringing hermeneutics into social science: Marx, Dilthey, Mannheim, Talcott Parsons, and Alfred Schutz.[83]

Gadamer's language about "the universality of the hermeneutical problem" raises questions at the same metacritical level as those which Peter Berger raises about the nature of sociology in his popular book *Facing Up to Modernity*. Berger sees sociology as unmasking otherwise hidden assumptions on which society rests; assumptions which, in Schutz's terminology, are unnoticed simply because they are taken for granted.[84] Gadamer also addresses the kind of questions raised by Peter Winch's book *The Idea of a Social Science*. Winch writes, "Connected with the realization that intelligibility takes many and varied forms is the realization that reality has no key."[85] He further observes, "The whole idea of logical relation is only possible by virtue of some sort of agreement between men and their actions, which is discussed by Wittgenstein."[86] Gadamer accepts the practical, life-related, community-orientated angle of approach which we also find in Schutz, Berger, and Winch. But the strand of conservatism which stresses the role of judgment, tradition, and practical wisdom indicates a withdrawal from the level of social relativism which these writers reach.

Gadamer's key concept of "effective-history" (*Wirkungsgeshichte*) calls attention to the operative force of tradition over those who belong to it. Gadamer writes: "History does not belong to us, but we belong to it. Long before we understand ourselves through the process of self-examination, we understand ourselves in a self-evident way in the family, society, and state in which we live. The focus of subjectivity is a distorting mirror."[87] Here the paradigm of apprehending truth is not the individual-centred rational reflection of the Enlightenment, but the context-related foundations (prejudices or pre-judgments) which are derived through the inter-subjective community of both past and present generations. These foundations constitute a person's "historical reality". Enlightenment rationalism invoked "critical reason" to distinguish between legitimate and false prejudices. But in so doing it suggested an artificial, abstract, and destructive antithesis between reason and authority. *Authority, seen in its proper sense, has nothing to do with abdication of reason.* Respect for authority rests on an entirely *rational* judgment that one is "aware of one's own limitations", and has reason to accept "that others have better understanding."[88]

In society we often accept and acknowledge this kind of authority as a reality when we seek the help of a teacher, a specialist, or a professional expert. But still more is at issue. In Romanticism, with its concern for classical origins and roots, authority could also be seen positively in relation to what could be learned from tradition. In hermeneutics "the main feature is not a distancing and freeing of ourselves from what has been transmitted. Rather, we stand always within tradition, and this is no objectifying process . . . It is always part of us . . . The abstract antithesis between tradition and historical research must be discarded."[89] Gadamer's conclusion about the relation between historical situatedness and tradition is expressed in terminology taken up by Richard Bernstein and by Georgia Warnke: it entails moving *beyond objectivism*; but it also entails going *beyond relativism*.[90]

It is more difficult however (as Bernstein, Weinsheimer, and Georgia Warnke agree) to determine from Gadamer's work by what criteria we are now to distinguish "true prejudices" from others. Gadamer relies at this point on his four key models of the game-world, the art-world, the "arising" of truth in conversational dialogue, and the practical virtues of common sense and judgment. But a particular difficulty arises in the case of interpreting texts because here the language of "conversation", and to a lesser extent "world", become quasi-metaphorical, even though they entirely make sense as part of the experience of reading and interpretation. In the end, Gadamer's written work in conjunction with some of his public oral comments suggests that much weight has to be placed on "hermeneutically trained", cultivated, and sensitive *judgment* in the context of tradition and effective-history, because *judgment is precisely the quality that comes into play when we can no longer "do it by the book" and follow methods and rules*. The post-Heideggerian, radically historical, meta-critical, side of Gadamer's work suggests that the rules run out. The conservative, traditional truth-conscious side of his work suggests that within a linguistic and radically-historical context, practical wisdom, conversation, and judgment have a positive part still to play. But this radically-historical context places the initiative *not* with human *consciousness*, but with the *"performance" of the text*, the art-work, or the utterance. Here the later Heidegger's contrast between being-as-concept and Being-as-event stands in the background. The *reality* of the text and its *truth* does not exist, as it were, apart from the moment of interaction and performance.

This still leaves the fundamental problem. How can we ever know whether our act of judgment was valid, or whether the experience of performance was an authentic one? Gadamer invites us both to look back to intersubjective tradition and forward to the "advance" that emerges from dialogue, and which moves towards "the anticipation of completeness". This provides a perspective, but the norms that might otherwise constitute criteria of good judgment *cannot in principle be separable from the historically-situated acts of judgment themselves*, because "every age has to understand a transmitted text *in its own way*, for the text is part of the tradition in which the age takes an objective interest and in which it seeks to understand itself".[91] The criterion cannot rest, for example, "in the contingencies of the author and (those for) whom he originally wrote . . . Not occasionally only, but always, the meaning of a text goes beyond its author"[92]

For understanding can no more be "reproductive" than a game can consist of exact duplications or repetitions of the *same* acts and events of play. Weinsheimer aptly observes: "No game is ever played twice identically, and for all this variety it is still the one game".[93] If a football game, or a game of cards, is turned into part of a stage-play "in becoming repeatable, it is simply not a game anymore."[94] For example, the original card game that is re-enacted in Pope's *Rape of the Lock* began as a game, but ceases to be a *game* when it follows the precise routines prescribed for it in the play. Hence, to prescribe *a criterion for right judgment in advance would constitute a return to method, to objectivity, and to a not-fully-historical understanding*. Conversely, however, to remove all rules *from the game itself*, so that it no longer *constrains the reactions and purposes* of the players and creates their world, *would constitute a move into relativism*. This represents Gadamer's attempt to offer a "universal" hermeneutic which avoids the *two opposite pitfalls of objectivism and relativism*.

It is now clear why Gadamer's hermeneutics have been consistently and repeatedly attacked on two fronts. Most notably Jürgen Habermas, while endorsing Gadamer's attack on positivism and rationalism, insists that the role ascribed by Gadamer to tradition verges on the naive, because it does not sufficiently allow for ideological distortion or for the kind of deception identified by psycho-analytic hermeneutics.[95] As we have seen, Emilio Betti attacks Gadamer for surrendering the notion of objectivity. Karl-Otto Apel approves Gadamer's emphasis on inter-subjectivity, but argues that he has compromised and relativized what is left of the notion of rationality. Apel writes "The strength of Gadamer's 'philosophical hermeneutics' lies in his critique of the objectivistic methodological ideal of historicism, but he goes too far when he disputes the meaning of the methodological-hermeneutic abstraction from the question of truth and equates the model of the judge or director with that of the interpreter.[96] Apel's reference to "methodological-hermeneutic abstraction" challenges Gadamer's assimilation of "criteria" into the acts of judgment themselves. Indeed, strikingly, Apel accuses Gadamer of a "scientistic" fallacy (!) because effectively Gadamer connives with the tendency in the natural sciences to reserve notions of "objectivity" to the sciences rather than to the humanities.[97] Apel firmly agrees with Gadamer that the problem of "understanding" is universal, but he argues that hermeneutics entails an *expanded* understanding of rationality, rather than one that moves in the direction of relativity.

On the other hand, Richard Rorty's evaluation comes from a different angle. Rorty approves of Gadamer's emphasis on the role of pre-judgment, tradition, effective-history, and the relativity of radical historical finitude. But Rorty urges that Gadamer does not go far enough in reducing "truth" to more pragmatic terms. Rorty sees hermeneutics as "an expression of the hope that the cultural space left by the demise of epistemology will not be filled".[98] Rorty places "edification" in the space left by truth, and effectively, replaces knowledge by Gadamer's *Bildung* or "cultivatedness". In his essay "Solidarity or Subjectivity" Rorty argues that adjudication between "traditions" can be carried out only on a pragmatic basis, since all norms, whether ethical or rational, remain relative to the traditions themselves.[99] Thus, although Rorty treats Gadamer as an ally in his own hermeneutical enterprise, as Georgia Warnke convincingly shows, his "neo-pragmatism" has quite different implications from those of the "universality of hermeneutics" in Gadamer. In his *Contingency, Irony, and Solidarity* (1989) Rorty stresses the contingency of language, of selfhood, and of the liberal community.[100]

Gadamer's work convincingly demonstrates that hermeneutical, historical, or contextual understanding radically relativizes the claims of any a-historical version of rationalism, such as the critical rationalism of the Enlightenment. Gadamer firmly establishes the fundamental nature of the problems which he addresses, including the universal role of hermeneutics, tradition, effective-history, and practical-reason-in-community, all of which were neglected or even ignored in rationalism. He also succeeds in underlining the decisive importance of intersubjectivity and community in relation to truth. Nevertheless the ambiguities which Rorty and others exploit in the direction of contextual relativism remain open to difficulties which we shall expand in later chapters. The kind of arguments which Apel, Ricoeur, and Pannenberg bring to bear about the role of "explanation", assertion or even normative frameworks need to be taken into account alongside Gadamer's work. From a theological viewpoint, it is, on one side, very seriously unsatisfactory that no criterion for textual interpretation can be found other than the "performance" of the text itself, alongside some role accorded to human judgment in the context of community and effective-history. On the other side, however, Gadamer is right to call attention to the role of practical wisdom within the community at points where "rules" or "methods" run out. Theological traditions must encourage, and allow for trained and cultivated "practical wisdom" or "pastoral judgment", especially where questions arise about the application of texts to new situations, within fresh temporal horizons.

Nevertheless, as Pannenberg has powerfully argued, Christian eschatology does, in the light of Christology, entail norms and criteria beyond those of the human judgments reflected in given traditions. In Christ and in the cross and resurrection of Christ, the end and goal of history is partially, provisionally, and proleptically anticipated. In this sense, as Pannenberg declares, "the text can only be understood in the context of the total history which binds the past to the present, and . . . also to the future horizon . . ." Biblical eschatology and apocalyptic, and not simply Hegel, speak of "the meaning of the present (being) illuminated in the light of the future".[102] History is "a totality presented from the perspective of an end", even if this is only "provisionally and proleptically accessible".[103] This is why Christian theological traditions have envisaged the last judgment, even if symbolically, as a definitive, public, and cosmic horizon in the light of which all "facts" assume their significance. But would not such a notion constitute special pleading for a concept of Christian theology? If anything may be said to characterize Pannenberg's thought, it is the conscious attempt to avoid some form of special pleading, as against the universal significance of theology in the light of generally accepted public criteria. How, then, does Pannenberg establish this approach, and claim to offer a metacritical account of knowledge? To Pannenberg's thoughts we now turn.

3. Pannenberg's Metacritical Unifying of a Hermeneutics of Universal History with the Scientific Status of Theology

Wolfhart Pannenberg (b. 1928) has consistently addressed metacritical questions which concern the foundations of knowledge. Even before the appearance of Gadamer's *Truth and Method*, he spoke of history as a whole as the comprehensive horizon of understanding and of Christian theology (1959), and in his *Theology and the Philosophy of Science* (German, 1973, English 1976) he proposes a unitary theory of knowledge in which hermeneutical understanding and scientific explanation belong together.[104] He shares with Gadamer, however, a distaste for the pretensions of a simplified positivism which purports to begin with foundational "facts" independently of hermeneutical understanding, and agrees with him that understanding is profoundly historical. In common with Betti, whose work we have discussed, as well as with Apel and Habermas, Pannenberg affirms the fundamental role of hermeneutics and hermeneutical understanding. But with them he also criticises Gadamer for under-rating the need for objectivity, and for by-passing questions of method on the assumption that these are incompatible with a genuinely metacritical hermeneutical theory. Pannenberg seeks a universal foundation for knowledge which transcends any particular, contingent, contextualization or actualization. He develops Gadamer's hermeneutics in the diametrically opposite direction to that which is travelled in Richard Rorty's social or contextual pragmatism.

In Pannenberg's view, a theological approach offers more convincing grounds than any other basis for wrestling with the problem of the foundations of knowledge at a metacritical level. Philosophically he is sympathetic with Hegel's view that meaning can be determined only in the light of the whole. An incomplete context leads to a distorted picture. Theology, because it speaks of God who is the creator and end of all, "includes all truth whatever. This universality of theology is unavoidably bound up with the fact that it speaks of God . . . Anyone who does not want to revert to a polytheistic or polydaemonistic stage of phenomenology of religion must think of God as the creator of all things. It belongs to the task of theology to understand all being in relation to God, so that without God they simply could not be understood."[105]

In insisting on *both* a universal metacritical approach *and* a historical-hermeneutical approach simultaneously Pannenberg was also, negatively, identifying some contrasting targets for attack; and, positively, exploring a particular philosophical tradition. Negatively, he was attacking first the "salvation-history" approach of the so-called biblical theology movement, comparing unfavourably "a ghetto of redemptive history" with "the universal correlative connections of human history."[106] Second, he was attacking the kind of positivism which was also under fire from Gadamer and from other writers. Such positivism, Pannenberg stated, "seems apt to exclude the transcendent" and amounts to "methodological anthropocentrism."[107]

In biblical interpretation this kind of positivism led to a view of historical enquiry which might seem to exclude the occurrence of any new or unexpected event. Novelty lay beyond the progress-reports of existing "laws" and beyond the analogies of interpretation projected by Troeltsch and others. How, then, could such an approach allow the resurrection of Jesus Christ to be located or designated as a historical event, rather than as a merely perspectival, non-cognitive, or non-referential implicate of faith? This was intimately bound up with Pannenberg's third target of attack, namely the driving of a wedge between fact and value, or between the Jesus of history and the Christ of faith. Here probably the most notorious and influential perpetrator of such dualism was Rudolf Bultmann, following in the steps of Martin Kähler. The whole Bultmannian school tends to reflect this dualism.

In positive terms, for Pannenberg the whole of reality remains essentially historical. The philosophy which he finds most constructive and congenial is a critically modified and theologically corrected version of Hegel's philosophy of history. This has implications for Pannenberg's view of the nature of hermeneutics. He writes: "History is the most comprehensive horizon of Christian theology. All theological questions and answers are meaningful only within the framework of the history God has with humanity and through humanity with the whole of creation – the history moving towards a future still hidden from the world, but already revealed in Jesus Christ."[108]

Hermeneutics is concerned with the "analysis of the interrelation of wholes and parts."[109] In one sense, as Gadamer argues, the horizon of meaning moves as the horizon of history and the horizons of readers expand. On the other hand, not only the community of interpretation but also the events which surround the birth of the text belong to a historical tradition, and it is fundamental to Pannenberg's hermeneutics that event and meaning, word and deed, tradition and interpretation, belong inextricably together. This is what Kähler and Bultmann tended to overlook. Thus in his well-known and influential essay "The Revelation of God in Jesus of Nazareth" (1967) Pannenberg urges, by contrast, that "we must reinstate today the original unity of facts and their meaning... (Every event) brings its own meaning... brings it with its context, which of course is always a context of tradition."[110] But the notion of tradition, with its implications concerning continuity and patterns of identifiable regularity, also points forward to "the eschatological event which binds history into a whole."[111] The knowledge of God is made possible by history: "One has to reckon with an intertwining both of prophetic words and of events."[112]

Events may surpass words, and thus give them a new meaning, even a new reference; but conversely words give to what would otherwise be bare events their significance as parts of a larger whole. This was the work of the prophets, especially "Deutero-Isaiah and the Deuteronomist." (cf. Deut. 18:9–22; Jer. 28:6–9).

This principle, however, can be extended until it embraces the whole of history. Pannenberg declares, "Only in the light of the End is the close proximity of the Creator to his creation revealed, and hence the true nature of his creation."[113] In contrast to Bultmann (and, we shall see, also in contrast to Ricoeur) Pannenberg insists, "Knowledge is not a stage beyond faith, but leads into faith . . . The act of faith or trust presupposes a knowledge of the trustworthiness of the partner."[114] But knowledge is corrigible and progressive as history moves on. Thus, "In a completely altered context, in a situation that has been radically transformed, a message cast in precisely the same words no longer means the same thing."[115] "Each individual entity has its meaning only in relation to the whole to which it belongs."[116]

It comes as no surprise that at this point Pannenberg alludes not only to parallels with, and differences from, Hegel, but also compares his approach with that of Gadamer. In particular he takes up Gadamer's discussion of universal history in Dilthey.[117] The fullest discussion of his relation to Gadamer comes in his essay "Hermeneutics and Universal History" (1963).[118] He comments: "Gadamer excellently describes the way in which the past and the present are brought into relation to each other in the process of understanding as a 'fusion of horizons' . . . A new horizon is formed."[119] Pannenberg also offers a cautiously positive evaluation of Gadamer's use of the notion of dialogue and conversation as *that out of which* some new or third thing arises above and beyond what each partner already brings. This model, however, has limitations as a model of *textual* interpretation. Gadamer's notion of an "unspoken" horizon of meaning offers some parallel to Pannenberg's idea of history as a totality presented from the perspective of the end.

In philosophical terms, Pannenberg's position in this particular area of debate comes close to that of Gadamer, including the use made for hermeneutics by Gadamer and by Ricoeur of Heidegger's notion of "possibility." Like Gadamer, he carefully qualifies his words to avoid following Hegel too closely, although unlike Gadamer he has a much more positive evaluation of assertions. Pannenberg writes: "The text can only be understood in connection with the totality of history which links the past to the present, and . . . also to the horizon of the future based on what is presently possible . . . The meaning of the present becomes clear only in the light of the future."[120] Pannenberg seeks significantly to modify Hegel's conception of history. The End of history "is itself only *provisionally* known."[121] Theologically "its end has become accessible in a provisional and anticipatory way that is to be gathered today from the history of Jesus and its relationship to the Israelite-Jewish tradition."[122]

Gadamer sees this argument as "a highly useful discussion of my book", and comments further: "There is really no dispute between Pannenberg and myself . . . Pannenberg does not propose to renew Hegel's claim either." The "only difference" is that the Christian theologian finds a "fixed point in the absolute historicity of the Incarnation".[123] But this "only difference" becomes crucial not only for theology but also for philosophical hermeneutics. For as we have briefly noted, and shall see further in more detail, without such a "fixed point" Gadamer's philosophy reflects a deep ambivalence which allows Rorty to develop it in one direction, Apel in another, and Habermas in a third direction. In particular Rorty attempts a development in terms of social or contextual pragmatism, which explicitly rejects metacritical argument as impossible, and substitutes a kind of social-narrative hermeneutics.

Pannenberg represents a diametrically opposite view. His volume *Theology and the Philosophy of Science* constitutes a careful *metacritical* argument for the *unity* of knowledge which *incorporates humeneutics*.[124] Pannenberg begins by taking up Augustine's argument that science and knowledge must serve wisdom. On the other hand, if theology claims to make truth-claims which relate to the "whole" as it reflects God's creation and activity, theology must work with "generally accepted criteria".[125] Christianity is not a sect. We cannot claim that there is *no sense at all* in which theology shares criteria of truth with sciences. Pannenberg agrees with Habermas that positivism can be challenged only by some paradigm of critical knowledge which will *embrace* and *include* it; not by that which attacks it "from without" or tries to by-pass it.[126]

Pannenberg critically discusses Karl Popper's modifications to a simplified form of positivism, including his notion that metaphysical or "scientifically unwarranted" assumptions are involved in scientific enquiry.[127] He reviews the dual role in Popper of "critical thought" and "openness" to the revision of hypotheses in the light of testing. But any over-simple notion of falsification must be modified in the light of T.S. Kuhn's work. It is an "illusion" that criteria of falsification can be applied without reference to wider contexts and bodies of knowledge, or at any time.[128] Theories are less "mirrors" of nature than explanatory devices which address issues of evidence. Even in the sciences, however, hypotheses entail elements of conjecture or *anticipation*. They imply "an anticipatory understanding of truth".[129] It is better to speak of this as critical rationalism than as positivism.

In the social sciences, equally, explanation and understanding belong together. Pannenberg expounds this thesis against the background of

Dilthey, Weber, Talcott Parsons, and Habermas. He comments, "A need for explanation arises wherever states of affairs are discovered which cannot be fitted into the existing theory in the field in question, but conflict with it."[130] Understanding, however does not always presuppose explanation, although it may sometimes require an explanatory framework.

Pannenberg traces the rise of hermeneutical theory (after its pre-history in Flacius and the post-Reformation period) in Schleiermacher, Dilthey, Heidegger, and Gadamer. Although he rejects several of Betti's arguments, Pannenberg fundamentally supports Betti in his criticism of Gadamer's "loss of objectivity."[131] This loss arises, he asserts, because Gadamer has followed Heidegger in "the existentialist devaluation of the statement."[132] Pannenberg does not deny Heidegger's point that propositions are embedded in wider frames of a "totality of involvements", just as he endorses Gadamer's language about an "unexpressed horizon of meaning". But there remains a conceivable and abstractable propositional content which can be "objectified" in the process of interpretation. Here Pannenberg reinforces the ground marked out in his earlier essay "Hermeneutic and Universal History." Interpretation transposes his horizon "into an explicit statement."[133]

Like Gadamer, then, Pannenberg stresses human historical finitude, and the hermeneutical dimensions of understanding which lie behind or within any claim to knowledge. But unlike Gadamer, Pannenberg assigns a more fundamental status to testable propositions or assertions, and argues for the scientific status of theology.[134] Yet this in no way constitutes a retreat from his earlier claims about universal history and Christian eschatology. E. Frank Tupper comments, "Pannenberg insists that the theological conception of history dare not be sacrificed because of the failure of the Hegelian solution. Instead it is essential to develop a conception of universal history which, in contrast to Hegel's, would preserve the finitude of human experience, the openness of the future, and the intrinsic validity of the particular. Pannenberg poses a conception of universal history wherein the end of history, which gathers history into a whole, is only known provisionally: the eschatological activity and destiny of Jesus of Nazareth constitutes the prolepsis of the *eschaton* wherein the meaning of the entirety of history is anticipated."[135]

Pannenberg's insistence that explanation and understanding belong together, together with his emphasis on the eschatological horizon of "possibility" identify some clear points of affinity with the hermeneutics of Paul Ricoeur, to whom we are about to turn. Allan Galloway comments, "True openness to the world consists in the fact that man can always see *beyond* any experience. . . . to new possibilities . . . Imagination is the front on which we are open to the radically new and so to the infinite 'beyond' of the world . . . The creativeness of imagination corresponds to what is new and unforeseeable in external events."[136]

This provides a very different account of the foundations of knowledge from that of positivism, and accounts for the controversy that surrounds Pannenberg's hermeneutical discussion of the New Testament material about the resurrection of Jesus. Within a positivistic framework there can be no room for genuine novelty. If interpretation depends entirely on analogies between past experience and the event or text to be interpreted, it is as if nothing new could ever be perceived to happen for the first time. We do have to hand existing parables, metaphors, or symbols. Thus, Pannenberg writes, "The familar experience of being awakened and rising from sleep serves as a parable for the completely unknown destiny expected for the dead."[137] But whenever the theory of truth espoused by positivism is static, unhistorical, and a-temporal, a hermeneutical and universal or metacritical understanding of truth takes account of its historical and temporal dimension. Thus in his important essay "What is Truth?" Pannenberg argues: *The truth of God must prove itself anew in the future* . . . The truth of God embraces all other truth."[138]

This emphasis on the temporal horizon of truth is identified by Pannenberg with the Hebrew-Jewish and biblical traditions in contrast to views of truth in Greek philosophy. He writes: "It is this historical feature that is completely lacking in the Greek idea of truth."[139] It is all the more surprising then, whatever the validity of claims about "Hebrew" and "Greek" ideas of truth, that J. Moltmann should accuse Pannenberg at this point of turning away from a biblical notion of truth to that of a "Greek cosmic theology" or a teleological construct of "reality in its totality."[140] Tupper is correct to include this among Moltmann's "illegitimate criticisms" of Pannenberg.[141] Both Moltmann and Pannenberg stress the importance of eschatology and promise, and the possibility of creative novelty in history. But Moltmann draws from this eschatology a hermeneutical *praxis* of liberation and social change, whereas Pannenberg directs the main focus of his attention of epistemological questions. This is distinct from, but not unrelated to, Moltmann's concerns about the cross and the work of Christ as the converse of presupposition of hope, in contrast to Pannenberg's concerns about the resurrection and the person of Christ. Moltmann sees eschatology in the context of social change and socio-critical hermeneutics; Pannenberg develops the concept to raise questions about the foundations of knowledge.

Perhaps nowhere is Pannenberg's emphasis on historical novelty clearer than in his two essays first on myth and then on "eschatology and the experience of meaning."[142] Pannenberg readily admits that the biblical writings contain "mythical themes." But these are transformed and re-applied, often to eschatology. Mythical themes play a large part in apocalyptic. But the language of myth is always transcended because myth carries with it a "cyclical" understanding of history, the world, or reality.[143] This is not the same as typological analogy. Pannenberg writes: "The element of historical novelty, which is the essential difference between the typological mode of thought . . . and mythological thought, is expressed above all in these themes of qualitative distinction between the future and the present."[144] "In primitive Christianity eschatology does not display mythical features."[145]

The importance and decisiveness of the horizon of eschatology may be suggested even by ordinary experiences in life: "What formerly seemed insignificant may perhaps appear later as of fundamental importance, and the reverse may be true."[146] Pannenberg appeals to the findings of Thomas Luckmann and other social theorists for the view that even in terms of a phenomenology of religion, "religion is concerned with the totality of the meaning of life."[147] In a dissertation entitled *Three Horizons: A Study in Biblical Hermeneutics with Special Reference to Wolfhart Pannenberg* (1987) James McHann argued that hermeneutical theory needed to move beyond the notion of "Two Horizons", to take account of the three horizons of "past, present, and future", and thereby to ground hermeneutics more adequately in ontology and eschatology.[148]

Pannenberg has developed a foundational metacritical theory that modifies and corrects Gadamer's hermeneutics while taking seriously the problem of historical finitude, historical understanding, and the contextual nature of hermeneutics within traditions and communities. This metacritical approach has developed elements in Gadamer (as we have already noted) in the opposite direction to that of Rorty's anti-metacritical social pragmatism. But like Apel, Habermas, and Ricoeur, Pannenberg places explanation and understanding together, seeing Gadamer as perpetuating the disjunction which stems from Dilthey.

In common with all of these thinkers, Apel, Gadamer, Habermas, Ricoeur and Rorty, Pannenberg questions the claims of traditional positivism. Like all of them, although in his own distinctive way, he seeks to bring together notions of knowledge and action. But Pannenberg is more deeply concerned with *the extra-linguistic realities of history*, and with *the interaction and intertwining of language and patterns of events in the context of historical traditions*. As we shall see in the next chapter, he is probably stronger at this point than Ricoeur, not least because of the pivotal importance of Christology for his work, and because linguistic reference can move beyond the intra-linguistic world for Pannenberg. Speech about God moves beyond merely speaking of human existence and thought. God is revealed in the deeds and words of Jesus of Nazareth, and we do not need to speak of "deeds", as Ricoeur sometimes does, in inverted commas or quotation marks, as if the term functioned only in a quasi-metaphorical or intra-linguistic sense.

Pannenberg's hermeneutics of textual meaning also advances the discussion. On the one hand, he takes seriously the historical horizon and context of the tradition to which the texts themselves bear witness. On the other hand, as the horizons of historical understanding move forward in history, these horizons may be enlarged. The explanatory or scientific dimension allows for historical reconstruction, although not of a positivistic kind, and encourages critical testing of hypotheses of meaning. The hermeneutical dimension resists the seduction of the text and its context to the level of a cognitive abstraction which is read off at some unfinished stage of history, for the meaning-potential of the text always transcends this. Tentatively in his work on the philosophy of sciences Pannenberg suggests that systems-theory and "related cybernetic considerations" can contribute to our understanding of the hermeneutical relation between the givenness of the past and the provisionality of the whole.[149]

If we move to the world of the New Testament, we find strong justification for identifying metacritical or foundational realities with futurity. As we have already argued in chapter VII, when the writer to the Hebrews describes faith as the *hypostasis* of that for which we hope (Heb. 11:1), the contrast remains a temporal one, not a spatial one. Even the notion of faith as the "conviction" (*elegkhos*) of things "not seen" probably alludes here to what is not seen because it has *not yet* come to pass (11:1). The Epistle contains a sentence which in Käsemann's words, "applies to the whole letter: "We have no lasting city, but we seek the city which is to come (13:13,14)."[150] In Heb. 4:10, the writer identifies the "city" of eschatological consummation as "the city with *foundations*." It is precisely "hope" which is said to constitute a foundational or fixed "anchor" (Heb. 6:19). In Hebrews this carries us into the realm of a more confessional theology. But as a principle of hermeneutical theory, Pannenberg has shown that it is not only coherent and intelligible, but deserves to be taken seriously in the widest possible context. It contributes to a theological understanding of the foundations of knowledge.

NOTES TO CHAPTER IX

1. David E. Klemm (ed.) *Hermeneutical Inquiry* I, 173.
2. David Tracy, in Robert M. Grant and D. Tracy, *A Short History of the Interpretation of the Bible* 2nd edn. Philadelphia: Fortress Press, 1984, 155.
3. Paul Ricoeur, *Hermeneutics and the Human Sciences*, Cambridge: Cambridge University Press, 1981, 76 (my italics).
4. Anthony C. Thiselton, *The Two Horizons*, 40–45, 293–326, 337–41, and 344–51.
5. Stephen Fowl, "The Canonical Approach of Brevard Childs", *Expository Times* 96, 1985, 173–76.
6. *Ibid* 176.

7. Joel C. Weinsheimer, *Gadamer's Hermeneutics. A Reading of "Truth and Method"*, New Haven: Yale University Press, 1985, 102 (my italics).
8. *Ibid* 110.
9. *Ibid* 108.
10. Georgia Warnke, *Gadamer. Hermeneutics, Tradition, and Reason*, Cambridge: Polity Press, 1987.
11. *Ibid* 139–66.
12. Richard J. Bernstein, *Beyond Objectivism and Relativism: Science, Hermeneutics and Praxis*, Oxford: Blackwell, 1983, 15–52.
13. R. Hollinger (ed.) *Hermeneutics and Praxis*, Indiana: University of Notre Dame Press, 1985, 277–94 (See also his essay in Bruce Wachterhauser, cited n.22).
14. Frank Stack, *The Experience of a Poem: Jung and Wallace Stevens*, London: Guild of Pastoral Psychology 1987, 11.
15. Robert Fowler, "Who is 'the Reader' in the Text?" *Semeia* 31, 1985, 5–23.
16. *Ibid* 9.
17. Robert Morgan, *Biblical Interpretation*, 7.
18. Hans-Georg Gadamer, *Truth and Method* 325–41.
19. Richard Rorty "A Reply to Dreyfus and Taylor" in *Review of Metaphysics* 34, 1980, 3–23.
20. Calvin O. Schrag, *Radical Reflection* xi, 97, and 126.
21. Richard J. Bernstein, *op.cit.* 1–11 *et passim*.
22. Bruce R. Wachterhauser (ed.) *Hermeneutics and Modern Philosophy*, New York: Albany State University of New York Press, 1986. This includes Hans-Georg Gadamer, "Text and Interpretation" 377–96.
23. Hans-Georg Gadamer, *Truth and Method* 218 and 219.
24. Martin Heidegger, *Discourse in Thinking*, Eng. New York: Harper & Row, 1966, 54 n.4 *et passim*.
25. *Ibid* 46, and *On the Way to Language*, 84.
26. M. Heidegger, *On the Way to Language*, 85.
27. *Ibid* 65.
28. Martin Heidegger, *An Introduction to Metaphysics*, Eng. New Haven: Yale University Press, 1959, 172 and 173; *On the Way to Language* 108; *Poetry, Language, and Thought*, New York: Harper & Row, 1971, 32–7 and 42 Cf. Anthony C. Thiselton, *The Two Horizons* 335–42.
29. Hans-Georg Gadamer, *Truth and Method* 92, 93 and 94.
30. Georgia Warnke, *op. cit.* 48.
31. Hans-Georg Gadamer, *Truth and Method*, 95 and 96.
32. *Ibid* 98.
33. *Ibid* 100.
34. *Ibid* 104 and 110.
35. Joel C. Weinsheimer, *op. cit.* 111.
36. H.-G. Gadamer, *Truth and Method*, 20.
37. *Ibid* 102–03.
38. *Ibid* 329: cf. 325–33.
39. *Ibid* 19–26.
40. *Ibid* 10–19, 29–39.
41. *Ibid* 245; German, *Wahrheit und Methode. Grundzüge einer philosophischen Hermeneutik*, Tübingen: Mohr, 2nd edn. 1965, 255.

42. *Ibid.*
43. Reiner Wiehl, "Heidegger, Hermeneutics, and Ontology" in Bruce R. Wachterhauser (ed.) *op cit.*, 468.
44. Hans-Georg Gadamer, *Philosophical Hermeneutics*, Berkeley: University of California Press, 1976, 3–17.
45. *Ibid* 10.
46. *Ibid* 11.
47. *Ibid* 13, 15.
48. *Ibid* 399.
49. *Ibid* 401.
50. *Ibid* 402 and 403.
51. *Ibid* 411.
52. *Ibid* 431.
53. *Ibid* 434.
54. Gershon Weiler, *Mauthner's Critique of Language*, Cambridge: Cambridge University Press 1970, 272, 273.
55. *Ibid* 271.
56. *Ibid* 331 (my italics).
57. L. Wittgenstein, *Tractatus Logico-Philosophicus*, Germ. and Eng. London: Routledge & Kegan Paul, 1961, 4.0031.
58. *Ibid* 4.002.
59. *Ibid* 5.6 (Wittgenstein's italics).
60. *Ibid* 4.01.
61. *Ibid* 4.04.
62. *Ibid* 4.26.
63. *Ibid* 6.41.
64. *Ibid* 4.1212 and 6.522.
65. G. Weiler, *op cit* 301.
66. L. Wittgenstein, *Philosophische Bemerkungen*, Oxford: Blackwell 1964, 54 (from the period 1929–30).
67. G. Weiler, *op cit* 298–99.
68. *Ibid* 304.
69. L. Wittgenstein, *On Certainty*, Oxford: Blackwell, 1969, sect.199.
70. *Ibid* sect. 204.
71. L. Wittgenstein, *Philosophical Investigations* sect. 242.
72. *Ibid* sect. 179.
73. *Ibid* sects 156–205.
74. Gerhard Ebeling, *Introduction to a Theological Theory of Language*, Eng. London: Collins 1973, 76.
75. Gerhard Ebeling, *God and Word*, Eng. Philadelphia: Fortress, 1967, 2.
76. Gerhard Ebeling, *Introduction to a Theological Theory of Language* 156 and 157.
77. Gerhard Ebeling, *God and Word* 17.
78. Zygmunt Bauman, *Hermeneutics and Social Science*, London; Hutchinson, 1978.
79. *Ibid* 58 (my italics).
80. *Ibid* 105; cf. 89–110.
81. Karl Mannheim, *Ideology and Utopia: Introduction to the Sociology of Knowledge*, Eng. London: Routledge and Kegan Paul, 1960.
82. Alfred Schutz and Thomas Luckmann, *The Structures of the Life-World* Eng.

London: Heinemann, 1974, Alfred Schutz, *Collected Papers*, (3 vols) The Hague: Nijhoff 1962–66; and Ronald R. Cox, *Schutz's Theory of Relevance: A Phenomenological Critique*, The Hague: Nijhoff, 1978.
83. Peter Berger and Thomas Luckmann, *The Social Construction of Reality*, London: Penguin edn. 1971 (1966) 13–61.
84. Peter Berger, *Facing Up to Modernity*, London: Penguin edn. 1979 (1977) 13–14.
85. Peter Winch, *The Idea of a Social Science and its Relation to Philosophy* London: Routledge and Kegan Paul, 1958, 102.
86. *Ibid* 126.
87. H-G. Gadamer, Truth and Method 245.
88. *Ibid* 248.
89. *Ibid* 250 and 251.
90. Hans-Georg Gadamer, *Kleine Schriften*, Tübingen: Mohr (3 vols.) 1967, I, 42; Richard Bernstein, *Beyond Objectivism and Relativism, passim*; and Georgia Warnke, *op cit* 81.
91. H-G. Gadamer *Truth and Method* 263.
92. *Ibid* 263–64.
93. Joel C. Weinsheimer, *op. cit.* 104.
94. *Ibid* 108.
95. Jürgen Habermas, *Zur Logik der Sozialwissenschaften*, Frankfurt a.M: Suhrkamp, 5th edn. 1982, with part-translation of "On Hermeneutics' Claim to Universality" (largely on Gadamer, but also his own hermeneutics) in Kurt Mueller-Vollmer (ed.) *op.cit.* 294–319.
96. Karl-Otto Apel, *Towards a Transformation of Philosophy*, 62–63.
97. Karl-Otto Apel, *Understanding and Explanation. A Transcendental-Pragmatic Perspective*, Cambridge, Mass; M.I.T. Press, 1984, xvi (from the introduction by Georgia Warnke).
98. Richard Rorty, *Philosophy and the Mirror of Nature*, 315.
99. Richard Rorty, "Solidarity or Objectivity" in John Rajchman and Cornel West (eds.) *Post-analytic Philosophy*, New York: Columbia University Press, 1985, 3–19.
100. Richard Rorty, *Contingency, Irony, and Solidarity*, Cambridge: Cambridge University Press, 1989, 3–69.
101. Wolfhart Pannenberg,"Hermeneutics and Universal History" in *Journal for Theology and the Church*, 4: History and Hermeneutic, Tübingen: Mohr, and New York: Harper & Row, 1967, 147; cf. 122–52.
102. *Ibid* 147.
103. *Ibid* 151.
104. Wolfhart Pannenberg, *Theology and the Philosophy of Science*, Eng. Philadelphia: Westminster Press, 1976; and *Basic Questions in Theology*, (3 vols.) Eng. London: S.C.M. 1970–73, vol.1, 15–80 (German *Kerygma und Dogma* 5, 1959, 218–37 and 259–88.).
105. W. Pannenberg, *Basic Questions in Theology* vol.1, 1.
106. *Ibid* 41; cf. 15–80; also part-translated in Claus Westermann (ed.), Essays in *Old Testament Hermeneutics*, Richmond: John Knox, 1963, 314–35.
107. W. Pannenberg, *Basic Questions in Theology*, vol.1, 39.
108. *Ibid* vol.1, 15.

109. W. Pannenberg, *Theology and the Philosophy of Science* 189.
110. W. Pannenberg, "The Revelation of God in Jesus of Nazareth" in James M. Robinson and John B. Cobb Jr. (eds.) *New Frontiers in Theology: III, Theology as History*, New York and London: Harper and Row, 1967, 127; cf. 101–33.
111. *Ibid* 122.
112. *Ibid* 120.
113. *Ibid* 113.
114. *Ibid* 129–30.
115. W. Pannenberg, "Response to the Discussion", *ibid* 222.
116. *Ibid* 242.
117. *Ibid* 243n.
118. W. Pannenberg, "Hermeneutic and Universal History" in *Basic Questions in Theology* 1, 96–136; a different translation appears in W. Pannenberg et al., *History and Hermeneutic: Journal for Theology and the Church* 4, New York: Harper and Row, and Tübingen: Mohr, 1967, 122–54 (German Z.Th.K. 60, 1963, 90–121).
119. W. Pannenberg, *Basic Questions in Theology* 1, 117.
120. *Ibid* vol.1, 129.
121. *Ibid* vol.1, 135 (Pannenberg's italics).
122. *Ibid*.
123. Hans-Georg Gadamer, "On the Scope and Function of Hermeneutical Reflection" in *Philosophical Hermeneutics*, 36–37; cf. 18–43.
124. Wolfhart Pannenberg, *Theology and the Philosophy of Science*, Eng. Philadelphia: Westminster Press, and London: Darton, Longman & Todd, 1976.
125. *Ibid* 13.
126. *Ibid* 27.
127. *Ibid* 40.
128. *Ibid* 57.
129. *Ibid* 70.
130. *Ibid* 152.
131. *Ibid* 165–69.
132. *Ibid* 179.
133. *Ibid* 184.
134. *Ibid* 358.
135. E. Frank Tupper, *The Theology of Wolfhart Pannenberg*, London: S.C.M. 1974 (Philadelphia: Westminster, 1973) 121.
136. Allan D. Galloway, *Wolfhart Pannenberg*, London: Allen & Unwin, 1973, 14 & 17.
137. Wolfhart Pannenberg, *Jesus – God and Man*, Eng. London: S.C.M. and Philadelphia: Westminster, 1968, 74.
138. W. Pannenberg, *Basic Questions in Theology* vol.2, 8; cf. 1–27.
139. *Ibid* 3œ.
140. Jürgen Moltmann, *Theology of Hope: On the Ground and Implications of a Christian Eschatology*, Eng. London: S.C.M. and New York: Harper and Row, 1967, 77; cf. further E. Frank Tupper, *op. cit.* 259–60, and James M. Robinson, *loc. cit.* 89–90.
141. E. Frank Tupper, *op. cit.* 259.
142. W. Pannenberg, *Basic Questions in Theology* vol.3, 1–79 and 192–210.

143. *Ibid* 58.
144. *Ibid* 63–4.
145. *Ibid* 68.
146. *Ibid* 201.
147. *Ibid* 203.
148. James C. McHann Jr., *The Three Horizons: A Study in Biblical Hermeneutics with Special Reference to Wolfhart Pannenberg*, University of Aberdeen Ph.D Dissertation, 1987, 40; cf. 14.
149. W. Pannenberg, *Theology and the Philosophy of Science* 131; cf. 132–55.
150. Ernst Käsemann, *The Wandering People of God. An Investigation of the Letter to the Hebrews*, Eng. Minneapolis: Augsburg, 1984, 23.

CHAPTER X

The Hermeneutics of Suspicion and Retrieval: Paul Ricoeur's Hermeneutical Theory

1. Human Fallibility, Hermeneutical Suspicion, and Freudian Psychoanalysis: Idols, Dreams, and Symbols

Paul Ricoeur (b. 1913) stands probably alone with Gadamer in the extent of his influence on, and importance for, late twentieth-century hermeneutical theory. Like Pannenberg, Apel, and Habermas, but unlike Gadamer and Rorty, Ricoeur seeks to bring together the two dimensions of "explanation" and "understanding". He recognizes that explanation alone can be reductive, but that understanding alone remains vulnerable to uncritical individual or corporate illusion or self-deception. Certainly he notes, with Habermas, Apel, and Pannenberg, that Gadamer has as a matter of principle left no metacritical or even critical procedure for testing the validity of traditions in effective-historical consciousness. For Ricoeur, hermeneutics properly remains a metacritical discipline, which embodies both the unmasking function of explanation and the creative function of understanding.

Where explanation is critical, socio-critical, or metacritical, understanding may nevertheless operate at a "post-critical" level. Explanation entails the *willingness to expose and to abolish idols* which are merely projections of the human will; understanding requires *a willingness to listen with openness* to symbols and to "indirect" language. The two major areas of hermeneutics, explanation and understanding, thus invite respectively metacritical or socio-critical *suspicion* which in turn bring about re-valuations, and also post-critical *retrieval* embodying openness towards a new "possibility" which may entail renewal or change. For humankind is fundamentally finite and deeply fallible, and yet is also able to reach "beyond" to what Heidegger termed "possibility".

A further reason for the immense importance and influence of Ricoeur's hermeneutical theory lies in its *constructively interdisciplinary* character. He began with interests in phenomenology and existentialism and moved into questions of interpretation in linguistic theory, psychoanalysis, structuralism, theories of texts, metaphor, and narrative and Christian theology and religions. In order to trace the development and evolution of Ricoeur's complex hermeneutical theory, it may be helpful to signpost chronologically aspects of his intellectual pilgrimage in his early years.

In the 1930s he was a student in Paris of Gabriel Marcel (1889–1973). Marcel's philosophical orientation is often described as that of Christian existentialism. Inter-personal understanding, Marcel stressed, is different from the more manipulatory knowledge of the sciences or technology. Persons are not objects, but presences, who are named and addressed as subjects. There are certain affinities at this point with Martin Buber. From Marcel, Ricoeur derived an interest in the problem of human subjectivity, and of the difference between abstract or scientific knowledge (which would contribute to the axis of "explanation" in Ricoeur's hermeneutics) and *participatory* apprehension (which would characterize the axis of understanding). He also derived a concern for the problems of human finitude, human fallibility, the human will, and distinctions between finitude, and guilt. A phenomenological approach to these issues seemed to be invited.

Ricoeur himself traces the next stage of his pilgrimage in his autobiographical reflections which formed part of an address to the University of Chicago in 1971, and is conveniently available in his book *The Rule of Metaphor*.[1] Loretta Dornisch uses this material as the basis for an introduction to Ricoeur in the volume of *Semeia* which is devoted to Ricoeur's hermeneutics.[2] During the war period 1939–45 Ricoeur became a prisoner of war in Germany, and used the occasion as an opportunity to study German philosophy intensively, especially the philosophies of Jaspers, Husserl, and Heidegger. Heidegger's notion of "possibility" would become a key concept for his narrative hermeneutics; Jaspers underlined the role of limit-situations, and the relation between psychology, illusion, and truth.

Ricoeur planned a trilogy under the general heading of *The Philosophy of the Will*. His major concern in this early period was to explore distinctions between the givenness of human finitude and the experience of human guilt. Existentialist writers, he comments, tended to view guilt simply as "a particular case of finitude, and for that reason beyond cure and forgiveness."[3] The first volume of his projected trilogy appeared in French in 1949 as *Le voluntaire et l'involuntaire*, and was translated into English in 1966 as *Freedom and Nature: The Voluntary and Involuntary*.[4] The second volume bore the general title *Finitude and Guilt*, but was published in French in 1960 as two separate books (translated into English, 1967): *Fallible Man* and *The Symbolism of Evil*.[5]

Ricoeur notes in his autobiographical reflections that his work on the symbolism of evil now exposed serious inadequacies in the phenomenological approach to language which he had hitherto presupposed and adopted. Phenomenology, he recalls, "tries to extract from lived experience the essential meanings and structures of purpose, project, motive, wanting, trying, and so on . . . (but) the consideration of the problem of evil brought into the field of research new linguistic perplexities."[6] Why does the language of sin and guilt draw so heavily, for example, on such metaphors as estrangement, wandering, burden, and bondage? These symbols and images are embedded, in turn, in given *contexts in primal narratives* which tell stories of prohibition, temptation, trespass, and exile. Therefore, Ricoeur comments, "I had to introduce a *hermeneutical dimension* into reflective thought."[7] Enquiry into the nature of human will thus raised questions about the structure of symbol; but questions about symbolism invited further fundamental reflection on hermeneutics and on the philosophy of language.

Symbols entail what Ricoeur calls "double meaning expressions." When we speak of guilt or of evil as "burden" or "bondage" we are extending our interpretation of the meaning of these terms from a spatio-temporal or empirical level to a trans-empirical or *metaphorical* level. But this leads Ricoeur to a further area of enquiry. Once we begin to reflect on the possibility of "layers" or "levels" of meaning, however this invites reflection on what has been said about layers of meaning in psychoanalytic theory. Both reflection on *will, "bad will", and guilt,* and also reflection on the *status and role of the symbols* which express these realities lead us, Ricoeur asserts, in the same direction of exploring *psychoanalysis.*

Psychoanalysis takes on the role of *critique*, parallel in some ways to a social *critique* of ideology in Habermas or in Marxist theory. Yet it also has a *linguistic* role. Moreover it does not belong exclusively to the axis of "explanation" rather than understanding. In psychoanalysis a patient is assisted in overcoming symptomatic behaviour *both* through an explanatory process which uses *causal* explanation, *and* through a deepened self-awareness in *understanding*. The *diagnostic* process offers a tool which entails both aspects. Ricoeur writes: "Psychoanalysis was also directly linked to linguistic perplexity . . . Are not dreams and symptoms some kind of indirect language?"[8]

In terms of the *explanatory* axis, however an intellectual challenge is involved, not least for religious faith. The kind of psychoanalysis pioneered by Freud also sought to interpret the symbols of religion and culture by *reducing* them. Ricoeur comments: "Freud was only one of the exponents of the reductive hermeneutic . . . Marx and Nietzsche, and before them Feuerbach, had to be understood as the fathers of this reductive method. The claim of psychoanalysis to explain symbols and myths as fruits of unconscious representations, as distorted expressions of the relation between libidinal impulses and the repressive structures of the super-ego, compelled me to enlarge my first concept of hermeneutics beyond a mere semantic analysis of double-meaning expressions."[9]

Ricoeur's detailed and constructive response to these issues appeared in a major treatment in 1965 under the title *De l'interpretation: Essai sur Freud*, translated into English as *Freud and Philosophy: An Essay on Interpretation*, in 1970.[10] In this substantial work Ricoeur examines the respective roles of a *reductive explanation* and a *constructive retrieval* of the original meaning of the symbol. He begins by placing Freud in the context of wider enquiries about language. Language, he points out, is the common meeting ground of Wittgenstein and English linguistic philosophy, of Heidegger and phenomenology, of Bultmann and biblical hermeneutics, of questions about myth, ritual, and belief, and of psychoanalysis. Freud invites us to look at dreams "for the various relations between desire and language."[11] *Dreams constitute models of "disguised, substitutive, and fictive expressions of human wishing or desire."*[12] Thus what has to be "interpreted" is *not the dream or dreamed*, but *the text of the dream as it is recounted*. Psychoanalysis aims to recover the primitive speech of desire. Thus dream provides a classic model of double meaning, in which both showing and hiding take place. In our second chapter above, we observed that Ricoeur sees this showing-hiding duality as also characterizing the revelation of the God who is both hidden and revealed.

Specifically, therefore, for Ricoeur "to interpret is to understand a double meaning."[13] A symbol is a double-meaning linguistic expression which requires an interpretation. In this respect Ricoeur believes that the definition of symbol found in such writers as Ernst Cassirer is too broad. It obscures a fundamental distinction between univocal and plurivocal signification. Thus all the major language concerning evil, its confession and removal, Ricoeur argues, uses terms which are capable of bearing a physical meaning but function in this context at a different level: a "spot" or "stain" is removed, washed, or wiped away. Sin is seen as "deviation" from a path, as a "wandering", as that which brings about "slavery". Hence Ricoeur takes up Freud's notion of "overdetermination" (also used in a different context by Louis Althusser) to denote an intermixture or overlapping of multi-signification which exhibits the "richness" or "plurivocal" nature of language, and makes interpretation, in principle, a task which is "perhaps interminable."[14]

Here we reach Ricoeur's central thesis in *Freud and Philosophy*, which also constitutes a fundamental principle for hermeneutics including biblical interpretation. Ricoeur writes: "Hermeneutics seems to me to be animated by this double motivation: *willingness to suspect, willingness to listen; vow of rigor, vow of obedience*. In our time we have not finished doing away with *idols* and we have barely begun to listen to *symbols*."[15] On the one hand, extreme iconoclasm may be involved in the path towards truth, authenticity, and faith. Disguises and masks must be stripped away. Here we find echoes of Jaspers as well as of Marcel. But we also need "faith that has undergone criticism, *postcritical* faith . . . It is a rational faith, for it interprets; but it is a faith because it seeks, through interpretation, a second naïveté . . . 'Believe in order to understand, understand in order to believe' . . . Its maxim is the 'hermeneutical circle' itself of believing and understanding."[16]

On this basis Ricoeur views the work of the "three masters of suspicion", Marx, Nietzsche, and Freud, in positive terms as "clearing the horizon for a more authentic word, for a new reign of Truth, not only by means of a 'destructive' critique, but by the invention of an art of *interpreting* . . . by an exegesis of meaning."[17] Fundamentally the task of hermeneutics is "to destroy the idols, to listen to the symbols."[18] Here the critique of language co-incides with "the crisis of reflection."

This brings us back to a second thesis which we have already noted, and which constitutes Ricoeur's most major point of disagreement with Gadamer. A hermeneutic of suspicion demands that we must retain *explanation alongside understanding* as the two key axes of hermeneutical enquiry. "Explanation" in the human sciences, however, represents what Gadamer has described as *method* and has pointedly and elaborately rejected. David Jasper sums up the point of contrast: "For Gadamer we must choose between truth or method. Ricoeur, on the other hand, suggests not an opposition, but a dialectical relationship..between explanation (method) and understanding (truth) which enable us more adequately to describe the tension between self and other, and to remain responsible to . . . explanatory methods."[19]

Ricoeur develops this principle in three directions: in relation to a philosophy of language; in relation to psychoanalytical interpretation and description; and in relation to structuralism. On language, for example, he comments that "as long as the logic of multiple meaning is not grounded in its reflective function, it necessarily falls under the blows of formal and symbolic logic. In the eyes of the logician, hermeneutics will always be suspected of fostering a culpable complacency towards equivocal meanings, of surreptitiously giving an informing function to expressions that have merely an emotive, hortatory, function."[20] For this reason from the period of *Freud and Philosophy* onwards Ricoeur becomes increasingly interested not only in Continental European approaches to language but also in Anglo-American linguistic philosophy and a broad philosophy of language.

Ricoeur noted that in the developing concern with structuralism in France, models were drawn from linguistics. Turning to linguistics and to semiotics he sought to examine "all semiological disciplines" and aimed to become "more competent in linguistic problems."[21] Although in some respects this broadens his critique and allows him to engage with the

French intellectual life of the day, this detour into structuralism also has the less happy effect of purporting to offer "explanatory" critiques which in practice remain primarily intra-linguistic devices. Indeed it is arguable that this excursion into structuralism had damaging effects on Ricoeur's theory on textuality.

In his critique of Freud, Ricoeur paid particular attention to the Freudian notions of "condensation" and "displacement". According to Freud, when the latent content of the dream-as-dreamed ("the dream-thoughts") are transposed into the manifest content of the dream-as-remembered (the "dream content" or dream-account), what is actually recounted may represent a "condensation" of the dream in a form which is "brief, meagre, and laconic." It may also reflect "displacement", in which sequences and images become transformed and "scrambled" by the repression of the censor, which protectively disguises the meaning of the symbols or images from the conscious mind. Psychoanalytical interpretation seeks to discover the deeper "text" below the dream-account, represented by the dream-thoughts. These Freudian categories were developed by Roman Jakobson in linguistics in terms of metaphor (condensation) and metonymy (displacement), and in psychoanalytical post-structuralism by Jacques Lacan. Condensation and displacement, Ricoeur agrees, "attest, on the plane of meaning, to an 'overdetermination' which calls for interpretation ... Each of the elements of the dream-content is said to be overdetermined when it is 'represented in the dream-thoughts many times over'".[22]

Freud describes the processes in terms of "forces": "A transference and displacement of psychical intensities occurs in the process of dream-formation."[23] But there is an ambiguity, Ricoeur argues, in Freud's account of symbolizing processes. Freud himself formulates his hypotheses with the use of much metaphorical language, including that of "repression" and "displacement", and seems eventually to forget its metaphorical status. One clear example is Freud's use of "cathexis" as an economic metaphor of investment, to denote sexual energy which is "invested" in another person or object.[24] But here, Ricoeur argues, "economic mechanism" and metaphors of "energy" perform *both* an explanatory (naturalistic) *and* hermeneutical (interpretative) function. One of Ricoeur's major conclusions is that "the analytic situation as such is irreducible to a description of observables ... Analytic experience bears a much greater resemblance to historical understanding than to natural explanation."[25] In this context Ricoeur initiates, in effect, tri-partite discussion between Husserl, Freud, and Hegel.[26]

In *Freud and Philosophy* Ricoeur moves hermeneutics away from Heidegger's philosophical individualism and from a phenomenological view of human consciousness. He examines the relation between individual consciousness and "narcissism" in Freud. On the one hand, consciousness "ceases to be what is best known, it becomes problematic."[27] There is nothing self-evident about Descartes' notion of *being* conscious rather than *becoming* conscious. On the other hand, individual consciousness embodies the "contrariety of narcissism, as the center of resistance to truth."[28] The Copernican revolution challenged the notion that humankind constituted the centre of the universe; the psychoanalytic revolution likewise challenges the notion that the ego is master in its own house.

The unconscious, however, is not a mere absence of consciousness; it is a potential source of meaning, separated from the conscious by a barrier. Ricoeur comments, "The meaning of the barrier is that the unconscious is inaccessible *unless the appropriate technique is used* . . . It is indeed *another text* that psychoanalysis deciphers, *beneath the text of consciousness*. Phenomenology shows that it is another *text*, but not that this text is *other*".[29] For phenomenological approaches confirm that our experience of language and the world has an inter-subjective dimension, and that "objectivity" arises when others make explicit that which is otherwise implicit in the subject.[30] Freud's distinctive contribution, Ricoeur argues, is to make clear that "the subject is never the subject one thinks it is."[31] But in critically interpreting Freud, he concludes, "The reflective re-interpretation of Freudianism cannot help but alter our notion of reflection: as the understanding of Freudianism is changed, so is the understanding of oneself."[32]

Towards the end of his book on Freud and interpretation Ricoeur returns to his central theme of the duality of the symbol as that which both hides and reveals, disguises and shows, conceals and discloses. This reflects, in turn, his hermeneutic of suspicion and of retrieval. Completely coherent with this is his view of the human subject as one in whom, below the threshold of consciousness, there lie both disguises and hidden springs of meaning. The *explanatory dimension alone* merely "demythizes" symbols and robs them of their richness. But explanation must supplement *hermeneutics*. Ricoeur concludes: "*The idols must die — so that symbols may live*"[33] He adds: "I attempt to construct the *yes* and the *no* which I pronounce about the psychoanalysis of religion." Freud separates *idols* from symbols, and this Ricoeur affirms. But Ricoeur also recognizes that Freudianism represents a *world-view*. This cannot be sustained as it stands, and Ricoeur rejects it. "'Symbols give rise to thought'; but they are also the birth of idols. That is why the critique of idols remains the condition of the conquest of symbols."[34] That is also why a hermeneutics of retrieval must be matched by a hermeneutic of suspicion. Ricoeur therefore concludes that the theories and procedures of Freud represent both an indispensibly positive contribution to hermeneutics, but also one which is to be questioned, corrected, and modified. They provide considerations which must be addressed with integrity at a metacritical level, but also as methodological tools for a hermeneutic of suspicion and retrieval.

2. Paul Ricoeur on Metaphor and Narrative: Possibility, Time, and Transformation

In his later writings, especially in *The Rule of Metaphor* (French 1975, English 1978) and *Time and Narrative* (3 volumes, French 1983–85, English 1984–88) Ricoeur focusses increasingly on the creative power of language not only in symbols but also particularly in metaphor and in narrative. While cerebral concepts and factual reports *reflect already-perceived actualities*, metaphors and narratives *create possible ways of seeing or understanding* the world and human life. This approach to metaphor and to narrative develops further some of the themes already present in his two earlier essays "The Hermeneutics of Symbols and Philosophical Reflection", which are published in his collection *The Conflict of Interpretations*.[35] Here he takes up the well-known principle which he invokes in *The Symbolism of Evil*, namely that "the symbol gives rise to thought", and which he describes as the "maxim that I find so appealing".[36] In this context Ricoeur is still directly addressing Freudian and psychoanalytical questions. He writes: "The plunge into the archaic mythologies of the unconscious brings to the surface new signs of the sacred. The eschatology of consciousness is always a creative repetition of its own archaeology."[37] In *The Rule of Metaphor* and in *Time and Narrative* the concern moves to the creative power of language. Metaphor produces *new possibilities* of imagination and vision; narrative creates *new configurations* which structure individual or corporate experience.

In his recent study *Biblical Narrative in the Philosophy of Paul Ricoeur*, Kevin J Vanhoozer (partly anticipated by David Klemm) correctly traces this emphasis on *possibility* to the philosophy of Martin Heidegger, and less directly to Kant.[38] As I observed in *The Two Horizons*, "Heidegger distinguishes the existential 'Being-possible' which is 'essential for Dasein' both from 'logical possibility' and 'from the contingency of something present-at-hand'."[39] In Heidegger's words, "Possibility as an *existentiale* is the most primordial and ultimate positive way in which Dasein is characterized ontologically."[40] Understanding, for Heidegger, involves, I had urged, "not seeing actual objects or situations so much as seeing their *possible* uses, *possible* contexts, *possible* ways of service."[41] Heidegger calls this "potentiality-for-Being." He writes: "Interpretation is grounded in *something we have in advance – in a fore-having (Vorhabe)* . . ."[42] Practical understanding that can issue in *decision* depends on an awareness of genuine *possibilities*. In this sense also Wittgenstein speaks of "understanding", especially in the context of mathematics, as "knowing how to go on".[43] Similarly in Ernst Bloch's philosophy of hope, as Vanhoozer notes in this context, hope appears as a "passion for the possible", or as an "ontology of the not-yet".[44]

If metaphor, therefore, presents *possibilty* rather than *actuality* it is arguable that metaphoric discourse can open up new understanding more readily than purely descriptive or scientific statement. Ricoeur's hermeneutics of metaphor also reflects the "turn" of the later Heidegger increasingly towards poetry and art, and his relative disparagement of scientific or conceptual thinking as merely "calculative".

In his essay "Metaphor and Symbol" in *Interpretation Theory* Ricoeur finds the essence of symbol and metaphor not only in the "semantic structure of having a double-meaning" entailing "the productive use of ambiguity" but also "semantic innovation" and "extension of meaning" which "structures and expresses a mood".[45] Ricoeur quotes Max Black with approval: "A memorable metaphor has the power to bring two separate domains into cognitive and emotional relation by using language directly appropriate for the one as a lens for seeing the other."[46] Ricoeur's language about "mood", however, also uses the vocabulary of Heidegger. In *Being and Time* Heidegger considers the hermeneutical role of "state-of-mind" (*Befindlichkeit*), "Being-attuned" (*die Stimmung*) and "mood" in a sense which Heidegger insists has an ontological status, and is more than mere subjective "feeling".[47] John Macquarrie discusses this double significance of "mood" or "feeling" in relation to the ontological claims of Schleiermacher, Rudolf Otto, and Paul Tillich.[48]

The heart of Ricoeur's theory of metaphor can be found in the following statement. In his introduction to *The Rule of Metaphor* Ricoeur writes: "Metaphor presents itself as a strategy of discourse that, while preserving and developing the creative powers of language, preserves and develops the *heuristic* power wielded by *Fiction*."[49] Nevertheless, he continues, metaphor "says something about reality"; its power does not depend on the suspension of all reference, even if we may need to speak of its double meaning as entailing what Jakobson terms a "split reference".[50]

As he elaborates his theory of metaphor in more detail, Ricoeur looks not so much to the philosophy of Heidegger as to theories of metaphor drawn from such writers as Nelson Goodman's *Languages of Art* (1968), and from Max Black's *Models and Metaphors* (1962). Indeed Ricoeur argues that the dual linking of "fiction" and "re-description" restores a recognition of Aristotle's key point in the *Poetics*, namely that a creative *poiēsis* (making) of language arises out of the connection between *mythos* and *mimēsis*. Aristotle's theory of metaphor constitutes the first of eight thematic studies in *The Rule of Metaphor*. Metaphor is viewed by Aristotle as being situated at the intersection of *rhetoric*, in which it functions as to persuade, and *poetics*, in which it functions to reconstruct human action. Aristotle defines metaphor as "giving the thing a name that belongs to something else . . ." (*Poetics* 1457b, 6–9). It entails a movement (*phora*) which constitutes a deviation *para to kurion*, from a current usage. But some modern theorists are misled, Ricoeur argues, by interpreting such "deviation" as necessarily implying a *substitution* theory of metaphor. Metaphor does not substitute "for an ordinary word which one could have found in the same place".[51] Even if Aristotle himself is ambiguous (as some claim) or inconsistent on this point, the notion of linguistic *interaction* is more important and more central to what Aristotle seeks to say than that of substitution. There is a transposition from one pole to another (*epiphora*). Thus: "The modern authors who say that to make a metaphor is to see two things in one are faithful to this feature".[52]

Ricoeur rejects, then, the tradition that views metaphor as mere ornament, together with the positivistic view, represented for example by Thomas Hobbes, that metaphor constitutes a generally misleading abuse of language, which encourages illusion. In the third study in *The Rule of Metaphor* Ricoeur moves beyond an approach that views metaphor in terms of *words*, to a theory of metaphor which sees the basic unit as the *sentence*. We move to the realm of metaphorical *discourse*. Up to this point, the novelty or distinctiveness of Ricoeur's approach has not yet genuinely appeared. The "pivotal text" (to use Ted Cohen's term) for the capacity of metaphor to convey *cognitive truth* rather than mere emotion was Max Black's essay on metaphor, first published in 1955; while the *creative power* of metaphor as "tensive language" or as "double language" was expounded by Philip Wheelwright in 1954 and especially 1962, and partly anticipated by Owen Barfield in 1947.[53]

Barfield, writing as a specialist in law rather than as a philosopher of language, drew an analogy between the creative transposition or extension set up by metaphor (which he called "tarning") and the use of legal fiction in the discourse of law. In order to extend what is already capable of expression and application under existing laws to new situations, not previously envisaged, we regularly need, he argues, to use the device of legal fiction. Fictional identities, locations, or situations may be postulated and "accepted" as hypotheses for the purpose of extending some established legal provision. Metaphor, Barfield argues, similarly extends language by using fictions, but fictions which have a second level of meaning. Barfield's work was re-printed in a collection of essays on language edited by Max Black, and this collection also included C.S. Lewis' essay on metaphor "Bluspels and Flalans".[54] Here Lewis carefully distinguishes between the merely illustrative or didactic function of what he called "pupil metaphors", and the indispensable conceptual creativity of "master metaphors" which expressed new and genuine perceptions of reality. Lewis argues that the suggestive power of "master" metaphor plays an untranslatable and irreducible part in the formation and development of concepts. The debate about whether metaphor can be translated or paraphrased has a long history, in which opposing positions are taken, for example, by W.M. Urban and Philip Wheelwright.[55]

Ricoeur is not therefore breaking new ground when he argues that metaphor makes new connections through the use of creative imagination. In his *Models and Metaphors* (1962) Max Black formulated the suggestive aphorism in the context of observations on the philosophy of science, that "Perhaps every science must start with metaphor and end with algebra; and perhaps without the metaphor there would never have been any algebra".[56] Mary Hesse (1966) also argues that the fertility of theories in the sciences lies in their ability to suggest possibilities usually through models that are more than merely logical extensions of formulae.[57] Ricoeur's more innovative and influential contributions emerge in his interweaving of this theory of metaphor with his approach to discourse and narrative. Narratives present *possibilities of human action*, as understood in terms of *a schema of time*. In his preface to the first volume of *Time and Narrative* Ricoeur observes that in the case of metaphor "innovation lies in the producing of a new semantic pertinence by means of an impertinent attribution ... With narrative, the semantic innovation lies in the inventing of another work of synthesis – a plot. By means of the plot, goals, causes, and chance *are brought together within the temporal unity of a whole and complete account*. It is this synthesis of the heterogeneous that *brings narrative close to metaphor*".[58]

Ricoeur informs us that his studies on metaphor and his extended work on narrative "form a pair: published one after the other, these works were conceived together".[59] In both cases he is concerned with "meaning-effects" and with "semantic innovation". While metaphor offers the tension of interaction between two contexts, narrative, as "living metaphor", draws creative power from "a feigned plot, that is, a new congruence in the organization of events".[60] The plot "grasps together" and "integrates into one whole and complete story multiple and scattered events, thereby schematizing the intelligible signification attached to the narrative taken as a whole".[61] But while a metaphor or a conceptual theme may transpose scattered aspects of thought into some coherent working structure, Ricoeur stresses that the narrative orders scattered sequential *experiences and events* into a *coherent structure of human time*. He writes: "The world unfolded by every narrative work is always a *temporal* world.... Time becomes human time to the extent that it is organized after the manner of a narrative; narrative, in turn, is meaningful to the extent that it portrays the features of temporal experience."[62]

The English title *Time and Narrative* may allow us too easily to forget that Ricoeur is drawing on established narrative theory or narratology in his distinction between *"plot"* as a *construct of human time* and *"story"* as a sequence of events, situations, and settings in *natural time*. The French title *Temps et Récit* (for which Vanhoozer suggests "Time and Telling") presupposes the kind of contrast formulated in narrative theory by Gérard Gennette and others between *histoire* and *récit*.[63] This is broadly parallel, in turn, with contrasts in other theorists between *story* and *narrative* or between *story* and *plot*; in Russian Formalism between fable (*fabula*) and plot (*sjuzhet*); or in the well-known title of Seymour Chatman's influential book, *Story and Discourse*.[64] Chatman writes: "Structuralist theory argues that each narrative has two parts: a story (*histoire*), the content or chain of events (actions, happenings) plus what may be called the existents (characters, items of setting); and a discourse (*discours*), that is, the expression, the means by which the content is communicated ... The fable is 'the set of events tied together' ... ; plot is 'how the reader becomes aware of what happened'."[65] Chatman's allusion to the contrast between *histoire* and *discours* reflects the terms used by Emile Benveniste.

The "telling" (*récit*) of the plot depends on an organizational construct which has as its organizing principle "human" time (narrative-time) rather than sequential time (*histoire*). The plot of a detective story, for example, may entail holding back information about sequentially prior events until the dénouement near the end. It may entail flash-backs of events perceived through the eyes of different witnesses as these are reconstructed, in turn, in accordance with the purposes of the narrator and the movement of the plot. In *Great Expectations* Charles Dickens witholds from the reader until the end information about the identity of Pip's benefactor, and this is essential to the movement of the *plot*, not to "natural" time.

Ricoeur insists that Aristotle's conceptions both of *mythos* and of *mimesis* should be thought of as "reconstruction", rather than as "imitation" of actions (*praxis*) in the world. The plot (*mythos*) embodies arguments (*logos*) organized in terms of human time. But in place of logical premises and conclusions, traversed by processes of logical inference, we are caught up and drawn along in a *movement* of human time which commences with "a beginning", moves through given patterns of events, and reaches a "conclusion" or "end". This transforms it into a coherent temporal *whole*. As Seymour Chatman observes, many plots can be made from the same story.[66] Ricoeur therefore insists that we must exclude from Aristotle's notion of *mimesis* any idea of "a copy or identical replica" of actions or events. It concerns, rather, "the organization of events by emplotment".[67]

Narrative components thus constitute not bare events in a sequence, but active contributions to the flow and movement of the plot. They both serve to build a whole, and also conversely they derive their significance from their place *within* this coherent whole. This "whole" now becomes the narrative-world of the reader. But when the reader is seized by this "re-figured" world, the narrative-effects, Ricoeur argues, become *revelatory and transformative*. Ricoeur declares: "The effects of fiction, revelation, and transformation are essentially the effects of reading".[68]

Like metaphor, narrative constructs a world of the *possible*. Further, just as Heidegger distinguished between mere logical possibility and the concrete possibility which relates to decision and hermeneutical understanding, so, too, in *Being and Time* Heidegger draws a careful distinction between "time" as sequential or natural time, and "temporality" (*Zeitlichkeit*) as human time. Temporality constitutes *Dasein's* experience in time "in an *existentiell* way".[69] Temporality, Heidegger argues, provides a necessary "ontological condition" for human existence in time.[70] Nevertheless Ricoeur is also critical of this section of *Being and Time*. In particular Ricoeur has a quite different standpoint from that of Heidegger's individual-centred or *Dasein*-centred hermeneutics. In his essay on Heidegger and the human subject, Ricoeur attacks, with justice, Heidegger's "*hermeneutics of the 'I am'*".[71] Even when the self comes into view in this section of *Being and Time* before it fades again from the later writings, the lone human subject remains at best "only a kind of anonymous self".[72] By contrast, in his own essay on "The Task of Hermeneutics" Ricoeur, while recognizing that historical finitude "excludes any overview, any final synthesis in the Hegelian manner" sees the hermeneutical goal in terms of an interaction in which "there is an horizon which can be . . . enlarged".[73]

In his essay "The Narrative Function" (1977) reprinted in *Semeia* Ricoeur identifies "the decisive concept of plot" as that which by having "a *particular directedness*" allows the readers to be "pulled forward" towards the conclusion as "the attracting pole of the process".[74] This does not mean that the conclusion is predictable; quite the reverse. But by following twists and surprises, the readers reach an understanding of the whole "configurational" structure which embodies a reflective judgment, including a "point of view".[75] Hermeneutical interaction takes place between the teller and the readers which does not leave the readers entirely unchanged.

At this point, however, as Kevin Venhoozer notes, questions arise about the relation between historical narrative and fictional narrative. Ricoeur believes that "the way has been paved for a full recognition of the fictional character of history by the general critique of the positivistic epistemology of history".[76] Whereas, he claims, for positivists, the historian's work is "to unearth facts", in contemporary epistemology history becomes "imaginative reconstruction".[77] The decisive new factor, Ricoeur believes, is the view of history as "a literary artifact" which has emerged from literary theory and from semiotics.[78] Hayden White, for example, speaks of the explanatory procedures of history which constitute "Metahistory" as those of literary Poetics, namely "explanation by emplotment".[79] The historian *makes* the story into a completed whole, and writes from a given vantage-point, perhaps adding a conceptual argument about "what it adds up to". Yet Ricoeur is unwilling to *identify* historical narrative with fiction. He states: "History is both a literary artifact *and* a representation of reality".[80] On the other hand, "fiction" and "representation of reality", Ricoeur insists, "are not antithetical terms".[81]

Ricoeur concludes: "Both history and fiction refer to human actions, although they do so on the basis of two different referential claims. Only history may articulate its referential claim in compliance with rules of evidence common to the whole body of science ... Fictional narratives may assert a referential claim of another kind, appropriate to the split reference of poetic discourse."[82] Fictional reference entails "redescription" of reality according to the symbolic structures of the fiction. Although, therefore, both fiction and history are "true", they are true in different senses. Ricoeur concludes his essay on the narrative function with a question formulated as a paradoxical turn to the rest of the argument: "Could we not say that by opening us to the different, history opens us to the possible; while fiction, by opening us to the unreal, brings us back to the essential?"[83]

Ricoeur insists that fiction has power "to re-make" reality, by ordering otherwise scattered aspects of the world into new configurations. Fictions can have revelatory and transforming power. But historical narrative may also transform readers, because, like fiction, it may also stand in contrast with the readers' actual present experience. Historical narrative, Ricoeur repeats, is also a "model" of the past; but "there is no original given with which to compare the model".[84] Historical narrative, unlike fictional narrative, invites other activities as well as narration. Ricoeur writes: "Historians are not simply narrators: they give reasons why they consider a particular factor *rather than some other* to be the sufficient cause of a given course of events."[85]

We come full circle, and return to Ricoeur's insistence, as against Gadamer, that hermeneutics calls for *both* explanation *and* understanding. Ricoeur argues: "History as a science removes the explanatory process from the fabric of the narrative and sets it up as a separate problematic."[86] But the important element, for a theory of reader-*effects*, is the "investigation of the relations between the writing of history and the operation of emplotment".[87]

Kevin Vanhoozer correctly underlines the close connection between this key notion of emplotment and the role of possibility and imagination in Ricoeur's philosophy of the human will. Vanhoozer observes: "Fiction ... is about possible ways of human being in the world ... Time becomes 'human' time only as one inhabits a constellation of historical and fictional worlds ... Without the prior imaginative appropriation of a possibility, the will would have no projects to realize."[88] Vanhoozer also expresses reservations about what he sees as Ricoeur's ambivalence concerning the relation between history and fiction. He notes: "Ricoeur fears that descriptive language stifles the passion for the possible by confining us within the limits of the present, and closes our imagination to the future."[89] It is not difficult to think of examples where fiction or fictive devices have brought about new cognitive apprehensions of truth. Vanhoozer cites the examples, in the context of Ricoeur's language about creative invention, from the history of painting, in which the invention of oil paint in the fifteenth century allowed Flemish painters to articulate the "luminosity" of the world, and the devices of impressionists also conveyed something of its fleetingness.[90]

Has Ricoeur, in the end, assigned such a decisive role to the transforming and revelatory power of plot-configuration and plot-movement in fictional models, that "reference" in historical narrative cannot reach beyond the intra-literary and intra-linguistic world of "refiguration"? Is Vanhoozer correct in seeing Ricoeur as approaching biblical narrative in a way similar to that of exponents of the new hermeneutic, in which "Ricoeur has merely transposed subjectivity into a new key", and ultimately the object of "reference" remains only the human self?[91] Vanhoozer identifies common ground between Ricoeur's approach to biblical narrative and David Tracy's approach to interpretation, whereby "Face to face with a classic, we have to admit that it is *we* who are being described"[92] In Tracy's words: "The referent (*sic*) of the text [of a classic] is to a *possible* way of being in the world, a vision of reality, a form of life".[93]

3. Metacriticism, Fiction, History, and Truth: Some Assessments Largely in the light of Speech-Act Theory

Vanhoozer rightly identifies an ambiguity in Ricoeur's account of the status of historical narrative and its relation to the power of fiction. But the ambiguity, it may be argued, is not a contradiction. It arises from a lack of consistent specificity about whether discussion is proceeding *at the interpretative, at the critical, or at the metacritical level.* Along with Gadamer (and with B. Wachterhauser, Richard Bernstein, Christopher Norris and others), Ricoeur rightly holds that hermeneutics constitutes a metacritical discipline. Whereas Schleiermacher and especially Dilthey, he observes, "construed hermeneutics as epistemology", this is "precisely what Heidegger and Gadamer place in question . . . Rather, it must be seen as an attempt *to dig beneath the epistemological enterprise itself,* in order to uncover its properly ontological condition."[94] If Schleiermacher's hermeneutics constituted a Copernican revolution in the hermeneutical theory, then the movement with which Ricoeur identifies himself as well as Gadamer and Habermas, represents a "second Copernican inversion".[95] In his careful discussion of the need for critical interaction between the hermeneutics of Gadamer and Habermas's critique of ideology, Ricoeur affirms the notion that "hermeneutics ultimately claims to set itself up as a critique of critique, or *meta-critique*."[96]

We have already underlined the point that in opposition to Gadamer, Ricoeur recognizes the need for *explanation* as well as human *understanding*. But this poses a dilemma. On the one hand, Ricoeur sympathizes with Gadamer that ultimately language itself (in some sense almost inter-subjective consensus) offers a more valid claim to constitute the bedrock uncovered by meta-critical exploration *than* "methods" *or* "explanations" which operate at a higher or more derivative level of abstraction. On the other hand, however, Gadamer's devaluation of method and explanation fails to provide criteria for the evaluation of evidence. It constitutes in some respects a retreat rather than an advance, and at the *critical* level explanation must come into play. Yet explanation, even if it functions as a criterion, remains also derivative. In the struggle against "methodological distanciation", Ricoeur writes, we "must always push the rock of Sisyphus up again; restore the ontological ground that methodology has eroded away."[97]

On the yonder side of criticism and metacriticism lies what Ricoeur calls "second naïveté". In his early work *The Symbolism of Evil* he writes that he is animated by "hope for a *re-creation* of language. *Beyond the desert of criticism*, we wish to be *called* again."[98] Second-order critical reflection about human consciousness of fault is derivative from the first-order experience of *confession* as "a blind experience, still embedded in the matrix of emotion, fear, anguish".[99] The philosopher does not "feel" these things "in their first naïveté; he 're-feels' them in a neutralized mode, in the mode of 'as if'."[100] As Mary Gerhart and others point out, inner experience can be interpreted only indirectly by what Ricoeur terms a "diagnostic" method. Ricoeur's work reflects Heidegger's discussion of the derivative nature of assertions. Like metaphor and narrative-plot, symbol and myth express human experience at a primordial level. First, *myth* utilizes cosmic symbols for the purpose of temporal narration. Second, *dreams*, as we noted in the context of Ricoeur's *Freud and Philosophy*, constitute symbolic texts. Third, *poetic imagination* creates narrative-plots which construe human experience in terms of human time and refigurations of the possible, which beckon us on.

In the case of Ricoeur's work on symbols and on dreams, it is relatively clear how his hermeneutic of suspicion interacts with his hermeneutic of retrieval and reconstruction. But this distinction remains fundamental to understanding also his more ambiguous interweaving of narrative-fiction and narrative-history. At the level of *language-effect* or *interpretation* Ricoeur is content to focus on a hermeneutic of reconstruction in which narrative-plot and narrative-movement provide power, engagement, and transformation for the reader. At this level Vanhoozer's question how we can distinguish adequately between a good metaphor and a bad one, or between narrative-fiction and narrative-report remains generally unanswered, largely because, for Ricoeur, *at this level* an answer is *unnecessary*. But Ricoeur is willing to address the question at a *critical* level and discusses what kinds of consideration might *count* as an answer at the *metacritical* level. At these levels, however, we are no longer engaged with the text.

At the critical level Ricoeur distinguishes history from fiction as that which is *constrained by the givenness of evidence*. We recall the title of Anthony E. Harvey's book, *Jesus and the Constraints of History* (1982). But all is not plain sailing. For Ricoeur follows Hayden White and others in arriving at a particular view of the nature of historical reconstruction. Building on the agreed modern consensus that no history-writing is value-free, Ricoeur goes much further, and assimilates the paradigm of historical enquiry onto a paradigm of literary construction. But this means that the argument has, in effect, become circular at the metacritical level. The critical layer of "explanation" threatens to become squeezed out from attention because at one level Ricoeur's main concern is with the meaning-*effect* of symbol, metaphor, and narrative in relation to human *possibility*, while at another level "beneath" explanation and "method" lies a philosophical theory which leaves us, in effect, trapped within our intralinguistic world in which the traditional notion of "reference" has been transposed into an internal relation within a phenomenological system.

The relation of these considerations to the structure of Ricoeur's hermeneutical theory as a whole receives helpful clarification from the constructive discussions of Ricoeur's hermeneutics by David E. Klemm and also by John B. Thompson.[101] Klemm underlines the extent of Ricoeur's indebtedness to Husserl and to Heidegger, and the central role of "the split between the poetic and the conceptual".[102] He observes: "What is characteristic of the *first naîveté* is immediacy of belief, and this immediacy always adheres to poetic texts (and therefore most especially religious texts). Characteristic of *critique* is mediation of the content of assertions through application of the criteria for knowledge established in critical idealism."[103] Productive and reconstructive imagination invites a "reflexive awareness of what he calls 'second naîveté' in hermeneutics". This constitutes, for Ricoeur, a dimension of *transformation* in which self-awareness is deepened and broadened. Klemm rightly concludes, however, that this raises the question "whether or not the hermeneutical consciousness can speak of the *truth or falsity* of the poetic language that it interprets ... Critical consciousness measures truth as the correspondence between thought and percept, whose locus is in judgment. And since in poetic language the metaphor suspends reference to the perceived world in order to redescribe reality, it must sacrifice its claim for truth-value in the narrow sense."[104]

Ricoeur offers a counter-reply to such criticisms by appealing to Heidegger's notion of truth as "letting-be", or "manifestation". I attempted to identify some of the limitations of this theory of truth elsewhere, and Klemm argues that Ricoeur's hermeneutical theory does not actually demand a full surrender of every aspect of the correspondence theory of truth.[105] But it is perhaps a mistake to seek a *comprehensive* theory of hermeneutics, or even of narrative-hermeneutics, in Ricoeur's writings. Ricoeur's stated aim is to shift attention from "behind" the text, which he sees largely as a distraction of Romanticist hermeneutics, to what takes place "in front of" the text. Here its revelatory function becomes apparent, characteristically through "split reference", through "double meaning", through "refiguration", or through what Kierkegaard had called indirect communication.

What is revealed is truth concerning the human self, or the construct of inter-subjective consciousness. Don Ihde comments, "For Ricoeur it is impossible that man may know himself directly or introspectively. It is only by a series of detours that he learns about the fullness and complexity of his own being . . . The emphasis on indirectness pervades the whole of Ricoeur's methodology . . . Hermeneutics refocusses this indirectness by developing . . . a set of reflections upon the expressions of equivocal symbols."[106] In Ricoeur's words: "*All* our relations with the world have an intersubjective dimension . . . All 'objectivity' is intersubjective, insofar as the implicit is what another can make explicit."[107]

But why is the hermeneutic of suspicion, which was so powerful in dealing with questions about "false consciousness" in the context of Freudian theory so much less in evidence as an effective tool for evaluating explanatory claims about historical narrative? Why is it that, even in his work on metaphor, Ricoeur invites Vanhoozer's comment: "Lacking in Ricoeur's otherwise brilliant rehabilitation of metaphor is any indication of how one may judge the difference between good and bad metaphors"?[108]

Part of the heart of the difficulty, we have argued already, springs from the particular view of nature of historiography and historical report which Ricoeur holds. But a further factor arises from the *particular role* which Ricoeur assigns *within* his hermeneutical system to the work of so-called "ordinary language" philosophy and to *speech-act* theory, with its contrast between force, propositional content, and presuppositions or "background." Ricoeur states: "I have become very attentive to the contribution of ordinary language analysis emanating from Wittgenstein, Austin, and Strawson, for the philosophy of action."[109] The particular value, he argues, of "ordinary language . . . following the work of Wittgenstein and Austin", is decisively to remind us that understanding takes place in an intersubjective context, and that language "has no fixed expressions independent of their contextual uses."[110] Language-uses are therefore "actualizations of its polysemic values".[111] It was on such grounds that I urged in *The Two Horizons* that Wittgenstein's philosophy of language and of understanding was profoundly hermeneutical.[112]

Wittgenstein, however, stressed two points, among many others. First, his own work offers a *descriptive* account of language-*uses* or language-*functions*. He writes, "We must do away with all *explanation*, and description alone (*nur Beschreibung*) must take its place."[113] He observes: "Philosophy simply puts everything before us ... The work of the philosopher consists in assembling reminders for a particular purpose."[114] In terms of Ricoeur's category-distinction between *explanation* and *understanding*, the work of Wittgenstein mainly comes under the heading of understanding. Wittgenstein explicitly states that his aim in his later work is to have "changed your way of seeing."[115] A brilliant commentary on this aspect of Wittgenstein's aims is offered by Stanley Cavell.[116] Wittgenstein's style, he argues, serves to prevent understanding which is unaccompanied by inner *change*. His work largely concerns the formation and *grammar of concepts*, which depend on patterns of inter-personal behaviour in life. The interwoven whole in a given particular instance can be thought of as a language-game. Wittgenstein writes: "When language-games change, then there is a change in concepts, and with the concepts the meanings of words change."[117]

The second point of emphasis which becomes relevant here concerns the scope of the *language-behaviour* which underlies the shape of the *concepts*. The whole, for Wittgenstein, includes not only the behaviour and stance of the hearer or reader, but also of the speaker. Wittgenstein's model language-games are usually taken from situations of oral or living speech. But Ricoeur believes that in the case of written texts, what the text presupposes about the purposes and situation of the author "behind" the text assumes at best a secondary or relatively minimal importance.

In speech-act theory, however, a succession of writers has drawn attention to the role of what Austin called "presuppositions", "implications", and "entailments", and Searle thought of as "Background". This includes "a set of extralinguistic, non-semantic, conventions", and also extralinguistic commitments, attitudes, and acts. This also relates to what François Recanati calls a "look behind the scenes".[118] Even if his approach is widely regarded as insufficiently sophisticated, Austin was rightly convinced that the "happy" functioning of language at the level which Ricoeur thinks of as occuring "in front of" the text depended on the existence of certain states of affairs "behind" the text.[119] A more sophisticated discussion lies to hand in J.R. Searle's helpful essay "The Logical Status of Fictional Discourse".[120] Searle carefully distinguishes between the operational effectiveness which may be shared by fictional and non-fictional texts, and *extratextual* factors which determine the different *bases upon which* the same operations may depend. Searle writes: "There is no textual property, syntactical or semantic, that will identify a text as a work of fiction. What makes it a work of fiction is, so to speak, the illocutionary stance that the author takes toward it".[121] This approach is also expounded convincingly and with philosophical rigour by Nicholas Wolterstorff, whose work we discuss later.

Searle readily concludes that *at the level of function* "serious (i.e. non-fictional) speech-acts can be conveyed by fictional texts . . . Almost any important work of fiction conveys a 'message' or 'messages' which are conveyed *by* the text but are not *in* the text."[122] We need only recall, he suggests, the notion of the "moral" of some children's stories or fables, or "tiresomely didactic authors such as Tolstoy" to appreciate the point. Nevertheless, at the level of *extra*-textual presuppositions which relate to human commitments and purposes, as well as to situations, a world of differences emerges. The speaker or writer tacitly makes *commitments in non-fictional discourse* which are inapplicable or irrelevant to the speech-acts of fictional texts. This point is underlined rigorously by Wolterstorff, and exemplified with logical notation.

Some of these presuppositions operate as tacit conventions. Searle invites us to consider two different sets of conventions which relate respectively to non-fictional and to fictional discourse. He suggests that we try to imagine these as the vertical and horizontal aspects of a system: "Vertical rules establish connections between language and reality . . . What makes fiction possible, I suggest, is a set of *extralinguistic* non-semantic conventions that break the connections between words and the world established by the rules mentioned earlier. Think of the conventions of fictional discourse as a set of horizontal conventions that break the conventions established by the vertical rules. They suspend the normal requirements established by these rules."[123] In what sense are these "normal requirements" extra-linguistic? The answer lies in the normal conditions of assertions which set up expectations that speakers or writers who are serious or "sincere" will "stand behind" their words. They imply certain *commitments, attitudes*, and *responsibilities*. We expound this feature further in Chapter XV, with further reference to Wolterstorff.

The development of Searle's argument exposes two crucial differences between Searle and Ricoeur. First Searle points out that the important role of tacit commitments in non-fictional discourse becomes clear when we are examining *illocutionary* speech-acts, but concealed when we view speech-acts as *perlocutions. In* establishing certain effects or meaning-forces the *speaker or writer* more clearly adopts a certain stance than when we ask only what *force or effect* is achieved *by* an utterance or a text (perlocutions). In the latter case, *intra-textual data alone* may in most cases (perhaps even in all cases) account for the textual *effect*. But this is precisely the boundary of Ricoeur's interest. His hermeneutics concern what occurs *in front of* the text, *not behind it*.

Ricoeur makes this quite explicit in two kinds of comment. First, he writes, "The difference between the *illocutionary* and the *prelocutionary* is nothing else than (*sic*) the presence in the former and absence in the latter of the intention to produce in the listener a certain mental act by means of which he will *recognize my intention*."[124] The point about "mental acts" need not detain us, since Searle has shown that this notion is not a necessary part of literary intention. Rather, he speaks of a purposive directedness on the part of a speaker or author; or of the author's stance or set of commitments in the context of the "Background".[125] (Again, we explore this issue further in chapter XVI.) But Ricoeur directs his major attention to the prelocutionary dimension of texts, restricting illocution to dialogic situations. Second, Ricoeur also insists that "in written texts the dialogic situation has been exploded . . . The text escapes the finite horizon lived by its author."[126] Thus, Ricoeur observes, "Hermeneutics begins where dialogue ends".[127]

The second crucial difference between Austin and Searle, on the one hand, and Ricoeur on the other, concerns what Searle regards as the indispensable role of certain extra-linguistic factors for answering a full range of questions about meaning. For Ricoeur, hermeneutics arises when there emerges a range of polyvalent meaning-*possibilities for the reader*. For Searle, accounts of meaning depend on *relations between two sets* of variable possibilities: variant *possibilities in the Background-situation* on which the text, narrative, or utterance rests, and possibilities which derive from its effective force or impact on the hearer or reader.

Building on the work of Austin and Searle, although also departing from Searle at certain key points, François Recanati examines in rigorous detail the distinction between language-force and language-content. In terms of the dimension which Ricoeur thinks of as "the front of" the text, Recanati believes that even assertions about states of affairs function with illocutionary force. But not all propositions are assertions. Propositions may occur where they lie embedded among other language-uses simply to be "mentioned" in a declarative mood either, for example, as assertions made by someone else, or as hypotheses, fictions, or other pragmatically neutral declarations.

Recanati follows R.M Hare in pointing out the ambiguity of what Frege and Russell indicated as "assertive force" by distinguishing in logical notation between "p", a pragmatically neutral propositional content, and "p", which could be used *both* as a mood-indicator *and* as a "neustic", i.e. to "indicate the speaker's 'subscription' to the proposition he utters in a certain mood".[128] Recanati is unwilling to follow Searle's precise method of distinguishing between "sentence meaning" and "speaker's meaning." Indeed here he stands further from Ricoeur than Searle does. Even the *force* of an utterance cannot be made fully explicit without reference to contextual influences outside the sentence-meaning or the textual meaning. Thus, while "declarative sentences are force-neutral", Recanati argues that Austin is quite close to Frege in urging that assertions have the *force* of an effective performance of an *illocutionary* act of assertion.[129] This cannot be reduced exhaustively and without remainder to its textual content or sentence-meaning. Recanati insists: "However explicit an utterance is, knowledge of its meaning is never sufficient to determine its illocutionary force in this sense, because the question of seriousness is never settled at the level of meaning, but requires *considering the context.*"[130] He concludes: "To say something, in the locutionary sense, is to act the performing of an illocutionary act; but if one seeks an understanding of the real pragmatic activity of the actors, as opposed to the character they play on the stage, one had better look *behind* the *scenes.*"[131]

In Recanati's theory of speech-acts, Ricoeur's "textual world" is rather like the action of a play: as an audience we may be moved and transformed by the play, but we cannot ask critical questions about its function and truth without breaking its spell, and looking behind the lines of the characters. In theory, Ricoeur's emphasis on "explanation" and on a hermeneutic of suspicion takes account of the problem. But in practice his theories of history and of language reduce and subordinate the role of this critical dimension in his narrative theory.

More recent speech-act theory, especially in linguistics, has given prominence to the notion of "conversational implicature", which was formulated initially by H.H. Grice in his lecture "Logic and Conversation" (1967) and published only in part.[132] Because Ricoeur rejects the model of dialogue or conversation as relevant only to oral situations, this area cannot feature effectively, or adequately in his theory of texts. Yet many writers, including Recanati and Levinson, recognize its importance, even if others, such as R.A. Van der Sandt, question its value. Conversation, Grice argued, is governed by tacit goals of co-operative communication, which entail four "maxims of conversation". It is axiomatic, he insisted, that conversation presupposes an *extra*-linguistic and *rational basis* which goes beyond merely intra-linguistic conventions. Certain attitudes and purposes may be presupposed that relate, in the context of a co-operative effort, to *commitments* to goals that concern truth, information, relevance, and the avoidance of ambiguity or obscurity. Conversational implicature, therefore, concerns factors *"behind"* the text which do not come within the scope of primary attention in Ricoeur's theory of textuality. Recanati observes, "The notion of conversational implicature sheds light on the mechanism by which people mean more than they literally say."[133] Speaker's meaning may be more than textual meaning.

Stephen Levinson develops Grice's theory of implicature in greater detail. It represents, he believes, "one of the single most important ideas in pragmatics."[134] In particular it has great *explanatory* power. Levinson examines and develops Grice's theory that figures of speech arise when the maxims of conversation are deliberately "flouted" or "exploited."[135] Levinson argues that traditionally both the *comparison* or *substitution* theory of metaphor (which Ricoeur rejects) and the *interaction* theory of metaphor (which Ricoeur accepts) "are both usually construed as *semantic* theories of metaphor". But these "fail to yield adequate accounts of the phenomena".[136] The development of language-change and the processes by which metaphors are born, live, and die, invite reflection on the *contextual assumptions* that lie *behind* them. For example, euphemisms, he argues, may begin as polite metaphors, but soon acquire the sense they originally implicated. He makes similar comments about honorifics.

For some linguisticians and philosophers, the notion of presupposition and its dependence on context is more problematic. In a full-scale study of this issue, Rob A. Van der Sandt (1988) attacks Grice's approach, together with those of L. Karttunen and G. Gazdar.[137] On the other hand, with enormous vigour and sophistication Quentin Skinner maintains the view (1988) that "there is a sense in which we need to understand why a certain proposition has been put forward if we wish to understand the proposition itself."[138] Although he departs from them clearly on matters of detail, Skinner defends the general perspectives adopted by Austin, Searle, and Stephen R. Schiffer. If, as Wittgenstein declared, "words are deeds", illocutionary acts, Skinner argues, are speaking *or writing* with a certain intended illocutionary force. "Serious utterances" depend on what Austin called "a total speech-act situation". To understand a speech-act, utterance, or text, "we need to grasp why it seemed worth making that precise move; to recapture the presuppositions and purposes that went into the making of it."[139] In the history of ideas, Skinner urges there can be no histories of concepts as such; there can only be histories of their *uses* in argument.

Quentin Skinner notes that one of his critics, John Keane, accuses him of adopting an "author-subject" approach, "thereby suggesting that I have yet to hear about the death of the author announced by Barthes and Foucault. It is true that these announcements strike me as a trifle exaggerated. I cannot agree with Keane that authors are nothing more than 'prisoners of the discourse within whose boundaries they take pen in hand'."[140] For there are moments when an author chooses to challenge or to subvert a convention, and to the extent that our social world is constituted by our concepts, any successful alteration in the *use* of a concept will at the same time constitute a change in our social world. Drawing on Wittgenstein's arguments about *behaviour*, Skinner responds to his critics that he has not returned to a pre-Gadamerian hermeneutics of empathy or mental processes. To understand the intentions of a man who is waving his arms in the next field, he argues, it is not necessary to identify ideas inside his head,

The Hermeneutics of Suspicion and Retrieval 367

but of grasping that there is a context of convention in which arm-waving can count as an act of warning.

This approach, with its implicit and explicit appeal back to Wittgenstein, brings us to the major difficulty about Ricoeur's understanding of metaphor. Wittgenstein draws a distinction between "picture" and application. The vulnerability of metaphor to the kind of attacks brought against it in the tradition from Nietzsche to Derrida depends on its disengagement from *use* which rests on *judgment*. Ricoeur is partly aware of this aspect by drawing such a firm distinction, in reply to such criticism, between living and dead metaphor. He allows that dead metaphor may trap us within illusions and may seem to reinforce them, but insists that living metaphor breaks the mould of illusion or "idolatry."

Nevertheless, as Vanhoozer concludes, there remains an ambivalence about the capacity of Ricoeur's role of "explanation" to offer adequate criteria concerning the relation between metaphor and truth, and Vanhoozer compares the more cognitively robust account of metaphor which he finds in the work of Janet Martin Soskice, to which we have already referred. If our theory of language places us within a fundamentally intra-linguistic world, in which the context of human behaviour, at least on the part of speakers or writers is at best secondary, we fall victim to the concern expressed by Wittgenstein. "A *picture* held us captive. And we could not get outside it, for it lay in our language, and language seemed to repeat it to us inexorably."[141] In such cases, the picture bewitches us into adopting a given logical grammar, and there is "a whole cloud of philosophy condensed into a drop of grammar."[142] Whether a picture or a metaphor is good or bad may well depend on how it is *applied*, and "Philosophy is a battle against the bewitchment of our intelligence by means of language."[143] In their more popular book entitled *Metaphors We Live By* Lakoff and Johnson trace the power of metaphorical language to invite us to understand and to experience one thing *as if* it were another. Their rational argument comes to be viewed *as* a war when we speak of attacking, defending, demolishing, shooting down, and wiping out an opponent.[144] The metaphor encourages confrontation and aggression. Pictures are powerful, but also seductive.

Ricoeur's "explanatory" role functions with some ambivalence in this context. At the metacritical level, a hermeneutic of suspicion seems to operate with more radical effect than more traditional rationalist criteria. In common with Jürgen Habermas Ricoeur sees the "seductive" role of the critique of ideology through Freud and others as more genuinely "critical" than traditional approaches which are associated with empiricism or rationalism can offer. Yet all this is weakened by an insistence in *practice* that the "reference" of the text occurs through what is projected in front of it, not through referential dimensions in what lives behind it. There is thus a one-sidedness in his approach, which might have been avoided if he had been persuaded by certain approaches in speech-act theory.

4. Some Consequences for Ricoeur's Approach to Biblical Hermeneutics

Ricoeur's approach to biblical texts has certain fundamental affinities with Kierkegaard's approach to "indirect communication." There is far more, of course, to Ricoeur's complex theory; but the focal point concerns the need for readers of texts to engage with "possibilities" that can be realized only through *decision* where there is a conflict of interpretations. Truth is bound up with the self-knowledge conveyed through interpretation, through an indirect detour through texts which open up *inter-subjective worlds of imagination* by means of symbol, metaphor, and narrative. They therefore carry the reader *beyond the merely individual* self. Here is a crucial difference from Kierkegaard. For Kierkegaard individual selfhood remained central. Ricoeur also ranks more highly than Kierkegaard the place to be assigned to the "objective" or explanatory modes of knowledge. Explanation takes its place alongside understanding. Thus, although the thrust of our argument in the previous section remains applicable to his general theory of texts, in biblical hermeneutics he does find a place, albeit not a major one, for the techniques of historical criticism.

But does the interaction of Ricoeur's hermeneutics of suspicion with his hermeneutics of retrieval allow us to speak of the truth of biblical texts, over and above their function of creating new ways of perceiving human selfhood? Once again, different comments and observations from Ricoeur seem to point in different directions, perhaps because the answer to the question can remain only a contextual one. In his essay "Hermeneutics and the Critique of Ideology" Ricoeur insists that Gadamer's hermeneutics and Habermas's critical theory *both* have validity up to a point, and are most fruitful where they "interpenetrate". We must affirm *both* Gadamer's ontology of prior understanding, for we belong to traditions, *and* Habermas's movement by a critique of ideology towards an eschatology of freedom, for tradition must undergo psycho-analytical and social criticism. John B. Thompson's helpful study *Critical Hermeneutics*, to which we have referred, compares Ricoeur and Habermas, and confirms the point.

Does all this take us further than the notion of *possibility*? Lynn Poland and David Klemm identify this other side of the problem. In the end, the interpreter must *wager* on possibility, which accords with the place of the *human will* in Ricoeur's philosophy, and in this respect brings Kierkegaard to mind again. Explanation and understanding, Lynn Poland observes, involve "the comparison and conflict of *possible* ways to construe the text's meaning. With regard to the biblical writings, this clearly implies that no appropriation is earned if it has not engaged with *possible seductive explanations* of the text. Beyond the question of appropriation lies the question of *truth* – can the respective understandings of existence of Shakespeare, Melville, and Auden all be true? The question of truth at this level, Ricoeur seems to suggest, lies *beyond the task of interpretation*; it is the province of *philosophical thought*."[145] David Klemm also underlines the largely intra-textual and intra-linguistic character of Ricoeur's criteria: "The most probable reading is the one that makes sense of the greatest number of details as they fit into a whole, and the one that renders all that can be brought forth by the text."[146] This may recall Schleiermacher's emphasis on the corrigibility of all interpretation; but it seems to go further.

Towards the end of his *Symbolism of Evil* Ricoeur writes: "How shall we get beyond the 'circle of hermeneutics'? By transforming it into a *wager*. I wager that I shall have a better understanding of man and of all beings if I follow the *indication* of symbolic thought. That wager then becomes the task of *verifying* my wager and saturating it, so to speak, with intelligibility."[147] To make such an act or wager on the basis of symbols, metaphor, and narrative, is to open the possibility of "a qualitative transformation of reflexive consciousness."[148] This is not the traditional direction of a belief founded on knowledge, but "on essentially Anselmian schema."[149] Loretta Dornisch comments, "When interpretations are in conflict even after the applications of the norms of truth, one must make a *commitment*; wager that one interpretation will give more meaning than another; one must profess a *faith*."[150]

In *this* direction Ricoeur does allow for "reference" on the part of the text. That is why in our second chapter above, on textuality and theology, we saw that Ricoeur can make room for the notion of the biblical text as *indirect address*. He is certainly not satisfied with the kind of structuralism that reduces a message or textual content to the mere interplay of semiotic codes. He declares: "Structuralism, to my mind, is a dead-end the very moment when it trusts any 'message' as the mere 'quotation' of its underlying 'code' . . . I call dead-end not all structural analysis, but only the one which makes it irrelevant . . . to return from deep structure to the surface structures."[151] In this respect, he adds, "The object of hermeneutics is not 'the text', but the text as discourse, or discourse as the text."[152]

These principles become evident in Paul Ricoeur's approach to biblical texts. The parables of Jesus reveal a symbolic interplay with the narrative of the Passion. Ricoeur writes, "As soon as the preaching of Jesus as the 'Crucified' is interwoven with the narratives of his 'deeds' and of his 'sayings', a *specific possibility* of interpretation is opened up by what I call here the establishment of a *'space* of intersignification."[153] But the proclamation of Jesus *cannot be more than a metaphor* or "parable of God", and thus a parabolic proclamation. Any other kind of "reference" remains at best a "model" which in turn is "qualified", in Ian Ramsey's phrase, by modifiers which transcend and point beyond models to allow for creative redescription or refiguration. There is a "transgression" by which biblical forms of discourse "point beyond their immediate signification toward the Wholly Other."[154]

Although he recognizes that "there is considerable evidence that Ricoeur feels close to Barth in his hermeneutical intent", Vanhoozer argues that at the most fundamental points Ricoeur has a very different orientation.[155] He writes, "Unlike Frei and Barth, Ricoeur reads the biblical narrative within a general theory of textual discourse."[156] A key statement occures in Ricoeur's essay "Biblical Hermeneutics" in *Semeia*. He writes: "What religious language does is *to redescribe*; what it redescribes is *human experience*. In this sense we must say that *the ultimate referent of the parables, proverbs, and eschatological sayings is* not *the Kingdom of God but human reality in its wholeness*."[157] In this respect, Ricoeur's work remains more akin with that of Norman Perrin, Dan-Otto Via, and J.D. Crossan, than with that of Barth. On the other hand two aspects of Barthian theology remain important for Ricoeur: the word of God is *eventful* within the time-horizon of the reader; and God is wholly *transcendent*, or wholly *Other*.

Lewis Mudge argues that Ricoeur stands closer to Barth than to Bultmann. What blocks us from hearing the word is not, as Bultmann argued, our incapacity to respond to myth or symbol: rather it is because our rejection of symbol, metaphor, and indirect communications of transcendence, has "deprived us of the possibility of articulating such realities as radical evil or grace-empowered hope."[158] We need to be open to the "diagnostic signs" (as Mary Gerhart notes) which indirectly reveal the human condition.[159] But Lynn Poland and Kevin Vanhoozer more convincingly trace closer parallels with Bultmann.[160] Ricoeur declares, "I would reproach Bultmann with not having sufficiently followed the Heideggerian 'path' . . . He has taken a short cut."[161] Ricoeur's own hermeneutical work functions, in his own words, "not at all as a rejection of Bultmann or even as a supplement to his work, but as somehow a foundation supporting it."[162] In the end, biblical narrative has human "existence" as its primary referent.

Although, for Ricoeur, revelation assumes the form of five modes of discourse, the prophetic, narrative discourse, the prescriptive, wisdom discourse, and hymnic discourse, "we cannot say that the idea of revelation is completely conveyed by this idea of communication between two persons. Wisdom, we have seen, recognizes a hidden God who takes as his mask, the anonymous and non-human course of events."[163] The Book of Job assumes a particular importance for Ricoeur, as does also the wisdom mode of discourse to which it belongs. In Job 42: 1–6, Job's questions are not "answered": "Job presupposes an unsuspected meaning which cannot be transcribed by speech or *logos* . . . What is revealed is the possibility of hope in spite of . . ."[164] Ricoeur concludes, "Wisdom intends every person in and through the few. Its themes are the limit-situations spoken of by Karl Jaspers . . . solitude, the fault, suffering, and death . . . The God who reveals himself is a hidden God, and hidden things belong to him."[165]

Vanhoozer's concluding evaluation of Ricoeur identifies some valid points. Ricoeur, he concludes, formulates a "'believing philosophy', rather than a theology."[166] Part of his constructive originality lies in his "rehabilitation of the imagination . . . the scope of my possibilities."[167] "However, Ricoeur is not principally a Proclaimer. His is the more humble task of 'making space' for this proclamation."[168] There is a deep ambivalence in his hermeneutics, which, Vanhoozer argues, can encourage "left-wing" or "right-wing" interpretation, just as Hegelians may be divided in their interpretation of Hegel.[169] The minimal interpretation would draw attention to Ricoeur's dialogue with Kant's "limits" and Heidegger's "possibility", and see Ricoeur's philosophical aims as standing, in Don Ihde's words, "in the Socratic tradition of seeking to understand oneself in understanding man."[170] But Ricoeur constantly rejects the individualism of a "narrow and narcissistic 'I' of immediate consciousness."[171] Engagement with texts expands our horizons.

If speech-act theory underlines one or two of the difficulties and limitations of Ricoeur's hermeneutics, this same approach also throws into relief some of its achievements. The creative emphasis in Searle and in Recanati of shaping the world to fit the eventful word of promise finds expression in Ricoeur's connection between "possibility" and eschatological hope.[172] Language is creative. "The precedence of the future", Don Ihde comments, signals "a hope engendered through the very opening provided by hermeneutic phenomenology in its uncovering of *possibilities* . . . 'the creative imagination of the possible' . . . Hope is the 'answer' to evil."[173] Ricoeur declares: "Psychoanalysis has its foundation in an archaeology of the subject, the phenomenology of the spirit in a teleology, and the phenomenology of religion in an eschatology."[174] The language of promise, of hope, and of eschatology has an important place in Ricoeur's biblical hermeneutics.

The horizons of religion including the biblical texts provide for Ricoeur a framework within which imaginative possibility performs the double function of a critique grounded in metacritical hermeneutical theory and also a creative advance through listening and affirmation. Towards the conclusion of his own anthology, edited by Reagan and Stewart, he returns to the theme of hermeneutics as having "a double edge and double function. It is an effort to struggle against idols . . . It is a critique of ideologies in the sense of Marx; it is a critique of all flights and evasions in the sense of Nietzsche; a struggle against childhood father and against securing illusions in the sense of psychoanalysis . . . This was the task of second Isaiah when he tied the preaching of Yahweh to the fight against the Baals."[175] But hermeneutics is "also an act of listening . . . to let speak a language which though addressed to us, we no longer hear."[176] This double event of destruction and call takes place in the parables of Jesus, which bring about "reorientation by disorientation . . . to listen to the Parables of Jesus, it seems to me, is to let one's imagination be opened to the new possibilities disclosed by the extravagance of these short dramas."[177]

The Book of Job, similarly, offers first what Ricoeur calls "this shattering of moral vision . . . the irreducibility of the evil of scandal to the evil of fault."[178] The "virulence" of the Book of Job surpasses that of any other culture, because it presupposed an unparalleled vision of the "ethical" God. But "the ethical vision is eaten away right down to the very core of action".[179] Job cries: "I wish to remonstrate with God" (Job 13:3); "Oh! If I knew where to find him" (23:3); "Who will make God listen to me?" (Job 31:35). Job "penetrates beyond any ethical vision to a new dimension of faith", but this is "the dimension of *unverifiable* faith."[180] In Job 38 and 42: 1–6 "the final theophany has explained nothing to him, but it has changed his view."[181]

In the introduction to the volume of *Semeia* which contains various studies suggested by Ricoeur's approach to Job (1981) Loretta Dornisch points out that Ricoeur does at times make use of a wide variety of "explanatory" tools to approach the text.[182] But in practice explanation is to dispel illusion and to serve understanding. The major function of biblical texts remains a perspectival and refigurational one. They project possible worlds which have the capacity to transform us, or to "change our view."[183] Whether this change accords with the truth about actual states of affairs beyond the worlds of texts and language, however, may need to remain, at least for the present, a matter of wager. But Ricoeur's respect for explanation and for metacritical reflection makes it an intelligent wager, not a blind one. What remains central for Ricoeur is the double function of hermeneutics: the hermeneutics of suspicion which unmasks human wish-fulfilments and shatters idols, and the hermeneutics of retrieval which listens to symbols and to symbolic narrative discourse. Where criticism operates, this is only to arrive at post-critical creativity on the yonder side of the critical desert.

NOTES TO CHAPTER X

1. Paul Ricoeur, *The Rule of Metaphor. Multi-disciplinary Studies of the Creation of Meaning in Language*, Eng. London: Routledge and Kegan Paul, 1978 (and Toronto: University of Toronto Press, 1977) 315–22.
2. Loretta Dornisch "Symbolic Systems and the Interpretation of Scripture: An Introduction to the Work of Paul Ricoeur" *Semeia* 4, 1975, 1–22.
3. Paul Ricoeur, *The Rule of Metaphor*, 315.
4. Paul Ricoeur, *Le voluntaire et l'involuntaire*, Paris: Aubier, 1949, Eng. *Freedom and Nature: The Voluntary and the Involuntary*, Evanston: Northwestern University Press, 1966.
5. Paul Ricoeur, *Fallible Man*, Eng. Chicago: Regnery, 1967; and *The Symbolism of Evil*, Eng. Boston: Beacon Press, 1967.
6. Paul Ricoeur, *The Rule of Metaphor* 316.
7. *Ibid*.
8. *Ibid* 317.
9. *Ibid* 318.
10. Paul Ricoeur, *De l'interpretation: Essai sur Freud*, Paris: Éditions du Seuil, 1965; Eng. *Freud and Philosophy. An Essay on Interpretations*, New Haven and London: Yale University Press; 1970.
11. Paul Ricoeur, *Freud and Philosophy* 5.
12. *Ibid*.
13. *Ibid* 8.
14. *Ibid* 19.
15. *Ibid* 27 (first italics mine; second italics, Ricoeur's).
16. *Ibid* 28.
17. *Ibid* 33.
18. *Ibid* 54.
19. David Jasper, "The Limits of Formalism and the Theology of Hope: Ricoeur, Moltmann and Dostoyevsky" in *Literature and Theology* 1, 1987, 4; cf. 1–10.
20. Paul Ricoeur, *Freud and Philosophy*, 52.
21. Paul Ricoeur, *The Rule of Metaphor* 318 and 319.
22. Paul Ricoeur, *Freud and Philosophy*, 93.
23. *Ibid* 94.
24. *Ibid* 147–51.
25. *Ibid* 374.
26. *Ibid* 387–88; cf.422.
27. *Ibid* 424.
28. *Ibid* 427.
29. *Ibid* 392 (Ricoeur's italics).
30. *Ibid* 386.
31. *Ibid* 420.
32. *Ibid*.
33. *Ibid* 531.
34. *Ibid* 543.
35. Paul Ricoeur, *The Conflict of Interpretations* 287–334.
36. *Ibid* 288.
37. *Ibid* 334.
38. Kevin J. Vanhoozer, *Biblical Narrative in the Philosophy of Paul Ricoeur. A Study in*

Hermeneutics and Theology, Cambridge: Cambridge University Press, 1990, 17–55; cf. David E. Klemm, *The Hermeneutical Theory of Paul Ricoeur: A Constructive Analysis*, London and Toronto: Associated University Presses, 1983, 27–44.
39. Anthony C. Thiselton, *The Two Horizons*, 163; cf. 161–68.
40. Martin Heidegger, *Being and Time*, 183.
41. Anthony C. Thiselton, *The Two Horizons*, 164.
42. Martin Heidegger, *Being and Time*, 191.
43. Ludwig Wittgenstein, *Philosophical Investigations* sects. 151 and 323.
44. Kevin J. Vanhoozer, *op. cit.* 24.
45. Paul Ricoeur, *Interpretation Theory: Discourse and the Surplus of Meaning*, Fort Worth: The Texas Christian University Press, 1976, 45, 47, 52, 55 & 60.
46. *Ibid* 67.
47. Martin Heidegger, *Being and Time*, 172–74 and 203.
48. John Macquarrie, *Studies in Christian Existentialism*, London: S.C.M., 1966, 30–42.
49. Paul Ricoeur, *The Rule of Metaphor*, 6 (Ricoeur's italics).
50. *Ibid*.
51. *Ibid* 19.
52. *Ibid* 24.
53. Ted Cohen, "Metaphor and the Cultivation of Intimacy" in Sheldon Sacks (ed.) *On Metaphor*, Chicago and London: University of Chicago Press, 1979, 3; cf. 1–10; Max Black, "Metaphor" rp. in *Models and Metaphors: Studies in Language and Philosophy*, Ithaca: Cornell University Press, 1962, 25–47; cf: "How Metaphors Work" in Sheldon Sacks (ed.) *op. cit.* 181–92; Philip Wheelwright, *The Burning Fountain: A Study in the Language of Symbolism*, Bloomington: Indiana University Press, 1954, and *Metaphor and Reality*, Bloomington: Indiana University Press, 1962 and 1968; and Owen Barfield, "Poetic Diction: A Study in Meaning", London: Faber & Faber, 1952.
54. Owen Barfield, "Poetic Diction and Legal Fiction", rp. in Max Black (ed.) *The Importance of Language*, Englewood Cliffs: Prentice Hall, 1963; cf. also C.S. Lewis "Bluspels and Flalansferes" in Max Black (ed.) *loc. cit.* This title alludes to two hypothetical metaphors relating to "blue spectacles" and to "Flatlanders".
55. For example, W.M. Urban, *Language and Reality*, New York and London: Allen and Unwin, 1939, chapters 9–10, argues that metaphorical language can be translated into non-metaphorical terms; Wheelwright argues that metaphor is irreducible and not inter-translatable, offering "a perpetual Something More...," *Metaphor and Reality*, 172.
56. Max Black, *Models and Metaphors*, 242.
57. Mary Hesse, *Models and Analysis in Science*, Notre Dame: University of Notre Dame Press, 1966, 30–55.
58. Paul Ricoeur, *Time and Narrative*, Eng. 3 vols., Chicago and London: University of Chicago Press, 1984–88, vol.1, ix (my italics).
59. *Ibid*.
60. *Ibid*.
61. *Ibid* x.
62. *Ibid* 3 (my italics).
63. Gérard Gennette, *Narrative Discourse Revisited*, Eng. Ithaca: Cornell University Press, 1988 (French 1983) 13–16.

64. Seymour Chatman, *Story and Discourse: Narrative Structure in Fiction and Film*, Ithaca: Cornell University Press, 1978, 19–22; Jonathan Culler, *The Pursuit of Signs*, "Semiotics, Literature, Deconstruction", London: Routledge & Kegan Paul, 1981 169–87; and Michael Toolan, *Narrative. A Critical Linguistic Introduction*, London and New York: Routledge, 1988, 12–14.
65. Seymour Chatman, *op. cit.* 19.
66. *Ibid* 43.
67. Paul Ricoeur, *Time and Narrative*, vol.1, 34.
68. Paul Ricoeur, *ibid* vol.3, 101.
69. Martin Heidegger, *Being and Time* 357.
70. Anthony C. Thiselton, *The Two Horizons* 181–84.
71. Paul Ricoeur, *The Conflict of Interpretations* 223 (his italics); cf. 223–35.
72. *Ibid* 232.
73. Paul Ricoeur, *Hermeneutics and the Human Sciences*, Eng. Cambridge: Cambridge University Press, 1981, 61–62.
74. Paul Ricoeur, "The Narrative Function", *Semeia* 13 (*The Poetics of Faith*), 1978, 181 and 182 (Ricoeur's italics); cf. 177–202.
75. *Ibid* 182–83.
76. *Ibid* 188.
77. *Ibid.*
78. *Ibid* 189.
79. *Ibid* 189–90; cf. Hayden White, *Metahistory: the Historical Imagination in Nineteenth-Century Europe*, Baltimore: Johns Hopkins University Press, 1973, and "The Historical Text as Literary Object", *Clio* 3, 1974, 277–303; and Louis O. Mink, "History and Fiction as Modes of Comprehension" in Ralph Cohen (ed.) *New Directions in Literary History*, Baltimore: Johns Hopkins University Press, 1974, 107–24.
80. Paul Ricoeur "The Narrative Function" *loc. cit.* 191.
81. *Ibid.*
82. *Ibid* 194–95.
83. *Ibid* 198.
84. Paul Ricoeur, *The Reality of the Historical Past*, Milwaukee: Marquette University Press, 1984 (The Aquinas Lecture) 32.
85. Paul Ricoeur, *Time and Narrative* vol.1, 186 (Ricoeur's italics).
86. *Ibid* 175.
87. *Ibid* 227.
88. Kevin J. Vanhoozer, *op. cit.* 103 and 104.
89. *Ibid* 282.
90. *Ibid* 97.
91. *Ibid* 140.
92. *Ibid* 158.
93. David Tracy, *The Analogical Imagination: Christian Theology and the Culture of Pluralism*, London: S.C.M., 1981, 123 (his italics); cf. 99–153.
94. Paul Ricoeur, "The Task of Hermeneutics" in *Hermeneutics and the Human Sciences*, 53 (my italics).
95. *Ibid* 54.
96. *Ibid* 76 (my italics).
97. *Ibid* 77.

98. Paul Ricoeur, *The Symbolism of Evil*, 349 (my italics).
99. *Ibid* 7.
100. *Ibid* 19.
101. David E. Klemm, *The Hermeneutical Theory of Paul Ricoeur. A Constructive Analysis*, Lewisburg: Bucknell University Press, and London and Toronto: Associated University Presses, 1983; and John B. Thompson, *Critical Hermeneutics: A Study in the Thought of Paul Ricoeur and Jürgen Habermas*, Cambridge: Cambridge University Press, 1981.
102. David E. Klemm, *op. cit.* 27–44 (cf. also 45–73) and 160; John B. Thompson, *op. cit.* 38–44 and 50.
103. David E. Klemm, *op. cit.* 160.
104. *Ibid* (Klemm's italics).
105. Anthony C. Thiselton, *The Two Horizons*, 160–61, 173–76, 199–200; (cf. further 411–15); and "Truth" in Colin Brown (ed.) *New International Dictionary of New Testament Theology* vol.3, Exeter: Paternoster and Grand Rapids: Zondervan, 1978, 874–902; and David E. Klemm, *op. cit.* 161–63.
106. Don Ihde, *Hermeneutic Phenomenology: The Philosophy of Paul Ricoeur*, Evanston: Northwestern University Press, 1971 (Studies in Phenomenology and Existential Philosophy) 7.
107. Paul Ricoeur, *Freud and Philosophy* 386 (his italics).
108. Kevin J. Vanhoozer, *op. cit.* 66.
109. Paul Ricoeur "Foreword" to Don Ihde, *op. cit.* xiv.
110. Paul Ricoeur, *The Rule of Metaphor*, 321–22.
111. *Ibid* 322.
112 Anthony C. Thiselton, *The Two Horizons* 33–40 and especially 357–85, and 407–15.
113. Ludwig Wittgenstein, *Philosophical Investigations* sect. 109 (his italics).
114. *Ibid* sects. 126–27.
115. L. Wittgenstein, *Zettel* sect. 461; cf. *Philosophical Investigations*, sect.144.
116. Stanley Cavell, "The Availability of Wittgenstein's Later Philosophy" in *Philosophical Review* 71, 1962, 67–93, also rp. in George Pitcher (ed.) *Wittgenstein: The Philosophical Investigations*, London: McMillan, 1968, 151–85.
117. L. Wittgenstein, *On Certainty* sect. 65.
118. J.L. Austin, *How to Do Things with Words*, 45–52; John R. Searle, *Intentionality* 141–59; and François Recanati, *Meaning and Force: the Pragmatics of Performative Utterances*, Eng., Cambridge: Cambridge University Press, 1987, 266.
119. J.L. Austin, *loc. cit.*.
120. John R. Searle, "The Logical Status of Fictional Discourse" in *Expression and Meaning*, 58–75.
121. *Ibid* 65.
122. *Ibid* 74.
123. *Ibid* 66.
124. Paul Ricoeur, *Interpretation Theory*, 18–19; cf. 14–16 (my italics).
125. John Searle, *Intentionality*, 1–36 *et passim*.
126. Paul Ricoeur, *Interpretation Theory*, 29–30.
127. *Ibid* 32.
128. F. Recanati, *op. cit.* 262.
129. *Ibid* 164.

130. *Ibid* 265 (my italics); cf. 226–28.
131. *Ibid* 266.
132. H.H. Grice, "Logic and Conversation" in P. Cole and J.L. Morgan (eds.) *Syntax and Semantics*, 3: Speech-Acts, New York: Academic Press, 1975, 41–58.
133. F. Recanati, *op. cit.* 121.
134. Stephen C. Levinson, *Pragmatics*, Cambridge: Cambridge University Press, 1983, 97.
135. *Ibid* 109.
136. *Ibid* 148.
137. Rob A. Van der Sandt, *Context and Presupposition*, London and New York: Helm, 1988, 104–222.
138. Quentin Skinner "A Reply to my Critics" in James Tully (ed.), *Meaning and Context: Quentin Skinner and his Critics*, Cambridge: Polity Press, 1988, 274.
139. *Ibid;* cf. 262.
140. *Ibid* 276.
141. L. Wittgenstein, *Philosophical Investigations* sect. 115.
142. *Ibid* 222.
143. *Ibid* sect. 55, *ibid* sect. 109.
144. George Lakoff and Mark Johnson, *Metaphors We Live By*, Chicago: Chicago University Press, 1980, 3–21 *et passim*.
145. Lynn Poland, *op. cit.* 178 (my italics).
146. David E. Klemm, *The Hermeneutical Theory of Paul Ricoeur*, 93.
147. Paul Ricoeur, *The Symbolism of Evil*, 355.
148. *Ibid* 356.
149. *Ibid* 357.
150. Loretta Dornisch, "Symbolic Systems and the Interpretation of Scripture: An Introduction to the Work of Paul Ricoeur", *Semeia* 4, 1975, 15–16 (my italics); cf. 1–21.
151. Paul Ricoeur, "Biblical Hermeneutics", *Semeia* 4, 1975, 65.
152. *Ibid* 67.
153. *Ibid* 105.
154. *Ibid* 108.
155. K.J. Vanhoozer, *op. cit.* 149.
156. *Ibid* 156.
157. Paul Ricoeur, "Biblical Hermeneutics" *loc. cit.* 127 (my italics).
158. Lewis S. Mudge, "Paul Ricoeur on Biblical Interpretation" in Paul Ricoeur, *Essays on Biblical Interpretation*, 8; cf. 1–40.
159. *Ibid* 12; cf. Mary Gerhart, "Paul Ricoeur's Notion of 'Diagnostics': its Function in Literary Interpretation", *Journal of Religion* 56, 1976, 137–56.
160. Lynn Poland, *op. cit.* 183–96; K.J. Vanhoozer, *op. cit.* 119–47.
161. Paul Ricoeur, "Preface to Bultmann" in *Essays on Biblical Interpretation*, 71; cf. 49–72.
162. *Ibid* 72.
163. Paul Ricoeur, "Toward a Hermeneutic of the Idea of Revelation" *loc. cit.* 89.
164. *Ibid* 87.
165. *Ibid* 85–6 and 93.
166. K.J. Vanhoozer, *op. cit.* 275.
167. *Ibid* 281.

168. *Ibid* 288.
169. *Ibid* 286.
170. Don Ihde, *Hermeneutic Phenomenology*, 11.
171. Paul Ricoeur, "Preface" *ibid* xvii.
172. Cf. John R. Searle, *Expression and Meaning* 3–4; F. Recanati, *op. cit.* 146–50 and chapter VIII, above.
173. Don Ihde, "Editor's Introduction" to Paul Ricoeur, *The Conflict of Interpretations* xxii.
174. Paul Ricoeur, *ibid* 23.
175. Paul Ricoeur, "Religion and Faith" in Charles E. Reagan and David Stewart (eds.) *The Philosophy of Paul Ricoeur: An Anthology of his Work*, Boston: Beacon Press, 1978, 234–35.
176. *Ibid* 235.
177. *Ibid* 244–45.
178. Paul Ricoeur, *The Symbolism of Evil*, 314.
179. *Ibid* 316.
180. *Ibid* 319 (Ricoeur's italics).
181. *Ibid* 321.
182. Loretta Dornisch, "The Book of Job and Ricoeur's Hermeneutics" in *Semeia* 19, 1981, 3–21, especially 9; cf. also Paul Ricoeur, "Philosophical Hermeneutics, and Biblical Hermeneutics" in François Bovon and Gregoire Rouiller (eds.) *Exegesis: Problems of Method and Exercises in Reading*, Eng. Pittsburgh: Pickwick Press, 1978, 321–39.
183. Cf. further Paul Ricoeur, "The Bible and the Imagination" in Hans Dieter Betz (ed.) *The Bible as a Document of the University*, Chico: Scholars Press, 1981, 49–75; and Mary Gerhart, "Imagination and History in Ricoeur's Interpretation Theory", *Philosophy Today* 23, 1979. 51–68; and *The Question of Belief in Literary Criticism: An Introduction to the Hermeneutical Theory of Paul Ricoeur*, Stuttgart: Akademischer Verlag Hans-Dieter Heinz, 1979.

CHAPTER XI

The Hermeneutics of Socio-Critical Theory: Its Relation to Socio-pragmatic Hermeneutics and to Liberation Theologies

1. The Nature of Socio-Critical Hermeneutics: Habermas on Hermeneutics, Knowledge, Interest, and an Emancipatory Critique

Socio-critical hermeneutics may be defined as an approach to texts (or to traditions and institutions) which seeks to penetrate beneath their surface-function *to expose their role as instruments of power, domination, or social manipulation. To use Habermas's terms, "critical" hermeneutics (which looks back to Marx) and "depth" hermeneutics (which looks back to Freud) aim to achieve the liberation of those over whom this power or social manipulation is exercised.* In the most authentic forms of socio-critical hermeneutical theory this is effected by establishing a metacritical or transcendental dimension distinct from the horizons of the texts or traditions in question, on the basis of which their manipulatory or oppressive functions and mechanisms can be made transparent.

It is clear that within Western traditions *certain ways* of reading and using the biblical writings, far from transforming readers, serve effectively to re-affirm pre-existing prejudices, traditions, attitudes, and social relationships. In such a context socio-critical hermeneutics becomes both a tool for potential *liberation* and rediscovery of truth, and also a weapon against individual and corporate self-deception. This may lead not only to the *liberation of persons*, but also to *liberation of the biblical texts*. Christopher Rowland and Mark Corner capture the double aspect in their recent title *Liberating Exegesis* (1990).[1] Socio-critical hermeneutics provides the theoretical hermeneutical framework for liberation hermeneutics, including, at the metacritical level, feminist and black hermeneutics.

Yet there is also a deep divide at this point between genuinely metacritical theory and more pragmatic versions of liberation hermeneutics. Some versions of feminist hermeneutics, for example, primarily take the form of a socio-pragmatic or narrative "reading" of texts "through the eyes of a female reader." Other strands in feminist hermeneutics draw deeply on social-critical theory at a metacritical level. Some approaches are ambivalent or even explicitly avoid theory. For example, as we noted in our Introduction, Rowland and Corner claim on the one hand that "It is certainly no longer possible to consider liberation theology's approach to problems of biblical interpretation without some understanding of the sociology of knowledge and the writings of Paul Ricoeur and Jürgen Habermas."[2] On the other hand, however, this single sentence constitutes their only reference to Ricoeur, and their consideration of Habermas is restricted to one quotation of eight lines, and a single brief comment. They commence their study with the explicit reservation that a "highly technical discussion of 'theology or *praxis*'" would represent an ironic self-contradiction, and most of their book focusses on concrete case-studies of liberation hermeneutics in various social contexts of socio-religious life.

Praxis is a slippery, but also technical, term. Philosophically it gained currency first from Aristotle, who set it in contrast, on one side, to *theōria*, and, on the other side, to *poiēsis*. Aristotle regarded it not simply as "action", but as moral or political action strictly under the guidance of *phronēsis*, namely practical reason or wisdom. But in the context of hermeneutics the more relevant consideration is the key role of *praxis* in the early philosophy of Karl Marx. The term occurs most frequently in his writings of the 1840s; but the methodological concept remains fundamental for all of Marx's work. In his full-length exposition and evaluation of this issue, Richard Bernstein concludes that for Marx *praxis* becomes not only "activity, production, labor . . . revolutionary practice" but also "relentless criticism."[3] It is an integral part of a "comprehensive and coherent theory of man and of his world." Paul Avis makes a similar point: "In its Marxist sense . . . *praxis* is more closely related to *theōria* than in Aristotle . . . It embodies *theōria*", even if it is also "dependent on *poiesis*."[4] Avis rightly concludes that in "critical philosophy" the theoretical dimension is less readily dissolved than it is in "critical theology."

Jürgen Habermas (b. 1929) stands as the most important and influential contemporary theorist of socio-critical hermeneutics. Since 1964 he has been professor of philosophy and sociology at Frankfurt. His major works include *Theory and Practice* (German, 1963; English, 1973); *Knowledge and Human Interests* (German, 1968; English 1971); *The Theory of Communicative Action* (2 vols., German, 1982; English 1984 and 1987); and *Der philosophische Diskurs der Moderne* (1985), which has issued in discussions with Lyotard about modernity and post-modernism.

Among his main English-speaking commentators, Stephen White, David Ingram, John Thompson, and Richard Bernstein agree in tracing a significant shift of development in his more recent writings.[5] The studies of T. McCarthy and R. Geuss were too early fully to note the turn.[6] Post-modernism encourages (and also moves beyond) the more pragmatic anti-metacritical notion of hermeneutics which we shall examine with particular reference to Richard Rorty. But along with Karl-Otto Apel, Habermas remains resolute in attempting to formulate a transcendental, metacritical, philosophical position which seeks *both* to affirm the *critical* or "quasi-transcendental" capacity of social theory grounded in intersubjective, social, communicative interaction, alongside, or over against, instrumental or technical reason, and *also* to retain some notion of the universal or *trans-contextual* nature of human rationality.

The dilemma with which Habermas wrestles is that if he wishes to offer a social critique of systems which include positivism, post-Enlightenment rationalism, and "modernity", he needs a transcendental frame within which to establish the validity of the critique; but if social practice and communicative interaction play the decisive part which Habermas's social theory ascribes to them, this frame will not be foundational, and will perhaps not even be a "frame". Stephen White describes this philosophical stance as "non-foundational universalism."[7] But it is the unsatisfactory nature of this solution which drives forward the later development of Habermas's thought. Bernstein poses sharply the dilemma posed by the interaction of philosophy and social theory: "To speak of 'the pathology of modernity' ... presupposes a normative standard for judging what is pathological ... Can we still, in our time, provide a rational justification for universal normative standards? Or are we faced with relativism, decisionism, or emotivism which holds that ultimate norms are arbitrary?"[8] This was the question posed especially by the work of Adorno and Horkheimer, to whom we shall return shortly. It lies behind Habermas's *Knowledge and Human Interests*, but is also addressed, with a more developed answer, in *The Theory of Communicative Action*.

In spite of Habermas's later reservations about the earlier work, *Knowledge and Human Interests* contains the fundamental critique of positivist theories of knowledge which also is basic to the hermeneutical theory of Gadamer, Ricoeur, Pannenberg, Apel, and Rorty. This work also affirms a *critique of hermeneutics* which will emerge in other writings in terms of Habermas's categorical rejection of Gadamer's claim (and by implication, *a fortiori*, of Rorty's) concerning the "universality" of hermeneutics. Habermas speaks of this critique of hermeneutics as "meta-hermeneutics!"[9] This aspect of the discussion emerges most clearly in his 1971 essay "The Hermeneutic Claim to Universality."[10] Here, in ways partly parallel to Ricoeur but also with differences from Ricoeur, Habermas discusses the relation between psychoanalysis, interpretation, and language, with reference to Freud and to Alfred Lorenzer. But while he endorses Gadamer's work on the nature of hermeneutical understanding as such, he rejects his claim concerning "the ontologically inevitable primacy of linguistic tradition . . . the ontological priority of linguistic tradition *over all possible critique*.[11]

The fundamental flaw in Gadamer's work, Habermas claims, is a social one: he presupposes that "the consensus on which authority is founded can arise and develop *free from force*. The experience of distorted communication contradicts this presupposition."[12] Max Weber showed how "force" could be "legitimated" as institutional authority, and the implication of the work of Marx and others is the need for a "depth hermeneutic."[13]

With this background concerning Habermas's evaluation of hermeneutical theory we may turn to *Knowledge and Human Interests*. In his preface to this volume, Habermas underlines the need for a critique of epistemology. But this is more than a hermeneutical critique: this "radical critique of knowledge is possible only as social theory."[14] Such a social framework is *implicit* in Marx, but not actually part of Marx's thought or of Marxism as such. In his later and fuller discussion of Marx's "metacritique" of Hegel, Habermas endorses the view that "labor or work is not only a fundamental category of human existence but also an epistemological category."[15]

This approach is possible because Habermas follows Kant, Hegel, and Marx, in attempting to establish a "critique" which metacritically elucidated the forms and categories which render *possible* the cognitive activity of the human subject. Hegel developed Kant's transcendental conditions of possibility in terms of a dialectic of historical process; Marx, in dialogue with Feuerbach transposed Hegel's reason, or *Geist*, into material categories of labour and production in relation to needs manifested in social life. In his *Introduction to the Critique of Political Economy* (1859) Marx made the key statement: "It is not men's consciousness which determines their existence, but on the contrary *their social existence which determines their consciousness*."[16] Social existence is then the substructure on which derivative modes of knowledge rest. This principle is often regarded as the point of departure for the modern sociology of knowledge; Zygmunt Bauman calls this Marxist principle "A programme of a hermeneutics-turned-sociology."[17]

In Habermas's critical theory, however, the status of knowledge and hermeneutics is more complex. He distinguishes between three fundamental cognitive interests: the technical, the practical, and the emancipatory. Habermas writes: "The approach of the empirical-analytic sciences incorporates a *technical* cognitive interest; that of the historical-hermeneutical sciences incorporates a *practical* one; the approach of critically orientated sciences incorporates the *emancipatory* cognitive interest . . ."[18]

Empirical or positivistic knowledge has its place as a method within the sciences, provided that it is seen as only one type of knowledge. As Bernstein comments, "it is not to be taken as the canonical standard for all forms of knowledge."[19] Here Habermas follows exponents of the hermeneutical tradition in relativizing "explanation" or empirical falsification as only one mode of knowledge, in contrast to "understanding." Elsewhere he endorses that aspect of Gadamer's hermeneutics which exposes the false objectivism which confuses scientific method with a "method" for understanding the whole of reality. Habermas observes: "Positivism stands or falls with the principle of scientism, that is that the meaning of knowledge is defined by what the sciences do."[20] But positivistic knowledge answers only *instrumental interests*. He stresses the limitations of Comte's positivism, and argues that even C.S. Peirce and Dilthey, although they saw these limitations were still "so much under the spell of positivism that they do not quite escape from objectivism."[21]

Dilthey did, however, open up and develop the notion of a historical-hermeneutical mode of understanding which presupposed pre-understanding, and "the intersubjectivity of the frame of reference" which made it possible.[22] Habermas endorses Dilthey's interweaving of hermeneutical understanding and "life". Intersubjective exchanges affect the other at the level of both language and action. Here, like Karl-Otto Apel, Habermas constructively appeals to the later Wittgenstein. He observes: "language and action interpret each other reciprocally; this is developed as Wittgenstein's concept of the language-game."[23] He thus affirms the role of hermeneutics for interpretative or inter-subjective interests. The goal here is interpersonal understanding and social co-operation, or what Habermas terms "practical" interest, as opposed to the "technical" interest of positivist science. Here Habermas's terminology is partly parallel (but not wholly so) with Gadamer's section under the title "The Hermeneutic Relevance of Aristotle."[24] Aristotle's *techné* relates to the act of material production; *praxis* relates to human communication; and *phronésis* to the critical self-reflection which guides them.

Here, however, Habermas parts company with the hermeneutical tradition of Dilthey and Heidegger, as we have seen. Hermeneutical understanding, in spite of Gadamer's claims, invites a transcendental critique, especially a social critique, in terms of what traditions can be tested in relation to their embodiment of *social force* and *epistemological distortion*. This demand for metacriticism places Habermas alongside Apel, and in more theological terms also suggests affinities with Pannenberg. Ricoeur's "hermeneutics of suspicion" can also be regarded as a psychosocial critique, although we noted that its full effectiveness in relation to metaphor and narrative held some ambivalence. The metacritical dimension, however, combines social theory and practice. As a critique of ideology, the "interest" which governs this critique is *emancipatory*.

Like Ricoeur, Habermas finds needed resources for this searching critique in Freudian psychoanalysis, drawing on Freud and on Alfred

Lorenzer. This approach coheres with the demand in Marxist social theory for *freedom*. Habermas writes: "The starting point of psychoanalytical theory is the experience of . . . the *blocking* force that stands in the way of the *free* and public communication of repressed contents . . . The unconscious impulses do not want to be remembered."[25] Habermas's extended discussion of Freud on repression and on the interpretation of dreams runs partly parallel to that of Ricoeur's longer discussions in *Freud and Philosophy*.[26] The critical frame takes the form of "depth-hermeneutics."[27]

Other resources for critical theory emerge in dialogue with Nietzsche and with Marx. One limitation of Marx was that "Marx was not able to see that power and ideology are distorted communication."[28] Nevertheless, as he saw, the key aim of critical self-reflection is *liberation* "from dependence on hypostatized powers. Self-reflection is determined by an *emancipatory cognitive interest*."[29]

This provides the climax of the argument in *Knowledge and Human Interests*. But, as David Ingram observes, in his more recent work "Habermas has largely abandoned the attempt to ground critical social theory in cognitive interests."[30] Habermas's dissatisfaction with his work is expressed in the postscript which he has added to the second edition of *Knowledge and Human Interests*. The two closely-related problems, which Bernstein calls the two "major flaws", concern the ambiguous *nature* and ambiguous *status* of Habermas's self-reflective critique: is this genuinely *transcendental*, or if it is derived from social theory is it *contingent* or *a posteriori*?[31] How can *engagement in a particular form of social or political struggle* be identified with transcendental reflection on necessary or *universal conditions* of knowledge? In Habermas's words in his "Postscript", "What is the sense in which we speak of a 'transcendental' foundation of knowledge . . . in the framework of a constitutive theory of experience?"[32]

None of this makes *Knowledge and Human Interests* any less relevant to socio-critical hermeneutics. Quite the reverse is the case. This work has served to *sharpen the issues* which are now re-addressed in Habermas's more recent two-volume work *The Theory of Communicative Action*. But whereas his partners in dialogue had previously been mainly critical philosophers (Kant and Hegel), positivists (Comte), hermeneutical theorists (Dilthey) and exponents of psycho-social metacritique (Freud, Marx, and Nietzsche), now Habermas turns in more detail to two other areas. On one side, he takes up *the relation between social theory and accounts of human rationality* with particular reference to Max Weber and to Talcott Parsons (as well as to Marx and to Durkheim). On the other side, he explores the area of Anglo-American *speech-act theory*, explicitly entering into dialogue with the later Wittgenstein and Austin, and presupposing categories of speech-act theory such as those used by Searle. To these two areas we now turn.

2. Habermas's Theory of Communicative Action in the Double Context of Social Theory in Marx, Weber, and Parsons, and Speech-Act Theory: Habermas and Biblical Interpretation

The nature and consequences of what has been termed Habermas's "linguistic turn" will become clearer if we return first to his development of an "emancipatory critique" against the background of Hegel, Marx, and the Frankfurt school of Adorno and Horkheimer. This is the context of *praxis* in which his discussion of relations between language, understanding, and social practice is carried out.

The key category of "liberation" or "emancipation" which is fundamental for socio-critical hermeneutics and liberation theology holds a central place for Marx. Marx takes up Hegel's dialectic of inter-relationship between *social encounters* (whether for bondage or for freedom), and *human knowledge*. Hegel writes that "self-consciousness . . . *is* only by being acknowledged or 'recognized'."[33] In order to gain this "recognition", Hegel argues, one consciousness may seek to *"dominate"* another. The one who is dominated, the slave, produces objects for the master, who consumes them. But by a *dialectical negation*, the *slave* may come to arrive at self-understanding through this very process of labour.[34] Behaviour motivated by forces outside the control of the self results in *alienation*; but self-motivating or self-affirming action promotes *freedom*. Marx comments in his 1844 Paris Manuscripts that here in this dialectic of negativity in his *Phenomenology* Hegel genuinely grasps the nature of "work".[35] When economic and social systems produce conflict in the form of alienation, when power becomes hostile and dominating, *alienated forms of labour and production must be unmasked*.

From the viewpoint of hermeneutical theory rudimentary affinities may be noted between existentialist notions of "de-personalization" which result in Bultmann's programme of "de-objectification", and Marxist and Weberian notions of depersonalization as "alienation" which result in a programme of "de-ideologization". This process of *liberation* through the unmasking of alienating socio-economic structures and mechanisms is hindered, Marx argued, by *ideologies*. Ideologies are socially determined, and serve to defend and *to justify external or established interests*. Thus a dialectic of liberation must include *a critique of ideology* which will expose it as an instrument of social oppression, or as a myth which is constituted by social factors.

This notion of an "emancipatory" critique was further explored and developed by the Frankfurt school of Theodor Adorno (1903–1969), Max Horkheimer (1893–1973), and Herbert Marcuse (1898–1979). Habermas became Assistant to Adorno in 1956. Adorno and Horkheimer urged that the rationalism of the Enlightenment had failed to bring about a liberation from the oppression of social interests of power and domination, to any extent which would have been comparable with the success of the "technical" sciences, or functional technology, in freeing humankind from servitude to the constraints of the natural world. The limitation of the Frankfurt critique, however, was that they could not offer a philosophical or social theory which could fully account for the *rationality of the critique itself.* For Habermas, this work intensified, rather than solved, this metacritical problem.

Habermas and his friend and collaborator Karl-Otto Apel both turned their attention to a different philosophical tradition, namely to the linguistic philosophy of the later Wittgenstein and Austin, and to speech-act theory as this was developed through Wittgenstein and Austin in the work of Searle and others. Apel had already argued that close parallels existed between the later Wittgenstein and the hermeneutical tradition in his *Analytical Philosophy of Language and the Geisteswissenschaften* (1967). In *The Theory of Communicative Action* Habermas argues for a "paradigm-shift" which locates "the foundations of social science in the theory of communication."[36] He sees the "three roots of communicative action" in the propositional, the illocutionary, and the expressive.[37] These reflect explicitly, he writes, the work of J.L. Austin on speech-acts, and more broadly the approach of the later Wittgenstein.[38].

The heart of the issue in *The Theory of Communicative Action* concerns the relation between *social practice, intersubjectivity, language, and system*, as seen in terms of a linguistic-behavioural paradigm. The hermeneutical tradition, including the speech-act approach of Wittgenstein and Austin, stresses the subjectivity of the human speaker and addressee as *agents who share a life world shaped by shared horizons and common behaviour-situations*. But some account must also be taken of language and social practice as *a system which transcends this contextual subjectivity*. These two aspects reflect a great methodological divide not only in linguistic theory (*speech-acts and hermeneutics vs structure and semiotic theory*) but also different traditions in modern sociology (*hermeneutical value-orientated* approaches vs. *structural-functional* quasi-objectivist approaches). The approach in terms of functional *systems* which most influences Habermas is the sociological theory of Talcott Parsons (1902–79).

Habermas now explicitly addresses the running debate in sociology about the relation between social theory and human rationality. As Bernstein observes, this work "reflects Habermas's long-standing conviction that critical theory must fuse together both philosophical and scientific-empirical dimensions of analysis . . . He supports his basic thesis by showing how Marx, Weber, Durkheim, Mead, Lukács, Horkheimer, Adorno and Parsons can all be seen as making contributions to (or are blended from aspects of) a comprehensive sociological theory grounded in a full understanding of rationality and rationalization processes."39

The splitting apart of the "life-world" (or the hermeneutical aspect) and the "system" (or scientific aspect) occur in a classic form in Max Weber (1864–1920). Weber wrestled with Dilthey's hermeneutical theory, and rightly saw that instrumental reason operates *within* a life-world and cannot evaluate it externally. But this led him to concentrate on the supposedly value-neutral methods of quantification and statistical description, and to limit the notion of rationality to *instrumental reason*. He leaves the fact-value dualism unresolved. We may note Zygmunt Bauman's comment: "When he had singled out . . . sociology as the answer to the problem of historical hermeneutics, he turn(ed) to a sociological method patterned on economics as the way to resolve all the tasks posited by historical understanding."40

Weber's work invited three kinds of responses. One was that of Georg Lukács who saw in his relativization of Enlightenment rationalism confirmation of his own Marxist social theory.41 A second, related, response was that of Adorno and Horkheimer, who developed his work into a diagnosis of the pathology of modernity. A third and very different direction was taken by Talcott Parsons, who extended and broadened the functional approach into a general theory of systems. This provided the working foundation for his view of rationality. The rational, for Parsons, is not historical and contingent but formal and logical. In his discussions of hermeneutics and social science, Bauman sees this approach as a logical extension of Husserl's programme. He writes: "Parsons assumes that essentially subjective human action can be understood objectively . . . Phenomenological inquiry into the transcendental structures of human action supplies the only, but solid, foundation to the whole of Parson's model of social system."42

Habermas wishes to embrace aspects of validity in all this work by exploring a model of *linguistic and behavioural interaction*. He draws not only on Wittgenstein and Austin, but also on George H. Mead's pragmatic social psychology. To speak a language is to perform an act, and the *performance of linguistic acts* depends on certain general *presuppositions* (as we have repeatedly urged in Chapters VIII and X above). These presuppositions relate to *social roles* in life. Here Habermas draws on Mead. He writes "Mead connects with the concept of *social role* the sense of a norm that simultaneously *entitles* group members to expect certain actions from one another in certain situations."43 Language, Habermas notes, has not only "the function of *reaching understanding*", but also of "*co-ordinating action and socializing actors* as well. Under the aspect of reaching understanding, communicative acts serve as the *transmission of culturally stored knowledge* ... Under the aspect of co-ordinating action the same communicative acts serve the *fulfilment of norms* appropriate to a given context.44 Social integration also takes place through this medium.

This "linguistic turn" to Habermas's critical theory exposes and makes transparent two complementary points. On the one hand, language is a matter of *action* by *social agents*; hence the approach which sees everything in terms of *system is one-sided and incomplete*. System ignores the dimension of human action and *contingent hermeneutic*. On the other hand, we cannot fully understand or *critically evaluate* the *inter-personal language-game as life-world without reference to the system which transcends it*. Each pole or axis represents a different dimension of human rationality. A "*communicative*" rationality may be distinguished from a "*purposive*" rationality.

Habermas draws from this some fundamental socio-critical implications. The *life-world* belongs to the *hermeneutical level of inter-personal understanding and co-operative behaviour*. In terms of our own discussion, it coheres with the hermeneutical nature of conversation and communication expounded by Gadamer, and which in *The Two Horizons* we argued in detail also characterized the work of the later Wittgenstein with his emphasis on the interweaving of language-games, forms of life, and patterns of behaviour which constitute traditions.45 But the hermeneutical dimension cannot operate at the level of *psycho-social critique*: for this, a standpoint is demanded in which *contextual-behavioural features are transcended in a larger system*. System provides a frame or *dimension for ideological and social critique*. As long as we remain at the level of the life-world, it may seem as if the surface-conversation of language and behaviour is, as it were, *all there is*. Habermas writes: "As long as they maintain a performative attitude, communicative actors cannot reckon with a systematic distortion of their communication."46

Habermas explains that if we confuse the system with the life-world, or remain within the horizons of the life-world, we cannot detect certain "fictions". In David Ingram's paraphrase, we cannot detect what, from the standpoint of critical social system, can be perceived as "loss of meaning ... lack of respect ... motivation vis-a-vis norms ... nihilism, alienation and neurosis."47 Without system, we stand under the illusion that language is transparent and conveys only its surface-meaning: and we uncritically believe that agents or subjects of speech-acts are entirely conscious of the motivations and constraints that drive them.48 This would be a hermeneutics of innocence.

System thus unmasks the external constraints that have repressed or dominated humankind, *denying freedom* and *imposing alienation*. These constraints, it is argued, may include the forces of the market economy and bureaucratic mechanisms. On the other hand, the actual co-operative venture of organizing action around genuinely shared values depends on participation in the life world. Life-world should not be reduced to system; neither should system be reduced to life-world.

Habermas can now offer a social diagnosis of the oppressions and alienations of social history and "modernity." With the emergence from tribal societies to national or state-orientated cultures, an original match between life-world and system became lost, and in modernity a *progressive "uncoupling" of system and life-world has taken place.*[49] Habermas identifies the more autonomous emergent sub-systems as bureaucratic mechanisms of the state apparatus, the market economy, and laws which preserve the interests of certain sub-groups at the expense of others. In tribal societies, "Systemic mechanisms have not yet become detached from institutions effective for social integration."[50] The concept of *role* is "unproblematic." But in place of the supposedly more "relativized" role dictated by distinctions of sex and generation in tribal society, when later cultures become orientated to production processes, a consequent socio-economic "authority of office" artificially locates personal "status" in terms of this production process.[51]

Habermas, as we might expect, sees a close "parallel" between this social analysis and Marxist theories which also ground social explanatory hypothesis in theories concerning production, labour, exchange-value, and dependent social roles. Although in a different sense from that of Weber, the primacy of socio-economic factors is decisive for questions about the nature of freedom. Habermas endorses Marx's argument concerning the "illusion" fostered by "the classics of political economy" that systemic imperatives were fundamentally "in harmony with the basic norms of a polity guaranteeing freedom and justice." Marx, he argues, revealed that a capitalist commodity structure presupposed norms or laws which made "a mockery of bourgeois ideals."[52]

An understanding of language as speech-acts based on social interaction embodying social roles offers firmer ground, but is also coherent with Marxist social theory. In 1929 the Soviet Marxist philosopher V.N. Vološinov (or M.M. Baxtin?) produced a philosophy of language which consciously adhered to Marxist-Leninist principles. (Whether "Vološinov" was actually Baxtin is discussed briefly below). Vološinov saw some value in Dilthey's hermeneutics, but made the criticism that Dilthey had made "*no provision for the social character of meaning.*[53] He insists: "Consciousness takes shape and being in the material of signs created by an organised group in the process of its social intercourse ... All ... forms of speech interchange operate in extremely close connection with the conditions of the social situation."[54] As we proceed to read Vološinov's pages, there emerges an almost uncanny anticipation of several of Habermas's basic theses in *The*

Theory of Communicative Action. Vološinov distinguishes between two kinds of approach to language. According to the first, "*Language is an activity, an unceasing process of creation . . . realized in individual speech-acts* (sic). . . ."[55] According to the second, "*language is a stable . . . system of normatively* (sic) *identical linguistic forms . . .*"[56] Neither offers a complete account without the other.

After detailed discussion of Saussure and the socio-ethical issues raised by the behavioural dimension, Vološinov states his central conclusion: "*The actual reality of language-speech is not the abstract system of linguistic forms, not the isolated monologic utterance, and not the psychophysiological act of its implementation, but the social event of interaction implemented in an utterance or utterances.* Thus, verbal interaction is the basic reality of language."[57] Vološinov now goes further. There are *three* modes of linguistic enquiry: first, we can explore "forms and types" of language; second, we can explore "speech performances"; third, we can undertake a "re-examination of this new basis of language forms in their usual linguistic presentation."[58] This will demonstrate their relation to "social custom . . . the social mileau . . . holiday, leisure time . . . the workshop . . . processes of labour and processes of commerce . . . Marxist philosophy of language should and must stand squarely on the utterance as . . . language-speech and as sociological structure."[59]

It is perhaps surprising that Habermas, who draws on a wealth of different traditions in philosophy, sociology, and linguistic theory, does not appear to allude to this work in either *Knowledge and Human Interests* of *The Theory of Communicative Action*. This is not to be explained on the basis of confusion about the possible identity of Vološinov: V.V. Ivanov declared in 1973 that the author of the work in question was in fact M.M. Baxtin, and some references speak either of Vološinov or of Baxtin, Bahtin, or Bakhtin. But the translators of the volume urge in the 1986 edition that this cannot be established, and none of these names seems to feature in Habermas's volumes which we have discussed.[60] Nevertheless Vološinov draws neither the fundamental socio-critical conclusions which Habermas draws concerning the transcendental conditions for knowledge and the basis of rationality, nor the more detailed conclusions of Habermas about the uncoupling of life-world and system. In the most fundamental respects Habermas's socio-critical theory remains distinctively his own. The approach of Vološinov overlaps with that of Habermas, but is not central to his concerns.

Habermas's later work remains a *hermeneutical* theory, in as much as he firmly takes account of hermeneutical understanding as a model of inter-personal communication, endorsing the positive hermeneutical implications offered by Dilthey, Betti, Gadamer, Ricoeur, and Apel, and from a different tradition, also the later Wittgenstein. But it is a pointedly *socio-critical* hermeneutic, because along with the hermeneutical dimension of life-world Habermas allows for a transcendental *critique* of understanding and social interaction in terms of social systems. This underlines the value of "unmasking" character as a socio-critical tool, but from a theological point of view leaves unanswered questions about the status which is claimed for social theory rather than for theology. There are points of affinity, for example, with Pannenberg's work which offers a more convincing metacritical foundation; but Pannenberg lacks the vigorous dynamics of social critique which is the distinctive contribution of socio-critical hermeneutics.

As a speculative but also fruitful working tool for biblical studies, my former colleague John Rogerson has taken up and explored Habermas's distinction between system and life-world. Avoiding Norman Gottwald's *causal* neo-Marxist "explanation" of religious legitimation in wholly social terms, Rogerson first considers the transition from tribalism to the monarchy in Israel in the light of Habermas's categories.[61] Instrumental knowledge led to success for David in building, fortification, agriculture, and related activities, but the new organization of labour disturbed the tribal system and brought about systemic change. Rational justification was linked to Davidic and monarchic legitimation in theological terms; but the Northern tribes held to a corporate identity and life-world which precluded the acceptance of the new system of rationalization. Rogerson comments, "In terms of Habermas's theory ... the system of political integration did not succeed in becoming part of the communicative life-world of the northern tribes."[62]

John Rogerson extends Habermas's conceptual tools to the narratives of creation and exodus. The primal scene (Gen. 1:26 – 2:25) projects a system and life-world of perfect communicative interaction between man and woman, and between God and humankind. But communicative harmony breaks down when Adam and Eve resort to recrimination and accusation and when Cain denies responsibility for his brother Abel (Gen. 3: 12,16; 4: 9, 10). Lamech escalates the cycle of retribution, violence, and disruption (Gen. 4: 24); Babel becomes a symbol of confusion, disruption, and fragmentation (Gen. 11: 7–9). There can be no freedom where there is such disruption between system and life-world. But Abraham emerges as a new focus for solidarity, which is potentially universal in scope: his election and blessing is for "all peoples on earth" (Gen. 12: 13). The Exodus story also has, in Rogerson's words, "strong communicative potential: those whom God has freed may not enslave each other or turn their brothers aside in time of need."[63] The sacrificial and penitential systems constitute means of restoring broken communication. Their social interdependence of persons based upon communicative interaction represents, in Rogerson's view, a great part of what it means "to be human."[64]

Rogerson expounds this principle further in terms of a social contrast between power-exploiting Kings and prophetic visions of a re-created world. The prophets look forward to a time when "The Lord ... will settle disputes ... they will beat their swords into ploughshares, and their spears into pruning hooks" (Isa. 2: 4). In the prophetic vision, a hitherto mismatched life-world becomes *re-matched* with the system. In the ambitions of power-seeking kings, *alienating* sub-systems are *imposed* on mis-matching life-worlds oppressively. In the prophetic vision, all humanity enjoys *freedom*.

Although, Rogerson concedes, Habermas's theory is speculative, it has potential, he believes, not only as a working tool but as a mediating way between more radical versions of liberation theology and the constraints of the socio-economic contexts of biblical scholars who have to work within the framework of market-economy forces and funding.[65] From the point of view of conceptual hermeneutic exploration, even more speculatively we may suggest a hypothesis about the application of these categories to New Testament theology.

If we approach issues, perhaps with equal speculation, but perhaps true to the situation in New Testament theology, we might suggest a different account of system and life-world. The human life-world, as we shall argue in detail in chapter XVI, may be shaped by criteria of relevance centred on the individual or corporate self. The human life-world of interactive communication is seen theologically as corporately fallible and structurally flawed by self-interest. Co-operative interaction *need* not always be for good, but may serve *corporate* self-interest. On the other hand Paul sees the law simultaneously as fulfilling two systemic functions. On the one hand, it serves as an *external transcendental value-frame, providing a critique of the human life-world*. In this respect "if it had not been for the law, I should not have known sin" (Rom. 7: 7); i.e. my relation to sin would have remained at a *pre-critical* narrative level. "The law is holy . . . just and good" (Rom. 7: 12); for it constitutes a necessary transcendental critical system. On the other hand, the system of the law *provokes conflict with the human life-world:* "Apart from the law, sin lies dead . . . but when the commandment came, sin revived . . . The very commandment which promised life proved to be death to me" (Rom. 7: 8–10).

In the face of this self-defeating, though necessary, system, Paul expounds the different basis and effects of the principle of grace which brings about new integration and new creation of the "one" (2 Cor. 5: 17). Repeatedly this is seen in terms of "freedom" from the system of the law (Rom. 8: 2; Gal. 5: 1). But this is not (as in a non-Pauline Pelagian view of freedom) a freedom to construct any kind of life-world. It is a creative transformation of the human life-world which brings about correspondence through the Holy Spirit between the eschatological system of divine love and purpose and the corporate life-world of communicative interaction that is in process of moving from mis-match to match. Whereas under the law, human life-world and legal system became split apart, divine grace does not destroy what the system represents, but integrates system and life-world within a new, transformed, whole. Herein lies the healing newness of the gospel as universal whole.

This constitutes a theological transposition of Habermas's social theory into a new and different key. But here Ricoeur's comments on Freud are apposite. Just as we may draw from Freud critical conceptual tools for hermeneutics without subscribing to his world-view, so Habermas invites utilization of categories which he finds fruitful for socio-critical theory. In Christian theology the law does offer a transcendental systemic critique of the human condition, but it gives rise to an ultimate flaw because system and life-world remain split apart. Paul writes: "If it had not been for the law I should not have known sin" (Rom. 7: 7). "The law is holy" (7: 12). But "the very commandments which promised life proved to be death for me ... For I do not do what I want" (7: 10,15). Nevertheless under grace the new community overcomes the disjunction: "the new has come" (2 Cor. 5: 17); "you are all one [person] in Christ Jesus (Gal. 3: 28).

Even if the specific details of this suggested analysis are not accepted, Habermas offers to hermeneutics a vigorous socio-critical conceptual apparatus for metacritical enquiry. He acknowledges the inevitability of metacritical questions, and rightly explores the extra-linguistic presuppositions of language in shared worlds of human behaviour. As Jonathan Culler acknowledges, he sees that social sciences must focus on language. It is not the fault of Habermas that Culler's own one-sided emphasis on system as against life-world forces him to part company from Habermas's interpretation of Wittgenstein, and to reject his claims about rational "norms".[66] Habermas rightly defends *the principle of the need to search for a transcendental basis* for hermeneutical criteria. In this respect his work stands together with Apel's hermeneutics in sharp contrast to the contextual social pragmatism of Rorty's hermeneutics. When we move on to examine the hermeneutics of liberation theologies and feminist theories, the effects of this contrast between socio-critical and socio-pragmatic programmes can be seen to be of key importance for evaluating their hermeneutical power and credibility. To Rorty and to Apel we therefore turn, as part of a comparative evaluation.

3. Richard Rorty's Socio-Pragmatic Contextualism vs. Karl-Otto Apel's Cognitive Anthropology as Transcendental Metacritique

Richard Rorty and Karl-Otto Apel invite appropriate comparison not least because they claim broadly the same kinds of philosophies and philosophical traditions as offering implied support for their hermeneutical conclusions.

Yet the philosophical and socio-ethical consequences of their respective systems sharply differ. Further, they represent polar opposite answers to the question of whether any metacritical evaluation can be offered of the norms presupposed by a community of interpretation that may be grounded in trans-contextual considerations outside the boundaries of the community itself. Both writers believe strongly in the importance of the later Wittgenstein and of the analytical philosophical tradition; both enter into dialogue with Gadamer and post-Kantian hermeneutics; both have an interest in Charles S. Peirce, Josiah Royce, and American pragmatic traditions.

In 1967 Richard Rorty edited a volume under the title *The Linguistic Turn* which included essays from Gilbert Ryle, John Wisdom, Richard Hare, J.O. Urmson, P.F. Strawson and other analytical philosophers. Rorty's questions, which he raised in a long introduction, included that of whether philosophy could ever do more than suggest "perspectival" changes.[67] The same year, 1967, Apel published his *Analytic Philosophy of Language and the Geisteswissenschaften*. Here he offered a critique of the early Wittgenstein, expounded Wittgenstein's *Blue and Brown Books* as "the hermeneutics of 'meaning intentions'", and defined Wittgenstein's language-games as "concrete unities of language-usage, of a form of life, and a certain way to see the world, *each different but still related to the others*".[68] They are *not autonomous*, and *do not invite radical relativism*. But they do, as Peter Winch argued, invite a *hermeneutical* approach to the social sciences.

Also in 1967 Apel published a German edition of the writings of C.S. Peirce and subsequently wrote a book on the thought of C.S. Peirce which appeared in 1975.[69] Apel's "chief thesis" in his essay on Peirce in *Towards a Transformation of Philosophy* is that "Peirce's philosophical approach may be understood as a semiotical transformation of Kant's transcendental logic."[70] Rorty enters into dialogue more explicitly with John Dewey than with Peirce, but the influence of American pragmatism is fundamental to his philosophy.

Rorty fastens onto, and develops, *one side* of the philosophical hermeneutics of Gadamer. This is the very aspect which Habermas, Apel, and Pannenberg believe to be Gadamer's weakest and most vulnerable aspect. In our assessment of Gadamer in chapter IX, we drew attention to *a tension and ambivalence* identified correctly by Joel Weinsheimer, Georgia Warnke, and Richard Bernstein. Alongside more "conservative" respect for cultivated judgment, Gadamer asserts, to borrow Weinsheimer's words, that "the work exists *nowhere but in its representations* . . . There can be *no determinate criterion* of correct interpretation."[71] Georgia Warnke writes that Gadamer's hermeneutics "show the way in which all forms of knowledge adhere to a set of historically produced norms and conventions."[72]

"Hermeneutics" is defined by Rorty as "not (*sic*) 'another way of knowing'" but "as another way of coping."[73] Knowledge cannot "mirror" nature as it is. Hermeneutics reveals that all *claims* to knowledge, indeed what is deemed to *count* as knowledge, arises only from within some given social tradition, in which the context of *convention* determines what is acceptable as "rational." Following Wilfrid Sellars, Rorty attacks the "myth of the given." Clearly there are close parallels with the later work of Stanley Fish in literary theory. In 1980 Fish writes: "Whereas I had once agreed with my predecessors on the need to control interpretation lest it overwhelm and obscure texts, facts, authors, and intentions, I now believe that *interpretation is the source of texts, facts, authors, and intentions.*"[74] In 1989 Fish writes that what seems "natural" is merely determined by a process which is "anything but natural", namely by "unreflective actions that follow from being embedded in a context of practice" shaped by social formation.[75]

We shall explore the consequences of such a philosophical position for literary theory further in chapters XIII and especially XIV. We may note here, however, that *literary* questions about *reading-communities* are closely interwoven with *socio-ethical* issues. Thus David Bleich in his book *The Double Perspective* (1988) criticizes Fish not for his emphasis on the reading-community (with which he agrees) but for identifying "norms" with the perceptions of an academic, male orientated-community, rather than with the two genders and all social backgrounds.[76] What *counts as* "rational" or "natural" is more broadly-based for Bleich, but nevertheless remains socially contextual.

Habermas, Apel, and Rorty, all draw on the traditions of the late Wittgenstein, Heidegger, and Dewey, as well as C.S. Peirce and Josiah Royce. But Rorty stresses those aspects which are compatible with a pragmatic behaviourism and which might be thought to encourage a consensus theory of truth. Apel and Habermas, as we have noted, are not content to dispense with universal, transcendental, or trans-contextual questions. Even within Wittgensteinian interpretation alone, two different correlative emphases have emerged. W. Hordern, Paul van Buren, and Henry Staten write as if Wittgenstein's language-games could be viewed as virtually self-contained contextual settings; Apel insists that these language-games *interact*, and I have argued this at length in *The Two Horizons*. If they did not overlap and interact, Wittgenstein's crucial appeal to public criteria of meaning would lose much of the force and significance which Wittgenstein assigns to it.[77] By contrast, in his recent *Contingency, Irony, and Solidarity* (1989) Rorty expresses the view that notions of truth as given rather than made depend on, or are facilitated by, "confining attention to single sentences as opposed to vocabularies", or by failing to move from "criterion-governed sentences within language-games to language games as wholes, games which we do not choose between by reference to criteria".[78] This calls for a "thoroughly Wittgensteinian" approach to language.[79]

Rorty expresses sympathy for two types of "historicist" thinkers. Both have helped us, he argues, to "substitute Freedom for Truth as the goal of thinking".[80] One strand he finds represented in Heidegger and in Foucault; this questions the ultimacy of human solidarity or social practice. The other is represented by Dewey and Habermas and gives primacy to the social dimension. But, as we have noted, Rorty rejects the search undertaken by Habermas for a transcontextual or transcendental critique of the social community. Rorty describes the view which has his greatest sympathy as that of "liberal ironist". Liberals, he explains, disown cruelty; but "for liberal ironists there is no answer to the question 'Why not be cruel?' – no noncircular theoretical backup for the belief that cruelty is horrible".[81] The only quality or value that can claim universality is precisely that of *renouncing* a universal critique or metacritique: "One of my aims in this book is to suggest the possibility of a liberal utopia: one in which ironism, in the relevant sense, is universal".[82] Much of my own discussion up to the end of the last chapter, addresses the status and consequences of such an aim for hermeneutical theory and for interpretative practice.

In his earlier work *Philosophy and the Mirror of Nature* (1979) Rorty identifies Wittgenstein, Heidegger, and Dewey, as "the three most important philosophers of our century."[83] Each of them, Rorty points out, in his earlier years tried to formulate a philosophy which was foundational, but each came to see in later years that his earlier effort had been self-deceptive. According to Rorty's own interpretation of these three philosophers, they expose the fact that the foundations of knowledge consist in nothing more than contextual social practices, language-games, or even social self-images.

In the central chapter of *Philosophy and the Mirror of Nature* Rorty appeals to Sellars critique of "givenness" in conjunction with Quine's critique of the basis of any distinction between necessary and contingent propositions. Rorty comments, "If we see knowledge as a matter of conversation and of social practice, rather than as an attempt to mirror nature, we will not be likely to envisage a metapractice which will be the critique of all possible forms of social practice."[84] Rationality, Rorty claims, is a property of "what society lets us say."[85] On the question of whether anything might count as rational criteria at the critical level he states, "*Nothing counts as justification unless by reference to what we already accept ... There is no way to get outside our beliefs and our language so as to find some test other than coherence..*[86] "Holism", as he calls this invites "a distrust of the whole epistemological enterprise."[87]

How, then, can we arbitrate between philosophies that spring from different traditions? Neither epistemology nor a theory of meaning can offer any foundation, "because the notion of philosophy as having foundations is as mistaken as that of knowledge having foundations."[88] Taking up Thomas Kuhn's notions of the social contexts of scientific paradigms, Rorty interprets philosophical progress not as the victory of rational argumentation over fallacy, but as "new philosophical paradigms nudging old problems aside."[89] This is *social* pragmatism because everything depends on the nature of the community in which given or acquired *social* norms of expectation assume the role normally ascribed to rationality and to argument in traditional epistemology.

This leads Rorty to re-define hermeneutics, withdrawing it more explicitly from epistemology. When we *think* that we understand what we are doing, we call it epistemology; we call it hermeneutics "where we do not understand what is happening, but are honest enough to admit it."[90] The matter of "getting it right" appears to take the form of an epistemological or rational task only on the basis of Whiggish *post factum* hindsight. In this sense, the history of science is profoundly hermeneutical. Questions of the assessment or legitimation of scientific knowledge remain historically contingent and *socially* conditioned.

Rorty draws what he sees as two constructive conclusions from this revaluation of philosophy and rationality. First, if criteria for understanding a culture remain relative to that culture, we need to respect "the hermeneutical discovery of how to translate them without making them sound like fools."[91] But this was already Wittgenstein's point in his observations about Frazer's *The Golden Bough*, and Wittgenstein's approach is developed in this way for social science by Peter Winch.[92] Second, his approach encourages pluralism and pragmatism. In the last chapter of *Philosophy of the Mirror of Nature* he offers his own gloss on Gadamer and the "*polemical*" character of the term "hermeneutics."[93] His gloss on Gadamer's notion of "effective-historical consciousness" is that it signifies "what we can get out of nature and history *for our own uses*.[94] His gloss on his use of *Bildung* is "finding new, better, more interesting, more fruitful, ways of speaking".[95] Rorty remains, however, committed to a "pragmatic" (*sic*) tradition of what he terms "peripheral" rather than "systematic" philosophers, namely (in his view) Dewey, Wittgenstein and Heidegger.[96]

At the end of his volume, Rorty explicitly rejects as "unfortunate" the attempts of Apel and Habermas to pursue hermeneutical theory in a less pragmatic, less context-relative, way.[97] Apel and Habermas are mistaken, he believes, in trying to seek some new sort of transcendental viewpoint. A "universal pragmatics" or a "transcendental hermeneutics" is "very suspicious." Rorty attacks the programmatic Postscript to Habermas's *Knowledge and Human Interests*, and insists that there can be no "synoptic way" of analyzing the functions which knowledge has in "universal" contexts of practical life.[98]

In his essay "Pragmatism and Philosophy" (1982) in *Consequences of Pragmatism* Rorty develops the view which he has already formulated that philosophy has more to do with "making" than with discovery of any given.[99] In chapters XIII and XIV we shall note how this view of knowledge and truth comes to dominate Stanley Fish's socio-pragmatic approach to literary texts, especially in his later work. It is not enough to say that what is perceived as "given" depends on how it is conditioned by prior interpretation. In his essay "Habermas and Lyotard on Postmodernity" (1984), Rorty effectively distances himself from Habermas, preferring John Dewey's notion of philosophy as making "clear and coherent the meaning of the daily detail", or "social engineering."[100] He shares with Jean-François Lyotard the "postmodern" attitude which is, in Lyotard's phrase, "*incredulous towards metanarrative*".[101] As Bernstein points out, "a great deal is at stake" in the confrontation between Lyotard's book *The Postmodern Condition*, with its post-structuralist and deconstructionist themes, and Habermas's "universal pragmatics" or theory of communicative action.[102] Although Rorty speaks of "splitting the difference" between Lyotard and Habermas, whereas Habermas aims to retrieve a critical or transcendental philosophy, Rorty and Lyotard share the "incredulous" antipathy of postmodernism towards all metacritical "theory."[103]

Rorty applies these pragmatic principles to the hermeneutics of textual meaning in his "Texts and Lamps" (1985).[104] Textual meaning is no more a "given" for Rorty than it is for Fish, and disputes about meaning can be cashed out in terms of differences of "interest" on the part of given communities of interpretation. Gadamer's hermeneutics have been radicalized into the contextually variable "givens" of social pragmatism.

We have seen that Habermas and Apel criticize Gadamer for a lack of critical and socio-critical dimension. But is this where Gadamer leads us? In a closely-argued chapter of her excellent book on Gadamer, Georgia Warnke demonstrates convincingly that Rorty's interpretation of Gadamer is too one-sided. In particular he ignores two crucial components of Gadamer's thought. First, Gadamer stresses the dimension of hermeneutical *dialogue* as that which transcends simply "our" interests. Georgia Warnke writes: "We can *learn* . . . we may be changed by what we learn. Hermeneutics is not as subjectivistic as Rorty makes it out to be."[105] In Gadamer's own words, in conversation a content "arises" or "emerges", which was not in our minds or assumptions beforehand; the speaker is "challenged"; we "see each other's point"; concepts are worked out "in common."[106] David Tracy sees this notion of "conversation" as a crucial resource in the face of the negative inroads of deconstructionism.[107]

Second, Georgia Warnke underlines Gadamer's emphasis on content or *die Sache*. While there is a sense in which texts "exist" only in their *actualization in different contexts*, it is at the same time *these same texts* that are actualized. It is simply not the case that a reading community within a given tradition "makes" what it counts as a text for its purposes. Rorty acknowledges that his view leads to a position which is "frankly ethnocentric"; but why, Georgia Warnke asks, should we not describe this view as "simply irrational?"[108] She is not impressed by his attempts to offer criteria from within social pragmatism in ethical terms. In response to his essay "Solidarity or Objectivity?" (1985), she argues that his socio-ethical claims are themselves falsifiable on pragmatic grounds.[109] She rightly concludes: "Gadamer's position offers options that Rorty's cannot."[110]

In his challenging book *Contest of Faculties* Christopher Norris draws attention to a third source of difficulty in Rorty's neo-pragmatist philosophy. As we have seen from his discussion of Habermas and Lyotard, Rorty sides with Lyotard's postmodernism against Habermas in explicitly rejecting as "incredulous" the notion that we can establish any dimension behind or beneath social practices by metacritical argumentation. But this gives rise to what Norris describes as "a sharp distinction between Rorty's avowed 'post-modernist' attitude and the kind of story he tells by way of backing it up."[111] Rorty's account of philosophy, Norris points out, effectively takes the form of a *narrative*. It is like a well-made narrative-plot, in which obstacles are overcome and finally surmounted. On Rorty's own terms, we must adhere to a narrative perspective, and avoid meta-narrative justification. It is "a straightforward persuasive account of how we (the bourgeois liberal intelligentsia) have put away the problems of traditional thought and have emerged at last as decent commonsense pragmatists."[112]

The problem about all this, Norris claims, is that it calls in question precisely the affinity with post-modernist critique that Rorty claims, in parts of his narrative, serve to carry it along. For post-modernism involves contrivance and "a manipulative stance *outside and above the story-line flow of events* ... A strong 'meta-narrative' tendency which precisely *undermines the naïve habit of trust in first-order 'natural' narration*.[113] Devastatingly Norris concludes that there is a *concealed authoritarianism* in Rorty's philosophy. He writes: "Under cover of its liberal-pluralist credentials, this narrative very neatly closes all exits except the one marked 'James and Dewey' ... It is this use of a *liberal rhetoric to frame an authoritative message* which marks the real kinship between Rorty's pragmatism and nineteenth-century narrative forms."[114]

Norris's allusion to Rorty's pragmatism and to the nineteenth century raises a fourth issue. We noted earlier that since the turn of the century pragmatism has held a fatal attraction for American thinkers which is identified, although in positive terms, by Robert S. Corrington in his book *The Community of Interpreters*. Corrington traces a distinctively American approach to hermeneutical theory in a direct line which began with C.S. Peirce and Josiah Royce, and continues by picking out from Gadamer those aspects which were consonant with a neo-pragmatic emphasis.[115] Peirce and Royce presupposed "the ontology of community" as their "answer" to an irreducible fallibility on the part of human judgments and concepts.[116] Royce sought criteria and goals of interpretation not in terms of correspondence with any "given", for none was available; but in terms of *effects* which "built up" (cf. Rorty's "edification") the "one beloved and united community". Although he writes before the publication of Corrington's book, and therefore independently of him, Christopher Norris also identifies this approach as a distinctively *American "pragmatist cultural politics"*, and Jonathan Culler identifies "the new pragmatism" with a complacency "appropriate to the Age of Reagan".[117]

Rorty acknowledges the close relation between pragmatism and American thought. Pragmatism appears to be the most socially comfortable philosophy for a continental culture which embraces within itself a wide pluriformity of ethnic and sub-cultural traditions. It is not surprising that Rorty and Fish are accorded intellectual leadership among those circles which welcome the suggestion that it is unnecessary, futile, and improper to ask questions about truth-values outside the social contexts in which they operate, other than to agree on a pragmatic universal such as "success" or "winning". This avoids undue competition and threat between diverse sub-cultures, and brands propagandists as pretentiously and naïvely elevating a tradition to a universal. It would presumably be grist to the mill of the social pragmatist to note that in cultures which are extended in time rather than space, contextual pragmatism has a less re-assuring ring. My work-place and home are adjacent to the Norman cathedral which houses the bones of Cuthbert and Bede. It becomes more difficult, as I stand beside their tombs, to think that their witness to truth operates only within a given social consensus in given centuries, rather than that a thread of continuity runs down thirteen centuries of tradition. The massive solidity of Durham Cathedral somehow relativizes my own social context, and asks questions of it *which come from beyond it.*

This very example calls our attention once again to the one-sidedness of Rorty's appeal to Gadamer and to Wittgenstein. The historical-temporal continuity of tradition constitutes for Gadamer a connecting stratum in which historically finite actualizations occur; these are not merely equal autonomous "moments" like the claims of sub-groups within a pluralistic culture. Similarly, Wittgenstein's language-games *inter-penetrate, overlap,* and exhibit *family resemblances*; just as the faith of pilgrims who visit the tombs of Cuthbert and Bede over the centuries overlap in criss-crossing testimonies to truth and in family resemblances alongside their historical particularities.

Norris sees the social powerlessness and philosophical vulnerability of Rorty's approach. Rorty, he urges, provides an example of how social pragmatism professes open-minded tolerance while in practice tending to privilege its own liberal cultural values. Its status quo philosophy of the present moment can only allow the oppressed to remain oppressed, for it offers no basis on which to challenge the status quo. A further area of concern is therefore identified by voices of protest. Cornel West speaks out for black American theology when he attacks the bland and inept incapacity of socio-pragmatic philosophy to offer socio-critical theory or norms for action. West asks: "Does Rorty's neo-pragmatism only kick the philosophical props from under bourgeois capitalist societies, and require no change in our cultural and political practices?"[118] West notes that Dewey himself, to whom Rorty so firmly appeals, acknowledges that wholesale relativist historicism has only four possible consequences: either a paralyzing scepticism, or the view that "might is right", or sheer intuitionism, or a self-situating contextualism. None of these four alternatives provides a critical theory for social action, as Rorty and Fish concede.

Rorty seeks painfully and unsuccessfully to address this moral dilemma in the last chapter of *Contingency, Irony, and Solidarity*. The liberal pluralist within him sees moral progress in the acknowledgement that even the most diverse people are somehow "like us". But the ironist within him can define a universal only in negative terms: neither we nor our institutions can really know what it is like for someone else to suffer loss or pain. Like the universal doubt of the ancient sceptics, the only universal is one of renunciation. But this seemingly humble and tolerant pluralism while simultaneously appearing to affirm minorities and the weak, in practice can offer no argument for constraints upon those who oppress them. Indeed Rorty acknowledges both at the beginning and at the end of this book that he simply has no answer of principle to the question "why not be cruel?" The mistake is to confuse the role of historical contingency and contextualism in challenging the status of some absolutized foundationalism outside time, place, and history, with a positive dialectical relation between contextual contingency and ongoing metacritical exploration and testing in the form of an open system. Habermas and Apel explore the possibility of such a system, in which neither contingent life-world nor explanatory system has the last word, but contribute to some interactive whole.

We shall now review the hermeneutics of Karl-Otto Apel, by way of contrast. But we have not left the debate about Rorty and socio-pragmatic hermeneutics behind. We shall see in the next chapter how the contrasting theories of socio-critical and socio-pragmatic hermeneutics give rise to a watershed in liberation theologies and in feminist hermeneutics. Then in chapters XIII and especially XIV we shall take up the five problematic areas which we have identified in connection with Rorty, and examine and develop them further as part of our critique of Stanley Fish. We shall see that far from claiming Wittgenstein as an advocate for their pragmatic and contextual theories, some of the arguments put forward by Rorty and Fish founder on Wittgenstein's philosophy of language. We shall also argue that, as Rorty anticipates, the consequences of their approach for Christian theology turn out to be bizarre. The very purpose for which "hermeneutics" first arose, namely to offer critical reflection on the basis of interpretation in order to constrain merely assertive or militant voices, in the name of rationality, and to replace anarchy by reflection, is actually undermined by their conclusions.

Karl-Otto Apel seeks to avoid these pitfalls, and rejects a theory of truth which can be reduced to social pragmatism. His aim is not to transpose epistemology into hermeneutics, but to work out "an *enlargement* (*sic*) of traditional 'epistemology' in terms of 'cognitive anthropology'."[119] He wants to *enlarge* Kant's transcendental question about "preconditions for the possibility of knowledge." Like Habermas, he finds this in "the living engagement of human beings . . . related to a specific cognitive interest."[120]

Apel's discussions of the later Wittgenstein are more extensive, more detailed and probably more close-knit than Rorty's. In his essay "Wittgenstein and the Problem of Hermeneutic Understanding" Apel allows that Wittgenstein's view of intention and meaning places question-marks against the "psychological" aspect of hermeneutics in Schleiermacher and Dilthey.[121] Nevertheless "repeatedly Wittgenstein explicitly repudiated behaviourism."[122] The upshot of Wittgenstein's work, for Apel, is that hermeneutical understanding *presupposes* "a public 'habit' or a social 'institution'."[123] Historical tradition provides a mediating continuum "between the disintegrating and the emerging language-games" as life moves forward historically.[124]

The cognitive interests of humankind, however, embrace *different modes of knowledge and understanding*. In 1973, before the publication of Habermas's book *The Theory of Communicative Action*, Apel expounded a "trichotomy of concepts: 'scientistics', 'hermeneutics', and 'the critique of ideology'."[125] Like Ricoeur (and against Gadamer), he argued that "explanation" and "understanding" were complementary.[126] Nevertheless empirical data are themselves "constituted in the context of a language-game."[127] In her helpful "Translator's Introduction" to Apel's volume *Understanding and Explanation*, Georgia Warnke sums up the point. She writes, "In summary, then, Apel differentiates three legitimate approaches to the social sciences, connected with three 'knowledge-constitutive' interests: deductive-nomological sciences correspond to a 'technological' interest in predicting and controlling behaviour; historical-hermeneutical sciences correspond to the interest in expanding communicative understanding; and critical-reconstructive sciences pursue an interest in emancipation from pathological or ideological impediments to understanding. In Apel's work this theory of interests is part of his transcendental-pragmatic transformation of Kantian philosophy."[128]

Whereas his book *Towards a Transformation of Philosophy* (two vols. German 1973, part in English, 1980) addresses the relation between intersubjectivity, cognitive interests, and transcendental conditions of knowledge, Apel's volume *Understanding and Explanation* (German 1979, English, 1984) addresses issues in contemporary social theory. He addresses the gulf between social theories which rely on the paradigm of general laws and causal explanations (Max Weber, Carl Hempel and "neo-positivists") and those which utilize hermeneutics (Dilthey, Peter Winch, Charles Taylor and "neo-Wittgensteinians"). Apel views Gadamer's work both as a vindication of the hermeneutical approach and as an unwitting confirmation of its inadequacy as a universal mode of knowledge or critical understanding. Apel also focusses much attention on Georg H. von Wright's discussion of the limits of Hempel's conception of causal explanation.[129] The givenness of intersubjectivity and social interaction leads to a "transcendental-pragmatic" theory which accounts for the possibility of explaining actions in terms of causal models. Without the hermeneutical dimension, scientific explanation alone in social science is paradoxical; but hermeneutics alone would be insufficiently critical.

This is closely parallel to Apel's discussion of historical explanation in *Towards a Transformation of Philosophy*. In both volumes he appeals to William Dray's arguments that historical explanation cannot wholly be subsumed under general laws. It transcends "deductive-nomological" explanation.[130] Contextual questions about pre-understanding cannot be ignored. But the explanatory and the hermeneutical "supplement one another."[131] Apel adds: "As Peirce recognized, the natural scientist's community of experiment always expresses a semiotic community of interpretation."[132]

Apel enters into dialogue with both Peirce and Royce in this context.[133] Peirce, Royce, and Gadamer, he urges, were right to call attention to the role of the social community in establishing conditions for the possibility of knowledge and language. But Gadamer was wrong to try to avoid any category of "methodological-hermeneutic abstraction." It is simply not good enough to equate the model of critical interpretation with that of a judge, director, or participants in a play or in a game.[134] Even in the model of conversation, something more than "listening" and "adjustment" takes place, because room must also be left for the evaluation of breakdown or possible distortion. In psychoanalytic theory the diagnosis and recognition of such breakdown and distortion is fundamental.

It is of interest, in comparing Rorty's hermeneutics with Apel's to note how seriously Apel also enters into dialogue with the American pragmatic tradition. Two essays hold particular significance: "From Kant to Peirce: the Semiotical Transformation of Transcendental Logic"; and Apel's "Scientism or Transcendental Hermeneutics? . . . the Interpretation of Signs in the Semiotics of Pragmatism."[135] Apel argues that the behaviourism and effective neo-positivism of Charles Morris is actually undermined by Morris's own work: the logic of signs can operate only within an inter-active social context, which is denoted by his "pragmatics" in distinction from "syntactics" and "semantics." Peirce saw that any theory of signs presupposes that there can be "no representation of something *as* something by a sign without *interpretation by a real interpreter*".[136] But this does not lead to a reductive or anti-transcendental account of meaning. Peirce was concerned with the *"meta-scientific rules of explication of meaning with reference to possible experimental experiences"*.[137] Peirce and more especially Royce implied a "transcendental hermeneutic interpretation of hermeneutics."[138] Explanation and understanding become *complementary* within this perspective. (We have already noted how firmly Ricoeur wishes to hold these together).

Apel concludes that Peirce and Royce did not necessarily abolish the possibility of a transcendental dimension in epistemology; but they transposed and called into question a narrowly traditional epistemology by revealing its "methodological solipsism."[139] Royce's notion of the hermeneutical mediation of tradition makes him, in one sense, "Royce the Hegelian". But his notion of a community of interpretation is founded in "purposive rational action that is valid for *all* people at *all* times." There are "norms of social interaction" which are "always presupposed in *all* purposive rational behaviour."[140] We may recall Wittgenstein's parallel observation about the common behaviour of humankind as the reference-point for language.

In close affinity with Habermas Apel declares that "the *historically constituted life-form of a given society*" (cf. Habermas's "life-world" and Wittgenstein's "language-game") transcends simply the normative "institutionalizing" of its own institutions (cf. Habermas's "sub-systems" and Wittgenstein's "training"). Apel continues: "It is also the 'meta-institution' of *all* dogmatically established institutions . . . the instance of *criticism for all unreflected social norms*".[141] Because languages are *inter-translatable*, and because language-games *overlap, merge, fall apart*, and *re-integrate*, these "meta-institutions" form part of a *"medium of unlimited communication"* (cf. Habermas's "general system" and Wittgenstein's "common behaviour of mankind").[142]

Apel has brought together hermeneutics, social theory, and the search for a transcendental dimension which will allow a psycho-social critique of societies and traditions which is not merely contextually internal to them. Therefore, unlike Rorty, he is not obliged to formulate a pragmatic pluralism or an ethnocentricity for his socio-critical theory. At the heart of the differences between Apel and Rorty are different readings and interpretations of Peirce, Royce, and most especially of Wittgenstein. Apel's standpoint is close to Habermas; but one advantage over Habermas is that his transcendental critique is less specifically bound up with certain social theories. On the other hand by the same token it may also be argued that Apel has left us with a level of generality which appeals much more to the theorist than to those engaged in actual social criticism or in liberation hermeneutics.

The significance of the comparison between Habermas, Apel, and Rorty, however, appears in its fullest light when we examine specific socio-critical systems of hermeneutics in the area of liberation theology. Latin American liberation hermeneutics, black hermeneutics, and feminist hermeneutics all bring together fundamental questions about the framework of knowledge, language, and understanding with specific practices of biblical interpretation and re-interpretation. But we do not leave behind the questions about transcendental or universal principles. Indeed perhaps the single most important question to pose to each strand of liberation hermeneutics is that of whether it embodies the kind of critical principle sought by Habermas and Apel, entailing a trans-contextual notion of rationality and rational norms, or whether the system collapses into the kind of socio-contextual pragmatism which we have observed and criticized in Rorty. It is also essential to keep in mind the issues raised by Apel about interactions, overlappings, and integration between growing language-games when we examine Stanley Fish's attempt to provide his own reader-response theory with a framework of socio-pragmatic philosophical theory. For all its dash and sparkle, Fish's philosophical theory remains vulnerable and inadequate. Apel's approach to Wittgenstein, to the nature of rationality, and to problems of interpretation, is more rigorous, by comparison. Like Habermas, Apel writes as a creative theorist of socio-critical hermeneutics.

NOTES TO CHAPTER XI

1. Christopher Rowland and Mark Corner, *Liberating Exegesis. The Challenge of Liberation Theology to Biblical Studies*, London: S.P.C.K. 1990.
2. *Ibid* 76; cf. 7, 8–34, and 78–9.
3. Richard J. Bernstein, *Praxis and Action*, Philadelphia: University of Pennsylvania Press, 1971, and London: Duckworth, 1972, 76; cf. esp. 11–83.
4. Paul D.L. Avis, "In the Shadow of the Frankfurt School: from 'Critical Theory' to 'Critical Theology'", *Scottish Journal of Theology* 35, 1982, 534; cf. 529–40.
5. Stephen K. White, *The Recent Work of Jürgen Habermas. Reason, Justice, and Modernity*, Cambridge: Cambridge University Press, 1988 and 1989, 1–4, 48–68; David Ingram, *Habermas and the Dialectic of Reason*, New Haven: Yale University Press, 1987, 6; Richard J. Bernstein (ed.), *Habermas and Modernity*, Cambridge:

Polity Press, 1985, 1–32; and John B. Thompson, *Critical Hermeneutics: A Study in the Thought of Paul Ricoeur and Jürgen Habermas*, Cambridge: Cambridge University Press, 1981, 71–111, and *Studies in the Theory of Ideology*, Cambridge: Polity Press, 1984, 279–302.
6. R. Geuss, *The Idea of a Critical Theory: Habermas and the Frankfurt School*, Cambridge: Cambridge University Press, 1981; and T. McCarthy, *The Critical Theory of Jürgen Habermas*, Cambridge, Mass.: M.I.T. Press, 1978.
7. Stephen K. White, *op. cit.* 129.
8. Richard J. Bernstein, *Habermas and Modernity*, 4.
9. Jürgen Habermas, "The Hermeneutic Claim to Universality" in Josef Bleicher, *Contemporary Hermeneutics*, 203.
10. Jürgen Habermas, "Der Universalitätsanspruch der Hermeneutik" in Karl-Otto Apel, J. Habermas et al., *Hermeneutik und Ideologiekritik*, Frankfurt: Suhrkamp, 1971, Eng. translation in J. Bleicher, *Contemporary Hermeneutics* 181–211.
11. *Ibid* 203 and 204 (my italics).
12. *Ibid* 207 (my italics).
13. *Ibid* 208.
14. Jürgen Habermas, *Knowledge and Human Interests*, Eng., London: Heinemann, 2nd edn. 1978, vii.
15. *Ibid* 28.
16. Karl Marx and Friedrich Engels, *Über Kunst und Literatur* (2 vols.), Berlin: Dietz, 1967–68, vol.1, 74.
17. Z. Bauman, *op. cit.* 58.
18. J. Habermas, *Knowledge and Human Interests*, 308.
19. R.J. Bernstein, *Habermas and Modernity*, 9.
20. J. Habermas, *Knowledge and Human Interests*, 67.
21. *Ibid* 69.
22. *Ibid* 142.
23. *Ibid* 168.
24. Hans-Georg Gadamer, *Truth and Method* 278–89.
25. J. Habermas, *Knowledge and Human Interests*, 229 and 231.
26. *Ibid* 214–73.
27. *Ibid* 272.
28. *Ibid* 282.
29. *Ibid* 310.
30. David Ingram, *op. cit.* 15.
31. Richard J. Bernstein, *Habermas and Modernity*, 12–13.
32. J. Habermas, *Knowledge and Human Interests*, 359.
33. Georg W.F. Hegel, *The Phenomenology of Mind*, Eng. London: Allen & Unwin, 2nd edn. 1949, 229 (Hegel's italics).
34. *Ibid* 239.
35. Karl Marx, *Writings of the Young Marx on Philosophy and Society*, (eds. L.D. Easton and K.H. Guddat) New York: Doubleday, Anchor Books, 1967, 321.
36. Jürgen Habermas, *The Theory of Communicative Action: The Critique of Functionalist Reason*, 2 vols., Eng. Cambridge: Polity Press, 1984 and 1987, vol.2, 3.
37. *Ibid* vol.2, 67.
38. *Ibid* 67–76.
39. Richard Bernstein, *Habermas and Modernity*, 21–22.

40. Z. Bauman, *Hermeneutics and Social Science*, 69; cf. 69–88.
41. J. Habermas, *The Theory of Communicative Action*, vol.1, 355–65.
42. Z. Bauman, *op. cit.* 131; cf. 131–47.
43. J. Habermas, *The Theory of Communicative Action*, vol.2, 37.
44. *Ibid* vol.2, 63 (Habermas's italics).
45. Anthony C. Thiselton, *The Two Horizons*, 33–40, 357–62, and 370–79.
46. J. Habermas, *The Theory of Communicative Action*, vol.2, 150.
47. David Ingram, *op. cit.* 118.
48. J. Habermas, *The Theory of Communicative Action*, 150–52.
49. *Ibid* 153–97.
50. *Ibid* 163.
51. *Ibid* 167.
52. *Ibid* 185.
53. V.M. Vološinov, *Marxism and the Philosophy of Language*, Eng. Cambridge, Mass: Harvard University Press, 1986 (1973), 27 (his italics).
54. *Ibid* 13 and 20.
55. *Ibid* 48 (Vološinov's italics).
56. *Ibid* 57 (Vološinov's italics).
57. *Ibid* 94 (Vološinov's italics).
58. *Ibid* 96.
59. *Ibid* 97.
60. *Ibid* viii-xi, by L. Matejka and I.R. Titunik.
61. John W. Rogerson, "'What Does it Mean to Be Human?' The Central Question of Old Testament Theology" in D.J.A. Clines, S.E. Fowl and S.E. Porter (eds.), *The Bible in Three Dimensions*, 285–98. Cf., for a *different* analysis of the relation between tribal life-world and theological system, Norman K. Gottwald, *The Tribes of Yahweh: A Sociology of the Religion of Liberated Israel, 1250–1050 B.C.E.*, New York: Orbis, 1979.
62. *Ibid* 291.
63. *Ibid* 294–95.
64. *Ibid* 287–88; cf. 285–98.
65. *Ibid* 286–87 and 295.
66. Jonathan Culler, *Framing the Sign. Criticism and its Institutions*, Oxford: Blackwell, 1988, 185–200 ("Habermas and Norms of Language").
67. Richard Rorty (ed.), *The Linguistic Turn: Recent Essays in Philosophical Method*, Chicago: Chicago University Press, 1967, 39; cf. 1–39.
68. Karl-Otto Apel, *Analytic Philosophy of Language and the Geisteswissenschaften*, Dordrecht: Reidel, 1967, 37, (Apel's italics).
69. Karl-Otto Apel, *Der Denkweg von Charles S. Pierce*, Frankfurt, a/M: Suhrkamp, 1975.
70. Karl-Otto Apel, *Towards a Transformation of Philosophy*, Eng. London and Boston: Routledge and Kegan Paul, 1980, 81.
71. Joel C. Weinsheimer, *Gadamer's Hermeneutics*, 110 and 111 (my italics); cf. Georgia Warnke, *Gadamer. Hermeneutics, Tradition, and Reason*, 156–76.
72. Georgia Warnke, *op. cit.* 139.
73. Richard Rorty, *Philosophy and the Mirror of Nature*, Princeton: Princeton University Press, 1979 and 1980, 356.
74. Stanley Fish, *Is There a Text in This Class?* 16.

75. Stanley Fish, *Doing What Comes Naturally: Change, Rhetoric, and the Practice of Theory in Literary and Legal Studies*, Durham: Duke University Press, 1989, ix; cf. 29, 104–5, and 121–28.
76. David Bleich, *The Double Perspective. Language, Literacy, and Social Relations*, Oxford and New York: Oxford University Press, 1988, 55.
77. Anthony C. Thiselton, *The Two Horizons*, 370–85. For the opposite view, cf. Paul van Buren, *Theological Explorations*, London: S.C.M. 1968; and *The Edges of Language*, London: S.C.M. 1972.
78. Richard Rorty, *Contingency, Irony, and Solidarity*, Cambridge: Cambridge University Press, 1989, 5.
79. *Ibid* 21.
80. *Ibid* xiii.
81. *Ibid* xv.
82. *Ibid.*
83. Richard Rorty, *Philosophy and the Mirror of Nature*, 5.
84. *Ibid* 171.
85. *Ibid* 174.
86. *Ibid* 178 (my italics).
87. *Ibid* 181.
88. *Ibid* 264.
89. *Ibid.*
90. *Ibid* 321.
91. *Ibid* 346.
92. L. Wittgenstein, "Bemerkungen über Frazers *The Golden Bough*" in *Synthese* 17, 1967, 233–53, cf. Peter Winch *The Idea of a Social Science and its Relation to Philosophy*, London and New York: Routledge & Kegan Paul, 1958.
93. R. Rorty, *loc. cit.* 357; cf. 357–72.
94. *Ibid* 359 (my italics).
95. *Ibid* 360.
96. *Ibid* 368.
97. *Ibid* 379.
98. *Ibid* 380–82.
99. Richard Rorty, *Consequences of Pragmatism*, Minneapolis: University of Minnesota Press, 1982, esp. "Pragmatism and Philosophy" which provides the introduction.
100. Richard Rorty, "Habermas and Lyotard on Postmodernity" in Richard J. Bernstein (ed.) *Habermas and Modernity*, Cambridge: Polity Press, 1985, 174–75; cf. 161–75. (Rp. from *Praxis International* 4, no.1, 1984).
101. *Ibid* 161.
102. Richard Bernstein, "Introduction", *ibid* 31; cf. also Richard Bernstein, "What is the Difference that Makes a Difference? Gadamer, Habermas, and Rorty" in B.R. Wachterhauser (ed.) *Hermeneutics and Modern Philosophy*, Albany: State University of New York Press, 1986.
103. Richard Rorty, "Habermas and Lyotard on Postmodernity" *loc. cit.* 161 and 174.
104. Richard Rorty, "Texts and Lamps", *New Literary History* 17, 1985, 1–16.
105. Georgia Warnke, *op. cit.* 146.
106. Hans-Georg Gadamer, *Truth and Method* 329 and 331.
107. David Tracy, *Plurality and Ambiguity: Hermeneutics, Religion, and Hope*, San Francisco: Harper and Row, 1987, 19–25 and 58–60.

108. Georgia Warnke, *op. cit.* 154.
109. Richard Rorty, "Solidarity or Objectivity?" in John Rajchman and Cornel West (eds.) *Post-Analytical Philosophy*, New York: Columbia University Press, 1985, 3–19. Cf. also his *Contingency, Irony, and Solidarity*, 189–98.
110. Georgia Warnke, *op. cit.* 156.
111. Christopher Norris, *Contest of Faculties. Philosophy and Theory after Deconstruction*, London & New York: Methuen, 1985, 158.
112. *Ibid* 157.
113. *Ibid* 158 (my italics).
114. *Ibid* 159 (my italics).
115. Robert S. Corrington, *The Community of Interpreters*, 1–29 and 43–46.
116. *Ibid* 2–4 and 11; cf. also 17 and 23.
117. Christopher Norris, *Contest of Faculties*, 162, and Jonathan Culler, *Framing the Sign*, 55. See further, C. Norris, *loc. cit.* 194–96.
118. Cornel West, "Afterword: the Politics of American Neo-Pragmatism" in J. Rajchman and Cornel West (eds.), *Post-Analytic Philosophy*, New York: Columbia University Press, 1985, 267. Cf. also Cornel West, *Prophetic Fragments*, Grand Rapids: Eerdmans, 1988.
119. Karl-Otto Apel, *Towards a Transformation of Philosophy*, 46 (my italics).
120. *Ibid* 49.
121. *Ibid* 27.
122. *Ibid* 29.
123. *Ibid* 33.
124. *Ibid* 37.
125. Karl-Otto Apel, "Scientistics, Hermeneutics, and the Critique of Ideology: Outline of a Theory of Science from a Cognitive-Anthropological Viewpoint", in *Towards a Transformation of Philosophy*, 46–76.
126. *Ibid* 58.
127. *Ibid* 55.
128. Karl-Otto Apel, *Understanding and Explanation. A Transcendental-Pragmatic Perspective*, Eng. Cambridge, Ma.: M.I.T., 1984, xx.
129. *Ibid* 83–178.
130. Karl-Otto Apel, *Towards a Transformation of Philosophy*, 54.
131. *Ibid* 58.
132. *Ibid*.
133. *Ibid* 58, 60, 80–92 and 101–35.
134. *Ibid* 62–71.
135. *Ibid* 77–92 and 93–135.
136. *Ibid* 103.
137. *Ibid* 107 (Apel's italics).
138. *Ibid* 112.
139. *Ibid* 113.
140. *Ibid* 117, 118 and 119.
141. *Ibid* 119 (my italics).
142. *Ibid* (my italics).

CHAPTER XII

The Hermeneutics of Liberation Theologies and Feminist Theologies: Socio-Critical and Socio-Pragmatic Strands

The present chapter continues the framework of discussion established in the previous chapter. Latin American liberation hermeneutics, black hermeneutics, and feminist hermeneutics tend to share certain major themes. First and foremost, they construct critiques of *frameworks of interpretation* which are used or presupposed in dominant traditions. From within liberation theologies, these frameworks may be perceived as Western, thought-centered, or bourgeois-capitalist; from within some black theologies, as white colonial, racist, or imperialist; from within some feminist theologies, as androcentric or patriarchal. These frameworks transmit pre-understandings and symbolic systems which perpetuate, it is argued, the ideologies of dominant traditions. Second, liberation, black, and feminist approaches offer alternative *re-interpretations of biblical texts from the standpoint of a particular context of experience and action*. This may take the form of a history of social oppression, or an exposition of "women's experience". Third, each approach seeks *critical* tools and resources to unmask those uses of biblical texts *which serve social interests of domination, manipulation, or oppression,* to expose them as what they are. Each claims to embody some *critical* principle, by means of which to reveal the *unjust* goals and bases of manipulative interpretative devices and procedures.

The evaluation of these hermeneutical claims brings us back therefore to the central question raised by the previous chapter. Do the hermeneutical systems constructed or utilized by liberation theologies or by feminist approaches function *pragmatically to filter out from the biblical text* any signal which does anything other than affirm the hopes and aspirations of a given social group; or do they embody a *genuine socio-critical principle which unmasks oppression as part of a larger trans-contextual critique*? Do they merely reflect back the horizons of the community of protest in self-affirmation, or do they offer a social critique under which all (or many) communities may experience correction, transformation, and enlargement of horizons?

1. The Major Concerns, Development, and Dual Character of Latin American Liberation Hermeneutics

Virtually all liberation hermeneutics reflects the concern of its exponents to stress *both its theoretical hermeneutical integrity and the grass-roots nature of its commitment to practical action.* Leonardo and Clodovis Boff of Brazil urge the point by use of a metaphor. They write: "Liberation theology may be compared to a tree. Those who see only professional theologians at work in it see only the branches of the tree. They fail to see the trunk, which is the thinking of priests and other pastoral ministers, let alone the roots beneath the soil that hold the whole tree – trunk and branches – in place. The roots are the practical living and thinking – though submerged and anonymous – going on in tens of thousands of base communities living out their faith and thinking in a liberating key."[1] Leonardo and Clodovis Boff explicitly distinguish between the "level" of liberation theology at which "professionals" elaborate "socio-analytical, hermeneutical, and theoretico-practical" issues, and other "levels" at which pastors judge and act, and people in base (almost always lay-led) communities live out the Christian gospel with an action-orientated commitment to liberation. What unites these levels is "a faith that transforms history . . . the basic content is the same".[2] We have already noted the argument of Rowland and Corner that a heavily theoretical liberation hermeneutics would be a contradiction in terms.

In 1984 Juan Luis Segundo of Uruguay distinguished, however, between two theologies of liberation. The first, or first line, represented largely university-trained theologians who were well versed in the critical, socio-critical, post-Freudian and neo-Marxist tools of suspicion and the critique of ideology. The second line, under the equally biblical and neo-Marxist constraint of *"doing"*, rather than merely "thinking" or "contemplating", increasingly sought not only to live among the deprived and oppressed, but also to learn from them.[3] Julio de Santa Ana speaks of theology's "moving home . . . with the people".[4] Carlos Mesters, a Dutchman who has worked mainly in Brazil, articulates this popular community emphasis as a major theme in his writing. He comments, "The Bible was taken out of the people's hands. Now they are taking it back. They are expropriating the expropriators: 'It is our book! It was written for us' . . . The Bible has moved to the side of the poor. One could almost say that it has changed its class status."[5]

Christopher Rowland and Mark Corner have documented the use of biblical material within the mainly lay-led Basic Christian Communities of Sao Paulo, Brazil.[6] Much use is made of the parables of Jesus. These are seen as invitations to change things on the basis of the goodness and justice of God. The parable of the lost sheep in Matt. 18:10–14 is perceived to stress that the church should not be over-concerned with "preservation" (the shepherd left the ninety-nine), but should serve the lost and helpless. The sheep and the goats in Matt. 25:31–46 are associated respectively with oppressed and oppressors. The "oppressors" are incredulous about the accusation of their lack of compassion, and seek to defend and to justify themselves. The sheep and the goats are divided by different political action. The birth narratives in Luke (Luke 1:26–2:51) lead to a narrative-discussion of the hardships, humiliations, and indignities experienced by mothers, together with the experiences of affirmation that God exalted an unprivileged mother to play a key role in his purposes.

As Rowland and Corner point out, there is little sense of "critical distance" or "historical understanding" among the Basic Christian Communities. The story of Cain and Abel (Gen. 4:1–26) is assimilated directly into the experience of struggle between the landed and landless, or the farmers and the shepherds. In Gen. 4:8–16 the oppressor becomes the oppressed, and in a reversal of values faces vengeance from the oppressed in a state of insecurity. Rowland and Corner appear plausibly to place this under Gadamer's model of a "fusion of horizons".[7] But when they suggest that this model is important for liberation hermeneutics, they do not note, or allude to, Gadamer's caveat: "The fusion of horizons . . . (is) not simply the formation of one horizon . . . Every encounter . . . involves the experience of tension between the text and the present. The hermeneutic task consists in not covering up this tension by attempting a naive assimilation but consciously bringing it out."[8] Only what was once respected as separate can subsequently become "fused".

Another documented source which adds point to this issue can be found in Ernesto Cardenal's transcripts of Bible study groups in Nicaragua, published under the title *Love in Practice: The Gospel in Solentiname* (4 volumes, Spanish, 1975 onwards, Eng. 1977–84). One extract contains a question concerning the Magnificat (Luke 1:46–55). What would Herod have thought of Mary's words? Rosita answers that he would say she was a communist. Laureano interposes: "The point isn't that they would just say the Virgin was a communist. She was a communist . . . That is the Revolution. The rich person or the mighty is brought down, and the poor person, the one who was down, is raised up." But was the promise that the poor would have good things only for then, for Mary's time? One of the young people in the group replied: "She spoke for the future . . . We are just barely beginning to see the liberation she announces."[9]

In spite of the observations of Boff, Mesters, and Rowland and Corner, however, the Latin American movement began with a crucial attention to theory. This gives to Latin American liberation hermeneutics, an arguably dual character. For the professional theologians who contributed to the intellectual foundation of liberation theology worked, for the most part, with a more complex hermeneutical system than that which later basic communities presupposed. A major example may be found in the hermeneutical theory of Juan Luis Segundo of Uruguay in his book *The Liberation of Theology* (1975). His theory of hermeneutics embodies no less than the following seven elements: (i) the *hermeneutical circle*; (ii) a general theory of human *perception* of reality; (iii) an elaboration of the principle of hermeneutical and *ideological suspicion*; (iv) a utilization of *Ricoeur's* evaluation of the hermeneutical role of Freud, Nietzsche, and Marx; (v) a critique of *Weber's* value-neutral notion of social analysis; (vi) a programme of *de-ideologizing* roughly parallel to Bultmann's demythologizing of cosmological objectivism; and (vii) an evaluation of hermeneutical relations between contingent or *particular acts of will* (especially in Karl Mannheim and James Cone) and *historical or rational universality*.[10]

Such a complex theoretical apparatus, however, is not peculiar to Segundo. The hermeneutical theory of J. Severino Croatto is also complex, drawing especially on Ricoeur; Hugo Assmann explores relations between hermeneutics and the critique of ideology; and J. Miguez Bonino and Clodovis Boff explore the relation between *praxis* in hermeneutics and the status of epistemological truth-claims.[11] Severino Croatto develops a hermeneutical theory which offers a critique of the situatedness of the interpreter or community of interpretation not simply in terms of historical-conditionedness but more explicitly in terms of the political significance of the symbolic signifying systems which are part of this situatedness. A political hermeneutic requires a framework which is neither supposedly apolitical nor tied to interests of privilege rather than commitment to liberation. But this suggests that the distinction between theory and practice is less sharp or clear-cut than might be supposed. Severino Croatto expresses in theoretical terms a principle which can be interpreted pragmatically when it is expressed in the language of Leonardo Boff. In his essay "What are Third World Theologies?" he writes: "Liberation theology makes a preferential and evangelical option for the oppressed; it tries to look at society from the standpoint of *what will help* in their liberation, and *through their eyes*."[12]

In the Latin American context, as Phillip Berryman observes, "theory" does not stand in opposition to "practice" in the same way as it does in American pragmatism or in British empiricism. He writes: "Theory is regarded as a tool for cutting through appearance to get at the heart of things . . . *Praxis* is poles apart from . . . 'practicality'."[13] We discussed the Marxist conception of *praxis* earlier in this book, noting especially the issues set forth by the early Marx in his eleven theses on Feuerbach of 1845, but published only after his death. We noted Richard Bernstein's careful comparisons between the use of the term in Aristotle and in

Marx, and Paul Avis's valid observation that in socio-critical theory the theoretical dimension of *praxis* is more readily included and given proper significance than in "critical" theologies. In the 1840s, Bernstein points out, the "left-wing" radical interpreters of Hegel found in *"praxis"* an inkling of the area where Hegel's system had somehow gone wrong. In this context A.V. Ciezkowski "seems to have coined this 'new' use of *'praxis'* (to denote) . . . a philosophy of practical activity . . . exercizing a direct influence on social life."[14]

Marx, however, Bernstein continues, was dissatisfied with the vagueness of even this notion, and developed a comprehensive *"theory of praxis"*. Although the centrality of this was lost from sight in traditional or official Marxism in the late 1940s and 1950s, it was revived by Sartre, among others and more recently in the Neo-Marxist or humanist-Marxist circle of the journal *Praxis* based in Yugoslavia. The key comment of Marx, to which writers constantly refer, is his eleventh thesis on Feuerbach: "The philosophers have only *interpreted* the world in various ways; the point is, to *change* it." But revolutionary *praxis* still needs, Marx insists, to be guided by concrete theoretical thought.

In a fascinating study of the relation between *action* and *theories* of action Bernstein traces a continuity between *praxis* in Marx, concrete *Existenz* in Kierkegaard and Sartre, practical judgment in Dewey, and behavioural action in post-Wittgensteinian analytical philosophy. For Wittgenstein, common patterns of *behaviour* serve as a frame of reference for conceptual formation and judgment. But this is not too far, Bernstein concludes, from Marx's broad principle that people *"are* what they *do* . . . their social *praxis* shapes and is shaped by the complex web of historical institutions and practices within which they function and work."[15] In Latin American hermeneutical theory one of the most sophisticated models which develops, and responds to, these issues is offered by Clodovis Boff in his book *Theology and Praxis: Epistemological Foundations* (Petrópolis, Brazil, 1978, Eng. 1987). Boff notes that not only Marxism but also post-modernist approaches reject the attempts of post-Enlightenment rationalism to abstract concepts, ideas, and criteria of knowledge from *socio-historical contingent* situations, practices, and states of affairs. Boff therefore seeks *to ground hermeneutical understanding in a dialectic between socio-historical contingencies in human society* and the claims of *theology* as a structural or coherent principle.

Against this broader background we may now trace the origins and development of Latin American Liberation hermeneutics. The first formal outline for a programme of liberation theology emerged in material produced in preparation for the major meeting of the Second Conference of Latin American Bishops at Medellín, Colombia, in 1968. The Peruvian theologian Gustavo Gutiérrez (b.1928) wrote the outline, which he then expanded and developed into his book *The Theology of Liberation* (Lima,

1971; Salamanca, 1972, English 1973).[16] This has become one of the two or three major classics for the movement. In the same year, another of the founder-thinkers of the movement, the Brazilian Hugo Assmann published *Opresión-Liberacion*, followed by the Mexican writer José Porfirio Miranda's book *Marx and the Bible*.[17] By 1975 major theological leaders of the movement included (in addition to those already mentioned) Severino Croatto (Argentina), Juan Luis Segundo (Uruguay), Leonardo Boff (Brazil), Enrique Dussel (Argentina), Carlos Mesters (Brazil) and J. Miguez Bonino (Argentina). In an otherwise largely Roman Catholic context, Rubem Alves, Julio de Santa Ana, Miguez Bonino, and Emilio Castro wrote from within Protestant traditions.

In *The Theology of Liberation* Gustavo Gutiérrez outlines what he considers to be four fundamental contributory factors both to liberation theology and to a wider understanding of the whole area. The first demands an empathetic understanding of the socio-economic situation of the poor in Latin America, and its relation to Christian love and faith as "a going out of one's self, a commitment to God and neighbour, a relationship with others."[18] This is the starting-point which is also given logical priority in "second line" liberation theology. Thus fifteen years later (1986) Leonardo Boff and Clodovis Boff begin their exposition of liberation theology with a narrative of extreme suffering in Northeastern Brazil, and list under the heading "Com-passion, 'suffering with'": five hundred million persons starving . . . one billion in absolute poverty . . ." They comment, "Without a minimum of 'suffering with' . . . liberation theology can neither exist nor be understood."[19]

Although the term "Third World" did not originate in 1955 Gustavo Gutiérrez dates a sense of self-conscious awareness of the collective predicament and hence of Third-World solidarity from the Afro-Asian Bandung conference of 1955. Yet while the Western capitalist and Eastern Marxist economies had their own ways of producing wealth, there was, Gutiérrez argues, still a spirit of optimism in the 1950s that aid for "development" held the key to the aspirations of the poor in the Third World. But by the middle of the 1960s it had become apparent that underdevelopment in the poorer nations constituted a permanent bi-product of development in the richer ones: the gap was widening, not narrowing. It was perceived that there must be "a radical break from the status quo . . . a profound transformation of the private property system . . . Liberation expresses the inescapable moment of radical change which is foreign to the ordinary use of the term *development*."[20]

Between 1960 and 1970 developed nations increased their wealth, Gutiérrez points out, by 50 percent, while the third world continued to struggle in poverty. Only Cuba, after the 1959 revolution, appeared to offer a counterexample of economic progress in Latin America, and this espoused Marxist principles. An increasing polarization between existing regimes and the aspirations of the poor led to violent political activity on both sides, which Helder Camara called "the spiral of violence". This spiral was vividly and tragically demonstrated in Camilo Torres's call for violent revolution on the part of fellow Roman Catholics, and his own violent death in 1966.

In contrast to earlier days of close association with colonialism from Europe and support for ruling regimes, the Latin American Roman Catholic Church associated itself increasingly with the poor. Gutiérrez comments, "The bishops of the most poverty-stricken and exploited areas are the ones who have denounced most energetically the injustices they witness."[21] The Episcopal Conference at Medellin affirmed such a stance, especially in the light of pronouncements about social justice in the Second Vatican Council. Pope Paul VI's Encyclical *Populorum Progressio* (1967) included a critique of economic order. The Latin American Church (including the Protestant Church) became committed to a programme of "consciousness-raising" (*concientización*). This term with its programmatic implications, first arose in the context of the work of Paulo Freire. Freire undertook literacy programmes in Brazil and later in Chile, working among the poor from the late 1950s. He brought together a theory of education with a philosophy of critical praxis in his book *Pedagogy of the Oppressed* (1972). Education, Freire urges, is not value-neutral; it sets people *free* by *changing what they count as "reality"*.

This brings us to the second area identified by Gustavo Gutiérrez as one of the four foundation-elements of liberation theology. *Karl Marx*, he writes, opened the door for a step on the road of "*critical thinking* . . . It made him (humankind) more aware of the *socio-economic determinants* of his ideological creations."[22] Gutiérrez invokes precisely the kind of *socio-critical* tools which we examined in the first two sections of the previous chapter in connection with Marx and Habermas. Fruitful psycho-socio-critical tools emerge, Gutiérrez believes, from Marx, Freud, and Marcuse, as well as additional advances from the philosophies of Hegel and Ernst Bloch, and the theologies of Moltmann and Johannes Metz.[23] Socio-critical tools are crucial because the church must be an "institution of social criticism".[24] Theology must be "a criticism of society" with "a critical attitude".[25] Socio-critical tools are needed because poverty is not simply a matter of an individual's economic status, but of the "oppressive and alienating" circumstances and structures which surround it and render it intolerable. Socio-critical reflection is part of *concientización*.

A third foundation-element for liberation theology springs directly, Gutiérrez argues, from the message of *biblical texts* concerning liberation. Gutiérrez is one of the first to identify what becomes a recurring theme in all liberation hermeneutics, namely *the central theme of the Exodus*. He refers us not only to the exodus narratives, but also to their interpretation in the prophets: "Awake, put on strength, O arm of the Lord . . . Was it not you who hacked the Rahab in pieces and ran the dragon through? Was it not you who dried up the sea . . . and made the ocean depths a path for the ransomed?" (Isa. 51:9,10; cf. Psalm 74:14; 87:4; 89:11). The initial chapters of Exodus describe "oppression": Egypt is a land of slavery (Ex. 13:3; 20:2; Deut. 5:6) and repression (Ex. 1:1–10). The narrative speaks of alienated work (Ex. 5:6–14), and of humiliations (Ex. 1:13,14).[26] But the word of God addresses the situation: "I have seen the misery of my people . . . I have heard their outcry . . . I have taken heed of their sufferings, and I have come down to rescue them" (Ex. 3:7–9).

Even so, Gutiérrez points out, the people have *not yet become fully aware* of their need for liberation from oppression. They criticize Moses for "bringing them out", and cry, "Leave us alone; let us be slaves to the Egyptians" (Ex. 14:11,12). There is need for "consciousness-raising", for "*concientización*". Gutiérrez comments: "A gradual pedagogy of successes and failures would be necessary for the Jewish people to become aware of the roots of their oppression, to struggle against it, and to perceive the profound sense of liberation to which they are called."[27] But God remains faithful to his creation; he is the Liberator or *goel* of Israel (Isa. 43:14; 47:4). Therefore the New Testament continues language concerning new creation (2 Cor. 5:17) and freedom (Gal. 5:1).

Fourthly and finally, the theological contribution to a theology of liberation also draws on the language of promise and of eschatology. Gustavo Gutiérrez alludes approvingly to the re-discovery of biblical eschatology by Johannes Weiss and Albert Schweitzer, and enters into dialogue with the theological work of Jürgen Moltmann and Johannes B. Metz. He also draws on the philosophy of hope formulated by Ernst Bloch. It is important for Gutiérrez that Bloch develops Marx's first thesis on Feuerbach. In Marx's words, it is the defect of earlier materialism that "actuality . . . is conceived only in the form of the object or perception (*Anschauung*), but not as sensuous human activity, practice (*Praxis*) . . ."[28] As we have already noted, Marx's eleventh thesis on Feuerbach declares: "Philosophers have only *interpreted* the world in various ways; the point is, to *change* it."[29] Gutiérrez comments: Bloch's hope "is an active hope which subverts the existing order . . . This ontology of what 'is not yet' is dynamic, in contrast to the static ontology of being."[30]

As Gutiérrez points out, Bloch's *The Principle of Hope* directly influenced Moltmann. Liberation from the present, Moltmann argues, rests on the promise which brings about "the reality which is coming . . . and hoped-for transformation."[31] "We are saved by hope; but hope that is seen is not hope . . ." (Rom. 8:24). Clearly in conscious parallel to Marx, Moltmann writes: "The theologian is not concerned merely to supply a different *interpretation* of the world . . . but to *transform* (states of affairs) in expectation of a divine transformation."[32]

In *The Crucified God* Moltmann turns from the subject of hope to the experience of suffering which gives hope its currency *as "hope"*. He explicitly combines what he sees as the socio-critical "negative dialectics" of Adorno and Horkheimer with a theology of the cross and of social action.[33] He writes: "Unless it apprehends *the pain of the negative*, Christian hope cannot be realistic and *liberating*."[34] The cross challenges all security-seeking "establishment" attitudes of politics, theology, or power. It criticizes attitudes which "push people who suffer to the fringes of society in order to withdraw undisturbed into its own small groups".[35] It invites "solidarity with the sufferings of the poor".[36] Moltmann's theology is not simply "Marxist": in an essay on Bloch he compares the silence of Marxism in the face of death with the Christian hope of resurrection and of "surprises" and novelty in history.[37] But he rejects any Christian theology or eschatology which has become de-coupled from social or political action. Thus on Teilhard's eschatology he comments, "For the sake of one starving child, I reject . . . this idea of evolution."[38]

In broader terms, Juan Luis Segundo summarizes these issues succinctly. Liberation theologians, he declares, suspect "that anything and everything involving *ideas*, including theology, is intimately bound up with the existing social situation in at least an unconscious way".[39] He continues: "If theology somehow assumes that it can respond to the new questions without changing its customary interpretation of the Scriptures, that immediately terminates the hermeneutical circle."[40] The hermeneutical circle presupposes, he declares, a commitment, "a *partiality*".[41] Ideological suspicion reveals that some biblical interpretations serve to maintain exploitation by the ruling classes; others become a weapon in the class struggle. The only "finality" or "universality" which is available is one of *action*, not of thought.[42]

This general suspicion of "ideas", which is intensified through dialogue with Marxism, finds two distinct forms of expression in hermeneutics. The more radical undergoes development into neo-Marxist or social-theory "materialist" hermeneutics, and we shall discuss this approach later in this chapter. Thus Carlos Mestos expresses unease over the role of the biblical "expert". He reflects: "We members of the clergy expropriated the Bible. . . . We took the Bible out of the hands of the common people, locked it with a key, and then threw the key away. But the people have found the key and are beginning again to interpret the Bible."[43] The method of interpretation, or hermeneutical "critical principle" which they use "is the only tool they have at hand: their own lives, experiences, struggles".[44] This rediscovery of the Bible as "our book" gives "a militancy that can overcome the world".[45]

The contrast between Mestos's approach and that of Segundo reflects a duality between a pragmatic and a critical approach. Can sheer commitment to liberation take a socio-critical form if the hermeneutical key to interpretation is only the *experiences* of a given community of interpretation? David Lochhead makes some crucial comments in his work "The Liberation of the Bible". He writes: "The group *must be free and able to distinguish the perspective of the group from the perspective of the text*."[46] The temptation is to rely on an "expert" for critical perspective; but what about the expert's own ideological perspectives? Yet if we do away with all the expert help, "we know the result. The group is then *dominated by the more aggressive representatives of the unofficial ideology of the group: the most pious or the most militant*."[47]

This is "domination" indeed; for the texts in such a situation have been manipulated to provide only positive signals for the aspirations and desires of the dominant sub-group. Yet *liberation* theology is not meant to imprison a community within the social pragmatism of its own existing practices. If *praxis* (which properly includes theory) becomes *practice* based on given *experience*, how can the future genuinely *liberate* rather than merely extend the *present*? If liberation hermeneutics are genuinely *social-critical* hermeneutics, texts will be transforming and horizons will be changing. We have come up against the socio-critical *vs.* socio-pragmatic issue again.

2. Parallels and Contrasts with Black Hermeneutics: the Varied Approaches of Cone, Boesak, Goba, Mosala, and other Writers.

The very wide range of hermeneutical approaches which we find in practice, if not in theory, in Latin American liberation hermeneutics is broadly matched by a corresponding diversity of approaches in black theology and in black hermeneutics. Both reflect a similar spectrum of perspectives, ranging from an emphasis on the immediacy of existential experience, at one end, through a variety of more critical or socio-critical sub-systems, to Marxist or "materialist" readings based on world-views at the other. One end of the spectrum focuses on life-world; the other, on system. This is not to overlook important differences between the Latin American, black, and neo-Marxist approaches. Latin American liberation theologies tend to focus especially on economic poverty and political powerlessness. Materialist readings embody Marxist suspicions of traditional interpretation as *idealist* and *thought-centred* constructions, and use Marxist theory not simply for a social analysis of the community's experience, but also as a *theory of the material conditions which produce biblical texts*. Finally, *black hermeneutics embody three quite distinct contexts*. Black theology in South Africa focusses on issues overshadowed by colonial history and the legacy of Apartheid; North American black theology finds expression in the historical memory of slavery and its aftermath; African hermeneutics in black African states mainly concerns *contextualization* and the relation between the Bible and African cultures.

All these movements (with the possible exception of African hermeneutics) stress experience and struggle as the context of hermeneutics. Latin American and black South African and North American hermeneutics tend to identify with similar themes in the biblical writings. They raise parallel questions about the relation between *narrative-experience* and the *immediacy* of the biblical text for Christian devotion and social action; yet both also search for a *socio-critical principle* of hermeneutics which will unmask those uses of the biblical texts which have been promoted in the interests of structures of wealth and power. Both also firmly reject the notion that mainstream biblical interpretation in Western universities and seminaries has been convincingly objective or value-neutral. Both perceive positivist or rationalist interpretations as inadequate and even deceptive. Many interpretative procedures, they argue, either serve an ineffective pluralism through pluralizing meaning, or serve the interests of socio-politically dominant groups. *The very pluralism of "academic" interpretations seems to postpone social critique in endless revisions of ideas.*

(i) The Experience of Oppression as a Hermeneutical Principle: "Black Experience"

Juan Luis Segundo makes common cause with the starting-point of James Cone's North American black theology. He supports Cone's assertion that "Black Theology must be consistent with the perspective of the black community . . . Black theologians must work in such a way as to destroy the corruptive influence of white thought by building a theology on the sources and norm that are appropriate to the black community."[48] Segundo sees Cone's book *A Black Theology of Liberation* (1970) as an example of a positive use of "the hermeneutical circle".[49]

In his later book *God of the Oppressed* (1975), Cone's black hermeneutics addresses "the problem of the particular and the universal in theological discourse".[50] The biblical texts remain *fundamental* but always relational to concrete *experience*. Cone writes: "The theologian is *before all else* an exegete simultaneously of Scripture and of existence . . . Scripture is not an abstract word . . . It is God's Word to those who are oppressed and humiliated in this world."[51] In response to questions about belief and "evidence", Cone asserts: "My reply is quite similar to the testimony of the Fathers and the Mothers of the Black Church: let me tell you a story . . ."[52] Theo Witvliet, commenting on this in his book *The Way of the Black Messiah*, sees both black narrative-experience and biblical narrative not as a tool of pragmatic affirmation but as a *critical* principle. He declares: "What Cone writes about the black story amounts to the best pages in *God of the Oppressed*. He recognizes that the theologian can speak only as a witness . . . The power of these stories is that they cannot be reduced to a private possession . . . They are capable of taking people outside their social context . . . Through them I am challenged to leave my own subjectivity behind, and enter into another domain of thought and action."[53]

Yet within both black theology and Latin-American theology there are also voices which question the adequacy of narrative-experience as a critical tool. In his recent book *Biblical Hermeneutics and Black Theology in South Africa* (1989), Itumeleng J. Mosala urges that only a *historical-materialist* reading of texts can be adequately critical for black South Africa.[54] He argues that the hermeneutics of Desmond Tutu and Allan Boesak turn out to be "idealist", and to depend ultimately on the *existential* interpretation used by white theologians to perpetuate *Western ideologies*.[55] A similar kind of criticism, also from a firmly Marxist viewpoint, is levelled by Alistair Kee against Clodovis Boff and other Latin American writers. Boff, Kee argues, *purports* to find in Marx "the exciting leading edge of modern critical thought", but in actuality collapses theology back into a "pre-modern" mode, which has "failed the people".[56]

Before we examine further parallels in concrete interpretations of specific biblical texts, some further account needs to be offered of the nature and development of black theology and the conscious emergence of distinctive black hermeneutics. As Mosala and B. Goba indicate, black theology in South Africa emerged in the context of the black consciousness movement during the late 1960s and early 1970s. Mosala further observes: "All major black theological studies in South Africa draw in some way on the work of James Cone . . . For Cone, the Word of God represents one structural pole of the biblical hermeneutics of black theology, while the black experience constitutes the other . . . The black experience of oppression . . . provides the epistemological lens through which to perceive the God of the Bible as the God of liberation."[57]

If we begin with James Cone, however, we must draw a careful distinction between his own North-American tradition of black theology and the wider range of theological and hermeneutical traditions of black South African theology. Further, the ethos of black African theology in black African states is yet different again. Cone begins from concerns about black power in his work *Black Theology and Black Power* (1969), and consistently addresses the issue of black consciousness. In *God of the Oppressed* (1975) he observes: "White people did everything within their power to define black reality, to tell us who we were . . . To be put in one's place, as defined by white society, was a terrible reality."[58] Cone sought "a new way of looking at theology" which would not embody "insensitivity to black pain and suffering".[59]

Two of the major components of this "new way" were the "social basis of theology" and a hermeneutics which would operate between the two poles of the biblical texts and black experience. Black experience is identified less in analysis than in story, which is "the history of individuals coming together in the struggle to shape life according to commonly held values".[60] The black American story is recorded in the tales, songs, and narratives of African slaves and their descendants. It is, as Theo Witvliet noted, a potentially critical tool, because in Cone's words, "story can serve as a check against ideological thinking".[61]

The biblical-textual pole of Cone's hermeneutics naturally identifies "liberation" passages in the texts: the exodus theme (especially Ex. 19:4,5); the social critique announced by the prophets; and the gospel of liberation declared by Jesus in his synagogue reading (Luke 4:18,19). The "experience" pole comes from the black story in terms of *content*. But in terms of theological *method* Paul Tillich's notion of the method of correlation plays at least a minor methodological role together with his understanding of "ultimate concern" in Cone's earlier *A Black Theology of Liberation* (1970).[62] Tillich refused to identify ultimate concern with any given theological content; it related to the Kierkegaardian passion of the infinite for "what concerns *us* (my italics) ultimately".[63] All theology, for Cone, must be passionate.[64] According to his "method of correlation", Tillich believes that "the Bible as such never has been the norm of systematic theology . . . The method of correlation . . . makes an analysis of the human situation out of which existential questions arise . . . Symbols used in the Christian message are answers to those questions."[65]

A hermeneutic which seeks to "understand" Jesus, and God through Jesus, must therefore formulate a Christology in terms of *"our"* questions and experience. For Cone, these are the questions of *black experience*, which includes not simply physiological skin-colour, but the wider psycho-social experience of being *"defined" by others* and inheriting a situation of inequality.[66] Hence he reaches a conclusion which, outside of the context of its argument, might seem even more polemical than it is. The significance of Jesus, he writes, "is not an abstract question. If Christ is to be existentially relevant . . . the Christological importance of Jesus Christ must be found in his blackness. If he is not black, as we are, then the resurrection has little significance for our times . . . Our being with him is dependent on his being with us in the oppressed black condition, revealing to us what is necessary for our liberation."[67] Cone refers not to "the *literal* colour of Jesus", but to an identity with oppressed people that identifies him as "not white".[68]

This notion of a "black Christ", however, is different from the more inclusive or universal approaches found in many African black theologies, and it would be true of many, but not all, black theologies in South Africa. John S. Mbiti's *New Testament Eschatology in an African Background* (1971) offers a hermeneutical translation of eschatology in relation to the horizons of the Akamba people in Kenya.[69] This work compares language used within the horizons of the biblical texts with functions of concepts within two modern horizons: those of European missionaries of the Africa Inland Mission who brought the gospel to the Akamba; and those of the Akamba people themselves. Mbiti argues for the importance of hermeneutical translation into the thought-forms of traditional African cultures. Broadly parallel approaches can be found in the work of Harry Sawyerr of Sierra Leone and subsequently by John Pobee of Ghana in his *Toward an African Theology* (1979).

It would be tempting to suggest that African hermeneutics stresses *contextualization* where Latin Americans speak of *praxis*, and where North American black theology speaks of *black experience*. But a recent survey on the use of the Bible in John Mbiti's more recent book *Bible and Theology in African Christianity* reviews such a diversity of approaches that such a generalization needs to be qualified.[70] Hermeneutics of a traditional evangelical kind are represented, and the emphasis on immediacy which we noted in *The Gospel in Solentiname* is reflected in Mbiti's descriptions of the Bible in African preaching and in oral communication.[71] "Black experience" plays some part in all strands of black hermeneutics. What varies is the status which it is accorded as a "critical principle" in dialogue with the text. We shall examine the principle further in our discussion of the role of "women's experience" in feminist hermeneutics.

(ii) The Divide between Mainstream and Materialist Black Hermeneutics
Black South African hermeneutics takes up the social, economic, and political themes which also characterize Latin American hermeneutics. In 1969 the all-black South African Students Organization initiated the black consciousness movement under Steve Biko, and from 1972 essays on black theology began to appear. John Mbiti initially strongly dissociated African theology from the movement, commenting that while African theology sprang from an experience of *joy* and *faith*, black theology was borne out of *pain*.[72] A sense of general Third World identity, however emerged with the formation in 1976 of the Ecumenical Association of Third World Theologians. Similarities and differences between African and South African black theology are charted by Patrick A Kalilombe from Malawi and by John Parratt who has worked in Botswana.[73] In his essay "Black Theology and African Theology – Soulmates or Antagonists?" Desmond Tutu argued that his own work represented both theologies.[74]

Black South African hermeneutics works largely out of the context of the struggle against the legacy of Apartheid, including the question of land-ownership among other issues. The black experience poignantly recalls that in Takatso Mofokeng's words, "When the white man came to our country he had the Bible and we had the land ... After the prayer, the white man had the land and we had the Bible."[75] In particular, behind the call for a *black* hermeneutics in South Africa lies an awareness that in 1942 the Afrikaner draft constitution spoke of the Afrikaner "national calling" as manifested in the history of the Voortrekkers, as one of "obedience to Almighty God and to His Holy Word". Hence black hermeneutics looks to a method which will not only exclude and unmask such an appeal to the biblical text, but would also operate as a counter-affirmation. The key question, then, for hermeneutical theory is whether *both* such approaches would be hermeneutics of socio-pragmatic affirmation, or whether any other approach would provide a new starting point.

The work of Desmond Tutu, Allan Boesak, and Manas Buthelezi represent more traditional "mainstream" black hermeneutics.[76] More recently Bonganjalo Goba and Itumeleng Mosala have drawn more consciously on socio-critical theory, although Mosala opts for a radical Marxist-materialist hermeneutic.[77] The 1985 declaration known as *The Kairos Document* sets in contrast, on the one hand "state" theology and "church" theology, and on the other a "return to the Bible ... for a message that is relevant to what we are experiencing in South Africa today".[78]

Allan Boesak offers an interpretation of the narrative of Cain and Abel, which Mosala regards as an example of "existential" hermeneutics, but which resonates with Latin American interpretation.[79] Cain rose up "against his brother" Abel and killed him (Gen. 4:8). Boesak focusses first on the notion of "brother" as "being human in community", to seek together "for true humanity", and then on Cain's curse (Gen. 4:12–16). Like landless people in South Africa, Cain the farmer no longer possesses the land. But it is the *oppressor* whom God has removed from the land. Boesak writes: "The story meant to tell us that the oppressors shall have no place on God's earth." Cain has lost his brother and his security; "and so whites remain anxious and fearful ... eaten up with anxiety ..." Can Cain's chain of evil, multiplied by Lamech, ever come to an end? On the one hand Jesus reversed the words of Lamech; but whether we can speak of forgiveness in South Africa cannot be answered "too hastily".[80]

Allan Boesak's book *Comfort and Protest* (1987) is an interpretation of the Book of Revelation. He writes: "The clue to understanding the Apocalypse as protest literature ... lies, I think, in Rev. 1:9: 'I, John, your brother, who share with you in Jesus the tribulation ... and patient endurance [of suffering].' This is the key. Those who do not know this suffering through oppression, who do not struggle together with God's people for the sake of the gospel ... shall have great difficulty understanding this letter from Patmos."[81] Thus the cry "How long before Thou wilt judge ... ?" (Rev. 6:9,10) speaks with the voice of the martyrs. "It is a cry of pain and anguish; it is a cry of protest. It is also a cry of hope ... It is a cry black South Africans who find their help in Yahweh have been uttering for a long time . . . under racist colonial oppression for almost three and a half centuries . . . through thirty-eight years of apartheid . . ."[82]

Christopher Rowland and Mark Corner explore the Apocalypse more generally as a "discourse for social criticism". They write: "The Apocalypse's dualism challenges the notion that human injustice is the centre of the universe by positing another horizon: at present, heaven . . . In Rev. 17–18 the state and public and private greed are thus de-centred . . ." The Apocalypse offers an "alternative horizon".[83]

Boesak's method entirely coheres with the hermeneutical approach of Severino Croatto in his interpretation of Exodus. The fundamental starting-point is "the *cry*" of an oppressed people: "I have seen the *affliction* of my people . . . and have heard their *cry*" (Ex. 3:7).[84] "The cry of the people . . . has come to me" (Ex. 3:9). The cry leads first to the people's beginning 'to be conscientized' . . . to embark on the path to liberation. "The word of God has a conscientizing function . . . Moses' understanding of his new commitment comes slowly" (Ex. 3:11; 4:1; 4:10,13).[85] Croatto declares: "Every hermeneutical circle runs in two directions: from the archetypal event to the existential present and vice-versa . . . Any 'memory' has meaning for me only if I am in some way involved in a *present-day* process of liberation."[86]

In his black hermeneutics Bonganjalo Gobo makes a parallel plea for "conscientization" and "hermeneutical praxis".[87] Gobo appeals both to the socio-critical hermeneutics of Habermas and to the work of Gustavo Gutiérrez.[88] The response to *The Kairos Document*, he writes, must be "to take sides with marginalized oppressed people" and to do so "in the context of the Black theological hermeneutics I am presenting". This takes the form of a "communal praxis . . . a unity based on our humanity and commitment to justice for all".[89] Gobo addresses his work to the black South African situation, but writes from Chicago.

Nevertheless for Itumeleng Mosala only a *materialist* reading of biblical texts can be radical enough to constitute a genuinely socio-critical hermeneutic. Mosala attacks Boesak's assumption "that there exists a 'gospel' that all social classes, genders, and races can recognize equally as representing the essential message of Jesus of Nazareth."[90] This assumption makes black theology "impotent" because it accepts the notion of the thought-content of the gospel independently of action and material causality, and thereby constitutes "useless sparring with the ghost of the oppressor, whom black theology has already embraced in the oppressor's most dangerous form, *the ideological form of the text.*"[91] Sociological and materialist readings, by contrast, take up the contradictory and conflicting social and political *forces and interests which lead to the production* of the biblical texts. The task of materialist hermeneutics is to unmask these for what they are.

Not surprisingly, Mosala appeals to the work of Norman Gottwald as a paradigm, including Gottwald's assessment that liberation theologies have not gone far enough in their social structural analysis of biblical texts. Mosala also appeals to the socio-political literary theory of Terry Eagleton. In specific terms, he selects Allan Boesak's interpretation of Gen. 4:1–16, which we have already examined, as "the most glaring example of this fighting of the class enemy with his own weapons".[92] There is nothing, he claims, in Boesak's "existential" interpretation to suggest that the landless and oppressed ever *will* find their situations reversed.

Mosala assigns Genesis 4:1–16 to the so-called J-document which is regularly associated with the scribes of the Davidic Solomonic era of Israelite monarchy. As it stands, Mosala writes, it is "a ruling-class author's attempt to validate this landlessness of the village peasants".[93] Such scribal work involved "the need for an ideological explanation of the creation in Israel of large estates (*latifundia*) which were privately owned, and the simultaneous large-scale dispossession of the majority of the peasant producers of Israel from their . . . inherited plots of land".[94] Cain the tiller of soil represents the "freeholding peasantry": the royal classes are represented by Abel. The text enlists divine pleasure on Abel's side, and Cain is dispossessed. The whole story is an ideological production.

Boesak's interpretation is virtually turned on its head, and some major points of contrast emerge. First, although Mosala claims that his interpretation offers a genuine socio-critical unmasking of exploitation and oppression, its level of critical abstraction deprives it of some immediacy and power at the level of narrative-resonance and existential rapport which, according to Boesak, Cone, and other writers, are fundamental for black experience and consciousness. We have moved back "behind" the text to a historical re-construction, but to one which entails some radically hypothetical assumptions. Paradoxically, Mosala rightly sees a need for a transcendental frame which will guarantee a genuinely critical dimension; but the key question remains of whether a materialist-Marxist reading actually provides such a transcendental or authentic frame.

Mosala is willing to press his socio-critical theory to the utmost limits. He attacks Desmond Tutu's hermeneutical procedure, for example, because Tutu is willing to call Jesus "Messiah" in the linguistic terms of Isaiah 11:1–7. This, Mosala suggests, "ignores the class basis of the text, as it now stands, in the royal ruling class ideology . . . *Messiah* is thoroughly royal". Messiahship is the product of interests of "a formerly Zion-based elite, a ruling-class people now displaced from Jerusalem".[95]

Mosala's materialist reading thus offers a more radical hermeneutic than the relatively milder neo-Marxist perspectives of most Latin American writers. He goes well beyond Miranda's work in *Marx and the Bible*. Miranda claims: "I am not reducing the Bible to Marx nor Marx to the Bible".96 Miranda's own concern is to use Marx as a source of social analysis to understand the situation of the oppressed, not to offer materialist readings. Thus, to select one example, Miranda does not seek to "de-ideologize" Rom. 1:16,17 in terms of its material "production"; but expounds Pauline "righteousness" in terms of "the justice of God" for those who have nothing in which to boast, but look to God to intervene.97

3. Further Examples of Marxist or "Materialist" Readings: Belo and Clévenot

The most widely-known example of a materialist reading is that of Fernando Belo's book *A Materialist Reading of the Gospel of Mark* (1974). This work, Belo writes, represents a passionate "body-to-body struggle with the text of the bourgeois-Christian ideology that for a number of years marked out the limits of my field of speech".98 Before Marxism had provided him with the right materialist tools, Belo was "imprisoned" in ideology. As Mosala would also argue, if faith, in the black African or Latin American worlds still survived social criticism as an "ideology", this transformed faith would actually still "contradict the practices aimed at liberation, in which Christians are now striving to take part".99 The motivation of Belo's materialist reading is therefore to support, not to undermine, liberation; but the notion of a "theology" of liberation might seem to Belo to reify an ideology based on interpretative thought-processes, rather than on a *praxis* of transformation.

Belo's search for a new language suggested that, in his words, "as a guide in the reading process I took Roland Barthes (to whom I later added Julia Kristeva)".100 Marxist categories provide the conceptual tools for identifying processes of *social formation and production* beneath the text, and for relating these to what the texts supposedly "say" or "represent". Belo, therefore, begins with questions about "modes of production", partly in dialogue with the work of Louis Althusser. Processes of what we earlier referred to as "demystification" in the work of Roland Barthes are further facilitated, Belo writes, by additional dialogue with Freud, Derrida, and Lacan. *These contribute to the dimension of critical suspicion which will make possible a genuinely socio-critical reading.*

One other major ingredient contributes to Belo's work. Mary Douglas had examined the Old Testament material about "clean" and "unclean" animals in Lev. 11 and Deut. 14 from a largely structuralist or socio-semiotic point of view. "Unclean" animals, she argued, are not "proper" animals within the semiotic system because they do not find a place within the semiotic system of Gen. 1. The meaning of "clean" and "unclean" draws its semantic currency from a structural system organized around the notion of *purity*. This system is distinct from the Deuteronomic system which revolves around behavioral *morality*.

Belo claimed to find dual "codes" reflecting a parallel duality of *socio-political interests* in the Gospel of Mark. The purity-pollution code of semiotic system persists in the socio-political interests of the *priestly* classes, represented by the dominant tradition of the Old Testament by the Jewish temple-establishment in the time of Jesus. But the Deuteronomic system of social justice and "egalitarian" interests also finds expression in the Markan texts. Jesus sides with the egalitarian Deuteronomic tradition against the socio-political interests of the privileged Jewish priesthood. Jesus has "authority", in the Markan texts as they stand, "over the pollution system . . . (and) over the debt system".[101] The destruction of the temple results, in the Markan texts, from a "subversion-displacement . . . and rejection of the Messiah by the chief priests, elders and scribes", which in turn "subverts the dominant practice . . . at the centre of the Jewish symbolic field".[102]

Belo's work is extremely demanding reading, not least because his interweaving of different layers of textual code operates in conjunction with the highly complex multiform theoretical framework within which Belo works. It is probably the most radical expression, to date, of Marxist-semiotic suspicion that the meaning of biblical texts, far from being transparent, demand a more fundamental de-ideologization and demythologization than has hitherto been attempted. It reflects a positive answer to Norman Gottwald's question: "does the class position of the biblical writers and biblical readers have something critical to do with how the Bible is interpreted?"[103] Similarly Sergio Rostagno questions the possibility of using "class-neutral" biblical interpretation. Without a class-commitment to the poor, Rostagno argues, "anything and everything can in fact be found in the text".[104]

The intensity, density, and complexity of Belo's approach is relaxed in Michel Clévenot's work *Materialist Approaches to the Bible*.[105] He draws on the Marxist theory used by Belo, but recognizes that materialist approaches represent a plurality of standpoints. Clévenot's work underlines the role of historical reconstruction as an indispensable tool for determining what socio-political forces operated to produce the text. Clévenot selectively underlines certain aspects of Belo's work, for the sake of reaching a wider readership who would be daunted by Belo's complexity. He distinguishes between a semiotic "gift" system, and the "purity" system. The "gift" system he associates with the ten Northern tribes of Israel and with the so-called E and D documents. Here "the spirit of the clan was ferociously democratic . . . hostile to all centralization . . . to all monopolizing of power".[106] The elitist priestly casts work with the purity system. But Jesus affirms the egalitarian system of gift. Thus in Mark 6:36,37, the disciples suggest "buying" something to eat, but Jesus replies: "*Give* them something to eat" (6:37). Clévenot sees this as "the negation of the merchant system that governs exchanges by money and the promotion of the system of the gift in which everything belongs to everyone."[107]

We may note that just as Mosala's interpretation of Gen. 4:2–16 consciously subverted and inverted the positive and negative role of Cain and Abel respectively, so in Clévenot the Davidic line is "unmasked" as the elitist holders of power, while the "rebellious" Northern tribes represent the true "Messianic" tradition. Materialist interpretation depends on the presence not only of internal contradictions within the biblical material, but also on an explicit identification of different conflicts as representing conflicting social interests on the part of different socio-political groups in the inter-play of power and labour which produces the texts.

Such is the diversity of hermeneutical theory and practice in liberation theologies that it would be unwise to suggest any general assessment which would include all cases. Nevertheless one or two broad comments may be made. First, the very *least* that is achieved is a necessary sensitizing of the pre-understanding with which we approach biblical texts. Does our own community of interpretation have vested interests in given interpretations? Have the particular texts before us been used as instruments for social manipulation or control, which are over-convenient for certain groups of interpreters? Until recently hermeneutical suspicion might duly fall on hierarchical claims for a status quo; but with egalitarian trends in socio-literary and socio-political ideologies, suspicion needs to be exercized in a *double* direction about vested interests.

Second, the relationship between *socio-critical* and *socio-pragmatic* hermeneutics is highlighted and intensified by Marxist theorists and by materialist readings of biblical texts. Any merely selective use of texts to encourage those who are oppressed can be perceived in principle to represent precisely the same strategy of hermeneutical method as the oppressors who use texts to legitimize their own programmes. Both in this case confront each other with socio-pragmatic methods. Without some *critical* hermeneutical tool, both sides in the struggle can continue to appeal to different texts to re-enforce and re-affirm their corporate identity and interests. The pragmatic approach simply escalates a polarization of conflict. But the notion that Marxist theory or materialist readings can provide a transcendental frame within which a theology of the text is itself relativized rests on a particular Marxist world-view. According to this view, such a theology is merely an ideological product of historical and social situations. But, as many of the Latin American theologians note, a social theory may not constitute an adequate basis for a transcendental world-view or critique. To transform materialist *methods* into a transcendental materialist *world-view* is itself incompatible with the standpoint of the biblical texts. Moreover it excludes the very openness to "listen" which Gadamer, Betti, and Ricoeur regard as indispensable for a hermeneutic of dialogue or retrieval.

Leonardo and Clodovis Boff are clear about the status of Marxism, even though Alistair Kee criticizes their evaluation as compromise. They write: "Liberation theologians ask Marx: 'What can you tell us about the situation of poverty and ways of overcoming it?' Here Marxists are submitted to the judgment of the poor, . . . not the other way round. Therefore liberation theology uses Marxism purely as an *instrument*, . . . borrows from Marxism certain 'methodological pointers'."[108]

Third, we have identified a range of attitudes towards the use of critical self-awareness and critical-social awareness in the various strands before us. Some tend towards a socio-pragmatic hermeneutic in simply screening out any signals from the text which would question their own enterprise or prior commitment. Where there is struggle, this may surrender the biblical texts to the status of instruments for sheer self-affirmation on both sides. But some systems do attempt to combine commitment to the texts and commitment to the oppressed within a frame which allows for questioning and appraisal. To argue that questioning and social criticism cannot even arise outside a given social theory or praxis is to discard the numerous issues which we have already addressed in our discussions of the respective strengths and weaknesses of Habermas, Apel, and Rorty.

In chapter XVI we shall take up Alfred Schutz's notion of criteria of relevance in an attempt to show that metacritical and socio-critical questions can and should be kept in view. But the basis for metacritical ranking is not some absolute Archimedian system. It entails dialogue and mutuality between the hermeneutical life-world and an enlarged open system centred on a theology of the cross.

4. The Nature and Development of Feminist Biblical Hermeneutics

Feminist hermeneutics brings together almost every major issue in hermeneutical theory. At the theoretical level it offers a major model of *socio-critical hermeneutics*. It rests on the principle that biblical texts have been interpreted in such a way as to promote and to legitimate secondary or oppressive social roles to women. Certain biblical texts, as mediated through many Christian traditions, are perceived in most strands of feminism to have been transposed into instruments of power, domination, and social control. A critical hermeneutical principle is sought which will unmask this "legitimating" social function to produce women's emancipation from these supposed norms and patterns. In this sense, as Elisabeth Schüssler Fiorenza argues, feminist hermeneutics is *also liberation hermeneutics*.[109]

Feminist writers approach biblical texts, however, at a variety of hermeneutical levels. The central philosophical premise is the priority of hermeneutics over positivism or rationalism. Feminist hermeneutics embodies a deep hermeneutic of suspicion that the conventional constructions of the history of biblical interpretation do *not represent value-neutral descriptions* of biblical history, traditions, and texts. All interpretation, it is argued, at least until very recently, has been mediated through male-dominated reading-communities. Thus Mary Ann Tolbert speaks of "the fiction of 'objective' scholarship."[110] Elisabeth Schüssler Fiorenza attacks "the dogma of value-neutral detached interpretation . . . the so-called objectivity and value-neutrality of academic theology."[111] T. Drorah Setel suspects the notion of "objective" enquiry.[112]

This recalls some of the basic questions which we addressed, in earlier chapters of this book. How are biblical texts re-contextualized within the framework of a tradition? Phyllis Trible identifies this as the first hermeneutical issue to be addressed in her book *God and the Rhetoric of Sexuality*. She begins by examining "the hermeneutics functioning within scripture."[113] But a hermeneutics of tradition must be supplemented by a hermeneutics of enquiry: what is *the status of the tradition* which constitutes a given context of understanding? Certain points of affinity with feminist hermeneutics may perhaps be detected in the Reformers' desire *both* to affirm authentic early Patristic tradition and yet *also to refuse to equate it* with a later fifteenth or sixteenth century ecclesial *magisterium*. This partially anticipates the ambivalent attitude of many feminists towards tradition. While androcentric tradition is destructive, it is urged, many aspects of tradition including women's "lost" place in it should be "retrieved." So great is this tension of positive and negative that many feminist writers part company with each other on this issue.

The desire to "retrieve" the place of women in traditions and texts accounts for much of the motivation for what might be thought of as the more "empirical" aspect of reformist feminist approaches to biblical texts. Many instances of feminist biblical interpretation focus on the study of biblical texts or Patristic traditions which speak positively of women. The minimal aim, although not usually the whole aim, is to retrieve those aspects of tradition which narrate a *more positive and less stereotyped* view of women than traditions might otherwise seem to suggest. Elizabeth Schüssler Fiorenza seeks, among other things, a "critical re-appropriation of the past.[114]

One classic study of this kind is the influential volume *Women of Spirit* (1979), edited by Rosemary Ruether and Eleanor McLaughlin. In this collection Elisabeth Schüssler Fiorenza re-examined literature of the second and third centuries, including such sources as *The Acts of Paul and Thecla*. The conclusion is urged that because of patriarchal bias, the dominant interpreters and transmitters of early tradition "transmitted only a fraction of the rich traditions about significant women and their contribution in early Christianity. Most of the egalitarian traditions of primitive Christianity are probably lost."[115] Rosemary Ruether argues that by the late Patristic age there were still women who were "writers, thinkers, scripture scholars" but had "no public voice."[116]

The distinction between textual content and a negative frame or context of tradition is applied in feminist hermeneutics to tensions within the biblical writings themselves. Janice Capel Anderson, for example, adopts a "literary" approach to Matthew within the framework of a feminist interpretative interest in which "the androcentric perspective of the Gospel" and its "patriarchal assumptions" are set in contrast to a different textual content.[117] The textual content in question portrays the initiative and faith of two women: the woman with the haemorrhage (Matt. 9: 20–22), and especially the Canaanite woman (Matt. 15: 21–28). "Both exhibit initiative and faith in their approach to Jesus . . . The Canaanite woman . . . calls Jesus Lord three times and worships him."[118] The women at Bethany and at the cross and at the tomb provide a "non-threatening contrast with the disciples."[119] With minor exceptions "women are portrayed favourably. The important roles of women and of Jesus' response to women supplicants strain the boundaries of the gospel's patriarchal worldview."[120] An appendix to the essay enumerating thirty-six references to women in Matthew's Gospel (although admittedly with some overlap) helps to *retrieve* a "lost" perspective.

A broadly parallel exercize in terms of Old Testament texts has been undertaken by J. Cheryl Exum.[121] She focusses attention on Ex. 1: 8–2: 10. In this text Pharaoh's attempts to take initiatives and to mould history are repeatedly foiled and frustrated by women who successively control the key events. After the imposition of affliction fails as a strategy, the centre of attention moves to the Hebrew midwives who refuse to obey Pharaoh, not out of fear of man, but out of fear of God (Ex. 1: 16, 20, 21). The midwives frustrate Pharaoh's second strategy. He makes a third attempt to shape events, but this is foiled by two women: Pharaoh's daughter and Moses's mother. Cheryl Exum comments: "The speech and action of women shape the contours of the story."[122]

There is more to this focus on women in the biblical texts, however, than the retrieval of lost aspects or silences in tradition. We have said that feminist hermeneutics includes the level of *socio-critical* hermeneutics. Reflecting the double hermeneutic of Paul Ricoeur, therefore, Elisabeth Schüssler Fiorenza combines historical reconstruction of an "explanatory" nature with a "sharpened . . . *'hermeneutic of suspicion'*".[123] Similarly Katharine

Doob Sakenfeld urges that the "beginning point, shared with all feminists studying the Bible, is appropriately a stance of *radical suspicion*."[124] In common with most strands of liberation hermeneutics Fiorenza believes that "all theology, willingly or not, is by definition always engaged for or against the oppressed."[125]

This brings us to the very heart of the major concern expressed in this chapter. What critical principle is used to unmask the objects of suspicion as instruments of social power, control, or interest? Further, is this critical principle a *transcendental critique which can operate transcontextually* or is it a *socio-pragmatic norm which can function only internally within the context of a given tradition*? It would be premature to offer an answer at this stage, but we shall argue in due course that different types of feminist hermeneutics invite different answers to this major question.

To come to terms with the feminist argument more fully it is worth recalling the dilemma posed by neo-Marxist hermeneutical theory. Marxists argue that only a *praxis* borne out of the experience of labour, production, and struggle for liberation from oppression can offer an ideological *critique*, because *bourgeois reflection does not provide the categories which are indispensable for the formulation of such a critique*. There is a close conceptual parallel here with feminist socio-critical hermeneutics. Rosemary Radford Ruether declares: "The androcentric bias of the male interpreters of the tradition, who regard maleness as normative humanity, not only erase women's presence in the past history of the community, but silence even the questions about their absence. *One is not even able to remark upon or notice women's absence*, since women's silence and absence is the norm."[126]

If what *counts* as a "norm" has in effect already been determined, what critical principle is still available by which it can be assessed? Rosemary Ruether defines the ideological critique of feminist hermeneutics as "the appeal to *women's experience*. It is precisely women's experience that has been shut out of hermeneutics . . . Women's experience explodes as a critical force, exposing classical theology, including its foundational tradition in scripture, as shaped by male experience rather than human experience."[127] This experience is not defined, however, solely with respect to the contribution of given biological, physiological, or psychological qualities, although these indeed play a positive contributory role. The experience includes *socio-cultural history of the experience of marginalization and "inferiorization"* imposed over generations by male-dominated societies and concomitant roles.

In order to elucidate what is meant by ascribing to "women's experience" the status of a *critical* principle, we must first observe how this principle operates at three different levels.

First, it becomes apparent that the hermeneutical function of biblical interpretation within the feminist movement is *not only to "retrieve" traditions for positive affirmation, but also to make them available as a contributory force for criticism of the present and for transformative action.* This is a major function, for example, of Phyllis Trible's book *Texts of Terror* (1984). This volume "recounts tales of terror *in memoriam* to offer sympathetic readings of abused women . . . It interprets stories of outrage . . . to pray that these terrors shall not come to pass again."[128] Thus is Gen. 16: 1–16 we find Hagar trapped in a circle of bondage. She knows that her unborn child will be a wanderer and a loner (Gen. 16: 11,12). In Gen. 21: 9–21, while God is on Israel's side, "with Hagar the reverse happens. God supports, even orders, her departure to the wilderness, not to free her from bondage, but to protect the inheritance of her oppressors."[129] Hagar's story "depicts oppression in three familiar forms: nationality, class, and sex . . . As a symbol of the oppressed . . . all sorts of rejected women find their stories in her. She is the faithful maid exploited, the black woman used by the male and abused by the female of the ruling class . . . the resident alien without legal recourse . . . the pregnant young woman alone . . . She is bruised for the iniquities of Sarah and Abraham; upon her is the chastisement that makes them whole."[130]

Phyllis Trible continues *Texts of Terror* with other examples: the rape of Tamar, in which Tamar's wise dignity stands in contrast to Amnon's brutal violence (2 Sam. 13: 1–22); an unnamed victim of sexual violence and murder (Judges 19: 1–30); and the daughter of Jepththah (Judges 11: 29–40) whose fate was forgotten by "patriarchal hermeneutics" in the biblical traditions, but in whose death "we are all diminished."[131] The kind of approach taken up in *Texts of Terror* is developed further by Alice L. Laffey in her book *Wives, Harlots, and Concubines: The Old Testament in Feminist Perspective* (1988 and 1990). She attacks both the implied superiority of male gender which she considers to be axiomatic for patriarchal culture which is usually presupposed in the Old Testament and also the stereotypification of women as wives and mothers, or in other "acceptable" roles defined in relation to men. She writes: "The underlying presupposition of feminist interpretation is that women are equal to men. It insists that all texts are to be interpreted by this principle . . . Interpreters have the obligation of unmasking . . . patriarchal bias."[131] Thus the Book of Ruth, she argues for example, is not simply to be read as a story about a woman's tenacity, loyalty, and courage (Ruth 1: 5–14; 2: 1–7,14–18; 4: 7–22) although it includes this. It is also a text which invites the reader to address "a challenge to the presuppositions of the patriarchal culture" which sees the promise of "sons" as the successful narrative closure, but nevertheless grounds the narrative in "woman's experience".

This partial parallel to *concientización* in Latin American liberation theology leads to the kind of understanding of "women's experience" which Rosemary Radford Ruether has identified as a critical hermeneutical principle. It is also worth noting in passing that Phyllis Trible makes extensive and successful use of the hermeneutics of imaginative rapport which is central to Schleiermacher's hermeneutics of understanding. Although in much current literary theory Schleiermacher, Dilthey and Betti are out of favour, we may recall from our chapter on Schleiermacher that he explicitly described this dimension as the "feminine" principle of hermeneutics. But I am not aware of any discussion of Schleiermacher's contribution in feminist hermeneutics.

The conceptual character of "women's experiences" can be explored further by reviewing the origins and development of the *modern* feminist movement both more generally and also more specifically as feminist theology in dialogue with biblical texts. One initial landmark for feminist hermeneutics was the publication of *The Woman's Bible* in 1895 and 1898 by Elizabeth Cady Stanton. It might be said that she broadly anticipated socio-critical hermeneutics, because her motivation for the production of this work sprang from her awareness that biblical texts can be used for the social control and manipulation of women and their social roles. Recently Ruth Page has evaluated her work in an essay reprinted in Ann Loades's *Feminist Theology* (1990). Another landmark was the appearance of Simone de Beauvoir's *The Second Sex* in 1949 (English, 1953), in which she raised questions concerning the relation between *symbolic conceptual* perception and women's *social roles*. She writes: "Humanity is male, and man defines woman not in herself but as relative to him . . . He is the subject . . . She is the Other."[132]

Modern feminism, for a time, perhaps especially in the 1960s, took either of two forms. One form advocated equality and liberation on the grounds of *similarities* between women and men; the other form argued for the same goals on the basis of *differences* between women and men, which demanded female self-expression and recognition as persons. In 1969, Kate Millett's book *Sexual Politics* articulated the widespread view that positions on the ladder of social power-structures were determined by sexual identity rather than by merit. The repressive structure of the patriarchal family unit was held responsible, and psychoanalysis and sociology put forward as *critical unmasking* principles, which therefore facilitated liberation. Germaine Greer's *The Female Eunuch* (1970) argued that the social roles imposed on women by the constraints of the family, education, work, and capitalist market-forces simply had the effect of *reducing* ("castrating") women as persons.

Elaine Marks and Isabelle de Courtivron offer a clear analysis of some major differences between American and French feminism.[133] Anglo-American feminism, they argue, is more empirical, and pragmatic, and focusses on socio-economic and socio-political liberation and equality. French feminism is more rigorously theoretical and radical, and is less concerned with "filling cultural silences" in past traditions. In essence, the heavy influence of post-modernism makes it more iconoclastic. Like Julia Kristeva it even suspects "the dogma" of *feminism*.[134] Marxist-related feminism "loudly proclaims the death of God, the death of man, the death of the privileged work of art."[135] This is because *in everything* up to now "only one sex has been represented . . . language, capitalism, socialism, monotheism . . ."[136] Paradoxically, since French feminists stress "theory" more than Anglo-American counterparts, there is also even a feminist sub-group (Marguerite Duras and others) who argue that "the will to theory is the most pernicious of male activities."[137]

Mary Daly's book *The Church and the Second Sex* (1968) took up Simone de Beauvoire's title in response to some of the documents of the Second Vatican Council. In *spite* of their fundamentally progressive character some documents seemed to address women only as wives, mothers, widows, daughters, or "religious" women; in other words, in terms of roles defined by their relation to men, rather than as persons in their own right. Mary Daly at first tried to work within the Roman Catholic church but became increasingly disillusioned with the church's lack of response. In *Beyond God the Father* (1973) she moves to a *post*-Christian "radical" feminism. She attacks what she perceives as the maleness of the God of the Bible and of the Hebrew-Christian tradition.[138] She takes up the issue which we have noted in French feminism about the social effects of the whole core symbolism of the Christian and Western tradition as lending legitimation to male-orientated culture. As we have also noted, she advocates a post-Christian separatism of "anti-church" and "sisterhood."

Mary Daly and Rosemary Radford Ruether effectively founded the women's caucus within the American Academy of Religion in 1971, from which a series of papers emerged. Phyllis Trible's paper "Depatriarchalizing in Biblical Tradition" appeared in 1973; and Letty Russell edited what she has modestly called a "premature" guide to feminist interpretation of the Bible in 1976 under the title *The Liberating Word*.[139] Here Letty Russell argued that God *transcends* all categories of male and female, and warned against sexual stereotyping.[140] This was followed in 1978 by Phyllis Trible's *God and the Rhetoric of Sexuality*. This begins with hermeneutical questions about re-contextualization of texts within the biblical traditions, and then explores the approach of literary and rhetorical criticism to a number of Old Testament passages. One major conclusion is that in Gen. 1: 26,27, language about the "image of God" refers not to "man" but to a plural humanity: "Humankind is synonymous with the phrase 'male and female' . . . Unity embraces sexual differentiation . . . 'Male and female' gives the clue for interpreting 'the image of God'."[141] The remainder of the argument turns on the validity of exploring "female" imagery in relation to God, especially on the basis of a metaphorical correlation between "womb" (Hebrew *rechem* or *racham*) and "compassion" (Hebrew *racham* or *rach^mim*).[142]

The history of this approach up to the beginning of the 1980s is traced by Dorothy Bass.[143] The 1980s witnessed a flood of studies. The primary sources for feminist hermeneutical theory during this period include: Elizabeth Schüssler Fiorenza's *In Memory of Her* (1983) and *Bread not Stone* (1984); Mary Ann Tolbert's collection *The Bible and Feminist Hermeneutics* (1983); Letty M. Russell's symposium *Feminist Interpretation of the Bible* (1985); Adela Yarbro Collins's collection *Feminist Perspectives in Biblical Scholarship* (1985); and Alice L. Laffey's *Wives, Harlots, and Concubines: The Old Testament in Feminist Perspective* (1988 and 1990). (Details have already been documented.)[144] In addition to essays included in these collections, Rosemary Ruether, Phyllis Trible, and Elizabeth Schüssler Fiorenza have also published individual papers in this area.[145] Ann Loades has collected together twenty-two extracts from feminist writers in her anthology *Feminist Theology* (1990).

It is difficult to know where to draw the boundary of literature relevant to feminist hermeneutics. Certainly within this boundary come works on conceptuality, language, social interaction and symbolic worlds. Here Rebecca S. Chopp has produced a provocative study which seeks to draw on post-structuralist and post-modernist views of language. Her book *The Power to Speak* appeared in 1989.[146] If, as Ursula King urges, "Feminism is about a different consciousness and vision, a radically changed perspective", the whole movement, and not just those who interact with biblical texts or theology, raises profound hermeneutical questions, in the sense that what is at stake is the possibility and validity of a claim to knowledge and a rational (or at least rationally justifiable) basis for action as perceived from within a given contextual horizon and from a given community of interpretation.[147] But here we return to the area of Gadamer, Pannenberg, Ricoeur, Habermas, Apel and Rorty, and to fundamental issues about whether all norms are contextually relative to a specific social history, or whether some larger interactive frame or open system may be deemed to operate for metacritical purposes.

Yet not all feminism would claim to demand such radical new vision. As Ursula King also observes, feminism is not a unitary movement, and consists of many different political and ideological orientations.[148] We may note, for example, the work of two British feminist studies which come from within a more conservative or evangelical framework: Mary Evans's *Women in the Bible* (1983) and Elaine Storkey's *What's Right with Feminism* (1985).

Elaine Storkey traces the roots of feminist tradition to the Reformation. Calvin, she notes, stressed the "companionable aspect" of marriage, in contrast to its function in terms of procreation. The Reformers applied marriage-laws equally to men and women.[149] Evangelical feminism embodies "a commitment to *others* . . ." Christian feminists look beyond *their* rights.[150] Like Phyllis Trible, she sees "humanity" in Gen. 1: 26,27, as "together created in the image of God . . . Together they are told to have dominion . . . and to exercize stewardship."[151] The word "helper" (Gen. 2: 18) is used for God's role in relation to humankind, so in no way implies a secondary role. Jesus does not uphold a male establishment, and offers "no male-dominant model".[152]

Elaine Storkey recognizes that feminism rightly addresses *structural* rather than only individual issues; but she also perceives the potential danger of an incipient "self-righteousness" as feminists accuse and blame external systems (patriarchy, capitalism, class-structure) rather than our common participation as men and women in corporate human fallenness. Christian feminists do not seek "a power struggle". But on the other side they do not wish to be assigned "a slot marked 'woman', and live their lives according to a set of prescribed cultural and essentially non-biblical values."[153] In this respect, Elaine Storkey concludes, liberation "is for men also." Grace delivers *both* women and men from outworn stereotypes.

This very high evaluation of the authority of biblical texts may also cohere with a very radical narrative of "women's experience" as one of oppression. In her moving essay "The Emergence of Black Feminist Consciousness" (1985) Katie Geneva Cannon traces a devastating and appalling history of the experience of Black women amidst abuse, coercion, and exploitation.[154] Yet she concludes: "The Bible is the highest source of authority for most Black women. In its pages Black women have learned how to refute the stereotypes . . . As an interpretative principle, the Black womanist tradition provides the incentive to chip away at oppressive structures . . . The Black womanist identifies with those biblical characters who hold onto life in the face of formidable oppression."[155]

We may sum up this part of our discussions by noting that, in spite of the enormous differences of perspective within feminist theology, feminist hermeneutics may be said to embody the same four basic features as those which Gustavo Gutiérrez identified as fundamental for an understanding of liberation theology. First, *feminist hermeneutics begins with women's experience.* We traced the nature of this in earlier traditions in the context of Phyllis Trible's *Texts of Terror*, but also in terms of secular feminist analysis initiated by such writers as Kate Millett and Germaine Greer, developed in French feminism, and portrayed in theology by such writers as Katie Cannon. A very high-profile general social analysis is offered by Susan Brooks Thistlethwaite, when she asserts: "All women (*sic*) live with male violence . . . A feminist biblical interpretation must have this consciousness at its center . . . It involves claiming self-esteem, taking control, and owning one's anger."[156]

Second, this category of woman's experience, understood in its fullest socio-historical sense, becomes *a critical principle*. In liberation hermeneutics "consciousness-raising" (*concientización*) interacts with the development of socio-critical tools, whether these are drawn from Marx, from Freud, from social theory, or from elsewhere. We shall shortly explore how far feminist hermeneutics becomes socio-*critical* rather than socio-*pragmatic*. The answer is not unitary but is variable, depending on which particular strands of feminism are under investigation.

Third, *biblical texts* may now speak in new ways, once hermeneutical pre-understanding has been informed by the first two steps of the process. We postpone for the present the question of whether the sequence of this process leads to truth or to distortion, although advocates of liberation hermeneutics are quick to point out that the process follows a hermeneutical circle, in which, it is to be hoped, initial "understandings" are revised and corrected. Although, to my knowledge, little attention, if any, has been given to illocutionary force in speech-act theory, the goal is for texts to *liberate*, not to provide reflection about liberation. It is also surprising that relatively little theoretical attention is given in feminist theory to the hermeneutical tradition of Schleiermacher, Dilthey, and Betti. For frequently in feminist interpretations of biblical texts, we encounter the use of empathetic imagination and *rapport*. For example the courage of the Hebrew midwives who feared God but not men becomes an existential self-involving source of courage (Ex. 1: 15–21); Moses's mother and the Pharaoh's daughter resonate as active and successful in the struggle against evil (Ex. 1: 22–2: 10).

The fourth area identified by Gutiérrez is that of *eschatology*. Rosemary Ruether and especially Letty Russell share this liberation perspective. Letty Russell asserts that feminist hermeneutics is not simply about "particular stories about women or particular female images of God. It is found in *God's intention for the mending of all creation* . . . The story of God's love-affair with the world leads me to a *vision of New Creation* that impels my life."[157]

5. The Use of Socio-Critical and Socio-Pragmatic Methods and Epistemologies in Feminist Hermeneutics: Ruether, Fiorenza, Tolbert, and other Writers

Our evaluation of feminist hermeneutics cannot cover more than selected aspects. But two areas entail such a high degree of hermeneutical complexity that no serious hermeneutical study could by-pass them. First, *every* example of socio-critical hermeneutical theory raises questions, not about "subjectivism", but about criticism: do the systems function as *socio-critical* ones *in the sense that they embody some trans-contextual, metacritical, or transcendental principle of critique*, or do they collapse into *socio-pragmatic* hermeneutics which, on the basis only of narrative-experience *within a given context, exclude all interpretative options in advance which would give any other signals than positive ones for the journey already undertaken?* It is important to note that we do not propose to argue that all feminist hermeneutics falls within the pragmatic category. The question in fact exposes distinctions in hermeneutical method between different strands *within* feminism. It is equally important to repeat again that the methodological contrast between socio-critical and socio-pragmatic *is not to be confused with a contrast between "objective" and "subjective"*. This contrast operates at a different level of critique.

This latter point deserves special note because Mary Ann Tolbert tends to move back and forth between those two different sets of contrasts in her attempt to offer a philosophical defence of the authority of feminist hermeneutics. She writes; "The most common objection to a *feminist* reading of a text . . . is that it is *subjective* . . . (But) *all* interpretations are 'subjective' . . . interpretation is always a subjective activity."[158] This is not the issue which we are addressing at this point.

Mary Ann Tolbert appeals to a diversity of interpretation in biblical studies of the kind identified and exemplified by the surveys of Albert Schweitzer on Jesus and on Paul, and to Bultmann's advocacy of the necessity of "pre-understanding" and "pre-supposition". But we examined *these* questions in our two chapters on the *hermeneutics of understanding*. We noted *why* such differences arose, and what were the *tools for this resolution* over a historical period. The questions raised in post-Gadamerian hermeneutics by Apel, Pannenberg, and Habermas, was whether such *hermeneutical* understanding must operate without recourse to some metacritical dimension, or whether Gadamer's "conversation" must simply "proceed" in whatever direction it proceeds. The different answers to this question are what distinguish Apel, Habermas, and Pannenberg, on one side, and Rorty, on the other. The question here is whether any *critical principle* involved by feminist hermeneutics is *trans-contextual* or *external to a given life-world*, and if so, in what sense? Does the community of interpretation accord an ontological or epistemological ultimacy to its own "interests" which preclude their being transcended by any other norm or criterion as a matter of confessional principle? Alternatively, does the community of interpreters settle for the epistemological pessimism which ends with the "recognition" that everyone can only "do what they do"?

We can make some firm progress by identifying a first parting of the paths within feminism. At first sight Mary Daly's "radical feminism" may appear to have cut loose from contextual dependency on a single tradition, since she firmly rejects any notion of the priority or privilege of Christian tradition. But on closer investigation, her own critical principle of "women's experience" and "the community of women" has to be understood in an *exclusive, internal* or *separist* sense. This is in contrast to Rosemary Radford Ruether and to Letty Russell, who both stress the *inclusive* nature of the criterion of woman and women's experiences as part of the wholeness of the new humanity. Letty Russell, we shall see, perceives a principle of "correlation" which offers a trans-contextual perspective.

Rosemary Radford Ruether carefully examines and evaluates Mary Daly's radical post-Christian feminism in her book *Sexism and God-Talk*.[159] She writes concerning Mary Daly's work: "The female utopia cultivates a women's culture . . . Eden can be restored only by subordinating the male to the female . . . The male consort of the Goddess is not her equal . . . but her son-lover."[160] Male objectifying rationality must be subordinated to female intuitive knowledge. Ultimately, Rosemary Ruether points out, Mary Daly promotes a "separatism", in which a culture of rape, war, and genocide typifies "male inhumanity." But such "enemy making" subverts feminism, because in Ruether's judgment "The dehumanization of the other ultimately dehumanizes oneself."[161] Mary Daly's system leaves no room for trans-contextual hermeneutical dialogue which might lead to what Apel calls the "enlargement" of rationality, or what Habermas identifies as critical interaction between life-world and system. Like Rorty, she is locked up inside corporate contextual boundaries within which everything must count as positive signals for the journey already in hand.

Rosemary Ruether elaborates her own universal concerns further in her two essays "Feminist Interpretation" and "The Future of Feminist Theology in the Academy." She firmly asserts that "women's experience" provides a critical hermeneutical key for feminist liberation. But she also declares, "Women cannot just reverse the sin of sexism . . . in a way that diminishes male humanity. Women . . . must search for a continually expanding definition of the inclusive humanity: inclusive of both genders, inclusive of all social groups and races. Any principle . . . that marginalizes one group of persons as less than fully human diminishes us all."[162] We must reject ruling norms, she urges, that simply come from *dominant* groups, and seek a genuine *mutuality*. My Durham colleague, Ann Loades expresses this universal concern succinctly: "The agenda is to get everyone to see that what has passed as 'universal' theology has been partial in its exclusion of women and their insights."[163] Ann Loades also addresses this point elsewhere in her book *Searching for Lost Coins* and in her *Feminist Theology: A Reader* (1990), although in this most recent volume she identifies with the concerns of Mary Daly with less reserve than her critical (as against pragmatic) perspective might lead us to expect.[164]

Letty Russell is no less explicit than Rosemary Ruether on this issue. For her, the "interpretive key" remains the affirmation of the full humanity of "women and all persons seen in the prophetic witness of scripture against injustice and dehumanization."[165] But although Elisabeth Schüssler Fiorenza speaks of "a discipleship of equals", Letty Russell rightly perceives a fundamental difference between herself and Rosemary Ruether on the one hand and Elisabeth Schüssler Fiorenza's ranking of norms and critical principles on the other. Letty Russell sees a "correlation" between the "biblical critical principle" and the "feminist critical principle." Such a correlation allows for something approaching a provisional transcendental principle. If it is more fluid and open to revision than Pannenberg's metacritical open system, and less complex than Habermas's socio-critical theory, it reflects some partial affinity with the "soft" transcendentalism of Apel, when its inclusive vision is combined with its eschatological dimension of new creation. It arguably moves beyond mere contextual social pragmatism, because it shares a proper hermeneutical concern that horizons of life-world and of experience *should be enlarged and transformed in dialogue with biblical texts and promissory language beyond* any experience-centred starting point.

Elisabeth Schüssler Fiorenza's orientation is more complex and ambivalent. She writes, "The locus or place of divine revelation and grace is not the Bible . . . but the *ekklesia* of women and the lives of women who live the 'option for our women selves'."[166] The "women-church" is "the movement of self-identified women and women-identified men in biblical religion . . . Its goal is *not simply the 'full humanity' of women* since humanity as we know it is male defined, but *women's self-affirmation, power,* and liberation from all patriarchal alienation, marginalization, and oppression."[167] Elisabeth Schüssler Fiorenza sees her community of interpretation as one which is fully committed to a very particular agenda, as her specific allusions to the political left and right indicate.

It is tempting to assume that Elisabeth Schüssler Fiorenza's subsequent comments in the essay to which we allude firmly place her hermeneutics into the category of contextual pragmatism. She gives her community "authority 'to choose and to reject' biblical texts", thereby filtering out any signals which do not promote the direction of the journey already undertaken.[168] If we ask why we should use the Bible at all, this is because "women . . . testify to a liberating experience with the Bible . . . All texts must be tested as to this feminist liberating content."[169] This looks like a pragmatic rejection of any trans-contextual meta-criterion. Feminist interpretations of the Bible, Fiorenza urges, cannot do other than operate with what amount to *internal* norms within feminist life-worlds or systems, because the Bible itself is already irremediably *selective*. It is "authored by men, written in androcentric language, reflective of male experience, selected and transmitted by male religious leadership. Without question the Bible is a male book."[170] Therefore, Fiorenza concludes, the biblical writings cannot provide a transcontextual critical principle; the needed critical dimension emerges from the experience of women. What guides the *interest* of interpretation tends to be that which retrieves women's experience and corporately affirms women readers.

Nevertheless to stop here would be too simple. Elisabeth Schüssler Fiorenza adds two crucial qualifications or caveats which distinguish her approach from straightforward socio-pragmatic relativism. First, even though the struggle of women for liberation and justice places conflict at "its hermeneutical centre", nevertheless "women's liberation struggle ... does not mean to advocate a separatist strategy".[171] The reason for Fiorenza's caution over the more universalist approach of Rosemary Ruether or the earlier work of Ann Loades is a fear that this universal critical principle might mean, at worst, "the integration of women into patriarchal ecclesial structures" in which traditions remained unchanged in substance, rather than inviting a full-blooded *"transformation of Christian symbols, traditions, and community"*[172] (her italics).

The second important caveat or qualification arises from Fiorenza's detailed work on the historical reconstruction of the life-worlds which lie behind some New Testament texts and texts of the Patristic era. To place feminist biblical interpretation at the bar of accepted norms of evaluation common to various strands in biblical scholarship is at once to move out of the socio-pragmatic ghetto, especially when a wider hermeneutic of suspicion also embraces *all* interpretative models. In principle this approach places the work of Fiorenza within the category of feminism warmly advocated by Janet Radcliffe Richards, in contrast to those types of feminists which claim that "reason" and "critical theory" remain male-generated or male-exclusive areas. In one of the strongest and most important contemporary discussions of feminism Janet Radcliffe Richards urges that whereas the latter type of feminism presses the claims of *a particular social group, namely women*, the other urges the pleas of the *universal principle of justice* even if it may do so with understandable but not exclusive attention to *a particular social group, namely women*. She observes: "Feminism is not concerned with a *group of people it wants to benefit*, but with a *type of injustice it wants to eliminate*"[173] (her italics). *Nothing could more clearly serve to distinguish socio-critical theory and practices from socio-pragmatic theory and practice.*

In her book *The Sceptical Feminist* (1980) Janet Radcliffe Richards singles out for special attack those feminists who reject the "universals" of rationality, argument, and critical theory. The notion, she urges, that to compete at the bar of reason with men is thereby to sell out to the domination of men in disguised form is the most insidious and self-destructive move that feminists can make, for it brings in by the back door the very self-image identified by

Simone de Beauvoir as "lacking a sense of the universal". It allows men sociologically to monopolize the rational, and yields to the questionable psychological hypothesis that women are "feelers" *rather than* "thinkers". Janet Radcliffe Richards sees feminism not as serving "a community of women", but as rectifying social injustices to women. The way forward, she urges, is to engage in socio-critical argument. Otherwise the oppressed use the tools of the opposition, namely those of pragmatic pressure, privilege, political rhetoric, and social manipulation. They use the enemy's tools and thereby revert back to a new kind of bondage and oppression, perhaps with different victims.

In this respect Fiorenza's appeal to historical biblical interpretation seems at first sight to place her firmly in the area of socio-critical enquiry, in spite of earlier apparent evidences to the contrary. But the empirical outworking of her supposedly open-handed historical approach is often deeply disappointing in the extent to which *she allows her own social and hermeneutical interest to determine not simply the weighting* of probability that a given historical hypothesis receives, but *even the very selection of hypotheses which are presented for serious consideration and evaluation*. Admittedly most biblical scholars find it difficult to escape some colouring of judgment projected by their own loyalties and hopes. John Barclay has recently offered a valid warning against "mirror reading" whereby one is tempted "to dress up Paul's opponents with the clothes of one's own theological foes".[174] But, as I have argued in my essay "The Morality of Christian Scholarship", *impartiality* differs from *neutrality*. A referee or a professional scholar is not expected to have neutral hopes about the outcome of an argument. But the one (perhaps the only) strength of traditional academic liberalism was the expectation that a referee or professional scholar *would with integrity apply the same rules of play to the opposition* as to the home side, even if the outcome was painful, uncomfortable, or disappointed one's hopes.[174a]

Admittedly liberalism has been supplanted and made obsolete in hermeneutics by the recognition that if much scholarly discourse in actuality already operates with "rules" laid down by the established or dominant tradition, playing by the rules does not always guarantee the impartial procedure supposed by liberals to be the case. *Reason operates within a tradition.* But much of the debate in this volume, especially with reference to Wittgenstein, to post-modernism, and to socio-critical and speech-act theory turns on whether this hermeneutical recognition actually invalidates the notion of trans-contextual "rules" of rational discourse; whether *all* system, even *open* system, dissolves into the context-relative contingencies of life-worlds; whether what counts as "mistakes" in language and argument can *never* be systematic but *always* exclusively relative to a given life-world.

In broad principle Elisabeth Schüssler Fiorenza's historical work on the New Testament accords with the norms generally accepted by biblical and historical specialists, rather than with narrower criteria internal to her social interests. But as we proceed to examine a series of concrete examples, a sense of unease about the even-handedness of this historical and exegetical work emerges. It is not simply that some scholars would offer a different weighting of *evaluation* to certain arguments; this could be accounted for by the distinctive perceptions which arise from different social traditions. A more serious problem concerns the *clearly selective discussions of different explanatory hypotheses which might account for the same textual and historical data.* An analogy may be suggested. In a review of the work of the conservative New Testament scholar Donald Guthrie, Stephen S. Smalley has observed that Guthrie always scrupulously brings to the attention of readers every face of the dice, but in the end readers can readily and unfailingly predict on what face the dice will eventually fall. But in the case of some examples from Fiorenza's work, the reader can not only predict the fall of the dice; those faces of the dice which might militate against the social interest of the main argument are not always identified or described. But such a method calls into question, at least at some decisive points, the genuinely socio-critical, rather than pragmatic, status of this work. The task of holding together a hermeneutic which is explicitly aggressive, namely a *hermeneutic of conflict* with genuine hermeneutical *openness* (of the kind advocated by Betti and Gadamer) imposes on the author herself an exceedingly demanding and perhaps impossible task.

One of the most striking examples arises from Fiorenza's handling of the different biblical narrative-traditions of the resurrection appearances of Jesus to the women. In her book *In Memory of Her*, Fiorenza attempts to develop the thesis put forward earlier in *Women of Spirit* that Luke "attempts to play down the role of women as proclaimers of the Easter kerygma by stressing 'that the words of the women seemed to the eleven an idle tale, and they did not believe them' (Luke 24:11)."[175] In her more extensive treatment, Fiorenza drives a wedge between the positive affirmation of women found both in Matthew and especially in John, and an allegedly negative and suppressive anti-feminist stance in the pre-Pauline tradition, in Paul, in Mark 16:1-8, and in Luke 24:1-11. In the Johannine tradition, Fiorenza writes, Mary Magdalene "becomes the *apostola apostolorum*, the apostle of the apostles. She calls Peter and the Beloved Disciple to the empty tomb.... In contrast to Mark 16:8 we are unambiguously told that Mary Magdalene went to the disciples and announced to them 'I have seen the Lord'."[176] In John, Jesus calls Mary by name (John 20:1-18; cf. 10:3,4). Mary Magdalene, Mary of Nazareth, the Samaritan woman, Martha, and Mary of Bethany become for John and his community "paradigms of apostolic discipleship" with "leadership in the Johannine communities".[177]

Fiorenza argues that "whereas Matthew, John, and the Markan appendix credit primacy of apostolic witness to Mary Magdalene, the Jewish Christian pre-Pauline confession in 1 Cor. 15:3–6 and Luke claim that the resurrected Lord appeared first to Peter. . . . The tradition of Mary Magdalene's primacy in apostolic witness challenged the Petrine tradition."[178] But if some texts stress the role of the women, while the others do not, what is the reason for this? Fiorenza is interested (*sic*) in pursuing only one set of questions: what gender-related evaluations of the status of women serve to address this problem? She does not seriously ask whether some other question might equally well, or perhaps more convincingly invite an alternative explanation for the same data, because such questions are not a major part of her agenda. But this weakens the credibility of her hypotheses as genuinely critical constructions.

One such alternative explanatory hypothesis was offered by Walter Künneth in his specialist treatise on the resurrection. Künneth wrote before the rise of feminist theology, and therefore in no way offers his work as a counter-response to feminist claims. His work in some respects anticipates that of Moltmann. For Künneth the central issue in the accounts of the resurrection appearances is that of *continuity of identity in the context of transformation and change*. It is correct to perceive this as the theological nerve-centre of New Testament theologies of resurrection. The entity whom God raises will assume a transformed mode of existence; but remains the very same entity as that which died (1 Cor. 15:35–44). Paul offers the analogy of the transformation of a seed into a transformed mode of existence as part of a harvest; or as a fruit or flower; but continuity of identity is also preserved. "What you saw is not the body which is to be . . . God gives it a body . . . to each kind of seed its own body" (1 Cor. 15:37). The role of the resurrection appearances also functions first of all to establish *continuity of identity* between the crucified Jesus and the transformed, exalted, Lord Christ. The importance of this continuity of identity as central to the kerygma has been stressed by James Dunn, by W. Pannenberg, and by numerous writers on this subject.

If the Christian kerygma, however, announces that the new humanity shares in this resurrection, continuity-contrast-transformation, we need not be surprised if the earliest texts also trace this same pattern of transformation and continuity in the experience of the earliest witnesses who proclaim it. This is precisely Künneth's point. *Peter denied Jesus*, and in his failure shared in the apparent "failure" of the cross; in and through the resurrection he was re-commissioned to the apostolic task as one who shared in fellowship with the Risen One after coming to the end of himself and his own strength, in need of resurrection. Künneth writes: "The second factor which illuminates the meaning of the appearances lies in the restoration of relations of fellowship between the Risen One and the disciples, and, *bound up with that* [my italics] in *the founding of the apostolate*" (Künneth's italics).¹⁷⁹ This is *one* reason Peter, who denied Jesus, "the twelve", who forsook him and fled, and Paul who persecuted him, occupy a special role as witness of the resurrection and of resurrection salvation in I Cor. 15:3–6. *Apostleship entails both weakness and suffering, and resurrection*. It is also, in Künneth's words, bound up with *the restoration of a broken relationship*.

Fiorenza has the raw material explicitly to hand to consider this hypothesis. For, ironically, she stresses again and again that while all of the texts point up the repeated *failures* of the men, the *women remain models of unfailing discipleship*. Yet she does not even consider the *possibility* that for the evangelists and for Paul to be a witness of the resurrection has something to do *with the birth of hope out of despair, as Moltmann also urges*. Fiorenza is committed to find *explanations which depend wholly on gender-differences*. But is this the issue in those traditions which stress the role and experience of Peter, the twelve, and Paul? Further, the Lukan verse on which Fiorenza places so much weight for an allegedly anti-feminist perspective ("these words seemed to them an idle tale and they did not believe them", Luke 24:11) is read by most specialists (and probably by most ordinary readers) as a rebuke to the unbelief of the *male* disciples. All of the women in my classes judged that the verse should be read in this way: the failure of the men is consistent with earlier accounts of their other failures.

Other alternative hypotheses might also have been considered. Willi Marxsen tries to argue (to my mind unconvincingly) that the kind of "seeing" to which 1 Cor. 15:3–8 alludes is of a different order from that of the encounters with Mary Magdalene. Marxsen speculates that the Mary narrative has behind it "a defence of the empty tomb" whereas supposedly "Paul is not here offering anything in the nature of factual evidence for the resurrection".¹⁸⁰ Contrary to Fiorenza, Marxsen sees the *Johannine* account as interrupting the Mary narrative in the interests of the primacy of Peter and of John, although I cannot find a reference to Marxsen in Fiorenza's thinly documented discussion. Ernest Best offers a constructive hypothesis concerning the difficulty of Mark 16:8 ("they fled from the tomb ... they said nothing to anyone"). His work appeared in 1983, and therefore could not have been used by Fiorenza. Best comments: "Mark turns thought on the resurrection away from the idea of a number of isolated and discrete appearances which Jesus made ... He can be present at all times with all who believe in him".¹⁸¹ Best therefore concludes that this passage *does not address social issues about gender*: "Mark does not appear to be feminist or anti-feminist".¹⁸²

None of these arguments has been presented as a means of devaluing or attacking Fiorenza's *final conclusions as such* (unless they do so incidentally). *The issue at stake is one of hermeneutical theory and method: does not the selectivity* of a small segment of gender-related explanatory hypotheses for historical or textual data erode claims to offer a genuinely critical rather than pragmatic-orientated enquiry, in which social interest takes precedence over hermeneutical openness and forecloses certain possibilities before they are examined? It would be no defence of such an approach to try to argue that *every* exegete in biblical interpretation does the same thing. Professional scholars evaluate one another's work partly in terms of evidence of judiciousness in giving due weight to a variety of alternative hypotheses, provided that these can claim genuine intellectual seriousness. Although empirical traditions of enquiry embody acknowledged weaknesses, there is some value in what is implied by the principle of falsification, namely: what kind of data or argument could count as evidence *against* the theory that is being advocated? Only when this question has been asked and answered, does the theory itself gain credible currency.

At the socio-pragmatic level it may well be the case that Fiorenza's work comes into its own as a way of calling attention to elements of tradition and memory that need to be retrieved and re-affirmed. Thus, even if the evidence for anti-feminist *Tendenz* in Mark, Luke, and the pre-Pauline tradition remains indecisive, Fiorenza's work points up the role of the women as the first witnesses to the resurrection appearances in Matthew and in John. Some of Fiorenza's work remains invaluable in setting the record straight; other aspects are more speculative and less firmly grounded in critical enquiry than she seems to concede; a third category performs a useful pragmatic function of affirming values which serve the needs of a particular hermeneutical situation and community, and in this way also serve the wider community.

This last aspect receives positive evaluation and theological approval as part of what amounts to a socio-pragmatic theology of community in Robert Morgan's recent essay "Feminist Theological Interpretation of the New Testament" published in *After Eve* (1990) under the editorship of Janet Martin Soskice. Morgan describes Fiorenza as the one feminist New Testament specialist who has made a major contribution. But he perceives the greatest value of her work to lie in offering *possibilities* "to neutralize dangerous texts by suggesting a less offensive but equally plausible exegesis".[183] He admits that "this sounds corrupt", but defends the pragmatic principle on the ground that sometimes "one exegesis looks as good as another".[184] Morgan also disarmingly concedes that his positive evaluation of Fiorenza's work arises more from its socio-theological or socio-pragmatic function than from its credentials as historical exegesis. He cites the example of her treatment of the obscure verse "a woman ought to have a (?) (Greek *exousia*, usually authority; R.S.V. veil) on her head because of the angels" (1 Cor. 11:10). He comments: "Nobody for sure knows what the phrase means, and Fiorenza is justified in choosing a plausible suggestion that happens to be more positive about women . . ."[185]

As an exercize in the affirmation of woman's history therefore Fiorenza's work successfully fulfils the socio-pragmatic aspects of the hermeneutical agenda. She is also justified in pointing out that some widely revered names in New Testament studies have undertaken historical enquiry under the motivation of a given theological or social interest or *Tendenz*. Rudolf Bultmann's particular philosophical and theological attitude towards history and faith did not hinder him from undertaking historical enquiry. But whether such an example actually inspires confidence is another matter. Bultmann's theological distaste for the objective clearly had some influence on his formulation of historical criteria. In a parallel way Fiorenza's debt to socio-pragmatic interest determines a direction and selectivity in her procedures of historical enquiry which causes it to slide at times between the pragmatic and the critically open.

This is confirmed by Fiorenza's own model of a "hermeneutic of remembrance".[186] At one level she constructively retrieves a lost tradition of the corporate memory of "struggles and victories of biblical women".[187] The purpose of such remembrance is to break "the hold of androcentric biblical texts over us".[188] To *complement* dominant traditions by recovering lost and neglected traditions to seek a trans-contextual wholeness which coheres with the goal of interpretation identified by Fiorenza in her Presidential address to the Society of Biblical Literature in 1987. This entailed a "global discourse seeking justice and well-being for all".[189] But there is also another side to this feminist hermeneutic of remembrance. It is pointedly a hermeneutic of *conflict*. Fiorenza cannot share, we noted, Rosemary Ruether's langauge about wholeness and universality lest this encourages re-introducing through the back door "the integration of women into patriarchal ecclesial structures".[190] Her goal is, rather, that of the *"transformation of Christian symbols, traditions, and community"*.[191]

This raises two distinct sets of conceptual issues. First, to what extent can a given tradition undergo transformation before it ceases to be *this* tradition, and from where do we derive norms appropriate to answer this question? This marks an area of debate not only between pragmatic and critical theory, but also sometimes between Christian feminism and so-called post-Christian feminism. On one side, it can achieve no more than a Pyrrhic victory to move boundaries if thereby genuine continuity of corporate identity is lost. On the other side, if a living corporate entity grows and develops, its contours will inevitably undergo degrees of transformation and invite re-definition. Second, does the "transformation" of which Fiorenza speaks come into being by imposing one community's values upon another in a hermeneutic of conflict, or by progress towards a universal commitment to a transcendental critique of justice and of the cross which speaks from beyond given context-bound communities in a hermeneutic of openness? The admitted danger of the latter model is that corporate self-deception can render interpretation insipid, bland, and inept, and unwittingly dissolve into the acceptance of some dominant tradition. On the other hand the danger of the former model is to reduce texts to merely instrumental devices which serve to provide pragmatic support for values and traditions already affirmed and espoused *prior to* engagement with the texts.

Here, once again, the self-contradictory nature of *socio-pragmatic* liberation theology comes to view: *the oppressed take up the tools of the oppressors.* Without a genuinely socio-critical hermeneutic, pragmatism merely changes the identity of the oppressed and of the oppressors, who continue to use instruments of selectivity, privilege, and manipulation even if in new and different ways. By contrast, openness to the critique of the cross, or to some trans-contextual correlation between open system and contingent life-world may serve to transform *all* horizons centred on the self to embrace greater and wider reality. Genuine *liberation* de-centres both the individual and corporate self; we explicitly explore this issue in chapter XVI. Meanwhile, we may note Susanne Heine's comment in her book *Women and Early Christianity* (1986) that "A position which refuses to adopt a critical detachment . . . sets one possible experience over against another possible experience."[192] Conflict is thus affirmed by socio-pragmatic method. Oppression is re-defined for different personnel, but not in principle ended. Susanne Heine's two volumes, *Women and Early Christianity* and its sequel *Christianity and the Goddesses* (Ger. 1987, Eng. 1988) represent a distinctive and positive evaluation of theological feminist concerns. But they offer a critique of current feminism and constitute a devastating attack on feminist uses of socio-pragmatic theory. She speaks of her own "degree of scorn . . . indeed sometimes of anger" concerning the supposedly "assured results of feminist scholarship. She sees social-pragmatism as a betrayal of the feminist case and calls for a different kind of theological feminism. We shall return to her work shortly.

Mary Ann Tolbert nevertheless attempts a defence of the kind of epistemology associated with socio-pragmatic theory and with Rorty as a defence of feminist hermeneutical theory. She firmly rejects the possibility of metacritical evaluation. We earlier noted her disclaimer to the effect that since *all* interpretations are "subjective", we cannot accuse feminist hermeneutics of any greater degree of subjectivism. We tried to disentangle questions about objectivity and subjectivity in acts and processes of interpretation from metacritical questions about what might be said to *count as* objectivity or subjectivity.

Nevertheless, after beginning with a rejection of the validity or relevance of the subject-objective distinction, Mary Ann Tolbert proceeds to unfold an argument which is closely parallel to that of Rorty. She does not recite the same philosophical narrative-accounts of Peirce, Dewey, and Wittgenstein. But on other grounds she accepts similar consequences for the status of epistemology, reason, and rationality, as those which Rorty traces. Reason is the functional tool by which a community advocates its rhetoric. Mary Ann Tolbert writes: "To admit that all scholarship is advocacy is not.. to chart new ground and invite anarchy. It is only to admit honestly what the case has been and still is. The criteria of public evidence, logical argument, reasonable hypotheses, and intellectual sophistication still adjudicate acceptable and unacceptable positions. Yet these criteria themselves raise additional problems. The 'public' who determine what is reasonable, who form a 'consensus view' are special interest groups with different canons of validity . . . No value-neutral position exists or ever has."[193]

We discuss in detail elsewhere (especially in connection with Rorty and with Fish) the dubious status of the notion that "reasonableness" is no more than a social construct. We have noted that Kuhn radically modified his initial language about the social context of scientific knowledge, and have begun to trace the consequences of failing to qualify a sociology-of-knowledge approach by other equally important considerations. These issues are expanded in chapters XIV and XV. It would be a tragedy, and a betrayal of feminist hermeneutics, to stake the ethical and rational defence of feminist hermeneutical theory on the broken reed of socio-pragmatic epistemology. We cannot even argue credibly that a sensitive social and socio-contextual awareness inevitably demands social pragmatism; for Apel and especially Habermas consciously formulate a *hermeneutic of social critique and liberation* which is designed precisely to ground social criticism and interpretation not in pragmatic relativism but in a wider theory of rationality and of reality. In chapter XI we observed that the most severe criticisms of Rorty's contextual relativism came not simply from white, male, scholars, but on the grounds of its social ineptitude from the black Afro-American thinker Cornel West; on the grounds of its irrationality from the woman writer Georgia Warnke; and on the grounds of a shallow innocence about a supposed choice between objectivism and relativism from Richard Bernstein and from Christopher Norris. These criticisms raise questions about the supposedly critical status of narrative experience, whether communal or individual, and we shall re-consider their force as against the socio-pragmatic claims of Stanley Fish, in chapter XIV.

As Norris points out, the very challenge of Rorty and Fish about the apparent "rightness" of our own community's story and corporate experience can be turned onto its head: why should "our" community experience *as such* claim any critical status as over against that of others? The potentially transforming effect of engagement with the "other" not least through biblical texts is to de-centre our pre-occupation with our own criteria of relevance by enlarging our horizons to embrace a wider understanding. Historically hermeneutics emerged as a critical discipline precisely to deliver and to free communities from being brow-beaten and placed under socio-political pressure by purely *instrumental* appeals to biblical texts *as supports for some prior interest*. Predominantly pragmatic uses of biblical texts have the status of exercizes in self-justification and potential manipulation, whether we are considering a dominant social tradition or a social minority, women or men, pietists or sceptics. Liberation hermeneutics cannot *liberate anyone* if it uses the oppressor's weapons.

6. Further Complexities in Feminist Hermeneutics: Parallels between Demythologizing and Depatriarchalizing

We now need to identify a second area of complexity which has less to do with hermeneutics as a theory of knowledge or understanding but more to do with hermeneutics as a programme of radical *re-interpretation*. Proposals have been made for various methods or programmes of *depatriarchalizing* the biblical texts. It is clear that this is essentially a *hermeneutical* issue, not least because of the obvious parallels with Bultmann's proposals for *demythologizing* biblical material and Latin American or neo-Marxist proposals about *de-ideologizing* the biblical texts. Since in *The Two Horizons* I devoted nearly a hundred pages to Bultmann and to a critique of his proposals, I hope that there is no need to retrace this ground other than in broad outline.[194] Three components in Bultmann's proposals and programme run closely parallel to some feminist programmes of *"depatriarchalizing"* the biblical texts. The clearest examples of parallels can be seen in Phyllis Trible's now classic study *God and the Rhetoric of Sexuality* (1978), which was one of the earliest pioneering studies of feminist hermeneutics. We may identify the following parallels.

(1) Bultmann has been at pains to argue that his proposals do not constitute an attempt to impose an alien philosophical frame or content onto the texts of the New Testament. He insisted that the biblical texts themselves *invited* such demythologizing.[195] This was the case, in his view, first because the New Testament presented an existential summons, to decision, whereas this kerygmatic thrust was masked by a pseudo-descriptive linguistic form or mythological vehicle. It appeared as if texts were asserting *objective* states of affairs about the world, when supposedly they were not. Phyllis Trible offers a parallel distinction between the two language-functions which interact in biblical images or metaphors. Drawing on the terminology of I.A. Richards (1936) she distinguishes between the *vehicle* of a metaphor (which is parallel

The Hermeneutics of Liberation

to Bultmann's notion of linguistic *form* or *myth*) and its *tenor* or thrust (which is equivalent to Bultmann's notion of *kerygma*).[196] Both writers believe that a virtually disposable or translatable linguistic *form* is *intended to serve, but can sometimes obscure, the thrust, purpose, or "point"* of a biblical text. *Male imagery in language about God provides a case-study.*

(2) Bultmann believes that hints of already demythologized language appear in some texts. The interpreter can discern tensions between different linguistic forms or imagery in the texts, and such tensions or "contradictions" invite translation into coherent discourse. Phyllis Trible detects, as a parallel, "hermeneutical clues" which reveal already-depatriarchalized imagery: God is portrayed by the use of a simile as like a pregnant woman (Isa. 42: 14); as like a mother (Isa. 66: 13); as like a midwife (Ps. 22: 9); and as like a mistress (Ps. 123: 2).[197] Phyllis Trible carefully speaks here of "semantic correspondence" rightly avoiding arguments from "etymology" in the light of James Barr's strictures in his book *The Semantics of Biblical Language*. She finds "semantic correspondence" between God's *compassion* (the *tenor*, *rachamim*), and the female *womb* (the *vehicle*, *rechem*).[198]

(3) In Bultmann's view the biblical writings reflect an outdated cosmology or mythological world-view. But this constitutes a "stumbling block" (*skandalon*) for the modern world. According to Paul (1 Cor. 1:18–23; 2:2) the *only skandalon* should be that of the cross. Bultmann's clear recognition that the gospel *is* a stumbling-block excludes the notion that Bultmann is simply a "liberal". He *explicitly rejects* "trimming the traditional Biblical texts" simply to make everything "more acceptable" as the *mistaken* way of *"liberalism"*.[199] His own main aim is *to remove a false framework which unnecessarily obscures the true message*. For many Feminist readers, *the supposedly geocentric cosmology of the Bible* provides a close parallel, especially in terms of its irrelevance to the biblical message, to *the supposedly androcentric sociology of the Bible*, which is deemed to be equally "not the point".

Phyllis Trible herself is more cautious about this large issue than many later writers. She is more concerned with the positive task of "searching for lost coins", a metaphor which Ann Loades later took up as a title for her earlier book on feminism.[200] But just as Bultmann urges not the "trimming down" of awkward texts in the manner of classical liberal theology, so many feminist interpreters see hermeneutics not as smoothing away difficult texts here and there, but as perceiving male-related or androcentric imagery or sociology as part of a dispensable stage-setting which is optional for the play. It is an unthought-through presupposition, not an assertion or statement. It is more akin to the method of projection used in an ancient map, rather than the content of what the map declares.

Such a programme of depatriarchalization embraces many of the strengths and weaknesses of Bultmann's programme of demythologization.

(1) First, as the early and later Wittgenstein and Gilbert Ryle often observed, the surface-appearances of language may put us on the wrong track; it may direct attention to the wrong thing. Wittgenstein reminds us that price-rises in butter cannot be understood as "an activity of butter". Bultmann worries that language about the Son of Man's "coming on the clouds" or the Lord's "descending from heaven with a cry" (1 Thess. 4:16) will direct attention to clouds and to skies rather than to divine vindication. Phyllis Trible sees male and female imagery as metaphorical *vehicles* for a *tenor* which these vehicles convey. *Male* imagery in language for God may unwittingly obscure the tenor for some readers, and direct attention to the wrong thing. For some women readers, she urges, *female* imagery needs to be underlined as a way of liberating them from being trapped and offended by the androcentric imagery which is used elsewhere.

Rudolf Bultmann and Phyllis Trible perform a constructive hermeneutical service in focusing questions about "the point" of a stretch of language to which we should direct primary attention. A difficulty, however, arises from the theory of language which both seem to presuppose. Bultmann pays grossly inadequate attention to the multi-functional nature of langauge: he is trapped within a Kierkegaardian either/or about descriptive and volitional utterances. But in 1941, when Bultmann wrote his classic essay, and in 1936, when I.A. Richards formulated the theory of metaphor on which Phyllis Trible heavily depends, it was customary to operate with a linguistic polarity between cognitive and emotive discourse. This was the era of the Vienna Circle, of A.J. Ayer's move towards logical positivism, and of polarizations in literary theory between fact-stating language and the expressive creativity of poetry and metaphor. Later theories of metaphor, such as that of Max Black, saw that cognitive truth could not always be disentangled from metaphor, and the "vehicle" merely discarded as dispensable or separable from the "tenor". Ricoeur's development of interactive theory, research on the status of cognitive models in the philosophy of science, and the recent work of Janet Martin Soskice underlines this point for issues about biblical language.

In post-Wittgensteinian and post-Gadamerian theory, language is not a container which has a separable identity from its content. Concepts, for Wittgenstein, reflect regularities of language-use; they are patterned *uses* of language. Wittgenstein observes, "Thinking is not an incorporeal process . . . which it would be possible to detach from speaking" rather as if one may detach a person's shadow.[201] In this respect, as we shall consider further in more detail, the line of thought suggested by I.A. Richards's theory of metaphor in terms as contrast between *vehicle* and *tenor* may not have been altogether helpful to the argument.

(2) The second area of difficulty concerns, what, in Bultmann's case, John Macquarrie has called (in the title of his book on this subject) "the scope of demythologizing".[202] Bultmann, we noted, rejects the path of

liberalism and of so-called theological modernism whereby biblical texts are trimmed down to accommodate them to the sensitivities of modern humanity. Instead, like Fiorenza, he calls for a transformation of the whole symbolic system. *Whatever* appears to constitute cosmological or quasi-objectifying language *must* be translated into existential challenge and address. But his "right-wing" critics, including John Macquarrie, Helmut Thielicke, and David Cairns, argue that he does not offer norms or criteria by which language about the resurrection of Christ, judgment, and the work of the Holy Spirit are included as signifying simply existential possibilities; while his "left-wing" critics, including Schubert Ogden, Karl Jaspers, and Herbert Braun complain equally that no rational norm exists according to which "God" should be regarded as more than a functional linguistic cipher, useful for expressing a sense of human finitude or gratitude for existence.[203]

In the same way, it is not entirely clear by what criterion, if any, we are to evaluate the status of supposedly androcentric imagery in relation to theological and ontological truth-claims. It is clear from the work of Phyllis Trible and from other Old Testament specialists that since both male and female *co-jointly* reflect and bear the image of God, any male or female imagery cannot function in a gender-exclusive way without violating what is claimed in biblical texts about the divine image. But claims of the so-called "radical" (now often "post-Christian") feminists, including most notably Mary Daly's earlier response to Phyllis Trible, are analogous to the claims of Bultmann's "left-wing" critics. Once we start on the road, why not go the whole way, and transpose the entire symbolic system into something different? Is not the whole system a "vehicle" which takes different forms and shapes, to be assessed by purely functional criteria? Such a move inevitably provokes the "right-wing" critics into re-affirming the absence of criteria for calling a halt as we descend the slope.

(3) The status of supposed evidence for internal processes of demythologizing or of depatriarchalizing already within the texts also remains ambivalent. Bultmann cannot have it both ways. *Either* myth, like dreams and symbols, arises from pre-critical imagery which precedes conscious judgment; *or* biblical writers use what Brevard Childs helpfully termed "broken myth" and were critically aware of the metaphorical status of their language. In the former case, examples of deliberate "demythologizing" in Paul and in John presupposes a level of critical consciousness that makes claims about raw myth unconvincing. In the latter case, the use of particular imagery against a socio-historical background that allowed, and provided for, choice, suggests that some conscious function, beyond mere historical conditioning, should be taken into account. Does language about "sunrise" *really* presuppose a geocentric world-view? Conversely, does langauge about divine judgment constitute *only* a call to responsibility?

The parallel issue is whether dominant gender-related imagery in biblical language about God represents no more than a socially pre-determined vehicle in relation to which complementary gender-related images signal conscious reflection; or whether it is impossible to assess where uncritical symbolic worlds become raised to the level of critical awareness, and therefore language-choice.

Elizabeth Achtemeier has put forward a case for the view that male or female imagery for divine presence and activity affirms a given theological perspective which is consciously chosen. In her carefully-argued essay "Female Language For God" (1986) *she urges that gender-related imagery cannot and should not be evaluated solely in pragmatic terms, as an optional vehicle which sets up favourable resonances for readers.*[204] The *concept* of God, not in the sense of human processes of conceptualization, but in the sense of *ontological identity and relation to the world* is bound up, she argues, with such imagery.

Elizabeth Achtemeier sees the issue as turning on a *theological* contrast between the transcendent God of prophetic revelation, and an unduly *immanental* notion of God as a presence which animates earth and nature. She writes: "It is not that the prophets *could not* imagine God as female; they were surrounded by peoples who so imagined their deities. It is rather that the prophets, as well as the Deuteronomists and Priestly writers and Jesus and Paul *would not* use such language because they had ample evidence from the religions surrounding them that female language for the deity results in a basic distortion of the nature of God and of his relation to his creation."[205]

This essay assumes a polemical vein, arguing that "feminist theologies themselves" substantiate such a claim. Thus Elizabeth Achtemeier quotes Dorothee Soelle's own appraisal of the story of the fall as "liberation": "Let us praise Eve . . . Without her curiosity we would not know what knowledge was."[206] Here she finds an example of immanentalism without an adequate theology of the fall and sin. She traces nature-immanentalism similarly in Rosemary Radford Ruether's *Sexism and God-Talk*. In this volume Rosemary Ruether speaks of "the root of the human image of the divine as the Primal Matrix, the great womb within which all things, Gods and humans, sky and earth, human and nonhuman beings are generated" (*sic*). On the last page of her book she celebrates "She in whom we live and move and have our being."[207] Elizabeth Achtemeier could also have cited, if she had wished, passages from *In Memory of Her*. Elisabeth Schüssler Fiorenza contrasts the prophetic and wisdom traditions. Wisdom was willing, unlike the prophets, "to integrate elements of . . . 'goddess cult', especially of Isis worship, into monotheism . . . They call on the goddess, doing so because they know that Isis, being *one*, is *all*" (first italics, Fiorenza's; second, mine).[208] Fiorenza's "retrieval" of tradition in *gnostic* writings and in *Montanism* also appears, in this light, a double-edged argument.

Susanne Heine writes on this subject with a wealth of research and meticulous argument which ranges from highly informed evaluations of Ugaritic, Canaanite, and gnostic myths to modern sociology of knowledge. She is deeply grieved and angered by *the unintended betrayal of feminism* by "the sisters who nevertheless have very much the same intentions as I do".[209] A considerable body of re-constructed feminist history of religions, she argues, cannot stand at the bar of genuinely scientific enquiry, and she views the sell-out to social pragmatism "with a degree of scorn, and indeed sometimes with anger" as a betrayal.[210] Issues about goddess-language, matriarchy, and depatriarchalizing receive very careful and rigorous evaluation. She argues with a high degree of complexity and sophistication, insisting that "without systematic reflection it is also easy to get entangled in avoidable dilemmas, simple contradictions, which lead a feminist theology that is insensitive to them into dangerous alliances with ideologies of the most varied kind: with antisemitism, with the libertinism of the so-called sexual revolution, with the anti-intellectualism of conservative social systems."[211] Without rigorous critical thinking in which "interest" is firmly disciplined, feminist transformations of traditions merely invite the patronizing response: "That's all right, if it helps them."[212]

Some of Susanne Heine's work in *Women and Early Christianity* appears to corroborate the claims of Elizabeth Achtemeier which we have just considered. She considers the work of Elaine Pagels, for example, who argued in *The Gnostic Gospels* (1979) that gnostic texts continually use sexual symbolism to describe God, presuppose the superiority of the feminine Sophia, and celebrate God as Father *and* Mother. Pagels sees the *orthodox rejection of gnosticism as anti-feminist.* Susanne Heine, on the other hand, traces deeper theological complexities. She insists that Pagel's work on gnostic texts shows inadequate sophistication and attention to contexts. The really distinctive theological feature of gnosticism, Heine concludes, is that "the self-understanding of a Gnostic can be most appropriately expressed by the statement 'Remember that you are a god'. All the Gnostic anthropology hangs on that: man has a spirit-self which is thought to be substantially divine."[213] Together with this, divine relations with the universe are perceived in terms of "emanations".

Nevertheless possible relations between immanentism and feminist interpretation are not Susanne Heine's main concern here. She argues, in the light of careful exegetical and contextual research, that "if one bears in mind the overall context of the Gnostic myth, the worthlessness of those androgynous conceptions for any feminist interest becomes evident. They exclusively have negative connotations! Sophia is certainly superior to the demiurge God, but she is merely one of the emanations of the highest light-God and the occasion of a fall . . . It is a feminine being which provokes all this disaster."[214] Heine concedes that at first sight it may seem to serve feminism to explore gnostic texts, but she concludes: "It does not help women where it combines this interest with an offence against historical honesty. On the contrary, it harms them, because it is easy for the opposition to repudiate the selected 'facts'."[215] What appears to be a depatriarchalizing movement in the gnostic texts turns out to be more complex and more problematic.

As Heine points out, second-century gnosticism claimed to offer the "true" meaning of the Christian tradition, with related adjustments to its language, imagery, and symbolic system. But thereby it entirely transposed its theology of God and its view of human nature In these broad terms Heine's study adds further caution to Elizabeth Achtemeier's anxieties about the theological consequences of linguistic change.

In her sequel *Christianity and the Goddesses*, Suzanne Heine turns her attention to Old Testament traditions and to myths of the goddesses in the Canaanite and Ugaritic background. She reviews the use of feminine imagery for God in the Old Testament. She writes: "The strongest statements about the motherhood of God appear in Deutero-Isaiah . . . Can a woman forget her sucking child, that she should have no compassion on the son of her womb? . . . I will not forget you" (Isa. 49: 15–16). 'Hearken to me O house of Jacob . . . who have been borne by me from your birth, carried from the womb' (Isa. 46: 3–4) . . . 'As one whom his mother comforts, so I will comfort you' (Isa. 66: 13).[216] God is also like a mother bird which teaches her young to fly (Deut. 32:11; cf. Ex. 19:4): like a hen who gathers her chickens under her wings (Ps. 17:8; 91:4; cf. Matt. 23:37); and carries the needy "as a nurse carries the sucking child" (Num. 11: 12). Analogies between creation and birth from the womb appear in Job 38: 3–9, 28–29.

Heine acknowledges that in feminist hermeneutics such examples can formulate "feminine features . . . as a counterbalance to a long tradition of one-sided stress in the masculinity of God."[217] But she adds: "The question remains whether that is honest and meaningful . . . *It is dangerous and contrary to basic feminist interests when a division of the male and female properties of God gives a boost to the usual stereotyping of roles.*"[218] *Such interpretations tend to perpetuate the notion that law, justice, anger, and power are "typically masculine"; while oversight, feeding, care and compassion are "typically feminine."*

Susanne Heine insists that apart from the image of birth and breast-feeding, "there is nothing against understanding physical care, love, illness, and mercy *as a fatherly attitude towards children. And is not a mother's love* also concerned to look strictly at a social life in *accordance with ethical maxims, fighting with children and for children if need be?*"[219] The motherhood of God, Heine observes, can be directed in anger and in discipline against the children: "I will fall upon them like a she-bear robbed of her cubs" (Hos. 13: 8).

With impressive scholarship Heine examines the precise nature of the goddess myths which belong to the early matriarchal cultures often focussed in feminist theologies. She scrutinizes available texts and sources, and especially the work of Heide Göttner-Abendroth. The Ugaritic texts discovered in 1929 at Ras Shamra depict sixteenth-century to thirteenth-century (or twelfth-century) myths of female deities. Anat is the sister-consort of Baal, who is subordinate to her. But Anat is no modern stereotype of "the feminine": "She fights, she wades in the blood of her opponents, is not sated with her killing; the heads she has cut off reach up to her waist. . . . She is filled with joy as she plunges her knees in the blood of heroes."[220] Anat without question delights in power, domination, and killing.

Socio-critical hermeneutics encourages questioning about the social order and social interests which texts may be deemed to presuppose or to legitimate. Heine points out that the gods and goddesses of the Ugaritic pantheon have no regard whatever for moral order, and she observes drily that if feminists prefer the society reflected in the Ugaritic Goddess-system to that of the Old Testament prophets they "would be in a bad position."[221] Eroticism and nature-cycles dissolve into a lawless chaos which may move either into ecstasy or into the abyss of destruction and extinction. Eros is a *martial* power; it entails *violence*. It is worlds-away from the feminist utopia of "'natural' gentleness and readiness for peace."[222]

Achtemeier and Heine thus offer at least two or three distinct theological and sociological reasons for caution over full-scale programmes of depatriarchalizing language about God. *If the ancient biblical writers did not begin with the gender stereotypes projected back by the modern world, their choice of gender-related images had a different significance from that presupposed in much current popular debate.* The use of "Father" in biblical traditions does not necessarily presuppose an anti-feminist social orientation: it is used analogically to designate the relation of care, compassion, authority, and social discipline which *both* parents, regardless of gender, can exercize towards their children. What makes the term offensive to some is the sociological assumption that it carried for the biblical writers the pre-determined stereotyping of a later age. On this basis the language is perceived to be exclusive.

Susanne Heine argues that such depatriarchalizing as Rachel Wahlberg's "creed for women" ("I believe in the Holy Spirit, the feminine Spirit of God") misses this argument.[223] Heine sees the use of feminine imagery for God in the Old Testament *not* as an indicator of early depatriarchalizing within the texts, but as the very reverse. "It is obvious", she comments, what "Hosea, Jeremiah, Deutero-Isaiah, Trito-Isaiah, Deuteronomy, the Priestly Writing . . . want to say" as they confront Canaanite myths, namely: "Why do you need a mother goddess? Yahweh, the father, judge, and warrior hero, can also give birth, breast-feed, care for, and have mercy. Even if a mother left her child, God would never leave his people."[224]

Susanne Heine is not insensitive to the hermeneutical barriers thrown up by male imagery. She therefore makes three key points about the nature of theological language. (1) She insists on the importance of negations in conjunction with imagery: God is Father, but he does *not beget*. "The *via negativa* dissociates God from all naive identifications with human reality."[225] (2) The very same biblical tradition that enjoins that universal justice and protects the weak from domination also portrays "the transcendent God" as "the critical principle."[226] God is not the "object" of our critique and choice; God made male-and-female in God's image; it is not for some part of humanity (whether men or women) to make God in theirs. (3) The analogical status of theological language means that "God's fatherhood transcends our experiences of fathers."[227] Negative childhood experiences of fathers or of mothers should lead not to the elimination of related imagery, but to a proliferation of biblical images in which each image is qualified and supplemented by others.

These valid and important points bring us back to the suggested parallel with the demythologizing debate. Bultmann confused the issue because he worked with three sometimes incompatible theories of myth. First he speaks of myth simply as *analogy*. But we cannot dispense with analogy in theology *as long as its analogical status is recognized*. This principle also applies to language about fatherhood. Second, he speaks of myth as conveying an *outdated cosmology*. But it is far from clear that language about the ascension or "coming down from heaven" really *asserted* a three-decker universe cosmology. What other options were available which might not imply *geocentrism as a doctrine*? The debate about *androcentric language* affords some parallel. Elizabeth Achtemeier and Susanne Heine have at very least offered good reasons why alternative modes of language might have invited even greater difficulties. Third, Bultmann speaks of myth as an *objectifying* use of language, which obscures its primary function. But in largely dispensing with the objective or descriptive function he has reduced the basis of its capacity to offer historical and *ontological truth-claims*. For example, divine judgment is a present or future process or state of affairs which cannot be cashed out exhaustively without loss as a call to human responsibility. Similarly, Susanne Heine expresses concern that "the transcendent God of the Bible is the critical principle". The direction of critique cannot be transposed without transforming ontological truth-claims about God into a purely functional system. Bultmann, in effect, goes a long way towards doing this by grounding Christology on the human experience of salvation, rather than salutation on Christology.

Post-modern feminist hermeneutics might more readily develop this option, and indeed Rebecca Chopp (1989) advocates precisely a post-modern hermeneutic which offers "emancipatory transformation."[228] She calls for a transformation of the entire socio-symbolic order, accepting the post-modernist Derridean and post-structuralist view that symbolic systems, because they are *systems*, promote *"hierarchical* oppositions." They thereby propagate "logocentrism."[229] Since in such a hierarchy, in Deborah Cameron's words, "men can be men only if women are unambiguously women", Rebecca Chopp concludes "women must develop new discourses for their lives . . . discourses of emancipatory transformation that proclaim the Word to and for the world."[230]

Rebecca Chopp describes her own hermeneutical theory as "a hermeneutic of marginality".[231] It is a "restless" hermeneutic, that leaves behind any foundationalism, and moves through the endless polyvalency of language.[232] Such a hermeneutic provides "space" for women from the outer margins.[233] Like Barthes and Derrida, she sees the function of scripture as "play" among images.[234] Jesus's reading of Isaiah in Luke 4: 16–21 offers a vision, but one which must also be "re-vision" and transformation. Using supposedly the "different logic" of post-modernism she argues that "women have been placed outside of words in order to continue the funding of words through the Word."[235] The scriptures, in this "hermeneutic of marginality" are to be "de-centered" in order to produce "an experience of emancipatory transformation."

Such an approach raises once again our earlier question about "the scope of demythologizing". It is difficult to establish adequate criteria for determining how far a tradition can be transformed before it ceases to remain *this* tradition. Post-modernism, by its very nature, cannot even sympathize with such a question; but Christian theology is in no position to ignore it.

What has emerged most clearly of all is that *feminist biblical hermeneutics is not one thing: it embodies a huge variety of methods, values, theologies, and interpretative strategies and goals.* It is quite impossible to offer a *generalizing* assessment of feminist hermeneutics; for each strand and each model deserves respect and separate evaluation in its own right. At its most fruitful and most essential, feminist hermeneutics offers an example of some effective *socio-critical models* of enquiry which have as their goal *the unmasking of the kind of illusions and interpretative assumptions or manipulations that support and appear to legitimize injustice or domination.* Richard Bauckham's recent book, *The Bible in Politics* (1989) is a sustained, though straightforward, study of the consistent attack mounted within the biblical texts themselves against institutionalized exploitation and oppression.[236]

Nevertheless, although Bauckham is correct to speak of "the constant Old Testament concern to protect the weak" and to exercise "power on behalf of the powerless" (Deut. 16:19; 2 Chron. 19:7; Job 29:15; Ps. 68:5; Amos 5:12), feminist theologians such as Fiorenza are rightly wary of the kind of "justice" that smacks of being patronized by the powerful.[237] It is therefore right that feminist hermeneutics *begins* by letting the horizons of biblical texts interact with horizons of *women's experience*. The narrative biography and autobiography with which we began contributes an essential component. This is not to stereotype; it is to follow the hermeneutical principle of Schleiermacher, Betti, and Gadamer that the *first step towards understanding is to listen, and to do so in openness*. The next stage is noted in work on feminist readings of Esther by my former colleague David Clines. He rightly takes up Elaine Showalter's observation: *"the hypothesis of a female reader changes our apprehension of a given text"*.[238] This relates to a necessary consciousness-raising identified in liberation hermeneutics in general, although it is not entirely alien to Dilthey's principle of self-awareness through interaction with the other.

When we move to the third stage, differences of strategy and method cannot be avoided. Some argue that "women's experience" constitutes the necessary critical principle of interpretation. Others urge the need for a broader-based socio-critical theory. Norman Gottwald, for example, argues that the way forward for feminist hermeneutics is to explore the causal social factors relating to work, status, and economics that "produce" biblical texts. He points to the implications of a contrast between "egalitarian" inter-tribal Israel and "elitist hierarchical Canaan".[239] Feminist hermeneutics thus provides a case-study for the competing strategies of *socio-critical and socio-pragmatic* philosophies.

Further, the complex debate about *depatriarchalizing* biblical and theological language leads along a route which initially was also travelled by the demythologizing debate, until more distinctive issues raised by each debate lead us along different paths. The theoretical issues thus form part of a larger and wider set of critical hermeneutical discussions. The aim of this chapter has been to set feminist hermeneutics in this wider context in hermeneutical theory, and also to present both sympathetically and critically the strengths and weaknesses of various models and strands within it. In as far as these raise or constitute questions about socio-critical and socio-pragmatic hermeneutics, and about relations between communities, traditions, texts, and interpretation, they constitute an integral part of the argument of this volume as a whole. No merely evaluative account of the strengths and weaknesses of the theoretical models which are utilized in feminist hermeneutics, however, should be allowed to obscure the basic issues which the movement seeks to address, and which we have set out clearly in section 4 of this chapter.

NOTES TO CHAPTER XII

1. Leonardo Boff and Clodovis Boff, *Introducing Liberation Theology*, Eng. London: Burns and Oates, 1987, 12.
2. *Ibid* 14.
3. Juan Luis Segundo, "The Shift within Latin American Theology" *Journal of Theology for Southern Africa*, 52, 1985, 17–29; "Two Theologies of Liberation", *The Month*, Oct. 1984, 321–27.
4. Julio de Santa Ana, "The Situation of Latin American Theology (1982–1987)" *Concilium: Theologies of the Third World, Convergences and Differences* (ed. L. Boff and V. Elizondo) Edinburgh: Clark, 1988, 52; cf. 46–53.
5. Carlos Mesters, "The Use of the Bible in Christian Communities of the Common People" in Norman Gottwald (ed.) *The Bible and Liberation. Political and Social Hermeneutics*, New York: Orbis, 1983, 119–33. Cf. further, Carlos Mesters, *Defenseless Flower. A New Reading of the Bible*, Eng. New York: Orbis, 1989 (Portuguese, 1983).
6. Christopher Rowland and Mark Corner, *Liberating Exegesis. The Challenge of Liberation Theology to Biblical Studies*, 9–19.
7. *Ibid* 22.
8. H.-G Gadamer, *Truth and Method*, 273.
9. Ernesto Cardenal, *Love in Practice: The Gospel in Solentiname* (4 vols.) Eng. New York: Orbis, 1977–84, vol.1, 30–31.
10. Juan Luis Segundo, *The Liberation of Theology*, Eng. Dublin: Gill & McMillan, 1977 (New York: Orbis, 1976) 7–38; cf. 231–40.
11. J. Severino Croatto, *Exodus. A Hermeneutics of Freedom*, Eng. New York: Orbis, 1981, 1–11; and *Biblical Hermeneutics: Towards a Theory of Reading as the Production of Meaning*, Eng. New York: Orbis, 1987; José Miguez Bonino, *Revolutionary Theology Comes of Age*, London: S.P.C.K. and Philadelphia: Fortress, 1975, 86–103; Clodovis Boff, *Theology and Praxis: Epistemological Foundations*, Eng. New York: Orbis, 1987. Boff's important book is critically discussed by David Cunningham, "Clodovis Boff and the Discipline of Theology", *Modern Theology* 6, 1990, 137–58.
12. Leonardo Boff, "What are Third World Theologies?" in *Concilium* (as cited) 1988, 11; cf. 3–13.
13. Phillip Berryman, *Liberation Theology*, London: Tauris, 1987, 85.
14. Richard J. Bernstein, *Praxis and Action*, xi.
15. *Ibid* 306.
16. Gustavo Gutiérrez, *A Theology of Liberation. History, Politics and Salvation*, Eng. New York: Orbis, 1973, and London: S.C.M. 1974.
17. José P. Miranda, *Marx and the Bible. A Critique of the Philosophy of Oppression*, Eng. New York: Orbis, 1974 and London: S.C.M., 1977.
18. Gustavo Gutiérrez, *op. cit.* 6.
19. Leonardo and Clodovis Boff, *op. cit.* 1–16.
20. Gustavo Gutiérrez, *op. cit.* 27 (his italics); cf. 26 and 82–84.
21. *Ibid* 106.
22. *Ibid* 30 (my italics).
23. *Ibid* 27–33; cf. 216–225.
24. *Ibid* 223.
25. *Ibid* 11.

26. *Ibid* 156.
27. *Ibid.*
28. Karl Marx, "Theses on Feuerbach", in L.D. Easton and K.H. Guddat (eds.) *Writings of the Young Marx on Philosophy and Society*, 400.
29. *Ibid* 402.
30. Gustavo Gutiérrez, *op. cit.* 216.
31. Jürgen Moltmann, *Theology of Hope*, Eng. London: S.C.M., 1967, 18.
32. *Ibid* 84 (Moltmann's italics).
33. Jürgen Moltmann, *The Crucified God. The Cross of Christ as the Foundation and Criticism of Christian Theology*, Eng. London: S.C.M. 1974, 5.
34. *Ibid.*
35. *Ibid* 9.
36. *Ibid* 19 and 25.
37. Jürgen Moltmann, *The Experiment Hope*, Eng. London: S.C.M. and Philadelphia: Fortress, 1975, 37 and 49; cf. 30–43.
38. J. Moltmann, "Response to the Opening Presentations" in Ewert H. Cousins (ed.), *Hope and the Future of Man*, Philadelphia: Fortress and London: Teilhard Centre, 1972, 56, 58 and 59; cf. 55–59.
39. Juan Luis Segundo, *The Liberation of Theology*, 8 (my italics).
40. *Ibid* 9.
41. *Ibid* 13.
42. *Ibid* 32.
43. Carlos Mestos, "The Use of the Bible in Christian Communities of the Common People", *loc. cit.* 125.
44. *Ibid.*
45. *Ibid* 128.
46. David Lochhead, "The Liberation of the Bible" *ibid* 81; cf. 74–93.
47. *Ibid* 81.
48. James H. Cone, *A Black Theology of Liberation*, New York and Philadelphia: Lippincott, 1970, 53; cf. 53–81, and Juan Luis Segundo, *The Liberation of Theology*, 29.
49. Juan Luis Segundo, *op. cit.* 25–36.
50. James H. Cone, *God of the Oppressed*, London: S.P.C.K. 1977 (New York: Seabury, 1975), 7.
51. *Ibid* 8.
52. *Ibid* 106.
53. Theo Witvliet, *The Way of the Black Messiah* Eng. London, S.C.M. 1987, 257 and 258.
54. Itumeleng J. Mosala, *Biblical Hermeneutics and Black Theology in South Africa*, Grand Rapids: Eerdmans, 1989, 4, 6, *et passim*.
55. *Ibid* 13–42.
56. Alistair Kee, *Marx and the Failure of Liberation Theology*, London: S.C.M. and Philadelphia: Trinity Press, 1990, 262 and 263.
57. I.J. Mosala, *op. cit.* 14 and 15.
58. James H. Cone, *God of the Oppressed*, 2.
59. *Ibid* 6.
60. *Ibid* 102.
61. *Ibid* 103.

62. James H. Cone, *A Black Theology of Liberation*, 50–53, 114–16.
63. Paul Tillich, *Systematic Theology* (3 vols.) London: Nisbet, 1953–64, vol.1,15.
64. James H. Cone, *op. cit.* 46.
65. Paul Tillich, *op. cit.* vol.1, 57 and 70.
66. James H. Cone, *A Black Theology of Liberation*, 218.
67. *Ibid* 213; cf. "The Black Christ", 212–19; and "God is Black", 120–25.
68. *Ibid* 218.
69. John S. Mbiti, *New Testament Eschatology in an African Background. A Study of the Encounter between New Testament Theology and African Traditional Concepts*, London: S.P.C.K. 1971 and 1978.
70. John S. Mbiti, *Bible and Theology in African Christianity*, Nairobi: Oxford University Press, 1986, 46–66.
71. *Ibid* 52–54.
72. Cf. Desmond M. Tutu, "Black Theology and African Theology - Soulmates or Antagonists?" in John Parratt (ed.) *A Reader in African Christian Theology*, London: S.P.C.K. 1987, 46–55.
73. Patrick A. Kalilombe, "Black Theology" in David F. Ford (ed.) *The Modern Theologians. An Introduction to Christian Theology in the Twentieth Century*, Oxford: Blackwell, 1989, 193–216; and John Parratt (ed.) *op. cit.*
74. John Parratt (ed.) *op. cit.* 54; cf. 46–55.
75. T.A. Mofokeng, "Black Christians, the Bible, and Liberation" in *The Journal of Black Theology* 2, 1988, 34. The article was drawn to my attention by Gerald O. West, *Biblical Interpretation in Theologies of Liberation: Modes of Reading the Bible in the South African Context of Liberation*, University of Sheffield Ph.D. Dissertation, 1989.
76. Desmond M. Tutu, "Black Theology and African Theology" in John Parratt (ed.) *loc. cit* and "The Theology of Liberation in Africa" in K. Appiah-Kubi and T. Sergio (eds.) *African Theology en Route*, New York: Orbis, 1979; Allan A. Boesak, *Black and Reformed: Apartheid, Liberation and the Calvinist Tradition*, New York: Orbis, 1984; and *Comfort and Protest: Reflections in the Apocalypse of John of Patmos*, Philadelphia; Westminster, 1987; and Manas Buthelezi "Towards Indigenous Theology in South Africa" in S. Torres and V. Fabella, *The Emergent Gospel: Theology from the Underside of History*, New York: Orbis, 1978.
77. Bonganjalo Goba, *An Agenda for Black Theology. Hermeneutics for Social Change*, Johannesburg: Skotaville, 1988; and Itumeleng J. Mosala, *Biblical Hermeneutics and Black Theology in South Africa*, Grand Rapids: Eerdmans, 1989 (as already cited).
78. The Kairos Theologians, *The Kairos Document: Challenge to the Church*, Grand Rapids: Eerdmans, 1986.
79. Allan A. Boesak, *Black and Reformed* 149–56.
80. *Ibid* 155–56.
81. Allan Boesak, *Comfort and Protest*, 38.
82. *Ibid* 68 and 69.
83. Christopher Rowland and Mark Corner, *op. cit.* 133, 135, and 142.
84. J. Severino Croatto, *Exodus. A Hermeneutics of Freedom*, Eng. New York: Orbis, 1981, 18.
85. *Ibid* 20.
86. *Ibid* 23.
87. Bonganjalo Gobo, *op. cit.* 16 and 18.

88. *Ibid* 44,45.
89. *Ibid* 117.
90. Itumeleng Mosala, *op. cit.* 27.
91. *Ibid* 28 (my italics).
92. *Ibid* 33.
93. *Ibid* 35.
94. *Ibid.*
95. *Ibid* 38.
96. José Porfirio Miranda, *Marx and the Bible. A Critique of the Philosophy of Oppression*, Eng. London: S.C.M. 1977 (New York: Orbis, 1974) 35.
97. *Ibid* 202–206.
98. Fernando Belo, *A Materialist Reading of the Gospel of Mark*, Eng. New York: Orbis, 1981, 1.
99. *Ibid.*
100. *Ibid* 3.
101. *Ibid* 108.
102. *Ibid* 202.
103. Norman K. Gottwald, "The Bible and Liberation: Deeper Roots and Wider Horizons" in *The Bible and Liberation*, 4; cf. 1–25.
104. Sergio Rostagno, "The Bible: Is an Interclass Reading Legitimate?" *ibid* 62; cf. 61–73.
105. Michel Clévenot, *Materialist Approaches to the Bible* Eng. New York: Orbis, 1985.
106. *Ibid* 29; cf. 17–34.
107. *Ibid* 78.
108. Leonardo and Clodovis Boff, *op. cit.* 28.
109. Elisabeth Schüssler Fiorenza, *In Memory of Her. A Feminist Theological Reconstruction of Christian Origins*, New York: Crossroad, and London: S.C.M. 1983, 6 and 16.
110. Mary Ann Tolbert (ed.), *The Bible and Feminist Hermeneutics: Semeia*, 28, 1983, 114; cf. 113–26.
111. Elisabeth Schüssler Fiorenza, *op. cit.* 5 and 6.
112. T. Drorah Setel, "Feminist Insights and the Question of Method" in Adela Yarbro Collins (ed.) *Feminist Perspectives on Biblical Scholarship*, Chico: Scholars Press, 1985, 35–42.
113. Phyllis Trible, *God and the Rhetoric of Sexuality*, Philadelphia: Fortress, 1978, 1; cf. 1–5.
114. Elisabeth Schüssler Fiorenza, *op. cit.* 42.
115. Elisabeth Schüssler Fiorenza, "Word, Spirit and Power: Women in Early Christian Communities" in Rosemary Ruether and Eleanor McLaughlin (eds.) *Women of Spirit: Female Leadership in the Jewish and Christian Traditions*, New York: Simon and Schuster, 1979, 57; cf. 30–70; and *In Memory of Her*, 55 and 80.
116. Rosemary Ruether and Eleanor McLaughlin (eds.) *op. cit.* 94.
117. Janice Capel Anderson, "Matthew: Gender and Reading", *Semeia* 28, 1983, 7; cf. 3–27.
118. *Ibid* 11, 15 and 16.
119. *Ibid* 18.
120. *Ibid* 21.

121. J. Cheryl Exum, "'You shall Let Every Daughter Live': A Study of Exodus 1:8 – 2:10", *Semeia* 28, 1983, 63–82.
122. *Ibid* 75.
123. Elisabeth Schüssler Fiorenza, *In Memory of Her*, xxiii (my italics).
124. Katharine Doob Sakenfeld, "Feminist Uses of Biblical Materials" in Letty M. Russell (ed.) *Feminist Interpretation of the Bible*, Oxford and New York: Blackwell, 1985, 55 (my italics); cf. 55–64.
125. Elisabeth Schüssler Fiorenza, *In Memory of Her*, 6.
126. Rosemary Radford Ruether, "Feminist Interpretation: A Method of Correlation" in Letty M. Russell (ed.) *op. cit.* 113 (my italics); cf. 111–24.
127. *Ibid* 112–13 (Reuther's italics).
128. Phyllis Trible, *Texts of Terror. Literary-Feminist Readings of Biblical Narratives*, Philadelphia: Fortress Press, 1984, 3.
129. *Ibid* 25.
130. *Ibid* 27–28; cf. also 107 and 108.
131. Alice L. Laffey, *Wives, Harlots, and Concubines: The Old Testament in Feminist Perspective*, London: S.P.C.K. 1990 (Fortress Press, 1988) 2–3. (On Ruth, cf. 209–10).
132. Simone de Beauvoir, *The Second Sex*: Introduction rp. in Elaine Marks and Isabelle de Courtivron (eds.) *New French Feminism: An Anthology*, Harvester Press, 1981, 44; cf. 41–56.
133. Elaine Marks and Isabelle de Courtivron (eds.) *op. cit.* ix-xiii *et passim*.
134. Julia Kristeva, *The Kristeva Reader*, esp. "Introduction" by Toril Moi, 1–23.
135. Elaine Marks and Isabelle de Courtivron (eds.) *op. cit.* xi.
136. *Ibid* xii.
137. *Ibid* xi.
138. Mary Daly, *Beyond God the Father: Toward a Philosophy of Women's Liberation*, Boston: Beacon Press, 1973.
139. Phyllis Trible, "Depatriarchalizing in Biblical Tradition". *Journal of the American Academy of Religion* 41, 1973, 35–42; and Letty M. Russell (ed.) *The Liberating Word. A Guide to Nonsexist Interpretation of the Bible*, Philadelphia: Westminster Press, 1976.
140. Letty M. Russell, *loc. cit.* 17–18; cf. 13–22.
141. Phyllis Trible, *God and the Rhetoric of Sexuality* 18 and 21.
142. *Ibid* 31–56.
143. Dorothy C. Bass, "Women's Studies and Biblical Studies: An Historical Perspective", *Journal for the Study of the Old Testament* 22, 1982, 10–11; cf. 3–71.
144. The exception is Elisabeth Schüssler Fiorenza, *Bread Not Stone*, Boston: Beacon Press, 1984.
145. Elizabeth Schüssler Fiorenza, "For Women in Men's Worlds: A Critical Feminist Theology of Liberation", *Concilium: Different Theologies, Common Responsibility* (ed. Claude Geffré, Gustavo Gutiérrez, and Virgil Elizondo) Edinburgh: Clark, 1984, 34; cf. 32–9; Phyllis Trible, "Feminist Hermeneutics and Biblical Studies", *The Christian Century*, Feb. 1982, 116–18. Rosemary Radford Ruether, "The Future of Feminist Theology in the Academy" *Journal of the American Academy of Religion* 53, 1985, 703–16.
146. Rebecca S. Chopp, *The Power to Speak: Feminism, Language, God*, New York: Crossroad, 1989.

147. Ursula King, *Women and Spirituality: Voices of Protest and Promise*, London: McMillan, 1989, 15.
148. *Ibid* 3.
149. Elaine Storkey, *What's Right with Feminism*, London: S.P.C.K. 1985, 138.
150. *Ibid* 141.
151. *Ibid* 153.
152. *Ibid* 154 and 158.
153. *Ibid* 164.
154. Katie Geneva Cannon, "The Emergence of Black Feminist Consciousness" in Letty M. Russell (ed.) *op. cit.* 30–40.
155. *Ibid* 39 and 40.
156. Susan B. Thistlethwaite, "Every Two Minutes: Battered Women and Feminist Interpretation" in Letty M. Russell (ed.) *op. cit.* 96; cf. 96–107.
157. Letty M. Russell (ed.) *op. cit.* 138.
158. Mary Ann Tolbert "Defining the Problem", *Semeia* 28, 1983, 117; cf. 113–26.
159. Rosemary Radford Ruether, *Sexism and God-Talk: Towards a Feminist Theology*, London: S.C.M. 1983, 228–34.
160. *Ibid* 229 and 230.
161. *Ibid* 231.
162. Rosemary Radford Ruether "Feminist Interpretation" in Letty M. Russell (ed.) *op. cit.* 116; cf. 111–24.
163. Ann Loades, "Feminist Theology" in David F. Ford (ed.) *The Modern Theologians. An Introduction to Christian Theology in the Twentieth Century* (2 vols.) Oxford: Blackwell, 1989, vol. 2, 250; cf. 235–52.
164. Ann Loades, *Searching for Lost Coins: Explorations in Christianity and Feminism*, London: S.P.C.K., 1987, 96–100; and *Feminist Theology. A Reader*, London: S.P.C.K., 1990, 186–89 and 192–93.
165. Letty Russell (ed.) *op. cit.* 139; cf. 137–46.
166. Elisabeth Schüssler Fiorenza, "The Will to Choose or to Reject: Continuing our Critical Work" in Letty M. Russell (ed.) *op. cit.* 128; cf. 125–46.
167. *Ibid* 126 (my italics).
168. *Ibid* 131.
169. *Ibid* 130 and 131.
170. *Ibid* 130.
171. Elisabeth Schüssler Fiorenza, "For Women in Men's Worlds: A Critical Feminist Theology of Liberation", *loc. cit.* 37.
172. *Ibid* 36.
173. Janet Radcliffe Richards, *The Sceptical Feminist. A Philosophical Enquiry*, London: Penguin edn. 1983 (1980) 17–18.
174. John Barclay, "Mirror-Reading a Polemical Letter: Galatians as a Test Case", *Journal for the Study of the New Testament* 31, 1987, 81; cf. 73–93.
174a. Anthony C. Thiselton, "The Morality of Christian Scholarship" in Mark Santer (ed.) *Their Lord and Ours: Approaches to Authority, Community, and the Unity of the Church*, London: S.P.C.K., 1982, 20–45.
175. Elisabeth Schüssler Fiorenza, *loc. cit.* 52; cf. *In Memory of Her* 315–34. Cf. also E.S. Malbon, "Fallible Followers: Women and Men in the Gospel of Mark", *Semeia* 29–48.
176. Elisabeth Schüssler, *In Memory of Her*, 332.

177. *Ibid* 333.
178. *Ibid* 332.
179. Walter Künneth, *The Theology of the Resurrection*, Eng. London: S.C.M. 1965, 89. See 89–91; cf. 92–149.
180. Willi Marxsen, *The Resurrection of Jesus of Nazareth*, Eng. London: S.C.M. 1970, 60 and 108.
181. Ernest Best, *Mark. The Gospel as Story*, Edinburgh: Clark, 1983, 74.
182. *Ibid* 73.
183. Robert Morgan, "Feminist Theological Interpretation of the New Testament" in Janet Martin Soskice (ed.) *After Eve* London: Collins and Marshall Pickering, 1990, 26; cf. 10–37.
184. *Ibid* 27.
185. *Ibid.*
186. Elisabeth Schüssler Fiorenza, "The Will to Choose or to Reject" in Letty M. Russell (ed.) *op. cit.* 134; and "Remembering the Past in Creating the Future: Historical-Critical Scholarship and Feminist Biblical Interpretation" in Adela Yarbro Collins (ed.) *op. cit.* 43–63.
187. Elisabeth Schüssler Fiorenza, "The Will to Choose or to Reject", *loc. cit.* 134.
188. Elisabeth Schüssler Fiorenza, "Remembering the Past", *loc. cit.* 61.
189. Elisabeth Schüssler Fiorenza, "The Ethics of Interpretation: Decentering Biblical Scholarship", *Journal of Biblical Literature* 107, 1988, 115; cf. 101–15.
190. Elisabeth Schüssler Fiorenza, "For Women in Men's Worlds: A Critical Feminist Theology of Liberation" *loc. cit.* 36.
191. *Ibid.*
192. Susanne Heine, *Women and Early Christianity: Are the Feminist Scholars Right?* Eng. London: S.C.M. 1987, 9.
193 Mary Ann Tolbert, "Defining the Problem", *Semeia* 28, 1983, 118; cf. 113–26.
194. Anthony C. Thiselton, *The Two Horizons* 205–92, esp. 252–75.
195. Rudolf Bultmann, *Kerygma and Myth*, vol.1, 25 and 210–211; cf. A.C. Thiselton, *The Two Horizons*, 262–63.
196. Phyllis Trible, *God and the Rhetoric of Sexuality*, 22, 33, 200 *et passim*. cf. also her essay "Depatriarchalizing in Biblical Interpretation" in Elisabeth Koltun (ed.) *The Jewish Woman. New Perspectives*, New York: Schocken Books, 1978, 217–40.
197. Phyllis Trible, *God and the Rhetoric of Sexuality*, 21–22.
198. *Ibid* 31–59; cf. 56 n.4.
199. Rudolf Bultmann, *loc. cit.* vol. 2, 182–83; cf. A.C. Thiselton, *The Two Horizons*,259.
200. Phyllis Trible, *op. cit.* 202.
201. Ludwig Wittgenstein, *Philosophical Investigations*, sect. 339.
202. John Macquarrie, *The Scope of Demythologizing: Bultmann and his Critics*, London: S.C.M. 1960, 11–22 and 222–29.
203. Schubert M. Ogden, "Bultmann's Project of Demythologization and the Problems of Theology and Philosophy", *Journal of Religion*, 37, 1957, 156–73, esp. 168.
204. Elizabeth Achtemeier, "Female Language for God: Should the Church Adopt it?" in Donald G. Miller (ed.) *The Hermeneutical Quest: Essays in Honor of James Luther Mays*, (Princeton Theological Monograph 4), Allison Park, Pa: Pickwick Press, 1986, 97–114.
205. *Ibid* 109 (Elizabeth Achtemeier's italics).

206. *Ibid* 107, and Dorothee Soelle, *The Strength of the Weak: Towards a Christian Feminist Identity*, Eng. Philadelphia: Westminster, 1984, 126.
207. Rosemary Radford Ruether, *Sexism and God-Talk*, 48–49 and 266; and Elizabeth Achtemeier, *loc. cit.* 100.
208. Elisabeth Schüssler Fiorenza, *In Memory of Her*, 133.
209. Susanne Heine, *Christianity and the Goddesses. Systematic Criticism of a Feminist Theology*, Eng. London: S.C.M. 1988, 8.
210. *Ibid.* 5.
211. *Ibid.* 8.
212. *Ibid.* 3.
213. Susanne Heine, *Women and Early Christianity*, 109.
214. *Ibid.* 121–22.
215. *Ibid.* 122.
216. Susanne Heine, *Christianity and the Goddesses*, 26.
217. *Ibid.* 28.
218. *Ibid.* (My italics).
219. *Ibid.* 29 (My italics).
220. *Ibid.* 46; cf. 51.
221. *Ibid.* 52.
222. *Ibid.* 65.
223. *Ibid.* 28.
224. *Ibid.* 28–29,.
225. *Ibid.* 34.
226. *Ibid.* 35.
227. *Ibid.* 37.
228. Rebecca S. Chopp, *The Power to Speak: Feminism, Language, God*, New York: Crossroad, 1989, 2, 43, *et passim*.
229. *Ibid.* 1–2.
230. *Ibid.* 2.
231. *Ibid.* 43.
232. *Ibid.* 8.
233. *Ibid.* 23.
234. *Ibid.* 41.
235. *Ibid.* 26.
236. Richard Bauckham, *The Bible in Politics. How to Read the Bible Politically*, London: S.P.C.K. 1989, esp. 41–72.
237. *Ibid.* 45–46.
238. D.J.A. Clines, "Reading Esther from Left to Right: Contemporary Strategies for Reading a Biblical Text" in David J.A. Clines, S.E. Fowl and S.E. Porter (eds.) *op. cit.* 40; cf. 31–52.
239. Norman K. Gottwald, 24 *The Tribes of Yahweh*, 797 n.628.

CHAPTER XIII

The Hermeneutics of Reading in the Context of Literary Theory

1. Problematic and Productive Aspects of the Literary Approach and the Legacy of the New Criticism

The turn towards literary theory in biblical studies constitutes one of the three most significant developments for biblical hermeneutics over the last quarter of a century. It is comparable in importance for biblical interpretation with the impact of post-Gadamerian hermeneutics and the emergence of socio-critical theory and related liberation movements. Yet some biblical specialists still seem to regard this turn to literary theory as little more than an optional icing on the cake. It is as if it meant only a matter of catching up on literary formalism, or supporting the waning interest in structuralism, or placing greater emphasis on the role of imagination and non-cognitive, indirect, or metaphorical, discourse.

As recently as in 1987, Christopher Tuckett's otherwise helpful volume entitled explicitly *Reading the New Testament: Methods of Interpretation* restricted all its observations about literary theory into half a dozen or so pages within a general chapter called "Other Approaches". In the event, "literary theory" in this book embodies little more than references to the formalism of Wellek and Warren, to E.D. Hirsch and to the work of Mary Ann Tolbert.[1]

Literary theory, for good or for ill, brings into biblical studies an intimidating and complicated network of assumptions and methods which were not in origin designed to take account of the particular nature of *biblical* texts. These carry with them their own agenda of deeply philosophical questions about the status of language, the nature of texts, and relations between language, the world, and theories of knowledge. In many cases they also presuppose, or are connected with, a socio-political agenda which is sometimes explicit (as in the case of David Bleich) and sometimes hidden. The notion, for example, that readers may be perceived as co-authors of texts is closely bound up with the kind of social agenda and social theories which lay behind motivations discussed in the previous two chapters. The authority of an author as a "canonical", "elitist", or "privileged" source of knowledge, for example, may be de-centred by spreading authorship and creation of meaning across a wider egalitarian reading-community. In his recent book on narrative Michael J. Toolan observes, "Narrators assert their authority to tell, to take up the role of knower or entertainer . . . in relation to the addressees' adopted role of learner or consumer. To narrate is to make a bid for a kind of power"[2] The very way in which, in narrative theory, a narrator is perceived to "focalize" a narrative and to project a narrative-world in which certain persons or objects are perceived as "other" from the point of view of the narrator and/or reader has the kind of *ideological* implications which we have been discussing in the previous chapter.[3]

In his significant book *Literary Criticism and the Gospels* (1989) Stephen D. Moore therefore rightly expresses the concern that more traditionalist biblical scholars should not regard the turn to literary theory as merely "light exercise – 'fluff', as one colleague puts it".[4] The literary theorists whose work is brought into biblical interpretation, Moore accurately observes, are "hugely muscled from long, strenuous workouts with Heidegger, Derrida, and de Man, Freud and Lacan, Saussurian semiology and Barthesian semioclasty, Foucault, French Nietzscheanism (Deluze, Lyotard et al.) French feminist theory . . . various Marxisms (the Frankfurt School, Althusser, Jameson) and various Pragmatisms (Rorty, Fish)."[5]

If there is any area at all in theology and biblical studies where attention to *method* and to *theory* is crucial, it is here. We recall Terry Eagleton's apt comment that hostility to *theory* means an opposition to other people's theories and an oblivion of one's own.[6] In terms of theories of meaning, the development of literary theories of various kinds since the rise of modern hermeneutical theory with Schleiermacher has brought with it some confusion. Initially the expressive approach associated with the Romanticism of Wordsworth and Coleridge ran broadly parallel with Schleiermacher's hermeneutic of understanding, as we have argued in chapter VI. The reaction against author-focussed theories of meaning reflected in literary formalism, however, transferred the focus from the hermeneutical life-worlds of authors to texts as linguistic systems. In effect, the hermeneutical tradition was exchanged for that of the semiotic system. Meaning arises from an interplay of different forces within a text, regardless of what an author might intend or readers might perceive. But when formalism, the new criticism, and structuralist approaches give way to post-structuralism, reader-response theories, and post-modernism, theories of meaning were disrupted once again. The focus shifted to variable context-relative perceptions and constructions of socially-conditioned reading-communities, whose expectations and norms were internal to their own social and semiotic conventions.

The Hermeneutics of Reading

On the basis of this most recent phase of development, the traditional attention to "the author's intention" in biblical studies is likely to be dismissed as naïve. If reader-orientated literary theory has become entangled with philosophical contextual relativism and post-modernism, *meanings of texts are not only contingently plural in the history of interpretation and textual reception; they are irreducibly plural in principle as a hermeneutical axiom.*

In this light it becomes clear why literary theory in biblical interpretation has nothing to do with "icing on the cake" or with "fluff". It provides the most radical challenge to traditional hermeneutical models which has yet arisen. We have already observed in detail in our extended discussions of Barthes, Derrida, and of deconstructionism (chapter III) that a further radical issue arises for biblical interpretation over the issue of whether textual meaning is generated only intralinguistically and inter-textually, or whether it also entails inter-subjective communicative action grounded in extra-linguistic states of affairs or behaviour, as Habermas, Searle, and Wittgenstein maintain. In chapter VIII we argued that effective speech-acts *depend on certain states of affairs being the case.* We shall pursue these questions further in subsequent chapters. Similarly it is arguable that "history" has a role in biblical texts that it is difficult for literary theory fully to accommodate. The convergence of deconstruction, post-modernism, and social relativism in literary theory creates a climate which is fraught with difficulties for biblical studies and for Christian theology.

Both the gains and the losses of the impact of literary theory on biblical interpretation are, equally, potentially huge. Before we begin to take steady stock of some of the gains, it is worth drawing attention to the sane and perceptive comments of Patrick Grant on this point, whose recent book *Reading the New Testament* (1989) reflects an equal awareness of the positive resources and perils offered by literary approaches. Grant helps to explain why too often traditionalists and post-modern theorists "talk past" each other, without really hearing each other. *Theories which stress the self-referring and unstable nature of texts and textual meanings form part of a distinctive agenda in which rhetorical interaction between context-relative socio-narrative communities stands in contrast to logically evaluative judgments which may be offered over against a community.* To express the point negatively, it is difficult to find room for the notion of biblical texts as offering *external norms of judgment over against their readers* in the context of these particular socio-literary philosophical theories.

Patrick Grant shows how for those theorists who are accustomed to handle poetic, imaginative, fictional, and metaphorical texts, the notion of self-referring textuality can readily assume the status of an axiom, while for those who have been schooled in a discipline in which history, incarnation, situations, and evidence are fundamental, such an approach, far from being axiomatic, is problematic. Each side "talks past" the other, because each side is tempted to think that it has "seen through" the claims of the other. Thus Grant makes the following very important (even if syntactically complex) statement. He writes: "Jacques Derrida's 'deconstruction' of philosophical texts sets out to show that philosophy is more like literature than philosophers assume. Like all writing, philosophy is *rhetorical* (my italics), and because it uses language (an endless network of signifiers the sense of which depends mainly on differences from other signifiers), it never manages to stabilize meaning, which is perpetually deferred . . . The notion that philosophers (and other writers) *always rely on metaphor understandably appeals to literary theorists because poets and critics have usually been quite open about the rhetorical nature of their discourse and the self-referencing element in imaginative writing. It is as if literary people have been onto the game all along, as the others are now coming to realise*" (my italics).[7]

Before we leave this point, we may note that for one of the most influential literary theorists, namely Stanley Fish, there can be no doubt that meaning becomes subsumed under "rhetoric", and in effect philosophy of language becomes subsumed under literary theory. Truth-claims rest on socio-pragmatic hermeneutical criteria internal to the persuasive techniques of given communities. Fish writes: "There is no single way of reading that is correct or natural, only 'ways of reading' that are extensions of community perspectives . . . Interpretation is the source of texts, facts, authors, and intention . . . all . . . *products* of interpretation.[8] "The reader's response is not *to* the meaning: it *is* the meaning."[9] (We discuss this later).

The definition of "literature" depends also on community conventions. Fish asserts, "What will, at any time, be recognized as literature is a function of a *communal decision* as to what will count as literature."[10] In his latest book *Doing What Comes Naturally* he adds, "'Rhetorical' is, of course, a master-word in the essays that make up this volume, and indeed the conclusion of this book (hardly a novel one) is finally that we live in a rhetorical world."[11] Once again, a whole agenda is determined in its shape by this approach. We shall note, for example, that whereas they agree that the reading-community determines what counts as "literature", John Searle and Nicholas Wolterstorff most firmly and rigorously insist that differences between "factual report" and "fiction" can be determined only with reference to an author's extra-linguistic commitments.[12] Such a notion would be unlikely to find any place in Fish's literary and philosophical agenda. It would find an important place, by contrast, in Wittgenstein's philosophical agenda. For Wittgenstein, at least in his later thought from *The Blue Book* onwards, the nature of linguistic cash-currency depends significantly on how it is "backed" by patterns of regularity in human behaviour, especially that of the speaking or writing agent.

We may now turn from more problematic issues, to which we shall return later, to consider some of the *productive* contributions brought to biblical interpretation from literary theory.

(1) We need not play down, although in the light of Schleiermacher it is not distinctive to literary theory, the re-emphasis brought by literary theory to *the use of imagination* in biblical reading. T.R. Wright (1988) and David Jasper (1987) underline this aspect, together with the Romanticist warning, which we earlier noted in Wordsworth (chapter VI) against shattering the *wholeness* of texts by atomistic dissection; although in a more recent work (1989) David Jasper also addresses more complex issues of theory.[13]

It is tempting to offer an anecdote which dates the struggle to recognize the place of "holistic" narrative study in biblical interpretation. My former colleague David M. Gunn, together with David Clines, was a pioneer in this endeavour when we worked together in the University of Sheffield in the early 1970s. The work of one of his doctoral candidates received ambivalent recognition by a colleague in another university, largely on the ground that the narrative "whole" which constituted the subject-matter of the doctoral dissertation was too large and over-ambitious, and too extensive to allow for the proper use of form-critical, source-critical, linguistic, and other "proper" Old Testament tools in sufficient detail. After some considerable discussion in the Faculty of Arts, in which the Department of Biblical Studies stood firmly together, the dissertation was re-examined and approved.

(2) A second line of approach which also operates at a modest level arises from greater *attention to metaphor*. George B. Caird used theories of metaphor to undertake a creative examination of New Testament eschatology. He undertook this in oral lectures at Oxford in 1969, but they did not achieve extended published form until he published *The Language and Imagery of the Bible* in 1980, four years before his untimely death.[14] I myself was strongly influenced by his oral comments to me on the need to explore models from other disciplines in order to move creatively beyond certain stalemates in New Testament studies. Caird was particularly sceptical about the mainstream view among specialists about Jesus' understanding of the future.

Nearest to Caird's own heart was the problem of the status of eschatological imagery. On the basis of the nature of metaphor, he felt unable to accept the widespread view in New Testament studies that Jesus was simply mistaken about the supposedly near-future timing of the end of the world. He examined the status of "day of the Lord" language in such passages as Amos 5: 18,20; Isa. 2: 12; 13: 6,9; Zeph. 1: 7,14; Jer. 46: 10; Ezk. 13: 5; and Joel 1: 15; 2: 1,2; 3: 14,21. In this light he further explored the linguistic function and status of language about the coming of the kingdom, or of the Son of Man (Mark 9: 1; Matt. 10: 23; Luke 17:

24).[15] Jesus, Caird concluded, along with other biblical figures "regularly used end-of-the-world language metaphorically to refer to that which they well knew was not the end of the world."[16]

(3) All three literary emphases which we have so far identified, namely imagination, wholeness, and metaphor, are taken up by Stephen Prickett in his *Words and the Word: Language, Poetics, and Biblical Interpretation* (1986).[17] His earlier work on Wordsworth and Coleridge makes him sensitive to Wordsworth's line which we quoted in our chapter on Schleiermacher, "we murder to dissect". But he goes further. Like David Gunn's literary work on Saul and on David, Prickett calls attention to *the role of ambiguity and indirectness* in the biblical texts. Prickett attacks both the translators of the Bible Society's *Good News Bible* and Kenneth Grayston's explanation of the principles behind the *New English Bible* for attempting to remove all ambiguities and sources of puzzlement and to aim at clarity and precision. For the biblical texts themselves, Prickett urges, are *not* in actuality "clear, simple, and unambiguous", and to offer an unambiguous translation imposes a modern cultural norm onto the ancient text.[18]

Prickett illustrates this principle from the Elijah narratives, especially the theophany at Horeb (1 Kings 19: 8–12). It is counter-productive to try to specify what the wind, the earthquake, and the "still small voice" mean; the key point is not the description of states of affairs but that Elijah came expecting one thing, and found another. God will not repeat the pyrotechnic display of Carmel. Elijah is re-commissioned in a persistent context of "ambiguous discontinuity".[19] Such ambiguity, as David Gunn and Robert Alter also argue, is sometimes sustained by *literary artifice*. This is often lost, Prickett urges, in what he regards as bland, unsubtle, packaged and over-neat attempts to "create in the receptor language an equivalent effect" to that of the source language in E.A. Nida's theory of translation by "dynamic equivalence".[20] In 1977 I myself made the very same point about turning the powerful metaphor "and the moon into blood" (Acts 2: 20) into a flat descriptive simile "red like blood"; or Paul's language "put on Christ" (Gal. 3:27) into the translation in Today's English Version of "take upon ourselves the qualities of Christ".[21]

For those who have been trained in the so-called new criticism of the 1950s little of this is especially startling. Ambiguities are set up by differing forces within the textual system; what superficially may appear as cognitive statement may on the basis of a "close reading" turn out to be paradox, metaphor, irony, or some other form of non-transparent discourse. In articles published in 1970 and in 1973 I argued for the open-ended texture and deliberate ambiguity of certain parables of Jesus (especially Luke 16: 1–8), of the identity of the Suffering Servant in Isaiah (Isa. 49:1 ff.; 50:4 ff.; 52:13–53:12), and of the Son of Man, and of apocalyptic language about "the desolating sacrilege" (Mark 13:14).[22] However, I had journeyed not by the shorter road of the new criticism; but by the more complex and winding way of the later Wittgenstein, with his emphasis on the important role performed by concepts with blurred edges, and the development of this approach in F. Waismann's linguistic philosophy.

A more decisive step taken by Prickett is his rejection of a theory of texts which fall under Umberto Eco's category of transmissive or "closed" texts. Prickett views the class of productive or "open" texts as more characteristic of biblical literature, because they invite the reader to engage actively in puzzling out an indeterminate meaning. But this takes us into the realm of reader-response theory, which constitutes the subject of the next chapter. Prickett moves here into deeper waters, endorsing the maxim of Roland Barthes that "once the author is removed, the claim to decipher a text becomes quite futile". We cannot "close the writing".[23] At this point my journey initially alongside Prickett takes a very different direction. My reservations about Barthesian theories of language were put forward in chapter III.

(4) A genuinely major advance through interaction with literary theory emerges in the theory of narrative. But before we examine the impact of narrative theory in more detail, it is worth calling attention to the early advance offered by Edwin M. Good in his excellent study *Irony in the Old Testament*, ahead of its time in 1965. This combines an awareness of issues about the shape of *narrative* with an incisive study of *the role of irony* as a literary device. Good argues that, given the "sophisticated subtlety" of irony, Old Testament writers may perhaps "have said something different from, or more complex than, what we had supposed".[24] Irony begins in conflict, creating a distance between pretence and reality. In comic irony the pretensions of the imposter are exposed as folly; in tragic irony an overstepping of the bounds of reality leads to disaster and to fall. Satire and parody, Good declares, provide a sub-category of irony in which *the pretence and conflict is exaggerated in order to ridicule it*. Parody uses the grand style for a trivial subject, and *incongruity is exposed*.

The story of Jonah offers an outstanding example of the exposure of incongruity through irony and satire, with elements of parody. Good observes: "The Book of Jonah is a satire. It portrays the prophet in order to ridicule him . . . Its basis is a perception of incongruity."[25] Incongruities abound. Jonah gives his testimony to the sailors that he believes in the God "who made the sea" (Jonah 1:9), yet he seeks to escape from God by taking ship to Tarshish (1:2). Inside the fish, Jonah uses the solemn liturgical metrical language of the psalmists, but "the author is emphasizing Jonah's humiliation in being transported back to his proper element inside the belly of a fish and then being summarily spat out . . . or vomited . . . a touch both of the miraculous and of the ludicrous."[26] At least twice Jonah prays to die, but is upset when this appears to be a genuine possibility.

A huge city (if three days journey represents something of the order of fifty miles) follows the precise rule-book for corporate repentance, and Jonah is dismayed. The narrator, in terms of more recent theories of narrative-time, only now discloses that it was because Jonah *feared a positive* response to his preaching that he originally sought to escape God's commission. Jonah is utterly self-centred, but uses all the right religious formulae: "You are a God gracious and merciful, slow to anger ... (Jon. 4:2; cf. Ex. 34:6; Ps. 86:15; 103:8); "I fear the God of Heaven ..." (Jon. 1:9).

The climactic irony concerns the episode of the great castor-oil plant. God "appoints" a plant to give Jonah the comfort of shade. But then God also "appoints" a worm to destroy the plant. At last the pretence and the irony is truly exposed: "You feel sorry for the plant, though you never toiled over it nor grew it ... But I, am I not to feel sorry for Nineveh, the great city ...?" (Jon. 4:10,11). Good observes: "For the first time Jonah has committed himself to something. His verbal commitments to God earlier in the story were, as we have seen, a mere spouting of rote phrases with no real relation to Jonah's real feelings. Now Jonah is willing to die for a castor-oil plant. Could any satirist have drawn his portrait more deftly?"[27]

Good turns his attention to the role of irony in other parts of the Old Testament. The tragedy of Saul offers a second notable example. Saul's tragic rejection is conveyed to him privately: "Saul has nothing left but keeping up appearances with the people ... This provides the thematic irony of the entire story. For Saul neglects his responsibilities to Yahweh in favour of public relations" (2 Sam. 15:21–30).[28] The theme of Saul as a figure of ambiguity and ultimately of dark tragedy is developed in another constructive study by my former Sheffield colleague David M. Gunn.[29] The story of Saul, he concludes, discloses "a picture of the dark side of God ... at some distance from the innocuous God of the ethical absolutes."[30]

(5) One of the key advances, we have observed, springs from a particular approach to biblical narrative. It is possible to distinguish within this movement three distinct contributory components, which in the case of many writers overlap. (a) The notion of the beginning, middle, and end, of a narrative structure has particular affinities with literary formalism. It often encourages an approach which is adopted by my friend and colleague R. Walter L. Moberly in his book *At the Mountain of God* (1983) and described by him as viewing "the text in its own right".[31] (b) But this does not commit its advocates to a more structural or even structuralist approach, in which the controlling forces which determine the shape of the narrative are judged to emerge from the dictates of a formal "narrative grammar". The inspiration behind this second approach comes not from the new criticism, but from the Russian formalist Vladimir Propp and especially the French structuralist Greimas. We consider their work later in this chapter. (c) A third and more productive strand emerges from the so-called narratology of

Gérard Genette, Tzvetan Todorov, Roland Barthes, and Seymour Chatman. We shall examine this approach in the next section.

One common effect of all three sub-categories of this literary approach to narrative is to sharpen contrasts in hermeneutics with historical-critical and especially source-critical approaches. As Alter, Moberly, and many others have pointed out, *literary considerations may suggest that apparent doublets or duplications, for example, may be due not to clumsy editing in conflating dual sources, but to a narrative technique of juxtaposing two foci of vision which may even stand in tension, because the vision as a whole transcends either of the two single strands of narrative as flat statements.* Thus the two accounts of the anointing and coming to power of David may perhaps portray, as Robert Alter urges, a process from two *"points of view"*: one focussing on divine election (1 Sam. 16:12,13), and the other on the activity of a human agent or hero (1 Sam. 17–2 Sam. 5:5).

Walter Moberly considers the theory of source-criticism since as far back as Richard Simon "the founding father of modern biblical study" whereby the duplicating or repetitive character of the flood narratives were construed as a tell-tale evidence of composite authorship or dual sources.[32] He examines Hebrew narrative style, and explores textual repetition, clashes of contrasts, uses of climax, symbolism and suspense, as *literary* phenomena. In his introduction to his own fuller study of Exodus 32–34, Moberly reviews the classic arguments of Richard Simon. Simon cited, for example, the repetitions in the flood narrative of "the waters increased" (Gen. 7:17,18) and "the waters prevailed" (7:18–20). But already in 1978 B.W. Anderson argued that this was to achieve an ascending *literary* effect, and Gordon Wenham offers similar observations.[33] Moberly observes, "The fact of repetition in itself provides no evidence of composite authorship; that could only be argued on the basis of other criteria."[34] Simon's theory rests on "literary insensitivity" and a degree of historical anachronism about literary conventions. Moberly's work also demonstrates that a good grasp of literary theory enhances, rather than detracts from, a perceptive theological approach.

2. A Closer Examination of Narrative Theory

In 1969 Tzvetan Todorov proposed the term "narratology" for the network of theories now associated with Gérard Genette, Seymour Chatman, Roland Barthes, and others including Todorov himself.[35] Their methodological distinctions and devices have become standard tools in narrative theory. Thus in our discussion of Ricoeur's hermeneutics of narrative, we noted the importance of the contrast in narrative theory between what Seymour

Chatman designated *story* (events as they occurred in "natural" sequence) and *discourse*.36 *Discourse* represents the story-as-told-in-the-telling, *a structured plot*, which has a shape which satisfies the goals of the telling. It is a *construct*. The story-discourse contrast roughly corresponds to V. Propp's contrast in Russian formalism between *fabula* and *sjuzhet*; or in Benveniste and in Barthes, between *histoire* and *discours*. Gérard Genette, for his own purposes, sub-divided and extended the contrast to include a third term.37

Genette's influential book *Narrative Discourse* (French 1972, English 1980) opens with a major discussion of the three key issues of "order", "duration" (for which he later prefers "speeds"), and "frequency".38 The order at the level of narrative-telling may not reflect the order of the story. There may be flash-backs or premature disclosures, or a withholding of some early event, as in *Great Expectations* or in many popular detective stories. The purpose of such re-ordering is not to deceive the reader, who is usually aware that conventions allow for such re-ordering. It is to facilitate movement, direction, suspense, surprise, imagination, or reader-engagement in the plot. Genette similarly examines the relative speed of story and narrative. In his *Narrative Discourse* he had written mainly of "duration", but in his later revaluation of his work in his *Narrative Discourse Revisited* (French 1983; Eng. 1988) Genette prefers to speak of narrative "speeds".39 Tempo and pace is to be assessed in terms of its ratio to other parts of the same narrative. The notion of "frequency" concerns the repeated textual telling of the same event.

The important point to note is that such narrative devices as flash-backs (what Genette calls *analepses*) and flash-forwards (Genette's *prolepses*) are conventions accepted by readers, and at least retrospectively, appreciated for what they are. If today we are viewing a television film, we trust that any re-casting of temporal sequence is not to deceive us about sequence, but to make some "point" which will add to our appreciation of the narrative as it unfolds, or as it reaches its closure. It would be intolerable if an Agatha Christie film began by describing the initial crime in all-inclusive detail, so that we began by knowing the identity of the villain.

These three narrative categories of order, tempo and repetition have now been used frequently to elucidate the interpretation of specific biblical texts. Wesley A. Kort, for example, in his *Story, Text, and Scripture* (1988) traces the build-up of tension in the Gospel of Mark as the first part of Mark's "formal-shaped" narrative assumes a rapid pace: Jesus is engaged with various people, performs diverse acts, addresses a variety of issues, and moves from place to place. Kort writes: "The pace of this section is very quick ... The pace slows remarkably as Jesus moves toward and approaches Jerusalem. His encounter on the way with blind Bartimaeus is presented in detail, with dialogue that retards the pace (Mark 10:46–52). The entry into the city is elaborately prepared for and executed; and a daily account is given of the story in the city. The day of crucifixion is carefully measured, and the process of dying is detailed by the hour" (Mark 15:16–39).[40] All this serves to place the emphasis on the passion, as if the narrator were using at this point a slow-motion camera. Ernest Best had also noted these differences of pace in his earlier book on Mark as story (1983).

As soon as we have become fully sensitive to the role and importance of literary and narrative conventions, we may be less hasty to assume that a clumsy editor or distant author attempted a photographic snapshot but somehow "got it wrong". A new set of questions arises. In his well-known book *The Art of Biblical Narrative* (1981) Robert Alter insists that Hebrew narratives presuppose "an elaborate set of tacit agreements between artist and audience about the ordering of the art-work".[41] Repetitions, for example, far from representing duplicate historical sources are no more "duplications" than different stories about fast-shooting sheriffs constitute duplications of a single film. He explicitly argues that the "doublet" of quite different accounts of David's introduction to Saul serve to effect a particular literary impact co-jointly. In the narrative of 1 Sam. 16 God is in control of events and directs Samuel to anoint David (1 Sam. 16:12,13), and the Spirit falls on David at the very moment when the Spirit departs from Saul (16:14). In the narrative of 1 Sam. 17–2 Sam. 5:5, David assumes the role of the narrative hero, and divine agency scarcely features at all. The two narratives serve to bring together the two dimensions of divine decree and the "brawling chaos" of everyday historical experience.[42]

Ronald Thiemann alludes to Alter's example alongside his own proposals about techniques of emplotment in Matthew as examples of narrative illumination through patterns of hiddenness and obscurity. Everything serves to "summon the reader to enter the world of the text".[43] Over-neat packages and over-sharp lines are avoided, for Matthew creates "narrative space for his readers within the Gospel story."[44] The promise of Christ's presence together with his commission in Matt. 28: 16–20 "shifts the flow of the narrative into the world of the reader".[45] We discuss Ronald Thiemann's narrative theology in greater detail in the last two chapters.

Narrative, as Wolfgang Iser's reader-response theory underlines, draws the reader to participate in constructing the meaning of the text. Narrative also, in Stephen Crites's words, creates "an inner bond among tellers and hearers. Stories are community-creating."[46] Thus in the parables of Jesus, as Ernst Fuchs long ago observed, the listener "may think together with Jesus . . . love provides in advance the sphere in which meeting takes place."[47] The Markan narrative, Kermode seeks to argue, turns readers either into "insiders" or into "outsiders".[48] The reader is invited to share a "point of view", and to be carried along in the forward movement of the narrative plot.

Wesley Kort follows Ricoeur in stressing *the coherent or ordered nature of the plot within the framework of narrative time*.⁴⁹ In Kort's view, narrative embodies four indispensable elements: character, which portrays human traits; plot, which carries forward coherent movement as temporal process; tone, which the teller of the tale projects for the reader; and atmosphere, which determines the boundaries of the narrative world.⁵⁰ He observes, "Narrative provides an underlying unity to human experience."⁵¹ *Narrative therefore constructs a coherent logic, but by presenting a plot temporally, concretely, and in terms of human inter-relations, it carries those readers along who might remain uninvolved or unimpressed by abstract logical argument, the force of which is atemporal.* In our closing chapters on hermeneutics and pastoral theology, we discuss the particular appeal of narrative-projection for particular types of readers and reading-situations. A tentative and speculative illustration may be suggested by the Myers-Briggs indicator which is based on Jungian distinctions among human types and temperaments. Even allowing for the limits imposed by crude quantification by the indicator, as well as its over-reliance on given polarities and presuppositions, it remains plausible to suggest that so-called "thinkers" (Ts) will more readily be drawn to *abstract logic* than "feelers" (Fs) who may be at home with the *temporal flow of person-related events structured by the logic of a narrative plot*. While so-called sensors (Ss) may be most at home with history-like "reporting" stories, "intuitive feelers" (NFs) may readily trace the *possibilities projected by narrative worlds, including metamorphical or allegorical narrative*, and so-called "intuitive thinkers" (NTs) may be drawn to the *complex possibilities* generated within what Wittgenstein termed *"logical space"*.

Kort illustrates the productive use of these narrative tools for reading and understanding with reference to specific biblical texts. The Exodus narratives offer a paradigm for his exploration of *plot*. The narratives are packed with events: the call of Moses (Ex. 3:1–4,17), confrontations with Pharaoh (Ex. 5:1–21), the plagues (Ex. 7:20–11:10), the preparations for flight and pursuit (14:5–18), and the parting of the sea (14:21–29). Patterns of conflict occur within a frame of forward-moving direction. The climax of the plot is the "exchange". Initially, and as tension builds, there is a separation or disjunction between the ultimate divine purpose and Israel's plight. But the tension is resolved in the unity of purpose and actuality. Conversely, for the Egyptians the movement begins with unity and ends with separation as this fate or destiny is disentangled from that of Israel.⁵²

In Kort's view, the narratives of Judges provide a particular focus for the part played by *character* in narrative. The stories are more episodic than might be expected if plot were the major concern, although there is a rhythmic pattern of wrongdoing, distress, a cry for help, and deliverance.⁵³ Kort observes, "The religious meaning of Judges arises primarily from the effect of contrasting a consistent function of deliverer with a wide diversity of character."[54] The deceitful Ehud (Judges 3:15–30) performs a parallel functional role within the structure of the narrative to the actions of Gideon who is repeatedly anxious about the need for proofs and signs (Judges 6:36–40).

Kort is one of a number of writers who, (like E.M. Good, Patrick Grant, and Frank Kermode) explore narrative approaches to Jonah and to Mark. Jonah, he suggests, acquires a narrative focus in terms of *atmosphere and boundaries*. The prophet cannot control the boundaries of what he would like to be his world. This expanding inclusiveness even extends to the role of intertextuality: "Jonah" may perhaps allude to the Jonah ben Amittai of II Kings 14:23–27; Jonah's prayers clearly employ the language of the Psalms; there are resonances, it is argued, with the prophetic ministry of Elijah.[55]

Mark, in a number of studies including that of David Rhoads and Donald Michie, is the so-called *"omniscient narrator"* who is party to privileged information, and who shares this *"point of view"* with the reader.[56] This places the reader above or ahead of the characters in the story, who are deprived of this perspective. Kort observes: "The narrator places the reader in a position that exceeds even that of the disciples in the story."[57] Mark is eager "to share privilege with the reader", and to take the reader into the narrator's confidence. This Markan tone holds together the human and divine, and universalizes the particular.

Kort's narrative approach to Mark, however, differs significantly at precisely this point from that of Frank Kermode's *Genesis of Secrecy* (1979). Kermode sees Mark as deliberately puzzling, and *in principle* polyvalent and ambiguous. Any Markan text can provoke a host of conflicting interpretations. Mark "banishes interpreters from its secret places."[58] Anyone outside "the guild", Kermode claims, *remains* an "outsider". Parables in Mark "require some interpretative action from the auditor; they call for completion . . . (but) interpretation . . . is bound to fail; it is an intrusion always, and always unsuccessful."[59]

The narrative, Kermode argues, only appears superficially to be perspicuous: "we are never inside it."[60] Paradoxes come together into an unresolvable set of knots: demons recognize Jesus, disciples do not; the law is now kept, now broken; tangles occur in "riddling parables."[61] The irreducible "given" is only "secrecy." Alluding to the tantalizing situation portrayed by Franz Kafka in *The Trial* Kermode concludes: "Hot for secrets, our only conversation may be with guardians who know less and see less than we can; and our sole hope and pleasure is the perception of a momentary radiance, before the door of disappointment is finally shut on us."[62]

It would be tempting to seek to offer a critique of Kermode's observations at this point. But we have not yet examined some of the theoretical issues which arise in the context of reader-response theory, and it is into this area that Kermode's approach has effectively brought us. I doubt whether Kermode's reading does full justice to the text of Mark, and the radically different reasons for "obscurity" in the Markan narrative which Ronald Thiemann identifies place a serious question mark against some of Kermode's arguments. Some of the theoretical issues involved will re-emerge in our critique of reader-response theory in the next chapter, and we shall develop some relevant points further in the final two chapters on hermeneutics and pastoral theology.

Meanwhile a number of other writers have undertaken further work on the temporal flow of narrative plot and the projection of narrative "points of view". Tannehill, Kelber, Jasper, and Best all offer contributions of this kind. The wholeness of the narrative assists the forward temporal flow of the narrative-plot.[63] In this respect Stephen Moore expresses hesitation about James Dawsey's book *The Lukan Voice: Confusion and Irony in the Gospel of Luke* (1986), in which Dawsey tries to utilize the notion of what Wayne Booth termed the "unreliable narrator".[64] Booth's term refers not to historical unreliability as such, but to the narrator's projection at times of a narrative "point of view" with which the readers are invited *not* to identify, but from which they are to *distance* themselves. This disrupts the unity of the narrative and the narrative-world. But Stephen Moore follows Robert Scholes and Robert Kellog in arguing that this particular narrative technique is a modern one, and therefore for the reading of Luke "almost two millenia out of time".[65]

We should not drive too sharp a wedge, however, between the concerns of narrative or literary theory and the aims of composition criticism or redaction criticism. Meier Sternberg's book *The Poetics of Biblical Narrative: Ideological Literature and the Drama of Reading* (1985) argues *at least in principle* for the complementary roles of ideological, historical, and aesthetic hermeneutics.[66] For Sternberg, a literary approach, far from excluding questions about the *theological, social, or ideological purpose of the writer*, accepts it as a given that biblical texts constitute "directed" literature which embodies truth-claims about ideas. Questions about history and setting may therefore operate alongside the use of literary tools. Sternberg accepts the importance of "interest", of the kind which we associated with Habermas and socio-critical hermeneutics in the previous two chapters. But he also remains sensitive to the additional dimensions addressed by literary studies and by literary theory.

Such an approach is warmly endorsed by Lynn Poland, Martin Warner, and others, at the recent Warwick conference on the Bible and literature, papers of which are published under the title *The Bible as Rhetoric* (1990).[67] Lynn Poland notes that Sternberg's description of the Bible as "ideological" literature stands in contrast to the tenet of literary formalism that art must be "purposeless" and "disinterested". But as her earlier book *Literary Criticism and Biblical Hermeneutics* demonstrates, she is well aware of the limitations of formalism, she shares Sternberg's goal of asking "how this (ideological) function of biblical narrative works with or against its historiographic and aesthetic functions".[68]

Hans Frei's influential book *The Eclipse of Biblical Narrative* (1974) draws on both the legacy of the new criticism in literary theory and on historical and theological hermeneutics, with particular reference to changes of hermeneutical perspective in the eighteenth century.[69] From the eighteenth century onwards, especially after the work of J.S. Semler and Anthony Collins, modern historical rationalist scholarship imposed a distinctively *modern* conceptual contrast onto the biblical narratives, one which, Frei claims, the biblical writers could or would not have made. Modern "propositional" approaches, such as Collins inherited from John Locke, imposed a sharp dualism between historical and fictional narrative, whereas biblical writers projected by "figuration" a "realistic" narrative that was "history-*like*" but not always or not necessarily "history". Frei urged that "the realistic or history-like quality of biblical narratives" should be seen "for the bearing it had *in its own right* (my italics) on meaning".[70]

We have already noted in chapter VIII that according to the speech-act theory of Searle, Recanati, and others, whether a projected narrative world presupposes certain extra-linguistic states of affairs will decisively condition the particular effects of the textual narrative. It is doubtful whether Frei's work pays sufficient attention to the logical differences entailed between purely intra-linguistic discourse and that which presupposes some kind of interaction between the linguistic system and extra-linguistic life-world. Certainly Searle and Wolterstorff demonstrate that the *force* of narrative texts (to use Recanati's particular terminology) or their *"count-generative"* nature (to use Wolterstorff's term) as acts of remembering, celebrating, social bonding, promising, or describing *differs according to the extra-linguistic behavioural commitments of a narrator or editor*. We discuss these points in the section on narrative in chapter XV, and have already noted some of the issues in our discussion of Ricoeur's narrative hermeneutics in chapter X.

Where Frei's narrative theory contributes most is in the warning against the *hermeneutically anachronistic assumption* that the relation between the linguistic and extra-linguistic worlds in biblical narrative takes the form of a series of *atomistic correspondences between logically elementary propositions containing object-words and components of states of affairs on the basis of ostensive reference*. Biblical narrative does not characteristically function in accordance with the picture theory of the early Wittgenstein, in which there is always a precise one-to-one correspondence between *logically atomic components of a narrative configuration* and relations between objects that constitute states of affairs in the extra-linguistic world. The very contrast, for example, *between natural time and narrative time*, not to mention the *organization of a narrative-structure in terms of a plot,* excludes an understanding of biblical narrative as a wooden or photographic mirror-reflection of states of affairs as these are depicted in logical atomism, or in theories of ostensive reference offered as comprehensive context-free systems of meaning.

3. Formalist and Structuralist Approaches to Biblical Narrative Texts

Formalism and structuralism approach texts as systems, whereas the hermeneutical tradition from Schleiermacher to Gadamer approaches them as life-worlds bounded by horizons of understanding. It becomes possible to abstract the text or the narrative as a system from the variable particularities of the flow of human life only by drawing an imaginary line of insulation between the text and its author, on one side, and between the text and its readers, on the other. The text and its narrative now achieve the artificial status of a system which has overcome the problem of hermeneutical contingency and particularity, and can be studied by "scientific" method as a self-contained "objective" or formal structure.

In our two early chapters on textuality we considered the notion that texts constitute quasi-autonomous formal structures, which, in Ricoeur's phrase, reflect "a double eclipse of the reader and the writer".[71] We noted Derrida's development of Saussure's model of formal structure to formulate a conception of the text as "a differential network".[72] We also observed further that in the new criticism of J.C. Ransom (1938) of Wellek and Warren (1942) and of Northrop Frye's *Anatomy of Criticism* (1957) the model of a text as a formal system abstracted from the life-world of the author and the reader was congenial to a method which stressed the disinterested operation of textual forces.

In the world of the early 1960s, the supposed "objectivity" of the first phase of structuralism appealed to an intellectual climate in France which was weary of the over-preoccupation with subjectivity in European existentialism. But in terms of *literary* and *narrative* theory the roots of structuralist approaches to narrative may be traced to Russian formalism. The search for a *formal "grammar"* of narrative is connected with the desire to achieve a deductive model capable of *quasi-scientific generalization.* It stands far removed from *hermeneutical* concerns about socio-historical factors of particularity and contingency. The foundational starting-point for a formal grammar or "morphology" of narrative is the seminal work of Vladimir I. Propp in 1928.

The possibility of generalizing about narrative-*form* has a *prima-facie* plausibility, especially for those generations who have had the misfortune to spend large stretches of their childhood in front of the television looking at Westerns. As Pierre Guiraud observes, in theatre or in film there are *standard roles*: the hero, the villain, the helper, the traitor, the confidant, and so on.[73] *Typified* categories embrace to standard patterns of action: the quest, the thwarting of love, punishment, vengeance, and reward. In 1928 Vladimir Propp published his *Morphology of the Folktale*, in which he traced common *formal patterns* which recurred in a hundred Russian folk-tales. Certain functions constitute *invariant* elements of the tale.

Although he used the term "functions", Propp found the stable invariables of quasi-scientific generality in the characters who performed them. Function is "an act of a character defined from the point of view of its significance for the course of the action".[74] Propp identified thirty-one such functions, which included such roles of performance as the hero, the provider (or "donor"), the villain, the princess (the "sought-for" person), the helper, and the "false hero".[75] Propp's work was translated into English in 1958, and into French in 1973, and became, in Kort's words, "a primer for the structural analysis of narrative".[76]

As we observed in chapter III, structuralism began to assume the shape of a wider theory when in 1929 the Prague Linguistic Circle argued on the basis of Saussure's work that linguistics should begin not with atomistic "facts" of language, but with the language-*system* (*langue*) on the basis of which selected speech-utterances (*parole*) achieved their meaning-currency. Colour-words and kinship patterns offer very clear paradigms: "orange" can be defined in terms of its relation between "red" on one side and "yellow" on the other within a colour spectrum or colour "field". In 1931 J. Trier declared that verbal meaning emerged "only within a field", and in 1933 N. Trubetzkoy, as we have already noted, proposed that this Saussurian model be extended to other academic disciplines. Roman Jakobson developed Saussure's contrast between syntagmatic (linear) and paradigmatic (substitutional) axes within the system, in terms of the *code* through which *messages* between the *sender* and *receiver* were communicated in a given *context* through some *contact* made possible by speech, writing, or other (e.g. electronic) media.

There is no need to re-trace the ground covered in our earlier chapter concerning Lévi-Strauss's application of these principles to kinship systems and to other social phenomena in his *Structural Anthropology* (1958). We observed how he worked with the notion of systems of internal binary oppositions in myth, such as those between heaven and earth, life and death, female and male, or God and the world. In the words of Jean-Marie Benoist: "A sign signifies only by virtue of the differential gap which associates it with other signs ... language (is) a self-referring system."[77] Benoist cites the parallel of the Bourbakist mathematicians who employed the notion of structure in their set theory: "For the mathematicians, knowledge of a mathematical object is not directed towards the isolated qualities of an entity, but to the formal properties of a system."[78]

Apart from Barthes, the only other figure comparable in formative influence to Propp for structuralist approaches to biblical narrative is Alexander J. Greimas (1966 and 1970).[79] Greimas began his work by exploring the subject-object system of differential within the "sentence". But he extended his construction of system to the larger unit of narrative, on the basis of Propp's work. Greimas developed the link between subject and object (in a propositional context) into what becomes transposed in narrative structure into an axis of desire and quest (the *subject* desires, or begins a quest for, the *object*); and an axis of communication (the *subject*, or *"sender"*, transmits the *object* to a *"receiver"*). To these four functional narrative-components, Greimas added two more: a *helper* and an *opponent*, who inter-relate on the plane of struggle. Greimas' "grammar" or morphology of narrative now has six components: subject and object, sender and receiver, and helper and opponent. These stand in differential relations of quest or desire, of communication, and of struggle.

David Greenwood observes that in contrast to Roland Barthes, Greimas consciously aims at a "scientific" approach to the narrative text.[80] He works deductively, applying a general model to particular texts. Greenwood argues that Todorov by contrast works inductively, looking for patterns in particular texts. Greimas is concerned not with textual meaning, but with the formal structures that underlie it and generate it: with the level of *langue*, not with the level of *parole*. The invariant formal narrative *actant-roles* which Greimas claims to identify are therefore invariables of "deep" structure. The "deep" structure arises from the givens of binary opposition identified by Lévi-Strauss. But the oppositions subject vs. object, opponent vs. helper, sender vs. receiver are structured in narrative along axes which construct the coherence of a narrative sequence or plot. In particular the notion of "contract" organizes the plot: the sender commands the receiver or hero to undertake some task or venture.[81] This contractual dimension is supplemented by dimensions of performance (trials, difficulties, struggles), and disjunction (departure, movement, return). These form basic invariables of a narrative "grammar".

In biblical interpretation Greimas' model has been widely influential. Roland Barthes, Dan Otto Via, Daniel Patte, and Jean Calloud are among those which have used it for the exploration of specific texts, along with other methods. Louis Marin combines a utilization of Greimas with the approach of Jacques Lacan. But perhaps the first major exploration of structuralist narrative grammar for biblical texts was undertaken in Roland Barthes' well-known essay, published in 1971, under the title "The Struggle with the Angel: Textual Analysis of Genesis 32:23–33".[82] The same year (1971) Barthes also published his essay "A Structural Analysis of a Narrative from Acts X-XI".[83]

Barthes drew on his own earlier work on structuralism and on his developing work on semiotic codes, but the wider influence of conceptual tools from Propp, from Lévi-Strauss, and from Greimas can also be seen. Barthes distinguishes between three types of enquiry: "*Where* the text comes from (historical-critical analysis) . . . *how* it is made (structural analysis) . . . (and) *how* it is unravelled . . . and which coded stages go into it" (textual analysis or theory of textuality).[84] Barthes follows Propp in noting that structural analysis calls "an inventory . . . of the characters involved in the narrative". He also notes Greimas' use of such an inventory "to classify their function . . . as subjects of a repetitive action: as a Sender, Seeker, Envoy . . . the *actantielle* analysis of which A.J. Greimas was the first to give the theory."[85] The organizational structure of the narrative flow also invites *sequential* analysis.

Barthes stresses that since the Jacob passage in Gen. 32: 23–33 consists mainly of *contingent* actions, priority should be accorded to a sequential analysis. The major differentials, however, generated by the structure emerge as "the crossing" (Gen. 32: 23–25); "the struggle" (32: 25–30); and "the change of names or the mutations" (32: 28–33). Three elements we may notice, reflect Greimas' respective categories of disjunction (departure, testing or struggle in the face of opponents or trials); and the contractual motif (change of names). Jacob is the hero of the quest, while God assumes the role of "provider" or "donor" (Propp) or "sender" (Greimas). But the very formulation of the structural pattern throws into relief a discordant and contingent feature. There is "an inversion of the expected relationship of forces".[86] It is God who "sends" Jacob contractually on the purposive quest; but it is also God who turns out to be both opponent and helper in the performance axis. Barthes comments: "That the sender may be the adversary is very rare . . . What interests me most in this famous crossing is not the 'folklorist' model, but the interactions, the *disruptions*, the *discontinuities* of legibility."[87]

In one direction Barthes has adopted the structuralist stance of viewing the text as a closed system. But already his emphasis on disruptive features which transcend formal patterns point not simply to heightened differentials created by a system, but to socio-historical factors which modify purely systemic forces. Barthes' approach to the structural analysis of Acts 10–11 underlines this aspect further. In this passage he identifies no less than twelve semiotic "codes", which are not simply codes of formal narrative grammar, but a series of interlocking and overlapping systems which arise from a variety of socio-linguistic conventions. Thus at the beginning of the Cornelius narrative he identifies a "narrative" code ("There was at Caesarea a man called Cornelius..."); "Caesarea" presupposes a "topographic" code (in which the term stands in operational differential from "Joppa", 10:5).[88] A so-called "onomastic" code sets up oppositions between the names "Cornelius" and "Peter" (10:5); the reference to the Italian Cohort (10:1) presupposes a "historical" code; and "the sixth hour" (10:9) functions on the basis of a "chronological" code.[89]

One upshot of the analysis is to see the mainspring of the text as concerning communication rather than quest.[90] But, as he declares near the beginning of his essay, Barthes' main interest lies in the structures or codes which make meaning "a Possible". He observes, "The meaning for me is *the very being of the possible*" (his italics).[91] But we argued in chapter III that issues could be clouded if we slide between the level of *langue* and the level of *parole* within the use of the one term "meaning". Syntactic semiotic and semantic *systems* differ from acts in pragmatics, in which meanings emerge in the context of *interrelationships* between *systems* and *life-worlds*. Admittedly without any notion of structure or system, the patterned (but revisable) regularities embodied in *langue* become dissolved. But without any adequate action-orientated anchorage of the text in the communicative inter-active life-world of speaker and hearer, we slide from one level of code to another, without any stable grounding in patterns of extra-linguistic behaviour.

A second leading figure also made a well-known contribution to structuralism in biblical interpretation co-jointly with Barthes in this same year (1971). In February 1971 the Protestant Theology Faculty of the University of Geneva invited two speakers, Roland Barthes from Paris, and Jean Starobinski from Geneva, to lead a dialogue on structuralism with biblical specialists and literary theorists. Jean Starobinski's paper, which has now (like that of Barthes on Gen. 32:23–33) become a classic for structuralist theory, was published in 1971 (English 1974) under the title "The Gerasene Demoniac: A Literary Analysis of Mark 5:1–20".[92]

Starobinski begins by adopting the typical structuralist strategy of viewing the text as a "narrative system", abstracted from the life-world of the writer or narrator. He also argues that the Markan narrative has no addressee; this has "the effect of universalizing its audience". Within the textual system of Mark 5:1–20, oppositions and polarities emerge. The world of the demoniac is savage, wild, violent, and fearful, and is associated with storm, mountains, nightfall, and the tombs (Mark 5:2–5,7,11; cf. 4:35–41). Violence, agitation, cries, and isolation characterize the world of the demoniac; but Jesus exchanges the man's nakedness for "clothing", his violent instability for a "right mind", and his isolation for "going home to his friends" (Mark 5:15,19). Savage chaos is exchanged for wholeness, coherence, and order.

Topographical locations and especially movements underline the binary contrasts. "The other bank becomes the homologue of an infernal 'other world'."93 The demons make a "triple crossing ... out of the man, into the bodies of the swine (*eis tous choirous*) *into the sea* (*eis* ten thalassan, 5:13)."94 Topographical indices signal a contrast of *"return to order"*, in which the plurality of "Legion" (5:9) returns into the chaotic abyss: "The journey of the demonic powers literally *crosses* that of Jesus" as the vertical fall of the pigs "contrasts with the horizontal journey of Christ".95 A residue of opposition is indicated by the plea of the Gerasene local people for Jesus to depart from their neighbourhood (5:17).

After these initial explorations in 1971, a flood of literature streamed into biblical studies offering structural analyses of this or that biblical narrative. The first two numbers of *Semeia* at its foundation in 1974 were wholly devoted to structural approaches to the parables, with main contributions from John Dominic Crossan, Dan O. Via, Norman Petersen and Robert Funk. In 1973 (English, 1976) Jean Calloud published his *Structural Analysis of Narrative*, using almost exclusively the methods and tools of Greimas, to examine the temptation narrative in Matt. 4:1–11.96

Calloud's detailed results were far from being earth-shattering. The first "lexie", "Jesus was led by the Spirit out into the wilderness to be tempted by the Spirit" (Matt. 4:1) embodies the formal elements of *departure* (disjunctive axis), *contractual* mandating (Jesus accepts the Spirit's leading) and *struggle* (to be tempted). "Being hungry" (4:2) corresponds to Propp's category of "lack"; and the devil's proposal to turn stones into bread (4:3) potentially casts the devil into the role of an anti-sender, or rival *sender* to God.97 The second temptation would identify *God's* "contract" ("scripture says ..."4:6) with the devil's proposed contractual mandate ("cast yourself down ..."). Over the whole extended narrative binary oppositions (presence vs. absence, satisfaction vs. lack, need vs. desire) add further differentials within the structure.98

Does Calloud aim to help us to understand the meaning of the temptation narrative? He tells us that his work is to show how units function *on the basis of system*, and how the narrative network is *organized*. But it may be doubted whether the enormous energy expended in applying Greimas' model in such detail offered much more than a mainly theoretical exercize. We shall note in due course the reservations expressed by some biblical scholars both about the usefulness of this approach, and about the capacity of this so-called "scientific" method to be submitted to criteria of verification. Meanwhile, however, these structuralist approaches to the New Testament (1973, 1974) were parallelled by Old Testament work. The same year that *Semeia* devoted its first two numbers to structuralism, the journal *Interpretation* offered a series of structuralist essays including articles by Robert Spivey, Richard Jacobson, Robert Culley, and work by Robert Polzin on Job, which he later expanded into the book *Biblical Structuralism*.99

Dan Otto Via and Daniel Patte have consistently worked over a period of time to apply structuralist approaches to biblical texts, in Via's case mainly to the parables of Jesus. His early work *The Parables: Their Literary and Existential Dimension* (1967) applied both the legacy of the new criticism and an existential hermeneutic to a number of parables.[100] Following Robert Funk, he brought to the attention of American readers the suggestive approach of Ernst Fuchs and the new hermeneutic.[101] In addition to the category of narrative-world and existential resonance, however, Via developed an understanding of parables in terms of *plot*. Tragedy is "a plot moving downward toward catastrophe and the isolation of the protagonist".[102] By contrast, "the category of comedy is being used in the broad sense of a plot that moves upwards toward the well-being of the protagonist".[103] Tragic plot shapes such parables as the parables of the talents (Matt. 25:14–30), the wedding garment (Matt. 22:11–14), and the ten maidens (Matt. 25:1–13). Thus the one-talent person recognizes only at the last moment the painful consequences of refusals to take any risk, and of construing oneself as an inevitable victim of other people's initiatives; while the maidens are finally confronted with the painful consequences of the assumption that someone else will always pay the bill.[104] On the other hand, the labourers in the vineyard (Matt. 20:1–16), the dishonest manager (Luke 16:1–9), and the prodigal son (Luke 15:11–32) represent examples of comic plot. For the prodigal son, the story ends festively with a well-being which exceeds his highest expectations.[105]

At this stage, Via's work offers a synthesis between the new criticism and hermeneutics. He moves to structuralist analysis in his *Kerygma and Comedy in the New Testament* (1975).[106] Via is sensitive to the limitations of those purely formalist or semiotic versions of structuralism that repress all historical questions. He distances himself from Barthes' comment about "immobilization of time", and concurs that Michel Foucault presents "an excessively anti-historical point of view".[107] Yet he also expresses a confidence that structuralism will "produce new knowledge".[108]

One example of Via's approach concerns the structural basis in which he believes certain biblical language operates in Pauline texts. Several structures, codes, or, as he calls them "axes" of structure may operate behind Paul's language about "letter and spirit" (2. Cor. 3:6). These include the axes of covenant, law, and power. Law would be perceived as "letter" if the structural basis from which it derives its meaning is a notion of works-justification by achievement: but within a structure of space or of justification by faith, law appears to signify "Spirit" (cf. Rom. 7:6,7; 8:2).[109] But Via integrates structural approaches with hermeneutical ones. For he speaks of the presuppositional dimension as "pre-understanding". Thus another "pre-understanding" which shapes the meaning of "letter" and "spirit" is the axis of power. The Spirit can be perceived to give power for life; within an achievement-orientated "pre-understanding" the letter works its power to produce death.[110]

We shall return to this question of the relation between structuralism and hermeneutics, with its transposition of the categories of "system" and "life-world" into a literary or interpretative key. In contrast to Via, Daniel Patte sets aside the hermeneutical tradition in successive volumes which begin with his *What is Structural Exegesis?* (1976). Patte explicitly recognizes and uses the influences of Saussure, Lévi-Strauss, Propp, Greimas, and Barthes, but rejects the hermeneutical models of Dilthey through to Gadamer on the ground that the biblical text "is *not* living language . . . no longer a speech". It is *not* "addressed to me".[111] Historical exegesis, he insists, does not lead in practice to hermeneutics.[112] Patte is concerned with the "meaning-effect" which he hopes to derive from structuralism. "Meaning-effect" is analogous to "sound-effect".[113]

The major problem here is the sheer predictability of the results produced in an era when Greimas' narrative grammar was thought to have objective or "scientific" status. Thus when Patte expounds at length not only the repeated story of Saussure, Propp, and Greimas, but the application of these structuralist categories, through Calloud, to the parable of the Good Samaritan (Luke 10:30–32), we can predict the outcome in general (which would, on its own terms, verify a "scientific" hypothesis, if it were not that the selectivity of the model embodies socio-contingent factors). The story begins with the "disjunction" of departure and journey; robbers take the role of "opponents"; the wounded man is "receiver"; while Patte designates as "helper" oil, wine, and "know-how"(!)[114] But how does this provide a basis for a better hermeneutic than other more traditional approaches?

Patte perseveres with this structural approach producing major works in 1978 (with Aline Patte), 1983, and 1987.[115] In his preface to the collection *Signs and Parables* (1978) he recognizes the possibility that the structuralists may in fact operate with a theory of meaning which "we may eventually wish to reject".[116] In their joint work D. and A. Patte acknowledge that Roland Barthes and Michel Foucault have moved on in their thought, and that they both firmly deny the possibility of establishing "a universal network of relations characteristic of narratives".[117] In *Structural Exegesis*, in *Paul's Faith and the Power of the Gospel,* and in *The Gospel according to Matthew,* Patte uses a much more broadly "structural" approach to determine the systems of "deep values or convictions" which make reality and convictions about reality what it is for those who hold them.

Structural exploration here aims to determine conditions for the *possibility* of *convictions* on the part of Paul and of Matthew.[118] Patte defines faith as "being held by a system of convictions".[119] Convictions are to be distinguished from beliefs. An inappropriate structure or frame (for example, the boundaries of revelation equated entirely with law) could absolutize revelation "into an idolatrous system of convictions".[120] Within such a structure, Jesus would be perceived as a scandal; but within a different structure, Christ means the manifestation of the power of God (Rom. 8:1–4).

In his very perceptive and helpful book *Reading the New Testament*, Patrick Grant describes Patte's work on Paul in this volume as reading "remarkably like a modern study of a literary text".[121] But how is this different from Via's recognition that the *frame* within which understanding operates is not simply a structural *system*, but also a hermeneutical *life-world*? A failure to recognize that enquiries about *system alone* without reference to *life-world* are not enough gives a very hollow ring to the extravagant claims of Erhardt Güttgemanns (1971, 1972, 1973, 1976). He claims to provide a method of approach which will replace the entire historical-hermeneutical tradition of European and Western biblical scholarship with a better "linguistic" theology. Güttgemanns presented his own development of the structural study of narrative drawing not only extensively on Propp and Greimas but also on N. Chomsky's generative linguistics. Not a person to make modest claims, Güttgemanns asserted "Traditional New Testament theology is to be rejected on the basis of linguistics, since it is not derived from a textual theory".[122] It is to be replaced by his own structuralist "generative poetics".

The development of structuralism *either* into post-structuralism and deconstructionism *or* into a semiotic theory which takes fuller account of socio-cultural contingent factors in human life-worlds, leaves Güttgemanns's theories stranded as products of an earlier formalist and pseudo-scientific phase of structuralism. What *counts as* system or as *semiotic code* is at least partly a matter of socially-contingent reading conventions. But once we recognize that the systems are not autonomous universalized networks but *frames* conditioned by socio-cultural factors, this leads, as Jonathan Culler has forcefully argued, to a shift of attention from "the text alone" to the role of the *reader*. Culler uses the term "framing" in this reader-orientated way in his recent book *Framing the Sign* (1988) to designate reader-context as well as text-context. Culler writes, "*Framing the Sign* has several advantages over *context*: it reminds us that framing is something we do; it hints of the frame-up . . . a major use of context".[123] To trace the limitations, difficulties, and effective demise of "structuralist" approaches (in contrast to post-structuralist and semiotic work) in biblical studies is thereby to begin to explore the growth and development of *reader*-orientated theories in biblical hermeneutics and in literary studies. To these two areas we now turn.

4. From Post-Structuralism to Semiotic Theories of Reading: Intertextuality and the Paradigm-Shift to "Reading"

Structuralism has largely become transposed into semiotic or into post-structuralist theories. Jonathan Culler expressed the key principle involved when he observes that as soon as the structural network is perceived to be nothing other than *conventions of reading*, the focus of attention *shifts to the reader*. Further, Culler writes, since *semiotics* concerns conventions on the basis of which signs become operative, semiotic enquiries in literary theory constitute *theories of reading*. Semiotics, he argues in his book *The Pursuit of Signs* (1981) takes account of how readers interpret texts, and "such a semiotics would be a theory of reading".[124]

In his earlier book *Structuralist Poetics* (1975) Culler had presented an argument for developing structuralism into a theory of *literary competence*, which could account for the myriad of possibilities found in literary texts. Literature can be "read" only on the basis of "possibilities". There is thus a parallel between the system of possibilities (*la langue*) which generate the event of performance (*parole*) and task of *"poetics"*, which is to formulate the conditions of *possibility* for acts of *"reading"*.[125]

Before we consider Culler's work more closely, however, it is perhaps worth drawing together a brief summary of some of the factors which precipitated the demise of structuralism in biblical studies, even though its influence in a different form continues to pervade more recent literary theory. In current works on biblical interpretation, post-structuralist or semiotic trends have led to an emphasis on "theories of *reading*" and on *inter-textuality*. The explosion of energy poured into "structuralist" approaches has dissipated in different directions.

First, we may remind ourselves that at the end of the 1950s and beginning of the 1960s structuralism emerged in a context of French intellectual history when reactions were strong against an over-long and dominant pre-occupation with existentialist subjectivity. Part of this reaction gave rise to a *quasi-objectivist* emphasis in early structuralism. Although hopes for a "science" soon crumbled, part of the general *reaction against the centredness of the human subject* still operates in an utterly different form in the semiotics of post-modernism as *a de-centering of the human subject*. This shift away from the human subject has been hastened by *post-Freudian psycho-analytical approaches to texts*, in which the capacity of the self for deception and illusion becomes a dominant motif in post-modernist hermeneutics. In addition to the general legacy and influence of Freud, the work of Jacques Lacan and others calls attention to these issues.

The optimism of objectivist early structuralism is well expressed in the essay by F. Bovon which commended "French structuralism" to biblical scholars in 1971. Bovon contrasts an existential concern with "the subject", "life", and "decision" in hermeneutics with "new logical and objective methods drawn from the natural sciences . . . One does not speak any more of historicity but of . . . systems".[126] But only four years later, in 1975, Jean-Marie Benoist speaks of the same "turn from the subject" in very different terms, which clearly point towards post-modernist developments. Benoist writes: "The subject, then, is just a point or stroke upon a mobile and dynamic graph, and so we cannot grant it . . . epistemological and philosophical supremacy . . .".[127] If post-structuralism shifts attention to the reader, this is not to the consciousness of the *individual* reader of formalist theory, but to the *conventions, cultural codes, and historically-conditioned expectations which constitute the reading-community as a socio-cultural phenomenon.*

Second, in mainstream biblical studies there has been not only scepticism at the theoretical level about the predictability or in some cases arbitrariness of the particular structural models which have been selected, but also impatience at the pragmatic level at the ratio of detailed labour to actual results. Stephen Moore candidly speaks of "those who were reduced to yawns or groans by biblical structuralism, semiotics, or discourse analysis".[128] Robert Culley responded to an earlier structuralist paper by Patte by asking, first, what could count as *verification* in this pseudo-scientific procedure, and second wherein its *usefulness* might be said to lie. Similarly Vern S. Poythress acknowledged the potential value of structuralism as an approach which opened new perspectives, but argued that it offers no criterion by which to evaluate the truth of its claims.[129] The *arbitrariness* of certain semiotic or structuralist categories came to be seen as precisely what they were: socio-historically conditioned conventions of reading, which represent only one possible network of generative conventions among others.

Third, the inevitable broadening and modifying in biblical studies of the earlier objectivist notions of structure developed by Greimas, Calloud, Güttgemanns and others begins to call in question how strictly more recent work can still be called "structuralist". Patte's recent work is at most on the borderline, and he uses the term "structural" rather than "structuralist". We noted Patrick Grant's comments that this work looked like an approach to "literary" texts in more general terms. Patte still insists, however, on a contrast between structural and hermeneutical approaches, although as early as 1975 Via had noted the close parallel, if not identity, between the notion of a structure within which a text was understood and *pre-understanding* in the hermeneutic tradition. Similarly in his earlier work *Meaning in Texts* (1978) Edgar V. McKnight in effect pressed structuralism into the service of hermeneutics; while in his more recent work *The Bible and the Reader* (1985) McKnight rightly sees the main significance of what he calls "the structural-semiotic approach" as paving the way for attention to *the role of the reader*. In this connection he alludes favourably to Geoffrey Hartman's "hermeneutic criticism", and negatively to Güttgemanns' tortuously complex apparatus as "simplistic".[130] He takes this reader-orientated approach further in his *Post-Modern Use of the Bible: The Emergence of Reader-Oriented Criticism* (1988).

Both strands weave a pattern together in Jonathan Culler's notion of "framing". Here the reader plays a key role in determining what counts as meaning in the processes of contextualization and re-contextualization which renders texts intelligible. The fundamental question, in this case, is whether structural semiotics has crumbled entirely into post-structuralism and post-modernist deconstruction, or whether it has the capacity to broaden into what Susan Wittig describes as "a larger apprehension of the total semiotic model – to an understanding of the relationships among the semantic, syntactic, and pragmatic axes of the communicative event".[131] Each of these two different directions would suggest a different understanding of hermeneutics.

In *The Pursuit of Signs* Jonathan Culler formulates a presupposition for the possibility of "reading" which is closely parallel to the more traditional hermeneutical notion of pre-understanding. This turns on the category or concept, developed from Julia Kristeva's work, of *intertextuality*. It may be argued that this concept is less subject-centred or consciousness-centred than hermeneutical pre-understanding; but hermeneutics *after* Heidegger, from *Gadamer onwards*, depends not on questions about *individual* consciousness only, but on *inter-subjectivity*. *Just as hermeneutics depends on the dialectic of the hermeneutical circle, so intertextuality moves between the two poles of langue and parole.* "Intertextuality" includes "presuppositions" in Culler's thought.

Culler argues that a text is intelligible "only in terms of a prior body of discourse ... the intertextual nature of any verbal construct".[132] He sees "formulating presupposition" and "describing intertextuality" as virtually synonymous.[133] He writes: "One function of inter-textuality is to allude to the paradoxical nature of discursive systems ... Everything in *la langue*, as Saussure says, must have first been in *parole*. But *parole* is made possible by *la langue*, and if one attempts to identify any utterance or text as a moment of origin one finds that they depend on prior codes."[134]

Culler argues, therefore, that intertextuality "has a double focus. On the one hand it calls attention to the importance of prior texts, insisting that the autonomy of texts is a misleading notion ... Yet ... 'intertextuality' leads us to consider prior texts as contributions to a code which makes possible the various effects of signification." Intertextuality thus becomes "less a name for a work's relation to particular prior texts than a designation of its participation in the discursive space of a *culture* ... the relationship between a text and the various ... *signifying practices of a culture.*"[135]

Schleiermacher had already seen at the beginning of the nineteenth century that hermeneutical pre-understanding implied the *corrigibility* of textual interpretation. In our chapters on Schleiermacher and on the application of a hermeneutic of understanding to biblical texts, we noted what implications this carried for "schools" of interpretation in New Testament Studies, and for the historical purposes of biblical exegesis. But, as Jonathan Culler points out, intertextuality in literary theory becomes a principle which seems to suggest *not only corrigibility, but irreducible polyvalency and radical indeterminacy as a matter of principle which the reader does not seek to overcome.* He examines Riffaterre's notion of intertextuality according to which literary works *always and endlessly refer to other literary works or texts, so that the boundaries of this intertextuality can never be established.*[136] Julia Kristeva's notion that a text simultaneously "absorbs" and "destroys" the other "texts of inter-textual space" undergoes development in the work of Harold Bloom. Bloom writes that the words of the literary text "refer to still other words, and so on into the densely overpopulated world of literary language".[137]

Culler notes, however, the difficulties of such views. They illustrate, he writes, *"the dangers that beset the notion of intertextuality: it is a difficult concept to use because of the vast and undefined discursive space it designates, but when one narrows it so as to make it more usable one either falls into a source study of a traditional . . . kind or else ends by naming particular texts as the pre-texts on grounds of interpretative convenience"*[138] (my italics). Culler constructively edges the discussion forward by *distinguishing between kinds of logical, literary, epistemological, and pragmatic "presupposition"* which might be used to determine *different understandings of intertextuality.* These *may* take the form of embracing other literary texts, but they *may* equally include extra-linguistic presuppositions of the kind discussed by Edward Keenan, namely pragmatic presuppositions relating to *"situation of utterance".*[139] Texts which convey *promises*, for example, relate to presuppositions which make the words intelligible and effective *"as* a speech act".[140]

If the "text", then, effectively includes this broad network as a condition of its intelligibility to readers, three lines of approach are suggested, each of which has been explored in biblical studies especially over the last ten years. First, the paradigm of *"reading"* in literary theory and questions about "reading competence" have tended to replace hermeneutical terminology about *"interpretation" and understanding.* Second, the whole question of *intertextuality* has assumed a new importance in biblical studies, and precisely the issues formulated by Jonathan Culler which we set out in the previous paragraphs have become an issue for exploration and discussion. The two volumes *Intertextuality in Biblical Writings* edited by Spike Draisma (1989) and *Echoes of Scripture in the Letters of Paul* by R.B. Hays (1989) presuppose and explore such questions and issues." Third, these questions lead us to see the importance of *reader-response* theories. Some theories, such as Iser's began in the context of a very different philosophical and literary climate; but most theories have now become merged *either* with these post-structuralist, post-modernist approaches *or* with a broader semiotics, whereby they also tend to become associated with a context-relativist or socio-pragmatic philosophy and hermeneutic.

5. The Paradigm of "Reading" in Biblical Studies and Intertextuality in Biblical Interpretation

The switch from the *hermeneutical* paradigm of *understanding* to the *literary* paradigm of *reading* did not originate in biblical studies simply with the decline of structuralist approaches. Quite the reverse is the case. Structuralist approaches carved such titles as "A Structuralist Reading of . . .", and, indeed biblical specialists had borrowed the notion of "close readings" from literary formalism and from the new criticism. But the widespread turn from "interpretation" to "reading" co-incides with a general interest in literary theory, and with a greater recognition of the role of the reader in interpretation. It marks a new awareness of the crucial part played by conventions of reading and by the purposes for which readers read texts, as well as reflecting the more general turn to the tools of literary theory.

A notable example of this paradigm-shift can be found in John Barton's widely-used book *Reading the Old Testament* (1984).[141] Barton explicitly enters into conversation with Jonathan Culler's earlier work in the context of his own emphasis on reading and reading-competence, as against interpretation and understanding.[142] Like Caird, nearly fifteen years earlier, Barton rightly sees the need to look beyond models exclusively used in biblical studies. "Reading", he urges, "depends crucially on decisions about *genre*, about what a text is to be read *as*" (his italics).[143] He then asserts: Instead of saying simply that methods of biblical study aim to assist *understanding* (my italics) of the text we may say that they aim to make the student *competent in reading* (Barton's italics) biblical material."[144] Following the Saussure-Chomsky usage in linguistics, Barton stresses that "competence" means "being in command of the conventions governing the use of a given language-system".[145] He draws comparisons between the respective conventions which govern the reading of commercial correspondence, poems, and novels. His discussion runs parallel to our expositions of semiotic code at the beginning of chapter III, above. Literary competence, he rightly concludes, develops "some sense of *what sorts of questions it makes sense to ask*" of a given text [146] (his italics).

Barton next expounds the variety of "methods" which are currently employed in Old Testament studies: literary (i.e. mainly source) analysis; form criticism of pre-literary oral material in largely stereotypical settings;

redaction criticism; the canonical approach of B.S. Childs; and the structuralist approaches of Propp and Barthes. Barton also describes the holistic method of David Clines' approach to the Pentateuch (to which we alluded in chapter VIII) as "structural", in a broader sense. Similarly, although he uses familiar parts of "structuralist equipment", J.A. Loader's work on Ecclesiastes remains structuralist "only in a very qualified sense".[147] The emphasis of the new criticism on "the text itself" or on the so-called autonomy of text invites comparison with B.S. Childs' claim about canon. Barton also notes close affinities between the assumptions of the new criticism about "the text in its own right" and Hans Frei's very influential work on narrative, to which we have also alluded under the heading of the legacy of the new criticism and narrative theory.

How does Barton utilize the notions of "reading" and "reading-competence" against this multiform background? Where he agrees, in effect, with Culler, is that *we cannot assess the success of one reading-model in terms of another*. For example, he declares: "A good deal of the criticism of structuralism in Old Testament scholarship is merely muddled, attacking structuralism as a failed attempt to achieve traditional historical-critical results. Such attacks wholly fail to engage with its real intentions. Conversely, both structuralists and canon critics often talk as though it were a flaw in (say) redaction criticism not to have allowed for the 'canonical' or 'structural' dimension or (worse) as though redaction critics had been dimly and fully groping after the insights now at least revealed."[148]

Barton's case, reiterated in his joint work with Robert Morgan (1988) is that questions about textual "meaning" cannot be asked or answered in abstraction from considerations about the *purpose* for which the text is *read*.[149] In line with the "common sense" approach which we earlier identified as often a particular contribution of the British tradition, Barton rejects all imperialist claims that any *single* model of meaning or method is applicable to *all* biblical texts for *all* reading purposes. This includes the "literary" approach itself with its tendency to work with non-referential intra-linguistic and inter-textual accounts of meaning, and to regard *all* biblical texts as "literary" texts. Hence Barton has hesitations about different versions of "text-immanent" readings as claims to constitute comprehensive models of reading, as well as about the presupposition that *all* biblical texts may be seen as "literary" texts. We cannot take it for granted, he rightly urges, that Frei's "literary" account of narrative hermeneutics embraces all biblical narratives.[150] Moreover for certain reading purposes, it is entirely proper to construe meaning in terms of the author's intention. Barton asserts: "Against strident denials of the importance of the author and his intentions, Hirsch's proposals seem to me eminently sane."[151]

Barton and Morgan tend to go further than this, however, on the basis of theories of reading-competence. Their work is convincing in stressing rightly that one kind of reading-model cannot be assessed in terms of another which presupposes a different *kind* of reading-competence. Barton and Morgan argue for the value of a variety of methods and models, each of which contributes something distinctive within the wider hermeneutical enterprise. But Barton also rejects the claim that any method could be applied to a text which would "elicit its 'true' meaning", on the ground that "what kind of meaning is the true one is variously defined".[152] Barton's "main conclusion" in *Reading the Old Testament* is that it is a mistake to talk about, or to aim at, "discovering the meaning of texts".[153] The notion of "one valid way of understanding the text" is a "fruitless quest".[154] This coheres with the thesis of the book co-written with his Oxford colleague Robert Morgan, that textual meaning depends almost entirely, or at least primarily, on the interpretative purpose, and "interpreters choose their own aims".[155]

I am not convinced that the second claim necessarily follows from the first. It does not seem *necessarily* to follow from what Barton has carefully expounded about literary competence (in my terminology, semiotic codes) in his first main chapter. In this first part of his argument Barton properly and convincingly elaborated the basic hermeneutical axiom that an understanding of codes develops "some sense of *what sorts of questions it makes sense to ask*" (his italics) of a text.[156] His examples included the absolutely valid principle that in a commercial letter which begins "Dear Sir . . .", it would *not* "make sense" to ask what degree of endearment is implied by "dear"; any more than "Yours faithfully" invites sensible questions about degrees or qualities of commitment or personal "faithfulness" on the part of the writer. But this presupposes (rightly) that some *appropriate match of writing-code and reading-code* is a prime hermeneutical aim in reading *this kind of text*. Barton fully recognizes that the mistake of applying literary-theory models to biblical texts *wholesale* lies precisely in the tendency of literary models to undervalue or even reject the *sometimes transmissive* function of texts as *media of a communicative content*.

At this point we must be cautious about making the same claims, or apply the same theories, in the case of *all* biblical texts. Biblical poetry, parables, and anonymous narratives do not operate in precisely the same terms as prophetic discourse or Pauline letters, although elements of each overlap with the other. But Barton's example of the commercial letter raises the issue not only of "matching up" writer-code and reader-code, but also of *whether this goal of aiming approximately to match codes should not have some privilege and priority, in cases where an epistemological dimension or disclosure-content of a biblical text is in question. The literary paradigm of "reading" has an advantage over more traditional hermeneutical theory in focussing attention on semiotic reading-competencies and the inter-active dimensions of reading between the reader and the text. But in exchanging it* for "understanding" the privileged status of its function at certain times and in given cases as an epistemological medium or disclosure-medium is in danger of being lost from view.

Is Barton's generous hospitality to a pluralism of methods fully compatible with this principle? I suggest that a tantalizing half-truth lies in the argument that "much harm has been done in biblical studies by insisting that there is, somewhere, a 'correct' method".[158] If by this Barton intends to say that each of the methods he discusses makes some positive contribution to textual elucidation, and that one method should not be judged in terms of the reading-competence appropriate to another, this argument is both correct and healthy. If by this, however, Barton means that the nature of given biblical texts offers no criteria by which we may *metacritically rank* what counts as meaning in a given context, or the most appropriate method *in some given case*, this unnecessarily places the emphasis on the reader to make his or her own "choices", without adequate reference to textual or to other given constraints. Reader-response theorists, especially Stanley Fish, would claim that this notion of "constraints" is *arbitrary, artificial, and illusory, whether they are perceived as textual constraints* or as *socio-critical constraints which offer a critique of the interests of a particular community of readers*. But Barton implies elsewhere in his work that he would not wish to stand precisely where Fish stands on the issue of meaning. I should be surprised if Barton wishes to share Fish's scepticism about whether anything can be *"given" in a text which is not provided by the interpreter*. Apart from the philosophical difficulties of contextual relativism, such a position would not cohere with Barton's other concerns about theology and about language.

The shift of paradigm from "understanding" or "interpretation" to *reading* offers some admitted advantages, but it also invites a shift of emphasis which may be regretted, unless the problems which it may raise are clearly noted. First, "reading" is to literary and to semiotic theorists what "interpretation" is to philosophers of language and to those concerned with epistemology. It is arguable that the models of meaning constructed by philosophers are more rigorous than those used in literary theory, and allow for greater attention to counter-examples which qualify theories, and to particular cases. Further, whereas literary theories apply to "literary" texts, philosophers especially in the tradition of Wittgenstein, seek answers about meaning only after establishing what counts as a "home" language-game in *settings of everyday life*. Many, perhaps most, of the biblical writings at one level remain "literary"; but it is even more fundamental to their *raison d'etre* that they reflect what human beings say and do, and how, in turn, they are addressed, *in everyday life*. This is not to deny that these texts are often also literary products, which are designed to produce certain *effects*, but *it is to deny that this latter aspect provides the primary, only, or supposedly most comprehensive model of meaning.*

Long ago, in the first decade of this century, Adolf Deissmann opened the debate about the Bible and "everyday" *vs.* "literary" language in the context of discoveries among the papyri. In his *Light from the Ancient East* he called attention to the *non*-literary character of much language in the New Testament. The subsequent course of the discussions has revealed literary, rhetorical, and non-literary aspects in New Testament texts. But the steps from art to artifice, and from artifice to artificiality, should be taken only with considerable caution and literary and rhetorical assumptions should not be assimilated too readily without careful evaluation. We need models of interpretation that leave *open* the question of whether parables about leaven, about weeds, about business deals, and so forth, are to be seen as springing from the soil of inter-personal communication anchored deeply and closely in everyday life; or whether they are part of a carefully constructed artifice designed to achieve rhetorical effects; whether in their broadest context they are to be understood as *both*, or whether it is in principle undecidable and simply "up to the *reader*" how they are read. "Reading" as a term without semantic opposition seems neutral and innocent; but as a contrastive term to "interpretation" or "understanding" the newer paradigm shifts the focus from epistemological communication and interpretative judgment to semiotic effect, with some considerable loss for biblical scholarship and for the status of the Bible itself.

Such a move also coheres too neatly with the trend towards social egalitarianism in an age which transfers any notion of "privileged" knowledge on the part of an author or a sacred text to the shared contributions of pluralist reading communities. In the commercial world too, the *consumer* decides what is to be offered and what is marketable, and *what is marketable becomes "what is"*. By contrast, the challenge *to understand* may necessitate *self-reorientation* of an individual or corporate nature. It may not be easy; and the reader, as Bonhoeffer comments in the context of a theology of the cross, may not be able to understand "on his or her own terms". The key issue, we shall argue in the next chapter, which arises from the work of Stanley Fish is whether a community of readers can be shaped and judged by texts, as it were, "from outside", or whether they must remain trapped in their own contextual relativism, hearing no prophetic summons from outside and beyond.

The current interest in some quarters in offering *"intertextual"* readings of biblical passages does not serve to re-stabilize this problem for biblical studies. Indeed, "intertextuality", as it most recently occurs in biblical interpretation looks to the post-modernism of Julia Kristeva and the later Barthes. It needs to be distinguished clearly from "*inner*-textuality" in the approach of Michael Fishbane (discussed briefly in chapter I) and especially from "*intra*-textuality" as the context of narrative theology associated with Hans Frei, with Lindbeck, and with Ronald Thiemann (discussed in chapter XV and elsewhere). It is a source of regret that many of those biblical specialists who have drawn *intertextuality* as a model for biblical research seem to owe more to Barthesian perspectives than to the careful and precise sub-categorizations and sympathetic but perceptive warnings put forward on this subject by Jonathan Culler, and noted in the previous section.

A recent volume published under the title *Intertextuality in Biblical Writings* (1989) in honour of Bas van Iersel largely adopts or presupposes a Barthesian approach to textuality, although some essays seem to suggest more simplistic models, almost allowing post-modernist perspectives to collapse into pre-modern, pre-critical, modes of thought.[159] (We noted in chapter IV that there were certain apparent parallels between pre-modern and post-modernist outlooks; but we also questioned how deeply these superficial parallels actually went.)

In their introduction to *Intertextuality in Biblical Writings*, W. Beuken and Ellen van Wolde stress that reading texts constitutes an act of *creativity*. As T. Todorov argues in the volume *The Reader in the Text*, reading is construal, or "construction".[160] Beuken and Wolde recall Barthes's notion of textuality in which texts are "threads", "nets", "webs", or "textures". Threads appear in the structure, and "texts refer to each other, chronologically backwards and forwards, semantically inwards and outwards ... Texts do not exist without other texts".[161] By introducing this into biblical interpretation, Beuken and van Wolde conclude, "We are entering a new road which leads us to new vistas".[162]

W.S. Vorster articulates a major theme of this volume, namely that, "The shift in focus from author-oriented to text and reader-orientated study of the New Testament texts simply compels us to look at matters such as intertextual relationships afresh".[163] In Vorster's view this may *include* source-influence studies, but is not the bare *fact* of allusions to other texts within texts; readers have been aware of this phenomenon since ancient times. The issue is *how* we regard these allusions: "All texts can be regarded as the re-writing of previous texts, and also as *reactions to texts*".[164] In the textual theory of Barthes and especially of Julia Kristeva, all texts "abort" and "transform" other texts, as if to form a mosaic. In Derridean terms, a text is a network of "Traces".

After this weighty theoretical beginning, Vorster turns to a specific example, namely to Mark 13: 5–37. But the "pre-texts" and the "co-texts" turn out to be a mixture of familiar and speculative ones. The "sacrilege that makes desolate" of Mark 13: 14 alludes, as has always been pointed out, to Daniel 12: 11; Mark 13: 26 probably alludes to the "clouds of heaven" and "one like a son of man" in Dan. 7: 13,14. But Vorster claims at least thirteen "possible allusions" to other Old Testament texts, as well as the relationships with gospel parallels in Matt. 24, Luke 21, and elsewhere.[165] Norman Perrin had spoken of such allusions as being "woven into the text".[166] The burden of Vorster's argument is that redaction-critical enquiry about the relation between redaction and tradition have gone as far as they can, especially with the work of R. Pesch. Nevertheless, he suggests, we can move forward if we view these relationships as a network of *equal importance*; as an "intertext" of "speeches about the future". The textual allusions and textual resonances thereby provide the *code* through which Mark 13 is to be read.

Especially when we recall our chapter above on pre-modern hermeneutics, this "new road which leads to new vistas" has some striking similarities with Patristic and pre-Reformation interpretation. Texts become *matrices* and *codes*. It is no accident that Tzvetan Todorov's *Symbolism and Interpretation* (Eng. 1982 French, 1978) represents a sustained defence of early Christian *allegory* on the basis of its status as *code*.[167] Like *semiotic code*, it constitutes *a generative matrix of polyvalent meaning*. Direct signs or literal discourse cannot "evoke"; such discourse remains *transparent*.[168] Todorov asserts: "If there were no allegory, there would be no God".[169] Todorov approves of Henri de Lubac's comment "Jesus changes the water of the letter to the wine of the spirit"; and of Richard of St. Victor's respective comparison of "history to wood" and of "allegory or mystical meaning to gold".[170]

The theme of *polyvalency* of language and *indeterminacy* of signs is precisely what James W. Voelz selects as the focus of his essay in the Bas van Iersel volume on intertextuality. Meaning becomes polyvalent because all meaning is identified not as *parole*, but as a further *matrix* which generates further meaning in its capacity as *langue*. This is the principle which we queried in the semiotics of Barthes in our discussion of deconstructionism. A new speech-utterance *(parole)* can *contribute* to the expansion or modification of the system which generated it, but does it *of itself* constitute a new generative system? Voelz insists: "Textual events or ideas are matrixed (*sic*) with other textual events or ideas", and these are not restricted "to the same level or . . . to the same text".[171] What a text means is whatever it *can* mean *for* the reading-community. Freyne thus observes elsewhere in this volume that all texts are dependent not just on other texts known and cited by the author, but indeed on all pre-texts whether the author is aware of them or not". In his volume *Echoes of Scripture in the Letters of Paul* (1989) R.B. Hays examines the role of intertextual relations with earlier scriptures in shaping the language of Romans and other Pauline passages. He considers the Pauline contrast between letter and Spirit in 2 Cor. 3:1–4:6 as contributing to a hermeneutical basis for such an exploration.[172]

Earlier we expressed some scepticism about the allegedly clear-cut contrast between systems in structuralism and pre-understanding in hermeneutics. In terms of Habermas's constructive conceptual contrast, is *system* here distinct from *life-world*? If intertextuality is perceived as a contributing factor to pre-understanding, as Culler suggests that it should do, then the notion is less problematic but also less novel. In *The Two Horizons* I discussed Heinrich Ott's claims that "dogmatics and exegesis stand in a relation of interaction with one another". Understanding by its very nature takes place at different levels".[173] For Ott this meant that faith is not "a stance of the isolated individual" but the communion of saints and "common understanding". Similarly Peter Stuhlmacher speaks of the horizon of interpretation as "the horizon of the Christian community's faith and experience . . . openness to an encounter with the truth of God coming to us from out of transcendence.[174] Pannenberg, we noted, spoke of potentially "universal" horizons. What is problematic about current notions of intertextuality is *not the huge scope* of the boundaries which have been enlarged, but the transposing of horizons of understanding into *matrices which generate an infinite chain of semiotic effects*. Stuhlmacher can speak of open horizons of experience towards transcendence, but, rather than giving the *reader* the last word, still speaks of "the self-sufficiency of the scriptural word".[175]

These claims about intertextuality raise two problems. First, is it appropriate to treat *all* biblical texts under this model? Second, is it legitimate to claim, with Vorster, that all intertextual signs have "equal importance"? Umberto Eco, we shall see, distinguishes "open" from "closed" texts. Clearly if we took as an example of a "text" a purely functional, transmissive, communicative model such as traffic signs, train signals, fever charts, or even legal wills, *in such instances it is not simply "up to the reader" to determine what "counts" as a code*. A private letter, such as Philemon, seems to fall within a quite different textual category in this respect from biblical poetry, or from a number of biblical narratives, or from passages in the Revelation of John which depend on Ezekiel and a history of interpretation of *inner*-textual symbol. But *this* is hardly "a new road . . . new vistas".

It is crucial to observe, however, that the van Iersel volume represents no more than one particular sample of intertextual research in biblical interpretation. With some relief, we may compare the equally well informed but more constructive approach of Patrick Grant. In order to set the scene for Grant's example of an intertextual approach to Mark 14:3–8, we may note the nature of his general evaluation of the Markan narrative.

Grant notes the contrast between Augustine's representational view of language, and the insistence in current literary theory that literary language undermines stable meanings. In Paul de Man's terms, sign and meaning never coincide.[176] Yet Augustine also experiences existential anguish, and times when confusion seemed to bar the road to mystery. Mark's Gospel, Grant suggests, sets us in "a turbulent middle ground whereby on the one hand we are summoned by the signs and promises to affirm a transcendent, beneficent reality, even as, on the other hand, we are warned against naive interpretations of signs."[177] We are invited "to read the narrative in a realist sense as a true revelation from God, providing us with re-assurance of an objective, transcendent, design for our salvation. But we are invited also to expect our hopes to be confounded, and our securities dashed. Christ himself, after all, was left in abandonment."[178] Grant concludes: "The cross is the sign which stands for the failure of signs to provide solace or certainty, and it is not just another play of the text. It is an event, the place of abandonment . . . where the rhetorical pattern of *katabasis* and *anabasis* is most vigorously turned inside out".[179]

Grant suggests that the anointing at Bethany (Mark 14: 3–8) provides an example of multivalency of meaning and intertextuality. Jesus's "interpretation" of the women's act of anointing him as "for burying" (14:8) may transcend the woman's own anticipation; but behind the act of anointing lie textual resonances concerning the anointing of kings (1 Sam. 10: 1; 2 Kings 9: 1–13) and of persons for tasks.[180] Yet the practice of leaving broken ointment-containers beside corpses at burial places makes the relation between the woman's purpose and Jesus's interpretation far from clear-cut and literalistic. The disciples interpret the act in accordance with what they perceive to be the mind of Jesus, namely concern for the poor. But their interpretation turns out to be "wrong". The episode of the anointing reflects an ambiguity of signs which belongs to the central theme of Mark's Gospel. But this "indeterminacy of signs", this interweaving of different levels of awareness, brings home to us "the instability of our plans and expectations", and shows "how elusive is the relationship between grace and understanding".[181]

Patrick Grant's approach may have affinities with some kinds of reader-response theory, but he does not imply that the reader is left to construct textual meaning without external or given constraints. Moreover, Grant pays meticulous attention to *the different textual functions and status of different texts within the New Testament.* In the Pauline epistles, for example, some texts signal the discontinuities of Paul's creative, burning, struggles; in other texts "Paul is clear and objective".[182] As Herbert M. Gale observed in a neglected book in 1964, Paul's conceptual formation often embodied metaphor.[183] Grant concludes: the langauge of the New Testament is "neither cheap nor simple", but offers "an elusive kind of knowledge which is strongly *critical of easy institutional answers* and attitudes . . . .In the last resort . . . . the New Testament is *intolerant of the merely fictive imagination* . . . We are drawn through the literature *towards the extra-literary*" (my italics).[184]

In reader-response theory, by contrast, *"knowledge"*, even "an elusive kind of knowledge", finds relatively little place among a volatile and variable array of context-relative reader-effects. It is not at all clear what role, if any, *"the extra-literary"* can perform; other than as social or conventional variables in reader-behaviour which shape *what the reading community itself constructs from its texts*. But reader-response theory takes varied forms, ranging from that of the moderate Iser to that of the explicitly immoderate Fish. To these issues we now turn.

NOTES TO CHAPTER XIII

1. Christopher Tuckett, *Reading the New Testament. Methods of Interpretation*, London: S.P.C.K., 1987, 175–80.
2. Michael J. Toolan, *Narrative. A Critical Linguistic Introduction*, London and New York: Routledge, 1988, 3.
3. *Ibid* 73.
4. Stephen D. Moore, *Literary Criticism and the Gospels: the Theoretical Challenge*, New Haven and London: York University Press, 1989, xviii.
5. *Ibid* xviii-xix.
6. Terry Eagleton, *Literary Theory: An Introduction*, Minneapolis: University of Minnesota Press, 1983, viii.
7. Patrick Grant, *Reading the New Testament*, London: MacMillan, 1989, 6.
8. Stanley Fish, *Is There a Text in this Class?*, 16–17.
9. *Ibid* 3 (Fish's italics).
10. Stanley Fish, *Is There a Text in this Class?*, 10.
11. Stanley Fish, *Doing What Comes Naturally. Change, Rhetoric, and the Practice of Theory in Literary and Legal Studies*, Oxford: Clarendon Press, 1989, 25.
12. Nicholas Wolterstorff, *Work and Worlds of Art*, Oxford: Clarendon Pess, 1980, 222–34 (discussed more fully in chapters XV and XVI), and John Searle's essay "The Logical Status of Fictional Discourse", in *Expression and Meaning* 58–75.
13. T.R. Wright, *Theology and Literature*, Oxford: Blackwell, 1988, 7–8; and David Jasper, *The New Testament and the Literary Imagination*, London: MacMillan, 1987, esp. 27–42 and 83–96. See further David Jasper, *The Study of Literature and Religion: An Introduction*, London: MacMillan, 1989.
14. George B. Caird, *The Language and Imagery of the Bible*, London: Duckworth, 1980. Caird worked closely with his Oxford colleague Stephen Ullmann, and also drew on the work of Barr. Cf. Stephen Ullmann, *Semantics. An Introduction to the Science of Meaning*, Oxford: Blackwell, 1962; and James Barr, *The Semantics of Biblical Language*, Oxford: Oxford University Press, 1961.
15. George B. Caird, *op. cit.* 243–71.
16. *Ibid* 256.
17. Stephen Prickett, *Words and the World: Language, Poetics, and Biblical Interpretation*, Cambridge: Cambridge University Press, 1986.
18. *Ibid* 6; cf. 4–36.
19. *Ibid* 12.
20. *Ibid* 31.
21. Anthony C. Thiselton, "Semantics and New Testament Interpretation" in I.H. Marshall (ed.) *New Testament Interpretation. Essays on Principles and Methods*, Exeter: Paternoster 1977, 93–95; cf. 75–104.

22. The example of the Servant, the "desolating sacrilege", and the Son of Man is discussed in Anthony C. Thiselton, "The Meaning of *Sarx* in 1 Cor. 1:5. A Fresh Approach in the Light of Logical and Semantic Factors" in *Scottish Journal of Theology* 26, 1973, 227–28; cf. 204–28. Cf. further "The Parables as Language-Event" in *Scottish Journal of Theology* 23, 1970, 437–68, esp. 453–61.
23. Stephen Prickett, *op. cit.* 26–27.
24. Edwin M. Good, *Irony in the Old Testament*, London: S.P.C.K. 1965, 10.
25. *Ibid* 41.
26. *Ibid* 46.
27. *Ibid* 53.
28. *Ibid* 72.
29. David M. Gunn, *The Story of King David: Genre and Interpretation*, Sheffield: J.S.O.T. Suppl. 6, 1978; and *The Fate of King Saul: An Interpretation of a Biblical Story*, Sheffield: J.S.O.T. Suppl. 14, 1980.
30. David M. Gunn, *The Fate of King Saul*, 130–31.
31. R.W.L. Moberly, *At the Mountain of God. Story and Theology in Exodus 32–34*, Sheffield: J.S.O.T. Press Suppl. 22, 1983, 29.
32. *Ibid* 29.
33. B.W. Anderson, "From Analysis to Synthesis: the Interpretation of Genesis 1–11" in *Journal of Biblical Literature* 97, 1978, 23–29; cf. Gordon J. Wenham, "The Coherence of the Flood Narrative" *Vetus Testamentum* 28, 1978, 336–48.
34. R.W.L. Moberly, *op. cit.* 30.
35. Tzvetan Todorov, *Grammaire du Décaméron*, The Hague: Mouton, 1969; and Gérard Genette, *Narrative Discourse Revisited*, Eng., Ithaca: Cornell University Press, 1988, 7.
36. Seymour Chatman, *Story and Discourse*, Ithaca: Cornell University Press, 1978, 19–42, *et passim*.
37. For a comparison cf. Michael J. Toolan, *op. cit.* 9–14.
38. Gérard Genette, *Narrative Discourse*, Eng. Ithaca: Cornell University Press, 1980, chapters 4–6.
39. Gérard Genette, *Narrative Discourse Revisited*, 33–37.
40. Wesley A. Kort, *Story, Text, and Scripture. Literary Interests in Biblical Narrative*, University Park and London: Pennsylvania State University Press, 1988, 44.
41. Robert Alter, *The Art of Biblical Narrative*, New York: Basis Books, 1981, 47.
42. *Ibid* 154; cf. 147–53.
43. Ronald Thiemann, "Radiance and Obscurity in Biblical Narrative" in Garrett Green (ed.) *Scriptural Authority and Narrative Interpretation*, Philadelphia: Fortress, 1987, 35–6; cf. 21–41.
44. *Ibid* 37.
45. *Ibid*.
46. Stephen Crites "The Spatial Dimensions of Narrative Truthtelling", *ibid* 101; cf. 97–120.
47. Ernst Fuchs, *Studies of the Historical Jesus*, Eng. London: S.C.M. 1964, 129.
48. Frank Kermode, *The Genesis of Secrecy. On the Interpretation of Narrative*, Cambridge, Mass., and London: Harvard University Press, 1979, 27–33, 44–47 *et passim*.
49. Wesley A. Kort, *op. cit.* 14–28.

50. *Ibid* 16–17.
51. *Ibid* 18; cf. 1–13.
52. *Ibid* 24–28.
53. *Ibid* 29.
54. *Ibid* 34.
55. *Ibid* 38.
56. *Ibid* 41.
57. *Ibid* 42.
58. Frank Kermode, *op. cit.* 34
59. *Ibid* 24 and 27.
60. *Ibid* 45.
61. *Ibid* 141.
62. *Ibid* 145.
63. Robert C. Tannehill, *The Narrative Unity of Luke-Acts: A Literary Interpretation*, vol. 1, *The Gospel According to Luke*, Philadelphia: Fortress, 1986, xiii; David Jasper, *op. cit.*, 2 and 20–21; and Werner Kelber, *Mark's Story of Jesus*, Philadelphia: Fortress, 1979, 11; and Ernest Best, *Mark: The Gospel as Story*, Edinburgh: Clark, 1983, 145.
64. James Dawsey, *The Lukan Voice: Confusion and Irony in the Gospel of Luke*, Macon: Mercer University Press, 1986; cf. Wayne C. Booth, *The Rhetoric of Fiction*, (2nd edn) Chicago: University of Chicago Press, 1983, 304–09.
65. Stephen D. Moore, *op. cit.* 33.
66. Meir Sternberg, *The Parables of Biblical Narrative: Ideological Literature and the Drama of Reading*, Bloomington: Indiana University Press, 1985.
67. Martin Warner (ed.) *The Bible as Rhetoric. Studies in Biblical Persuasion and Credibility*, London and New York: Routledge (Warwick Studies in Philosophy and Literature) 1990, 1–47.
68. Lynn Poland, "The Bible and the Rhetorical Sublime" *ibid* 29; cf. 29–47.
69. Hans Frei, *The Eclipse of Biblical Narrative. A Study in Eighteenth and Nineteenth Century Hermeneutics*, New Haven: Yale University Press, 1974, 1–16 *et passim*.
70. *Ibid* 16; cf. 41–85, esp. 56 and 75–85.
71. Paul Ricoeur, *Hermeneutics and the Human Sciences* 147; cf. above, chapter V, section 1.
72. Jacques Derrida, "Living On/Border Lines" *loc. cit.* 73.
73. Pierre Guiraud, *Semiology*, Eng. London and Boston: Routledge and Kegan Paul, 1975, 77–81.
74. Vladimir I. Propp, *Morphology of the Folktale*, (2nd edn) Austin and London: University of Texas Press, 1968, 21.
75. *Ibid* 26–53.
76. Wesley Kort, *op. cit.* 65.
77. Jean-Marie Benoist, *The Structural Revolution*, Eng. London: Wiedenfeld and Nicholson, 1978, 3.
78. *Ibid* 7.
79. Alexander J. Greimas, *Sémantique Structurale*, Paris: Larousse, 1966; and *Du Sens*, Paris: Seuil, 1970.
80. David C. Greenwood, *Structuralism and the Biblical Text*, Berlin, New York, and Amsterdam: Mouton, 1985, 63; cf. 64–73.
81. See further, Terence Hawkes, *Structuralism and Semiotics*, 87–95, Susan Wittig (ed.) *Structuralism. An Interdisciplinary Study*, Pittsburgh: Pickwick Press, 1975, 15–17;

and Corina Galland, "An Introduction to the Method of A.J. Greimas" in Alfred M. Johnson (ed.) *The New Testament and Structuralism*, Pittsburgh: Pickwick Press, 1976, 1–26.
82. Roland Barthes, "The Struggle with the Angel: Textual Analysis of Genesis of 32:23–33" in R. Barthes et al., *Structural Analysis and Biblical Exegesis: Interpretational Essays*, Eng. Pittsburgh: Pickwick Press, 1974 (French 1971) 21–33.
83. Roland Barthes "A Structural Analysis of a Narrative from Acts X-XI" in Alfred M. Johnson Jr. (ed.) *Structuralism and Biblical Hermeneutics. A Collection of Essays*, Eng. Pittsburgh: Pickwick Press, 1979, 109–44.
84. Roland Barthes, "The Struggle with the Angel" *loc. cit.* 22.
85. *Ibid* 23.
86. *Ibid* 28.
87. *Ibid* 31 and 33 (my italics).
88. Roland Barthes, "A Structural Analysis of Narrative from Acts X-XI" *loc. cit.* 123–26.
89. *Ibid* 126–28.
90. *Ibid* 137.
91. *Ibid* 118.
92. Jean Starobinski, "The Gerasene Demoniac: A Literary Analysis of Mark 5:1–20" in R. Barthes, F. Bovon, et al., *Structural Analysis and Biblical Exegesis*, Pittsburgh: Pickwick Press (Pittsburgh Theological Monograph 3) 1974, 57–84.
93. *Ibid* 59.
94. *Ibid* 68.
95. *Ibid* 63.
96. Jean Calloud, *Structural Analysis of Narrative*, Eng. Philadelphia: Fortress, and Missoula: Scholars Press, 1976 (French 1973) 49–108.
97. *Ibid* 50–55.
98. *Ibid* 59–64; 83–89.
99. Robert M. Polzin, "The Framework of Job", *Interpretation*, 28, 1974, 182–200; and *Biblical Structuralism. Method and Subjectivity in the Study of Ancient Texts*, Philadelphia: Fortress, and Missoula: Scholars Press, 1977; and Robert C. Culley, "Structural Analysis: Is it done with Mirrors?" *Interpretation* 28, 1974, 165–81.
100. Dan Otto Via Jr., *The Parables, their Literary and Existential Dimension*, Philadelphia: Fortress, 1967.
101. Anthony C. Thiselton, *The Two Horizons*, 347–52.
102. Dan O. Via, *op. cit.* 110.
103. *Ibid* 145.
104. *Ibid* 116–20 and 126.
105. *Ibid* 169.
106. Dan Otto Via, *Kerygma and Comedy in the New Testament. A Structuralist Approach to Hermeneutics*, Philadelphia: Fortress, 1975.
107. *Ibid* 4.
108. *Ibid* 7.
109. *Ibid* 54.
110. *Ibid* 55.
111. Daniel Patte, *What is Structural Exegesis?* Philadelphia: Fortress, 1976, 5.
112. *Ibid* 13.
113. *Ibid* 21.

114. *Ibid* 41–46.
115. Daniel Patte, *Paul's Faith and the Power of the Gospel. A Structural Introduction to the Pauline Letters*, Philadelphia: Fortress, 1983, 238; *The Gospel according to Matthew: A Structural Commentary on Matthew's Faith*, Philadelphia: Fortress, 1987; and with Aline Patte, *Structural Exegesis: From Theory to Practice*, Philadelphia: Fortress, 1978.
116. Jean Calloud *et al.*, *Signs and Parables. Semiotics and Gospel Texts*, Eng. Pittsburgh: Pickwick Press, 1978, xvii.
117. Daniel and Aline Patte, *op. cit.* 9.
118. Daniel Patte, *Paul's Faith and the Power of the Gospel*, 11; cf. 273.
120. *Ibid* 285 cf. 281–90.
121. Patrick Grant, *op. cit.* 7.
122. Erhardt Güttgemanns, "Linguistic-Literary Critical Foundation of a New Testament Theology" rp. in *Semeia* 6, 1976, 196; cf. 181–215, from *Linguistica Biblica* 13/14, 1972, 2–18. Cf. further his "What is 'Generative Poetics'?" *Semeia* 6, 1976, 1–22.
123. Jonathan Culler, *Framing the Sign: Criticism and its Institutions*, Oxford: Blackwell, 1988, ix.
124. Jonathan Culler, *The Pursuit of Signs. Semiotics, Literature, Deconstruction*, London: Routledge and Kegan Paul, 1981, 50; cf. *Structuralist Poetics : Structuralism, Linguistics, and the Study of Literature*, London: Routledge and Kegan Paul, 1975, viii.
125. Jonathan Culler, *Structuralist Poetics*, 30.
126. François Bovon "French Structuralism and Biblical Exegesis" in R. Barthes *et al.*, *Structural Analysis and Biblical Exegesis*, 4; cf. 4–20.
127. Jean-Marie Benoist, *op. cit.* 216.
128. Stephen D. Moore, *op. cit.* xvi.
129. Robert C. Culley, "Response to Daniel Patte" in Daniel Patte (ed.) *Semiology and Parables. An Exploration of the Possibilities Offered by Structuralism for Exegesis*, Pittsburgh: Pickwick Press, 1976, 156–57; cf. 151–58; and Vern S. Poythress, "Philosophical Roots of Phenomenological and Structuralist Literary Criticism", *Westminster Theological Journal* 41, 1978–79, 165–71.
130. Edgar V. McKnight, *The Bible and the Reader. An Introduction to Literary Criticism*, Philadelphia: Fortress Press, 1985, 5–8 and xvi. cf. *Meaning in Texts: the Historical Shaping of a Narrative Hermeneutic*, Phiiladelphia: Fortress Press, 1978, 235–312; and *Post-Modern Use of the Bible: The Emergence of Reader-Oriented Criticism*, Nashville: Abingdon, 1988.
131. Susan Wittig (ed.) *Structuralism: An Interdisciplinary Study*, Pittsburgh: Pickwick Press, 1975, 19.
132. Jonathan Culler, *The Pursuit of Signs*, 101.
133. *Ibid* 102.
134. *Ibid* 103.
135. *Ibid*.
136. *Ibid* 105.
137. *Ibid* 107; cf. Harold Bloom, *Poetry and Repression*, New Haven: Yale University Press, 1976, 1–3.
138. *Ibid* 109.
139. *Ibid* 116 (my italics).
140. *Ibid* 117 (my italics).

141. John Barton, *Reading the Old Testament. Method in Biblical Study* London: Darton, Longman and Todd, 1984; cf. also John Barton, "Reading the Bible as Literature: Two Questions for Biblical Critics", *Literature and Theology* 1, 1987, 135–63.
142. John Barton, *Reading the Old Testament*, 204–06; cf. 19 and 181–82.
143. *Ibid* 6 (Barton's italics).
144. *Ibid* 11.
145. *Ibid* 12.
146. *Ibid* 17.
147. *Ibid* 131.
148. *Ibid* 199.
149. Robert Morgan with John Barton, *Biblical Interpretation*, 7, 215, 221 *et passim*.
150. John Barton, *Reading the Old Testament* 163–67.
151. *Ibid* 191; cf. 167–70; 175–79; and 191–94.
152. *Ibid* 205.
153. *Ibid*.
154. *Ibid* 207.
155. Robert Morgan with John Barton, *op. cit.* 287.
156. John Barton, *Reading the Old Testament*, 17.
157. *Ibid* 4.
158. *Ibid* 5.
159. Spike Draisma (ed.) *Intertextuality in Biblical Writings. Essays in Honour of Bas van Iersel*, Kampen: Kok, 1989.
160. Tzvetan Todorov, "Reading as Construction" in Susan R. Suleiman and Inge Crosman (eds.) *The Reader in the Text. Essays on Audience Interpretation*, Princeton: Princeton University Press, 1980, 67–82.
161. Spike Draisma (ed.) *op. cit.* 7.
162. *Ibid*.
163. Willem S. Vorster, "Intertextuality and Redaktionsgeschichte" *ibid* 16; cf. 15–26.
164. *Ibid* 20.
165. *Ibid* 23.
166. Norman Perrin, *The Kingdom of God in the Teaching of Jesus*, London: S.C.M., 1963, 133.
167. Tzvetan Todorov, *Symbolism and Interpretation*, Eng. Ithaca: Cornell University Press, 1982.
168. *Ibid* 125.
169. *Ibid* 129.
170. *Ibid*.
171. Spike Draisma (ed.) *op. cit.* 30–31.
172. R.B. Hays, *Echoes of Scripture in the Letters of Paul*, New Haven: Yale University Press, 1989.
173. Anthony C. Thiselton, *The Two Horizons* 323–24; cf. Heinrich Ott, "What is Systematic Theology?" in James M. Robinson and J. Cobb Jr. (eds.) *New Frontiers in Theology I: The Later Heidegger and Theology*, New York: Harper, 1963, 94 and 102.
174. Peter Stuhlmacher, *Historical Criticism and Theological Interpretation of Scripture. Towards a Hermeneutics of Consent*, Eng. Philadelphia: Fortress, 1977, 89.
175. *Ibid* 88.
176. Patrick Grant, *op. cit.* 18.

177. *Ibid* 19.
178. *Ibid.*
179. *Ibid* 21.
180. *Ibid* 15.
181. *Ibid* 128.
182. *Ibid* 86 and 87.
183. Herbert M. Gale, *The Use of Analogy in the Letters of Paul*, Philadelphia: Westminster Press, 1964, 18–19 *et passim*.
184. Patrick Grant, *op. cit.*, 132.

CHAPTER XIV

The Hermeneutics of Reading in Reader-Response Theories of Literary Meaning

In the previous chapter we traced a shift of focus in literary theory from formalism, the new criticism, and earlier structuralism, with their emphasis on textual system, to post-structuralism, reader-response theory, and post-modernist approaches, in which the emphasis has moved from the text itself to readers and to reading communities. *Reader-response theories call attention to the active role of communities of readers in constructing what counts for them as "what the text means".*

From the point of view of biblical interpretation a potentially positive contribution is offered by any theoretical hermeneutical model which places an emphasis on *the role of readers as participatory and active.* Some reader-response theorists, most notably Wolfgang Iser, draw on a theory of perception to establish the role of readers in *filling in or completing* a textual meaning which would otherwise remain only potential rather than actual. At first sight this has strong affinities with our arguments in chapter II about the *concrete actualizations of texts within the time-horizons of readers.* In theological terms, such a theory seems to cohere with expectations that reading the biblical text should constitute not an exercize for passive spectators, but *an eventful and creative process.*

Nevertheless reader-response theories also embrace a wide variety of theoretical assumptions. Some raise acute philosophical difficulties about the role of the communication of *knowledge* in transmissive or communicative texts, and the capacity of texts to shape or to transform the expectations of readers *from outside their community.* They invite the possible collapse of critical or socio-critical interpretation into *social-pragmatic* reading which serves only to affirm *prior community norms.* The most polemical and radical statement of a socio-pragmatic context-relative reader-response theory comes from the pen of Stanley Fish. Norman Holland sees engagements or "transactions" with texts as explicating and affirming readers' prior identities.

Although there are strong affinities between Fish's philosophical position and that of Richard Rorty, Fish is unsuccessful in his attempt to ground his context-relative literary theory in an adequate or convincing philosophy of language. I shall argue in this chapter that if "meaning" is subsumed within the prior horizons of the reading-community, *we no longer stand where, with Gadamer, we construe engagements between readers and texts as interaction between two horizons, each of which is first to be respected before a fusion of these two horizons can take place.* Moreover, Fish's recent counterarguments against standard criticisms of his work depend on *an undue polarization between formalist and anti-formalist philosophies of language.* The thrust of his essay "Going Down the Anti-Formalist Road" (1989) entirely misses the points made by Wittgenstein about concepts with blurred edges, family resemblances, and the common behaviour of humankind.[1] Wittgenstein in effect *rejects* Fish's artificial alternative that *either* we have a formal system (like the *Tractatus*) *or* there are no inter-penetrating or overlapping regularities of a stable nature which transcend the boundaries of a single language-game or context-relative social community. The supposed alternative of *either* formal system *or* social relativism without trans-contextual critique is a false one.

Before we attempt to expose the untenable nature of Fish's philosophy of language and its negative consequences for biblical interpretation and for Christian theology, we may first survey theories of reader-response which are less sweeping and more modest in their claims. We commence with the moderate theory of Wolfgang Iser. Stanley Fish attacks Iser on grounds of inconsistency; but Iser's angle of approach has stimulated some creative reflection in biblical studies. Fish's provocative and aggressive onslaught on Iser appears in his essay "Why No One's Afraid of Wolfgang Iser", reprinted in his volume *Doing What Comes Naturally.*[2]

1. Wolfgang Iser's Theory of Reader-Interaction and its Utilization in Biblical Studies

The philosophical background to Wolfgang Iser's literary theory is drawn partly from Roman Ingarden, who was a disciple of Husserl. Its significance for biblical interpretation has been explored by Susan Wittig, Jouette Bassler, James Resseguie and Robert Fowler, among others, whose work we shall examine. Following Ingarden, Iser pointed out that objects of perception are not perceived by the consciousness of the human subject exhaustively, but *in terms of those aspects which are presented.* A measure of *incompleteness* is involved in all perception. The perceiving subject "fills in" what is missing by *construing* what is not "given" in Husserl's phenomenological consciousness.

Ingarden expanded this model of "filling out a schema". The clearest example in theories of aspective perception is that of perceiving a three-dimensional object. We do not "see" the back or all the sides of the object;

but we *construe* what lies beyond immediate perception. Iser pointed out that this principle applies and can even be extended in literary narrative. The text often does not specify whether an object has certain properties (for example whether a table is wooden or plastic, or has three or four legs) but we regularly "fill in" what we *presuppose* and *construe*. The notion of the reader's activity in "filling in *blanks*" in the text becomes a central theme in Iser's theory.

Iser draws from Ingarden the notion that the reader "*actualizes*" and "*concretizes*" dimensions of meaning that are otherwise only *potential* rather than actual. Iser writes, "Effects and responses are properties neither of the text nor of the reader; the text represents a potential effect that is realized in the reading process".[3] While reading-processes entail the *re-organization* or "grouping" of "thought-systems" invoked by the text, the literary work remains for Iser a potentially communicative act. It impinges on the extra-linguistic world. To describe the reading-process is to bring to light "operations which the text activates within the reader".[4] These utilize the reader's imagination, perceptions, and capacity both to "assemble" and to "adjust and even differentiate his own focus".[5]

Even more fundamentally, Iser distinguishes explicitly between a theory of reader-response, which "has its roots in the text", and a "theory of reception" which arises from a history of readers' judgments. Thus, unlike the later Fish, he does not question the "givenness" of stable constraints in textual meaning, but underlines their potential and indeterminate status independent of actualization by the reading process. Iser first formulated his notion of indeterminacy and potentiality in 1970 (Eng. 1971).[6] "*Actualization*" is the result of "interaction" between the text and the reader.[7]

In the previous section we asked whether Barton's "competent" reader would not share a *matching of code* with the text's author. Iser argues that interpretative codes will inevitably reflect something of a reader's own culture: this historically-conditioned reader is the "real" reader. By contrast, the technical category of "the ideal reader" would need "to have an identical code to that of the author . . . The ideal reader would also have to share the intentions underlying this process".[8] Such a reader, however, remains *hypothetically* "ideal" rather than empirically actual, because this person would thus in principle grasp the textual meaning *exhaustively and without remainder*. He or she is therefore a fictional being. The best that we can seek is literary or reading "competence", which will allow the reader's role to be performed, but in different ways. Iser's terminology of the construct of this typified "competent" reader, whose empirical token exemplifications are variable, is "the implied reader".[9]

On matters of detail Iser distinguishes his position from that of Ingarden, but stipulates that his own concept of "the *blank*" designates "a vacancy in the overall system of the text, the filling of which brings about an interaction of textual patterns". Part of the "completion", for Iser, involves the building up and establishing of "connections" between different segments of the text. Throughout his long chapter on "How Acts of Constitution Are Stimulated" Iser explores two axes of interaction: the possibility of infinite polyvalency is to be "narrowed down" by an appropriate reading competence which is aware of textual features such as interconnections and code; on the other hand, his theory sees the text-reader interaction as "the productive matrix which enables the text to be meaningful in a variety of different contexts".[10] Helpfully, Iser stresses the "narrowing down" aspect with reference especially to "expository texts", and the "productive matrix" aspect especially in relation to "literary" texts.[11]

Iser's approach offers a broad parallel, as we have observed (although not in all respects) with our comments about the *actualization* of biblical texts within the time-horizon of the hearer or reader (above, in chapter II). In more detailed terms, attempts have been made by several writers to apply this model to specific biblical texts. In *Semeia* 9 (1977), devoted to "polyvalent narration", Susan Wittig explores the semiotic perspectives offered by C.S. Peirce and by Charles Morris, noting the role of Morris's pragmatic or "rhetorical" axis between sender and receiver.[12] Polyvalency, she argues, is generated first by different perspectives on the part of successive receivers; second, by multiple codes which produce multiple significations; and third by interactive relations between more than one semiotic system. A parable draws together in polyvalent tension the referential or "literal" semiotic system of the everyday world and the system contributed by the reader who becomes co-author with the text of a "duplex connotative system".[13]

The first and longer part of Susan Wittig's argument draws on semiotic theory. But then she turns to the phenomenology of the act of reading, and at this point takes up the approach of Wolfgang Iser. She observes: "The lack of syntactic or semiotic connections and the omission of detail . . . invite the reader to establish his own connections . . . when the text does not offer it".[14] She considers as an example the opening of the parable of the prodigal son (Luke 15:11). The dimensions of "application" or metaphorical extension is "unstated". But this coheres, she argues, with the *purpose* of such a parable. This purpose is "not to create one particular meaning, but *to create the conditions under which the creation of meaning can be defined and examined by each perceiver*" (her italics).[15] In other words, the parable exposes self-knowledge, because *how* the reader completes the meaning constitutes part of the parable's self-involving disclosure-function. A parallel emerges with Robert Funk's earlier comments on the hermeneutics of parables. Funk took the same parabolic examples (Luke 15:11–32) and argued that the text itself *transforms the audience* into one of two reactive categories: by their *response* the audience identify *themselves* either as pharisaic "righteous" elder-son critics, or as repentant younger sons who return.[16]

A second exemplification of Iser's models in biblical interpretation is offered by James L. Resseguie in his article "Reader-Response Criticisms and the Synoptic Gospels" (1984).[17] Like Susan Wittig, Resseguie underlines the role of reader-involvement, and the reader's part in "filling gaps" in the text in his or her own way.[18] He seeks to find a place for *both* the possibility of "infinite" variations of actualization, *and* a measure of constraint on the part of the text. He explores the narrative of the rich man who came eagerly to Jesus but after hearing his words "went away sorrowful; for he had great possessions" (Mark 10: 22; cf. 10: 17–22). In line with the constraints of the text, Resseguie attends to the Markan context; but in line with an emphasis on the role of the reader, he calls attention to the part played by wealth for the reader and by his or her own axioms about wealth.

This corresponds precisely to the dual aspect or alleged ambivalence of Iser's theoretical model which draws down the wrath and scorn of Stanley Fish. Which is the master: the text or the reading-community? Fish's crushing review of Wolfgang Iser's work in his essay "Why No One's Afraid of Iser", forcefully elaborates the argument that Iser tries to have his cake and eat it too. Iser admits that meaning, (to the satisfaction of pluralists) is "there" only when it is "read", actualized and interpreted; but Iser also imagines (to the satisfaction of objectivists or traditionalists) that meaning is a concretization of what was potentially "there" in the text. So neither traditionalists nor pluralists need "fear" Iser, because he has the "ability to embrace contradiction cheerfully".[19]

Before we consider this criticism in more detail, we may note that Robert M. Fowler (1981) and Jouette M. Bassler (1986) also raise questions about Markan narratives on the basis of this kind of reader-response model. They distinguish between reader-effects which would belong to the process or activity of reading the Markan text temporally *for the first time*, and the effects of *second and subsequent* readings which retrospective perspectives and knowledge bring to the text from outside its own temporal framework of narrative-time.

Both writers pay particular attention to the feeding miracles and references to bread in the Markan text (Mark 6: 30–44; 8: 1–10; 14: 22). In his suggestive book *Loaves and Fishes*, Robert Fowler questions the assumption that within the linear and temporal reading-process, readers of Mark were expected to project *back* onto Mark 6 and Mark 8 *later* material about the Last Supper. Fowler comments *"As the author has structured his work, Jesus' last meal with his disciples in Mark 14 presupposes the earlier feeding stories and not vice versa"*.[20] Fowler reflects: "Often the verbal similarities between 6: 41, 8: 6, and 14: 22 are noted and used to justify the discovery of 'eucharistic' overtones in the two feeding stories". But if we follow *reading-processes* generated and designed by Mark, such an approach "is to stand the gospel on its head".[21]

Fowler reaches the conclusion that the traditional feeding story of Mark 8, subsequently reflected in Mark 6: 30–44, originally contained no reference to fish as well as to loaves. This aspect of his argument is open to question.[22] But Fowler's approach achieves success in pin-pointing potential differences of expectation about Jesus on the part of the reader from those of the disciples in the narrative. However we account for the two narratives of Mark 6: 30–44 and Mark 8: 1–10, we can hardly doubt that the disciples' question in 8: 4: "How can one feed these people with bread here in the desert?" has an impact *which invites incredulity on the part of the reader who has just read Mark* 6.[23] How can those who have recently witnessed a feeding miracle entertain doubts about what Jesus could do in a closely parallel situation? Can readers still share such obtuse underestimations of Christology? In Fowler's view, Mark himself has inserted Mark 6 prior to the traditional story of Mark 8, *in order to heighten the reader's responses to Jesus against the contrasting background and clear inadequacy of the disciples' expectations.*

Iser's theoretical model provides the tools for such an approach, and Fowler acknowledges the value of Iser's work on anticipation and retrospection in reading processes. Iser, Fowler observes, shows that "during the process of reading there is an active interweaving of anticipation and retrospection".[24] The reading process entails both guesses about what is to come, and reflection over what is past.

Jouette Bassler also traces the twists and turns by which the Markan text seems to provoke the reader to struggle with apparently insoluble puzzles. To keep the reader in some measure of suspense and in the dark allows the reader initially to share the disciples' sense of puzzlement about Jesus. Narrative "gaps" generate and heighten reader-involvement and reader-activity, as the reader wrestles with a text which, until the end, constitutes an incomplete jig-saw.[25] The release of information, the putting together of the pieces of the puzzle, comes to be achieved by the text and the reader gradually, until the eucharist and the cross in Mark 14 bring about a *retrospective* understanding of the significance of the long struggle with the text. In a metaphorical sense, Iser's claim in his earlier book *The Implied Reader* (1974) is thereby vindicated, that the *work* is "more" than the *text*. Iser writes: "The text only takes on life when it is realized ... The convergence of text and reader bring the literary work into existence".[26]

R. Alan Culpepper's book *Anatomy of the Fourth Gospel* (1983) combines elements of Iser's conceptual tools with other methodological elements drawn from the narrative theories of Gérard Genette and Seymour

Chatman.[27] It also utilizes standard apparatus from the new criticism, such as "point of view", plot development, irony, and so forth. Culpepper's focus of interest is not on John as a "window" onto the Johannine community but as a "mirror" in which to see the world. The Johannine text calls the reader to make *moves*: through the "narrator" the "author" sends signals which establish expectations, distance, and intimacy, and powerfully affect the reader's sense of identification and involvement . . . The implicit purpose of the gospel narrative is to alter irrevocably the reader's perceptions of the ideal world . . . to 'see' the world as the evangelist sees it".[28]

Culpepper introduces the working distinctions of Seymour Chatman which we have noted: distinctions between narrative time and natural sequence, between story and discourse, and between narrator and narrative, together with Wayne Booth's distinction between an author and the "implied author". The implied author is the literary construct which determines how or what we read. The narrator communicates directly with the reader; the implied author must be inferred from the narrative. In this terminology our "author" of the Epistle to the Hebrews in chapter VII above would in certain respects be the "implied" author, although in other respects it remains difficult to distinguish such an entity from the voice that directly addresses us as preacher or writer. Culpepper concedes that only from time to time is such a distinction clear in John. In John 21:24 the "implied author" is identified as the beloved disciple. Since the beloved disciple is a witness, the gospel "daring in its perspective" establishes an authority and "point of view" for the narrator.[29]

Culpepper expounds the relevance of such literary categories as narrative time, plot-development, and characterization in John. We have considered the roles which these can play in our discussion of narrative theory. Culpepper turns more specifically to reader-response aspects in his examination of Johannine "implicit commentary" as a rhetorical device. Here John regularly employs "misunderstandings" by narrative characters. The standard examples include John 2:19–21, "this temple"; 3:3–5, "born anew"; 4:10–15, "living water"; 4:31, "food"; 6:32–35, "bread from heaven"; 6:51, "my flesh"; 7:33, "where I am"; 8:31–35, "make you free"; and ten other instances (including the well-known "sleep" in 11:11–15 and "lifted up" in 12:32–34).[30]

These aspects also entail the "silent" communication of the implied author's smile, wink, or raising of eyebrows in instances of Johannine irony over such subjects as the origins of Jesus (1:46; 7:52 "Are you from Galilee?"), or the *double entendre* of the "good wine saved to the end", or the pharisees' bland question about whether they are to be presumed "blind", like the blind man (9:39). Culpepper expounds the role of dramatic irony, of symbolism, and of misunderstanding, for stimulating the reader into making his or her own response. In language which in a different context would remind us of Dilthey's hermeneutics, Culpepper concludes that the modern reader must enter imaginatively, if need be even by "pretense", into what the evangelist assumed his first-century readers knew or thought. In Iser's words the "implied reader" (i.e. the construct-reader for whom the text operates) "embodies all those predispositions necessary for a literary work to exercize its effect", and finds in the text "invitations to shared perceptions".[31]

Although it is arguable that Iser's reader-response theory contributes only one component within a wider range of literary tools including formalism and narrative theory, Culpepper's work demonstrates, like that of Fowler and others, the value of placing an emphasis on *reading processes* not only in terms of temporal, sequential, and rhetorical features, but *also more broadly as a focus for hermeneutical questions about reader-engagement, interaction, and self-involvement.*

Nevertheless Iser's theoretical model, and by implication the work of those who adopt it as a tool of biblical interpretation, receives some criticism, as we have already noted. We have observed that Stanley Fish, with little restraint, attacked Iser for attempting to satisfy both "objectivists" who still believe in textual "givens", and pluralists who view meaning as constructs determined by the agenda and expectations of *readers*. On this ground, Fish insists, Iser "embraces contradiction", and therefore he need not be "feared" either by conservatives or by radicals. In his work on Mark 10:17–22 Resseguie has attempted a similar dialectical balance between constraint and construction. But here Stephen Moore and Stanley Porter firmly take sides with Fish against Resseguie. Moore insists that Resseguie "follows Iser the critic into deep contradiction".[32] On this same basis Stanley Porter dismisses Iser as "notoriously ambiguous", views the related work of Norman Petersen (discussed below) as "particularly disappointing", and remains highly critical of the approach of Resseguie as well as the work of Jeffrey Lloyd Staley (1988) who has "taken his cue from Resseguie".[33] Disarmingly Porter concedes that he is partly dazzled because compared with Fish "few are as insightful and plain brilliant"(!)[34] Porter is reluctant even to use the term "reader-response theory" of Iser, Resseguie, Fowler, Petersen, or Staley, because Fish supposedly represents *genuine* reader-response theory (i.e. readers are not constrained by textual "givens").

In practice three major factors separate Fish's category of reader-response theory from that of Iser. First, the reason why Fish opposes the supposedly self-contradictory nature of Iser's approach so vehemently is doubtless because with the zeal of the convert Fish perceives it as a position which he himself formerly held, but has now "seen through". His is a conversion theology, in which values prior to conversion, retrospectively, are painted in over-drawn colours. This helps to explain the aggressive missionary tone of his writing which is so noticeable as to attract attention in a special paper, namely Susan R. Horton's article "The Experience of Stanley Fish's Prose".[35] He traces his own pilgrimage from the end of *Surprised by Sin* (1967) and *Self-Consuming Artifacts* (1972) when he believed that given texts may draw readers along certain paths, to 1980, when his book *Is There a Text in this Class?* appeared. By now Fish had come to "cease worrying" about how much respectively the text or the reader contributed to interpretation: there was *nothing "in" the text to interpret, because everything is interpretation.*[36] Fish complains that Iser still sees the interpretative relationship as "one of script to performer", whereas Fish himself urges that we cannot "speak meaningfully of a text that is simply there, waiting for a reader who is, at least potentially, wholly free".[37]

A second major difference arises from the contrast between Iser's focus on the *individual reader* and Fish's notion of *communities of readers*. Fish insists that "there is no subjective element of reading because the observer is never individual in the sense of unique or private, but is always the product of categories of understanding that are his *by virtue of his membership in a community of interpretation*" (my italics). [38]

The third point of contrast emerges in a radical difference of attitude and evaluation towards both a philosophy of perception and a philosophy of language. Iser seeks to ground and build a theory of reading on the basis not only of pragmatic assumptions about how reading seems to work, but on *philosophical* issues about the *nature of human perceptions*, the processes of *construal* and *projection*, and relations between perception and *language*. We may entertain some reservations about Husserl's phenomenology, and about the philosophical status of some of the theory which Iser draws from Husserl and from Ingarden. But it is difficult to perceive the same level of rigorous *philosophical* argument in the claims of Stanley Fish. Indeed, as Patrick Grant and others have observed in comments which we have taken up in previous chapters, certain theories of "literary" meaning sometimes rest on the illusion that *philosophy*, after Rorty and Derrida, can be *subsumed under literary theory itself*. But this assumption is a disastrous mistake, and leads to consequences which we shall explicate towards the end of this chapter. The huge claims made by Fish to the effect that the social community *constructs or determines what counts as given*, and his scorn for Iser's philosophical view that reading or perception *conditions what counts as given* are not supported by a philosophical rigour proportionate to the size of the claim.

2. Umberto Eco's Semiotic and Text-Related Reader-Response Theories and their Implications for Biblical Texts

Whereas Iser drew on a *philosophy of perception*, and Fish (as Culler rightly observes) draws on contextual *pragmatism*, Umberto Eco lays a careful foundation for his own reader-response theory by a *rigorous examination of principles of semiotics*. Thus Eco's book *The Role of the Reader: Explorations on the Semiotics of Texts* (1981) draws on theoretical foundations which he laid in his earlier work *A Theory of Semiotics* (1976). Some aspects are then developed further in his *Semiotics and the Philosophy of Language* (1984).[39] A major step forward arises from Eco's recognition at the beginning of his *A Theory of Semiotics* that semiotic theory needs to include *both* a theory of *codes*, which comes under the heading of *signification*, *and* a semiotics of *sign-production* which comes under the heading of *communication*. This contrast is *not* to be identified, he insists, simply with the distinction between syntactics and pragmatics; and it does not correspond precisely to the difference between *langue* and *parole*. Eco writes: "One of the claims of the present book is to overcome these distinctions, and to outline a theory of codes which takes into account even rules of discursive competence, text formation, contextual and circumstantial (or situational) disambiguation therefore proposing a semantics which solves within its own framework many problems of the so-called pragmatics".[40]

The *signification-system* arises on the basis of codes of social convention, but the *communication-process* "exploits" the sign-system physically to produce expressions for a variety of practical purposes. Signification has logical primacy in the sense that "every act of communication to or between human beings ... presupposes a signification system as its necessary condition. It is possible ... to establish a semiotics of signification independently of a semiotics of communication: but it is impossible to establish a semiotics of communication without a semiotics of signification".[41]

Wittgenstein made a parallel point by means of an analogy, shared partly with Saussure. To know the rules of chess and to set out the pieces on the board in a certain way (cf. *langue*, system, signification, structure) is not yet to make an actual chess *move* (cf. *parole*, speech-act-in-life-world, language-*use*, communication *act*). Wittgenstein observes: "Naming is so far not a move in the language-game – any more than putting a piece in its place on the board is a move in chess ... *Nothing* has so far been done, when a thing is named".[42] Eco's understanding of semantic fields and of semiotic systems has a parallel with Wittgenstein's perceptive observations: these are *conditions of signification* which are activated in what other writers might term hermeneutical life-worlds or speech-acts, in which *interaction occurs* between the *code system* of the writer or sender, and the *code-system* of the reader or receiver.

Eco makes a fundamental advance in his notion of *understanding*, which arises from *"the absence of reliable pre-established rules"* to an extent which *permits readers to make over-generalized assumptions about the code which a given text presupposes*.43 Such a principle has crucial importance for biblical interpretation. We noted, for example, in chapters II and III, that modern readers could all too easily come to ancient texts with over-generalized assumptions which blurred important differences between the codes of first-century apocalyptic (e.g. uses of symbols in the Book of Revelation) and modern narrative or media accounts of events. As we shall shortly note, Norman Petersen takes up this kind of consideration of code in his article on Mark and the reader.

One major strength of Eco's theoretical approach, which is invaluable for biblical hermeneutics, concerns *his recognition of the very wide range of models which constitute "texts", ranging from the simplest functional transmissive system in engineering through to complex matrices of productive systems of "literary" meaning*. Eco's introductory example of a semiotic system rightly begins with a very simple model. In this respect it is like Wittgenstein's simplified model language game of communication between two builders by ostensive reference. Eco describes the functional and transmissive "reading" of the pointer of a dial on a control panel which is mechanically linked to a floating buoy in order to indicate water-level or fuel-level. Even in this example, "reading" the dial rests on a social convention; but one which is so widespread today that it is virtually trans-cultural (except in cultures which have no plumbing or traffic vehicles). An ancient culture might not recognize the basis on which the signifying system functions, but almost all modern cultures would presuppose the code which allowed the pointer to communicate data.

Differences between and within codes may entail *"sub-codes"*. Eco points out the purely transmissive function of indicating a high water-level as a *fact* differs from communicating some *judgments* about its *significance*, namely what level constitutes a "flood warning" or a "danger level". *Sub-codes may entail a professional training* (just as Wittgenstein also rightly addressed the role of "training" in communicating and on understanding).44 This "training" becomes a matter of "reader-competency" when we consider more "productive" or literary texts, as Culler and Barton note. Barton rightly observes that *reader-competency* demands a sufficient mastery of code to allow communicative or productive reading in the case of biblical texts.

At this point Eco takes up a useful methodological distinction embodied in the semiotic theory of Jurij Lotman.45 Lotman distinguishes between categories of texts which function primarily to *transmit* or to *communicate* meanings, and those which serve to *generate* or to *produce* meanings. He speculates that this contrast represents a difference of *cultural* perspective. The former reflects a *"handbook"* culture, and operates with generally *stable* meanings. In this case, literary texts may embody *multiple coding*. In such cases *how texts are read* will depend largely on the *reader's choice of de-coding systems*. Thus, following Lotman, Eco concludes that when "re-readings" produce changes of code, this *modifies the very meaning* of the text or work. Petersen, we shall shortly note, makes this kind of observation about the reading of Mark. We have already called attention to Fowler's comments on the difference between "reading" Mark sequentially in a temporal mode for the first time, and second or subsequent re-readings which presuppose a retrospective "timeless" frame.

Lotman's working contrast forms part of the foundation of Eco's work on reader-response theory and reading-processes in his book *The Role of the Reader*. It also features in his book *Semiotics and the Philosophy of Language* especially in the distinctions in his own sign-theory between "communication signs" (emblems, street signs, trademarks) and indirect or "premonitory signs" (metaphors, traces, even ancient ruins). *The former presuppose matching codes; the latter incorporate multiple interpretation.* In principle the latter can expand into an *outward-moving, growing, labyrinth*. In terms of the former category the *semantic* function of the *encyclopedia* exhibits *"markers"*; in terms of the latter category *temporal advance* characterizes the "infinity" of chains of signs and language-systems in the *dictionary*, the function of which is to catch momentary *"transient revaluations" of pragmatic language-uses*.[46] Only "cultural inertia" slows these changes sufficiently to make them adequately stable as "dictionary meanings" or as working definitions.

In *The Role of the Reader*, Eco stresses that in poetry and in literary texts generative strategies aim at "imprecise or undetermined response" on the basis of intertextual competence. Some texts invite *"the co-operation" of their readers by compelling "interpretative choices"*.[47] Arguably many biblical parables, a number of narratives, many parts of the wisdom literature, and biblical apocalyptic precipitate reader-activity of this kind. *But Eco does not categorize all texts in the same way. Every text envisages, or "selects" by its nature, a "model reader". This is the construct-reader who shares the ensemble of codes presupposed by the author.* In comments closely parallel to those of Culler or even Bultmann on "pre-understanding" and "presupposition", Eco suggests by way of example that a text which speaks of "chivalry" presupposes a knowledge of the tradition of Romantic chivalry on the part of the *"model reader"*.

In instances in which a reader-response invited by a text is indeterminate, it is not of great concern whether the reader shares the author's code. But other texts fall into a different category. Eco observes: "Those texts (which) aim at arousing a precise response on the part of more or less empirical readers ... are in fact open to any possible 'aberrant' de-coding. A text so immoderately 'open' to every possible interpretation will be called a *closed* one."⁴⁸ Eco offers examples of "closed texts" which pull the reader along a *pre-determined path* in order to arouse specific emotions and effects. These include mass-advertizing formats, comic strips and soap-opera romances or Westerns. By contrast, James Joyce's *Finnegans Wake* represents an *open* text which embodies *generative processes* within its own structure. Some texts are conceived for a general audience. These might include political speeches or scientific instructions. In others, however, the author or reader may be necessarily specific (for example in the case of a private letter); or the reader may be a construct (an "open" letter); or both author and readers may do no more than perform actantial roles. In such instances, even in such a phrase as "I tell you . . ." references to author and reader are no more than textual strategies.⁴⁹ The most distinctive advantage of *open* texts, Eco believes, is their greater capacity to resist "aberrant" or mis-matching codes.

Eco distinguishes between differing reader-processes which relate to language *about states of affairs*, unverifiable hypotheses which would be empirical in principle (i.e. *counterfactual conditionals*), and *fiction*. In a series of ten diagrammatic structures or boxes, Eco schematizes a number of combinations of selected responses that a reader might choose to make to different kinds of texts. *In some cases, questions about empirical truth-claims would be invited; in other instances forecasts and "inferential walks"; in fictional stories, questions about narrative plot and actantial structures.* "Switching" from box to box may be entailed in reading-processes.⁵⁰ But throughout the processes code, and changes of code, remain paramount.

Like Wolfgang Iser, Eco demonstrates the role of the reader in filling out or "blowing up" (his term) some textual characterizations or events, and reducing or "narcotizing" others. *The reader has to be helped "to select the right frames, to reduce them to manageable format, to blow up and to narcotize given semantic properties* of the lexemes to be amalgamated, and to establish the isotopy according to which he decides to interpret the linear text manifestation so as to *actualize* (my italics) the discursive structure of a text."⁵¹ In the case of narrative a reader will be invited to wonder about the next step of a given story. This may pose a decision, or disjunction of probabilities, and *different choices may have different values*. Many of the parables of Jesus fall into Eco's category of offering the reader "solutions he does not expect, *challenging every overcoded intertextual frame as well as the reader's predictive indolence.*"⁵² "Open" narrative-texts allow for the widest possible range of interpretative proposals.

William Ray rightly calls attention to Eco's affinities with Ingarden and Iser. Like Iser, Eco avoids "both pure objectivism and pure subjectivism".⁵³ Ray comments: "The hermeneutical circle is thus thoroughly embedded in Eco's model of reading".⁵⁴ But in Ray's own view, this position is unsatisfactory. He categorizes Eco's supposedly "dubious generic distinction between 'open' and 'closed' texts" as leading to "an impasse".55 Ray's criticism of Eco runs parallel to Fish's attack on Iser. Eco, he claims, tries to have the best of both worlds. But Eco's careful correlation between *different kinds of texts* and *different reading-roles* seems to be more meticulously and convincingly grounded in rigorous semiotic theory that the "literary" approaches of Ray and Fish. As Tremper Longman observes, there is a difference between claiming that there are as many "interpretations" of texts as there are readers, and attempting to establish what active processes readers undertake *"in interaction with the text"* (Longman's italics).56

Eco's approach to reader-response theory offers a positive resource for biblical interpretation, and moves beyond the work of Iser, although Iser's work retains its distinctive elements. On the other hand, as against Ray and other advocates of purely "literary" theories of texts and of meaning, Eco's recognition of the *constraints operative on readers in the case of communicative* (less clearly, of "productive") *texts* places him in a different category in relation to biblical studies from Fish, Bleich, Holland, and Culler. Although Porter (partly because he is seduced by aspects of the claims of Fish) finds Petersen's reader-response approach to biblical texts "particularly disappointing", numerous affinities may be traced between Norman Petersen's article "The Reader in the Gospel" (1984) and Eco's theoretical system. The most frequent criticism brought against Eco by some literary theorists is the claim that, in the end, "constraints" are achieved only by returning to the notion of "system" in a way which reflects more structuralist perspectives.

Petersen does not allude to Eco's theory in explicit terms, but he shares much of the same terminology. He writes: "Reader-response criticism warns actual readers to be wary of . . . seduction by an undercoded text . . . to seek the always at least implied reader before jumping, as it were, into the text and its context."57 He scrutinizes the text of Mark for instances in which "the reader" is encoded in the text itself. One example is the well-known "wink" in Mark 13:14 "let the reader understand". The framing of language about the elect under persecution in the apocalyptic discourse also, Petersen argues, allows readers to recognize themselves as "encoded in the text".58 At the same time, perspectives that seem to be "for us" may not always be the same as those which are conveyed to the implied reader of Mark. Some passages share perspectives which are clearly "for" readers of various kinds: the voice at the baptism of Jesus (Mark 1:11) and probably the whole of the introduction (Mark 1:1–15) is "for" the reader alone. Petersen draws a contrast between "non-authorial" readers, and "authorial" readers who constitute "participants in the communicative transaction".59

The value of Eco's approach remains deeper and far broader than the specific area which Petersen's article explores. But Petersen's observations on the text of Mark indicate at least one possible direction of exploration of this theoretical model for biblical interpretation. For Porter such an approach remains "particularly disappointing" because its reader-response theory is not full-blooded and radical enough; indeed, in Porter's view, Iser's model (and presumably Eco's, which he does not discuss) do not deserve the name "reader-response" theory at all. We may now move into this more radical area of reader-response theory, where the work of Stanley Fish seems virtually to dominate discussion, but where Holland and Bleich also deserve attention. Here also, although he rejects the term "reader-response theory" as a description of his work, Jonathan Culler's rigorous semiotic emphasis on reader-competency invites further attention, in addition to our discussion of his work in the previous chapter, in which we examined Culler's concept of intertextuality.

3. Differences among more Radical Reader-Response Theories: The Psychoanalytical Approach of Holland and the Socio-Political Approach of Bleich

A number of standard studies and introductions trace the divergencies which exist within what is commonly called reader-response theory. The most widely known introductions to these theories are probably those of Elizabeth Freund (1987), Jane P. Tompkins (1980), and the volume jointly edited by Susan R. Suleiman and Inge Crosman (1980).[60] Jane Tompkins traces a reader-orientated development from Riffaterre, Iser, and Poulet, to Fish, Culler, Holland, Bleich, and Walter Michaels.[61] Elizabeth Freund compares the "implied reader" of Booth and Iser, the "model reader" of Eco, Riffaterre's "super-reader", Culler's "ideal reader" and Fish's "interpretative community".[62] We have already suggested above that whereas Iser's approach draws on a philosophical phenomenology of perception through Ingarden and Husserl, Eco draws primarily on semiotic theory, Culler draws on post-structuralist and semiotic explorations of reader-competency, and Fish on socio-pragmatic conclusions arrived at in the context of a personal pilgrimage. In contrast to all of these, David Bleich operates largely with socio-political and educational concerns, while Norman Holland works on the basis of psychoanalytic theory and other broader psychological observations. We shall endeavour to underline *differences* within a broadly shared common emphasis on the decisive role of readers in interpreting texts between Holland, Bleich, Culler, and Fish.

Norman Holland's earlier approaches (1968, 1973 and 1975) draw on a psycho-analytical perspective in the tradition of Freud.[63] Interaction between the self and features of a text as *"other"* set in motion certain *strategies on the part of the reader's conscious self.* We may recall our earlier discussions in chapter X of Paul Ricoeur's utilization of Freud's work in the context of interpreting dreams and symbols. Patterns of *desire* (cf. Ricoeur on the will) on the part of the self give rise to strategies of *self-protection and concealment*, and thus to *overdetermination of meaning*. Multiple meaning-effects emerge, in other words, which can be attributed to conflicts, ambiguities, and overlapping causes within the self. Holland describes *the active operation of these defensive strategies as "transactions" between the self and the other.* In processes of reading, readers shape their strategies and perceptions in *ways which serve their patterns of desire, and what they construct reflects and serves their own unique identity.* Holland summarizes the devices which constitute strategies of reading set in motion by the self's defence of its identity under the acronym "DEFT": Defences, Expectations, Fantasies, and Transformations.

Holland's approach shares with Iser's theory an emphasis on the role of *the individual reader,* in contrast to community-centred stress on *communities of readers* which characterizes the theories of Bleich, Culler and Fish. Holland also attempts to support his theories by experimental observational psychological research. In his book entitled 5 Readers Reading (1975) he compares the *different quasi-empirical responses* made by five different readers to the same texts. He concluded that these different responses could be significantly correlated with the readers' respective differences of identity, including their narrative experiences and personality types.

The contribution to *biblical hermeneutics* by Holland's theoretical model takes both a positive and a negative form. (i) On the positive side, the ways in which readers read biblical texts produce not only understanding of texts, but often no less produce an increased awareness, with appropriate hermeneutical sensitivity, of self-perception and self-identity. Further, as existentialist and narrative theories of hermeneutics underline, *a self-awareness and a strengthening of an individual and corporate identity as one who has a stake in the texts and that to which they bear witness constitutes an important reader-effect in the case of biblical texts.*

(ii) If the *implications* of Holland's theory are adequately noted, this approach also underlines, negatively, *the urgent need for a hermeneutic of suspicion in reading biblical texts.* In an important statement Holland observes: *"We use the literary work to symbolize and finally to replicate ourselves"* (my italics).[64] But if this is the case, the reading of biblical texts, as Paul Ricoeur so cogently argues, *can result in idolatry. We can project our own interests, desires, and selfhood onto that which the biblical text proclaims.* We can thereby unwittingly re-create and *"construct" God in our own image through our reading-processes.*

(iii) We should note in passing how Holland's theory, by its very affinity with certain individualist strands within religious or Christian pietism, offers a warning about innocent subjective reading in *traditions of pietism*. Very often in religious groups an individual is encouraged to "frame" the biblical text with reference to the narrative history of personal testimony, and to "read" the text as "what the text *means to me*". If this is undertaken within a frame of corporate evaluation and testing, the life-experience in question may enhance pre-understanding and weave meaning and textual force with emotional warmth and practices in life. But without any principle of *suspicion*, in Gadamer's terminology a *premature* fusion of horizons will take place *before* readers have listened in openness with respect for the tension between the horizons of the text and the horizon of the reader. The textual horizon has collapsed into that of the reader's narrative biography, and is unable to do more than to speak back his or her own values and desires.

(iv) This example exposes the ultimately *socio-pragmatic* status of Holland's theoretical model. In the end, if "we use the literary work . . . *to replicate ourselves*", as in Fish and in Rorty the text can never transform us and correct us "*from outside*". There can be no prophetic address "from beyond". This may still leave room for a measure of *creativity and surprise* in *literary* reading. For *in such cases it does not profoundly matter whether it is ultimately the self* who brings about its own creative discoveries. But in the case of many biblical texts, theological truth-claims constitute more than triggers to set self-discovery in motion (even if they are not less than this). If such concepts as "grace" or "revelation" have any currency, texts of this kind speak not *from the self* but *from beyond the self*.

David Bleich approaches reader-response theory from a different angle. His developing and especially his later work is characterized less by psychoanalytic concerns than by a *socio-literary and socio-political context of interests*. Like Holland, Bleich's earlier work focusses on "subjective" reading and on human "subjectivity"; but in contrast to Holland *within a framework of a theory of intersubjectivity*. His early book *Readings and Feelings* (1975) explores psychological and psychotherapeutic categories, and in his book *Subjective Criticism* (1978) Bleich also shares Holland's view that reading-processes are processes in which readers "re-symbolize" texts. Differences in these reading-processes and their strategies emerge and grow from "personal and communal subjectivity".[65] Like Fish, Bleich firmly emphasizes the creative role of community interests, goals, and epistemological assumptions in shaping or in determining how readers within a community read; but his notion of *what constitutes a genuine community of readers* distances him from Fish in major ways.

This issue becomes sharply clear in Bleich's later work *The Double Perspective: Language, Literacy, and Social Relations* (1988).[66] The "double perspective" enhances the wholeness of the dualities of male and female, individual and communal, subjective and inter-subjective, academy and classroom, the institutional and the personal, the traditional and the creative. Bleich attacks Fish for appearing to presuppose that a "community of readers" means an *academic* community rather than one from the classroom. Fish is allegedly *too elitist*, while Culler is supposedly *too immersed in theory* to handle the issues of "reading" in the everyday world. Fish's so-called elitism, Culler's supposed absorption in theory, and several major philosophers of language, in the end suffer the same general criticism: they are tied to the lecture-hall of the university, and ignore "the actual human use of texts and language, which would mean bringing in consideration, from the history, psychology, and sociology of literacy".[67] Far from representing everyday models of reading-processes, post-modernist deconstructionist and post-structuralist theories of reading present what occurs only in an "academic fraternity with a French accent".[68] It thereby intensifies individualistic elitism, and has only a veneer of social orientation.

Bleich's "double" perspective includes the need for a co-jointly male and female community of readers. His later work in this respect makes a major contribution to feminist hermeneutics, which we discussed in chapter XII. Bleich writes: "The work of the feminist movement, particularly its epistemological thinking, puts intersubjectivity in a light which, perhaps now in retrospect, explains many of Husserl's frustrations: his academic community was thoroughly and profoundly masculine . . . What can intersubjectivity ever mean *if the fundamental relations of the two genders remain in the background of cultural inquiry* and under the political rug?"[69]

This general observation may be evaluated in a positive light for issues in biblical hermeneutics. In a recent doctoral dissertation Mark Labberton notices the coherence of such a general reader-orientated approach with the *theological* principle that reading biblical texts is an activity of the *whole* community, including the "*ordinary*" reader; not an exclusively male or white or "professional" and elitist activity. Bible reading embraces "Jew and Greek, slave and free, male and female" (cf. Gal. 3: 28). Labberton entitles his work *Ordinary Bible Reading: The Reformed Tradition and Reader-Orientated Criticism* (1990).[70] He traces the development of the theological tradition of attending to the role of the "ordinary" reader in reading biblical texts from Calvin and from Reformation theology. Whereas prior to around 1540 literacy was largely restricted to a social intellectual elite, Labberton offers evidence for the view that in Calvin's Strasbourg the literacy rate increased dramatically over a wide urban population. From being a "professional" activity, reading became amateur, private, and democratic".[71] Calvin believed that divine revelation through the biblical texts embodied a principal of "accommodation" to ordinary people; thus through the texts God spoke "like a nurse".[72] We may note the contrast between post-modernist notions of literary polyvalency and "productivity" and Calvin's insistence that biblical texts do not propound enigmas to keep readers in suspense.73

For Calvin, however, as for Luther, "ordinary reading" did not preclude the necessity for instruction or for pastoral guidance. Reformation theology, at least in its mainstream forms, is not equivalent to social or theological egalitarianism. Calvin assigned a positive role "to the learned who are experienced and versed in scripture, and in particular to duly ordained pastors".74 But in the era after the Reformation itself a more scholastic Protestant rationalism arguably began to lose sight of the fundamentally corporate nature of interpretation, to which persons of all kinds could contribute. Reading became over-intellectualized. Andrew Kirk underlines these points in his writings on Latin American liberation theology, including his book *Liberation Theology* (1979).

Labberton recognizes the value of reader-orientated theory in restoring neglected attention to the role of ordinary readers in the encounter between biblical texts and whole communities. Such theory *corrects a rationalist over-emphasis on the "professional" interpreter. It also calls attention to the fallacy of assuming that "natural" meaning would be perceived as "natural" from within any* given *tradition as if the notion were context-free.* Labberton recognizes the value of Bleich's approach for the emphasis on "ordinary" readers in the whole community, and of the work of Culler and Fish for underlining the fallacy of objectivist notions of "natural" or "plain" meaning. Nevertheless he is uncomfortable with the accompanying shift of primacy from texts to readers, and seeks some intermediate position. No doubt Fish would greet this attempt with the severity and scorn which he directs at Iser for attempting a similar task.

Nevertheless we cannot follow Bleich and Fish in their slide into socio-pragmatic hermeneutics. The clearest proof that Bleich's theory degenerates from ethics to pragmatism emerges in his exposition of his feminist hermeneutic in wholly pragmatic terms. Indeed, after introducing promising aspects for feminist theory, Bleich not only risks stereotyping gender differences, but also sells out critical theory from its capacity to support the feminist case in ways which, we noted in chapter XII, cause Susanne Heine and Janet Radcliffe Richards, exasperation, anguish, and almost despair. *For the outcome of Bleich's argument is that to include women fully in hermeneutics we must replace critical theory and rational discourse by pragmatic, instrumental, rhetoric.*

Bleich claims not only that Husserl's notion of intersubjectivity is "masculine", but that the major philosophical tradition from Husserl to Derrida rests on the "masculine" qualities of "individualism, strong boundaries, adversarial attitudes.75 Bleich similarly rejects the model of *gender-neutral reading* advocated by Louise Rosenblatt as itself *so abstract as to constitute a sell-out to a "masculine" ploy. Any metacritical hermeneutic would, on this basis,* become "masculine" in tone. *The rigorous work of Wittgenstein and Gadamer, and even the claims of Derrida, are said to utilize and focus on the allegedly masculine notion of rules.* In Wittgenstein and in Gadamer, Bleich tries to argue, "the game idea is part of the ethical and psychosocial mentality of the academy".[76]

Bleich devotes some ten pages of *The Double Perspective* to arguing that the philosophies of language expounded and defended by Gadamer, Barthes, Derrida, Hegel, and Wittgenstein are "governed by individualist and masculinist ideology".[77] The most tragic feature of these pages is not simply the misunderstanding of the central role of community and creativity in Gadamer and in Wittgenstein but more especially the attempt to *transpose truth-questions into a social pragmatism based partly on the questionable psychological stereotypifications of gender arrived at by J. Piaget.* Piaget observes: "Girls . . . have a more 'pragmatic' attitude towards rules".[78] But, in the first place, in the tradition of Jung, any "P" ("perceiving") or "F" ("feeling") type of human agent, *whether male or female*, is likely to emphasize "relationships" more than "abstract principles", as against any "J" type ("judicial" or "judgmental") or "T" type ("thinking") who may accord primacy to "rules" also *whether male or female*. *Males or females* may *equally* fall under Jungian categories of "thinkers" as against "feelers". In terms of critical theory, the views of Jung, Piaget, or other observational psychologists remain *unproven and certainly provide no basis for assessing the truth of any given philosophy of language or theories of hermeneutics.* In the second place, as we have seen, Susanne Heine and Janet Radcliffe Richards regard such surrender of critical theory in the name of feminism as a *betrayal of feminism*, as if to imply that women could not compete in cognitive discourse and critical theory. Some observational psychologists, if their research is to be trusted, seem to suggest that the *maximum* gender-correlation of "T" to "F" would be around 6:4, and we must then allow for sociological conditioning, on top of this. There is apparently no gender correlation between Jungian "P" types and "J" types or between "S" types (sensors) and "N" types (those who readily intuit or project possibilities).

Presumably Bleich would offer the counter-reply that academic or *"elitist"* women should not call the tune for *other* women. But this would shift the ground of the debate. The very same principle applies to *men*. Is Wittgenstein wrong because he is an intellectual? Further, if we determine the validity of *truth-claims* about the nature of language and texts in terms of *socially egalitarian pragmatic* criteria we have surrendered philosophy, linguistics, hermeneutics and theology, to certain contingent hypotheses in sociology and psychology. In practice Bleich's *literary* theory is bound up with a familiar *socio-political agenda. Egalitarian social politics dictate the de-privileging of the author, the de-privileging of academic interpreters, and even the de-privileging of a literary or theological canon of "classics", in order to make the whole mixed community co-authors of texts*: everyone constructs, and no construction is "better" than another *because critical theory would already prejudice an answer in favour of the elite*. Once again, socio-pragmatic theory disintegrates into the anarchy in which *the most militant pressure-group actually carries the day about what satisfies their pragmatic criteria of "right" reading*. It is no accident that reason creates "order", while socio-pragmatic egalitarianism is "anti-hierarchical".

4. Further Observations on the Reader-Orientated Semiotics of Culler and on the Social Pragmatism of Fish

We have already examined Jonathan Culler's approach to questions of *reading-competency* and to *inter-textuality* in the previous chapter. It is unnecessary therefore to reconsider his reader-orientated theory in the same length as that accorded to other theorists in this chapter. Indeed, largely because he wishes to dissociate himself from the pragmatic stance of Bleich and especially of Fish, Culler is not at ease with the term "reader-response theory" as a description of his work. Nevertheless his approach strongly stresses the constitutive role of the "competences" of a reading community as determinative for textual meaning, as we have already seen. We have also already noted the use made of his work by John Barton in his book on reading the Old Testament, as well as the relation between his work on intertextuality and biblical studies. We need not therefore pursue further Culler's significance for biblical interpretation; but his place among the other theorists considered in this present chapter invites further comment.

Initially, like Eco, Culler bases his approach on semiotic theory. But consistent development in the direction of the role of the reader can be traced from *Structuralist Poetics* (1975) through *The Pursuit of Signs* (1981) to *Framing the Sign* (1988). Jane Tompkins offers an initial summarizing observation: "If meaning is no longer a property of the text but a product of the reader's activity the question to answer is not 'what do these poems mean?' or even 'what do poems do?' but 'how do readers make meaning?' Jonathan Culler's *Structuralist Poetics* provides an answer to this question based on the central insights of French structuralism from Saussure to Derrida".[78] Culler's central concern in his work of 1988, *Framing the Sign* is to enquire how signs are "constituted (framed) by various discursive practices, institutional arrangements, systems of value, semiotic mechanisms".[79]

It will not do, Culler argues, simply to claim that the "context" of a text determines its meaning rather than these semiotic or institutional features, because it is these that determine how we "frame" the sign, where "framing is determining, setting off the object or event *as* . . ." what we perceive it to be. Far from viewing this as shifting the focus to the psychological subject, as Holland's earlier work had done, Culler applies and extends the *semiotic emphasis on system* rather than a hermeneutics of life-world. This remains the case even although in *The pursuit of Signs* he is sympathetic with the view that the notion of inter-textuality has close parallels with hermeneutical presupposition or pre-understanding, and may function like Searle's idea of "Background". He asserts: "Words prove to be not tools . . . but machines, with complex internal structures that can generate results not always predictable to their users".[80]

In our Introduction to this volume we cited Jonathan Culler's comment in his *Framing the Sign* that pragmatic literary theory, and in effect socio-pragmatic hermeneutics, reflects a cultural "complacency" which is "altogether appropriate to the age of Reagan".[81] Elsewhere he speaks of the complacency of "neo-pragmatism". Such a comment not only underlines the potentially passé nature of a phase which may not survive for long on such flimsy theoretical foundations, but also indicates Culler's conscious distancing of himself from the kind of positions held by Fish, Bleich, and Rorty. Culler would no doubt view Bleich's complaint that he is too theory-centred as a confirmatory affirmation of his approach. A certain parallel may be suggested between Culler's work and the critical quest for a *transcendental* hermeneutics which began with Schleiermacher and which reaches its climax in Gadamer, Ricoeur, Apel, and Habermas. Thus in his earlier book *Structuralist Poetics* Culler makes it clear by *"Poetics"* he means *the conditions for the possibility of processes of reading.*[82] In a parallel way hermeneutical theory in the Schleiermacher tradition offers critical reflection on *conditions for the possibility of understanding.*

In *The Pursuit of Signs*, however, Culler demonstrates that the *subject-matter* of his concern is quite different from that of Schleiermacher and his hermeneutical successors. Culler's focus of interest lies less on understanding a supposed textual "content" in its own right, than perceiving the "conventions", "operations" and "procedures" by which a given system may function operatively for a given community of readers.[83] In his book *On Deconstruction* (1982) Culler accepts Roland Barthes's view that a literary work embodies endless interacting layers of semiotic code or system, with the result that it may offer no stable, identifiable, centre or meaning-content.[84] In *Framing the Sign* Culler argues that even contextualization, in the sense of "framing", does *not arrest* "the play of signs", because *how* a text is contextualized or *re-*contextualized remains variable in relation to decisions, conventions, and strategies on the part of communities of readers. In his other works Culler concludes: "There are no final meanings" that bring this process to closure.[85] Interpretation, he writes, is not a matter of "recovering" meaning, but of participating as readers in the play of *possible* meanings to which a text gives access.[86]

We have already noted that Culler compares the double axes of *langue* and *parole* with the endless process of interaction between understanding and pre-understanding in the *hermeneutical circle*. One major difficulty with Culler's work arises precisely from this inter-relation between *langue* and *parole*, as it does in Barthes. He seems to give priority to the axes of *langue, system*, and *linguistic competence* or *possible* meaning, as over against *parole, actual* language-*use*-in-life-world, and linguistic *performance* (in spite of Ray's claim to the contrary).[87] What "we do" in Culler's judgment is expressed in the title *Framing the Sign*. This may include the artificial manipulation of a "frame-up". This may regularly entail "*naturalizing*" the text, namely giving it a place "in the world which our culture defines ... to bring it within the modes of order which culture makes available".[88] Here we come near to the hermeneutical insight that we *begin* by contextualizing a text in terms of the familiar as an implicate of "pre-understanding". But in Schleiermacher and in Betti, and in a different way in Gadamer, further interaction with the text enlarges this horizon and may potentially transform it. If all the weight in reader-orientated hermeneutics is placed on prior expectations, codes, conventions, horizons, *out of which meaning is determined and constructed* it is difficult to see how the text can transform or correct the horizons of reading communities "*from outside*".

This is precisely the issue that comes to a head prominently and explicitly in the work of Stanley Fish. *The major contribution of Fish is his unflinching acceptance of what is entailed, or not entailed, in socio-pragmatic hermeneutics.* Especially in the volume of essays published under the title *Doing What Comes Naturally* (1989) Fish anticipates and checks out every possible move which critics of his pragmatic relativism might make. He disarmingly accepts what has to be accepted, and relishes his opponents' confusion when some (by no means all) of his counterarguments take, in effect, the form: "So, what?" Fish is more interested in the "*non-consequences*" of his theory than in its consequences.

The key issue, namely whether texts can challenge or transform communities of readers "*from outside*" is identified as a watershed in Fish's important essay "Going Down the Anti-Formalist Road" (1989). Fish writes: "Once you start down the anti-formalist road, there is no place to stop ..." As soon as we grasp the *contextual pragmatic* relativity of criteria of meaning *to social presuppositions and interests*, "the general conclusion that follows from this is that *the model in which a practice is altered or reformed by constraints brought in from the outside . . . never in fact operates. . . . Theory has no consequences"* (my italics).[89]

Fish, we earlier noted, did not begin his literary pilgrimage from this point. In *Surprised by Sin* (1967) he focussed on the capacity of texts (especially in this study, of John Milton's *Paradise Lost*) to lead readers along paths that invite re-valuation of the reader's own perceptions. They invite reader-awareness. In *Self-Consuming Artifacts. The Experience of Seventeenth-Century Literature* (1972) Fish traces alternative reading-strategies which may characterize relations between readers and texts.[90] The supposed "objectivity" of the text as that which *controls* strategy is an illusion; different strategies of reading represent different *things which readers do with* texts. Thus where *readers* may have *cognitive* reading-*expectations*, it is likely that this will give rise to a rhetorical strategy of *discursive* reading; *readers'* quests for self-knowledge, or their *expectations* that the text will enhance self-awareness, may dictate a strategy of "*dialectical*" reading-processes. At this stage in his development of theory (1972) Fish experienced a genuine *tension* between the notion that a text "out there" somehow *constrained* interpretation (and therefore invited quasi-objective questions about style, genre, or purpose) and his growing awareness that *readers' own strategies, goals, assumptions, and expectations* seem to determine what *counts for them as* reading or interpretation.

Fish looks back on this period of "worry" from a later vantage-point in his introductory essay to *Is There a Text in this Class?* (1980). He entitles his autobiographical reflections "How I Stopped Worrying and Learned to Love Interpretation".[91] By this stage (1980) he has come to "see through" the illusion that any "meaning" resided *in* the text at all. Interpretation as "reading meaning" is *constructed* by what Fish terms "the authority of interpretive communities". This alone determines what *counts as* interpretation. The notion that texts have meanings is illusory, at least in the sense of their lying "innocently" in the text itself. Fish comments on his own earlier mistaken assumptions: "I did what critics always do: I 'saw' what my interpretive principles permitted or directed me to see, and then I turned around and attributed what I had 'seen' to a text and an intention. What my principles direct me to 'see' are readers performing acts."[92]

Textual meanings, Fish therefore declared, "do not lie innocently in the world; rather, they are themselves *constituted* by an interpretive act. The facts one points to are still there (in a sense that would not be consoling to an objectivist) but only as a consequence of the interpretive (man-made) model that has called them into being."[93] It is thus operationally justifiable, and even necessary if confusion is to be avoided, to *replace* the question "What does this *mean*?" by the question "What does this *do*?" In a key sentence (already noted earlier)

Fish writes: "The reader's response is not *to* the meaning; it *is* the meaning".94

The later work undertaken by Fish between 1980 and 1989 consolidates and defends this position. Everything hinges on "social and institutional circumstances".95 Thus in the large volume of twenty-two essays published under the title *Doing What Comes Naturally* Fish includes his notoriously polemical review of Wolfgang Iser's work (1981) in which he attacks Iser for stopping half-way on the journey to a consistent reader-response theory; Fish also attacks Owen Fiss's essay "Objectivity and Interpretation" (1982) in "Fish v. Fiss"; and he argues that Ronald Dworkin "repeatedly falls away from his own best insights into the fallacies (of pure objectivity and pure subjectivity) he so forcefully challenges".96 He discusses the nature of change in social frameworks of thought partially with reference to Thomas Kuhn and to Richard Rorty.97 A unifying theme emerges in the contrast between formalist systems and socio-contingent pragmatic contexts of life. Fish views performative utterances as "contingent . . . [they] cannot be formally constrained".98 But he detects an ambivalence in J.L. Austin which gives rise to the development of speech-act theory either in a formalist direction (Jerrold Katz) or in contingent-pragmatic terms (H.P. Grice and Mary L. Pratt).99

These twenty-two essays offer a panoramic view of diverse twists and turns in contemporary debate. The relation between social institutions and institutional, legal, or performative *force* receives a particular focus in Fish's critique of H.L.A. Hart's philosophy of law.100 As we saw in chapter VIII in our discussion of Austin, Evans, and Searle, what count as "institutional" facts offer a foundation on which certain illocutions and speech-acts can become operative. In these terms there is *prima facie* plausibility in Fish's observations that concerning the "temporally contingent nature of our 'fundamental' assumptions".101 In many of these essays, where his concerns are broader than his earlier work on literary "meaning" and literary texts, *Fish seems often to be an ally in the hermeneutical enterprise, with its emphasis on the historical contingency of the life-world as against a purely formal system.*

Nevertheless we have argued repeatedly in this volume that *sociopragmatic hermeneutics ultimately betrays the function which hermeneutics arose to perform.* Fish includes in this volume of essays a very brief skirmish with Habermas, and it is clear that he cannot entertain the possibility of a genuinely critical, socio-critical, metacritical, or transcontextual hermeneutic. He cannot journey with Habermas or with Apel in the quest for any principle that would *relate* the life-world to a broader system, however loose and open such a system might be. For Fish has committed himself: it is *either* formalism *or* radical pragmatic *anti*-formalism. There is no place to stand, according to Fish, between the two extremes. This is Fish's fatal error.

5. What Fish's Counterarguments Overlook about Language: Fish and Wittgenstein

Wittgenstein was as eager as Fish to shake off the illusion of formal or "ideal" language, "as if our logic were, so to speak, a logic for a vacuum".[102] In retrospect Wittgenstein writes that logic of a purely *formal* kind is "*a priori* order: that is, the order of *possibilities* . . . It is *prior* to all experience . . . a *super*-order . . . *super*-concepts . . .' (Wittgenstein's italics).[103] This was the formalist view that Wittgenstein had presented in his early systematic work on the philosophy of logic under the title *Tractatus Logico-Philosophicus*.[104] Wittgenstein later comments in his *Philosophical Investigations*: "The *pre-conceived idea* of crystalline purity can only be removed by turning our whole examination round . . . A *picture* held us captive . . . The confusions which occupy us arise when language is like an engine idling, not when it is doing work."[105]

By contrast with formalist theories of language, Wittgenstein insists that the meaning of such terms as "proposition", "language", and even "meaning" itself depends on "the language-game in which they are to be applied".[106] Wittgenstein observes in his book *On Certainty* "When language-games change, then there is a change in concepts, and with the concepts the meanings of words change".[107] Rush Rhees comments on Wittgenstein's approach: "Speaking is not *one thing*, and 'having meaning' is not *one thing* either".[108] Wittgenstein notes in his *Zettel*: "What determines . . . our concepts is . . . the whole hurly-burly of human actions, the background against which we see any action."[109] Finally, in his *Remarks on the Foundations of Mathematics* he writes: "The kinds of use we feel to be 'the point' are connected with the role that such-and-such a use has in our whole life."[110]

Wittgenstein's own journey "down the anti-formalist road" seems in the light of primary sources and secondary literature to be altogether more intense and philosophically serious than Fish's account of his journey in "How I stopped Worrying . . ." Through struggle Wittgenstein passed through the so-called middle period of the *Philosophische Bemerkungen* (1929–30; published in 1964) and earlier parts of *Philosophical Grammar* (1929–34; published in 1974) to the later period of *The Blue and Brown Books* (1933–35; published in 1958), his major work *Philosophical Investigations* (Part I, 1936–45, Part II, 1947–49; first edition, 1953), and *On Certainty* (1950–51, published in 1969). Major studies of Wittgenstein's thought shed additional light on how a view of meaning emerged which is neither formalist nor purely contextual-pragmatic. In addition to the first-generation assessments from Norman Malcolm (1958, 1967) and from Rush Rhees (1970), and the early work of George Pitcher (1964), special note may be taken of the critical studies offered by Anthony Kenny (1975), David Pears (1971), A. Janik and S. Toulmin (1973), and Gordon P. Baker and P.M. Hacker (3 vols 1983, 1988, 1990), among others.[111] In *The Two Horizons* I devoted two detailed chapters and part of a third chapter to Wittgenstein's relation to hermeneutical theory, and in this connection also alluded to the work of Apel.[112]

If both Fish and Wittgenstein see the illusions of formalism, however, their respective methods in distancing themselves from it are entirely different. In *Doing What Comes Naturally* Fish consciously "sets up" Ruth Kempson's formalist approach to language purely as a foil for his own *either/or*.[113] For Fish it becomes a matter of *necessity* to reject formalism and to espouse its supposed opposite as a way of being doctrinally *consistent* (in contrast to Iser, Fiss, and numerous similar targets of attack). But Wittgenstein has had enough of doctrine and personal narrative ("A picture held us captive"). His method of achieving liberation from this formalist "picture" which had "held him captive" is expressed in his *Philosophical Investigations* under the maxim: "Don't say: 'There *must* be . . .' but *look* and see whether there is . . . Don't think, but look" (Wittgenstein's italics).[114] Further, whereas Fish sees the alternative to formalism as that of socially conditioned norms *internal to given communities*, in the *Zettel* Wittgenstein observes: "The philosopher is not *a citizen of any community of ideas. This is what makes him into a philosopher*" (my italics).[115] This is different from Fish's socio-pragmatic language about convictions which arise from Kempson's "story" and from "my story".

When he *looked at* language, Wittgenstein observed that *some* language-games could be thought of in entirely context-relative terms, but *for the most part* "we see a complicated network of similarities overlapping and criss-crossing".[116] In other words, although social practices of given communities do indeed provide a background which contextually shapes concepts and meanings, *overlappings and interpenetration also offer certain criss-crossings which constitute trans-contextual bridges*. Sufficient bridging can occur for Wittgenstein to suggest that in many cases a trans-contextual frame of reference for meanings can be found in *"the common behaviour of mankind"*.[117]

It is not the case, as Fish suggests it is, that we must choose between the sharply-bounded crystalline purity of formalist concepts and the unstable concepts of contextual pragmatism. Concepts may function with a measure of operational stability, but with "blurred edges". Differences of social context and practice may *push or pull them into relatively different shapes*, but do not necessarily change their stable *identity*. For Wittgenstein, as for F. Waismann, "concepts with blurred edges" are situated on middle ground along the road from formalism to pragmatism.[118]

The fundamental philosophical weakness in Fish's polarizing of his two alternatives lies in failure to come to terms with the major transcendental questions which stem from Kant, in which very careful and rigorous attention is given to the working distinction between how the knowing human subject or agent *conditions* raw data and what this subject or agent *constructs* independently of raw data. *Do social contexts condition or do they construct social realities, including texts?* Beyond the Kantian philosophical tradition, the tradition of Hegel which passes on through Gadamer to Habermas wrestles with a parallel tension between the contextually-historically finite and the broader continuum or frame which finite historical phenomena presuppose.

Fish, as a lawyer and literary critic, "sees through" what has long preoccupied the minds of the great philosophers, endeavouring to move quickly, with little or no reference to the deeper philosophical background, to fairly brief skirmishes with Habermas and with Toulmin, and with passing appeals for support to Thomas Kuhn and to Richard Rorty. (He does not seem to note that Kuhn has substantially modified his earlier claims about the socio-contextual nature of knowledge in science in his later book of essays, *The Essential Tension*, 1977).[119] In an essay with the promising title "Critical Self-Consciousness, or Can We Know What We're Doing?" Fish dismisses as untenable or as self-contradictory the "universal pragmatics" or socio-critical theory of Habermas. Fish argues that "the insight of historicity – the fashioned or *constructed* nature of *all* forms of thought and organization" (my italics) relativizes Habermas's claim to offer *critical* theory.[120] He insists that the counterarguments and defences put forward by Habermas merely "re-start" the argument again and again, and that critical theory, rather than solving the problem, simply re-instates it.

Like Rorty, Fish only "listens" to that aspect of post-Hegelian, post-Gadamerian philosophy which recognizes exclusively the internal instrumental function of reason within social traditions on the basis of a doctrine that all rationality operates at this single level, and can never explore outside socially-determined boundaries in order to provide broader or deeper metacritical reflection. It is precisely here, however, that we return to Wittgenstein, and to his overlapping language-games. *If* our vision is *always internal to our own language-games*, how could Wittgenstein declare: "One learns the game by *watching* how others play"?[121] Why does Wittgenstein recognize the *specific* cultural relativity of *some* language-games, while insisting that the contextual conditions for the operability of *other* language-games lie simply in being "a *living human being*"?[122] Why does he see so many conceptual meanings as simply grounded in "ordinary intercourse with others" (like Apel's universal intersubjectivity) rather than as context-specific (like Rorty's local traditions)?[123] How would it make sense for Wittgenstein to say: "The common behaviour of mankind is the system of reference by means of which we interpret an unknown language"?[124]

Fish offers some recognition in his latest counterarguments designed to forestall criticism, to the notion that the social roles which arise from contextual institutions may overlap or interpenetrate. Practices and communities, he acknowledges, are not "pure". For example, he suggests, "My way of being a parent is all mixed with my way of being a teacher", or we may bring together two community-traditions in the very notion of "black academics".[125] Feminist academics likewise bring to their work and to their "reading" more than one set of community interests, presuppositions, and expectations.[126] But Fish does not develop this fundamental point in the direction adopted by Karl-Otto Apel. He refines the concept of "reading community" but insists that we cannot gain access thereby to norms or criteria "outside" the community.

The key difficulty is that while he recognizes variables in contingencies of social history, Fish holds to a pragmatic *doctrine* whereby *all* texts depend for *all* meaning on what socio-contextual boundaries construct by internal community norms and practices. Wittgenstein, by contrast, observes diversity among different "texts" and among different examples of "meaning". In the well-known language-game of "Wittgenstein's builders" meanings are created by ostensive reference *only because "this narrowly circumscribed region" presupposes a given communicative situation between these two builders*. It is context-specific.[127] But in his *Culture and Value* Wittgenstein envisages a different example. Two people, this time, share a joke. Wittgenstein writes: "One of them has used certain somewhat unusual words and now they both break out into a sort of bleating. That might appear *very* extraordinary to a visitor coming from quite a different environment. Whereas we find it completely *reasonable*" (his italics).[128] In the case of laughter, the "meaning" of this "institutional" or social behaviour is trans-contextual or trans-cultural.

The principle, however, can be extended. What about language which expresses pain?[129] Its *embeddedness in universal pain-behaviour* makes it artificially forced to say: "Only these reading-communities which experience pain like *this* construct *this* kind of meaning for pain in texts." How are we to evaluate language about remorse, sincerity, or lying? Wittgenstein sees these as having *stable* meanings in the context of *human* behaviour as such. In his *Zettel* he makes this point clearly. Human beings *as human beings* (not *as* academics or *as* women) "reflect on the past"; but "can a dog feel ... remorse?"[130] In the *Investigations* he seems to make the same point about sincerity: "Why can't a dog simulate pain? Is he too honest? ... A dog cannot be a hypocrite, but neither can he be sincere."[131] This is not to deny the role of education and learning. Thus, for example, "lying is a language-game that needs to be learned like any other one".[132] But *this* tradition of learning weaves in and out through a multitude of socio-cultural communities.

Wittgenstein's arguments about "private language" (in the strictly technical sense of the term) can be applied at a corporate level to interaction between communities of interpretation. Wittgenstein's point is that *without an intersubjective "checking" or testing process*, there would be no way in which language-users could tell the difference between uses or meanings that were "correct", and those which "seemed" correct. There would be no difference between a "mistake" and a "*systematic mistake*". Wittgenstein declares: "It is not possible to obey a rule privately; otherwise *thinking* one was obeying the rule would be the same thing as *obeying* it" (my italics).[133] But this principle can be extended to checking or to testing inter-contextual currency-values *between* communities of readers. "*Hard*" currency can be measured and transacted across national or contextual boundaries; "*soft*" currency meets *only internal demands* in accordance with internal norms. Its pragmatic value is culture-bound. Like the currency of some Eastern Block countries at the time of writing, *soft* currency depends on internal subsidies which, when removed, makes them uncompetitive and unusable for our international business. But language, too, can acquire an inflated currency in relation to internal norms, where such criteria as "literary productivity" operate without reference to inter-contextual or trans-contextual human practices and communicative currency-rates. The need for some behavioural "backing" for linguistic currency is explored by Wittgenstein especially in his *Blue Book*.

In the light of all this, we may look again at the standard criticisms of socio-pragmatic hermeneutics and at Fish's disarming disclaimers in his "Going Down the Anti-Formalist Road".

(i) Fish readily concedes Cornel West's criticism that pragmatism can offer no effective socio-critical assessment for social action. He agrees: "The thesis that theory goes nowhere (except in the contingent ways of all rhetorics) is itself a thesis that can go nowhere."[134] Jonathan Culler, as we have noted, understandably views such a position as "complacent", because it would be tolerable only if one had supreme confidence that one's theory was not itself corrigible in the light of further enquiry and research. While Habermas genuinely takes on board the dimension of historical and hermeneutical contingency, Rorty (as West notes) insists that everyone else must share his own evaluation of social narrative as marking out pragmatic anti-metacritical ground, and he seems unable to "see" the possibility of inter-contextual *exploration*. While Wittgenstein *goes on* "looking", exploring and enquiring, Rorty (and Fish) propound a pragmatic *doctrine* which offers only ghetto-like consistency *on its own terms*. In the end Fish argues that philosophical sterility does not really matter because society and social theory is "propped up", in his view, not by critical thought, theory, or philosophy, but by "the material conditions" of everyday life.[135] Social relations, dollars, and military security thus provide the nearest thing to a metacritical principle; hence Culler associates this pragmatic "complacency" with "the age of Reagan". Pragmatic hermeneutics has more than a touch of Hollywood and John Wayne: "A man's gotta do what a man's gotta do" (given the community's conventions); but we cannot *ask* metacritical questions about whether the community's conventions are testable or right (even if they sometimes glorify retaliation or oppress conquered races) because we cannot get *"outside"* the film without perceiving it *as* a film.

(ii) This brings us precisely to the second standard criticism. *Sociopragmatic philosophy can never be more than narrative philosophy.* This is why Fish's key essay in *Is There a Text in This Class?* remains narrative testimony about shifting convictions. Rorty's style in *Philosophy and the Mirror of Nature* reflects this narrative style: it is the re-telling of the story of a particular tradition of philosophy, with a retrospective "pointing up" of what supports pragmatic doctrine. Richard Bernstein and Christopher Norris both engage brilliantly, as we have seen, with the self-contradictory nature of this mode of argument as a claim to *philosophize*.[136] Norris acutely observes that Rorty offers, on the basis of his own pragmatic premise, *"just one story among many"*; but that he [and Fish] could still try to have "the last word against anyone who wanted philosophy to be *more* than just a story . . . Under cover of its liberal-pluralist credentials, this narrative very neatly closes all exits except the one marked 'James and Dewey'. The rejection of a meta-narrative standpoint goes along with *a refusal to entertain any serious alternative account of what philosophy ought to be. It is this use of a liberal rhetoric to frame an authoritative message* which marks the real kinship between Rorty's pragmatism and nineteenth-century narrative forms."[137]

(iii) In chapter XI we drew attention to Georgia Warnke's careful discussion concerning the trans-contextual nature of rationality in relation to assessments of Gadamer and of Rorty. Such an approach coheres with Wittgenstein's observations about overlappings and criss-crossings among contextual language-games, about publicly accessible criteria of meaning, and about *the philosopher's status as a citizen of no particular given community*. Wittgenstein's work unmasks Fish's attempts to "set up" formalism in a way which superficially invites a re-bound into social pragmatism. For while Wittgenstein shares Fish's disillusionment with formalism, whether there is any "place to stop" along the anti-formalist road depends not on pragmatic (anti-formalist) *doctrine*, but on *noticing what kinds of language, what kinds of texts, and what kinds of meanings are at issue*. In a *large class* of cases (though not in all cases) it is simply doctrinaire to claim that "meaning" can be reduced exhaustively and without remainder to what the internal norms and conventions of given communities simply construct. The meaning-currency of *many* texts (not all texts) draws its cash-value from the backing of the intersubjective world out of which it is spoken or written, and in many cases (though not all) its system of reference is the common behaviour of humankind.

(iv) We observed among the difficulties of David Bleich's social pragmatism that a radical or exclusive emphasis on the role of the reading-community in *constructing* meaning *collapses "the two horizons" of hermeneutics into one single horizon*. This violates the concern for listening, openness, and dialogue, which stands at the heart of hermeneutical theory from Schleiermacher to Betti, and from Gadamer to Ricoeur. In social pragmatism a hermeneutics of suspicion can have little effective value as a *critical principle*; nor can the effort to *"respect the other"*, in such a way as to present a *premature* "fusion of horizons", in which the reading-community *constructs* an image or projection of itself as "the meaning of the text". Ricoeur identifies this latter process, in cases of sacred texts, as idolatrous. We need to look more closely therefore at the impact which Fish's model might have in biblical studies or in Christian theology.

6. The Major Difficulties and Limited Value of Fish's Later Theory for Biblical Studies and for Theology

Those who have attempted to utilize Fish's model of interpretation for biblical studies have focussed largely on two major issues: (i) the problematic status of the traditional notion of "the meaning of a text"; and (ii) the supposedly controlling or decisive role of community interests and expectations on the part of readers in "constructing" textual meaning, or at very least, on constructing what *counts as* textual meaning.

Three essays deserve particular attention, two of which occur in the volume *The Bible in Three Dimensions* (1990), which celebrates forty years of biblical studies in the University of Sheffield. All the authors of the three essays in question are former doctoral research students of Sheffield, contemporary with my teaching there.

Mark Brett has written extensively on canon criticism, but in this volume he confines his attention largely to hermeneutical questions about the role played by *interpretative interests and goals*.[138] His essay "Four or Five Things to Do with Texts" offers perhaps an indirect allusion to Fish's theoretical model in which *readers "do things with" texts*, rather than simply find themselves *addressed by* texts. There is also a legitimate recognition, shared with Fish, that what appears to be the "natural" way of understanding a text depends in practice largely on the goals, expectations, assumptions, stance, and interests of given communities of readers. Brett pays particular attention to the contrast between more traditional goals within the humanist paradigm which takes account of the purposes of authors of texts and more recent materialist readings represented in the work of Norman K. Gottwald and of F. Frick. In the latter case, a *social-scientific causal explanation* of the social guides the agenda of hermeneutical enquiry.[139] Brett rightly concludes that diversities of goals produce diversities of readings; but he does not seek to engage closely with metacritical questions about *whether* or *how* these goals or interests should be ranked. Thus he stands broadly in the tradition of hermeneutical enquiry which we have associated with John Barton and Robert Morgan, whose work I discuss also in this same Sheffield volume.

Stephen Fowl, whose book *The Story of Christ in the Ethics of Paul* (1990) began as a Sheffield doctoral dissertation under my supervision, entitles his essay "The Ethics of Interpretation or What's Left Over after the Elimination of Meaning".[140] Here he draws heavily on Jeffrey Stout's article "What is the Meaning of a Text?" (1982).[141] Stout has philosophical sympathies with W.V. Quine, who has also influenced Rorty. But the particular strategy adopted by Stout anticipates that used by Fish in his "Anti-Formalist Road" essay of 1989. Stout associates the search for meanings in texts with what amounts to a hidden formalism, or more strictly a hidden essentialism; it is "searching for the essence of meaning, or the core of the concept".[142] He claims to look behind these three questions to what prompts them, namely the interests of the enquiring community. Hence he re-formulates the hermeneutical agenda "if need be, by eliminating reference to meaning."[143] Looking partly to Quine, he believes that to explicate meaning is to eliminate it.

We have already demonstrated from Wittgenstein's observations in our discussions in the previous section that the whole issue of what constitutes "meaning" is far more complex and subtle than such a crude polarization of supposed alternatives allows. Nevertheless Fowl finds himself drawn along by the logic of the choices imposed by Stout and parallelled in Fish. He writes: *"I would like to propose that we in Biblical Studies give up discussions of meaning and adopt Stout's position"* (my italics).[144] That Fowl moves towards the pragmatic contextualism of Rorty and Fish emerges from his scepticism about *metacritical* evaluation: he believes that there is no way "of adjudicating between competing conceptions of textual meaning."[145] If deciding between meanings is a critical task, deciding between "conceptions of textual meaning" is a metacritical one; but Fowl seems to exclude this possibility.

Nevertheless Fowl is ultimately ambivalent about the status of metacritical hermeneutics. He recognizes, on one side, that he opens the door to pluralism and relativism. In one sense, he believes, this is both inevitable and healthy. But he adds two qualifications which conflict radically with the social pragmatism of Rorty and Fish. First, among the "interests" of given communities, one guiding goal may be to reconstruct the intentions of the author of the text. (In Schleiermacher's view, this would have been to recover its "meaning", provided that provisional reconstructions *(parole)* were successively tested and checked against the critical linguistic or systemic axis of the intersubjective language-system *(langue)*, and placed in dialogue together within this broad contextual frame). Second, Fowl rightly *(pace* Fish) seeks a *socio-critical frame* within which to constrain an otherwise relativist pluralism, which he finds in *ethics (pace* Fish). A socio-political concern for justice is to be sought in a context of openness. He appeals to the paper of Elizabeth Fiorenza discussed above as a model for this kind of approach.

This cautious ambivalence towards metacritical reflection saves Fowl from falling prey to the Stout-Rorty-Fish socio-pragmatic hermeneutic which he otherwise proposes to substitute for traditional enquiries about meaning. But the very ambivalence of this position will satisfy neither the pragmatists nor those who seek more complex and adequate accounts of meaning and theories of hermeneutics. By contrast, Stanley Porter, also a former research student, shows no ambivalence and less caution in sharing Fish's company down the anti-formalist road towards social pragmatism. Porter seems to combine some of Fish's scepticism about extra-linguistic "givens" in texts with socio-political concerns about communities of scholars and their social interests.

In his article "Why Hasn't Reader-Response Criticism Caught On in New Testament Studies?" (1990) Porter shares Fish's view that the kind of reader-response theory which takes serious account of a historical givenness or which seeks some extra-linguistic context relating to situations behind the text is half-baked and disappointing.[146] Thus in a series of negative criticisms Porter sees Petersen's article on reading codes as "particularly disappointing"; while Fowler's work "subordinates the reader's involvement" by leaning too heavily both on the first "historical" readers and on the kind of "implied reader" associated with Iser who is "notoriously ambiguous".[147] Fowler is "formalistic" in his over-all result; Resseguie "pulls back" from Fish's model; and Staley has "taken his cue from Resseguie".[148] Culpepper sees the ambiguities in Iser's theory, but nevertheless belongs to the "generally disappointing" story in biblical studies of a lack of nerve in following where Fish leads. There is supposedly still a "clear fixation with formalism", and a dominant insistence on "historical concerns.[149] Porter concludes: "Reader-response criticism . . . in New Testament Studies . . . is definitely lagging behind developments in the secular literary field."[150]

On two points I agree with Porter. He pleads for biblical specialists to have less second-hand dependence "upon secular scholars for their theoretical grounding".[151] To contribute to this need is one purpose of the present volume. Porter also pleads for a greater diversity of hermeneutical models to be utilized in Biblical studies. This also represents a need to which the present volume provides a response. Nevertheless, to go to Fish for such freedom and multiformity is to offer a remedy worse than the problem. *Almost all current calls for the use of a greater variety of strategies in biblical hermeneutics seem to presuppose that these strategies cannot be ordered and ranked metacritically in relation to different tasks or to the nature of different texts.* But if strategies reflect interests, and if interests reflect world-views and values, we cannot simply say of pluralism "Well, there it is!" Least of all can those who espouse Christian theology settle for the central doctrine of social pragmatism (and doctrine it is) that there is no possibility of reforming or correcting a community "from outside".

Already there is too strong a suggestion in Porter's article that socio-political factors govern what approach to "meaning" is welcome within what he calls "the biblical guild". Porter is troubled by the influence of those "who occupy important seats of power . . . and control . . . influential study groups".[152] No doubt such potential scepticism about the use of socio-pragmatic criteria of truth is not unrelated to the belief that "Fish's concept of interpretive communities appears to be one of the strategic concepts which will have to be utilized if reader-response criticism is going to emerge fully in New Testament studies."[153]

We have demonstrated, however, in the previous section and elsewhere that we cannot operate with socio-pragmatic models as a major, let alone as a comprehensive, theory of hermeneutics. Its greatest weakness, at least in the version advocated by Fish, lies in its inadequacy as a philosophy of language. But it is time to conclude by noting its disastrous entailments for Christian theology. We identify five in particular.

(i) If textual meaning, is the *product* of a community of readers, as Fish concedes, texts cannot reform these readers "from outside". In this case *The Reformation* then becomes a dispute over alternative community life-styles. It *has nothing to do with retrieving authentic meanings of biblical texts, let alone texts which address communities "from beyond"*. (ii) *Prophetic address* as that which comes "from beyond" virtually against human will is either illusory or to be explained in terms of pre-conscious inner conflict. It is really, after all, an address which coheres with the deepest hopes or expectations of a community, though it might not seem like this. *It is not, in the end, an address*: the community itself has created the word. (iii) Such notions as *grace* or *revelation must* (by pragmatic doctrine) be illusory, because Rorty tells us that there are no "givens". (iv) *The message of the cross* remains a *linguistic construct* of a tradition. Some gnostics already claimed this in the second or third centuries. (v) It would be impossible to determine what would *count as a systematic mistake in the development of doctrine*. Pragmatism allows only the view that what gave rise to *our* past and present must somehow have broadly been right. Social pragmatism accepts only social winners as criteria of truth.

Porter is right to suggest that in biblical studies we need to undertake a first-hand, not a second-hand, assessment of theoretical models formulated in secular literary theory. We have seen in these last two chapters that the gains and contributions can be potentially enormous; some mistakes and losses could be disastrous. There are few reader-response theorists who have nothing to tell us. Iser's work on the active role of readers, Eco's work on codes and texts, Holland's theories about self-identity, and Bleich's reminders about ordinary people in communities of readers, all have something very important to say. Culler's work on reader-competency and Fish's warnings about the context-relative status of so-called "natural" meanings, all assist hermeneutical self-awareness. Fish also reminds us that boundaries between texts and interpretative traditions are by no means sharp and clear-cut.

Nevertheless the notion that biblical texts do not transform readers "from beyond", or that they merely evoke "constructions" drawn from the hitherto undiscovered inner resources of the reading community does not cohere readily with Christian theology. Theology cannot dispense with metacritical reflection. But, more than this, socio-pragmatic hermeneutics transposes the meaning of texts into projections which are *potentially idolatrous* as instruments of self-affirmation. *Such a model transposes a Christian theology of grace and revelation into a phenomenology of religious self-discovery.* Paul Ricoeur calls us "to destroy the idols, and to listen to symbols."[154] This, he argues, is the goal of hermeneutics.

CHAPTER XIV

1. Stanley Fish, "Going Down the Anti-Formalist Road", in *Doing What Comes Naturally*, 1–33.
2. Stanley Fish, "Why No One's Afraid of Wolfgang Iser" *ibid* 68–86.
3. Wolfgang Iser, *The Act of Reading: A Theory of Aesthetic Response*, Baltimore and London: Johns Hopkins University Press, 1978 and 1980, ix.
4. *Ibid.*
5. *Ibid* x.
6. Wolfgang Iser, "Indeterminacy and the Reader's Response in Prose Fiction" in J. Hillis Miller (ed.) *Aspects of Narrative: Selected Papers from the English Institute*, New York: Columbia University Press, 1971, 1–45.
7. W. Iser, *The Act of Reading* 21.
8. *Ibid* 29.
9. *Ibid* 38.
10. *Ibid* 231; cf. 180–230.
11. *Ibid* 183–85.
12. Susan Wittig, "A Theory of Multiple Meanings", *Semeia* 9, 1977, 75–105.

13. *Ibid* 84.
14. *Ibid* 95.
15. *Ibid* 95–96.
16. Robert W. Funk, *Language, Hermeneutic and Word of God. The Problem of Language in the New Testament and Contemporary Theology*, New York: Harper and Row, 1966, 17.
17. James L. Resseguie, "Reader Response Criticism and the Synoptic Gospels", *Journal of the American Academy of Religion* 52, 1984, 307–24.
18. *Ibid* 308.
19. Stanley Fish, *Doing What Comes Naturally*, 69–70; cf. 68–86.
20. Robert Fowler, *Loaves and Fishes: the Function of the Feeding Stories in the Gospel of Mark*, Chico: Scholars Press, 1981, 134–35.
21. *Ibid* 134.
22. *Ibid* 83.
23. *Ibid* 93–96.
24. *Ibid* 171.
25. Jouette M. Bassler, "The Parable of the Loaves", *Journal of Religion* 66, 1986, 167; cf. 157–72.
26. Wolfgang Iser, *The Implied Reader: Patterns of Communication in Prose Fiction from Bunyan to Beckett*, Baltimore: Johns Hopkins University Press, 1974, 274–75.
27. R. Alan Culpepper, *Anatomy of the Fourth Gospel: A Study in Literary Design*, Philadelphia: Fortress Press, 1983, 6–9, 20–27, 54–70 *et passim*.
28. *Ibid* 4.
29. *Ibid* 48.
30. *Ibid* 161–62.
31. *Ibid* 209 and 233.
32. Stephen D. Moore, *op. cit.* 103.
33. Stanley E. Porter, "Why Hasn't Reader-Response Criticism Caught On in New Testament Studies?" in *Literature and Theology* 4, 1990, 280, 281 and 282; cf. 278–92.
34. *Ibid* 282.
35. Susan R. Horton, "The Experience of Stanley Fish's Prose on The Critic as Self-Creating, Self-Consuming, Artifices", *Genre* 10, 1977, 449 and 452; cf. 443–53.
36. See Fish's introductory autobiographical essay in *Is There a Text in This Class?* 1–17.
37. Stanley Fish, *Doing What Comes Naturally* 69–70 and 83.
38. *Ibid* 83.
39. Umberto Eco, *A Theory of Semiotics*, Bloomington: Indiana University Press, 1976; *The Role of the Reader: Explorations in the Semiotics of Texts*, London: Hutchinson, 1981; and *Semiotics and the Philosophy of Language*, London: MacMillan, 1984.
40. Umberto Eco, *A Theory of Semiotics*, 4.
41. *Ibid* 9.
42. L. Wittgenstein, *Philosophical Investigations* sect. 49; cf. sects. 22 and 33.
43. Umberto Eco, *A Theory of Semiotics* 135.
44. *Ibid* 56.
45. *Ibid* 136–39.
46. Umberto Eco, *Semiotics and the Philosophy of Language*, 68–86.

47. Umberto Eco, *The Role of the Reader*, 4.
48. *Ibid* 8.
49. *Ibid* 9–11.
50. *Ibid* 14–17.
51. *Ibid* 27.
52. *Ibid* 33.
53. William Ray, *Literary Meaning: From Phenomenology to Deconstruction*, Oxford: Blackwell, 1984, 134.
54. *Ibid* 137.
55. *Ibid* 134.
56. Tremper Longman III, *Literary Approaches to Biblical Interpretation*, Grand Rapids: Academie and Leicester: Apollos, 1987, 38.
57. Norman R. Petersen, "The Reader in the Gospel" in *Neotestamentica* 18, 1984, 41; cf. 38–51.
58. *Ibid* 45.
59. *Ibid* 40.
60. Elizabeth Freund, *The Return of the Reader: Reader-Response Criticism*, London and New York: Metheun, 1987; cf. Jane P. Tompkins (ed.) *Reader-Response Criticism. From Formalism to Post-Structuralism*, Baltimore and London: Johns Hopkins University Press, 1980; and Susan R. Suleiman and Inge Crosman (eds.) *The Reader in the Text: Essays in Audience and Interpretation*, Princeton: Princeton University Press, 1980.
61. Jane P. Tompkins (ed.) *op. cit.* esp. xiv-xxiv.
62. Elizabeth Freund, *op. cit.* 7.
63. Norman Holland, *Poems in Persons: An Introduction to the Psychoanalysis of Literature*, New York: Norton, 1973; 5 Readers Reading, New Haven: Yale University Press, 1975; and "Recovering 'the Purloined Letter': Reading as Personal Transaction" in Susan Suleiman and Inge Crosman (eds.) *op. cit.* 350–70; cf. further Norman Holland, *The Dynamics of Literary Response*, New York: Oxford, 1968; "Literary Interpretation and Three Phases of Psychoanalysis" in *Critical Inquiry* 3, 1976, 221–33; and "Transactive Criticism: Re-Creation through Identity", in *Criticism* 18, 1976, 334–52.
64. Norman Holland, "Transactive Criticism: Re-Creation through Identity" *loc. cit.* 342.
65. David Bleich, *Subjective Criticism*, Baltimore: Johns Hopkins University Press, 1978, 66; cf. *Readings and Feelings. An Introduction to Subjective Criticism*, Urbana: National Council for the Teaching of English, 1975.
66. David Bleich, *The Double Perspective. Language, Literacy, and Social Relations*, New York: Oxford University Press, 1988.
67. *Ibid* 17; cf. also 319.
68. *Ibid*.
69. *Ibid* 55 (my italics).
70. Mark Labberton, *Ordinary Bible Reading: The Reformed Tradition and Reader-Orientated Criticism*, Ph.D. Dissertation, University of Cambridge, 1990, esp. 1–33, 86–8, 130–61 and 187–213.
71. *Ibid* 10–13.
72. John Calvin, *Institutes*, I, 13.1.
73. M. Labberton, *op. cit.* 18–24; cf. Calvin on Deut. 30:11.

74. Cf. Calvin on Acts 15:30, and M. Labberton, *op. cit.* 24–33.
75. David Bleich, *The Double Perspective* 25.
76. *Ibid* 16.
77. *Ibid* 24; cf. 16–25.
78. Jane Tompkins, *op. cit.* xvii.
79. Jonathan Culler, *Framing the Sign*, ix.
80. *Ibid* 95.
81. *Ibid* 55.
82. Jonathan Culler, *Structuralist Poetics: Structuralism, Linguistics, and the Study of Literature*, Ithaca: Cornell University Press, 1975.
83. Jonathan Culler, *The Pursuit of Signs*, 5.
84. Jonathan Culler, *On Deconstruction: Theory and Criticism After Structuralism*, Ithaca: Cornell University Press, 1982, 22.
85. Jonathan Culler, *The Pursuit of Signs*, 188.
86. Jonathan Culler, *Structuralist Poetics*, 247.
87. William Ray, *op. cit.* 114; but Ray also claims the centrality of "literary competence" in Culler; cf. 113.
88. Jonathan Culler, *Structuralist Poetics*, 137.
89. Stanley Fish, *Doing What Comes Naturally*, 2 and 14.
90. Stanley Fish, *Self-Consuming Artifacts. The Experience of Seventeenth-Century Literature*, Berkeley: University of California Press, 1972.
91. Stanley Fish, *Is There a Text in this Class?* 1–17.
92. *Ibid* 12.
93. *Ibid* 13.
94. *Ibid* 3.
95. *Ibid* 371.
96. Stanley Fish, *Doing What Comes Naturally*, 88; cf. 68–86; 87–119; 120–40.
97. *Ibid* 143 and 157–59; cf. 141–60, and 485–94.
98. *Ibid* 489; cf. 471–502.
99. *Ibid* 61–67; cf. 37–60.
100. *Ibid* 503–524.
101. *Ibid* 523–24.
102. L. Wittgenstein, *Philosophical Investigations*, sect. 81.
103. *Ibid* sect. 97.
104. L. Wittgenstein, *Tractatus Logico-Philosophicus*, Germ. & Eng., London: Routledge & Kegan Paul, 1961. See further his *Notebooks* 1914–16, Eng. Oxford: Blackwell, 1961.
105. L. Wittgenstein, *Philosophical Investigations*, sects. 108, 115 and 132.
106. *Ibid* sect. 96.
107. L. Wittgenstein, *On Certainty*, Germ. and Eng., Oxford: Blackwell, 1969, sect. 65.
108. Rush Rhees, *Discussions of Wittgenstein*, London: Routledge & Kegan Paul, 1970, 75; cf. 71–84 (first italics, Rhees's; second, mine).
109. L. Wittgenstein, *Zettel*, sect. 567.
110. L. Wittgenstein, *Remarks on the Foundations of Mathematics*, Germ. and Eng., Oxford: Blackwell, 1956, I, 8, sect. 16.
111. Anthony Kenny, *Wittgenstein*, London: Penguin Books, edn. 1975; David Pears, *Wittgenstein*, London: Collins, 1971; George Pitcher, *The Philosophy of*

Wittgenstein, Englewood Cliffs: Prentice Hall, 1964; Allan Janik and Stephen Toulmin, *Wittgenstein's Vienna*, London: Wiedenfeld & Nicolson, 1973; Gordon P. Baker and P.M. Hacker, *Analytical Commentary on Wittgenstein's Philosophical Investigations* (3 vols) I; Understanding and Meaning; II, Rules, Grammar and Necessity; III, Meaning and Mind, Oxford: Blackwell, 1983, 1988 and 1990.
112. Anthony C. Thiselton, *The Two Horizons*, chapters XIII and XIV; cf. also chapter II, and the relevant studies of Karl-Otto Apel (cited in chapter XI, above).
113. S. Fish, *Doing What Comes Naturally*, 1–6.
114. L. Wittgenstein, *Philosophical Investigations* sect. 66; cf. sects. 126–30.
115. L. Wittgenstein, *Zettel* sect. 455; cf. sect. 452.
116. S. Fish, *loc. cit.* 3.
117. L. Wittgenstein, *Philosophical Investigations* sect. 206; cf. sect. 281.
118. *Ibid* sect. 71.
119. S. Fish, *Doing What Comes Naturally* 471–502, esp. 487; cf. also Thomas S. Kuhn, *The Essential Tension. Selected Studies in Scientific Tradition and Change*, Chicago: University of Chicago Press, 1977, esp. 293–319.
120. S. Fish, *Doing What Comes Naturally*, 455; cf. 436–70.
121. L. Wittgenstein, *Philosophical Investigations*, sect. 54 (my italics).
122. *Ibid* sect. 281 (my italics); cf. sect. 360.
123. *Ibid* sect. 420.
124. *Ibid* sect. 206.
125. S. Fish, *loc. cit.* 31.
126. *Ibid* 31–32.
127. *Ibid* sects. 2 and 3.
128. Ludwig Wittgenstein, *Culture and Value*, 78.
129. L. Wittgenstein, *Philosophical Investigations* sects. 281–351; cf. *Zettel* sects. 532–42.
130. L. Wittgenstein, *Zettel* sects. 518 and 519.
131. L. Wittgenstein, *Philosophical Investigations*, sect. 250 and ii, 229.
132. *Ibid* sect. 249; cf. *Zettel* sects. 89 and 90.
133. L. Wittgenstein, *Philosophical Investigations*, sect. 202; cf. Anthony C. Thiselton, *The Two Horizons*, 385.
134. S. Fish, *Doing What Comes Naturally*, 27.
135. *Ibid* 28.
136. Christopher Norris, *The Contest of Faculties: Philosophy and Theory after Deconstruction*, London and New York: Methuen, 1985, 139–66 *et passim*; Richard Bernstein, *Habermas and Modernity* 3–10, 19–23.
137. Christopher Norris, *loc. cit.* 159 (my italics).
138. Mark G. Brett, "Four or Five Things to Do with Texts. A Taxonomy of Interpretative Interests" in D.J.A. Clines, S.E. Fowl and S.E. Porter (eds.) *The BIble in Three Dimensions*, 357–77; cf. also Mark G. Brett, *Biblical Criticism in Crisis? The Impact of the Canonical Approach in Old Testament Studies*, Cambridge: Cambridge University Press, 1991.
139. Mark Brett, "Four or Five Things to Do with Texts", *loc. cit.* 362–65.
140. Stephen E. Fowl, "The Ethics of Interpretation or What's Left Over after the Elimination of Meaning", *loc. cit.* 379–98.
141. Jeffrey Stoutt, "What is the Meaning of a Text?" in *New Literary History* 14, 1982, 1–12.

142. *Ibid* 4.
143. *Ibid* 2.
144. Stephen E. Fowl, *loc. cit.* 380.
145. *Ibid*.
146. Stanley E. Porter, "Why Hasn't Reader-Response Criticism Caught On in New Testament Studies?" in *Literature and Theology* 4, 1990, 278–92.
147. *Ibid* 280 and 281.
148. *Ibid* 281 and 282.
149. *Ibid* 283–85.
150. *Ibid* 290.
151. *Ibid*.
152. *Ibid* 289.
153. *Ibid* 287.
154. Paul Ricoeur, Freud and Philosophy, 54.

CHAPTER XV

The Hermeneutics of Pastoral Theology: (I) Ten Ways of Reading Texts in Relation to Varied Reading-Situations

Biblical interpretation and pastoral theology both address issues of *contingency and particularity* as well as questions about theological coherence. Both are concerned with *life-worlds, situations and horizons*. Paul Ballard observes: "Pastoral theology is reflection on the pastoral situation. The pastoral situation is by definition *particular in time and space*."[1] Don Browning notes that pastoral theology is informed by an ethical vision, but "mediated to individuals and groups in all their situational, existential, and developmental *particularity*."[2] Similar language could be found in David Tracy, Edward Farley, and Thomas Groome.[3] Browning also observes that these contingent particularities become more diverse in the light of today's pluralism. Pastoral theology, he urges, addresses "the *diversity* found in the public world outside the church" as well as "*diverse* publics within specific churches".[4]

A *prima facie* case exists, then, for claiming that the task of hermeneutical understanding, in contrast to that of scientific, generalizable, quantifiable, theoretical explanation, embraces pastoral theology as well as biblical studies. If the particularities of the "first" horizon of the biblical text provide a primary focus for biblical specialists, the particularities of the "second" horizon of present situations and readers offer a primary focus for pastoral specialists. But this raises a difficulty. As Edward Farley and others point out, such an assignment of professional sub-disciplines within theology splits apart and fragments a single hermeneutical task. The practical character of theology as "*habitus*", or as wisdom-based action, he argues, "appear(s) to be defeated from the start by the dispersion of theology into independent areas of scholarship".[5]

The criticism which is addressed to many biblical specialists on the basis of this artificial division of labour is predictable. Biblical scholars who concentrate on the historical aspects of their task are accused of becoming locked up into the past. In the first quarter of this century, Karl Barth and Rudolf Bultmann raised powerful voices of protest against the limitations of a merely historical "liberal" exegesis which left the task of biblical interpretation only half done. Recently Robert Morgan, as we have noted, renews the protest against a slippage which moves from using *historical method as part of a larger hermeneutical task* to substituting a *historical aim as the goal of hermeneutics*. This reduces biblical texts to the status of instrumental "sources" for historical reconstruction.[6] This protest about using texts simply as "sources" reflects Bultmann's point in his *Theology of the New Testament*, except that Bultmann's interests are more narrowly kerygmatic, while Morgan addresses a wider pluralism.

By the same token, however, a less familiar but *by no means less important mirror-image argument can be put forward about pastoral theology*. Might it be that many pastoral theologians, by concentrating on the segment of the process that concerns the *present*, have fallen into *the very same trap of objectifying pastoral phenomena in ways which give privilege to the present as over against the biblical text?* Just as some biblical specialists ignore the meaning-*effects* of texts for present situations, might it not also be the case that some pastoral theologians tend to ignore historical factors that relativize present criteria of relevance, as if these were not in process of *shifting and undergoing transformation through encounter with biblical texts and with Christian traditions?*

I am extremely cautious about George Lindbeck's tendency to locate the meaning of biblical texts in intralinguistic or "intratextual" categories to the exclusion of presuppositional and extra-linguistic contextual factors about states of affairs in the world. But on the issue of what he calls "the direction of interpretation" Lindbeck's work serves to question this tendency to give privilege to the present in a necessary way. He writes: "It is the religion instantiated in Scripture which defines being, truth, goodness, and beauty, and the non-scriptural exemplifications of these realities need to be transformed into figures (or types or antitypes) of the scriptural framework . . . It is the text, so to speak, which absorbs the world, rather than the world the text."[7] Lindbeck cites the example of the relation between the cross and human suffering. It is inadequate, he argues, to objectify present suffering and then to see the cross as a figurative representation of it; rather, the cross addresses present suffering *in ways which transform it into cruciform suffering*.

Even Lindbeck, however, tends to do less than justice to the particularities of different biblical horizons and types of texts, speaking too often only about biblical texts-in-general. But the flow of interpretation between the horizons of biblical texts and the horizons of pastoral situations assumes different forms and different functions as the two sets of *particularities* change. One reason why so many books on hermeneutics remain unsatisfying is that generalization too often either restricts work to theory alone or becomes trivial because it articulates only what can be universally observed about general patterns. But didactic texts, narrative texts, poetic texts, boundary-situation texts, apocalyptic texts, promissory texts, and so forth, perform *different, though often overlapping, hermeneutical functions, especially in relation to different reading-situations.*

In the review of models and resources set out below, an attempt is made for the equal benefit of biblical interpretation and of pastoral theology to outline the diversity of some of the models which we have already discussed, and *to propose paradigmatic or optimal reader-situations in relation to which their most distinctive hermeneutical functions most readily become apparent.* Our discussions of socio-pragmatic and metacritical hermeneutics signal our awareness of the complexity of speaking of "optimal" reader-situations: the discussion must first be allowed to stand on its own feet and to speak for itself before we refer back to this.

In the case of the first three models some further theoretical issues also need brief consideration. For certain residual theoretical issues which we have not yet fully explored come to a head in the present context of discussion. Misunderstandings still initiate appeals to the theoretical model of *reconstruction*, and especially to the role played by *"author's intention"* in related approaches. It is a mistake, however, either to construe "intention" as a matter of "having certain mental processes" which can usually be observed only by introspection, or of assigning the *same role* to intention in different kinds of texts. We begin, then, by drawing some *points of contrast* between *particular examples* of biblical texts and of reading situations which invite the use of a *reconstructionist* model as a resource, and a different type of biblical text and reading-situation which invites, by contrast, the use of an *existentialist* model. Most textual examples are fresh ones, but in the case of the first model we refer back to the example of I Cor. 8:1–11:1 and 11:17–22, to which we alluded earlier in chapter VII.

1. Life-Worlds, Intentional Directedness, and Enquiring Reading in Reconstructionist Models

We saw in chapters VI and VII that *the hermeneutics of understanding*, developed by Schleiermacher, Dilthey, and Betti, entailed *much more than historical reconstruction*. In pastoral terms, the emphasis placed by Schleiermacher on what he called the "feminine" quality of creative immediacy of understanding, by Dilthey on imaginative empathy and rapport, and by Betti on openness, listening, patience, and respect for "the other", describe qualities which relate as closely to pastoral sensitivity towards persons as to the understanding of biblical texts. For these theorists it would be wide of the mark to associate "listening skills" exclusively with pastoral theology and comparative, critical "objective" distance with historical biblical studies. Inter-personal understanding embraces understanding the processes that lie behind production of communicative language as a means of understanding persons. But understanding remains a single, complex, interactive, process, in which the interpreter's own developing understanding undergoes constant revision, modification, and correction.

The work of Schleiermacher and of Dilthey often suffers unfair criticism on the ground that it is impossible "to step into someone else's shoes" or "to think his or her thoughts"; still less, to reconstruct that person's *intentions*. But I argued in chapter VI that Schleiermacher's close attention to language as both system (cf. Saussure's *langue*) and as temporal speech-act or event (cf. Saussure's *parole*), together with complex and careful qualifications which are very often overlooked, does not compel us to tie Schleiermacher's hermeneutics with psychologizing notions of intentionality, as if to imply that these represent mental processes to be observed by introspection. It is possible to accept Bauman's antithetical polarity between "thinking the thoughts of others" and "sharing in a form of life" *only* if we interpret the former in a psychologistic rather than linguistic-interactive way.[8] Schleiermacher and Dilthey saw *flow-of-life* (cf. Wittgenstein's term "stream of life") as a hermeneutical key, and to "re-live" the life-experiences which led to the production of the text was for them to reconstruct its life-world and to seek to enter it by sharing in its form (cf. Wittgenstein's "form-of-life").

This angle of approach helps us to see *why in the case of many biblical texts* (not all) *it is necessary to include the work of historical reconstruction*. This has nothing *directly* to do with allegedly falling prey to the genetic fallacy: Schleiermacher does not imagine that enquiries about antiquarian *origins as such* provide answers to all hermeneutical questions. His *reason* for historical enquiry arises from the task of determining the *life-world in relation to which the text draws its currency*. It is closely parallel to Searle's technical notion of "Background", which, in Searle's terminology is "pre-intentional . . . a set of pre-conditions of Intentionality . . . the biological and cultural resources that I must bring to bear on this task."[9] Searle insists that situational Background has nothing directly to do with mental states; it concerns *pre-conditions* (cf. Schleiermacher's pre-understanding) for meaning. It is against the *Background*, Searle observes, that "I can intend to peel an orange, but I cannot in that way intend to peel a rock or a car."[10] As Wittgenstein observes in his *Zettel*, often the grammar of meaning "is embedded in a situation from which it takes its rise".[11] It operates "under particular circumstances . . . Only in the stream of thought and life do words have meaning."[12]

Explicitly for Wittgenstein and for Searle, and implicitly for Schleiermacher, "to intend" a linguistic meaning is emphatically *not to perform some action or process separable from the linguistic act or process itself.* It is not, in this sense, an "*act*" at all. Wittgenstein points out that the imperative: "Intend to . . ." would be as far-fetched as the imperative, "Laugh heartily at this joke".[13] *Intention is better understood adverbially: to write with an intention is to write in a way that is directed towards a goal.* Searle identifies a linguistic category within which the criterion of intention, far from involving psychological hypotheses, coincides precisely with the criterion used for effective performative force. In expressive illocutions, such as, "I apologize . . .", "I congratulate . . .", and "I thank . . ." the *directedness* of the utterance is *internal to its meaning and force.*[14] No one could imagine that some second shadow-process called intention was involved; but nor could it be denied that as illocutions these embody intentions of writers or of speakers. But why should this understanding of intention be restricted to this paradigm only?

We may summarize a defence of the model used in the hermeneutics of understanding, then, and its traditional role in biblical studies, by calling attention to four theoretical features. First, *in many cases* (not necessarily all) a *reconstruction of the stream of life, life-world, or extra-linguistic context which surrounds a text* is indispensable to understanding its meaning. *This is not a "genetic" fallacy.* Second, it is *inaccurate and misleading to associate historical reconstruction with a restriction of method to scientific positivism or rationalism.* Schleiermacher, Dilthey, and Betti have roots in Romanticism which disclaim the adequacy of purely rationalist enquiry. Dilthey's paradigm of *life* had little to do with Descartes's scientific model of mathematics; indeed he argued that in Locke's subject "no real blood flowed". Third, *many* (not all) *biblical texts address a directed goal* which may rightly be identified as its author's intention, provided that intention is understood only "adverbially". This is *not an example of the "intentional fallacy".* A mistakenly psychologistic dimension is avoided if we follow Leith and Myerson in seeing as a feature of the category of texts under discussion "some feeling of address towards another . . ."[15] Fourth, it is a common mistake to claim that Schleiermacher gives priority to *authors over texts.* We quoted Schleiermacher's words from his *Compendium* of 1819, confirmed by his marginal notes of 1828, that "to understand what is said in the context of the language with its possibilities" [cf. the semiotic system] and the communicative act "in the thinking of the speaker" [cf. *parole* as communication of the author's thought] constitute *"two hermeneutical tasks* [which] *are completely equal".*[16] Well ahead of his time, Schleiermacher perceived that which of these two axes received primary emphasis remained a *matter of interpretative strategy.*

As a footnote for pastoral theology we may also note that Dilthey's struggle over the hermeneutical relation between the general and the particular lay behind his articulation of "re-discovering the 'you' in the 'me'," and of "putting myself in your place".[17] On the one hand it remains a principle of pastoral theology and indeed of Christian love that one should try to put oneself into someone else's place, whether one seeks simply to understand, or to "do to others what you would have them do to you"

(Matt. 7:12). On the other hand, to measure others by our own feelings, experiences, norms, and life-world may fail to take adequate account of *differences as well as similarities* between ourselves and others. For Emilio Betti these differences are what lead to a call for openness, patience, tolerance, and respect for the other. In psychoanalytical hermeneutics further complicating factors which arise from self-deception and from pre-conscious conflicts within the self also demand a more complex model than Dilthey could formulate in his era. But this does not entirely invalidate the model in principle.

In spite of Schleiermacher's emphasis on the two-sided nature of interpersonal understanding, this theory is clearly orientated more specifically towards authors and texts than towards readers, even though, we saw in chapter VI, Schleiermacher is aware of the dimensions of textual effects. This model stands in contrast, in this respect, to existential or reader-response models. By definition, it demands of readers initial sympathy with the directedness of the text, and willingness to engage in the use of imagination and critical reflection.

This model operates characteristically in cases in which biblical texts serve primarily as *transmissive and communicative vehicles to express the thought of an author towards a given directedness* (though Schleiermacher's Romanticist emphasis on imagination has relevance to "open" or to "productive" literary biblical texts). Paul's pastoral and didactic advice on issues about the administration of the Lord's Supper (1 Cor. 11:17–22) and on food offered to idols (1 Cor. 8:1–11:1), which we reviewed in chapter VII provide classic examples of communicative texts. If the most difficult or most characteristic problems about meaning and understanding in some "productive" texts such as the Book of Revelation arise for modern readers from complexities of semiotic code and from intertextual framing, in 1 Corinthians the key lies in historical reconstruction of the life-world within which the language acquires its proper currency. Jerome Murphy O'Connor's outstanding use of archaeological research together with the valuable socio-historical reconstruction undertaken by Gerd Theissen offer important resources, together with other contributions such as those of J.C. Hurd, R.A. Horsley, and Peter Marshall.[18]

Theissen and Murphy O'Connor, we may recall from chapter VII, reconstruct the social life-world in which certain groups came to be thought of as "the weak" and "the strong" (1 Cor. 8:9), and in which "divisions" occurred not only in more everyday settings but even at the Lord's Supper (1 Cor. 1:12; 11:17,18). Those who were poor had few opportunities to eat meat, unless they were invited to someone's house as a guest, or unless they attended a festal meal in honour of a hellenistic-oriental deity in the temple precincts. Slaves would also end their work later than others. The size of available meeting-space suggested by archaeological reconstruction underlines the possibility that meeting in separate houses would provide conditions for the development of differences of ethos in the groups to which 1:12 alludes. In the house-gathering, those who were free to arrive earlier for the Lord's Supper would make their way to the *triclinium*, where they would recline in comfort with the host for a leisured meal. Those whose work, including duties as slaves, kept them late, could only later crowd into the *atrium*, where they would feel like second-class guests, or like an overflow meeting in the annex. All this forms part of the life-world which constitutes a "Background" (in Searle's sense) for understanding the text as a communicative work.

Inter-textual allusions may fill out our understanding of this life-world, within this particular theoretical model not as productive codes or matrices of meaning, but as sources of understanding of the life-world. C.A. Pierce alludes to the "weak" in the gospels. If they were conditioned to think of pseudo-deities as realities, to eat meat against their conscience could inflict *pain* or *damage* on the "weak" even if only because their conscience was oversensitive (1 Cor. 8:11–13).[19] To cause the weak to stumble would be like harming "the little ones" of the gospels (Matt. 18:6). By contrast, the more intellectual "strong", who "had knowledge" could appeal with justice to credal theology: "There is no God but one . . . one God, the Father, from whom all things come . . ., one Lord, Jesus Christ, through whom all things come" (1 Cor. 8:6). Hence "we know that an idol is nothing" (8:4). But although he shares their "correct" theology, Paul insists that *love* provides a working criterion more fundamental here than "knowledge": "Love builds; knowledge (*gnosis*) inflates" (8:1).

In *this* example textual meaning can be optimally determined only with reference to the *directedness* of its author's thought through a *communicative text*. This operates *in relation to the Background of a given life-world* in interaction with readers who are prepared to think *within its frame of reference*. It would do violence to this directedness to claim that such an account of "meaning" is in no way "given" by the text, but only "constructed" in the light of the interests of the community of interpretation, perhaps in this case the biblical guild or the church. The claim, expressed by Robert Morgan, that "texts, like dead men and women, have no rights" may seem plausible only if we believe that a text's directedness is a reading-construct, and follow Barthes, and others, about the "death of the author" in literary texts.[20]

If an artifact is directed towards meeting a design-specification, it is true only in a trivially descriptive, uninformative, sense that we *can* use the artifact for any different purpose of our own. Someone *could* use a chisel as a screwdriver, but a craftsman *would* not; someone *could* use the Mona Lisa as a surface for graffiti, but most people would respect its given uniqueness, and to do this would for most people constitute some kind of violation. *Some* texts are not design-specific or direction-specific, but others are.

2. Disruptions of Passive Reading in Existentialist Models

Much of the argument concerning existential hermeneutics in chapter VIII reflected our concern to demonstrate its *limitations*. We alluded to the values and limits of the model with particular reference to early New Testament confessions of Christ as Lord (1 Cor. 12:3). The cash-currency of such confessions can be seen in existential attitudes of surrender, obedience, reverence, and devotion. To confess Christ as Lord, as Bultmann rightly observes, is to let the care of oneself go, to place oneself entirely in the sovereign hands of the one who is "Lord": "If we live, we live to the Lord; and if we die, we die to the Lord . . ." (Rom. 14:7). Yet, as speech-act models show so clearly, the self-involving dimensions of direction and commitment depend on a certain state of affairs, namely that God has appointed or declared Christ Lord in the resurrection (Rom. 1:3,4). In this respect Christ is Lord, irrespective of our human response.

Nevertheless existentialist hermeneutics reflect far more than a dimension of practical human will and language-effect. If we go back to Kierkegaard, existential critique entails above all *a discontinuity and description of communal habituations of meanings* which depend on convention. *These models speak especially to those situations which Karl Jaspers identified as boundary situations.* In this respect, they do not share the social and communal perspectives of socio-pragmatic or even speech-act models. Understanding in the genuinely existentialist model is precisely *not* determined in terms of *the expectations of a reading community*. Equivocation and ambiguity characterizes a text, of a kind which can be resolved only by an *individual decision*. Biblical texts become *individuating* vehicles. This principle operates in the case of Bultmann's sermon on the text "Adam, where art thou?" (Gen.3:9). Adam can no longer hide among the "trees" of anonymity and the crowd. In his sermon Acts 17:31, Bultmann translates universal judgment into individual existential responsibility: "Man stands before God alone . . . in stark loneliness".[21]

In terms of *pastoral theology*, this existentialist model speaks not only to readers who, in situation or in personality-type, relate *more readily to doing than to reflection*, but also to those who perceive themselves *as loners or as outsiders*. On one side it is partly those for whom the *shared habits, practices, and expectations of the reading-community somehow ring hollow*, for whom existential models may optimally offer a potential resource. Conversely, on the other side, if *these* readers find *affirmation* in such existentialist readings those who unthinkingly equate faith with mere *passive acceptance of the religious conventions of a particular sub-culture or group* may be roused to perceive the dimension of *individual obedient venture* in a transforming reading which gives birth to more authentic faith.

A well-known example of this model of reading biblical texts arises from Kierkegaard's struggle to come to terms with the meaning of Abraham's command to slay the son of promise (Gen. 22:1–19). Virtually the whole of his *Fear and Trembling* (1843) wrestles with this passage and *compares how it will be "understood" by different readerships.* The wider background to his approach lies in his belief that Hegel's notion of "the System" offers only an arm-chair spectator approach to participatory faith and to decision. Such an approach cheapens faith, and encourages second-hand, and therefore illusory, understanding. From the viewpoint of *generality*, it remains perfectly possible to pour out speech *about* Abraham and *about* Abraham's faith; but to admire it and to praise it is not to *understand* it. In *Point of View for my Work as an Author* Kierkegaard saw his own task as that of showing what it is to *live* the gospel, rather than to *think about* it.

Kierkegaard's narrower and more specific "pre-understanding" was shaped also by a sharpened awareness of different "levels" of interpretation, none of which can grasp the full meaning of a paradoxical phenomenon independently of other levels. His broken engagement with Regine Olsen, which Kierkegaard terminated two years before *Fear and Trembling* brought this home to him. A merely *conventional* understanding of this broken engagement suggested that it constituted an unjustified violation of social norms, just as a *conventional* understanding of Abraham's potential act of slaying Isaac suggested the worst kind of murder. But even a trans-conventional "reading" which "suspended the ethical" in the light of the individual could still miss the heart of the paradox and thereby *hide* the truth. If Kierkegaard or if Abraham become "heroically resigned" to their sacrifice, the sharp edge of choice-in-the-face-paradox has been blunted. Such a reading-strategy may *conceal unworthy* motivations. Only where these various levels intersected in order to be transcended could the command to slay the son of promise be understood as inviting *an act of faith*.

Kierkegaard's model is different from Schleiermacher's. On the approach of different interpreters Kierkegaard writes with tongue-in-cheek that "if the interpreter had known Hebrew, then perhaps it might have been easy for him to understand the story of Abraham."[22] Even Isaac could not "understand" the demeanour and conduct of Abraham; while Abraham himself "left his worldly understanding behind and took with him only faith".[23] Abraham's agony lay in "disappointed expectation". Time had stretched out inordinately as he had waited for the fulfilment of the divine promise for Isaac's birth; and then abruptly he was called upon to negate the very hopes that had reversed years of hope that had been disappointed. "Now all the horrors of the struggle were to be concentrated in one moment . . . 'Take now thy son, thine only son Isaac whom thou lovest . . . Offer him there for a burnt offering' (Gen. 22:2) . . . what *meaning* could there be in it if Isaac was to be sacrificed?"[24] Yet Abraham "believed the ridiculous . . .

He knew that no sacrifice was too hard when God demanded it – and he drew the knife."[25]

Understanding runs its head against the limits of the conventional community world. In terms of *pragmatic contingency*, the act of obedience destroys the possibility of blessing mediated through Abraham's line; in terms of *"universals"* it violates universal ethical principles through an act of murder. But Kierkegaard will not collapse the paradox into a "justification" or "understanding" of one side at the expense of the other: if he becomes "resigned" to the death of Isaac, Abraham has thereby surrendered his faith in God's promise of blessing. So the paradox cannot be resolved in this way.

Thereby Abraham's dilemma exposes the illusion of Hegel's "system": some things refuse to be systematized. Moreover, as in the case of his own decision about Regine Olsen, some decisions can only be enacted, apart from the expectations and conventions of the crowd. In his *Purity of Heart* Kierkegaard writes: "The most ruinous evasion of all is to be hidden in the crowd in an attempt to get away from hearing God's voice as an individual."[26] A paradox that transcends logic and community norms seems to reach into the absurd. But Abraham "acts on the strength of the absurd . . . As a single individual he is higher than the universal. The paradox cannot be mediated. On the strength of the absurd he got Isaac back."[27]

In broad terms this does not presuppose an exegesis radically different from the kind of historical exegesis which we find among Old Testament specialists. Gerhard von Rad and Bruce Vawter also stress the unwavering character of Abraham's faith in the divine promise (cf. also Rom. 4:19–22; Hebs. 11:17–19); the inexorable demand for obedience; and the turmoil generated by the need for such a decision. Vawter adds that a textual pre-history may include a prohibition against human sacrifice, and that this may remain in the suggestion that "there were sacrifices that he (God) did not want at all."[28] Kierkegaard's own existential and anti-Hegelian pre-understanding, however, sharpens what it is at stake in the lonely subjectivity of creative decision, where packaged assumptions and passively-accepted conventions of understanding run out in the face of some unpredicted event or demand.

In this respect existentialist hermeneutics shares with speech-act theory an emphasis or strong emphasis on the self-involvement of readers. Genuine and creative understanding, as opposed to that of passive acquiescence to convention, Kierkegaard maintained, *never leaves the reader unchanged, uninvolved, or untransformed.* Existential hermeneutics reminds us of this with reference both to textual effects *on* readers, and also with reference to persons *within* texts. Thus Dan Otto Via brings out from Matt.25:14–30 that the one-talent man who refused to take any risk wanted *to remain unchanged in an unchanged situation.* He *would not venture*, but insisted on *perceiving himself as the victim* of his employer's demand for action.[29] He did not want the risk of novel opportunities, and so the inbuilt "internal" judgment was that he would remain permanently without them, permanently inactive.

Geraint Vaughan Jones likewise shows how the Prodigal Son's remorse, nostalgia, and longing for return *changes him into a different person* from the defiant young man who left home demanding his "rights" (Luke 15:11–32). In his experience of alienation the son lost the dignity of personhood by becoming anonymous and unwanted (when his money ran out) in a strange land. But on his return his father restored to him his dignity as a person by placing a ring on his finger and shoes on his feet, and by celebrating his return.[30] D.D. Evans, we have noted, also underlines the role of self-involvement. He examines the creation accounts (Gen 1:1–2:25, cf. Ps.8:4–9). These are not simply flat descriptions of "objective" creative processes (though they are not less) but involve all human readers in recognizing their own creatureliness, responsibility, and roles as created beings, including stewardship of ecological resources. In the broad sense, Gen. 22:1–19, Matt. 25:14–30, Lk. 15:11–30, and Gen 1:1–2:25 all *involve* readers; but in different ways, at different levels, and with different demands.

3. Drawing Readers into Biblical Narrative-Worlds: Four Theories of Narrative in Relation to Reading-Situations

Narratives which project "worlds" to be entered by readers offer hermeneutical advantages not provided by most other categories of texts. Readers have become habituated to enter narrative-worlds almost every day, through television or through fiction. They often suspend their own belief-systems or even their customary moral defences for the sake of being carried along by the flow of the story. Resistances or prejudices become weaker, or even provisionally lifted, although in such contexts as ecclesial or propagandist settings non-verbal cues may reinstate them. Millions choose to become caught up in the temporal life-flow of plots and sub-plots on television or in popular literature even when the same regularities of narrative grammar are employed (discussed above in the context of the work of Propp, Greimas, and others, in chapter XIII). In chapter XIII we also discussed the role played by flash-backs, by pre-views, by speeding up or slowing down narrative-time, by suspense, by surprise, and by point of view. Often, in Propp's language, a hero struggles with a villain: helpers assist the hero while opponents hinder the quest or struggle; closure brings victory, restoration of fortunes, return, or love and marriage.

In terms of pastoral theology, the functions of narrative are manifold. We select four. (1) In the classic parable-form, exemplified in Nathan's parable of the rich man who took his poor neighbour's lamb (II Sam. 12:1–6) *narrative can catch readers off-guard*. Because the narrative entices them into its world and enthrals them, they become unconsciously exposed to viewpoints, judgments, and reversals of assumptions which in other modes of discourse would have called explicitly for conscious willingness to be "open" and to "listen to the text". Narrative can *reverse expectations which initially would be hostile* to its viewpoint. In different reading-situations narrative may achieve a second function.

(2) Because actions and characters are unfolded through narrative-time which can be slowly focussed or made more urgent, the *possibility of grasping personal identities* arises in narrative more readily than in less temporally-orientated modes of understanding. Personhood emerges as life unfolds; it is not to be defined in terms of a set of generalizing properties. For *pastoral theology* this has key consequences for understanding self-identity (as Crites argues) and more especially, as Stroup and Thiemann urge, for reaching some understanding of the identity of God in Christ.

(3) Narrative-worlds also stimulate *imagination and exploration* of *possible* worlds, as Ricoeur has stressed.

(4) Further, they may overlap with *self-involving speech-acts* in which *illocutions become operative*. Here Nicholas Wolterstorff's work becomes very important. This sub-categorization of narrative, invited by the questions raised about the present situations of readers by pastoral theology, stands in need of further brief theoretical exposition, and practical instanciation.

(1) In Gadamer, (partly following the later Heidegger) "worldhood" is grounded ontologically in the *pre-judgments* of language and effective-history. Ernst Fuchs draws on the notion of narrative-world to trace the hermeneutical function of the parable of the labourers in Matt. 20:1–16.[31] The audience is caught up in the good fortune of those who successively find employment in difficult times, and in the suspense of waiting to see what those who had worked longest will receive for their wages. The shared presuppositions on which the momentum of the plot is constructed encourage the audience to expect a *"just"* reward. But this pre-conception is shattered: the crowd is deeply shocked, and *feels* it, by the way in which grace supercedes justice. This narrative-dynamic, Fuchs urges, functions quite differently from any bald theological *statement*; from "the pallid requirement of belief in God's kindness".[32] The story-world engages with different people at a deeper-than-intellectual level. Moreover, Fuchs urges, in his *love* Jesus uses narrative to prepare a *place of meeting* which is not merely a confrontation of "viewpoints" or of "ideas"; grace

is not simply a "doctrine" to be prematurely rejected. Like the world of Gadamer's "conversation", the hearer is led into sharing presuppositions which allow fresh understanding and avoid a premature dismissal of ideas. (I have discussed this in greater detail in *The Two Horizons* and elsewhere under the heading of "the new hermeneutic").

(2) In narrative theology which draws on categories used in literary theory, the notion of *narrative-coherence on the basis of narrative-time* assumes a special importance. Stephen Crites, David Kelsey, and Stanley Hauerwas, stress the *primordial character of narrative as an expression of human experience and, still more fundamentally, of human personhood and of individual and corporate identity*.33 For human experience is *temporal*; it is orientated towards, and organized in terms of, a temporal history. Our earlier study in chapter X of Ricoeur's narrative theory, and in chapter XIII of narrative-time in Seymour Chatman and in Genette, confirms that *narrative provides an organizational coherence and structure which is operational in terms of temporal flow rather than in terms of abstract logic*. Narrative in Crites's view is bound up with our understanding of *identity*. In the story we encounter a "tensed unity" of a temporal experience which is more than bare natural succession. On this basis George Stroup declares: "Christian narrative, therefore, assumes a literary form akin to that of confession or religious autobiography."34 He writes: "Christian narrative emerges from the collision between an individual's identity narrative and the narratives of the Christian community."35 He uses the term "collision" because encounter in faith with texts or with traditions may "transform" a person's identity. As we have seen, in the work of David Kelsey and Frances Young this transformation of personal identity is a function of reading biblical texts.

George Stroup spells out further implications of this approach. Reading narrative-texts "is not simply a matter of meditation and self-discovery"; understanding revelation entails "an activity . . . in relation to an 'other' called 'God'". The narrative-history of the Christian community provides the context in which the individual encounters God . . ."36 William Hordern pointed out in his work on Wittgenstein and religious language that stories identify the personhood of persons in ways impossible for abstract, generalizing, thought or for scientific treatises or philosophical essays. He writes: "A young man does not fall in love with a specimen of the class of females, aged twenty, good-looking, likeable, socially adjusted, and so on. On the contrary, he falls in love with Mary Jones, and his love is directed precisely to those aspects of Mary that make her unique. Here is the distinction between love and lust."37 To categorize a person in terms of qualities may help in identification (e.g. in a police search) but they constitute categories of an *object*. We can best describe their *personhood* by telling stories about what they did on some particular occasions, what peculiarities of action they have performed, and so forth. This perspective is important for Ronald Thiemann and in the same way, Stroup insists, "the Markan Gospel constitutes a *narrative text*: it is "neither a treatise on christology nor a doctrinal discussion", because it provides "*a narrative in which his (Christ's) identity emerges from those events that make up his personal history.*"38

Narrative biblical texts, in this sense, witness to the personhood of God more effectively by proclaiming *a history of the acts of God* than abstract theological language which rehearses Aristotelian-like "divine attributes" of righteousness, holiness, and love. Ronald F. Thiemann develops this point further than Stroup, characterizing biblical narrative-texts as conveying divine hiddenness and divine identity: "God's complex identity is presented through narrative accounts of his action which stress both his immanence and his transcendence, his presence and his hiddenness."39 The narrative of Jesus portrays God's hidden but active power.

(3) This kind of narrative theology, however, accounts for only one particular segment of a wider variety of functions ascribed to narrative in broader literary and semiotic theory. Stories can be told for one purpose, and re-told for another. In folk-literature one narrative becomes superimposed onto another, and inter-textual relations begin to form productive "texts" that can offer polyvalent readings. Robert Alter, as we have noted in chapter XIII, sees conscious artistic plurality and internal tension in the stories of David's rise to kingship, and David Clines, as we noted in chapter III, sees layered texts in Job which undermine any dogmatic conclusion by deconstructing the narrative-texts which seem to lead to it. Here the temporal logic carries readers with it in different ways and with different effects, although "narrative" only thinly and perhaps superficially frames the genre of wisdom discourse.

In chapter X we examined in detail Ricoeur's use of Heidegger's technical notion of *possibility* for his theory of narrative. Narratives project *possible* worlds which engage the imagination by providing strategies of projection for *future* action. We need not enlarge further here on the ground already covered, except to note its relevance to pastoral theology. In this model, narrative *stimulates the imagination*, and offers constructs which project possibilities for *future action*. They *activate* the eschatological call of Christian pilgrimage, in the sense of beckoning onwards towards new future action, or in some cases also warning readers of projected possibilities to be avoided. They provide a resource by which readers can transcend the present.

(4) In literary theory, the distinction between narrative and flat description rests on contrasts between plot and natural sequence, or between narrative-time and natural-time. In the philosophy of language a more logically rigorous distinction performs the same function. In his meticulously-argued and creatively important book *Works and Worlds of Art* (1980) Nicholas

Wolterstorff develops conceptual tools found in speech-act theory. He distinguishes between a propositional content (*p*) which functions as *description*, and illocutions which convey a content with a certain force (*F*). We discussed the importance of this distinction for Searle and Recanati in chapter VIII. But Wolterstorff designates this force axis more strictly in these examples as "*mood-actions*". Just as D.D. Evans distinguished between *causal* and *institutional* force in his Austinian "logic of self-involvement", so Wolterstorff distinguishes between the *causal* generation of the world of art through uses of its physical materials and the "*count-generation*" which transforms narrative-elements into the events and characterizations of the coherent "world" of a narrative-plot.[40] *Count-generation* therefore includes *more than the linguistic or narrative conventions themselves*. Like Searle, Wolterstorff ascribes "rights and responsibilities" to authors as *agents* who exercize these to project the art-world.[41]

In his book *Art in Action* (1980) and more rigorously in *Works and Worlds of Art*, Wolterstorff follows Searle in drawing out the fundamental philosophical consequences which flow from the difference between *descriptive* language and the projection of a narrative-world in which a "*mood-stance*" generates assertions, questions, expressions, or promises.[42] In fiction, the fictive mood-stance "consists of *presenting*, of *offering for consideration* certain states of affairs" for reflection, exploration, edification, cathartic cleansing, or for sheer delight.[43] But whereas fiction neither affirms nor denies a propositional content (*p*), the liar and the historian both take up an assertive stance, even if the historian also projects a narrative-world.[44] This world presupposes assertive truth-claims, rather than simply providing bare "description".[45] For Wolterstorff, as for Searle, however, *the status of authors as human agents capable of assuming commitments and responsibilities remains fundamental*. We cannot speak here, as in the Gadamerian, semiotic, or Barthesian models, of the death of the author who simply falls from view in written narrative texts.

The effect of readers' participation in narrative-worlds may be *transforming*, on the basis of any of these four sub-categories of narrative theory. But they operate in different ways: they may subvert, entice, create conditions for the possibility of identity and identification, stimulate imagination and project future possibilities, or project worlds which potentially set in motion illocutions. They may also convey self-involving descriptions from a point of view, nourish social solidarity by corporate remembrance and celebration, may affirm, challenge, or create pre-conditions for the next step in the process of understanding. According to Frank Kermode and Graham Shaw, narrative can also perform the potentially more divisive function of manipulating the reader into either becoming an "insider" by accepting the authority and secrets of the narrator and the narrator's circle, or remaining an "outsider" for whom the narrative remains unintelligible. But Thiemann and Stroup examine parallel considerations to reach a different conclusion, and it is time to move from theory to concrete instanciation.

(1) There is no need to set out in detail other examples which correspond to the function ascribed by Fuchs of the parable of the labourers in the vineyard (Matt. 20:1–16). Robert Funk and especially J.D. Crossan have identified a category of "parables of reversal". Crossan pays particular attention to the parable of the good Samaritan (Luke 10:30–37). Parable, here, to use his particular term, *subverts* "world".[46] It changes the network of assumptions and *transforms the pre-understanding* which hearers or readers are likely to have brought to the parable. In *The Two Horizons* I drew particular attention to W. Wink's interpretation of the parable of the pharisee and the tax collector as a parable of reversal (Luke 18:9–14). Our twentieth-century assumptions about "pharisees" tend to turn the parable hermeneutically onto its head: *we* are thankful not to be "even as this pharisee". But to the earliest audiences and readers, "pharisees" would be perceived not as hypocrites but as exemplifications of devotion. What is reversed in the narrative-world is the reader's expectations about the status of the genuinely devout before God.[47]

Many narratives, however, *found and create*, rather than subvert, *worlds*. The Exodus narratives of release from bondage to liberty (Ex. 12:31–15:21) are more than bare description, for they embody a plot and unfold through narrative time, with coherence and closure (Ex. 12:31–14:31). We observed these characteristics in Wesley Kort's discussion of the texts of Exodus. They also function *to celebrate* the events they tell, strengthening thereby the *community bonds* of those who share in "remembrance" and liturgical recital of these events (Ex. 15:1–27). In the New Testament, the texts of certain parables, as well as the plots of the gospel narratives themselves, found worlds. But it is important to distinguish between a hermeneutic of narrative-worlds and that of allegorical interpretation. The narrative world coheres together, and can draw in the outsider as it carries the reader along in a single process. Allegorical interpretation demands a series of individual atomistic interpretative jumps from one level to another, in which only "insiders" have the key to make the right jumps from coded language to reality. Here the function becomes mainly cognitive and much narrower.

(2) Functions of narratives may be diverse, even in the case of the same biblical narrative. The Book of Esther offers an example. The following "readings" do not necessarily compete with one another. John Goldingay is sympathetic with G. Gerlemann's reading of the Book of Esther as a diaspora version of the new exodus.[48] It projects a narrative-world in which every Jew, in whatever situation, is invited to take responsibility, even at personal risk, to assist the Jewish people. David Gunn argues that one special strength of the narrative-worlds of Ruth and of Esther is that they merge much more readily with the worlds and horizons of most modern readers

than "the grandiose world of parting seas and tumbling walls and floating axe-heads".⁴⁹ David Clines offers five or six distinct reading-strategies for Esther (1990) in addition to the exegesis of his earlier commentary on the book (1984).⁵⁰ Vashti's story offers a satire on the power of the Persian king, but also portrays the courage of a woman in the face of an oppressive power-structure. In literary formalist terms it embodies a plot in which tension and struggle achieve resolution. In structuralist terms, the *subject*, Esther, is assisted by a *helper*, Mordecai, and hindered by an *opponent*, Haman, in the quest for the *object* of deliverance, in relation to which the Jews stand as *receiver*. Semiotic systems embody "alimentary" codes or types of feasting and fasting, a code of clothing, and a topographical code of power. The story offers two kinds of socio-critical readings: a feminist and a materialist critique of power-structures (Esther 1:3; 1:18–19; 2:3, 8:11; 10:3).⁵¹

(3) Ronald Thiemann selects the Gospel of Matthew as an example of narrative-texts which hold together the identification of Jesus Christ with a recognition of divine hiddenness (1985, 1987). Matthew's narrative presents "a uniquely identifying description of God". The Matthean goal is "to identify Jesus . . . Emmanuel, the Son of God, the one who enacts God's intention to save his people."⁵² In Matt. 1:1–4:16, Thiemann argues, Jesus' formal identity is specified as the Son of God who fulfils the divine mission and promise, while 4:18–20:34 specify the individual personal identity of Jesus, which is not without some degree of ambiguity. Finally Matt. 21:1–28:20 connects the formal and personal identifications. Jesus receives divine authority (28:18), and through the unity of his person and mission with God (3:17; 17:5; 26:36–46) identifies God as his Father and as the God of promise who enacts his intentions in Jesus. The extension of the final promise (28:20) "functions to carry the world of the Gospel narrative into that of the reader . . . Precisely as the narrative provides its definitive identification of God and Jesus, it also functions as a promise of direct address . . . Thus the discourse functions . . . as an invitation to enter the world of the text."⁵³

Thiemann's approach to Matthew runs parallel with Stroup's observations on the text of Mark. Stroup urges: "Mark clearly demonstrates that one cannot know who Jesus is apart from the narrative of his personal history."⁵⁴ Stroup argues that the question of Jesus's identity is prompted by the authority which Jesus exercizes in the narrative texts (Mark 1:24 – "Have you come to destroy us? I know who you are"): "The question of Jesus's identity is intensified by the issue of his authority . . . 'Who can forgive sins but God alone?'" (Mark 2:7).⁵⁵

The work of Stroup and of Thiemann looks back in part to the seminal work of Hans Frei in 1967, later re-published with a new introduction under the new title *The Identity of Jesus Christ* (1975). There is hiddenness in the gospel texts, because as the witness to God Jesus "points away from himself".[56] But for believing readers, whom Frei distinguishes from unbelievers and also from pilgrims, the identity of Jesus Christ is given in and through the narrative texts, together with the presence of Christ which is one with his identity.[57]

(4) Wolterstorff's speech-act account of worlds of art invites questions about the status of illocutionary forces generated in or by narrative-worlds. In some cases the narration of a story *counts as* an act of description; in other cases it *counts as* an act of exploration, suggestion, or promise. In earlier times conservative interpreters tended to assume that *all* biblical narration *counted as* referential description. But a number of conservative writers feel free nowadays to allow such issues to be determined through enquiry about *genre* and *hermeneutical functions*. Thus Sidney Greidanus argues that in the case of Job and Jonah "the historical referent is *hermeneutically* inconsequential" (his italics), whereas "the historical referent of the Exodus narrative ... is indispensable".[58] In the Westminster Theological Seminary symposium *Inerrancy and Hermeneutic* (1988) Tremper Longman III argues not only that Job contains "literary artifice", but also that "the Scriptures are multi-functional", and that Alter is right to draw attention to "conventions of biblical storytelling".[59] Literary artifice can be "true". In biblical narrative, Longman allows, point of view, ordering of time, characterization, and the organization of plot all play a part that prohibits a strict antithesis between literature and history.

In terms of the vocabulary used by Wolterstorff for broader philosophical questions, we may say that the creation-narratives in Gen. 1:1; 2:25 are more than "cause-generated" texts; their act of projecting a narrative of creation *counts as* an act of ascribing a status and role to humankind, as well as counting as an assertion about origins and existence.[60] The language does not simply represent, but represents *as*: it represents humankind *as* creaturely beings, *as* stewards of created resources, *as* authorized to eat produce and to pro-create. In D.D. Evans's language, the creation accounts assign institutional *roles* to humankind in relation to each other and to God. In Wolterstorff's terminology, these narrative-texts embody more than an *assertive* "mood-stance": they *authorize* certain patterns of action (1:29; 2:16); they *evaluate and celebrate* all creation as "good" (Gen. 1:12; 1:18; 1:21; 1:31); they *direct* (1:28; 2:17).[60] The performative illocutionary acts of giving and blessing (1:28,29) take the form of address.

Some writers trace complex, even socially divisive and theologically authoritarian functions to some kinds of narrative texts. Frank Kermode, as we have noted, believes that the text of Mark is "endlessly plural" and in the end remains a source of "disappointment" unless the reader counts for Mark as an "insider". Graham Shaw develops this insider-outsider contrast explicitly as a "pastoral" theology approach to Mark.[62] Mark, he claims, is deliberately *manipulative*. Shaw associates Jesus, as the bringer of freedom, with Tolstoy's "anarchistic" view of the Kingdom of God. But Mark, he attempts to argue, uses the "insider" point of view of a narrative of secrecy to beguile readers into accepting the authority of Mark and his circle as custodians of the secret tradition. Paul's claims about apostolic authority, he writes, are at least open: "We may even look back rather wistfully at the undisguised egotism of Paul's letters: the self-assertion in Mark's Gospel is considerably more devious."[63] For Mark uses the secrecy motif, Shaw claims, "to establish not the authority and prestige of Jesus . . . but the authority and prestige of his present representatives".[64] The privilege of sharing the secrets of the omniscient narrator, and of eavesdropping behind closed doors, is conferred on a select group by those who have privileged access to it.

Shaw's approach remains unconvincing, not least because Thiemann and others have offered more plausible explanations for the so-called secrecy element or "obscurity" of the Markan text. Thiemann rejects the over-polarized sharply-bounded contrast between "totally perspicuous" and "totally indeterminate" meaning that is utilized, he believes, by Nietzsche, Derrida, and Kermode with misleading effects.[65] With Richard Bernstein he rejects the polarized alternative either "fixed foundation" or "forces of darkness that envelop us".[66] In parallel fashion we rejected the same kind of polarization in Fish between logical formalism on one side and social pragmatism with its contextual pluralism at the other end of the "anti-formalist road". In biblical narrative there is mystery and hiddenness, because the God of whom they speak, and who speaks through them, remains transcendent and "other". But there is also disclosure, and this disclosure includes, as Thiemann argues, identity and promise.

The functions of narrative-worlds as hermeneutical resources for pastoral theology, we may conclude, are *manifold*; but they embody certain patterns. Supposedly self-sufficient or indifferent readers who might be unwilling to engage adequately with didactic or informational texts in openness and with a positive willingness to listen may find themselves unexpectedly enticed into a narrative-world which has the effect of subverting some of their prior values and assumptions. Narrative-worlds, under our first sub-category of theory and examples, may also found and create values as well as subverting them. Within another sub-category narrative-text may serve to carry forward certain questions about personal identity. In Christian tradition and history, the narrative-world of the Fourth Gospel has often had the effect of inviting, and giving birth to, faith. For the structure around which its plot is organized is the temporal flow of ascending narrative-sequence of witnesses to the identity of Christ as the Word of God, and Christological discourse and Christological confession punctuate this narrative flow.

Literary theories and models of narratives demonstrate the multiformity of their possible functions for a multiformity of possible reading-situations.

But here the narrative-world often (but not always) constitutes a *possible world* which projects *future possibilities for action and scenarios for imaginative exploration*. Speech-act approaches to "count-generated" narrative-worlds which embody stances that initiate a *more specific range of acts*. These may also perform multiform tasks for different readers, but within a different category: they may *offer pardon* to the guilty, may *liberate* the oppressed, may *comfort* the sorrowing, may *warn* the over-confident, or may *pledge promises* to those who are trustful.

Among this multitude of positive functions, however, *some* cannot so easily remain fully operative for readers who *already know the closure* of the narrative (as Fowler has observed). The parable of the labourers in the vineyard (Matt. 20:1–16) can hardly produce tension and shock for those who already know its outcome. A further point may be made about the propositional content (*p*) as against the force (*F*) of such parables. Robert Funk and others have criticized Adolf Jülicher for *abstracting a cognitive content* to reconstruct "the teaching of Jesus", and thereby undermining the hermeneutical function of many parables. J. Jeremias has been criticized on the same ground. But it is legitimate to isolate *p* from *F* for *given purposes*, provided that it is also recognized clearly that such a process *transposes* the narrative into a *different hermeneutical function* in which it no longer operates *to project a narrative world*. Such "readings" are *entirely retrospective*. On the other hand, narratives that are *re-told as familiar narratives within the community* can assume *other* productive narrative-functions. The labourers in the vineyard (Matt. 20:1–16) may become a *celebratory narrative* for a worshipping community that has already given up all claims for justice, and knows that it owes its existence and its nature entirely to grace. Meanwhile, the original hermeneutical function of the parable to bring about shock and reversal remains *ready to be re-activated when a new pastoral situation emerges* which allows and invites this fundamental operative effect. In a memorable metaphor to which I have alluded elsewhere, Fuchs observes: "the hermeneutical principle for understanding the cat is the mouse."[67] Textual narrative cats await the varied mouse-situations which re-activate them.

4. Biblical Symbols: Productive and Spiritual Reading, with Questions partly from Freud and Jung for Pastoral Theology

The biblical texts abound in images. Northrop Frye observes in *The Great Code*: "City, mountain, river, garden, tree, oil, fountain, bread, wine, bride, sheep . . . recur so often that they clearly indicate some kind of unifying principle."[68] But is image the same as symbol? In twentieth-century Christian theology two very influential writers on symbol in theology contribute significantly to this area, namely Paul Tillich and Paul Ricoeur. Tillich expounds his view of symbol against the background of Jung's psychology and Jung's theory of archetypes; Ricoeur, as we saw in chapter X above, participates in a dialogue about the status of symbol with Freud and with the psycho-analytical tradition.

For Ricoeur, as we have seen, symbols constitute "double meaning" expressions.[69] To speak of evil as a "burden" or as "bondage" is to interpret these terms within a trans-empirical framework so that they operate at a higher or second level of meaning. Evil in this way can be symbolized as a blot or stain, and sin as deviation from a path. Two consequences follow from this for Ricoeur. First, symbols invite *critical* interpretation. For multi-signification allows room for self-deception and for the projection of human will to create values which might serve self-interest. Freudian psychoanalysis we noted, offers one type of critical tool.[70] Second, symbols may *creatively* give rise to thought and to understanding in a "second naïvety". The critical dimension is explanatory; the creative dimension is hermeneutical. Symbol thus represents components which, in sentence form, become metaphor, and in sequences of metaphor become narrative.

Where Ricoeur, in continuity with Freud, stresses the *"double meaning"* nature of symbol, with its capacity either to deceive the self or creatively to transcend it, Tillich, in continuity with Jung, stresses the *participatory and integrative* function of symbols. As Wayne Rollins observes, Jung noted in his earliest work the "emotion-laden" character of certain words for his psychiatric patients.[71] For Freud and for Jung equally, dreams constitute symbolic texts. In Freud's analysis, dream-symbols can *disguise the repressed wishes* or contents of the unconscious; in Jung's view, they *compensate for one-sided or absent features* in consciousness, and perform a constructive role in the movement towards maturity and integration.[72] Thus where Ricoeur focusses on the contrast between deceptive disguise and creative revelation, Tillich focusses on the contrast between the fragmenting character of conceptual subject-object language and the integrating power of the wholeness disclosed through symbol.[73]

As his research on dreams developed, Jung became convinced that certain recurring images and patterns reported in dreams reflected parallels and similarities found in a diversity of mythic and historical materials from cultures which differed widely in geographical and chronological origin. In 1919 Jung revived the term *archetype* from second-century Egyptian gnosticism to denote the "patterning tendency" which he attributed to the human psyche not simply as an unconscious reservoir of images for the individual, but on the basis of what he termed the "collective" or universal consciousness of humankind.[74] He also spoke of "primordial images". *Archetypal images*, in Jung's view, include the masculine figures of the father, the ominous giant or ogre, the hero or noble knight; and the wise old man; the feminine figures include the mother, the princess, the wicked queen, and the wise old woman. But Jung also worked on the development of individuation: the process of "becoming one's own self". In the earlier part of our lives, he believed, we promote those features which our orientations already emphasize as "established": as technical thinkers, as feelers, as sensors, or as intuitive thinkers. In the later part of our development, however, sides of the self hitherto undeveloped call for attention. Aspects which Jung calls "contra-sexual" ingredients and "shadow" aspects need to be integrated with those other elements to which earlier life has accorded prominence. The path to integration lies not in bare rational reflection and in the manipulation of concepts, but in the healing power of deeper forces, including especially the power of symbols.[75]

In Jung's view, biblical texts offer such a resource when they are *more than vehicles for the conscious thought-processes of an argument*. Their integrative and healing power operates optimally when they evoke "the depths of God . . . not taught by human wisdom" (1 Cor. 2:10,13). Image, figure, parable, dark saying, poetry, or whatever presupposes the inadequacy of plain descriptive speech or rational argument functions, for Jung, with this kind of effect, especially if it evokes *feelings* at the deepest level. Jung finds some typical examples in the Book of Revelation: "But I saw a beast rising out of the sea, with ten horns and seven heads, with ten diadems upon its horns . . . let him who has understanding reckon the number of the beast, for it is a human number, its number is six hundred and sixty-six" (Rev. 13:1,18). Numerology in Revelation provides further examples of symbols. The "four corners of the earth" (Rev. 7:1) and "the four living creatures" (Rev. 6:1) denote wholeness or completeness; the number seven denotes perfection ("the seven spirits of God", Rev. 4:5, cf. Rev. 3:1; "the seven seals", Rev. 6:1; "the seven bowls", 15:1). "The tree" symbolizes physical and spiritual growth and well-being rooted in the divine (Psalm 1:3, Prov. 11:30) and becomes a source of life identified with the cross (1 Pet. 2:24, Rev. 22:2).

Paul Tillich takes up this Jungian approach and develops it not only for his systematic theology, but also for his exposition of the principle of correlation which shapes his hermeneutics and his pastoral theology. Tillich writes: "Religious symbols . . . are a representation of that which is unconditionally beyond the conceptual sphere." They transcend the realm "that is split into subjectivity and objectivity".[76] Symbol "grasps our unconscious as well as our conscious being. It grasps the creative ground of our being."[77] The main function of the symbol, therefore, is "the opening up of levels of reality which otherwise are hidden".[78] Symbol thus provides a pre-conceptual bridge between the human psyche and what is symbolized. Tillich asserts: "Every symbol is two-edged. It opens up reality, and it opens the soul."79 "It opens up hidden depths of our own being."80 Following Jung, again, Tillich declares that symbols "grow out of the individual or collective unconscious and cannot function without being accepted by the unconscious dimension of our being."81

All this dwells on meaning-*effects* in biblical texts as sources of integration and healing power. Like Norman Holland's work on the formation and recognition of *identity* through reading, and David Bleich's emphasis on *feeling*, this approach demonstrates the *power* of symbols to achieve certain operative effects in terms of *reader-response*. Paul Ricoeur has firmly pointed out, however, that to determine whether symbols achieve any more than *pragmatic self-affirmation or wish-fulfilment* a critical hermeneutic of suspicion needs to operate interactively with *post*-critical attention to symbol. Indeed Tillich admits that in principle symbols can destroy as well as create. Symbols, as Wittgenstein constantly remarks about pictures, can be *variously interpreted*. Indeed, while many post-modernists affirm the role of symbols in relation to socio-symbolic worlds, the dependence of sign on inherited patterns of belief and practice makes it a prime category for "de-mystification" of a Barthesian or a materialist kind. Freud's attitude to myths was different from Jung's. Whereas Jung immersed himself in a variety of religious traditions, including gnosticism and mediaeval alchemy, Freud dismissed religious myth and the occult as "the black tide of mud". The status of a symbol may appear different from *outside* the symbolic system: its direction of power may depend on how it operates within traditions of habituated interpretation.

For this reason the symbol in biblical texts may remain *primary as a vehicle of power*, but always context-dependent and in this sense *derivative as a vehicle of truth*. It functions on the basis of traditions of interpretation which have been established in the light of critical reflection, including the use of communicative and didactic texts, and narrative-texts which offer patterns of personal identification. In pastoral theology this suggests at least two particular functions. First, with a stable tradition of interpretation established on other grounds, symbols provide material *for healing and integrative meditation in the tradition of lectio divina or spiritual reading*. In Jung's language, they nourish the human soul. Second, they may also provide *exploratory resources for enquiring readers* outside given traditions, *provided that* it is recognized, as Ricoeur rightly insists, that without a hermeneutic of suspicion they *may* operate only as windows on the human unconscious, or on the social history of arbitrary conventions inherited and transmitted in given societies.

These two principles require some further brief elucidation, defence, and exemplification. In meditative "spiritual reading" the power of the eschatological symbols in the Apocalypse may be perceived within the Christian tradition to convey truth. They function as both communicative and productive texts: "The river of the water of life" flows from God's throne (Rev. 22:1); "the leaves of the tree were for the healing of the nations" (22:2); "His name shall be on their foreheads" (22:14). Without some structure of interpretation provided by a tradition, however, "water" and other symbols can be variously understood. In primitive mythology water spawns life, but water may also destroy by drowning, or bring oblivion in the river Lethe, and in depth psychology may be associated with the feminine unconscious.[82] In the Book of Revelation, however, as Caird, Beasley-Murray, and others point out, the river of the water of life reflects primarily the restoration at the End-time of the primal river of Eden (Gen. 2:9,10) together with a further allusion to the river-symbolism of Ezekiel (Ezk. 47:1-12).[83]

If "spiritual reading", then, is undertaken with particular reference to the boundaries of the Christian canon or of a stable Christian tradition of interpretation we arrive at an example of the kind of *lectio divina* which we discussed in chapter IV. The non-cognitive feeling-related dimensions of symbol may operate productively and healingly because a community has already established an interpretative tradition which embodies cognitive hermeneutical judgments. In this sense, in spiritual reading the power of symbols remains primary while their meaning and truth derives from other interpretative factors. All symbols and "pictures" whether in Eastern Orthodox or Western charismatic traditions, retain a measure of ambiguity as matrices of multivalent meaning unless or until these operate in the light of some interpretative judgment of "seeing as". But for readers who see symbols *as symbols*, these interpretations are not conscious acts; they are "given" either, according to some theorists, along with the tradition which the readers inherit; or, according to different theorists, well up from the unconscious.

Nevertheless symbols engage more than intellect, emotion, and imagination. In psychiatry, Rollo May urges, symbol "is given its power and character as a symbol by the *total situation of the patient's life at that moment.*"[84] It is this investment of the self and of the total situation at a given time which makes symbol especially important for pastoral theology. Jung argued that engaging with the biblical texts and their symbols entailed asking questions both about the text and also "The meanings of the text *in the personal life of the reader*"[85]

This brings us explicitly to pastoral theology and to reading situations. Jung insisted that symbols in biblical texts could perform healing and interpretive functions for varieties of readers. But this cannot apply in every case, unless, two principles are acknowledged: first, the interactive plurality of biblical symbols is recognized; and, second their effect is acknowledged to be ambivalent, even if also very powerful. The symbol of "father" represents a classic case. Dominique Stein, for example, expresses "unease" about the symbol of God as father.[86] Freud, as we know, saw the father-figure as representing both a plea for protection and a desire to kill and to displace, which at the infantile level gave rise to projecting a super-father figure beyond attack. But fatherhood of this kind is left behind in maturity. Hence Stein views the father symbol as one implying *psychological regression.* Yorick Spiegel, in the same volume as that in which Stein writes, addresses the problems of sociology, where language concerning authority-figures, whether father or king may be associated with so-called pre-egalitarian political romanticism.[87] In Spiegel's view this symbol is *sociologically regressive.* Elisabeth Moltmann-Wendel follows Mary Daly in calling for "a replacement of the Father . . . . His activities reflect predominantly male actions . . . The God whom Jesus proclaimed is rooted in the matriarchal Sophia tradition."[88] Moltmann-Wendel rejects the implied *maleness* of the symbol. For Daphne Hampson the symbol is destructive and irretrievable, for this reason, and in the end untranslatable.[89] We discussed hermeneutical issues about *depatriarchalizing* and the proposed use of matriarchal "goddess" language in chapter XII.

Elisabeth Moltmann-Wendel qualifies "father" with such a multitude of conceptual caveats that it can no longer function as *pre-conceptual symbol.* Its effective emasculation and conscious re-interpretation transpose it into a highly conceptualized abstract and cognitively qualified language-function. The effect and perhaps the goal here, whatever we may make of it, has been to *neutralize the power* of a symbol, because *in her reading-situation* Elisabeth Moltmann-Wendel found it not simply powerful, but also *powerfully destructive.*

If *all* symbols receive this treatment, the biblical texts would function with less immediacy and power, and all symbols would be transposed into concepts. The process of reducing symbolic polyvalency by a conceptual removal of ambiguity inevitably reduces symbolic power and the capacity of symbols for integrative shaping. Hence the more traditional and effective response in pastoral theology has been neither to eliminate symbols nor to qualify the varying effects of symbols by cerebralizing them. Unwanted or destructive resonances have been neutralized by embracing the reciprocal mutuality of a plurality of symbols within the biblical texts. Specific reading-situations call for an *avoidance of an obsessive pre-occupation with single isolated symbols.* For example, for a reader who suffers from over-burdened problems of guilt, an obsessive focus on the symbol of judge and judgment could become a destructive and disintegrating force. Yet alongside conceptual discourse about release and forgiveness, speech-acts and symbols which express freedom from guilt would perform a decisive function. The power of the sin-bearing sacrificial substitute or the abrogation of the bill of debt offers a healing resource for such a situation. (Col. 2:14; II Cor. 5:18–20; Hebs. 9:12–14).

Othmar Keel reviews the variety of symbolic resources offered by Old Testament texts, especially the Psalms, in the cultural settings of Ancient Near-Eastern traditions.[90] God is a fortress and a rock, and a "height that offers refuge" (Psalm 31:2; 46:7,11; 48:2,3; 61:3). The symbol draws on images of an impregnable fortress built on a hill, to which people could withdraw from smaller towns in times of attack (1 Sam. 13:6; Jer. 4:29). God is a lamp (Ps. 18:29; 2 Sam. 22:29) whose presence and word is light (Ps. 36:9; 119:105), and from whom flow the fountains of life. He offers intimate shelter, like a bird, under his wings (Ps. 17:8; 36:7; 57:1; 61:4; 63:7; 91:4). God is a welcoming host who protects his guests and fills their cups (Ps. 23:5; 63:5). He is a trustworthy shield (Ps. 7:10; 18:2; 28:7; 33:20).[91] God provides a defence against destructive forces also portrayed in symbol: against the pit, against the desert, against the raging storm, against the night, and against collapse into dust (Ps. 16:10; 49:9; 63:1; 90:3; 104:29; 107:5, 29–30).

The power and potential multivalency of symbols also becomes evident in the Fourth Gospel. Johannine material is organized around certain structured themes which before the discoveries of the Dead Sea Scrolls at Qumran, were often prematurely ascribed to "hellenistic dualism": life, death (John 1:4; 10:10; 11:23) light, darkness (1:5; 3:19; 8:12; 9:5) truth, falsehood (8:32; 14:6); Spirit, creaturely humanity (3:6; 6:63). To these may be added such familiar symbolic imagery as that of the good shepherd (John 10:11), the bread of life (6:35), the door (10:7), and the true vine (15:1). Most readers have a deep personal investment in such symbols: from early childhood doors which are open or shut signal access and welcome or exclusion and loneliness; light removes fear of unknown nocturnal terrors or fear of losing one's way; the figure of the good shepherd is rooted in images of caring, tender, wisdom, usually idealized and thus immunized against "bad" experiences which may colour symbols such as father.

Nevertheless in the Johannine texts contextualizing settings and textual allusions also constrain meaning by situation-directedness in ways which may be perceived by some readers, but not by others. Light, for example, is *used* by John in a consciously double way to signify *both* "shedding light upon" persons and situations in judgment (a more likely meaning of *phōtizō* in 1:9 than the R.S.V. "enlightens every man") and illuminating and enlightening them. Light, in John, chases away the fears and terror of darkness, but only by first exposing everything as what it is, i.e. by act of judgment.

In Lotman's terminology, Johannine symbols function partly as elements of communicative texts; partly as elements of productive texts. In the tradition of Clement of Alexandria and Origen from the late second century onwards, John was seen as "the spiritual gospel". This Patristic notion of the "spiritual" gospel called attention to the Johannine use of day-to-day objects or events (water, wine, bread, light, birth, doors, shepherding, foot-washing) to convey trans-empirical or transcendent truth. In philosophical terms John does not use "religious language" but uses ordinary language for "religious" purposes. In *this* sense John remains a sacramental gospel: the outward and extra-linguistic everyday world provides signs and symbols of invisible and transcendent realities. This is different from claiming that John has an obsessive pre-occupation with the *particular examples* of the two dominical sacraments of baptism and holy communion. In view of the omission of their institution, among other factors, it is doubtful whether John is "sacramental" in this second and narrower sense.

Nevertheless symbols, models and events in John serve most characteristically to articulate Christology. The divine *logos* is enfleshed in Jesus and in identifiable patterns of word and deed. Traditions found in the Old Testament already provide a frame of reference for the understanding of such language as "bread", "vine", and "shepherd". This background provides a semiotic code which allows them to function communicatively as well as productively. On the one hand *the symbols remain sufficiently multivalent for readers to see their own lives and wellbeing at stake in them*. On the other hand they are also sufficiently situation-specific within a variety of patterns of traditions to function *communicatively as well as productively* in a text which has an explicitly *situation-directed goal*: "that you may believe that Jesus is the Christ . . . and that you may have life in his name" (John 20:31).

5. Models Five through to Eight on Variable Reader-Effects: Semiotic Productivity, Reader-Response, Socio-Pragmatic Contextualization, and Deconstruction

The fifth of our ten theoretical models to be considered is that of semiotic productivity. The impact of semiotic theory on biblical interpretation has two quite different effects for pastoral theology. On one side, it is possible for the interpreter to stand *outside the semiotic system* of codes through which textual meaning is perceived to be generated. In this case a socio-critical or political assessment of the semiotic system may be offered as a critique of the institutional structures in which it is embedded. "Materialist" readings by Michel Clevenot, socio-political readings by Norman Gottwald, and "demystifying" interpretations of texts by Roland Barthes offer examples. But on the other side, readers can stand *inside the semiotic system*. If a straight match of shared code between the author and the reader occurs, a clear-cut communicative or transmissive process of understanding may be set in motion. But self-conscious enquiries about semiotic codes generally arise when the codes are *mis-matched*, or, more typically, when *two or more semiotic systems operate simultaneously in the texts*. As in the case of symbol or metaphor, different levels of reading or interpretation may be entailed, and the text may fall into the category described by J. Lotman and by U. Eco as "productive" or "generative". Here the "first" reading can become a code or matrix for "second" and subsequent readings.

A semiotic approach shares with structuralism and with literary formalism the presupposition of a model in which meaning is generated by a language-*system* rather than by the conscious choices, judgments, and goals of an author as an *agent* who determines how such a system *is put to operational use*. As structuralism gave way to a post-structuralist phase, such a perspective remained congenial to post-modernist, post-Freudian, and post-Marxist *suspicions of consciousness*. It also reflects post-modernist diagnoses of the arbitrary role of *social conventions* as devices which mask power-interests of those in control in communities. The status of semiotic systems remains a fundamental philosophical and theological issue; it is not simply one for literary theorists, social historians, or biblical interpreters. *Precisely the symbols which Jung and Tillich see as integrating personhood through interaction with the unconscious also betray the social conventions of organized codes relative to cultures. "Archetypal images", in Jung's terminology, of the king, and the son, or of the prince and the princess, constitute functions within a gender-system or a hierarchical power-system.* Hero and villain, trickster and wise counsellor, trial and restoration, represent semiotic components within a directed structure of quest.

Even if one adopts the standpoint, advocated in these chapters, that most (not necessarily all) biblical texts are optimally understood with reference to a directedness willed by an author towards a situational context for which some reconstructive imagination and enquiry is invited, we may nevertheless ask: what gains, if any, can be achieved for readers by drawing a boundary round the text which excludes its author and situation *for purposes of hermeneutical strategy?* John Barton reminds us that support for such an approach comes "from a most surprising source: an essay by C.S. Lewis". Lewis argues (1939) that a passage such as Isa. 13:19–22a cannot be attributed to any single human individual, and has nothing to do with the personality or intentions of the author. It is like a work of art which takes on new colours never foreseen or intended by the artist. We can have poetry without the poet. In his small book *An Experiment in Criticism* (1961) C.S. Lewis defends the older formalist theory of reading texts "in their own right" rather than as expressions of what the author wills to communicate or the reader wishes to "use".[92]

Barton recognizes that this approach, for all its apparent dignifying of "the text alone" in practice transfers the onus for interpretation and understanding, and even in a sense co-authoring, onto the reader. Barton observes: "Lewis is saying, in effect, that the meaning (or at any rate *a* valid meaning) of the text is constituted by our conventions for reading it, by the expectations we bring to it."[93] Once semiotic systems are perceived not only to generate meaning on the basis of systems without agents (other than readers) or on the basis of interactions with other systems or matrix-generators, we move into the area of reader-response theories, as Susan Wittig's work on polyvalent meaning in the parables of Jesus demonstrates.

But here, from the point of view of philosophy of language as well as for pastoral theology, some complex issues arise. As Stephen Schiffer observes at the very beginning of his book *Meaning* the logical grammar of "Seymour meant something" is different from that of "That mark means something".[94] In the former case, a human agent usually produces meaning by *doing* something, by *performing an act entailing choices and uses*, by drawing on the repertoire of some prior linguistic or semiotic system. *Simply within the system* a human artifact, such as a signal flag, produces meaning not at this *systemic* level by virtue of some action but by virtue of its conventional status within some inherited semiotic code.[95] The flag "means" something *potentially*. But if it is selected from a box, and waved by a human agent, the human agent "means" something by this *use* of the flag at the *operational* level. The ambiguity of the active and derivative sense of "means" can be illustrated from traffic signs in the highway code. Signs for falling rocks or for pedestrians crossing "mean" potentially in a booklet only as *possibilities*: when a human agent selects them from others and places them by a cliff or a crossing their meaning becomes *operational by virtue of the agent's action*. Learning about the semiotic system is *learning about the possibilities which conventions can generate*. In Wittgenstein's simile there is all the difference between *watching* a board-game and learning its rules than actually *moving* a piece in the game.[96] The latter is the analogue of *operational* meaning; the former, only of systemic or *potential* meaning.

What, then, does this suggest for pastoral theology or for varied reading-situations? It suggests at least two considerations. First, it enhances readers' understandings of the contrast used by Lotman and Eco between productive and communicative texts. To use one semiotic system as a matrix to generate meaning within a further system produces complex and sometimes novel effects. The Book of Revelation utilizes the texts of Ezekiel, Daniel, Isaiah, Zechariah, and other texts to generate productive, symbolic, imagery. George Caird calls attention to its surrealist kaleidoscopic dream-like texture with the warning that we should not attempt "*to unweave the rainbow*"; these texts have "evocative and emotive power".[97] In apocalyptical imagery, *everything is at stake for the reader*. The Apocalypse uses Ezk. 1:5,16–18 as a matrix for productive imagery about "four living creatures... full of eyes inside and out" (Rev. 4:8). The voice which speaks "with the sound of many waters" (Rev. 1:13) evokes a sense of awe at God's unutterable transcendence on the basis of Ezk. 43:2. *To transpose these texts, as some popular translations tend to do, into mere communicative description of an omniscient intelligence or a super-human voice has reductionist effects.*

Nevertheless Revelation remains *also* a communicative text which presupposes, in its directedness towards oppressed readers, some overlapping or even sharing of codes. As Beasley-Murray notes, many of the images represent recognizable stereotyped cartoons or caricatures, like John Bull or Uncle Sam, within traditions used in apocalyptic literature of the day.[98] Readers knew that "144,000" (Rev. 14:1) does not stand in a semiotic system of mathematics in which the adjacent semantic choice would be 143,999. In these texts a *productive* axis signals that *everything, including one's own life, is at stake*, while a *communicative* axis conveys a message concerning *God's sovereign purposes and modes of action in relation to reading-situations of oppression, suffering and marginalization. The text is multi-functional.*

Second, to review the options offered by the signal-flags which lie in a box might suggest that the availability of systems constrain *what possibilities might exist* for communication. This brings us back to our earlier discussion in chapter III of the so-called Whorfian language hypothesis. The embodiment of linguistic habits and conventions in systems offer a provisional and approximate guide to what can *more readily* be said, or can be said *only with difficulty*. The notion that language-communities remain entirely trapped within their own semiotic systems is a fallacy popularized by Whorf but disproved by research on inter-translatability in general theoretical linguistics, as can be evidenced in the work of John Lyons, David Crystal, and others. Moreover, more than one semiotic system may function interactively. Systems of semantic networks and socio-symbolic worlds may overlap but may also generate different repertoires of choices for authors and for readers in different socio-cultural situations. Care is needed in this respect to note what has been transposed when modern Western readers unconsciously perhaps presuppose that biblical texts operate with corresponding systems to those of Western conventions.

In the symbolic worlds of much modern popular Western culture, for example, the word "spiritual" often functions in a system in which the term opposes "physical". But the ancient hellenistic-oriental world embodied systems in which "spiritual" opposed a variety of possible semantic contrasts. Some in first-century Corinth saw it as standing in opposition to the "ordinary" status of people who possessed no special religious gifts. But in Pauline and in earliest Christian thought the semiotic system which was presupposed determined the semantic boundaries of "spiritual" with reference to the Holy Spirit, and as therefore reflecting the character of Christ. Hence 1 Corinthians, I have argued elsewhere

(1973, 1978) exhibits a conflict of semantic networks and of the persuasive definitions which these may generate: the Corinthians claim to be "spiritual" in a way that Paul seeks to re-define in more Christological terms related to the work of the Holy Spirit. Further, Paul's language about a "spiritual body" (1 Cor. 15:44) becomes unintelligible on the basis of modern Western assumptions about the semantic role of "spirit".[99] For Paul, the resurrection mode of existence is "spiritual" not because the main "point" has to do with spiritual *vs.* physical (the R.S.V. *misses* the point of the Greek *pneumatikos* vs. *psychikos* in I Cor. 15:44), but because the Holy Spirit has transformed this mode in accordance with the Spirit's own character.

While we must be cautious about the danger of imposing a Whorfian or Barthesian philosophy of language onto semiotic systems, the issue sheds considerable light on reasons for *differences of reader-expectations*. The shape of the semiotic system offers a *tentative and provisional* indicator of *probable* habits of expectation and attitude within a linguistic world. We must bear in mind, however, that the shape of a language-game determines *not always actual moves* but degrees of *difficulties, possibilities,* or even *probabilities* of moves. In the end, as Searle and Schiffer stress, what counts is the action of agents on the basis of what Schiffer terms "shared knowledge", and Wittgenstein calls "agreements in judgments".[100] This lies behind Wittgenstein's celebrated simile "If a lion could talk, we could not understand him".[101] In our discussion of Stanley Fish's contextual relativism in the previous chapter, we noted that for Wittgenstein communicative meaning rested on frameworks which varied from "the common behaviour of mankind" or "being a living human being" to given "narrowly circumscribed" forms of life.

The sixth theoretical model to be considered may be examined under this same general heading, *namely Reader-response Theory*. In chapter XIV we traced significant differences of theory between the various formulations of reader-response theory found in Iser, Eco, Culler, Holland, Bleich, and Fish. We considered some specific examples of readings of biblical texts especially within the first two sub-categories. Susan Wittig's work on the parables (1977) included a reading of the parable of the Prodigal Son (Luke 15:11–32), and drew on the theory of Wolfgang Iser. Similarly we examined Resseguie on Mark 10:17–22 and modern readers; Robert Fowler and Jouette Bassler on Mark 6:30–44; Mark 8:1–10; and Mark 14:22; Norman Petersen on readers, reading, and codes in Mark (especially Mark 1:1–15 and Mark 13:14); and Alan Culpepper on the Johannine narrative. Alan Culpepper's work on the Johannine narrative-text, we saw, places the activity of the reader within the frame of narrative theory in Genette, Chatman, and others, as well as that of Iser's reader-response theory. Petersen's dual emphasis on semiotics and on reader-processes runs parallel to the interests which we examined in the work of Umberto Eco.

These approaches contribute to discussions in pastoral theology in as far as they serve to clarify issues about the nature of reading-processes *within the time-horizons of readers*. In common with the reception-theory of Hans Robert Jauss, Iser, Eco, Holland, Fish and others give attention to the role played by *expectation, construction, projection, and surprise in processes of engagement between readers and texts*. For pastoral theology it is constructive to identify what may be entailed in the *activity* of readers and reading. To repeat an analogy that may be in danger of being overworked, the musical score *must be played*, whether by a soloist, or by a chorus, or orchestra as a temporal process which is of an *eventful nature*. As we have argued already in chapters II and IX, no two performances will be identical, but it still makes sense to speak of a *good* performance as being one which *includes both faithfulness to the score (pace* Fish*), and a creativity which transcends merely wooden, mechanical, or repetitive routine*. Readers are invited to perform active and creative roles in reading-processes.

We noted in the previous chapter the critical comments of Fish on the half-hearted and allegedly self-contradictory nature of Iser's position. We also observed Porter's parallel assessment that Fish, rather than Iser, provided the "real" reader-response theory which he believes that biblical interpreters need. What is the positive value of these claims for pastoral theology? At very least they focus attention on the goals of interpretation *presupposed within given communities, and unmask what are often viewed as "natural" meanings or "natural" norms as community-relative constructions of convention and habit*. These are born out of *routinization*. A community of readers, it is urged, so repeatedly and consistently presupposes certain habits of reading that what in actuality represent no more than context-relative or community-relative assumptions and practices become elevated to the supposed status of universal principles.

Reader-response theory could in principle stop short of contextual pragmatism, and offer a positive critical tool for pastoral theology by inviting provisional and corrigible metacritical reflection on the status of the critical norms used within a community. This becomes an increasingly urgent task in relation to pluralistic cultures and theologies. But the literary theorists who see most clearly the problematic nature of this area seem also to be determined to transpose this model of reading into a narrative philosophy which, to recall the admirable comment of Christopher Norris cited above, makes "use of a liberal rhetoric to frame an authoritative message", pressing its claims "under cover of its liberal-pluralist credentials". The entailments for pastoral theology demand urgent and clear exposure, and to this task we now turn.

That segment of reader-response theory which comes under the heading of *socio-pragmatic hermeneutical theory constitutes a distinct, and seventh, model from among our ten*. The theory seems to explain so much, and may seem initially or superficially to liberate exegesis of biblical texts from control by communities of realists, sectarians, or conversely from an agenda fixed by the biblical guild of historical and lexicographical specialists. It enlarges and universalizes Robert Morgan's observation that "some disagreements about what the Bible means stem not from obscurities in the texts, but from conflicting aims of the interpreters".[102] It seems to provide an intellectual and philosophical explanation for the gut-level feeling shared equally by many right-wing conservatives and left-wing radicals, that not only is the ideal of disinterested scholarship an outdated liberal illusion; but also that all biblical exegesis can be *predicted by socio-political typifications* of "conservative", "neo-liberal", "radical", "historical-critical", "moderate", or "pleasing the Board and the Constituency" goals of interpretation.

There can be little doubt that *some* communities and *some* individuals do allow such interests to shape the agenda with which they come to biblical texts. A deeply ingrained habit of mind and fierce loyalty to a given tradition *provides a sincere but illusory belief that what they perceive as meaning is "natural", "plain", and "given"*. Honesty can hardly be at issue if a community's presuppositions *make them blind to other options which are before their eyes. In the context of pastoral theology either sustained scepticism and unbelief or blinkered and closed loyalty to given pietist or doctrinaire theological traditions may have the same effect*. A corporate context-relative mind-set elevates "our church" or "the modern world" to the status of a trans-contextual universal.

Pastorally it is crucially important to provide an individual with the hermeneutical understanding to dislodge and to disentangle the claims of a given sub-cultural group to be sole custodians of the "natural" meanings of biblical texts, especially if in practice these claims are founded not on painstaking exegesis and hermeneutical reflection but on exegetical *fiats* arising from a need to defend community-interests. But *it is precisely here that socio-pragmatic hermeneutics reveals its pastoral inadequacy*. For if *all* claims to patient exegesis are merely internally generated by communities governed by interests, *no claim can be ranked in relation to any other claim* except among those who share the same ethnocentric interests.

Socio-pragmatic theory rests on the same kind of desire to cut the knot, or avoid "the slippery slope" as ultra-fundamentalism. As we saw in the previous chapter, we are offered a false polarization between *either* formalism and old-fashioned liberal impartiality *or* the end of the anti-formalist road in which socio-political conventions swallow up all pretensions to achieve a standpoint outside one's own reading community. But to say, rightly, that no one can fully *reach* the goal of impartiality does not logically entail the proposition that no one can begin to travel along the road toward more critical openness. He or she can enter into dialogue with other traditions with special reference to the points at which overlapping and criss-crossings between community-boundaries occur. Fish is aware that we live with multiple roles: as parents, teachers, home-owners and so on.[103] But this ought to make him more sympathetic, rather than less sympathetic, to the human capacity to distinguish between what Alan Montefiore terms "neutrality" and "impartiality".[104] As members of a family or city, sports referees will hardly be "neutral" in their wishes for a team's success. But in applying the same rules to each side, they are trusted to be impartial. In a study entitled "The Morality of Christian Scholarship" (1982) I developed this distinction for Christian academic commitment and openness.[105] Some indication of the *possibility* of trans-contextual openness lies in the experience of *pain and distress* which we feel when respect for truth forces us to abandon a cherished belief *even though colleagues and our ecclesial or social community may hold these beliefs, or may set some different agenda for us.*

This critical self-consciousness is what is often misleadingly and mistakenly called the "individualism" of the Protestant Reformation. T.F. Torrance, we noted, ascribes to the Reformation a *repentant readiness* to re-valuate all pre-conceptions. When the *meaning* of the biblical texts, especially Rom. 1:17, opened a new world for Luther, more was at stake than exchanging one set of community-interests and expectations for another. The process of anguish, pain, disruption, discontinuity, emancipation, joy, and freedom was more than a phenomenon of social history to be accounted for in social terms, even though no doubt social historians can offer purely causal hypotheses. It would be more accurate to say that a world of textual meanings *constructed the community* of the Reformation than that the Protestant communities of the Reformation *"constructed" the meanings of the texts.*

Nevertheless, two reading-situations, each the converse of the other, stand especially *to gain* from a consideration of the socio-pragmatic model. On the one hand, some, as we have observed, find themselves oppressed and under pressure because sometimes contrary to their own judgments or instincts, certain biblical textual "meanings" are imposed on them by a community as the only *natural, obvious, or plain* meaning of the text. Rorty and Fish are right to insist that *what counts as "natural" is relative to assumptions, habits of reading, expectations and norms held within the community of readers.* We have referred to the work of Mark Labberton in which he sees this perspective as a necessary corrective to undue objectivism in some Protestant communities. On the other side, socio-pragmatic hermeneutics addresses those individuals *who underestimate the role of community-contexts* in one direction for *shaping their own individual reading-habits* and in another direction, for providing a *stable and affirming framework* within which as individuals, they may explore texts. Reading remains in principle a corporate rather than individual activity. On one side sharing common readings of texts nourishes social bonding; on the other side, a sense of expectancy within a gathered or worshipping community heightens the actualizations of texts, as we noted in chapter II.

We may now move on to consider *the eighth of our ten models, namely that of deconstruction.* We have already discussed deconstructionist theory in detail with reference to Barthes and to Derrida. We noted several specific examples of the application of deconstructionism to biblical texts. The most illuminating example was found in the work of my former colleague, David Clines, on Job (1990) with particular reference to Job 42:7–17. We also compared Crossan's work on some of the parables of Jesus, as well as on the relation between the Ezra tradition and Ruth 1:16; 4:17–22; and on parts of Ecclesiastes (e.g. Eccles. 2:16; 9:11). Although these examples from Crossan are not technically "deconstruction" in the fullest sense, they offer examples of iconoclasm in the tradition of a Barthesian and Derridean approach to texts.

The *reader situation* which deconstructionist models address emerges from what Clines calls the *craving of the heart for fixed dogma*. Within such a horizon everything is expected to be fixed, sharply-bounded and absolute. In this case it does not help, Clines urges, to try to "cure the problem of a dogma with another dogma. Whenever you have a case of dogma eat dogma, you always have one dogma surviving and snapping at your heels". Deconstruction "loosens our attachment to any one of them *as dogma*" (his italics).[106] In pastoral theology a very fine and delicate line needs to be drawn between the legitimate and necessary use of *coherent formulations in creeds* for the stable transmission of traditions which maintain some consistency of theological identity and a doctrinaire scholasticism in which an *obsession with doctrine* can become an end in itself that even displaces faith and restricts personal growth by placing boundaries everywhere. For this reason Anglicanism, especially the Church of England as evidenced in its Doctrine Commission's Report *Believing in the Church* (1981) stresses that continuity of corporate belief embraces *both* the role played by scripture and the creeds *and* an identifiable continuity in patterns of *worship*, patterns of *ministry*, and patterns of *life*.[107] Presbyterian ecclesiology does not reject this wider notion of coherence and identity.

Nevertheless although deconstructionist theories have some value, by definition they remain primarily negative and context-dependent. They function with a degree of prophetic protest where tradition has become *fossilized* and no longer serves the vision which it emerged to articulate, or in reader-situations where understanding has become exclusively tied to some *single controlling paradigm* as a fixed centre. But "undoing" in Paul de Man, and "play" in Derrida, involves something more radical than correcting traditions. Many writers seem to be tempted to try to cash-out the value of deconstruction for biblical studies by an over-selective attention to those which it shares with certain other literary movements. Thus E.V. McKnight draws attention to its stress on "warring forces of signification" and on the capacity "of the signified to become in turn a signifier".[108] But these characteristics are not exclusive to deconstructionism. Formalism uncovered warring "textual forces", and semiotics explores productive texts.

Part of the problem lies in a pre-occupation with the *sign system* at the expense of the *human life-world*. In a recent volume edited by Stephen Prickett, Kevin Hart identifies these two approaches as "two ways of playing the game" in current theory.[109] The premise that meaning arises from the system, may beg the question of *how* it arises; and the conclusion that meaning is arbitrary and pluriform rests on glossing over the role of human agents in constraining, judging and choosing, *from* the *possibilities* of the system. Amos Wilder, we noted in chapter III, received praise from Crossan for bringing a high degree of literary sensitivity to biblical studies; but Wilder expresses the greatest possible reserve towards an approach which forgets that in most or many biblical texts "the witness in the word was *inseparable from the witness in action and behaviour*". "The word was made flesh" (Jn.1:14).

Indeed this may suggest one last point in this area for pastoral theology, which we shall shortly develop in connection with speech-act theory. Radical indeterminacy and the dissolution of communicative intelligibility comes about when human behaviour fails to provide a frame of reference for interpretation. We have several times recalled Wittgenstein's observation that "the common behaviour of mankind is the system of reference by means of which we interpret an unknown language". In the case of language which reflects beliefs, neither belief nor the role of the human agent can be "de-centred" without self-contradiction. For, in terms of perspectives shared by Wittgenstein, Austin, Polanyi, and others, in certain instances the expression "*p* is true" *includes* "an explicit personal accreditation – my personal backing or signature – which I give to *p*".[110] This "backing" needs to be evidenced in the public arena of life. In the New Testament it is *kerygma* and *confession*. Its nature and implications for language and for texts bring us to speech-act models in hermeneutical theory and in the practice of reading.

Clear affinities and parallels exist between the respective roles of system, tradition, and contextually shifting life-worlds in theories of literature and issues about system, identity or continuity of tradition, and contextual relativism in theology. If we may compare a spectrum of possible views, at one end of the spectrum theological identity and tradition can be defined in terms of a *system of thought abstracted* from the historical *flow of life*, in which the system has very *sharp boundaries* and little flexibility. Even minor deviations transgress the edges of the credal system. At the other end of the spectrum theological tradition and identity virtually collapse and dissolve, as *each new contextual life-world shapes it into some new form which cannot be assessed from outside its new context.* The boundaries of traditions now become uncertain.

Some elements in Catholic theologies lay emphasis on institutional mechanisms to bridge contexts and to provide continuity of structure; some congregational or charismatic theologies tend to leave the issue of continuity on one side, and may even attempt to engage with biblical texts without reference to the issues raised by history, historical distance, and tradition. In contrast to both of these views, Anglican theologies tend to insist (*pace* Fish) that *neither a formalist system abstracted from life nor contextual relativism in which trans-contextual identity is dissolved* addresses the problem. In the interweaving of thought and historical life, a stable continuity can be found in patterns which operate in differing contexts in life like Wittgenstein's *"concepts with blurred edges"*. In the dialogue between the contextual and the universal, the fallible church *points beyond itself and its own context* to that which lies beyond it, especially to the divine promise of the future, and the universals of the cross and the resurrection. In the language of Habermas and of Pannenberg life-world interacts with system, in a way which promotes both stable identity and historical movement.

NOTES TO CHAPTER XV

1. Paul H. Ballard, "Pastoral Theology as Theology of Reconciliation", *Theology* 91, 1988, 375 (my italics); cf. 375–80.
2. Don S. Browning, "Pastoral Theology in a Pluralist Age" in Don S. Browning (ed.) *Practical Theology*, San Francisco: Harper & Row, 1983, 187 (my italics); cf. 187–202.
3. Edward Farley, "Theology and Practice Outside the Clerical Paradigm" in Don S. Browning (ed.) *Practical Theology*, San Francisco: Harper and Row, 1983, 21–41; David Tracy, "The Foundations of Practical Theology" *ibid* 61–82; and Thomas H. Groome, *Christian Religious Education. Sharing our Story and Vision*, San Francisco: Harper and Row, 1980.
4. Don S. Browning, *Religious Ethics and Pastoral Care*, Philadelphia: Fortress, 1983, 17.
5. Edward Farley, "Theory and Practice Outside the Clerical Paradigm", *loc. cit.* 23 and 30.
6. Robert Morgan (with John Barton) *op. cit.* 287.
7. George Lindbeck, *The Nature of Doctrine. Religion and Doctrine in a Postliberal Age*, London: S.P.C.K. 1984, 118.
8. Zygmunt Bauman, *op. cit.* 217.
9. John R. Searle, *Intentionality* 143.
10. *Ibid* 144.
11. L. Wittgenstein, *Zettel* sects. 67 and 116.
12. *Ibid* sect. 173.
13. *Ibid* sect. 51. .
14. John R. Searle, *Intentionality* 173; cf. 166–76.

15. Dick Leith and George Myerson, *op. cit.* 170.
16. F.D.E. Schleiermacher, *Hermeneutics: The Handwritten Manuscripts*, 98–99.
17. W. Dilthey, *op. cit.* 7, 191.
18. Mostly cited above; cf. especially J. Murphy-O'Connor, *St Paul's Corinth*, 1983; and "Food and Spiritual Gifts in 1 Cor. 8:8", *Catholic Biblical Quarterly*, 41, 1979, 292–98, and "Freedom or the Ghetto (1 Cor. VIII.1-13, X.23 – XI.1)", *Revue Biblique* 85, 1978, 543–74; R.A. Horsley, "Consciousness and Freedom among the Corinthians: 1 Cor. 8–10" in *Catholic Biblical Quarterly* 40, 1978, 574–89; and G. Thiessen, *The Social Setting of Pauline Christianity: Essays on Corinth*, Eng. London: S.C.M., 1982.
19. C.A. Pierce, *Conscience in the New Testament*, London: S.C.M., 1955.
20. Robert Morgan (with John Barton) *op. cit.* 7.
21. Rudolf Bultmann, *This World and Beyond. Marburg Sermons*, London: Lutterworth Press, 1960, 21.
22. Søren Kierkegaard, *Fear and Trembling: Dialectical Lyric by Johannes de silentio*, Eng. (ed. A. Hannay) London: Penguin edn. 1985, 44.
23. *Ibid* 45 and 50.
24. *Ibid* 52, 53.
25. *Ibid* 54, 55.
26. S. Kierkegaard, *Purity of Heart is to Will One Thing*, London: Collins (Fontana edn.) 1961, 163.
27. S. Kierkegaard, *Fear and Trembling*, 85; cf. Anthony C. Thiselton, "Kierkegaard and the Nature of Truth", *Churchman* 89, 1975, 85–107. .
28. Bruce Vawter, *On Genesis: A New Reading*, New York: Doubleday, 1977, 254, 255, and 258.
29. Dan Otto Via, *The Parables: their Literary and Existential Dimension*, 113–22.
30. Geraint Vaughan Jones, *The Art and Truth of the Parables*, London: S.P.C.K., 1964, 167–205.
31. Ernst Fuchs, *Studies of the Historical Jesus*, 32–38 and 154–56.
32. *Ibid* 33–37.
33. Stephen Crites, "The Narrative Quality of Experience", *Journal of the American Academy of Religion* 39, 1971, 291–311; and Stanley Hauerwas, *A Community of Character*, Notre Dame: University of Notre Dame Press, 1981; and David H. Kelsey "Biblical Narrative and Theological Anthropology" in Garrett Green (ed.) *Scriptural Authority and Narrative Interpretation*, Philadelphia: Fortress Press, 1987, 121–43.
34. George W. Stroup, *The Promise of Narrative Theology*, London: S.C.M. 1984 (John Knox, 1981) 91.
35. *Ibid*.
36. *Ibid* 202.
37. William Hordern, *Speaking of God. The Nature and Purpose of Theological Language*, London: Epworth Press, 1965, 147.
38. George W. Stroup, *op. cit.* 163 (my italics).
39. Ronald F. Thiemann, *Revelation and Theology. The Gospel as Narrated Promise*, Notre Dame: University of Notre Dame Press, 1987 (1985), 89.
40. Nicholas Wolterstorff, *Works and Worlds of Art*, Oxford: Clarendon Press, 1980, 3–8 and 202–15.
41. *Ibid* 205 .

42. Nicholas Wolterstorff, *Art in Action: Towards a Christian Aesthetic*, Grand Rapids: Eerdmans, 1980, esp. 122–55, and *Works and Worlds of Art*, 222–31.
43. N. Wolterstorff, *Works and Worlds of Art*, 233.
44. *Ibid* 231; cf. 232–34.
45. *Ibid* 239.
46. J.D. Crossan, *In Parables*, 64 and *The Dark Interval* 55, 106–07 and 121–22.
47. Anthony C. Thiselton, *The Two Horizons* 12–16; cf. W. Wink, *The Bible in Human Transformation. Toward a New Paradigm for Biblical Study*, Philadelphia: Fortress Press, 1973, 42–43.
48. John Goldingay, *Theological Diversity and the Authority of the Old Testament*, Grand Rapids: Eerdmans, 1987, 51–52.
49. David M. Gunn, "Reading Right: Reliable and Omniscient Narrator, Omniscient God, and Foolproof Composition in the Hebrew Bible" in David J.A. Clines, S.E. Fowl and S.E. Porter (eds.) *op. cit.* 63; cf. 53–64.
50. David J.A. Clines, "Reading Esther from Left to Right", *ibid* 31–52.
51. *Ibid* 40–46.
52. Ronald Thiemann, *Revelation and Theology. The Gospel as Narrative Promise*, Notre Dame: University of Notre Dame Press, 1987, 113.
53. *Ibid* 142 and 143.
54. George W. Stroup, *op. cit.* 161.
55. *Ibid* 157.
56. Hans Frei, *The Identity of Jesus Christ. The Hermeneutical Bases of Dogmatic Theology*, Philadelphia: Fortress Press, 1975, 164–65.
57. *Ibid* 3–9.
58. Sidney Greidanus, *The Modern Preacher and the Ancient Text. Interpreting and Preaching Biblical Literature*, Leicester: Inter Varsity Press, and Grand Rapids: Eerdmans, 1988, 194 and 195.
59. Harvie M. Conn (ed.) *Inerrancy and Hermeneutics. A Tradition, A Challenge, A Debate*, Grand Rapids: Baker, 1988, 140, 148 and 149; cf. 137–49.
60. On "count-generation" cf. Nicholas Wolterstorff, *op. cit.* 202–15.
61. *Ibid* 226–231 on mood-stance and stance-indicators.
62. Graham Shaw, *The Cost of Authority. Manipulation and Freedom in the New Testament*, London: S.C.M. 1983, vii-viii.
63. *Ibid* 257.
64. *Ibid* 256.
65. Ronald F. Thiemann, "Radiance and Obscurity in Biblical Narrative" in Garrett Green (ed.) *op. cit.* 25.
66. *Ibid* 26.
67. Ernst Fuchs, *Hermeneutik*, Tübingen: Mohr, 4th edn. 1970, 110.
68. Northrop Frye, *The Great Code*, xiii.
69. Paul Ricoeur, *Interpretation Theory*, 45, and 55–57; and cf. also *The Conflict of Interpretations* 287–334.
70. Paul Ricoeur, *Freud and Philosophy* 93–94, 420, and 543 *et passim*..
71. Wayne G. Rollins, *Jung and the Bible*, Atlanta: John Knox Press, 1983, 18–20.
72. *Ibid* 24–26, 37–40; and Paul Ricoeur, *Freud and Philosophy*, 5; cf. *The Rule of Metaphor*, 318. .
73. Tillich's major discussions of symbol occur in addition to his *Systematic Theology*, Eng. London: Nisbet (3 volumes) 1953, 1957, and 1964, in *Dynamics of Faith*,

London: Allen and Unwin, 1957, esp. 42–47; *Theology of Culture*, New York: Oxford University Press, Galaxy edn. 1964, 53–67; and "The Meaning and Justification of Religious Symbols" and "The Religious Symbol" in Sidney Hook (ed.) *Religious Experience and Truth*, Edinburgh: Oliver and Boyd, 1961 (New York: University, 1961) 3–11 and 301–21, also rp. in F.W. Dillistone (ed.) *Myth and Symbol*, London: S.P.C.K. 1966, 15–34.
74. Wayne G. Rollins, *op. cit.* 74; cf. 72–92.
75. Carl Gustav Jung, *Man and his Symbols*, New York: Doubleday, 1971; cf. Jolande Jacobi, *Complex, Archetype, Symbol in the Psychology of C.G. Jung*, Eng. Princeton: Princeton University Press, 1959; and Hans Schaer, *Religion and the Cure of Souls in Jung's Psychology*, Eng. New York: Pantheon, 1950.
76. Paul Tillich, "The Religious Symbol" in Sidney Hook (ed.) *op. cit.* 303.
77. Paul Tillich, *The Shaking of the Foundations*, London: S.C.M. 1962, 86.
78. Paul Tillich, *Theology of Culture*, 56.
79. *Ibid.*
80. Paul Tillich, *Dynamics of Faith*, 43.
81. *Ibid*; cf. *Theology and Culture* 57–58.
82. The huge variety of possible symbolic interpretation which is evident from ancient and modern sources can be seen in such works as J.E. Cirlot, *A Dictionary of Symbols*, Eng. London: Routledge & Kegan Paul, 2nd edn., 1971 (New York: Vail-Ballou Press, 1983).
83. G.R. Beasley-Murray, *The Book of Revelation* London: Marshall, Morgan & Scott, 1974, 330–31; and G.B. Caird, *The Revelation of St John the Divine*, London: Black, 1966, 280–81. .
84. Rollo May, "The Significance of Symbols" in Rollo May (ed.) *Symbolism in Religion and Literature*, New York: Braziller, 1960, 18 (my italics); cf. 11–49.
85. Wayne G. Rollins, *Jung and the Bible*, 101 (my italics).
86. Dominique Stein, "The Murder of the Father and God the Father in the Work of Freud" in Johannes-Baptist Metz and Edward Schillebeeckx (eds.) *God as Father? Concilium*, Edinburgh: Clark, and New York: Seabury Press, 1981, 11–18.
87. Yorick Spiegel, "God the Father in the Fatherless Society" *ibid* 3–10.
88. Elisabeth Moltmann-Wendel, *A Land Flowing with Milk and Honey. Perspectives on Feminist Theology*, Eng. London: S.C.M. 1986, 91 and 101.
89. Daphne Hampson, *Theology and Feminism*, Oxford: Blackwell, 1990, 86–96.
90. Othmar Keel, *The Symbolism of the Biblical World. Ancient Near Eastern Iconography and the Book of Psalms*, Eng. New York: Seabury Press, 1978.
91. *Ibid* 179–92, 222–25.
92. C.S. Lewis, *An Experiment in Criticism*, Cambridge: Cambridge University Press, 1961, 5–13, 16–39 *et passim*; see also John Barton, *Reading the Old Testament*, 194.
93. *Ibid* 196.
94. Stephen R. Schiffer, *Meaning*, Oxford: Clarendon Press, 1972, 1.
95. Cf. *ibid* 1–16, 118–55.
96. L. Wittgenstein, *Philosophical Investigations* sects. 30, 31, and 49.
97. George B. Caird, *The Revelation of St John the Divine*, 25 (my italics).
98. G.R. Beasley-Murray, *The Book of Revelation*, 16.
99. Anthony C. Thiselton, "The Meaning of *Sarx* in 1 Corinthians 5:5. A Fresh Approach in the Light of Logical and Semantic Factors", *Scottish Journal of Theology*

26, 1973, 204–28; and "Realized Eschatology at Corinth", *New Testament Studies* 24, 1978, 510–26.
100. Stephen R. Schiffer, *op. cit.* 154; cf. 118–55.
101. L. Wittgenstein, *Philosophical Investigations II*, xi, 223.
102. Robert Morgan (with John Barton) *op. cit.* 8.
103. Stanley Fish, *Doing What Comes Naturally* 30–32.
104. Alan Montefiore (ed.) *Neutrality and Impartiality. The University and Political Commitment*, Cambridge: Cambridge University Press, 1975, 12.
105. Anthony C. Thiselton, "The Morality of Christian Scholarship" in Mark Santer (ed.) *Their Lord and Ours: Approaches to Authority, Community, and the Unity of the Church*, London: S.P.C.K. 1982, 20–45.
106. David J.A. Clines, "Deconstructing the Book of Job" *loc. cit.* 79. David Clines has re-printed the essay in somewhat altered form in D.J.A. Clines, *What Does Eve Do to Help? And Other Readerly Questions to the Old Testament*, Sheffield: J.S.O.T. Suppl. 94, 1990, 103–26.
107. The Doctrine Commission of the Church of England, *Believing in the Church: the Corporate Nature of Faith*, London: S.P.C.K. 1981 esp. 1–8 (John V. Taylor), 45–78 (A.C. Thiselton), 108–58 (J.V. Taylor and N.T. Wright), and 286–302 (A.E. Harvey).
108. Edgar V. McKnight, *The Bible and the Reader*, 93–94.
109. Kevin Hart, "The Poetics of the Negative" in Stephen Prickett (ed.) *Reading the Text. Biblical Criticism and Literary Theory*, Oxford: Blackwell, 1991, 289; cf. 281–340.
110. Dallas M. High, *Language, Persons and Belief: Studies on Wittgenstein's Philosophical Investigations and Religious Uses of Language*, New York: Oxford University Press, 1967, 142.

CHAPTER XVI

The Hermeneutics of Pastoral Theology: (2) Further Reading-Situations, Pluralism, and "Believing" Reading

1. Some Implications of Speech-Act Models for Enquiring and Believing Reading (Ninth Model); and the Socio-Critical Quest to Transcend Instrumental Uses of Texts (Tenth Model)

In the Introduction I set out how I came to be concerned about language-*effects*. In Ricoeur's metaphor, effects focus on what occurs "in front of" the biblical text, in contrast to the author's situation "behind it" or forces generated internally "within it". But I also expressed deep reservations about the pragmatic tradition which reduces meaning to *de facto* reader-effects in which by definition we cannot conceive of systematic mistakes, for the meaning *is* what the reader *makes of* the text. How are these two standpoints to be reconciled?

In speech-act theory, which constitutes the ninth model to be explored in this discussion, the determinant for the effects which an utterance or written communicative message produces is *the nature of the act which the agent who speaks or writes performs*. It has the quality of *directedness* which, in Searle and other post-Wittgensteinian theorists denotes the "adverbial" intentionality of the speech-act. The effects are performative or illocutionary, in a very large class of cases, within the extra-linguistic world. Normally their directedness implies either that they are addressed to a specific situation or that they apply to types or patterns of situation. *Promises*, characteristically, are seldom indiscriminate (though they can be; for example, by politicians in elections). They carry with them commitments to action on behalf of specific persons, types of persons, or all persons, or on behalf of persons in given patterns of situation. *Authorizations* are directed towards those who are designated as addressed, and who fall within certain institutional categories or extra-linguistic situations. Acts of *forgiveness and liberation* likewise presuppose appropriate conditions: a situation of recognized guilt or bondage; a desire to enjoy and to take advantage of freedom; and so on.

In contextual pragmatism and in reader-response hermeneutics the kinds of processes and effects which are envisaged differ both in their nature and in their bases from those which we have just outlined. In the case of speech-act theory, the initiating, enabling, or creative act does not originate with the reader, except in the case of such sub-categories as acts of praise, confessions, or prayers. (We leave aside, for the present, the distinctively theological question of whether such acts are responsive components within the frame of a divine-human-divine dialogue). In liturgical texts, for example in the Psalms, *readers* are invited to perform illocutionary acts which carry commitments and responsibilities beyond the saying of the words themselves. But these transcend social convention: they entail extra-linguistic pledges or attitudes, or other "backing". By contrast in reader-response theory the effects are determined by the contingent social horizons themselves which define the community of readers to which a reader belongs. If any act of will is involved, this can be traced only to routinizations which originated in the corporate will of the community; otherwise meaning is either simply causally generated, or count-generated by virtue of conventions alone. But speech-acts entail performance-acts which carry extra-linguistic consequences.

The basis of operative effect is strikingly different in speech-act theory. In the case of *promises* or *authorizations* (and even non-fictional acts of assertion) *something is at stake in the extra-linguistic attitudes and commitments of the speaker or writer*. In the case of *prayers, confessions*, or utterances of repentance or of faith, *something is at stake in the extra-linguistic attitudes or commitments of those readers* who participate in the speech-act character of the text as a speech-act. Here it begins to emerge that certain qualities characterize *"believing" reading*. It is not that believers understand some new propositional content unknown to unbelievers or to enquirers; it is that they participate in the *count-generated act*, to borrow Wolterstorff's term. They perceive themselves as *recipients or addressees* of directed acts of commitment, or of promise. They perceive the utterances in question as carrying with them illocutionary and extra-linguistic *consequences*.

In theological terms, readers may perceive themselves as liberated, empowered, authorized, forgiven and loved in the operation of the text. The theological basis for such illocutionary language lies to hand in the broad notion of covenant, which, whatever its sociological origins in the Old Testament, runs through the later Old Testament writings to become central in the New Testament. The shedding of blood focussed in the pre-Pauline *paradosis* of the Lord's Supper is expressed in terms of "the new covenant in my blood" (1 Cor. 11:25, cf. Mark 14:24; Matt. 26:28). In the theology of the Epistle to the Hebrews there is a play on the performative effect of covenant and legal testament by means of the same dual-purpose Greek word *diathēkē* (Hebrews 9:15; cf. 7:22; 8:8). Law and promise for Paul both reflect performative and self-involving dimensions of covenant (Gal. 3:17). The logical issue is not whether the propositional content of a promise is true or false in Galations 3, but whether its force is "void" or operative (3:17).

This presupposes, however, a *directedness* on the part of texts. In chapter II we alluded more generally to the dimension of *inter-personal address*. In our discussion of intention we alluded to post-Wittgensteinian notions of adverbial "directedness" as characterizing not "intention" but the quality of addressing an utterance or a text to a person, persons, or situation "intentionally", i.e. with some degree of context-specificity and involvement of will. If the word of God is perceived as above all an act of divine love, expressing divine purpose or evaluation, this word has the status of an expression of the divine *will*. To read this word only as religious phenomenology is very much like Austin's example of pseudo-promise and pseudo-response as in the example: "Willie promises, don't you Willie?" It describes a *third-person* assumption about the *possibility* of a first-person promise.

In pastoral theology, then, these linguistic and logical issues become crystallized into questions about what a reader *stakes* in the reading of biblical texts. Does the text "O God in thee I trust" (Psalm 25:2) come to be read as an affirmation or self-involving act of trust? Does it count-generate acts of renewed faith, or does it merely generate a portrayal of the Psalmists's trust? The logical direction of fit between language and reality is, to use Searle's and Recanati's terminology, opposite in each case. If the words express only the Psalmist's trust, they reflect a *word-to-world* direction of fit; if they commit the reader to an act of trust, they embody a *world-to-word* direction of fit. The latter is not force-neutral. It functions *as a self-involving illocutionary act, which carries practical consequences for the life and behaviour of the reader.*

The difference between a force-neutral reading and a self-involving illocutionary reading of "O God, in thee I trust" *does not* (as Searle and Wolterstorff rightly insist about intention and count-generated acts) consist in some supposed second shadow-action or mental process or vocal or emotional intensity; it lies in the capacity of the same linguistic act to *count* as a commissive and as an expressive act which also carries self-involving consequences in practical life. Wittgenstein observes that the locution "I am in pain" is compatible with saying "It's all right; it has gone off now"; but if I say "I love you" – "oh it has gone off now" the behaviour surrounding the speech-act would make it empty. "One does not say: 'That was not true pain, or it would not have gone off so quickly'."[1] To say "In thee I trust" as a self-involving illocution invites the test that the succession of attitudes and behaviour in which it is embedded will not consist predominantly in fear, doubt, or undue self-reliance. One *could* say: "That was not true trust, or it would not have gone off so quickly".

By the same logic, pledges of love ascribed to God or to Christ in biblical texts can be interpreted with the same propositional content either as force-neutral narrative projections in which God is *described as* making pledges by biblical writers (cf. Austin's "he promises, don't you, Willie?") or as *commissive-expressive illocutions in which a pattern of consequences is locked into its illocutionary force*. Dallas High regularly uses the term "personal backing" to describe the logical asymmetry between first-person and third-person utterances identified by Wittgenstein in such examples as "I love; he loves"; "we mourn; they mourn"; "I believe; she believes".[2] One can say "he believes it but it is false"; but not "I believe it but it is false", because "I believe", like "I love", carries *consequences which constrain possible future language and behaviour*. If it is possible to speak of divine love or divine promise as involving constraints, this may be expressed theologically as the voluntary constraints of covenant faithfulness.

In the case of speech-acts of promise, several further consequences may be involved. First, usually some degree of specificity in the semantic boundaries of a propositional content belong to the internal grammar of what makes a promise a promise. One cannot say "I promise to . . ." without specifying some kind of content, how ever vague, conditional, or imprecise. To do so would be to make the promise meaningless or void. When a politician pledges a promise to "go forward into the future" we rightly question whether this is a *promise* of anything. Second, promises carry implications about the extra-linguistic status and situation of the speaker or writer, and addressee. It is empty to promise to "give x" if x is not the speaker's to give. Austin's lectures *How to Do Things with Words* abound in such examples. As he conceded, although performatives operate in terms of *force*, their function remains dependent on issues about the *truth* of certain states of affairs.

Some critical theorists regard such an approach as over-simple. Derrida offers a critique of Austin's approach, and Stanley Fish, in turn, evaluates Derrida's assessments of Austin in his essay "With the Compliments of the Author: Reflections on Austin and Derrida".[3] Clearly Austin's notion, shared by Searle, that an author's real-life public commitments "stand behind" the illocutionary force of speech-acts contradicts Derrida's axiom about "orphaned" or "distanced" speech in written texts, and differs from Barthes's principle about the "death of the author". Fish observes that in Austinian traditions of speech-act theory "distanced or orphaned speech" together with "fictional speech" are regarded "as deviations from the full presence and normative contextuality of face-to-face communication".[4]

Derrida's line of approach is to argue that what Austin views and discusses as a series of *contingent* explanations for *"infelicities"*, (i.e. for conditions that render illocutions "hollow", "void", or inoperative) are actually not contingent but systematic and constitutive for the structure on which they rest. Derrida quotes Austin against Austin himself on the "infelicities" of *all* speech-acts. Fish predictably subsumes everything under "distinctions between different kinds of interpretive practice". The key issue turns on *what we think that "context" means*. Fish asserts: "It is the difference between thinking of a context as something *in* the world and thinking of a context as a construction *of* the world, a construction that is itself performed under contextualized conditions. Under the latter understanding one can no longer have any simple (that is non-interpretative) recourse to context in order to settle disputes or resolve doubts about meaning, *because contexts*, while they are productive of interpretation, are *also products of interpretation*" (first italics, Fish's; second, mine).5

This largely represents a re-formulation of the issues which we have discussed exhaustively in chapter XIV. We examined how Fish's philosophy of language failed to address certain perceptions about language formulated by Wittgenstein. Among many more complex issues, Wittgenstein appeals to observable regularities in extra-linguistic behaviour as "backing" to prevent the inflation of merely internal linguistic currency, in which *systematic* mistakes would become uncheckable, and the distinction between "correct" and *"seems* correct" would begin to dissolve. Wittgenstein is aware that, as he drily observes, statements (p) can always be transposed into the form of constructions: *"I think that p."*, as if these simply reflected our states of mind. But such transposition of philosophical grammar does not exercise a purchase on life, except as an expression of personal backing or personal stake in the assertion. We need not re-trace the arguments of chapter XIV. Here our primary concern is with *theology*. If "context *in* the world" can be reduced exhaustively and without remainder to a *"construction of* the world", we cannot speak of divine action or revelation *in history* in any way that systematically sustains a clear-cut contrast between revelation and idolatry. *Distinctions ultimately collapse between idolatry and faith; between trust in what is worthy of trust and credulity about what is empty but plausible; between worship of community-projections and worship in response to that which addresses us from beyond.*

In biblical literature, as we have argued in chapter VIII, the performative utterances pronounced by Jesus presuppose a Christology. Many examples of promise presuppose states of affairs both on the part of a speaker or writer and the addressee. The invitation "Let him who is thirsty come, let him who desires take the water of life without price" (Rev. 22:17) operates as an *invitation* only if the power to relieve thirst can be exercized, and the addressee perceives himself or herself as being in need. Ronald Thiemann elucidates the extra-linguistic dimensions of the promissory force of the gospel narratives admirably. He writes: "To acknowledge the narrative as God's promise is to confess that Jesus the crucified lives."[6] Promise and acknowledgement or confession presuppose the states of affairs on the basis of which they become operative. Stephen Schiffer identifies this presuppositional background as a sphere of "mutual knowledge" which provides a condition for meaning.[7] All this is far removed from the operational basis of reader-response theory. Speech-act theory, unlike reader-response theory vigorously resists the notion that textual meaning may be equated with readers' intra-linguistic constructs.

The tenth of the ten models under discussion is that of *socio-critical theory*, or socio-critical approaches as metacritical hermeneutics. Socio-critical models also seek to disengage texts and their uses from wish-fulfilments or social constructs which serve only to affirm and to legitimate individual or social interests. Few comments expose more sharply the difference between socio-pragmatic and socio-critical perspective in general than the observation of Janet Radcliffe Richards who, we recall, writes as a feminist who fights "on two fronts." On one side she affirms the need for feminist goals and concerns. On the other side she asserts: "Feminism is not concerned with *a group of people it wants to benefit*, but with *a type of injustice it wants to eliminate*" (her italics).[8] On this basis, feminist hermeneutics would not seek to use texts *instrumentally to serve interests already pre-determined*, but *transcendentally* to explore *trans-contextual criteria* that would define and evaluate in what justice would consist. The approach would be socio-critical, not socio-pragmatic.

This exposes the heart of the *theological* problem implicit in the contemporary trend to welcome a wide plurality of interpretative purposes and interests *without the further task of metacritical ranking*. Many respected colleagues seem to adopt this pluralism. Thus John Barton writes that we are no longer entitled to speak of *"correct"* methods or *"successful"* procedures: "The basic flaw . . . .. is the belief that the question 'How should we read the Old Testament?' can be answered."[9] It is a different matter when Robert Morgan writes: "Several *different* aims are *legitimate*. It is these, not the different *methods*, which provide the best guide through the contemporary maze, because they focus attention on the central problem of biblical interpretation in the West today: The tension between uses of the Bible as scripture in religious contexts and the frequently non-religious aims of modern biblical scholarship."[10] The "legitimacy" of *various* aims is not being called into question. But: *if interests determine how we read the text, and if any interest represents as good a candidate as another, how can biblical texts do more than instrumentally serve interests rather than shape, determine, and evaluate them? How can they unmask oppressive interests if the status of a socio-critical reading is* ranked no higher than a socio-pragmatic reading which serves the interests of the oppressor?

The problem, in this case, is that pragmatic hermeneutics is *diametrically opposed in practice* to the deepest theoretical concerns which lie behind liberation hermeneutics: those whose readings of texts win the day can only be the power groups: the most militant, the most aggressive, the most manipulative.

By contrast, Rowland and Corner remind us that the challenge of liberation hermeneutics is that of how biblical texts may transform *the horizons and the situations of those who have been marginalized*. They refer, for example, to "the subversive memory" of the Apocalypse, "with its alternative horizon beckoning towards a different future." The forces which undergird oppression and injustice are "shown to be unstable and destined to defeat (Rev. 17:16) . . . In contrast the apparent fragility of the witness of those who follow the way of Jesus is promised ultimate vindication (Rev. 7 and 14)."[11] But the Book of Revelation does more than offer dreams of the future. It encourages the faithful to create some ethical distance from the typical behaviour of an oppressive society (Rev. 2:14,20) and resists compromise. Rowland and Corner, however, offer an important contribution when they attack the assumption that liberation "readings" address *only the reading-situations of the oppressed*. They write: "The First World is already intimately involved in the patterns of oppression in the Third World . . . The issue of poverty is not a national one, but an international one."[12] On the other hand, they also trace the importance of narrative-texts and narrative-worlds for the base communities of Latin America and for black theology.

The value of the approach offered by Rowland and Corner lies precisely in this area of the relation between liberation hermeneutics and the reading-situations which it addresses. But the socio-critical and metacritical dimension of theory does not emerge clearly from their work. C. René Padilla addresses metacritical issues in the volume which he co-edits (with Mark Branson) on hermeneutics in the Americas (1986). From a liberation perspective, he observes, the hermeneutical agenda in many more traditional North American circles seems to be determined, and seriously restricted by a hierarchy of interests in which the long-standing "fundamentalism/ liberalism controversy" still persists in shaping hermeneutical interests.[13] In the same volume Pinnock calls attention to the responsibility of theology to explore universals: "to ask about the cause of the whole."[14]

In his *Marx and the Bible* Miranda identifies Paul's universal concern about "the righteousness of God" (Rom. 1:18-3:20) with God's setting to rights the injustice which characterizes corporate human structures.[15] This justice or righteousness is "manifested apart from law" (Rom. 3:21,28), because the "law" of human societal institutions and power-structures cannot achieve this divine justice. The world awaits the justice of the new creation. The experience of the righteousness of God, Miranda concludes, is societal rather than individual. It may be the case that at various points, as Andrew Kirk argues, Miranda "finishes his exegesis of the Old and New Testaments by almost equating biblical and Marxist hope."[16] But in terms of critical theory Miranda urges that biblical texts should themselves "modify our hierarchy of values"; otherwise the Bible "cannot tell us anything new."[17] Socio-critical hermeneutics, then, brings into sharpest possible focus the two axes of trans-contextual critique or trans-contextual system and the particularities and relevances of concrete life-worlds. In Habermas system and life-world represent the two basic axes of metacritical hermeneutics. In the Branson-Padilla volume, where Pinnock calls for reflection on universals, Linda Mercadante argues in her essay of formal response that the key issue remains one of "relevancy" as "really addressing the situation in all its particularity."[18]

2. "The Present Situation" in Hermeneutical Approaches to Pastoral Theology and to Social Science: Criteria of Relevance in Alfred Schutz and the Critique of the Cross

The plea that biblical texts will be allowed to constitute a framework which "absorbs the world rather than the world the text" comes from writers as utterly diverse as Lindbeck and Miranda; and we have observed that David Kelsey and Frances Young ascribe to biblical texts as Christian scripture the capacity *"to shape persons' identities so decisively as to transform them"* (Kelsey's italics).[19] But in pastoral theology many writers and teachers tend to allow reflection to revolve round the present situation. At the beginning of this chapter we noted several definitions of pastoral theology offered by specialists in the field, including Paul Ballard (1988) and Don Browning (1983). Don Browning observes: "It is the primary task of pastoral theology to bring together theological ethics and the social sciences to articulate a normative vision of the human life cycle"; while David Deeks writes in his book on pastoral theology (1987) "Pastoral theology begins with the search we all make for meaning in life."[20] In our introduction to chapter XV we expressed reservations about a tendency to grant too great a privilege to the present situation, as if this provided the one fixed point around which theological reflections should revolve in pastoral theology. We shall now formulate a more sustained argument to this effect. The argument involves the following stages.

(i) Hermeneutical theory exposes the fundamental problem posed in biblical, systematic, and pastoral, theology which stems, as we noted above, from a professional division of labour. Edward Farley identifies this disjunction. The practical character of theological endeavour, he complains, is "defeated from the start by the dispersion of theology into independent areas of scholarship."[21] Nicholas Lash's telling comparison with the "relay-race" model of hermeneutics which we note shortly, confirms this diagnosis. Biblical scholars of a certain kind assume that they can package "what the text meant" and pass it on to the systematic and pastoral theologians as if it were an entity abstractable from the whole hermeneutical process itself. Thus a single hermeneutical process of understanding the interactive horizons of past and present is split apart and segmented into "stages" in which biblical specialists are tempted to regard the texts as "objects" of historical-past enquiry; systematicians are tempted to abstract doctrine from its double-sided historical contingency; and pastoral theologians are tempted to absolutize the present as the key determinant of "relevancy" for assessing what sources and traditions of the past can meaningfully address the present.

We have already traced how biblical scholarship was challenged, especially from 1919, to question whether the past could be objectivized and be "understood" in abstraction from hermeneutical questions about the relation between the past and the present. This was the force of Karl Barth's vigorous protestations in his commentary on Romans to the effect that Jülicher and Harnack offered no more than prolegomena to exegesis, and Bultmann took up this point. As Gareth Jones insists, unlike Barth, Bultmann does not disown the liberalism of Harnack, Wrede, and Herrman, but he does reject the adequacy of their methods.[22] We have also noted in detail that more recently the Oxford biblical specialists John Barton and Robert Morgan have attacked the inadequacy of a purely "historical paradigm". Similarly the Cambridge theologian Nicholas Lash attacks the simplistic tendency to regard biblical specialists as aiming at "description" (or "what the text meant") as against systematic theologians who supposedly aim at "hermeneutics" (or "what the text means"). Such a view, he rightly asserts, "comes dangerously close to endorsing the positivist myth that exegesis is not yet interpretation".[23] This is the context of Lash's allusion to the "relay-race" model.

If hermeneutical theorists rightly attack those biblical scholars who adhere to a seemingly innocent descriptivism, *should not the same challenge be addressed to those pastoral theologians who begin with bare "description" of the present situation in abstraction from its past and future context of theological founding and theological promise?* Might we not justly conclude about some methods of pastoral psychology and the use of sociological data that this, equally, can come *"dangerously close to endorsing the positivist myth that it [social and pastoral analysis] is not yet interpretation"?* (to re-apply Lash's terminology). We shall examine this point more closely in these remaining pages by means of a short discussion of the relation between hermeneutics and the social sciences.

On the other hand, the relation between biblical material and the present situation *cannot be regarded as fully symmetrical.* One test question is this: would it be the same, in principle, *to de-centre the present situation as a criterion* of theological relevance and truth as *to de-centre the biblical texts and their witness to Christ and to the cross as a criterion* of relevance and truth? Much of the argument of the remaining pages serves to elucidate the lack of symmetry between these two perspectives.

Here we return to Lindbeck's argument, noted above. Each in his own way, Lindbeck, Frei, Thiemann, Stroup, and indeed also Miranda, makes this point. In chapter IX we saw the crucial importance for theology of Pannenberg's argument that the *present* can be *understood* only in the light of the *past history of traditions* as these move towards the *promised goal of the future* revealed in a provisional and preliminary way in the resurrection of Christ. For Moltmann, too, the future promise of God may itself bring *transforming discontinuities which transform the meaning of the present in the light of a new future.* What is common to all these seven writers whom we have named is their shared belief that *divine promise shapes both the nature of reality and how the present is to be understood.* In arguments distinctive to this present volume we noted in chapter VIII, and elaborated further in this current chapter that *promissory biblical texts as operating with illocutionary force in terms of a "world-to-word" direction of correspondence creatively and transformingly de-centre the present situation as a fixed or immutable point of reference.*

(ii) In urging the importance of hermeneutical theory not only for biblical interpretation but also for pastoral theology, we may usefully call attention to the controversy over method which hermeneutical theory has engendered in the social sciences. For often the over-privileging of the present in pastoral theology goes hand in hand with a particular reliance on, or sympathy with, the more functional approaches in social sciences which utilize quasi-scientific models of quantifiable responses and generalizable typifications in social, psychological, and educational theory.

In his excellent study *Hermeneutics and Social Sciences* Zygmunt Bauman traces the varying relations between the two disciplines from Dilthey's hermeneutical understanding of the social life-world, through Marx, Weber, Talcott Parsons, Mannheim and Schutz to Schutz's colleague and former pupil, Luckmann, and to Luckmann's well-known collaborator Peter Berger. In chapter XI we noted Marx's contrast between historical understanding rooted in social processes and the ideological nature of "descriptive" objectivism. Weber saw the hermeneutical problem focussed by Dilthey, but attempted to achieve scientific status for social theory by deliberately restricting its agenda *to the sphere of instrumental reason.* By this means social science could adopt the models of economics, with its use of quantifiable statistical patterns. Habermas, as we also saw in chapter XI, viewed this as a disastrous *splitting apart of system from life-world.*

Talcott Parsons widened this disjunction by his structural-functional approach. From the standpoint of hermeneutics and of Habermas, the subjectivities and particularities of human *agents* become typified by Parsons into role-*responses* by *actors.* Responses can be measured; whereas personal agency includes areas more difficult to chart. Karl Mannheim took a very different path. He fully recognized the problem of contextual relativism, but over-pressed it into an ethnocentric account of human rationality. Each age, culture, or social class, he urged, can be assessed or understood only with reference to its own internal norms. "Utopianism" occurs when the norms of a future age are applied to the past. "Ideology" imposes past norms on the present or the future. Mannheim is often said to have laid the foundations of the sociology of knowledge. Through Schutz and Luckmann this finds expression in the well-known and popularly influential book by Berger and Luckmann, *The Social Construction of Reality* (1966), which bears the sub-title "A Treatise in the Sociology of Knowledge". What people often take for granted as "reality", they argue, are "social constructions" transmitted through typifications. They write: "The social reality of everyday life is thus apprehended in a continuum of typifications . . . structured in terms of relevances".[25] Among these social and linguistic habits, texts and religions, among other phenomena, can be perceived to function as "legitimating formulas" which eventually become embedded and perceived as "external and coercive fact".

It would be a mistake, however, to suggest that we have to choose between the sociology of knowledge of Mannheim or Berger and the more instrumental quasi-positivist systemic approach of Parsons. Once again Habermas reminds us of the consequences of splitting explanatory system from hermeneutical life-world. Towards the end of his masterly survey *Hermeneutics and Social Science* Bauman argues that the task of hermeneutics for social science is that of *"constructing a form of life of a 'higher order' which will incorporate previous* [ones] *as . . . sub-forms"* (his italics).[26] This can be achieved, he explains, "by spotting the general in the particular, by enlarging both the alien and one's own experience so as to construct a large system in which each 'makes sense' to the other".[27] It will be apparent that Bauman shares some of the major operational hermeneutical tools which Wittgenstein, Habermas, and Apel also share. Bauman follows Habermas (and, we noted in chapter XI, Apel) in arguing that hermeneutical understanding rests ultimately on *"a broader basis of intersubjectivity which forms of life could share"* (his italics).[28]

From a theological viewpoint it is not surprising that Bauman is more cautious than Habermas about the limitations of what he calls "sociological hermeneutics". This social frame can function mainly as a *negative* critique to expose systematic distortion in understanding between sub-forms of life. Its positive contribution is to ensure, as Wittgenstein expresses it, that we understand enough "to go on", or in David Tracy's terminology, following Gadamer, that "conversation" may continue. Bauman's main points are that: (a) understandings of "present situations" are always interactive understandings, *always on the move*; and (b) that *in principle* the present is to be understood as a sub-form of life to be contextualized within the *larger or "higher"* frame or form of life, shared by the interpreter, that transcends *both* horizons of particularity. This is true to the angle of approach of Habermas and Gadamer, and implicitly even if not explicitly, in Wittgenstein.

We understand the present by *incorporating it within some larger frame*; we do not "understand" simply by making "the present situation" equivalent to the horizon of understanding. It would be over-simple to transpose this into a well-worn polarization between "Bible-centred" and "experience-centred" orientations in theology; it arises from deeper and wider questions about the very nature of understanding, and the relativizations of the present within the larger frame of past, present, and future. Along the way, it also explodes an over-simplified model of pastoral theology as "study of the objective data" of sociological, psychological, and educational description, as that which in turn determines "relevance" in and for theology. Such description would never be value-neutral. Moreover theology itself is co-extensive with the larger frame of biblical and eschatological horizons within which sources and interpretations of both past and present operate.

(iii) The next step in the argument takes us decisively further forward. We observed in our review of socio-critical and liberation hermeneutics in this present chapter that a theological concern about universals (as voiced by Pinnock) seemed to stand in hermeneutical tension with a concern for particulars and for *"relevancy"* (as voiced by Linda Mercadante). At first sight the importance of *"relevancy"* seems to call strongly for decisive emphasis on the present situation and its particularities. But a careful examination of one of the most important sociological expositions of this concept seems to suggest a surprising conclusion, which brings us back to questions about *enlarged horizons* and eventually to universals. The work to which we refer is the important contribution of Alfred Schutz. His work on criteria of relevance appears in his *Collected Papers* (Eng. 1962, 1964, 1966) and in his *Reflections on the Problem of Relevance* (Eng. edn.1970).[29] An excellent critical commentary on this area has been provided by Ronald R. Cox (1978).

Alfred Schutz developed the category of *life-world* which he found in Husserl, and, less directly, Dilthey. Like Husserl and Dilthey, Schutz was concerned about the status of "objective" understanding of the subjectivities of persons and of social actions and agencies. He parted company from

Husserl, however, in refusing to "bracket out" the pre-reflexive life-world, but by beginning with it. The life-world yields routine patterns which we scarcely notice because we take them for granted. Retrospectively we assign meaning to *what is relevant to particular purposes at hand by processes of typification.* In his specialist critique of Schutz's theory of relevance, Ronald Cox urges that "systems of relevance" move on and undergo change "as we work toward our purposes and goals"; they apply "until further notice".[30] Even more important, because typifications gloss over unique particularities, the *group* becomes fundamental in *sharing* systems of relevance. Hence: *the emerging of new purposes and new interests in the context of a new or wider social interaction and fresh information-inputs will produce new criteria of relevance and revise prior typifications.*

A concrete illustration will illuminate the principle. We may envisage *the transformation of criteria of relevance brought about by the experience of loving another person.* Examples from everyday life abound on all sides. A young person may share with an "in-group" interests in rock music and motorbikes. He or she falls in love with someone whose peers from a different "in-group" reflect typifications and relevances drawn from an enthusiasm for classical music and English cathedrals. If the two persons are really "in love", each of them will discover that his or her criteria of relevance *rapidly expand and become transformed.* Further, their *prior typifications of each other's relevances will be shattered and disengaged from mere stereotypes.*

In theological terms, however, love represents the major transforming force of all systems and criteria of relevance. Interests which have hitherto gathered round the self as a system of self-centred relevance begin to be re-grouped and re-ranked round the self of another, or even the Other. Ultimately, and in the sharpest theological terms, a person may share in the experience to which Paul alludes: "The love of God is poured into our hearts through the Holy Spirit, who has been given to us" (Rom. 5:5). In this case, the outgoing love from the heart of God to his creation *will constitute a new motive-force that re-defines criteria of relevance for the believer: the goal of transformation into the image of Christ is to see the world through the eyes and interests of God's purposes for the world.*

We saw, however, from the work of Frei, Thiemann, Stroup, and others that biblical narrative texts played a decisive part in allowing and enabling readers *to identify* God's personhood and purposes through Christ. Most sharply and pointedly of all, in Christian theology these come to a focus in the cross and resurrection of Christ. The enfleshment of the divine Word in Christ and in the event of the cross constitute the extra-linguistic reality on which promissory and other illocutionary forces and transforming effects depend for their operative validity. We could not conceive of *this foundation reality* as no more than "symmetrical" with subsequent moments in the hermeneutical process, least of all simply "the present situation". *The cross transforms present criteria of relevance: present criteria of relevance do not transform the cross. Salvation is pro-active, not re-active, in relation to the present.*

Current fashions in theological education have, oddly, appealed sometimes to hermeneutical theory in order to place disproportionate weight on "understanding the present situation" at the expense of time and energy devoted to understanding biblical texts and the stable tradition of pastoral case-studies which we call historical theology. One move is to appeal to Latin American hermeneutics and to Paulo Freire's notion of *concientización*. If this means primarily allowing an active *engagement* between the horizons of biblical texts and present horizons, this is all to the good. But often in practice it means a separate exercise of sociological reflection on the present in which the full resources of biblical and historical-theological horizons are not yet brought into full play.

Another move is to appeal to the contrast in hermeneutical theory between the instrumental rationalism of Enlightenment "method" and a Gadamerian or neo-Marxist emphasis on the practical dimensions of understanding. This emphasis lies behind Thomas Groome's approach to Christian education. He rightly rejects an objectivist "spectator theory of knowledge".[31] He engages with Dilthey's notion of the life-world, and with its development in Habermas. Groome seeks "a *praxis* way of knowing" which remains "life-centred", in contrast to a pre-occupation with "ideas" or mere sources of ideas.[32] The Christian story and the Christian vision then assume the role of a partner of in dialogue in a process which Groome calls "a dialectical hermeneutic".[33]

There remains, however, a deep ambivalence in Groome about "the present". He writes: "The 'present' is the only time that actually exists for us, and within the present reside the heritage of the past and the possibility of the future . . . The present is a source of knowledge *in its own right* (my italics). The concern for the present is an expression of the creative dimension of educational activity".[34] We may appreciate Groome's concern that those who learn experience *living* encounter with the past in which they make it their own. But in hermeneutical terms he embraces one half of Gadamer (the "Rorty" half) without entirely adequate attention to the other. First, Gadamer is so very careful to stipulate that we cannot appropriate the horizons of the past in the present without the utmost critical endeavour to respect their distance and difference in the first place. Second, the pre-judgments of the interpreter, which are anchored in the broader historical life-flow of "universal history" are more important and more fundamental than the conscious judgments in which "the 'present' is the only time that actually exists for us" (to use Groome's phrase). To shift the ontological priority from historical reality to the enactments of present finite acts of social understanding comes near to interpreting Gadamer along the lines followed by Rorty.

In spite of Groome's insights, this approach places the emphasis within the hermeneutical process at a point which is unnecessarily restricting for Christian theology. His work has a positive place as a warning against a theology which is objectivist, disengaged, over-cerebral, or antiquarian. But any emphasis on "the present situation" must very clearly seek an understanding of the present which allows it to be perceived within the broadest possible horizons from the very outset of the hermeneutical process of identifying what *counts as* "present experience" of a relevant nature. We may recall some words of C.H. Dodd. He writes: "We may well turn away from the narrow scene of individual experience at the moment, to the spacious prospect . . . in the Bible . . . Here we trace the long history of a community which through good fortune and ill tested their belief in God, and experimented too in varieties of beliefs, with the result that the 'logic of facts' drove deeper and deeper the conviction that while some ways of thinking of God are definitely closed, this way lies open and leads on and on . . . The factor of historical tradition cannot be excluded."[35] The sentences were written in 1928.

3. The Transformation of Criteria of Relevance and Power in the New Horizons of the Cross and Resurrection: Towards a New Understanding of Hermeneutical Pluralism

Ever since the work of Dilthey it has been recognized that hermeneutics arises from interaction or dialectic between the general and the particular, the universal and the contingent, the critical and shifting horizons of life-worlds. Objectivism and a pre-occupation with wholly "scientific" deductive and inductive generalizations about texts collapses the tension into a scientific, positivist, or formalist-doctrinal, system. Contextual relativism, social pragmatism, and deconstructionism, collapses the tension into a socio-contingent, fluid, life-world, in which horizons constantly shift simply in accordance with the flow of life as it is.

Among other writers, Pannenberg and Moltmann see that such a collapse would represent a *betrayal of the critical character of Christian theology* as that which offers a *critique* of life, and *not merely a descriptive reflection of it as it is*. Similarly Habermas and Apel view such a collapse as selling out the possibility of a genuinely *social critique of human life* to settle for mere pragmatic affirmation of the interests of the present community at the present moment.

In this closing section I shall argue that *in one sense hermeneutical pluralism is inevitable* because, on the basis of the historical situatedness of the interpreter and his or her reading-community *within a prior life-world,* to use John Barton's strikingly clear comment, *we cannot assess one reading-model in terms of another.* To seek to *impose* some universal model, or even to impose a model onto other readers as "primary" would be to operate in the same authoritarian terms that social pragmatists use but disguise as liberal pluralism. On the other hand, *Christian theology would move into self-contradiction if it ceased to evaluate the prohibition of idolatry, the message of the cross, and the universality of eschatological promise as merely context-relative*; as the *product* or *construction* of a particular social culture with no claim to offer a *universal critique* of life and thought, and even a *metacritique* of other criteria of thought, understanding, and action.

We need to explore both of these axes of life-world and trans-contextual critique before we can fully grasp the degree of complexity with which they interact in a theory of hermeneutics which is compatible with Christian theology. In the background to this final discussion the influence of Pannenberg, Moltmann, Habermas, and Wittgenstein, all play a part in approaching questions about how life-worlds and horizons relate to open systems, and Searle, Wolterstorff, and Schutz offer fundamental insights about the relation between pluralism, metacriticism, and self-involving, transforming, language within a life-world.

The example of the young couple whose criteria of relevance and interest become transformed when they fall in love, and when they interact with each other's "group", brings into focus one way of understanding the relation between metacritique and pluralism. In one sense their experience affirms the reality and inevitability of pluralism: what, up to that moment, they had taken for granted as the *only* obvious way of understanding and evaluating the world has become relativized as no more than one option among others. But in another sense, their love-relationship has now *enlarged* their understanding, with the result that their former interests and stereotypifications appear from their new and transformed vantage-point to be relatively *narrow, ill-informed,* and *self-centred.* Whether or not they have ever encountered the term "metacritical", their new attitudes will at very least imply fresh *judgments,* including *re-assessments* of earlier *criteria* of relevance, i.e. a *critical re-ranking* of their earlier *critical norms.*

Nevertheless the battle has not yet been won by the systematist against the pluralist. For, to extend the analogy, this couple may become disillusioned with their relationship and drift apart. The motor-bike enthusiast may come to rationalize what had come to be perceived as an *enlarged* life-world in which the self had become de-centred for the sake of the other as an artifice and delusion, in which the life-world imposed the instrumental self-interests of the other in ways which would have proved to be oppressive of the self's freedom. Indeed the motor-bike enthusiast now "sees through" classical music as a bourgeois artifact designed to maintain the living-standards of professional middle-class musicians. All the while we remain at the level of *the life-world alone*, the transcending of pluralism will remain relative and temporary.

From this angle hermeneutical pluralism seems "right". For a reader who retains a commitment to thoroughly Marxist criteria of relevance, biblical texts *can* only be read as socio-literary indicators of causal socio-historical processes which "produce" them as devices which reflect and serve given socio-political interests and conditions of society. But is the recognition of the inevitability of such pluralism the same as the belief that each life-world is self-contained, and incapable of metacritical ranking in terms of a trans-contextual theory? Probably *few confusions have more seriously damaged the contemporary debate than the confusion between recognizing the inevitability of contextual pluralism at the level of establishing critical norms and the mistaken assumption that to attempt to move in the direction of a provisional and corrigible meta-critical ranking of such norms is thereby to deny this inevitability.*

In relation to the metacritical claims of Christian theology we may attempt at this point to approach the problem from the other end. On what basis, if any, does Christian theology seek to call into question the realities of social contextualism? We may briefly formulate and identify three fundamental principles which we shall then explicate and elaborate. (i) The *prohibition against idolatry and the reality of the cross seem by definition to lose their currency if they are deemed to operate only in relation to given cultures and contexts.* They are paradigm cases of trans-contextual claims. Yet undeniably they both emerge *from within a particular tradition of events and expectations* which has socio-contingent historical features; namely the history of the Jewish people and of Old Testament thought. (ii) We shall explore the argument that the integrity and directedness of biblical texts themselves become maximized when we recognize their *illocutionary force as address, promise, liberation, pardon, and commission*. Yet clearly to read "bless the Lord, O my soul, and forget not all his benefits, who forgives all your iniquity" (Ps. 103:2,3) with the illocutionary force of *an act of praise and thanks* falls within the socio-theological category of "believing reading", and in this respect seems context-relative to given reader-situations. (iii) The biblical texts witness to a *universal horizon of eschatological promise* in which it is pledged that the world is to be transformed in accordance with what Searle terms "a world-to-word" direction of fit. But again, whether this *counts as* world-changing promise may seem to depend on beliefs about the status of the texts which operate in given community-contexts.

(i) *Every tradition in the New Testament about the cross challenges any context-relative or ethnocentric understanding of its status:* the cross impinges equally on "Jew and Greek, slave and free, male and female" (Gal. 3:28).

It reverses all contextual traditions of wisdom including scribal authorities, wisdom traditions, philosophical world-views, and religious hunger for pragmatic criteria (I Cor. 1:18–25). Christ cannot be parcelled out (I Cor. 1:13). The single new creation embraces all in one new person (II Cor. 5:17; Eph. 2:15); for all merely contextual criteria of relevance, especially criteria centred on the individual or corporate self, share a single all-embracing crucifixion (Rom. 6:3–11). Baptism constitutes the sign of oneness that transcends ethnocentric division in the one baptism (Mark 10:38; Eph. 4:4,5). The cup which proclaims the cross (I Cor. 11:26) is, like the bread, one (I Cor. 10:16,17). Whereas Paul underlines the *transcending of ethnic relativity* in the cross, the writer to the Hebrews stresses its *temporal finality*, as finished, entire, complete, and definitive, and wholly incapable of future revision (Hebs. 1:3; 5:9; 6:19,20; 7:11–28; 8:5,6; 9:11–14,26; 10:12,14; 11:1). John disengages Christology from context-relative criteria by providing a *cosmic and universal* ontological frame for the gospel narrative (John 1:1–5,9–14; cf. 8:12,58; 11:25; 20:28,31).

The major hermeneutical point about the cross, however, lies in *its discontinuity with contextual or self-centred criteria of relevance; rather, it establishes new criteria of relevance*. George Stroup speaks here of the "collision" of identity which occurs when the transforming power of the cross addresses humankind. Stephen Crites and Ronald Thiemann make similar points, as we have noted. But the point is made most powerfully by J. Moltmann. Moltmann rightly urges that *the cross and the resurrection have a capacity to transcend and to surprise all prior human expectations which are projected forward simply on the basis of present states of affairs*. Moltmann writes in his *Theology of Hope*: "The experience of the cross of Christ means ... the experience of the god-forsakenness of God's ambassador ... The experience of the appearance of the crucified one as the living Lord ... means the experience of the nearness of God in the God-forsaken one ... the revelation of the identity and continuity of Jesus in the total contradiction of cross and resurrection ... A continuity in radical discontinuity, or an identity in total contradiction."[36]

In his later book *The Crucified God* Moltmann expands the notion of the cross, far from representing "answer" to a religious quest, as a *critique*: it *criticizes* and *reforms* the church from beyond its boundaries (*pace* Fish) and "develops ... beyond a criticism of the church into a criticism of society".[37] *It becomes a socio-critical principle*, which by apprehending "the pain of the negative" gives meaning to hope which lies beyond it, and which is not merely generated by present values. It thereby offers not only new horizons, but "a new self ... 'Whoever seeks to gain his life will lose it, but whoever loses his life will preserve it' ... self-emptying for the sake of others."[38] As if he were looking over his shoulder at socio-pragmatic hermeneutics, Moltmann writes of sharing in the cross as leaving "behind the circle of those who share and re-inforce" one's own opinions, seeking individual or corporate self-preservation at all costs. For the person who shares crucifixion with Christ, there is alienation "from the wisdom, religion, and power politics of his society".[39]

In this sense, the cross and resurrection stand not only as a critique of human self-affirmation and power, but also as a *meta-critique which assesses other criteria, and which transforms the very concept of power*. The power of the cross lies *precisely not in rhetorical self-assertion or manipulation* (I Cor. 2:1–5). Graham Shaw's account of Mark presupposes that Mark has entirely misunderstood the cross. The power of the cross does *not lie in what merely overwhelms us as impressive* (II Cor. 8 through to 13). It is *power-in-weakness* (I Cor. 1:23–25) because it is derived from "a Christ crucified" (I Cor. 1:23). *It revaluates self-affirming, manipulative, dominating power as self-destructive.*

Nevertheless, it remains the case that the cross can be *seen as* complete, perfect, sufficient, and final *within the specificity of the traditions of promise and fulfilment* reflected in the Old Testament, with its axioms about sacrifice, sin, and atonement; in Paul, with his distinctive theology of being crucified and raised with Christ as a single new humanity; and in Hebrews, John, and other Christian contexts of interpretation. From the standpoint of pluralism these appear "privileged", and in the end a conflict of truth-claims may be inevitable. Here theological interests are best served by encouraging pluralities of readings, since each reading answers the agenda reflected in a life-world, and one mode of reading may lead to another. But this does not entail abandoning a metacritical judgment about the universal status of theology, as a matter of principle, as Pannenberg insists. In any case, the cross and the message of the resurrection will be deemed conspicuously to *transcend* in terms of creative surprise what was simply otherwise "in" the tradition which first framed the message.

(ii) We may also explore the claim, which outside Jewish-Christian traditions will be regarded as speculative and subjective, that *the biblical texts themselves function with greatest integrity and coherence with their directedness when they function* (where appropriate) *as illocutionary acts of address, promise, commission, decree, praise, celebration, pardon, liberation, and authorization*. It would be a mistake to assume that "unbelieving", "enquiring", and "believing" reading may always diverge in their understandings of what Searle and Recanati term "the propositional content" in the case of communicative or transmissive texts. But they undeniably diverge in what Evans calls their reader-*involvement*; in what Searle and Recanati call their illocutionary *force*; and in what Wolterstorff calls their *count-generation*. As Wolterstorff points out, it is *not* simply reading-conventions or community-conventions (*pace* Culler and Fish) that determine whether "an act A will count as an act B... At the centre of the phenomenon of act A counting as act B is not the existence of rules and conventions, also not the existence of intentions, but rather the acquisition of rights and responsibilities" (even though admittedly "convention" and "intention" "play a role").[40]

This brings us to a key question for the present discussion. Does the actual operation of illocutionary force depend on factors extrinsic to the beliefs of readers? As we have seen from Searle the operational status of directives may differ from those of expressives, and commissives may share in either or both sets of conditions. A psalm of praise (*expressives, behabitives*) may be read *as an act of praise* only if the reader has certain beliefs and certain patterns of attitude and response. But a *directive or verdictive* biblical text may operate as an *act of commanding or act of pardon* not on the basis of *whether the reader recognizes it as such*, but on the basis of *what status and authority stands behind the text*. Wolterstorff emphasizes that the general principle of count-generation does not *depend on* subjective beliefs. He writes: "*One act may count as another even though no one counts it as the other* . . . Counting as is a matter of prima facie rights and responsibilities, not a matter of *according* and *acting in accord with* rights and responsibilities" (first italics mine, second set, Wolterstorff's).[41]

An analogy might be suggested. If a judge who is duly appointed pronounces a terrorist either sentenced or pardoned in a court sitting in due process, the prisoner and those associated with the cause may claim "not to recognize this court". *De facto* pluralist readings, by the same token, will not necessarily "recognize" parables of Jesus or epistles of Paul *as declaratory and verdictive acts of pardon* in this or that reading-situation. Within the metacritical frame of Christian theology the illocutionary status of decrees, promises, commissions, acquittals or commands *does not depend on whether readers have certain beliefs about* them. But *de facto* they *will not and probably cannot be "read" in this self-involving performative way from within horizons and life-worlds in which different beliefs set a different hermeneutical agenda*. In relation to the *internal norms of these horizons and life-worlds* non-illocutionary readings would be "right" in a pluralist sense. Within the frame of a Christian theological system they would *also* be "wrong" in a metacritical sense. For socio-pragmatic theorists such as Rorty and Fish, whether we "recognize the court" is *always* a matter of internal relative norms. Whether someone "is" a terrorist or a freedom-fighter must, in pragmatic theory, always remain a matter of interpretation on the basis of the *internal* norms of dominant or ascendent communities at any given time; even if this criterion masquerades as a universal ethical criterion sanctioned by international law.

The first and the second principles come together in the New Testament understanding of "proclaiming" (*kēryssō*) the message of the cross. In his book *The Risk of Interpretation* (1987) Claude Geffré rightly notes the interactive relation between narrative description of states of affairs and a "preaching addressed to" hearers and readers as "performative statements" (*sic*).[42] Both dimensions characterize the proclamation of the cross and the resurrection. Thus brief exclamatory confessions "The Lord has risen indeed" (Luke 24:34) constitute in the words of J. Delorme and C. Geffré, acts which "proclaim faith rather than state it . . . language is not [a] neutral instrument."[43] As Vernon Neufeld argued, early Christian confessions are neither purely expressions of personal stance nor purely descriptive statements, but they portray states of affairs to which the speaker stakes his or her personal signature. In the language of Wittgenstein and of High, the speaker "stands behind" the words giving *a pledge and personal backing* that he or she is prepared to undertake commitments and responsibilities that are entailed in extra-linguistic terms by the proposition which is asserted. This is part of what "believing reading" of biblical texts entails for the Christian community.

(iii) Christian theology also sees the cross and resurrection of Christ as the ground of possibility and affirmation of an eschatology of promise, of which the resurrection constitutes the firstfruits. For the earliest Christians the apocalyptic and eschatological context of the resurrection proclaimed its cosmic status and therefore its universal significance. It heralded nothing less than new creation. Nevertheless history continued, and Christian understanding still operated within a temporal-historical-contingent frame in which the church could make fallible judgments, which in turn could be corrected as horizons expanded with experience which moved towards the future. On the one hand, as Pannenberg rightly insists, the resurrection and Christology provide a "centre" for a universal horizon which transcends this or that context-relative life-world. On the other hand, it does not deliver Christian interpretation from fallibility, and from the need to revise understanding as horizons temporally expand.

Nevertheless because of the definitive nature of eschatological promise affirmed in Christ, it remains no longer adequate to speak as if competing or divergent life-worlds could not be evaluated within some broad quasi-systemic frame. Because understanding remains fallible and corrigible, such a system, even one focussed on Christology and resurrection as its centre, does not constitute a closed system. Indeed, the very notion of a closed system is more likely to represent some idolatrous distortion than that which reflects the ongoing creativity of the living God. Nevertheless the cross, we have said, relativizes and calls into question the respective corporate claims and corporate self-interests of Jews and Gentiles, male and female, slave and free. As Paul argues throughout Romans, it places Jewish Christian and Gentile Christian, Jew and Gentile, precisely on the same footing as debtors to divine grace. On such a basis different cultural traditions are to "accept one another" (Rom. 15:7).

The decisive factor in determining the hermeneutical significance of this universal eschatological horizon is the dimension of promise and of the unrevisable divine evaluation which is expressed in language about the last judgment. Social contingency and hermeneutical life-world remain a necessary context of understanding in so far as the significance of all human life and expressions of communication and production remain provisional until the definitive verdicts of last judgment. Only at the last day will the "criss-crossings and overlappings" between interpenetrating language-games and life-worlds be portrayed within the frame of a definitive general system, when God will be all in all, and all assessment and significance will be fully "public". Meanwhile, evaluations from within the horizons of life-worlds remain provisional and open to misunderstanding and to revision.

Promise, nevertheless, springs from a creative relation to this eschatological goal, as that which God wills for his world. In contrast to reader-response theory and to socio-pragmatic models of hermeneutics, it does not "create" by facilitating mere human "construction" of meaning from unrealized inner resources of corporate or individual imagination and anticipation or projection. Once again, in this connection we recall Ricoeur's warnings about projections of interpretation which can be *idolatrous*. By contrast, divine promise transforms the world-as-it-is in accordance with the word of promise: in Searle's language, in a world-to-word direction of fit.

Christian pilgrimage, as the Epistle to the Hebrews makes clear, consists in thought, faith, and patterns of action which are shaped in accordance with such promise. Reading biblical texts opens these horizons of promise. These are not simply reading-constructs, even though readers are invited to become active in reading-processes, listening in openness to the text and seeking new awareness of the role played by their own agenda, interests, expectations, assumptions, and goals. Rather, the texts enlarge reader-horizons to form new horizons. The de-centering of the self which is brought into play by the message of the cross may not be entirely comfortable. As we noted from Bonhoeffer's words in our first chapter the cross as the place of meeting with God may not be at first "agreeable" because it may not "fit" with my own initial criteria of relevance and life-world of social interests. But daily encounter with biblical texts, especially as vehicles of address from God, may transform these horizons in accordance with the creativity of divine promise. Reading-processes may lead to transformation and surprise.

At some levels this may simply reflect the re-ordering of self-discovery which secular literary and hermeneutical theory has assisted us to understand. Charles Winquist speaks of "the variety of levels" at which this self-discovery can take place. This may involve what Winquist calls "a transformation of consciousness ... a re-ordering of values and a new perception of meanings".⁴⁴ But emphatically it may involve much more, because, to take up our earlier quotation from Bonhoeffer, God is not necessarily "a God who in some way corresponds to me, is agreeable to me, fits in with my nature".⁴⁵ Partly for this reason Paul regards even prayers, even human address to God, as evidence of the Holy Spirit's initiating communication *through* persons to God (Rom. 8:15,16). It is arguable that the Spirit initiates "communicative" prayer-texts in recitals of praise of God's saving acts or in articulate intercessions. We might speculate about the Spirit's invitation of "productive" prayer texts in hymns, poetry, exclamatory celebration or "private tongues" (I Cor. 14:2–25). But if address *to* God can be understood as initiated by the Holy Spirit, how much more in the case of address *from* God? In a co-operative shared work, the Spirit, the text, and the reader engage in *a transforming process*, which enlarges horizons and creates *new horizons*.

That *into which* readers are transformed in this reading-process remains partly but not wholly hidden. The promissory horizon of future destiny which beckons the reader is described by Paul as "beholding the glory of the Lord ... being transformed (*metamorphoumetha*) from glory to glory into the image (*eikōn*) of Christ" (II Cor. 3:18). In the hermeneutical terminology of Habermas, the *life-world which is bounded by the readers' present horizons* is in process of transformation towards *new horizons which form an open system* because the system constitutes a transcendental metacritique. Nevertheless, the system, if such it is, remains *open* towards the future, and is therefore still a horizonal life-world, because "it does not yet appear what we shall be, but we know that when Christ appears we shall be like him, for we shall see him as he is" (1 John 3:2).

NOTES TO CHAPTER XVI

1. L. Wittgenstein, *Zettel* sect. 504.
2. Dallas M. High, *op. cit.* 124; cf. 146–63.
3. Stanley Fish, *Doing What Comes Naturally* 37–67; cf. 488–92.
4. *Ibid* 40.
5. *Ibid* 52.
6. Ronald Thiemann, "Radiance and Obscurity in Biblical Narrative", *loc. cit.* 38.
7. Stephen Schiffer, *op. cit.* 30–42 *et passim*.
8. Janet Radcliffe Richards, *The Sceptical Feminist*, 17–18; cf. 11.
9. John Barton, *Reading the Old Testament*, 207.
10. Robert Morgan (with John Barton) *op. cit.* 271 (his italics).
11. Christopher Rowland and Mark Corner, *op. cit.* 141, 142, and 147.
12. *Ibid* 157 and 163.
13. Mark L. Branson and C. René Padilla (eds.) *Conflict and Context: Hermeneutics in the Americas*, Grand Rapids: Eerdmans, 1986, 22.

14. *Ibid* 47.
15. J. Miranda, *Marx and the Bible* 162–63; cf. 178.
16. J. Andrew Kirk, *Liberation Theology: An Evangelical View from the Third World*, London: Marshall, Morgan, and Scott, 1979, 88.
17. J. Miranda, *op. cit.* 123.
18. Mark L. Branson and C. René Padilla (eds.) *op. cit.* 61.
19. George Lindbeck *op. cit.* 118; and David Kelsey *op. cit.* 91.
20. Don Browning, "Pastoral Theology in a Pluralistic Age", *loc. cit.* 187; and David Deeks, *Pastoral Theology: An Inquiry*, London: Epworth Press, 1987, 67.
21. Edward Farley, "Theology and Practice Outside the Clerical Paradigm" in Don S. Browning (ed.) *op. cit.* 30.
22. Gareth Jones, *Bultmann. Towards a Critical Theology*, Cambridge: Polity Press, 1991, 19.
23. Nicholas Lash, "What Might Martyrdom Mean?" in N. Lash, *Theology on the Way to Emmaus*, London: S.C.M. 1986, 77; cf. 75–92 (also in *Ex Auditu*, vol. 1).
24. Peter Berger and Thomas Luckmann, *The Social Construction of Reality. A Treatise in the Sociology of Knowledge*, London and New York: Penguin University Books edn. 1971 (1966), 47 and 59.
25. *Ibid* 76.
26. Zygmunt Bauman, *op. cit.* 217.
27. *Ibid* 218.
28. *Ibid* 240.
29. Alfred Schutz, *Collected Papers* (3 vols), The Hague: Nijhoff, 1962, 1964, and 1966; and *Reflections on the Problem of Relevance* (ed. R.M. Zaner) New Haven: Yale University Press, 1970.
30. Ronald R. Cox, *Schutz's Theory of Relevance: A Phenomenological Critique*, The Hague: Nijhoff, 1978, 3 and 5.
31. Thomas H. Groome, *Christian Religious Education. Sharing our Story and Vision*, San Francisco: Harper and Row, 1980, 145.
32. *Ibid* 147–49.
33. *Ibid* 174.
34. *Ibid* 8.
35. C.H. Dodd, *The Authority of the Bible*, London: Nisbet, 1928, 298–99.
36. J. Moltmann, *Theology of Hope*, 198–99; cf. 201.
37. Jürgen Moltmann, *The Crucified God*, 4.
38. *Ibid* 15 and 17.
39. *Ibid* 24.
40. Nicholas Wolterstorff, *Works and Worlds of Art*, 205.
41. *Ibid* 213.
42. Claude Geffré, *The Risk of Interpretation. On Being Faithful to the Christian Tradition in a Non-Christian Age*, Eng. New York: Paulist Press, 1987, 85.
43. *Ibid* .
44. Charles E. Winquist, *Practical Hermeneutics. A Revised Agenda for the Ministry*, Chico: Scholars Press, 1980, 17 and 36.
45. Dietrich Bonhoeffer, *Meditating on the Word, op. cit.* 44 and 45.

BIBLIOGRAPHY

(* denotes selection of key primary sources for modern hermeneutical theory)

Aageson, J.W. "Scripture and Structure in the Development of the Argument in Romans 9–11" *Catholic Biblical Quarterly* 48, 1986, 268–89.
—— "Typology, Correspondence, and the Application of Scripture in Romans 9–11" *Journal for the Study of the New Testament* 31, 1987, 51–72.
Abercrombie, Nicholas, *Class, Structure and Knowledge: Problems in the Sociology of Knowledge*, Oxford: Blackwell, 1980.
Abraham, M.H., "How to Do Things with Texts", *Partisan Review*, 44, 1978, 566–88.
Achtemeier, Elizabeth, "Female Language for God: Should the Church Adopt it?" in Donald G. Miller (ed.) *The Hermeneutical Quest: Essays in Honour of James Luther Mays*, (Princeton Theological Monograph 4), Allison Park, Pa: Pickwick Press, 1986, 97–114.
—— *The Old Testament and the Proclamation of the Gospel*, Philadelphia: Westminster Press, 1973.
Achtemeier, Paul J., "Omne verbum sonat: The New Testament and the Oral Environment of Late Western Antiquity", *Journal of Biblical Literature* 109, 1990, 3–27.
Ackroyd, P.R. et. al. (eds.), *The Cambridge History of the Bible* (3 vols.), Cambridge: Cambridge University Press, 1963, 1969 and 1970.
Aichele, G., *The Limits of Story*, Philadelphia: Fortress Press and Chico: Scholars Press (S.B.L. Semeia Studies), 1985.
Albano, Peter J., *Freedom, Truth and Hope: the Relationship of Philosophy and Religion in the Thought of Paul Ricoeur*, New York: University Press of America, 1987.
Alter, Robert *The Art of Biblical Narrative*, New York: Basic Books, 1981.
Alter, Robert and Kermode, Frank (eds.), *The Literary Guide to the Bible*, London: Collins, 1987.
Altizer, T.J.J. et. al., *Deconstruction and Theology*, New York: Crossroad, 1982.
Anderson, B.W., "From Analysis to Synthesis: the Interpretation of Genesis 1–11" in *Journal of Biblical Literature* 97, 1978, 23–29.
Anderson, Janice Capel, "Matthew, Gender and Reading", *Semeia* 28, 1983, 3–27.
Apel, Karl-Otto, *Analytic Philosophy of Language and the Geisteswissenschaften*, Dordrecht: Reidel, 1967.*
—— (with Habermas, J. et. al.), *Hermeneutik und Ideologiekritik*, Frankfurt: Suhrkamp, 1971.*
—— *Der Denkweg von Charles S. Pierce*, Frankfurt, a/M: Suhrkamp, 1975.
—— *Towards a Transformation of Philosophy*, Eng. London and Boston: Routledge and Kegan Paul, 1980.*
—— *Understanding and Explanation. A Transcendental-Pragmatic Perspective*, Cambridge, Mass: M.I.T. Press, 1984.*
Arens, E. *Kommunikative Handlungen: die paradigmatische Bedeutung der Gleichnisse Jesu für eine Handlungstheorie*, Düsseldorf: Patmos 1982.

Armogathe, J.-R. (ed.), *Le Grand Siècle et la Bible*, Paris: Beauchesne, 1989.
Atkinson, James, *The Great Light, Luther and the Reformation*, Grands Rapids: Eerdmans, and Exeter: Paternoster, 1968.
Auerbach, Eric, *Mimesis: The Representation of Reality in Western Literature*, Eng. Princeton: Princeton University Press, 1953.
Aurelio, T., *Disclosures in den Gleichnissen Jesu: Eine Anwendung der disclosure-Theorie von I.T. Ramsey*, Frankfurt a/M: Lang, 1977.
Austin, J.L., *Philosophical Papers*, Oxford: Clarendon Press, 1961.
—— *How to do Things with Words*, Oxford: Clarendon Press, 1962 (2nd edn. Cambridge Mass.: Harvard University Press, 1975).*
Avis, Paul D.L., "In the Shadow of the Frankfurt School: from 'Critical Theory' to 'Critical Theology'", *Scottish Journal of Theology* 35, 1982, 529–40.
Bailey, Ken E., *Poet and Peasant*, Grand Rapids: Eerdmans, 1976.
Baird, J. Arthur, *Audience Criticism and the Historical Jesus*, Philadelphia: Westminster, 1969.
Baker, David L., *Two Testaments, One Bible*, Leicester: Inter-Varsity Press, 1976.
Baker, Gordon P. and Hacker, P.M., *Analytical Commentary on Wittgenstein's Philosophical Investigations* (3 vols.) I, Understanding and Meaning; II, Rules, Grammar and Necessity; III, Meaning and Mind, Oxford: Blackwell, 1983, 1988 and 1990.
Ballard, Paul H., "Pastoral Theology as Theology of Reconciliation", *Theology* 91, 1988, 375–80.
Bar-Hillel, Y., "On Habermas' Hermeneutic Philosophy of Language", *Synthese* 26, 1973, 1–12.
Barbour, Ian, *Myths, Models, and Paradigms. The Nature of Scientific and Religious Language*, London: S.C.M., 1974.
Barclay, John, "Mirror-Reading a Polemical Letter: Galatians as a Test Case", *Journal for the Study of the New Testament* 31, 1987, 73–93.
Barnard, Leslie W., "To Allegorize or Not to Allegorize?" *Studia Theologica* 36, 1982, 1–10.
Barnes, Barry, *Interests and the Growth of Knowledge*, London and Boston: Routledge & Kegan Paul, 1977.
Barr, James, *The Semantics of Biblical Language*, Oxford: Oxford University Press, 1961.
—— *The Bible in the Modern World*, London: S.C.M., 1973.
—— *Holy Scripture: Canon, Authority, Criticism*, Oxford: Clarendon Press, 1983.
—— "The Literal, the Allegorical, and Modern Biblical Scholarship", *Journal for the Study of the Old Testament* 44, 1989, 3–17.
Barrett, C.K., "The Interpretation of the Old Testament in the New" in P.R. Ackroyd and C.F. Evans (eds.) *The Cambridge History of the Bible*, Cambridge: Cambridge University Press, 1970, 377–411.
Barth, Karl, *Protestant Theology in the Nineteenth Century*, Eng. London: S.C.M., 1972.
—— *The Theology of Schleiermacher. Lectures at Göttingen 1923–24.*, Eng. Grand Rapids: Eerdmans, 1982.
Barth, Markus, *The People of God*, Sheffield: J.S.N.T.S. 5, 1983.
—— *Conversation with the Bible*, New York: Holt, Rinehart and Winston, 1964.
Barthes, Roland, *On Racine*, Eng. New York: Hill and Wang, 1964.
—— *Elements of Semiology* Eng. London: Jonathan Cape, 1967.*
—— *Writing degree Zero*, Eng. London: Jonathan Cape, 1967.*

—— "Introduction to the Structural Analysis of Narrative", *New Literary History* 6, 1974 (Fr. 1966, from *Communications* 8).

—— *Mythologies*, Eng. London: Jonathan Cape, 1972.*

—— "The Struggle with the Angel: Textual Analysis of Genesis of 32:23–33" in R. Barthes et. al., *Structural Analysis and Biblical Exegesis: Interpretational Essays*, Eng. Pittsburgh: Pickwick Press, 1974 (French 1971), 21–33.*

—— *S/Z*, Eng. London: Jonathan Cape, 1975.

—— *The Pleasure of the Text*, Eng. London: Jonathan Cape, 1975.

—— "From Work to Text" in Josué V. Harari (ed), *Textual Strategies. Perspectives in Post-Structuralist Criticism*, Ithica: Cornell University Press, 1979, 73–81.*

—— "A Structural Analysis of a Narrative from Acts X-XI" in Alfred M. Johnson Jr. (ed.), *Structuralism and Biblical Hermeneutics. A Collection of Essays*, Eng. Pittsburgh: Pickwick Press, 1979, 109–44.*

—— *Criticism and Truth*, Eng. Minneapolis: University of Minnesota Press, 1987.

Barton, John, *Reading the Old Testament. Method in Biblical Study*, London: Darton, Longman and Todd, 1984.

—— "Reading the Bible as Literature: Two Questions for Biblical Critics", *Literature and Theology* 1, 1987, 135–63.

—— *People of the Book? The Authority of the Bible in Christianity*, London: S.P.C.K., 1988.

Bartsch, H.-W, (ed.) *Kerygma und Mythos. Ein theologisches Gespräch* (6 vols.), Hamburg: Reich & Heidrich, 1948 onwards.

Bass, Dorothy C., "Women's Studies and Biblical Studies: An Historical Perspective", *Journal for the Study of the Old Testament* 22, 1982, 3–71.

Bassler, Jouette, M., "The Parable of the Loaves", *Journal of Religion* 66, 1986, 157–72.

Battles, Ford Lewis, "God was Accommodating Himself to Human Capacity" *Interpretation* 31, 1977, 19–38.

Battles, Ford L. and Wevers, Richard, *A Concordance to Calvin's Institutio* 1559, Grand Rapids: Calvin College and Eerdmans (n.d. continuing).

Bauckham, Richard, *The Bible in Politics. How to Read the Bible Politically*, London: S.P.C.K., 1989.

Bauman, Zygmunt, *Hermeneutics and Social Science. Approaches to Understanding*, London: Hutchinson, 1978.

Beisser, Friedrich, *Claritas Scripturae bei Martin Luther*. Göttingen, Vandenhoeck & Ruprecht, 1966.

Beker, J. Christiaan, *Paul the Apostle. The Triumph of God in Life and Thought*, Edinburgh: Clarke, Philadelphia: Fortress, 1980.

Belo, Fernando, *A Materialist Reading of the Gospel of Mark*, Eng. New York: Orbis Books, 1981.*

Belsey, Catherine, *Critical Practice*, London: Methuen, 1980.

Benoist, Jean-Marie, *The Structural Revolution*, Eng. London: Wiedenfeld and Nicholson, 1978.

Berger, Klaus, *Die Gesetzesauslegung Jesu. Ihr historischer Hintergrund im Judentum und im Alten Testament*, Neukirchen-Vluyn: Neukirchener, 1972.

—— "Wissenssoziologie und Exegese des Neuen Testaments" *Kairos* 19, 1977, 124–33.

Berger, Peter and Luckmann, Thomas, *The Social Construction of Reality*, London: Penguin edn. 1971 (1966).

Berger, Peter, *Facing Up to Modernity*, London: Penguin edn. 1979 (1977).
Berkouwer, G.C., *Studies in Dogmatics: Holy Scripture*, Eng. Grand Rapids: Eerdmans 1975.
Berlin, Adele, *Poetics and Interpretation of Biblical Narrative*, Sheffield: Almond, 1983.
Bernstein, Richard, J., *Praxis and Action*, Philadelphia: University of Pennsylvania Press, 1971, and London: Duckworth, 1972.
────── *Beyond Objectivism and Relativism: Science, Hermeneutics, and Praxis*, Oxford: Blackwell, 1983.*
────── (ed.), *Habermas and Modernity*, Cambridge: Polity Press, 1985.
────── "What is the Difference that Makes a Difference? Gadamer, Habermas and Rorty" in Bruce R. Wachterhauser (ed.) *Hermeneutics and Modern Philosophy*, Albany: State University of New York Press, 1986.
Berryman, Phillip, *Liberation Theology*, London: Tauris, 1987.
Best, Ernest, *From Text to Sermon: Responsible Use of the New Testament in Preaching*, Atlanta: John Knox, 1978.
────── *Mark: The Gospel as Story*, Edinburgh: Clark, 1983.
Betti, Emilio, *Allgemeine Auslegungslehre als Methodik der Geisteswissenschaften*, Tübingen: Mohr, 1967.*
────── *Die Hermeneutik als allgenmeine Methodik der Geisteswissenschaften*, 2nd edn., Tübingen: Mohr, 1972.*
Birch, D., *Language, Literature, and Critical Practice*, London: Routledge, 1989.
Black, Max, "Linguistic Relativity: the Views of Benjamin Lee Whorf", *Philosophical Review* 68, 1959, 228–38.
────── *Models and Metaphors: Studies in Language and Philosophy*, Ithaca: Cornell University Press, 1962.
────── (ed.), *The Importance of Language*, Englewood Cliffs: Prentice Hall 1963.
Blackman, E.C., *Biblical Interpretation* London: Independent Press, 1957.
Blank, G.K., "Deconstruction: Entering the Bible through Babel", *Neotestamentica* 20, 1986, 61–67.
Bleich, David, *Readings and Feelings. An Introduction to Subjective Criticism*, Urbana: National Council for the Teaching of English, 1975.*
────── "The Logic of Interpretation", *Genre* 10, 1977, 363–94.
────── *Subjective Criticism*, Baltimore: Johns Hopkins University Press, 1978.
────── *The Double Perspective. Language, Literacy and Social Relations*, Oxford and New York: Oxford University Press, 1988.*
Bleicher, Josef, *Contemporary Hermeneutics. Hermeneutics as Method, Philosophy, and Critique*, London: Routledge & Kegan Paul, 1980.
────── *The Hermeneutical Imagination. Outline of a Positive Critique of Scientism and Sociology*, London and Boston: Routledge & Kegan Paul, 1982.
Bloom, Harold, *Poetry and Repression*, New Haven: Yale University Press, 1976.
──────, Paul de Man, et. al., *Deconstruction and Criticism*, London: Routledge & Kegan Paul, 1979.
Bloomfield, Leonard, *Language*, London: Allen & Unwin 1935 (1933).
Boeckh, Philip August, *On Interpretation and Criticism*, Eng. Norman, Oklahoma: University of Oklahoma Press, 1968. The longer German text was edited after Boeckh's death: *Enzyklopädie und Methodologie der philologischen Wissenschaften*, 2nd edn. Leipzig: Teubner, 1886.*
Boesak, Allan A., *Black and Reformed: Apartheid, Liberation and the Calvinist Tradition*, New York: Orbis, 1984.

―――― *Comfort and Protest: Reflections in the Apocalypse of John of Patmos*, Philadelphia: Westminster, 1987.
Boff, Clodovis, *Theology and Praxis: Epistemological Foundations*, Eng. New York: Orbis, 1987.*
Boff, Leonardo and Boff, Clodovis, *Introducing Liberation Theology*, Eng. London: Burns and Oates, 1987.
Boff, Leonardo and Elizondo, V. (eds.), *Concilium: Theologies of the Third World: Convergences and Differences*, Edinburgh: Clark, 1988.
Bonhoeffer, Dietrich, *Meditating on the Word*, Cambridge, Mass.: Cowley Publications, 1986.
Bonino, José Miguez, *Revolutionary Theology Comes of Age*, London: S.P.C.K. and Philadelphia: Fortress, 1975.
Bonsirven, J., *Exégèse rabbinique et exégèse paulinienne*, Paris: Beauchesne, 1939.
Booth, Wayne C., *The Rhetoric of Fiction*, (2nd edn.) Chicago: University of Chicago Press, 1983.
Boring, M. Eugene, "The Christology of Mark: Hermeneutical Issues for Systematic Theology" in *Christology and Exegesis: New Approaches: Semeia* 30, 1985, 125–54.
Bornkamm, Heinrich, *Luther in Mid-Career 1521–30*, London: Darton, Longman, & Todd, 1983.
―――― *Luther and the Old Testament*, Eng. Philadelphia: Fortress, 1969.
Borsch, Frederick H. (ed.), *Anglicanism and the Bible*, Wilton: Morehouse Barlow 1984.
Bostock, Gerald, "Allegory and the Interpretation of the Bible in Origen", *Journal of Literature and Theology* I, 1987, 39–53.
Bovon, François, "French Structuralism and Biblical Exegesis" in R. Barthes *et al.*, *Structural Analysis and Biblical Exegesis*, Eng. Pittsburgh: Pickwick Press, 1974, 4–20.
―――― *Exegesis. Problems of Method and Exercizes in Reading*, Eng. Pittsburgh: Pickwick Press, 1978.
Braaten, Carl and Clayton, Philip (eds.), *The Theology of Wolfhart Pannenberg*, Minneapolis: Augsburg, 1988.
Brandt, Richard, *The Philosophy of Schleiermacher*, New York: Greenwood Press, 1968 (1941).
Branson, Mark L. and Padilla, C. René (eds.), *Conflict and Context: Hermeneutics in the Americas*, Grand Rapids: Eerdmans, 1986.
Breck, John, "Theoria and Orthodox Hermeneutics" *St. Vladimir's Theological Quarterly* 20, 1976, 195–219.
―――― *The Power of the Word in the Worshipping Church*, New York: St. Vladimir's Seminary Press, 1986.
Brett, Mark G., "Four or Five Things to Do with Texts. A Taxonomy of Interpretive Interests" in D.J.A. Clines, S.E. Fowl and S.E. Porter (eds.) *The Bible in Three Dimensions*, Sheffield: J.S.O.T., 1990.
―――― *Biblical Criticism in Crisis? The Impact of the Canonical Approach in Old Testament Studies*, Cambridge: Cambridge University Press, 1991.
Brown, Colin, *Christianity and Western Thought. A History of Philosophies, Ideas and Movements*, vol. 1., Leicester: Apollos, 1990.
Brown, Raymond, "The *Sensus Plenior* in the Last Ten Years" *Catholic Biblical Quarterly* 25, 1963, 262–85.
Brown, Raymond E., *Biblical Exegesis and Church Doctrine*, New York: Paulist Press, 1985.

Browning, Don S., *Religious Ethics and Pastoral Care*, Philadelphia: Fortress, 1983.
────── (ed.), *Practical Theology*, San Francisco: Harper & Row, 1983.
Brueggemann, Walter, *The Bible Makes Sense*, Atlanta: John Knox, 1977.
────── *The Creative Word. Canon as a Model for Biblical Education*, Philadelphia: Fortress, 1982.
Bruce, F.F., *This is That: The New Testament Development of Old Testament Themes*, Exeter: Paternoster, 1968.
────── *The Epistle of Paul to the Galatians. A Commentary on the Greek Text*, Grand Rapids: Eerdmans, 1982.
Bryant, D.J., *Faith and the Play of Imagination. On the Role of Imagination in Religion*, Macon: Mercer University Press, 1989.
Buckley, J.J., "The Hermeneutical Deadlock between Revelationists, Textualists and Functionalists" *Modern Theology* 6, 1990, 325–39.
Buckley, Walter, *Sociology and Modern Systems Theory*, Englewood Cliffs: Prentice Hall, 1967.
Bultmann, Rudolf, *Theology of the New Testament* (2 vols.) Eng. London: S.C.M. 1952 and 1955.
────── *This World and Beyond. Marburg Sermons*, London: Lutterworth Press, 1960.
────── "New Testament and Mythology" in Hans Werner Bartsch (ed.) *Kerygma and Myth* (2 vols.), Eng. 2nd edn. London: S.P.C.K., 1964 & 1962.*
────── *Existence and Faith. Shorter Writings of Rudolf Bultmann*, Eng. London: Fontana edn. 1964.*
────── *Glauben und Verstehen. Gesammelte Aufsätze* (4 vols.) Tübingen: Mohr, 1964–5. Part translated as *Faith and Understanding I*, Eng. London: S.C.M. 1969.*
Buren, Paul van, *The Edges of Language*, London: S.C.M. 1972.
Burnham, F.B. (ed.), *Postmodern Theology. Christian Faith in a Pluralist World*, San Francisco: Harper and Row, 1989.
Buss, Martin J. (ed.), *Encounter with the Text. Form and History in the Hebrew Bible*, Missoula: Scholars Press (S.B.L. Semeia Suppl.), 1979.
Caird, George B., *The Language and Imagery of the Bible*, London: Duckworth, 1980.
Calloud, Jean, *Structural Analysis of Narrative*, Eng. Philadelphia: Fortress, and Missoula: Scholars Press, 1976 (French 1973).
────── et al., *Signs and Parables. Semiotics and Gospel Texts*, Eng. Pittsburgh: Pickwick Press, 1978.
Calvin, John, *Institutes of the Christian Religion*, Eng. (2 vols.) Edinburgh: Clarke, 1957.
────── *Commentaries*, (Library of Christian Classics 23) London: S.C.M., 1958.
Cannon, Katie Geneva, "The Emergence of Black Feminist Consciousness" in Letty M. Russell (ed.) *Feminist Interpretation of the Bible*, Oxford and New York: Blackwell, 1985, 30–40.
Caputo, John D., *Radical Hermeneutics: Repetition, Deconstruction and the Hermeneutical Project*, Bloomington: Indiana University Press, 1987.
Cardenal, Ernesto, *Love in Practice: The Gospel in Solentiname* (4 vols.) Eng. New York: Orbis, 1977–84.
Carmody, Denise Lardner, *Biblical Woman. Contemporary Reflections on Scriptural Texts*, New York: Crossroads, 1989.
Carroll, R.P., "Sisyphean Task of Biblical Transformation", *Scottish Journal of Theology* 30, 1977, 501–21.
Carson, D.A. (ed.), *Biblical Interpretation and the Church: Text and Context*, Exeter: Paternoster, 1984.

―――― and H.G.M. Williamson (eds.), *It is Written: Scripture Citing Scripture: Essays in Honour of Barnabas Lindars*, Cambridge: Cambridge University Press, 1988.
―――― and Woodbridge, J.D. (eds.), *Scripture and Truth*, Grand Rapids: Zondervan, 1983.
―――― and Woodbridge, J.D. (eds.), *Hermeneutics, Authority and Canon*, Leicester: Inter- Varsity Press, 1986.
Cavell, Stanley, "The Availability of Wittgenstein's Later Philosophy" in *Philosophical Review* 71, 1962, 67–93, also rp. in George Pitcher (ed.) *Wittgenstein: The Philosophical Investigations*, London: McMillan, 1968, 151–85.
―――― *Must We Mean What We Say?*, Cambridge: Cambridge University Press, 1976.
Chapman, J. Arundel, *An Introduction to Schleiermacher*, London: Epworth Press, 1932.
Chase, Frederic H., *Chrysostom, A Study in the History of Biblical Interpretation*, Cambridge: Deighton, Bell & Co., 1887.
Chatman, Seymour, *Story and Discourse: Narrative Structure in Fiction and Film*, Ithaca: Cornell University Press, 1978.
Childs, Brevard S., *Myth and Reality in the Old Testament*, London: S.C.M., 1962.
―――― *Introduction to the Old Testament as Scripture*, London: S.C.M., 1979.
―――― *The New Testament as Canon: An Introduction*, London: S.C.M., 1984.
―――― "Critical Reflections on James Barr's Understanding of the Literal and the Allegorical" *Journal for the Study of the Old Testament*, 46, 1990, 3–9.
Chilton, Bruce D., *A Galilean Rabbi and his Bible: Jesus' own Interpretation of Isaiah*, London: S.P.C.K., 1984.
Chladenius, Johann Martin, *Einleitung zur richtigen Auslegung Vernünftiger Reden und Schriften*, rp. Düsseldorf: Stern, 1969, part (chapters 4 and 8) translated in Kurt Muellner-Vollmer (ed.) *The Hermeneutics Reader: Texts of the German Tradition from the Enlightenment to the Present*, Oxford: Blackwell, 1986, 55–71.
Chopp, Rebecca S., *The Power to Speak: Feminism, Language, God*, New York: Crossroad, 1989.
Church of England Doctrine Commission Report, *Believing in the Church: The Corporate Nature of Faith*, London: S.P.C.K., 1981.
―――― *We believe in God*, London: Church House Publishing, 1987.
―――― *We Believe in the Holy Spirit*, London: Church House Publishing, 1991.
Clarke, D.S., *Principles of Semiotic*, London & New York: Routledge & Kegan Paul, 1987.
Clévenot, Michel, *Materialist Approaches to the Bible*, Eng. New York: Orbis, 1985.
Clines, David J.A., *The Theme of the Pentateuch*, Sheffield: J.S.O.T. Press Suppl. 11, 1978.
―――― "Nehemiah 10 as an Example of Early Jewish Biblical Exegesis" in *Journal for the Study of the Old Testament* 21, 1981, 111–17.
―――― "Deconstructing the Book of Job" in Martin Warner (ed.) *The Bible as Rhetoric. Studies in Biblical Persuasion and Credibility*, London and New York: Routledge, 1990, 65–80. also revised and reprinted in *What Does Eve Do to Help?* (as cited below).
―――― *What Does Eve Do To Help? And Other Readerly Questions to the Old Testament*, Sheffield: J.S.O.T. Suppl. 94, 1990.
Clines, David J.A., Fowl, S.E. and Porter, S.E. (eds.), *The Bible in Three Dimensions: Essays in Celebration of Forty Years of Biblical Studies in the University of Sheffield*, Sheffield: Sheffield Academic Press (J.S.O.T. Suppl. Ser. 87), 1990.

Cohen, L. Jonathan, *The Diversity of Meaning*, London: Methuen, 2nd edn. 1966.
Collins, Adela Yarbro (ed.), *Feminist Perspectives on Biblical Scholarship*, Chico: Scholars Press, 1985.
Collins, R.F., "On Reading the Scriptures" *Emmanuel* 96, 1990, 70–73 and 98–101.
Combrink, H.J.B., "Multiple Meaning and/or Multiple Interpretation of a Text" *Neotestamentica* 18, 1984, 26–37.
Cone, James H., "Biblical Revelation and Social Existence" *Interpretation* 28, 1974, 422–40.
—— *God of the Oppressed*, London: S.P.C.K., 1977 and New York: Seabury, 1975.*
—— *A Black Theology of Liberation*, New York and Philadelphia: Lippincott, 1970.*
Conn, Harvie, M. (ed.), *Inerrancy and Hermeneutics. A Tradition, A Challenge, A Debate*, Grand Rapids: Baker, 1988.
Corrington, Robert S., *The Community of Interpreters: On the Hermeneutics of Nature and the Bible in the American Philosophical Tradition*, Macon Ga: Mercer University Press, 1987.
Court, John M., *Myth and History in the Book of Revelation*, London: S.P.C.K., 1979.
Courtivron, Isabelle de and Marks, E. (eds.), *New French Feminism: An Anthology*, Harvester Press, 1981.
Cox, Ronald R., *Schutz's Theory of Relevance: A Phenomenological Critique*, The Hague: Nijhoff, 1978.
Cranfield, Charles E.B., *A Critical and Exegetical Commentary on the Epistle to the Romans* (2 vols.), Edinburgh: Clark 1975 and 1979.
Crites, Stephen "The Narrative Quality of Experience", *Journal of the American Academy of Religion*, 39, 1971, 291–311.
Croatto, J. Severino, *Exodus. A Hermeneutics of Freedom*, Eng. New York: Orbis, 1981.*
—— *Biblical Hermeneutics: Towards a Theory of Reading as the Production of Meaning*, Eng. New York: Orbis, 1987.*
Cronbach, Abraham, "Unmeant Meanings of Scripture", *Hebrew Union College Annual* 36, 1965, 99–122.
Crossan, John Dominic, *In Parables. The Challenge of the Historical Jesus*, New York: Harper and Row, 1973.
—— *The Dark Interval. Towards a Theology of Story*, Niles: Argus Communications, 1975.*
—— *Raid on the Articulate. Comic Eschatology in Jesus and Borges*, New York: Harper and Row, 1976.
—— "Waking the Bible", *Interpretation* 32, 1978, 269–85.
—— "A Metamodel for Polyvalent Narration", *Semeia* 9, 1977, 105–47.
—— *Finding is the First Act: Trove Folktales and Jesus' Treasure Parable*, Missoula: Scholars Press and Philadelphia: Fortress Press, 1979 (*Semeia Supplements* 9).
—— *Cliffs of Fall: Paradox and Polyvalence in the Parables of Jesus*, New York: Seabury Press, 1980.*
—— "A Structuralist Analysis of John 6", in Richard A. Spencer (ed.) *Orientation by Disorientation. Studies in Literary Criticism and Biblical Literary Criticism in Honour of W.A. Beardslee*, Pittsburgh: Pickwick Press, 1980, 235–49.
—— (ed.) "The Book of Job and Ricoeur's Hermeneutics", *Semeia* 19, 1981, 41–46.

―――― *A Fragile Craft: the Work of Amos Niven Wilder* (S.B.L. Centennial 1980) Chicago: Scholars Press, 1981.
―――― "Difference and Divinity" in Robert Detweiler (ed.) *Derrida and Biblical Studies, Semeia* 23, 1982, 29–40.
―――― "Kingdom and Children. A Study in the Aphoristic Tradition", *Semeia* 29, 1983.
―――― *In Fragments. The Aphorisms of Jesus*, New York: Harper, 1983.
Crystal, David, *Linguistics, Language and Religion*, London: Burns and Oates, 1965.
Culler, Johnathan, *Structuralist Poetics: Structuralism, Linguistics, and the Study of Literature*, London: Routledge and Kegan Paul, 1975 and Ithaca: Cornell University Press, 1975.*
―――― *The Pursuit of Signs. Semiotics, Literature, Deconstruction*, London: Routledge and Kegan Paul, 1981.*
―――― *On Deconstruction: Theory and Criticism After Structuralism*, Ithaca: Cornell University Press, 1982.*
―――― *Framing the Sign: Criticism and its Institutions*, Oxford: Blackwell, 1988.*
Culley, Robert C., "Structural Analysis: Is it done with Mirrors?" *Interpretation* 28, 1974, 165–81.
―――― "Response to Daniel Patte" in Daniel Patte (ed.), *Semiology and Parables. An Exploration of the Possibilities Offered by Structuralism for Exegesis*, Pittsburgh: Pickwick Press, 1976, 151–58.
Culpepper, R. Alan, *Anatomy of the Fourth Gospel: A Study in Literary Design*, Philadelphia: Fortress Press, 1983.
Cunningham, David, "Clodovis Boff and the Discipline of Theology", *Modern Theology* 6, 1990, 137–58.
Curtin, T.R., *Historical Criticism and the Theological Interpretation of Scripture. The Catholic Discussion of a Biblical Hermeneutic 1958–83*, Rome: Pontifica Universitas Gregoriana, 1987.
Daly, Mary, *Beyond God the Father: Toward a Philosophy of Women's Liberation*, Boston: Beacon Press, 1973.
Davies, W.D., *Paul and Rabbinic Judaism. Some Rabbinic Elements in Pauline Theology* (1948) 4th edn., Philadelphia: Fortress, 1980; London: S.P.C.K., 1981.
Dawsey, James, *The Lukan Voice: Confusion and Irony in the Gospel of Luke*, Macon: Mercer University Press, 1986.
Dawsey, J.M., "The Lost Front Door into Scripture: Carlos Mesters, Latin American Liberation Theology, and the Church Fathers", *Anglican Theological Review* 72, 1990, 292–305.
Deeks, David, *Pastoral Theology: An Inquiry*, London: Epworth Press, 1987.
Demetz, Peter, et al., *The Disciplines of Criticism: Essays in Literary Theory, Interpretation and History*, New Haven: Yale University Press, 1968, 193–225.
Denis, A.M., "Foi et exégèse: reflexions sur les fondements theologiques de l'exégèse", *New Testament Studies*, 20, 1973, 45–54.
Derrida, Jacques, *Speech and Phenomena, and Other Essays on Husserl's Theory of Signs*. Eng. Evanston: North Western University Press, 1973 (Fr. 1967).*
―――― *Writing and Difference*, Eng. London: Routledge and Kegan Paul, 1978, (Fr. 1967).*
―――― *Of Grammatology*, Eng. Baltimore London: Johns Hopkins University Press, 1976 (Fr. 1967).*
―――― *La Dissémination*, Paris: Seuil, 1972.

—— (with Julia Kristeva and others), "Positions", *Diacritics*, Diacritics 3, 1973, 33–46 (Fr. 1972).

—— *Marges de la philosophie*, Paris: Minuit, 1972; part translated as "The White Mythology: Metaphor in the Text of Philosophy", *New Literary History*, 6, 1974, 5–74.*

—— *Spurs: Nietzsche's Styles* Eng. Chicago: Chicago University Press, 1972.

—— *The Truth in Painting* Eng. Chicago: University of Chicago Press, 1987.

—— "Living On"/"Border Lines" in Harold Bloom, Paul de Man, Jacques Derrida et al., *Deconstruction and Criticism*, London: Routledge and Kegan Paul, 1979, 75–176.

—— "Of an Apocalyptic Tone Recently Adopted in Philosophy" in *Semeia* 23, 1982, 63–97.

—— *Signéponge* New York: Columbia University Press, 1984.

—— et al., *The Ear of the Other: Otobiography, Transference, Translation*, (ed. C.V. McDonald) Eng. New York: Schocken Books, 1985.

—— *De l'esprit: Heidegger et la question* Paris: Galilee, 1987.

—— *The Post Card. From Socrates to Freud and Beyond* Eng. Chicago: University of Chicago Press, 1987.

Detweiler, Robert, *Story, Sign and Self: Phenomenology and Structuralism as Literary-Critical Methods*, Philadelphia: Fortress and Missoula: Scholars Press, 1978.

—— (ed.), *Derrida and Biblical Studies: Semeia* 23, 1982.

Dillistone, F.W., *The Power of Symbolism in Religion and Culture*, New York: Crossroad, 1986.

Dilthey, Wilhelm, *Gesammelte Schriften V: Die geistige Welt. Einleitung in die Philosophie des Lebens*, and *VII: Der Aufbau der Geschichtlichen Welt in den Geisteswissenschaften*, Stuttgart, Leipzig and Berlin: Teubner, 1927 and 1962.*

—— Vol. VII partly translated in "The Development of Hermeneutics" in H.P. Rickman (ed.) *Selected Writings*, Cambridge: Cambridge University Press, 1976, and part selections in K. Mueller-Vollmer (ed.) *The Hermeneutics Reader*, Oxford: Blackwell, 1986, 149–64.

—— "Types of World-View and Their Development in the Metaphysical Systems" (1911), Eng. in David E. Klemm, *Hermeneutical Inquiry* (2 vols.), Atlanta: Scholars Press, 1986, vol. 2.*

Donfried, Karl P. (ed.), *The Romans Debate: Essays on the Origins and Purpose of the Epistle*, Minneapolis: Augsburg, 1977.

Doohan, L., "Scripture and Contemporary Spirituality", *Spirituality Today* 42, 1990, 62–74.

Dornisch, Loretta, "Symbolic Systems and the Interpretation of Scripture: An Introduction to the Work of Paul Ricoeur", *Semeia* 4, 1975, 1–22.

—— "The Book of Job and Ricoeur's Hermeneutics", in *Semeia* 19, 1981, 3–21.

Dörrie, H., "Zur Methodik antiker Exegese" *Zeitschrift für die Neutestamentliche Wissenschaft* 65, 1974, 121–38.

Draisma, Spike (ed.), *Intertextuality in Biblical Writings. Essays in Honour of Bas van Iersel*, Kampen: Kok, 1989.

Dreisbach, D.F., "Paul Tillich's Hermeneutic", *Journal of the American Academy of Religion* 43, 1975, 84–94.

Dreyfus, Hubert L., "Holism and Hermeneutics", *Review of Metaphysics* 34, 1980, 3–55.

Drury, John (ed.), *Critics of the Bible, 1724–1873*, Cambridge: Cambridge University Press, 1989.
Duffield, Gervase E. (ed.), *The Work of William Tyndale*, Appleford: Sutton Courtenay Press and Philadelphia: Fortress, 1965.
—— (ed.), *The Work of Thomas Cranmer*, Appleford: Sutton Courtenay and Philadelphia: Fortress, 1965.
Dufrenne, Mikel, *Phénoménologie de l'expérience esthétique*, Paris: Universitaires de France, 1953.
Dugmore, C.W. (ed.), *The Interpretation of the Bible*, London: S.P.C.K., 1944.
Duke, J.O., *The Prospects for Theological Hermeneutics: Hegel versus Schleiermacher*, Vanderbilt University Ph.D. Dissertation, 1975, Ann Arbor: University Microfilms, 1979.
Dunn, James D.G., *Unity and Diversity in the New Testament. An Inquiry into the Character of Earliest Christianity*, London: S.C.M., 1977.
—— *Christology in the Making: A New Testament Inquiry into the Origins of the Doctrine of the Incarnation*, London: S.C.M., and Philadelphia: Westminster, 1980.
—— "Levels of Canonical Authority", *New Horizons in Biblical theology* 4, 1982, 13–60 (also rp. in *The Living Word*, 1987,141–76.
—— *The Living Word*, London: S.C.M., 1987.
—— *Romans* (Word Biblical Commentary 38, 2 vols.) Dallas: Word, 1988.
Du Plessis, J.G., "Some Aspects of Extralingual Reality and the Interpretation of Texts" *Neotestamentica* 18, 1984, 80–93.
—— *Clarity and Obscurity. A Study in Textual Communication of the Relation between Sender, Parable and Receiver in the Synoptic Gospels*, Stellenbosch: University of Stellenbosch D.Theol. Dissertation, 1985.
—— "Pragmatic Meaning in Matthew 13:1–23", *Neotestamentica* 21, 1987, 42–56.
—— "Why did Peter Ask his Question and How Did Jesus Answer Him? Or: Implicature in Luke 12:35–48," *Neotestamentica* 22, 1988, 311–34.
—— "Speech Act Theory and New Testament Interpretation with Special Reference to G.N. Leech's Pragmatic Principles", in P.J. Hartin and J.H. Petzer (eds) *Text and Interpretation. New Approaches in the Criticism of the New Testament*, Leiden: Brill, 1991, 129–42.
Dussel, Enrique D., "Historical and Philosophical Presuppositions for Latin American Theology" in Rosino Gibellini (ed.) *Frontiers of Theology in Latin America*, London: S.C.M., 1980, 184–212.
Dwyer, Philip, *Sense and Subjectivity. A Study of Wittgenstein and Merleau-Ponty*, Leiden: Brill, 1990.
Eagleton, Terry, *Literary Theory: An Introduction*, Minneapolis: University of Minnesota Press and Oxford: Blackwell, 1983.
—— "J.L. Austin and the Book of Jonah" in Regina M. Schwartz (ed.) *The Book and the Text. The Bible and Literary Theory*, Oxford: Blackwell, 1990, 231–36.
Ebeling, Gerhard, "Hermeneutik" in *Die Religion in Geschichte and Gegenwart* 3rd edn. Tübingen: Mohr vol. III, 1959, cols. 242–62.
—— *Introduction to a Theological Theory of Language*, Eng. London: Collins, 1973.
Eco, Umberto, "Social Life as a Sign System" in David Robey (ed) *Structuralism: An Introduction*, Oxford: Clarendon Press, 1973, 57–72.
—— *A Theory of Semiotics*, Bloomington: Indiana University Press, 1976.*
—— *The Role of the Reader: Explorations in the Semiotics of Texts*, London: Hutchinson, 1981.*

────── *Semiotics and the Philosophy of Language*, London: MacMillan, 1984.
Elizondo, Virgil and Greinacher, N. (eds.), *Women in a Men's Church: Concilium 134*, Edinburgh: Clark, 1980.
Elliott, J.H., "Social-Scientific Criticism of the New Testament: More on Methods and Models" *Semeia* 35, 1986, 1–33.
Ellingsen, M., *The Integrity of Biblical Narrative. Story in Theology and Proclamation*, Minneapolis: Fortress, 1990.
Ellis, M.H. and Maduro. O (eds.), *The Future of Liberation Theology. Essays in Honor of Gustavo Gutiérrez*, New York: Orbis, 1989.
Engelmann, Paul, *Letters from Ludwig Wittgenstein*, Oxford: Blackwell, 1967.
Erasmus, Desiderius, *The Praise of Folly*, Eng. Chicago: Packard, 1946.
Evans, Donald D., *The Logic of Self-Involvement. A Philosophical Study of Everyday Language with Special Reference to the Christian Use of Language about God as Creator*, London: S.C.M., 1963.*
Evans, Gillian R., *The Language and Logic of the Bible: the Earlier Middle Ages*, Cambridge: Cambridge University Press, 1984.
────── *The Language and Logic of the Bible: the Road to the Reformation*, Cambridge: Cambridge University Press, 1985.
Exum, J. Cheryl, "'You shall Let Every Daughter Live': A Study of Exodus 1:8 - 2:10", *Semeia* 28, 1983, 63–82.
Fann, K.T. (ed.), *Symposium on J.L. Austin*, London: Routledge & Kegan Paul, 1969.
Farley, Edward, "Theology and Practice Outside the Clerical Paradigm" in Don S. Browning (ed.) *Practical Theology*, San Francisco: Harper and Row, 1983, 21–41.
Farrar, Frederic W., *History of Interpretation*, Grand Rapids: Baker, rp. 1961.
Fatio, B. and Fraenkel, P. (ed.), *Histoire de l'exégèse au XVIe Siècle*, Geneva: Droz, 1978.
Fatum, L., "Women, Symbolic Universe and Structures of Silence. Challenges and Possibilities in Androcentric Texts", *Studia Theologica* 43, 1989, 61–80.
Fawcett, Thomas, *The Symbolic Language of Religion*, London: S.C.M., 1970.
Fee, Gordon D., *The First Epistle to the Corinthians*, Grand Rapids: Eerdmans, (N.I.C.N.T.), 1987.
────── "Issues in Evangelical Hermeneutics" *Crux* 26, 1990, 21–26 and 35–42.
Ferguson, Duncan S., *Biblical Hermeneutics. An Introduction*, London: S.C.M., 1986.
Fiorenza, Elisabeth Schüssler, "Word, Spirit and Power: Women in Early Christian Communities" in Rosemary Ruether and Eleanor McLaughlin (eds.) *Women of Spirit: Female Leadership in the Jewish and Christian Traditions*, New York: Simon and Schuster, 1979, 30–70.
────── *In Memory of Her. A Feminist Theological Reconstruction of Christian Origins*, New York: Crossroad and London: S.C.M., 1983.*
────── "'You are not to be Called Father': Early Christian History in a Feminist Perspective" in Norman K. Gottwald (ed.) *The Bible and Liberation: Political and Social Hermeneutics*, New York: Orbis, 1983, 394–417.
────── *Bread Not Stone*, Boston: Beacon Press, 1984.
────── "For Women in Men's Worlds: A Critical Feminist Theology of Liberation", *Concilium: Different Theologies, Common Responsibility* (ed. Claude Geffré, Gustavo Gutiérrez, and Virgil Elizondo) Edinburgh: Clark, 1984, 32–9.
────── "The Will to Choose or to Reject: Continuing our Critical Work" in Letty M Russell (ed.) *Feminist Interpretation of the Bible*, Oxford and New York: Blackwell, 1985, 125–46.*

───── "The Ethics of Interpretation: Decentering Biblical Scholarship", *Journal of Biblical Literature* 107, 1988, 101–15.*
───── "Biblical Interpretation and Critical Commitment" *Studia Theologica*, 43, 1989, 5–18.*
───── "Text and Reality – Reality or Text: The Problem of a Feminist and Social Reconstruction Basis Of Texts" *Studia Theologica* 43, 1989, 19–34.*
Firth, J.R., *Papers in Linguistics, 1934–51*, London: Oxford University Press, 1957.
Fish, Stanley, *Surprised by Sin: The Reader in Paradise Lost*, London & New York: MacMillan, 1967.
───── *Self-Consuming Artifacts: The Experience of Seventeenth Century Literature*, Berkeley: University of California Press, 1972.
───── *Is There a Text in This Class? The Authority of Interpretive Communities*, Cambridge, Mass: Harvard University Press, 1980.*
───── *Doing What Comes Naturally: Change, Rhetoric, and the Practice of Theory in Literary and Legal Studies*, Oxford: Clarendon Press, 1989.*
Fishbane, Michael, *Biblical Interpretation in Ancient Israel*, Oxford: Clarendon Press, 1985.
Florovsky, Georges, *Bible, Church, Tradition: An Eastern Orthodox View*, Belmont: Nordland Publishing Co., 1972.
Fokkema, D.W. and Kunne-Ibsch, Elrud, *Theories of Literature in the Twentieth Century. Structuralism, Marxism, Aesthetics of Reception, Semiotics*, London: Hurst, 1978.
Ford, David F. (ed.) *The Modern Theologies. An Introduction to Christian Theology in the Twentieth Century.* (2 vols.) Oxford: Blackwell, 1989.
Foreman, Terry H., *Religion as the Heart of Humanistic Culture. Schleiermacher as Exponent of Bildung in the Speeches on Religion of 1799* (Dissertation for Yale Ph.D.) Ann Arbor: University Microfilms, 1977.
Forstman, Jack, *A Romantic Triangle: Schleiermacher and Early German Romanticism*, Missoula: Scholars Press (A.A.R. Studies in Religion 13), 1977.
Fowl, Stephen, "The Canonical Approach of Brevard Childs", *Expository Times*, 96, 1985, 173–76.
───── "The Ethics of Interpretation or What's Left Over after the Elimination of Meaning" in D.J. Clines, S.E.Fowl and Stanley Porter (eds.), *The Bible in Three Dimensions*, Sheffield: J.S.O.T. Press, 1990, 379–98.
Fowler, Robert, *Loaves and Fishes. The Function of the Feeding Stories in the Gospel of Mark*, Chico: Scholars Press, 1981.
───── "Who is 'the Reader' in the Text?" *Semeia* 31, 1985, 5–23.
Frei, Hans W., *The Eclipse of Biblical Narrative. A Study in Eighteenth and Nineteenth Century Hermeneutics*, New Haven and London: Yale University Press, 1974.*
───── *The Identity of Jesus Christ. The Hermeneutical Bases of Dogmatic Theology*, Philadelphia: Fortress Press, 1975.
Freiday, Dean, *The Bible: Its Criticism, Interpretation, and Use in Sixteenth and Seventeenth Century England*, Pittsburgh: Catholic and Quaker Studies no. 4, 1979.
Freund, Elizabeth, *The Return of the Reader: Reader-Response Criticism*, London and New York: Methuen, 1987.
Froehlich, Karlfried, *Biblical Interpretation in the Early Church*, Eng. Philadelphia: Fortress, 1984.
Frye, Northrop, *The Great Code. The Bible and Literature*, New York and London: Harcourt Brace Jovanovich, 1982.
Fuchs, Ernst, *Studies of the Historical Jesus*, Eng. London: S.C.M., 1964.
───── *Hermeneutik*, Tübingen: Mohr, 4th edn., 1970.

——— *Marburger Hermeneutik*, Tübingen: Mohr, 1968.
Funk, Robert W., *Language, Hermeneutic and Word of God*, New York: Harper and Row, 1966.*
——— (ed.) *Schleiermacher as Contemporary; Journal for Theology and the Church* 7, New York: Herder, 1970.
——— *The Poetics of Biblical Narrative*, Sonoma: Polebridge Press, 1988.
Fyall, Robert, "How God Treats His Friends: God, Job, and Satan", Unpublished Seminar Paper, Durham, 1990.
Gadamer, Hans-Georg, *Truth and Method*, Eng. London: Sheed & Ward, 1975.*
——— *Kleine Schriften*, Tübingen: Mohr (4 vols.), 1967, 1972 and 1977.*
——— *Philosophical Hermeneutics*, Berkeley: University of California Press, 1976 (part translation of *Kleine Schriften* vols. 1–3).*
——— "The Problem of Language in Schleiermacher's Hermeneutics" *Journal for Theology and the Church* 7, 1970, 68–95.
——— "On the Scope and Function of Hermeneutical Reflection" *Continuum* 8, 1970, 77– 95, rp. in *Philosophical Hermeneutics*, 18–42.*
——— *Reason in the Age of Science*, Eng. Cambridge, Mass.: M.I.T. Press, 1981.
——— "Text and Interpretation" in B. R. Wachterhauser (ed.) *Hermeneutics and Modern Philosophy*, New York: Albany State University of New York Press, 1986, 377–96.*
Gale, Herbert M., *The Use of Analogy in the Letters of Paul*, Philadelphia: Westminster Press, 1964.
Galloway, Allan D., *Wolfhart Pannenberg*, London: Allen & Unwin, 1973.
Geffré, Claude, *The Risk of Interpretation. On Being Faithful to the Christian Tradition in a Non-Christian Age*, Eng. New York: Paulist Press, 1987.
Genette, Gérard, *Narrative Discourse*, Eng. Ithaca: Cornell University Press, 1980.
——— *Narrative Discourse Revisited*, Eng. Ithaca: Cornell University Press 1988 (French 1983).
Gerhart, Mary, "Paul Ricoeur's Notion of 'Diagnostics': its Function in Literary Interpretation", *Journal of Religion* 56, 1976, 137–56.
——— "Imagination and History in Ricoeur's Interpretation Theory", *Philosophy Today* 23, 1979, 51–68.
——— *The Question of Belief in Literary Criticism: An Introduction to the Hermeneutical Theory of Paul Ricoeur*, Stuttgart: Akademischer Verlag Hans-Dieter Heinz, 1979.
Gerrish, B.A., *A Prince of the Church. Schleiermacher and the Beginning of Modern Theology*, London: S.C.M., 1984.
Geuss, R., *The Idea of a Critical Theory: Habermas and the Frankfurt School*, Cambridge: Cambridge University Press, 1981.
Gibellini, Rossino (ed.), *Frontiers of Theology in Latin America*, London: S.C.M., 1980 and New York: Orbis, 1979.
Gier, Nicholas, F., *Wittgenstein and Phenomenology: A Comparative Study of the Later Wittgenstein, Husserl, Heidegger and Merleau-Ponty*, Albany: State University of New York Press, 1981.
Goba, Bonganjalo, *An Agenda for Black Theology. Hermeneutics for Social Change*, Johannesburg: Skotaville, 1988.*
Godsey, John D., "The Interpretation of Romans in the History of the Christian Faith", *Interpretation* 34, 1980, 3–16.
Goldberg, Michael, *Theology and Narrative. A Critical Interpretation*, Nashville: Abingdon, 1981.
Goldingay, John, "Luther and the Bible", *Scottish Journal of Theology*, 35, 1982, 33–58.

—— "Interpreting Scripture", *Anvil* 1, 1984, 261–81.
—— *Theological Diversity and the Authority of the Old Testament*, Grand Rapids: Eerdmans, 1987.
Good, Edwin M., *Irony in the Old Testament*, London: S.P.C.K., 1965.
Goodenough, R., *An Introduction to Philo Judaeus*, 2nd edn., Oxford: Blackwell, 1962.
Goppelt, Leonhard, *Typos: The Typological Interpretation of the Old Testament in the New*, Eng. Grand Rapids: Eerdmans, 1982.
Gottwald, Norman K., *The Tribes of Yahweh: A Sociology of the Religion of Liberated Israel, 1250–1050 B.C.E.*, New York: Orbis, 1979.
—— (ed.), *The Bible and Liberation: Political and Social Hermeneutics*, New York: Orbis, 1983.*
Grabner-Haider, Anton, *Semiotik und Theologie: Religiöse Rede zwischen analytischer und hermeneutischer Philosophie*, Munich: Kösel Verlag, 1973.
Grant, Patrick, *Reading the New Testament*, London: MacMillan, 1989.
Grant, R.M., *The Letter and the Spirit*, London: S.P.C.K., 1957.
—— and Tracy, David, *A Short History of the Interpretation of the Bible*, 2nd edn., Philadelphia: Fortress, 1984.
Grayston, Kenneth, "They Set Us in New Paths: A Century of New Testament Commentaries", *Expository Times* 100, 1988, 84–87.
Green, Garrett (ed.), *Scriptural Authority and Narrative Interpretation*, Philadelphia: Fortress, 1987.
Greenwood, David C., *Structuralism and the Biblical Text*, New York and Amsterdam: Mouton, 1985.
Greer, Rowan A. (ed.), *Origen: An Exhortation to Martyrdom, Prayer and Selected Works*, London: S.P.C.K., 1979.
Greidanus, Sidney, *The Modern Preacher and the Ancient Text. Interpreting and Preaching Biblical Literature*, Leicester: Inter-Varsity Press and Grand Rapids: Eerdmans, 1988.
Greimas, Alexander J., *Sémantique Structurale*, Paris: Larousse, 1966, and Seuil, 1970.
Grice, H.P., "Logic and Conversation" in P. Cole and J.L. Morgan (eds.) *Syntax and Semantics*, 3: Speech-Acts, New York: Academic Press, 1975, 41–58.
—— "Meaning" in P.F. Strawson (ed.) *Philosophical Logic*, Oxford: Oxford University Press, 1971, 39–48.
—— "Utterance-Meaning, Sentence-Meaning, and Word-Meaning" in J.R. Searle (ed.), *The Philosophy of Language*, London: Oxford University Press, 1971, 54–70.
Groome, Thomas H., *Christian Religious Education. Sharing our Story and Vision*, San Francisco: Harper and Row, 1980.
Gros Louis, Kenneth R.R., *Literary Interpretations of Biblical Narratives* (2 vols.), Nashville: Abingdon, 1974 and 1982.
Gruenler, Royce Gordon, *New Approaches to Jesus and the Gospels: A Phenomenological and Exegetical Study of Synoptic Christology*, Grand Rapids: Baker, 1982.
Gudorf, C.E., "Liberation theology's Use of Scripture. A Response to the First World Critics" *Interpretation* 41, 1987, 5–18.
Guiraud, Pierre, *Semiology*, Eng. London and Boston: Routledge and Kegan Paul, 1975.
Gunn, David M., *The Story of King David: Genre and Interpretation*, Sheffield: J.S.O.T. Suppl. 6, 1978.
—— *The Fate of King Saul: An Interpretation of a Biblical Story*, Sheffield: J.S.O.T. Suppl. 14, 1980.

Gunneweg, A.H.J., *Understanding the Old Testament*, Eng. London: S.C.M., 1978.
Gutiérrez, Gustavo, *A Theology of Liberation History, Politics and Salvation*, Eng. New York: Orbis, 1973 and London: S.C.M., 1974.*
Güttgemanns, Erhardt, *Studia Linguistica Neotestamentica. Gesammelte Aufsätze zur linguistischen Grundlage einer Neutestamentlichen Theologie*, Beiträge zur evangelischen Theologie Bd. 60, Münich: Kaiser, 1971.
—— "Linguistic-Literary Critical Foundation of a New Testament Theology" rp. in *Semeia* 6, 1976, 181–215, from *Linguistica Biblica* 13/14, 1972, 2–18.
—— "'Text' und 'Geschichte' als Grundkategorien der Generativen Poetik", *Linguistica Biblica*, 11, 1972, 2–12.
—— "What is 'Generative Poetics'?" *Semeia* 6, 1976, 1–22.
—— *Candid Questions Concerning Gospel Form Criticism*, Eng. Pittsburgh: Pickwick Press, 1979.
Habermas, Jürgen, *Knowledge and Human Interests*, Eng. London: Heinemann, 2nd edn. 1978.*
—— *Zur Logik der Sozialwissenschaften*, Frankfurt a/M: Suhrkamp, 5th edn. 1982. The essay on Gadamer and the universality of hermeneutics is translated in Kurt Mueller-Vollmer (ed.) *The Hermeneutics Reader* (as cited), 294–319.*
—— *The Theory of Communicative Action: The Critique of Functionalist Reason*, 2 vols., Eng. Cambridge: Polity Press, 1984 and 1987.*
—— *Theory and Practice*, Eng. Boston: Beacon Press, 1973.
Hagner, Donald A., "The Old Testament in the New" in Samuel Schultz and Morris A. Inch (eds.), *Interpreting the Word of God. Festschrift in Honor of Steven Barabas*, Chicago: Moody Press, 1976, 78–104.
Hampson, Daphne, *Theology and Feminism*, Oxford: Blackwell, 1990.
Hancher, Michael, "Performative Utterances, the Word of God, and the Death of the Author", in *Semeia* 41, 1988, 27–40.
Hanson, Anthony T., *The New Testament Interpretation of Scripture*, London: S.P.C.K., 1980.
—— *The Living Utterances of God: The New Testament Exegesis of the Old*, London: Darton, Longman and Todd, 1983.
—— *The Paradox of the Cross in the Thought of Paul*, Sheffield: J.S.N.T. Suppl. 17, 1987.
Hanson, Anthony T. and Hanson, Richard P.C., *The Bible without Illusions*, London: S.C.M. and Philadelphia: Trinity Press, 1989.
Hanson, Richard P.C., *Tradition in the Early Church*, London: S.C.M., 1962.
Harari, Josué V. (ed.), *Textual Strategies. Perspectives in Post-Structuralist Criticism*, Ithaca: Cornell University Press, 1979.
Harran, Marilyn J. (ed.), *Luther and Learning. The Wittenberg University Luther Symposium*, Selinsgrove: Susquehanna University Press and London: Associated University Press, 1985.
Hart, Ray L. *Unfinished Man and the Imagination: Towards an Ontology and a Rhetoric of Revelation*. New York: Herder, 1968.
Hartin, P.J., and Petzer, J.H., (eds.) *Text and Interpretation. New Approaches in the Criticism of the New Testament*, Leiden: Brill, 1991.
Hartin, P., "Angst in the Household: A Deconstructive Reading of the Parable of the Supervising Servant (Luke 12:41–48)", *Neotestamentica* 22, 1988, 373–90
Harvey, David, *The Condition of Postmodernity. An Enquiry into the Origins of Cultural Change*, Oxford: Blackwell, 1989 (1980).

Hauerwas, Stanley, *A Community of Character*, Notre Dame: University of Notre Dame Press, 1981.
Hawkes, Terence, *Metaphor*, London: Methuen, 1972.
—— *Structuralism and Semiotics*, London: Methuen, 1977.
Hawthorne, Gerald F. and Betz, Otto (eds.), *Tradition and Interpretation in the New Testament: Essays in Honor of E. Earle Ellis*, Grand Rapids: Eerdmans and Tübingen: Mohr, 1987.
Hays, R.B., *Echoes of Scripture in the Letters of Paul*, New Haven: Yale University Press, 1989.
Heal, Jane, "On the Phrase 'Theory of Meaning'" in D.L. Boyer, P. Grim, and J.T. Sanders (eds.), *The Philosophers Annual* 2, Oxford: Blackwell, 1979, 111–27.
Hegel, Georg W.F., *The Phenomenology of Mind*, Eng. London: Allen & Unwin, 2nd edn. 1949.
Heidegger, Martin, *Being and Time*, Eng. Oxford: Blackwell, 1962.*
—— *An Introduction to Metaphysics*, Eng. New Haven: Yale University Press, 1959.
—— *The Question of Being*, Eng. New York: Vision, 1958.
—— *Discourse on Thinking*, Eng. New York: Harper & Row, 1966.
—— *Poetry, Language and Thought*, New York: Harper & Row, 1971.*
—— *On the Way to Language*, Eng. New York: Harper & Row, 1971.*
—— *On Time and Being*, Eng. New York: Harper & Row, 1972.
Heine, Susanne, *Women and Early Christianity: Are the Feminist Scholars Right?*, Eng. London: S.C.M., 1987.
—— *Christianity and the Goddesses. Systematic Criticism of a Feminist Theology*, Eng. London: S.C.M., 1988.
Hervey, Sándor, *Semiotic Perspectives*, London: Allen and Unwin, 1982.
Hesse, Mary, *Models and Analysis in Science*, Notre Dame: University of Notre Dame Press, 1966.
Hesselgrave, David J., *Communicating Christ Cross-Culturally*, Grand Rapids: Zondervan, 1978.
High, Dallas M., *Language, Persons and Belief: Studies on Wittgenstein's Philosophical Investigations and Religious Uses of Language*, New York: Oxford University Press, 1967.
Hirsch Jr., E.D., *Validity in Interpretation*, New Haven: Yale University Press, 1967.*
—— "Three Dimensions of Hermeneutics", *New Literary History* 3, 1972, 245–61.
—— "Current Issues in Theory of Interpretation", *Journal of Religion* 55, 1975, 298–312.*
—— *The Aims of Interpretation*, Chicago: University of Chicago Press, 1976.*
Hodges, H.A., *The Philosophy of Wilhelm Dilthey*, London: Routledge & Kegan Paul, 1952.
Hofius, Olfried, *Katapausis. Die Vorstellung vom endzeitlichen Ruheort im Hebräerbrief*, Tübingen: Mohr, 1970.
Hofmann, Dietram, *Die geistige Auslegung der Schrift bei Gregor dem Grossen*, Münsterschwarzach: Vier-Türme Verlag, 1968.
Holland, Norman, *The Dynamics of Literary Response*, New York: Oxford, 1968.
—— *Poems in Persons: An Introduction to the Psychoanalysis of Literature*, New York: Norton, 1973.*
—— *5 Readers Reading*, New Haven: Yale University Press, 1975.*
—— "Literary Interpretation and Three Phases of Psychoanalysis" in *Critical Inquiry* 3, 1976, 221–33.

—— "Transactive Criticism: Re-Creation through Identity", in *Criticism* 18, 1976, 334-52.*

—— "Stanley Fish, Stanley Fish", *Genre* 10, 1977, 433-41.

—— "Re-Covering 'The Purloined Letter': Reading as a Personal Transaction" in Susan R. Suleiman and Inge Crosman (eds.) *The Reader in the Text. Essays on Audience and Interpretation*, Princeton: Princeton University Press, 1980, 350-70.

Hollinger, R. (ed.), *Hermeneutics and Praxis*, Indiana: University of Notre Dame Press, 1985.

Holmberg, Bengt, *Paul and Power: The Structure of Authority in the Primitive Church as Reflected in the Pauline Epistles*, Coniectanea Biblica, Lund: Gleerup, 1978 and Philadelphia: Fortress, 1980.

—— *Sociology and the New Testament. An Appraisal*, Minneapolis: Fortress, 1990.

Holub, Robert C., *Reception Theory. A Critical Introduction*, London: Methuen, 1984.

Homans, P., "Psychology and Hermeneutics: an Exploration of Basic Issues and Resources", Journal of Religion 55, 1975, 327-47.

Hooker, Morna D., "Interpreting the Bible: Methods Old and New", *Epworth Review* 17, 1990, 69-77.

Hooker, Richard, *Works*, Oxford: Oxford University Press, 1886.

Hordern, William, *Speaking of God. The Nature and Purpose of Theological Language*, London: Epworth Press, 1965.

Horgan, M.P., *Pesharim: Qumran Interpretations of Biblical Books*, Washington: Catholic Biblical Quarterly Monograph, 1979.

Horsley, R.A., "Consciousness and Freedom among the Corinthians: 1 Cor. 8-10" in *Catholic Biblical Quarterly* 40, 1978, 574-89.

Horton, Susan R., "The Experience of Stanley Fish's Prose or the Critic as Self-Creating, Self-Consuming, Artificer", *Genre* 10, 1977, 443-53.

Howard, George, *Crisis in Galatia: A Study in Early Christian Theology*, Cambridge: Cambridge University Press (S.N.T.S.M.S. 35) 1979.

Howard, Roy J., *Three Faces of Hermeneutics. An Introduction to Current Theories of Understanding*, Berkeley: University of California Press, 1982.

Hoy, David Couzens, *The Critical Circle: Literature, History and Philosophical Hermeneutics*, Berkeley: University of California Press, 1982.

—— "Must We Say What We Mean? The Grammatological Critique of Hermeneutics" in Bruce R. Wachterhauser (ed.) *Hermeneutics and Modern Philosophy*, New York: Albany State University of New York Press, 1986, 397-415.

Hughes, F.W., "Feminism and Early Christian History", *Anglican Theological Review* 69, 1987, 287-99.

Hughes, Graham, *Hebrews and Hermeneutics. The Epistle to the Hebrews as a New Testament Example of Biblical Interpretation*, Cambridge: Cambridge University Press, 1979.

Hummel, Horace D., "The Outside Limits of Lutheran Confessionalism in Contemporary Biblical Interpretation", *The Springfielder* 35, 1971, 103-25, 264-73 and 1972, 37-53 and 212-22.

Hurd Jr., John C., *The Origin of I Corinthians*, London: S.P.C.K., 1965.

Husserl, Edmund, *Logical Investigations* (2 vols.), Eng. London: Routledge & Kegan Paul, 1976 (First German edn. 1900-01).

Huyssen, Andreas, *After the Great Divide. Modernism, Mass Culture, Post-Modernism*, Bloomington: Indiana University Press, 1986.

Ihde, Don, *Hermeneutic Phenomenology: The Philosophy of Paul Ricoeur*, Evanston: Northwestern University Press, 1971 (Studies in Phenomenology and Existential Philosophy).

Ingarden, Roman, *The Literary Work of Art. An Investigation on the Borderlines of Ontology, Logic, and Theory of Literature*, Eng. Evanston: Northwestern University Press, 1973.

—— *The Cognition of the Literary Work of Art*, Eng. Evanston: Northwestern University Press, 1973.

Ingram, David, *Habermas and the Dialectic of Reason*, New Haven: Yale University Press, 1987.

Iser, Wolfgang, "Indeterminacy and the Reader's Response in Prose Fiction" in J. Hillis Miller (ed.) *Aspects of Narrative: Selected Papers from the English Institute*, New York: Columbia University Press, 1971, 1–45.*

—— *The Implied Reader: Patterns of Communication in Prose Fiction from Bunyan to Beckett*, Baltimore: Johns Hopkins University Press, 1974.*

—— *The Act of Reading: A Theory of Aesthetic Response*, Baltimore and London: Johns Hopkins University Press, 1978 and 1980.*

Jacobi, Jolande, *Complex, Archetype, Symbol in the Psychology of C.G. Jung*, Eng. Princeton: Princeton University Press, 1959.

Jacobson, Richard, "The Structuralists and the Bible", *Interpretation* 28, 1974, 146–64.

Jameson, Fredric, *The Political Unconscious. Narrative as a Socially Symbolic Act*, Ithaca: Cornell University Press, 1981.

Janik, Allen and Toulmin, Stephen, *Wittgenstein's Vienna*, London: Wiedenfeld and Nicolson, 1973.

Jasper, David, "The New Testament and Literary Interpretation", *Religion and Literature* 17, 1985, 1–10.

—— "The Limits of Formalism and the Theology of Hope: Ricoeur, Moltmann and Dostoyevsky" in *Literature and Theology* 1, 1987, 1–10.

—— *The New Testament and the Literary Imagination*, London: MacMillan, 1987.

—— *The Study of Literature and Religion: An Introduction*, London: MacMillan, 1989.

Jauss, Hans Robert, *Towards an Aesthetic of Reception*, Eng. Minneapolis: University of Minnesota Press, 1982.*

—— *Aesthetic Experience and Literary Hermeneutics*, Eng. Minneapolis: University of Minnesota Press, 1982.

Jeanrond, Werner, "The Theological Understanding of Texts and Linguistic Explication", *Modern Theology* 1, 1984, 55–66.

—— "The Impact of Schleiermacher's Hermeneutics on Contemporary Interpretation Theory" in David Jasper (ed.) *The Interpretation of Belief: Coleridge, Schleiermacher, and Romanticism*, London: MacMillan, 1986, 81–96.

—— *Text and Interpretation as Categories of Theological Thinking*, Eng. Dublin: Gill and MacMillan, 1988.

Jewett, Robert, *Christian Tolerance. Paul's Message to the Modern Church*, Philadelphia: Westminster, 1982.

—— *Paul's Anthropological Terms. A Study of their Use in Conflict Settings*, Leiden: Brill, 1971.

—— *Letters to Pilgrims. A Commentary on the Epistle to the Hebrews*, New York: Pilgrim Press, 1981.

Johnson, Alfred M. (ed.), *New Testament and Structuralism*, Pittsburgh: Pickwick Press, 1976.

Johnson, Anthony L., "Jakobsonian Theory and Literary Semiotics: Toward a Generative Typology of the Text", *New Literary History* 14, 1982, 33–61.
Johnson, Cedric B., *The Psychology of Biblical Interpretation*, Grand Rapids: Zondervan, 1983.
Johnson, Elliott E., *Expository Hermeneutics: An Introduction*, Grand Rapids: Academie, 1990.
Johnston, Robert K. (ed.), *The Use of the Bible in Theology: Evangelical Options*, Atlanta: John Knox, 1985.
Jones, Gareth, *Bultmann. Towards a Critical Theology*, Cambridge: Polity Press, 1991.
Jones, Geraint Vaughan, *The Art and Truth of the Parables*, London: S.P.C.K., 1964.
Jones, O.R. (ed.), *The Private Language Argument*, London: MacMillan, 1971.
Juhl, P.D., *Interpretation. An Essay in the Philosophy of Literary Criticism*, Princeton: Princeton University Press, 1980.
Jung, Carl Gustav, *Man and his Symbols*, New York: Doubleday, 1971.
Kairos Theologians, The, *The Kairos Document: Challenge to the Church*, Grand Rapids: Eerdmans, 1986.
Kaiser, Walter C., *Biblical Exegesis for Preaching and Teaching*, Grand Rapids: Baker, 1981.
——— *The Uses of the Old Testament in the New*, Chicago: Moody Press, 1985.
Kalilombe, Patrick A., "Black Theology" in David F. Ford (ed.) *The Modern Theologians. An Introduction to Christian Theology in the Twentieth Century*, Oxford: Blackwell, 1989, 193–216.
Käsemann, Ernst, *Perspectives on Paul*, London: S.C.M. and Philadelphia: Fortress, 1971.
——— *The Wandering People of God. An Investigation of the Letter to the Hebrews*, Eng. Minneapolis: Augsburg, 1984.
Kee, Alistair, *Marx and the Failure of Liberation Theology*, London: S.C.M. and Philadelphia: Trinity Press, 1990.
Keegan, Terence, *Interpreting the Bible. A Popular Introduction to Biblical Hermeneutics*, New York: Paulist Press, 1985.
Keel, Othmar, *The Symbolism of the Biblical World. Ancient Near Eastern Iconography and the Book of Psalms*, Eng. New York: Seabury Press, 1978.
Kelber, Werner, *Mark's Story of Jesus*, Philadelphia: Fortress, 1979.
——— *The Oral and the Written Gospel: The Hermeneutics of Speaking and Writing in the Synoptic Tradition, Mark, Paul and Q*, Philadelphia: Fortress Press, 1983.
——— "Biblical Hermeneutics and the Ancient Art of Communication", *Semeia* 39, 1987, 97–105.
——— "Gospel Narrative and Critical Theory", *Biblical Theology Bulletin* 18, 1988, 130–36.
Kelsey, David, *The Uses of Scripture in Recent Theology*, London: S.C.M., 1975.
——— "Biblical Narrative and Theological Anthropology" in Garrett Green (ed.) *Scriptural Authority and Narrative Interpretation*, Philadelphia: Fortress Press, 1987, 121–43.
Kenny, Anthony, *Wittgenstein*, London: Penguin Books, edn. 1975.
Kermode, Frank, *The Genesis of Secrecy. On the Interpretation of Narrative*, Cambridge, Mass., and London: Harvard University Press, 1979.
Kierkegaard, Søren, *The Point of View for my Work as an Author*, Princeton: Princeton University Press, 1941 (rp. New York, 1962).
——— *The Attack upon "Christendom"*, Eng. Princeton: Princeton University Press, 1944.

—— *Purity of Heart is to Will One Thing*, London: Collins (Fontana edn.), 1961.
—— *The Concept of Irony*, Eng. London: Collins, 1966.
—— *Concluding Unscientific Postscript to the Philosophical Fragments*, Eng. Princeton: Princeton University Press, 1941.
—— *Fear and Trembling: Dialectical Lyric by Johannes de Silentio*, Eng. (ed. A. Hannay), London: Penguin edn., 1985 (also with *The Sickness unto Death*, New York: Fontana edn., 1954).*
Kimmerle, Heinz, "Hermeneutical Theory or Ontological Hermeneutics" in *Journal for Theology and the Church*, 4: History and Hermeneutic, Tübingen: Mohr and New York: Harper and Row, 1967, 107–121.
King, Ursula, *Women and Spirituality: Voices of Protest and Promise*, London: MacMillan, 1989.
Kirk, J. Andrew, *Liberation Theology: An Evangelical View from the Third World*, London: Marshall, Morgan and Scott, 1979.
Kisiel, T., "Ideology Critique and Phenomenology", *Philosophy Today* 14, 1970, 151–60.
Klemm, David E., *The Hermeneutical Theory of Paul Ricoeur. A Constructive Analysis*, Lewisburg: Bucknell University Press, and London and Toronto: Associated University Presses, 1983.
—— (ed.), *Hermeneutical Inquiry: I, The Interpretation of Texts, and II, The Interpretation of Existence* (2 vols.), Atlanta: Scholars Press (A.A.R. Studies in Religion, 43), 1986.
Korshin, Paul, J., *Typologies in England 1650–1820*, Princeton: Princeton University Press, 1982.
Kort, Wesley, A., *Narrative Elements and Religious Meanings*, Philadelphia: Westminster, 1975.
—— *Story, Text, and Scripture. Literary Interests in Biblical Narrative*, University Park and London: Pennsylvania State University Press, 1988.
Kraft, Charles H., *Christianity vs Culture*, New York: Orbis, 1979.
Kraus, Hans-Joachim, "Calvin's Exegetical Principles", *Interpretation* 31, 1977, 8–18.
Krentz, Edgar, *The Historical-Critical Method*, Philadelphia: Fortress Press, 1975.
Kristeva, Julia, *Revolution in Poetic Language*, Eng. New York: Columbia University Press, 1984.
—— Selected Writings in Toril Moi (ed.) *The Kristeva Reader*, New York: Columbia University Press, 1986.
—— "The System and the Speaking Subject", *Times Literary Supplement*, 12 Oct., 1973, 1249–52; rp. in *The Kristeva Reader*, 25–32.
—— *In the Beginning was Love: Psychoanalysis and Faith*, Eng. New York: Columbia University Press, 1987.
Kugel, James L. and Greer, Rowan A., *Early Biblical Interpretation*, Philadelphia: Westminster, 1986.
Kuhn, Thomas S., *The Structure of Scientific Revolutions* 2nd revd. edn., Chicago: Chicago University Press, 1970.
—— *The Essential Tension: Selected Studies in a Scientific Tradition and Change*, Chicago: University of Chicago Press, 1977.
Kümmel, Werner G., *The New Testament: History of the Investigation of its Problems*, Eng. London: S.C.M., 1972.
Küng, H. and Tracy, D. (eds.), *Paradigm Change in Theology. A Symposium for the Future*, Eng. New York: Crossroad, 1989.

Labberton, Mark, *Ordinary Bible Reading: The Reformed Tradition and Reader-Orientated Criticism*, Ph.D. Dissertation, University of Cambridge, 1990.
Lacan, Jacques, *The Four Fundamental Concepts of Psychoanalysis*, Eng. London: Penguin edn. 1979.
Laeuchli, Samuel, *The Language of Faith: An Introduction to the Semantic Dilemma of the Early Church*, London: Epworth Press, 1965.
LaFargue, M., "Are Texts Determinate? Derrida, Barth [sic] and the Role of the Biblical Scholars", *Harvard Theological Review*, 81, 1988, 341–57.
Laffey, Alice L., *Wives, Harlots, and Concubines: The Old Testament in Feminist Perspective*, London: S.P.C.K., 1990 and Fortress Press, 1988.
Lakoff, George and Johnson, Mark, *Metaphors We Live By*, Chicago: Chicago University Press, 1980.
Lampe, Geoffrey W.H. and Woollcombe, K.J., *Essays on Typology*, London: S.C.M., 1957.
Lan, K.P., "The Feminist Hermeneutics of Elisabeth Schüssler Fiorenza: An Asian Feminist Response", *East Asian Journal of Theology* 3, 1985, 147–53.
Lapointe, R., "La valeur linguistique du Sitz im Leben", *Biblica* 52, 1971, 469–87.
——— "Hermeneutics Today", *Biblical Theology Bulletin* 2, 1972, 107–54.
Larkin Jr., William J., *Culture and Biblical Hermeneutics. Interpreting and Applying the Authoritative Word in a Relativistic Age*, Grand Rapids: Baker, 1988.
Lash, Nicholas, "What Might Martyrdom Mean? in N. Lash, *Theology on the Way to Emmaus*, London: S.C.M., 1986, 75–92.
Lategan, B.C., "Current Issues in the Hermeneutical Debate", *Neotestamentica* 18, 1984, 1–17.
Lategan, B.C., "Reception Theory and Practice in Reading Romans[13]", in P.J. Hartin and J.H. Petzer (eds.) *Text and Interpretation. New Approaches in the Criticism of the New Testament*. Leiden: Brill, 1991, 145–70.
Lategan, Bernard and Vorster, Willem, *Text and Reality: Aspects of Reference in Biblical Texts*, Atlanta: Scholars Press, 1985.
Lawson, Hilary, *Reflexivity. The Post-Modern Predicament*, London: Hutchinson, 1985.
Leach, Edmund, "Structuralism in Social Anthropology" in David Robey (ed.) *Structuralism. An Introduction*, Oxford: Clarendon Press, 1973, 37–56.
Leech, Geoffrey, *Principles of Pragmatics*, London and New York: Longman, 1983.
Leith, Dick and Myerson, George, *The Power of the Address: Explorations in Rhetoric*, London and New York: Routledge, 1989.
Lentricchia, Frank, *After the New Criticism*, Chicago: University of Chicago Press, 1980.
Lévi-Strauss, Claude, *Structural Anthropology*, Eng. London and New York: Basic Books, 1963.
Levinson, Stephen C., *Pragmatics*, Cambridge: Cambridge University Press, 1983.
Lewis, C.S., *An Experiment in Criticism*, Cambridge: Cambridge University Press, 1961.
Lindbeck, George, *The Nature of Doctrine. Religion and Doctrine in a Postliberal Age*, London: S.P.C.K., 1984.
Linnemann, Eta, *Parables of Jesus. Introduction and Exposition*, Eng. London: S.P.C.K., 1966.
Loades, Ann, *Searching for Lost Coins: Explorations in Christianity and Feminism*, London: S.P.C.K., 1987.
——— "Feminist Theology" in David F. Ford (ed.) *The Modern Theologians. An Introduction to Christian Theology in the Twentieth Century* (2 vols.) Oxford: Blackwell, 1989, vol. 2, 235–52.

―――― (ed.), *Feminist Theology. A Reader*, London: S.P.C.K., 1990.
Lochhead, David, "The Liberation of the Bible" in Norman Gottwald (ed.) *The Bible and Liberation. Political and Social Hermeneutics*, New York: Orbis, 1983, 74–93.
Longenecker, Richard N., *Biblical Exegesis in the Apostolic Period*, Grand Rapids: Eerdmans, 1975.
―――― "Three Ways of Understanding Relations between the Testaments" in Gerald F. Hawthorne and Otto Betz (eds.) *Tradition and Interpretation in the New Testament: Essays* in Honor of E. Earle Ellis, Grand Rapids: Eerdmans and Tübingen: Mohr, 1987.
Longman III, Tremper, *Literary Approaches to Biblical Interpretation*, Grand Rapids: Academie and Leicester: Apollos, 1987.
Lotman, Jurij, *The Structure of the Artistic Text*, Eng. Ann Arbor: University of Michigan Press, 1977.
Louth, Andrew, "The Hermeneutical Question Approached through the Fathers", *Sobornost* 7, 1978, 541–549.
―――― *Discerning the Mystery. An Essay on the Nature of Theology*, Oxford: Clarendon Press, 1983.
Lundin, Roger, Thiselton, Anthony and Walhout, Clare, *The Responsibility of Hermeneutics*, Exeter: Paternoster and Grand Rapids: Eerdmans, 1985.
Luther, Martin, *Luther's Works* (ed. J.J. Pelikan and H.T. Lehmann), St. Louis, Philadelphia: Concordia Publishing House, 1955.
―――― *On the Bondage of the Will*, Eng. Edinburgh: Clarke, 1957.
Lyons, John, *Introduction to Theoretical Linguistics*, Cambridge: Cambridge University Press, 1968.
―――― *Semantics* (2 vols.), Cambridge: Cambridge University Press, 1977.
Mack, B.L., *Rhetoric and the New Testament*, Minneapolis: Fortress Press, 1990.
Macky, P.W., *The Centrality of Metaphors to Biblical Thought. A Method for Interpreting the Bible*, Lampeter: Mellen, 1990.
Macquarrie, John, *The Scope of Demythologising: Bultmann and his Critics*, London: S.C.M., 1960.
―――― *Studies in Christian Existentialism*, London: S.C.M., 1966.
Mailloux, Steven, "Reader-Response Criticism?" *Genre* 10, 1977, 413–31.
Man, Paul de, "Rhetoric of Temporality" in C. Singleton (ed.) *Interpretation: Theory and Practice*, Baltimore: The Johns Hopkins University Press, 1969, 171–209.
―――― *Allegories of Reading*, New Haven: Yale University Press, 1979.
Mannheim, Karl, *Ideology and Utopia: Introduction to the Sociology of Knowledge*, Eng. London: Routledge and Kegan Paul, 1960.
Margerie, B. de, *Introduction a l'histoire de l'exégèse* (3 vols.), Paris: Les Editions du Cerf, 1980–83.
Marlé, René, *Introduction to Hermeneutics*, Eng. London: Burns & Oates, 1967.
Marshall, Peter, *Enmity in Corinth: Social Conventions in Paul's Relations with the Corinthians*, Tübingen: Mohr, 1987.
Marx, Karl, *Writings of the Young Marx on Philosophy and Society*, (eds. L.D. Easton and K.H. Guddat), New York: Doubleday, Anchor Books, 1967.
May, Rollo (ed.), *Symbolism in Religion and Literature*, New York: Braziller, 1960.
Mbiti, John S., *New Testament Eschatology in an African Background. A Study of the Encounter between New Testament Theology and African Traditional Concepts*, London: S.P.C.K., 1971 and 1978.
―――― *Bible and Theology in African Christianity*, Nairobi: Oxford University Press, 1986.

McCarthy, T., *the Critical Theory of Jürgen Habermas*, Cambridge, Mass.: M.I.T. Press, 1978.
McEvenue, S.E. and Meyer, B.F. (eds.), *Lonergan's Hermeneutics: its Development and Application*, Washington: Catholic University of America Press, 1989.
McFague, Sallie, *Speaking in Parables: A Study in Metaphor and Theology*, Philadelphia: Fortress Press, 1975.
—— *Metaphorical Theology. Models of God in Religious Language*, Philadelphia: Fortress Press, 1982.
McGrath, Alister E., *The Genesis of Doctrine. A Study of the Foundations of Doctrinal Criticism*, Oxford: Blackwell, 1990
McHann Jr., James C., *The Three Horizons: A Study in Biblical Hermeneutics with Special Reference to Wolfhart Pannenberg*, University of Aberdeen, Ph.D. Dissertation, 1987.
McKim, Donald K., *What Christians Believe about the Bible*, Nashville: Abingdon, 1985.
McKim, Donald (ed.), *A Guide to Contemporary Hermeneutics. Major Trends in Biblical Interpretation*, Grand Rapids: Eerdmans, 1986.
McKnight, Edgar V., *The Bible and the Reader. An Introduction to Literary Criticism*, Philadelphia: Fortress Press, 1985.
—— *Meaning in Texts: the Historical Shaping of a Narrative Hermeneutic*, Philadelphia: Fortress Press, 1978.
—— *Post-Modern Use of the Bible: The Emergence of Reader-Oriented Criticism*, Nashville: Abingdon, 1988.
—— "New Criticism and Old" *Journal of the American Academy of Religion*, 57, 1989, 385–91.
McNally, R.E., *The Bible in the Early Middle Ages*, Atlanta: Scholars Press, 1986 (1959).
Meeks, Wayne A. (ed.), *The Writings of St. Paul: Norton Critical Edition*, London & New York: Norton 1972.
—— "A Hermeneutics of Social Embodiment", *Harvard Theological Review*, 79, 1986, 176–86.
Megivern, James J. (ed.), *Bible Interpretation* (Official Catholic Teachings), Wilmington: McGrath, 1978.
Meier, John P., *The Vision of Matthew: Christ, Church, and Morality in the First Gospel*, New York: Paulist Press, 1979.
Meiland, Jack W., *The Nature of Intention*, London: Methuen, 1970.
Merill, A.L. and Overholt, T.W. (eds.), *Scripture in History and Theology: Essays in Honour of J.C. Rylaarsdam*, Pittsburgh: Pickwick Press, 1977.
Mesters, Carlos, "The Use of the Bible in Christian Communities of the Common People" in Norman Gottwald (ed.) *The Bible and Liberation. Political and Social Hermeneutics*, New York: Orbis, 1983, 119–33.
—— *Defenseless Flower. A New Reading of the Bible*, Eng. New York: Orbis 1989 (Portugese 1983).
Michalson, Gordon E., *Lessing's 'Ugly Ditch': A Study of Theology and History*, Pennsylvania State University Press, 1985.
Michel, Otto, *Paulus und seine Bibel*, Gütersloh: Bertelsmann, 1929.
Mickelsen, A. (ed.), *Women, Authority and the Bible*, Downers Grove: Inter-Varsity, 1986.
Miller, Donald G. (ed.), *The Hermeneutical Quest:* Essays in Honor of James Luther Mays, Allison Park: Pickwick Press, 1986.
Mink, Louis O., "History and Fiction as Modes of Comprehension" in Ralph Cohen (ed.) *New Directions in Literary History*, Baltimore: Johns Hopkins University Press, 1974, 107–24.

Miranda, José P., *Marx and the Bible. A Critique of the Philosophy of Oppression*, Eng. New York: Orbis, 1974 and London: S.C.M., 1977.*
Misgeld, Dieter, "Discourse and Conversation: The Theory of Communicative Competence and Hermeneutics in the Light of the Debate between Habermas and Gadamer", *Cultural Hermeneutics* 4, 1977, 321–44.
Miskotte, Kornelis H., *When the Gods are Silent*, Eng. London: Collins, 1967.
Mitchell, W.J.T., (ed.) *The Politics of Interpretation*, Chicago and London: Chicago University Press, 1983.
Moberly, R.W.L., *At the Mountain of God. Story and Theology in Exodus 32–34*, Sheffield: J.S.O.T. Press Suppl. 22, 1983.
Molina, David De-Newton (ed.), *On Literary Intention*, Edinburgh: Edinburgh University Press, 1976.
Moltmann, Jürgen, *Theology of Hope: On the Ground and Implications of a Christian Eschatology*, Eng. London: S.C.M. and New York: Harper and Row, 1967.
——— *The Crucified God. The Cross of Christ as the Foundation and Criticism of Christian Theology*, Eng. London: S.C.M., 1974.
——— *The Experiment Hope*, Eng. London: S.C.M. and Philadelphia: Fortress, 1975.
——— "Response to the Opening Presentations" in Ewert H. Cousins (ed.), *Hope and the Future of Man*, Philadelphia: Fortress and London: Teilhard Centre, 1972, 55–59.
——— *Theology Today*, Eng. London: S.C.M. and Philadelphia: Trinity Press, 1988.
Moltmann-Wendel, Elisabeth, *A Land Flowing with Milk and Honey. Perspectives on Feminist Theology*, Eng. London: S.C.M., 1986.
Moore, Stephen D., *Literary Criticism and the Gospels: the Theoretical Challenge*, New Haven and London: York University Press, 1989.
——— "Doing Gospel Criticism As/With a 'Reader'", *Biblical Theology Bulletin*, 19, 1989, 85–93.
——— "The 'Post-' Age Stamp: Does it Stick? Biblical Studies and the Post-Modernism Debate", *Journal of the American Academy of Religion*, 57, 1989, 543–59.
Morgan, Robert (with John Barton), *Biblical Interpretation*, Oxford: Oxford University Press, 1988.
Morris, Charles W., *Writings on the General Theory of Signs*, The Hague: Mouton, 1971.
Mosala, Itumeleng J., *Biblical Hermeneutics and Black Theology in South Africa*, Grand Rapids: Eerdmans, 1989.*
Muddiman, John, *The Bible: Fountain and Well of Truth*, Oxford: Blackwell, 1983.
Mueller-Volmer, Kurt (ed.), *The Hermeneutics Reader: Texts of the German Tradition from the Enlightenment to the Present*, Oxford: Blackwell, 1986 and Continuum Publishing, 1985.
Munck, Johannes, *Paul and the Salvation of Mankind*, Eng. London: S.C.M., 1959.
Murphy, Roland, *Theology, Exegesis and Proclamation*, New York: Herder, 1971.
Murphy-O'Connor, J., "Food and Spiritual Gifts in 1 Cor. 8:8", *Catholic Biblical Quarterly*, 41, 1979, 292–98.
——— "Freedom or the Ghetto (1 Cor. VIII.1–13, X.23–XI.1)", *Revue Biblique* 85, 1978, 543–74.
——— *St. Paul's Corinth: Texts and Archeology*, Wilmington: Glazier, 1983.
Neill, Stephen and Wright, Tom, *The Interpretation of the New Testament 1861–1986*, Oxford: Oxford University Press, 2nd edn., 1988.
Netherlands Reformed Church, *The Bible Speaks Again*, Eng. London: S.C.M., 1969.

Neufeld, Vernon H., *The Earliest Christian Confessions*, Leiden: Brill, 1963.
Neuhaus, R.J. (ed.), *Biblical Interpretation in Crisis: The Ratzinger Conference on the Bible and Church*, Grand Rapids: Eerdmans, 1989.
Neusner, Jacob, "Introduction: Metaphor and Exegesis" in *Semeia* 27, 1983, 37–116.
Nicholson, Ernest W., *God and His People: Covenant and Theology in the Old Testament*, Oxford: Clarendon Press, 1986.
Nida, Eugene A., "The Implications of Contemporary Linguistics for Biblical Scholarship", *J.B.L.* 91, 1972, 73–89.
Niebuhr, R., *Schleiermacher on Christ and Religion: A New Introduction*, New York: Scribner, 1964.
Nikiprowetsky, V., *Le commentaire de l'écriture chez Philon d'Alexandrie*, Leiden: Brill, 1977.
Nineham, Dennis, *The Use and Abuse of the Bible. A Study of the Bible in an Age of Rapid Cultural Change*, London: MacMillan, 1976.
Noll, Mark A., *Between Faith and Criticism. Evangelicals, Scholarship, and the Bible in America*, San Francisco: Harper & Row, 1987.
Norris, Christopher, *Deconstruction. Theory and Practice*, London: Methuen, 1982.
—— *Contest of Faculties. Philosophy and Theory after Deconstruction*, London & New York: Methuen, 1985.
—— *Derrida*, London: Fontana, 1987.
Ogden, Schubert M., "Bultmann's Project of Demythologization and the Problems of Theology and Philosophy", *Journal of Religion* 37, 1957, 156–73.
Olthuis, James H., *A Hermeneutics of Ultimacy*, New York: University Press of America, 1987.
O'Neill, J.C., *The Bible's Authority. A Portrait Gallery of Thinkers from Lessing to Bultmann*, Edinburgh: Clark, 1991.
Ong, W.J., "Maranatha: Death and Life in the Text of the Book", *Journal of the American Academy of Religion* 45, 1977, 419–49.
—— "Text as Interpretation: Mark and After", *Semeia* 39, 1987, 7–26.
Ott, Heinrich, "What is Systematic Theology?" in James M. Robinson and J. Cobb Jr. (eds.) *New Frontiers in Theology: I The Later Heidegger and Theology*, New York: Harper & Row, 1963, 77–111.*
Otte, Klaus, *Das Sprachverständnis bei Philo von Alexandrien: Sprache als Mittel der Hermeneutik*, Tübingen: Mohr, 1968.
Padilla, C. René, "The Interpreted Word: Reflections on Contextual Hermeneutics" (1981), rp. in D.K. McKim (ed.) *A Guide to Contemporary Hermeneutics*, Grand Rapids: Eerdmans, 1986, 297–308.
Pagels, Elaine H., *The Johannine Gospel in Gnostic Exegesis: Heracleon's Commentary on John*, Nashville & New York: Abingdon Press, 1973.
—— *The Gnostic Paul: Gnostic Exegesis of the Pauline Letters*, Philadelphia: Fortress, 1975.
Painter, John, *Theology as Hermeneutics. Rudolf Bultmann's Interpretation of the History of Jesus*, Sheffield: Sheffield Academic Press, 1987.
Palmer, Richard E., *Hermeneutics. Interpretation Theory in Schleiermacher, Dilthey, Heidegger, and Gadamer*, Evanston: Northwestern University Press, 1969 (Studies in Phenomenology and Existential Philosophy).
—— "Toward a Postmodern Interpretive Self Awareness", *Journal of Religion* 55, 1975, 313–26.

―――― "What are We *Doing* When We Interpret a Text? – Variations on the Theme of Hermeneutic *Handeln*", *Eros* 7, 1980, 1–45.
Pannenberg, Wolfhart, *Jesus – God and Man*, Eng. London: S.C.M. and Philadelphia: Westminster, 1968.
―――― "Hermeneutics and Universal History" in *Journal for Theology and the Church*, 4: History and Hermeneutic, Tübingen: Mohr and New York: Harper & Row, 1967, 122–52.*
―――― *Basic Questions in Theology* (3 vols.), Eng. London: S.C.M., 1970, 1971 & 1973.*
―――― *Theology and the Philosophy of Science*, Eng. Philadelphia: Westminster Press and London: Darton, Longman & Todd, 1976.*
―――― *Metaphysics and the Idea of God*, Eng. Edinburgh: Clark, 1990.
Parker, T.H.L., *Calvin's New Testament Commentaries*, London: S.C.M., 1971.
Patte, Daniel, *Early Jewish Hermeneutic in Palestine*, Missoula: Scholars Press, 1975.
―――― *What is Structural Exegesis?*, Philadelphia: Fortress, 1976.
―――― *Paul's Faith and the Power of the Gospel. A Structural Introduction to the Pauline Letters*, Philadelphia: Fortress, 1983.
―――― *The Gospel according to Matthew: A Structural Commentary on Matthew's Faith*, Philadelphia: Fortress, 1987.
―――― "Speech Act Theory and Biblical Exegesis", *Semeia* 41, 1988, 85–102.
―――― *Structural Exegesis for New Testament Critics*, Minneapolis: Fortress, 1990.
―――― *The Religious Dimension of Biblical Texts. Greimas's Structural Semiotics and Biblical Exegesis*, Atlanta: Scholars Press (S.B.L. Semeia Studies), 1990.
Patte, Daniel and Patte, Aline, *Structural Exegesis: From Theory to Practice*, Philadelphia: Fortress, 1978.
Pears, David, *Wittgenstein*, London: Collins, 1971.
Peirce, Charles S., *The Collected Papers of Charles Sanders Peirce*, (eds. Charles Hartshorne and Paul Weiss), Cambridge, Mass.: Harvard University Press, 1934–36.
Pelikan, Jaroslav, *Luther's Works: Companion Volume, Luther the Expositor*, St. Louis: Concordia, 1959.
Perkins, P., "Crisis in Jerusalem? Narrative Criticism in New Testament Studies", *Theological Studies* 50, 1989, 296–313.
―――― "Commentaries: Windows to the Text", *Theology Today*, 46, 1990, 393–98.
Perrin, Norman, *Jesus and the Language of the Kingdom. Symbol and Metaphor in New Testament Interpretation*, London: S.C.M., 1976.
Peters, T., "Truth in History: Gadamer's Hermeneutics and Pannenberg's Apologetic Method" *Journal of Religion* 55, 1975, 36–56.
Petersen, Norman R., *Literary Criticism for New Testament Critics*, Philadelphia: Fortress Press, 1978.
―――― "The Reader in the Gospel" in *Neotestamentica*, 18, 1984, 38–51.
―――― *Rediscovering Paul. Philemon and the Sociology of Paul's Narrative World*, Philadelphia: Fortress, 1985.
Peterson, Thomas D., *Wittgenstein for Preaching. A Model for Communication*, Lanham: University Press of America, 1980.
Pitcher, George, *The Philosophy of Wittgenstein*, Englewood Cliffs: Prentice Hall, 1964.
Platts, Mark de Bretton, *Ways of Meaning: An Introduction to a Philosophy of Language*, London and Boston: Routledge & Kegan Paul, 1979.
Poland, Lynn M., *Literary Criticism and Biblical Hermeneutics: A Critique of Formalist Approaches*, Chicago: Scholars Press, 1985 (A.A.R. Academy Series 48).

Polanyi, Michael and Prosch, Harry, *Meaning*, Chicago: Chicago University Press, 1975.
Polzin, Robert M., "The Framework of Job", *Interpretation* 28, 1974, 182–200.
—— *Biblical Structuralism. Method and Subjectivity in the Study of Ancient Texts*, Philadelphia: Fortress and Missoula: Scholars Press, 1977.
Popkin, Richard H., *The History of Scepticism from Erasmus to Spinoza*, Berkeley: University of California Press, 1979.
Porter, Stanley E., "Wittgenstein's Classes of Utterance and Pauline Ethical Texts", *Journal of the Evangelical Theological Society* 32, 1989, 85–97.
—— "Why Hasn't Reader-Response Criticism Caught On in New Testament Studies?" in *Literature and Theology* 4, 1990, 278–92.
Poulet, Georges, "Phenomenology of Reading", *New Literary History* 1, 1969, 53–68.
Poythress, Vern S., "Philosophical Roots of Phenomenological and Structuralist Literary Criticism", *Westminster Theological Journal* 41, 1978–79, 165–71.
—— "Ground-Rules of New Testament Interpretation", *Westminster Theological Journal* 41, 1978–79, 190–201.
—— "Divine Meaning of Scripture", *Westminster Theological Journal* 48, 1986, 241–79.
—— "What Does God Say Through Human Authors?" in Harvey M. Conn (ed.) *Inerrancy and Hermeneutic. A Tradition, A Challenge, A Debate*, Grand Rapids: Baker, 1988, 81–99.
—— *Science and Hermeneutics. Implications of Scientific Method for Biblical Interpretation*, Grand Rapids: Academie Books and Leicester: Apollos, 1988.
Pregeant, Russell, *Christology beyond Dogma: Matthew's Christ in Process Hermeneutic*, Missoula: Scholars Press, 1978.
Preus, J.S., *From Shadow to Promise: Old Testament Interpretation from Augustine to the Young Luther*, Cambridge: Harvard University Press, 1969.
Prickett, Stephen, *Words and the World: Language, Poetics, and Biblical Interpretation*, Cambridge: Cambridge University Press, 1986.
—— (ed.) *Reading the Text: Biblical Criticism and Literary Theory*, Oxford: Blackwell, 1991.
Propp, Vladimir I., *Morphology of the Folktale*, (2nd edn.), Eng. Austin and London: University of Texas Press, 1968.
Quasten, Johannes, *Patrology*, Eng. Westminster: Christian Classics, 1984 (1950).
Quine, W.V.O., *Word and Object*, Cambridge, Mass.: M.I.T. Press, 1960.
Rad, Gerhard von, *Old Testament Theology* (2 vols.), Eng. Edinburgh: Oliver & Boyd, 1965.
Ramm, Bernard, *Protestant Biblical Interpretation* 3rd edn., Grand Rapids: Baker, 1970.
Rajchman, John and West, Cornel (eds.), *Post-Analytic Philosophy*, New York: Columbia University Press, 1985.
Rand, Richard, in Jacques Derrida, *Signéponge*, New York: Columbia University Press, 1984.
Raschke, Carl A., *The Alchemy of the Word: Language and the End of Theology*, Missoula: Scholars Press, 1979 (A.A.R. Studies in Religion 20).
Ray, William, *Literary Meaning: From Phenomenology to Deconstruction*, Oxford: Blackwell, 1984.
Reagan, Charles E. and Stewart, David (eds.), *The Philosophy of Paul Ricoeur: An Anthology of his Work*, Boston: Beacon Press, 1978.

Recanati, François, *Meaning and Force. The Pragmatics of Performative Utterances*, Eng. Cambridge: Cambridge University Press, 1987.
Redeker, Martin, *Schleiermacher's Life and Thought*, Eng. Philadelphia: Fortress Press, 1973.
Resseguie, James L., "Reader Response Criticism and the Synoptic Gospels", *Journal of the American Academy of Religion* 52, 1984, 307–24.
Reu, M., *Luther and the Scriptures*, Columbus, Ohio: Wartburg Press, 1944.
Reumann, John (ed.), *Studies in Lutheran Hermeneutics*, Philadelphia: Fortress, 1979.
Reumann, John, *Variety and Unity in New Testament Thought*, Oxford: Oxford University Press, 1991.
Reventlow, Henning Graf, *The Authority of the Bible and the Rise of the Modern World*, Eng. London: S.C.M., 1984.
Rhees, R., *Discussions of Wittgenstein*, London: Routledge & Kegan Paul, 1970.
Rhoads, David and Michie, Donald, *Mark as Story*, Philadelphia: Fortress Press, 1982.
Richards, Janet Radcliffe, *The Sceptical Feminist. A Philosophical Enquiry*, London: Penguin edn., 1983.
Riches, John K. and Millar, A., "Interpretation: A Theoretical Perspective and Some Applications", *Numen* 28, 1981, 29–53.
Ricoeur, Paul, *Le voluntaire et l'involuntaire*, Paris: Aubier, 1949, Eng. *Freedom and Nature: The Voluntary and the Involuntary*, Evanston: Northwestern University Press, 1966.
―――― *Fallible Man*, Eng. Chicago: Regnery, 1967.
―――― *The Symbolism of Evil*, Eng. Boston: Beacon Press, 1969 (1967).*
―――― *Freud and Philosophy: An essay on Interpretation*, Eng. New Haven: Yale University Press, 1970.*
―――― *The Conflict of Interpretations. Essays in Hermeneutics* (ed. Don Ihde), Evanston: Northwestern University Press, 1974.*
―――― *Interpretation Theory. Discourse and the Surplus of Meaning*, Fort Worth: Texas Christian University Press, 1976.*
―――― "Biblical Hermeneutics" *Semeia* 4, 1975, 29–148.*
―――― *The Rule of Metaphor. Multi-disciplinary Studies of the Creation of Meaning in Language*, Eng. London: Routledge and Kegan Paul, 1978 and Toronto: University of Toronto Press, 1977.*
―――― "Philosophical Hermeneutics, and Biblical Hermeneutics" in François Bovon and Gregoire Rouiller (eds.) *Exegesis: Problems of Method and Exercises in Reading*, Eng. Pittsburgh: Pickwick Press, 1978, 321–39.*
―――― "The Narrative Function" *Semeia* 13, 1978, 177–202.*
―――― *Hermeneutics and the Human Sciences*, Cambridge and New York: Cambridge University Press, 1981.*
―――― *Essays on Biblical Interpretation* (ed. L.S. Mudge), London: S.P.C.K., 1981.*
―――― "The Bible and the Imagination" in Hans Dieter Betz (ed.) *The Bible as a Document of the University*, Chico: Scholars Press, 1981, 49–75.*
―――― *The Reality of the Historical Past*, Milwaukee: Marquette University Press, 1984 (The Aquinas Lecture).*
―――― *Time and Narrative*, Eng. 3 vols., Chicago and London: University of Chicago Press, 1984–88.*
―――― "Interpretative Narrative" in Regina M. Schwartz (ed.) *The Book and the Text. The Bible and Literary Theory*, Oxford: Blackwell, 1990, 237–57.

Robbert, G.S., *Luther as Interpreter of Scripture*, St. Louis: Concordia, 1982.
Robey, David (ed.) *Structuralism. An Introduction*, Oxford: Clarendon Press, 1973.
Robinson, James M. and Cobb Jr., John B. (eds.), *New Frontiers in Theology: II, The New Hermeneutic*, New York: Harper and Row, 1964.
—— *New Frontiers in Theology: III, Theology as History*, New York: Harper and Row, 1967.
Robinson, R.B., *Roman Catholic Exegesis Since Divino Afflante Spiritu: Hermeneutical Implications*, Atlanta: Scholars Press (S.B.L. Dissertation Ser. III), 1988.
Rogers, Jack B., "The Book that Reads Us" *Interpretation* 39, 1985, 388–401.
Rogers, Jack B. and McKim, Donald K., *The Authority and Interpretation of the Bible. An Historical Approach*, San Francisco: Harper & Row, 1979.
Rogerson, John W., *Old Testament Criticism in the Nineteenth Century: England and Germany*, London: S.P.C.K., 1984.
—— "'What Does it Mean to Be Human?' The Central Question of Old Testament Theology" in D.J.A. Clines, S.E. Fowl and S.E. Porter (eds.), *The Bible in Three Dimensions*, Sheffield: Sheffield Academic Press, 1990, 285–98.
Rohrbaugh, Richard L., *The Biblical Interpreter. An Agrarian Bible in an Industrial Age*, Philadelphia: Fortress, 1978.
Rollins, Wayne G., *Jung and the Bible*, Atlanta: John Knox Press, 1983.
Rorty, Richard (ed.), *The Linguistic Turn: Recent Essays in Philosophical Method*, Chicago: Chicago University Press, 1967.
Rorty, Richard, *Philosophy and the Mirror of Nature*, Princeton: Princeton University Press, 1980 (1979).*
—— "A Reply to Dreyfus and Taylor" in *Review of Metaphysics* 34, 1980, 3–23.*
—— *Consequences of Pragmatism*, Minneapolis: University of Minnesota Press, 1982.*
—— "Habermas and Lyotard on Postmodernity" in Richard J. Bernstein (ed.) *Habermas and Modernity*, Cambridge: Polity Press, 1985, 161–75 (1984).*
—— "Texts and Lamps", *New Literary History* 17, 1985, 1–6.*
—— *Contingency, Irony and Solidarity*, Cambridge: Cambridge University Press, 1989.*
Rowland, Christopher, "Reading the New Testament Sociologically: An Introduction" *Theology* 88, 1985, 358–64.
Rowland, Christopher and Corner, Mark, *Liberating Exegesis. The Challenge of Liberation Theology to Biblical Studies*, London: S.P.C.K., 1990.
Ruether, Rosemary and McLaughlin, Eleanor (eds.), *Women of Spirit: Female Leadership in the Jewish and Christian Traditions*, New York: Simon and Schuster, 1979.
Ruether, Rosemary Radford, *Sexism and God-Talk: Towards a Feminist Theology*, London: S.C.M., 1983.
—— "The Future of Feminist Theology in the Academy", *Journal of the American Academy of Religion*, 53, 1985, 703–16.
Runia, K., "Some Crucial Issues in Biblical Interpretation" *Calvin Theological Journal* 24, 1989, 300–15.
Russell, Letty M. (ed.), *The Liberating Word. A Guide to Nonsexist Interpretation of the Bible*, Philadelphia: Westminster Press, 1976.
—— *Feminist Interpretation of the Bible*, Oxford and New York: Blackwell, 1985.
Sacks, Sheldon (ed.), *On Metaphor*, Chicago and London: University of Chicago Press, 1979.
Said, Edward, "The Problem of Textuality: Two Exemplary Positions", *Critical Inquiry*

4, 1978, 673-714 (on Derrida and Foucault).
—— *The World, The Text, and the Critic*, Cambridge, Mass: Harvard University Press, 1983.
Sakenfeld, K.D., "Feminist Biblical Interpretation" *Theology Today* 46, 1989, 154-68.
Sallis, John (ed.), *Deconstruction and Philosophy. The Texts of Jacques Derrida*, Chicago: University of Chicago Press, 1987.
Sanders, E.P., *Paul and Palestinian Judaism. A Comparison of Patterns of Religion*, London: S.C.M., 1977.
Sanders, J., *Torah and Canon*, Philadelphia: Fortress, 1972.
—— *Canon and Community*, Philadelphia: Fortress, 1984.
Sandmel, Samuel, *Philo of Alexandria. An Introduction*, Oxford: Oxford University Press, 1979.
—— *Philo's Place in Judaism* 2nd edn., New York: Ktav, 1971.
Sandt, Rob A. van der, *Context and Presupposition*, London and New York: Helm, 1988.
Santa Ana, Julio de "The Situation of Latin American Theology (1982-1987)" *Concilium: Theologies of the Third World, Convergences and Differences* (ed. L. Boff and V. Elizondo), Edinburgh: Clark, 1988.
Sartre, Jean-Paul, *Qu'est-ce que la littéature?* Paris: Gallimard, 1948.
Saussure, Ferdinand de, *Course in General Linguistics*, Eng. London: Owen, 1960.
—— *Cours de linguistique générale (édition critique)* by R. Engler, Wiesbaden: Harasowitz, 1967.
Sawyer, John F.A., "Context of Situation and *Sitz im Leben*", *Proceedings of the Newcastle- upon-Tyne Philosophical Society* 1, 1967, 137-47.
—— "The 'Original Meaning of the Text' and Other Legitimate Subjects in Semantic Description" in G. Brekelmans (ed.) *Questions disputées d'Ancien Testament*, Gembloux: Duculot, 1974, 63-70.
Scalise, C.J., "The 'Sensus Literalis': A Hermeneutical Key to Biblical Exegesis", *Scottish Journal of Theology* 42, 1989, 45-65.
Schaer, Hans, *Religion and the Cure of Souls in Jung's Psychology*, Eng. New York: Pantheon, 1950.
Schiffer, Stephen R., *Meaning*, Oxford: Clarendon Press, 1972.
Schillebeeckx, E., "La crise du language de la foi comme problème herméneutique" *Concilium* 85, 1973, 33-46.
—— *The Understanding of Faith: Interpretation and Criticism*, London: Sheed & Ward, 1974.
Schleiermacher, F.D.E., *On Religion, Speeches to its Cultural Despisers*, Eng. New York: Harper edn., 1958.
—— *Hermeneutik: Abhandlung der Heidelberger Akademie der Wissenschaften*, Heidelberg: Carl Winter, 1959.*
—— "Die Weinachtsfeier. Ein Gespräch", rp. in Schleiermacher's *Werke* IV, Aalen: Scientia Verlag, 1967 (From the 2nd Leipzig edn. of 1928), 475-532.
—— *Hermeneutik und Kritik. Mit einem Anhang sprachphilosophischer Texte Schleiermachers* (ed. Manfred Frank), Frankfurt a/M: Suhrkamp, 1977.*
—— *Hermeneutics: The Handwritten Manuscripts* edited by H. Kimmerle, Eng. Missoula: Scholars Press, 1977 (A.A.R. Text and Translation series 1, Tr. by J. Duke and J. Forstman).*
Schmidt, James, *Maurice Merleau-Ponty. Between Phenomenology and Structuralism*, London: MacMillan, 1985.

Schneidau, H.N., "Let the Reader Understand" *Semeia* 39, 1987, 135–45.
Schneiders, Sandra M., "The Paschal Imagination: Objectivity and Subjectivity in New Testament Interpretation", *Theological Studies* 43, 1982, 52–68.
────── "Church and Biblical Scholarship in Dialogue" *Theology Today* 42, 1985, 353–58.
Scholer, D.M., "Issues in Biblical Interpretation" *Evangelical Quarterly*, 60, 1988, 5–22.
Scholes, Robert, *Structuralism in Literature*, New Haven: Yale University Press, 1974.
────── *Semiotics and Interpretation*, New Haven: Yale University Press, 1982.
────── *Textual Power*, New Haven: Yale University Press, 1985.
Schrag, Calvin O., *Radical Reflection and the Origins of the Human Sciences*, West Lafayette: Purdue University Press, 1980.
Schröer, H., "Bibelauslegung durch Bibelgebrauch: Neue Wege 'Praktischer Exegese'", *Evangelische Theologie* 45, 1985, 500–15.
Schultz, Samuel J. and Inch, Morris A. (eds.), *Interpreting the Word of God. Festschrift in Honor of Steven Barabas*, Chicago: Moody Press, 1976.
Schutz, Alfred, *Collected Papers* (3 vols.), The Hague: Nijhoff, 1962, 1964 and 1966.
────── *Reflections on the Problem of Relevance* (ed. R.M. Zaner), New Haven: Yale University Press, 1970.
────── and Luckmann, Thomas, *The Structures of the Life-World*, Eng. London: Heinemann, 1974 and The Hague: Nijhoff, 1962–66.
Schütz, J.H., *Paul and the Anatomy of Apostolic Authority*, Cambridge: Cambridge University Press, 1975 (S.N.T.S.M. 26).
Schwartz, R.M. (ed.), *The Book and the Text. The Bible and Literary Theory* Oxford: Blackwell, 1990.
Schweitzer, Albert, *Paul and his Interpreters. A Critical History*, London: Black, 1912.
────── *The Mysticism of Paul the Apostle*, Eng. London: Black, 1931.
Scott, C.E., "Gadamer's *Truth and Method*", *Anglican Theological Review* 59, 1977, 63–78.
Searle, John R., *Speech Acts. An Essay in the Philosophy of Language*, Cambridge: Cambridge University Press, 1969.*
────── *Expression and Meaning. Studies in the Theory of Speech Acts*, Cambridge: Cambridge University Press, 1979.*
────── *Internationality. An Essay in the Philosophy of Mind*, Cambridge: Cambridge University Press, 1983.*
Searle, John R., Kiefer, Ferenc and Bierwisch, Manfred (eds.), *Speech-Act Theory and Pragmatics*, Dordrecht, London and Boston: Reidel, 1980.*
Searle, John R. and Vanderveken, Daniel, *Foundations of Illocutionary Logic*, Cambridge: Cambridge University Press, 1985.*
Sefler, George F., *Language and the World: A Methodological Synthesis Within the Writings of Martin Heidegger and Ludwig Wittgenstein*, Atlantic Highlands: Humanities Press, 1974.
Segundo, Juan Luis, *The Liberation of Theology*, Eng. Dublin: Gill & McMillan, 1977 and New York: Orbis, 1976.*
────── "Two Theories of Liberation", *The Month*, Oct. 1984, 321–27.
────── "The Shift within Latin American Theology" *Journal of Theology for Southern Africa*, 52, 1985, 17–29.
Senft, Christophe, "Ferdinand Christian Baur: Methodological Approach and Interpretation of Luke 15: 11–32" in François Bovon and Grégoire Rouiller (eds.)

Exegesis: Problems of Method and Exercises in Reading, Eng. Pittsburgh: Pickwick, 1978, 77–96.
Seung, T.K., *Structuralism and Hermeneutics*, New York: Columbia University Press, 1982.
Shaw, Graham, *The Cost of Authority. Manipulation and Freedom in the New Testament*, London: S.C.M., 1983.
Sheppard, G.T., "Biblical Hermeneutics: The Academic Language of Evangelical Identity", *Union Seminary Quarterly Review* 32, 1977, 81–94.
Shotwell, Willis A., *the Biblical Exegesis of Justin Martyr*, London: S.P.C.K., 1965.
Showalter, Elaine (ed.), *The New Feminist Criticism. Essays on Women, Literature and Theory*, London: Virago Press, 1986.
Silberman, Lou H., "Reflections on Orality, Aurality, and Perhaps More", *Semeia* 39, 1987, 1–6.
Silva, Moisés, *Biblical Words and their Meaning. An Introduction to Lexical Semantics*, Grand Rapids: Academic Books, 1983.
Silverman, Hugh J. and Ihde, Don (eds.), *Hermeneutics and Deconstruction*, Albany: State University of New York, 1985.
Singleton, C (ed.), *Interpretation: Theory and Practice*, Baltimore: Johns Hopkins University Press, 1969.
Smalley, Beryl, *The Study of the Bible in the Middle Ages*, 3rd edn., Oxford: Blackwell, 1983.
Smart, James D., *The Interpretation of Scripture*, London: S.C.M., 1961.
——— *The Strange Silence of the Bible in the Church: A study in Hermeneutics*, London: S.C.M. and Philadelphia: Westminster Press, 1970.
Soelle, Dorothee, *The Strength of the Weak: Towards a Christian Feminist Identity*, Eng. Philadelphia: Westminster, 1984.
Soskice, Janet Martin, *Metaphor and Religious Language*, Oxford: Clarendon Press, 1985, 158.
——— (ed.), *After Eve*, London: Collins and Marshall Pickering, 1990.
Spencer, Richard A. (ed.), *Orientation by Disorientation. Studies in Literary Criticism and Biblical Literary Criticism in Honor of W.A. Bearsdlee*, Pittsburgh: Pickwick Press, 1980.
Spiegel, Y., *Psychoanalytische Interpretationen biblischer Texte*, Munich: Kaiser, 1972.
Stack, Frank, *The Experience of a Poem: Jung and Wallace Stevens*, London: Guild of Pastoral Psychology, 1987.
Stanton, Graham N., *The Gospels and Jesus*, Oxford: Oxford University Press, 1989.
——— (ed.), *The Interpretation of Matthew*, Philadelphia: Fortress and London: S.P.C.K., 1983.
Starobinski, Jean, "The Gerasene Demoniac: A Literary Analysis of Mark 5:1–20" in R. Barthes, F. Bovon, et. al., *Structural Analysis and Biblical Exegesis*, Pittsburgh: Pickwick Press (Pittsburgh Theological Monograph 3), 1974, 57–84.
Staten, Henry, *Wittgenstein and Derrida*, Lincoln and London: University of Nebraska Press, 1984.
Stein, Dominique, "The Murder of the Father and God the Father in the Work of Freud" in Johannes-Baptist Metz and Edward Schillibeeckz (eds.) *God as Father? Concilium*, Edinburgh: Clark and New York: Seabury Press, 1981, 11–18.
Stein, S.J., "The Quest for the Spiritual Sense: the Biblical Hermeneutics of Jonathan Edwards", *Harvard Theological Review* 70, 1977, 99–113.
Stendahl, Krister, *Paul Among Jews and Gentiles and Other Essays*, London: S.C.M., 1977 and Philadelphia: Fortress, 1976.

——— *Meanings: the Bible as Document and as Guide*, Philadelphia: Fortress Press, 1984.
Sternberg. Meir, *The Poetics of Biblical Narrative: Ideological Literature and the Drama of Reading*, Bloomington: Indiana University Press, 1985.
Storkey, Elaine, *What's Right with Feminism*, London: S.P.C.K., 1985.
Stout, Jeffrey, "What is the Meaning of a Text?" *New Literary History*, 14, 1982, 1–12.
Stroup, George W., *The Promise of Narrative Theology*, London: S.C.M., 1984 (John Knox, 1981).
Stuhlmacher, Peter, *Historical Criticism and Theological Interpretation of Scripture. Towards a Hermeneutics of Consent*, Eng. Philadelphia: Fortress, 1977.
——— "Adolf Schlatter's Interpretation of Scripture" *New Testament Studies* 24, 1978, 433– 46. Sturrock, John (ed.), *Structuralism and Since: From Lévi Strauss to Derrida*, Oxford: Oxford University Press, 1979.
Suleiman, Susan R. and Crosman, Inge (eds.), *The Reader in the Text: Essays on Audience and Interpretation*, Princeton: Princeton University Press, 1980.
Suskind, Hermann, *Der Einfluss Schellings auf die Entwicklung von Schleiermachers System*, Tübingen: Mohr, 1909.
Swartley, Willard M, *Slavery, Sabbath, War and Women. Case Issues in Biblical Interpretation*, Scottdale: Herald Press, 1983.
Swidler, Leonard, *Biblical Affirmations of Women*, Philadelphia: Westminster Press, 1979.
Swinburne, Richard, "Meaning in the Bible" in S.R. Sutherland and T.A. Roberts (eds.) *Religion, Reason and the Self. Essays in Honour of H.D. Lewis*, Cardiff: University of Wales Press, 1989, 1–33.
Sykes, Stephen W., *The Identity of Christianity: Theologians and the Essence of Christianity from Schleiermacher to Barth*, Philadelphia: Fortress Press, 1984.
Tallis, Raymond, *Not Saussure. A Critique of Post-Saussurean Literary Theory*, London: MacMillan, 1988.
Tannehill, Robert, *Dying and Rising with Christ. A Study in Pauline Theology*, Berlin: Töpelmann, 1967.
——— *The Narrative Unity of Luke-Acts: A Literary Interpretation*, vol. 1, *The Gospel According to Luke*, Philadelphia: Fortress, 1986.
Taylor, Charles, "Interpretation and the Sciences of Man", *Review of Metaphysics* 25, 1971, 3–51.
Taylor, Mark C., *Deconstructing Theology*, New York: Crossroad and Chico: Scholars Press, 1982 (A.A.R. Studies in Religion 28).
——— *Erring: A Postmodern A/Theology*, Chicago: University of Chicago Press, 1984.
——— "Masking: Domino Effect" in "On Deconstructing Theology: A Symposium on *Erring: a Postmodern A/Theology*", *Journal of the American Academy of Religion* 54, 1986, 547– 57.
Taylor, Mark C. (ed.), *Unfinished...Essays in Honor of Ray L. Hart*, Chico: J.A.A.R. Thematic Issue 48, 1981.
Theissen, Gerd, *The Social Setting of Pauline Christianity. Essays on Corinth*, Eng. Philadelphia: Fortress, 1982, 121–43.
——— *Psychological Aspects of Pauline theology*, Eng. London: S.C.M., 1987.
Thiel, John E., *God and World in Schleiermacher's Dialektik und Glaubenslehre*, Bern, Frankfurt a/M.: Lang, 1981
Thielicke, Helmut, *The Evangelical Faith I*, Eng. Grand Rapids: Eerdmans, 1974.

Thiemann, Ronald F., *Revelation and Theology. The Gospel as Narrated Promise*, Notre Dame: University of Notre Dame Press, 1987 (1985).
—— "Radiance and Obscurity in Biblical Narrative" in Garrett Green (ed.) *Scriptural Authority and Narrative Interpretation*, Philadelphia: Fortress, 1987, 21–41.
Thils, G. and Brown, R.E. (eds.), *Exégèse et Theologie. Les saintes écritures et leur interpretation théologique*, Gembloux: Duculot, 1968.
Thiselton, Anthony C., "The Parables as Language-Event: Some Comments on Fuchs's Hermeneutics in the Light of Linguistic Philosophy", *Scottish Journal of Theology*, 23, 1970, 437–68.
—— "The Meaning of *Sarx* in 1 Cor. 5:5. A Fresh Approach in the Light of Logical and Semantic Factors" in *Scottish Journal of Theology* 26, 1973, 204–28.
—— "The Supposed Power of Words in the Biblical Writings", *Journal of Theological Studies* n.s. 25, 1974, 282–99.
—— "Kierkegaard and the Nature of Truth", *Churchman* 89, 1975, 85–107.
—— "Explain, Interpret" in Colin Brown (ed.) *The New International Dictionary of New Testament Theology*, Exeter: Paternoster and Grand Rapids: Zondervan, (3 vols. 1975–8) vol. 1, 573–84.
—— "Semantics and New Testament Interpretation" in I.H. Marshall (ed.) *New Testament Interpretation*, Grand Rapids: Eerdmans and Exeter: Paternoster Press, 1977, 75–104.
—— "The New Hermeneutic" in I.H. Marshall (ed.) *New Testament Interpretation*, Grand Rapids: Eerdmans and Exeter: Paternoster, 1977, 308–33.
—— "Realised Eschatology at Corinth", *New Testamtent Studies* 24, 1978, 510–26.
—— "Structuralism and Biblical Studies: Method or Ideology?" *Expository Times* 89, 1978, 329–35.
—— "Truth" in Colin Brown (ed.) *New International Dictionary of New Testament Theology* vol. 3, Exeter: Paternoster and Grand Rapids: Zondervan, 1978, 874–902.
—— "Schweitzer's Interpretation of Paul", *Expository Times* 90, 1979, 132–37.
—— *The Two Horizons: New Testament Hermeneutics and Philosophical Description with Special Reference to Heidegger, Bultmann, Gadamer, and Wittgenstein*, Grand Rapids: Eerdmans and Exeter: Paternoster, 1980.
—— "Knowledge, Myth and Corporate Memory" in *Believing in the Church: Essays by Members of the Church of England Doctrine Commission*, London: S.P.C.K., 1981, 45–78.
—— "The Morality of Christian Scholarship" in Mark Santer (ed.) *Their Lord and Ours: Approaches to Authority, Community, and the Unity of the Church*, London: S.P.C.K., 1982, 20–45.
—— "Sign, Symbol" in J.G. Davies (ed.) *New Dictionary of Liturgy and Worship*, London: S.C.M., 491–2.
—— "Address and Understanding: Some Goals and Models of Biblical Interpretation as Principles of Vocational Training", *Anvil* 3, 1986, 101–18.
—— "Speaking and Hearing" in Mark A. Noll and David F. Wells (eds.), *Christian Faith and Practice in the Modern World*, Grand Rapids: Eerdmans, 1988, 139–51.
—— "On Models and Methods: A Conversation with Robert Morgan" in David J.A.Clines, Stephen E. Fowl, and Stanley E. Porter (eds.) *The Bible in Three Dimensions: Essays in Celebration of Forty Years of Biblical Studies in the University of Sheffield*, Sheffield: Sheffield Academic Press (J.S.O.T. Suppl. Ser. 87) 1990,

337–56.

——— "Meaning" in R.J. Coggins and J.L.Houlden (eds.) *A Dictionary of Biblical Interpretation*, London: S.C.M., and Philadelphia: Trinity Press, 1990, 435–38.

——— Walhout, Clare and Lundin, Roger, *The Responsibility of Hermeneutics*, Grand Rapids: Eerdmans and Exeter: Paternoster, 1985.

Thompson, John B., *Critical Hermeneutics: A Study in the Thought of Paul Ricoeur and Jürgen Habermas*, Cambridge: Cambridge University Press, 1981.

——— *Studies in the Theory of Ideology*, Cambridge: Polity Press, 1984.

Thorne, Barrie, Kramer, Cheris, and Henley, Nancy (eds.), *Language, Gender, and Society*, Rowley, Mass.: Newbury House, 1983.

Tillich, Paul, *Systematic Theology* (3 vols.), London: Nisbet, 1953–64.

——— *Theology of Culture*, New York: Oxford University Press, Galaxy edn., 1964.

——— "The Meaning and Justification of Religious Symbols" and "The Religious Symbol" in Sydney Hook (ed.) *Religious Experience and Truth*, Edinburgh: Oliver and Boyd, 1961 (New York University, 1961), 3–11 and 301–21, also rp. in F.W. Dillistone (ed.) *Myth and Symbol*, London: S.P.C.K., 1966, 15–34.

Todorov, Tzvetan, "Reading as Construction" in Susan R. Suleiman and Inge Crosman (eds.) *The Reader in the Text. Essays on Audience Interpretation*, Princeton: Princeton University Press, 1980, 67–82.

——— *Symbolism and Interpretation*, Eng. Ithaca: Cornell University Press, 1982.

——— *Theories of Symbol*, Eng. Ithaca: Cornell University Press, 1984.

Tolbert, Mary Ann (ed.), *The Bible and Feminist Hermeneutics: Semeia* 28, 1983.

Tolbert, Mary Ann, "Protestant Feminists and the Bible: On the Horns of a Dilemma" *Union Seminary Quarterly Review* 43, 1989, 1–17.

Tollinton, R.B., *Selections from the Commentaries and Homilies of Origen*, London: S.P.C.K., 1929.

Tompkins, Jane P. (ed.), *Reader-Response Criticism. From Formalism to Post-Structuralism*, Baltimore and London: Johns Hopkins University Press, 1980.

Toolan, Michael J., *Narrative. A Critical Linguistic Introduction*, London and New York: Routledge, 1988.

Toon, Peter, *The Right of Private Judgment. The Study and Interpretation of Scripture in Today's Church*, Portland: Western Conservative Baptist Seminary, 1975.

Torrance, James, "Interpretation and Understanding in Schleiermacher's Theology: Some Critical Questions", *Scottish Journal of Theology* 21, 1968, 268–82.

Torrance, Thomas F., *Theological Science*, Oxford: Oxford University Press, 1969.

——— "Hermeneutics according to F.D.E. Schleiermacher", *Scottish Journal of Theology* 21, 1968, 257–67.

——— *The Hermeneutics of John Calvin*, Edinburgh: Scottish Academic Press, 1988.

Torjesen, Karen Jo, *Hermeneutical Procedure and Theological Method in Origen's Exegesis*, Berlin: Walter de Gruyter, 1986.

Torres, S. and Fabella, V., *The Emergent Gospel: Theology from the Underside of History*, New York: Orbis, 1978.

Torres, Sergio and Eagleson, John (eds.), *The Challenge of Basic Christian Communities*, New York: Orbis, 1981.

Tracy, David, *Blessed Rage for Order: the New Pluralism in Theology*, New York: The Seabury Press, 1975.

——— "Modes of Theological Argument" *Theology Today* 33, 1977, 387–95.

——— *The Analogical Imagination: Christian Theology and the Culture of Pluralism*, London: S.C.M., 1981.

―――― "The Foundations of a Practical Theology" in Don S. Browning (ed.) *Practical Theology*, San Francisco, 1983, 61–82.

―――― "Certainty in the Interpretation of Religion: the Question of Radical Pluralism" *New Literary History* 15, 1983–4, 289–309.

―――― *Plurality and Ambiguity: Hermeneutics, Religion and Hope*, San Francisco: Harper and Row, 1987.

Trible, Phyllis, "Depatriarchalizing in Biblical Tradition", *Journal of the American Academy of Religion* 41, 1973, 35–42; also in Elisabeth Koltun (ed.), *The Jewish Woman. New Persectives*, New York: Schocken Books, 1978, 217–40.

―――― *God and the Rhetoric of Sexuality*, Philadelphia: Fortress, 1978.

―――― "Feminist Hermeneutics and Biblical Studies", *The Christian Century*, Feb. 1982, 116– 18.

―――― *Texts of Terror. Literary-Feminist Readings of Biblical Narratives*, Philadelphia: Fortress Press, 1984.

Trigg, Joseph W., *Origen: The Bible and Philosophy in the Third-century Church*, London: S.C.M., 1983.

―――― *Biblical Interpretation* (Message of the Fathers of the Church, 9), Wilmington: Glazier, 1988.

Tuckett, Christopher, *Reading the New Testament. Methods of Interpretation*, London: S.P.C.K., 1987.

Tully, James (ed.), *Meaning and Context: Quentin Skinner and his Critics*, Cambridge: Polity Press, 1988.

Tupper, E. Frank, *The Theology of Wolfhart Pannenberg*, London: S.C.M., 1974 and Philadelphia: Westminster, 1973.

Turner, G., "Pre-Understanding and New Testament Interpretation", *Scottish Journal of Theology* 28, 1975, 227–42.

Tuttle, Howard N., *Wilhelm Dilthey's Philosophy of Historical Understanding*, Leiden: Brill, 1969.

Tutu, Desmond M., "The Theology of Liberation in Africa" in K. Appiah-Kubi and T. Sergio (eds.), *African Theology en Route*, New York: Orbis, 1979.

―――― "Black Theology and African Theology – Soulmates or Antagonists?" in John Parratt (ed.) *A Reader in African Christian Theology*, London: S.P.C.K., 1987, 46–55.

Uffenheimer, B. and Reventlow, Henning Graf (eds.), *Creative Biblical Exegesis. Christian and Jewish Hermeneutics through the Centuries*, Sheffield: Sheffield Academic Press (J.S.O.T. Suppl. 59), 1988.

Ullmann, Stephen, *Semantics. An Introduction to the Science of Meaning*, Oxford: Blackwell, 1962.

Urban, W.M., *Language and Reality*, New York and London: Allen and Unwin, 1939.

Van Aarde, A. G., "Narrative Criticism" in P.J. Hartin and J.H. Petzer (eds.) *Text and Interpretation. New Approaches in the Criticism of the New Testament*, Leiden: Brill, 1991, 101–28.

VanderGoot, Henry, *Interpreting the Bible in Theology and Church*, Toronto: Edwin Mellen, 1984.

Vanderveken, Daniel, "Illocutionary Logic and Self-Defeating Speech Acts" in J.R. Searle, F. Kiefer, and M. Bierwisch (eds.), *Speech Act Theory and Pragmatics*, Dordrecht and Boston: Riedel 1980, 247–72.

Vanhoozer, Kevin J., *Biblical Narrative in the Philosophy of Paul Ricoeur. A Study in Hermeneutics and Theology*, Cambridge: Cambridge University Press, 1990.

Vawter, Bruce, *Biblical Inspiration*, Philadelphia: Westminster and London: Hutchinson, 1972.
—— *On Genesis: A New Reading*, New York: Doubleday, 1977.
Via Jr., Dan Otto, *The Parables. Their Literary and Existential Dimension*, Philadelphia: Fortress, 1967.
—— *Kerygma and Comedy in the New Testament. A Structuralist Approach to Hermeneutics*, Philadelphia: Fortress, 1975.
Villiers, P.G.R. de, "New Testament Scholarship in South Africa", *Neotestamentica* 23, 1989, 119–24.
Virkler, Henry A., *Hermeneutics. Principles and Processes of Biblical Interpretation*, Grand Rapids: Baker, 1981.
Voelz, J.W., "The Problem of 'Meaning' in Texts" *Neotestamentica* 23, 1989, 33–43.
Vogels, W., *Reading and Preaching the Bible: A New Semiotic Approach*, Wilmington: Glazier, 1986.
Vološinov, V.M., *Marxism and the Philosophy of Language*, Eng. Cambridge, Mass.: Harvard University Press, 1986 (1973).
Vorster, N.S., "The Reader in the Text: Narrative Material" *Semeia* 48, 21–39.
Wadsworth, M. (ed.), *Ways of Reading the Bible*, Sussex: Harvester Press and New Jersey: Barnes and Noble, 1981.
Wachterhauser, B.R. (ed.), *Hermeneutics and Modern Philosophy*, New York: Albany State University of New York Press, 1986.
Walhout, Clarence, Lundin, Roger and Thiselton, Anthony C., *The Responsibility of Hermeneutics*, Grand Rapids: Eerdmans and Exeter: Paternoster, 1985.
Wallace, M.I., *The Second Naïveté. Barth, Ricoeur, and the New Yale Theology* (Studies in American Biblical Hermeneutics), Macon: Mercer University Press, 1990.
Walsh, Katherine and Wood, Diana (eds.), *The Bible in the Medieval World: Essays in Memory of Beryl Smalley*, Oxford: Blackwell, 1985.
Walton, Kendall L., "How Remote are Fictional Worlds from the Real World?" *Journal of Aesthetics and Art Criticism* 38, 1978, 11–23.
—— "Fearing Fictions" in D.L. Boyer, P. Grim, and J.T. Sanders (eds.) *The Philosophical Annual* 2, Oxford: Blackwell, 1979, 191–214.
Warner, Martin (ed.), *The Bible as Rhetoric. Studies in Biblical Persuasion and Credibility*, London and New York: Routledge (Warwick Studies in Philosophy and Literature) 1990.
Warnke, Georgia, *Gadamer. Hermeneutics, Tradition and Reason*, Cambridge: Polity Press, 1987.
Watson, Francis, *Paul, Judaism and the Gentiles. A Sociological Approach*, Cambridge: Cambridge University Press (S.N.T.S.M. 56), 1986.
Wedderburn, A.J.M., *The Reasons for Romans*, Edinburgh: Clark, 1988.
Weiler, Gershon, *Mauthner's Critique of Language*, Cambridge: Cambridge University Press, 1970.
Weinsheimer, Joel C., *Gadamer's Hermeneutics. A Reading of "Truth and Method"*, New Haven: Yale University Press, 1985.
Wellek, René and Warren, Austin, *Theory of Literature*, London: Penguin Books, 1973 (1949).
West, Cornel, "After Word: the Politics of American Neo-Pragmatism" in J. Rajchman and Cornel West (eds.), *Post-Analytic Philosophy*, New York: Columbia University Press, 1985.
—— *Prophetic Fragments*, Grand Rapids: Eerdmans, 1988.

West, Gerald O., *Biblical Interpretation in Theologies of Liberation: Modes of Reading the Bible in the Southern African Context of Liberation*, University of Sheffield Ph.D. Dissertation, 1989.
Westerholm, S., "'Letter and Spirit': the Foundation of Pauline Ethics" *New Testament Studies* 30, 1984,229–48.
Westermann (ed.), *Essays in Old Testament Hermeneutics*, Richmond: John Knox, 1963.
Wheelwright, Philip, *The Burning Fountain: A Study in the Language of Symbolism*, Bloomington: Indiana University Press, 1954.
―――― *Metaphor and Reality*, Bloomington: Indiana University Press, 1962 and 1968.
White, Hayden, *Metahistory: the Historical Imagination in Nineteenth-Century Europe*, Baltimore: Johns Hopkins University Press, 1973.
White, Hugh C. (ed.), *Speech Act Theory and Biblical Criticism, Semeia* 41, 1988.
White, Stephen K., *The Recent Work of Jürgen Habermas. Reason, Justice, and Modernity*, Cambridge: Cambridge University Press, 1988 and 1989.
Whorf, Benjamin L., *Language, Thought and Reality: Selected Writings of Benjamin Lee Whorf*, ed. J.B. Carroll, Cambridge Mass.: M.I.T. Press, 1956.
Whybray, R.N., "On Robert Alter's *The Art of Biblical Narrative*", *Journal for the Study of the Old Testament* 27, 1983, 75–117.
Wilder, Amos N., *Jesus' Parables and the War of Myths. Essays on Imagination in the Scriptures*, Philadelphia: Fortress, 1982.
Wiles, Maurice F., *The Divine Apostle. The Interpretation o St. Paul's Epistles in the Early Church*, Cambridge: Cambridge University Press, 1967.
Williams, J.G., "Exegesis-Eisegesis: is There a Difference?", *Theology Today* 30, 1973, 218–27.
Williams, Raymond B., "Origen's Interpretation of the Old Testament and Lévi-Strauss' Interpretation of Myth" in A.L. Merrill and T.W. Overholt (eds.) *Scripture in History and Theology: Essays in Honour of J.C. Rylaarsdam*, Pittsburgh: Pickwick Press, 1977, 279–99.
Williams, Robert, *Schleiermacher the Theologian. The Construction of the Doctrine of God*, Philadelphia: Fortress, 1978.
―――― "Schleiermacher, Hegel, and the Problem of Concrete Universality", *Journal of the American Academy of Religion* 56, 1988, 473–96.
Williamson, Ronald, *Philo and the Epistle to the Hebrews*, Leiden: Brill, 1970.
Wilson, B.A., "Hirsch's Hermeneutics: a Critical Examination", *Philosophy Today* 22, 1978, 20–33.
Wilson, R. McL., "Of Words and Meanings" *Journal for the Study of the New Testament* 37, 1989, 9–15.
Wilmer, Richard H., "Hooker on Authority", *Anglican Theological Review* 32, 1951, 102–8.
Wimbush, V.L., "Historical/Cultural Criticism as Liberation: A Proposal for an African American Biblical Hermeneutic" *Semeia* 47, 1989, 43–55.
Wimsatt, William K., "Genesis: A Fallacy Re-visited" in Peter Demetz *et al.*, *The Disciplines of Criticism: Essays in Literary Theory, Interpretation and History*, New Haven: Yale University Press, 1968, 193–225.
Wimsatt, William K. and Beardsley, Monroe, "The Intentional Fallacy" in W.K. Wimsatt, The Verbal Icon: studies in the Meaning of Poetry, New York: Noonday Press, 1966 (1954).
Winch, Peter, *The Idea of a Social Science and its Relation to Philosophy*, London: Routledge & Kegan Paul, 1958.

Wink, W., *The Bible in Human Transformation. Toward a New Paradigm for Biblical Study*, Philadelphia: Fortress Press, 1973.
—— *Transforming Bible Study*, Nashville: Abingdon, 1980.
—— *Unmasking the Power*, Philadelphia: Fortress, 1986.
Winquist, Charles E., *Practical Hermeneutics. A Revised Agenda for the Ministry*, Chico: Scholars Press, 1980.
—— *Epiphanies of Darkness: Deconstruction in Theology*, Philadelphia: Fortress Press, 1986
Wittgenstein, Ludwig, *Notebooks* 1914–16, Eng. Oxford: Blackwell, 1961.
—— *Tractatus Logico-Philosophicus*, Germ. & Eng., London: Routledge & Kegan Paul, 1961.
—— *Philosophische Bemerkung* (1929–30), Oxford: Blackwell, 1964.
—— *Philosophical Grammar* (1929–34), Oxford: Blackwell, 1974.*
—— *The Blue and Brown Books* 2nd edn. Oxford: Blackwell, 1969.*
—— *Remarks on the Foundations of Mathematics*, Germ. and Eng., Oxford: Blackwell, 1956.
—— *Philosophical Investigations* (1936–49), Germ. & Eng. Oxford: Blackwell, 3rd edn. 1967.*
—— *Lectures and Conversations on Aesthetics, Psychology, and Religious Belief*, Oxford: Blackwell, 1967.
—— *Zettel*, Germ. and Eng. Oxford: Blackwell, 1967.*
—— "Bemerkungen über Frazers *The Golden Bough*" in *Synthese* 17, 1967, 233–53.*
—— "Notes for Lectures on Private Experience and 'Sense Data'" in *Philosophical Review* 77, 1968, 271–320.*
—— *On Certainty*, Germ. and Eng. Oxford: Blackwell, 1969.*
—— *Culture and Value*, Eng. and Germ. 2nd edn. Oxford: Blackwell, 1980.*
Wittig, Susan (ed.) *Structuralism: An Interdisciplinary Study*, Pittsburgh: Pickwick Press, 1975.
—— "A Theory of Multiple Meanings" *Semeia* 9, 1977, 75–105.
Witvliet, Theo, *The Way of the Black Messiah*, Eng. London: S.C.M., 1987.
Wolfson, Harry A., *Philo* (2 vols.) Cambridge: Harvard University Press, 1947.
Wolterstorff, Nicholas, *Art in Action: Towards a Christian Aesthetic*, Grand Rapids: Eerdmans, 1980.
—— *Works and Worlds of Art*, Oxford: Clarendon Press, 1980.
Wood, Charles M., *Theory and Understanding. A Critique of the Hermeneutics of Joachim Wach*, Missoula: Scholars Press and A.A.R., 1975.
Wood, A. Skevington, *The Principles of Biblical Interpretation as Enunciated by Irenaeus, Origen, Augustine, Luther and Calvin*, Grand Rapids: Zondervan, 1967.
—— *Captive to the Word: Martin Luther, Doctor of Sacred Scripture*, Exeter: Paternoster, 1969.
Worton, Michael, and Still, Judith (eds.), *Intertextuality: Theories and Practices*, Manchester: Manchester University Press, 1990.
N.T. Wright, *The Messiah and the People of God: A Study in Pauline Theology with Particular Reference to the Argument of the Epistle to the Romans*. D. Phil. Thesis, Oxford: University of Oxford, 1980.
—— "Jesus, Israel, and the Cross" in K.H. Richards (ed.) *Society of Biblical Literature Seminar Papers*, Atlanta: Scholars Press, 1985, 75–95.
—— *The Climax of the Covenant. Christ and the Law in Pauline Theology*. Edinburgh: Clark, 1991.

Wright, T.R., *Theology and Literature*, Oxford: Blackwell, 1988.
Wuellner, W., "Is There an Encoded Reader Fallacy?" *Semeia* 48, 1989, 41–54.
Wunderlich, Dieter, "Methodological Remarks on Speech-Act Theory" in J.R.Searle, F. Kiefer, and M. Bierwisch (eds.), *Speech-Act Theory and Pragmatics*, Dordrecht: Reidel, 1980, 291– 312.
Young, Frances, *The Art of Performance. Towards a Theology of Holy Scripture*, London: Darton, Longman, and Todd, 1990.
Young, Frances, and Ford, David, *Meaning and Truth in* 2 *Corinthians*, London: S.P.C.K., 1987.
Young, Robert (ed.), *Untying the Text: A Post-Structuralist Reader*, London: Routledge & Kegan Paul, 1981.
Ziman, John M., *Public Knowledge: An Essay Concerning the Social Dimension of Science*, Cambridge: Cambridge University Press, 1968.
Zuck, John E., "The New Hermeneutic Language: A Critical Appraisal" *Journal of Religion* 52, 1972, 397–416.
———— "Tales of Wonder: Biblical Narrative, Myth and Fairy Stories" *Journal of the American Academy of Religion* 44, 1976, 299–308.

INDEX OF AUTHORS

Aageson, J.W. 149, 163
Achtemeier, Elizabeth 456–460
Adorno, T.W. 381, 385–87, 418
Allen, Stuart 193
Alt, A 305
Alter, Robert 50, 476, 479, 481, 569, 573
Althusser, Louis 131, 347, 427, 472
Altizer, Thomas 119
Alves, Rubem 415
Ambrose 183
Anderson, B.W. 432, 479
Anscombe, Elizabeth 294
Anselm of Canterbury 142, 144–45, 183, 209, 369
Apel, Karl-Otto 7, 11, 12, 28, 87, 88, 113, 128, 148, 253, 314, 318, 329–31, 334, 337, 344, 381, 383, 386, 390, 393, 394–98, 401–05, 430, 437, 440–42, 451, 536, 539, 541–43, 607, 611
Aquinas, Thomas 183
Arendt, Hannah 315
Arens, E. 17, 289, 291
Aristobulus 159
Aristotle 61, 82, 104, 122, 145, 192, 194, 315, 321, 352–53, 355, 380, 383, 413
Assman, Hugo 413, 415
Ast, F. 22, 197–98, 209, 214–16, 221

Athanasius 154
Atkinson, James 180
Auden, W.H. 369
Augustine 83, 146, 183, 192, 263, 277, 334, 506
Aurelio, T. 17, 289, 290
Austin, John L. 16, 17, 18, 20, 32, 70, 261, 272–74, 275, 278, 282–84, 286, 290–300, 304, 313, 361–62, 364–66, 384, 386–87, 539, 591, 599, 600, 601
Avis, Paul 380, 414
Ayer, A.J. 21, 37, 91, 113, 217, 454

Bailey, Ken 43
Baird, J. Arthur 273
Baker, Gordon P. 541
Bakhtin (see Baxtin)
Ballard, Paul 556, 604
Balthaser, Hans Urs von 167
Balzac, Honoré de 98
Barclay, J. 444
Barfield, Owen 353
Barnard, Leslie 157
Barr, J. 453
Barrett, C.K. 163, 237
Barth, Karl 209, 212, 220, 225, 229–30, 272, 276, 278, 370, 556, 605
Barth, Markus 32, 70, 301
Barthes, Roland 21, 47, 57, 75, 81, 82, 83, 91, 92–103, 117, 119, 122, 124, 127–29, 145, 288,

366, 427, 461, 473, 477, 479, 480, 488–90, 492–93, 500, 503, 504, 534, 536–37, 562, 582, 590, 600
Barton, J. 499–506, 517, 525, 535, 547, 583, 602, 612
Bass, D. 437
Bassler, J. 516, 519, 520, 586
Battles, F.L. (with Richard Wevers) 185
Bauckham, R. 461
Bauman, Zygmunt 198, 325, 382, 387, 559, 606–08
Baur, Ferdinand Christian 197, 233, 242, 254, 258
Bavinck, H. 184
Baxtin, M.M. 389, 390
Beale, G.K. 150
Beardsley, M. 59
Beasley-Murray, G.R. 579, 585
Beauvoir, S. de 435–36, 444
Bede 183
Beisser, Friedrich 182–84
Beker, J. Christiaan 24, 239, 240, 242
Belo, Fernando 48, 427–28
Benoist, J.M. 487, 496
Benveniste, Emile 298, 355, 480
Berger, Peter 326, 327, 606–07
Bergson, H. 321

Berkouwer, G.C. 184
Berlin, Adele 50
Berlin, B. 103
Bernstein, Richard 25, 315, 318, 327, 358, 380–82, 387, 394, 398, 413, 451, 545, 574
Berryman, Phillip 413
Best, Ernest 71, 288, 447, 481, 484
Betti, Emilio 4, 10, 24, 33, 49, 196, 247, 251–53, 313, 329, 331, 335, 390, 430, 435, 439, 448, 462, 537, 546, 558, 560, 561
Beuken, W. 504
Black, Max 103, 352, 353, 354, 454
Blackman, E.C. 164
Bleich, David 15, 60, 61, 395, 471, 528–36, 546, 550, 578, 586
Bleicher, Josef 253
Bloch, Ernst 351, 416–18
Bloom, Harold 88, 104, 115
Bloomfield, Leonard 87, 90
Boeckh, Philip August 22, 59, 197, 198, 215, 216
Boesak, A. 421, 424–26
Boethius 192, 193
Boff, C. 411–15, 430
Boff L. 411–13, 430
Bonhoeffer, Dietrich 34, 74, 503, 618, 619
Bonino, J. Miguez 413, 415
Booth, Wayne 60, 484, 521, 529
Borges, Jorges Luis 118
Boring, Eugene 288
Bornkamm, G. 246, 286, 287
Bornkamm, Heinrich 182, 190

Bostock, G. 163, 167, 172
Bousset, Wilhelm 239, 285
Bovon, François 62, 495, 496
Brandt, Richard 213, 227, 229
Braun, Herbert 455
Breck, John 64
Brett, Mark 546, 547
Brooks, Cleanth 115
Brown, Raymond 306
Browning, Don 556, 604
Bruce, F.F. 163, 256, 257
Buber, Martin 73, 345
Buchanan, George Wesley 265
Bullinger, Heinrich 194–95
Bultmann, Rudolf 10, 17, 24, 44, 45, 159, 161, 239, 243, 236, 251, 259, 272, 274–76, 278–82, 313, 332, 347, 370, 385, 413, 440, 449, 452–54, 460, 526, 556–57, 563, 605
Bunyan, John 157, 170
Buren, van Paul 395
Buthelezi, Manas 424

Cadbury, H.J. 257
Caird, G.B. 16, 41, 475, 499, 579, 584
Cairns, D. 455
Calloud, Jean 488, 491, 493, 496
Calvin, John 9, 23, 61, 164, 179, 180, 185–94, 207, 257, 275, 437, 533
Cameron, Deborah 461
Cannon, Katie Geneva 438
Caputo, John 51, 145
Cardinal Ernesto 412
Carnap, Rudolf 87
Carson, D.A. 150
Cassirer, Ernst 347

Castro, Emilio 415
Cavell, Stanley 362
Cerfaux, L. 284
Chapman, J. Arundel 210
Chatman, Seymour 15, 355, 479, 480, 521, 568, 586
Childs, Brevard 36, 37, 41, 314, 455, 500
Chilton, Bruce 151
Chladenius, Johann Martin 61, 195, 196–97, 214
Chomsky, N. 88, 91, 494, 499
Chopp, Rebecca S. 437, 461
Chrysostom, John 142, 172, 191
Cicero 61, 185
Ciezkowski, A.V. 414
Clement of Alexandria 146, 153, 165, 166–67, 171, 180, 581
Clement of Rome 165, 263
Clévenot, Michel 428–29, 582
Clines, David J.A. 9, 40, 114, 120–21, 124, 304, 462, 475, 500, 569, 590
Cohen, Ted 276, 353
Coleridge, S.T. 472, 476
Colet, John 186
Collingwood, R.G. 276
Collins, Adela Yarboro 473
Comte, A. 383, 384
Cone, James H. 413, 420–22, 426
Conn, Harvie M. 594 n.59
Conzelmann, H. 246
Corner, Mark 3, 379, 380, 411, 412, 425, 603
Corrington, Robert S. 12, 84, 87, 399, 400
Court, John M. 81

Courtivron, Isabelle de (with Marks, Elaine) 435
Cox, Ronald R. 608
Cranfield, Charles E.B. 237
Cranmer, Thomas 194
Crites, Stephen 481, 567–68, 614
Croatto, J. Severino 413, 415, 425
Cronbach, Abraham 44
Crosman, Inge 60, 529
Crosman, Robert 60
Crossan, John Dominic 51, 65, 88, 114, 115–20, 124, 126, 129, 157, 290, 370, 570–71, 591
Crystal, David 585
Culler, Jonathan 15, 27, 38, 42, 101, 393, 400, 494, 495, 497–500, 504, 506, 524–26, 528–30, 532–33, 535–37, 544, 545, 550, 586, 615
Culley, Robert 491, 496
Cullmann, Oscar 284
Culpepper, R. Alan 520–22, 548, 586
Cupitt, Don 126
Cyril of Alexandria 146

Daly, Mary 436, 440, 441, 455, 580
Dannhauer, J.C. 194, 214
Dante 144
Davies, W.D. 239
Dawsey, James 484
Deeks, David 604
Deissmann, Adolf 238, 239, 243, 302, 503
Delorme, J. 617
de Man, Paul 88, 104, 111, 115, 130, 472, 506, 590
Demosthenes 185

Derrida, Jacques 21, 47, 51, 57, 58, 75, 83, 88, 89, 91, 99, 101, 103–32, 145, 288, 318, 323, 367, 427, 461, 472–74, 486, 523, 533, 535, 574, 582–92, 590, 600–01
Descartes, R. 36, 91, 143, 145, 147, 186–87, 230, 321, 350, 570
Detweiler, Robert 97
Dewey, J. 394–99, 401, 414, 451, 545
Dibelius, M. 243
Dickens, Charles 355
Dilthey, Wilhelm 4, 7, 10, 33, 45, 113, 145, 196, 198, 205, 206, 213, 247–56, 258, 261, 266, 267, 276, 279, 313, 318, 322, 326, 333, 335, 337, 358, 383–84, 387, 389, 390, 402, 435, 439, 462, 493, 522, 558–61, 606, 608, 610–11
Dodd, C.H. 65, 146, 164, 611
Dornish, Loretta 345, 369, 372
Douglas, Mary 427
Draisma, Spike 498
Dray, William 403
Dreyfus, Hubert 125, 317
Droysen, J.G. 318
Duke, James 208, 217, 226
Dunn, James 36, 237, 241, 242, 284, 285, 287, 446
Duras, Marguerite 436
Durkheim 384, 387
Dürr, L. 292
Du Plessis, J.G. 17, 283, 289–91
Dussel, Enrique 415
Dworkin, Ronald 539

Dwyer, P. 92

Eagleton, Terry 131, 426, 474
Ebeling, G. 11, 184, 194, 286, 314, 325
Eberhard, J.A. 212
Eco, Umberto 9, 15, 20, 41, 47, 66, 82, 131, 157–58, 160, 166, 477, 506, 524–29, 535, 550, 583, 584, 586, 587
Ehrmann, J. 117
Eichholz, Georg 239
Eichrodt, W. 305
Eliezer, Rabbi 145
Eliot, T.S. 115, 116
Ellis, E. Earle 163
Engelmann, Paul 53 (n.23)
Epicurus 182
Erasmus, Desiderius 23, 61, 180–82, 186
Ernesti, J.A. 195, 214
Euripedes 160
Evans, Donald D. 16, 272, 274–75, 278, 282–84, 290, 292, 296, 298, 300, 615
Evans, Gillian R. 23, 144, 191–93
Evans, Mary 437, 539, 566, 570, 573
Exum, J. Cheryl 432

Fann, K.T. 292
Farley, Edward 556, 605
Farrar, Frederick 156, 163
Fee, Gordon D. 254, 255
Felde, Johannes von 195, 214
Ferguson, Duncan 171
Feuerbach, L. 346, 413, 414, 417
Feyerabend, Paul 148
Fichte, J.G. 213, 227, 229
Fiorenza, Elizabeth Schussler 431–33,

437, 442–49, 455, 456, 462, 548
Firth, J.R. 61
Fish, Stanley 7, 12, 15, 19, 27, 50, 60, 61, 87, 125, 395, 398, 400–02, 405, 451, 474, 502–03, 515–19, 522–24, 528–31, 533, 535–50, 574, 586–92, 600–01, 615–16
Fishbane, Michael 19, 39–41, 125, 503
Fisher, G.P. 211
Fiss, Owen 539–541
Flacius (Matthias Flacius Illyricus) 194–95, 335
Florovsky, Georges 64
Foerster, Werner 153
Fokkema, D.W. 92, 97
Ford, David F. 468 (n.163)
Foreman, T. 213
Forstman, Jack 210, 217, 226
Foucault, M. 366, 396, 472, 492, 493
Fowl, Stephen E. 314, 547–48
Fowler, Robert M. 282, 316, 519–20, 522, 526, 548, 575, 586
France, R.T. 286
Frege G. 364–65
Frei, Hans 26, 195, 370, 485–86, 500, 503, 572–73, 606, 609
Freiday, Dean 191
Freire, Paulo 416, 610
Freud, Sigmund 14, 47, 48, 51, 92–94, 104, 105, 110–12, 143, 198, 228, 259–60, 343–51, 361, 367, 379, 381–84, 393, 413, 439, 472, 495, 529–31, 575–80
Freund, Elizabeth 529
Freyne, S. 505

Frick, F. 547
Friedman, Shamma 125
Frye, Northrop 60, 91, 143, 144, 486, 575
Fuchs, Ernst 16, 34, 115, 119, 248, 273, 292, 314, 325, 481, 492, 567–68, 576
Funk, Robert W. 65, 70, 116, 290, 491, 492, 518, 570, 572, 575
Fyall, Robert 14

Gadamer, Hans-Georg 1, 3, 6, 8, 10–12, 17, 24, 33, 38, 46, 61, 88, 113, 123, 128, 145–47, 186, 222, 232, 251–53, 256, 313–31, 332–35, 337, 344, 348, 357–59, 366, 368, 381–83, 388, 390, 394, 397–403, 412, 430, 437, 440, 445, 462, 486, 493, 497, 516, 531, 534, 536, 542, 545–46, 567–68, 570, 608, 610
Gale, Herbert M. 507
Galloway, Allan 335
Garrett, Clive 276
Gazdar, G. 366
Geffré, Claude 616, 617
Genette, Gérard 15, 355, 479–80, 520, 568, 586
George, Stefan 107
Gerhart, Mary 359, 370
Gerlemann, G. 571
Gerrish, B.A. 210, 211
Geuss, R. 381
Goba, Bonganjalo 421, 424–25
Goldingay, John 189, 571
Good, Edwin M. 477, 483
Goodenough, E.R. 159
Goodman, Nelson 352
Goppelt, L. 150, 162
Göttner-Abendroth, Heide 459

Gottwald, Norman K. 391, 426–28, 462, 547, 582
Grant, Patrick 72, 473, 474, 483, 494, 496, 506, 507, 523
Grant, R.M. (with Tracy, David) 164
Grayston, Kenneth 476
Greenwood, D. 488
Greer, Germaine 435, 438
Greer, R.A. (with Kugel, J.L.) 171
Gregg, R.C. (with Groh, D.E.) 154
Gregory the Great 183
Greidanus, Sidney 573
Greimas, Alexander J. 15, 91, 97, 478, 487–94, 496, 566
Grether, O. 292
Grice, H.P. 38, 59, 289, 291, 365, 366, 539
Grobel, K. 153
Groh, D.E. (with Gregg, R.C.) 154
Groome, Thomas 556, 610
Guiraud, Pierre 487
Gunn, David M. 475–78, 571
Gunneweg, A.H.J. 166
Guthrie, Donald 261, 445
Gutiérrez, Gustavo 414–17, 425, 438–39
Güttgemanns, Erhardt 91, 494–97

Habermas, Jürgen 3, 7, 11, 12, 15, 23, 25, 28, 48, 103, 113, 148, 313, 315, 318, 329, 331, 334–35, 337, 344, 346, 358, 367, 368, 379–93, 395–99, 401–02, 404, 405, 416, 425, 430, 437, 440,

442, 451, 473, 484, 505, 536, 539, 542, 544, 592, 604, 607, 608, 610–12
Hacker, P.M. 541
Hagner, Donald A. 53, n.21
Hampson, Daphne 580
Hancher, Michael 288
Hanson, Anthony T. 149, 157, 302, 303
Hanson, Richard P.C. 146, 156, 164, 166, 171
Harari, J.V. 113
Hare, R.M. 364, 394
Harnack, Adolf von 155, 170, 242, 605
Harran, Marilyn J. 189
Hart, H.L.A. 539
Hart, Kevin 591
Hartin, P.J. 122
Hartman, Geoffrey 88, 104, 111, 115, 497
Hartmann, Nicolai 251, 252
Harvey, Anthony E. 360
Harvey, David 88
Hauerwas, Stanley 568
Hays, R.B. 498, 505
Hegel, G.W.F. 88, 100, 105, 113, 247, 250–52, 276, 315, 319, 321, 330–35, 349, 356, 371, 382, 384, 385, 414, 416, 534, 542, 565
Heidegger, Martin 17, 24, 33, 44, 45, 51, 104–10, 115, 119, 121, 123, 125–27, 147, 196, 249, 272–74, 276, 279–83, 288, 294, 313, 315, 318–21, 325–26, 328, 333, 335, 344, 345, 347, 349, 351, 352, 356, 358–61, 370–71, 383, 395–97, 472, 497, 567, 569

Heine, Susanne 450, 457–60, 533, 534
Hempel, Carl 403
Heraclitus Stoicus 158
Herder, J.G. 198, 210, 215, 226, 227, 250
Herrmann, Wilhelm 276, 605
Hertz, Heinrich 276
Hervey, Sándor 87, 95, 97
Hesiod 145, 158
Hesse, Mary 148, 354
High, Dallas M. 617
Hill, David 150, 286
Hillel, Rabbi 145
Hippocrates 82
Hippolytus 153, 263
Hirsch, E.D. 13, 37, 127, 471, 500
Hjelmslev, L. 94
Hobbes, Thomas 83, 186, 353
Hock, Ronald 257, 258
Hodges, H.A. 247
Hofius, Olfried 262
Holland, Norman 15, 87, 515, 529–33, 536, 550, 578, 586–87
Holmberg, P. 241
Homer 122, 145, 158, 160
Hooker, Morna 150
Hooker, Richard 186, 194
Hordern, W. 395, 568
Horgan, M.P. 151
Horkheimer, M. 381, 385–87, 418
Horsley, R.A. 561
Horton, Susan R. 523
Howard, George 239
Hoy, David Couzens 51
Hubbard, B.J. 286
Hugh of St Victor 183
Hughes, Graham 263
Humboldt, Wilhelm von 102, 197, 318, 322
Hume, David 88, 247
Hummel, Horace D. 189

Hurd, J.C. Jr 254, 561
Husserl, E. 33, 104–06, 147, 196, 249, 279, 318–19, 326, 345, 349, 360, 387, 516, 523, 529, 532–33, 608
Huyssen, Andrew 103

Iersel, Bas van 504, 506
Ihde, Don 361, 371
Illyricus, Matthias Flacius 194–95, 335
Ingarden, Roman 516, 523, 529
Ingram, David 380, 384, 388
Irenaeus 22, 146–47, 148–57, 165, 166, 195, 247
Iser, Wolfgang 9, 58, 60, 61, 66, 289, 481, 498, 508, 515–24, 527–30, 539, 541, 548, 586 87
Ishmael, Rabbi 145
Ivanov, V.V. 390

Jacob, E. 293
Jakobson, Roman 47, 86, 90, 94, 98, 349, 352, 487
James, William 84, 399, 545
Jameson, Fredric 95, 472
Janik, A. 541
Jasper, David 348, 475, 484
Jaspers, Karl 276, 279, 345, 348, 371, 455, 563
Jauss, Hans Robert 33, 60, 587
Jeanrond, Werner G. ii, 19, 61–62
Jeremias, J. 575
Jerome 263
Jewett, Robert 240, 241, 259, 262, 281
Johnson, Elliott E. 13, 367

Jones, Geraint Vaughan 566
Jones, Gareth 605
Jonge, M. de (with von der Woude, A.S.) 271 (n.141)
Joyce, James 98, 527
Jülicher, Adolf 65, 575, 605
Juhl, P.D. 38
Jung, C.G. 315, 534, 575-80, 583
Justin Martyr 152, 155

Kafka, Franz 483
Kähler, Martin 332
Kaiser, Walter C. 37
Kalilombe, Patrick A. 423
Kant, Immanuel 88, 145, 186, 196, 198, 205, 212, 213, 231, 247-49, 252, 319, 323, 351, 371, 382, 384, 394, 402, 403, 542
Karlstadt, Andreas 184, 188
Karttunen, L. 366
Käsemann, E. 239, 241, 262
Katz, Jerrold 539
Kay, P. (with B. Berlin) 103
Keane, John 366
Kee, Alistair 421, 430
Keel, Othmar 581
Keenan, Edward 498
Kelber, Werner 56, 70-72, 484
Kellog, Robert 484
Kelly, J.N.D. 156, 260
Kelsey, David 29, 568, 604
Kempski, Jürgen von 88
Kempson, Ruth 541
Kenny, Anthony 541
Kermode, Frank 481, 483-84, 570, 573-74

Kierkegaard, S. 66, 111, 120, 121, 145, 243, 272-74, 276-79, 288, 294, 319, 361, 368, 414, 563-66
Kimmerle, Heinz 206, 208
King, Ursula 437
Kirk, Andrew 533, 604
Kittelson, James 189
Klemm, David 3, 35, 313, 351, 360, 361, 368-69
Knox, W.L. 239
Kort, Wesley A. 480-83, 487, 571
Kramer, Werner 283
Krentz, Edgar 186
Kristeva, Julia 38, 42, 81, 82, 88, 90, 91, 93, 112, 128-29, 427, 436, 497, 498, 503-04
Kugel, J.L. (with Greer, R.A.) 171, 451
Kuhn, Thomas S. 148, 334, 397, 539, 542
Kunne-Ibsch, E. 92, 97
Künneth, Walter 446, 447

Labberton, Mark 532-33, 589
Lacan, Jacques 93, 112, 128, 131, 349, 427, 472, 488, 495
Laeuchli, Samuel 23, 27, 152, 153
Laffey, Alice L. 434, 437
Lakoff, George (with Johnson, M.) 367
Lampe, G.W. (with Woollcombe, K.) 163
Lash, Nicholas 605
Lategan, Bernard (with Vorster, W.) 67
Lawson, Hilary 113
Leach, Edmund 91
Leech, Geoffrey 32, 41, 284, 289, 291

Leith, Dick (with Myerson, G.) 69, 131, 560
Lentricchia, Frank 13, 60, 110
Lévi-Strauss, Claude 90-91, 93, 98, 171, 487, 489, 493
Levinson, Stephen 282, 284, 304, 365, 366
Lewis, C.S. 172, 353, 583-84
Lindbeck, George 503, 557, 604, 606
Linnemann, Eta 170
Lipsius, Richard 256
Loader, J.A. 500
Loades, Ann 435, 437, 441, 443, 453
Locke, John 83, 189, 247, 485, 560
Lockhead, David 419
Longenecker, Richard N. 142, 149, 151, 164
Longman, Tremper 528, 573
Lorenzer, Alfred 381, 384
Lotman, Jurij 41, 525-26, 581, 583-84
Louth, Andrew 155-57, 166
Lubac, Henri de 505
Lücke, F. 206
Luckmann, Thomas 326, 337, 606-07
Lüdemann, Hermann 256
Lukács, Georg 387
Lundin, Roger 131
Luther, Martin 9, 23, 35, 156, 158, 164, 179-90, 193, 194, 248, 257, 533, 589
Luz, Ulrich 149
Lyons, John 55, 61, 83, 585
Lyotard, J.F. 103, 113, 380, 398-99, 472

McCarthy, T. 381
McHann, James Jr 26, 251, 337
Mackintosh, H.R. 229
McKnight, Edgar V. 496, 590
McLaughlin, Eleanor (with Ruether, Rosemary Radford) 431
Macquarrie, John 281, 352, 454, 455
Malcolm, Norman 540
Malinowski, B. 91
Mannheim, Karl 326, 413, 607
Manson, T.W. 254, 262, 273
Marcel, Gabriel 73, 345, 348
Marcion 154, 155
Marcuse, Herbert 386, 416
Marin, Louis 488
Marks, Elaine (with Isabelle de Courtivron) 435
Marquart, Kurt 190
Marshall, Peter 254, 258, 561
Marshall, I. Howard 296
Martinet, A. 94, 95
Marx, Karl 14, 47, 92, 100, 143, 325, 346, 348, 372, 379–85, 387, 389–91, 413–14, 416, 427, 430, 439, 606, 613
Marxsen, Willi 447
Mauthner, Fritz 106, 145, 318, 323–24
May, Rollo 579
Mbiti, John S. 422–23
Mead, George H. 387
Meeks, Wayne 242, 243
Meier, John P. 288
Melanchthon, Philipp 61, 191
Mercadante, Linda 604, 608

Merleau-Ponty, Maurice 92, 97, 100–01, 116
Mesters, Carlos 411, 412, 415, 418
Metrodonus of Lampsacus 158
Metz, Johannes 416, 417
Mezger, Manfred 248
Michel, Otto 163, 286
Michaels, Walter 529
Michalson, Gordon E. 207, 230
Michie D. (with Rhoads, D.) 483
Miller, J. Hillis 111
Millett, Kate 435, 438
Milton, John 144, 538
Miranda, José Porfirio 415, 426–27, 603–04, 606
Moberly, R. Walter 478, 479
Mofokeng, Takatso A. 423
Moltmann, Jürgen 336, 416–18, 446, 606, 611, 612, 614
Moltmann-Wendel, Elisabeth 580
Montefiore, Alan 589
Moore, Stephen D. 472, 484, 496, 522
Morgan, Robert 49, 57–58, 62, 66, 157, 272, 317, 448, 500, 501, 547, 556–57, 562, 588, 602, 605
Morris, Charles W. 87, 119, 404, 518
Mosala, Itumeleng J. 421, 424–27, 429
Mudge, Lewis 370
Mueller-Vollmer, Kurt 3, 197
Munck, Johannes 238, 239, 254, 255
Münzer, Thomas 188

Murphy-O'Connor, Jerome 254, 255, 258, 261, 561
Myerson, George (with Leith, Dick) 69, 131, 560

Nagarjuna 119
Nestorius 146, 276
Neufeld, Vernon 244, 617
Neusner, Jacob 125
Nicholson, Ernest 305
Nida, E.A. 476
Niebuhr, Richard R. 231
Nietzsche, Friedrich 14, 47, 51, 91, 93, 104–08, 110–12, 121, 127, 130, 143, 243, 278, 346, 348, 367, 372, 384, 413, 574
Norris, Christopher 88, 111, 130, 350, 399, 400, 451, 545, 587
Noth, M. 305
Novalis 210

Ogden, Schubert 455
Ong, Walter 56, 70–71
Origen 23, 142, 144, 146, 153, 157, 162–65, 167–73, 183, 263, 581
Ott, Heinrich 265, 506
Otte, Klaus 160, 162
Otto, Rudolf 210, 226, 352
Overbeck, Franz 155, 256

Padilla, C. René (with Branson, Mark) 603
Page, Ruth 435
Pagels, Elaine 22, 152, 156, 165, 457
Palmer, Richard 125, 127, 224
Pannenberg, Wolfhart 11, 12, 25, 238, 250, 251, 253, 282, 330, 331–38,

Index of Authors

344, 381, 383, 391, 394, 437, 440, 442, 446, 506, 592, 606, 611–12, 615
Parker, T.H.L. 185, 191
Parratt, John K. 423
Parsons, Talcott 335, 384–87, 606, 607
Patte, D. 151, 486, 492–94, 496
Pears, David 541
Peirce, Charles S. 12, 47, 75, 83, 84, 86, 88, 105, 124, 383, 394, 399, 400, 518
Pelikan, Jaroslav 182
Perlitt, L. 305
Perrin, Norman 67, 287, 370, 504
Pesch, R. 505
Petersen, Norman 57, 58, 68, 258, 491, 522, 525–26, 528, 548, 586
Pfleiderer, Otto 256
Philo of Alexandria 159–63, 164, 169, 171
Piaget J. 534
Picard, Raymond 95
Pierce, C.A. 403–05, 562
Pindar, 160
Pinnock, C. 503, 604, 608
Pitcher, George 540
Plato 104, 105, 107, 110, 145, 158–60, 321
Plessis, J.G. du 17, 283, 289–91
Plutarch 159
Pobee, John 423
Poland, Lynn 115–16, 119, 368–70, 424
Polanyi, Michael 251, 591
Polzin, Robert M. 491
Pope, Alexander 328
Popkin, Richard H. 180, 334
Popper, Karl 334
Porter, Stanley 522, 528–29, 548–50, 587

Poulet, Georges 529
Pound, Ezra 115
Poythress, Vern 75, 197, 496
Prabhu, Joseph 119
Pratt, Mary L. 539
Prickett, Stephen 475, 477, 591
Propp, V. 97, 478, 480, 486–89, 491, 493, 494, 500, 566

Quine, W.V.O. 87, 396, 547

Racine, J. 95
Rad, Gerhard von 163, 292, 565
Radcliffe-Brown, A. 91
Ramm, Bernard 184
Ramsey, Ian T. 73, 274, 370
Ransom, J.C. 486
Raschke, Carl 88, 123
Ray, William 527–28, 537
Recanati, François 2, 19, 24, 26, 32, 38, 41, 69, 274, 282–85, 287, 291–99, 302–04, 362–65, 371, 485, 570, 615
Redeker, Martin 206, 209, 211
Reid, J.K.S. 303
Reid, Thomas 321
Reimarus, Hermann S. 186
Resseguie, James L. 516, 519, 522, 548, 586
Reu, M. 190
Reumann, John 190
Reventlow, Henning Graf 181, 186
Rhees, Rush 540
Rhoads, D. (with Michie, D.) 288, 483
Richards, Janet Radcliffe 443–44, 533–34, 602

Richards, I.A. 452–54
Richardson, Alan 161
Rickert, H. 253
Rickman, H.P. 247
Ricoeur, Paul 3, 5, 9, 11, 14, 26, 27, 36, 38, 48, 56, 58, 67, 69–74, 112, 114, 123, 126, 220, 228, 288–90, 313, 330, 333, 335, 337, 344–78, 380, 381, 383–84, 390, 393, 402–04, 413, 430, 432, 437, 454, 479, 482, 485–86, 530, 536, 546, 550, 567–69, 576, 578, 597, 618
Riffaterre, M. 38, 42, 498, 529
Robinson, James M. 248
Rogerson, John W. 196, 391–92
Rohrbaugh, Richard 42
Rollins, Wayne G. 576
Rorty, Richard 7, 12, 15, 87, 113, 315, 317–18, 329, 331, 334, 337, 344, 381, 393–401, 402–05, 437, 440–41, 450, 451, 472, 515, 523, 531, 536, 539, 542, 544–49, 589, 610, 616
Rostagno, Sergio 428
Rosenblatt, L. 533
Rousseau, J.J. 211
Rowland, Christopher 3, 379, 380, 411, 412, 425, 603
Royce, Josiah 12, 84, 87, 88, 394, 395, 399, 400, 403–05
Ruether, Rosemary Radford 431–34, 436–38, 441–43, 449, 456
Rupert of Deutz 142, 144, 145, 158, 183

Russell, Bertrand 37, 364
Ryle, Gilbert 394, 454

Sakenfeld, Katherine
    Doob 433
Sanders, J.A. 36
Sanders, E.P. 24, 245,
    246, 281, 300–03
Sandmel, Samuel
    159, 161
Sandt, Rob A. van der
    365, 366, 411, 413, 415
Santa Ana, Julio de 411
Sapir, E. 89, 102
Sartre, Jean-Paul 414
Saussure, Ferdinand de
    21, 23, 47, 75, 83–89,
    91, 93, 94, 98, 99–101,
    104, 106, 119, 125,
    127, 217–18, 291, 390,
    486–87, 499, 524,
    555, 559
Sawyerr, Harry 423
Schelling, F. 213, 227
Schiffer, Stephen R. 366,
    584, 586, 602
Schlegel, Friedrich
    209–11, 226, 227
Schleiermacher, F.D.E.
    4, 5, 10, 23, 24,
    44, 49, 59, 62, 173,
    196–98, 204–43,
    246–47, 249–50,
    252–55, 258, 261,
    266–67, 313, 318–19,
    322, 335, 352, 358,
    369, 402, 435, 439,
    462, 474–76, 486,
    497, 536–37, 546, 548,
    558–61, 564
Schmidt, James 100, 101
Schoeps, Hans Joachim
    243, 244
Scholes, Robert 91, 484
Schrag, Calvin 278, 318
Schrenk, G. 263
Schutz, Alfred 326, 327,
    430, 606–09, 612

Schütz, John H. 241
Schweitzer, Albert 24,
    239, 244, 255–56, 302,
    417, 440
Searle, John R. 2, 13, 17,
    19, 24, 26, 32, 38, 41,
    45, 59, 69, 115, 147,
    223, 274, 282–304,
    307, 313, 362–66, 371,
    385, 386, 473, 479,
    485, 536, 539, 558–63,
    570, 586, 599, 612–13,
    615–16, 618
Segundo, Juan Luis 411,
    413, 415, 418, 420
Sellars, Wilfrid 395, 396
Semler, Johann Salomo
    186, 195–96, 212, 485
Setel, T.D. 431
Seung, T.K. 101
Shaftesbury, Earl of 321
Shakespeare, William 369
Shaw, George Bernard
    243
Shaw, Graham 48, 570,
    573–74, 615
Shklovski, Viktor 34,
    89, 117
Shotwell, Willis 152
Showalter, Elaine 462
Silberman, Lou 70, 71
Simon, Richard 196, 479
Skinner, B.F. 87
Skinner, Quentin 366
Smalley, Stephen S. 445
Smart, James D. 188
Smith, D. Moody 149
Smith, Joseph 154
Socrates 321, 371
Soelle, Dorothee 456
Sophocles 160
Soskice, Janet Martin 42,
    67, 367, 454
Spiegel, Yorick
    580
Spinoza, B. 22, 186, 196,
    212–13
Spitz, Lewis 189

Spivak, Gayatri 104, 109,
    111, 112
Spivey, Robert 491
Stach, Frank 315
Staley, Jeffrey Lloyd
    522, 548
Stanton, Elizabeth
    Cady 435
Stanton, Graham N. 150,
    275, 287–88
Starobinski, Jean 490
Staten, Henry 115, 395
Stein, Dominique 579–80
Stendahl, Krister 239,
    243, 245, 246, 256,
    257, 281, 300–01
Sternberg, Meir 484, 485
Still, Judith 38
Storkey, Elaine 437, 438
Stout, Jeffrey 61, 66,
    547–48
Strawson, P.F. 291,
    361, 394
Stroup, George W.
    567–69, 572, 606,
    609, 614
Stuhlmacher, Peter 506
Sturrock, John 98
Suleiman, Susan 60, 529
Suskind, H. 213, 227
Swinburne, Richard 36

Tallis, Raymond 101, 127
Tannehill, Robert C. 302,
    303, 484
Taylor, Charles 317
Taylor, Mark C. 119,
    121–23, 127
Teilhard de Chardin 418
Tertullian 146, 152,
    155, 263
Theagenes of Rhegium
    158
Theissen, Gerd
    43, 241, 254,
    260, 561
Theodore of Mopsuestia
    142

Index of Authors

Thielicke, Helmut 230, 455
Thiemann, Ronald F. 481, 484, 503, 567, 568–70, 572–74, 601, 606, 609, 614
Thiselton, Anthony C. 3, 10–11, 16, 17, 32, 103, 106, 238–39, 244, 251, 275–76, 280, 289, 292–93, 476–77, 506, 589
Thistlethwaite, Susan Brooks 438
Thompson, John B. 360, 368, 380
Tillich, Paul 229, 352, 422, 538, 576–78
Todorov, Tzvetan 22, 97, 479, 488, 504–05
Tolbert, Mary Ann 290, 431, 437, 440, 450–51, 471
Tollinton, R.B. 167
Tolstoy, Leo 363, 574
Tompkins, Jane P. 529, 535
Toolan, Michael J. 472
Torjesen, Karen 23, 167–68
Torrance, T.F. 185, 186, 192, 193, 257, 589
Torres, Camilio 416
Toulmin, S. 541, 542
Tracy, David 66, 131, 313, 317, 358, 398, 556, 608
Trible, Phyllis 19, 431, 434–37, 438, 452–55
Trier, J. 89, 487
Troeltsch, E. 332
Trubetzkoy, N. 90, 487
Tuckett, Christopher 471
Tupper, E. Frank 335, 336
Turretinus, Jean A. 195
Tuttle, Howard 249

Tutu, Desmond 421, 423, 424, 426
Tyndale, William 186, 190–91, 194

Urban, W.M. 354
Urmson, J.O. 274, 394

Valla, Laurentius 186
Vanderveken, Daniel 304
Vanhoozer, Kevin J. 74, 351, 354, 356–59, 361, 367, 370, 371
Vawter, Bruce 565
Via, Dan Otto 290, 370, 488, 491–94, 565
Vico, G.B. 321
Voelz, James W. 505
Vološinov, V.N. 389–90
Vorster, W.S. 67, 289, 504–06

Wach, Joachim 214
Wachterhauser, B. 318, 358
Wadsworth, Michael 20, 125
Wahlberg, Rachel 459
Waismann, F. 477, 541
Warner, Martin 484
Warnke, Georgia 25, 147, 314, 320, 327, 329, 394, 398–99, 402, 451, 545
Warren, Austin (with Welleck R.) 58, 59, 471, 486
Watson, Francis 301
Weber, Max 241, 251, 252, 305, 326, 335, 382, 384–87, 389, 403, 413, 606
Wedderburn, A.J.M. 301
Weiler, G. 323, 324
Weinsheimer, Joel C. 314, 320, 327–28, 394
Weiss, Johnnes 256, 283, 417

Welleck, René (with Warren, A.) 58, 59, 471, 486
Wenham, Gordon 479
Werner, Martin 244, 245
West, Cornel 401, 451, 544
Westerholm, S. 192
Wevers, Richard with Battles, Ford L. 185
Wheatley, Jon 275
Wheelwright, Philip 67, 353, 354
White, Hayden 356, 360
White, Hugh C. 32, 288
White, Stephen 380, 381
Whiteley, D.E.H. 260, 284
Whorf, B.L. 102, 103, 585
Wiehl, Reiner 321
Wikenhauser, Alfred 302, 303
Wilder, Amos N. 129
Wiles, Maurice 245
Williams, Raymond 171
Williamson, H.G.M. 40
Williamson, Ronald 164, 264
Wimsatt, W.K. (with Beardsley, M.) 59
Winch, Peter 148, 326, 327, 394, 397, 403
Winquist, Charles 618
Wisdom, John 394
Wittgenstein, Ludwig 6, 9, 12–13, 16, 17, 20, 21, 22, 37, 45, 70, 88, 89, 92, 102, 115, 124–31, 145, 206, 217–19, 244, 253, 291, 300, 318, 323–26, 347, 351, 361–62, 366–67, 383–84, 386–88, 390, 393–97, 400–05, 414, 444, 451, 454, 473, 474, 477, 482, 485, 502, 516, 524–25,

534, 540–47, 559, 568, 578, 584, 586, 591–92, 599, 601, 607–08, 612, 617
Wittig, Susan 290, 497, 516, 518–19, 584, 586
Witvliet, Theo 420, 422
Wolde, Ellen van 504
Wolf, Christian 195
Wolf, Friedrich A. 22, 197, 209, 214
Wolfson, H. 159
Wolterstorff, Nicholas 290, 363, 474, 485, 570–75, 598–99, 612, 615–16
Wood, Skevington 156
Woollcombe, K. (with Lampe G.W.) 163
Wordsworth, William 210, 211, 474, 475
Worton, Michael 38
Woude, A.S. van der (with de Jonge M.) 271 (n.141)
Wrede, W. 605
Wright, N.T. 303
Wright, T.R. 475
Wunderlich, Dieter 296, 299

Yorck, Graf 318
Young, Frances 3, 29, 568, 604

Zeno 158, 160
Zimmerli, W. 292

INDEX OF SUBJECTS

An asterisk (*) indicates pages on which meanings of technical terms (italicized) are explained. In some cases more than one explanation of terms occurs when different writers use the same term with different meanings. Italicized pages represent main discussions. This index thus provides over 200 glossary entries in addition to others.

Abraham 240, 273, 564
Absence*, absence of signatory, 83, 104, 109*, 119
Abstraction 316. See method, mathematics, system.
Abyss 109
Academic community 2, 4, 189, 532, 549, 550, 588. See ordinary readers, biblical guild, egalitarianism.
Accommodation 532
Actant, actant-role* 488*
Acts, action 130, 180, 248, 337. See speech-acts, *parole*, social action, communicative action, language-game.
Actualization* 11–12*, 31*, 34, 63–68, 320, 331, 361, 398, 400, 515, 517–19, 527
Address 69, 72, 74, 276, 294, 549, 560, 573, 613, 615–19
Aesthetic theory 131
Affirmation 412. See self-affirmation.
African theologies 423. See black hermeneutics.
Agents, authors or human subject as, 474, 570, 584, 591
Agrarian society 42
Alexandrian culture 264
Alienation* 385*, 416
Allegorical interpretation* 11, 22, 118, 141–46, 157–59*, 160–73, 181, 183–94, 226, 505

Ambiguity 53, 352, 530. See blurred edges, paradox, point of view, productive texts, metaphors.
American feminism 435. See feminism, feminist hermeneutics.
American hermeneutics, American pragmatic tradition, 84, 87, 399–400, 403
Anagogical meaning* 144*, 183*
Analepsis* 480*
Analogy, analogical language, 73, 250, 460
Analytic tradition 394. See linguistic philosophy.
Anarchy 131
Androcentric language, androcentric socio-symbolic worlds, 431, 433, 443, 453, 457, 460. See gender-system, feminist hermeneutics, father, de-patriarchalizing.
Anglican theology 194, 590, 592.
Anointing at Bethany 507
Anonymous texts 254, 261–67. See death of the author, and author.
Anthropomorphism, anthropomorphic understanding, 39, 110, 158, 161, 171, 332
Anticipation 520. See expectation, horizon of expectation.
Antiochene Fathers 171
Anti-formalist road 516. See formalism, socio-pragmatic hermeneutics.
Antitype 163. See type, typology.

Apartheid 420, 423, 425. See black hermeneutics.
Apocalypse of John 80, 123, 424, 425, 506, 584, 603
Apocalyptic, apocalyptic texts, 80, 114, 239, 256, 282, 285, 330, 336, 525, 528, 557, 617. See eschatology.
Apocryphon of John 153
Apostleship, apostolic testimony, 69, 152, 154, 446–47
Application 127–28, 158, 169, 367. See reading, pastoral theology.
Arbitrariness of signs 83, 104. See sign, semiotics, difference, code.
Archetype* 576–77*, 583
Arianism 154
Art 10, 94, 115, 213, 219–200, 226, 313–15, 327, 352, 481
Argentina 415
Ascension 263
Aspect, aspective perception, 516
Assertions 181–82, 283–307, 333. See propositions, propositional content.
Atmosphere in narrative 483
Atomistic exegesis, atomistic language, 156, 301
Atonement 19, 300–03, 615
Attitudes 274. See responsibilities, behavitives, expressives, commissives.
Audience-orientated interpretation 84, 87. See reader-response theory and reading.
Author, author as agent, 55–58, 197, 216–17, 225, 228, 232, 288, 290, 364, 366, 395, 570. See author's intention.
Author's intention 38, 59, 62, 195, 206, 290, 486, 500, 558–61, 600. See intention.
Authority 147, 194, 284, 286–91, 299, 300, 327, 382, 428, 438, 442, 448, 472, 521, 572, 611
Authorization 2, 6, 18, 29, 286–91, 597–99, 615

Autonomy of text 58–63, 67, 497, 500. See New Criticism, semiotics, formalism, death of the author, structuralism, reading, texts.

Background*, pre-intentional Background* 45–46*, 147, 233, 266, 362–63, 536, 540, 559, 562
Backing for currency of language 544, 598–602. See personal backing, first-person utterances, promise, action, illocution, commissives, extra-linguistic states of affairs, behaviour.
Bandung Conference 415
Baptism 614
Base communities 411–17
Behavitives* 284*, 287, 295–96*, 299*, 616
Behaviour 130, 362, 366, 402, 404, 414, 474, 576
Behavioural psychology 87
Being 104, 106, 107, 108, 120, 122
Being-in-Christ 245, 302
"Behind the text" in hermeneutics 57, 59, 215, 227, 232, 361, 365
"Believing" reading* 598*, 599–614, 615–17*, 618–19
Betrayal of feminism 450, 457. See feminism.
"Better understanding than the author"* 197–98, 227, 252, 258–61*
Bewitchment of intelligence 102
Biblical guild 549, 588. See academic community, ordinary readers.
Bildung (culture) 213, 321, 329, 397
Binary oppositions 90, 94, 491. See structuralism, myth.
"Black Christ" 422
Black consciousness 421
Black feminist consciousness 438
Black hermeneutics 2, 7, 14, 27, 48, 379, 410–18, 419–27, 603
Black power 421
Bland effect 450. See routinization.
Bless, blessing 32, 292, 299, 573
Blurred edges, concepts with, 131, 477, 516, 541, 592

Index of Subjects 675

"Bottomless chess board". See chess.
Boundary situations, see limit situations.
Bourgeois interests 389, 410, 433. See Marxism, interests, class-ideology.
Brazil 411, 415
Bricoleur 91
British philosophical tradition 3, 500
Broken myth 41, 455
Buddhism 119
Bureaucracy 389

Calculative thinking 319. See method, science, scientific method, statistics, mathematics.
Calvin College ii, 193
Calvinist tradition 179, 185–94, 532
Canaanite religion 457
Canon, canonical levels of meaning* 36–42*, 96, 110, 320, 472, 500
Canon, literary canon as *vs* post-modernist egalitarianism 534
Case law 117
Cathexis* 349*
Causal force, cause-generation (as *vs* institutional force, count-generation), 274, 290. See force, illocutions, count-generation.
Celebration, celebration of Christmas, 130, 210, 571
Centre 111, 119, 242. See difference, de-centred.
Certainty 181
Change. See transformation.
Characterization 482–83
Chess 85, 102, 108, 128, 524
Choices of speaking subject, meaning as choice, 99. See *parole*, language-use, agent.
Christian community 2, 266, 506. See community of readers.
Christian education. See theological education.
Christian theology, Christian faith, 2, 33, 62–64, 549, 550, 564, 611–19. See theology, faith, Christology, God.

Christology, Christological texts, Christological confession, 2, 18, 67, 68, 75, 125, 160, 180, 188, 229, 231, 245, 264, 282, 283–91, 298, 306, 337, 422, 460, 520, 569, 572–74, 601, 614–19
Ciceronian method 191
Circularity of language 323
Claritas scripturae* 18, 23, 179–86*, 190–94
Clarity 93, 241
Class ideology, class struggle, 418, 426, 428. See oppression, domination, power, bourgeois-interests, interests.
Classical-humanist paradigm of textuality 55, 58
Classroom and reading 531
Close reading* 476*, 499
Closed texts* 527*
Closure 571
Clothes-system as semiotic structure 55, 81, 82, 94, 572
Co-author 99, 471, 535, 584. See reading, reader-response theory, egalitarianism.
Code in semiotic theory* 80–81*, 82–103, 124, 428, 489–90, 501, 505, 518, 524–25, 527, 536, 550, 583–85
Cognitive truth, cognitive content, 244, 454. See truth.
Coherence 239
Collective unconscious 578
Colonial history, colonial oppression, 416, 420, 425
Colour-words and colour perception 83, 85, 103, 487
Comedy 117
Commentary 61, 191
Commissives* 284*, 287, 293–96, 299*, 599, 615–16
Commission 286, 299
Commitments 17, 26, 312, 274–75, 290, 365, 369, 418, 485, 570, 597–604, 616–18
Common behaviour of humankind 386, 404, 541, 586

Common sense 92, 94, 194, 314, 321
Communication signs* 526*
Communicative action, communication, 13, 28, 100, 289, 380–93, 517, 583. See transmissive texts, matching codes, inter-personal communication, language-games, speech-acts.
Community-building language 481, 589
Community-norms 515. See socio-pragmatic hermeneutics.
Community of readers, community of interpretation 65, 88, 143, 152, 317, 321, 332, 394, 398, 403, 523. See reader-response theory, convention.
Comparative method 223
Composition 249
Conceptual formation, conceptual tools, 107, 393, 414, 456. See language games.
Concientización* (consciousness-raising) 416*, 417, 425, 434, 439, 610.
Condensation* 112*, 129, 349*
Conditions of possibility 43, 100–01, 197. See transcendental philosophy.
Confess, confession, 299, 591, 616–18. See personal backing, Christology.
Configurational structure 356
Conflict 450
Connotative semiotics 96, 97
Consciousness, conscious self, 10, 38, 97, 111–114, 125, 187, 207, 227, 248, 257, 259, 319, 320, 328, 349–50, 382, 385, 389, 583–84. See Freud, unconscious, post-modernism, psychoanalytical interpretation, speaking subject, subjectivity.
Consumer-approach 503
Contemplation 142
Context, contextualization, 6, 17, 25, 61, 181, 188, 224–25, 261, 330, 420, 423, 536, 599, 601. See more specifically:

context as frame 15, 494, 497*, 535–37
context-free 173
context of experience 410
context of practice 395
context of situation* 53, 61, 67, 75, 251, 261, 364–65
context of understanding 148–56. See tradition, effective-history.
context of utterance 304
context-specific 558–62, 597–602
contextual Background. See Background.
contextual inference 295
contextual pragmatism. See contextual relativism, social pragmatism.
contextual relativism 393–405, 535–50. See socio-pragmatic theory.
Contingency 250. See historical finitude.
Continuity 154, 592. See tradition.
Contract 488
"Contradiction"* (as de-contextualized propositional content) 19*, 429, 453
Controlling paradigm 124. See paradigm, metaphor.
Convention 12, 17, 50, 80–113, 143, 292, 323, 363, 395, 480–81, 499, 524, 536
Conversation 131, 219, 317, 388
Conversational implicature* 289, 291, 365*
Cooking as framing a semiotic system 81, 90. See clothes, furniture.
Co-production of author and reader 197. See co-author.
Corinthian correspondence 241, 254, 255
Corporate identity 530. See identity.
Corporate nature of interpretation 191, 233, 238, 533. See community of readers.
Corporate self-interest 392, 450
Corrigibility 24, 219, 238
Cosmology 460

Co-texts 504
Count-generation* 290, 485, 570*, 573, 575, 598–99, 615
Counterfactual conditionals* 527*
Covenant 17, 32, 43, 73, 166, 246, 297, 300, 305, 598–601
Creation, creation accounts, 160, 274–75, 391
Creativity, creative processes, creative understanding, 5, 8, 9, 205, 213, 220, 227, 230, 247, 353, 504, 515, 565
Creator 331, 333. See creation.
Creeds 8, 9, 36, 156, 260, 590–91. See tradition, continuity, habituation, confession, Christology, routinization.
Criteria, criteria of rationality, 89, 326, 330, 334, 396. See metacritical hermeneutics, public criteria of meaning, systematic mistake.
Criteria of relevance* 8, 392, 430, 452, 557, 604–11*, 612–19
Critical distance 412
Critical principle, critical test, critical philosophy, critical thought, 23, 25, 145, 180, 182, 186, 189, 223, 334, 380, 410, 416, 433
Critical theory, critical hermeneutics. See socio-critical theory, socio-critical hermeneutics, Frankfurt School.
Critique: see above and more specifically:
 critique of criteria, i.e. metacritique, 346–50. See metacriticism.
 critique of the cross 28, 614–19. See cross of Christ.
 critique of epistemology 382. See knowledge, truth.
 critique of hermeneutics 381. See radical hermeneutics.
 critique of historical reason 198, 248
 critique of ideology 358, 367, 368, 372, 383, 385–86, 402, 411, 413. See socio-critical theory.
 critique of language 24, 106, 145, 315, 318–19, 322–30, 348. See language.
 critique of semiotics 82, 91, 129. See post-modernist semiotics.
Cross of Christ 28, 35, 71, 154, 241, 243, 276, 282, 302, 336, 432, 446, 520, 527, 577, 592, 606–19
Crossing (in structuralism) 491
Culture, cultural system, cultural tradition, 44, 81–82, 90, 93, 124, 213, 249. On cultural relativism, see social pragmatism.

Dasein 277, 336
Day of the Lord 475. See eschatology, apocalyptic.
Dead metaphor 367. See metaphor.
Death of the author* 99*, 122, 366, 562, 570, 600. See autonomy of the text, reading, the New Criticism, post-modernism.
Death 418
De-centred self 6, 611–19. See criteria of relevance, new horizons, cross of Christ, power, interests.
Deception, self-deception, disguise, 28, 35, 228, 259, 347–50. See illusion, psycho-analytical hermeneutics, post-modernism.
Deconstruction, deconstructionism*, 15, 50–51*, 84–108, 109–10*, 111–14, 115*, 116–32, 318, 398, 473–74, 494, 505, 590–92. See undoing, post-modernism, semiotics, deferment.
Declaratives* 284*, 295–96*, 299*, 365
Defamiliarization* 117*. See routinization, surprise, expectation, horizon of expectation, reception theory.
Defensive strategies 530
"Defined by others" in race or gender 422

Degrees of understanding 266
De-habitualization 34. See creative understanding.
De-ideologizing 94, 413, 427–28, 452–62. See ideology, critique of ideology.
Demystifying, demystification*, 94*, 427, 578
Demythologizing, demythologization*, 158–63*, 281, 413, 428, 452–62
De-objectification 158, 159, 281
Depatriarchalizing 436, 452–62, 579–80. See father, gender, feminist hermeneutics.
De-privileging of the author 534. See egalitarianism, canon of literature.
Depth hermeneutics 379, 382, 384
Description 295, 362. See propositions, assertions, objectivism, hermeneutics of innocence, world-to-word direction of fit.
Despair 277
Destruktion 109
Development of doctrine 549. See tradition.
Diachronic linguistics 101
Diagnostic method* 346–59*, 370
Dialectical theology 276
Dialogue 315, 317, 321, 327, 333, 364, 398. See conversation.
Dictionary meanings 526
Didache 165
Didactic material 219
Différence, différance, deferment*, 83*, 85, 88, 99, 101, 105*, 125
Differential network 57, 86, 104, 487. See semiotics.
Directedness of texts* 13, 45*, 50, 59, 297, 356, 558–62, 583, 597–601. See intention, promise, author, address.
"Direction of fit". See world-to-word direction of fit.
Directives* 284*, 295–96*, 299*, 616
Disclosure. See revelation.
Discourse, discourse analysis, 369, 496

Disembodiment 69. See incarnation, extra-linguistic world, backing, Background.
Displacement* 112*, 349*
Dispositional analysis of belief 244
Disruption of community convention 273, 391, 563–66, 589
Distanciation* 56–57*, 70–71*, 359
Distortion, distorted communication, 326, 382, 384, 403
Divinatory axis of understanding 223, 228, 241, 246, 250
Doceticism 7, 69
Doctrinal centre, dogma, 239, 590
Domination* 325, 385–86*, 410, 419, 430, 443, 459–60, 615. See power, interest.
Doubt 143, 182, 186
Double eclipse of reader and writer 56, 486. See autonomy of texts.
Double meaning expressions* 346–47*, 576. See metaphor.
Double perspective 531
Doublets 479, 481
Dream, dream-symbols, dream-text, 14, 346–50, 359, 384, 530, 576
Duplications 479, 481
Durham Cathedral 400
Dynamic equivalence 476

Eastern Orthodox Church 64, 65
Ecclesiastes 114, 117
Écrivain* 98*
Eden 161, 179
"Edification" 329, 400
Educational training 252. See Christian education, theological education.
Effective-history (Wirkungsgeschichte)* 325–30*
Effective-historical consciousness 344, 397
Egalitarianism 131, 428–29, 432, 462, 472, 503, 533–35
Elitism 93, 426, 428–29, 472, 532
Emancipatory critique* 7, 383–86*. See socio-critical theory, liberation hermeneutics.

Empathy (Hineinversetzen)* 248*. See imagination.
Empiricism 367. See logical positivism, scientific method, facts.
Encoding 528. See code, semiotic code.
Enlargement of horizons 356, 402, 410, 607–19. See horizons, new horizons.
Enlightenment, the, 212, 215, 327. See rationalism.
Enticing role of narrative 567
Epistemology 180, 325, 397, 402, 404, 450, 501–02. See knowledge.
Epistle of Ignatius 165
Erasure* 108–09*, 122
Essence, essentialism, 106. See formalism, blurred edges, language-game.
Ethics 372, 548. See justice, oppression, love, power.
Ethnocentricity 12, 27, 399–405, 588, 613–15. See social pragmatism.
Evangelical feminism 438
Evil, guilt, 345–48
Exegesis, exegetical method, 237, 238, 266, 313. See commentary.
Exercitives* 274, 284*, 287, 295–96*, 299*
Eventfulness of textual meaning 64
Existential hermeneutics, existentialism, "existence", 10, 24, 119, 149, 223, 249, 256, 272 82, 285, 288, 301, 306, 419, 421, 424, 426, 563–66
Exodus, the Exodus narratives, 391, 416–19, 422, 425, 482, 571
Expectation 520, 521, 530, 537, 563, 567–68, 571, 586, 614
Experience as a hermeneutical principle 419–27, 430–52
Explanation (as *vs* understanding)* 335, 344*, 383, 402, 404
Expressives* 284*, 295–96*, 299*, 599, 616
Extra-linguistic commitments 362, 597–604. See commitments, commissives.

Extra-linguistic states of affairs, extra-linguistic world, 2, 7, 17, 21, 26, 55, 67, 98–101, 290, 301, 337, 362–64, 393–94, 485, 548, 597–604

Fabric of traces 104. See traces, textuality.
Facts 275–76, 319, 322, 331–32, 395, 458, 474, 611
Faith 333, 339, 369, 372, 423, 564. See Christian faith.
Falsification 122, 383, 447
Family resemblances 400
Father, fatherhood, 46, 458, 577, 579–80. See depatriarchalizing.
Feeding miracles 519
Feeling, feelings, 210, 352, 577–78. See divinatory axis, imagination, romanticist hermeneutics.
Feminine, the, 5, 210, 223, 237, 579. See feminist hermeneutics.
Feminine imagery, of God, 458–59. See feminist hermeneutics.
Feminism 435–36, 440
Feminism, betrayal of, 534
Feminist hermeneutics* 2, 7, 14, 27, 124, 379, 380, 393, 401, 410–29, 430–31*, 432–70, 532–35, 572, 602
Fiction, fictionality, fictiveness*, 26–7*, 128–30, 289–90, 352–54*, 355–61, 362–63*, 364–72, 388, 485, 527, 566, 570*
Field semantics 90, 488–89
"Filling in" 515–17, 519
Film 81, 315–16, 487
Finality 614. See eschatology.
Finished work of Christ 303
Finitude, finite situatedness, 6, 25, 118, 345. See historical finitude, contingency.
First-person utterances 70, 73, 591, 600. See backing, personal backing, commissives, promise.
Flash-backs 355, 566
"Floating" narrative 266
Flood narratives 479

Flow of human life 249, 250.
See stream of life, life-world,
language-game.
Flux 122
Food offered to idols 241, 561
Food-system (in semiotics) 94. See
clothes-system, furniture-system.
Force, illocutionary-force-indicators*,
294–96*, 299*. See illocutions.
Force, linguistic*, 19*, 41*, 47, 85,
286, 295, 363–65, 599–602
Force-neutral language 296, 599
Forgiveness 286, 299, 580
Form criticism 272
Form of life 89, 237, 253, 388,
394, 607
Formalism, literary formalism*, 50*,
75, 130, 471, 486–87, 539, 547,
548, 574, 583, 592. See anti-
formalism, system, new criticism,
autonomous texts.
Foundationalism 401
Foundations of human studies 250,
315, 327
Foundations of knowledge 180, 250,
322–38, 384, 396
Four senses of mediaeval
interpretation 183, 190, 193
Framing* 15, 494*, 497, 535–37
Frankfurt School 385–87, 472
French classicism 93
French feminism 435, 472
Freudian categories, Freudian
methods, 5, 106, 125, 126, 259,
346–50, 495. See unconscious,
dream, symbol, psychoanalytical
hermeneutics.
Functional semiotics 87
Furniture-system in semiotics 81, 94.
See clothes-system, food-system.
Fusion of horizons 333, 412. See
horizon, premature fusion of
horizons.
Future 333, 335, 337–38, 606–19.
See eschatology, universal history.

Game 10, 99, 117, 320, 327–29,
403, 534

Geisteswissenschaften * 248*, 394
Gender, gender-system, 395,
430–70, 532–35, 583. See feminist
hermeneutics.
Gender-correlation with thinkers and
feelers 534
"Genetic fallacy" 59, 559
Generality, "general truths", 65, 213,
217, 225, 250, 278
*Generative matrices, generative models**,
39*, 96, 504–07, 583–85. See
generative poetics, productive texts,
intertextuality, semiotics.
Generative poetics * 91*, 491
Given, givenness, give, 63, 87, 108,
109, 110, 345, 360, 395, 396,
398, 400, 502, 517, 522–23, 548,
562, 588
Gnosticism, gnostic interpretation, 7,
142, 152–56, 165–66, 457, 459
God, 331–37, 370, 422, 446, 453–55,
458, 460, 505, 507, 530, 563,
567–69, 572–73, 577, 599, 600,
609, 611, 613–19
Goddess-language 456–59
Gospel of Truth 152–53
Grace 7, 9, 34, 132, 180, 190,
239–40, 263, 276, 281, 290, 370,
392–93, 438, 507, 531, 549, 567.
See give, givenness.
"Grammatical" hermeneutics 206–33
Grammatology* 51, 104–06*, 107–13
Gregorian system 193
Guilt 345, 580. See evil.

Habituated patterns of reading,
563–65, 589. See routinization,
expectation, convention, tradition.
Handbook culture 526
Heart 259
Hellenistic Judaism 160
Heracleon 165
Hermeneutics * 28*, 31*, 48*, 145*,
194*, 214, 279*, 325, 331, 348*,
372, 395*, 397*, 402
hermeneutical awareness 4
hermeneutical canons
253

Index of Subjects

hermeneutical circle* 195*, 204,
  215*, 221–22*, 232–33, 237–47,
  249, 253, 280, 413, 418, 420,
  439, 527, 537
hermeneutical goals 42, 62, 66,
  169, 204, 218, 224, 546–620.
  See interests.
hermeneutical pluralism 113,
  612–18. See interests, meaning.
hermeneutical principle,
  hermeneutical key, 240
hermeneutical spiral 222
hermeneutical trouble-making 145.
  See radical hermeneutics.
hermeneutics of conflict 445, 449
hermeneutics of enquiry 179–203
hermeneutics of innocence 13, 59,
  92, 94, 388
hermeneutics of liberation 379–470
hermeneutics of marginality* 461*
hermeneutics of metacriticism
  313–409
hermeneutics of reading 471–555
hermeneutics of remembrance 449
hermeneutics of retrieval 14,
  344–58
hermeneutics of self-involvement
  272–312. See self-involvement,
  backing, illocutions.
hermeneutics of social critique 451.
  See socio-critical hermeneutics.
hermeneutics of suspicion* 13–14*,
  111, 126, 146, 197, 228,
  344–51, 359, 372, 383,
  431–32, 530
hermeneutics of tradition 22,
  142–78. See also effective
  history.
hermeneutics of trust 146
hermeneutics of understanding 23,
  197– 271, 435, 558–62
hermeneutics-turned-sociology 392
Hero, hero figure, 487, 566, 577, 583
Hierarchical structures 583. See
  power, egalitarianism.
History 68, 322–38, 356, 473, 485
  historical explanation 226,
  403

historical finitude, historicality,
  25, 232, 252, 276, 279, 280,
  315, 335
historical interpretation 226
historical methods 57, 557
historical necessity 254
historical reconstruction 158,
  214, 224, 261, 266, 360, 426,
  428, 443
historical report 290
historical understanding 248,
  349, 387
"history-like" narrative 26–27*, 49,
  485*. See fictionality.
Holism* 125*, 246, 396
Hollywood 545
Holy Spirit 64, 167, 168, 182, 188,
  208, 220, 241–45, 259, 260, 273,
  281, 392, 455, 492, 505, 585–86,
  609, 617–19
Holy Trinity 233
Homeric writings 145, 158
Hope 338, 371, 417–18, 424, 447.
  See eschatology, promise.
Horizon* 33–4, 41, 44–6*, 147, 196,
  338, 556, 607
horizon of expectation 34–6*, 44*,
  61, 65. See expectation.
horizon of meaning 332
horizon of otherness 36. See new
  horizons.
horizon of the present 267. See
  present.
horizon of understanding 332
Humanist learning 189, 193
Humanities 329. See *Geisteswissenschaften*, academic community.
Hymns, hymnic forms, 73, 114, 619
Hyponoia* 159*
Hypothesis of female reader, 462

Iconoclasm 8, 9, 21, 51, 93, 114,
  116–19, 122–24, 130, 347, 436
Ideal reader* 517*, 529
Identity 515, 530, 567, 572,
  604, 614
Identity of Jesus Christ 56, 188, 285,
  288, 572

Ideology, ideologies, ideological critique*, 93, 384, 385–86*, 410, 418, 426–27, 433, 484, 606, 607*
Idol, idolatry, 5, 6, 14, 26, 113, 116–17, 123, 132, 344, 347, 350, 372, 530, 601, 613
Illocution, illocutionary act, illocutionary language*, 16–19*, 41*, 43–44*, 286*, 287–92, 293*, 294–307, 364–65, 366, 386, 567, 569–70, 573, 597–601, 606, 613. See speech-act, backing, personal backing, first-person utterances, Background.
Illusion 82, 277, 326, 344, 353, 372, 389, 495, 576. See deception, psychoanalytical hermeneutics, truth.
Image of God 436
Imagination, imaginative rapport, 9, 184, 223, 243, 247–51, 253, 290, 322, 335, 351, 354, 357, 359, 471, 475, 558–59. See empathy, divinatory axis, possibility.
Implicatures* 290*. See conversational implicatures.
Implied author* 521*
Implied reader* 517*, 522, 528, 529, 548
Incarnation of Christ, incarnational theology, 114–15, 240, 243, 277, 334, 473
Indeterminacy 107. See pluralism, blurred edges, meaning, productive texts.
Indirect communication 66, 74, 277, 344, 361, 368–69
Individualism, individual consciousness, 38, 143, 186, 230, 371
Infelicities* 601*
"In front of the text" 5, 26, 57, 351–58, 361, 597
"In" groups, insiders *vs* outsiders, 481, 483, 571, 609. See stereotypification.
"Inner-biblical exegesis", inner-textuality*, 39*, 125, 503*

Innocence 451, 503, 531, 605. See hermeneutics of innocence.
Input text* 22*
Institutional facts, institutional role, 128, 285–87, 290, 292, 299, 539, 573
Instrumental reason 387, 391, 533, 606–07
Integration, integrative power, 405, 576–77
Intention, intentionality, intention as directed will, or *directedness of texts**, 13*, 37, 38, 56, 59, 106, 185, 294, 297, 364, 548, 558–61*, 597–600. See author's intention.
intention as adverbial 560
"intentional fallacy" 59, 560
Interactive theory of metaphor 366. See metaphor.
Interdisciplinary approaches 16, 344–45
Interests, power-interests, social interests*, 6, 7, 12*, 28, 93, 143, 316, 317, 326, 385–86*, 398, 413, 425, 429, 433, 440, 447, 484, 530, 546–49, 588, 609, 612–18
Internal norms, internal criteria, 545. See socio-pragmatic hermeneutics.
Inter-personal address, inter-personal communication, 43, 56, 68, 73, 114, 197, 207, 217, 272, 390, 599
Interpretation 10, 22, 28, 66, 151, 170, 186. See hermeneutics.
interpretation of interpretation 110, 121, 127
interpretation of Saussure 92
interpretative strategies 228, 261
Inter-subjectivity, inter-subjective world, inter-subjective judgement, 13, 28, 41, 87, 97, 100, 114, 126, 128, 156, 172, 217, 252, 315, 318, 323–30, 383, 386, 497, 531, 544
Intertextuality*, 27, 28*, 38–9*, 41, 51, 81*, 97, 100–02, 114, 125, 129, 171–72, 217, 473, 495–96, 497*, 498–502, 503*, 504–08, 535
Intertranslatability 103, 585

Intratextuality, intra-linguistic world*,
  16, 38, 67, 258, 295, 348, 358,
  367, 503*
Introduction to the New Testament
  208
Introspection 248
Intuition, intuitive understanding,
  215, 223. See divinatory
  understanding.
Inventio* 61*
Inversion of creative process 252
Irony* 58, 117, 476*, 521
Isaiah Targum 151
Israel 281, 301, 305

Jewish allegorical interpretation
  159–63
Job, Book of, 73, 114, 372
Johannine irony 521
Joke, in linguistic behaviour, 543
Jonah, Book of, 33, 477–78
Judgments 16, 89, 102, 128, 314,
  321, 325, 328, 367, 414
Jungian psychology, Jungian theory,
  534, 576–80. See symbols.
Justice 411, 425, 449, 548, 602–04.
  See socio-critical hermeneutics.

Kairos Document 424–25
Kantian critique 212, 403, 542
Kenya 423
Kingdom of God 118, 287, 370
Kinship terms, kinship system,
  90, 487
Knowledge 84, 98, 104, 107, 153,
  180, 187, 192, 205, 213, 231, 330,
  333–37, 388, 395, 402, 437, 455
Knowledge, foundations of, 181–85,
  313–38, 397, 515
"Know how to go on" 351

Labour 385, 391, 429
Ladder-image 324
Language 206–28, 283–307, 322–31,
  344–73 *et passim.*
  language-behaviour 55. See
  behaviour, speech-acts.

language-games 17, 88, 102,
  324–25, 362, 388, 394–96, 400,
  402, 502, 524
language-system, langue*, 23*, 47,
  83*, 86*, 89, 91, 96, 99, 127,
  218, 232, 291, 488–90, 495,
  505, 526, 548, 559
language-uses, parole*, 23*, 47, 83*,
  86*. See *langue.*
Last judgment 618
Law 245, 392–93
Lectio divina* 22, 142–45*, 158, 183,
  578–80
Legal fiction* 353*
Legal texts 2, 32
Legisign* 86*
Letter 168, 192
Letter of Aristeas 159
Lexeme* 98*
Lexicography 195. See also dictionary
  meanings.
Liberal irony, liberal rhetoric,
  liberal-pluralist credentials, 396,
  399, 545, 587
Liberation hermeneutics, liberation
  theology, 7, 14, 379–470. See also
  Latin American hermeneutics,
  black hermeneutics, feminist
  hermeneutics, socio-critical
  hermeneutics.
Liberation* 383–86*, 613–19.
  See emancipatory critique, and
  socio-critical hermeneutics.
Life, lived experience (Erlebnis)*, 45,
  114, 115, 198, 223, 247–48*,
  251, 276
Life-world* 7, 12, 20, 23, 25, 32,
  237, 247–52, 261, 276, 319, 326,
  386–93*, 401, 419, 556, 606–09
Light 69, 581
Limits of language 323. See language.
Limit-situations 73, 345, 371, 563
Linguistics 83, 348
Linguistic competence 89. See
  reading competence.
Linguistic philosophy 347, 348, 386,
  477. See philosophy of language,
  speech-act theory.

Linguistic relativity 102. See inter-translatability.
"*Linguistic theology*"* 494*. See generative poetics.
Listen, listening, 5, 207, 347, 372, 403, 430, 462, 558–59. See openness.
Literacy 532. See orality, oral speech.
"*Literal meaning*"* 167, 172–73*, 181–84, 190, 192. See meaning, allegorical interpretation.
Literary canon 534
Literary productivity. See productive texts, intertextuality.
Literary theory 15, 50, 57, 92–103, 130, 471– 555
"Literature", "literary" meaning*, 26, 48, 474*, 503
Liturgical texts, liturgical contexts, 64–5, 285, 571, 590, 598
Loci 191
Logic 104, 106, 111, 122, 124, 290, 323–24
 logical asymmetry 600
 logical atomism 486
 logical necessity 86
 logical positivism 21, 87, 92, 113, 454
 logic of contradiction 122
 logic of promise 294. See promise.
Logocentrism* 83*, 104, 115, 323, 461
Logos principle 167, 169
Lord, Christ as, 260, 283, 298, 306
Lord's Supper 255, 561, 598–99
Love, acts of love, 9, 18, 69, 153, 273, 294, 299, 300, 392, 415, 599, 609–13
Luke, Luke-Acts, 248, 273, 286
Luther's hermeneutics 179– 90

Macro-speech-act 291
Magisterium 146, 179, 180, 182, 431
Male imagery 454, 460. See father, depatriarchalization.
Manipulation of readers 48, 399, 410, 429, 444, 450, 452, 603, 615. See power, domination, narrative, author, egalitarianism.

Marcionite interpretation 152, 154–55, 171
Marginality, marginalization 461, 585. See oppression, socio-critical hermeneutics.
Mark, Mark's narrative 71, 285, 286, 288, 480–81, 506, 519
Marked (unmarked) terms 95
Marxist theory, Marxist hermeneutics, Marxist philosophy of language, 14, 95, 382, 388–90, 414–19, 427–30, 603– 04
Mary Magdalene 445
Masculine gender-relatedness 210, 223, 237, 533–34. See male imagery, gender, depatriarchalizing, father, feminist hermeneutics.
Master code 95. See code, semiotics.
Master metaphors* 353*. See metaphor.
Match of code, matching codes*, 501, 525– 26*, 582. See code, semiotics.
Materialist readings* 14, 48, 417–18, 421, 425–26*, 427–30, 547, 582. See Marxist hermeneutics, positivism, social sciences.
Mathematics, mathematical models, 81, 187, 488, 585
Matriarchy 457. See feminist hermeneutics.
Matrices of meaning. See intertextuality, "productive" texts.
Matthew's interpretation, Matthew's Christology, 150, 286–88
Meaning, meanings*, 13*, 20, 21, 25, 36– 38*, 40, 42, 50, 55, 59–62, 66, 85, 95, 111, 113, 124, 127, 157, 218, 249, 255, 295, 297, 326, 337–38, 364–68*, 398, 402, 474, 500–01, 504, 515, 535, 538, 540–46, 558–60*, 584–86, 589
meaning and intention 558–60*. See intention, author's intention.
meaning as against significance* 13*, 36– 38*
meaning as against "unmeant" meaning* 44*

Index of Subjects

meaning as meaning-effect* 13*, 84, 87, 354, 389, 399–400*, 493–99, 529–46. See socio-pragmatic hermeneutics, pragmatism.
Meaning as meaning-system. See semiotics, *langue*.
Meaning as reference 192
Meaning as use. See language-game, *parole*, Background.
Mechanical interpretation 220
Mediaeval interpretation, mediaeval tradition, 144, 157, 183, 190, 192
Melchizedek 265
"Mental processes" 558–59
Metacriticism, metacritical hermeneutics, metacritical theory, metacritique*, 5, 6, 11, 25, 48*, 51, 57*, 279, 313–14, 315–18*, 319–38, 358–59, 379–409, 440, 602–04, 612–29
Metalanguage, metalinguistic*, 94, 96*
Metanarratives 398–99
Metaphor 9, 58, 67, 110–11, 116, 119, 157, 345–46, 349, 351–58, 360–61, 366–68, 454, 475–76, 507, 576
Metaphysics, metaphysics of presence, 83, 106–07, 110, 120, 122
Methods, methods, 6, 11, 24, 97, 125, 130, 191, 204, 251, 314, 319, 348, 359, 383, 472, 610
method of correlation 422
method of projection 453
methods of science. See science, scientific method.
Metonymy 112, 349
Militancy, militant pressure-groups, 419, 603
Mimesis 355
Mishnah 151
Mistakes (in interpretation) 17, 21, 28, 444, 544. See systematic mistakes.
Misunderstanding 196, 205, 220, 228
Model language-game 525. See language-game.
Model reader* 526*, 529

Models and qualifiers 73, 96
Modernity 380, 387, 389
Montanism 457
Mood-indicator* 364*
Mood-stance, mood-actions*, 570*, 573
Morphology of narrative 486. See narrative grammar.
Motherhood of God 458
Motor-bike enthusiast 612–13
Music, musical code, musical texts, 31, 80, 99, 104, 129–30, 210, 212, 587
Mutual understanding 252
Myers-Briggs type indicator 482
"Mystic writing pad"* 112*
Mystification* 82*
Myth, mythologies, 90, 93, 95, 116, 171, 276, 281–82, 336–37, 347, 351, 359, 452–54, 457, 460. See demythologizing.
Mytheme * 90*

Nailing one's colours to the mast 244. See backing, personal backing, illocutions.
Naming 102
Narcissism 349, 350, 371
Narrative, narrative theory, narratology*, 73, 354–58, 380, 477, 478–80*, 479–94, 566–75
narrative experience 419–27
narrative gaps 520
narrative grammar* 97, 486–94*
narrative hermeneutics 288, 334, 345, 361, 399, 527
narrative philosophy 545, 587
narrative theology* 481, 568–69*
narrative speed, narrative tempo*, 50, 480–81*
narrative-time* 354–57*, 358–68, 485, 521, 568, 571
narrative-world 32, 68, 170, 266, 288, 315, 482, 566–75
narrator's point of view 72, 356, 521
"Natural" meaning, naturalness, 47, 50, 82, 93–94, 183, 185,

395–96, 456, 474, 533, 587–88
Nature-immanentism 456
Negation (of force or of propositional content) 294
Negative dialectics 418
Negative theology* 120*
Neo-Kantianism 272, 276
Neo-pragmatism 329, 400, 536. See pragmatism, socio-pragmatic, hermeneutics.
Neustic* 364–65*
New Creation 392–93, 439, 614, 617, 619
New Criticism* 49–50*, 58– 60*, 65, 96, 115, 472, 476, 484, 500, 521. See formalism, autonomy of text.
New hermeneutic* 11, 34*, 119, 313, 314, 325, 567–68
New horizons 1–29, 618–19. See horizon, transformation, enlarged horizons.
Nietzschean critique of metaphysics 110
Non-verbal language 55
Norms 330, 388, 393–94. See socio-pragmatic hermeneutics.
North American black theology 420–23

Objectification 248–50, 252, 276, 279
Objectivism 60, 183, 318–19, 383
Objectivity 82, 91, 97, 147, 251–52, 329, 331, 350, 361, 431, 539
Obscurity 241, 289, 484, 574. See *claritas scripturae*, transcendence.
Old Testament, use of in the church, 148–57, 229
"*Omniscient narrator*"* 483*, 574
Ontology, ontological, 10, 165, 285, 288, 314, 337, 358, 368, 440, 455, 610. See reality.
ontology of community 400, 417
Ontotheology 88
Openness* 4, 24, 26, 33*, 251–53*, 334–35, 344, 445, 450, 506, 558–60, 588–89, 618. See listening.

Open system 25, 99, 148, 401, 442, 444, 619. See system.
Open texts* 477, 527*. See productive texts.
Oppression, oppressors, oppressive structures of power, 7, 379, 386, 392, 401, 410–70, 602–04. See power, interest, domination.
Orality, oral hermeneutics, oral speech, 56, 70, 71, 83, 104, 423
Ordinary readers 532, 550.
See academic community, egalitarianism, community of readers.
Orphaned speech* 600*. See death of the author.
Ostensive reference 26, 485–86, 526, 543.
Other, texts as the, 35–36, 248–49, 348, 370, 529–30
Output text* 22*
Outside, correction from, 515, 537, 543, 549. See socio-pragmatic hermeneutics.
Overcoding, overcoded intertextual frames*, 527*
Overdetermination* 14*, 112, 347*, 349, 530
Overlapping and criss-crossing 541, 545. See language-games, trans-contextual communication.

Pain, pain-language, pain-behaviour, 300, 543, 599
Paper currency, paper money, 126
Parables, parables of Jesus, 17, 26, 67, 115–20, 273, 290, 372, 411, 481, 492, 527, 567– 68, 571
Paradigmatic relations* 85*, 90, 94
Paradigm shift 28, 58, 60, 314, 315, 386, 397
Paradox 58, 67, 117, 118, 130, 480, 564
paradox of scepticism, paradox of semioclasm, 97, 127
Parole* 23, 47, 83*, 86*, 89, 91, 101, 125, 128, 217–18, 232, 291. See language-use, *langue*.

Parody 117
Participation, participatory language, 19, 251, 301, 303
Particularity, particular case, 217–18, 224–25, 279. See contingency.
Passive reading 536–66. See convention, system.
Pastoral theology* 4, 5, 33, 556*, 557–603, 604*, 605–20
   pastoral application 22, 171
   pastoral concern, pastoral sensitivity, 168–73, 191, 266, 558–59
   pastoral dialogue, pastoral judgment, 238, 239, 330, 333, 556
   pastors, ordained ministers, 189, 244, 411, 533, 590
Patience 33
Patriarchal culture, patriarchy, 432, 434, 438. See depatriarchalization, father, feminist hermeneutics.
Pattern-recognition 86
Paul, Pauline texts, 237–47, 253–67, 273
   Paul as pastor
   Paul as "second founder" of Christianity 243
Pentateuch 304–06
Perception 103, 112, 126, 523, 529. See also colour, colour-perception.
Performance 314, 328, 330, 387. See actualization.
Performative language, performative force*, 16–19*, 276, 286, 290, 388. See illocution, speech act, promise.
Perlocutionary acts* 293*, 363–64
Personal backing, personal accreditation, 544, 591, 598–601, 615–18. See first-person utterances, self-involvement, commissives, illocutions, promise.
Persons, persons as agents, 243–44, 266, 345. See agents, subjectivity, inter-personal communication.
Perspicuity 23, 179. See *claritas scripturae*.
Persuasive definition 152

Pesher interpretation 151
Phenomenology, phenomenological method, 97, 107, 319, 345–47, 387, 518, 523
Philonic interpretation 159–63
Philology 214
Philosophy. philosophical methods, philosophical foundations, 101, 106, 112, 127, 129, 131, 362, 367, 369, 396, 399, 474, 523, 541, 545
   philosopher not a citizen of any community of ideas 541
   philosophical hermeneutics 216–17, 318–30, 334
   philosophy of language 115, 118, 324, 348, 402, 502, 515, 523, 534, 540–46, 549. See linguistic philosophy.
   philosophy of law 539
   philosophy of logic 540
   philosophy of science 354. See science, scientific method.
Photography 93
Pictures 367, 578–79
Pietism, pietist interpretation*, 179, 185, 193*, 211, 229, 276, 288, 530
Platonic idealism 162, 264
Play*, textual play, semiotic play*, 99, 110–11*, 117–19, 122, 125, 129, 130–31*, 142, 314, 365, 461, 536, 590
Pleasure 130, 131
Plot* 354–55*, 481, 482*, 484, 488, 521, 527, 571–73
Pluralism, plurivalence*, 5, 96, 130, 315, 397, 473, 549, 612–18*. See deferral, difference, interest, life-world.
Poetics* 352–53*, 356, 495*, 496–99, 536*. See generative poetics, post-structuralism, system.
Poetry, poetic vision, 107, 129, 325, 352, 386, 454, 499, 506, 557
Poièsis 352
Point of view* 479, 481–84*. See narrative theory.
Political ideology, political left, 81, 94, 129, 413, 419. See ideology.

Polyvalent meaning 131, 172, 498, 505, 518. See polyvalent narration, pluralism, semiotics, play, meaning.
Polyvalent narration* 119*
Poor, poverty, 411–12, 415–16, 418, 430, 603. See oppression, socio-critical hermeneutics.
Positivism 329, 331–32, 334, 336–37, 353, 382, 383, 605
Possibility, the possible, 100–01, 333, 351–58, 360, 368, 569. See conditions for possibility, transcendental questions.
Post-Christian feminism 436, 449
Post-critical naïveté, post-critical retrieval*, 344, 348*, 359*, 372. See second naïveté.
Post-Gadamerian hermeneutics* 11–16*, 51, 272, 278
Postmodernism* 9, 15, 50–51*, 60, 112, 157, 314, 320–21, 380–81, 398, 399, 414, 436–37, 444, 461
Post-structuralism* 28, 349, 437, 472, 495–99*
Power, power-structures, 6, 69, 93, 240, 384, 386, 392, 429–30, 459, 472, 615. See oppression, interests.
power-in-weakness 615
Practical reason, practical wisdom, 315, 321, 325–28, 330, 380. See *praxis*.
Pragmatic, pragmatism, pragmatic hermeneutics*, 7, 12*, 27, 84, 393–99, 445, 448, 533, 538–50, 587–90. See socio-pragmatic hermeneutics.
pragmatic doctrine 543–45
Pragmatics (as *vs* semantics or syntactics) 41*, 87*, 128, 365, 366*, 490, 524. See speech-act theory, extra-linguistic world.
Prague Linguistic Circle 89–90
Praise 73, 282, 299, 598, 615
Praxis* 336, 380, 383, 385, 413–14*, 417, 419, 433, 610–11
Prayer 64, 598

Preaching 212, 299. See pastors, pastoral theology, proclamation.
Pre-critical interpretation, pre-modern interpretation, 142–48, 315
Pre-intentional Background 45. See Background.
Pre-judgments 321. See effective-history, tradition, pre-understanding, Background.
Premature fusion of horizons 531. See horizons, fusion of horizons.
Premonitory signs* 526*
Present, "present situation", 333, 337, 401, 556–57, 604–11. See criteria of relevance, universal history.
Pressure 444, 452
Presupposition* 45*, 282, 291, 362, 366, 387, 453, 497, 526. See Background, pre-understanding, intertextuality.
Pre-texts 504, 505
Pre-understanding (Vorverständnis)* 44–46*, 314, 383, 429, 496–97, 526, 537, 564. See Background, presupposition, intertextuality.
Principle of correlation 577
Private interpretation 191
Private language* 13*, 17, 21*, 216, 544
Productive texts* 20*, 41*, 96, 525, 544, 583–85. See open texts, intertextuality, semiotics, play, literary meaning.
Projection 344, 523, 530, 587. See idolalry, socio-pragmatic hermeneutics, narrative-world.
Prolepsis* 480*
Promise, logic of promise*, 2, 18, 19, 25, 32, 43, 70, 123, 264, 287, 293–308*, 336, 371, 417, 442, 564, 575, 597–602, 605–06, 613–19
Prophetic address, prophetic discourse, 73, 114, 549
Propositions 294, 323, 324, 335, 364, 366, 396, 485
propositional content 41, 295, 305, 361, 364, 575, 615–16
Protest literature 424

Index of Subjects

Provisionality of interpretation 219, 222, 231. See corrigibility.
Psychoanalytical interpretation, psychoanalytical hermeneutics*, 93, 96, 111, 329, 346–50*, 371–72, 381–84, 403, 435, 495, 529–31, 561. See Freudian theory, unconscious, consciousness.
Psychological regression 580
Psychological ("technical") hermeneutics* 206–33* (in Schleiermacher)
Psychologistic interpretation 223, 267, 559. See mental processes.
Public criteria of meaning, public domain*, 12, 16, 21*, 26*, 45, 88, 102, 126, 129, 162, 166, 191, 193, 395, 402, 545
Purity-pollution semiotic code 428

Qualitative misunderstanding 221
Quantification 387
Qumran 151

Rabbinic interpretation 145, 151
Radical hermeneutics* 51*, 145, 318
Radical historical finitude* 318–30*. See historical finitude.
Ranking of criteria 316–17, 602–03, 612–14. See metacriticism, criteria of relevance.
Rationality* 11*, 152, 278, 326, 381, 384, 387, 402, 405, 441, 443, 451, 545
Rationalism* 6, 11*, 24, 143, 182, 186, 318, 321, 327, 329–30, 367, 386, 396
Reader, reading*, 2, 15–16*, 28*, 32*, 56, 84, 91, 96, 172, 315, 355, 462, 495–555
  ideal reader* 517*, 529
  implied reader* 517*
  model reader* 526*
  reader-competency* 525, 535–37*
  reader-effects 168–73, 208, 229, 357
  reader-response theory* 9, 15, 17, 60–61*, 125, 208, 277, 472, 474, 484, 515–55*, 586–87

reading community 64, 395, 474
reading situations 96, 272, 558–620
super-reader 529
Reality 122, 126, 131, 247, 322–38, 355–72, 606–19. See ontology.
Reason 147, 187, 189, 194, 196, 318–30, 443–44, 451
Reception theory 33, 60, 517, 587
Receptivity (*Empfänglichkeit*) 252
Reconstruction 251–53, 275, 359, 558–62. See historical reconstruction.
Re-contextualization* 36–42*, 436, 497. See context, contextualization.
Redaction criticism 484, 500
Reductive explanation 346–50
Reference, referential meaning 17, 66, 104, 130, 290, 352, 357, 367. See ostensive reference, meaning, extra-linguistic world.
Re-figuration* 357–58*, 361, 370
Reflexion, reflexivity, 119, 120, 320, 369. See post-modernism, semiotics.
Reformers, Reformation, 179–94, 239, 533, 549, 589
Relativism 314, 318, 381, 394, 547. See contextual relativism, social pragmatism.
Relay race model of hermeneutics 605
Relevance 326, 365, 604–19. See criteria of relevance.
Re-living 247–53, 248*
"Re-orientation by disorientation" 372
Repression, repressed wishes, 349, 384, 576
Re-ranking of criteria 612–14. See ranking of criteria, metacriticism.
Responsibility 274, 282, 290, 570, 615–16. See commitment.
Resurrection, resurrection of Christ, 69, 244–45, 263, 284–85, 289, 302, 332, 336, 418, 445–47, 586, 609–19
Retrieval* 347*

Retrospective interpretation 519–20, 575
Revelation 56, 72, 74, 88, 264, 289, 332, 370, 442, 507, 532, 549, 568, 576, 601
Rhetoric, rhetorical distance, 352, 451, 474
Ritual 55, 90, 93
Romantic triangle 210
Romanticist hermeneutics, Romanticism* 10, 56, 204, 209–11*, 213, 220, 226, 229, 237, 247, 472
Routinization* 8, 10, 587*, 598
Rule of faith 142. See tradition, creed, context of understanding.
Rule, linguistic, 128, 324, 534. See language-game, system, *langue*, game.
Russian formalism 89, 355, 486. See formalism.

Sachkritik 158
Salvation-history 239, 331
Scepticism 88, 127, 180, 182, 401, 588. See paradox of scepticism.
Science, sciences, 101, 126, 249, 279, 319, 322, 329, 334, 345, 352, 382, 383, 386, 403, 488, 495–96, 542
  scientific method, scientific paradigm, 97, 126, 237, 251, 320, 321, 331, 397, 486, 491
  scientific world-view 97. See positivism.
Second naïveté 359, 376. See post-critical naïveté.
Selfhood, self-identity, 368, 530, 550, 567
  self-affirmation, self-interest, 392, 410, 430, 550, 578, 612–13, 615. See social pragmatism, pragmatism, the cross.
  self-deception 228, 344, 379. See deception, illusion, psychoanalytical hermeneutics.
  self-emptying, de-centred self, 614–15. See transformation, the cross.

  self-involvement, logic of, hermeneutics of, 192, 274–307, 564–66, 615–18
  self-referential, self-referring system, 38, 42, 119, 123, 473, 487. See intra-linguistic world, semiotics, system.
Semantics, semantic breakdown, 27, 61, 97, 226, 354
Semiotic code* 31, 80–81*, 82–103. See code, semiotics.
Semiotic productivity 582–86. See productive texts, intertextuality.
Semiotics, semiotic system, semiotic theory*, 2, 13, 21, 47–48*, 80–81*, 82–113, 427, 472, 578, 524, 535–37, 578. See system.
Semitic colouring 224
Sensus communis 321
Septuagint 160, 224
Sexual politics, sexism, 435, 441. See gender, feminism, feminist hermeneutics.
Signs, sign-systems*, 47*, 55, 82–84*, 110, 123, 248, 404, 536–37, 584. See semiotics, system, *langue*, meaning, significance.
sign-behaviour 87
sign-icon* 86*
sign-index* 86*
sign-punning 109
Signal, signal flag, 506, 584
Significance* 13*, 36–38* (as *vs* meaning), 47, 80* (as signification), 90, 94, 330. See semiotics, meaning.
Silence 64, 73, 116, 194
Situation, situation of utterance, 42, 62, 244, 249, 498. See context of situation.
Slavery 420. See oppression, domination, power.
Social critique 368, 379–470. See socio-critical theory, socio-critical hermeneutics.
social action 401, 418
social agents 388
social behaviour 80, 81

social bonding 589
social code 81
social construction 607
social control 435
social criticism 368, 381, 388, 410, 416, 420, 430, 544
social integration 388–89
social interaction 248
social norms 128. See internal norms.
social psychology 387
social roles 387, 389, 435
Social Sciences 148, 248–49, 251, 325, 326, 386–87, 393–94, 397, 402, 604–11. See sociology.
Socio-critical hermeneutics, socio-critical theory*, 2, 5, 6, 7, 12*, 14, 27, 28*, 92, 93, 128,143, 379*, 380–470, 515, 602–04
Socio-economic factors 389, 392, 416
Socio-historical conditions 41–44
Socio-linguistic context 207, 531
Sociology 241, 252, 325, 326, 386–90, 435, 605. See social sciences.
sociological hermeneutics* 607–08*
sociology of knowledge 56, 258, 326, 380, 382, 451, 457, 607–09
sociology of literacy 532
Socio-political hermeneutics, socio-political agenda, 428, 471, 529, 531–35
Socio-pragmatic hermeneutics, social pragmatism*, 6, 12*, 27*, 337, 380, 396–98*, 419, 433,443, 448, 457, 529–50, 587–90. See contextual relativism.
socio-pragmatic affirmation 424, 515, 531. See self- affirmation.
Solipsism 126, 208, 216, 404
Son of Man 287, 475–76, 504
Sound effect 493
Speaking subject 127–28
Speech-acts, speech-act theory*, 2, 16–19*, 24, 32, 274–75, 282, 283–312, 361–63, 364–67*,386, 389, 390, 439, 498, 559–60, 591, 597– 604. See illocutions, first-person utterances, performative language, force, Background, promise, personal backing, stake in the text.
Speech and writing 72
Speech aphasia 90
Spiritual reading* 22, 142–45*, 192, 578–82. See *lectio divina*, believing reading, symbol, allegorical interpretation, four senses.
Spirit. See Holy Spirit.
Split reference 352
Staggered systems 96
Stake in the text, personal stake, 530, 581, 584. See personal backing, believing reading.
Statistics 322
Steno-symbol 67
Stereotypification 98, 431, 434, 436, 458–59, 462, 533–34, 585, 608–13. See feminist hermeneutics, black hermeneutics, social critique, "in" group, criteria of relevance.
Stoic interpretation 158
Story* 97, 116, 355*, 419–27, 479–81*, 521. See narrative, discourse.
Stream of life 67, 127, 218, 250, 559
Structural-functional social science* 607*
Structuralism* 91, 97, 369, 471, 487–88*, 489–94, 535. See system, meaning, narrative-grammar, *langue*.
Structure 80, 83, 85, 91. See system, *langue*.
Struggle with the angel 489–90
Style-less (zero-degree) writing 93
Sub-apostolic writings 165– 67
Sub-codes* 525*. See codes.
Sub-conscious 259. See unconscious.
Subjectivity 63, 125, 230, 277, 440, 450, 495, 565
Sub-systems, sub-cultures, sub-forms, 389, 392, 400, 607
Suffering servant 476

Super-reader 529. See reader, reading.
Surprise 480, 587, 614. See horizon of expectation.
Suspicion 5, 143, 259, 413. See hermeneutics of suspicion.
Symbols, symbolism* 14, 67, 86, 98, 345–50*, 410, 437, 521, 576–82
Syntactics* 87*
Syntagmatic relations* 85*, 90, 487
System* 7, 12, 23, 83, 85, 118, 122, 127, 193, 266, 276, 278, 386–93*, 419, 486–87, 496, 505–06, 516, 525, 536–37, 559, 583, 607–18. See semiotics, life-world, open system, *langue*, metacriticism.
Systematic mistakes, criteria for, 544, 549, 601
Systematic theology 22, 238, 243, 313. See theology.

Talmud 123, 125, 151
Targumic traditions 151
Technical reason, technology, 318, 380, 383, 386. See instrumental reason, calculative thinking.
Tempo (narrative speed)* 480–81*
Temporal horizons, temporal reading processes, 106, 114, 264, 519. See time, time horizons.
Tenor, as *vs* vehicle, 453
Tension (e.g. between text and other, or within text) 49, 58, 256, 412
Tensive language, tensive symbol, 67, 353
Texts, textuality*, 15*, 19–20*, 32, 49*, 55–58*, 59–97, 98*, 99–141, 219, 228, 232, 328, 333, 345, 349, 399, 471, 497, 517, 528
textual constraints 502. See socio-pragmatic hermeneutics.
textual forces 476. See formalism.
textual play 131. See play.
textual strategies 527. See postmodernism, interests.
texture, text as, 124–25, 129, 504. See intertextuality, postmodernism.

Theological education 556–57, 604–11
Theology 331–38. See Christian theology, systematic theology, pastoral theology, the cross, resurrection.
Theophany 476
Theory* 3, 412, 413–14*, 436, 472, 532, 536, 544, 586. See *praxis*.
theory of knowledge 231, 247, 331, 381. See epistemology.
Thinking 207, 216, 225, 454
Third world, third-world identity, 411–27, 603
Time, temporality, 31, 64–65, 106, 264, 279, 351–58, 479–86, 519. See narrative time.
time-consciousness 106. See effective history, historical finitude.
time-horizons, temporal horizons, 21, 31, 64–68, 164, 168, 370, 515, 587. See actualizations, performances.
"Timeless" propositions, "timeless" truth, 44, 161, 215. See context-free utterances.
Token* (*vs* type) 86*
Tools of the oppressors 450. See oppression, militancy, pressure, domination.
Topographic code 490
Traces, tracks, 105, 108, 504
Tradition* 9, 22, 25, 42, 64, 88, 100, 102, 146–48*, 149–73, 179, 182–86, 194, 272, 314, 320, 322–24, 325–27*, 328–38, 382, 388, 400, 431, 444, 590. See effective history, community.
tradition as context of understanding 148–56
Traffic signals 53, 506, 584
Training 17, 102, 128, 325, 404, 525
Transaction 515, 530
Transcendence 112–18, 370, 572
Transcendental hermeneutics, transcendental philosophy, transcendental critique*, 89, 113,

145, 205*, 213, 279, 318, 393–96, 397*, 398– 405*, 426, 433, 440, 449, 618–19. See conditions for possibility, Kantian philosophy, metacriticism.
Trans-contextual bridges, trans-cultural critique, 88, 395, 440–41, 541, 604, 613–19. See overlapping, inter-penetration, metacriticism, socio-critical hermeneutics.
Transforming, transformation of texts, transforming reading*, 2, 39–41*, 355, 359–60, 392, 414, 418, 427, 443, 449, 461, 504, 530, 565–68, 606–19. See outside, correction from, cross, resurrection, Holy Spirit, new horizons, speech-act theory, promise.
Transient revaluations 526
Transmissive texts* 20, 41, 501, 525–26*. See inter-personal communication, productive texts.
Transposition* 42*, 248*, 353. See intertextuality.
Tribal society 389, 391
Trinitarian language 260. See Holy Trinity, Holy Spirit.
Tropological sense 193
Trust 143, 283, 285, 599
Truth, truth-claims, 110–13, 130–31, 182, 275–77, 285, 314–15, 323, 327, 329, 331–38, 350, 360, 368–69, 395–96, 398, 413, 484, 527, 550, 564, 581
Two horizons 515, 546. See horizon, fusion of horizons, premature fusion of horizons.
Two Testaments, the, 148–52, 167, 170
Tyndale's biblical interpretation 190–91
Type (vs token)* 86*
Type, typology (vs antitype, allegory)*, 144, 155*, 163–64*, 336
Type, Typification* 252*, 258, 261, 265, 326, 487, 588, 606– 13. See stereotypification.

Ugaritic texts 459
Ultimate concern 229, 421
Ultrafundamentalism 588
"Unbaptism" 293
Unconscious 93, 111–12, 129, 198, 227–28, 259, 346, 384, 576, 583. See psychoanalytical hermeneutics, Freudian theory, postmodernism.
Understanding (*Verstehen*)* 10, 14, 23, 28, 32, 204, 210, 218, 248*, 325, 335, 337, 402, 440, 528. See hermeneutics of understanding.
"Undoing" 590. See deconstruction.
University 4, 189, 532. See academic community, theological education, hermeneutics, *Geisteswissenschaften*, science, social sciences.
Universals, universality* 14, 25, 42*, 213, 322, 323–24, 330–38, 391, 396, 443, 449, 460, 608–19
universal history 330–38, 610
universality of hermeneutics 322– 30
universal pragmatics 397–404
universal principle of justice 443, 460
universal status of theology 330–38, 608–19
Utopianism* 326, 607*

Vehicle (vs tenor in metaphor)* 452– 54*
Verbal carnival 98
Verdictives* 284*, 295–96*, 299*, 616. See declaratives.
Verification 496
Via negativa 120, 460
Violence 416, 434, 438, 459

Wager 369, 372
Wax nose, biblical text as, 189
Western tradition of philosophy. See philosophy.
Westerns 487, 527
Whole, wholeness, vision of the whole, 211, 216, 228, 249, 269, 331, 338, 355, 393. See divinatory axis of understanding.

wholeness of Pauline thought 244
wholeness of scripture 154–55, 194
Whorfian hypothesis 102
Will, wish-fulfilments, 111, 297, 345–46, 372, 506, 602
Wisdom, wisdom literature, wisdom mode, 11, 25, 73, 117, 181, 282, 315, 321, 371, 380. See practical reason, transcendence.
Witness 114, 306–07. See first-person utterances, personal backing.
Wittgenstein's builders 543
Word and deed 69, 70, 75. See extra-linguistic world, linguistic behaviour, speech-act.
Word of God 187, 230. See actualization, revelation.
*Word-to-world direction of fit** 291–307*, 599–602. See propositions, propositional content.
World, worldhood, 10, 279, 294, 313, 322, 567

world of art 319. See art, count-generation.
*world-to-word direction of fit** 291–307*, 599–602, 606–19. See promise.
world as projected narrative-world. See narrative-world, count-generation.
Worship, worshipping community, 21, 64–65, 169, 263, 299, 590. See liturgical texts, liturgical context.
*"Writerly text"** 98*
Writing, written texts, 27, 83, 104, 112, 248. See grammatology, oral hermeneutics.

Yugoslavian circle 414

Zen Buddhist Koans 88, 119
*Zero-degree style** 93*

INDEX OF BIBLICAL REFERENCES

Genesis		11:7–9	391	3:7–9	417
1:1–2:25	566, 573	12:1–3	304	3:9	425
1:2	39	12:1–8	160	3:11	425
1:3	296	12:7	304	4:1	425
1:5, 16	169	12:13	391	4:10, 13	425
1:12	573	12:50	304	5:1–21	482
1:18	573	14:18–20	265	5:6–14	417
1:21	573	15:4, 5	304	6:1–9	305
1:26	153	15:6	240	6:3, 6–8	305
1:26, 27	391, 436, 438	16:01	304	7:20–11:10	482
1:26–2:25	566	16:11, 12	434	12:31–14:31	571
1:27	160	16:15	163	12:31–15:21	571
1:28	573	17:1–11	304	13:3	417
1:28, 29	573	17:17, 18	304	14:5–18	482
1:13	573	17:19, 20	204	14:11, 12	417
2:2	159	19:30–38	155	14:21–29	482
2:7	160	21:2	163	15:1–27	571
2:8	161, 169	21:9–21	434	15:2	305
2:9, 10	579	22:1–19	273, 564, 566	17:11, 12	155
2:11	161	22:2	564	19:3	159
2:13	161	22:16–18	304	19:4	458
2:16	573	26:3, 24	304	19:4, 5	422
2:17	573	27:33–37	292	19:5, 8	305
2:18	438	28:15	304	19:18	159
3:1	162	31:49	44	20:2	417
3:1–6	155	32:23–25	489	20:5	153
3:8	160, 169	32:23–33	490	20:8–11	151
3:9	563	49:11	155	20:19	151
3:12, 16	391			24:26	151
4:1–16	426	**Exodus**		34:6	478
4:2–16	429	1:1–10	417	34:6, 7	40
4:8	424	1:8–2:10	432	34:10	305
4:9, 10	391	1:13, 14	417		
4:12–16	424	1:15–21	439	**Leviticus**	
4:11	165	1:16, 20, 21	432	6:5, 6	40
:17	160	1:22–2:10	439	11:3	159
4:24	391	3:1–4:17	482	25:1–55	40
6:15	169	3:6, 10	305	26:34, 35	40
7:17–20	479	3:7	425	26:40, 43, 46	305

27:23, 30	305	13:1–22	434	8:4			287
		15:21–30	478	8:4–6			37
Numbers		22:29	581	8:4–9			566
10:11, 12, 29	305			16:10			581
11:12	458	**I Kings**		17:8		458, 581	
23:20	292	15:11–15	39	18:1, 2			300
		19:8–12	476	18:2, 29			581
Deuteronomy		21:1–29	42	22:9			453
4:2	182			23:5			581
5:6	417	**II Kings**		24:1		42, 259	
6:4	9	9:1–13	507	25:2			599
6:5, 6	73	14:23–27	483	28:7			581
16:19	462			31:2			581
18:9–22	333	**II Chronicles**		33:20			581
25:4	164	14:1–4	39	36:7, 9			581
32:11	458	19:7	462	38:2			169
		30:18, 19	299	39:7, 12			282
Joshua		36:18–21	40	40:2, 3			282
1:2–5, 13, 14	64			44:6			187
2:1	155	**Nehemiah**		46:7, 11			581
2:18, 21	165	10:31–40	40	48:2, 3			581
6:2	64			57:1			581
10:12	64	**Esther**		61:3, 4			581
11:23	64	1:3, 18, 19	572	63:1, 5, 7			581
		2:3	572	65:5–8			286
Judges		8:11	572	68:5			462
3:15–30	483	10:3	572	74:13, 14			41
6:36–40	483			74:14			417
11:29–40	434	**Job**		75:1			299
19:1–30	434	1:1–3	121	78:2			166
		13:3	372	86:15			478
Ruth		23:3	372	87:4			417
1:5–14	434	23:8	74	89:8, 9			286
1:16	117, 590	29:15	462	89:11			417
2:1–7, 14–18	434	30:20	74	90:3			581
4:7–22	434	31:35	372	91:4		171, 458	
4:17–22	117, 590	38	372	95:7			46
		38:3–9	458	103:2, 3			613
I Samuel		38:8–11	286	103:8			478
10:1	507	38:28, 29	458	104:26			41
16:7	259	41:1	41	104:29			581
16:12, 13	479, 481	42:1–6	74, 371, 372	107:5			581
16:14	481	42:7–17	121, 590	107:23–32			286
17–2 Samuel 5:5	479, 481	42:10–17	65	107:29–30			581
				110:4			265
II Samuel		**Psalms**		114:2			144
7:13	187	1:3	577	118:7			44
12:1–6	567, 581	7:10	581	118:22			150

Index of Biblical References

119:105	181, 581	**Ezekiel**		**Matthew**	
123:2	453	1:5, 16–18	584	1:1–4:16	572
136:26	42	11:19	73	3:17	572
		13:5	475	4:1–11	491
Proverbs		43:2	585	4:6	491
1:7	42	47:1–12	579	4:8	169
8:25	282			4:18–20:34	572
11:30	577	**Daniel**		5:3–6	34
21:9	172	2:4, 7, 16, 28	151	5:17, 18–20	150, 151
22:20	168	5:7–16	151	5:21–26	150
		7:13, 14	287, 504	5:21–37	285
Ecclesiastes		9:2	39	5:39–41	117
2:16	117, 590	12:11	504	6:11	170
9:11	117, 590			7:12	73
12:13	65	**Hosea**		8:22	285
		6:7	305	8:23–27	286
Isaiah		8:1	305	9:2	286, 298, 299
2:4	392	13:8	459	9:20–22	432
2:12	475			10:23	475
5:1, 2	164	**Joel**		10:39	34
13:6, 9	475	1:15	475	11:25	187
13:19–22a	583	2:1, 2	475	12:22–30	286
29:14	150	2:28–36	149	12:28	67
31:4, 5	37	3:14, 21	475	13:1–9	118
42:14	453			13:13	166
43:14	417	**Amos**		13:18–23, 44	118
45:18	39	5:12	462	13:45, 46	166
46:3, 4	458	5:18–20	475	13:46	154
47:4	417			15:21–28	432
49:1	476	**Jonah**		17:5	572
49:15–16	458	1:2–9	33, 477, 478	18:6	562
50:4	476	4:1–11	33	18:12–14	153
51:9, 10	41, 417	4:2	478	20:1–15	34
52:13–53:12	476	4:10, 11	478	20:1–16	170, 492, 567, 571, 575
61:2, 3	37				
66:13	453, 458	**Nahum**		21:1–28:20	572
		1:2, 3	40, 41	22:11–14	492
Jeremiah				23:37	458
2:1, 2	73	**Habakkuk**		24	504
3:12	73	1:1, 2a	151	25:1–13	492
4:27	73	1:5	150	25:14–30	492, 565, 566
4:29	581			26:28	598
25:9–12	39, 40	**Zephaniah**		26:36–46	572
25:11, 12	39	1:7, 14	475	27:35	66
28:6–9	333			28:16–20	481
31:3	300	**Zechariah**		28:18	572
46:10	475	3:2	300	28:18–20	286, 288
		4:10	171	28:19, 20	287

Mark							
1:1	288	4:18, 19	422	4:31	521		
1:1–15	586	5:20	286	4:39	306		
1:11	528	6:20–22	34	5:32, 33, 37	306		
1:15	285	6:29	117	6:1–14	69		
1:24	572	8:22–25	286	6:32–35	521		
1:25	286	10:5	299	6:35	69, 581		
2:5	286	10:29–37	34	6:35, 41	120		
2:7	572	10:30–32	493	6:51	521		
2:21, 22	285	10:30–37	117, 170, 571	6:52–66	120		
3:1–6	150	11:14, 15	286	6:63	581		
3:23–27	286	11:17–23	286	6:68	306		
4:1–9	122	11:20	67	7:33	521		
4:3–20	118	11:31, 32	285	7:43	306		
4:35–41	286, 490	14:16–24	118	7:52	521		
5:1–20	490	15:11–32	118, 166, 290, 492, 518, 566, 586	8:12	69, 181, 581		
5:9	491	15:22	166	8:12, 58	614		
5:13, 17	491	16:1–8	476	8:18	306		
5:15, 19	490	16:1–9	492	8:31–35	521		
6:30–44	519, 520, 586	16:19–31	118	8:32	581		
6:36, 37	429	17:33	34, 475	9:1–11	69		
6:41	520	18:9–14	34, 118, 571	9:5	581		
8:1–10	519, 520, 586	20:17	150	9:39	306		
8:4, 6	520	21	504	10:3, 4	521		
8:35	34	23:33	66	10:7, 10, 11	581		
9:1	475	24:1–11	445	11:1–44	69, 306		
10:17–22	519, 522, 586	24:11	445, 447	11:11–15	521		
10:22	519	24:27	149	11:23	581		
10:31	34	24:27, 45	150	11:25	69, 306		
10:38	614	24:34	617	11:38–44	69		
10:46–52	480			12:25	34, 614		
12:1–9	164	**John**		12:32–34	521		
13	505	1:1	114	13:5–17	69		
13:5–37	504	1:1–5, 9–14	614	14:6	307, 581		
13:14	476, 504, 528, 586	1:1–18	307	14:6–9	74		
13:26	504	1:4, 5	581	14:26	307		
14	519, 520	1:7, 8, 15, 32	306	14:27	299		
14:3–8	506, 507	1:14	115, 307, 591	15:1	581		
14:22	519, 520, 586	1:46	521	15:27	306		
14:24	598	2:11	69	16:8	306		
15:16–39	481	2:19–21	521	16:13	307		
15:24	66	3:3–5	521	19:18	66		
16:1–8	445	3:6, 19	581	20:1–18	445		
16:8	445, 447	3:26	306	20:21	69		
		3:32, 33	306	20:23	299		
Luke		4:7–26	165	20:28	306		
1:1–4	68	4:10–15	521	20:28, 31	614		
3:1, 2	67	4:23	165	20:30	69		
				20:31	306, 307, 582		

Index of Biblical References

21:24	306, 521	8:27	259	8:1	43, 152, 241, 562
		8:29	302	8:1–13	43, 257
Acts		9:1–11:36	301	8:1–11:1	241, 558, 561
2:1–14	149	9:2	259	8:4	9, 173, 562
2:14–36	273	9:3	257	8:6	260, 562
2:15–21	149	10:1, 6	259	8:7	43
2:16	151	10:9	284	8:9	561
2:20	476	11:22	246	8:10	255
7:48	264	11:33	181	8:11–13	562
9:1–30	261	14:1	240	9:1–19	70
10:1, 5	490	14:7	563	9:9, 10	164
10:9	490	14:7, 8	283	9:12–23	69
10 and 11	489	14:15	240	9:20–23	273
13:2–28:31	261	15:1, 7	240	10:1–4	164, 170
13:41	150	15:7	617	10:1–13	163
14:15–18	273	16:1–4	257	10:16, 17	614
17:22–31	273	16:18	259	10:19–11:1	43
17:31	563			11:10	448
		I Corinthians		11:16	240
Romans		1:12	197, 254, 255	11:17, 18	561
1:1	283		561, 562	11:17–22	558, 561
1:3, 4	563	1:13	614	11:20–22	255
1:4	260, 284	1:18	150	11:23–25	260
1:16, 17	427	1:18, 23, 24	34	11:25	598
1:17	35, 589	1:18–25	614	11:26	614
1:18–3:20	603	1:19	150	12:1	152
1:21, 28	259	1:23	298, 615	12:3	260, 283, 563
2:5	259	1:23–25	615	12:4–11	64
3:21, 28	603	2:1–5	615	12:12	153
4:19–22	565	2:2	453	13:10	153
4:25	260	2:4	168	14:2–25	619
5:2	263	2:6, 7	152	14:30	255
5:5	259, 609	2:10, 13	577	15:3–5	148, 260
5:12–21	163, 302	2:15	152	15:3–8	446, 447
6:3–11	614	3:1	152	15:4	298
6:4	172, 245	4:4	284	15:20	244, 302
6:8	245, 302	4:5	259	15:22–27, 45	302
6:11	302, 303	4:9–13	258	15:37	446
7	246	4:11, 12	70	15:44	446, 586
7:6–12	392, 393, 492	4:15	46	15:46	160
7:7–25	246, 301	4:17	240		
7:8–10	392	4:18	299	**II Corinthians**	
7:10–15	393	4:19, 20	69	1:9, 12, 24	69
8:1–4	494	6:9, 10	246	3:1–4:6	505
8:2	392, 492	7:1–11:1	244	3:6	168, 192, 492
8:7	281	7:17	240	3:14	154, 166
8:14–17, 26, 27	260	7:22, 23, 32	283	3:14, 15	259
8:15, 16	619	7:37	259	3:17	260

3:18	619	4:17	300	5:1–10	154
4:2–12	69			5:6, 8	154
4:7–15	70, 241	**Philippians**		5:9	614
4:10	302	1:1	283	5:11–16:12	262
4:10–12	245	2:5–11	263	6:19	338
5:9	283	2:11	284	6:19, 20	614
5:14, 15	241, 303	3:3–7, 9	281	7	521
5:17	256, 392, 393, 417, 614	3:4–7	246	7:1–3	164
		3:4–16	261	7:11–28	614
5:18–20	580	3:10–11	245	7:22	599
6:3–10	69, 241	4:2, 3	257	7:25	263
6:3–13	70			7:27	264
7:1	173	**Colossians**		8:5	264
10:11	70	1:15	260	8:5, 6	614
10:18	284	1:15, 19	74	8:8	599
11:7–15	70	2:14	580	9:11–14, 26	614
11:21–33	261			9:12	264
11:23–27	257	**I Thessalonians**		9:12–14	580
11:29, 30	257	1:5	69	9:15	599
12:9, 10	257	2:4	259	9:24	264, 265
12:9, 15	69	2:7	69	9:26, 28	264
12:13–16	70	2:8, 9	70, 71	10:10	264
13:4	69	4:16	454	10:12, 13	263
		4:17	285	10:12, 14	614
Galatians				10:22	263
1:10	283	**II Thessalonians**		10:26–39	262
1:11–2:21	261	3:8, 9	70	11:1	264, 338, 614
2:20	172, 245, 302	**Hebrews**		11:4–40	265
3:6	240	1:1	264	11:8	262
3:11	281	1:2	154	11:8, 9	265
3:17	599	1:2, 3	74	11:17–19	565
3:27	476	1:3	264, 614	12:1, 2	265
3:28	261, 302, 393, 613	1:4	154	12:1–17, 25–29	262
4:4	149	1:9	154	13:13	262
4:9	257	2:1–4	262	13:13, 14	338
4:21–24	169	2:7, 8	37	13:14	262
4:22–24	192	2:9, 11, 14	154	13:20	263
4:24–26	163, 164	2:16	154		
4:28, 31	163	3:2	154	**James**	
5:1	392, 417	3:7, 15	46	2:14–26	64
6:11, 12	257	3:7–19	262		
6:17	245	4:3, 8	262, 263	**I Peter**	
		4:7	46	2:7	150
Ephesians		4:8, 9	164	2:24	577
2:15	614	4:9	262		
4:4, 5	614	4:10	338	**II Peter**	
4:7–13	64	4:14–16	262	1:19	181
4:8–10	263	4:16	263	1:20, 21	191

John

1:2	306
3:2	619
4:14	306
5:6, 9	306

Revelation

1:9	424
1:13	585
2:14, 20	603
3:1	577
3:1–3	123
4:5	577
4:8	282, 585
6:1	577
6:3, 5, 7	123
6:9, 10	424
7:1	577
7:4	81
9:10	81
11:1, 2	81
12:3–17	41
13:1, 18	577
14	585
15:1	577
16:13	41
17:1	123
17:16	603
17:18	425
21:9	123
22:1	579
22:2	577, 579
22:14	579
22:17	123, 601

INDEX OF ANCIENT EXTRA-BIBLICAL SOURCES

Aristotle (IV B.C.)
   Poetics   1457b, 6-9   352
Athanasius (IV A.D.)
   Or. contra Arianos   III:29   175 n.46
Barnabas, *Epistle of*, (II A.D.)
       9:8   165
       10:1–12   165
Chrysostom, John (IV–V A.D.)
       IX:531 D   178 n.140
       X:675 A   178 n.138
Clement of Alexandria (II–III A.D.)
   Fragments   V   177 n.112
   Stromata   I:12:56   146
       V:12   177 n.108
       V:21:4   177 n.107
       VI:15   177 n.109
Clement of Rome (I A.D.)
   I Clem.   13:7   165
Cyril of Alexandria (V A.D.)
   Epistles   1 and 4   146, 173
Evang. Ver. (II A.D.)
       18:40   153
       23:16–21   152
       25:2,3   153
       32:4,5   153
Heraclitus of Ephesus (VI–V B.C.)
   Fragments   125   122
Heraclitus Stoicus (I B.C. – I A.D.)
   Quaest. Homericae   22   175
Homer (VIII–VII B.C.)
   Iliad   XI, 624 and 641   122
Irenaeus (II A.D.)
   Adv. Haereses   I:8:1   175 n.56
       I:9:2   175 n.60
       I:11:1   175 n.58
       II:5:2   175 n.58
       II:27   175 n.63
       II:28:3   175 n.56
       IV:26:1   175 n.48
       IV:26:2   174 n.34

	IV:27:1	174 n.35
	IV:28:1	175 n.51
	IV:33:6	175 n.49
Proof Ap. Pr.	34	175 n.53
	36	175 n.49
	46	175 n.52
	57	175 n.54
Justin (II A.D.)		
Apologia	I:32	175 n.55
	I:46	174 n.33
Dialogues	54	175 n.55
Origen (III A.D.)		
Contra Celsum	II:69	178 n.137
	IV:41	177 n.126
Homilies	on Ex. 5:1	178 n.127
De Principiis	IV:I	168
	IV:1:6	167
	IV:1:7–20	173 n.1
	IV:1:7	177 n.119
	IV:1:11	177 n.120
	IV:2:3	167
	IV:3:1	177 n.125
	IV:3:1–2	177 n.126
Philokalia	VI:2	176 n.69
Philo (I A.D.)		
De agricultura	96,97	176 n.89
De congr. quaer erud. grat.	1–6	176 n.83
De ebrietate	36	176 n.81
De migratione Abr.	93	176 n.90
De mutatione nom.	8	176 n.78
De plantatione	8	176 n.82
De posteritate Caini	11, 14	176 n.79
Legum allegoriae	III:12, 16	176 n.80
Quis rer. div. her.	53	176 n.78
Plato (IV B.C.)		
Ion	534 D	176 n.73
Qumran (II – I B.C.)		
	I Qp. Hab. 1:1–21	51
	4 Q. Florilegium	265
	11 Q Melch.	165
Thomas, Gospel of, (I–II A.D.)		
log		76, 109

PATERNOSTER DIGITAL LIBRARY
Titles in this series

C.K. Barrett
Church, Ministry and Sacraments in the New Testament

George R. Beasley-Murray
Baptism in the New Testament

George R. Beasley-Murray
Jesus and the Kingdom of God

Tim Bradshaw
The Olive Branch
An Evangelical Anglican Doctrine of the Church

F.F. Bruce
(Revised by David F. Payne)
Israel and the Nations
The History of Israel from the Exodus to the Fall of the Second Temple

F.F. Bruce
Men and Movements in the Primitive Church
Studies in Early Non-Pauline Christianity

F.F. Bruce
Paul
Apostle of the Free Spirit

F.F. Bruce
The Spreading Flame
The Rise and Progress of Christianity from its First Beginnings
to the Conversion of the English

R.E. Clements
Wisdom in Theology

James D.G. Dunn
Christian Liberty
A New Testament Perspective

Mary J. Evans
Woman in the Bible
An Overview of all the Crucial Passages on Women's Roles

Edward William Fudge
The Fire that Consumes
The Biblical Case for Conditional Immortality

C.E. Gunton
Christ and Creation
A Summary Dogmatic Christology

Trevor A. Hart and Daniel Thimell (Editors)
Christ in Our Place
The Humanity of God in Christ for the Reconciliation of the World

Morna D. Hooker
Not Ashamed of the Gospel
New Testament Interpretations of the Death of Christ

I. Howard Marshall
Biblical Inspiration

I. Howard Marshall (Editor)
New Testament Interpretation
Essays on Principles and Methods

I. Howard Marshall
Last Supper and Lord's Supper
A Comprehensive Study of Recent Work on the Lord's Supper in the New Testament

I. Howard Marshall
Luke – Historian and Theologian

I. Howard Marshall
Kept by the Power of God
A Study of Perseverance and Falling Away

Leon Morris
The Cross in the New Testament
A Book-by-Book Study of the Central Fact of Christianity

Vinoth Ramachandra
The Recovery of Mission
Beyond the Pluralist Paradigm

Deryck Sheriffs
The Friendship of the Lord
An Old Testament Spirituality

David W. Smith
Transforming the World?
The Social Impact of British Evangelicalism

W. A. Strange
Children in the Early Church
Children in the Ancient World, the New Testament and the Early Church

Anthony C. Thiselton
The Two Horizons
New Testament Hermeneutics and Philosophical Description With Special Reference to Heidegger, Bultmann, Gadamer and Wittgenstein

Anthony C. Thiselton
New Horizons in Hermeneutics
The Theory and Practice of Transformaing Biblical Reading

John Wenham
Easter Enigma
Are the Resurrection Accounts in Conflict?

H.G.M. Williamson
Variations on a Theme
King, Messiah and Servant in the Book of Isaiah

Christopher J.H. Wright
God's People in God's Land
Family, Land and Property in the Old Testament

www.ingramcontent.com/pod-product-compliance
Lightning Source LLC
Chambersburg PA
CBHW071710300426
44115CB00010B/1374